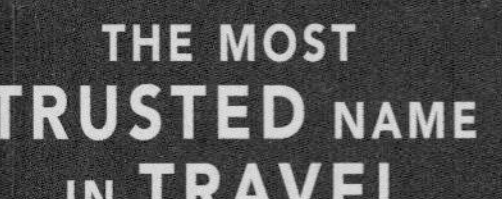
THE MOST TRUSTED NAME IN TRAVEL

Frommer's®

ITALY 2018

...abeth Heath,
...chelle
...d Strachan

FrommerMedia LLC

Published by:
Frommer Media LLC

Frommer's Italy 2018
ISBN 978-1-62887-344-3 (paper), 978-1-62887-345-0 (e-book)

Editorial Director: Pauline Frommer
Editor: Alexis Lipsitz
Production Editor: Lindsay Conner
Cartographer: Liz Puhl
Photo Editor: Meghan Lamb

For information on our other products or services, see www.frommers.com.

Frommer Media LLC also publishes its books in a variety of electronic formats. Some content that appears in print may not be available in electronic formats.

Manufactured in China

5 4 3 2 1

FROMMER'S STAR RATINGS SYSTEM

Every hotel, restaurant and attraction listed in this guide has been ranked for quality and value. Here's what the stars mean:

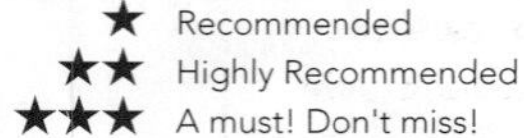

AN IMPORTANT NOTE

The world is a dynamic place. Hotels change ownership, restaurants hike their prices, museums alter their opening hours, and busses and trains change their routings. And all of this can occur in the several months after our authors have visited, inspected, and written about, these hotels, restaurants, museums and transportation services. Though we have made valiant efforts to keep all our information fresh and up-to-date, some few changes can inevitably occur in the periods before a revised edition of this guidebook is published. So please bear with us if a tiny number of the details in this book have changed. Please also note that we have no responsibility or liability for any inaccuracy or errors or omissions, or for inconvenience, loss, damage, or expenses suffered by anyone as a result of assertions in this guide.

CONTENTS

LIST OF MAPS

ABOUT THE AUTHORS

Stephen Brewer has been savoring Italian pleasures ever since he sipped his first cappuccino while a student in Rome many, many years ago (togas had just gone out of fashion). He has written about Italy for many magazines and guidebooks and remains transported in equal measure by Bolognese cooking, Tuscan hillsides, the Bay of Naples, and the streets of Palermo.

A long-time contributor to Frommer's guides, **Elizabeth Heath** has served as editor-in-chief to several regional magazines, and writes articles on travel, business, celebrities, politics, and lifestyle for online, local, regional, and national outlets. Liz fell in love with Italy on her first visit 17 years ago. She now lives in the green hills of Umbria with her family, plus five dogs, several hundred olive trees, and acres of grapevines. She writes about the peculiarities of life in the Italian countryside in her award-winning blog, "My Village in Umbria."

Stephen Keeling has been traveling to Italy since 1985 and covering his favorite nation for Frommer's since 2007. He has written for *The Independent, Daily Telegraph,* various travel magazines, and numerous travel guides as well as the award-winning *Frommer's Guide to Tuscany & Umbria*. Stephen resides in New York City.

Michelle Schoenung is an American journalist and translator in Milan who relocated to the Belpaese in 2000 for what was to be a yearlong adventure. Almost 2 decades later, she is pleased that Milan has evolved into a much more international and cosmopolitan city and has shed its image of merely being a foggy northern Italian business hub. Her writings and translations have appeared in magazines and books in the United States and Italy. In her free time, she likes to read, run, travel, and explore the city with her two rambunctious Italian-American *bambini*.

Donald Strachan is a travel journalist who has written about Italy for publications worldwide, including *National Geographic Traveler, The Guardian, Sunday Telegraph,* CNN.com, and many others. He has also written several Italy guidebooks for Frommer's, including *Frommer's EasyGuide to Rome, Florence, and Venice*. He lives in London, England. For more, see www.donaldstrachan.com.

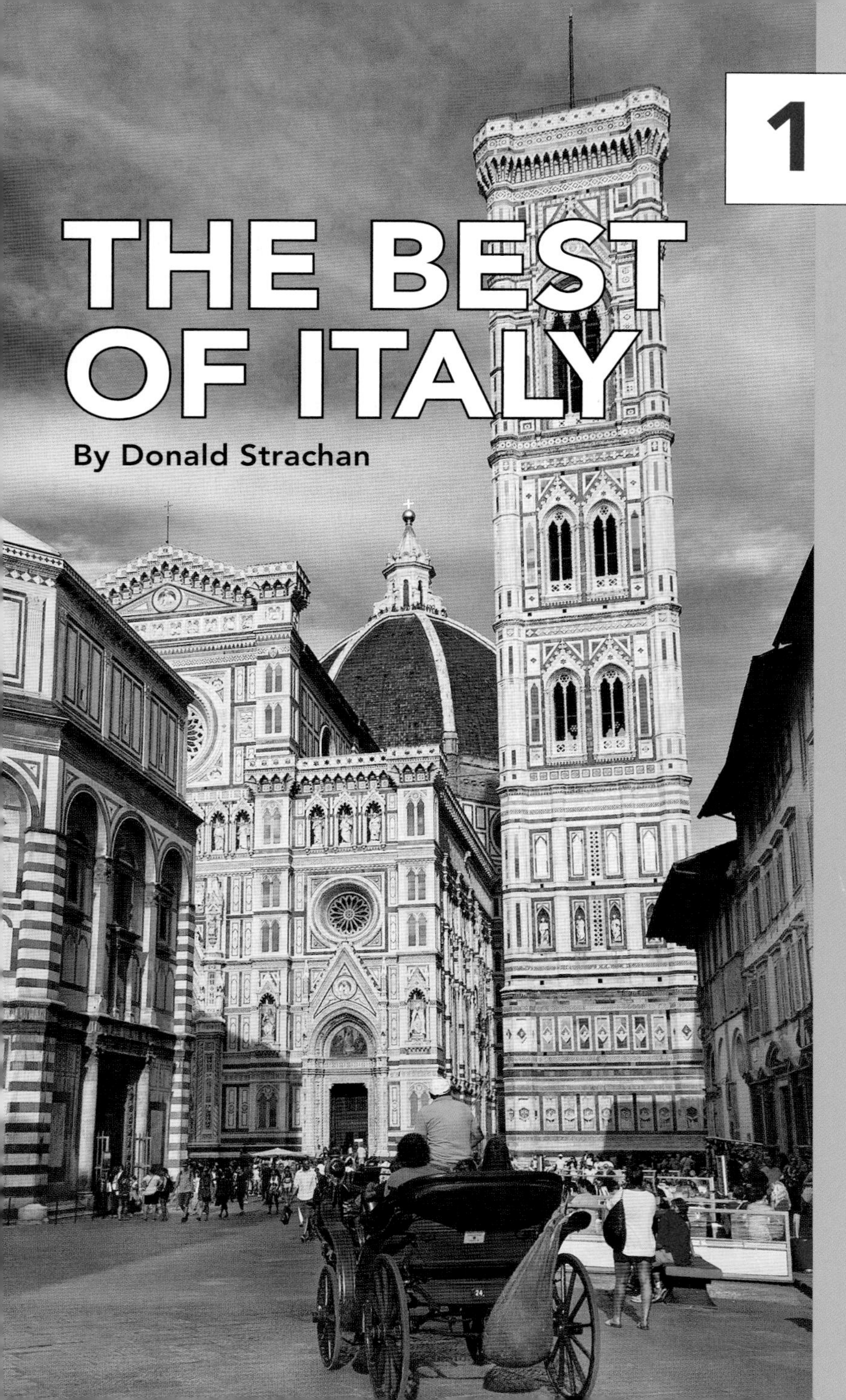

1 THE BEST OF ITALY

By Donald Strachan

Just speak the word "Italy," and you can already see it. The noble stones of ancient Rome and the Greek temples of Sicily. The wine hills of Piedmont and Tuscany, the ruins of Pompeii, and the secret canals and crumbling palaces of Venice. For centuries, visitors have come here looking for their own slice of *la dolce vita,* and for the most part, they have found it.

Nowhere in the world is the impact of the Renaissance felt more than in its birthplace, **Florence,** whose vast repository of art includes works left by Masaccio, Botticelli, Leonardo da Vinci, Michelangelo, and many, many others. Much of the "known world" was once ruled from **Rome,** a city supposedly founded by twins Romulus and Remus in 753 B.C. There's no place with more artistic treasures—not even **Venice,** a seemingly impossible floating city whose beauty and history was shaped by its centuries of trade with the Byzantine and Islamic worlds to the east.

Of course, there's more. Long before Italy was a country, it was a loose collection of city-states. Centuries of alliance and rivalry left a legacy of art and architecture in **Verona,** with its Shakespearean romance and intact Roman Arena; and in **Mantua,** which blossomed during the Renaissance under the Gonzaga dynasty. **Padua** and its sublime Giotto frescoes are within easy reach of Venice, too. In **Siena,** ethereal art and Gothic palaces survive, barely altered since the city's 1300s heyday.

A millennium earlier, the eruption of Vesuvius in A.D. 79 preserved **Pompeii** and **Herculaneum** under volcanic ash. They remain the best places to get close-up with everyday life in the Roman era. The buildings

PREVIOUS PAGE: **Florence's Duomo.** BELOW: **Dining Italian style at alfresco cafe near the church of Santa Maria Assunta in Monteriggioni.**

of ancient Greece still stand at **Paestum,** in Campania, and at sites on **Sicily,** the Mediterranean's largest island. Cave dwellings, frescoed rupestrian churches, and even a rock cathedral honeycomb one side of **Matera,** in Basilicata.

The corrugated, vine-clad hills of the **Chianti** and the cypress-studded, emerald-green expanses of the **Val d'Orcia** serve up iconic images of **Tuscany.** Adventurous walkers of all ages can hike between the coastal villages of the **Cinque Terre,** where you can travel untroubled by the 21st century. Whether it's seafood along the Sicilian coast, pizza in **Naples,** pasta in **Bologna,** pesto in **Genoa,** or the red Barolo and Barbaresco wines of **Piedmont,** your taste buds are in for an adventure of their own. **Milan** and Florence are centers of world fashion. Welcome to *La Bella Italia.*

ITALY'S best AUTHENTIC EXPERIENCES

- **Dining Italian style:** There is probably no pastime more cherished than eating. No genuinely "national" cuisine dominates: Each region and city has its own recipes handed down over the generations. If the weather is fine and you're dining outdoors, perhaps with a view of a medieval church or a vineyard, you'll find the closest thing to food heaven. *Buon appetito!*
- **Exploring Rome's Mercato di Testaccio:** In 2012 the old Testaccio Market made way for a glass-paneled, modernist beauty, across the street from Rome's MACRO museum. Mingle with busy *signore* whose trolleys are chock-full of celery, carrots, and onions for the day's *ragù*, grab a slice of focaccia or some Roman street food, and soak up the authentic flavors of the Eternal City. See p. 152.

Catching an opera at Verona's Roman Arena.

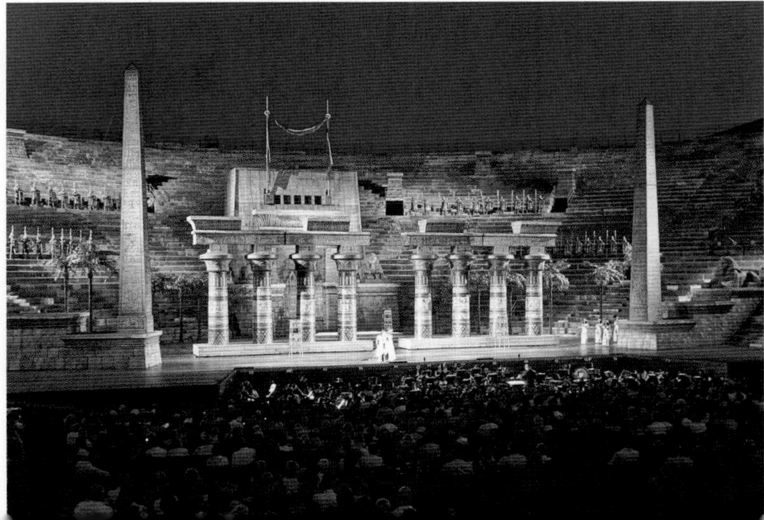

- **Cicchetti and a spritz in Venice:** *Cicchetti*—tapas-like small servings, usually eaten while standing at a bar—are a Venetian tradition. To make the experience complete, accompany the *cicchetti* with a spritz made with Aperol and sparkling prosecco wine from the Veneto hills. Your options are numerous, but some of the best spots to indulge are on the San Polo side of the Rialto Bridge. See p. 430.
- **Catching an opera at Verona's Arena:** In summer, Italians enjoy their opera under the stars. The setting for Italy's largest and most famous outdoor festival is the ancient Arena di Verona, a site that's grand enough to accommodate as many elephants as might be needed for a performance of "Aïda." See p. 453.
- **Slowing down to Italy pace:** Nothing happens quickly here: Linger over a glass of wine from the Tuscan hills, slurp a gelato made with seasonal fruit, enjoy the evening *passeggiata* (ritual walk) just like the locals. They call it Slow Food for a reason.

ITALY'S best RESTAURANTS

- **Ottava Nota** (Palermo): Palermo's old Arab quarter, the Kalsa is buzzing once again, especially at this place, which takes a creative angle on Sicilian cuisine. Ingredients come straight from the city's famous produce markets. See p. 745.
- **Trattoria dal Biassanot** (Bologna): Just about every restaurant in Bologna lays claim to the original sauce *alla bolognese,* but many connoisseurs agree this is the best. Under the wood beams of a gracious bistro, you can sample light-as-a-feather pastas, then mop the plate clean with their homemade bread. See p. 358.
- **Taverna San Giuseppe** (Siena): A long, brick-vaulted room from the 12th century is the atmospheric setting for hand-rolled *pici* with a *ragù* of *cinghiale* (wild boar), ricotta-filled *gnudi*, and other expert takes on Tuscan comfort food. This is a place many travelers long remember as their best meal in Italy. See p. 242.
- **Ai Artisti** (Venice): Venice's culinary rep is founded on the quality of the catch at its famous fish market. Both *primi* and *secondi* at Ai Artisti feature the freshest fish from the lagoon and farther afield. See p. 436.

ITALY'S best HOTELS

- **Villa Spalletti Trivelli** (Rome): Recent upgrades have only enhanced the unique experience of staying in a neoclassical mansion in the middle of the capital. Opulence plus impeccable, understated service comes at a price, of course. When our lottery numbers come up, we will be booking a stay here—a long one. See p. 131.
- **Santa Caterina** (Amalfi): Another favorite splurge on the peninsula, Santa Caterina is not outrageously posh, just magically transporting,

with a setting in citrus groves above the sea. Ceramic tiles, a smattering of antiques, and sea-view terraces grace the rooms, and a garden path and elevator descend to a private beach. Shoulder season rates and special offers help bring the cost out of the stratosphere. See p. 657.

- **Palazzo Tolomei** (Florence): A palace where Raphael once stayed—and perhaps even gifted its former owners a painting in lieu of rent—sounds grand, and you won't be disappointed. The Renaissance layout and a baroque redecoration from the 1600s are intact. See p. 204.
- **La Bandita Townhouse** (Pienza): In huge, loftlike guest quarters, distressed leather armchairs, slinky divans, and freestanding tubs are set against honey-colored stone walls and old beams. Complementing this contemporary twist on a Tuscan village home are a lovely garden and views over dreamy Val d'Orcia countryside. See p. 254.
- **Fra I Sassi Residence** (Matera): Staying in a cave is an experience in itself, especially when accommodations are as stylish and comfortable as these. All open onto a meandering, sunny terrace that provides a front-row seat on a sculpture-like cluster of cave dwellings that tumble down surrounding cliffs. See p. 702.

ITALY'S best FOR FAMILIES

- **Climbing Pisa's wonky tower** (Tuscany): Are we walking up or down? Pleasantly disoriented kids are bound to ask as you spiral your way to the rooftop-viewing balcony atop one of the world's most famous pieces of botched engineering. Pisa is an easy day trip from Florence, and 8 is the minimum age for heading up its *Torre Pendente,* or Leaning Tower. See p. 297.
- **Acquario di Genova** (Liguria): After museums, churches, palaces, and more museums, Genoa's aquarium is a welcome change of direction, for everyone in the family. It may not be as large as some North American super-aquariums, but it is beautifully designed (by architect Renzo Piano) and houses sharks, seals, and much weird and wonderful sea life, as well as a hummingbird sanctuary and great educational exhibits. See p. 547.
- **Exploring underground Naples**: There is more to Naples than you can see at eye level. Head below its maze of streets to see the remains of ancient Greek and Roman cities. As well as the Ágora and Forum, families can tour catacombs used for centuries to bury the Christian dead and tunnels that sheltered refugees from the cholera epidemic of 1884 and the bombs of World War II. See p. 577.
- **A trip to an artisan gelateria**: Blue "Smurf" or bubble-gum-pink flavors are a pretty clear indication of color enhancers, and ice crystals or grainy texture are telltale signs of engineered gelato. Gelato in fluffy heaps, however pretty, have been built with additives and air pumped into the blend—so steer clear. Authentic *gelaterie* produce good stuff

Bottlenose dolphins swim in Genoa's Acquario di Genova.

from scratch daily, with fresh seasonal produce and less bravado, along with a short ingredient list posted proudly for all to see. Check "Where to Eat" and "Gelato" sections in individual chapters for our favorites: Rome (p. 140) and Florence (p. 215) have several genuine gelato artisans. Believe us when we say: You will taste the difference.

ITALY'S most OVERRATED

- **Campo de' Fiori** (Rome): Yes, the piazza is stunning: It's the only square in Rome without a church, and the Renaissance light bounces off ochre and burnt-sienna facades. But between 8am and 3pm, it is a busy market where goods are geared toward (and priced for) tourists, not locals. Wait for the departure of the last boisterous pigeons and the vendors selling aprons embossed with the sculpted abs of Michelangelo's "David", and grab a slice of real Rome at sunset, when Campo de' Fiori reclaims its local, intimate, old Rome face. See p. 151.
- **Ponte Vecchio** (Florence): Sorry, lovers, but this isn't even the prettiest bridge in Florence, let alone one of the world's great spots for romantics. It's haphazard by design, packed at all hours, and hemmed in by shops that cater mostly to tourism. For a special moment with a loved one—perhaps even to "pop the question"—head downstream one bridge to the Ponte Santa Trínita. Built in the 1560s by Bartolomeo Ammanati, its triple-ellipse design is pure elegance in stone. At dusk, it is also one of Florence's best spots to photograph the Ponte Vecchio…if you must. See p. 184.
- **Capri** (Campania): We hate to say anything bad about such an enchanting beauty, but Capri falls victim to its justified popularity. Arrive in midsummer on a day excursion, corral through the gardens of Augustus, ride a boat through the Blue Grotto, shell out 5€ for a bottle of water. You will wish you could spend the night here, to enjoy the scenery and sparkling-white towns after the day-trippers leave, or to walk the scented flower paths early on a spring morning. Any of which, of course, you can and should do. See p. 670.

ITALY'S best MUSEUMS

- **Vatican Museums** (Rome): The 100 galleries that constitute the Musei Vaticani are loaded with papal treasures accumulated over the centuries. Musts include the Sistine Chapel, such ancient Greek and Roman sculptures as "Laocoön" and "Belvedere Apollo," the frescoed *stanze* executed by Raphael (among which is his "School of Athens"), and endless collections of Greco-Roman antiquities and Renaissance art by European masters. See p. 78.
- **Galleria degli Uffizi** (Florence): This U-shaped High Renaissance building designed by Giorgio Vasari was the administrative headquarters, or *uffizi* (offices), for the dukes of Tuscany when the Medici called the shots around here. It's now the crown jewel of Europe's fine-art museums, housing the world's greatest collection of Renaissance paintings, including iconic works by Botticelli, Leonardo da Vinci, and Michelangelo. See p. 176.
- **Accademia** (Venice): One of Europe's great museums houses an unequaled array of Venetian paintings, exhibited chronologically from the 13th to the 18th century. Walls are hung with works by Bellini, Carpaccio, Giorgione, Titian, and Tintoretto. See p. 407.
- **Museo Archeologico Nazionale** (Naples): Come to see the mosaics and frescoes from Pompeii and Herculaneum—the original of the much-reproduced "Cave Canem" ("Beware of the Dog") mosaic is here, as are the Villa of the Papyri frescoes. Much else awaits you, including the "Farnese Bull"—which once decorated Rome's Terme di Caracalla—and some of the finest statuary to survive from ancient Europe. See p. 591.

Michelangelo's Sistine Chapel, Vatican Museums.

- **Museo Egizio** (Turin): With a dazzling new refit unveiled in 2015, Turin's Egyptology museum has doubled in size and now has the finest collection of Egyptian artifacts outside Cairo. See p. 515.
- **Santa Maria della Scala** (Siena): The building is as much the star as the collections. This was a hospital from medieval times until it closed in the 1990s, and its frescoed wards, ancient chapels and sacristy, and labyrinthine basement floors were gradually revealed for public viewing. See p. 237.

ITALY'S best FREE THINGS TO DO

- **Getting rained on in Rome's Pantheon:** People often wonder whether the 9m (30-ft.) oculus in the middle of the Pantheon's dome has a glass covering. Visit this ancient temple in the middle of a downpour for your answer: The oculus is open to the elements, transforming the interior into a giant shower on wet days. In light rain, the building fills with mist, but during a full-fledged thunderstorm, the drops come down in a perfect shaft, splattering on the polychrome marble floor. Come on Pentecost to be rained on by a cloud of rose petals. See p. 100.
- **Surrendering to the madness of a Palermo market:** In Sicily's capital—a crossroads between East and West for some 2,000 years—the chaotic, colorful street theater is a vignette of a culture that often feels more Middle Eastern than European. The Vucciria isn't what it was, however: Focus on the Capo and Ballarò markets. See p. 747.
- **Watching the sun rise over the Roman Forum:** A short stroll from the Capitoline Hill down Via del Campidoglio to Via di Monte Tarpeo brings you to a perfect outlook: The terrace behind the Michelangelo-designed square provides a momentary photo op when the sun rises

The Pantheon, Rome's best-preserved ancient building.

behind the Temple of Saturn, illuminating the archaeological complex below in pink-orange light. Early risers can reward themselves with breakfast in the bakeries of the nearby Jewish Ghetto. See chapter 4.

- **Discovering you're hopelessly lost in Venice:** You haven't experienced Venice until you have turned a corner convinced you're on the way to somewhere, only to find yourself smack against a canal with no bridge, or in a little courtyard with no way out. All you can do is shrug, smile, and give the city's maze of narrow streets another try, because getting lost in Venice is a pleasure. See chapter 9.
- **Driving the Amalfi Coast:** The SS163, "the road of 1,000 bends," hugs vertical cliffs and deep gorges, cutting through olive groves, lemon terraces, and whitewashed villages—against a background of the bluest ocean you can picture. One of the world's classic drives, it provokes fear, nausea, and wonder in equal doses; the secret is to make sure someone else is at the wheel. Someone you trust. See p. 652.

ITALY'S best ARCHITECTURAL LANDMARKS

- **Brunelleschi's dome** (Florence): It took the genius of Filippo Brunelleschi to work out how to raise a vast dome over the huge hole in Florence's cathedral roof. Though rejected for the commission to cast the bronze doors of the Baptistery, Filippo didn't sulk. He went away and became the city's greatest architect, and the creator of one of Italy's most recognizable landmarks. See p. 175.
- **The Gothic center of Siena** (Tuscany): The shell-shaped Piazza del Campo stands at the heart of one of Europe's best-preserved medieval cities. Steep, canyonlike streets, icons of Gothic architecture like the Palazzo Pubblico, and Madonnas painted on gilded altarpieces transport you back to a time before the Renaissance. See p. 225.
- **Pompeii** (Campania): When Mt. Vesuvius blew its top in A.D. 79, it buried Pompeii under molten lava and ash, ending the lives of perhaps 35,000 citizens and suspending the city in a time capsule. Today, still under the shadow of the menacing

Detail of a preserved fresco from Pompeii.

volcano, this poignant ghost town can be coaxed into life with very little imagination. See p. 620.

- **Valley of the Temples, Agrigento** (Sicily): The Greeks built these seven temples overlooking the sea to impress, and their honey-colored columns and pediments still do. Seeing these romantic ruins—some, like the Temple of Concordia, beautifully preserved; others like the Temple of Juno, timeworn but still proud—is an experience of a lifetime. See p. 777.
- **Castel del Monte** (Puglia): If the 13th-century castle that Frederick II built above the fertile Puglian plains looks familiar, that's because it appears on Italy's 1-cent coin. This tall octagon is embellished with eight octagonal towers, a fanciful masterpiece that merges Islamic and Gothic influences. See p. 705.

best UNDISCOVERED ITALY

- **The aperitivi spots and craft-beer bars of Rome:** Don't confuse *aperitivo* with happy hour: Predinner cocktails tickle appetites and induce conversation and flirting. The best *aperitivi* bars allow free access to all-you-can-eat buffets if you buy one drink. And Romans are increasingly turning to artisan-brewed beers for that one drink. See "Entertainment & Nightlife," in chapter 4.
- **Drinking your coffee al banco:** Italians—especially city dwellers—don't often linger at a piazza table sipping their morning cappuccino. For them, a *caffè* is a pit stop: They stand at the counter (*al banco*), throw back the bitter elixir, and continue on their way, reinforced by a hit of caffeine. You will also save a chunk of change drinking Italian style, at least 50% less than the sit-down price, even in the baroque surrounds of Turin's Piazza San Carlo. See p. 154.
- **Genoa's handsome center:** Don't be fooled by a rough, industrial exterior: Genoa has Italy's largest *centro storico,* with architecture that rivals Venice. A restored old port, the Palazzo Reale, and the *palazzi* of Strada Nuova are just a few of the highlights in a trading city that got wealthy from the sea. See chapter 11.
- **The art at Padua's Cappella degli Scrovegni:** Step aside, Sistine Chapel. Art lovers armed with binoculars behold this scene in awe, the cycle of frescoes by Giotto that revolutionized 14th-century painting. It is considered the most important work of art leading up to the Renaissance, and visiting is an unforgettable, intimate experience. See p. 449.
- **The canals of Treviso:** Venice's near-neighbor has canals of its own, and much thinner crowds, even in peak season. Its atmospheric old fish market occupies an island, and city churches are adorned with medieval artworks by Tommaso da Modena. This is also the place to try recipes that use Treviso's prized red radicchio. See chapter 9.

- **The view from T Fondaco dei Tedeschi:** This newly opened Venice department store—renovated by stellar architect Rem Koolhas, no less—was once an elegant *palazzo* beside the Grand Canal. The views from its free rooftop deck are even more spectacular than the opulent goods inside. See p. 405.

ITALY'S best ACTIVE ADVENTURES

- **Seeing Ferrara on two wheels:** Join the bike-mad *Ferraresi* as they zip along narrow, cycle-friendly lanes that snake through the city's old center, past the Castello Estense and the Renaissance elegance of Palazzo Schifanoia. You can also bike a circuit atop the city's medieval walls. See p. 361.
- **Kayaking around Venice:** At around 120€ per day, seeing Venice from a kayak is not cheap. But if you want to get a unique angle on the palaces and quiet canalside corners of Italy's fairy-tale floating city, there is nothing quite like it. See p. 394.
- **Riding the Monte Bianco Skyway, Valle d'Aosta:** In Italy's far northwestern corner, you can catch a revolving cable car and travel high on Europe's tallest mountain, departing from the hiking, biking, and skiing resort of Courmayeur. Standing 4,810m (15,780 ft.), Monte Bianco ("Mont Blanc" to the French) guards the border between France and Italy and is flanked by perilous glaciers and

Riding the Monte Bianco Skyway, Valle d'Aosta.

jagged granite peaks, all visible from cableways that opened in 2015. It's pricey, but unforgettable. See p. 536.

- **Walking the Cinque Terre** (Liguria): The 3-mile path from Corniglia to Vernazza and the 2-mile section from Vernazza to Monterosso are the most rewarding in terms of sheer beauty. Narrow paths are surrounded by terraced vineyards, as well as olive and lemon groves that seem to hover over a sapphire Mediterranean Sea. This coastal path is best tackled in the early morning, before the crowds. Out of season, you might even have it to yourself. See p. 566.

ITALY'S best NEIGHBORHOODS

- **Testaccio, Rome:** The relaxed atmosphere of this working-class, all-Roman neighborhood is a perfect wind-down from the sightseeing hype and the crowds. Its appeal for travelers is growing, with museums, industrial design and architecture, lively nightlife, and especially culinary highlights, including the relocated Mercato di Testaccio. See chapter 4.
- **San Frediano, Florence:** Most Florentines have abandoned their *centro storico* to the visitors, but the Arno's Left Bank in San Frediano has plenty of local action after dark. Dine at **iO** (p. 214), slurp a gelato

Shopping for antiques on Via San Gregorio in Spaccanapoli, Naples.

by the river at **La Carraia** (p. 216), then drink until late at **Diorama** (p. 222) or catch an acoustic gig at **Libreria-Café La Cité** (p. 220).

- **Spaccanapoli, Naples:** It's sometimes said Naples is Italy on overdrive, and the city goes up another gear in the narrow, crowded, laundry-strung lanes of its *centro storico.* Gird your loins, watch your wallet, and forget about a map—just plunge into the grid and enjoy the boisterous scene as you browse shops selling everything from *limoncello* and carved nativity scenes to fried snacks and the world's best pizza. It's a European *souk*. See chapter 12.
- **Cannaregio, Venice:** This residential neighborhood has silent canals, elegantly faded mansions, and hidden churches graced by Tiepolo paintings. Here, too, is the old Ghetto Nuovo, a historic area of Jewish bakeries, restaurants, and synagogues. It's all a great escape from the chaos around San Marco. See chapter 9.
- **Navigli, Milan:** The city is still riding high on a post-Expo wave, and nowhere exudes it more than the regenerated Navigli neighborhood. Its hub is the Darsena, once Milan's canal port, now home to a market, shops, and bars. It's also the place where Milanese come together after dark for summer concerts, Christmas markets, or to watch the game on a big screen. See chapter 10.
- **Sasso Barisano and Sasso Caveoso, Matera:** Inhabited for more than 3,000 years, clusters of cave dwellings carved into limestone cliffs create one of Italy's weirdest architectural spectacles. The primitive, earth-hued assemblage of houses, churches, and monasteries pile one atop the other along a jumble of twisting stepped streets. They now house some unique restaurants and hotels, too. See chapter 14.

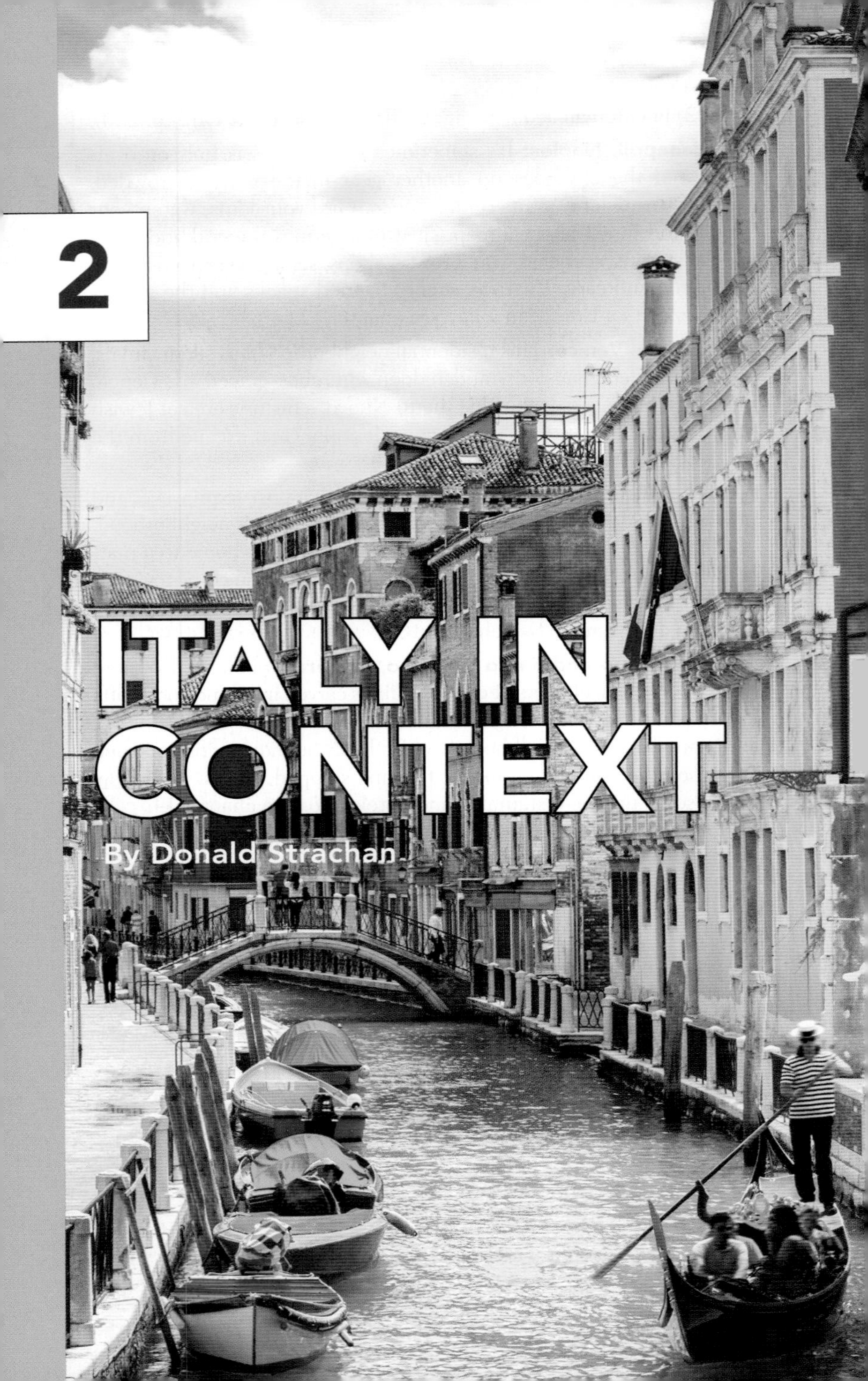

2

ITALY IN CONTEXT

By Donald Strachan

Many of the stereotypes you have heard about this charming country are accurate. Children are fussed over wherever they go; food and soccer are treated like religion; the north–south divide is alive and well; and (alas) bureaucracy is a frustrating feature of daily life for families and businesses. Some stereotypes, however, are wide off the mark: Not every Italian you meet will be open and effusive. Every now and then—but rarely in the South—they do taciturn pretty well, too. This chapter provides a little historic and cultural background to help you understand what makes Italy tick.

The most important thing to remember is that, for a land so steeped in history—3 millennia and counting—Italy has only a short history *as a country*. In 2011 it celebrated its 150th birthday. Prior to 1861, the map of the peninsula was in constant flux. War, alliance, invasion, and disputed successions caused that map to change color as often as a chameleon crossing a field of wildflowers. Republics, mini-monarchies, client states, Papal states, and city-states, as well as Islamic emirates, colonies, dukedoms, and Christian theocracies, roll onto and out of the pages of Italian history with regularity. In some regions, you'll hear languages and dialects other than Italian. It all combines to form an identity that's often more regional than it is national.

This confusing history explains why your Italian experience will differ wildly if you visit, say, Turin rather than Matera. (And why you should visit both, if you can.) The architecture is different; the food is different; the legends and important historical figures are different, as are the issues of the day. And the people are different: While the north–south schism is most often written about, cities as close together as Florence and Siena can feel very dissimilar. Milan to Naples is just

An elaborate Carnevale costume, Piazza San Marco, Venice.

cuisine AROUND THE COUNTRY

Italians know how to cook—just ask any of them. But be sure to leave plenty of time: Once Italians start talking food, it's a while before they pause for breath. Italy doesn't really have a unified national cuisine; it's more a loose grouping of regional cuisines that share a few staples, notably pasta, bread, tomatoes, and pig meat cured in many ways. On a **Rome** visit, you'll encounter authentic local specialties such as *saltimbocca alla romana* (literally "jump-in-your-mouth"—thin slices of veal with sage, cured ham, and cheese) and *carciofi alla romana* (artichokes cooked with herbs, such as mint and garlic), and a dish that's become ubiquitous, *spaghetti alla carbonara*—pasta coated in a silky sauce made with egg, *pecorino romano* (ewe's milk cheese) and cured pork (*guanciale*, cheek, if it's authentic).

To the north, in **Florence** and **Tuscany,** you'll find seasonal ingredients served simply; it's almost the antithesis of "French" cooking, with its multiple processes. The main ingredient for almost any savory dish is the local olive oil, prized for its low acidity. The typical Tuscan pasta is wide, flat *pappardelle,* generally tossed with a game sauce such as *lepre* (hare) or *cinghiale* (boar). Tuscans are fond of their own strong ewe's milk pecorino cheese, made most famously around the Val d'Orcia town of Pienza. Meat is usually the centerpiece of any *secondo:* A *bistecca alla fiorentina* is the classic main dish, a T-bone-like cut of meat. An authentic *fiorentina* should be cut only from the white Chianina breed of cattle. Sweet treats are also good here, particularly Siena's *panforte* (a dense, sticky cake); *biscotti di Prato* (hard, almond-flour biscuits for dipping in dessert wine, also known as *cantuccini*); and the *miele* (honey) of Montalcino.

Emilia-Romagna is the country's gastronomic center. Rich in produce, its school of cooking first created many pastas now common around Italy: tagliatelle, tortellini, and cappelletti (made in the shape of "little hats"). Pig also comes several ways, including in Bologna's mortadella (rolled, ground pork) and *prosciutto di Parma* (cured ham). Served in paper-thin slices, it's deliciously sweet. The distinctive cheese Parmigiano–Reggiano is made by hundreds of small producers in the provinces of Parma and Reggio Emilia.

Probably the most famous dish of **Lombardy** is *cotoletta alla milanese* (veal cutlet dipped in egg and breadcrumbs and fried in olive oil)—the

over 4 hours by train, but the experience is like two different worlds. This chapter aims to help you understand why.

ITALY TODAY

The big news for many North American travelers to Italy is the recent favorable movement in exchange rates. The 2015 edition of this guide listed the U.S. dollar/euro exchange rate at $1.37. At time of writing, it's hovering around $1.06. That change makes everything in Italy instantly 20% cheaper for U.S. visitors. (Canadians have been less fortunate, their dollar moving less dramatically from $1.51 to $1.39 in the same period.) If the dollar is your currency, congratulations: You picked a good time to visit.

Many Italians have not been so lucky. One reason for the euro's plunge is a stubbornly slow European recovery from the global financial

Germans call it Wienerschnitzel. *Osso buco* is another Lombard classic: shin of veal cooked in a ragout sauce. **Piedmont** and Turin's iconic dish is *bagna càuda*—literally "hot bath" in the Piedmontese language, a sauce made with olive oil, garlic, butter, and anchovies, into which you dip raw vegetables. Piedmont is also the spiritual home of *risotto,* particularly the town of Vercelli, which is surrounded by rice paddies.

Venice is rarely celebrated for its cuisine, but fresh seafood is usually excellent, and figures heavily in the Venetian diet. Grilled fish is often served with red radicchio, a bitter leaf that grows best in nearby **Treviso.** Two classic Venetian non-fish dishes are *fegato alla veneziana* (liver and onions) and *risi e bisi* (rice and fresh peas).

Liguria also turns toward the sea for its inspiration, as reflected by its version of bouillabaisse, *burrida* flavored with spices. But its most famous food is pesto *alla genovese,* a sauce made with fresh basil, hard cheese, olive oil, and crushed pine nuts, which is used to dress pasta, fish, and many other dishes.

So many Neapolitans moved to the New World that the cookery of **Campania**—including pizza and spaghetti with clam sauce—is very familiar to North Americans. Mozzarella is the local cheese, the best of it *mozzarella di bufala,* made with milk from water buffalo, a species first introduced to Campania from Asia in the Middle Ages. Mixed fish fries (a *fritto misto*) are a staple of many a lunch table, and genuine Neapolitan pizza is in a class of its own. The cuisine of **Basilicata** and **Puglia** is founded on peasant simplicity: pasta, often made without egg, tossed with oil and seasonal vegetables or garbanzo beans, for example. The region is known for its Senise peppers—which when dried become sweeter and piquant—and spicy or fennel-spiked Lucanica sausage. Seafood is ubiquitous along the regions' long coastline.

Sicily has a distinctive cuisine, with strong flavors and aromatic sauces. One staple is *pasta con le sarde* (with pine nuts, wild fennel, spices, chopped sardines, and olive oil). In fact, fish is good and fresh pretty much everywhere (local swordfish is excellent). Classic desserts include *cannoli,* cylindrical pastry cases stuffed with ricotta and candied fruit (or chocolate). Sicilian *gelato* and homemade pastries are among the best in Italy.

crisis, known here as the *crisi*. It had a disastrous effect on Italy's economy, causing the deepest recession since World War II. Public debt had grown to alarming levels—as high as €1,900 trillion. As a result, 2011 and 2012 saw Italy at the center of a European banking crisis that almost brought about the collapse of the euro currency, and concerns about major Italian banks rumbled on through 2017. In 2015, many Italians were beginning to see light at the end of their dark economic tunnel—a little, at least—only to face a return to stagnation in 2017. Italy has, in effect, experienced no GDP growth in well over a decade.

Populism has become a feature of national politics. A party led by activist comedian Beppe Grillo—the *MoVimento 5 Stelle* (Five Star Movement, or M5S)—polled around a quarter of the vote in 2013 elections. By early 2014, in the post-electoral shakedown, former Florence mayor Matteo Renzi became Italy's youngest prime minister—at 39 years of age—heading a coalition of the center-left led by his Democratic Party (PD). He resigned in late 2016, after defeat in a referendum on wide-ranging electoral reform. The PD remained in power, however, with Paolo Gentiloni taking over as prime minister.

It has not been easy sailing for M5S, either: Their candidate, Virginia Raggi, was elected Rome's first female mayor, but her administration has encountered multiple problems since she took office in 2016. Opinion polling through early 2017 showed Italians still favoring the PD government's reformism over rivals' policies, but with a slim lead over M5S. The next general election is scheduled for 2018.

Italy's population is aging, and a youth vacuum is being filled by immigrants, especially those from Eastern Europe, notably Romania (whose language is similar to Italian) and Albania, as well as from North Africa. Italy has had scant colonial experience, nor does it have the "melting pot" history of the New World. Tensions were inevitable, and discrimination is a daily fact of life for many minorities. Change is coming—in 2013, Cécile Kyenge became Italy's first black government minister, and black footballer Mario Balotelli has been one of the country's biggest sports stars. But it is coming too slowly for many. The plight of migrant refugees arriving from North Africa and Syria through 2016 added yet another layer of complexity to Italy's relationship with immigration, and left the country's temporary immigration centers bursting at the seams. Further recent signs of a changing society include the 2016 legalization of same-sex civil unions.

While others arrive, a "brain drain" continues to push young Italians to seek opportunities abroad. The problem is especially ingrained in rural communities and on the islands, where the old maxim, "it's not what you know, it's who you know," applies more strongly than ever in these straitened times. Prospects for everyone will improve if and when Italy puts the worst of its economic turmoil behind it. From top to toe, highlands to islands, fingers are firmly crossed that the good times are coming around again.

THE MAKING OF ITALY

Prehistory to the Rise of Rome

Of all the early inhabitants of Italy, the most extensive legacy was left by the **Etruscans.** Archaeologists continue to debate exactly where they came from, and the inscriptions they left behind (often on graves in *necropoli*) are of little help: The Etruscan language has never been fully deciphered by scholars. Whatever their origins, within 2 centuries of appearing on the peninsula around 800 B.C., they had subjugated the lands now known as Tuscany (to which they left their name) and Campania, along with the **Villanovan** tribes that lived there.

From their base at **Rome,** the Latins remained free until they too were conquered by the Etruscans around 600 B.C. The new overlords

Lungarno degli Acciaiuoli Street in Florence.

introduced gold tableware and jewelry, bronze urns and terracotta statuary, and the art and culture of Greece and Asia Minor. They also made Rome the government seat of Latium. "Roma" is an Etruscan name, and the early, perhaps mythical kings of Rome had Etruscan names: Numa, Ancus, even Romulus.

The Etruscans ruled until the **Roman Revolt** around 510 B.C., and by 250 B.C. the Romans and their allies had vanquished or assimilated the Etruscans, wiping out their language and religion. However, many of the former rulers' manners and beliefs remained and became integral to what we now understand as "Roman culture."

Meanwhile, the **Greeks**—who predated both the Etruscans and the Romans—had built powerful colonial outposts in the south, notably in Naples, founded as Greek "Neapolis." Remains of the *Àgora*, or market square, survive below **San Lorenzo Maggiore** (p. 592), in the old center of the city. The Greeks left behind stone monuments above ground too, including at the **Valley of the Temples,** Agrigento, Sicily (p. 777).

If you want to see remnants of Etruscan civilization, Rome's **Museo Nazionale Etrusco** (p. 110) and the Etruscan collection in Rome's **Vatican Museums** (p. 78) are a logical starting point. Florence's **Museo Archeologico** (p. 190) houses one of the greatest Etruscan bronzes yet unearthed, the "Arezzo Chimera." There are also fine Etruscan collections in **Volterra,** Tuscany (p. 277) and **Orvieto,** Umbria (p. 333). Mary Beard's excellent book "SPQR" is packed with insight on the rise of Ancient Rome.

The Roman Republic: ca. 510–27 B.C.

After the Roman Republic was established around 510 B.C.—it's impossible to be precise—the Romans continued to increase their power by conquering neighboring communities in the highlands and forming alliances with other Latins in the lowlands. They began to give to their allies, and then to conquered peoples, partial or complete Roman citizenship, with a corresponding obligation of military service. This further increased Rome's power and reach. Citizen colonies were set up as settlements of Roman farmers or military veterans, including both **Florence** and **Siena.**

The stern culture of the Roman Republic was characterized by belief in the gods, the necessity of learning from the past, the strength of the family, education through reading and performing public service, and most importantly, obedience. The all-powerful Senate presided as Rome defeated rival powers one after another and came to rule the Mediterranean. The Punic Wars with **Carthage** (in modern-day Tunisia) in the 3rd century B.C. were a temporary stumbling block, as Carthaginian general **Hannibal** (247–182 B.C.) conducted a devastating campaign across the Italian peninsula, crossing the Alps with his elephants and winning bloody battles by the shore of **Lago Trasimeno,** in Umbria, and at Cannae, in Puglia. In the end, however, Rome prevailed.

No figure was more towering during the late Republic, or more instrumental in its transformation into the Empire (see below), than **Julius Caesar,** the charismatic conqueror of Gaul—"the wife of every husband and the husband of every wife," according to scurrilous rumors reported by 1st-century historian Suetonius. After defeating the last resistance of the Pompeians in 45 B.C., he came to Rome and was made dictator and consul for 10 years. Conspirators, led by Marcus Junius Brutus, stabbed him to death at the Theater of Pompey on March 15, 44 B.C., the "Ides of March." The site (at Largo di Torre Argentina) is best known these days as the home of a photogenic feral cat colony.

The conspirators' motivation was to restore the power of the Republic and topple dictatorship. But they failed: **Mark Antony,** a Roman general, assumed control. He made peace with Caesar's willed successor, **Octavian,** and after the Treaty of Brundisium dissolved the Republic, found himself married to Octavian's sister, Octavia. This marriage, however, didn't prevent him from also marrying Cleopatra in 36 B.C. A furious Octavian gathered the legions and defeated Antony at the **Battle of Actium** on September 2, 31 B.C. Cleopatra fled to Egypt, followed by Antony, who committed suicide in disgrace a year later. Cleopatra, unable to seduce his successor and thus retain her rule of Egypt, followed suit with the help of an asp. The permanent end of the Republic was nigh.

The Campidoglio, on the Capitoline Hill.

Many of the standing buildings of ancient Rome date to periods after the Republic, but parts of the **Roman Forum** (p. 90) were built under the Republic, including the **Temple of Saturn.** The adjacent **Capitoline Hill** and **Palatine Hill** have been sacred religious and civic places since the earliest days of Rome. Rome's best artifacts from the days of the Republic are housed inside the **Musei Capitolini** (p. 86). The greatest exponent of political oratory in the period was **Marcus Tullius Cicero** (106–43 B.C.), who wrote widely on philosophy and statesmanship. He was killed after expressing outspoken opposition to Mark Antony, in his "Philippics."

The Roman Empire in Its Pomp: 27 B.C.–A.D. 395

Born Gaius Octavius in 63 B.C., and later known as Octavian, **Augustus** became the first Roman emperor in 27 B.C. and reigned until A.D. 14. His autocratic rule ushered in the *Pax Romana,* 2 centuries of peace. In Rome you can still see the remains of the **Forum of Augustus** (p. 89) and admire his statue in the **Vatican Museums** (p. 78).

By now, Rome ruled the entire Mediterranean world, either directly or indirectly. All political, commercial, and cultural pathways led straight to Rome, a sprawling city set on seven hills: the Capitoline, Palatine, Aventine, Caelian, Esquiline, Quirinal, and Viminal. It was in this period that **Virgil** wrote his epic poem, "The Aeneid," which supplied a grandiose founding myth for the great city and its empire. Also in this prosperous era, **Ovid** composed his erotic poetry and **Horace** wrote his "Odes."

The emperors brought Rome to new heights. But without the checks and balances formerly provided by the Senate and legislatures, success led to corruption. These centuries witnessed a steady decay in the ideals and traditions on which the Empire had been founded. The army became a fifth column of unruly mercenaries, and for every good emperor (Augustus, Claudius, Trajan, Vespasian, and Hadrian, to name a few) there were several cruel, debased, or incompetent tyrants (Caligula, Nero, Caracalla, and many others).

After Augustus died (by poison, perhaps), his widow, **Livia**—a shrewd operator who had divorced her first husband to marry Augustus—set up her son, **Tiberius,** as ruler through intrigues and poisonings. A series of murders and purges ensued, and Tiberius, who ruled during Pontius Pilate's trial and crucifixion of Christ, was eventually murdered in his late '70s. Murder was so common that a short time later, **Domitian** (ruled A.D. 81–96) became so obsessed with the possibility of assassination that he had the walls of his palace covered in mica so that he could see behind him at all times. (He was killed anyway.)

Excesses ruled the day—at least, if you believe tracts written by contemporary chroniclers with all kinds of bias: **Caligula** supposedly committed incest with his sister, Drusilla, appointed his horse to the Senate, lavished money on egotistical projects, and proclaimed himself a god. Caligula's successor, his uncle **Claudius,** was poisoned by his final

EARLY ROMAN emperors

Caligula (r. A.D. 37–41): Young emperor whose reign of cruelty and terror ended when he was assassinated by his Praetorian guard

Nero (r. A.D. 54–68): The last emperor of the Julio-Claudian dynasty was another cruel megalomaniac. He killed his own mother and was blamed—probably unjustly—for starting the Great Fire of Rome (A.D. 64)

Vespasian (r. A.D. 69–79): First emperor of the Flavian dynasty, who built the Colosseum (p. 88) and lived as husband-and-wife with a freed slave, Caenis

Domitian (r. A.D. 81–96): Increasingly paranoid authoritarian and populist who became fixated on the idea that he would be assassinated—and was proven right

Trajan (r. A.D. 98–117): Virtuous soldier-ruler who presided over the moment Rome was at its geographically grandest scale, and also rebuilt much of the city

Hadrian (r. A.D. 113–138): Humanist, general, and builder who redesigned the Pantheon (p. 100) and added the Temple of Venus and Roma to the Forum

Marcus Aurelius (r. A.D. 161–180): Philosopher-king, and the last of the so-called "Five Good Emperors," whose statue is exhibited in the Musei Capitolini (p. 86)

wife—his niece Agrippina the Younger—to secure the succession of **Nero,** her son by a previous marriage. Nero's thanks were to later murder not only his mother but also his wife (Claudius's daughter) and his rival, Claudius's 13-year-old son, Britannicus. Also an enthusiastic persecutor of Christians, Nero committed suicide with the cry, "What an artist I destroy!"

By the 3rd century, rivalry and corruption had become so prevalent that there were 23 emperors in 73 years. Few, however, were as twisted as **Caracalla,** who, to secure control, had his brother Geta slashed to pieces while Geta was in the arms of his mother, the former empress Julia Domna.

Constantine the Great became emperor in A.D. 306, and in 330 he made Constantinople (or Byzantium) the new capital of the Empire, moving administrative functions away from Rome altogether, partly because the menace of possible barbarian attacks in the west had increased. Constantine was the first Christian emperor, allegedly converting after he saw the "True Cross" in a dream, accompanied by the words "in this sign shall you conquer." He defeated rival emperor Maxentius and his followers at the **Battle of the Milivan Bridge** (A.D. 312), a victory that's remembered by Rome's triumphal **Arco di Costantino** (p. 84). Constantine formally ended the persecution of Christians with the **Edict of Milan** (A.D. 313).

It was during the Imperial period that Rome flourished in architecture, advancing in size and majesty far beyond earlier cities built by the Greeks. **Classical orders** were simplified into forms of column capital: **Doric** (a plain capital), **Ionic** (a capital with a scroll), and **Corinthian** (a capital with flowering acanthus). Much of this advance in building

Trajan's Column.

prowess was due to the discovery of a form of concrete and the fine-tuning of the arch, which was used with a logic, rhythm, and ease never before seen. Many of these monumental buildings still stand in Rome, notably **Trajan's Column** (p. 90), the **Colosseum** (p. 88), and Hadrian's **Pantheon** (p. 100). Elsewhere in Italy, Verona's **Arena** (p. 453) bears witness to the kinds of crowds that the brutal sport of gladiatorial combat could draw. Three **Roman cities** have been preserved, with street plans and, in some cases even buildings remaining intact: doomed **Pompeii** (p. 620) and its neighbor **Herculaneum** (p. 616), both buried by Vesuvius's massive A.D. 79 eruption, and Rome's ancient seaport, **Ostia Antica** (p. 156). It was at Herculaneum that one of Rome's greatest writers perished, **Pliny the Elder** (A.D. 23–79). It's thanks to him, his nephew, **Pliny the Younger,** the historians **Tacitus, Suetonius, Cassius Dio,** and **Livy,** and satirist **Juvenal,** that much of our knowledge of ancient Roman life and history was not lost.

The surviving Roman **art** had a major influence on the painters and sculptors of the Renaissance (see below). In Rome itself, look for the marble bas-reliefs (sculptures that project slightly from a flat surface) on the **Arco di Costantino** (p. 84), the sculpture and mosaic collections at the **Palazzo Massimo alle Terme** (p. 112), and the gilded equestrian statue of Marcus Aurelius at the **Musei Capitolini** (p. 86). The Florentine Medici rulers were avid collectors of Roman statuary, much now at the **Uffizi** (p. 176). Naples's **Museo Archeologico Nazionale** (p. 591) houses the world's most extraordinary collection of Roman art, preserved for centuries under the lava at Pompeii.

The Fall of the Empire through the "Dark Ages"

The Eastern and Western sections of the Roman Empire split in A.D. 395, leaving the Italian peninsula without the support it had once received from east of the Adriatic. When the **Goths** moved toward Rome in the early 5th century, citizens in the provinces, who had grown to hate the bureaucracy set up by **Emperor Diocletian,** initially welcomed the invaders. And then the pillage began.

Rome was first sacked by **Alaric I,** king of the Visigoths, in A.D. 410. The populace made no attempt to defend the city, other than trying in

ALL ABOUT vino

Italy is the largest **wine**-producing country in the world; as far back as 800 B.C. the Etruscans were vintners. However, it wasn't until 1965 that laws were enacted to guarantee consistency in winemaking. Quality wines are labeled **"DOC"** (Denominazione di Origine Controllata). If you see **"DOCG"** on a label (the "G" means *garantita*), it denotes an even better quality wine region. **"IGT"** (Indicazione Geografica Tipica) indicates a more general wine zone—for example, "Umbria"—but still with mandatory quality control.

Tuscany: Tuscan red wines rank with some of the finest in the world. **Sangiovese** is the prince of grapes here, and **chianti** from the hills south of Florence is the most widely known sangiovese wine. The premium zone is **Chianti Classico,** where a lively ruby-red wine partners with a bouquet of violets. The Tuscan south houses two even finer DOCGs: mighty, robust **Brunello di Montalcino,** a garnet-red ideal for roasts and game; and almost purple **Vino Nobile di Montepulciano,** which has a rich, velvet body. End a meal with the Tuscan dessert wine called **vin santo,** which is often accompanied by hard *biscotti* to dunk into your glass.

Veneto and Lombardy: Reds around Venice and the Lakes vary from light and lunchtime-friendly **Bardolino** to **Valpolicella,** which can be particularly intense if the grapes are partly dried before fermentation to make an **Amarone.** White, garganega-based **Soave** has a pale amber color and a velvety flavor. **Prosecco** is the classic Italian sparkling white, and the base for both a Bellini and a Spritz (joints that use Champagne are doing it wrong!).

Piedmont: The finest reds in Italy probably hail from the vine-clad slopes of Piedmont, particularly those made from the late-ripening **Nebbiolo** grape in the Langhe hills south of Alba. The big names—with big flavors and big price tags—are **Barbaresco** (brilliant ruby red with a delicate flavor) and **Barolo** (also brilliant ruby red, and gaining finesse when it mellows into a velvety old age).

The South and Sicily: From the volcanic soil around Vesuvius, the wines of **Campania** have been extolled for 2,000 years. Homer praised **Falerno,** straw yellow in color. The key DOCG wines from Campania these days are **Greco di Tufo** (a mouth-filling, full white) and **Fiano di Avellino** (subtler and more floral). The wines of **Sicily**—once called a "paradise of the grape"—were extolled by the ancient poets, and table wines here are improving after a drop in quality (though not quantity). Sicily is also the home of **Marsala,** a fortified wine first popularized by British port traders and now served with desserts; it also makes a great sauce for cooking veal.

vain to buy him off (a tactic that had worked 3 years earlier); most people fled into the hills. The feeble Western emperor **Honorius** hid out in **Ravenna** the entire time, which from A.D. 402 he had made the new capital of the Western Roman Empire.

More than 40 troubled years passed. Then **Attila the Hun** invaded Italy to besiege Rome. Attila was dissuaded from attacking, thanks largely to a peace mission headed by Pope Leo I in A.D. 452. Yet relief was short-lived: In A.D. 455, **Gaiseric,** king of the **Vandals,** carried out a 2-week sack that was unparalleled in its savagery. The empire of the West lasted for only another 20 years; finally, in A.D. 476, the sacks and chaos ended the once-mighty city, and Rome itself was left to the popes, though it was ruled nominally from Ravenna by an Exarch from Byzantium (aka Constantinople).

Although little detailed history of Italy in the immediate post-Roman period is known—and few buildings survive—it's certain that the spread of **Christianity** was gradually creating a new society. The religion was probably founded in Rome about a decade after the death of Jesus, and gradually gained strength despite early (and enthusiastic) persecution by the Romans. The best way today to relive the early Christian era is to visit Rome's Appian Way and its Catacombs, along the **Via Appia Antica** (p. 118). According to Christian tradition, it was here that an escaping Peter encountered his vision of Christ. The **Catacombs** (p. 118) were the first cemeteries of the Christian community of Rome, housing the remains of early popes and martyrs.

We have Christianity, along with the influence of Byzantium, to thank for the appearance of Italy's next great artistic style: the **Byzantine.** Painting and mosaic work in this era was very stylized and static, but also ornate and ethereal. The most accomplished examples of Byzantine art are found in the churches of **Ravenna** (p. 370). Later buildings in the Byzantine style include Venice's **Basilica di San Marco** (p. 398).

The Middle Ages: 9th Century to the 14th Century

A ravaged Rome entered the Middle Ages, its population scattered. A modest number of residents continued to live in the swamps of the **Campus Martius.** The seven hills—now without water because the aqueducts were cut—stood abandoned and crumbling.

The Pope turned toward Europe, where he found a powerful ally in **Charlemagne,** king of the Franks. In A.D. 800, Pope Leo III crowned him emperor. That didn't mean Rome was back in the big-time, however: Charlemagne ruled his empire from Aachen, in what's now northwest Germany. And although Charlemagne pledged allegiance to the church and looked to Rome and its pope as the final arbiter in most religious and

A Growing Taste for Beer

Italy will always be known, and adored, for its wine. But one gastronomic trend to watch for as you travel is the growth in popularity of artisanal beer, especially among the young. Although supermarket shelves are still stacked with mainstream brands like Peroni and Moretti, smaller stores and bars increasingly offer craft microbrews (known as *birre artigianali*). Italy had fewer than 50 breweries in 2000. That figure was almost 500 by 2016, and is still rising. Craft-beer consumption has more than tripled since 2012, according to data released by brewers' association Unionbirrai. You'll even find quality beers on the hallowed shelves of the occasional wine vendor.

cultural affairs, he also launched Western Europe on a course toward bitter opposition to papal meddling in affairs of state.

The successor to Charlemagne's empire was a political entity known as the **Holy Roman Empire** (A.D. 962–1806). The new Empire defined the end of the Dark Ages but ushered in a long period of bloody warfare. Magyars from Hungary invaded northeastern Lombardy and, in turn, were defeated by an increasingly powerful **Venice.** This was the great era of Venetian preeminence in the eastern Mediterranean; it defeated naval rival **Genoa** in the 1380 Battle of Chioggia; great buildings like the **Doge's Palace** (p. 402) were built; its merchants reigned over most of the eastern Mediterranean, and presided over a republic that lasted for a millennium. The Lion of St. Mark—symbol of the city's dominion—can be seen as far away as **Bergamo** (p. 483), close to Milan.

Rome during the Middle Ages was a quaint backwater. Narrow lanes with overhanging buildings filled many areas that had once been showcases of imperial power. The forums, mercantile exchanges, temples, and theaters of the Imperial era slowly disintegrated. It remained the seat of the Roman Catholic Church, and the state was almost completely controlled by priests, who began an aggressive expansion of church influence and acquisitions. The result was an endless series of power struggles. Between 1378 and 1417, competing popes—one in Rome, another **"antipope"** in Avignon—made simultaneous claims to the legacy of St. Peter.

Normans gained military control of Sicily from the Arabs in the 11th century, divided it from the rest of Italy, and altered forever the island's ethnic makeup. The reign of **Roger II of Sicily** (r. A.D. 1130–54) is remembered for religious tolerance and the multiracial nature of the court, as well as its architecture. The **Palazzo dei Normanni** (p. 739), in Palermo, and nearby **Monreale** (p. 748), are just two among many great projects the Normans left behind.

In the mid–14th century, the **Black Death** ravaged Europe, killing perhaps a third of Italy's population; the unique preservation of Tuscan towns like **San Gimignano** (p. 272) and **Siena** (p. 225) owes much to the fact that they never fully recovered after the devastation dished out by the 1348–49 plague. Despite such setbacks, Italian **city-states** grew wealthy from Crusade booty, trade, and banking. The **Florin,** a gold coin minted in Florence, became the first truly international currency for centuries, and dominated trade all over the continent.

The medieval period marks the beginning of building in stone on a mass scale. Flourishing from A.D. 800 to 1300, **Romanesque** architecture took its inspiration and rounded arches from Ancient Rome. Architects built large churches with wide aisles to accommodate the masses. Pisa's **Campo dei Miracoli** (1153–1360s; p. 295) is typical of the Pisan-Romanesque style, with stacked arcades of mismatched columns in the cathedral's facade (and wrapped around the **Leaning Tower of Pisa**), and blind arcading set with diamond-shaped lozenges. The influence of Arab architecture is obvious; Pisa was a city of seafaring merchants.

Romanesque **sculpture** was fluid but still far from naturalistic. Often wonderfully childlike in its narrative simplicity, the works frequently mix biblical scenes with the myths and motifs of local pagan traditions that were being incorporated into medieval Christianity. The 48 relief panels of the bronze doors of the **Basilica di San Zeno Maggiore** in Verona (p. 453) rank among Italy's greatest surviving examples of Romanesque sculpture. The exterior of Parma's **Baptistery** (p. 479) has Romanesque friezes by Benedetto Antelami (1150–1230).

As the appeal of Romanesque and Byzantine faded, the **Gothic** style flourished from the 13th to the 15th centuries. In architecture, the Gothic was characterized by flying buttresses, pointed arches, and delicate stained-glass windows. These engineering developments freed architecture from the heavy, thick walls of the Romanesque and allowed ceilings to soar, walls to thin, and windows to proliferate.

Although the Gothic age continued to be religious, many secular buildings also arose, including palaces designed to show off the prestige of various ruling families. Siena's civic **Palazzo Pubblico** (p. 233) and many of the great buildings of **Venice** (see chapter 9) date from this period. **San Gimignano** (p. 272), in Tuscany, has a preserved Gothic center. Milan's **Duomo** (p. 466) is one of Europe's great Gothic cathedrals.

Painters such as **Cimabue** (1251–1302) and **Giotto** (1266–1337), in Florence, **Pietro Cavallini** (1259–ca. 1330) in Rome, and **Duccio di Buoninsegna** (ca. 1255–1319) in Siena, began to lift art from Byzantine rigidity and set it on the road to realism. Giotto's finest work is his fresco cycle at Padua's **Cappella degli Scrovegni** (p. 449); he was the true harbinger of the oncoming Renaissance, which would forever change art and architecture. Duccio's 1311 "Maestà," now in Siena's **Museo dell'Opera Metropolitana** (p. 175), influenced Sienese painters for centuries. Ambrogio Lorenzetti painted the greatest civic frescoes of the Middle Ages—his "Allegories of Good and Bad Government" in Siena's

Siena's scallop-shell-shaped Piazza del Campo, fronting the Palazzo Pubblico.

Palazzo Pubblico (p. 233)—before he succumbed to the Black Death, along with almost every significant Sienese artist of his generation.

The medieval period also saw the birth of literature in the Italian language, which itself was a written version of the **Tuscan dialect,** primarily because the great writers of the age were Tuscans. Florentine **Dante Alighieri** wrote his "Divine Comedy" in the 1310s. Boccaccio's "Decameron"—a kind of Florentine "Canterbury Tales"—appeared in the 1350s.

Renaissance & Baroque Italy

The story of Italy from the dawn of the Renaissance in the early 15th century to the "Age of Enlightenment" in the 17th and 18th centuries is as fascinating and complicated as that of the rise and fall of the Roman Empire.

During this period, **Rome** underwent major physical changes. The old centers of culture reverted to pastures and fields, and great churches and palaces were built with the stones of Ancient Rome. Cows grazed on the crumbling Roman Forum. The city's construction boom did more damage to the ancient temples than any barbarian sack had done. Rare marbles were stripped from Imperial-era baths and used as altarpieces or sent to lime kilns for "recycling." So enthusiastic was the popes' destruction of Imperial Rome, it's a genuine miracle that anything is left.

Milan was a glorious Renaissance capital, particularly under the Sforza dynasty and Ludovico "Il Moro" (1452–1508), patron of Leonardo da Vinci. Smaller but still significant centers of power included the Gonzaga family's **Mantua** (p. 488) and the Este clan's **Ferrara** (p. 361).

This era is best remembered because of its art, and around 1400 the most significant power in Italy was the city where the Renaissance began: **Florence** (see chapter 5). Slowly but surely, the **Medici** family rose to become the most powerful of the city's ruling oligarchy, gradually usurping the powers of the guilds and the republicans. They reformed law and commerce, expanded the city's power by taking control of neighbors such as **Pisa,** and sparked a "renaissance," or rebirth, in painting, sculpture, and architecture. Christopher Hibbert's "The Rise and Fall of the House of Medici" is the most readable detailed account of the era.

Under the patronage of the Medici (as well as other powerful Florentine families), innovative young painters and sculptors went in pursuit of more expressiveness and naturalism. **Donatello** (1386–1466) cast the first freestanding nude since antiquity (a bronze now in Florence's **Museo Nazionale del Bargello,** p. 179). **Lorenzo Ghiberti** (1378–1455) labored for 50 years on two sets of doors for Florence's **Baptistery** (p. 170), the most famous of which were dubbed the "Gates of Paradise." **Masaccio** (1401–28) produced the first painting that realistically portrayed linear perspective, on the nave wall of **Santa Maria Novella** (p. 188).

Next followed the brief period that's become known as the **High Renaissance:** The epitome of the Renaissance man, Florentine **Leonardo da Vinci** (1452–1519), painted his "Last Supper," now in Milan's **Santa Maria delle Grazie** (p. 472), and an "Annunciation" (1481), now hanging in Florence's **Uffizi** (p. 176) alongside countless Renaissance masterpieces from such great painters as Paolo Uccello, Sandro Botticelli, Piero della Francesca, and others. **Raphael** (1483–1520) produced a sublime body of work in his 37 years.

Skilled in sculpture, painting, and architecture, **Michelangelo** (1475–1564) and his career marked the apogee of the Renaissance. His giant "David" at the **Galleria dell'Accademia** (p. 190) in Florence is the world's most famous statue, and the **Sistine Chapel** frescoes lure millions to the **Vatican Museums** (p. 78) in Rome.

Meanwhile in Venice, the father of the Venetian High Renaissance was **Titian** (1485–1576); known for his mastery of color and tone, he was the true heir to the great Venetian painters **Gentile Bellini** (1429–1507), **Giorgione** (1477–1510), and **Vittore Carpaccio** (1465–1525). Many of their masterpieces can be seen around **Venice** (see chapter 9).

As in painting, Renaissance **architecture** stressed proportion, order, classical inspiration, and mathematical precision. **Filippo Brunelleschi** (1377–1446), in the early 1400s, grasped the concept of "perspective" and provided artists with ground rules for creating the illusion of 3D on a flat surface. Ross King's "Brunelleschi's Dome" tells the story of his greatest achievement, the crowning of Florence's cathedral with that iconic ochre dome. Even **Michelangelo** took up architecture late in life, designing the Laurentian Library (1524) and New Sacristy (1524–34) at Florence's **San Lorenzo** (p. 188). He moved south (just as art's center of gravity did) to complete his crowning glory, the soaring dome of Rome's **St. Peter's Basilica** (p. 76).

The third great Renaissance architect—the most influential of them all—was **Andrea Palladio** (1508–80), who worked in a classical mode of columns, porticoes, pediments, and other ancient-temple-inspired features. His masterpieces include fine churches in Venice.

In time, the High Renaissance gradually evolved into the **baroque.** Stuccoes, sculptures, and paintings were carefully designed to complement each other—and the space itself—to create a unified whole. The baroque movement's spiritual home was Rome, and its towering figure was **Gian Lorenzo Bernini** (1598–1680), the greatest baroque sculptor, an accomplished architect, and a more-than-decent painter as well. Among many fine, flowing sculptures, you'll find his best in Rome's **Galleria Borghese** (p. 108) and **Santa Maria della Vittoria** (p. 112). Baroque architecture is especially prominent in the South: in the churches and devotional architecture of **Naples** (p. 577) and in **Siracusa** (p. 762), Sicily. **Turin** (p. 510) under the Savoys was remodeled by the baroque architecture of **Guarino Guarini** (1624–83) and **Filippo Juvarra** (1678–1736). In music, the most famous of the baroque composers is Venetian **Antonio Vivaldi** (1678–1741), whose "Four Seasons" is among the most regularly performed classical compositions of all time.

In painting, many baroque artists mixed a kind of super-realism based on using everyday people as models and an exaggerated use of light

Milan's Duomo.

and dark—a technique called *chiaroscuro*—with compositional complexity and explosions of dynamic fury, movement, and color. The period produced many fine painters, notably **Caravaggio** (1571–1610). Among his masterpieces are a "St. Matthew" (1599) cycle in Rome's **San Luigi dei Francesi** (p. 99) and "The Acts of Mercy" in **Pio Monte della Misericordia** (p. 590), Naples. The baroque era also had an outstanding female painter in **Artemisia Gentileschi** (1593–1652): Her brutal "Judith Slaying Holofernes" (1620) hangs in Florence's **Uffizi** (p. 176).

Frothy and ornate, **rococo** art was the baroque taken to flamboyant extremes, and had few serious proponents in Italy. **Giambattista Tiepolo** (1696–1770) was arguably the best of the rococo painters, and specialized in ceiling frescoes and canvases with cloud-filled heavens of light. He worked extensively in Venice and the northeast. For rococo building—more a decorative than an architectural movement—look no further than Rome's **Spanish Steps** (p. 106) or the **Trevi Fountain** (p. 107).

At Last, a United Italy: The 1800s

By the 1800s, the glories of the Renaissance were a fading memory. From Turin to Naples, chunks of Italy had changed hands many, many times—between the Austrians, the Spanish, and the French, among autocratic thugs and enlightened princes, between the noble and the merchant classes. The 19th century witnessed the final collapse of many Renaissance city-states. The last of the Medici, Gian Gastone, had died in 1737, leaving Tuscany in the hands of foreign Lorraine and Habsburg princes.

French emperor **Napoleon** brought an end to a millennium of republican government in **Venice** in 1797, and installed puppet or client rulers across the Italian peninsula. During the **Congress of Vienna** (1814–15), which followed Napoleon's defeat by an alliance of the British, Prussians, and Dutch, Italy was once again divided.

Political unrest became a fact of Italian life, some of it spurred by the industrialization of the north and some by the encouragement of insurrectionaries like **Giuseppe Mazzini** (1805–72). Europe's year of revolutions, **1848,** rocked Italy, too, with violent uprisings in Lombardy and Sicily. After decades of political machinations and intrigue, and thanks to the efforts of statesman **Camillo Cavour** (1810–61) and rebel general **Giuseppe Garibaldi** (1807–82), the Kingdom of Italy was proclaimed in 1861 and **Victor Emmanuel (Vittorio Emanuele) II** of Savoy became its first monarch. The kingdom's first capital was **Turin** (1861–65), seat of the victorious Piedmontese, followed by **Florence** (1865–71).

The establishment of the kingdom, however, didn't signal a complete unification of Italy because Latium (including Rome) was still under papal control and Venetia was held by Austria. This was partially resolved in 1866, when Venetia joined the rest of Italy after the **Seven Weeks' War** between Austria and Prussia. In 1871, Rome became the capital of the newly formed country, after the city was retaken on September 20, 1870. Present-day **Via XX Settembre** is the very street up which patriots advanced after breaching the city gates. The **Risorgimento**—the "resurgence," Italian unification—was complete.

Political heights in Italy seemed to correspond to historic depths in art and architecture. Among the few notable practitioners of this era, the most well-known is probably Venetian **Antonio Canova** (1757–1822), Italy's major neoclassical sculptor, who became notorious for painting both Napoleon and his sister Pauline as nudes. His best work is in Rome's **Galleria Borghese** (p. 108). Tuscany also bred a late-19th-century precursor to French Impressionism, the **Macchiaioli** movement; see their works in the "modern art" galleries at Florence's **Palazzo Pitti** (p. 194).

THE A-LIST OF italian novels AVAILABLE IN ENGLISH

- Alessandro Manzoni, "The Betrothed" (1827)
- Alberto Moravia, "The Conformist" (1951)
- Giuseppe Tomasi di Lampedusa, "The Leopard" (1958)
- Elsa Morante, "History: A Novel" (1974)
- Italo Calvino, "If on a Winter's Night a Traveler" (1979)
- Umberto Eco, "Foucault's Pendulum" (1988)
- Niccolo Ammaniti, "I'm Not Scared" (2001)
- Elena Ferrante, "Neapolitan Novels" (2012–15)

Via dei Fori Imperiali, built in 1932 on the orders of Benito Mussolini.

If art was hitting an all-time low, **music** was experiencing its Italian golden age. It's **opera** for which the 19th century is largely remembered. *Bel canto* composer **Gioachino Rossini** (1792–1868) was born in Pesaro, in the Marches, and found fame in 1816 with "The Barber of Seville." The fame of **Gaetano Donizetti** (1797–1848), a prolific native of Bergamo, was assured when his "Anna Bolena" premiered in 1830. Both were perhaps overshadowed by **Giuseppe Verdi** (1813–1901), whose arias from such operas as "Rigoletto" and "La Traviata" took on profound nationalist symbolism, and have since become some of the most whistled tunes on the planet.

The 20th Century: Two World Wars & One Duce

In 1915, Italy entered **World War I** on the side of the Allies. Italy joined Britain, Russia, and France to help defeat Germany and the traditional enemy to the north—now known as the Austro-Hungarian Empire—and so to "reclaim" Trentino and Trieste. (Mark Thompson's "The White War" tells the story of Italy's catastrophic campaign.) In the aftermath of wartime carnage, Italians suffered further with rising unemployment and horrendous inflation. As in Germany, a deep political crisis led to the emergence of a dictator.

On October 28, 1922, **Benito Mussolini,** who had started his Fascist Party in 1919, knew the country was ripe for change. He gathered 30,000 Black Shirts for his **March on Rome.** Inflation was soaring and workers had just called a general strike, so rather than recognize a state under siege, **King Victor Emmanuel III** (1900–46) proclaimed Mussolini as the new government leader. In 1929, Il Duce—a moniker Mussolini began using from 1925—defined the divisions between the Italian government and the Pope by signing the Lateran Treaty, which granted political, territorial, and fiscal autonomy to the microstate of **Vatican City.** During the Spanish Civil War (1936–39), Mussolini's support for Franco's Fascists, who had staged a coup against the elected government of Spain, helped seal the Axis alliance between Italy and Nazi Germany. Italy was inexorably and disastrously sucked into **World War II.**

Deeply unpleasant though their politics were, the Fascist regime did sponsor some remarkable **rationalist architecture.** It's at its best in Rome's planned satellite community, **EUR** (p. 117). In a city famed for Renaissance works, Florence's **Santa Maria Novella station** (1934) is another masterpiece—of modernism. Today the station has a plaque commemorating Jews who were sent from the terminus to their deaths in Nazi Germany. The 20th century's towering figure in music was **Giacomo Puccini** (1858–1924), a master of *verismo* ("realism"), a reaction to the dominant Romantic movement of the 1800s. His operas "Tosca" (1900), "Madame Butterfly" (1904), and the unfinished "Turandot" (1924) still pack houses worldwide. He's celebrated with a museum and opera festival in **Lucca,** Tuscany (p. 284).

After defeat in World War II, Italy's people voted for the establishment of the First Republic—overwhelmingly so in northern and central Italy, which counterbalanced a southern majority in favor of keeping the monarchy. Italy quickly succeeded in rebuilding its economy, in part because of U.S. aid under the **Marshall Plan** (1948–52). By the 1960s, as a member of the European Economic Community (founded by the **Treaty of Rome** in 1957), Italy had become one of the world's leading industrialized nations, and prominent in the manufacture of automobiles and office equipment. Fiat (from Turin), Ferrari (from Emilia-Romagna), and Olivetti (from northern Piedmont) were known around the world.

The country was plagued, however, by economic inequality, including between the industrially prosperous North and the depressed South. During the late 1970s and early 1980s, it was also rocked by domestic terrorism: These were the so-called **Anni di Piombo (Years of Lead),** during which extremists of the left and right bombed and assassinated with impunity. Conspiracy theories became an Italian staple diet; everyone from a shadow state to Masonic lodges to the CIA was accused of involvement in what became, in effect, an undeclared civil war. The most notorious incidents were the kidnap and murder of Prime Minister **Aldo Moro** in 1978 and the **Bologna station bombing,** which killed 85 in 1980. You'll find a succinct account of these murky years in Tobias Jones's "The Dark Heart of Italy."

The postwar Italian **film industry** became celebrated for its innovative directors. **Federico Fellini** (1920–93) burst onto the scene with his highly individual style, beginning with "La Strada" (1954) and going on to such classics as "The City of Women" (1980). His "La Dolce Vita" (1961) seems to define an era in Rome. The gritty "neorealism" of the controversial **Pier Paolo Pasolini** (1922–75) is conveyed most vividly in "Accattone" (1961), which he wrote and directed.

In the early 1990s, many of the country's leading politicians were accused of corruption. These scandals uncovered during the judiciary's **Mani Pulite (Clean Hands)** investigations—often dubbed **Tangentopoli** ("Bribesville")—provoked a constitutional crisis, ushering in the **Second Republic** in 1992.

Resonant events in recent Italian history have also centered on religion. As much of the world watched and prayed, **Pope John Paul II** died in April 2005, at the age of 84, ending a reign of 26 years. A doctrinal hardliner next took the papal throne as **Pope Benedict XVI.** He was succeeded by the surprisingly liberal **Pope Francis** in 2013, after Benedict became the first pope to resign since the 1400s.

WHEN TO GO

The best months for traveling in much of Italy are from **April to June** and **mid-September to October**: Temperatures are usually comfortable, rural colors are rich, and the crowds aren't too intense (except around Easter). From **July through early September** the country's holiday spots teem with visitors. **Easter, May,** and **June** usually see the highest hotel prices in Rome and Florence.

August is the worst month in many places: Not only does it get uncomfortably hot, muggy, and crowded, but seemingly the entire country goes on vacation for at least 2 weeks. Many Italians take off the entire month. Plenty of family-run hotels, restaurants, and shops are closed (except at the spas, beaches, and islands, where most Italians head). Paradoxically, you will have many urban places almost to yourself if you visit in August. Turin and Milan in particular can seem virtual ghost towns, and even excellent hotels there are heavily discounted. (Florence and Rome are no longer as quiet as they once were.) Just be aware that many fashionable restaurants and nightspots are closed for the whole month.

From **late October to Easter,** many attractions operate on shorter winter hours, and some hotels are closed for renovation or redecoration, though inconvenience is much less likely if you are visiting a city. Many family-run restaurants take a week or two off sometime between **November and February;** spa and beach destinations become padlocked ghost towns.

Weather

It's warm all over Italy in summer; it can be very hot in the south, and almost anywhere inland. Landlocked cities on the plains of Veneto, Lombardy, and Emilia-Romagna, and in Tuscany and Umbria, feel stifling during a July or August hot spell. The higher temperatures (measured in Italy in degrees Celsius) usually begin everywhere in May, often lasting until sometime in October. Winters in the north of Italy are cold, with rain and snow. A biting wind whistles over the mountains into Milan, Turin, and Venice. Florence likewise, though less regularly. In Rome and the south the weather is warm (or at least, warm-ish) almost all year, averaging 10°C (50°F) in winter. But even here chilly snaps are possible, as widespread freezing temperatures and heavy snow in early 2017 showed.

The rainiest months pretty much everywhere are usually October and November.

Italy's Average Daily High Temperature & Monthly Rainfall

ROME	JAN	FEB	MAR	APR	MAY	JUNE	JULY	AUG	SEPT	OCT	NOV	DEC
TEMP. (°F)	55	56	59	63	71	77	83	83	79	71	62	57
TEMP. (°C)	12	13	15	17	21	25	28	28	26	21	16	13
RAINFALL (IN.)	3.2	2.8	2.7	2.6	2	1.3	.6	1	2.7	4.5	4.4	3.8

FLORENCE	JAN	FEB	MAR	APR	MAY	JUNE	JULY	AUG	SEPT	OCT	NOV	DEC
TEMP. (°F)	49	53	60	68	75	84	89	88	81	69	58	50
TEMP. (°C)	9	11	15	20	23	28	31	31	27	20	14	10
RAINFALL (IN.)	1.9	2.1	2.7	2.9	3	2.7	1.5	1.9	3.3	4	3.9	2.8

VENICE	JAN	FEB	MAR	APR	MAY	JUNE	JULY	AUG	SEPT	OCT	NOV	DEC
TEMP. (°F)	42	47	54	61	70	77	81	81	75	65	53	44
TEMP. (°C)	6	8	12	16	21	25	27	27	24	18	11	7
RAINFALL (IN.)	2.3	2.1	2.2	2.5	2.7	3	2.5	3.3	2.6	2.7	3.4	2.1

Public Holidays

Offices, government buildings (though not usually tourist offices), and shops in Italy are generally closed on: January 1 (*Capodanno,* or New Year); January 6 (*La Befana,* or Epiphany); Easter Sunday (*Pasqua*); Easter Monday (*Pasquetta*); April 25 (Liberation Day); May 1 (*Festa del Lavoro,* or Labor Day); June 2 (*Festa della Repubblica,* or Republic Day); August 15 (*Ferragosto,* or the Assumption of the Virgin); November 1 (All Saints' Day); December 8 (*L'Immacolata,* or the Immaculate Conception); December 25 (*Natale,* Christmas Day); December 26 (*Santo Stefano,* or St. Stephen's Day). You'll often find businesses closed for the annual daylong celebration dedicated to a local patron saint (for example, on January 31 in San Gimignano, Tuscany).

Historic gondolas open Venice's Regata Storica.

Italy Calendar of Events

JANUARY

Festa di Sant'Agnese, Sant'Agnese Fuori le Mura, Rome. In this ancient ceremony, two lambs are blessed and shorn; their wool is used later for *palliums* (Roman Catholic vestments). January 21.

FEBRUARY

Carnevale, Venice. At this riotous time, theatrical presentations and masked balls take place throughout Venice and on islands in the lagoon. The balls are by invitation only (except the Doge's Ball), but the street events and fireworks are open to everyone. www.carnevale.venezia.it. The week before Ash Wednesday, the beginning of Lent.

Festival della Canzone Italiana (Festival of Italian Popular Song), San Remo, Liguria. At this 6-day competition, major artists perform previously unreleased Italian songs. www.sanremo.rai.it. Late February.

MARCH

Festa di San Giuseppe, the Trionfale Quarter, Rome. A decorated statue of the saint is brought out at a fair with food stalls, concerts, and sporting events. Usually March 19.

APRIL

Holy Week, nationwide. Processions and age-old ceremonies, some from pagan days, some from the Middle Ages. The most notable procession is led by the Pope, passing the Colosseum and Roman Forum; a torch-lit parade caps the observance. Beginning a week before Easter Sunday; sometimes late March but often April.

Easter Sunday (Pasqua), Piazza San Pietro, Rome. In an event broadcast around the world, the Pope gives his blessing from the balcony of St. Peter's.

Scoppio del Carro (Explosion of the Cart), Florence. At this ancient observance, a cart laden with flowers and fireworks is drawn by three white oxen to the Duomo. At the noon Mass, a mechanical dove detonates it. Easter Sunday.

MAY

Maggio Musicale Fiorentino (Florentine Musical May), Florence. Italy's oldest and most prestigious music festival emphasizes music from the 14th to the 20th centuries, and presents ballet and opera. www.maggiofiorentino.it. Late April to end of June.

Giro d'Italia, nationwide. Road cycling is second only to soccer in national sporting affections. One of Europe's three great endurance races, this month-long event celebrated its 100th staging in 2017. www.giroditalia.it.

Mille Miglia, Brescia, Lombardy. Vintage and classic cars depart Brescia and spend 4 days parading around the towns and cities of northern and central Italy as part of the annual "1000 Miles." www.1000miglia.eu. Mid-May.

Concorso Ippico Internazionale (International Horse Show), Piazza di Siena, Rome. Top-flight international equestrian show held in the Villa Borghese. www.piazzadisiena.it. Late May.

JUNE

Festa di San Ranieri, Pisa, Tuscany. The city honors its patron saint with candlelit parades, followed the next day by eight-rower teams competing in 16th-century costumes. June 16 and 17.

Calcio Storico (Historic Football), Florence. A revival of a raucous 15th-century form of football, pitting four teams in medieval costumes against one another. The matches usually culminate on June 24, the feast day of St. John the Baptist. Late June.

Gioco del Ponte, Pisa, Tuscany. Teams in Renaissance costume take part in a long-contested "push-of-war" on the Ponte di Mezzo, which spans the River Arno. Last Sunday in June.

Arena di Verona Opera Festival, Verona, Veneto. The 20,000-seat remains of Verona's Roman-era amphitheater is the venue for Italy's most famous outdoor opera season, now over 100 years old. www.arena.it. Late June to late August.

Biennale Arte, Venice. One of the most famous recurring art events in the world takes place every 2 years (in odd-numbered years). Even-numbered years see related events, including Biennale Architettura. www.labiennale.org. June to November.

JULY

Il Palio, Piazza del Campo, Siena, Tuscany. Palio fever grips this Tuscan hill town for a wild and exciting horse race dating from the Middle Ages. Pageantry, costumes, and the celebrations of the victorious *contrada* (sort of a neighborhood social club) mark the spectacle. It's a "no rules" event: Even a horse without a rider can win the race. July 2.

Umbria Jazz, Perugia, Umbria. One of Europe's top jazz festivals always attracts top-class artists. www.umbriajazz.com. July.

Puccini Festival, Torre del Lago, Tuscany. An outdoor lakeside venue is the stage for the Tuscan maestro's blockbuster operas. www.puccinifestival.it. Mid-July to mid-August.

Festa del Redentore (Feast of the Redeemer), Venice. This festival marks the lifting of a plague in 1576, with fireworks, pilgrimages, and boating. www.redentorevenezia.it. Third Saturday and Sunday of July.

AUGUST

Il Palio, Piazza del Campo, Siena, Tuscany. See July (above). This second annual staging is dedicated to the Assumption of the Virgin Mary. August 16.

Venice International Film Festival, Venice. Ranking second after Cannes, this festival brings together stars, directors, producers, and filmmakers from all over the world to the Palazzo del Cinema on the Lido. Although many seats are reserved for jury members, the public can attend, too. www.labiennale.org/en/cinema. Late August to early September.

SEPTEMBER

Regata Storica, Grand Canal, Venice. A maritime spectacular: Many gondolas participate in the canal procession, although gondolas don't race in the regatta itself. www.regatastoricavenezia.it. First Sunday in September.

Festa di San Gennaro, Naples, Campania. The cathedral is the focal point for this celebration in honor of the city's patron saint. Three times a year a solemn procession is followed by the miraculous "liquefaction" of the holy blood. September 19, December 16, and 1st Sunday in May.

Palio di Asti, Asti, Piedmont. Riders race for Italy's "second" Palio around the central square of a provincial Piedmont town. Expect medieval pageantry and daring horsemanship in an event with 800 years of history. Third Sunday in September.

DECEMBER

La Scala Opera Season Opening, Teatro alla Scala, Milan. At the most famous house of them all, the season begins each December 7, the feast day of Milan's patron, St. Ambrose. It runs into the following July, then September to mid-November. Even though opening-night tickets are almost impossible to find, it is worth a try. www.teatroallascala.org.

Christmas Blessing of the Pope, Piazza San Pietro, Rome. Delivered at noon from the balcony of St. Peter's Basilica, the Pope's words are broadcast to the faithful around the globe. December 25.

SUGGESTED ITALY ITINERARIES

3

By Donald Strachan

Italy is vast and treasure-filled, so it's hard to resist the temptation to pack too much into too short a time. This is a dauntingly diverse destination, and you can't even skim the surface in 1 or 2 weeks—so relax, and don't try. If you're a first-time visitor with little touring time on your hands, we suggest you go just for the classic cities: Rome, Florence, and Venice could be packed into 1 very busy week, better yet in 2.

How can you accomplish that? Well, for starters, Italy has well-maintained highways (called *autostrade*). You'll pay a toll to drive on them (p. 796), but it's much quicker to use them than to trust your limited time to the minor roads, which can be *much* slower going.

The country also boasts one of the most efficient high-speed rail networks in Europe. Rome, Bologna, and Milan are the key hubs of this 21st-century transportation empire—for example, from Rome's Termini station, Florence can be reached in only 95 minutes. If you're city-hopping between Rome, Florence, and Venice, you need never rent a car, as key routes are served by comfortable, quick trains. You'll only require a rental car for rural detours.

The itineraries that follow introduce some of our favorite places. The pace may occasionally be a bit breathless for some visitors, so consider skipping a stop to take some chill-out time—after all, you're on vacation. Of course, you can also use any itinerary as a jumping-off point to develop your own custom-made adventure. *Buon viaggio!*

The baroque Trevi Fountain, a tourist gathering spot in Rome.

THE REGIONS IN BRIEF

Although bordered on the northwest by France, on the north by Switzerland and Austria, and on the northeast by Slovenia, Italy is largely surrounded by the sea. It isn't enormous; the peninsula's slender boot shape gives the impression of a much larger area. Here's a brief rundown of the cities and regions covered in this guide. See the inside front cover for a map of Italy by region.

FACING PAGE: **Vatican Museums.**

ROME & LATIUM The region of **Latium** ("Lazio" in Italian) is dominated by **Rome,** capital of both the ancient empire and modern Italy. Much of the "civilized world" was once ruled from here, starting from when Romulus and Remus are said to have founded Rome, in 753 B.C. No place has more artistic monuments, or a bigger buzz—not even Venice or Florence.

FLORENCE, TUSCANY & UMBRIA **Tuscany** is one of Italy's most culturally and politically influential provinces. The development of Italy without Tuscany is simply unthinkable; in fact, today's Italian language is essentially an update of the medieval Florentine dialect. Nowhere in the world is the impact of the Renaissance still felt more fully than in **Florence,** the repository of artistic works by Masaccio, Leonardo da Vinci, Michelangelo, and many others. The main Tuscan destinations beyond Florence are the smaller cities of **Lucca, Pisa,** and especially **Siena,** Florence's great historical rival, as well as the **Chianti** winelands. Neighboring **Umbria** is a land of rolling green hills and olive groves, where the pace of life is sedate. It has outstanding art sights in **Perugia** and the former Etruscan stronghold of **Orvieto.**

BOLOGNA & EMILIA-ROMAGNA Italians don't agree on much, but one national consensus is that the food in **Emilia-Romagna** is the best in Italy. Probably. The regional capital, **Bologna,** also has museums, churches, and a fine university with roots in the Middle Ages. Among the region's other cities, none is nobler than Byzantine **Ravenna,** with mosaics dating to the time when it was capital of a Roman Empire in decline.

VENICE & THE VENETO Northeastern Italy is one of Europe's treasure troves, encompassing **Venice** (certainly the world's most unusual city) and the surrounding **Veneto** region. Aging, decaying, and sinking into the sea, Venice is so alluring we almost want to say visit it even if you have to skip Rome and Florence. Also recommended are the art cities of the "Venetian Arc": **Verona,** with its Shakespearean romance and intact Roman amphitheater hosting a famous summer opera festival; and **Padua,** with its Giotto frescoes on the walls of the Cappella degli Scrovegni.

LOMBARDY, PIEDMONT & THE LAKES Flat, fertile, and prosperous, **Lombardy** is dominated by **Milan.** However, despite Leonardo's "Last Supper," the La Scala opera house, shopping, and some major museums, Milan doesn't have the sights of Rome, Florence, or Venice. Still, Expo 2015 left a legacy of much improved tourist services, and its crop of artworks is impressive. You'll find charm (and a more manageable area to cover) in the nearby cities of **Bergamo** and **Mantua.** Also competing for your time should be the photogenic lakes of **Como** and **Garda.**

Piedmont's largest city, **Turin,** is the home of the Fiat empire. Its best-known sight is the Sacra Sindone (Holy Shroud), which some Christians believe is the cloth in which Christ's crucified body was wrapped.

LIGURIA Comprising most of the **Italian Riviera,** the region of **Liguria** incorporates the major historical seaport of **Genoa,** charming, upscale resorts such as the harbor at **Portofino,** and Italy's best coastal hiking, among the traditional villages of the **Cinque Terre.**

CAMPANIA, PUGLIA & BASILICATA **Campania** encompasses both the fascinating anarchy of **Naples** and the elegant beauty of **Capri** and the **Amalfi Coast.** The region has sites identified in ancient mythology (lakes defined as the entrance to the Kingdom of the Dead, for example) as well as some of the world's most renowned ruins, at **Pompeii** and **Herculaneum.** Cave dwellings that pepper **Matera,** in **Basilicata**—the *Sassi*—have been inhabited almost continuously since the Paleolithic Era. Over the centuries, streets and staircases, troglodyte homes, and even a 13th-century cathedral have been hewn from the rock. These days you can walk, dine, and stay in the Sassi, one of Europe's most remarkable neighborhoods. **Puglia** (sometimes called "Apulia" in English) is home to the conical *trulli* houses of **Alberobello** and the Valle d'Itria, and the baroque architecture of **Lecce**—sometimes nicknamed (just a little ambitiously) "the Florence of the South."

SICILY The largest island in the Mediterranean Sea, **Sicily** has a unique mix of bloodlines and architecture from medieval Normandy, Aragónese Spain, Moorish North Africa, Ancient Greece, Phoenicia, and Rome. Cars and fashionable people clog the lanes of its capital, **Palermo.** Areas of ravishing beauty and eerie historical interest include **Syracuse** (Siracusa in Italian), **Taormina,** and the ruins at **Agrigento** and **Selinunte.** Sicily's ancient ruins are rivaled only by those of Rome itself.

THE BEST OF ITALY IN 1 WEEK: ROME, FLORENCE & VENICE

Let's be realistic: It's impossible to see these storied cities properly in a week. However, a fast, efficient rail network along the Rome–Florence–Venice line makes it surprisingly easy to see a handful of the best that these elegant, art-stuffed cities have to offer. This weeklong itinerary treads the familiar highlights, but there's a reason why they are the country's most visited sights: They're sure to provide memories that will last a lifetime.

DAYS 1, 2 & 3: Rome: Capital, Ancient & Modern ★★★

You could spend forever in the Eternal City, but 3 days is enough to catch a flavor of it. There are two essential areas to focus on in a short visit. The first is the legacy of Imperial Rome, such as the **Forum, Campidoglio,** and **Colosseum** (p. 88). Bookend **DAY 1** with the Forum and Colosseum (one first, the other last) to avoid the busiest crowds; the same ticket is good for both. On **DAY 2,** tackle **St. Peter's Basilica** and the **Vatican Museums** (p. 78), with a collection unlike any other in the world that, of course, includes Michelangelo's **Sistine Chapel.** On **DAY 3,** it's a toss-up: Choose between the underground catacombs of the **Via Appia Antica** (p. 118); or spend

the day wandering the **Centro Storico** (p. 97) and the **Tridente** (p. 103), on the well-trod streets connecting Piazza Navona, the Pantheon, the Spanish Steps, the Trevi Fountain and more. Spend your evenings in the bars of **Campo de' Fiori** or **Monti** (p. 65) and the restaurants of **Trastevere** (p. 66) or **Testaccio** (p. 67). Toward the end of your third day, catch the late train to Florence. Make sure you've booked tickets in advance: Walk-up fares are much more expensive than advanced tickets on the high-speed network.

DAYS 4 & 5: Florence: Cradle of the Renaissance ★★★

You have 2 whole days to explore the city of Giotto, Leonardo, Botticelli, and Michelangelo. Start with their masterpieces at the **Uffizi**

(p. 176; you should definitely pre-book tickets), followed by the **Duomo** complex (p. 174): Scale Brunelleschi's ochre dome, and follow up with a visit to the nearby **Battistero di San Giovanni** (p. 170), the revamped **Museo dell'Opera del Duomo** (p. 171), and **Campanile di Giotto** (p. 174). Start **DAY 5** with "David" at the **Accademia** (p. 190). For the rest of your time, spend it getting to know the intimate murals of **San Marco** (p. 191), paintings hanging at the **Palazzo Pitti** (p. 194), and Masaccio's revolutionary frescoes in the **Cappella Brancacci** (p. 197). In the evenings, stay south of the Arno, in San Frediano or San Niccolò, for lively wine bars and more creative restaurants than you generally find in the historic center. Leave on an early train on the morning of **DAY 6.**

DAYS 6 & 7: Venice: City that Defies the Sea ★★★

You'll ride into the heart of Venice on a *vaporetto* (water bus), taking in the **Grand Canal,** the world's greatest thoroughfare. Begin the sightseeing at **Piazza San Marco** (p. 405). The **Basilica di San Marco** is right there, and after exploring it, visit the nearby **Palazzo Ducale** (**Doge's Palace;** p. 402) before walking over the **Bridge of Sighs.** Begin your evening with the classic Venetian *aperitivo,* an Aperol spritz, followed by *cicchetti* (Venetian tapas) before a late dinner. Make **DAY 7** all about the city's unique art: the **Gallerie dell'Accademia** (p. 407), the modern **Peggy Guggenheim Collection** (p. 409), and **San Rocco** (p. 412). Catch a late train back to Rome. Or add another night . . . You can never stay too long in Venice.

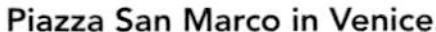

Piazza San Marco in Venice.

THE BEST OF ITALY IN 2 WEEKS

It's obviously difficult to see the top sights of Italy—and to see them properly—in just 2 weeks. But in this itinerary, we show you some of the best of them. We'll go beyond the well-trodden (and spectacular) Rome–Florence–Venice trail to include the southern region of Campania, specifically Pompeii, which has Europe's most precious Roman ruins. Additional stops in the center and north are Pisa (for the Leaning Tower and more) and Verona (the city of lovers since "Romeo and Juliet").

DAYS 1, 2 & 3: Rome ★★★

Follow the itinerary suggested in "The Best of Italy in 1 Week," above.

DAY 4: Naples ★★

Leave Rome early so that you can take in the major attractions of Naples, the historic "capital" of southern Italy. There is an unparalleled collection of ancient artifacts at the **Museo Archeologico Nazionale** (p. 591), plus Titians and Caravaggios at the **Museo e Gallerie Nazionale di Capodimonte** (p. 594). After dark, wander **Spaccanapoli**—the old center's main east–west thoroughfare—then make a date with a **pizzeria:** Neapolitans stake a reasonable claim that pizza was invented here. After dinner, stroll the **Mergellina** boardwalk to enjoy the breezes and views of the Bay of Naples. Stay overnight in Naples, the first of 3 nights based here.

DAY 5: Pompeii ★★

On **DAY 5,** take the Circumvesuviana train 24km (15 miles) south of Naples to spend a day wandering **Europe's best-preserved Roman ruins** at **Pompeii** (p. 620). Be sure to pack water and lunch, because onsite services aren't great. The city was buried for almost 2,000 years, having suffered instant devastation when nearby Vesuvius erupted in A.D. 79. Some of the great archaeological treasures of Italy—including the patrician **Casa dei Vettii** and the frescoed **Villa dei Misteri**—are here. Return to Naples for the night.

DAY 6: The Amalfi Coast ★★

On the morning of **DAY 6,** rent a car and drive 49km (30 miles) south of Naples along A3 until you see the turnoff for **Sorrento.** At Sorrento, head east along the curvy **Amalfi Drive,** of which Andre Gide said: "[There is] nothing more beautiful on this earth." The drive winds around the twisting, steep coastline to the southern resorts of **Positano** and **Amalfi,** either of which would make an idyllic stopover to extend your stay. Allow at least 3 hours for this drive because it can be slow moving. Alternatively, do the death-defying Amalfi Coast drive as part of an organized tour from Naples.

DAYS 7 & 8: Florence ★★★

Jump on the early high-speed train from Naples to Florence (journey time: 3 hrs.), then follow the itinerary suggested in "The Best of Italy in 1 Week," above. You'll be staying in Florence for the next 4 nights.

DAY 9: Gothic Siena ★★★

It's just over an hour to Siena on the *rapida* bus from Florence's bus station (p. 163). Leave early and set out immediately on arrival for **Piazza del Campo,** the shell-shaped main square, including its art-filled **Museo Civico** (inside the **Palazzo Pubblico;** p. 233). This is a quick visit, but you still have time to squeeze in a look at the **Duomo** (p. 253) and **Museo dell'Opera Metropolitana,** where you'll find Sienese master Duccio's giant "Maestà" painting. Stop on the Campo for an early evening drink and then head to a restaurant in Siena's atmospheric back streets. Reserve an early table: The last bus back to Florence departs around 8:45pm (Sun 7:10pm).

DAY 10: Off-Kilter Pisa ★★

Most trains between Florence and Pisa take around an hour. On arrival, hop aboard the LAM Rossa bus outside Pisa Centrale Station, heading to the **Campo dei Miracoli** ("Field of Miracles"). The set-piece piazza here is one of the most photographed slices of real estate on the planet—and home to the **Leaning Tower** (p. 297), of course. You can visit the **Duomo,** with its Arab-influenced Pisan-Romanesque facade, the **Battistero** with its carved pulpit and crazy acoustics, and the rest of the piazza's monuments and museums on the same combination ticket. You should book a slot ahead of time if you want to climb the Leaning Tower, however. For dining *alla pisana,* head away from the touristy piazza. The "real Pisa" lies in the warren of streets around the market square, **Piazza delle Vettovaglie.** Finish your visit with a stroll along the handsome promenade beside the **River Arno.** The last train back to Florence usually leaves at 10:30pm (though the 9:30pm train is quicker).

DAYS 11 & 12: Venice ★★★

Set your alarm clock for an early start: It takes around 2 hours to reach Venice from Florence aboard the high-speed train. Follow the itinerary suggested in "The Best of Italy in 1 Week," above.

DAY 13: Romantic Verona ★★★

Although he likely never set foot in the place, Shakespeare placed the world's most famous love story, "Romeo and Juliet," here. Wander **Piazza dei Signori** and take in another square, **Piazza delle Erbe,** before descending on the **Arena di Verona** (p. 453): It's the world's best-preserved gladiatorial arena, and is still packed out for monumental open-air opera performances in summer. Head back to Venice for the night. It is well worth booking your round-trip tickets ahead of time for a high-speed Frecciarossa or Frecciabianca train between Venice and Verona—the journey is just 1 hour, 10 minutes, compared with around 2 hours for a local train service.

DAY 14: Milan ★★

You should also prebook a fast train connection between Venice and Milan, a journey of between 2¼ and 2½ hours. The most bustling city in Italy isn't only about industry and commerce. Milan possesses one of Europe's great Gothic cathedrals, the **Duomo** (p. 466). Its **Biblioteca-Pinacoteca Ambrosiana** houses one of Italy's great art collections. The city of St. Ambrose also hosts the **Pinacoteca di Brera** (p. 471), a treasure trove of painting, laden with masterpieces from the likes of Mantegna and Piero della Francesca. Book ahead, too, to view Leonardo's fading but still magnificent "**Last Supper"** (p. 472). Stay overnight here if you are flying home or onward: It is one of Europe's major transportation hubs.

ITALY FOR FAMILIES

Italy is probably the friendliest family vacation destination in all Europe. Practically, it presents few challenges. If you're traveling by rental car with young children, be sure to request safety car seats ahead of time. Let the rental company know the age of your child and they will arrange for a seat that complies with EU regulations. Rail travelers should remember that reduced-price family fares are available on much of the high-speed network; ask when you buy your tickets or use a booking agent.

As you tour, don't go hunting for "child-friendly" restaurants or special kids' menus. There's always plenty available for little ones anywhere you dine, even dishes that aren't offered to grown-up patrons. Never be afraid to ask if you have a fussy eater in the family. Pretty much any request is met with a smile.

Perhaps the main issue for travelers with children is spacing your museum visits so that you get a chance to see the masterpieces without having young kids suffer a meltdown after too many paintings of saints. Remember to punctuate every day with a **gelato** stop. Italy makes the world's best ice cream, and you will even find soy flavors for anyone with lactose intolerance. We also suggest limiting long, tiring day trips out of town, especially by public transportation. And end your trip in Venice, which for most kids is every bit as magical as a Disney theme park.

DAY 1: Rome's Ancient Ruins ★★★

History is on your side here: The wonders of **Ancient Rome** (p. 84) should appeal as much to kids (of almost any age) as to adults. There are gory tales to tell at the **Colosseum** (p. 88), where the bookshop has a good selection of city guides aimed at kids. After that, they can let off steam wandering the **Roman Forum** and the **Palatine Hill.** (The ruins of the **Imperial Forums** can be viewed at any time.) Cap the afternoon by exploring the **Villa Borghese** (p. 108), a large park in the heart of Rome where you can rent bikes. For dinner, head for some crispy crusts at an authentic Roman **pizzeria.**

DAY 2: Rome: Living History ★★★

Head early to **St. Peter's Basilica** (p. 76). The kids will find it spooky wandering the Vatican grottoes, and few can resist climbing up to Michelangelo's dome at 114m (375 ft.). After time out for lunch, begin your assault on the **Vatican Museums** and the **Sistine Chapel.** Even if your kids don't like art museums, they are sure to gawk at the grandeur. Later in the day head for the **Spanish**

Steps (a good spot for upscale souvenir shopping; see p. 149) before wandering over to the **Trevi Fountain.** Let them toss coins into the fountain, which is said to ensure a return to Rome—perhaps when they are older and can fully appreciate the city's many more artistic attractions.

DAY 3: Rome: Underground ★★★

There are, literally, layers of history below the city streets, and kids will love exploring the catacombs of the **Via Appia Antica** (p. 118), the first cemetery of Rome's Christian community, and where the devout practiced their faith in secret during periods of persecution. **Context Travel** (p. 121) runs an excellent family tour of the city's subterranean layers, which takes in **San Clemente** (p. 94) and **Santi Giovanni e Paolo.** It costs 285€ per party. Eat more **pizza** before you leave; Rome's pizzerias are matched only by those in Naples, to the south, and our next recommended stops all lie to the north. Leave on a late afternoon train to Florence.

DAYS 4 & 5: Florence ★★★

Florence is usually thought of as more of a grown-up city, but there's enough here to fill 2 family days, with day trips. With multiple nights here, renting an apartment will give you more space to spread out. Check out **GoWithOh.com** or **HomeAway.com** for a good selection of quality places. Close to the Duomo, **Residence Hilda** (p. 207) is a family-friendly hotel that rents large, apartment-style rooms with kitchenettes.

Begin with the city's monumental main square, **Piazza della Signoria,** now an open-air museum of statues. The **Palazzo Vecchio** (p. 183) dominates one side; you can all tour it with special family-friendly guides, including a docent dressed as Cosimo de' Medici. You won't want to miss the **Uffizi.** With young children, you could turn your visit into a treasure trail of the museum's collection by first visiting the shop to select some postcards of key artworks. On the second morning, kids will delight in climbing to the top of Brunelleschi's dome on the **Duomo** for a classic panorama. Get there early—queues lengthen through the day. If kids and adults have still more energy to burn, climb the 414 steps up to the **Campanile di Giotto,** run around in the **Giardino di Boboli,** and cross the **Ponte Vecchio** at dusk. With older, fit children, you could add another day here, to allow time to see the Chianti hills on two wheels (see p. 168 for bike-tour info).

DAY 6: Pisa & its Leaning Tower ★★

If your kids are 7 or under, you should consider skipping **Pisa** (p. 292): 8 is the minimum age for the disorienting ascent up the bell tower of Pisa's cathedral, which more commonly goes by the name the **Leaning Tower.** Kids will enjoy the hyperreal monuments of the **Campo dei Miracoli** and learning about the city's Galileo links: The scientist was born here, and supposedly discovered his law of pendulum motion while watching a swinging lamp inside the **Duomo.** Take the kids to taste a local specialty, *cecina*, a pizzalike garbanzo-bean flatbread served warm. Your daylong visit complete, whiz up the coast on the fast train to Genoa. There is a luggage storage facility *(deposito bagagli)* at Pisa Centrale station.

DAYS 7 & 8: Genoa & the Riviera di Levante ★★

The industrial city-seaport of Genoa is home to one of Italy's most popular family attractions: The **Acquario di Genova** (p. 547), Europe's largest aquarium, where you can all enjoy a trip around the world's

Genoa's Aquarium, a top attraction for families.

oceans. It requires a half-day to see properly, so get in early, and then head out to the **Riviera di Levante** (p. 557), a coastline of pretty ports and rocky coves east of the city. Our favorite base around here is romantic **Portofino,** where you can easily kill your second day in Liguria beside the azure sea. **Santa Margherita Ligure** is a more budget-friendly alternative, with fewer crowds and a laid-back vibe.

DAYS 9 & 10: Lake Garda ★★

Slow down for a couple of days by Italy's biggest inland lake, perhaps basing yourself at photogenic **Sirmione** (p. 506). Take a ferry trip, hire a pedal boat or kayak, eat simple grilled lakefish, and generally enjoy lakeside life. In Sirmione you can scramble up high on the ramparts of the **Castello Scaligero,** then ride the little train out to the Roman ruins at the **Grotte di Catullo,** supposedly once a villa inhabited by the poet Catullus (ca. 84 B.C.–ca. 54 B.C.). For active families with more time to spend, **Riva del Garda** (p. 507), close to the lake's northernmost point, is one of Europe's major windsurfing/sailboarding centers.

Fresh seafood is one of many reasons to visit Italy's coastal cities.

DAYS 11, 12 & 13: Venice: City on the Lagoon ★★★

In Venice, the fun begins the moment you arrive and take a *vaporetto* ride along the **Grand Canal.** Head straight for **Piazza San Marco** (p. 405), where children will delight in feeding the pigeons and riding the elevator up the great **Campanile.** Catch the mosaics inside the **Basilica di San Marco,** which dominates the square. At the **Palazzo Ducale,** stroll over the infamous **Bridge of Sighs.** As in Florence, make time for some art: Visit the **Gallerie dell'Accademia** (p. 407) and **San Rocco,** where kids view the episodic Tintoretto paintings like a picture book. If it's summer, save time for the beach at **Lido** (p. 418) and perhaps for getting a different angle on Venice's canals, from the seat of a **gondola** (p. 395).

A WHISTLESTOP WEEK-OR-SO FOR FOOD & WINE LOVERS

Italy has one of Europe's great cuisines—or rather, make that *several* of Europe's great cuisines. The nation's history as a collection of independent city-states and noble fiefdoms has left a diverse legacy in food. Each regional cuisine is committed to its own local produce and artisanal specialties, with treasured recipes handed down through generations.

Italy is also the world's biggest wine producer. Although much of the output is undistinguished (if perfectly drinkable) table wine, some of the icons of world wine also hail from here. Our itinerary takes in three of the great Italian red wine zones: **Montepulciano,** whose noble wine was known to the Etruscans; the **Chianti,** probably the first legally defined wine zone in the world; and **Piedmont,** whose robust reds Barolo and Barbaresco command top prices at restaurants around the world.

DAYS 1 & 2: Rome ★★★

Italy's capital is packed with restaurants offering cuisine from pretty much everywhere in the Italian peninsula. The **Trastevere, Monti,** and **Testaccio** neighborhoods are great for dining and drinks after dark. While here, sample traditional Roman dishes like pasta with *cacio e pepe* (sheep's milk cheese and black pepper); *spaghetti alla carbonara* (similar but enriched with egg yolk plus added *guanciale,* cured pork cheek) or *alla gricia* (also with *guanciale* and *pecorino* cheese, but no egg); *saltimbocca alla romana*—literally, "jump in the mouth," a veal cutlet with prosciutto and sage; and *coda alla vaccinara* (stewed oxtail with tomatoes and celery). **Gelato** is either Florentine or Sicilian in origin, depending on who you ask, but in Rome you'll find some of the country's best (see p. 140). The city also has some of Italy's best craft beer bars (see p. 155). You'll need a rental car for your next leg. Collect it on your second afternoon and head north to Tuscany, to leave yourself a full day at your next stop.

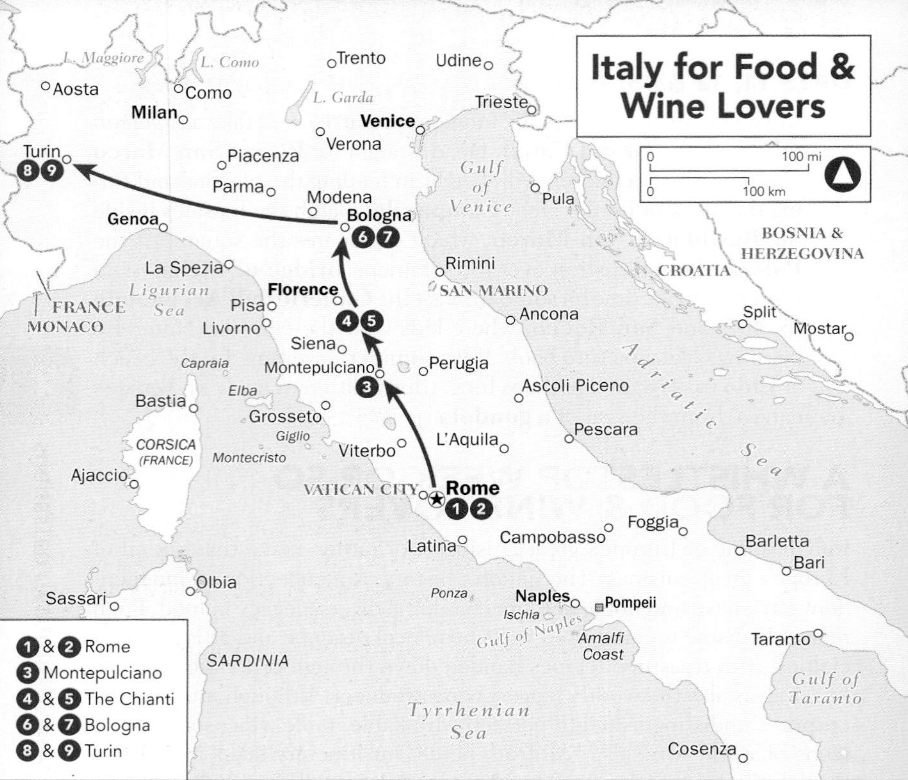

DAY 3: Montepulciano ★★

Begin with a walk up the handsome, steep Corso from the town gate to **Piazza Grande,** monumental heart of the *comune*. Here you'll find the **Palazzo Comunale** (climb it for a panorama of the surrounding winelands) and **Cattedrale.** Oenophiles should head to the **Consorzio del Vino Nobile di Montepulciano** office, where you can taste vintages from small producers and seek advice for nearby wineries to visit. Our favorite cellar in the center is **Gattavecchi.** End the evening at **Acquacheta** (p. 251), where the menu's all about beef—"*bistecca numero uno,*" is how Contucci winemaker Adamo describes it to us. Other local delicacies include sheep's milk cheese, *pecorino di Pienza*.

DAYS 4 & 5: The Chianti ★★★

Pick a base close to **Greve in Chianti** (p. 245) to lodge right at the heart of Tuscany's largest quality wine region. Sangiovese-based Chianti is a diverse wine: Chianti Classico denotes grapes from the original (and best) growing zone, and tasting opportunities abound at cellars such as **Villa Vignamaggio** and **Castello di Volpaia.** Book ahead if you require a tour anywhere. The Chianti is also

Vineyards in Tuscany.

famed for its butchers, where you can buy everything from cuts of fresh beef (ideal if you're staying in a villa) to salami made from a local breed of pig, the *Cinta Senese*. **Falorni,** in Greve, is outshone perhaps only by **Dario Cecchini,** in nearby Panzano. Also look out for Tuscan extra virgin olive oil. This local elixir is famed for its low acidity, and is among Italy's best.

DAYS 6 & 7: Bologna ★★

You've arrived in Italy's gastronomic capital. Leave the rental car here; it's easy to continue onward by train. The agricultural plains of Emilia-Romagna are Italy's breadbasket. So much of the produce we think of as typical "Italian food" hails from here: cured prosciutto and Parmigiano-Reggiano cheese from Parma and Reggio nell'Emilia; the finest balsamic vinegar from Modena; mortadella and tortellini (filled pasta) from Bologna itself. Foodies should browse Bologna's markets, the **Mercato delle Erbe** and the **Quadrilatero,** a warren of lanes with enticing food shops. Make a dinner reservation at a restaurant specializing in classic Bolognese cooking; see p. 356 for our picks.

DAYS 8 & 9: Turin ★

Snowcapped alpine peaks dot the horizon north and west of the Piedmontese capital, and the cooking in Italy's northwest reflects the heartier and hardier mountain folk that live on the city's doorstep. Nearby Vercelli is Italy's rice capital—the town is surrounded by paddy fields—and *risotto* is at its best here. There's also a noticeable Ligurian current in Torinese food: Basil-based pesto is superb and the favorite slice-on-the-go isn't pizza but *farinata*, garbanzo bean flour flatbread dusted with rosemary or pepper. The **Langhe Hills** (p. 531), south of the city, are famed for blockbuster red wines and white truffles. Sweet vermouth was also invented in Turin; the classic local labels are slightly bitter Punt e Mes ("point and a half" in Piedmontese) and vanilla-rich Carpano Antica Formula.

HISTORIC CITIES OF THE NORTH

Often overshadowed by blockbusters like Rome and Florence, the cities of northern Italy make an excellent itinerary for return visitors to the country. Each city on our tour has a center with refined architecture, and a history of independence—as well as struggle with and eventual subjection to the great regional powers, particularly Venice. The logical starting point is Milan, gateway to Italy for flights from across the globe. Spend a day there, collect your rental car or rail tickets—all train connections on this tour are easy—and set off early. The endpoint is Venice, where we recommend you extend your stay by as many days as you can; see chapter 9 for full coverage of the city.

DAYS 1 & 2: Milan ★★ & Turin ★★

See Milan under "The Best of Italy in 2 Weeks," above. Spend **DAY 2** taking a day trip by train to **Turin** (p. 510). The city of Fiat and football (meaning soccer) has a handsome baroque center, the finest Egyptian collection outside of Cairo at the **Museo Egizio** (p. 515), and views of the Alps from the top of the **Mole Antonelliana** tower (p. 515). It also has a food culture every bit as refined as Bologna's; Turin is the city of vermouth and on the doorstep of the Piedmont wine-growing region, so you need not go thirsty. You can complete the rail journey between the cities in as little as 45 minutes: There's no need to relocate your base from Milan, if you prefer to minimize changes of lodging.

DAY 3: Bergamo ★★

Whether you arrive by train or car, alight in the **Lower Town** (Città Bassa) and ascend to the **Upper Town** (Città Alta) in style, on the town's century-old funicular railway. **Piazza Vecchia** (p. 486) is the architectural heart of the Upper Town. Beyond the arcades you'll find the Romanesque **Basilica di Santa Maria Maggiore** and the Renaissance **Cappella Colleoni,** with its frescoed ceiling by Venetian

Juliet's Balcony in Verona.

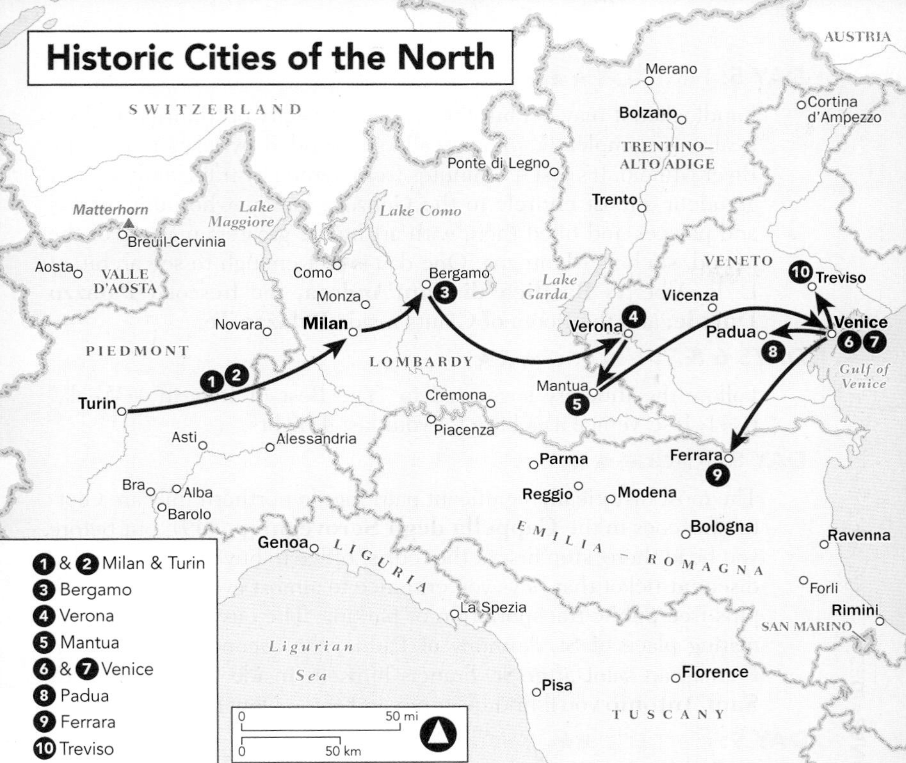

rococo painter Tiepolo. You should also make time for the **Accademia Carrara** (p. 484), with its exceptional collection of northern Italian painting. Bergamo was the birthplace of composer Donizetti and has a lively cultural (largely operatic) program. You needn't relocate from your Milanese base: Bergamo is an easy daytrip from Milan (50 min. by train), though it makes a delightfully serene overnight stop, too.

DAY 4: Verona ★★

A visit to northern Italy's most renowned small city (see p. 450) is less about ticking off sights than about soaking up the elegance of a place eternally associated with Shakespeare's doomed lovers, Romeo and Juliet. If you're here in summer, make straight for the box office at the **Arena di Verona;** Italy's most intact Roman amphitheater hosts monumental outdoor operatic productions, which you shouldn't miss. There's often last-minute tickets available, especially on weekdays; see *Aïda* if you can, the opera that opened the festival in 1913, and is still most associated with it. Your roaming should also take you to the **Basilica di San Zeno Maggiore,** one of Italy's most important Romanesque churches. Use Verona as a base for 2 nights and see Mantua as a day visit.

DAY 5: Mantua ★★★

Landlocked it may be, but the Renaissance city of Mantua (p. 488) is almost completely, romantically surrounded by lakes fed by the River Mincio. It's just 45 minutes from Verona by train, and owes its grandeur almost entirely to the Gonzaga family, who built piazzas and palaces and filled them with art by the greatest masters of the period, such as Mantegna. One day is just enough to see architect L. B. Alberti's **Basilica di Sant'Andrea,** the frescoed **Palazzo Ducale,** and the Room of Giants inside **Palazzo Te.**

DAYS 6 & 7: Venice ★★★

Follow the itinerary suggested in "The Best of Italy in 1 Week," p. 41. Use Venice as a base for your last 4 nights.

DAY 8: Padua ★★

The most historically significant paintings in northern Italy are Giotto's frescoes in the **Cappella degli Scrovegni** (p. 449), but before you head there, stop first at the tourist office to buy a PadovaCard, a discount ticket that buys you entrance to almost everything in town plus free public transportation or parking. The city is also the final resting place of St. Anthony of Padua, the second-most eminent Franciscan saint after St. Francis himself. Inside the **Basilica di Sant'Antonio** you'll find his tomb and some Donatello bronzes.

DAY 9: Ferrara ★★

Like nearby Mantua, this small, stately city of cyclists owes its grandeur to one despotic family. In Ferrara (p. 361) it was the Este dukes who held sway from the 1200s to the 1500s, ruling the city from the **Castello Estense.** Elsewhere in the center, check out the facade of the Gothic-Romanesque **Duomo** and the **Palazzo dei Diamanti,** another Este creation, named for the 9,000 diamond-shaped stones adorning its facade. Ferrara is a 1½ hour train ride from Venice.

DAY 10: Treviso ★★

It's not far (a half-hour by train) from Venice to its small northern neighbor, a geographical fact exploited by the powerful Venetians, who dominated Treviso for over 450 years from the 14th century. They left a rich architectural legacy—plus canals, of course. The pace here is sedate. You'll have ample time to catch up with paintings left by **Tomaso da Modena,** including at frescoed **Santa Lucia** church (p. 454), before enjoying a glass of the local prosecco around **Piazza dei Signori,** the medieval city's pretty heart.

ITALY'S ANCIENT RUINS

Italy itself isn't old. As a unified country, it only recently passed the 150-year mark. But the peninsula is rightly considered one of the cradles of European civilization. Michelangelo and the Renaissance, Gothic

architecture, even the Byzantine mosaics of Ravenna: These are relatively recent moments in Italian time. Even the Romans were not the first civilization to leave a mark here. There are ancient buildings still standing that owe their construction to expatriates from classical Greece.

DAYS 1, 2, 3 & 4: Sicily ★★★

As Greek Syracuse, modern-day **Siracusa** (p. 762) was one of the cultural hotspots of the ancient Mediterranean: Dramatist Aeschylus was a visitor, and lyric poet Sappho was exiled here toward the end of the 7th century B.C. A ruined Doric **Temple of Apollo** stands in town, and the **Parco Archeologico della Neapolis** (p. 766) has a Greek theater still used to host dramas each summer. The southwest of Sicily has another cluster of ruins. If the main reason for your visit is to see Greek remains, you should probably make your base over there for at least half your time on Sicily. Allow a couple of days to tour coastal **Selinunte** (p. 780), **Segesta** (p. 751), and the Valley of the Temples at **Agrigento** (p. 777). The visit-worthy mosaics of the **Villa Romana del Casale** (p. 776) lie almost midway between the two. You should rent a car for your time on Sicily. Catania, 67km (41 miles) north of Siracusa, is well connected by air with Rome (1 hr., 15 min. flight).

DAYS 5, 6 & 7: Rome ★★★

Rome is to ancient ruins as Coke is to fizzy brown liquids: This is the brand that counts when it comes to archaeology. Rome was the epicenter of a republic and empire that for centuries ruled most of Europe and Asia Minor, as well as much of North Africa and the Middle East. Spend **DAY 5** walking ancient Rome's civic and spiritual heart, the **Forum** (p. 90). The same ticket gets you into the **Colosseum** (p. 88). Between visits to those two, it makes sense to see the **Imperial Forums, Trajan's Markets,** and the city's best artifact collection, at the **Musei Capitolini** (p. 86), whose newest wing houses an equestrian bronze of philosopher-emperor Marcus Aurelius (r. A.D. 161–180). As well as the key archaeological sites, museums display an array of relics dug up here over the centuries: Add the ancient collections of the **Vatican Museums** (p. 78) and the busts and Roman art at **Palazzo Massimo alle Terme** (p. 112) to your to-do list for **DAY 6**. The ruins of Rome's former seaport, **Ostia Antica** (p. 156), stand a short train journey from the city—a comfortable half-day roundtrip for **DAY 7**. On the way back into the city, jump off at the Circo Massimo Metro stop to visit the **Terme di Caracalla** (p. 86) baths complex, and to admire for one last time the view of the **Palatine Hill** from the Circus Maximus. You could probably spend a month here just looking at the remnants of Ancient Rome.

DAYS 8, 9 & 10: Naples & Campania ★★

Ancient Naples—established as the fishing port of Parthenope, then refounded as Neapolis in the 6th century B.C.—was a key settlement in Magna Graecia, or "Greater Greece." Dating to a later period, the Roman towns of **Pompeii** and **Herculaneum** (p. 616) were preserved for centuries under the ash and lava after Vesuvius's cataclysmic eruption in A.D. 79. Remnants of the ancient world remain even in Naples's chaotic 21st-century *centro storico*: In the excavations below **San Lorenzo Maggiore** (p. 592), walk around the remains of the Roman Forum and Greek *Ágora* (market). Naples's **Museo Archeologico Nazionale** (p. 591) preserves wall art from Pompeii and Roman statuary, including the "Farnese Bull." West of Naples, the amphitheater at **Pozzuoli** (p. 607) was the third-largest

Ruins of the Temple of Apollo in Syracuse, Sicily.

in the Roman world. Leave Naples on the high-speed Frecciarossa or Italo service late on day 10: It is just under 3 hours to Florence by rail. If you have a little more time, the **Amalfi Coast** (p. 652) makes an even more scenic base for exploring the ruins of Campania.

The Amalfi Coast.

DAYS 11 & 12: Florence ★★

Florence made its name and its fortune during the Renaissance, in the 1400s and 1500s, and much of the center's art and architecture dates from that period. However, the **Museo Archeologico** (p. 190) displays relics from a civilization that predated even the Romans around here: the Etruscans. So many visitors to Florence zero in on Michelangelo & co. that you may have the "Arezzo Chimera" and the museum's other precious objects to yourself. Parts of a Roman theater uncovered below the **Palazzo Vecchio** (p. 183) are now open to the public, too. High on a hill to the north is a settlement that first rose under the Etruscans: **Fiesole** (p. 198), an easy 20-minute bus journey from Florence. Now little more than an overgrown village, it has a preserved Roman theater, a surviving stretch of Etruscan wall, and an archaeological area where visitors can roam among the stones.

DAY 13: Verona ★★

It seems a little harsh to label the **Arena di Verona** (p. 453) "a ruin." This city's enormous amphitheater is the best preserved in Italy. Come in summer—and book ahead—to experience one of Europe's most atmospheric outdoor opera festivals.

4

ROME

By Elizabeth Heath

Catching that first breathtaking glimpse of the Colosseum. Shopping at a colorful, chaotic outdoor market. Eating a piping-hot, paper-thin pizza fresh from a wood-fired oven. Marveling as residents young and old go about their daily business amid some of Western art's greatest creative endeavors, the Catholic Church's most sacred monuments, and the world's most iconic historic sites. Exploring winding streets laid out before the time of Christ, which still bear the names of medieval guilds and are lined with faded Renaissance palaces. Stumbling upon a church, a temple, or a fountain that has stood for centuries—or even millennia. This is Rome, after all. There are few places on earth where the layers of time are so overlapped, intersected, and palpable.

As a visitor to Rome, you will be constantly reminded of this city's extraordinary history. Take the time to get away from the crowds to explore the intimate piazzas and lesser basilicas in the back streets of Trastevere and the *centro storico*. Indulge in eno-gastronomic pursuits at coffee bars, trattorias, enotecas and gelaterias. Have a picnic in Villa Borghese or climb to the top of the Gianicolo for million-dollar views. Rome is so compact that without planning too much, you'll end up stumbling across its monuments and its simpler pleasures.

Walk the streets of Rome, and the city will be yours.

ESSENTIALS

Getting There

BY PLANE Most flights arrive at Rome's **Leonardo da Vinci International Airport** (www.adr.it; ✆ **06-65951**), popularly known as **Fiumicino,** 30km (19 miles) from the city center. (If you're arriving from other European cities, you might land at Ciampino Airport, discussed below. After you leave Passport Control, you'll see a **tourist information desk,** staffed Monday through Saturday from 8:15am to 7pm. A ***cambio*** (money exchange) operates daily from 7:30am to 11pm, but you're ahead to hit the ATM (see "FastFacts" in chapter 16).

There's a **train station** in the airport. To get into the city, follow the signs marked treni for the 31-minute shuttle ride to Rome's main station, **Stazione Termini.** The shuttle runs from 6:23am to 11:23pm for 14€ one-way (free kids 12 and under). On the way to the train, you'll pass a

FACING PAGE: **The Roman Colosseum, once the site of gladiator contests and wild animal fights.**

yellow machine dispensing tickets (cash or credit), or you can buy them at the Trenitalia window near the tracks. When you arrive at Termini, get out of the train quickly and try to grab a baggage cart. Do watch out for pickpockets at Termini.

A **taxi** from da Vinci airport to the city costs a flat-rate 48€ for the 1-hour trip, depending on traffic (hotels tend to charge 50€–60€ for pickup service). The expense might be worth it if you have a lot of luggage. Note that the flat rate is applicable from the airport to central Rome and vice-versa, but only if your central Rome location is inside the Aurelian Walls (most hotels are). Otherwise, standard metered rates apply, which can bump the fare to 75€ or higher. There are also surcharges for large luggage, Sunday and holiday rides, and more than 4 passengers.

If you arrive at **Ciampino Airport** (www.adr.it/ciampino; ✆ **06-65951**), you can take a Terravision bus (www.terravision.eu; ✆ **06-4880086;** first bus at 8:15am, last bus at 12:15am) to Stazione Termini. This takes about 45 minutes and costs 4€. A **taxi** from here costs a flat rate of 30€, provided you're going to a destination within the old Aurelian Walls. Otherwise, you'll pay the metered fare, but the trip is shorter (about 40 min.).

BY TRAIN OR BUS Trains and buses (including trains from the airport) arrive in the center of old Rome at **Stazione Termini,** Piazza dei Cinquecento. This is the train, bus, and subway transportation hub for all of Rome, and it is surrounded by many hotels, especially budget ones.

If you're taking the **Metropolitana** (subway), follow the illuminated red-and-white M signs. To catch a bus, go straight through the outer hall and enter the sprawling bus lot of **Piazza dei Cinquecento.** You will also find a line of **taxis** parked out front. Note that taxis now charge a 2€ supplement for any fares originating at Termini, plus 1€ for each bag in the trunk. This is official city policy. Use the official taxi queue right in front of the station; don't go with a driver who approaches you or get into any cab where the meter is "broken."

The station is filled with services. A money exchange window is located close to the end of platform 14, and an ATM is at the end of platform 24. **Informazioni Ferroviarie** (in the outer hall) dispenses information on rail travel to other parts of Italy. There is also a **tourist information booth,** plus baggage services, newsstands, clean public toilets, and snack bars. ***Tip:*** Be wary of young men/women lingering around ticket machines offering to help you. They will expect a tip. At worst, they will be distracting you so that an accomplice can pick your pocket.

BY CAR From the north, the main access route is the **Autostrada A1.** This highway links Milan with Naples via Bologna, Florence, and Rome. At 754km (469 miles), it is the longest Italian autostrada and is the "spinal cord" of Italy's road network. All the autostrade join with the **Grande Raccordo Anulare,** a ring road encircling Rome, channeling traffic into the congested city. ***Tip:*** Long before you reach this road, you should study a map carefully to see what part of Rome you plan to enter and

roma **PASSES**

If you plan to do serious sightseeing in Rome (and why else would you be here?), the **Roma Pass** (www.romapass.it) is worth considering. For 38.50€ per card, valid for 3 days, you get free entry to the first two museums or archaeological sites you visit; "express" entry to the Colosseum (though sometimes this line is longer than the regular line); discounted entry to all other museums and sites; free use of the city's public transport network (bus, Metro, tram, and railway lines; airport transfers not included); a free map; and free access to a special smartphone app. ***Note:*** The Vatican Museums are not part of the pass plan.

If your stay in Rome is shorter, you may want to opt for the **Roma Pass 48 Hours** (28€), which offers the same benefits as the 3-day pass, except that only the first museum you visit is free and the ticket is valid for just 48 hours.

The free transportation perk with the Roma Pass is not insignificant, if only because it saves you the hassle of buying paper tickets. In any case, do some quick math; if you plan to visit a lot of sites and dash around the city on public transport, it's probably worth the money.

You can buy either of the Roma passes online (www.romapass.it) and pick them up at one of the city's Tourist Information Points; you can also order in advance by phone, with a credit card, at ✆ **06-060608.** Roma Passes are also sold directly at Tourist Information Point offices (see below) or at participating museums and ATAC subway ticket offices.

A good alternative may be the **Archaeologia Card** (www.coopculture.it/ticket_office.cfm), which for 25€ (buy at the first site you visit) grants admission to the following nine sites for up to 7 days: the Colosseum, Palatine Museum and Roman Forum, Palazzo Massimo alle Terme, Palazzo Altemps, Crypta Balbi, the Baths of Diocletian, Cecilia Metella, Villa dei Quintili, and the Baths of Caracalla. With this pass, however, transport is not included, so if you plan to do a lot of sightseeing, the Roma Pass is a much better value.

Finally, you should note that the Colosseum, Roman Forum, and Palatine Hill are included under one ticket for 12€, good for 2 days and available for purchase online (plus small fee) or at the sites. Likewise, the four museums of the Museo Nazionale Romano offer a combo ticket good for 2 days that costs 7€.

mark your route accordingly. Route signs along the ring road tend to be confusing. Also consider an international smartphone data plan so you can access GPS information while traveling.

Warning: Return your rental car immediately on arrival, or at least get yourself to your hotel, park your car, and leave it there until you leave Rome. Think twice before driving in Rome—the traffic, as well as the parking options, can be nightmarish. In any case, most of central Rome is a **ZTL (Zona Traffico Limitato),** off-limits to nonresidents and rigorously enforced by cameras. You will almost certainly be fined; the ticket might arrive at your home address months after your trip.

Visitor Information

Information, online access, maps, and the Roma Pass (see above) are available at **Tourist Information Points** maintained by **Roma Capitale**

Mercato Centrale in Termini Station.

(www.turismoroma.it) around the city. They're staffed daily from 9:30am to 7pm, except the one at Termini (daily 8am–6:45pm), which is located in "Centro Diagnostico" hall (Building F) next to platform 24; there's often a long line at this one. Additional offices are at **Via Nazionale 183,** near the Palazzo delle Esposizioni; on **Piazza delle Cinque Lune,** near Piazza Navona; on **Via dei Fori Imperiali** (for the Forum); on **Via Marco Minghetti,** at the corner of Via del Corso, at **Castel Sant'Angelo** (Piazza Pia), and in Trastevere on **Piazza Sidney Sonnino.** There are also information points at Fiumicino and Ciampino airports.

City Layout

The bulk of what you'll want to visit—ancient, Renaissance, and baroque Rome (as well as the train station)—lies on the east side of the **Tiber River (Fiume Tevere),** which curls through the city. However, several important landmarks are on the other side: **St. Peter's Basilica** and the **Vatican, Castel Sant'Angelo,** and the colorful **Trastevere** neighborhood. Even if those last sights are slightly farther afield, Rome has one of the most compact and walkable city centers in Europe.

That doesn't mean you won't get lost from time to time (most newcomers do). Arm yourself with a detailed street map of Rome (or a smartphone with a hefty data plan). Most hotels hand out a pretty good version of a city map.

The Neighborhoods in Brief

Much of the historic core of Rome does not fall under easy or distinct neighborhood classifications. Instead, when describing a location, the frame of reference is the name of the nearest large monument or square, like St. Peter's or Piazza di Spagna. Street numbers usually run consecutively, with odd numbers on one side of the street, evens on the other. However, in centro, the numbers sometimes run up one side and then run back down on the other side (so #50 could be potentially opposite #308).

VATICAN CITY & THE PRATI **Vatican City** is technically a sovereign state, although in practice it is just another part of Rome. The **Vatican Museums, St. Peter's,** and the **Vatican Gardens** take up most of the land area, and the popes have lived here for 6 centuries. The neighborhood north of the Vatican—called Borgo Pio—is removed from the more happening scene of ancient and Renaissance Rome, and getting to and from those areas can be time-consuming. Borgo Pio is also rather dull at night and contains few, if any, of Rome's finest restaurants. **Prati**, a middle-class neighborhood east of the Vatican, may be a better choice, thanks to its smattering of affordable hotels and shopping streets, and the fact that it boasts some excellent places to eat.

CENTRO STORICO & THE PANTHEON One of the most desirable (and busiest) areas of Rome, the **Centro Storico** ("Historic Center") is a maze of narrow streets and cobbled alleys dating from the Middle Ages and filled with churches and palaces built during the Renaissance and baroque eras. The only way to explore it is by foot. Its heart is **Piazza Navona,** bustling with sidewalk cafes, *palazzi,* street artists, musicians, and pickpockets.

Slightly less chaotic than Piazza Navona but still abuzz with crowds, a cafe scene, and nightlife is the nearby area around the **Pantheon,** which remains from ancient Roman times and is surrounded by a district built much later. South of Corso Vittorio Emanuele is the lively square of **Campo de' Fiori,** home of the famous produce market and the colorful hub of a neighborhood of mostly Renaissance-era palaces and apartments. West of Via Arenula lies one of the city's most intriguing districts, the old Jewish **Ghetto,** where restaurants far outnumber hotels.

ANCIENT ROME, MONTI & CELIO Although no longer the heart of the city, this is where Rome began, with the **Colosseum, Palatine Hill, Roman Forum, Imperial Forums,** and **Circus Maximus.** This area offers only a few hotels—most of them inexpensive to moderate in price—and not a lot of great restaurants. Many restaurant owners here have their eyes on the tour-bus crowd, whose passengers are often herded in and out so fast they don't know whether the food is good or bad. Just beyond the Circus Maximus is the **Aventine Hill,** south of the Palatine and close to the Tiber, now rather posh residential quarter—with great city views. You will get much more of a neighborhood feel if you stay in **Monti** (Rome's oldest *rione,* or quarter) or **Celio**, respectively located north and south of the Colosseum. Both also have good dining, aimed at locals as well as visitors, and Monti especially has plenty of life from *aperitivo* o'clock and into the wee hours.

TRIDENTE & THE SPANISH STEPS The northern part of Rome's center is sometimes known as the Tridente, so-called for the trident shape of the roads leading down from **Piazza del Popolo**—Via di Ripetta, Via del Corso, and Via del Babuino. The star here is unquestionably **Piazza di Spagna,** which attracts Romans and tourists alike to idly sit on its celebrated **Spanish Steps.** Some of Rome's most upscale shopping streets fan out from here, including **Via Condotti.** This is the most upscale part of Rome, full of expensive hotels, designer boutiques, and chic restaurants.

VIA VENETO & PIAZZA BARBERINI In the 1950s and early 1960s, **Via Veneto** was the swinging place to be, as la Dolce Vita celebrities paraded along the tree-lined boulevard to the delight of paparazzi. The street is still the site of luxury hotels, cafes, and restaurants, although it's no longer such a happening spot, and the restaurants are mostly overpriced tourist traps.

To the south, Via Veneto comes to an end at **Piazza Barberini** and the magnificent **Palazzo Barberini,** begun in 1623 by Carlo Maderno and later completed by Bernini and Borromini.

VILLA BORGHESE & PARIOLI **Parioli** is Rome's most elegant residential section, a setting for some excellent restaurants, hotels, museums, and public parks. It attracts those who shun the Spanish Steps and the overly commercialized Via Veneto. Geographically, Parioli is framed by the green spaces of the **Villa Borghese** to the south and the **Villa Glori** and **Villa Ada** to the north. Adjacent to Prati but across the Tiber to the east; it's considered one of the safest districts in the city. All that being said, Parioli is not exactly central, so it can be a hassle as a base if you're dependent on public transportation.

AROUND STAZIONE TERMINI The main train station adjoins **Piazza della Repubblica,** and is for many visitors their first introduction to Rome. Much of the area is seedy and filled with gas fumes from all the buses and cars, plus a fair share of weirdos. If you stay here, you might not score the typical Rome charm, but you'll have a lot of affordable options and a convenient location, near the city's transportation hub and not far from ancient Rome. There is a fair amount to see here, including the **Basilica di Santa Maria Maggiore,** the artifacts at **Palazzo Massimo alle Terme,** and the **Baths of Diocletian.**

The neighborhoods on either side of Termini (Esquilino and Tiburtino) have been slowly cleaning up, and some streets are now attractive. Most budget hotels on the Via Marsala side occupy one or more floors of a *palazzo* (palace); many of their entryways are drab, although they are often charming upstairs or at least clean and livable. In the area to the left of the station as you exit, the streets are wider, the traffic is heavier, and the noise level is higher—and a little caution is needed late at night.

TRASTEVERE In a Roman shift of the Latin *Trans Tiber,* Trastevere means "across the Tiber." This once-medieval working-class district has been gentrified and is now overrun with visitors from all over the world. It started to transform in the 1970s when expats and other bohemians discovered its rough charm. Despite being most definitely on the tourist map, Trastevere retains its youthful, boho appeal, with dance clubs, offbeat shops, sidewalk vendors, pubs, and little *trattorie* and wine bars. Trastavere has places to stay—mostly rather quaint rentals and Airbnbs—and excellent restaurants and bars, too.

The area centers on the ancient churches of **Santa Cecilia** and **Santa Maria in Trastevere,** and remains one of Rome's most colorful quarters, even if a bit overrun.

TESTACCIO & SOUTHERN ROME In A.D. 55, Emperor Nero ordered that Rome's thousands of broken amphorae and terracotta roof tiles be stacked in a pile to the east of the Tiber, just west of today's Ostiense Railway Station. Over the centuries, the mound grew to a height of around 61m (200 ft.) and then was compacted to form the centerpiece for one of the city's most unusual working-class neighborhoods, **Testaccio.** Houses were built on the perimeter of the amphorae mound and caves were dug into its mass to store wine and foodstuffs. Once home to slaughterhouses and Rome's former port on the Tiber, Testaccio is now known for its authentic Roman restaurants. It's also one of Rome's liveliest areas after dark.

Farther south and east, the **Via Appia Antica** is a 2,300-year-old road that has witnessed much of the history of the ancient world. By 190 B.C., it extended from Rome to Brindisi on the southeast coast. Its most famous sights are the **Catacombs,** the graveyards of early Christians and patrician families. This is one of the most historically rich areas of Rome, great for a day trip but not a convenient place to stay.

Getting Around

Central Rome is perfect for exploring on foot, with sites of interest often clustered together. Much of the inner core is traffic-free, so you will need to walk whether you like it or not. However, in the most tourist-trod parts of the city, walking may be uncomfortable because of the crowds, uneven cobblestones, heavy traffic, and narrow (if any) sidewalks.

BY SUBWAY The **Metropolitana (Metro)** (www.romametropolitane.it; ✆ **06-454640100**) is the fastest way to get around, operating daily from 5:30am to 11:30pm (until 12:30am on Sat). A big red **m** indicates the entrance to the subway. If your destination is close to a Metro stop, hop on, as your journey will be much faster than by taking surface transportation. There are currently three lines: **Line A** (orange) runs southeast to northwest via Termini, Barberini, Spagna, and several stations in Prati near the Vatican; **Line B** (blue) runs north to south via Termini and stops in Ancient Rome; and a third, **Line C** (green), which is currently under construction and should be completed by 2021, will ultimately run from Monte Compatri in the southeast to Clodio/Mazzini (just beyond the Ottaviano stop on Line A). The oft-delayed portion from Piazza Lodi to San Giovanni is scheduled to be in operation by September 2017.

Tickets are 1.50€ and are available from *tabacchi* (tobacco shops), many newsstands, and vending machines at all stations. Booklets of tickets are available at newsstands, *tabacchi* and in some terminals. You can also buy a **pass** on either a daily or a weekly basis (see "By Bus & Tram," below). To open the subway barrier, insert your ticket. If you have a

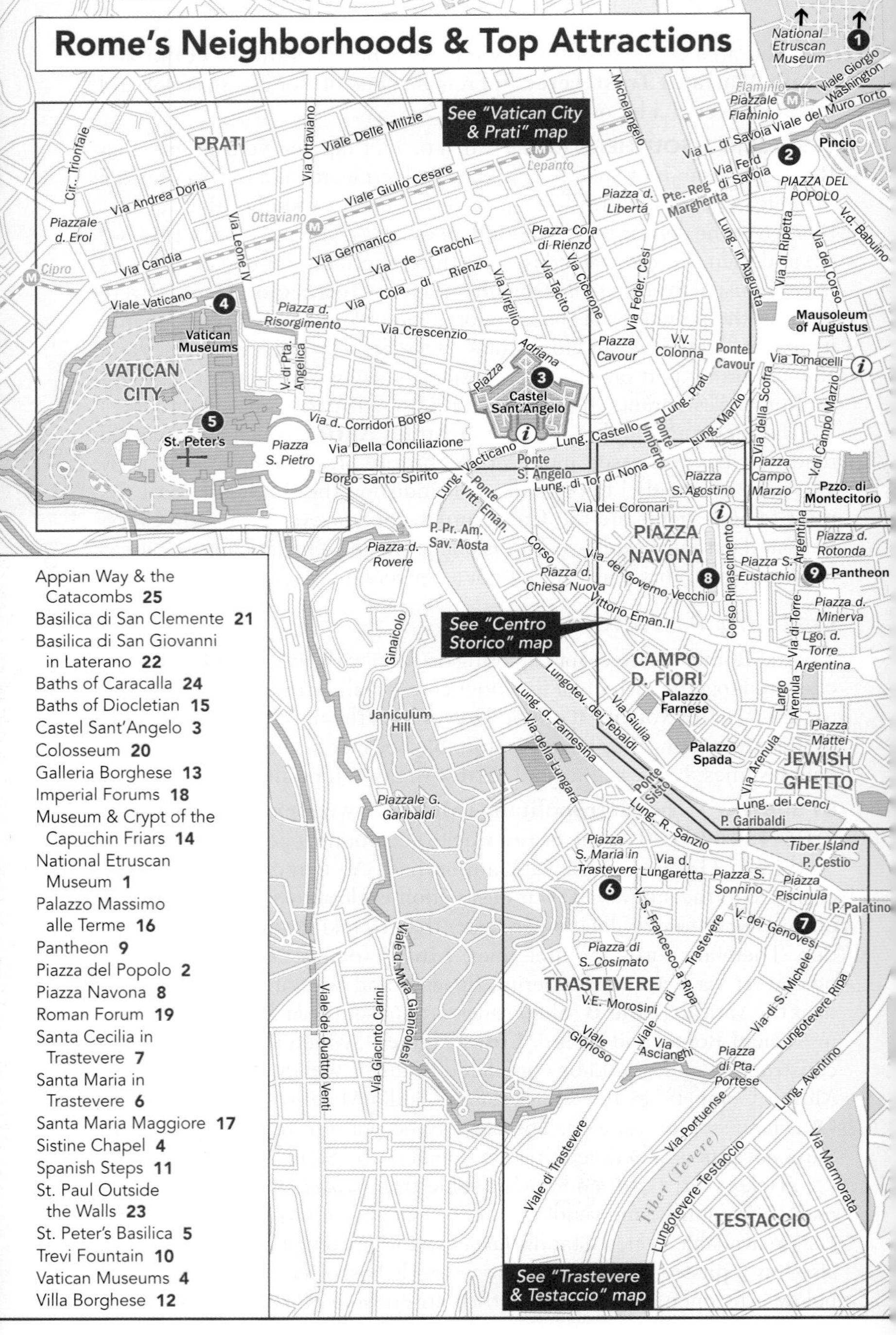

Rome's Neighborhoods & Top Attractions
See "Vatican City & Prati" map
See "Centro Storico" map
See "Trastevere & Testaccio" map
National Etruscan Museum 1
Pincio 2
PIAZZA DEL POPOLO
Mausoleum of Augustus
Castel Sant'Angelo 3
Vatican Museums 4
St. Peter's 5
Piazza S. Pietro
VATICAN CITY
PRATI
PIAZZA NAVONA 8
Pantheon 9
Pzzo. di Montecitorio
CAMPO D. FIORI
Palazzo Farnese
Palazzo Spada
JEWISH GHETTO
Tiber Island
Janiculum Hill
Piazzale G. Garibaldi
TRASTEVERE
Piazza S. Maria in Trastevere 6
7
TESTACCIO
Tiber (Tevere)
Appian Way & the Catacombs 25
Basilica di San Clemente 21
Basilica di San Giovanni in Laterano 22
Baths of Caracalla 24
Baths of Diocletian 15
Castel Sant'Angelo 3
Colosseum 20
Galleria Borghese 13
Imperial Forums 18
Museum & Crypt of the Capuchin Friars 14
National Etruscan Museum 1
Palazzo Massimo alle Terme 16
Pantheon 9
Piazza del Popolo 2
Piazza Navona 8
Roman Forum 19
Santa Cecilia in Trastevere 7
Santa Maria in Trastevere 6
Santa Maria Maggiore 17
Sistine Chapel 4
Spanish Steps 11
St. Paul Outside the Walls 23
St. Peter's Basilica 5
Trevi Fountain 10
Vatican Museums 4
Villa Borghese 12

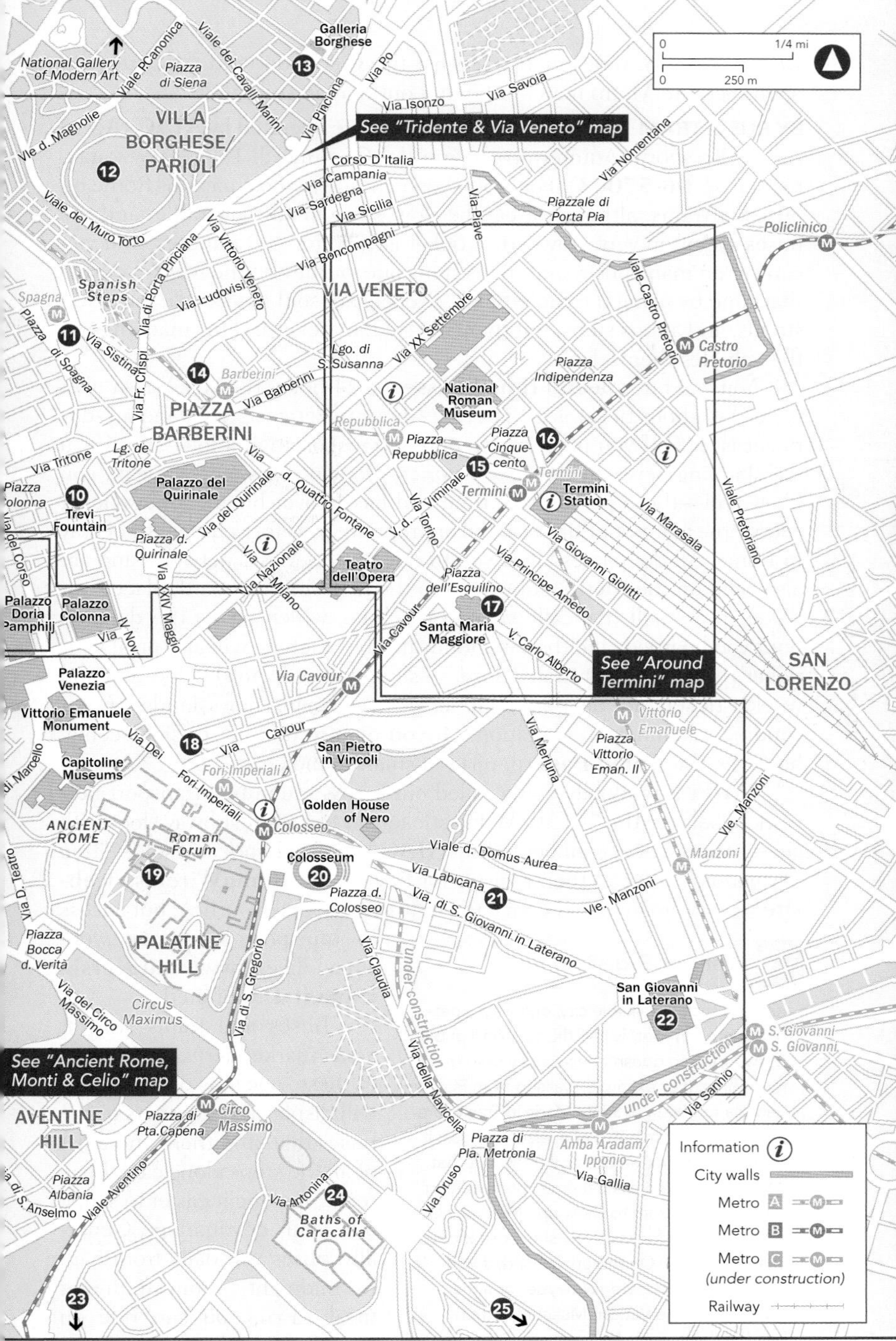
National Gallery of Modern Art
Viale P.Canonica
Piazza di Siena
Viale dei Cavalli Marini
Galleria Borghese
Via Pinciana
Via Po
Via Isonzo
Via Savoia
VILLA BORGHESE/ PARIOLI
Vle d. Magnolie
See "Tridente & Via Veneto" map
Corso D'Italia
Via Campania
Via Nomentana
Via Sardegna
Via Sicilia
Via Piave
Piazzale di Porta Pia
Viale del Muro Torto
Via Vittorio Veneto
Via di Porta Pinciana
Via Boncompagni
Policlinico
Spanish Steps
Spagna
Via Ludovisi
VIA VENETO
Via XX Settembre
Viale Castro Pretorio
Piazza di Spagna
Via Sistina
Via Fr. Crispi
Lgo. di S.Susanna
Castro Pretorio
Barberini
Piazza Indipendenza
PIAZZA BARBERINI
Via Barberini
National Roman Museum
Repubblica
Piazza Repubblica
Piazza Cinquecento
Via Tritone
Lg. de Tritone
Via d. Quattro Fontane
Piazza Colonna
Palazzo del Quirinale
Via del Quirinale
Via Viminale
Termini
Termini Station
Via Marasala
Trevi Fountain
Via Torino
V. d. Viminale
Viale Pretoriano
Via del Corso
Piazza d. Quirinale
Via Nazionale
Via Giovanni Giolitti
Teatro dell'Opera
Via Principe Amedo
Via Milano
Piazza dell'Esquilino
Palazzo Doria Pamphilj
Palazzo Colonna
Via XXIV Maggio
Via IV Nov.
Santa Maria Maggiore
V. Carlo Alberto
Via Cavour
See "Around Termini" map
SAN LORENZO
Palazzo Venezia
Vittorio Emanuele
Vittorio Emanuele Monument
Via Merluna
Piazza Vittorio Eman. II
Via Dei Fori Imperiali
San Pietro in Vincoli
Capitoline Museums
Fori Imperiali
Vle. Manzoni
ANCIENT ROME
Golden House of Nero
Colosseo
Roman Forum
Viale d. Domus Aurea
Colosseum
Manzoni
Via Labicana
Piazza d. Colosseo
Via. di S. Giovanni in Laterano
Via D. Teatro
Piazza Bocca d. Verità
PALATINE HILL
Via di S. Gregorio
Via Claudia
under construction
Via del Circo Massimo
Circus Maximus
San Giovanni in Laterano
S. Giovanni
Via della Navicella
See "Ancient Rome, Monti & Celio" map
Via Sannio
AVENTINE HILL
Piazza di Pta.Capena
Circo Massimo
Piazza di Pla. Metronia
Amba Aradam/ Ipponio
Via Gallia
Piazza Albania
Viale Aventino
Via Antonina
Via Druso
Via di S.Anselmo
Baths of Caracalla
Information
City walls
Metro A
Metro B
Metro C (under construction)
Railway
0 1/4 mi
0 250 m
10
11
12
13
14
15
16
17
18
19
20
21
22
23
24
25

Roma Pass (p. 63), touch it against the yellow dot and the gates will open. See the Metro map on the tear-out map in this guide.

BY BUS & TRAM Roman buses and trams are operated by **ATAC** (Agenzia del Trasporto Autoferrotranviario del Comune di Roma; www.atac.roma.it; ✆ **06-57003**). For 1.50€ you can ride to most parts of Rome on buses or trams, although it can be slow going in all that traffic, and the buses are often very crowded. A ticket is valid for 100 minutes, and you can get on many buses and trams (plus one journey on the Metro) during that time by using the same ticket. Tickets are sold in *tabacchi*, at newsstands, and at bus stops, but there are seldom ticket-issuing machines on the vehicles themselves.

You can buy **special timed passes:** a 24-hour (ROMA 24H) ticket is 7€; a 48-hour ticket is 12.50€; a 72-hour ticket costs 18€; and a 7-day ticket is 24€. If you plan to ride public transportation a lot—and if you are skipping between the *centro storico,* Roman ruins, and Vatican, you likely will—these passes save time and hassle over buying a new ticket every time you ride. Purchase the appropriate pass for your length of stay in Rome. All the passes allow you to ride on the ATAC network, and are also valid on the Metro (subway). On the first bus you board, place your ticket in a small (typically yellow) machine, which prints the day and hour you boarded, and then withdraw it. The machine will also print your ticket's time of expiration (*"scad."*—short for scadenza). One-day and weekly tickets are also available at *tabacchi,* many newsstands, and at vending machines at all stations. If you plan to do a lot of sightseeing, however, the **Roma Pass** (p. 63) is a smarter choice.

Wi-Fi is gradually being rolled out across the public transport network. Look for the "ATAC WiFi" sticker on the tram/subway doors. To access the service, connect to the "ATAC WiFi" network and select "free navigation"; you can then register for free on the **RomaWireless website** (www.romawireless.com). You only get 2 hours of surfing, but access to transport assistance websites like **www.muoversiaroma.it** is unlimited.

Buses and trams stop at areas marked *fermata.* At most of these, a yellow or white sign will display the numbers of the buses that stop there and a list of all the stops along each bus's route, making it easier to scope out your destination. Generally, buses run daily from 5am to midnight. From midnight until dawn, you can ride on special night buses (look for

Walk or Ride?

Rome is such a walkable city, one where getting there (on foot) is half the fun. And public transportation doesn't necessarily save that much time. (For example, walking from Piazza Venezia to Piazza di Santa Maria in Trastevere takes about 25 minutes at a leisurely pace; it takes 12 minutes via bus and tram, but that doesn't include potential time spent waiting for the bus or tram to show up.) My take? On a nice day and for relatively short distances, enjoy the stroll. On the other hand, if you want to save your steps (maybe for a marathon tour of the Vatican Museums), then head to the nearest Metro, tram, or bus stop.

Rome's Key Bus Routes

First, know that any map of the Roman bus system will likely be outdated before it's printed. Many buses listed on the "latest" map no longer exist; others are enjoying a much-needed rest, and new buses suddenly appear without warning. There's always talk of renumbering the whole system, so be aware that the route numbers we've listed might have changed by the time you travel. Second, take extreme caution when riding Rome's overcrowded buses—pickpockets abound! This is particularly true on bus no. 64, a favorite of visitors because of its route through the historic districts and thus also a favorite of Rome's pickpocketing community. This bus has earned various nicknames, including the "Pickpocket Express" and "Wallet Eater."

Although routes may change, a few reliable bus routes have remained valid for years in Rome:

- **40 (Express):** Stazione Termini to the Vatican via Via Nazionale, Piazza Venezia and Piazza Pia, by the Castel Sant'Angelo
- **64:** The "tourist route" from Termini, along Via Nazionale and through Piazza Venezia and along Via Argentina to Piazza San Pietro in the Vatican (***Head's up:*** It's also known as the Pickpocket Express.)
- **75:** Stazione Termini to the Colosseum
- **H:** Stazione Termini via Piazza Venezia and the Ghetto to Trastevere via Ponte Garibaldi

the "n" in front of the bus number), which run only on main routes. It's best to take a taxi in the wee hours—if you can find one. Call for one (see "By Taxi," below) in a pinch. **Bus information booths** at Piazza dei Cinquecento, in front of Stazione Termini, offer advice on routes.

BY TAXI Don't count on hailing a taxi on the street. If you're going out, have your hotel call one. At a restaurant, ask the waiter or cashier to dial for you. If you want to phone for yourself, try the **city taxi service** at ✆ **06-0609** (which will redirect to the nearest taxi stand, but you have to state the name of your location), or one of these **radio taxi numbers:** ✆ **06-6645,** 06-3570, or 06-4994. You can also text a taxi at ✆ **366-6730000** by writing "Roma [address]" as the message. Taxis on call incur a surcharge of 3.50€. Larger taxi stands are at Piazza Venezia (east side), Piazza di Spagna (Spanish Steps), the Colosseum, Corso Rinascimento (Piazza Navona), Largo Argentina, the Pantheon, Piazza del Popolo, Piazza Risorgimento (near St. Peter's), and Piazza Belli (Trastevere).

The meter begins at 3€ (Mon–Fri 6am–10pm) for the first 3km (1¾ miles) and then rises 1.10€ per kilometer. The first suitcase is free. Every additional piece of luggage costs 1€. On Saturday and Sunday between 6am and 10pm the meter starts at 4.50€; from 10pm to 6am every day the meter starts at 6.50€. Trips from Termini incur a 2€ surcharge. Avoid paying your fare with large bills; invariably, taxi drivers claim that they don't have change, hoping for a bigger tip. Italians don't tip taxi drivers like Americans do and, at most, will simply round up to the nearest euro. If the driver is really friendly or helpful, a tip of 1€ to 2€ is sufficient. Many taxis accept credit cards, but it's best to check first, before getting on.

As in the rest of the world, taxi apps have caught on in Rome. The main app for official city taxis is **it Taxi** (www.ittaxi.it), which is run by Rome's largest taxi company, **3570** (www.3570.it). It allows users to pay directly from the app using a credit card or PayPal. **Uber** (www.uber.com) is also available in Rome.

BY CAR All roads might lead to Rome, but you probably won't want to drive once you get here. Because the reception desks of most Roman hotels have at least one English-speaking person, call ahead to find out the best route into Rome from wherever you are starting out. You will want to get rid of your rental car as soon as possible, or park in a garage.

If you want to rent a car to explore the countryside around Rome or drive to another city, you will save money if you reserve before leaving home (see chapter 16). If you decide to book a car here, **Avis** (www.avis.com; ✆ **06-4814373**), **Maggiore,** an Italian company (www.maggiore.it; ✆ **06-4880049;** Metro: Termini), and several other agencies have desks inside Stazione Termini. **Hertz** is just down the street at Via Giovanni Giolitti 34 (www.hertz.com; ✆ **06-4740389;** Metro: Termini).

Note that rental cars in Italy may be smaller than what you are used to, including in terms of trunk space. Make sure you consider both luggage size and the number of people when booking your vehicle.

[Fast FACTS] ROME

Banks In general, banks are open Monday to Friday 8:30am to 1:30pm and 2:30 or 2:45 to 4pm. Lines can be painfully slow, and many banks do not do currency exchange.

Business hours Most Roman shops open at 10am and close at 7pm from Monday to Saturday. Smaller shops close for 1 or 2 hours at lunch, and may remain closed Monday morning and Saturday afternoon. Most restaurants are closed for *riposo* (rest) 1 day per week, usually Sunday or Monday.

Dentists **American Dental Arts Rome,** Via del Governo Vecchio 73 (near Piazza Navona; www.adadentistsrome.com; ✆ **06-6832613**), uses the latest technology, including laser dental techniques.

Doctors Call the U.S. Embassy at ✆ **06-46741** for a list of English-speaking doctors. All big hospitals have emergency rooms (*pronto soccorso*). You'll find English-speaking doctors at the privately run **Salvator Mundi International Hospital,** Viale delle Mura Gianicolensi 67 (in the Gianicolo neighborhood; www.salvatormundi.it; ✆ **06-588961**). For medical assistance, the **International Medical Center** is on 24-hour duty at Via Firenze 47 (near Piazza della Repubblica; www.imc84.com; ✆ **06-4882371;** Metro: Repubblica). Well east of centro, the **Rome American Hospital,** Via Emilio Longoni 69 (www.hcitalia.it/romeamericanhospital; ✆ **06-22551**), has English-speaking doctors on duty 24 hours. A more personalized service is provided 24 hours a day by **Medi-Call Italia,** Via Cremera 8 (www.medi-call.it; ✆ **06-8840113;** Bus: 86), which can arrange for a qualified doctor to make a house call at your hotel or anywhere in Rome. Fees begin at around 100€ per visit and can go higher if a specialist or specialized treatments are necessary.

Embassies & Consulates See chapter 16.

Emergencies

To call the police, dial ✆ **113;** for an ambulance ✆ **118;** for a fire ✆ **115.**

Internet Access

Most Roman hotels have Internet access—broadband connections in guest rooms, a hotel-wide wireless network, or an Internet terminal in the lobby. The Internet cafe/tearoom **Gran Caffè La Caffettiera,** Piazza di Pietra 65 (www.grancaffelacaffettiera.com; ✆ **06-6798147**), near the Pantheon, has great atmosphere.

Mail

Stamps *(francobolli)* for the *Poste Italiane* can be purchased at post offices or at most tobacco shops and hotel reception desks. It costs 2.20€ to mail a postcard to the U.S. You can buy special stamps at the **Vatican City Post Office,** adjacent to the information office in St. Peter's Square (Mon–Fri 8:30am–7pm, Sat until 6pm).

Newspapers & Magazines

You can buy major publications including *The New York Times International Edition* and *The Times of London* at most newsstands. The English-language expat magazine *Wanted in Rome* (www.wantedinrome.com) comes out every 2 weeks and lists current events and shows. If you read Italian, *Time Out* has a Rome edition and *La Repubblica* publishes the pull-out "TrovaRoma" every Thursday.

Pharmacies

Farmacie are recognizable by their neon green or red cross signs. Most pharmacies are open from 8:30am to 1pm and 4 to 7:30pm, though some stay open later. Farmacia Piram at Via Nazionale 228 is open 24 hours. All closed pharmacies have signs in their windows indicating any open pharmacies nearby.

Police

Dial ✆ **113.**

Safety

Violent crime is virtually nonexistent in Rome's touristed areas, though pickpocketing is a common problem. Men should keep their wallets in their front pocket or inside jacket pocket. Purse snatching happens on occasion, by young men speeding by on Vespas. Keep your purse on the wall side of your body and place the strap across your chest. Don't lay anything valuable on alfresco tables or chairs, where it can be grabbed up. Sadly, *Romani*, or *Roma* gypsies, often enlist children to beg desperately for money, and many are trained to pick pockets. Other pickpockets dress like typical businesspeople, so always be suspicious of anyone who tries to "befriend" you in a tourist area. In general, Rome is quite safe—walking alone at night is usually fine anywhere in the *centro storico.*

EXPLORING ROME

Rome's ancient monuments are a constant reminder that this was one of the greatest centers of Western civilization. In the heyday of the Empire, all roads led to Rome, with good reason. It was one of the first cosmopolitan cities, importing slaves, gladiators, great art, and even citizens from the far corners of the world. Despite its brutality and corruption, Rome left a legacy of law, a heritage of art, architecture, and engineering, and a canny lesson in how to conquer enemies by absorbing their cultures.

But ancient Rome is only part of the spectacle. The Vatican has had a tremendous influence on making the city a tourism center. Although Vatican architects stripped down much of the city's ancient glory during the Renaissance, looting ruins (the Forum especially) for their precious marble, they created more treasures and occasionally incorporated the old into the new—as Michelangelo did when turning Diocletian's Baths

St. Peter's Basilica and the Vatican, viewed from the Tiber River.

complex into a church. And in the years that followed, Bernini adorned the city with baroque wonders, especially his glorious fountains.

Bypassing the Lines

The endless lines outside Italian museums and attractions are a fact of life. But reservation services can help you avoid the wait, at least for some major museums. Buying a **Roma Pass** (p. 63) is a good start; holders can use a special entrance at the Colosseum, and for your first two (free) museums, you can skip the line (so choose busy ones).

For the **Vatican Museums,** buy an advance ticket at **http://bigliet teriamusei.vatican.va**; you'll pay an extra 4€ but you'll skip the line at the entrance (which can be very, very long). St. Peter's is not included in the perk: There is no way to jump the line there, unless you book a private or group tour (p 121).

Coopculture (www.coopculture.it) operates an online ticket office, which allows you to skip the line at many sites, including the Colosseum and the Forum, with a booking fee of 1.50€ and 2€ to print tickets.

St. Peter's & the Vatican

VATICAN CITY

The world's smallest sovereign state, **Vatican City** is a truly tiny territory, comprising little more than St. Peter's Basilica and the walled headquarters of the Roman Catholic Church. There are no border controls, though the city-state's 800 inhabitants (essentially clergymen and Swiss Guards) have their own radio station, daily newspaper, tax-free pharmacy and petrol pumps, postal service, and head of state—the Pope. The Pope had always exercised a high degree of political independence from the rest of Italy, formalized by the 1929 Lateran Treaty between Pope Pius XI and the Italian government to create the Vatican. The city is still protected by the flamboyantly uniformed (designed by Michelangelo) Swiss Guards, a tradition dating from when the Swiss, known as brave soldiers, were often hired out as mercenaries for foreign armies. Today the Vatican

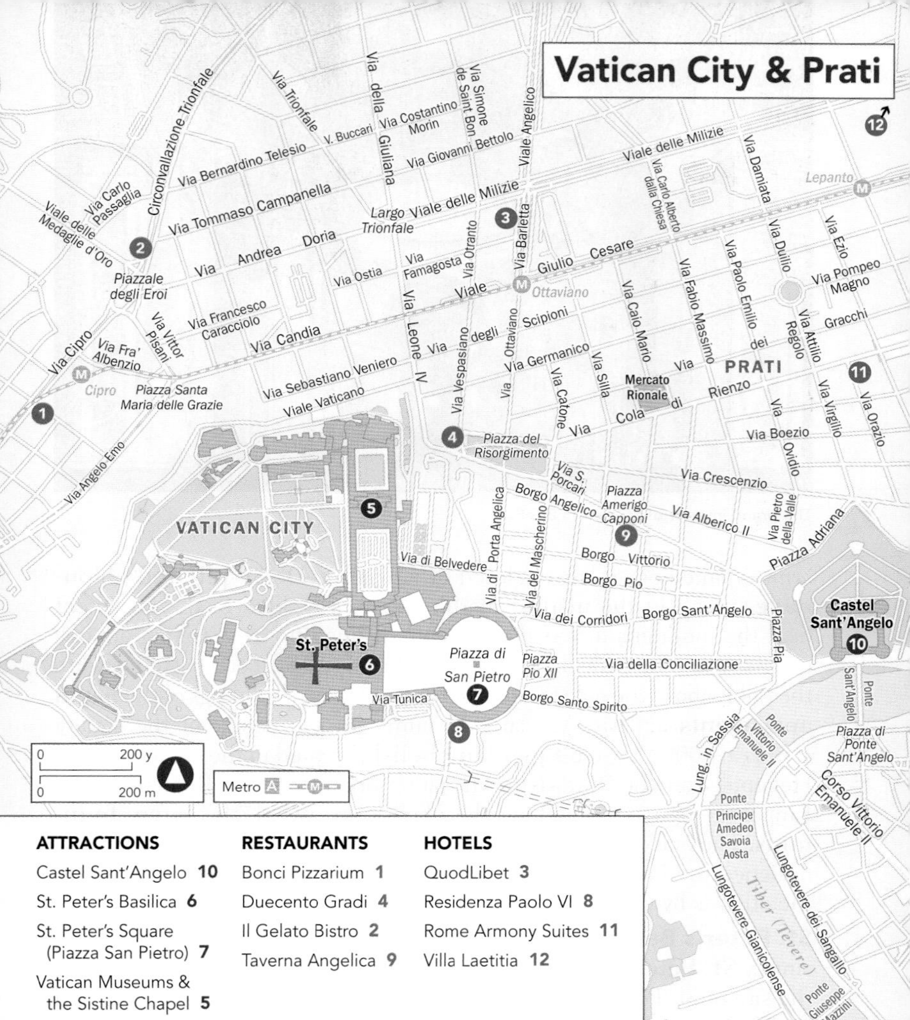

remains the center of the Roman Catholic world, the home of the Pope—and the resting place of St. Peter. **St. Peter's Basilica** is obviously one of the highlights, but the only part of the Apostolic Palace itself that you can visit independently is the **Vatican Museums,** the world's biggest and richest museum complex.

On the left side of Piazza San Pietro, the **Vatican Tourist Office** (www.vatican.va; ✆ **06-69882019;** Mon–Sat 8:30am–7:30pm) sells maps and guides that will help you make sense of the treasures in the museums; it also accepts reservations for tours of the Vatican Gardens.

The only entrance to St. Peter's for tourists is through one of the glories of the Western world: Bernini's 17th-century **St. Peter's Square (Piazza San Pietro).** As you stand in the huge piazza, you are in the

The grand interior of St. Peter's Basilica.

arms of an ellipse partly enclosed by a majestic **Doric-pillared colonnade.** Stand in the marked marble discs embedded in the pavement near the fountains to see all the columns lined up in a striking optical/geometrical play. Straight ahead is the facade of St. Peter's itself, and to the right, above the colonnade, are the dark brown buildings of the **papal apartments** and the Vatican Museums. In the center of the square stands a 4,000-year-old **Egyptian obelisk,** created in the ancient city of Heliopolis on the Nile delta and appropriated by the Romans under Emperor Augustus. Flanking the obelisk are two 17th-century **fountains.** The one on the right (facing the basilica), by Carlo Maderno, who designed the facade of St. Peter's, was placed here by Bernini himself; the other is by Carlo Fontana.

St. Peter's Basilica ★★★ CHURCH The Basilica di San Pietro, or simply **St. Peter's,** is the holiest shrine of the Catholic Church, built on the site of St. Peter's tomb by the greatest Italian artists of the 16th and 17th centuries. One of the lines on the right side of the piazza funnels you into the basilica, while the other two lead to the underground grottoes or the dome. Whichever you opt for first, you must be **properly dressed**—a rule that is very strictly enforced.

In Roman times, the Circus of Nero, where St. Peter is said to have been crucified, was just to the left of where the basilica is today. Peter was allegedly buried here in A.D. 64, and in A.D. 324 Emperor Constantine commissioned a church to be built over Peter's

A St. Peter's Warning

St. Peter's has a hard-and-fast dress code that makes no exceptions: **Men and women in shorts, above-the-knee skirts, or bare shoulders** are not admitted to the basilica, period. I've occasionally seen guards handing out disposable cloaks for the scantily clad, but don't count on that: Cover up or bring a shawl. The same holds for the Roman Necropolis and the Vatican Museums.

tomb. That structure stood for more than 1,000 years. The present basilica, mostly completed in the 1500s and 1600s, is predominantly High Renaissance and baroque. Inside, the massive scale is almost too much to absorb, showcasing some of Italy's greatest artists: Bramante, Raphael and Michelangelo. In a church of such grandeur—overwhelming in its detail of gilt, marble, and mosaic—you can't expect much subtlety. It is meant to be overpowering.

Going straight into the basilica, the first thing you see on the right side of the nave—the longest nave in the world, as clearly marked in the floor along with other cathedral measurements—is the chapel containing Michelangelo's graceful **"Pietà" ★★★.** Created in the 1490s when the master was still in his 20s, it clearly shows his genius for capturing the human form. (The sculpture has been kept behind reinforced glass since an act of vandalism in the 1970s.) Note the lifelike folds of Mary's robes and her youthful features; although she would've been middle-aged at the time of the Crucifixion, Michelangelo portrayed her as a young woman to convey her purity.

Further inside the nave, Michelangelo's dome is a mesmerizing space, rising high above the supposed site of St. Peter's tomb. With a diameter of 41.5m (136 ft.), the dome is Rome's largest, supported by four bulky piers decorated with reliefs depicting the basilica's key holy relics: St. Veronica's handkerchief (used to wipe the face of Christ); the lance of St. Longinus, which pierced Christ's side; and a piece of the True Cross.

Under the dome is the twisty-columned **baldacchino ★★**, by Bernini, sheltering the papal altar. The ornate 29m-high (96-ft.) canopy was created in part, so it is said, from bronze stripped from the Pantheon. Bernini sculpted the face of a woman on the base of each pillar; starting with the face on the left pillar (with your back to the entrance), circle the entire altar to see the progress of expressions from the agony of childbirth through to the fourth pillar, where the woman's face is replaced with that of her newborn baby.

Just before you reach the dome, on the right, the devout stop to kiss the foot of the 13th-century **bronze of St. Peter ★**, attributed to Arnolfo di Cambio. Elsewhere the church is decorated by more of Bernini's lavish sculptures, including his monument to Pope Alexander VII in the south transept, its winged skeleton writhing under the heavy marble drapes.

An entrance off the nave leads to the Sacristy and the **Historical Museum (Museo Storico)** or **treasury ★**, which is chock-full of richly jeweled chalices, reliquaries, and copes, as well as the late-15th-century bronze tomb of Pope Sixtus IV by Pollaiuolo.

You can also head downstairs to the **Vatican grottoes ★★**, with their tombs of the popes, both ancient and modern (Pope John XXIII got the most adulation until the interment of **Pope John Paul II** in 2005). Behind a wall of glass is what is considered to be the tomb of St. Peter.

After you leave the grottoes, you find yourself in a courtyard and ticket line for the grandest sight in the basilica: the climb to **Michelangelo's**

Fontana Della Pigna in the courtyard of the Vatican Museum.

dome ★★★, about 114m (375 ft.) high. You can walk all the way up or take the elevator as far as it goes. The elevator saves you 171 steps, and you *still* have 320 to go after getting off. After you've made it to the top, you'll have a scintillating view over the rooftops of Rome and even the Vatican Gardens and papal apartments.

Visits to the **Necropolis Vaticana ★★** and St. Peter's tomb itself are restricted to 250 persons per day on guided tours (90 min.) You must send a fax or e-mail 3 weeks beforehand, or apply in advance in person at the Ufficio Scavi (✆/fax **06-69873017;** e-mail: scavi@fsp.va; Mon–Fri 9am–6pm, Sat 9am–5pm), which is located through the arch to the left of the stairs up from the basilica. For details, check **www.vatican.va**. Children 14 and under are not admitted to the Necropolis.

Piazza San Pietro. www.vatican.va. ✆ **06-69881662.** Basilica (including grottoes) free. Necropolis Vaticana (St. Peter's tomb) 13€. Stairs to the dome 5€; elevator to the dome 7€; sacristy (with Historical Museum) free. Basilica (including grottoes and treasury) Oct–Mar daily 7am–6:30pm, Apr–Sep daily 7am–7pm. Dome Oct–Mar daily 8am–5pm, Apr–Sept daily 8am–6pm. Metro: Ottaviano/San Pietro, then a 10 min. walk; or take bus 40, 46, or 62 to Piazza Pia/Traspontina, then about a 10 min. walk.

Vatican Museums & the Sistine Chapel ★★★ MUSEUM Nothing else in Rome quite lives up to the awe-inspiring collections of the **Vatican Museums,** a 15-minute walk from St. Peter's out of the north side of Piazza San Pietro. It's a vast treasure store of art from antiquity and the Renaissance gathered by the Roman Catholic Church through the centuries, filling a series of ornate Papal palaces, apartments, and galleries leading to one of the world's most beautiful buildings, the justly celebrated **Sistine Chapel**.

Note that the Vatican dress code also applies to its museums (no sleeveless blouses, no miniskirts, no shorts, no hats allowed), though it tends to be less rigorously enforced than at St. Peter's. **Guided tours** are a good way to get the most out of a visit, and are the only way to visit the **Vatican Gardens.**

Obviously, one trip will not be enough to see everything here. Below are previews of the main highlights, showstoppers, and masterpieces on display (in alphabetical order).

APPARTAMENTO BORGIA (BORGIA APARTMENTS) ★ Created for Pope Alexander VI (the infamous Borgia pope) between 1492 and 1494, these rooms were frescoed with biblical and allegorical scenes by Umbrian painter Pinturicchio and his assistants. Look for what is thought to be the earliest European depiction of Native Americans, painted little more than a year after Columbus returned from the New World and Alexander had "divided" the globe between Spain and Portugal.

COLLEZIONE D'ARTE CONTEMPORANEA (COLLECTION OF MODERN RELIGIOUS ART) ★ Spanning 55 rooms of almost 800 works, these galleries contain the Vatican's concession to modern art. There are some big names here and the quality is high, and themes usually have a spiritual and religious component: Van Gogh's "Pietà, after Delacroix" is here, along with Francis Bacon's eerie "Study for a Pope II." You will also see works by Paul Klee ("City with Gothic Cathedral"), Siqueiros ("Mutilated Christ No. 467"), Otto Dix ("Road to Calvary"), Gauguin ("Religious Panel"), Chagall ("Red Pietà"), and a whole room dedicated to Georges Rouault.

MUSEI DI ANTICHITÀ CLASSICHE (CLASSICAL ANTIQUITIES MUSEUMS) ★★★ The Vatican maintains four classical antiquities museums, the most important being the **Museo Pio Clementino ★★★**, crammed with Greek and Roman sculptures in the small Belvedere Palace of Innocent VIII. At the heart of the complex lies the Octagonal Court, where highlights include the sculpture of the Trojan priest **"Laocoön" ★★★** and his two sons locked in a struggle with sea serpents, dating from around 40 B.C., and the exceptional **"Belvedere Apollo" ★★★** (a 2nd-c. Roman reproduction of an authentic Greek work from the 4th c. B.C.), the symbol of classic male beauty and a possible inspiration for Michelangelo's "David." Look out also for the impressive gilded bronze statue of **"Hercules"** in the Rotonda, from the late 2nd century A.D., and the **Hall of the Chariot,** containing a magnificent sculpture of a chariot combining Roman originals and 18th-century work by Antonio Franzoni.

The **Museo Chiaramonti ★** occupies the long loggia that links the Belvedere Palace to the main Vatican palaces, jam-packed on both sides with more than 800 Greco-Roman works, including statues, reliefs, and sarcophagi. In the **Braccio Nuovo ★** ("New Wing"), a handsome Neoclassical extension of the Chiaramonti sumptuously lined with colored marble, lies the colossal statue of the **"Nile" ★**, the ancient river portrayed as an old man with his 16 children, most likely a reproduction of a long-lost Alexandrian Greek original.

Vatican Museums: Buy the Book

The Vatican Museums have overpacked galleries and few descriptive labels. To help you make sense of the incredible riches, pick up the **detailed guide** sold at the Vatican Tourist Office (14€), on the left side of the Piazza San Pietro

The **Museo Gregoriano Profano ★★,** built in 1970, houses more Greek sculptures looted by the Romans (some from the Parthenon), mostly funerary steles and votive reliefs, as well as some choice Roman pieces, notably the restored mosaics from the floors of the public libraries in the **Baths of Caracalla** (p. 86).

MUSEO ETNOLOGICO (ETHNOLOGICAL MUSEUM) ★★ Founded in 1926, this astounding assemblage of artifacts and artwork is from cultures around the world, from ancient Chinese coins and notes, to plaster sculptures of Native Americans and ceremonial art from Papua New Guinea.

MUSEO GREGORIANO EGIZIO ★★ Nine rooms are packed with plunder from Ancient Egypt, including sarcophagi, mummies, pharaonic statuary, votive bronzes, jewelry, cuneiform tablets from Mesopotamia, inscriptions from Assyrian palaces, and Egyptian hieroglyphics.

MUSEO GREGORIANO ETRUSCO ★★ The core of this collection is a cache of rare Etruscan art treasures dug up in the 19th century, dating from between the 9th and the 1st centuries B.C. The Romans learned a lot from the Etruscans, as the highly crafted ceramics, bronzes, silver, and gold on display attest. Don't miss the **Regolini-Galassi tomb** (7th c. B.C.), unearthed at Cerveteri. The museum is housed within the *palazzettos* of Innocent VIII (reigned 1484–92) and Pius IV (reigned 1559–65), the latter adorned with frescoes by Federico Barocci and Federico Zuccari.

PINACOTECA (ART GALLERY) ★★★ The great painting collections of the Popes are displayed in the Pinacoteca, including work from all the big names in Italian art, from Giotto and Fra' Angelico to Perugino, Raphael, Veronese, and Crespi. Early medieval work occupies Room 1, with the most intriguing piece a keyhole-shaped wood panel of the "Last Judgment" by Nicolò e Giovanni, dated to the late 12th century. **Giotto** takes center stage in Room 2, with the "Stefaneschi Triptych" (six panels) painted for the old St. Peter's basilica between 1315 and 1320. **Fra' Angelico** dominates Room 3, his "Stories of St. Nicholas of Bari" and "Virgin with Child" justly praised (check out the Virgin's microscopic eyes in the latter piece). Carlo Crivelli features in Room 6, while decent works by Perugino and Pinturicchio grace Room 7, though most visitors press on to the **Raphael salon ★★★** (Room 8), where you can view five paintings by the Renaissance master. The best are the "Coronation of the Virgin," the "Madonna of Foligno," and the vast "Transfiguration" (completed shortly before his death). Room 9 boasts Leonardo da Vinci's **"St. Jerome with the Lion" ★★**, as well as Giovanni Bellini's "Pietà." Room 10 is dedicated to Renaissance Venice, with Titian's "Madonna of St.

Nicholas of the Frari" and Veronese's "Vision of St. Helen" being paramount. Don't skip the remaining galleries: Room 11 contains Barocci's "Annunciation," while Room 12 is really all about one of the masterpieces of the baroque, Caravaggio's **"Deposition from the Cross"** ★★.

STANZE DI RAFFAELLO (RAPHAEL ROOMS) ★★ In the early 16th century, Pope Julius II hired the young Raphael and his workshop to decorate his personal apartments, on the second floor of the Pontifical Palace. Completed between 1508 and 1524, the **Raphael Rooms** now represent one of the great artistic spectacles inside the Vatican.

The **Stanza dell'Incendio** served as the Pope's high court room and later, under Leo X, a dining room. Most of its lavish frescoes have been attributed to Raphael's pupils. Leo X commissioned much of the work here, which explains the themes (past Popes with the name Leo). Note the intricate ceiling, painted by Umbrian maestro and Raphael's first teacher, Perugino.

Raphael is the main focus in the **Stanza della Segnatura,** originally used as a Papal library and private office and home to the awe-inspiring **"School of Athens"** ★★★ fresco, depicting primarily Greek classical philosophers such as Aristotle, Plato, and Socrates. Many of the figures are thought to be based on portraits of Renaissance artists, including Bramante (on the right as Euclid, drawing on a chalkboard), Leonardo da Vinci (as Plato, the bearded man in the center), and even Raphael himself (in the lower-right corner with a black hat). On the wall opposite stands the equally magnificent "Disputa del Sacramento," where Raphael used a similar technique; Dante Alighieri stands behind the pontiff on the right, and Fra' Angelico poses as a monk (which in fact, he was) on the far left.

The **Stanza d'Eliodoro** was used for the private audiences of the Pope and was painted by Raphael immediately after he did the Segnatura. His aim here was to flatter his papal patron, Julius II: The depiction of the pope driving Attila from Rome was meant to symbolize the contemporary mission of Julius II to drive the French out of Italy. Finally, the **Sala di Costantino,** used for Papal receptions and official ceremonies, was completed by Raphael's students after the master's death, but based on his designs and drawings. It's a jaw-dropping space, commemorating four major episodes in the life of Emperor Constantine.

SISTINE CHAPEL ★★★ Michelangelo labored for 4 years (1508–12) to paint the ceiling of the Sistine Chapel; it is said he spent the entire time on his feet, paint dripping into his eyes. But what a result! Thanks to a massive restoration effort in the 1990s, the world's most famous fresco is today as vibrantly colorful and filled with roiling life as it was in 1512. And the chapel is still of central importance to the Catholic Church: This is where the Papal Conclave meets to elect new popes.

The "Creation of Adam," at the center of the ceiling, is one of the best known and most reproduced images in history, the outstretched hands of God and Adam—not quite touching—an iconic symbol of not just the Renaissance but the Enlightenment that followed. Nevertheless, it is somewhat ironic that this is Michelangelo's best-known work: The artist always regarded himself as a sculptor first and foremost.

The endless waiting in order to get into the chapel inevitably makes the sense of expectation all the greater, but despite the tour groups and the crowds, seeing the frescoes in person is a truly magical experience.

The ceiling **frescoes** are obviously the main showstoppers, though staring at them tends to take a heavy toll on the neck. Commissioned by Pope Julius II in 1508 and completed in 1512, they primarily depict nine scenes from the Book of Genesis (including the famed "Creation of Adam"), from the "Separation of Light and Darkness" at the altar end to the "Great Flood" and "Drunkenness of Noah." Surrounding these main frescoes are paintings of 12 people who prophesied the coming of Christ, from Jonah and Isaiah to the Delphic Sibyl. Once you have admired the ceiling, turn your attention to the altar wall. At the age of 60, Michelangelo was summoned to finish the chapel decor 23 years after he finished the ceiling work. Apparently saddened by leaving Florence, and depressed by the morally bankrupt state of Rome at that time, he painted these dark moods in his "Last Judgment," where he included his own self-portrait on a sagging human hide held by St. Bartholomew (who was martyred by being flayed alive).

Yet the Sistine Chapel isn't all Michelangelo. The southern wall is covered by a series of astonishing paintings completed in the 1480s: "Moses Leaving to Egypt" by Perugino, the "Trials of Moses" by Botticelli, "The Crossing of the Red Sea" by Cosimo Rosselli (or Domenico Ghirlandaio), "Descent from Mount Sinai" by Cosimo Rosselli (or Piero di Cosimo), Botticelli's "Punishment of the Rebels," and Signorelli's "Testament and Death of Moses."

On the right-hand northern wall are Perugino's "The Baptism of Christ," Botticelli's "The Temptations of Christ," Ghirlandaio's "Vocation of the Apostles," Perugino's "Delivery of the Keys," Cosimo Rosselli's "The Sermon on the Mount" and "Last Supper." On the eastern wall, originals by Ghirlandaio and Signorelli were painted over by Hendrik van den Broeck's "The Resurrection" and Matteo da Lecce's "Disputation over Moses" in the 1570s.

Vatican City, Viale Vaticano (a long walk around the Vatican walls from St. Peter's Sq.). www.museivaticani.va. ✆ **06-69884676.** 16€ adults, 8€ children 6–13, free for children 5 and under; 2-hr. tours of Vatican Gardens 32€ (no tours Wed or Sun). Mon–Sat 9am–6pm (ticket office closes at 4pm). Also open Fri 7–11pm (late Apr–July, Sept–Oct) per online booking. Also open last Sun of every month 9am–2pm (free admission). Closed Jan 1 and 6, Feb 11, Mar 19, Easter, May 1, June 29, Aug 14–15, Nov 1, and Dec 25–26. Advance tickets (reservation fee 4€) and guided tours (32€ per person) through www.bigliettieriamusei.vatican.va. Metro: Ottaviano or Cipro–Musei Vaticani; bus 46 stops in front of the entrance.

Castel Sant'Angelo ★★ CASTLE/PALACE This bulky cylindrical fortress on the Vatican side of the Tiber has a storied, complex history, beginning life as the mausoleum tomb of Emperor Hadrian in A.D. 138,

Seeing the Vatican at Night...or for Breakfast

Vatican Museum visitors now have an extraordinary opportunity to stroll through the galleries after sunset, at least on Friday nights from 7pm to 11pm (last entrance at 9:30) during the high tourist season, from the last Friday in April through July and the first Friday in September through the end of October. These **twilight visits** allow access to important collections, including the Pio-Clementine Museum, the Egyptian Museum, the Upper Galleries (candelabra, tapestries and maps), the Raphael Rooms, the Borgia Apartments, the Collection of Modern Religious Art, and the Sistine Chapel. Early birds should consider booking a **breakfast tour** of the Vatican. Starting at 7 or 7:15am (before the official opening time), breakfast visits cost more than regular tickets, but include a buffet breakfast and a far more tranquil visitor experience. Booking online is mandatory for both types of tours; visit **www.biglietteriamusei.vatican.va**.

and later serving as a castle (Pope Clement VII escaped the looting troops of Charles V here in 1527), papal residence in the 14th century, and military prison from the 17th century (Puccini used the prison as the setting for the third act of "Tosca"). Consider renting an audio guide at the entrance to help fully appreciate its various manifestations. The ashes and urns of Hadrian and his family have long since been looted and destroyed, and most of what you see today relates to the conversion of the structure into fortress and residence by the popes from the 14th century.

From the entrance a stone ramp *(rampa elicoidale)* winds its way to the upper terraces, from which you can see amazing views of the city and enjoy a coffee at the outdoor cafe. The sixth floor features the **Terrazza dell'Angelo,** crowned by a florid statue of the Archangel Michael cast in 1752 (location of the tragic denouement in "Tosca").

From here you can walk back down through five floors, including the Renaissance apartments (levels 3–5) used by some of Rome's most infamous Popes: Alexander VI (the Borgia pope) hid away in the castle after the murder of his son Giovanni in 1497, overwhelmed by grief (although his vows of moral reform were short-lived). The art collection displayed throughout is fairly mediocre by Rome standards, although there are a few works by Carlo Crivelli and Luca Signorelli, notably a "Madonna and Child with Saints" from the latter.

Below the apartments are the grisly dungeons **("Le Prigioni")** used as torture chambers in the medieval period, and utilized especially enthusiastically by Cesare Borgia. The castle is connected to St. Peter's Basilica by **Il Passetto di Borgo,** a walled 800m (2,635-ft.) passage erected in 1277 by Pope Nicholas III, used by popes who needed to make a quick escape to the fortress in times of danger, which was fairly often. Fans of Dan Brown will recognize it from his novel *Angels & Demons*. Note that the dungeons, Il Passetto, and the apartments of Clement VII are usually only open on summer evenings (July–Aug Tues–Sun 8:30pm–1am; free 50-min. tours with admission, English tour at

papal AUDIENCES

When the pope is in Rome, he gives a public audience every Wednesday beginning at 10:30am (sometimes 10am in summer). If you want to get a good seat near the front, arrive early—security begins to let people in between 8 and 8:30am. Audiences take place in the Paul VI Hall of Audiences, although sometimes St. Peter's Basilica and St. Peter's Square are used to accommodate a large attendance in the summer. With the ascension of Pope Francis to the Throne of Peter in 2013, this tradition continues. You can check on the Pope's appearances and the ceremonies he presides over, including celebrations of Mass, on the Vatican website (www.vatican.va). Anyone is welcome, but you must first obtain a **free ticket;** without a reservation you can try the Swiss Guards by the Bronze Doors located just after security at St. Peter's (8am–8pm in summer and 8am–7pm in winter). You can pick up tickets here up to 3 days in advance, subject to availability.

If you prefer to reserve a place in advance, download a request form at www.vaticantour.com/images/Vatican_Ticket_request.pdf or www.vatican.va and fax it to the **Prefecture of the Papal Household** at ✆ **06-69885863.** Tickets can be picked up at the office located just inside the Bronze Doors from 3 to 7:30pm on the preceding day or on the morning of the audience from 8 to 10:30am.

At noon on Sundays, the Pope speaks briefly from his study window and gives his blessing to the visitors and pilgrims gathered in St. Peter's Square (no tickets are required for this). From about mid-July to mid-September, the Angelus and blessing historically takes place at the Pope's summer residence at Castel Gandolfo, some 26km (16 miles) out of Rome. Though Pope Francis has mostly shunned this summer retreat for being too decadent, he has made it more accessible to visitors. The residence is accessible by Metro and bus as well as a new train service that leaves from the Roma San Pietro station. Visit biglietteriamusei.vatican.va for information on seeing Castel Gandolfo by train.

10:30pm) or by written request by e-mail at **pm-laz@beniculturali.it**. Classical music and jazz concerts are also held in and around the castle in summer (Wed, Fri–Sun 9:30pm).

Lungotevere Castello 50. www.castelsantangelo.com. ✆ **06-6819111.** 10€. Tues–Sun 9am–7:30pm. Bus: 23, 40, 62, 271, 280, 982 (to Piazza Pia).

The Colosseum, Forum & Ancient Rome

THE MAJOR SIGHTS OF ANCIENT ROME

Your sightseeing experience will be enhanced if you know a little about the history and rulers of Ancient Rome: See p. 73 for a brief rundown.

Arch of Constantine (Arco di Costantino) ★★ MONUMENT

The photogenic triumphal arch next to the Colosseum was erected by the Senate in A.D. 315 to honor Constantine's defeat of the pagan Maxentius at the Battle of the Milvian Bridge (A.D. 312). Many of the reliefs have nothing whatsoever to do with Constantine or his works, but they tell of the victories of earlier Antonine rulers (lifted from other, long-forgotten memorials).

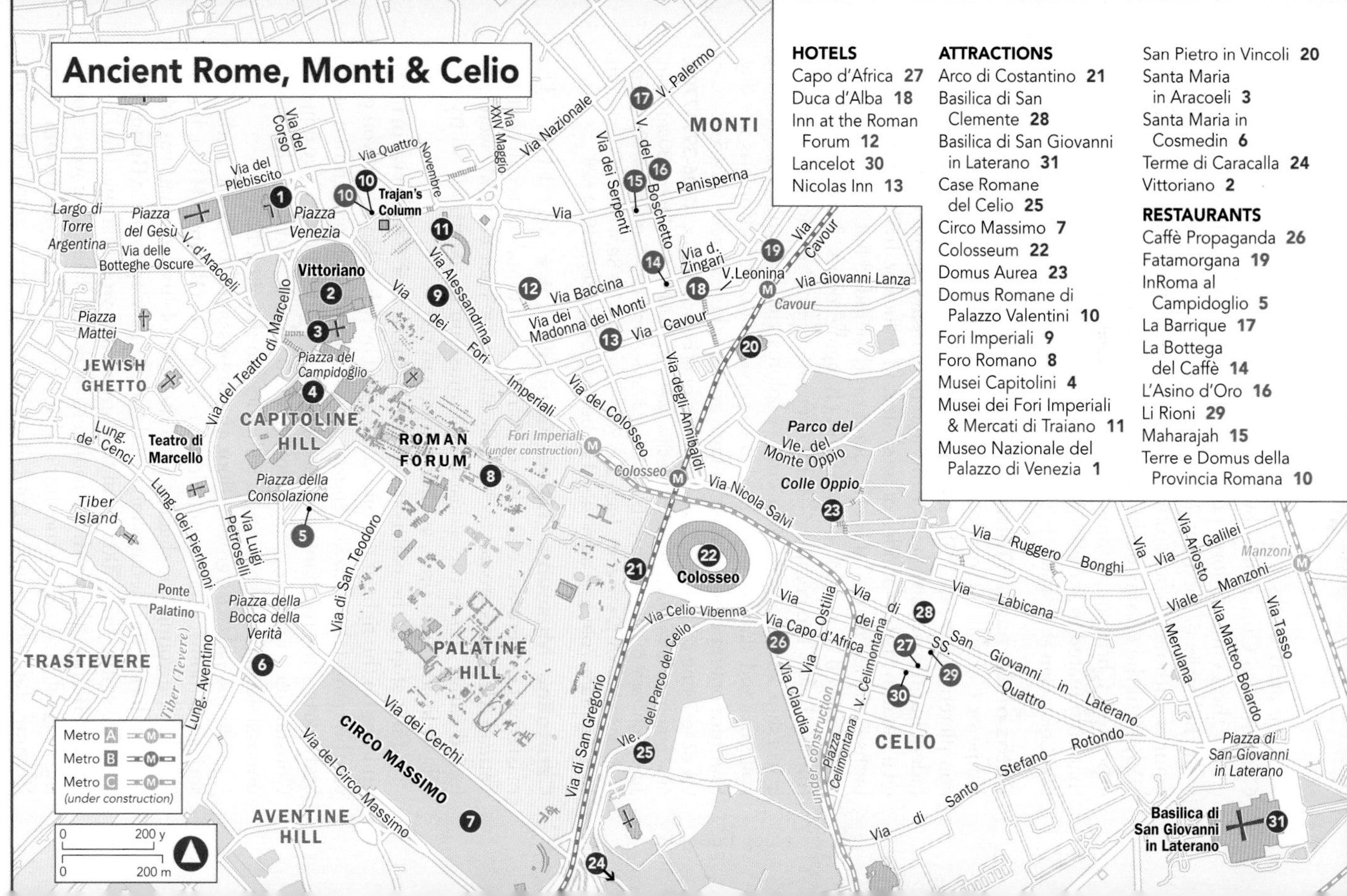
Ancient Rome, Monti & Celio
HOTELS
Capo d'Africa 27
Duca d'Alba 18
Inn at the Roman Forum 12
Lancelot 30
Nicolas Inn 13
ATTRACTIONS
Arco di Costantino 21
Basilica di San Clemente 28
Basilica di San Giovanni in Laterano 31
Case Romane del Celio 25
Circo Massimo 7
Colosseum 22
Domus Aurea 23
Domus Romane di Palazzo Valentini 10
Fori Imperiali 9
Foro Romano 8
Musei Capitolini 4
Musei dei Fori Imperiali & Mercati di Traiano 11
Museo Nazionale del Palazzo di Venezia 1
San Pietro in Vincoli 20
Santa Maria in Aracoeli 3
Santa Maria in Cosmedin 6
Terme di Caracalla 24
Vittoriano 2
RESTAURANTS
Caffè Propaganda 26
Fatamorgana 19
InRoma al Campidoglio 5
La Barrique 17
La Bottega del Caffè 14
L'Asino d'Oro 16
Li Rioni 29
Maharajah 15
Terre e Domus della Provincia Romana 10
MONTI
CAPITOLINE HILL
ROMAN FORUM
PALATINE HILL
CIRCO MASSIMO
AVENTINE HILL
JEWISH GHETTO
TRASTEVERE
CELIO
Colosseo
Vittoriano
Trajan's Column
Teatro di Marcello
Parco del Colle Oppio
Tiber Island
Tiber (Tevere)
Basilica di San Giovanni in Laterano
Metro A
Metro B
Metro C (under construction)
0 200 y
0 200 m

The arch marks a period of great change in the history of Rome. Converted to Christianity by a vision on the eve of battle, Constantine ended the centuries-long persecution of the Christians, during which many followers of the new religion had been put to death in a gruesome manner. Although Constantine didn't ban paganism (which survived officially until the closing of the temples more than half a century later), he espoused Christianity himself and began the inevitable development that culminated in the conquest of Rome by the Christian religion.
Btw. Colosseum and Palatine Hill. Metro: Colosseo.

Baths of Caracalla (Terme di Caracalla) ★★ RUINS Named for Emperor Caracalla, a particularly unpleasant individual, the baths were completed in A.D. 217 after his death. The richness of decoration has faded, but the massive brick ruins and the mosaic fragments that remain give modern visitors an idea of its scale and grandeur. In their heyday, the baths sprawled across 11 ha (27 acres) and included hot, cold, and tepid pools, as well as a *palestra* (gym) and changing rooms. A museum in the tunnels below the complex—built over an even more ancient *mithraem*, a worship site of an eastern cult—explores the hydraulic and heating systems (and slave power) needed to serve 8,000 or so Romans per day. Summer operatic performances here are an ethereal treat (p. 153).
Via delle Terme di Caracalla 52. www.archeoroma.beniculturali.it. ✆ **06-39967700.** 6€ (combined ticket with Tomb of Cecilia Metella, p. 119). Oct Mon 8:30am–2pm, Tues–Sun 9am–6:30pm; Nov–Feb 15 Mon 8:30am–2pm, Tues–Sun 9am–4:30pm; Feb 16–Mar 15 Mon 8:30am–2pm, Tues–Sun 9am–5pm; Mar 16–Sept Mon 8:30am–2pm, Tues–Sun 9am–7pm. Last admission 1 hr. before closing. Bus: 118 or 628.

Capitoline Museums (Musei Capitolini) ★★ MUSEUM The masterpieces here are considered Rome's most valuable (recall that the Vatican Museums are *not* technically in Rome). They certainly were collected early: This is the oldest public museum *in the world.* So try and schedule adequate time, as there's much to see.

First stop is the courtyard of the **Palazzo dei Conservatori** (the building on the right of the piazza designed by Michelangelo, if you enter via the ramp from Piazza Venezia). It's scattered with gargantuan stone body parts—the remnants of a massive 12m (39-ft.) statue of the emperor Constantine, including his colossal head, hand, and foot. It's nearly impossible to resist snapping a selfie next to the giant finger.

On the *palazzo*'s ground floor, the unmissable works are in the first series of rooms. These include "Lo Spinario" **(Room III),** a lifelike bronze of a young boy digging a splinter out of his foot that was widely copied during the Renaissance; and the "Lupa Capitolina" **(Room IV),** a bronze statue from 500 B.C. of the famous she-wolf that suckled Romulus and Remus, the mythical founders of Rome. The twins were not on the original Etruscan statue, but added in the 15th century. **Room V** has Bernini's famously pained portrait of "Medusa," even more compelling when you see its writhing serpent hairdo in person.

Before heading upstairs, go toward the new wing at the rear, which houses the original equestrian **statue of Marcus Aurelius ★★★**, dating to around A.D. 180—the piazza outside, where it stood from 1538 until 2005, now has a copy. There's a giant bronze head from a statue of Constantine (ca. A.D. 337) and the foundations of the original Temple of Jupiter that stood on the Capitoline Hill since its inauguration in 509 B.C.

The second-floor **picture gallery ★** is strong on baroque oil paintings. Masterpieces include Caravaggio's "John the Baptist" and "The Fortune Teller" (1595) and Guido Reni's "St. Sebastian" (1615).

A tunnel takes you under the piazza to the other part of the Capitoline Museums, the **Palazzo Nuovo,** via the **Tabularium ★★**. This was built in 78 B.C. to house ancient Rome's city records, and was later used as a salt mine and then as a prison. Here, the moody *galleria lapidaria* houses a well-executed exhibit of ancient portrait tombstones and sarcophagi, many of their poignant epitaphs translated into English, and provides access to one of the best balcony **views ★★★** in Rome: along the length of the Forum toward the Palatine Hill.

Much of the Palazzo Nuovo is dedicated to statues that were excavated from the forums below and brought in from outlying areas like Hadrian's Villa in Tivoli (p. 159). If you're running short on time at this point, head straight for the 1st-century **"Capitoline Venus" ★★**, in Room III—a modest girl covering up after a bath—and in Rooms IV and V, a chronologically arranged row of distinct, expressive busts of Roman emperors and their families. Another favorite is the beyond handsome **"Dying Gaul" ★★**, a Roman copy of a lost ancient Greek work. Lord Byron considered the statue so lifelike and moving that he mentioned it in his poem "Childe Harold's Pilgrimage."

Piazza del Campidoglio 1. www.museicapitolini.org. ✆ **060608.** 12€; up to 15€ during special exhibits. Daily 9:30am–7:30pm. Last entry 1 hr. before closing. Bus: 40, 44, 60, 63, 64, 70, 118, 160, 170, 628, 716 or any bus that stops at Piazza Venezia.

Circus Maximus (Circo Massimo) ★ HISTORIC SITE Today mostly an oval-shaped field, the once-grand circus was pilfered by medieval and Renaissance builders in search of marble and stone—it's a far cry from its *Ben-Hur*-esque heyday. What the Romans called a "circus" was a large arena ringed by tiers of seats and used for sports or spectacles. At one time, 300,000 Romans could assemble here, while the emperor observed the games from his box high on the Palatine Hill.

When the dark days of the 5th and 6th centuries fell, the Circus Maximus seemed a symbol of the ruination of Rome. The last games were held in A.D. 549 on the orders of Totilla the Goth, who had seized Rome twice. He lived in the still-glittering ruins on the Palatine and apparently thought the chariot races in the Circus Maximus would lend his rule credibility. After 549, the Circus Maximus was never used again, and the demand for building materials reduced it, like so much of Rome, to a great dusty field, now used mostly for big-name rock concerts.

Guided tours of a newly-opened archaeological area are available with reservation only (✆ **060608;** 5€). ***Tip:*** If you're crunched for time, bypass the Circus Maximus and instead take in the emperor's-eye views of the arena from atop the Palatine Hill.

Btw. Via dei Cerchi and Via del Circo Massimo. Metro: Circo Massimo. Bus: 81, 118, 160.

Colosseum (Colosseo) ★★★ ICON No matter how many pictures you've seen, the first impression you'll have of the Colosseum is amazement. Its massive bulk looks as if it has been plopped down among the surrounding buildings, and not the other way around.

Your first view of the Flavian Amphitheater (the Colosseum's original name) will be from the outside, and it's important to walk completely around its 500m (1,640-ft.) circumference. It doesn't matter where you start, but do the circle and look at the various stages of ruin before delving in. Note the different column styles on each level. An ongoing conservation makeover, funded by the Italian design house Tod's, helped eliminate nearly 2,000 years of soot from the monument's exterior; restoration efforts have now shifted to the structure's underground vaults and passageways.

The partially reconstructed wooden floor once covered the hypogeum, the place where gladiators and beasts waited their turn in the arena. Vespasian ordered the construction of the elliptical bowl in A.D. 72; it was inaugurated by Titus in A.D. 80. The stadium could hold as many as 87,000 spectators by some counts, and seats were sectioned on three levels, dividing the people by social rank and gender. Some 80 entrances allowed the massive crowds to be seated within a few minutes, historians say. Most events were free, but all spectators had to obtain a terracotta disc, called a *tessera,* to enter.

The Colosseum was built for gladiator contests and wild animal fights, but when the Roman Empire fell, it was abandoned and eventually overgrown. You'll notice on the top of the "good side," as locals call it, a few remaining supports. These once held the canvas awning that sheltered guests from rain or summer sun. Much of the ancient travertine that once sheathed its outside was used for palaces like the nearby Palazzo Venezia and Palazzo Cancelleria near the Campo de' Fiori.

Note: The same ticket that you buy for the Colosseum includes admission to the Forum and Palatine Hill, and is valid for 2 days.

Piazzale del Colosseo. www.archeoroma.beniculturali.it. ✆ **06-39967700.** 12€ (includes Roman Forum & Palatine Hill). Nov–Feb 15 daily 8:30am–4:30pm; Feb 16–Mar 15 daily 8:30am–5pm; Mar 16–31 daily 8:30am–5:30pm; Apr–Aug daily 8:30am–7:15pm; Sept daily 8:30am–7pm; Oct daily 8:30am–6:30pm. Last entry 1 hr. before closing. Guided tours (45 min.) in English daily at 10:15 and 11:15am, 12:30, 1:45, and 3pm (also 4:15 and 5:15pm depending on seasonal hours). Tours 5€. Metro: Colosseo. Bus: 51, 75, 85, 87, 118.

Imperial Forums (Fori Imperiali) ★ RUINS Begun by Julius Caesar to relieve overcrowding in Rome's older forums, the Imperial Forums were, at the time of their construction, flashier, bolder, and more

THREE free views TO REMEMBER FOR A LIFETIME

The Forum from the Campidoglio
Standing on Piazza del Campidoglio, outside the Musei Capitolini (p. 86), walk around the right side of the Palazzo Senatorio to a terrace overlooking the best panorama of the Roman Forum, with the Palatine Hill and Colosseum as a backdrop. At night, the ruins look even more haunting when the Forum is dramatically floodlit.

The Whole City from the Janiculum Hill
From many vantage points in the Eternal City, the views are panoramic. But one of the best spots for a memorable vista is the Janiculum Hill *(Gianicolo)*, above Trastevere. Laid out before you are Rome's rooftops, peppered with domes ancient and modern. From up here, you will understand why Romans complain about the materials used to build the 19th-century Vittoriano (p. 97)—it's a white shock in a sea of rose- and honey-colored stone. Walk 50 yards north of the famous balcony (favored by tour buses) for a slightly better angle, from the Belvedere 9 Febbraio 1849. Views from the 1612 Fontana dell'Acqua Paola are also splendid, especially at night.

The Aventine Hill & the Priori dei Cavalieri di Malta The mythical site of Remus's original settlement, the Aventine *(Aventino)* is now a leafy, upscale residential neighborhood—but also blessed with some magical views. From Via del Circo Massimo walk through the gardens along Via di Valle Murcia, and keep walking in a straight line. Along your right side, gardens offer views over the dome of St. Peter's. When you reach Piazza dei Cavalieri di Malta, look through the keyhole of the Priory gate (on the right) for a "secret" view of the Vatican.

impressive than their predecessors. This site conveyed the unquestioned authority of the emperors at the height of their absolute power.

Alas, Mussolini felt his regime was more important than the ancient one, and issued the controversial orders to cut through centuries of debris and buildings to carve out Via dei Fori Imperiali, thereby linking the Colosseum to the 19th-century monuments of Piazza Venezia. Excavations under his Fascist regime uncovered countless archaeological treasures. Most ruins more recent than imperial Rome were destroyed—*argh!*

The best view of the Forums is from the railings on the north side of Via dei Fori Imperiali; begin where Via Cavour joins the boulevard. (Visitors are not permitted down into the ruins.) Closest to the junction are the remains of the **Forum of Nerva,** built by the emperor whose 2-year reign (A.D. 96–98) followed the assassination of the paranoid Domitian. You'll be struck by how much the ground level has risen in 19 centuries. The only really recognizable remnant is a wall of the Temple of Minerva with two fine Corinthian columns. This forum was once flanked by that of Vespasian, which is now gone.

The next along is the **Forum of Augustus ★★**, built to commemorate Emperor Augustus's victory over Julius Caesar's assassins, Cassius and Brutus, in the Battle of Philippi (42 B.C.).

Ruins of the Temple of the Dioscuri in the Roman Forum.

Continuing along the railing, you'll see the vast, multilevel semicircle of **Trajan's Markets ★★**, essentially an ancient shopping mall whose arcades were once stocked with merchandise from the far corners of the Roman world. You can visit the part that has been transformed into the **Museo dei Fori Imperiali & Mercati di Traiano** (see p. 94).

In front of the Markets, the **Forum of Trajan ★★** was built between A.D. 107 and 113, designed by Greek architect Apollodorus of Damascus (who also laid out the adjoining market building). Many statue fragments and pedestals bear still-legible inscriptions, but more interesting is the great Basilica Ulpia, whose gray marble columns rise roofless into the sky. This forum was once regarded as one of the architectural wonders of the world. Beyond the Basilica Ulpia is **Trajan's Column ★★★**, in magnificent condition, with an intricate bas-relief sculpture depicting Trajan's victorious campaign.

The **Forum of Julius Caesar ★★**, the first of the Imperial Forums to be built, lies on the opposite side of Via dei Fori Imperiali, adjacent to the Roman Forum. This was the site of the stock exchange as well as the Temple of Venus.

Along Via dei Fori Imperiali. Metro: Colosseo. Bus: 51, 75, 85, 87, 118.

Roman Forum (Foro Romano) & Palatine Hill (Palatino) ★★★

RUINS Traversed by the **Via Sacra (Sacred Way) ★**, the main thoroughfare of ancient Rome, the Roman Forum flourished as the center of religious, social, and commercial life in the days of the Republic, before it gradually lost prestige (but never spiritual draw) to the Imperial Forums (see above).

You'll see ruins and fragments, some partially intact columns, and an arch or two, but you can still feel the rush of history here. That any semblance of the Forum remains today is miraculous: It was used for years as a quarry (as was the Colosseum). Eventually it reverted to a *campo vaccino* (cow pasture). Excavations in the 19th century and later in the 1930s began to bring to light one of the world's most historic spots.

By day, the columns of now-vanished temples and the stones from which long-forgotten orators spoke are mere shells. Weeds grow where a triumphant Caesar was once lionized. But at night, when the Forum is silent in the moonlight, it isn't difficult to imagine Vestal Virgins still guarding the sacred temple fire.

You can spend at least a morning wandering the ruins of the Forum. Enter via the gate on Via dei Fori Imperiali, at Via della Salara Vecchia. Turn right at the bottom of the entrance slope to walk west along the old Via Sacra toward the arch. Just before it on your right is the large brick **Curia ★★**, the main seat of the Roman Senate, built by Julius Caesar, rebuilt by Diocletian, and consecrated as a church in A.D. 630.

The triumphal **Arch of Septimius Severus ★★** (A.D. 203), is the next important sight, displaying time-bitten reliefs of the emperor's victories in what are now Iran and Iraq. During the Middle Ages, Rome became a provincial backwater, and frequent flooding of the Tiber helped bury (and thus preserve) most of the Forum. Some bits did still stick out aboveground, including the top half of this arch, which was used to shelter a barbershop!

Just to the left of the arch, you can make out the remains of a cylindrical lump of rock with some marble steps curving off it. That round stone was the **Umbilicus Urbus,** considered the center of Rome and of the entire Roman Empire; the curving steps are those of the **Imperial Rostra ★**, where great orators and legislators stood to speak and the people gathered to listen. Nearby, a much-photographed trio of fluted columns with Corinthian capitals supports a bit of architrave from the corner of the **Temple of Vespasian and Titus ★★** (emperors were routinely turned into gods upon dying).

Start heading to your left toward the eight Ionic columns marking the front of the **Temple of Saturn ★★** (rebuilt in 42 B.C.), which housed the first treasury of Republican Rome. It was also the site of one of the Roman year's biggest annual blowout festivals, the December 17 feast of Saturnalia, which, after a bit of tweaking, Christians now celebrate as Christmas. Turn left to start heading back east, past the worn steps and stumps of brick pillars outlining the enormous **Basilica Julia ★★**, built by Julius Caesar. Farther along, on the right, are the three Corinthian columns of the **Temple of the Dioscuri ★★★**, dedicated to the Gemini twins, Castor and Pollux. Forming one of the most photogenic sights of the Roman Forum, a trio of columns supports an architrave fragment. The founding of this temple dates from the 5th century B.C.

Beyond the bit of curving wall that marks the site of the little round **Temple of Vesta** (rebuilt several times after fires started by the sacred flame within), you'll find the reconstructed **House of the Vestal Virgins** (A.D. 3rd–4th c.). The temple was the home of the consecrated young women who tended the sacred flame in the Temple of Vesta. Vestals were girls chosen from patrician families to serve a 30-year-long priesthood. During their tenure, they were among Rome's most venerated citizens, with unique powers such as the ability to pardon condemned criminals. The cult was quite serious about the "virgin" part of the job description—if one of Vesta's earthly servants was found to have "misplaced" her virginity, the miscreant Vestal was buried alive, because it was forbidden to shed a Vestal's blood. (Her amorous accomplice was merely flogged to death.) The overgrown rectangle of their gardens is lined with broken, heavily worn statues of senior Vestals on pedestals.

The path dovetails back to Via Sacra. Turn right, walk past the so-called "Temple of Romulus," and then left to enter the massive brick remains of the 4th-century **Basilica of Constantine and Maxentius ★★** (Basilica di Massenzio). These were Rome's public law courts, and their architectural style was adopted by early Christians for their houses of worship (the reason so many ancient churches are called "basilicas").

Return to the path and continue toward the Colosseum. Veer right to the Forum's second great triumphal arch, the extensively rebuilt **Arch of Titus ★★** (A.D. 81), on which one relief depicts the carrying off of treasures from Jerusalem's temple. Look closely and you'll see a menorah among the booty. The war that this arch glorifies ended with the expulsion of Jews from the colonized Judea, signaling the beginning of the Jewish Diaspora throughout Europe. You can exit behind the Arch to continue on to the Colosseum, or head up to the Palatine Hill.

Accessing the **Palatine Hill ★★** (Palatino), where Romulus, after dispatching with his twin brother Remus, founded Rome around 753 B.C., is done via the **Imperial Ramp**. A secret passageway built by Emperor Domitian in the 1st century A.D., the 11m-tall (36 ft.) switchback ramp allowed the assassination-paranoid ruler to go back and forth undetected between his palace and the forum below. (He was murdered anyway.) Later, emperors and other ancient bigwigs built their palaces and private entertainment facilities up here.

A Tip for Absorbing the Ancient Ambience

Even though they're all included in the same admission fee, the ruins of the Colosseum, Roman Forum and Palatine Hill are quite a lot to take in on a single day, particularly in the heat of the Roman summer. We recommend that you take advantage of the 2-day window your admission ticket allows, and see the Forum and Palatine on your first day, then save the Colosseum for first thing in the morning on day 2, before the crowds pile in.

NERO'S golden HOUSE ★★★

After the Great Fire of 64 A.D., charismatic, despotic Emperor Nero staged a land grab to facilitate construction of his *Domus Aurea*, or Golden House, a massive, gilded villa complex covering all or parts of the Palatine, Esquiline, and Caelian hills and displaying a level of ostentation and excessiveness unheard of even among past emperors. After his death by noble suicide in 68 A.D., a campaign to erase all traces of Nero from the imperial city ensured that the palace was stripped of its gold, marble, jewels, mosaics and statuary and intentionally buried under millions of tons of rubble. It remained buried until the Renaissance, when young artists, including Raphael, descended into its "grottos" (actually the vaulted ceilings) to study the fanciful frescoes—the term grotesque (*grotto-esque*) was coined here. Later excavations, both haphazard and scientific, revealed the scale and richness of the villa, but also subjected it to catastrophic moisture damage. After a years-long closure for restoration and restabalization, the Domus Aurea is once again open for tours—but only if you time your trip well and plan ahead. Guided tours (16€; www.coopculture.it/en) of the scaffolded underground site (hardhats required) are offered on **Saturdays and Sundays only**, and with advance reservations. The tour includes a spectacular virtual reality experience that in itself is worth the visit.

Underground tour of Nero's Domus Aurea.

Upon exiting at the top of the ramp, visitors are presented with a sprawling, mostly crowd-free archaeological garden, with plenty of shady spots for picnicking and cooling off in summer.

The Palatine was where the first settlers built their huts under the direction of Romulus. In later years, the hill became a patrician residential district that attracted such citizens as Cicero. In time, however, the area was gobbled up by imperial palaces and drew an infamous roster of tenants, such as Livia (some of the frescoes in the House of Livia are in miraculous condition), Tiberius, Caligula (murdered here by members of his Praetorian Guard), Nero, and Domitian. A museum houses some of the most important finds from hill excavations.

Only the ruins of its former grandeur remain today, but it's worth the climb for the panoramic views of both the Roman and the Imperial

Forums, as well as the Capitoline Hill, the Colosseum and Circus Maximus. You can also enter from here, and do the entire tour in reverse.

Forum entrance at Via della Salara Vecchia 5/6. ✆ **06-39967700.** 12€ (includes Colosseum). Nov–Feb 15 daily 8:30am–4:30pm; Feb 16–Mar 15 daily 8:30am–5pm; Mar 16–31 daily 8:30am–5:30pm; Apr–Aug daily 8:30am–7:15pm; Sept daily 8:30am–7pm; Oct daily 8:30am–6:30pm. Last entry 1 hr. before closing. Metro: Colosseo. Bus: 51, 75, 85, 87, 118.

Museum of the Imperial Forums (Museo dei Fori Imperiali & Mercati di Traiano) & Trajan's Markets ★ RUINS/MUSEUM Built on three levels, Emperor Trajan's Market (call it the World's First Shopping Mall) housed 150 shops and commercial offices. Grooves still evident in the thresholds allowed merchants to slide doors shut and lock up for the night. You're likely to have the covered, tunnel-like market halls mostly to yourself—making the ancient past feel all the more present in this overlooked site. The Museum of the Imperial Forums occupies a converted section of the market, and has excellent visual displays that help you imagine what these grand public squares and temples used to look like. All in all, it's home to 172 marble fragments from the Fori Imperiali; here are also original remnants from the Forum of Augustus and Forum of Nerva.

Via IV Novembre 94. www.mercatiditraiano.it. ✆ **060608.** 11.50€. Daily 9:30am–7:30pm. Last admission 1 hr. before closing. Bus: 40, 60, 64, 70, 170.

OTHER ATTRACTIONS NEAR ANCIENT ROME

Basilica di San Clemente ★★ CHURCH This isn't just another Roman church—it's one of the best places to understand the city's complex evolution from pagan to Christian. In A.D. 4th century, a church was built over a 1st century house, beside which stood a temple dedicated to Mithras (a deity of Eastern origins). Down in the eerie grottos (which you explore on your own), are well-preserved frescoes from the 9th to the 11th centuries. The Normans destroyed this lower church, and a new one was built in the 12th century. Its chief attraction is the mosaic from that period adorning the apse, as well as a chapel honoring St. Catherine of Alexandria with frescoes by Masolino.

Via San Giovanni in Laterano (at Piazza San Clemente). www.basilicasanclemente.com. ✆ **06-7740021.** Basilica free; excavations 10€. Mon–Sat 9am–12:30pm and 3–6pm; Sun 12:15–6pm. Last entry 30 min. before closing. Metro: Colosseo. Bus: 51, 85, 87, 117. Tram: 3.

Basilica di San Giovanni in Laterano ★ CHURCH This church (not St. Peter's) is the cathedral of the diocese of Rome, where the Pope comes to celebrate Mass on certain holidays. Built in A.D. 314 by Constantine, it has suffered the vicissitudes of Roman history, forcing many overhauls. Only parts of the baptistery remain from the original.

The present building is characterized by an 18th-century facade by Alessandro Galilei (statues of Christ and the Apostles ring the top). Note that a 1993 terrorist bomb caused severe damage to the facade. Borromini gets the credit for the interior, built for Pope Innocent X. In a purportedly misguided attempt to redecorate, frescoes by Giotto were destroyed; remains attributed to Giotto were discovered in 1952 and are now on display against the first inner column on the right.

Across the street is the **Santuario della Scala Santa (Palace of the Holy Steps),** Piazza San Giovanni in Laterano 14 (✆ **06-7726641**). Allegedly, its 28 marble steps were originally at Pontius Pilate's villa in Jerusalem, and Christ climbed them the day he was brought before Pilate. The steps were brought from Jerusalem to Rome by Constantine's mother, Helen, and they've been in this location since 1589. Today pilgrims from all over the world come here to climb the steps on their knees. This is one of the holiest sites in Christendom, although some historians say the stairs might date only from the 4th century.

Piazza San Giovanni in Laterano 4. ✆ **06-69886433.** Free. Daily 7am–6:30pm. Metro: San Giovanni.

Case Romane del Celio ★ RUINS The 5th-century Basilica of SS. Giovanni e Paolo stands over a residential complex consisting of Roman houses of different periods. A visit provides you with a unique picture of how generations of Romans lived. Preserved at the labyrinthine site is a residence from the 2nd century A.D., a single home of a wealthy family, and a 3rd-century-A.D. apartment building for artisans.

According to tradition, this was the dwelling of two Roman officers, John and Paul (not the Apostles), who were beheaded during the reign of Julian the Apostate (361–63), when they refused to serve in a military campaign. They were later made saints, and their bones were said to have been buried at this site. The two-story construction also contains a small museum with finds from the site and fragmentary 12th-century frescoes.

Piazza Santi Giovanni e Paolo 13 (entrance on Clivo di Scauro). www.caseromane.it. ✆ **06-70454544.** Admission 8€ adults, 6€ ages 12–18. Thurs–Mon 10am–1pm and 3–6pm. Metro: Colosseo or Circo Massimo. Bus: 75, 81, 118. Tram: 3.

Domus Romane di Palazzo Valentini ★★★ RUINS/EXHIBIT One of Rome's newest attractions is thousands of years old—and this sleeper is its most well-presented archaeological site. Visitors descend underneath a Renaissance palazzo and, from a glass floor, peer down into the remains of several upscale Roman homes. With innovative use of 3-D projections, the walls, ceilings, floors. and fountains of these once grand houses spring back to colorful life, offering a captivating look at lifestyles of the ancient rich and famous.

Via Foro Traiano 85 (near Trajan's Column). www.palazzovalentini.it; ✆ **06-22761280.** 13.50€. Wed-Mon 9:30am–6:30pm. Timed entrance, with guided tours in English several times daily; reservations suggested. Metro: Colosseo. Bus: 40, 63, 70, 81, 83, 87, or any bus to Piazza Venezia. Tram: 8.

Museo Nazionale del Palazzo di Venezia ★ MUSEUM Best remembered today as Mussolini's Fascist headquarters in Rome, the palace was built in the 1450s as the Rome outpost of the Republic of Venice—hence the name. Today, several of its rooms house an eclectic mix of European paintings and decorative and religious objects spanning the centuries; highlights include Giorgione's enigmatic "Double Portrait" and some early Tuscan altarpieces.

Via del Plebiscito 118. www.museopalazzovenezia.beniculturali.it. ✆ **06-6780131.** 5€. Tues–Sun 8:30am–7:30pm. Bus: 30, 40, 46, 62, 64, 70, 87, or any bus to Piazza Venezia. Tram: 8.

St. Peter in Chains (San Pietro in Vincoli) ★ CHURCH This recently renovated church was founded in the 5th century to house the chains that supposedly bound St. Peter in Palestine (preserved under glass below the main altar). But the drawing card is the tomb of Pope Julius II, with one of the world's most famous sculptures: **Michelangelo's "Moses"** ★★. Michelangelo was to have carved 44 magnificent figures for the tomb. That never happened, but the Pope was given a great consolation prize—a figure intended to be "minor" that's now numbered among Michelangelo's masterpieces. Also take a quick look at the unusual "skeleton tombs," in the left aisle.

Piazza San Pietro in Vincoli 4A. ✆ **06-97844952.** Free. Spring–summer daily 8:30am–12:30pm and 3:30–7pm (fall–winter to 6pm). Metro: Colosseo or Cavour. Bus: 75.

Santa Maria in Aracoeli ★ CHURCH On the Capitoline Hill, this landmark church was built for the Franciscans in the 13th century. According to legend, Augustus once ordered a temple erected on this spot, where a prophetic sibyl forecast the coming of Christ. Highlights include a coffered Renaissance ceiling and the tomb of Giovanni Crivelli (1432) carved by the great Renaissance sculptor Donatello. The church is also known for the **Cappella Bufalini** ★ (first chapel on the right), frescoed by Pinturicchio with scenes illustrating the life and death of St. Bernardino of Siena. A chapel behind the altar contains the **Santo Bambino,** a devotional wooden figure of the Baby Jesus, which is venerated annually in a Christmas Eve ceremony.

You have to climb a long flight of steep steps (completed in 1348 to celebrate the end of the Black Plague in Rome) to reach the church, unless you're already on neighboring Piazza del Campidoglio, in which case you can cross the piazza and climb the steps on the far side of the Musei Capitolini (p. 86).

Scala dell'Arcicapitolina 12. ✆ **06-69763838.** Free. Daily 9am–12:30pm and 3–6:30pm (fall–winter to 5:30pm). Bus: 30, 40, 46, 62, 64, 70, 87, or any bus to Piazza Venezia.

Santa Maria in Cosmedin ★ CHURCH People line up outside this little church not for great art treasures, but to see the **"Mouth of Truth,"** a large disk under the portico. As Gregory Peck demonstrated to Audrey Hepburn in the film *Roman Holiday*, the mouth is supposed to chomp down on the hands of liars. The purpose of this disk is unclear. It may have been an ancient drain cover, though one hypothesis says that it was one of Rome's many "talking statues." If you wanted to rat someone out, all you'd have to do was drop an anonymous note into the open mouth. The church itself was erected in the 6th century but was subsequently rebuilt. A Romanesque bell tower was added at the end of the 11th century. Our take? Save this hokey photo op until you've seen everything else you want to see in Rome.

Piazza della Bocca della Verità 18. ✆ **06-6787759.** Church free; though there is sometimes a 2€ fee for a photo of the Mouth of Truth. Summer daily 9:30am–5:50pm; winter daily 9:30am–4:50pm. Bus: 23, 81, 118, 160, 280, 715.

> **All Roads Lead to... Piazza Venezia**
>
> Love it or loathe it, the massive Vittoriano monument at Piazza Venezia is a helpful landmark for visitors to get their bearings, and almost every bus line convenient to tourists stops here. Streets fanning out from the piazza lead to Termini Station, the Colosseum, the Trevi Fountain, and across the Tiber to the Vatican. You get the picture—it's a handy place from which to orientate.

Vittoriano (Altare della Patria) ★ MONUMENT It's impossible to miss the white marble Vittorio Emanuele monument that dominates Piazza Venezia. The city's most flamboyant and, frankly, disliked landmark was built in the late 1800s to honor the first king of a united Italy. It has been compared to everything from a wedding cake to a Victorian typewriter, and has been ridiculed because of its harsh white color in a city of honey-gold tones. An eternal flame burns at the Tomb of the Unknown Soldier. For a panoramic view over the city, glass elevators whisk you to the **Terrazza delle Quadrighe (Terrace of the Chariots) ★**.

Piazza Venezia. ✆ **06-6780664.** Elevator 7€. Daily 9:30am–6:45pm. Bus: 30, 40, 46, 62, 64, 70, 87, or any bus to Piazza Venezia.

Centro Storico & the Pantheon

CENTRO STORICO

Just across the Tiber from the Vatican and Castel Sant'Angelo lies the true heart of Rome, the **Centro Storico,** or "historic center," the triangular wedge of land that bulges into a bend of the river. Although the area lay outside the Roman city, it came into its own during the Renaissance, and today its streets and alleys are crammed with piazzas, elegant churches, and lavish fountains, all buzzing with scooters and people. It's a wonderful area in which to wander and get lost.

Fountain of the Four Rivers in Piazza Navona.

PIAZZA NAVONA & NEARBY ATTRACTIONS

Rome's most famous square, **Piazza Navona ★★★**, is a gorgeous baroque gem, lined with cafes and restaurants and often crammed with tourists, street artists, and pigeons by day and night. Its long, thin shape follows the contours of the old Roman Stadium of Domitian, where chariot races once took place, still a ruin until a mid-17th-century makeover by Pope Innocent X. The twin-towered facade of 17th-century **Sant'Agnese in Agone** lies on the piazza's western side, while the **Fontana dei Quattro Fiumi (Fountain of the Four Rivers) ★★★** opposite is one of three great fountains in the square, this one a typically exuberant creation of Bernini and topped with an Egyptian obelisk. The four stone personifications below symbolize the world's greatest rivers: the Ganges, Danube, de la Plata, and Nile. It's fun to try to figure out which is which. (***Hint:*** The figure with the shroud on its head is the Nile, so represented because the river's source was unknown at the time.) At the south end is Bernini's **Fontana del Moro (Fountain of the Moor)** and the 19th-century **Fontana di Nettuno (Fountain of Neptune**.

Art lovers should make the short walk from the piazza to **Santa Maria della Pace ★★** on Arco della Pace, a 15th-century church given the usual baroque makeover by Pietro da Cortona in the 1660s. The real gems are inside, beginning with Raphael's **"Four Sibyls" ★★** fresco, above the arch of the Capella Chigi, and the **Chiostro del Bramante (Bramante cloister) ★**, built between 1500 and 1504 and the Renaissance master's first work in the city. The church is normally open on Monday, Wednesday, and Saturday 9am to noon, while the cloister opens daily 10am to 8pm (to 9pm Sat and Sun). The church is free, but admission to the cloister (www.chiostrodelbramante.it), which hosts temporary art exhibitions, costs 10€ and up, depending on the exhibit.

Palazzo Altemps ★★ MUSEUM Inside this 15th-century *palazzo,* today a branch of the National Museum of Rome, is one of Rome's most charming museums. It's rarely crowded yet houses some of Rome's most famous private and public art collections. Much of it was once part of the famed **Boncompagni Ludovisi Collection,** created by Cardinal Ludovico Ludovisi (1595–1632) and sold at auction in 1901.

Among the highlights is the **"Ludovisi Ares" ★★**, a handsome 2nd-century copy of an earlier Greek statue of Mars (Ares to the Greeks). Equally renowned is the **"Ludovisi Gaul" ★**, a marble depiction of a Gaulish warrior plunging a sword into his chest, looking backwards defiantly as he supports a dying woman with his left arm. Also worth a look is the **"Ludovisi Throne,"** a sculpted block of white marble, thought to date from the 5th century B.C., depicting Aphrodite rising from the sea.

Piazza di Sant'Apollinare 46. www.archeoroma.beniculturali.it/en/museums; ✆ **06-39967700.** 7€ (good for 3 days; also valid at Palazzo Massimo, Palazzo Altemps, Baths of Diocletian, Crypta Balbi); 17 and under free. Tues–Sun 9am–7:45pm. Last entry 1 hr. before closing. Bus: C3, 70, 81, 87, 492, 628.

San Luigi dei Francesi ★★ CHURCH For a painter of such stratospheric standards as Caravaggio, it is impossible to be definitive in naming his "masterpiece." However, the **"Calling of St. Matthew" ★★**, in the far-left chapel of Rome's French church, must be a candidate. The panel dramatizes the moment Jesus and Peter "called" the customs officer to join them, in Caravaggio's distinct *chiaroscuro* (extreme light and shade) style. Around the same time (1599–1602) Caravaggio also painted the other two St. Matthew panels in the Capella Contarelli—including one depicting the saint's martyrdom. Other highlights inside include Domenichino's masterful "Histories of Saint Cecilia" fresco cycle.

Via di Santa Giovanna d'Arco 5. www.saintlouis-rome.net. ✆ **06-688271.** Free. Mon–Fri 9:30am–12:45pm; Sat 9:30am–12:15pm; Sun 11:30–12:45pm, plus daily from 2:30–6:30pm. Bus: C3, 70, 81, 87, 492, 628.

THE PANTHEON & NEARBY ATTRACTIONS

The Pantheon stands on **Piazza della Rotonda,** a lively square with cafes, vendors, and great people-watching.

The Pantheon ★★★ HISTORIC SITE Stumbling onto Piazza della Rotunda from the dark warren of streets surrounding it will likely leave you agape, marveling at one of ancient Rome's great buildings, and the only one that remains intact. The Pantheon ("Temple to All the Gods") was originally built in 27 B.C. by Marcus Agrippa but was entirely reconstructed by Hadrian in the early 2nd century A.D. This remarkable building, 43m (142 ft.) wide and 43m (142 ft.) high (a perfect sphere resting in a cylinder) is among the architectural wonders of the world, even today. Hadrian himself is credited with the basic plan. There are no visible arches or vaults holding up the dome; instead they're sunk into the concrete of the building's walls. The ribbed dome outside is a series of almost weightless cantilevered bricks.

Animals were once sacrificed and burned in the center, with the smoke escaping through the only means of light, the oculus, an opening at the top 5.5m (18 ft.) in diameter. The interior was richly decorated, with white marble statues ringing the central space in its niches. Nowadays, apart from the jaw-dropping size of the space, the main items of interest are the tombs of two Italian kings (Vittorio Emanuele II and his successor, Umberto I) and artist **Raphael** (fans still bring him flowers), with its poignant epitaph. Since the 7th century, the Pantheon has been used as a Catholic church, the **Santa Maria ad Martyres,** informally known as "Santa Maria della Rotonda."

Piazza della Rotonda. www.turismoroma.it/cosa-fare/pantheon. ✆ **06-68300230.** Free. Mon–Sat 9am–7:30pm; Sun 9am–6pm. Bus: 40, 46, 62, 64, 70, 81, 87, 492, 628 to Largo di Torre Argentina.

Santa Maria sopra Minerva ★★ CHURCH Just one block behind the Pantheon, Santa Maria sopra Minerva is Rome's most significant Dominican church and the only major Gothic church downtown. The facade is in Renaissance style (the church was begun in 1280 but worked on until 1725), but inside, the arched vaulting is pure Gothic. The main art treasures here are the "Statua del Redentore" (1521), a statue of Christ by **Michelangelo** (just to the left of the altar), and a wonderful fresco cycle in the **Cappella Carafa** (on the right before the altar), created by Filippino Lippi between 1488 and 1493 to honor St. Thomas Aquinas. Devout Catholics flock to the tomb of **Saint Catherine of Siena** under the high altar—the room where she died in 1380 was reconstructed by Antonio Barberini in 1637 (far left corner of the church). **Fra' Angelico,** the Dominican friar and painter, also rests here, in the **Cappella Frangipane e Maddaleni-Capiferro**. A delightful elephant statue by **Bernini** holds up a small obelisk in the piazza in front of the church.

Piazza della Minerva 42. www.basilicaminerva.it. ✆ **06-69920384.** Free. Mon–Fri 6:40am–7pm; Sat 6:40am–12:30pm, 3:30–7pm; Sun 8am–12:30pm, 3:30pm–7pm.

Crypta Balbi ★ MUSEUM/RUINS This branch of the National Museum of Rome houses the archaeological remains of the vast portico belonging to the 1st-century-B.C. **Theatre of Lucius Cornelius Balbus,** discovered here in 1981. The ground floor's exhibits chronicle the history of the site through to the medieval period and the construction of the Conservatorio di Santa Caterina della Rosa. The second floor ("Rome from Antiquity to the Middle Ages") explores the transformation of the city between the 5th and 9th centuries, using thousands of ceramic objects, coins, lead seals, bone and ivory implements, precious stones, and tools found on the site. The museum helps decode the complex layers under Rome's streets, but given its comprehensive collections, it's recommended for history buffs.

Via delle Botteghe Oscure 31. www.archeoroma.beniculturali.it/en/museums. ✆ **06-39967700.** 7€ adults (good for 3 days and valid for Palazzo Massimo, Palazzo Altemps, Crypta Balbi, Baths of Diocletian); 17 and under free. Tues–Sun 9am–7:45pm. Bus: C3, H, 40, 46, 62, 64, 70, 81, 87, 492, 780. Tram: 8.

Galleria Doria Pamphilj ★★ ART MUSEUM One of the city's finest rococo palaces, the Palazzo Doria Pamphilj is still privately owned by the aristocratic Doria Pamphilj family, but their stupendous art collection is open to the public.

The *galleria* winds through the old apartments, the paintings displayed floor-to-ceiling among antique furniture and richly decorated walls. The Dutch and Flemish collection is especially strong; it includes a rare Italian work by Pieter Brueghel the Elder, "Battle in the Port of Naples," and his son Jan Brueghel the Elder's "Earthly Paradise with Original Sin." Among the best Italian works are two paintings by Caravaggio, the moving "Repentant Magdalene" and his wonderful "Rest on the Flight into Egypt," hanging near "Salome with the Head of St. John," by Titian. There's also Raphael's "Double Portrait," an "Annunciation" by Filippo Lippi, and a "Deposition from the Cross" by Vasari. The gallery's real treasures occupy a special room: Bernini's bust of the Pamphilj **"Pope Innocent X" ★**, and **Velázquez's celebrated, enigmatic painting ★★** of the same man. Make sure you grab a free audio guide at the entrance—it's colorfully narrated by Prince Jonathan Doria Pamphilj himself.

Via del Corso 305 (just north of Piazza Venezia). www.dopart.it. ✆ **06-6797323.** 12€ adults, 8€ students. Daily 9am–7pm, last entry 6pm. Bus: 64 or any to Piazza Venezia.

CAMPO DE' FIORI

The southern section of the Centro Storico, **Campo de' Fiori** is another neighborhood of narrow streets, small piazzas, and ancient churches. Its main focus remains the piazza of **Campo de' Fiori ★★** itself, where a touristy but delightful open-air market runs Monday through Saturday, selling a dizzyingly colorful array of fruits, vegetables, and spices as well as cheap T-shirts and handbags from early in the morning until midday.

(Keep an eye on your purse or wallet here.) From the center of the piazza rises a statue of the severe-looking monk **Giordano Bruno,** a reminder that heretics were occasionally burned at the stake here: Bruno was executed by the Inquisition in 1600. Curiously this is the only *piazza* in Rome that doesn't have a church in its perimeter.

Built from 1514 to 1589, the **Palazzo Farnese ★**, on Piazza Farnese just to the south of the Campo, was designed by Sangallo and Michelangelo, among others, and was an astronomically expensive project for the time. Its famous residents have included a 16th-century member of the Farnese family, plus Pope Paul III, Cardinal Richelieu, and the former Queen Christina of Sweden, who moved to Rome after abdicating. During the 1630s, when the heirs couldn't afford to maintain the *palazzo,* it was inherited by the Bourbon kings of Naples and was purchased by the French government in 1874; the French Embassy is still located here, so the building is closed to the general public, though small group visits are sometimes offered (www.inventerrome.com). For the best view of it, cut west from Via Giulia along any of the narrow streets—we recommend Via Mascherone or Via dei Farnesi.

Palazzo Spada/Galleria Spada ★ MUSEUM Built around 1540 for Cardinal Gerolamo Capo di Ferro, Palazzo Spada was purchased by the eponymous Cardinal Spada in 1632, who then hired Borromini to restore it—most of what you see today dates from that period. Its richly ornate facade, covered in high-relief stucco decorations in the Mannerist style, is the finest of any building from 16th-century Rome. The State Rooms are closed (the Italian Council of State still meets here), but the richly decorated courtyard and corridor, Borromini's masterful illusion of perspective *(la prospettiva di Borromini),* and the four rooms of the **Galleria Spada** are open to the public. Inside you will find some absorbing paintings, such as the "Portrait of Cardinale Bernardino Spada" by Guido Reni, and Titian's "Portrait of a Violinist," plus minor works from Caravaggio, Parmigianino, Pietro Testa, and Giambattista Gaulli.

Piazza Capo di Ferro 13. www.galleriaspada.beniculturali.it. ✆ **06-6874893.** 5€. Mon–Sun 8:30am–7:30pm. Bus: H, 23, 63, 280, 780. Tram: 8.

THE JEWISH GHETTO

Across Via Arenula, Campo de' Fiori merges into the old **Jewish Ghetto ★★,** established near the River Tiber by a Papal Bull in 1555, which required that all the Jews in Rome live in one area. Walled in, overcrowded, prone to floods and epidemics, and on some of the worst land in the city, it was an extremely grim place to live. After the Ghetto was abolished in 1882, its walls were finally torn down and the area largely reconstructed. In the waning years of WWII, Nazis sent more than 1,000 Roman Jews to concentration camps; only a handful returned.

The **Via Portico d'Ottavia** forms the heart of a flourishing Jewish Quarter, with Romans flocking here to sample the **Roman-Jewish and Middle Eastern food** for which the area is known.

The **Great Synagogue of Rome** (Tempio Maggiore di Roma; www.romaebraica.it; ✆ **06-6840061**) was built from 1901 to 1904 in an eclectic style evoking Babylonian and Persian temples. The synagogue was attacked by terrorists in 1982, and since then has been heavily guarded by *carabinieri*, a division of the Italian police armed with machine guns.

Museo Ebraico di Roma (Jewish Museum of Rome) ★ MUSEUM On the premises of the Great Synagogue of Rome, this museum chronicles the history of not only Roman Jews but Jews from all over Italy. There are displays of works of 17th- and 18th-century Roman silversmiths, precious textiles from all over Europe, and a number of parchments and marble carvings that were saved when the Ghetto's original synagogues were demolished. Admission includes a guided English-language tour of the synagogue.

Via Catalana. www.museoebraico.roma.it. ✆ **06-6840061.** 11€ adults, 5€ students, free for children 10 and under. Apr–Sept Sun–Thurs 10am–6pm and Fri 10am–4pm; rest of year Sun–Thurs 10am–5pm and Fri 9am–2pm.

The Tridente & the Spanish Steps

The northern half of central Rome is known as the **Tridente** thanks to the trident shape formed by three roads—Via di Ripetta, Via del Corso, and Via del Babuino—leading down from **Piazza del Popolo.** The area around **Piazza di Spagna** and the **Spanish Steps** was once the artistic quarter of the city, attracting English poets Keats and Shelley, German author Goethe, and film director Federico Fellini (who lived on Via Margutta). Institutions such as Antico Caffè Greco and Babington's Tea Rooms are still here (see p. 142), but between the high rents and the throngs of tourists and shoppers, you're unlikely to see many artists left.

PIAZZA DEL POPOLO

Elegant **Piazza del Popolo ★★** is haunted with memories. Legend has it that the ashes of Nero were enshrined here, until 11th-century residents began complaining to the pope about his imperial ghost. The **Egyptian obelisk** dates from the 13th century B.C.; it was removed from Heliopolis to Rome during Augustus's reign (it once stood at the Circus Maximus).

The current piazza was designed in the early 19th century by Valadier, Napoleon's architect. Standing astride the three roads that form the "trident" are almost-twin baroque churches, **Santa Maria dei Miracoli** (1681) and **Santa Maria di Montesanto** (1679). The stand-out church, however, is at the piazza's northern curve: the 15th-century **Santa Maria del Popolo ★★**, with its splendid baroque facade modified by Bernini between 1655 and 1660. Inside, look for Raphael's mosaic series the

"Creation of the World" adorning the interior dome of the **Capella Chigi** (the second chapel on the left). **Pinturicchio** decorated the main choir vault with frescoes such as the "Coronation of the Virgin." The **Capella Cerasi** (to the left of the high altar) contains gorgeous examples of baroque art: an altarpiece painting of "The Assumption of Mary" by Carracci, and on either side two great works by Caravaggio, "Conversion on the Road to Damascus" and "The Crucifixion of Saint Peter."

Tourists gather on the Spanish Steps.

MAXXI (National Museum of the XXI Century Arts) ★ MUSEUM Ten minutes north of Piazza del Popolo by tram, leave the Renaissance far behind at MAXXI, a masterpiece of contemporary architecture with bending and overlapping oblong tubes designed by the late Zaha Hadid. The museum is divided into two sections, MAXXI art and MAXXI architecture, primarily serving as a venue for temporary exhibitions of contemporary work in both fields (although it does have a small permanent collection). The building is worth a visit in its own right.

Via Guido Reni 4a. www.fondazionemaxxi.it. ✆ **06-3201954.** 12€ 31 and over, 8€ ages 30 and under, 4€ students, free children 13 and under. Tues–Fri and Sun 11am–7pm; Sat 11am–10pm. Metro: Flaminio, then tram 2.

Museo dell'Ara Pacis ★★ MUSEUM The "Altar of Peace" was created in 9 B.C. to honor the achievements of (soon-to-be-Emperor) Augustus in subduing tribes north of the Alps. The temple-like marble monument was later lost to memory, and though signs of its existence were discovered in the 16th century, it wasn't until the 1930s that the ancient monument was fully excavated. After World War II it lay virtually abandoned until the 1970s, but true restoration began in the 1980s. The ultra-modern museum building containing it, finished in 2006 to a design by American architect Richard Meier, is one of the most effective showcases of Imperial Rome.

The exhibit complex housing the *Ara Pacis* provides context, with interactive displays in English. You get great views of the huge, overgrown

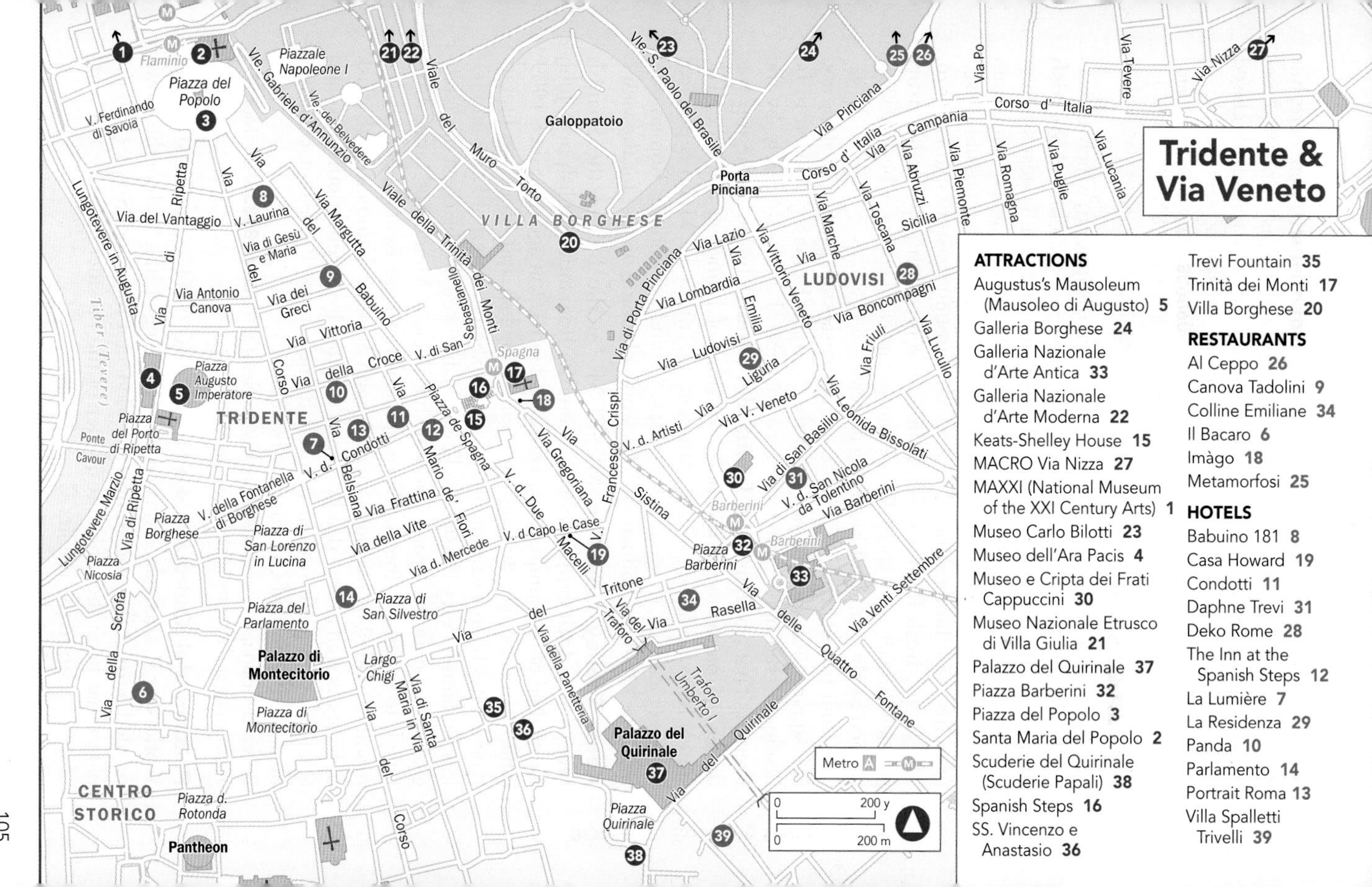
Tridente & Via Veneto
ATTRACTIONS
Augustus's Mausoleum (Mausoleo di Augusto) 5
Galleria Borghese 24
Galleria Nazionale d'Arte Antica 33
Galleria Nazionale d'Arte Moderna 22
Keats-Shelley House 15
MACRO Via Nizza 27
MAXXI (National Museum of the XXI Century Arts) 1
Museo Carlo Bilotti 23
Museo dell'Ara Pacis 4
Museo e Cripta dei Frati Cappuccini 30
Museo Nazionale Etrusco di Villa Giulia 21
Palazzo del Quirinale 37
Piazza Barberini 32
Piazza del Popolo 3
Santa Maria del Popolo 2
Scuderie del Quirinale (Scuderie Papali) 38
Spanish Steps 16
SS. Vincenzo e Anastasio 36
Trevi Fountain 35
Trinità dei Monti 17
Villa Borghese 20
RESTAURANTS
Al Ceppo 26
Canova Tadolini 9
Colline Emiliane 34
Il Bacaro 6
Imàgo 18
Metamorfosi 25
HOTELS
Babuino 181 8
Casa Howard 19
Condotti 11
Daphne Trevi 31
Deko Rome 28
The Inn at the Spanish Steps 12
La Lumière 7
La Residenza 29
Panda 10
Parlamento 14
Portrait Roma 13
Villa Spalletti Trivelli 39
Metro
0
200 y
0
200 m
Piazza del Popolo
Flaminio
Piazzale Napoleone I
Vle. Gabriele d'Annunzio
Vle. del Belvedere
Viale del Muro Torto
Galoppatoio
Vle. S. Paolo del Brasile
Via Pinciana
Porta Pinciana
VILLA BORGHESE
Viale della Trinità dei Monti
Via di Porta Pinciana
LUDOVISI
TRIDENTE
CENTRO STORICO
Via Vittorio Veneto
Via Veneto
Corso d' Italia
Via Tevere
Via Po
Via Nizza
Via Lucania
Via Puglie
Via Romagna
Via Piemonte
Via Abruzzi
Via Sicilia
Via Toscana
Via Marche
Via Campania
Via Boncompagni
Via Lucullo
Via Friuli
Via Leonida Bissolati
Via Lazio
Via Lombardia
Via Emilia
Via Ludovisi
Via Liguria
V. d. Artisti
Via di San Basilio
V. d. San Nicola da Tolentino
Via Barberini
Via Venti Settembre
Via delle Quattro Fontane
Via Rasella
Via del Tritone
Via Sistina
Via Francesco Crispi
Piazza Barberini
Barberini
Via Gregoriana
V. d. Due Macelli
V. d Capo le Case
Via d. Mercede
Via del Traforo
Traforo Umberto I
Via della Panetteria
Via del Quirinale
Piazza Quirinale
Palazzo del Quirinale
Via del Corso
Via di Santa Maria in Via
Largo Chigi
Piazza di San Silvestro
Piazza del Parlamento
Palazzo di Montecitorio
Piazza di Montecitorio
Piazza d. Rotonda
Pantheon
Via della Scrofa
Piazza Nicosia
Piazza Borghese
Piazza di San Lorenzo in Lucina
V. della Fontanella di Borghese
Via della Vite
Via Frattina
Via Mario de' Fiori
Piazza de Spagna
Spagna
Via Condotti
V. d. Belsiana
Via della Croce
V. di San Sebastianello
Via Vittoria
Via dei Greci
Via del Babuino
Via Margutta
Via di Gesù e Maria
V. Laurina
Via del Vantaggio
Via Antonio Canova
Via di Ripetta
Piazza Augusto Imperatore
Piazza del Porto di Ripetta
Ponte Cavour
Lungotevere in Augusta
Lungotevere Marzio
Tiber (Tevere)
V. Ferdinando di Savoia

ruin of **Augustus's Mausoleum (Mausoleo di Augusto)** from here, but the 1st-century-B.C. tomb itself—where urns with the ashes of emperors Augustus, Caligula, Claudius, Nerva, and Tiberius once rested—is closed to the public.

Lungotevere in Augusta. www.en.arapacis.it. ✆ **06-060608.** 10.50€. Daily 9:30am–7:30pm (last entry 6:30pm). Metro: Spagna. Bus: C3, 70, 81, 87, 280, 492, 628, 913.

PIAZZA DI SPAGNA

The undoubted highlight of Tridente is **Piazza di Spagna,** which attracts hordes of Romans and tourists alike to lounge on its celebrated **Spanish Steps (Scalinata della Trinità dei Monti) ★★**, the largest stairway in Europe, and enjoy the view onto "Fontana della Barcaccia," a fountain shaped like an old boat, the work of Pietro Bernini, with a possible assist from his more famous son, sculptor and fountain-master Gian Lorenzo. The Steps, fresh from a 1.5-million-euro renovation paid for by luxury jeweler Bulgari, are especially enchanting in early spring, when they are framed by thousands of blooming azaleas.

Built from 1723 to 1725, the monumental stairway of 135 steps and the square take their names from the Spanish Embassy (it used to be headquartered here), but were actually funded, almost entirely, by the French. That's because the **Trinità dei Monti** church at the top was under the patronage of the Bourbon kings of France at the time. The stately baroque facade of the 16th-century Trinità dei Monti is perched photogenically at the top of the Steps, behind yet another Roman obelisk, the "Obelisco Sallustiano." It's worth climbing up just for the views.

Keats-Shelley House ★ MUSEUM At the foot of the Spanish Steps is the 18th-century house where the Romantic English poet John Keats died of consumption on February 23, 1821 at age 25. Since 1909, when it was bought by well-intentioned English and American literary types, it has been a working library established in honor of Keats and fellow Romantic Percy Bysshe Shelley, who drowned off the coast of Viareggio with a copy of Keats' works in his pocket. Mementos range from kitsch to extremely moving. The apartment where Keats spent his last months, tended by his close friend Joseph Severn, shelters a death mask of Keats as well as the "deadly sweat" drawing by Severn. Both Keats and Shelley are buried in their beloved Rome, at the Protestant cemetery near the Pyramid of Cestius, in Testaccio.

Piazza di Spagna 26. www.keats-shelley-house.org. ✆ **06-6784235.** 5€. Mon–Sat 10am–1pm and 2–6pm. Metro: Spagna.

Palazzo del Quirinale ★★ HISTORIC SITE Until the end of World War II, this palace was home of the king of Italy; before the crown resided here, it was the summer residence of the pope. Since 1946 the palace has been the official residence of the President of Italy, but parts of it are open to the public.

Although it can't compare to Rome's major artistic showstoppers (there's little art or furniture in the rooms), the palace's baroque and

Art in the Pope's Stables

Across from the Palazzo del Quirinale, the **Scuderie del Quirinale** or **Scuderie Papali,** Via XXIV Maggio 16 (www.scuderiequirinale.it; ✆ **06-39967500**), originally 18th-century stables for the pope's horses, now function as remarkably atmospheric art galleries hosting temporary exhibitions ranging from the likes of Frida Kahlo to Japanese Buddhist sculpture. The galleries are usually open Sunday to Thursday 10am to 8pm and Friday and Saturday 10am to 10:30pm, but often close between exhibitions; check the website. Admission is 12€.

neoclassical walls and ceilings are quite a spectacle. Few rooms anywhere are as impressive as the richly decorated 17th-century **Salone dei Corazzieri,** the **Sala d'Ercole** (once the apartments of Umberto I but completely rebuilt in 1940), and the tapestry-covered 17th-century **Sala dello Zodiaco.** Despite its Renaissance origins, this *palazzo* is rich in associations with ancient emperors and deities. The colossal statues of the "Dioscuri," Castor and Pollux, which now form part of the fountain in the piazza, were found in the nearby Baths of Constantine; in 1793 Pius VI had an ancient Egyptian obelisk moved here from the Mausoleum of Augustus. The sweeping view of the city from the piazza, which crowns the highest of the seven ancient hills of Rome, is itself worth the trip.
Piazza del Quirinale. www.quirinale.it. ✆ **06-39-96-7557.** 1.50€ booking fee. Reservations must be made at least 5 days prior to visit. Tues–Wed and Fri–Sun 9:30am–4pm. Metro: Barberini. Bus: C3, 40, 60, 62-64, 70, 71, 80, 83, 85, 492.

Trevi Fountain (Fontana di Trevi) ★★ MONUMENT As you elbow your way through the summertime crowds around the **Trevi Fountain,** it's hard to believe that this little piazza was nearly always deserted before 1950, when it began "starring" in films. The first was *Three Coins in the Fountain*, and later it was the setting for an iconic scene in Fellini's

The Trevi Fountain.

1960 masterpiece *La Dolce Vita.* It was also where Audrey Hepburn gets her signature haircut in *Roman Holiday*. To this day, thousands of euros worth of coins are tossed into the fountain daily.

Supplied with water from the Acqua Vergine aqueduct and a triumph of the baroque style, the fountain was completed in 1762. The design centers on the triumphant figure of Neptune, standing on a shell chariot drawn by winged steeds and led by a pair of tritons. Two allegorical figures in the side niches represent good health and fertility. Thanks to the Roman fashion house Fendi, a 2015 cleaning of the fountain has restored the Trevi's travertine marble to a gleaming white.

> **Coin Toss: A Guaranteed Return to Rome?**
>
> The custom of tossing a coin into the Trevi Fountain to ensure your return to Rome apparently only works if you use correct form: With your back to the fountain, toss a coin with your right hand over your left shoulder. Works for me every time!

On the southwestern corner of the piazza is an unimpressive church, **SS. Vincenzo e Anastasio,** with a strange claim to fame. Within it are the relics (hearts and intestines) of several popes.

Piazza di Trevi. Metro: Barberini. Bus: C3, 51, 53, 62, 63, 71, 80, 83, 85, 160, 492.

Villa Borghese & Parioli

Villa Borghese ★★, in the heart of Rome, is not actually a villa but one of Europe's most elegant parks, 6km (3¾ miles) in circumference. It's home to the Galleria Borghese in the former Villa Borghese Pinciana (which really is a villa). Cardinal Scipione Borghese created the park in the 1600s. Umberto I, king of Italy, acquired it in 1902 and presented it to the city of Rome. With landscaped vistas, the greenbelt is crisscrossed by roads, but you can escape from the traffic and seek a shaded area under a tree to enjoy a picnic or relax. On a sunny weekend, it's a pleasure to stroll here and see Romans at play, relaxing or inline skating. The park has a few casual cafes and food vendors. You can also rent bikes or Segways here. In the northeast area of the park is a **zoo;** the park is also home to a few outstanding museums.

Galleria Borghese ★★★ ART MUSEUM On the far northeastern edge of the Villa Borghese, the Galleria Borghese occupies the former Villa Borghese Pinciana, built between 1609 and 1613 for Cardinal Scipione Borghese, an early patron of Bernini and an astute collector of work by Caravaggio. Today the gallery displays much of his collection and a lot more besides, making this one of Rome's great art treasures. It's also one of Rome's most pleasant sights to tour, thanks to the curators' mandate that only a limited number of people be allowed in at a time (see the last paragraph of this section for more on that).

The ground floor is a **sculpture gallery** par extraordinaire, housing Canova's famously risqué statue of Paolina Borghese, sister of Napoleon and wife of the reigning Prince Camillo Borghese (when asked if she was uncomfortable posing nude, she reportedly replied, "No, the studio was heated."). The genius of Bernini reigns supreme in the following rooms, with his "David" (the face of which is thought to be a self-portrait) and **"Apollo and Daphne" ★★** both seminal works of baroque sculpture. Look also for Bernini's Mannerist sculpture next door, "The Rape of Persephone." Caravaggio is represented by the "Madonna of the Grooms," the shadowy "St. Jerome," and the frightening **"David Holding the Head of Goliath" ★★**.

Upstairs lies a rich collection of paintings, including Raphael's graceful "Deposition" and his sinuous "Lady with a Unicorn." There's also a series of self-portraits by Bernini, and his lifelike busts of Cardinal Scipione and Pope Paul V. One of Titian's best, **"Sacred and Profane Love" ★**, lies in one of the final rooms.

Important information: No more than 360 visitors at a time are allowed on the ground floor, and no more than 90 are allowed on the upper floor, during set 2-hour windows. **Reservations are essential,** so call ✆ **06-32810** (Mon–Fri 9am–6pm; Sat 9am–1pm). You can also make reservations by visiting **www.tosc.it**, or stopping by in person on your first day to reserve tickets for a later date. If you are having problems making a reservation in advance, ask your hotel to help out. English labeling in the museum is minimal. Guided tours of the galleries in English cost an extra 6.50€, but failing that, opt for an **audio guide.**

Piazzale del Museo Borghese 5 (off Via Pinciana). www.galleriaborghese.it. ✆ **06-32810.** 15€ (includes 2€ booking fee); 18 and under 2€. Audio guides 5€. Tues–Sun 8:30am–7:30pm. Bus: C3, 53, 61, 89, 160, 490, 495, 590, 910.

MACRO Via Nizza ★★ MUSEUM Rome's contemporary art museum was recently expanded to occupy an entire block of early-1900s industrial buildings, formerly the Peroni beer factory, located near the Porta Pia gate of the Aurelian walls. Designed by French architect Odile Decq, the museum hosts contemporary art exhibits with edgy installations, visuals, and multimedia events. Another branch of the museum is housed in a converted slaughterhouse in Testaccio (p. 117).

Via Nizza 138. www.museomacro.org. ✆ **06-671070400.** 13.50€ (combined ticket with MACRO Testaccio). Tues–Sun 10:30am–7pm. Last entry 1 hr. before closing. Bus: 38, 60, 62, 66, 80, 82, 88-90. Tram: 3, 19.

Museo Carlo Bilotti ★ ART MUSEUM Fans of Greek-born Italian surrealist **Giorgio de Chirico** should make a pilgrimage to this small modern art gallery, created thanks to the generosity of Carlo Bilotti, an Italian-American collector who donated 23 artworks to Rome in 2006. Housed in a 16th-century palace in the Villa Borghese, the museum consists of two small rooms, and though the work is good, we recommend it for art aficionados only. Works to look out for include the elegant "Portrait of Tina and Lisa Bilotti" by Andy Warhol, a rare restrained piece by the Pop Art master; and Larry Rivers' depiction of Carlo Bilotti himself.

De Chirico dominates Room 2, with 17 paintings from the second half of the 1920s through to the 1970s.

Villa Borghese, at Viale Fiorello La Guardia. www.museocarlobilotti.it. ✆ **06-0608.** Free. June–Sept Tues–Fri 1pm–7pm, Sat–Sun 10am–7pm; Oct–May Tues–Fri 10am–4pm, Sat–Sun 10am–7pm. Metro: Flaminio. Bus: C3, 61, 89, 160, 490, 495, 590. Tram: 2.

Museo Nazionale Etrusco di Villa Giulia (National Etruscan Museum) ★★★ MUSEUM The great Etruscan civilization was one of Italy's most advanced, although it remains relatively mysterious, in part because of its centuries-long rivalry with Rome. Rome definitively conquered the Etruscans by the 3rd century B.C., and though they adopted certain aspects of Etruscan culture, including religious practices, engineering innovations, and gladiatorial combat, gradual Romanization eclipsed virtually all the Etruscans' achievements.

This museum, housed in the handsome Renaissance Villa Giulia, built by Pope Julius III between 1550 and 1555, is the best place in Italy to learn about the Etruscans, thanks to a cache of precious artifacts, sculptures, vases, monuments, tools, weapons, and jewels; the vast majority of it from tombs. Fans of ancient history could spend several hours here, but for those with less time, the most striking attraction is the stunning **Sarcofago degli Sposi (Sarcophagus of the Spouses) ★★,** a late 6th-century-B.C. terracotta funerary monument featuring a life-size bride and groom, supposedly lounging at a banquet in the afterlife (Paris's Louvre has a similar monument). Equally fascinating are the **Pyrgi Tablets,** gold-leaf inscriptions in both Etruscan and Phoenician from the 5th century B.C., and the **Apollo of Veii,** a huge painted terracotta statue of Apollo dating to the 6th century B.C. The **Euphronios Krater** is also here, a renowned and perfectly maintained red-figured Greek vase from the 6th century B.C. that returned home from New York's Metropolitan Museum of Art after a long legal battle.

Piazzale di Villa Giulia 9. www.villagiulia.beniculturali.it. ✆ **06-3226571.** 8€. Tues–Sun 8:30am–7:30pm. Bus: C3, 982. Tram: 2, 3, 19.

Galleria Nazionale d'Arte Moderna (National Gallery of Modern Art) ★ ART MUSEUM Housed in the monumental Bazzani Building constructed in 1911, this "modern" art collection ranges from unfashionable neoclassical and Romantic paintings and sculpture to better 20th-century works. Quality varies, but fans should seek out van Gogh's "Gardener" and "Portrait of Madame Ginoux" in Room 15, the handful of Impressionists in Room 14 (Cézanne, Degas, Monet, and Rodin), and Klimt's harrowing "Three Ages" in Room 16. Surrealist and Expressionist works by Miró, Kandinsky, and Mondrian appear in Room 22, and Pollock's "Undulating Paths" and Calder's "Mobile" hold court in Room 27. One of Warhol's "Hammer and Sickle" series is tucked away in Room 30.

The museum is primarily a showcase for **modern Italian painters,** a group inevitably laboring under the mighty shadow of their Renaissance and baroque forebears. Be sure to check out rooms dedicated to

Giacomo Balla (no. 34), Giacomo Manzù (no. 35), Renato Guttuso (no. 37), and Pino Pascali (no. 40).

Viale delle Belle Arti 131. www.gnam.beniculturali.it. ✆ **06-322981.** 10€, free children 17 and under. Tues–Sun 8:30am–7:30pm. Bus: 61, 160, 490, 495. Tram: 3 or 19.

Via Veneto & Piazza Barberini

Piazza Barberini lies at the foot of several streets, among them Via Barberini, Via Sistina, and Via Vittorio Veneto. It would be a far more pleasant spot were it not for the traffic swarming around its principal feature, Bernini's **Fountain of the Triton (Fontana del Tritone) ★**. For more than 3 centuries, the figure sitting in a vast open clam has been blowing water from his triton. To one side of the piazza is the aristocratic facade of the **Palazzo Barberini,** named for one of Rome's powerful families; inside is the **Galleria Nazionale d'Arte Antica** (see below). The Barberini reached their peak when a son was elected pope as Urban VIII; he encouraged Bernini and gave him patronage.

As you walk up **Via Vittorio Veneto,** look for the small fountain on the right corner of Piazza Barberini—it's another Bernini, the **Fountain of the Bees (Fontana delle Api).** At first they look more like flies, but they're the bees of the Barberini, the crest of that powerful family complete with the crossed keys of St. Peter above them. (Keys were always added to a family crest when a son was elected pope.)

Museo e Cripta dei Frati Cappuccini (Museum and Crypt of the Capuchin Friars) ★★ RELIGIOUS SITE/MUSEUM One of the most mesmerizingly macabre sights in all Christendom, this otherwise restrained museum dedicated to the Capuchin order ends with a series of six chapels in the crypt, adorned with the skulls and bones of more than 3,700 Capuchin brothers, woven into mosaic "works of art." Some of the skeletons are intact, draped with Franciscan habits; others form lamps and ceiling friezes. The tradition of the friars dates to a period when Christians had a richly creative cult of the dead and great spiritual masters meditated and preached with a skull in hand. Whatever you believe, the experience is a mix of spooky and meditative. The entrance is halfway up the first staircase on the right of the church of the Convento dei Frati Cappuccini, completed in 1630 and rebuilt in the early 1930s.

Note: Because this site is located within a church, it maintains a strict dress code—no short pants or skirts and no bare arms.

Beside the Convento dei Frati Cappuccini, Via Vittorio Veneto 27. www.cappuccini viaveneto.it. ✆ **06-88803695.** 8.50€, 4€ ages 17 and under. Daily 9am–7pm, last entry 6:30pm. Metro: Barberini. Bus: C3, 53, 61, 63, 80, 83, 160, 590.

Galleria Nazionale d'Arte Antica (National Gallery of Ancient Art) ★★ ART MUSEUM On the southern side of **Piazza Barberini,** the grand **Palazzo Barberini** houses the Galleria Nazionale d'Arte Antica, a trove of Italian art mostly from the early Renaissance to late baroque periods. Some of the art on display is wonderful, but the building itself is the main attraction, a baroque masterpiece begun by Carlo Maderno in 1627 and completed in 1633 by Bernini, with additional work by Borromini (notably a whimsical spiral staircase). The **Salone di Pietro da Cortona** in the center is the most captivating space, with a trompe l'oeil ceiling frescoed by Pietro da Cortona, a depiction of "The Triumph of Divine Providence."

The museum has intriguing works, including Raphael's "La Fornarina," a baker's daughter thought to have been the artist's lover (look for Raphael's name on her bracelet); paintings by Tintoretto and Titian (Room 15); a portrait of English King Henry VIII by Holbein (Room 16); and a couple of typically unsettling El Grecos in Room 17, "The Baptism of Christ" and "Adoration of the Shepherds." Caravaggio dominates room 20 with the justly celebrated "Judith and Holofernes" and **"Narcissus" ★★**.

Via delle Quattro Fontane 13. www.barberinicorsini.org. ✆ **06-4814591.** 7€; combined with Palazzo Corsini 9€. Tues–Sun 8:30am–7pm; last entry 6pm. Metro: Barberini. Bus: C3, 61-63, 80, 83, 85, 160, 492, 590.

Around Stazione Termini

Palazzo Massimo alle Terme ★★ MUSEUM A third of Rome's assortment of ancient art can be found at this branch of the Museo Nazionale Romano; among its treasures are a major coin collection, extensive maps of trade routes (with audio and visual exhibits on the network of traders over the centuries), and a vast sculpture collection that includes portrait busts of emperors and their families, as well as mythical figures like the Minotaur and Athena. But the real draw is on the second floor, where you can see some of the oldest of Rome's **frescoes ★★**; they depict an entire garden, complete with plants and birds, from the Villa di Livia a Prima Porta. (Livia was the wife of Emperor Augustus and was deified after her death in A.D. 29.)

Largo di Villa Peretti. www.archeoroma.beniculturali.it. ✆ **06-39967700.** 7€ (good for 3 days; also valid at Palazzo Massimo, Palazzo Altemps, Baths of Diocletian, Crypta Balbi); 17 and under free. Tues–Sun 9am–7:45pm. Last entry 1 hr. before closing. Metro: Termini or Repubblica. Bus: 40, 64, or any bus that stops at Termini.

Santa Maria della Vittoria ★ CHURCH This pretty little baroque church has the classic Roman travertine facade and an ornate interior. But a visit here is all about one artwork: Gian Lorenzo Bernini's **"Ecstasy of St. Teresa" ★★★**. Crafted from marble between 1644 and 1647, it shows the Spanish saint at the moment of her ecstatic encounter with an angel (the so-called "Transverberation"). To say Bernini's depiction is a little on the erotic side would be an understatement. The Cornaro family, who sponsored the chapel's construction, is depicted as witnesses to the moment from a "balcony" on the right.

Via XX Settembre 17 (at Largo S. Susanna). www.chiesasantamariavittoriaroma.it. ✆ **06-42740571.** Free. Mon–Sat 8:30am–noon and 3:30–6pm; Sun 3:30–6pm. Metro: Repubblica. Bus: 60-62, 66, 82, 85, 492, 590, 910.

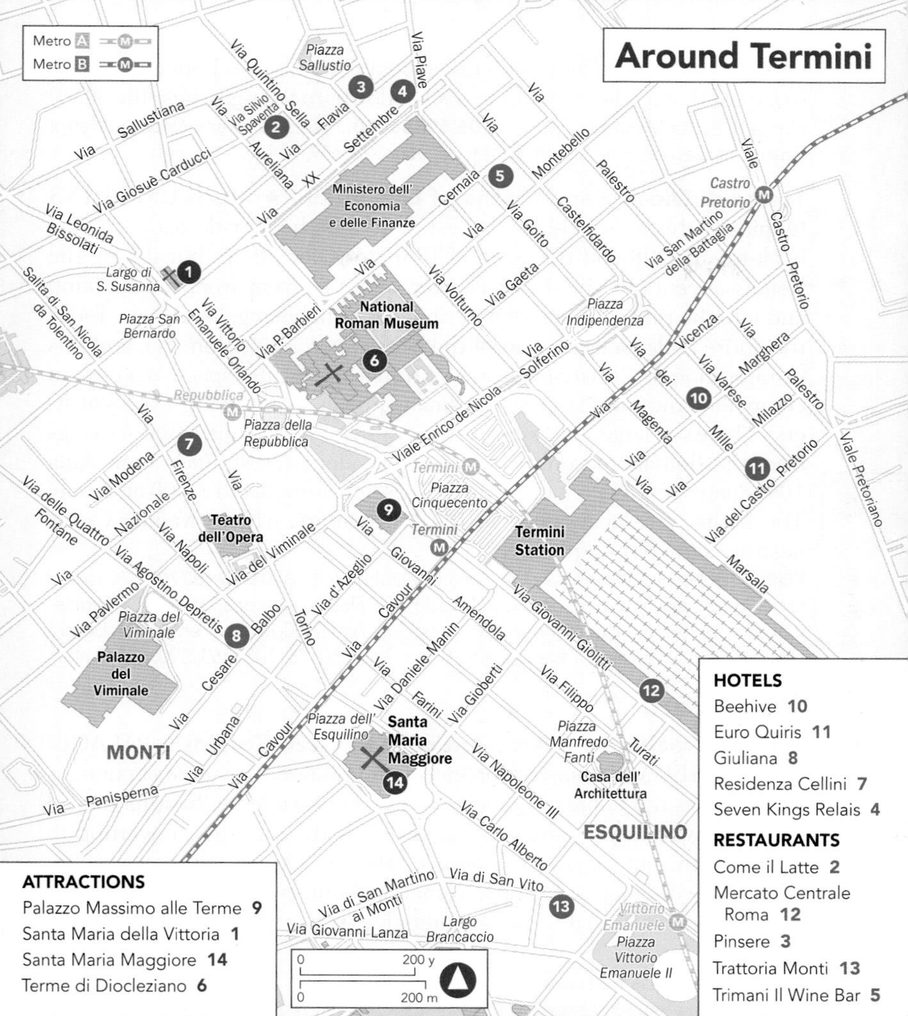

Santa Maria Maggiore (St. Mary Major) ★★ CHURCH This majestic church, one of Rome's four papal basilicas, was founded by Pope Liberius in A.D. 358 and rebuilt on the orders of Pope Sixtus III from 432 to 440. Its 14th-century **campanile** is the city's loftiest. Much doctored in the 18th century, the church's facade isn't an accurate reflection of the treasures inside. The basilica is noted for the 5th-century Roman mosaics in its nave, and for its coffered ceiling, said to have been gilded with gold brought from the New World. The church also contains the **tomb of Bernini,** Italy's most important baroque sculptor–architect. The man who changed the face of Rome with his elaborate fountains is buried in a tomb so simple that it takes a sleuth to track it down (to the right, near the altar). Piazza di Santa Maria Maggiore. ✆ **06-69886800.** Free. Daily 7am–6:45pm. Metro: Termini or Cavour. Bus: C3, 16, 70, 71, 75, 360, 590, 649, 714.

Terme di Diocleziano (Baths of Diocletian) ★ MUSEUM/RUINS Originally this spot held the largest of Rome's hedonistic baths (dating back to A.D. 298 and the reign of Emperor Diocletian), but during the Renaissance a church, a vast cloister, and a convent were built around and into the ruins—much of it designed by Michelangelo, no less. Today the entire hodgepodge is part of the Museo Nazionale Romano, and this juxtaposition of Christianity, ancient ruins, and exhibit space makes for a compelling museum stop that's usually quieter than the city's blockbusters. There's a large collection of inscriptions and other stone carvings from the Roman and pre-Roman periods, alongside statuary. Only Aula 10 remains of the vast baths, which once accommodated 3,000 at a time. The baths were abandoned in the 6th century, when invading Goths destroyed the city's aqueducts.

Viale E. di Nicola 78. www.archeoroma.beniculturali.it. ✆ **06-39967700.** 7€ (good for 3 days; also valid at Palazzo Massimo, Palazzo Altemps, Baths of Diocletian, Crypta Balbi); 17 and under free. Tues–Sun 9am–7:30pm. Last entry 1 hr. before closing. Metro: Termini or Repubblica. Bus: C3, 16, 50, 75, 105, 360, 590, 649, 714.

Trastevere

Galleria Nazionale d'Arte Antica in Palazzo Corsini ★ PALACE/ART MUSEUM Palazzo Corsini first found fame (or more accurately, notoriety) as the home of Queen Christina of Sweden. Christina moved to Rome when she abdicated the Swedish throne after converting to Catholicism, but her most famous epithet is "Queen without a realm, Christian without a faith, and a woman without shame," which stemmed from her open bisexuality. Several other big names stayed in this beautiful

Santa Maria Square in Trastevere.

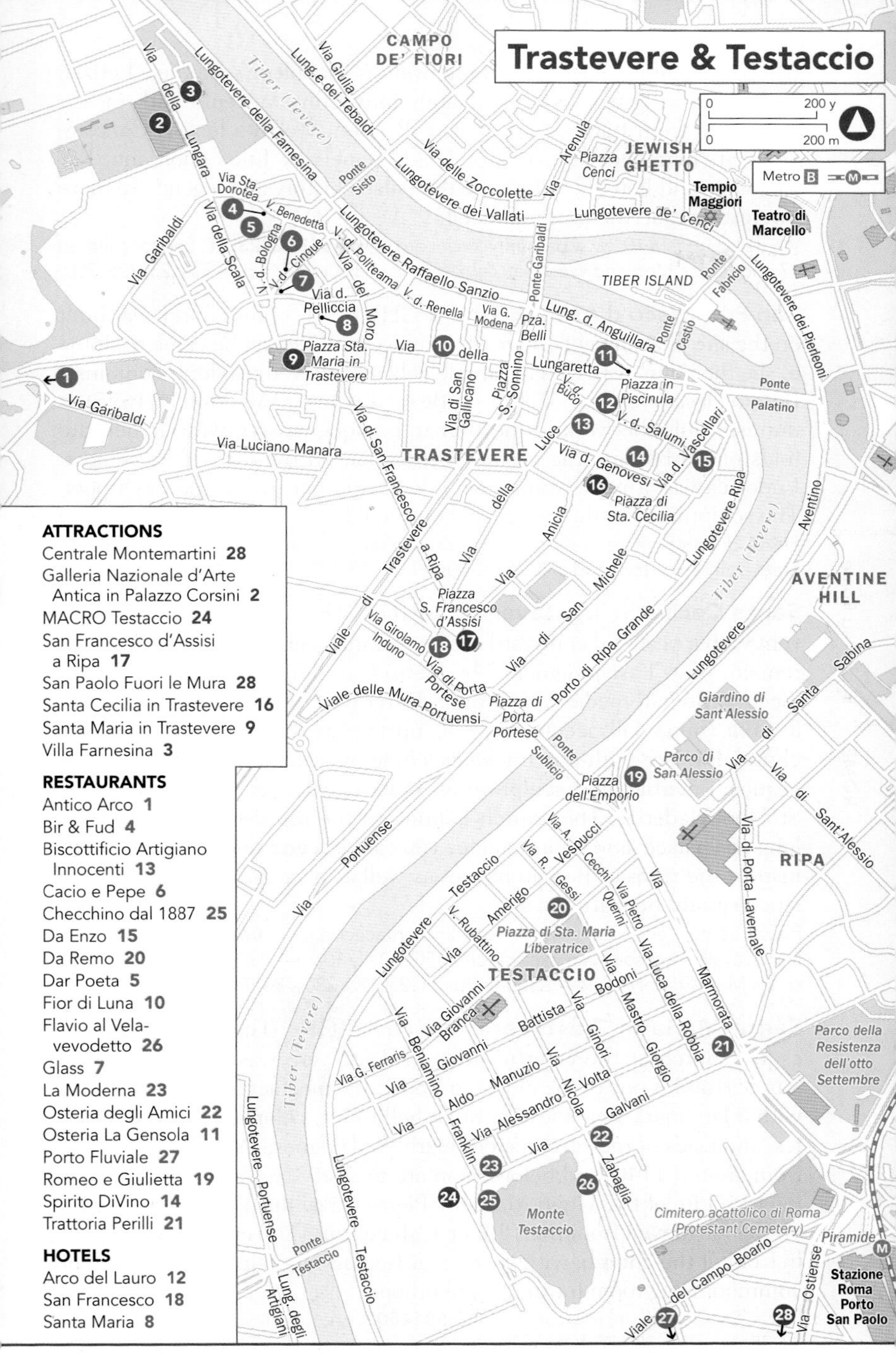
Trastevere & Testaccio
0
200 y
0
200 m
Metro
CAMPO DE' FIORI
JEWISH GHETTO
Tempio Maggiori
Teatro di Marcello
TIBER ISLAND
TRASTEVERE
AVENTINE HILL
RIPA
TESTACCIO
Tiber (Tevere)
Via della Lungara
Lungotevere della Farnesina
Via Giulia
Lung.e dei Tebaldi
Via delle Zoccolette
Lungotevere dei Vallati
Lungotevere de' Cenci
Piazza Cenci
Via Arenula
Ponte Sisto
Via Sta. Dorotea
V. Benedetta
Via della Scala
Via Garibaldi
V. d. Bologna
V. d. Cinque
Via d. Pelliccia
Via del Moro
V. d. Politeama
Lungotevere Raffaello Sanzio
V. d. Renella
Via G. Modena
Pza. Belli
Ponte Garibaldi
Lung. d. Anguillara
Ponte Cestio
Ponte Fabricio
Lungotevere dei Pierleoni
Piazza Sta. Maria in Trastevere
Via della Lungaretta
Piazza in Piscinula
V. d. Buco
V. d. Salumi
Via d. Vascellari
Ponte Palatino
Via di San Gallicano
Piazza S. Sonnino
Via Luciano Manara
Via di San Francesco a Ripa
Via della Luce
Via d. Genovesi
Piazza di Sta. Cecilia
Via Anicia
Lungotevere Ripa
Lungotevere Aventino
Viale di Trastevere
Piazza S. Francesco d'Assisi
Via di San Michele
Via Girolamo Induno
Via di Porta Portese
Viale delle Mura Portuensi
Piazza di Porta Portese
Porto di Ripa Grande
Ponte Sublicio
Giardino di Sant'Alessio
Via di Santa Sabina
Parco di San Alessio
Via di Sant'Alessio
Piazza dell'Emporio
Via Portuense
Via A. Vespucci
Via R. Gessi
Via A. Cecchi
Via Pietro Querini
Via di Porta Lavernale
Lungotevere Testaccio
Via Amerigo
V. Rubattino
Piazza di Sta. Maria Liberatrice
Via Luca della Robbia
Via Marmorata
Via Giovanni Branca
Via Giovanni Battista Bodoni
Via Mastro Giorgio
Via Ginori
Via Beniamino Franklin
Via G. Ferraris
Via Aldo Manuzio
Via Nicola Zabaglia
Via Alessandro Volta
Via Galvani
Parco della Resistenza dell'otto Settembre
Lungotevere Portuense
Monte Testaccio
Cimitero acattolico di Roma (Protestant Cemetery)
Piramide
Ponte Testaccio
Lung. degli Artigiani
Viale del Campo Boario
Via Ostiense
Stazione Roma Porto San Paolo
ATTRACTIONS
Centrale Montemartini 28
Galleria Nazionale d'Arte Antica in Palazzo Corsini 2
MACRO Testaccio 24
San Francesco d'Assisi a Ripa 17
San Paolo Fuori le Mura 28
Santa Cecilia in Trastevere 16
Santa Maria in Trastevere 9
Villa Farnesina 3
RESTAURANTS
Antico Arco 1
Bir & Fud 4
Biscottificio Artigiano Innocenti 13
Cacio e Pepe 6
Checchino dal 1887 25
Da Enzo 15
Da Remo 20
Dar Poeta 5
Fior di Luna 10
Flavio al Velavevodetto 26
Glass 7
La Moderna 23
Osteria degli Amici 22
Osteria La Gensola 11
Porto Fluviale 27
Romeo e Giulietta 19
Spirito DiVino 14
Trattoria Perilli 21
HOTELS
Arco del Lauro 12
San Francesco 18
Santa Maria 8

palace, including Michelangelo as well as Napoleon's mother, Letizia. Today one wing houses a moderately interesting museum with mostly the runoff from Italy's national art collection. Worth a look is Caravaggio's "St. John the Baptist" (1606) and panels by Luca Giordano, Fra' Angelico, and Poussin; otherwise the palace history and legend are more interesting than the museum itself.

Via della Lungara 10. www.barberinicorsini.org. ✆ **06-68802323.** 5€, free for children 17 and under. Mon and Wed–Sat 2–7:30pm; Sun 8:30am–7:30pm. Bus: 23, 125, 280.

San Francesco d'Assisi a Ripa ★ CHURCH This church was built on the site of a convent where St. Francis stayed when he came to Rome to see the pope in 1219. His simple cell is preserved inside. It contains a Bernini treasure: The "Tomb of Beata Ludovica Albertoni" (1675) is unmistakably the work of the Roman baroque master, with its delicate folds of marble and the ecstatic expression on the face of its subject. Ludovica was a noblewoman who dedicated her life to the city's poor. The sculpture is in the last chapel on the left.

Piazza di San Francesco d'Assisi 88. www.sanfrancescoaripa.com. ✆ **06-5819020.** Free. Daily 8am–1pm and 2–7:30pm. Bus: H, 23, 75, 115, 125m, or 280. Tram: 3 or 8.

Santa Cecilia in Trastevere ★ CHURCH A still-functioning convent with a peaceful courtyard garden, Santa Cecilia contains the partial remains of a "Last Judgment," by Pietro Cavallini (ca. 1293), a masterpiece of Roman medieval painting. (Enter to the left of the main doors; a *suora* (nun) will accompany you upstairs to see it.) Inside the airy church is a late-13th-century baldacchino by Arnolfo di Cambio, and an exquisite marble altar sculpture of Santa Cecilia (ca. 1600) carved by Stefano Maderno. The church is built on the reputed site of Cecilia's long-ago palace, and for a small fee you can descend under the church to inspect the ruins of Roman houses as well as peer through a gate at the stucco grotto beneath the altar.

Piazza Santa Cecilia 22. www.benedettinesantacecilia.it. ✆ **06-45492739.** Church free; Cavallini frescoes and excavations 2.50€. Daily 10am–12:30pm and 4–6pm. Frescoes Mon–Fri only 10am–12:30pm. Bus: H, 23, 125, 280, 780. Tram: 8.

Santa Maria in Trastevere ★★ CHURCH This ornate Romanesque church at the colorful heart of Trastevere was founded around A.D. 350 and is one of the oldest in Rome. It's spectacular inside and out, with a landmark Romanesque brick bell tower, colorful frescoes, mosaics, and loads of recycled ancient marbles. The mosaics on the apse date from around 1140, and below them are the 1293 mosaic scenes depicting the "Life of the Virgin Mary" by Pietro Cavallini. The faded mosaics on the facade are from the 12th or 13th century. The eponymous square in front of the church, with its ancient Roman fountain, acts as a kind of common living room for the neighborhood.

Piazza Santa Maria in Trastevere. ✆ **06-5814802.** Free. Daily 7:30am–9pm. Bus: H, 23, 75, 115, 125, 280, 780. Tram: 8.

Villa Farnesina ★ HISTORIC HOME Originally built for Sienese banker Agostino Chigi in 1511, this elegant villa was acquired by the Farnese family in 1579. With two such wealthy Renaissance patrons, it's hardly surprising that the interior decor is top drawer. Architect Baldassare Peruzzi began the decoration, with frescoes and motifs rich in myth and symbolism. He was later assisted by Sebastiano del Piombo, Sodoma, and, most notably, Raphael. Raphael's **"Loggia of Cupid and Psyche"** ★★ was frescoed to mark Chigi's marriage to Francesca Ordeaschi—though his assistants did much of the work. The ornamental gardens are perfumed and colorful in the spring and summer.

Via della Lungara 230. www.villafarnesina.it. ✆ **06-68077268.** 6€. Mon–Sat 9am–2pm; 2nd Sun of month 9am–5pm. Bus: 23, 125, 280.

Testaccio & Southern Rome

Centrale Montemartini ★★ MUSEUM The renovated boiler rooms of Rome's first thermoelectric plant now house a grand collection of Roman and Greek statues, creating a unique juxtaposition of classic and industrial archaeology. The 19th-century powerhouse was the first public plant to produce electricity for the city. Striking installations include the vast boiler hall, a 1,000-square-meter (10,764-sq-ft.) room where statues share space with a complex web of pipes, masonry, and metal walkways. Equally striking is the Hall of Machines, where two towering turbines stand opposite the reconstructed pediment of the Temple of Apollo Sosiano, which illustrates a famous Greek battle. Unless you run across a school group, this place is never crowded, and it provides an intimate look at the ancient world, despite the cavernous setting.

Via Ostiense 106. www.centralemontemartini.org. ✆ **06-0608.** 7.50€. Tues–Sun 9am–7pm. Last entry 30 min. before closing. Metro: Garbatella. Bus: 23 or 792.

MACRO Testaccio ★ MUSEUM The Testaccio outpost of Rome's contemporary art museum is housed—appropriately for this former meatpacking neighborhood—in a converted slaughterhouse. The edgy programs and exhibits are a mix of installations, visuals, events, and

Mussolini's City of the Future

South of the city center, the outlying **EUR suburb** ★ (the acronym stands for *Esposizione Universale Romana*) was designed and purpose-built by Mussolini in the Fascist era to stage the planned World Fair of 1942—canceled, thanks to World War II. Though never completed, EUR's mix of rationalist and classical-inspired elements will enthuse anyone with a serious interest in architecture. Perfect symmetry and sleek marble-lined avenues house a number of museums, corporate headquarters, and office agglomerates, connected to the *centro* by both subway and the modern thoroughfare Via Cristoforo Colombo. The residential area that later grew around the EUR business district is not particularly exciting, but it is verdant and quiet—a nice getaway from bustling central Rome.

special viewings. Opening times are made for night owls: Make a late visit before going on to Testaccio's bars and restaurants.

Piazza Orazio Guistiniani 4. www.museomacro.org. ✆ **06-671070400.** 14.50€ (combined ticket with MACRO Via Nizza). Tues–Sun 2–8pm. Last entry 30 min. before closing. Bus: 23, 83, 280, 673, 719. Tram: 3.

San Paolo Fuori le Mura (St. Paul Outside the Walls) ★★ CHURCH The giant Basilica of St. Paul, whose origins date from the time of Constantine, is Rome's fourth great patriarchal church. It was erected over the tomb of St. Paul and is the second-largest church in Rome after St. Peter's. The basilica fell victim to fire in 1823 and was subsequently rebuilt—hence the relatively modern look. Inside, translucent alabaster windows illuminate a forest of single-file columns and mosaic medallions (portraits of the various popes). Its most important treasure is a 12th-century marble candelabrum by Vassalletto, who's also responsible for the remarkable cloisters containing twisted pairs of columns enclosing a rose garden. Miraculously, the baldacchino by Arnolfo di Cambio (1285) wasn't damaged in the fire; it now shelters the tomb of St. Paul the Apostle.

Via Ostiense 190 (at Piazzale San Paolo). www.basilicasanpaolo.org. ✆ **06-69880800.** Basilica free; cloisters 4€. Basilica daily 7am–6:30pm. Cloisters daily 8:30am–6:15pm. Metro: Basilica di San Paolo. Bus: 23, 769, 792.

The Via Appia (Appian Way) & the Catacombs

Of all the roads that led to Rome, **Via Appia Antica** (begun in 312 B.C.) was the most famous. It stretched all the way to the seaport of Brindisi, through which trade with Greece and the East was funneled. (According to Christian tradition, it was along the Appian Way that an escaping Peter encountered the vision of Christ, causing him to go back into the city to face martyrdom.) The road's initial stretch in Rome is lined with the monuments and ancient tombs of patrician Roman families—burials were forbidden within the city walls as early as the 5th century B.C.—and, below ground, miles of tunnels hewn out of the soft *tufa* stone that hardens on exposure to the air.

These tunnels, or catacombs, were where early Christians buried their dead. A few are open to the public, so you can wander through musty-smelling tunnels whose walls are gouged out with tens of thousands of now mostly empty burial niches, including small niches made for children. Early Christians referred to each chamber as a *dormitorio*—they believed the bodies were only sleeping, awaiting resurrection (which is why they could not observe the traditional Roman practice of cremation). In some you can still discover the remains of early Christian art. The obligatory guided tours feature occasionally biased history, plus a dash of sermonizing, but the guides are very knowledgeable.

The Appia Antica park is a popular Sunday picnic site for Roman families, following the half-forgotten pagan tradition of dining in the presence of one's ancestors on holy days. The Via Appia Antica is closed

A Noble Survivor

Of all the monuments on the Appian Way itself, the most impressive is the **Tomb of Cecilia Metella ★**, within walking distance of the catacombs. The cylindrical tomb, clad in travertine and topped with a marble frieze, honors the wife of one of Julius Caesar's military commanders from the republican era. Why such an elaborate tomb for a figure of relatively minor historical importance? Other mausoleums may have been even more elaborate, but Cecilia Metella's earned enduring fame simply because her tomb has remained while the others have decayed. Part of the reason is its symbiotic relationship with the early-14th-century **Castle Caetani** attached to the rear. For centuries, the tomb survived being plundered for building materials because of the castle, which was built to guard the road and collect tolls; in later eras, the castle was spared because it was attached to the romantic ruin of the tomb. Admission to the tomb, on a combined ticket with the Baths of Caracalla (p. 86), is 6€, free for children 17 and under.

to cars on Sundays, left for the picnickers, bicyclists, and inline skaters. See **www.parcoappiaantica.it** for more, including downloadable maps.

To reach the catacombs area, take bus no. 218 from the San Giovanni Metro stop or the 118 from Colosseo or Circus Maximus. ***Tip:*** The 118 runs more frequently than the 218 and deposits you closer to the catacombs, but there's no service on Sundays. If you are in a hurry to accommodate your visit to the catacombs, take a cab (p. 62).

Catacombe di San Callisto (Catacombs of St. Callixtus) ★★ RELIGIOUS SITE/TOUR "The most venerable and most renowned of Rome," said Pope John XXIII of these funerary tunnels. These catacombs are often packed with tour-bus groups, but the tunnels are phenomenal. They're the first cemetery of Christian Rome, burial place of 16 popes in the 3rd century. They bear the name of the deacon St. Callixtus, who served as pope from A.D. 217–22. The network of galleries is on four levels and reaches a depth of about 20m (65 ft.), the deepest in the area. There are many sepulchral chambers and almost half a million tombs of early Christians.

Entering the catacombs, you see the most important crypt, that of nine popes. Some of the original marble tablets of their tombs are preserved. Also commemorated is St. Cecilia, patron of sacred music (her relics were moved to her church in Trastevere during the 9th century; see p. 116). Farther on are the Cubicles of the Sacraments, with 3rd-century frescoes.

Via Appia Antica 110–26. www.catacombe.roma.it. ✆ **06-5130151.** 8€ adults, 5€ children ages 7–15. Thurs–Tues 9am–noon and 2–5pm. Closed late Jan to late Feb. Bus: 118 or 218.

Catacombe di Domitilla ★★★ RELIGIOUS SITE/TOUR The oldest of the catacombs is the hands-down winner for most enjoyable experience. Groups are relatively small (in part because the site is not directly on the Appian Way), and guides are entertaining and personable.

The catacombs—Rome's longest at 17km (11 miles)—were built below land donated by Domitilla, a noblewoman of the Flavian dynasty who was exiled from Rome for practicing Christianity. They were rediscovered in 1593, after a church abandoned in the 9th century collapsed. The visit begins in the sunken church founded in A.D. 380, the year Christianity became Rome's state religion.

There are fewer "sights" here than in the other catacombs, but this is the only catacomb where you'll still see bones; the rest have emptied their tombs to rebury the remains in inaccessible lower levels. Elsewhere in the tunnels, 4th-century frescoes contain some of the earliest representations of Saints Peter and Paul. Notice the absence of crosses: It was only later that Christians replaced the traditional fish symbol with the cross. During this period, Christ's crucifixion was a source of shame to the community. He had been killed like a common criminal.

Via delle Sette Chiese 282. www.domitilla.info. ✆ **06-5110342.** 8€ adults, 5€ children ages 6–14. Wed–Mon 9am–noon and 2–5pm. Closed mid-Dec to mid-Jan. Bus: 30, 671, 714, 716 (to Piazza dei Navigatori) or bus 218.

Catacombe di San Sebastiano (Catacombs of St. Sebastian) ★

RELIGIOUS SITE/TOUR Today the tomb and relics of St. Sebastian are in the ground-level basilica, but his original resting place was in the catacombs beneath it. Sebastian was a senior Milanese soldier in the Roman army who converted to Christianity and was martyred during Emperor Diocletian's persecutions, which were especially brutal in the first decade of the 4th century. From the reign of Valerian to that of Constantine, the bodies of Saints Peter and Paul were also hidden in the catacombs, which were dug from the soft volcanic rock (*tufa*). The church was built in the 4th century and remodeled in the 17th century.

In the tunnels and mausoleums are mosaics and graffiti, along with many other pagan and Christian objects, as well as four Roman tombs

Lake at Villa Borghese.

ORGANIZED tours

Forget the flag-waving guides leading a herd of dazed travelers around monuments. A better class of professionally guided tours delivers topnotch insider expertise, focused themes, and personalized attention, plus perks such as skipping long admission lines and having bespoke after-hours experiences.

One of the leading tour operators in Rome, **Context Travel ★** (www.contexttravel.com; ✆ **800/691-6036** in the U.S., or 06-96727371) uses local scholars—historians, art historians, preservationists—to lead their small-group walking tours around Rome's monuments, museums, and historic piazzas, as well as on culinary walks and excellent family programs. Custom-designed tours are also available. Prices of the regular tours are high, beginning at about 60€ for 2 hours, but most participants consider them a highlight of their trip.

Walks of Italy (www.walksofitaly.com; ✆ **06-95583331**) also runs excellent guided tours of Rome starting from 39€, and more in-depth explorations of the Colosseum, Vatican Museums, and Forum go for 59€ to 125€.

Enjoy Rome, Via Marghera 8a (www.enjoyrome.com; ✆ **06-4451843**), offers a number of "greatest hits" walking tours, plus an early-evening tour of the Jewish Ghetto and Trastevere and a bus excursion to the Catacombs and the Appian Way that visits a ruined ancient aqueduct that most Romans, let alone tourists, never see. Tours cost 30€ to 50€ per person, but entrance fees are not included.

The team at **Through Eternity** (www.througheternity.com; ✆ **06-7009336)** are art historians and architects; what sets them apart is their theatrical delivery, helped along by the dramatic scripts that many of the guides seem to follow. It can be a lot of fun, but it's not for everyone. Through Eternity also offers twilight tours, food tours, and after-hours tours of the Vatican, allowing you to see its treasures without fighting the crowds (it's a tremendous experience). A 5-hour tour of the Vatican is 79€; most other tours range from 39€ to 119€.

The Roman Guy (www.theromanguy.com, ✆ **06-342-8761859**) provides knowledgeable guides who explain thousands of years of history in an engaging, informal way. They offer small-group (most about 10 people) tours and private tours of the Colosseum (including dungeons), Vatican Museums, Catacombs, and food tours of Trastevere, among a few others. Prices start from 59€ per person for a small-group tour to much more for exclusive VIP access and/or private excursions.

with their frescoes and stucco fairly intact, found in 1922 after being buried for almost 2,000 years.

Via Appia Antica 136. www.catacombe.org. ✆ **06-7850350.** 8€ adults, 5€ children 6–15. Mon–Sat 10am–4:30pm. Closed Nov 26–Dec 26. Bus: 118 or 218.

Especially for Kids

There's a real Jekyll and Hyde quality to exploring Rome with kids. On the one hand, it's a capital city, big, busy, and hot, and with dodgy public transportation. On the other, the very best parts of the city for kids—Roman ruins, subterranean worlds, and *gelato*—are aspects you'd want to explore anyway. Seeing Rome with kids doesn't demand an itinerary redesign—at least, if you're willing to skip some marquee museums. And despite what you have heard about its famous seven hills, much of the center is mercifully flat, and pedestrian.

Food is pretty easy too: Roman **pizzas** are some of the best in the world—see "Where to Eat" (p. 135) for our favorites. Ditto the ice cream, or *gelato* (p. 140). Restaurants in any price category will be happy to serve up a simple *pasta al pomodoro* (pasta with tomato sauce), and kids are welcomed virtually everywhere.

The city is shorter on green spaces than many European cities, but the landscaped gardens of the **Villa Borghese** have plenty of space for kids to let off steam. Pack a picnic or rent some bikes (p. 108). The **Parco Appia Antica** (www.parcoappiaantica.it) is another favorite, especially on a Sunday or holiday when the old cobbled road is closed to traffic. The park's **Catacombs** (p. 118) are eerie enough to satisfy young minds, but also fascinating Christian and historical sites in their own right.

Museums, of course, are trickier, though my 5-year-old was recently enthralled by several galleries of gory Renaissance paintings depicting biblical murders and sacrifices. You can probably get kids fired up more easily for the really ancient stuff. Make the bookshop at the **Colosseum** (p. 88) an early stop; it has a good selection of guides aimed at under-12s, themed on gladiators and featuring funny or cartoonish material. The **Musei Capitolini** (p. 86) invites kids to hunt down the collection's treasures highlighted on a free leaflet—it'll buy you a couple of hours to admire the exhibits and perhaps see them from a new and unexpected angle, too. The multiple levels below **San Clemente** (p. 94) and the **Case Romane del Celio** (p. 95) are another draw for small visitors.

Aspiring young gladiators may want to spend 2 hours at the **Scuola Gladiatori Roma (Rome Gladiator School),** where they can prepare for a duel in a reasonably authentic way. You can book through **Viator.com**.

Kids will also likely enjoy some of the cheesier city sights—at the very least these will make some good family photos to share on Facebook or Instagram. Build in some time to place your hands in the Bocca della Verità, at **Santa Maria in Cosmedin** (p. 96), to throw a coin in the **Trevi Fountain** (p. 107), and to enjoy watching the feral cats relaxing amid the ruins of **Largo di Torre Argentina.** A cat sanctuary here provides basic healthcare to Rome's many strays.

If you want to delve deeper into the city as a family, check out the tours on **Context Travel**'s family program (see Organized Tours, p. 121), such as walks, workshops, and tours of museums and underground Rome. The 2- to 3-hour tours are pricey (300€–425€ per family) but first-rate, and you will have the docent all to yourselves.

WHERE TO STAY

Hotels in Rome's *centro storico* are notoriously overpriced, and all too often the grand exteriors and lobbies of historic buildings give way to bland modern rooms. Our selections here made the cut because they offer unique experiences, highly personalized service, or extreme value—and in many cases all of the above.

Room rates vary wildly depending on the season, and last-minute deals are common. For example, a room at a hotel we classify as "expensive" might be had for as low as 99€ if said hotel has empty beds to fill. Always book directly with the hotel—you'll usually get a better rate and the chance to build some rapport with reception staff.

Breakfast in all but the highest echelon of hotels is often a buffet with coffee, fruit, rolls, and cheese. It's not always included in the rate, so check the listing carefully. If you are budgeting and breakfast is a payable extra, skip it and go to a nearby cafe-bar, where a caffè and *cornetto* will likely be much cheaper.

Most hotels are heated in the winter, but not all are air-conditioned in summer, which can be vitally important during a stifling July or August. Be sure to check before you book if it's important to you.

SELF-CATERING APARTMENTS

If you're planning to stay in Rome for more than 3 days, rental apartments have some great virtues: They're cheaper than standard facilities (and often more memorable), and they let you save money by preparing at least some of your own meals.

Nearly every vacation rental in Rome—and there are tens of thousands of them—is owned and maintained by a third party (that is, not the rental agency). That means that the decor and flavor of the apartments, even in the same price range and neighborhood, can vary widely. Every reputable agency, however, puts multiple photos of each property they handle on its website, so you'll have a sense of what you're getting into. The photos should be accompanied by a list of amenities. Goliath booking sites **www.airbnb.com** and **vrbo.com,** platforms that allow individuals to rent their own apartments to guests, have thousands of listings in Rome.

It's standard practice for local rental agencies to collect 30% of the total rental amount upfront to secure a booking. When you get to Rome and check in, the balance of your rental fee is often payable in cash only. Upon booking, the agency should provide you with detailed "check-in" procedures. Sometimes, you're expected to call a cell or office phone when you arrive, and then the keyholder will meet you at the property at the agreed-upon time. ***Tip:*** Before the keyholder disappears, make sure you have a few numbers to call in case of an emergency. Otherwise, most apartments come with information sheets that list neighborhood shops and services. Beyond that, you're on your own, which is what makes an apartment stay such a great way to do as the Romans do.

RECOMMENDED AGENCIES **Cross Pollinate** (www.cross-pollinate.com; ✆ **06-99369799**), a multi-destination agency with a roster of apartments and B&Bs in Rome, was created by the American owners of the Beehive Hotel in Rome. Each property is inspected before it gets listed. **GowithOh** (www.gowithoh.com; ✆ **800/567-2927** in the U.S.) is a hip rental agency that covers 12 European cities, Rome among them. **Eats & Sheets** (www.eatsandsheets.com; ✆ **06-83515971**) is a small boutique collective comprising two B&Bs (near the Vatican and Colosseum) and a dozen or so beautiful apartments for rent, most in the *centro storico*. **Roman Reference** (www.romanreference.com; ✆ **06-48903612**) offers no-surprises property descriptions (with helpful and diplomatic tags like "better for young people") and even includes the "eco-footprint" for each apartment. You can expect transparency and responsiveness from the plain-dealing staff. **Rental in Rome** (www.rentalinrome.com; ✆ **06-3220068**) has an alluring website—with video clips of the apartments—and the widest selection of midrange and luxury apartments in the *centro storico* zone (there are less expensive ones, too). **Bed & Breakfast Association of Rome** (www.b-b.rm.it) handles both B&Bs and self-catering apartments.

MONASTERIES & CONVENTS

Staying in a convent or a monastery can be a great bargain. But remember, these are religious houses, which means the decor is most often stark and the rules extensive. Cohabitating is almost always frowned upon—though marriage licenses are rarely required—and unruly behavior is not tolerated (so, no staggering in after too much *limoncello* at dinner). Plus, there's usually a curfew. Most rooms in convents and monasteries do not have private bathrooms, but ask when making your reservation in case some are available. However, if you're planning a mellow, "contemplative" trip to Rome, and you can live with these parameters, convents and monasteries are an affordable and fascinating option. The place to start is **www.monasterystays.com**, which lays out all your monastic options for the Eternal City.

Around Vatican City & Prati

For many, this is a rather dull area to be based in. It's well removed from the ancient sites, and though Prati has some good restaurants, the area overall is not geared to nightlife. But if the main purpose of your visit centers on the Vatican, you'll be fine here, and you will be joined by thousands of other pilgrims, nuns, and priests (see map p. 75).

EXPENSIVE

Residenza Paolo VI ★★ The only hotel actually within the Vatican state, Residenza Paolo is plugged into the walls of an Augustinian

> **A Note on a *Notte* in Rome**
>
> The Rome City Council applies a sojourn tax of 3€ to 7€ (depending on hotel class) per day, per person. Many hotels will request this fee in cash upon check-in; this is perfectly normal. Children ages 10 and under are exempt.

monastery, where it's been based since 1886. As a result, there's no city sales tax. Taking breakfast on the rooftop terrace is a special treat, as this narrow strip overlooks St. Peter's Square—if your timing's right, you'll see the Pope blessing crowds on Sunday. (There's bar service on the terrace from 4pm onwards.) Old-worldy rooms feature tile or hardwood floors, heavy drapes, Oriental rugs, and quality beds. And like their in-Rome-proper rival hotels, square footage is at a premium in many of the standard guest rooms. There's a 15% discount on bookings 3 or more nights.
Via Paolo VI 29. www.residenzapaolovi.com. ✆ **06-684870.** 35 units. 151€–400€ double, includes breakfast. Metro: Ottaviano. **Amenities:** Bar; room service.

Villa Laetitia ★★★ This elegant hotel overlooking the River Tiber is the work of Anna Fendi, member of the Roman fashion dynasty and a nifty designer in her own right. Thanks to Anna, the rooms are anything but traditional, despite the 1911 villa setting surrounded by tranquil gardens. The decor features bold patterns on the beds and floors and modern art on the walls. Splurge for the black and white Giulio Cesare suite, with a round leather bed and blissful garden views. Standard rooms are on the snug side, but most have kitchenettes. Look for great last-minute rates on the hotel website.
Lungotevere delle Armi 22–23. www.villalaetitia.com. ✆ **06-3226776.** 20 units. 139€–340€ double, includes breakfast. Metro: Lepanto. **Amenities:** Restaurant; bar; babysitting; bike rentals; fitness room; room service; Wi-Fi (free).

MODERATE

QuodLibet ★★★ The name is Latin for "what pleases," and we'll be frank: Everything pleases us here. This upscale B&B boasts spacious rooms, gorgeous artwork and furnishings, and generous, memorable breakfasts (served on the roof terrace, which offers evening bar service). All the rooms are set on the fourth floor of an elegant building (with elevator and A/C), so it's quieter than many places. It's located just a 10-minute walk from the Vatican Museums, and a block from the Metro. Charming, conscientious hosts Agostino and Gianluca possess a deep knowledge of Rome and what will interest visitors. A top pick!
Via Barletta 29. www.quodlibetroma.com. ✆ **06-1222642.** 4 units. 80€–170€ double, includes breakfast. Metro: Ottaviano. **Amenities:** Wi-Fi (free).

Rome Armony Suites ★★ A warning: Rome Armony Suites is almost always booked up months in advance, so if you're interested, book early. Why so popular? The answer starts with service; owner Luca is a charming, sensitive host, especially helpful with first-time visitors to Rome. Rooms are big, plush, clean, and modern, with minimalist decor, tea and coffee facilities, and a fridge in each unit. Final, major perk: free loaner smartphones loaded with maps and tourist info, to help guests get the most out of their visit; calls to the U.S. and Canada included, too.
Via Orazio 3. www.romearmonysuites.com. ✆ **348-3305419.** 5 units. 65€–150€ double, includes breakfast. Metro: Ottaviano. **Amenities:** Wi-Fi (free).

Ancient Rome, Monti & Celio

There aren't many hotel rooms on earth with a view of a 2,000-year-old amphitheater, so there's a definite "only in Rome" feeling to lodging on the edge of the ancient city (see map, p. 85). The negative to staying in this area—and it's a big minus—is that the streets adjacent to those ancient monuments have little life outside tourism. There's a lot more going on in **Monti,** Rome's oldest "suburb" (only 5 min. from the Forum), which is especially lively after dark. **Celio** has more of a neighborhood vibe, a local, gentrified life quite separate from tourism.

EXPENSIVE

Capo d'Africa ★★ Twin palm trees guard the entrance to this elegant boutique hotel, located in the heart of Imperial Rome and set in an early-20th-century *palazzo*. Guests are welcomed as if they were in a relaxed and unpretentious Roman home, albeit one with sweeping vistas from the manicured roof terrace (where you eat breakfast), chic design, and an upscale vibe. Light-filled rooms are spacious, smart, and modern, with cherrywood furniture, touches of glass and chrome, incredibly comfy beds, marble bathrooms, and lots of cupboard space. For a truly unforgettable stay, book a studio suite, which comes with a welcome bottle of wine and a private terrace with ethereal views of the Colosseum.

Via Capo d'Africa 54. www.hotelcapodafrica.com. ✆ **06-772801.** 65 units. 185€–325€ double, includes breakfast. Bus: 53, 85, 87. Tram: 3. **Amenities:** Restaurant; bar; exercise room; loaner bikes; room service; Wi-Fi (free).

The Inn at the Roman Forum ★★★ This small hotel is tucked down a medieval lane, on the edge of Monti, with the forums of several Roman emperors as neighbors. Rooms are tastefully luxurious, with ethnic silks, soothing tones, and spacious bathrooms. The posh fifth-floor Master Garden Rooms have private patios surrounded by flowers and greenery, ochre walls, and busts of emperors, and a plush apartment with a kitchen sleeps up to six people. The hotel's **roof lounge** has views of the Campidoglio, and for archaeology buffs there's an ancient Roman *cryptoporticus* behind the lobby. The inn isn't cheap, but the views alone more than make up for it.

Via degli Ibernesi 30. www.theinnattheromanforum.com. ✆ **06-69190970.** 20 units. 190€–790€ double, includes breakfast. Metro: Cavour. **Amenities:** Bar; concierge; room service; Wi-Fi (free).

MODERATE

Duca d'Alba ★★ Located on one of the main drags of hip Monti, with all the nightlife and authentic dining you'll need, Duca d'Alba strikes a fine balance between old-world genteelism and 21st-century amenities. Rooms in the main building are snug and contemporary, with modern furniture and gadgetry but tiny bathrooms. If you want to spring for slightly higher rates, the spacious annex rooms next door have a *palazzo* character, with terracotta floors, oak and cherry furniture, and soundproofed street-facing rooms. Second-floor rooms are the brightest.

Via Leonina 14. www.hotelducadalba.com. ✆ **06-484471.** 27 units. 102€–205€ double, includes breakfast. Metro: Cavour. **Amenities:** Bar; babysitting; Wi-Fi (free) .

Lancelot ★ Expect warmth and hospitality from the minute you walk in the door. The staff, all of whom have been here for years, are the heart and soul of Lancelot, and the reason why the hotel has so many repeat guests. The room decor is simple, and most of the units are spacious, immaculately kept, and light-filled, thanks to large windows. Sixth-floor rooms have private terraces overlooking Ancient Rome—well worth springing for. What makes this place truly remarkable are the genteel, chandelier-lit common areas for meeting other travelers, *Room With A View*–style. Unusual for Rome, Lancelot also has private parking, for which you'll need to book ahead.

Via Capo d'Africa 47. www.lancelothotel.com. ✆ **06-70450615.** 60 units. 130€–216€ double; 280€–330€ suite, includes breakfast. Bus: 53, 85, 87. Tram: 3. **Amenities:** Restaurant; bar; Wi-Fi (free).

Nicolas Inn ★ This tiny B&B, run by a welcoming American–Lebanese couple, makes a convenient base for those who want to concentrate on Rome's ancient sights—the Colosseum and the Forum are both just blocks away. Rooms are a good size and decorated with wrought-iron beds, cool tiled floors, and heavy wooden furniture. Best of all, light floods in through large windows. Guests take breakfast at a local cafe—with unlimited espresso. Downers: no children under 5, and no credit cards accepted.

Via Cavour 295. www.nicolasinn.com. ✆ **06-97618483.** 4 units. 95€–180€ double, includes breakfast at nearby cafe. Metro: Cavour or Colosseo. **Amenities:** Airport transfer (60€); concierge; Wi-Fi (free).

The Centro Storico & Pantheon

There's nothing like an immersion in the atmosphere of Rome's lively Renaissance heart, though you'll pay for *location, location, location*. Expect to do a lot of walking, but that's a reason many visitors come here in the first place—to wander and discover the glory that was and is Rome. Many restaurants and cafes are an easy walk from the hotels here.

EXPENSIVE

Del Sole al Pantheon ★ For history and atmosphere, it's hard to beat a place that's been hosting wayfarers since 1467, with past guests including Jean-Paul Sartre and Simone de Beauvoir, as well as the 15th-century Italian poet Ludovico Ariosto and at least one Hapsburg king. Rooms are decorated in a lavish period decor, with lots of brocade drapery, fine fabrics, and classic furniture. Each room comes equipped with air-conditioning and satellite TV, and some feature views of the Pantheon. Suites offer separate bedrooms and Jacuzzi tubs.

Piazza della Rotonda 63. www.hotelsolealpantheon.com. ✆ **06-6780441.** 25 units. 205€–414€ double, includes breakfast. **Amenities:** Bar; concierge; garden; Wi-Fi (free).

Raphael ★★★ Planning on proposing? This ivy-covered palace, just off Piazza Navona, is an ideal choice for a special-occasion stay, with luxurious rooms, enthusiastic staff, and a roof terrace with spectacular views across Rome. It's a gorgeous hotel, highlighted by 20th-century artwork inside, including Picasso ceramics and paintings by Mirò, Morandi, and De Chirico scattered across the property. The standard rooms are all decorated in Victorian style, with antique furnishings and hardwood floors. Some prefer staying in the quirky Richard Meier–designed executive suites, which blend modern and Asian design and feature oak paneling, contemporary art, and Carrara marble. A haute organic, vegetarian restaurant will leave even diehard carnivores sated.
Largo Febo 2, Piazza Navona. www.raphaelhotel.com. ✆ **06-682831.** 49 units. 250€–710€ double, includes breakfast. **Amenities:** Restaurant; bar; babysitting; concierge; room service; Wi-Fi (free).

MODERATE

Fontanella Borghese ★ Occupying two floors of a palazzo that once belonged to the Borghese family, this is a noble address (equidistant from the Pantheon, Spanish Steps, and Piazza del Popolo) at sort-of plebeian prices. It's not a fancy place, but the classically decorated, family-friendly rooms are bright and spacious, with high ceilings, parquet floors, and well-organized, if unremarkable, bathrooms.
Largo Fontanella Borghese 84. www.fontanellaborghese.com; ✆ **06-68809504.** 29 units. 100€–205€ double, includes breakfast. Metro: Spagna. **Amenities:** Wi-Fi (free).

Hotel Adriano ★★★ Secluded in a maze of small alleyways, but just 5 minutes from the Pantheon, the Adriano occupies an elegant 17th-century *palazzo*. The rooms boast an incredibly stylish and trendy modern design, with designer furniture carefully chosen for each room. The hotel drips with atmosphere and even includes the **Gin Corner,** a trendy cocktail bar specializing in…you guessed it. Note that if you opt for an "annex" room (in the "Domus Adriani"), this is quite a different experience, more akin to a self-catering apartment.
Via di Pallacorda 2. www.hoteladriano.com. ✆ **06-68802451.** 78 units. 80€–394€ double, includes breakfast. Bus: C3, 70, 81, 87. **Amenities:** Bar; babysitting; bikes; concierge; gym; Wi-Fi (free).

Residenza Canali ai Coronari This cozy little guesthouse (in a meticulously restored historic building) is on a blink-and-you'll-miss-it pedestrian alleyway in Rome's antiques district. Furnishings are warm and classic, and rooms are bright and surprisingly spacious. The Honeymoon Suite has a private terrace overlooking the terracotta rooftops near Piazza Navona. There are no surprises here, just clean, up-to-date facilities, good prices, and amiable staff.
Via dei Tre Archi 13. www.residenzacanali.com; ✆ **06-68309541.** 10 units. 120€–260€ doubles; online specials often much lower. **Amenities:** Wi-Fi (free).

Residenza in Farnese ★★ This little gem is tucked away in a 15th-century mansion across the street from the Palazzo Farnese, within stumbling distance of Campo de' Fiori but still reasonably quiet. Most rooms are spacious and artsy, with tiled floors and a vaguely Renaissance theme. Standard rooms are on the small side but come with free mini-bars, and prices are usually on the low end of the range shown here. The complimentary breakfast spread is downright generous.

Via del Mascherone 59. www.residenzafarneseroma.it. ✆ **06-68210980.** 31 units. 110€–310€ double, includes breakfast. **Amenities:** Airport transfer (free with min. 4-night stay); bar; concierge; room service; Wi-Fi (free).

Teatro di Pompeo ★★ History buffs will appreciate this small B&B, literally built on top of the ruins of the 1st-century Theatre of Pompey, where on the Ides of March Julius Caesar was stabbed to death (p. 20). The lovely breakfast area is actually part of the arcades of the old theater, with the original Roman walls. The large rooms themselves are not Roman in style, but feel authentic nonetheless, with wood-beam ceilings, cherrywood furniture, and terracotta-tiled floors. Some rooms have a view of the internal courtyard, while others overlook the small square. All are quiet despite the Campo de' Fiori crowds right behind the hotel. Staff members are extremely helpful, and all speak English. ***Tip:*** Avoid the Trattoria Der Pallaro restaurant next door; it's a tourist trap.

Largo del Pallaro 8. www.hotelteatrodipompeo.it. ✆ **06-68300170.** 13 units. 110€–220€ double, includes breakfast. **Amenities:** Bar; babysitting; room service; Wi-Fi (free).

INEXPENSIVE

Mimosa ★ This budget stalwart in the heart of the *centro storico* enjoys great word of mouth, so book early. Decor is hodgepodge at best, but the rooms are bright and air-conditioned (not a given at this price point), and the larger units are suitable for families with small children. A location this close to the Pantheon at these prices is hard to beat. Mention Frommer's for a 10% discount.

Via di Santa Chiara 61. www.hotelmimosa.net; ✆ **06-68801753.** 11 units. 59€–154€ double, includes breakfast. **Amenities:** Wi-Fi (free).

Tridente, the Spanish Steps & Via Veneto

The heart of the city is a great place to stay if you're a serious shopper or enjoy the romantic, somewhat nostalgic locales of the Spanish Steps and Trevi Fountain. But expect to part with a lot of extra euro for the privilege. This is one of the most elegant areas in Rome (see map, p. 105); we've found you a few bargains (and some worthy splurges).

EXPENSIVE

Babuino 181 ★★ Leave Renaissance and baroque Italy far behind at this sleek, contemporary hotel, with relatively spacious rooms and apartment-size suites outfitted with Frette linens, iPod docks, and Nespresso machines. Bathrooms are heavy on the marble and mosaics, and

A balcony view from the Inn at the Spanish Steps.

shuttered windows with hefty curtains provide a quiet and perfectly blacked-out environment for light sleepers. A surcharged breakfast buffet is served on the rooftop terrace, which doubles as a cocktail bar at night. Via del Babuino 181. www.romeluxurysuites.com/babuino. ✆ **06-32295295.** 24 units. 170€–430€ double. Metro: Flaminio or Spagna. **Amenities:** Bar; babysitting; concierge; room service; Wi-Fi (free).

Deko Rome ★★★ Honeymooners love Deko Rome, but then, so does everyone who stays here. This exceptionally warm and welcoming place is a true boutique hotel (just nine rooms), occupying the second floor of an early-20th-century *palazzo.* The interior blends antiques, vintage '60s pieces, and modern design for rooms that are chic in a way that's happily retro and quite comfortable; plus each room comes with an iPad and flatscreen TV. Add the friendly, fun owners (Marco and Serena) and excellent location near Via Veneto, and Deko is understandably hugely popular. It fills up quickly—reservations must be made months in advance. Via Toscana 1. www.dekorome.com. ✆ **06-42020032.** 9 units. 140€–230€. Rates include breakfast. Metro: Barberini. Bus: 910 (from Termini). **Amenities:** Bar; babysitting; Wi-Fi (free).

The Inn at the Spanish Steps ★★★ Set in one of Rome's most desirable locations on the famed Via dei Condotti shopping street, this lavish guesthouse is the epitome of luxe. Rooms are fantasias of design and comfort, some with parquet floors and cherubim frescoes on the ceiling, others decked out with wispy fabrics draping plush, canopied beds; upgraded units have swoon-worthy views of Piazza di Spagna. Swank standard perks include flatscreen TVs, iPod docks, Jacuzzi tubs, double marble sinks, curling irons, pet amenities, and so forth. Rooms located in the annex building tend to be larger than the ones in the main building. The perfectly manicured rooftop garden provides beautiful views, to be enjoyed at breakfast—where there's a generous buffet spread—or at sunset, with complimentary happy-hour snacks.

Via dei Condotti 85. www.atspanishsteps.com. ✆ **06-69925657.** 24 units. 230€–750€ (and way up) double, includes breakfast. Metro: Spagna. **Amenities:** Bar; babysitting; concierge; room service; Wi-Fi (free).

Portrait Roma ★★★ Fashionistas with money to spare, look no further than this boutique all-suites hotel run by the Ferragamo-owned Lungarno hotel group. Swanky and uncluttered are the keywords here, but warmth and amusing Italian flair aren't lacking in the ultra-stylish pink and grey suites, which come with kitchenettes. The roof terrace, with its overstuffed cushions, romantic candlelight, and exclusive company, is the epitome of modern Roman fabulousness. The superb staff (aka the "lifestyle team") anticipate your needs before you do.

Via Bocca di Leone 23. www.lungarnohotels.com/portrait-roma; ✆ **06-69380742.** 14 units. Suites from 480€, includes breakfast. Metro: Spagna. **Amenities:** Bar; concierge; room service; Wi-Fi (free).

Villa Spalletti Trivelli ★★★ This really is an experience rather than a hotel, an early-20th-century neoclassical villa remodeled into an exclusive 14-room guesthouse, where lodgers mingle in the gardens or the great hall, as if invited by an Italian noble for the weekend. There is no key for the entrance door; ring a bell and a staff member will open it for you, often offering you a glass of complimentary prosecco as a welcome. Onsite is a Turkish bath, a sizeable and modern oasis for those who want extra pampering, while rooms feature elegant antiques and Fiandra damask linen sheets, with sitting areas or separate lounges. And the minibar? All free, all day. A newly opened rooftop lounge boasts Jacuzzis and a bar serving light fare.

Via Piacenza 4. www.villaspalletti.it. ✆ **06-48907934.** 14 units. 450€–900€ double, includes breakfast. Metro: Barberini. **Amenities:** Restaurant; bar; concierge; exercise room; room service; Jacuzzis; sauna; Wi-Fi (free).

MODERATE

Daphne Trevi ★★ In a neighborhood with a lot of overpriced, underwhelming hotels, this above-average boutique option, in an 18th-century building minutes from Trevi Fountain, is a good value even in the summer. What rooms lack in size they make up for with sleek modern design and spotless bathrooms with mosaic tiles (two rooms share a bathroom). A 5th-floor covered terrace is the setting for an ample breakfast buffet with lots of home-baked goodies, as well as evening cocktails and occasional happy hours. The young owner/managers are happy to help you plan your days in Rome and your onward journey.

Via di San Basilio 55. www.daphne-rome.com. ✆ **06-87450086.** 10 units. 90€–240€ double, includes breakfast. Metro: Barberini. **Amenities:** Concierge; Wi-Fi (free).

Hotel Condotti ★ This cozy hotel can be a tremendously good deal depending on when you stay and how far out you book. For your money you'll get a clean, unpretentious room, though the common areas aim higher, with marble floors, antiques, tapestries, and a Venetian-glass chandelier. Standard rooms are tight; you'll get a bit more space and modernity in the nearby annex rooms. Overall it's worth considering for its proximity to the Spanish Steps.

Via Mario de' Fiori 37. www.hotelcondotti.com. ✆ **06-6794661.** 16 units. 142€ –320€, includes breakfast. Metro: Spagna. **Amenities:** Bar; babysitting; bikes; room service; Wi-Fi (free).

La Lumière ★ You won't be checking in for chic design or innovation—this traditional hotel just off Via dei Condotti smacks of middle-class comforts, from rooms with matchy-matchy color schemes, wood floors, and warm lighting to the glassed-in roof terrace or open-air patio where breakfast and evening libations are served. For all but highest season and holidays, it's a winner on the price/location ratio.

Via Belsiana 72. www.lalumieredipiazzadispagna.com; ✆ **06-69380806.** 10 units. 110€–350€ double, includes breakfast. Metro: Spagna. **Amenities:** Bar; Wi-Fi (free).

La Residenza ★ Considering its location just off Via Veneto, this hotel—hosting guests since 1936—is a smart deal. Renovated, modern rooms retain a touch of Art Deco appeal, and are all relatively spacious, with a couple of easy chairs or a small couch in addition to a desk. Families with children are especially catered to, with quad rooms and junior suites on the top floor featuring a separate kids' alcove with two sofa beds, and an outdoor terrace with patio furniture. The breakfast buffet is excellent and includes quality charcuterie and cheeses, homemade breads, and pastries.

Via Emilia 22–24. www.hotel-la-residenza.com. ✆ **06-4880789.** 29 units. 165€–300€ double, includes breakfast. Metro: Barberini. **Amenities:** Bar; babysitting; room service; Wi-Fi (free).

INEXPENSIVE

Casa Howard ★★ Cross the threshold of either of these two stylish, intimate guesthouses (about a 4-minute walk from one another), and you've been let in on a wonderful secret. Colorful, themed rooms features luxe fabrics like Toile de Jouy and Shanghai silk, fresh flowers, and non-cookie-cutter furnishings. Each house has a Turkish bath. Breakfast is served in-room, and kids are welcomed. Such luxury, at these prices, is unheard of in Rome.

Via Capo le Case 18 and Via Sistina 149. www.casahoward.com; ✆ **06-69924555.** 10 units. 69€–199€ double, includes breakfast. Metro: Spagna or Barberini. Bus: 117. **Amenities:** Wi-Fi (free).

Panda ★ Panda has long been popular among budget travelers, so it books up quickly. Rooms are spare, but not without some old-fashioned charm, like characteristic Roman *cotto* (terracotta) floor tiles, frescoed ceilings, and exposed beams. Most rooms are a bit cramped, but for these prices in this neighborhood they remain a very, very good deal.

Outside your doorstep are several great cafes and wine bars where you can start the day with espresso and end your evening with a nightcap.
Via della Croce 35. www.hotelpanda.it. ✆ **06-6780179.** 28 units (8 with shared bath). 85€–130€ double with bath. Metro: Spagna. **Amenities:** Wi-Fi (free).

Parlamento ★ Set on the top floors of a 17th-century *palazzo,* this is one of the best budget deals in the area. All of its rooms have private bathrooms and are equipped with satellite TVs, desks, exposed beams, and parquet or terracotta floors; renovated "boutique" rooms add modern decor. Breakfast is served on the rooftop terrace—you can also chill up there with a glass of wine in the evening. The Trevi Fountain, Spanish Steps, and Pantheon are all within a 5- to 10-minute walk.
Via delle Convertite 5 (at Via del Corso). www.hotelparlamento.it. ✆ **06-69921000.** 21 units. 134€–248€ double, includes breakfast. Metro: Spagna. **Amenities:** Bar; concierge; room service; Wi-Fi (free).

Around Termini

Known for its concentration of cheap hotels, the Termini area (see map, p. 113) is about the only part of the center where you can score a high-season double for under 100€. The streets around **Termini** station are not the most picturesque, and parts of the neighborhood are downright seedy, but it's very convenient for access to most of Rome's top sights. Termini is where Rome's Metro lines intersect, and buses and trams to every part of the city leave from the concourse outside.

The area has some upscale hotels, but if you have the dollars to spend on a truly luxe hotel, choose a prettier neighborhood.

MODERATE

Residenza Cellini ★★ For every rule, there's an exception, and in this case, spending a little more near Termini pays off at Cellini. The feeling of refinement begins the second you walk through the door to find a vase of fresh lilies in the elegant, high-ceilinged hall. Antique-styled rooms are proudly 19th century, with thick walls (so no noise from your neighbors), solid furnishings, and handsome parquet floors. Beds have memory-foam mattresses, and bathrooms come with Jacuzzi tubs or jetted showers. Air-conditioning keeps rooms cool all summer. Service is topnotch and wonderfully personal.
Via Modena 5. www.residenzacellini.it. ✆ **06-47825204.** 18 units. 80€–210€ double. Metro: Repubblica. **Amenities:** Babysitting; concierge; room service; Wi-Fi (free).

Seven Kings Relais ★★ This striking hotel has a slightly retro feel, kitted out with dark wooden furniture, chocolate-brown bedspreads, and modern tiled floors. Rooms are also unusually large—especially nos. 104, 201, and 205. Despite its location right on one of Rome's busiest thoroughfares, street noise is minimal—an external courtyard and modern soundproofing see to that. Breakfast is a 24-hour self-service bar with tea, coffee, and biscuits. Management has several nearby properties, run through **Roma Termini Suites** (www.romaterminisuites.com).

Via XX Settembre 58A. www.sevenkingsrelais.com. ✆ **06-42917784.** 13 units. 50€–200€ double. Metro: Repubblica. **Amenities:** Babysitting; Wi-Fi (free).

INEXPENSIVE

Beehive ★★ Conceived as part hostel and part hotel, the Beehive is an utterly cheerful lodging experience. The eco-minded American owners offer rooms for a variety of budgets. Some have private bathrooms, others have shared facilities or are actual six-bed dorms—but all are decorated with flair, adorned with artwork or flea-market treasures. The garden with trees and secluded reading/relaxing spaces is the biggest plus. There's also a concerted effort when it comes to minimal impact and eco-conscious practices. A buzzy cafe offers breakfast a la carte, as well as occasional, budget-friendly vegan/vegetarian meals. The Beehive's "Other Honey"—Clover and Cacaia guesthouses—is a smart option for a group of traveling friends. They feature private rooms and shared bathrooms and are located a 10-minute walk from the original B&B.

Via Marghera 8. www.the-beehive.com. ✆ **06-44704553.** 28 units. 60€–100€ double; 20€–35€ dorm beds. Metro: Termini or Castro Pretorio. **Amenities:** Restaurant; garden; lounge; Wi-Fi (free).

Euro Quiris ★ There's not a frill in sight at this one-star a couple of blocks north of the station. Rooms are on the 5th floor and simply decorated with functional furniture, but they are spotless, and mattresses are a lot more comfortable than you should expect in this price bracket. Bathrooms are ensuite, too. The friendly reception staff dispenses sound local knowledge, including tips on where to have breakfast in cafes nearby. No credit cards are accepted, and you'll pay extra for A/C.

Via dei Mille 64. www.euroquirishotel.com. ✆ **06-491279.** 9 units. 40€–160€ double. Metro: Termini. **Amenities:** Wi-Fi (free).

Giuliana ★★ The Santacroce family and their staff bend over backwards to make you feel welcome at this moderate-priced inn near the station and Santa Maria Maggiore. Basic but comfy rooms, most done up in crimson and buttercream, come with surprisingly large bathrooms. Breakfast is a simple affair, but the hotel is a good value for this side of the (train) tracks.

Via Agostino Depretis 70. www.hotelgiuliana.com; ✆ **06-4880795.** 11 units. 54€–160€ double, includes breakfast. Metro: Termini or Repubblica. **Amenities:** Bike rentals; concierge; Wi-Fi (free).

Trastevere

This was once an "undiscovered" neighborhood—but no longer. Being based here does give some degree of escape from the busy (and pricey) *centro storico,* however. And there are bars, shops, and restaurants galore among its narrow cobblestone lanes (see map, p. 115). The panorama from the **Gianicolo** (p. 89) is also walkable from pretty much everywhere in Trastevere.

MODERATE

Santa Maria ★★ The lovely Santa Maria is built around a 16th-century cloister, now a relaxing courtyard fragrant with orange trees. Cheerful rooms, some with exposed brick walls and beamed ceilings, are mostly on the ground floor. Free breakfast and loaner bikes, a roof garden, and a cocktail bar all make this charmer a stand-out in hotel-deprived Trastevere.

Vicolo del Piede 2. www.htlsantamaria.com. ✆ **06-5894626.** 19 units. 99€–260€ double, includes breakfast. Tram: 8. Bus: 23, 125, 280, 780, or H. **Amenities:** Bar; bikes; Wi-Fi (free).

INEXPENSIVE

Arco del Lauro ★★ Hidden in Trastevere's snaking alleyways, this serene little B&B occupies the ground floor of a shuttered pink *palazzo*. Bright rooms have parquet floors, plush beds, and simple decor, with a mix of modern and period furnishings. Rooms can't be defined as large, but they all feel spacious thanks to lofty wood ceilings. Breakfast is taken at a nearby cafe; there's also coffee and snacks laid out around the clock. No credit cards.

Via Arco de' Tolomei 29. www.arcodellauro.it. ✆ **06-97840350.** 6 units. 85€–145€ double, includes breakfast at nearby cafe. Bus: 23, 125, 280, 780, or H. Tram: 8. **Amenities:** Wi-Fi (free).

San Francesco ★ There's a local feel to staying here that has disappeared from much of Trastevere, perhaps because it's at the very edge of the neighborhood, close to the Porta Portese gate in an area that hasn't been gentrified or over-exploited. All rooms are bright, with color-washed walls and modern tiling. Doubles are fairly small, but the bathrooms are palatial. The grand piano in the lobby adds a touch of old-time charm; a top-floor garden with a bar overlooks terracotta rooftops and pealing church bell towers. Book a "charity room," and the hotel will match your 2€ donation to help Rome's shelter dogs.

Via Jacopo de Settesoli 7. www.hotelsanfrancesco.net. ✆ **06-48300051.** 24 units. 79€–171€ double. Bus: 44 or 125. **Amenities:** Bar; babysitting; Wi-Fi (free).

WHERE TO EAT

Rome remains a top destination for food lovers and today offers more dining diversity than ever. Though many of its *trattorie* haven't changed their menus in a quarter of a century (for better or worse), the city has an increasing number of creative spots with chefs willing to revisit tradition.

Restaurants generally serve lunch between 12:30 and 2:30pm, and dinner between 7:30 and 10:30pm. At all other times, most restaurants are closed—though a new generation is moving toward all-day dining, with a limited service at the "in-between" time of mid-afternoon.

If you have your heart set on any of these places below, we seriously recommend *reserving ahead of arrival*. Hot tables go quickly, especially on high-season weekends—often twice: once for the early-dining tourists, and then again by locals, who dine later, typically around 9pm.

A ***servizio*** (tip or service charge) is almost always added to your bill or included in the price. Sometimes it is marked on the menu as *coperto e servizio* or *pane e coperto* (bread, cover charge, and service). You can leave extra if you wish—a couple of euros as a token. Don't go overboard, however, and watch out for unsavory practices. More than once we have overheard waitstaff telling foreign tourists that service *wasn't* included, when the menu clearly stated (in Italian) that it was.

Near Vatican City

For restaurant locations, see map p. 75. If you just want a quick, tasty sandwich before or after your Vatican safari, **Duecento Gradi ★★,** is a topnotch panino joint with lots of yummy choices, right across from the Vatican walls at Piazza Risorgimento 3 (www.duecentogradi.it; ✆ **06-39754239;** Sun–Thurs 10–2am; Fri–Sat 11pm–5am).

EXPENSIVE

Taverna Angelica ★★ MODERN ITALIAN/SEAFOOD In a sea of overpriced, touristy restaurants near St. Peter's, Angelica serves up surprisingly good and justly priced (though not cheap) fare. Specialties include spaghetti with crunchy bacon and leeks, *fettuccine* with king prawns and eggplant, turbot with crushed almonds, and a black-bread-encrusted lamb with potato flan. Seafood is fresh and simply cooked, from octopus carpaccio to sea bream with rosemary. Save room for the delicious, non-run-of-the-mill dessert options. Reservations are required.

Piazza A. Capponi 6. www.tavernaangelica.it. ✆ **06-6874514.** Main courses 20€–24€; pastas 10€–14€. Daily 6pm–midnight; also Sun noon–3:30pm. Closed 10 days in Aug. Metro: Ottaviano.

MODERATE

Bonci Pizzarium ★★★ PIZZA Celebrity chef Gabriele Bonci has always had a cult following in the Eternal City. And since he's been featured on TV shows overseas and written up by influential bloggers, you can expect long lines at his pizzeria. No matter—it's worth waiting (and walking 10 minutes west of the Vatican Museums) for some of the best pizza you'll ever taste, sold by the slice or by weight. His ingredients are fresh and organic, the crust is perfect, and the toppings often experimental (try the mortadella and crumbled pistachio). There's also a good choice of Italian craft IPAs and wheat beers, and wines by the glass. There are only a handful of stand-up tables inside and benches outside for seating, and reservations aren't taken. Bonci also has a counter at Termini's Mercato Centrale (see p 145).

Via della Meloria 43. www.bonci.it. ✆ **06-39745416.** Pizza 12€–14€ for large tray. Daily 11am–10pm. Metro: Cipro.

INEXPENSIVE

Il Gelato Bistrò ★★★ GELATO Claudio Torcè's artisanal shop is credited with starting a natural, gluten-free gelato movement in Rome, but what makes this place really enticing (and why it doesn't really fit on our recommended "classic" gelato list; p. 140) are its savory flavors (out of a total 150). These are especially good during the happy hour *aperitivo* (dubbed *aperigelato*), when wine and cocktails are served. Prepare for gelato made from bell peppers, chili, green tea—even oyster and smoked salmon—paired with crudités, cold cuts, and sushi. Purists can still get an incredible chocolate and pistachio, too.

Circonvallazione Trionfale 11/13. ✆ **06-39725949.** Cup from 2.50€. Tues–Fri 8am–1am, Sat–Sun 9am–1am, Mon 7am–4pm. Metro: Cipro.

Ancient Rome, Monti & Celio

For restaurant locations, see map p. 85. For a cappuccino, a quick bite, or aperitivo snacking, head to the epicenter of Monti, **La Bottega del Caffè ★** (✆ **06-4741578**) on lively Piazza Madonna dei Monti, open from 8am to the wee hours. When we hanker for something other than Italian food, we head to **Maharajah ★★**, an elegant Northern Indian eatery at Via dei Serpenti 124 (www.maharajah.it; ✆ **06-4747144**).

MODERATE

Caffè Propaganda ★ MODERN ITALIAN This all-day eatery—part lively Parisian bistro, part cocktail bar—is a safe bet for scoring a good meal within eyeshot of the Colosseum. Diners lounge on caramel-colored leather banquettes and choose from a diverse menu that mixes Roman classics such as *carbonara* (pasta with cured pork, egg, and cheese) with familiar international dishes like Caesar salad (or an 18€ hamburger). Desserts are Instagram-worthy affairs. After dark, confident bartenders shake up Propaganda's signature cocktails. Service is relaxed by North American standards, so only eat here if you have time to linger.

Via Claudia 15. www.caffepropaganda.it. ✆ **06-94534255.** Main courses 11€–20€. Tues–Sun 12:30pm–3:30pm, 7pm–midnight. Metro: Colosseo. Bus: C3, 75, 81, 118. Tram: 3.

InRoma al Campidoglio ★ ITALIAN Once a club for Rome's film industry, InRoma sits on a cobbled lane opposite the Palatine Hill. Though the place rests on its cinematic laurels a bit too heavily, it still serves up authentic Roman and regional cuisine. Meals might start with *caprese di bufala affumicata* (salad of tomatoes and smoked buffalo mozzarella) followed by classic Roman pastas like *all'amatriciana* (cured pork, tomato, and pecorino) or a main course of *tagliata* (beef strip steak) with a red wine reduction. The ambience inside is fairly generic; we recommend the terrace for a table to remember.

Via dei Fienili 56. www.inroma.eu. ✆ **06-69191024.** Main courses 10€–20€. Daily 11:45am–4pm and 6:30–11:30pm. Bus: C3, H, 81, 83, 160, 170, 628.

La Barrique ★★ MODERN ROMAN This cozy, contemporary *enoteca* (wine bar with food) has a kitchen that knocks out fresh farm-to-table fare that complements the well-chosen wine list. The atmosphere is lively and informal, with rustic place settings and friendly service—as any proper *enoteca* should be. Dishes come in hearty portions on a daily-changing menu. Expect the likes of *bocconcini di baccalà* (salt-cod morsels), crispy on the outside and served with a rich tomato dipping sauce; or *crostone* (a giant crostino) topped with grilled burrata cheese, chicory, and cherry tomatoes.

Via del Boschetto 41B. ✆ **06-47825953.** Main courses 10€–16€. Mon–Fri 12:30–2:30pm; Mon–Sat 6:30–11:30pm. Metro: Cavour.

L'Asino d'Oro ★★ CONTEMPORARY UMBRIAN/ROMAN This isn't your typical Roman eatery. Helmed by Lucio Sforza, a renowned chef from Orvieto, L'Asino d'Oro offers a seriously refined take on the flavors of central Italy without a checked tablecloth in sight; instead, the setting is contemporary with a Scandinavian feel thanks to the light-wood interior. As for the food, it's marked by creativity and flair, in both flavor and presentation. Expect bizarre pairings and flavor combos—like *lumache in umido piccante al finocchietto selvatico* (snail stew with wild fennel) or fettuccine in duck liver and *vin santo* sauce—but they work!

Via del Boschetto 73. ✆ **06-48913832.** Main courses 13€–17€. Tues–Sat 12:30–2:30pm, 7:30–11pm. Closed last 2 weeks in Aug. Metro: Cavour.

Terre e Domus della Provincia Romana ★★ CONTEMPORARY ROMAN Located in the stunning Palazzo Valentini (see p 95), opposite Trajan's Column, with sleek, modern decor and floor-to-ceiling windows overlooking the Vittoriano and Trajan Markets, this enoteca strictly showcases only the best in local wines and foods, using produce grown at the Rebibbia prison in Rome. It's also a training ground for apprentice chefs and servers. The menu lists traditional Roman classics plus seasonal, vegetable-driven dishes—a welcome break from the pizza, pasta, and pork circuit.

Foro di Traiano 82–84. www.palazzovalentini.it. ✆ **06-69940273.** Main courses 10€–15€. Daily 7:30am–12:30am. Metro: Cavour. Bus: 80, 85, 87, 175.

INEXPENSIVE

Li Rioni ★★ PIZZA This fab neighborhood pizzeria is close enough to the Colosseum to be convenient, but just distant enough to avoid the dreaded "touristy" label that applies to so much dining in this part of town. Roman-style pizzas baked in the wood-stoked oven are among the best in town, with perfect crisp crusts. There's also a bruschetta list (from around 4€) and a range of salads. Outside tables can be cramped, but there's plenty of room inside. If you want to eat late, booking is essential or you'll be fighting with hungry locals for a table.

Via SS. Quattro 24. www.lirioni.it. ✆ **06-70450605.** Pizzas 6€–9€. Wed–Mon 7pm–midnight. Metro: Colosseo. Bus: C3, 51, 85, 87. Tram: 3.

Ristorante da Pancrazio, built on the ruins of the Theatre of Pompey.

Centro Storico & the Pantheon

For restaurant locations, see map p. 99. Vegetarians looking for massive salads (or anyone who just wants a break from all those heavy meats and starches) can find great food at the neighborhood branch of **L'Insalata Ricca,** Largo dei Chiavari 85 (www.linsalataricca.it; ✆ **06-68803656;** daily noon–midnight).

EXPENSIVE

Da Pancrazio ★ ROMAN Built over the ruins of the 1st-century B.C. Theatre of Pompey (where Julius Caesar was infamously murdered), and with various dining rooms and spaces decked out with charming historical decor and archaeological finds, Da Pancrazio, opened in 1922, turns out reliable Roman fare. Still, the setting here may be more stunning than the cuisine. Look for classics like *abbacchio al forno con patate* (baked lamb with potatoes) or *spaghetti alla carbonara.* Be sure to ask to see the ruins in the basement.

Piazza del Biscione 92. www.dapancrazio.it. ✆ **06-6861246.** Main courses 10€–24€. Thurs–Tues 12:30–3pm and 7:30pm–11pm. Closed 3 weeks in Aug. Bus: H, 40, 46, 62-64, 780. Tram: 8.

Osteria dell'Antiquario ★ MODERN ITALIAN/ROMAN This cozy *osteria* ticks off all the boxes: candlelit tables, a romantic setting on a quiet terrace overlooking Palazzo Lancillotti, and traditional Roman fare with some inventive detours, such as swordfish carpaccio, or linguini with asparagus, pistachios, and a citrus infusion. Fresh fish here is especially good, and lobster features prominently. This is a good spot to consider the full monty of *antipasto, primo,* and *secondo.*

Piazzetta di S. Simeone 26–27, Via dei Coronari. www.osteriadellantiquario.it. ✆ **06-6879694.** Main courses 14€–18€. Thurs–Tues noon–11pm (no midday closure); Sept–June. Closed July and Aug. Bus: 70, 81, 90.

GETTING YOUR FILL OF gelato

Don't leave town without trying one of Rome's outstanding **ice-cream parlors.** However, choose your gelato carefully: Don't buy close to the tourist-packed piazzas, and don't be dazzled by vats of brightly (and artificially) colored, air-pumped gelato. The best gelato is made only from natural ingredients, which impart a natural color—if the pistachio gelato is bright green, for example, rather than gray-green, move on. Take your cone *(cono)* or small cup *(coppetta)* and stroll as you eat—sitting down on the premises is usually more expensive. The recommended spots below are generally open mid-morning to late, sometimes after midnight on summer weekends. Cones and small cups cost between 2.50€ and 4€.

One of Rome's oldest artisan gelato makers, **Gelateria Alberto Pica** ★★★ (Via della Seggiola 12; ✆ **06-6868405;** Bus: H, 63 or 780; Tram 8) produces top-quality gelato churned with ingredients sourced locally, including wild strawberries grown on the family's countryside estate.

At the fabulous (and gluten-free) **Fatamorgana** ★★★ (Piazza degli Zingari 5, Monti; www.gelateriafatamorgana.it; ✆ **06-86391589;** Metro: Cavour), creative flavors are the hallmark, as is a firm commitment to seasonal and organic ingredients. This is the place to go bold, to try inventive flavors like delicate lavender and chamomile, say, or zingy avocado, lime, and white wine. Flavors change daily.

In the Termini area, tiny but sleek **Come il Latte** ★★★ (Via Silvio Spaventa 24; www.comeillatte.it; ✆ **06-42903882;** Metro: Repubblica or Castro Pretorio) turns out artisan gelatos in flavors ranging from salted caramel (yes please!), to mascarpone and crumbled cookies; fruit flavors change according to season and focus on indigenous Italian flavors, such as fig, persimmon, and Sorrento limon. Committed to short-supply-chain sustainability, the charming gelateria adds props like an American drinking fountain and old-school vat containers.

Trastevere's best artisan gelato, **Fior di Luna** ★★★ (Via della Lungaretta 96; www.fiordiluna.com; ✆ **06-64561314;** Bus: H or 780/Tram: 8), is made with natural and Fair Trade produce. The stars are the incredibly rich chocolate flavors, spiked with fig or orange or made with single *cru* cocoa, or the perfect pistachio. House-made chocolate bars make a great souvenir—if they last until you get home.

Enjoying gelato.

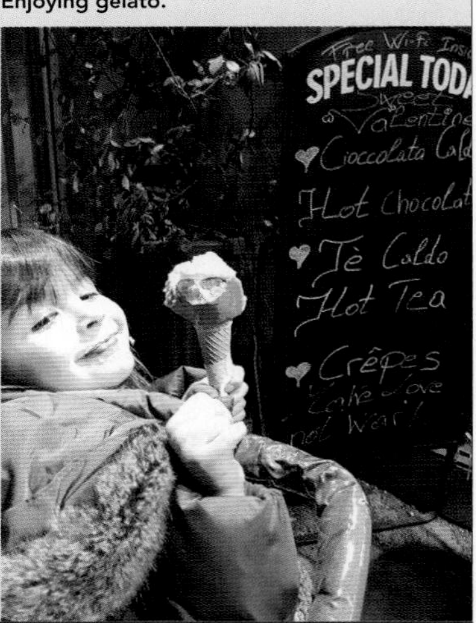

MODERATE

Alfredo e Ada ★★ ROMAN No menus here, just the waiter—and it's usually owner Sergio explaining, in Italian, what the kitchen is preparing that day. Look for Roman trattoria classics like eggplant parmigiana, artichoke lasagna, excellent carbonara, or tripe. The whole place oozes character, with shared tables, scribbled walls festooned with drawings, and the house wine poured into carafes from a tap in the wall. With only five tables, it's best to make a reservation or get here early. This sort of place is becoming rare in Rome—enjoy it while you can.

Via dei Banchi Nuovi 14. ✆ **06-6878842.** Main courses 10€–18€. Tues–Sat noon–3pm and 7–10:30pm. Closed Aug. Bus: 40, 46, 62, 64, 916.

Antica Hostaria Romanesca ★ ROMAN It's very easy to eat badly on Campo de'Fiori, which makes this authentic spot with ringside seats on the piazza such a pleasant surprise. Romanesca does dependable, old-school Roman fare at low prices, including a gloriously juicy *pollo con i peperoni* (stewed chicken with peppers) and *agnello abbacchio a scottadito*, lamb chops hot off the grill. Locals snatch up the tables after 9pm, so a reservation is advised.

Campo de' Fiori 40 (east side of square). ✆ **06-6864024.** Main courses 10€–15€. Daily noon–3pm, 7–11pm. Bus: 30, 40, 46, 62, 64, 70, 81, 87, 492. Tram: 8.

Armando al Pantheon ★ ROMAN/VEGETARIAN You know you're sure of your place in the Roman culinary pantheon (sorry, couldn't resist) when you opt to take Saturday nights and Sundays off. Despite the odd hours and a location just a few steps from the *actual* Pantheon, this family-run trattoria serves as many locals as tourists. Chef Armando Gargioli took over the place in 1961, and his sons now run the business. Roman favorites to look out for include *cacio e pepe*, marinated artichokes, and the Jewish-influenced *aliciotti all'indivia* (endive and roasted anchovies; Tues and Fri only). A Roman rarity: Vegetarians get their own, fairly extensive, menu.

Salita dei Crescenzi 31. ✆ **06-68803034.** Main courses 11€–25€. Mon–Fri 12:30–3pm and 7–11pm; Sat noon–3pm. Closed Sat night, Sun, Aug. Bus: 40, 46, 62, 64, 70, 81, 87, 492, 628. Tram: 8.

La Campana ★★ ROMAN/TRADITIONAL ITALIAN Family atmosphere and a classic Roman elegance permeate the spacious, well-lit rooms of this venerable address, feeding guests since 1518 and Rome's oldest restaurant. The atmosphere is convivial yet refined, with a lovely mixture of regulars and locals. The broad selection of *antipasti* is displayed on a long table at the entrance, and the daily menu features authentic *cucina romana* classics like pasta with oxtail ragout, tripe, gnocchi, *cacio e pepe,* and myriad vegetarian choices. The wine list includes interesting local labels, and the staff and service are impeccable.

Vicolo della Campana 18. www.ristorantelacampana.com. ✆ **06-6875273.** Main courses 10€–22€. Tues–Sun 12:30–3pm and 7:30–11pm. Metro: Spagna. Bus: 70, 81, 87, 280, 492, 628.

Nonna Betta ★★ ROMAN/JEWISH Though not strictly kosher, this is the only restaurant in Rome's old Jewish quarter historically owned and managed by Roman Jews. Traditional dishes include delicious *carciofi alla giudia:* deep-fried artichokes served with small morsels like battered cod filet, stuffed and fried zucchini flowers, carrot sticks, and whatever vegetable is in season. Don't forego the *baccalà* with onions and tomato or the tagliolini with chicory and mullet roe. Middle Eastern specialties such as falafel and couscous are on the menu, and all desserts are homemade, including a stellar cake with pine nuts.

Via del Portico d'Ottavia 16. www.nonnabetta.it. ✆ **06-68806263**. Main courses 10€–20€. Wed–Mon 11am–5pm and 6–11pm. Bus: H, 23, 63, 280, 780. Tram 8.

Retrobottega ★★ ROMAN Fresh, modern, and progressive, the somewhat misnamed Retrobottega is a nice contrast to the well-worn streets of the touristy heart of town. This culinary laboratory, founded by four young, accomplished chefs, is an intimate but convivial choice. Most seats surround the open kitchen and customers interact directly with the chefs—there is no waitstaff. The day's offerings focus on local, seasonal, responsibly sourced ingredients and unexpected pairings, like asparagus and fennel, or pasta with octopus ragú.

Via della Stelletta 4. www.retro-bottega.com. ✆ **06-68136310.** Main courses 10€–19€. noon–midnight. Bus: 30, 70, 81, 87, 186, 492, 628.

INEXPENSIVE

Antico Forno Roscioli ★★ BAKERY The Rosciolis have been running this celebrated bakery for three generations since the 1970s, though bread has been made here since at least 1824. Today it's the home of the finest crusty sourdough in Rome, assorted cakes, and addictive pastries and biscotti, as well as exceptional Roman-style *pizza bianca* and *pizza rossa* sold by weight. This is largely a takeout joint, with limited seating—and the wider range of pizza toppings is only available from noon to 2:30pm. Around the corner is the unmissable **Roscioli restaurant and *salumeria* deli** at Via dei Giubbonari 21 and, at Via Cairoli 16, **Roscioli Caffè,** the latest outpost of the family empire, which offers breakfast treats, cappuccini, and palate-pleasing panini.

Via dei Chiavari 34. www.anticofornoroscioli.it. ✆ **06-6864045.** Pizza from 5€ (sold by weight). Mon–Sat 7am–7:30pm. Tram: 8.

La Montecarlo ★★ PIZZA Dirt-cheap and immensely popular among Romans, Montecarlo feels like a big party: Efficient, flirtatious servers sling piping-hot, thin-crusted pies, and the wine and beer flow freely. Sure, they serve other fare, but seriously, come for the pizza.

Vicolo Savelli 11 (at Corso Vittorio Emanuele II). www.lamontecarlo.it; ✆ **06-6861877.** Pizzas 6€–10€. Tues–Sun lunch and dinner. Bus: 40, 46, 62, 64, 916.

Tridente, the Spanish Steps & Via Veneto

For restaurant locations, see map p. 105. The historic cafes near the Spanish Steps are saturated with history but, sadly, tend to be overpriced tourist traps, where mediocre cakes or even a cup of coffee or tea will cost 5€. Nevertheless, you may want to pop inside the two most celebrated institutions: **Babington's Tea Rooms** (www.babingtons.com; ✆ **06-6786027;** daily 10am–9:30pm), established in 1893 at the foot of the Spanish Steps by a couple of English *signore,* and **Caffè Greco,** Via dei Condotti 86 (www.anticocaffegreco.eu; ✆ **06-6791700;** daily

9am–8pm), Rome's oldest bar, which opened in 1760 and has hosted Keats, Ibsen, Goethe, and many other historical *cognoscenti*.

EXPENSIVE

Al Ceppo ★★ MARCHIGIANA/ROMAN The setting of this Parioli dining institution is an elegant 19th-century parlor, with dark wood furnishings, chandeliers, fresh flowers, family portraits on the walls, and an open kitchen with a wood-stoked hearth. The owners are from the Le Marche region northeast of Rome, and regional classics are represented here: *marchigiana*-style rabbit, fish stews, fresh seafood, and porchetta, all artfully prepared and presented. You'll also find veal, pork, and a variety of pastas. This is destination dining. If the braised beef cheek is on the menu, don't forego that mystical experience.

Via Panama 2 (near Piazza Ungheria). www.ristorantealceppo.it. ✆ **06-8419696.** Main courses 19€–42€. Tues–Sun 12:30–3pm and 7:30–11pm. Closed last 2 weeks in Aug. Bus: 52 or 910. Tram: 3 or 19.

Imàgo ★★★ INTERNATIONAL The views of Rome from this 6th-floor hotel restaurant are jaw-dropping, the old city laid out before you, glowing pink as the sun goes down. The food is equally special. Chef Francesco Apreda's reinterpretation of Italian cuisine borrows heavily from Indian and Japanese culinary schools. The Michelin-star menus change seasonally, but may include red onion and foie gras risotto, sake-glazed black cod, or even grilled pigeon with mango, lentils, and turmeric. Reservations are essential; jackets required for the gentlemen.

In Hotel Hassler, Piazza della Trinità dei Monti 6. www.imagorestaurant.com. ✆ **06-69934726.** Main courses 33€–49€; 10-course tasting menu 150€; 6-course vegetarian menu 120€. Daily 7–10:30pm. Metro: Spagna.

Metamorfosi ★★★ MODERN ITALIAN For our money, this is the place to have your blow-the-vacation-budget meal in Rome. This prestigious Michelin star–awarded restaurant is a feast for the eyes and the taste buds. The minimalistic decor balances the astonishing creations. Chef Roy Caceres, a native of Colombia, likes to tell a story with each beautifully crafted dish, from exquisite risotto and pasta preparations to elegant meat and fish interpretations. Be prepared for egg-yolk ravioli with precious white truffle, "encased" risotto with mushrooms and hazelnut, or lamb with red mole sauce, avocado, and chia seeds. The tasting menus are always full of delightful surprises.

Via Giovanni Antonelli 30/32. www.metamorfosiroma.it. ✆ **06-8076839.** Main courses 27€–40€. 10–course tasting menu 130€; 6–course menu 100€. Mon–Fri 12:30–2:30pm and 8–10:30pm; Sat 8–10:30pm. Bus: 168, 715, 910.

MODERATE

Canova Tadolini ★★ ROMAN Few restaurants are as steeped in history as this place. Antonio Canova's sculpture studio was kept as a workshop by the descendants of his pupil Adamo Tadolini until 1967, and even today it's littered with tools and sculptures in bronze, plaster, and marble. The whole thing really does seem like a museum, with tables squeezed between models, casts, drapes, and bas-reliefs. The pasta menu features tasty versions of *spaghetti alle vongole* and *alla carbonara,* while entrees might include seabass with a lemon crust or sliced skirt steak salad with arugula and cherry tomatoes.

Via del Babuino 150A–B. www.canovatadolini.com. ✆ **06-32110702.** Main courses 11€–30€. Mon–Sat noon–8:30pm (bar/cafe from 8am). Metro: Spagna.

Colline Emiliane ★★ EMILIANA-ROMAGNOLA This family-owned restaurant tucked in an alley beside the Trevi Fountain has been serving traditional dishes from Emilia-Romagna since 1931. Service is excellent and so is the food: Classics include *tortelli di zucca* (pumpkin ravioli in butter sauce) and magnificent *tagliatelle alla Bolognese*, the mother of all Italian comfort foods. Save room for the chocolate tart or lemon meringue pie. Reservations are essential.

Via degli Avignonesi 22 (off Piazza Barberini). www.collineemiliane.com. ✆ **06-4817538.** Main courses 14€–22€. Tues–Sun 12:45–2:45pm; Tues–Sat 7:30–10:45pm. Closed Sun in July and all of Aug. Metro: Barberini.

Il Bacaro ★ MODERN ITALIAN Il Bacaro's romantic and low-key setting on a hidden back street offers respite from the traffic and tourist crush. Insanely delicious *primi* and *secondi* (like *tortelli* with *taleggio* cheese and pumpkin or grouper with porcini mushrooms) are a welcome departure from the usual Roman fare. Desserts revolve around mousses paired with Bavarian chocolate, hazelnuts, caramel, and pistachio. The 600-label wine list features well-priced varietals from all over Italy. Try to get a prized sidewalk table on a balmy summer evening.

Via degli Spagnoli 27 (near Piazza delle Coppelle). www.ilbacaroroma.com. ✆ **06-6872554.** Main courses 12€–22€. Daily noon–midnight (no midday closure). Metro: Spagna.

Around Termini

For restaurant locations, see map p. 113. Mostly catering to dazed travelers toting wheeled suitcases and crumpled maps, restaurants around Termini don't have to be good in order to bring in business. Following are some of our favorite exceptions to that norm.

MODERATE

Trattoria Monti ★★ REGIONAL/MARCHE Word is definitely out on this cozy, plain-Jane trattoria near Termini station. But that just means you need to reserve in advance to sample outstanding, hearty pastas and meat dishes from the Marche region. You will remember the *tortello al rosso d'uovo*, a large, delicate ravioli filled with spinach, ricotta, and egg yolk, for the rest of your life. You also may discover a few new favorites among the territory's underappreciated wines.

Via di San Vito 13A (at Via Merulana). ✆ **06-4466573.** Main courses 12€–22€. Tues–Sat 1–2:45pm and 8–10:45pm; Sun lunch only. Metro: Cavour or Vittorio Emanuele. Bus: 50, 71, 105, 360, 590, 649. Tram: 5 or 14.

Trimani Il Wine Bar ★ MODERN ITALIAN This small bistro and well-stocked wine bar (with a 20-page wine list!) attracts white collars and wine lovers in a modern, relaxed ambience, accompanied by smooth jazz. The refined entrees might include rabbit stuffed with asparagus or Luganega sausage with a zucchini puree. The wines-by-the-glass list changes daily. If you just want a snack to accompany your vino, cheese and salami platters range from 9€ to 13€. The selection at Trimani's vast wine shop next door boggles the oenophilic mind.

Via Cernaia 37B. www.trimani.com. ✆ **06-4469630.** Main courses 10€–18€. Mon–Sat 11:30am–3pm and 5:30pm–midnight. Closed 2 weeks in mid-Aug. Metro: Repubblica or Castro Pretorio.

INEXPENSIVE

Mercato Centrale Roma ★★ GOURMET MARKET This ambitious, three-story gourmet pavilion has certainly upped the quality of food choices in Termini Station, with purveyors of everything from gourmet pizza to chocolate to truffles, a wine bar, and a high-end restaurant. Other ventures have tried and failed at the same location, but today's vendors are topnotch and the space is inviting. Even if you don't have a train to catch, it's worth having lunch or a quick snack here.

Via Giovanni Giolitti 36 (in Termini Station). www.mercatocentrale.it/roma; no phone. Daily 7am–midnight. Metro: Termini.

Pinsere ★★ PIZZA *Pinsa* is an ancient Roman preparation: an oval focaccia made with a blend of four organic flours and olive oil that's left to rise for 2 to 3 days. The result is a fragrant, feather-light single-portion snack. The small Pinsere bakery always has an assortment of pies ready to pop in the oven, and also bakes them to order. Favorites come with pureed pumpkin, smoked cheese, and pancetta; classic tomato, basil, and *bufala;* or the surprising combo of ricotta, fresh figs, raisins, pine nuts, and honey. There's also a good choice of salads and soups, plus bottled beers and soft drinks. Food to go only.

Via Flavia 98. www.pinsereroma.com. ✆ **06-42020924.** Pinsa 3.50€–5.50€. Mon–Fri 9am–4pm. Metro: Castro Pretorio. Bus: 60-62, 66, 82, 492, 590, 910.

Trastevere

For restaurant locations, see map p. 114. Popular craft-beer bar **Bir & Fud** ★ (p. 155) also serves pizzas and traditional snacks like *supplì* (fried rice croquettes filled with mozzarella and tomato sauce) to hungry drinkers. It serves dinner daily and lunch Thursday through Sunday. Hearts and taste buds soar at **Biscottificio Artigiano Innocenti** ★★ (Via della Luce 21 (✆ **06-5803926**), where Stefania and her family have been turning out delicate handmade cookies and cakes since the 1920s.

EXPENSIVE

Antico Arco ★★★ CREATIVE ITALIAN This well-known address for new Italian cuisine consistently delivers exquisite dishes made with the finest local and seasonal ingredients. Creative and artistic plates like carbonara with black truffle or crispy duck with artichoke and passion fruit are accompanied by excellent wine and topnotch service. A full meal here makes for a special night out (reservations are essential), but you can also just come to the restaurant's wine bar; a few glasses of vino and some finger food here pair nicely with the rapturous *centro storico* views from the nearby terraces of the Janiculum Hill.

Piazzale Aurelio 7 (at Via San Pancrazio). www.anticoarco.it. ✆ **06-5815274.** Main courses 15€–35€. Daily noon–midnight (no midday closure). Bus: 115 or 125.

Glass ★★★ CONTEMPORARY ROMAN In an industrial-chic setting of exposed brick, stark white walls, and polished floors, Michelin-starred chef Cristina Bowerman and partner Fabio Spada serve refined food using high-quality ingredients. The menu changes seasonally, but expect carefully prepared shellfish, aromatic dishes such as sumac-scented lamb with Stilton cheese and fennel, or an entire tasting menu devoted to precious white truffles. This is one of Rome's hottest tables—reservations are essential. See page 149 for news on the duo's latest venture, **Romeo e Giulietta.**

Vicolo del Cinque 58. www.glass-restaurant.it. ✆ **06-58335903.** Main courses 26€–50€; fixed-price menus 85€–140€. Tues–Sun 7:30–11:30pm. Closed 2 weeks in Jan, 2 weeks in July. Bus: 125.

Spirito DiVino ★★ ROMAN/SLOW FOOD In a medieval synagogue on a 2nd-century street (which you can visit on a cellar tour), the Catalani family does exceptional modern plates (like an appetizer salad of raisins, walnuts, pomegranate, and marinated duck) as well as ancient Roman cuisine (like *maiale alla mazio,* a favorite pork dish of Julius Caesar's), food as warm and comforting as the ambience. Finish with the delicately perfumed lavender panna cotta, a cream-based dessert.

Via dei Genovesi 31 (at Vicolo dell'Atleta). www.ristorantespiritodivino.com. ✆ **6-5896689.** Main courses 12€–26€. Mon–Sat 7–11pm. Bus: H, 23, 44, 125, 280. Tram: 8.

MODERATE

Cacio e Pepe ★ ROMAN This ultra-traditional trattoria, complete with paper tablecloths, a TV showing the game, the owner chatting up the ladies, and a bustling crowd of patrons waiting to be seated, is a Trastevere neighborhood stalwart. Start with cheapo plates of fried tidbits, from rice *suppli* to cod to vegetables, then move on to the namesake pasta *cacio e pepe* or other classic Roman pasta dishes, such as *amatriciana* or *carbonara*—be ready for hearty portions. For *secondo*—if you have room left—keep it simple; consider *polpette* (stewed meatballs), *saltimbocca alla romana* (veal cutlets with sage and ham), or grilled meats, all sold at reasonable prices.

Vicolo del Cinque 15. www.osteriacacioepepe.it. ✆ **06-89572853.** Main courses 9€–19€. Daily 7pm–midnight; Sat and Sun 12:30–3pm. Bus: 23, 125, 280. Tram: 8.

Da Enzo ★★ ROMAN This down-homey, non-touristy, family-run trattoria serves traditional Roman cuisine in a friendly and relaxed atmosphere. A few outdoor tables look out on some of Trastevere's characteristic alleyways. *Cucina romana,* including classic carbonara, *amatriciana,* and *cacio e pepe,* win the gold, but do consider the ravioli stuffed with ricotta and spinach or the house meatballs braised in tomato sauce. Local wines can be ordered by the jug or glass, and desserts (try the mascarpone with wild strawberries) come served in either full or half portions, a good thing considering Enzo's hefty servings.

Via dei Vascellari 29. www.daenzoal29.com. ✆ **06-5812260.** Main courses 9€–15€. Mon–Sat 12:30–3pm and 7:30–11pm. Bus: 125.

Osteria La Gensola ★★★ SEAFOOD/ROMAN This family-run restaurant is considered one of the best seafood destinations in Rome. The ambience is warm and welcoming, like a true Trastevere home; decor is cozy, with soft lighting and a life-size wood-carved tree in the middle of the main dining room. Fish-lovers come for the trademark spaghetti with sea urchin, the fish-forward *amatriciana,* and traditional Roman cuisine with a marine twist. The grill churns out succulent beefsteaks, among non-fish dishes. Reservations are a must on weekends.

Piazza della Gensola 15. www.osterialagensola.it. ✆ **06-58332758.** Main courses 15€. Daily 12:30–3pm and 7:30–11:30pm. Bus: 125.

INEXPENSIVE

Dar Poeta ★ PIZZA Ranking among the best pizzerias in Rome, "the poet" is a fine place to enjoy a classic Roman pizza margherita (tomato sauce, mozzarella, and fresh basil) or a more creative combo like the *patataccia* (potatoes, creamed zucchini, and *speck* [a smoked prosciutto]). The lines are long to eat in, but you can also order takeout. The decadent dessert calzone is filled with fresh ricotta and Nutella.

Vicolo del Bologna 45. www.darpoeta.com. ✆ **06-5880516.** Pizzas 5€–9€. Daily noon–midnight. Bus: 23, 125, 280.

Testaccio

The slaughterhouses of Rome's old meatpacking district (see map p. 115) have been transformed into art venues, markets, and the museum **MACRO** (p. 117), but restaurants here still specialize in (though are not limited to) meats from the *quinto quarto* (the "fifth quarter")—the leftover parts of an animal after slaughter, typically offal like sweetbreads, tripe, tails, and other goodies you won't find on most American menus. This is an area to eat *cucina romana*—either in the restaurants below or from street-food stalls in the **Nuovo Mercato di Testaccio** (p. 152). Food-themed tours of Rome invariably end up here.

EXPENSIVE

Checchino dal 1887 ★★ ROMAN Often mischaracterized as an offal-only joint, this establishment, opened in 1887 across from Rome's now-defunct abattoir, is a special-night-out type of place, serving wonderful *bucatini all'amatriciana* and veal saltimbocca—as well as hearty plates of spleens, lungs, and livers. Checchino is a pricier choice than most of the other restaurants in this area, but Romans from all over the city keep coming back when they want the real thing.

Via di Monte Testaccio 30 (at Via Galvani). www.checchino-dal-1887.com; ✆ **06-5746316.** Main courses 12€–27€. Set menus 40€–65€. Tues–Sat 12:30–2:45pm and 8pm–midnight. Sun 12:30–3pm. Closed Aug and last week in Dec. Metro: Piramide. Bus: 83, 673, 719. Tram: 3.

MODERATE

Flavio al Velavevodetto ★★ ROMAN Flavio's plain dining room is burrowed out of the side of Rome's most unusual "hill": a large mound made from amphorae discarded during the Roman era (see p. 67). Besides worthy in the city to try classic Roman pastas like *cacio e pepe,* and *quinto quarto* entrees at fair prices. *Polpette al sugo* (meatballs in red sauce), *coda alla vaccinara* (oxtail), and *involtini* (stuffed rolled veal) are good for sharing. The homemade *tiramisù* wins the gold.

Via di Monte Testaccio 97–99. www.ristorantevelavevodetto.it. ✆ **06-5744194.** Main courses 9€–20€. Daily 12:30–3pm and 7:45–11pm. Metro: Piramide. Bus: 83, 673, 719. Tram: 3.

Osteria degli Amici ★★ MODERN ROMAN This intimate and friendly *osteria,* on the corner of nightclub central and the hill of broken amphorae, serves both traditional Roman classics and creative iterations. Claudio and Alessandro base their menu on produce from the nearby market and their combined experience cooking in famous kitchens around the world. Signature musts include fish- and seafood-based pastas and mains, golden-fried mozzarella *in carrozza,* and a range of pastas, from classic *carbonara* to *paccheri* tubes with shrimp, mint, and zucchini. Let the honest vino flow and leave room for the apple tartlet with cinnamon gelato.

Via Nicola Zabaglia 25. www.osteriadegliamiciroma.it. ✆ **06-5781466.** Main courses 14€–18€. Wed–Mon noon–3pm and 8pm–midnight. Metro: Piramide. Bus: 83, 673, 719. Tram: 3.

Porto Fluviale ★ MODERN ITALIAN This multifunctional restaurant—part trattoria, part street-food stall, part pizzeria—can accommodate pretty much whatever you fancy. The decor is vaguely industrial, with a daytime clientele made up of families and white collars—the vibe gets younger after dark. From the various menus, best bets are the 30 or so *ciccheti,* small plates that allow you to taste the kitchen's range. You can share a few platters of *carpaccio di baccalà* (thin slices of salt cod), *maialino* (roasted suckling pig with pureed apple and rosemary), and *burrata e pomodori* (mozzarella with a creamy milky filling, served with tomatoes). Skip the pizzas; they're fairly nondescript.

Via del Porto Fluviale 22. www.portofluviale.com. ✆ **06-5743199.** Main courses 8€–19€; set lunch 12€–20€. Daily 10:30am–2am (Fri and Sat to 3am). Metro: Piramide. Bus: 23, 673, 715, 716.

Wherefore art thou Romeo?

Rome's foodies and journalists are buzzing over newly-opened **Romeo e Giulietta,** the most ambitious venture yet from dynamic duo Cristina Bowerman and Fabio Spada of Glass (p. 146) fame. A former car showroom in Testaccio has been transformed into 2,000sqm (21,500 sq ft) of ultramodern space, with seating for 500 (!), plus standing noshing/cocktail space for hundreds more. Romeo showcases Michelin-starred Chef Bowerman's inventive takes on street food, cooking up dishes like a foie gras hot dog, cappuccino of roasted carrots, and pork tacos with lettuce "shells" and haberñero sauce. Giuletta is an old-school pizzeria with wood-fired ovens turning out thin and crispy Roman-style pizza and thick Neopolitan pies. Next door, **Frigo** is a gelateria "laboratory" with flavors to delight both traditional and risk-taking palates. Head to Piazza dell'Emporio (www.romeo.roma.it; ✆ **06-32110120;** Metro: Piramide. Bus: 23, 75, 280, or 716. Tram: 3).

Trattoria Perilli ★★ ROMAN Dine elbow to elbow with locals and enjoy the old-school atmosphere at this beloved institution of Roman *ristorazione*. With zero pretense, Perilli's formally attired waitstaff serve unadulterated renditions of Roman classics. The dishes are reliable, from pasta standbys like *carbonara* and *cacio e pepe* to grilled meats to that most English of Italian desserts, *zuppa inglese* (literally "English soup," or trifle). This is a fun and reasonably affordable place to go for a real four-course meal of *antipasto*, *primo*, *secondo*, and *dolce*.

Via Marmorata 39 (at Via Galvani). ✆ **06-5742415.** Entrees 11€–18€. Thurs–Tues 12:30–3pm and 7:30–11pm. Reservations recommended. Metro: Piramide. Bus: 23, 75, 280, 716. Tram: 3.

INEXPENSIVE

Da Remo ★★ PIZZA Mentioning "Testaccio" and "pizza" in the same sentence elicits one typical response from locals: Da Remo, a Roman institution. In the summer especially, come early or be prepared to wait for a table. Every crisp-crusted, perfectly foldable pizza is made for all to see behind open counters. The most basic ones (margherita and marinara) start at around 7€. If it's too crowded on a summer evening, order your pizza for takeout and eat it in the park across the street.

Piazza Santa Maria Liberatrice 44. ✆ **06-5746270.** Pizzas 7€–15€. Mon–Sat 7pm–1am. Bus: 83, 673, 719.

SHOPPING

Rome offers retail temptations of every kind. In our limited space below we've summarized streets and areas known for their shops. Keep in mind that the monthly rent on the famous streets is very high, and those costs are passed on to you. Nonetheless, a stroll down some of these streets presents a cross-section of the most desirable wares in Rome. Note that **sales** usually run twice a year, in January and July.

The Top Shopping Streets & Areas

AROUND PIAZZA DI SPAGNA Most of Rome's haute couture and seriously upscale shopping fans out from the bottom of the Spanish Steps. **Via Condotti** is probably Rome's poshest shopping street, where you'll find Prada, Gucci, Bulgari, and the like. A few more down-to-earth stores have opened, but it's still largely a playground for the super-rich. Neighboring **Via Borgognona** is another street where both the rents and the merchandise are chic and ultra-expensive, but thanks to its pedestrian-only access and handsome baroque and neoclassical facades, it offers a nicer window-browsing experience. Shops are more densely concentrated on **Via Frattina,** the third member of this trio of upscale streets. Chic boutiques for adults and kids rub shoulders with ready-to-wear fashions, high-end chains, and a few tourist tat vendors. It's usually thronged with shoppers who appreciate the lack of motor traffic.

VIA COLA DI RIENZO The commercial heart of the Prati neighborhood, this long, straight street runs from the Tiber to Piazza Risorgimento and is known for stores selling a variety of merchandise at reasonable prices—from jewelry to fashionable clothing, bags, and shoes. Among the most prestigious is the historic Roman perfume store, **Bertozzini Profumeria dal 1913,** at no. 192 (✆ **06-6874662**). The department store **Coin** is at no. 173 (with a large supermarket in the basement), the largest branch of venerable gourmet food store **Castroni** at no. 196 (www.castroni.it), and the smaller, more selective gourmet grocery **Franchi** at no. 200 (www.franchi.it).

VIA DEL CORSO With less of a glamour quotient (and less stratospheric prices) than Via Condotti or Via Borgognona, Via del Corso boasts affordable styles aimed at younger consumers. Occasional gems are scattered amid international shops selling jeans and sports equipment. The most interesting stores are toward the Piazza del Popolo end of the street (**Via del Babuino** here has a similar profile). The farther south you walk (towards the Vittoriano monument), the more narrow the sidewalks—and generally, the more tacky the stores. If you are shopping with young children, the upper part of Via del Corso (from Piazza Colonna to Piazza del Popolo) is largely car-free, save for taxis.

VIA DEI CORONARI An antique-lover's souk. If you're shopping, or just window-shopping for antiques or vintage-style souvenir prints, then spend an hour walking the length of this pretty, pedestrian-only street.

CAMPO DE'FIORI Though the campo itself is now chockablock with restaurants, the streets leading up to it, notably **Via dei Giubbonari** and **Via Dei Baullari,** offer edgy and often one-of-a-kind fashions. Boutiques go in and out of business with dizzying frequency, but something interesting is always popping up.

VIA MARGUTTA This beautiful, tranquil street is home to numerous art stalls and artists' studios—Federico Fellini used to live here—though all the stores tend to offer the same sort of antiques and mediocre paintings

Upscale shopping on Via Condotti.

these days. You have to shop hard to find real quality. Highlights include **Bottega del Marmoraro** at no. 53b, the studio of master stonecarver Sandro Fiorentini, and **Saddlers Union** (at no. 11; www.saddlersunion.com) for exquisite handmade leather items.

MONTI Rome's most fashion-conscious central neighborhood has a pleasing mix of artisan retailers, vintage boutiques, and honest, everyday stores frequented by locals, with not a brand name in sight. Roam the length of **Via del Boschetto** for one-off fashions, designer ateliers, and unique homewares. In fact, you can roam in every direction from the spot where Via del Boschetto meets **Via Panisperna.** Turn on nearby **Via Urbana** or **Via Leonina,** where boutiques jostle for space with cafes that are ideal for a break or light lunch. Via Urbana also hosts the weekend **Mercatomonti** (see "Rome's Best Markets," below).

Rome's Best Markets

Campo de' Fiori ★ Central Rome's food market has been running since at least the 1800s. It's no longer the place to find a produce bargain and it tends to attract more tourists (and souvenir vendors) than locals these days, but it's a genuine slice of Roman life in one of its most attractive squares. The market runs Monday through Saturday 7am to 1 or 2pm. Campo de' Fiori. No phone. Bus: H, 40, 46, 62-64, 280, 780. Tram: 8.

Eataly ★★ Not strictly a market, but a four-floor homage to Italian food. Thirty different breads, 25 shelving bays of pasta, two aisles of olive oil . . . and that's just scratching the surface of what's under this one roof. Browse the cookbooks, chocolate, local wines, beer, and cheese, or stop for a meal in one of the ingredient-themed restaurants and food bars (although prices are a little steep). This foodie heaven is open daily from 9am to midnight. You can eat to your heart's content here. Piazzale XII Ottobre 1492. www.roma.eataly.it. ✆ **06-90279201.** Metro: Piramide.

Mercatomonti ★★ Everything from contemporary glass jewelry to vintage cameras, handmade clothes for kids and adults, and one-off designs are sold here in the heart of trendy Monti, in a commandeered parking garage (where else?). The market runs Saturdays and Sundays 10am to 6pm. Via Leonina 46. www.mercatomonti.com. No phone. Metro: Cavour.

Nuovo Mercato di Testaccio (New Testaccio Market) ★★ In 2012, the old Testaccio market building was replaced by this daringly modernist, sustainably powered market building. It's the best place to go produce shopping with the Romans. It has everything you need to pack a picnic—cheese, cured meats, seasonal fruit—as well as meat, fish, and fresh vegetables (ideal if you are self-catering in the city). There are also clothes and kitchenware stalls, but the food is the star. Sample the street food at **Mordi e Vai ★★**, Box 15 (www.mordievai.it; ✆ **339-1343344**). The market runs Monday through Saturday 6am to 2:30pm. Btw. Via Luigi Galvani and Via Aldo Manuzio (at Via Benjamin Franklin). www.mercatoditestaccio.it. No phone. Metro: Piramide. Bus: 83, 673, 719.

Nuovo Mercato Trionfale (New Trionfale Market) ★★★ This modern, working-class structure houses more than 250 stalls that more than make up for its rather unattractive exterior. Vendors sell top-choice local produce, meat, fish, cheese, eggs, baked goods, and spices, as well as household wares. A handful of stalls specializing in international ingredients sell everything from okra and pomelo to habañero chilis and hopia. If you plan to shop, bring cash; only a few fishmongers and butchers here accept credit cards. The market runs Monday through Saturday 7am to 2pm (till 5pm Tues and Fri). Via Andrea Doria 3. ✆ **06-39743501.** Tram: 19. Metro: Cipro or Ottaviano.

Porta Portese ★ Trastevere's vast weekly flea market stretches all the way from the Porta Portese gate along Via di Porta Portese to Viale di Trastevere. You have to wade through a lot of junk (and a sea of humanity), but there are good stalls for vintage housewares, clothing, and collectibles. Expect to find everything. It runs Sundays from dawn until midafternoon. Via di Porta Portese. No phone. Tram: 8.

ENTERTAINMENT & NIGHTLIFE

Even if you don't speak Italian, you can generally follow the listings of special events and evening entertainment in ***La Repubblica***, a leading national newspaper published in Rome. ***Wanted in Rome*** (www.wantedinrome.com) has listings of opera, rock, English-language cinema showings, and such and gives an insider look at expat Rome. **Un Ospite a Roma** (www.unospitearoma.it), available both online and in print, free at concierge desks and tourist centers, offers details on what's happening. Free magazine and website ***Romeing*** (www.romeing.it) is worth consulting for events on the contemporary scene.

Unless you're dead set on making the Roman nightclub circuit, try what might be a far livelier and less expensive option—sitting late at night on **Via Veneto, Piazza della Rotonda, Piazza del Popolo,** or one of Rome's other piazzas, all for the (admittedly inflated) cost of an espresso or a Campari and soda. If you're a clubber who likes it loud and late, jump in a cab to **Monte Testaccio** or **Via del Pigneto** and bar-hop wherever takes your fancy. In Trastevere, there's always a bit of life

Rome, Illuminated

When the sun goes down, Rome's palaces, ruins, fountains, and monuments are bathed in a theatrical white light. During your stay in Rome, be sure to make time for a memorable evening stroll past the solemn pillars of old temples or the cascading torrents of Renaissance fountains glowing under the blue-black sky.

The **Fountain of the Naiads** ("Fontana delle Naiadi") on Piazza della Repubblica, the **Fountain of the Tortoises** ("Fontana della Tartarughe") on Piazza Mattei, the **Fountain of Acqua Paola** ("Fontanone") at the top of the Janiculum Hill, and the **Trevi Fountain** (p. 107) are particularly beautiful at night. The **Capitoline Hill** (or Campidoglio) is magnificently lit after dark, with its Renaissance facades glowing like jewel boxes. The view of the Roman Forum seen from the rear of Piazza del Campidoglio is perhaps the grandest in Rome (see "Three Free Views to Remember for a Lifetime" box, p. 89). If you're across the Tiber, the Vatican's **Piazza San Pietro** (p. 75) is impressive at night without the crowds. The combination of illuminated architecture, baroque fountains, and sidewalk shows makes **Piazza Navona** (p. 98) even more delightful at night.

on **Via Politeana** where it meets **Piazza Trilussa.** In the *centro storico,* a nice *aperitivo-cena* scene unfolds along **Via del Governo Vecchio.**

Performing Arts & Live Music

While Rome's music scene doesn't have the same vibrancy as Florence's, nor the high-quality opera of Milan's La Scala or **La Fenice** in Venice (p. 446), classical music fans are still well catered to. In addition to the major venues featured below, be on the lookout for concerts and one-off events in churches and salons around the city. Check **www.operainroma.com** for a calendar of opera and ballet staged by the Opera in Roma association at the **Chiesa Evangelica Valdese,** Via IV Novembre 107. The **Pontificio Instituto di Musica Sacra,** Piazza Sant'Agostino 20A (www.musicasacra.va; ✆ **06-6638792**), and **All Saints' Anglican Church,** Via del Babuino 153 (www.accademiadoperaitaliana.it; ✆ **06-7842702**), both regularly run classical music and operatic evenings.

Alexanderplatz Jazz Club ★ A stalwart of Rome, Alexanderplatz has been the home of Rome's jazz scene since the early 1980s. If there's a good act in the city, you will find it here. Via Ostia 9. www.alexanderplatzjazzclub.com. ✆ 06-39742171. Cover usually 10€. Metro: Ottaviano. Bus: 23, 70, 180, 492, 913, 990.

Auditorium–Parco della Musica ★★ This exciting multipurpose center for the arts, designed by Renzo Piano, brings a refreshing breath of modernity to Rome. The schedule features lots of aging rock stars and singer-songwriter acts, as well as traditional orchestras. Great cafes and a bookstore on-site, too. Viale Pietro de Coubertin 30. www.auditorium.com. ✆ 06-80241281. Bus: 53, 168, 910. Tram: 2D.

Teatro dell'Opera di Roma ★★ This is where you'll find marquee operas such as *La Traviata, Carmen,* and *Tosca,* plus ballet and classical concerts from top-rank orchestras. This is the venue to see such ballets as *Giselle, Il Lago dei Cigni (Swan Lake)*, and *Lo Schiaccianoci (The Nutcracker)*. In summer the action moves outdoors for unforgettable open-air operatic performances at the ruined **Baths of Caracalla** (p. 86). Piazza Beniamino Gigli 1 (at Via del Viminale). www.operaroma.it; ✆ 06-4817003 (box office). Tickets 25€–150€. Metro: Repubblica.

Cafes

Remember: In Rome and everywhere else in Italy, if you just want to drink a quick coffee and bolt, walk up to *il banco* (the bar), order *"un caffè, per favore"* or *"un cappuccino,"* and don't move. They will make it for you to drink on the spot. It will cost more (at least double) to sit down to drink it (if you're in high-traffic, touristy areas—which you'll most likely be!), and outdoor table service is the most expensive way to go. Even in the heart of the city center, a short coffee *al banco* should cost no more than 1€; add around .30€ for a *cappuccino*. Expect to pay up to five times that price if you sit outdoors on a marquee piazza. Most cafes in the city serve a decent cup of coffee, but here's a small selection of places worth hunting down.

With its shabby-chic interior and namesake fig tree backdrop to charming outdoor seating where locals play chess at tables with mismatched chairs, **Bar del Fico ★** (Piazza del Fico 26; www.bardelfico.com; ✆ **06 6880 8413**) is one of Rome's most beloved aperitivo spots and coveted see-and-be-seen nightlife destinations. **Sant'Eustachio il Caffè ★★** (Piazza Sant'Eustachio 82; www.santeustachioilcaffe.it; ✆ **06-68802048**) roasts its own Fair Trade Arabica beans over wood. The unique taste and bitter kick to its brews draws a friendly crowd a few deep at the bar. (Unless you ask, the coffee comes with sugar.) Debate still rages among Romans as to whether the city's best cup of coffee is served at Sant'Eustachio or **Tazza d'Oro ★,** near the Pantheon (Via degli Orfani 84; www.tazzadorocoffeeshop.com; ✆ **06-6789792**). Jacketed baristas work at 100mph at **Spinelli ★** (Via dei Mille 60; no phone; weekdays only), a no-nonsense locals' cafe. Join the throng at the bar for a morning *cappuccino* and *un cornetto* (a croissant) filled with jam, *crema* (pastry cream), Nutella, or white chocolate. A cold-food buffet is served at lunch.

Outdoor cafes dot the streets of Rome.

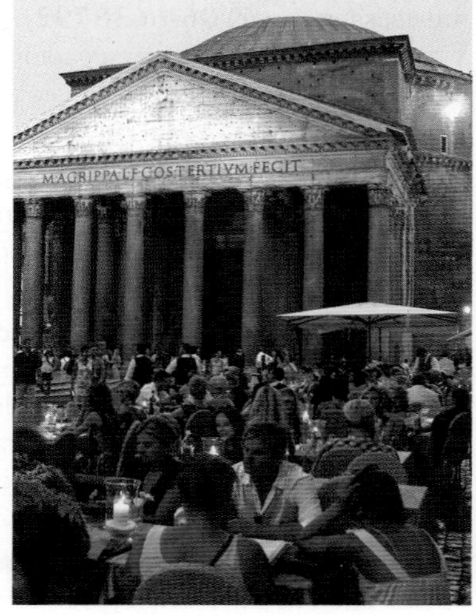

Wine Bars, Cocktail Bars & Craft Beer Bars

For Rome's most creative modern cocktails in a casual environment, visit **Caffè Propaganda** (p. 137).

APERITIVO CULTURE

The mass social phenomenon of the *aperitivo* (happy hour—and so much more) can be a great way to meet, or at least observe the particular ways of, real Romans. It started in hard-working northern cities like Milan, where you'd go to a bar after leaving the office and, for the price of one drink (usually under 10€), get access to an unlimited buffet of high-quality food—like chunks of *parmigiano*, cured meats, fresh green salad, or other pasta salads. Luckily for Rome, the custom trickled down here, and now the city is filled with casual little places to drop in for a drink (from 6 or 7pm onward) and eat to your heart's content all these tasty finger foods. All the places listed here are fine for families, too—Italian kids love *aperitivo* (minus the alcohol)!

Look for signs in the window and follow your nose. The **Monti** neighborhood is a good place to begin. The **Terre Domus Enoteca Provincia di Roma** (see below) also does good *aperitivo*.

Ai Tre Scalini ★ This little *bottiglieria* (wine bar) is the soul of Monti. There's a traditional menu, as well as a wine list sourced from across Italy. Arrive early or call for a table: This place is usually jammed. Via Panisperna 251. ✆ **06-48907495.** Metro: Cavour.

Barnum Café ★★ An honest-to-goodness cocktail bar (with wine and crafts beers to boot), Barnum attracts a grown-up crowd getting mellowly buzzed—making it a nice alternative to the nighttime antics at Campo de'Fiori. It's also a good morning stop for caffe and cornetti. Via del Pellegrino 87. www.barnumcafe.com. ✆ 06-64760483. Bus: 40, 46, 62, 64, 916.

Bir & Fud ★ Around 15 beers on tap (most of them Italian craft brews, some as strong as 9%) as well as carb-heavy snacks like pizza and *supplì* (fried rice balls). It's 5€ for a small beer. Via Benedetta 23. www.birandfud.it. ✆ **06-5894016.** Bus: 23, 125, 271, 280.

Cavour 313 ★★ A wine bar that's as traditional and genuine as you will find this close to the ancient ruins serves over 30 wines by the glass (from 3.50€) as well as cold cuts, cheese, and vegetable platters, or excellent carpaccio. Closed Sunday in summer. Via Cavour 313. www.cavour313.it. ✆ **06-6785496.** Metro: Colosseo and Cavour.

Freni e Frizioni ★★ Trastevere's "Brakes and Clutches" is a former mechanics garage turned nighttime hot spot, with an ethnic-inflected *aperitivo* spread (think curried risotto). On the adjacent square, an effervescent crowd lounges against stone walls and parked *motorini*. Via del Politeama 4–6 (near Piazza Trilussa). www.freniefrizioni.com; ✆ **06-45497499.** Bus: 23, 125, 280, or H. Tram: 8.

La Bottega del Caffè ★ Beers, wine, cocktails, *aperitivo*—there's a little of everything at one of Monti's busiest neighborhood bars. Piazza Madonna dei Monti 5. ✆ **06-64741578.** Metro: Cavour.

Litro ★★ A wonderful addition to Rome's dining/drinking scene: a wine bar in Monteverde Vecchio (residential area above Trastevere) that serves natural wines, cocktails, and snacks sourced from Lazio-based purveyors of cured meats and cheeses, plus bruschetta and stellar alcoholic sorbets. An entire menu is devoted to mezcal, tequila's smoky cousin. Via Fratelli Bonnet 5. www.vinerialitro.it. ✆ **06-45447639.** Bus: 75, 982.

NO.AU ★ Tricked out a little like a Barcelona cava bar and located right in the old center, this place has craft beers from local brewer Birra del Borgo on tap plus a selection of wines, from around 5€ a glass. NO.AU (pronounced "knowhow," almost) is set back in a narrow alley, a little escape from the chaos. Closed Monday. Piazza di Montevecchio 16. http://noauroma.wordpress.com. ✆ **06-45652770.** Bus: 30, 46, 62, 64, 70, 81, 87, 571.

Open Baladin ★★ If anyone ever tells you that "Italians don't do good beer," send them to this bar near the Ghetto. A 40-long row of taps lines the bar, with beers from their own Piedmont brewery and across Italy. Via degli Specchi 5–6. www.openbaladin.com. ✆ **06-6838989.** Tram: 8.

Salotto42 ★★ It's all fancy cocktails and well-chosen wines at this über-hip "bookbar" set opposite the columned facade of 2nd-century Hadrian's Temple (near the Pantheon). This makes for a classy after-dinner stop. It also does shared plates, fresh juices, smoothies, and infused teas. Piazza di Pietra 42 (off Via del Corso). www.salotto42.it; ✆ **06-6785804.** Bus: 51, 62, 63, 80, 83, 85, 117, 160, 492, 628.

Stravinskij Bar ★ An evening at this award-winning cocktail bar inside one of Rome's most famous grand hotels is always a regal affair. Mixology, ingredients, and canapés are all topnotch. Inside Hotel de Russie, Via del Babuino 9. ✆ **06-32888874.** Metro: Spagna.

SIDE TRIPS FROM ROME

Ostia Antica ★★

24km (15 miles) SW of Rome

The ruins of Rome's ancient port are a must-see for anyone who can't make it to Pompeii. It's an easier day trip than Pompeii, on a similar theme: the chance to wander around the preserved ruins of an ancient Roman settlement that has been barely touched since its abandonment.

Ostia, at the mouth of the Tiber, was the port of Rome, serving as the gateway for riches from the far corners of the Empire. Founded in the 4th century B.C., it became a major port and naval base under two later emperors, Claudius and Trajan. A prosperous city developed, full of temples, baths, theaters, and patrician homes.

Ostia flourished between the 1st and 3rd centuries and survived until around the 9th century before it was abandoned. It became little

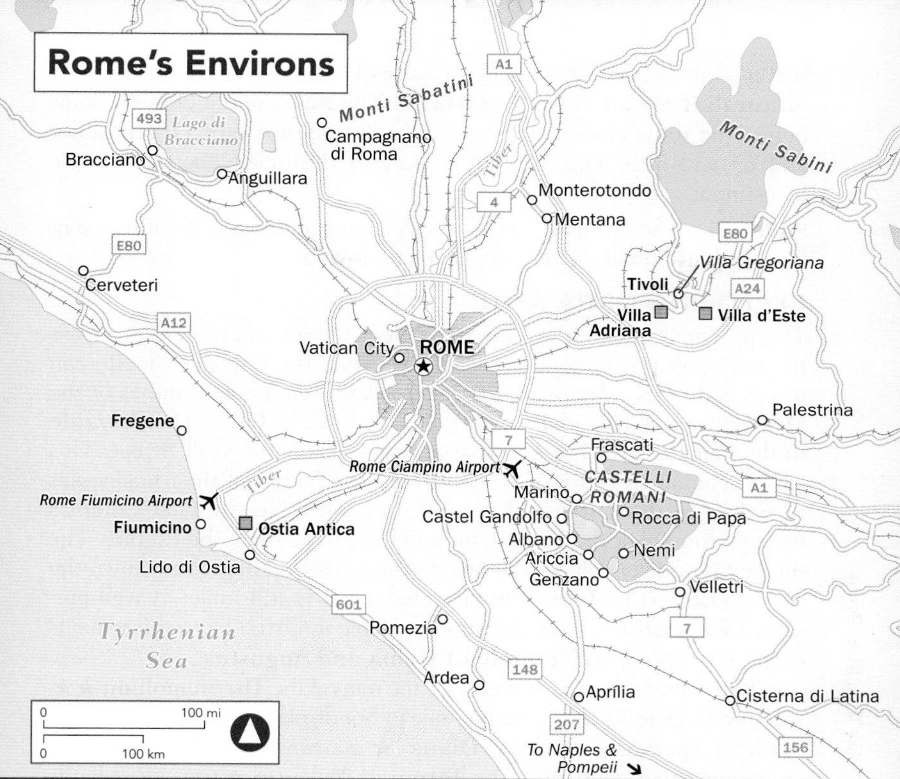

more than a malaria bed, a buried ghost city fading into history. A papal-sponsored commission launched a series of digs in the 19th century; however, the major work of unearthing was carried out under Mussolini's orders from 1938 to 1942. The city is only partially dug out today, but it's believed that all the chief monuments have been uncovered. It has quite a few impressive ruins—this is no dusty field like the Circus Maximus.

Note: Ostia is a mostly flat site, but the Roman streets underfoot are all clad in giant basalt cobblestones—wear comfortable walking shoes.

ESSENTIALS

GETTING THERE Take the Metro to Piramide, changing lines there for the Lido train to Ostia Antica. (From the platform, take "Air Terminal" exit and turn right at the top of the steps, where the station name changes to Porta San Paolo.) Departures to Ostia run every half-hour; the trip is 25 minutes and included in the price of a Metro single-journey ticket or **Roma Pass** (see p. 63). It's just a 5-minute walk to the excavations from the Metro stop: Exit the station, walk over the footbridge, and continue straight until you reach the car park. The ticket booth is to the left.

VISITOR INFORMATION The site opens daily at 9am. Closing times vary seasonally, ranging from 7:15pm in high season (April–Aug) to

4:30pm off-season (Nov–Feb 15); check at **www.ostiaantica.beniculturali.it** or call ✆ **06-56350215.** The ticket office closes 1 hour before the ruins close. Admission costs 8€, free for ages 17 and under and 65 and over. The 2€ map on sale at the ticket booth is a wise investment.

PARKING The car park, on Viale dei Romagnoli, costs 2.50€ per day, but it is fairly small. Arrive early if you're driving.

EXPLORING OSTIA ANTICA

The principal monuments are all labeled. On arrival, visitors first pass the *necropoli* (burial grounds, always outside the city gates in Roman towns and cities). The main route follows the giant cobblestones of the **Decumanus** ★ (the main street) into the heart of Ostia. The **Piazzale delle Corporazioni** ★★ is like an early version of Wall Street: This square contained nearly 75 corporations, the nature of their businesses identified by the patterns of preserved mosaics. Nearby, Greek dramas were performed at the **Teatro,** built in the early days of the Empire. The theater as it looks today is the result of much rebuilding. Every town the size of Ostia had a **Forum** ★, and the layout is still intact: A well-preserved **Capitolium** (once the largest temple in Ostia) faces the remains of the 1st-century-A.D. **Temple of Roma and Augustus**.

Elsewhere in the grid of streets are the ruins of the **Thermopolium** ★★, which was a bar; its name means "sale of hot drinks." An *insula* (a Roman block of apartments), **Casa Diana** ★ remains, its rooms arranged around an inner courtyard. The **Terme di Nettuno** ★ was a vast baths complex; climb the building at its entrance for an aerial view of its well-preserved mosaics.

WHERE TO EAT

There is no real need to eat by the ruins—a half-day here should suffice, and Ostia is within easy reach of Rome's city center. The obvious alternative is a picnic; the well-stocked food emporium **Eataly** (see p. 151) is just a couple of minutes from the Lido platform at Piramide Metro station, making it easy to grab provisions when you make the Metro interchange. There are perfect picnic spots beside fallen columns or old temple walls. If you crave a sit-down meal, **Allo Sbarco di Enea,** Viale dei Romagnoli 675 (✆ **06-5650034**), has a trattoria menu and a shaded garden. There's also a snack and coffee bar at the site.

Tivoli & the Villas ★★

32km (20 miles) E of Rome

Perched high on a hill east of Rome, ancient Tivoli has always been something of a retreat from the city. In Roman times it was known as Tibur, a retirement town for the wealthy; during the Renaissance it again became the playground of the rich, who built their country villas here. To do justice to the gardens and villas that remain—especially if the Villa Adriana is on your list, as indeed it should be—set out early.

ESSENTIALS

GETTING THERE Tivoli is 32km (20 miles) east of Rome on Via Tiburtina, about an hour's drive with traffic (the Rome–L'Aquila *autostrada*, A24, is usually faster). If you don't have a car, take Metro Line B to Ponte Mammolo. After exiting the station, transfer to a Cotral bus for Tivoli (www.cotralspa.it). Cotral buses depart every 15 to 30 minutes during the day. Villa d'Este is in Tivoli itself, close to the bus stop; to get to Villa Adriana you need to catch a regional bus from town.

EXPLORING TIVOLI AND THE VILLAS

Villa Adriana (Hadrian's Villa) ★★★ HISTORIC SITE/RUINS Globe-trotting Emperor Hadrian spent the last 3 years of his life in grand style. Less than 6km (3¾ miles) from Tivoli, between 118 and 134 A.D. he built one of the greatest estates ever conceived, filling acre upon acre with architectural wonders he'd seen in his travels. Hadrian erected theaters, baths, temples, fountains, gardens, and canals, filling palaces and temples with sculpture, some of which now rest in the museums of Rome. In later centuries, barbarians, popes, and cardinals, as well as anyone who needed a slab of marble, carted off much that made the villa so spectacular. But enough of the fragmented ruins remain to inspire a real sense of awe.

The most outstanding remnant is the **Canopo ★★★,** a re-creation of the Egyptian town of Canopus with its famous Temple of the Serapis. The ruins of a rectangular area, **Piazza d'Oro,** are still surrounded by a double portico. Likewise, the **Edificio con Pilastri Dorici (Doric Pillared Hall)** remains, with its pilasters with bases and capitals holding up a Doric architrave. The apse and the ruins of some magnificent vaulting are found at the **Grandi Terme (Great Baths),** while only the north wall remains of the **Pecile ★,** otherwise known as the *Stoà Poikile di Atene* or "Painted Porch," which Hadrian discovered in Athens and had reproduced here. The best is saved for last—the **Teatro Marittimo ★★★,** a circular theater in ruins, with its central building enveloped by a canal spanned by small swing bridges.

Largo Marguerite Yourcenar 1, Tivoli. www.villaadriana.beniculturali.it. ✆ **0774-312070.** 8€. Daily 9am–sunset (about 7:30pm in May–Aug, 5pm Nov–Jan, 6pm Feb, 6.30pm Mar and Oct, and 7pm Apr and Oct). Bus: 4 from Tivoli.

Villa d'Este ★★ PARK/GARDEN Like Hadrian centuries before, Cardinal Ippolito d'Este of Ferrara ordered this villa built on a Tivoli hillside in the mid-16th century. The dank Renaissance structure, with its second-rate paintings, is not that interesting; the big draw for visitors is the **spectacular gardens ★★★**, designed by Pirro Ligorio.

As you descend the cypress-studded garden slope you're rewarded with everything from lilies to gargoyles spouting water, torrential streams, and waterfalls. The loveliest fountain is the **Fontana dell Ovato ★★**, by Ligorio. Nearby is the most spectacular engineering achievement: the **Fontana dell'Organo Idraulico (Fountain of the Hydraulic Organ) ★★**, dazzling with music and water jets in front of a baroque chapel (the fountain "plays" every 2 hours from 10:30am).

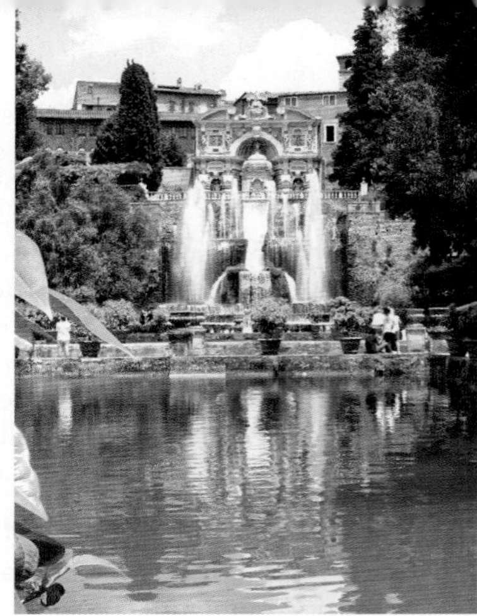

The musical Fountain of the Hydraulic Organ and fishpond, Villa d'Este.

The moss-covered **Fontana dei Draghi (Fountain of the Dragons),** also by Ligorio, and the so-called **Fontana di Vetro (Fountain of Glass),** by Bernini, are also worth seeking out, as is the main promenade, lined with 100 spraying fountains. The garden is worth hours of exploration, but it involves a lot of walking, with some steep climbs.

Piazza Trento 5, Tivoli. www.villadestetivoli.info. ✆ **0774-312070.** 8€. Tues–Sun 8:30am to 1 hr. before sunset. Bus: Cotral service from Ponte Mammolo (Roma–Tivoli); the bus stops near the entrance.

Villa Gregoriana ★ PARK/GARDEN Villa d'Este dazzles with artificial glamour, but the Villa Gregoriana relies more on nature. Originally laid out by Pope Gregory XVI in the 1830s, the main highlight is the panoramic waterfall of Aniene, with the trek to the bottom studded with grottoes and balconies that open onto the chasm. The only problem is that if you do make the full descent, you might need a helicopter to pull you up again (the climb back up is fierce). From one of the belvederes, there's a view of the **Temple of Vesta** on the hill.

Largo Sant'Angelo, Tivoli. www.visitfai.it/parcovillagregoriana. ✆ **0774-332650.** 7€. Apr–Oct Tues–Sun 10am–6:30pm; Mar, Nov, and Dec Tues–Sun 10am–4pm. Bus: Cotral service from Ponte Mammolo (Roma–Tivoli); the bus stops near the entrance.

WHERE TO EAT

Tivoli's gardens make for a pleasant picnic place (see **Eataly,** p. 151), but if you crave a sit-down meal, **Antica Trattoria del Falcone,** Via del Trevio 34 (✆ **0774-312358**), is a dependable option in Tivoli. Just off Largo Garibaldi, it's been open since 1918 and specializes in excellent pizza, Roman pastas, and roast meats. It's open daily lunch and dinner.

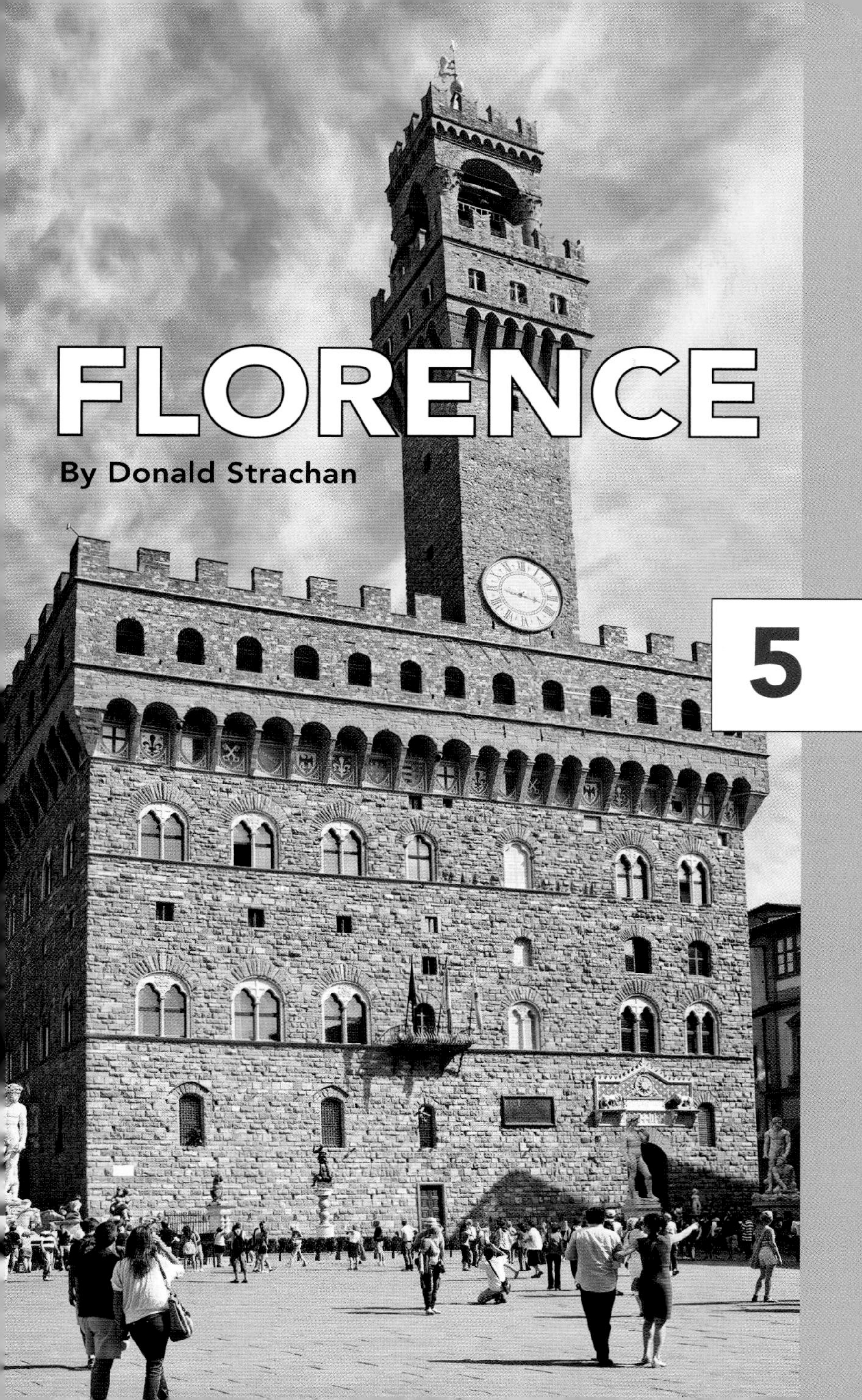

FLORENCE
By Donald Strachan
5

Botticelli, Michelangelo, and Leonardo da Vinci all left their mark on Florence, the city that was the cradle of the Renaissance. With Brunelleschi's dome as a backdrop, travelers follow the River Arno to the Uffizi Gallery (Florence's foremost art museum) to soak in centuries of great painting. They wander across the iconic Ponte Vecchio, take in the tangle of Oltrarno's medieval streets, and then sample seasonal Tuscan cooking in a Left Bank trattoria. Here is how to uncover the art of fine living in this masterpiece of a city.

Michelangelo's "David" stands tall (literally) behind the doors of the **Accademia,** and the delicate paintings of Fra' Angelico are in the convent of **San Marco.** Works by Donatello, Masaccio, and Ghiberti fill churches and museums. Once the Medici's home, **Palazzo Pitti** is stuffed with paintings by Raphael and Titian, and backed by the fountains of the **Boboli Garden**—where opera debuted in the 1590s.

But it's not just about the art. Florentines love to shop, too, and Italy's leather capital offers a bounty of handmade gloves, belts, bags, and shoes sold from workshops and high-toned stores, as well as at tourist-oriented **San Lorenzo Market.** You can splurge on designer wear from fashion houses along **Via de' Tornabuoni**—the home of Gucci, Pucci, and Ferragamo—or tap into the city's taste for vintage clothes.

As for Florentine cuisine, it's increasingly cosmopolitan, but flavors are often still Tuscan at heart. Even in fine restaurants, meals might kick off with ***ribollita*** (seasonal vegetable stew) before moving onto the chargrilled delights of a ***bistecca alla fiorentina*** (Florentine beefsteak on the bone), all washed down with a **Chianti Classico.** A plate of cold cuts and pecorino cheese makes a classic light lunch, or for the adventurous, ***lampredotto alla fiorentina*** (a sandwich of cow's stomach stewed in tomatoes and garlic). When you've dined to your fill, retire to a wine bar in the **Oltrarno,** or to one of the edgier joints of **San Frediano.** Lovers of opera, classical music, theater, and jazz will find entertainment, too.

ESSENTIALS

Getting There

BY PLANE Several European airlines serve Florence's **Amerigo Vespucci Airport** (www.aeroporto.firenze.it/en; ✆ **055-306-15** switchboard, 055-306-1300 for flight info), also called **Peretola,** just 5km (3 miles) northwest of town. There are no direct flights to or from the

United States, but you can make connections through London, Paris, Amsterdam, Frankfurt, and other major European cities. **Busitalia**'s half-hourly **Vola in Bus** shuttles between the airport and downtown's bus station at Via Santa Caterina da Siena 17 (www.fsbusitalia.it; ✆ **800-373760**), beside the train station, taking 20 to 30 minutes and costing 6€ one-way or 10€ round-trip. Metered **taxis** line up outside the airport's arrival terminal and charge a flat rate of 22€ to the city center (24€ on holidays, 25€ after 10pm; additional 1€ per bag).

The closest international airport with seasonal direct flights to North America is Pisa's **Galileo Galilei Airport** (www.pisa-airport.com; ✆ **050-849-300**), 97km (60 miles) west of Florence. Inaugurated in 2017, its **PisaMover** automatic transit service runs every 5 to 8 minutes from the airport terminal direct to Pisa Centrale station, where you can catch a state rail service to Florence (50–80 min.; 8.40€). A taxi from the airport costs around 10€. Alternatively, six daily buses operated by **Terravision** (www.terravision.eu) connect downtown Florence with Pisa Airport in just over 1 hour. One-way tickets are 5€ adults, 4€ children ages 5 to 12; round-trip fares are 10€ and 8€. Around 16 daily **Autostradale** buses (www.airportbusexpress.it) run a similar service (13.50€ adults; 4.75€ children 2–12).

BY TRAIN Florence is Tuscany's rail hub, with regular connections to all of Italy's major cities. To get here from Rome, take a high-speed **Frecciarossa** or **Frecciargento** train (1½ hr.; www.trenitalia.com) or rival high-speed trains operated by **Italo** (www.italotreno.it; p. 798). High-speed trains run to Venice (2 hr.) via Bologna and Padua.

Most Florence-bound trains roll into **Stazione Santa Maria Novella,** Piazza della Stazione, which you'll see abbreviated as **S.M.N.** The station is an architectural masterpiece, albeit one dating to Italy's Fascist period, rather than the Renaissance; it lies on the northwestern edge of the city's compact historic center, a 10-minute walk from the Duomo and a brisk 15-minute walk from Piazza della Signoria and the Uffizi.

BY CAR The **A1 autostrada** runs north from Rome past Arezzo to Florence and continues to Bologna, and **unnumbered superhighways** run to and from Siena (the *SI-FI raccordo*) and Pisa (the so-called *FI-PI-LI*). To reach Florence from Venice, take the A13 southbound then switch to the A1 at Bologna.

Driving *to* Florence is easy; the problems begin once you arrive. Almost all cars are banned from the historic center for much of the time; only residents or merchants with special permits are allowed into this clearly marked, camera-patrolled *zona a trafico limitato* (the "ZTL"). You can enter the ZTL to drop off baggage at your hotel or go direct to a prebooked parking garage (either can organize a temporary ZTL permit when provided with your license plate). Usual ZTL hours are Monday to Friday 7:30am to 8pm, Saturday 7:30am to 4pm.

Your best bet for overnight or longer-term parking is one of the city-run garages. The best deal—better than many hotels' garage rates—is at the **Parterre parking lot** under Piazza Libertà at Via Madonna delle Tosse 9 (✆ **055-5030-2209**). It's open round the clock, costs 2€ per hour, or 10€ for the first 24 hours, 15€ for the second, then 20€ per day; it's 70€ for up to a week's parking. Find more info on parking at **www.firenzeparcheggi.it**.

Don't park your car overnight on the streets in Florence without local knowledge; if you're towed and ticketed, it will set you back substantially, and the headaches to retrieve your car are beyond description. If this happens to you, start by calling the vehicle removal department (**Recupero Veicoli Rimossi**) at ✆ **055-422-4142.**

Visitor Information

TOURIST OFFICES The most convenient tourist office is at Via Cavour 1R (www.firenzeturismo.it; ✆ **055-290-832**), two blocks north of the Duomo. The office is open Monday through Friday from 9am to 1pm. Its free map is quite adequate for navigation purposes; there's no need to upgrade to a paid version.

The train station's nearest tourist office (✆ **055-212-245**) is opposite the terminus at Piazza della Stazione 4. With your back to the tracks, take the left exit, cross onto the concrete median, and bear right; it's across the busy road junction ahead. The office was renovated in 2017 and is usually open Monday through Saturday 9am to 7pm, Sunday 9am to 2pm. This office gets crowded; unless you're really lost, go to the Via Cavour office (see above) on a weekday morning.

Another helpful office is under the Loggia del Bigallo on the corner of Piazza San Giovanni and Via dei Calzaiuoli (✆ **055-288-496**); it's open Monday through Saturday from 9am to 7pm and Sunday to 2pm.

WEBSITES The official Florence tourism website, **www.firenzeturismo.it**, contains a wealth of reasonably up-to-date information. At the "Tools" section of the site, you can download the latest opening hours for major city sights, as well as themed apps, maps, and a monthly events calendar. The best-informed city **blogs** are written in Italian by locals: **Io Amo Firenze** (www.ioamofirenze.it) is handy for reviews of the latest eating, drinking, and events in town. For one-off exhibitions and culture, **Art Trav** (www.arttrav.com) is an essential bookmark, and written in English. The city itself maintains a useful events portal: Visit **http://eventi.comune.fi.it**. For more Florence info, go to **www.frommers.com/destinations/florence**. Listings magazine websites are covered in the "Entertainment & Nightlife" section, p. 220.

City Layout

Florence is a smallish city, sitting on the Arno River and petering out to olive-planted hills rather quickly to the north and south, but extending

Locating Addresses: The Red & the Black

The address system in Florence has a split personality. Private homes, some offices, and hotels are numbered in black (or blue), but businesses, shops, and restaurants are numbered independently in red. (That's the theory anyway; in reality, the division between black and red numbers isn't so clear-cut.) The result is that 1, 2, 3 (black) addresses march up the block numerically oblivious to their 1R, 2R, 3R (red) neighbors. You might find the doorways on one side of a street numbered 1R, 2R, 3R, 1, 4R, 2, 3, 5R. The color codes occur only in the *centro storico* and other old sections of town; outlying districts didn't bother with this confusing system.

farther west and east along the Arno valley with suburbs and light industry. It has a compact center that is best negotiated on foot. No two major sights are more than a 25-minute walk apart, and most of the hotels and restaurants in this chapter are in the relatively small ***centro storico* (historic center),** a compact tangle of medieval streets and *piazze* (squares) where visitors spend most of their time. The bulk of Florence, including the majority of tourist sights, is north of the river, with the **Oltrarno,** an old working artisans' neighborhood, hemmed in between the Arno and the hills on the south side.

The Neighborhoods in Brief

THE DUOMO The area surrounding Florence's gargantuan cathedral is as central as you can get. The Duomo itself is halfway between the two monastic churches of Santa Maria Novella and Santa Croce, as well as at the midpoint between the Uffizi Gallery and the Ponte Vecchio to the south and San Marco and the Accademia (home of Michelangelo's "David") to the north. The streets south of the Duomo make up a medieval tangle of alleys and tiny squares heading toward **Piazza della Signoria.** This is one of the oldest parts of town, and the streets still vaguely follow a grid laid down when the city was a Roman colony. The site of the Roman city's forum is today's **Piazza della Repubblica,** controversially "modernized" in the 1800s.

The Duomo neighborhood is, understandably, one of the most hotel-heavy parts of town, offering a range from luxury inns to student dives and everything in between. Because several places around here rest on the laurels of a sublime location, you need to be choosy. The same goes—even more so—for dining in the area.

PIAZZA DELLA SIGNORIA This is the city's civic heart and perhaps the best base for museum hounds: The Uffizi Gallery, Palazzo Vecchio, Bargello sculpture collection, and **Ponte Vecchio** are all nearby. It's a well-polished part of the tourist zone but still retains the narrow medieval lanes where Dante grew up. The few blocks just north of the Ponte Vecchio have reasonable shopping, but unappealing modern buildings were planted here to replace those destroyed in World War II. The entire neighborhood can be stiflingly crowded in peak season—**Via Por Santa Maria** is one to avoid—but in those moments when you catch it empty of tour groups, it remains the romantic heart of pre-Renaissance Florence. As with the Duomo neighborhood, you need to be *very* choosy when picking a restaurant or even an ice cream shop around here.

SAN LORENZO & THE MERCATO CENTRALE This wedge of streets between the train station and the Duomo, centered on the Medici's old family church of **San Lorenzo,** is market territory. The vast indoor **Mercato Centrale** food market is here, and many of the streets are filled daily with stalls hawking leather and other souvenirs: **San Lorenzo Market.** It's a colorful neighborhood, blessed with many budget hotels and a growing choice of good, affordable dining spots, but it's not the quietest part of town.

PIAZZA SANTA TRÍNITA This piazza sits just north of the river at the south end of Florence's shopping mecca, **Via de' Tornabuoni,** home to Gucci, Armani, and more. It's a quaint, well-to-do (and still medieval) neighborhood in which to stay, even if you don't care about haute couture. If you're an upscale shopping fiend, there's no better place to be.

SANTA MARIA NOVELLA This neighborhood, bounding the western edge of the *centro storico,* has two characters: an unattractive zone around the train station, and a nicer area south of it between the church of Santa Maria Novella and the river. In general, the train-station area is the least appealing part of town in which to base yourself. The streets are mostly

Piazza Santa Maria Novella.

heavily trafficked and noisy, and you're a little removed from the medieval atmosphere. This area does, however, have more good budget options than any other quarter, especially along **Via Faenza** and its tributaries. Try to avoid staying on heavily trafficked **Via Nazionale.**

The situation improves dramatically as you move east into the San Lorenzo area (see above), or pass Santa Maria Novella church and head south toward the river. **Piazza Santa Maria Novella** and its tributary streets have several stylish hotels.

SAN MARCO & SANTISSIMA ANNUNZIATA On the northern edge of the *centro storico,* these two churches are fronted by *piazze*: **Piazza San Marco,** a busy transport hub; and **Piazza Santissima Annunziata,** the most architecturally unified square in the city. The neighborhood is home to Florence's university, the **Accademia**, the San Marco paintings of Fra' Angelico, and quiet streets with some hotel gems. The walk back from the heart of the action isn't as far as it looks on a map, and you'll likely welcome the escape from tourist crowds.

SANTA CROCE The art-filled church at the eastern edge of the *centro storico* is the focal point of one of the most genuine neighborhoods in the center. Few tourists roam east beyond **Piazza Santa Croce,** so if you want to feel like a local, head here. The streets around the **Mercato di Sant'Ambrogio** have an appealing feel, and they get lively after dark. The Santa Croce area boasts some of the best restaurants and bars in the city—*aperitivo* time is vibrant along **Via de' Benci. Via Pietrapiana** and the northern end of **Via de' Macci** are both lively.

THE OLTRARNO, SAN NICCOLÒ & SAN FREDIANO "Across the Arno" is the artisans' neighborhood, still dotted with workshops. It began as a working-class neighborhood to catch the overflow from the expanding medieval city on the opposite bank, and later became a chic area for aristocrats to build palaces with countryside views. The largest of these, the **Pitti Palace,** became the home of Tuscany's grand dukes and today houses a set of paintings second only to the Uffizi in scope.

The Oltrarno's lively tree-shaded center, **Piazza Santo Spirito,** is lined with bars and close to some great restaurants (and lots of nightlife, too). West of here, the neighborhood of **San Frediano** gets ever more fashionable, and **San Niccolò** at the foot of Florence's southern hills has popular bars. You may not wish to stay around here—the hotel range isn't great—but when evening draws nigh, cross the river to eat and drink better, at better prices, than you'll generally find in the *centro storico.*

Getting Around

Florence is a **walking** city. You can stroll between the two top sights, Piazza del Duomo and the Uffizi, in 5 minutes or so. The hike from the most northerly major sights, San Marco and the Accademia, to the most southerly, the Pitti Palace across the Arno, should take no more than 30 minutes. From Santa Maria Novella eastward to Santa Croce is a flat 20- to 30-minute walk. But beware: **Flagstones,** some of them uneven, are everywhere. Wear sensible shoes with good padding and foot support.

BY BUS & TRAM You'll rarely need to use Florence's efficient **ATAF bus system** (www.ataf.net; © **800-424-500** in Italy) since the city is so compact. Bus tickets cost 1.20€ and are good for 90 minutes, irrespective of how many changes you make. A 24-hour pass costs 5€, a 3-day pass 12€, and a 7-day pass 18€. Tickets are sold at *tabacchi* (tobacconists), automatic machines, some bars, and most newsstands. ***Note:*** Once on board, validate a paper ticket in the box near the rear door to avoid a steep fine. Since traffic is restricted in most of the center, buses make runs on principal streets only, except for four tiny electric bus lines (*bussini* services C1, C2, C3, and D) that trundle about the *centro storico*. The most useful lines to outlying areas are no. 7 (for Fiesole) and nos. 12 and 13 (for Piazzale Michelangelo). Buses run from 7am until 9 or 9:30pm daily, with a limited night service on a few key routes. **Tram** line T1 (www.gestramvia.com) runs until after midnight, connecting Santa Maria Novella station with the Opera di Firenze, Cascine Park, and Florence's southwestern suburbs. Lines T2 (to the airport) and T3 are under construction.

BY TAXI Taxis aren't cheap, and with the city so small and the one-way system forcing drivers to take convoluted routes, they aren't an economical way to get about. They're most useful to get you and your bags between the train station and a hotel. It's 3.30€ to start the meter (which rises to 5.30€ on Sun; 6.60€ 10pm–6am), plus 1€ per bag or for a fourth passenger in the cab. There are taxi stands outside the train station, on Borgo San Jacopo, and in Piazza Santa Croce; otherwise, call **Radio Taxi SOCOTA** at © **055-4242** or **Radio Taxi COTAFI** at © **055-4390.** For the latest taxi information, see **www.4242.it**.

BY BICYCLE & SCOOTER Many of the bike-rental shops in town are located between San Lorenzo and San Marco. They include **Alinari,** Via San Zanobi 38R (www.alinarirental.com; © **055-280-500**), which rents city bikes (2.50€ per hour; 12€ per day) and mountain bikes (3€ per hour; 18€ per day). It also hires out 125cc scooters (15€ per hour; 55€ per day). Another renter with similar prices is **Florence by Bike,** Via San Zanobi 54R (www.florencebybike.it; © **055-488-992**). Make sure to use a lock (one will be provided with your rental): Bike theft is common.

BY CAR Trying to drive in the *centro storico* is a frustrating, useless exercise, and moreover, for most of the time unauthorized cars will be fined if they enter the **ztl.** You need a permit to do anything beyond dropping off and picking up bags at your hotel. Park your vehicle in one of the underground lots on the center's periphery and pound the pavement. (See "By Car" under "Getting There," p. 163.)

[Fast FACTS] FLORENCE

Business Hours Hours mainly follow the Italian norm (see chapter 16). In Florence, however, many larger and more central shops stay open through the midday *riposo* or nap (note the sign *orario nonstop*).

Doctors Tourist-oriented **Medical Service Firenze** is at Via Roma 4, in the city center (www.medicalservice.firenze.it; ✆ **055-475-411**). It's open for walk-ins Monday to Friday 11am to noon, 1 to 3pm, and 5 to 6pm; Saturday 11am to noon and 1 to 3pm only. **Dr. Stephen Kerr** has an office at Piazza Mercato Nuovo 1 (www.dr-kerr.com; ✆ **335-836-1682** or 055-288-055), with office hours Monday through Friday from 3 to 5pm without an appointment (appointments are available 9am–3pm). The consultation fee is 60€, or 48€ if you show a student ID card.

Hospitals The most central hospital is **Santa Maria Nuova,** a block northeast of the Duomo on Piazza Santa Maria Nuova (✆ **055-69-381**), with an emergency room *(pronto soccorso)* open 24 hours. There is a comprehensive guide to medical services, including specialist care, on the official Florence city website: See **www.firenzeturismo.it**.

Internet Access Every hotel we recommend now offers free wireless Internet. If you have your own laptop or smartphone, several bars and cafes also offer free Wi-Fi to anyone buying a drink or snack. There's free Wi-Fi upstairs at the **Mercato Centrale** (p. 213), too, and outdoors in Piazza del Duomo.

Mail & Postage Florence's **main post office** (✆ **055-273-6481**), at Via Pellicceria 3, off the southwest corner of Piazza della Repubblica, is open Monday through Friday from 8:20am to 7:05pm, Saturday 8:20am to 12:35pm.

Newspapers & Magazines Florence's national daily paper, "La Nazione," is on sale everywhere. "The Florentine" (www.theflorentine.net) is the city's monthly English-language publication, widely available at bars, cafes, and bookstores. Overseas English-language newspapers are also available: Try the newsstands at the station or the booth under the arcade on the western side of Piazza della Repubblica. You will find the "Financial Times," "Wall Street Journal," and London "Guardian," alongside the usual "The New York Times International Edition."

Pharmacies There is a 24-hour pharmacy (also open Sun and state holidays) in **Stazione Santa Maria Novella** (✆ **055-216-761;** ring the bell opposite taxi rank btw. 11pm and 7am). On holidays and at night, look for the sign in any pharmacy window telling you which ones are open locally.

Police To report a crime or passport problems, call the *questura* (police headquarters) at ✆ **055-49-771.** Lost property should find its way to the *Ufficio oggetti ritrovati*: ✆ **055/334802. *Note:*** It is illegal to knowingly buy fake goods anywhere in the city (and yes, a "Louis Vuitton" bag at 10€ counts as *knowingly*). You may be served a hefty on-the-spot fine if caught.

Safety As in any city, plenty of pickpockets are out to ruin your vacation, and in Florence you'll find light-fingered youngsters (especially around the train station), but otherwise you're safe. Steer clear of the Cascine Park after dark, when you may run the risk of being mugged; likewise both the area around Piazza Santo Spirito and in the backstreets behind Santa Croce after all the nightlife has gone off to bed. See chapter 16 for more safety tips.

EXPLORING FLORENCE

Most museums accept cash only at the door. **Precise opening times can change** without notice, especially at city churches (for example, the Baptistery sometimes remains open until 11pm in summer). The tourist office maintains an up-to-date list of hours. Note, too, that the **last admission** to the museums and monuments listed is usually between 30 and 45 minutes before the final closing time.

Piazza del Duomo

The cathedral square is always crowded—filled with tourists and caricature artists during the day, strolling crowds in the early evening, and students strumming guitars on the Duomo's steps at night. The piazza's vivacity amid the glittering facades of the cathedral and the Baptistery doors keep it an eternal Florentine sight—and now that it has been closed to traffic for almost a decade, it's a more welcoming space than ever.

Battistero (Baptistery) ★★★ CHURCH In choosing a date to mark the beginning of the Renaissance, art historians often seize on 1401, the year Florence's powerful wool merchants' guild held a contest to decide who would receive the commission to design the **North Doors ★★** of the Baptistery to match its Gothic **South Doors,** cast 65 years earlier by Andrea Pisano. The era's foremost Tuscan sculptors each cast a bas-relief bronze panel depicting their own vision of the "Sacrifice of Isaac." Twenty-two-year-old Lorenzo Ghiberti, competing against Donatello, Jacopo della Quercia, and Filippo Brunelleschi, won. He spent the next 21 years casting 28 bronze panels and building his doors. The restored originals are now inside the **Museo dell'Opera del Duomo** (see below).

The result so impressed the merchants' guild—not to mention the public and Ghiberti's fellow artists—that they asked him in 1425 to do the **East Doors ★★★**, facing the Duomo, this time giving him the artistic freedom to realize his Renaissance ambitions. Twenty-seven years later, just before his death, Ghiberti finished 10 dramatic Old Testament scenes in gilded bronze, each a masterpiece of Renaissance sculpture and some of the finest examples of low-relief perspective in Italian art. Each illustrates episodes in the stories of Noah (second down on left),

The ornate facade of Florence's Duomo.

DISCOUNT tickets FOR THE CITY

It may seem a little odd to label the **Firenze Card** (www.firenzecard.it) a "discount" ticket. It costs 72€. Is it a good buy? If you are planning a busy, museum-packed break here, the Firenze Card is a good value. If you only expect to see a few highlights, skip it.

For culture vultures out there, the card (valid for 72 hr.) allows one-time entrance to 60-plus sites; including some that are free anyway, but also the Uffizi, Accademia, Cappella Brancacci, Palazzo Pitti, Brunelleschi's dome, San Marco, and many more. In fact, *everything* we recommend in this chapter is included with the card, even sites in Fiesole (p. 198). It gets you into much shorter lines, and takes ticket prebooking hassles out of the equation—another saving of 3€ to 4€ for busy museums, above all the Uffizi and Accademia. The **FirenzeCard+** add-on (5€) includes up to 3 days' bus travel (which you likely won't use) and free Wi-Fi (which you might).

Don't buy a Firenze Card for anyone ages 17 and under: They can always enter via the express queue with you. Those under 17 gain free admission to civic museums (such as the Palazzo Vecchio) and pay only the "reservation fee" at state-owned museums (it's 4€ at the Uffizi, for example). Private museums and sights have their own payment rules, but it's very unlikely to add up to 72€ per child.

The Opera del Duomo has dispensed with single-entry tickets to its sites in favor of a value *biglietto cumulativo*, the **Grande Museo del Duomo** ticket. It covers Brunelleschi's dome (including the now **obligatory** booking of a time slot), the Baptistery, Campanile di Giotto, the revamped Museo dell'Opera, and crypt excavations of Santa Reparata (inside the cathedral) for 15€, 3€ for children ages 6 to 11. It also gets you into the Duomo without queuing (in theory). In Florence, buy it at the ticket office almost opposite the Baptistery, on the north side of Piazza San Giovanni. Just this square and its single ticket can fill a busy half-day, at least. See **www.ilgrandemuseodel duomo.it** for more details, to buy online ahead of arrival, and to book a time slot for the dome.

Moses (second up on left), Solomon (bottom right), and others. The panels mounted here are also copies; the originals are in the **Museo dell'Opera del Duomo.** Years later, Michelangelo was standing before these doors and someone asked his opinion. His response sums up Ghiberti's accomplishment as no art historian could: "They are so beautiful that they would grace the entrance to Paradise." They've been nicknamed the Gates of Paradise ever since.

The building itself is ancient. It is first mentioned in city records in the 9th century and was probably already 300 years old by then. Its interior is ringed with columns pilfered from ancient Roman buildings and is a riot of mosaic-work above and below. The floor was inlaid in 1209, and the ceiling was covered between 1225 and the early 1300s with glittering **mosaics ★★**. Most were crafted by Venetian or Byzantine-style workshops, which worked off designs drawn by the era's best artists. Coppo di

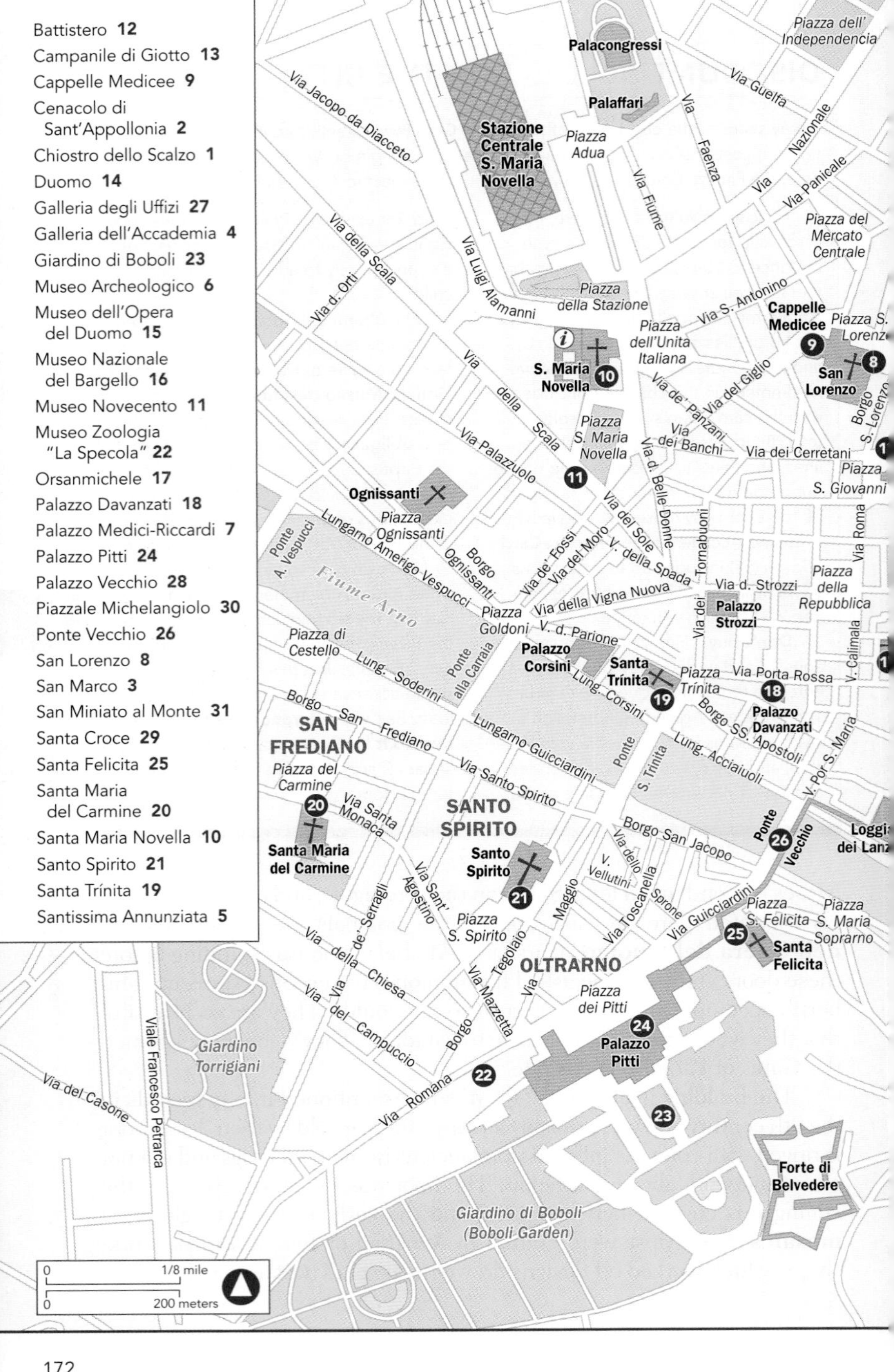

Battistero 12
Campanile di Giotto 13
Cappelle Medicee 9
Cenacolo di Sant'Appollonia 2
Chiostro dello Scalzo 1
Duomo 14
Galleria degli Uffizi 27
Galleria dell'Accademia 4
Giardino di Boboli 23
Museo Archeologico 6
Museo dell'Opera del Duomo 15
Museo Nazionale del Bargello 16
Museo Novecento 11
Museo Zoologia "La Specola" 22
Orsanmichele 17
Palazzo Davanzati 18
Palazzo Medici-Riccardi 7
Palazzo Pitti 24
Palazzo Vecchio 28
Piazzale Michelangiolo 30
Ponte Vecchio 26
San Lorenzo 8
San Marco 3
San Miniato al Monte 31
Santa Croce 29
Santa Felicita 25
Santa Maria del Carmine 20
Santa Maria Novella 10
Santo Spirito 21
Santa Trínita 19
Santissima Annunziata 5
Palacongressi
Palaffari
Stazione Centrale S. Maria Novella
Piazza dell' Independencia
Via Guelfa
Via Jacopo da Diacceto
Piazza Adua
Via Faenza
Via Nazionale
Via Panicale
Via Fiume
Piazza del Mercato Centrale
Via della Scala
Via Luigi Alamanni
Via d. Orti
Piazza della Stazione
Via S. Antonino
Cappelle Medicee
Piazza S. Lorenzo
Piazza dell'Unita Italiana
S. Maria Novella
San Lorenzo
Borgo S. Lorenzo
Via del Giglio
Via de' Panzani
Via dei Banchi
Piazza S. Maria Novella
Via Palazzuolo
Via dei Cerretani
Piazza S. Giovanni
Ognissanti
Piazza Ognissanti
Via d. Belle Donne
Via del Sole
Via Roma
Lungarno Amerigo Vespucci
Borgo Ognissanti
Via de' Fossi
Via del Moro
V. della Spada
Via Tornabuoni
Ponte A. Vespucci
Fiume Arno
Via della Vigna Nuova
Via d. Strozzi
Piazza della Repubblica
Piazza Goldoni
V. d. Parione
Palazzo Strozzi
Via dei Tornabuoni
Piazza di Cestello
Lung. Soderini
Ponte alla Carraia
Palazzo Corsini
Santa Trínita
Piazza Trínita
Via Porta Rossa
V. Calimala
Lung. Corsini
Palazzo Davanzati
Borgo San Frediano
SAN FREDIANO
Lungarno Guicciardini
Borgo SS. Apostoli
Via Por S. Maria
Ponte S. Trinita
Lung. Acciaiuoli
Piazza del Carmine
Via Santo Spirito
Via Santa Monaca
SANTO SPIRITO
Borgo San Jacopo
Ponte Vecchio
Loggia dei Lanzi
Santa Maria del Carmine
Santo Spirito
Via Sant' Agostino
Via de' Serragli
V. Vellutini
Via dello Sprone
Via Toscanella
Via Maggio
Via Guicciardini
Piazza S. Felicita
Piazza S. Maria Soprarno
Piazza S. Spirito
Santa Felicita
Via della Chiesa
Via Tegolaio
OLTRARNO
Via Mazzetta
Piazza dei Pitti
Via del Campuccio
Borgo
Palazzo Pitti
Giardino Torrigiani
Viale Francesco Petrarca
Via del Casone
Via Romana
Forte di Belvedere
Giardino di Boboli (Boboli Garden)
0 1/8 mile
0 200 meters

Florence Attractions
San Marco
Santissima Annunziata
Galleria dell' Accademia
Museo Archeologico
Ospedale degli Innocenti
Palazzo Medici-Riccardi
Palazzo Pucci
Ospedale S. Maria Nuova
Teatro d. Pergola
Santa Maria Maddalena dei Pazzi
Sinogoga (Museo Ebraico)
Duomo
Piazza del Duomo
Bargello
Badia
Teatro Verdi
Casa di Buonarroti
Carceri delle Murate
Archivo di Stato
Palazzo Vecchio
Uffizi
Santa Croce
Biblioteca Nazionale
SANTA CROCE
SAN NICCOLÒ
Piazzale Michelangelo
Fiume Arno
Giardino dei Semplici
Giardino della Gherardesca
Piazza Donatello
Piazza d'Azeglio
Piazza Cesare Beccaria
Piazza S. Croce
Piazza dei Cavalleggeri
Piazza Piave
Piazza G. Poggi
Piazza F. Ferrucci
Piazza San Marco
Piazza della SS. Annunziata
Piazza Brunelleschi
Piazza S. M. Nuova
Piazza Sant' Ambrogio
Piazza L. Ghiberti
Piazza S. Firenze
Piazza della Signoria
Piazza Mentana
Lungarno delle Grazie
Lung. della Zecca Vecchia
Lung. P. Giraldi
Lungarno Torrigiani
Lungarno Serristori
Lungarno B. Cellini
Ponte alle Grazie
Ponte A. Vespucci
Viale Antonio Gramsci
Viale Giovanni Amendola
Viale della Giovine Italia
Viale G. Poggi
Viale Michelangiolo
Via di Belvedere
Via del Monte alle Croci
Via dei Bastioni
Via di S. Niccolo
Via dei Renai
Via de' Bardi
Via Ghibellina
Via dell' Agnolo
Via della Colonna
Via Giuseppe Giusti
Via dell'Oriuolo
Via del Corso
Borgo degli Albizi
Via Pietrapiana
Borgo la Croce
Via de' Pandolfini
Borgo de' Greci
Via dei Neri
Corso dei Tintori
Borgo S. Croce
Via Cavour
Via Ricasoli
Via dei Servi
Via Guelfa
Via de' Ginori
Via dei Martelli
Via dei Pucci
Via M. Bufalini
Via S. Egidio
Borgo Pinti
Via Fiesolana
Via de' Pepi
Via dei Pilastri
Via di Mezzo
Via della Mattonaia
Via A. Manzoni
Via F. Paolieri
Via G. Verdi
Via de' Macci
Via di San Giuseppe
Via Pietro Thouar
Via de' Malcontenti
Via Tripoli
Via Laura
Via degli Alfani
Via della Pergola
Via G. Capponi
Via P. Cappone
Via G. La Farini
Via J. Nardi
Via B. Varchi
Via L. C. Farini
Via G. Carducci
Via Cesare Battisti
Via della Dogana
Via San Gallo
Via XXVII Aprile
V. S. Reparata
V. degli Arazzieri
Via del Proconsolo
V. d. Studio
Via Dante Alighieri
Cimatori
V. d. Vigna Vecchia
Via V. Magliabechi
Via de' Benci
Lung. Gen. Diaz
Via Buonarroti
Via Allegri
V. M. Buonarroti

Giotto's Bell Tower.

Marcovaldo drew sketches for an over 7.8m-high (26-ft.) "Christ in Judgment" and a "Last Judgment" that fills over a third of the ceiling. Bring binoculars if you want a closer look.

Piazza San Giovanni. www.ilgrandemuseodelduomo.it. ✆ **055-230-2885.** 15€ Grande Museo del Duomo ticket. Mon–Sat 8:15–10:15am and 11:15am–7:30pm; Sun (and 1st Sat of month) 8:30am–1:30pm. Bus: C2.

Campanile di Giotto (Giotto's Bell Tower) ★★ ARCHITECTURE In 1334, Giotto started the cathedral bell tower but completed only the first two levels before his death in 1337. He was out of his league with the engineering aspects of architecture, and the tower was saved from falling by Andrea Pisano, who doubled the thickness of the walls. Pisano also changed the design to add statue niches—he even carved a few of the statues himself—before quitting the project in 1348. Francesco Talenti finished the job between 1350 and 1359. The **reliefs** and **statues** in the lower levels—by Andrea Pisano, Donatello, Luca della Robbia, and others—are all copies; the weatherworn originals are housed in the Museo dell'Opera (see below). We recommend climbing the 414 steps to the top; the **view ★★** is memorable as you ascend, and offers the best close-up of Brunelleschi's dome in the entire city.

Piazza del Duomo. www.ilgrandemuseodelduomo.it. ✆ **055-230-2885.** 15€ Grande Museo del Duomo ticket. Daily 8:15am–6:30pm. Bus: C2, 14, 23.

Duomo (Cattedrale di Santa Maria del Fiore) ★★ CATHEDRAL By the late 13th century, Florence was feeling peevish: Its archrivals Siena and Pisa sported flamboyant new cathedrals while it was saddled with the tiny 5th- or 6th-century cathedral of Santa Reparata. So, in 1296, the city hired Arnolfo di Cambio to design a new Duomo, and he raised the facade and the first few bays before his death (around 1310). Work continued under the auspices of the Wool Guild and architects Giotto di Bondone (who concentrated on the bell tower) and Francesco Talenti (who expanded the planned size and finished up to the drum of the dome). The facade we see today is a neo-Gothic composite designed by Emilio de Fabris and built from 1871 to 1887.

The Duomo's most distinctive feature, however, is its enormous **dome ★★★** (or *cupola*), which dominates the skyline and is a symbol of Florence itself. The raising of this dome, the largest in the world in its

A MAN & HIS dome

Filippo Brunelleschi, a diminutive man whose ego was as big as his talent, managed in his arrogant, quixotic, and brilliant way to invent Renaissance architecture. Having been beaten by Lorenzo Ghiberti in the contest to cast the **Baptistery** doors (see p. 170), Brunelleschi resolved that he would rather be the top architect than the second-best sculptor and took off for Rome to study the buildings of the ancients. On returning to Florence, he combined subdued gray *pietra serena* stone with smooth white plaster to create airy arches, vaults, and arcades of perfect classical proportions, in his own variant on the ancient Roman orders of architecture. He designed **Santo Spirito,** the elegant **Ospedale degli Innocenti,** a chapel at **Santa Croce,** and a new sacristy for **San Lorenzo,** but his greatest achievement was erecting the dome over Florence's cathedral.

The Duomo—at that time the world's largest church—had already been built, but nobody had figured out how to cover the daunting space over its center without spending a fortune. No one was even sure whether they could create a dome that would hold up under its own weight. Brunelleschi insisted he knew how, and once granted the commission, revealed his ingenious plan, which may have been inspired by close study of Rome's **Pantheon** (p. 100).

He built the dome in two shells, the inner one thicker than the outer, both shells thinning as they neared the top, thus leaving the center hollow and removing a good deal of the weight. He also planned to construct the dome of giant vaults with ribs crossing them, and dovetailed the stones making up the actual fabric of the dome. In this way, the walls of the dome would support themselves as they were erected. In the process of building, Brunelleschi found himself as much an engineer as architect, constantly designing winches and hoists to carry the materials (plus food and drink) faster and more efficiently up to the level of the workmen.

His finished work speaks for itself, 45m (148 ft.) wide at the base and 90m (295 ft.) high from drum to lantern. For his achievement, Brunelleschi was accorded the honor of a burial inside Florence's cathedral.

time, was no mean architectural feat, tackled by Filippo Brunelleschi between 1420 and 1436 (see "A Man & His Dome," below). You can climb up between its two shells for one of the classic panoramas across the city—something that is not recommended for claustrophobes or anyone with no head for heights. Booking a time slot to climb the dome is now **compulsory:** Queues can be extremely long.

The cathedral is rather spartan inside, though check out the optical-illusion equestrian "statue" of English mercenary soldier Sir John Hawkwood on the north wall, painted in 1436 by Paolo Uccello.

Piazza del Duomo. www.ilgrandemuseodelduomo.it. ✆ **055-230-2885.** Church free; Santa Reparata and cupola with 15€ Grande Museo del Duomo ticket. Church Mon–Wed and Fri 10am–5pm; Thurs 10am–4:30pm; Sat 10am–4:45pm; Sun 1:30–4:45pm. Cupola Mon–Fri 8:15am–7pm; Sat 8:15am–5:40pm; Sun 1–4pm. Bus: C1 or C2.

Museo dell'Opera del Duomo (Cathedral Works Museum) ★★

ART MUSEUM Florence's Cathedral Museum reopened in 2015

after a major overhaul, now with double the space to show off what is Italy's second-largest collection of devotional art after the Vatican Museums (p. 78). The site itself is significant: It once housed the workshop where Michelangelo sculpted his statue of "David." The museum's prize exhibit is the centerpiece: The original **Gates of Paradise ★★★** cast by Lorenzo Ghiberti in the early 1400s (see "Baptistery," p. 170). You can see them in a lifesize re-creation of their original space on the piazza, and read from interpretation panels that explain their Old Testament scenes. Ghiberti's Baptistery **North Doors ★★** have also been moved inside (and will be joined in the future by Pisano's South Doors).

Also here is a Michelangelo **"Pietà" ★★** that nearly wasn't. Early in the process he had told students that he wanted this "Pietà" to stand at his tomb, but when he found an imperfection in the marble, he began attacking it with a hammer (look at Christ's left arm). The master never returned to the work, but his students later repaired the damage. The figure of Nicodemus was untouched—legend has it, because it was a self-portrait of the artist—a Michelangelo myth that, for once, is probably true. Elsewhere are works by Donatello—including his restored **"Magdalen" ★**—Andrea del Verrocchio, and Luca della Robbia.

Piazza del Duomo 9 (behind cathedral). www.ilgrandemuseodelduomo.it. ✆ **055-230-2885.** 15€ Grande Museo del Duomo ticket. Daily 9am–7:30pm. Closed 1st Tues of month. Bus: C1.

Around Piazza della Signoria & Santa Trínita

Galleria degli Uffizi (Uffizi Gallery) ★★★ ART MUSEUM There is no collection of Renaissance art on the planet that can match the Uffizi. Period. For all its crowds and other inconveniences, the Uffizi remains a must-see. And what will you see? Some 60-plus rooms and marble corridors—built in the 16th century as the Medici's private offices, or *uffici*—all packed with famous paintings, among them Giotto's "Ognissanti Madonna," Botticelli's "Birth of Venus," Leonardo da Vinci's "Annunciation," Michelangelo's "Holy Family," and many, many more.

Start with **Room 2** for a look at the pre-Renaissance, Gothic style of painting. Compare teacher and student with Cimabue's "Santa Trínita Maestà," painted around 1280, and Giotto's **"Ognissanti Madonna" ★★★** done in 1310. The similar subject and setting for both paintings shows how Giotto transformed Cimabue's iconlike Byzantine style into something more human. Giotto's Madonna looks like she's sitting on a throne, her clothes emphasizing the curves of her body, whereas Cimabue's Madonna and angels float in space, like portraits on coins, with stiff positioning. Also worth a look-see: Duccio's **"Rucellai Madonna" ★** (1285), a founding work of the ethereal Sienese School of painting.

Room 3 showcases the Sienese School at its peak, with Simone Martini's dazzling **"Annunciation" ★★** (1333) and Ambrogio Lorenzetti's "Presentation at the Temple" (1342). The Black Death of 1348 wiped out this entire generation of Sienese painters, and most of that city's population along with them. **Room 7** shows Florentine painting at its most decorative, in a style known as "International Gothic." The iconic work is Gentile da Fabriano's **"Procession of the Magi" ★★★** (1423). The line to see the newborn Jesus is full of decorative and comic elements, and is even longer than the one waiting outside the Uffizi.

Room 8 displays works by **Filippo Lippi** from the mid–15th century. His most celebrated, **"Madonna and Child with Two Angels" ★★**, dates from around 1465. The background, with distant mountains on one side and water on the other, framing the portrait of a woman's face, was shamelessly stolen by Leonardo da Vinci 40 years later for his "Mona Lisa." Lippi's work was also a celebrity scandal. The woman who modeled for Mary was said to be Filippo's lover—a would-be nun called Lucrezia Buti whom he had spirited away from a convent before she took vows—and the child looking toward the viewer the product of their union. That son, Filippino Lippi, became a painter in his own right, and some of his works hang in the same room. However, it was Filippo's student (who would, in turn, become Filippino's teacher) who would go on to become one of the most famous artists of the 15th century. His name was Botticelli.

The unflattering profiles of the Duke Federico da Montefeltro of Urbino and his duchess, done by **Piero della Francesca** around 1465, were recently moved to a new home in **Room 9.** The subjects are portrayed in a starkly realistic way—the duke exposes his warts and his crooked nose, which was broken in a tournament. This focus on earthly, rather than Christian, elements recalls the secular teachings of Greek and Roman times, and is made all the more vivid by depiction (on the back) of the couple riding chariots driven by the humanistic virtues of faith, charity, hope, and modesty (for her) and prudence, temperance, fortitude, and justice (for him).

A major renovation completed in late 2016 split **Rooms 10 to 14** into two separate spaces (despite the numbering, this had been one room since 1978). The entire area remains devoted to the works of Sandro Filipepi, better known by his nickname "Little Barrels," or Botticelli. Botticelli's 1485 **"Birth of Venus" ★★** hangs like a billboard you have seen a thousand times. Venus's pose is taken from classical statues, while the winds Zephyr and Aura blowing her to shore, and the muse welcoming her are from Ovid's "Metamorphosis." Botticelli's 1478 **"Primavera" ★★★**, its dark, bold colors a stark contrast to filmy, pastel "Venus," defies definitive interpretation. But again it features Venus (center), alongside Mercury, with the winged boots, the Three Graces, and the goddess Flora. Botticelli's "Adoration of the Magi" contains a self-portrait of the artist. He's the one in yellow on the far right.

Leonardo da Vinci's **"Annunciation" ★★★** anchors **Room 15.** In this painting, though completed in the early 1470s while Leonardo was still a student in Verrocchio's workshop, da Vinci's ability to orchestrate the viewer's focus is already masterful: The line down the middle of the brick corner of the house draws your glance to Mary's delicate fingers, which themselves point along the top of a stone wall to the angel's two raised fingers. Those, in turn, draw attention to the mountain in the center of the two parallel trees dividing Mary from the angel, representing the gulf between the worldly and the spiritual. Its unusual perspective was painted to be viewed from the lower right.

As soon as you cross to the Uffizi's west wing—past picture windows with views of the Arno River to one side and the perfect, Renaissance perspective of the Uffizi piazza to the other—you're walloped with another line of masterpieces. Among the highlights of this "second half" is Michelangelo's 1505–08 **"Holy Family"** ★. The twisting shapes of Mary, Joseph, and Jesus recall those in the Sistine Chapel in Rome for their sculpted nature and the bright colors. The torsion and tensions of the painting (and other Michelangelo works) inspired the next generation of Florentine painters, known as the **Mannerists.** Andrea Del Sarto, Rosso Fiorentino, and Pontormo are all represented in the revamped **Sale Rosse (Red Rooms)** downstairs. Here too, the Uffizi has a number of Raphaels, including his often-copied **"Madonna of the Goldfinch"** ★★ (Room 66), with a background landscape lifted from Leonardo and Botticelli.

Titian's reclining nude **"Venus of Urbino"** ★★ (Room 83) is another highlight of the later works. It's no coincidence that the edge of the curtain, the angle of her hand and leg, and the line splitting floor and bed all intersect at the forbidden part of her body. The **Sale Gialle (Yellow Rooms)** feature paintings by Caravaggio, notably an enigmatic **"Bacchus"** ★, and many by the 17th- to 18th-century *caravaggieschi* artists who aped his *chiaroscuro* (bright light and dark shadows) style. Greatest among them was Artemisia Gentileschi, a rare female painter from this period. Her **"Judith Slaying Holofernes"** ★ (ca. 1612) is one of the bloodiest paintings in the gallery, and shares Room 90 with Caravaggio.

Rooms 46 to 55 showcase the works of foreign painters in the Uffizi. The best among the so-called **Sale Blu (Blue Rooms)** is the Spanish gallery, with works by Goya, El Greco's "Sts. John the Evangelist and Francis" (1600), and Velázquez's **"Self-Portrait"** ★. **Room 49** displays some of Rembrandt's most familiar portraits and self-portraits.

If you find yourself flagging at any point (it happens to us all), there is a **coffee shop** at the far end of the west wing. Prices are in line with the piazza below, plus you get a great close-up of the Palazzo Vecchio's facade from the terrace. Fully refreshed, you can return to discover works by the many great artists we haven't space to cover here: Cranach and Dürer; Giorgione, Bellini, and Mantegna; and Uccello, Masaccio, Bronzino, and Veronese. There are original Roman statues and friezes,

too, notably in a room dedicated to the Medici garden at San Marco. In short, there is nowhere like the Uffizi anywhere in Italy, or the world.
Piazzale degli Uffizi 6 (off Piazza della Signoria). ✆ **055-23885.** (Reserve tickets at www.firenzemusei.it or ✆ 055-294-883.) 8€ (12.50€ during a temporary exhibition). Tues–Sun 8:15am–6:50pm. Bus: C1 or C2.

Museo Nazionale del Bargello (Bargello Museum) ★★
MUSEUM This is the most important museum anywhere for Renaissance **sculpture**—and often inexplicably quieter than other museums in the city. In a far cry from its original use as the city's prison, torture chamber, and execution site, the Bargello now stands as a three-story art museum containing some of the best works of Michelangelo, Donatello, and Ghiberti, as well as of their most successful Mannerist successor, Giambologna.

In the ground-level Michelangelo room, you'll witness the variety of his craft, from a whimsical 1497 **"Bacchus" ★★** to a severe, unfinished "Brutus" of 1539. "Bacchus," created when Michelangelo was just 22, genuinely looks drunk, leaning back a little too far, his head off kilter, with a cupid about to bump him over. Nearby is Giambologna's twisting **"Mercury" ★**, about to take off, propelled by the breath of Zephyr.

Upstairs an enormous vaulted hall is filled with some of Donatello's most accomplished sculptures, including his original "Marzocco" (from outside the Palazzo Vecchio; p. 183), and **"St. George" ★**, from a niche on the outside of Orsanmichele. Notable among them is his bronze **"David" ★★** (which some think might actually be a "Mercury"), done in 1440, the first freestanding nude sculpture since Roman times. The classical detail of these sculptures, as well as their naturalistic poses and reflective mood, is the essence of the Renaissance style.

Advance Reservations for the Uffizi, Accademia & More

If you're not buying a cumulative ticket (see "Discount Tickets for the City," p. 171), you should bypass the hours-long line at the Uffizi by reserving a ticket and an entry time in advance. The easiest way is through **Firenze Musei** (✆ **055-294-883** Mon–Fri 8:30am–6:30pm, Sat until 12:30pm) at **www.firenzemusei.it**. You should also reserve for the Accademia (another interminable line, to see "David"). It's possible, but usually not necessary, for the Galleria Palatina in the Pitti Palace, the Bargello, and several others, too. There's a 3€ fee (4€ for the Uffizi or Accademia, where a reservation is very strongly advised); you can pay by credit card. You can also reserve in person, in Florence, at a kiosk in the facade of Orsanmichele, on Via dei Calzaiuoli (Mon–Sat); or at a desk inside the bookshop **Libreria My Accademia,** Via Ricasoli 105R (✆ **055-288-310**), almost opposite the museum (open Tues–Sun). You can reserve, for the Uffizi only, at the Uffizi itself; do so at the teller window inside entrance number 2. The Uffizi's ticket collection point is across the piazza, at entrance number 3.

Interior courtyard of the Uffizi Gallery.

Side by side on the back wall are the contest entries submitted by Ghiberti and Brunelleschi for the commission to do the Baptistery doors in 1401. With the "Sacrifice of Isaac" as their biblical theme, both displayed innovative use of perspective. Ghiberti won the contest, perhaps because his scene is more thematically unified. Brunelleschi could have ended up a footnote in the art history books, but instead he gave up the chisel and turned his attentions to architecture instead, which turned out to be a wise move (see "A Man & His Dome," p. 175).

Via del Proconsolo 4. ✆ **055-238-8606.** 4€ (8€ during temporary exhibitions; free 1st Sun of month). Daily 8:15am–1:50pm (until 5pm during exhibitions). Closed 1st, 3rd, and 5th Mon, and 2nd and 4th Sun of each month. Bus: C1 or C2.

Orsanmichele ★★ CHURCH/ARCHITECTURE This bulky structure halfway down Via dei Calzaiuoli looks more like a Gothic warehouse than a church—which is exactly what it was, built as a granary and grain market in 1337. After a miraculous image of the Madonna appeared on a column inside, the lower level was turned into a shrine and chapel. The city's merchant guilds each undertook the task of decorating one of the outside Gothic tabernacles around the lower level with a statue of their guild's patron saint. Masters such as Ghiberti, Donatello, Verrocchio, and Giambologna all cast or carved masterpieces to set here (those remaining are mostly copies, including Donatello's "St. George").

In the dark interior, an elaborate Gothic stone **Tabernacle ★** (1349–59) by Andrea Orcagna protects a luminous 1348 "Madonna and

PIAZZA DELLA signoria

When the medieval Guelph party came out on top after a long political struggle with the Ghibellines, they razed part of the old city center to build a new palace for civic government. It's reputed that the Guelphs ordered architect Arnolfo di Cambio to build what we now call the **Palazzo Vecchio** (see p. 183) in the corner of this space but to be sure that not an inch of the building sat on cursed former Ghibelline land. This odd legend was probably fabricated to explain Arnolfo's quirky off-center architecture.

The space around the *palazzo* became the new civic center of town, L-shaped **Piazza della Signoria ★★**, named after the oligarchic ruling body of the medieval city (the "Signoria"). Today, it's an outdoor sculpture gallery, teeming with tourists, postcard stands, horses and buggies, and expensive outdoor cafes. If you want to catch the square at its serene best, come by 8am.

The statuary on the piazza is particularly beautiful, starting on the far left (as you're facing the Palazzo Vecchio) with Giambologna's equestrian statue of "Grand Duke Cosimo I" (1594). To its right is one of Florence's favorite sculptures to hate, the **"Fontana del Nettuno"** ("Neptune Fountain"; 1560–75), created by Bartolomeo Ammannati as a tribute to Cosimo I's naval ambitions but nicknamed by the Florentines "Il Biancone," or "Big Whitey." The **porphyry plaque** set in the ground in front of the fountain marks the site where puritanical monk Savonarola held the Bonfire of the Vanities: With fiery apocalyptic preaching, he whipped Florentines into a frenzy, and hundreds filed into this piazza, arms loaded with paintings, clothing, and other effects that represented their "decadence." They threw it all onto the flames.

To the right of Neptune is a long, raised platform fronting the Palazzo Vecchio known as the *arringheria,* from which soapbox speakers would lecture to crowds (we get our word "harangue" from this). On its far left corner is a copy (original in the Bargello) of Donatello's **"Marzocco,"** symbol of the city, with a Florentine lion resting his raised paw on a shield emblazoned with the city's emblem, the *giglio* (lily). To its right is another Donatello replica, **"Judith Beheading Holofernes."** Farther down is a man who needs little introduction, Michelangelo's **"David,"** a 19th-century copy of the original now in the Accademia. Near enough to David to look truly ugly in comparison is Baccio Bandinelli's **"Hercules and Cacus"** (1534). Poor Bandinelli was trying to copy Michelangelo's muscular male form but ended up making his Hercules merely lumpy.

At the piazza's south end is one of the square's earliest and prettiest embellishments, the **Loggia dei Lanzi ★★** (1376–82), named after the Swiss guard of lancers *(lanzi)* whom Cosimo de' Medici stationed here. The airy loggia was probably built on a design by Andrea Orcagna, spawning another of its many names, the Loggia di Orcagna (yet another is the Loggia della Signoria). At the front left stands Benvenuto Cellini's masterpiece in bronze, **"Perseus" ★★★** (1545), holding out the severed head of Medusa. On the far right is Giambologna's **"Rape of the Sabines" ★★**, one of the most successful Mannerist sculptures in existence, and a piece you must walk all the way around to appreciate, catching the action and artistry of its spiral design from different angles. Talk about moving it indoors, safe from the elements, continues . . . but for now, it's still here.

Orsanmichele church with older icon of the "Madonna and Child" by Bernardo Daddi.

Child" painted by Giotto's student Bernardo Daddi, to which miracles were ascribed during the Black Death of 1348–50.

Tip: Most Mondays (10am–5pm) you can access the upper floors, which house many of the original sculptures that once adorned Orsanmichele's exterior niches. Among the treasures of this so-called **Museo di Orsanmichele ★** are a trio of bronzes: Ghiberti's "St. John the Baptist" (1412–16), the first life-size bronze of the Renaissance; Verrocchio's "Incredulity of St. Thomas" (1483); and Giambologna's "St. Luke" (1602). Climb up one floor further, to the top, for an unforgettable 360° **panorama ★★** of the city.

Via Arte della Lana 1. ✆ **055-210-305.** Free, donations accepted. Daily 10am–5pm. Bus: C2.

Palazzo Davanzati ★★ PALACE/MUSEUM One of the best-preserved 14th-century palaces in the city offers a glimpse into domestic life during the medieval and Renaissance period. It was originally built for the Davizzi family in the mid-1300s, then bought by the Davanzati clan; the latter's family tree, dating back to the 1100s, is emblazoned on the wall of the ground-floor courtyard. The palace's painted wooden ceilings and murals have aged well (even surviving World War II damage), but the emphasis remains not on the decor, but on providing visitors with insights into medieval life for a noble Florentine family: feasts and festivities in the **Sala Madornale;** a private, internal well to secure water supply when things in Florence got sticky; and magnificent bedchamber frescoes from the 1350s, which recount, comic-strip style, "The Chatelaine of Vergy," a 13th-century morality tale. An interesting footnote:

In 1916, a New York auction of furnishings from this very same palace launched a "Florentine style" trend in U.S. interior design circles.
Via Porta Rossa 13. ✆ **055-238-8610.** 2€. Daily 8:15am–1:50pm. Closed 2nd and 4th Sun, and 1st, 3rd, and 5th Mon of each month. Bus: C2.

Palazzo Vecchio ★★ PALACE The core of Florence's fortresslike town hall was built from 1299 to 1302 to the designs of Arnolfo di Cambio, Gothic master builder. The palace was home to the various Florentine governments (and home today to the city government). When Duke Cosimo I and his Medici family moved to the *palazzo* in 1540, they redecorated: Michelozzo's 1453 **courtyard ★** was left architecturally intact but frescoed by Vasari with scenes of Austrian cities, to celebrate the 1565 marriage of Francesco I de' Medici and Joanna of Austria.

A grand staircase leads up to the **Sala dei Cinquecento ★**, named for the 500-man assembly that met here in the pre-Medici days of the Florentine Republic. It's also the site of the greatest fresco cycle that ever wasn't. Leonardo da Vinci was commissioned in 1503–05 to paint one long wall with a battle scene celebrating Florence's victory at the 1440 Battle of Anghiari. Always trying new methods and materials, he decided to mix wax into his pigments. Leonardo had finished painting part of the wall, but it wasn't drying fast enough, so he brought in braziers stoked with hot coals to try to hurry the process. As onlookers watched in horror, the wax in the fresco melted under the heat and colors ran down the walls to puddle on the floor. The search for what remains of his work continues; some hope was provided in 2012 with the discovery of pigments similar to those used by Leonardo in a cavity behind the current wall.

Michelangelo was supposed to paint a fresco on the opposite wall, but he never got past the preparatory drawings before Pope Julius II called him to Rome to paint the Sistine Chapel. Vasari and his assistants covered the bare walls from 1563 to 1565, with subservient frescoes exalting Cosimo I and the military victories of his regime, against Pisa (on the near wall) and Siena (far wall). Opposite the door you enter is Michelangelo's statue of **"Victory" ★**, carved from 1533 to 1534 for Pope Julius II's tomb but later donated to the Medici.

The first series of rooms on the upper floor is the **Quartiere degli Elementi,** frescoed with allegories and mythological characters, again by Vasari. Crossing the balcony overlooking the Sala dei Cinquecento, you enter the **Apartments of Eleonora di Toledo ★**, decorated for Cosimo's Spanish wife. Her **private chapel ★★★** is a masterpiece of mid–16th-century fresco painting by Bronzino. Under the coffered ceiling of the **Sala dei Gigli** is Ghirlandaio's fresco of "St. Zenobius Enthroned," with figures from Republican and Imperial Rome, and Donatello's original **"Judith and Holofernes" ★** bronze (1455), one of his last works. In the palace basement are the **Scavi del Teatro Romano ★**, the remnants of Roman Florentia's theater, upon which the medieval palace was built, with remains of the walls and an intact paved street.

Vasari's Corridor

The enclosed passageway that runs along the top of the Ponte Vecchio is part of the **Corridoio Vasariano (Vasari Corridor) ★**, a private elevated link between the Palazzo Vecchio and Palazzo Pitti, and now hung with the world's best collection of artists' self-portraits. Duke Cosimo I found the idea of mixing with the hoi polloi on his way to work distressing—and assassination was a real danger—so he commissioned Vasari to design his V.I.P. route in 1565. Walking the corridor is often possible, although it is now scheduled to remain closed until June 2018. Inquire at the tourist office for the latest news.

The Vasari Corridor along the banks of the Arno.

Visitors can also climb the **Torre di Arnolfo ★★**, the palace's crenellated tower. If you can bear small spaces and 218 steps, the views from the top of this medieval skyscraper are sublime. The 95m (312-ft.) Torre is closed during bad weather; the minimum age to climb it is 6, and children ages 17 and under must be accompanied by an adult.

Piazza della Signoria. www.museicivicifiorentini.comune.fi.it. ✆ **055-276-8325.** Palazzo or Torre 10€; admission to both, or to Palazzo plus Scavi 14€; admission to all 18€. Palazzo/Scavi: Fri–Wed 9am–7pm (Apr–Sept until 11pm); Thurs 9am–2pm. Torre: Fri–Wed 10am–5pm (Apr–Sept 10am–9pm); Thurs 10am–2pm. Bus: C1 or C2.

Ponte Vecchio ★ ARCHITECTURE The oldest and most famous bridge across the Arno, the Ponte Vecchio was built in 1345 by Taddeo Gaddi to replace an earlier version. Overhanging shops have lined the bridge since at least the 12th century. In the 16th century, it was home to butchers, until Duke Ferdinand I moved into the Palazzo Pitti across the river. He couldn't stand the stench, so he evicted the meat cutters and moved in gold- and silversmiths, and jewelers, who occupy it to this day.

The Ponte Vecchio's fame saved it in 1944 from the Nazis, who had orders to blow up all the bridges before retreating out of Florence as

The Ponte Vecchio spans the River Arno.

Allied forces advanced. They couldn't bring themselves to reduce this span to rubble, so they blew up the ancient buildings on either end instead to block it off. Not so discriminating was the **Great Arno Flood** of 1966, which severely damaged the shops. A private night watchman saw waters rising alarmingly and called many of the goldsmiths at home. They rushed to remove their valuable stock before it was washed away. Via Por Santa Maria/Via Guicciardini. Bus: C3 or D.

Santa Trínita ★★ CHURCH Beyond Bernardo Buontalenti's late-16th-century **facade** lies a dark church, rebuilt in the 14th century but founded by the Vallombrosans sometime before 1177. The third chapel on the right has what remains of detached frescoes by Spinello Aretino, found under Lorenzo Monaco's 1424 "Scenes from the Life of the Virgin" frescoes covering the next chapel along. In the right transept, Ghirlandaio frescoed the **Cappella Sassetti ★** in 1483 with a cycle on the "Life of St. Francis," but he set all the scenes against Florentine backdrops and peopled them with portraits of contemporary notables. His "Francis Receiving the Order from Pope Honorius" (in the lunette) takes place under an arcade on the north side of Piazza della Signoria. You'll recognize the Loggia dei Lanzi in the middle, and on the left, the Palazzo Vecchio (the Uffizi now between them hadn't been built yet).

The south end of the piazza leads to the **Ponte Santa Trínita ★★**, Florence's most graceful bridge. In 1567, Ammannati built a span here that was set with four 16th-century statues of the seasons, in honor of the marriage of Cosimo II. After the Nazis blew up the bridge in 1944, it was rebuilt, and all was set into place—save the head on the statue of Spring, which remained lost until a team dredging the river in 1961 found it by accident. If you want to photograph the Ponte Vecchio, head here at dusk.

Catch an Exhibition at the Strozzi

The Renaissance **Palazzo Strozzi ★★**, Piazza Strozzi (www.palazzostrozzi.org; ✆ **055-264-5155**), and basement **Strozzina** are Florence's major spaces for temporary and contemporary art shows, and have been experiencing a 21st-century renaissance of their own. Hits of recent years have included 2012's "Americans in Florence: Sargent and the New World Impressionists" and Bill Viola's "Electronic Renaissance" in 2017. There's always plenty going on including talks, late-night events, late-night openings (usually Thurs), and discovery trails aimed at 5- to 9-year-olds. Check the website for the latest exhibition news.

Piazza Santa Trínita. ✆ **055-216-912.** Free. Mon–Sat 8:30am–noon and 4–6pm; Sun 8:30–10:45am and 4–6pm. Bus: C3, D, 6, 11.

Around San Lorenzo & the Mercato Centrale

Until the market's controversial—and *perhaps* temporary—move in 2014, the church of San Lorenzo was lost behind the leather stalls and souvenir carts of Florence's vast **San Lorenzo street market** (see "Shopping," later in this chapter). In fact, a bustle of commerce characterizes the whole neighborhood, centered on both the tourist market and the nearby **Mercato Centrale**, whose upper floor became a must-see foodie destination when it opened in 2014 (see p. 213).

Cappelle Medicee (Medici Chapels) ★ MONUMENT/MEMORIAL When Michelangelo built the New Sacristy between 1520 and 1533 (finished by Vasari in 1556), it was to be a tasteful monument to Lorenzo the Magnificent and his generation of relatively pleasant Medici. When work got underway on the adjacent **Cappella dei Principi (Chapel of the Princes)** in 1604, it was to become one of Italy's most god-awful and arrogant memorials, dedicated to the grand dukes, whose ranks include some of Florence's most decrepit tyrants. Fittingly, the Cappella dei Principi is an exercise in bad taste, a mountain of cut marbles and semiprecious stones—jasper, alabaster, mother-of-pearl, agate, and the like—slathered onto the walls and ceiling with no regard for composition and still less for chromatic unity. The pouring of ducal funds into this monstrosity lasted until the rarely conscious Gian Gastone de' Medici drank himself to death in 1737, without an heir. Teams kept doggedly at the thing, and they were still finishing the floor in 1962. Judge for yourself.

Michelangelo's **Sagrestia Nuova (New Sacristy) ★★**, built to jibe with Brunelleschi's Old Sacristy in San Lorenzo proper (see below), is much calmer. (An architectural tidbit: The windows in the dome taper as they get near the top to fool you into thinking the dome is higher.) Michelangelo was supposed to produce three tombs here (perhaps four) but ironically got only the two less important ones done. So, Lorenzo de' Medici ("the Magnificent")—wise ruler of his city, poet of note, grand patron of the arts, and moneybags behind much of the Renaissance—ended up with a mere inscription of his name next to his brother Giuliano's on a plain marble slab against the entrance wall. They did get one genuine Michelangelo sculpture to decorate their slab, an unfinished **"Madonna and Child" ★**.

On the left wall of the sacristy is Michelangelo's **"Tomb of Lorenzo" ★**, duke of Urbino (and Lorenzo the Magnificent's grandson), whose seated statue symbolizes the contemplative life. Below him on the curves of the tomb stretch "Dawn" (female) and "Dusk" (male), a pair of Michelangelo's most famous sculptures. This pair mirrors "Day" (male) and "Night" (female) across the way. Observing "Dawn" and "Night" suggests that Michelangelo perhaps hadn't seen too many naked women.

Piazza Madonna degli Aldobrandini (behind San Lorenzo, where Via Faenza and Via del Giglio meet). ✆ **055-238-8602.** 6€ (9€ during temporary exhibitions; free 1st Sun of month). Daily 8:15am–1:50pm. Closed 1st, 3rd, and 5th Mon, and 2nd and 4th Sun of each month. Bus: C1, C2, 22.

Palazzo Medici-Riccardi ★ PALACE Built by Michelozzo in 1444 for Medici "godfather" Cosimo il Vecchio, this is the prototype Florentine *palazzo,* on which the more overbearing Strozzi and Pitti palaces were later modeled. It remained the Medici private home until Cosimo I officially declared his power as duke by moving to the city's civic nerve center, the Palazzo Vecchio. A door off the courtyard leads up a staircase to the **Cappella dei Magi,** the oldest chapel to survive from a private Florentine palace; its walls are covered with dense and colorful Benozzo Gozzoli **frescoes ★★** (1459–63), classics of the International Gothic style. The walls depict an extended "Journey of the Magi" to see the Christ child, who's being adored by Mary in the altarpiece.

Via Cavour 3. www.palazzo-medici.it. ✆ **055-276-0340.** 7€ adults (10€ during temporary exhibition), 4€ ages 6–12. Thurs–Tues 8:30am–7pm. Bus: C1, 14, 23.

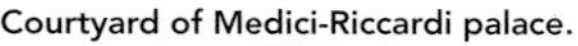

Courtyard of Medici-Riccardi palace.

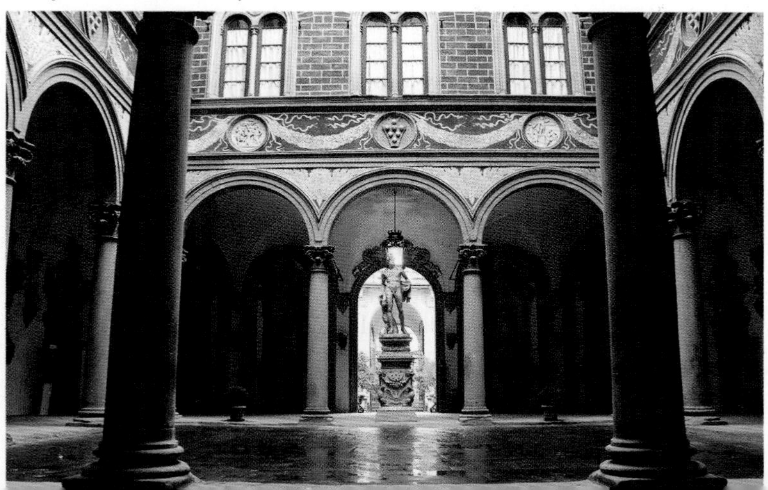

San Lorenzo ★ CHURCH A rough brick anti-facade fronts what is most likely the oldest church in Florence, founded in A.D. 393. It was later the Medici family's parish church, and Cosimo il Vecchio, whose wise behind-the-scenes rule made him popular with the Florentines, is buried in front of the high altar. The plaque marking the spot is inscribed pater patriae, "Father of the Homeland." Off the left transept, the **Sagrestia Vecchia (Old Sacristy) ★** is one of Brunelleschi's purest pieces of early Renaissance architecture. The focal sarcophagus contains Cosimo il Vecchio's parents, Giovanni di Bicci de' Medici and his wife, Piccarda Bueri. A side chapel is decorated with a star map showing the night sky above the city in the 1440s—a scene that also features, precisely, in Brunelleschi's Pazzi Chapel in Santa Croce. On the wall of the left aisle is Bronzino's huge fresco of the **"Martyrdom of San Lorenzo" ★**. The poor soul was roasted on a grill in Rome.

Piazza San Lorenzo. www.operamedicealaurenziana.org. ✆ **055-214-042.** Church 6€. Mon–Sat 10am–5pm; Mar–Oct also Sun 1:30–5pm. Bus: C1.

Near Piazza Santa Maria Novella

The two squat obelisks in **Piazza Santa Maria Novella ★**, resting on Giambologna tortoises, once served as turning posts for "chariot" races held here from the 16th to the mid–19th century. This former down-at-heel part of the center now has some of Florence's priciest hotels.

Museo Novecento ★ MUSEUM Inaugurated in 2014, this museum covers 20th-century Italian art in a multitude of media. Crowds are often sparse—let's face it, you're in Florence for the 1400s, not the 1900s. But that's no reflection on the quality of the collection, which spans 100 years of visual arts. Exhibits include works by major names such as De Chirico and Futurist Gino Severini, and closer examinations of Florence's role in fashion and Italy's relationship with European avant-garde art. Our favorite spot, though, is the top-floor **screening room ★★** where a 20-minute film-clip montage shows Florence as seen by a century of filmmakers, from Arnaldo Ginna's 1916 "Vita Futurista" to recent films such as "Room with a View" and "Tea with Mussolini."

Piazza Santa Maria Novella 10. www.museonovecento.it/en. ✆ **055-286-132.** 8.50€. Apr–Sept daily 11am–8pm (closes 2pm Thurs, 11pm Fri); Oct–Mar daily 11am–7pm (closes 2pm Thurs). Bus: 6 or 11.

Santa Maria Novella ★★ CHURCH Of all Florence's major churches, the home of the Dominicans is the only one with an original **facade ★★** that matches the era of the church's greatest importance. The lower Romanesque half was started in the 1300s by architect Fra' Jacopo Talenti. Renaissance architect and theorist Leon Battista Alberti finished the facade, adding a classically inspired top that not only went seamlessly with the lower half but also created a Cartesian plane of perfect geometry. Inside, **Masaccio's "Trinità" ★★★** (ca. 1425) is the first painting ever to use linear mathematical perspective. Florentine citizens and artists flooded in to see the fresco when it was unveiled, many remarking in awe that it seemed to punch a hole back into space, creating a chapel out of a flat wall. Frescoed chapels by Filippino Lippi and others fill the **transept.**

The **Sanctuary ★** behind the main altar was frescoed after 1485 by Ghirlandaio with the help of his assistants and apprentices, probably including a young Michelangelo. The left wall is covered with a cycle on the "Life of the Virgin," and the right has a "Life of St. John the Baptist." The works are also snapshots of the era's fashions and personages, full of portraits of the Tornabuoni family who commissioned them.

For many years the church's frescoed cloisters were treated as a separate site; they have now been reunited, all now accessible on one admission ticket. (Although, confusingly, there are two separate entrances, through the church's garden and via the tourist office at the rear, on Piazza della Stazione.) The **Chiostro Verde (Green Cloister) ★★** was partly frescoed between 1431 and 1446 by Paolo Uccello, a Florentine painter who became increasingly obsessed with the mathematics behind perspective. His Old Testament scenes include a "Universal Deluge," which ironically was badly damaged by the Great Arno Flood of 1966. Off the cloister, the **Spanish Chapel ★** is a complex piece of Dominican propaganda, frescoed in the 1360s by Andrea di Bonaiuto. The **Chiostro dei Morti (Cloister of the Dead) ★** is one of the oldest parts of the convent, and was another area badly damaged in 1966. Its low-slung vaults were decorated by Andrea Orcagna and others. From 2017, visitors have also been permitted access to the **Chiostro Grande** (Florence's largest cloister) and the papal apartments, frescoed by Florentine Mannerist Pontormo.

Piazza Santa Maria Novella/Piazza della Stazione 4. www.smn.it. ✆ **055-219-257.** 5€. Mon–Thurs 9am–5:30pm (Apr–Sept until 7pm); Fri 11am–5:30pm (Apr–Sept until 7pm); Sat 9am–5:30pm (July–Aug until 6:30pm); Sun 1–5:30pm (July–Aug noon–6:30pm). Bus: C2, 6, 11, 22.

Near San Marco & Santissima Annunziata

Cenacolo di Sant'Apollonia ★ ART MUSEUM Painter Andrea del Castagno (1421–57) learned his trade painting the portraits of condemned men in the city's prisons, and it's easy to see the influence of his apprenticeship on the faces of the Disciples in his version of **"The Last Supper,"** the first of many painted in Florence during the Renaissance. This giant fresco, completed around 1447, covers an

Seeing "David" Without a Reservation

The wait to get in to see "David" can be an hour or more if you didn't reserve ahead or buy a Firenze Card (p. 171). Try getting there before the museum opens in the morning or an hour or two before closing time.

entire wall at one end of the former convent refectory. Judas is banished to the other side of the communal table. Above Castagno's "Last Supper," his "Crucifixion," "Deposition," and "Entombment" complete the sequence.

Via XXVII Aprile 1. ✆ **055-238-8608.** Free. Daily 8:15am–1:50pm. Closed 1st, 3rd, and 5th Sat and Sun of each month. Bus: 1, 6, 11, 14, 17, 23.

Chiostro dello Scalzo ★ ARCHITECTURE You'll need luck to catch this place open, but it is well worth the short detour from San Marco if you do. Between 1509 and 1526 Mannerist painter Andrea del Sarto frescoed a cloister belonging to a religious fraternity dedicated to St. John the Baptist, who is the theme of an unusual monochrome (*grisaille*) fresco cycle. This place is usually blissfully empty, too.

Via Cavour 69. ✆ **055/238-8604.** Free. Mon, Thurs, 1st, 3rd, and 5th Sat, and 2nd and 4th Sun of each month 8:15am–1:50pm. Bus: 1 or 17.

Galleria dell'Accademia ★★ ART MUSEUM **"David"** ★★★—"Il Gigante"—is much larger than most people imagine, looming 4.8m (16 ft.) on top of a 1.8m (6-ft.) pedestal. He hasn't faded with time, either; the marble still gleams as if it were unveiling day in 1504. Viewing the statue is a pleasure in the bright and spacious room custom-designed for him after his move to the Accademia in 1873, following 300 years of pigeons perching on his head in Piazza della Signoria. Replicas now take the abuse there, and at Piazzale Michelangiolo. The spot high on the northern flank of the Duomo, for which he was originally commissioned, stands empty.

But the Accademia is not only about "David"; you will be delighted to discover he is surrounded by an entire museum stuffed with notable Renaissance works. Michelangelo's unfinished **"Prisoners"** ★★ statues are a contrast to "David," with their rough forms struggling to emerge from the raw stone. Michelangelo famously said that he tried to free the sculpture within from the block, and you can see this clearly here. Rooms showcase paintings by Perugino, Filippino Lippi, Giotto, Giovanna da Milano, Andrea Orcagna, and others.

Via Ricasoli 60. ✆ **055-238-8609.** (Prebook tickets at www.firenzemusei.it or ✆ 055-294-883.) 12.50€ (17€ during a temporary exhibition). Tues–Sun 8:15am–6:50pm. Bus: C1, 1, 6, 14, 19, 23, 31, 32.

Museo Archeologico (Archaeological Museum) ★ MUSEUM If you can force yourselves away from the Renaissance, rewind a millennium or two at one of the most important archaeological collections in central Italy, which has a particular emphasis on the **Etruscan** period. You will need a little patience, however: The collection is not easy to navigate, and exhibits have a habit of moving around, but you will easily find the **"Arezzo Chimera"** ★★, a bronze figure of a mythical lion–goat–serpent dating to the 4th century B.C. It is perhaps the most important bronze sculpture to survive from the Etruscan era, and at time of writing, it was displayed alongside the "Arringatore," a life-size bronze of an orator dating to the 1st century, just as Etruscan culture was being subsumed by Ancient Rome. On the top floor is the **"Idolino" ★**, an exquisite and slightly mysterious, lithe bronze. The collection is also strong on Etruscan-era *bucchero* pottery and funerary urns, and Egyptian relics that include several sarcophagi displayed in a series of eerie galleries. With other travelers so focused on medieval and Renaissance sights in the city, you may have the place almost to yourself.

Piazza Santissma Annunziata 9b. ✆ **055-23-575.** 4€ (free 1st Sun of month). Tues–Fri 8:30am–7pm; Sat–Mon 8:30am–2pm. Closed 2nd and 4th Sun of each month. Bus: 6, 19, 31, 32.

San Marco ★★★ ART MUSEUM We have never understood why this place is not constantly mobbed; perhaps because it showcases the work of Fra' Angelico, Dominican monk and Florentine painter in a style known as "International Gothic." This is the most important collection in the world of his altarpieces and painted panels, residing in the former 13th-century convent the artist-monk once called home. Seeing it all in one place allows you to appreciate how his decorative impulses and the sinuous lines of his figures place his work right on the cusp of the Renaissance. The most moving and unusual is his **"Annunciation" ★★★**, but a close second are the intimate frescoes of the life of Jesus—painted not on one giant wall, but scene by scene on the individual walls of small monks' cells that honeycomb the upper floor. The idea was that these scenes, painted by both Fra' Angelico and his assistants, would aid in the monks' prayer and contemplation. The final cell on the left corridor belonged to the firebrand preacher Savonarola, who briefly incited the populace of the most art-filled city in the world to burn their "decadent" paintings, illuminated manuscripts, and anything else he felt was a worldly betrayal of Jesus's ideals. (Ultimately, he ran afoul of the pope.) You'll see his notebooks, rosary, and what's left of the clothes he wore in his cell, as well as an anonymous panel painted to show the day in 1498 when he was burned at the stake in Piazza della Signoria. There is much more Fra' Angelico secreted around the cloisters, including a **"Crucifixion" ★** in the Chapter House. The former Hospice is now a gallery dedicated to Fra' Angelico and his contemporaries; look out especially for his **"Tabernacolo dei Linaioli" ★★** and a seemingly weightless **"Deposition" ★★**.

Piazza San Marco 3. ✆ **055-238-8608.** 4€. Mon–Fri 8:15am–1:50pm; Sat–Sun 8:15am–4:50pm. Closed 1st, 3rd, and 5th Sun and 2nd and 4th Mon of each month. Bus: C1, 1, 6, 7, 10, 11, 14, 17, 19, 20, 23, 25, 31, 32.

Santissima Annunziata ★ CHURCH In 1233, seven Florentine nobles had a spiritual crisis, gave away all their possessions, and retired to the forest to contemplate divinity. In 1250, they returned to what were then fields outside the city walls and founded a small oratory, proclaiming they were Servants of Mary (the "Servite Order"). Their oratory was enlarged by Michelozzo (1444–81) and later redesigned in the baroque style. The main art interest is the **Chiostro dei Voti (Votive Cloister),** designed by Michelozzo with Corinthian-style columns and decorated with some of the city's finest **Mannerist frescoes ★★** (1465–1515). Rosso Fiorentino provided an "Assumption" (1513) and Pontormo a "Visitation" (1515) just to the right of the door. Their master, Andrea del Sarto, contributed a "Birth of the Virgin" (1513), in the far-right corner, one of his finest works. To the right of the door into the church is a damaged but still fascinating "Coming of the Magi" (1514) by del Sarto, who included a self-portrait at the far right, looking out at us from under his blue hat.

In an excessively baroque **interior** is a huge tabernacle hidden under a mountain of *ex votos* (votive offerings). It was designed by Michelozzo to house a small painting of the "Annunciation." Legend holds that this painting was started by a friar who, vexed that he couldn't paint the Madonna's face as beautifully as it should be, gave up and took a nap. When he awoke, he found an angel had filled in the face for him.

On **Piazza Santissima Annunziata ★★** outside, flanked by elegant Brunelleschi porticos, is an equestrian statue of Grand Duke Ferdinand I by Giambologna. It was his last work, cast in 1608 after his death by his student Pietro Tacca, who also did the two fountains of fantastical mermonkey-monsters. The **Museo degli Innocenti ★** also reopened on the square in 2016, with a collection dedicated to one of the oldest child-focused institutions in Europe.

You can also stay right on this spectacular piazza, at one of our favorite Florence hotels, the **Loggiato dei Serviti** (p. 207).

Piazza Santissima Annunziata. ✆ **055-266-181.** Free. Cloister: daily 7:30am–12:30pm and 4–6:30pm. Church: daily 4–5:15pm. Bus: 6, 19, 31, 32.

Around Piazza Santa Croce

Piazza Santa Croce is pretty much like any grand Florentine square—an open space ringed with souvenir and leather shops and thronged with tourists. Once a year (during late June) it's covered with dirt and violent, Renaissance-style soccer is played on the piazza in the tournament known as **Calcio Storico Fiorentino.**

Santa Croce ★★ CHURCH The center of Florence's Franciscan universe was begun in 1294 by Gothic master Arnolfo di Cambio to rival the church of Santa Maria Novella being raised by the Dominicans across the city. The church wasn't consecrated until 1442, and even then it remained faceless until the neo-Gothic **facade** was added in 1857. This art-stuffed complex demands 2 hours of your time to see properly.

The Gothic **interior** is vast, and populated with the tombs of famous Florentines. Starting from the front door, immediately on the right is the tomb of the most venerated Renaissance master, **Michelangelo Buonarroti,** who died in Rome in 1564 at the ripe age of 89. The pope wanted him buried in the Eternal City, but Florentines managed to sneak his body back to Florence. Two berths along from Michelangelo's monument is a pompous 19th-century cenotaph to **Dante Alighieri,** one of history's great poets, whose "Divine Comedy" even laid the basis for the modern Italian language. (Exiled from Florence, Dante is buried in Ravenna—see p. 375.) Elsewhere are monuments to philosopher **Niccolò Machiavelli, Gioacchino Rossini** (1792–1868), composer of "The Barber of Seville," sculptor **Lorenzo Ghiberti,** and scientist **Galileo Galilei** (1564–1642).

The right transept is richly decorated with **frescoes.** The **Cappella Castellani** was frescoed with stories of saints' lives by Agnolo Gaddi. Agnolo's father, Taddeo Gaddi—one of Giotto's closest followers—painted the **Cappella Baroncelli ★** (1328–38) at the transept's end. The frescoes depict scenes from the "Life of the Virgin," and include an "Annunciation to the Shepherds," the first night scene in Italian fresco. Giotto himself frescoed the two chapels to the right of the high altar. Whitewashed over in the 17th century, they were uncovered in the 1800s and inexpertly restored. The **Cappella Peruzzi ★** is a late work with many references to antiquity, reflecting Giotto's trip to Rome's ruins. The more famous **Cappella Bardi ★★** appeared in the movie "A Room with a View"; key panels, featuring episodes in the life of St. Francis, include the "Trial by Fire Before the Sultan of Egypt" on the right wall; and, one of Giotto's best-known works, the "Death of St. Francis," in which monks weep and wail with convincing pathos.

Michelangelo's tomb in the church of Santa Croce.

Outside in the cloister is the **Cappella Pazzi ★,** one of Filippo Brunelleschi's architectural masterpieces (faithfully finished after his death in 1446). Giuliano da Maiano probably designed the porch that now fronts the chapel, set with glazed terracottas by Luca della Robbia. The chapel is one of Brunelleschi's signature pieces, decorated with his trademark *pietra serena* gray stone. It is the defining example of and model for early Renaissance architecture. Curiously, the ceiling of the smaller dome depicts the same night sky as the Old Sacristy in San Lorenzo (p. 188). In the church **Sacristy** is a Cimabue **"Crucifix"** ★ that was almost destroyed by the Arno Flood of 1966. It became an international symbol of the ruination wreaked that November day.

Piazza Santa Croce. www.santacroceopera.it. ✆ **055-246-6105.** 8€ adults, 6€ ages 11–17. Mon–Sat 9:30am–5pm; Sun 2–5pm. Bus: C1, C2, C3.

The Oltrarno, San Niccolò & San Frediano

Museo Zoologia "La Specola" ★ MUSEUM The wax anatomical models are one reason this museum may be the only one in Florence where kids eagerly drag their parents from room to room. Creepy collections of threadbare stuffed-animal specimens transition into rooms filled with lifelike human bodies suffering from dismemberments, flayings, and eviscerations. These wax models served as anatomical illustrations for medical students studying at this scientific institute from the 1770s. Grisly plague dioramas in the final room were created from wax in the early 1700s to satisfy the lurid tastes of Duke Cosimo III.

Via Romana 17. www.msn.unifi.it. ✆ **055-275-6444.** 6€ adults, 3€ children 6–14 and seniors 65 and over. June–Sept daily 10:30am–5:30pm; Oct–May Tues–Sun 9:30am–4:30pm. Bus: 11, 36, 37.

Palazzo Pitti (Pitti Palace) ★★ MUSEUM/PALACE Although built by and named after a rival of the Medici—the merchant Luca Pitti—in the 1450s, this gigantic *palazzo* soon came into Medici hands. It was the Medici family's principal home from the 1540s, and continued to house Florence's rulers until 1919. The Pitti contains five museums, including one of the world's best collections of canvases by Raphael. Out back are elegant Renaissance gardens, the **Boboli** (see below).

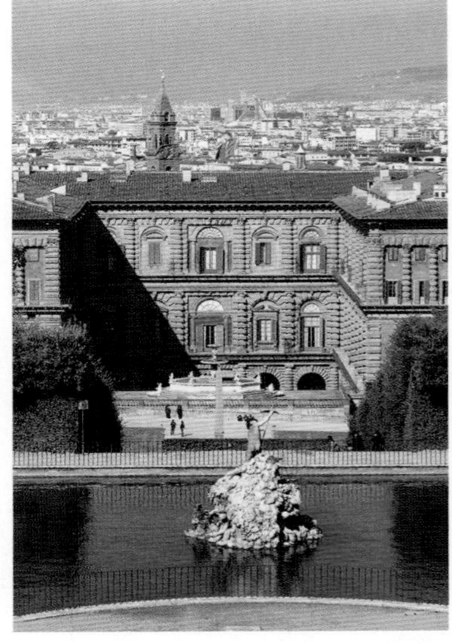
The Pitti Palace and Boboli Garden.

In the art-crammed rooms of the Pitti's **Galleria Palatina** ★★, paintings are displayed like cars in a parking garage, stacked on walls above each other in the "Enlightenment" method of exhibition. Rooms are alternately dimly lit, or garishly bright; this is how many of the world's great art treasures were seen and enjoyed by their original commissioners. You will find important historical treasures amid the Palatina's vast and haphazard collection; some of the best efforts of Titian, Raphael, and Rubens line the walls. Botticelli and Filippo Lippi's **"Madonna and Child"** ★ (1452) provide the key works in the **Sala di Prometeo (Prometheus Room).** Two giant versions of the "Assumption of the Virgin," both by Mannerist painter Andrea del Sarto, dominate the **Sala dell'Iliade (Iliad Room).** Here you will also find another Biblical woman painted by Artemisia Gentileschi, "Judith." The **Sala di Saturno (Saturn Room)** ★ is stuffed with Raphaels; in the **Sala di Giove (Jupiter Room)** you'll find his sublime, naturalistic portrait of **"La Velata"** ★★, as well as **"The Ages of Man"** ★. The current attribution of the painting is awarded to Venetian Giorgione, though that has been disputed.

At the **Appartamenti Reali (Royal Apartments)** you get a feeling for the conspicuous consumption of the Medici Grand Dukes, and their Austrian and Belgian Lorraine successors—and see some notable paintings in their original, ostentatious setting. Italy's first king lived here for several years during Italy's 19th-century unification process—when Florence was Italy's second capital, after Turin—until Rome was finally conquered and the court moved there. Much of the stucco, fabrics, furnishings, and general decoration is in thunderously poor taste, but you should look for Caravaggio's subtle canvas **"Knight of Malta"** ★.

The Pitti's "modern" gallery, the **Galleria d'Arte Moderna** ★, has a good collection, this time of 19th-century Italian paintings with a focus on Romanticism, Neoclassical works, and the **Macchiaioli**, a school of Italian painters who worked in an "impressionistic style" before the French Impressionists. If you have limited time, head straight for the major works of the latter, in Sala 18 through 20, which displays the Maremma landscapes of **Giovanni Fattori** ★ (1825–1908).

The Pitti's pair of lesser museums—the **Galleria del Costume** (Costume Gallery) and **Museo degli Argenti** (Museum of Silverware)—combine to show that wealth and taste do not always go hand in hand. One thing you will notice in the Costume Gallery is how much smaller locals were just a few centuries ago.

Piazza de' Pitti. Galleria Palatina, Appartamenti Reali, and Galleria d'Arte Moderna: ✆ **055-238-8614;** reserve tickets at www.firenzemusei.it or ✆ **055-294-883.** 8.50€ (13€ during temporary exhibitions). Tues–Sun 8:15am–6:50pm. Museo degli Argenti and Galleria del Costume: ✆ **055-238-8709.** 7€ (includes Giardino di Boboli and Giardino Bardini; 10€ during a temporary exhibition). Same hours as Giardino di Boboli; see below. Bus: C3, D, 11, 36, 37.

Giardino di Boboli (Boboli Garden) ★★ PARK/GARDEN The statue-filled park behind the Pitti Palace is one of the earliest and finest Renaissance gardens, laid out mostly between 1549 and 1656 with box hedges in geometric patterns, groves of ilex (holm oak), dozens of statues, and rows of cypress. Just above the entrance through the courtyard of the Palazzo Pitti is an oblong **amphitheater** modeled on Roman circuses, with a **granite basin** from Rome's Baths of Caracalla and an **Egyptian obelisk** of Ramses II. In 1589 this was the setting for the wedding reception of Ferdinand de' Medici and Christine of Lorraine. For the occasion, the family commissioned entertainment from Jacopo Peri and Ottavio Rinuccini, who decided to set a classical story entirely to music and called it "Dafne"—the world's first opera. (Later, they wrote a follow-up hit, "Erudice," performed here in 1600; it's the first opera whose score has survived.) At the south end of the park, the **Isolotto ★** is a dreamy island in a pond full of huge goldfish, with Giambologna's "L'Oceano" sculptural composition at its center. At the north end, down around the end of the Pitti Palace, are fake caverns filled with statuary, attempting to invoke a classical sacred grotto. The most famous, the **Grotta Grande,** was designed by Giorgio Vasari, Bartolomeo Ammannati, and Bernardo Buontalenti between 1557 and 1593; dripping with phony stalactites, it's set with replicas of Michelangelo's unfinished "Prisoners" statues. You can usually get inside on the hour (but not every hour) for 15 minutes.

Entrance via Palazzo Pitti. ✆ **055-238-8791.** 7€, includes Giardino Bardini, Museo degli Argenti, and Museo del Costume (10€ during temporary exhibitions). Nov–Feb daily 8:15am–4:30pm; Mar daily 8:15am–5:30pm; Apr–May and Sept–Oct daily to 6:30pm; June–Aug to 7:30pm. Closed 1st and last Mon of month. Bus: C3, D, 11, 36, 37.

Piazzale Michelangiolo (Michelangelo) ★ SQUARE This newly pedestrianized, panoramic piazza is on the itinerary of every tour bus. The balustraded terrace was laid out in 1869 to give a sweeping **vista ★★** of the entire city, spread out in the valley below and backed by the green hills of Fiesole beyond. The bronze replica of "David" here points directly at his original home, outside the Palazzo Vecchio.

Viale Michelangelo. Bus: 12 or 13.

San Miniato al Monte ★★ CHURCH High atop a hill, its gleaming white-and-green marble facade visible from the city below, San Miniato is one of the few ancient churches of Florence to survive the centuries virtually intact. The current building began to take shape in 1013, under the auspices of the powerful Arte di Calimala guild, whose symbol, a bronze eagle clutching a bale of wool, perches on the **facade ★★**. Above the central window is a 13th-century mosaic of "Christ Between the Madonna and St. Minias" (a theme repeated in the apse). The **interior** has a few Renaissance additions, but they blend in well with the overall medieval aspect—an airy, stony space with a raised choir at one end, painted wooden trusses on the ceiling, and tombs interspersed with inlaid marble symbols of the zodiac paving the floor. Below the choir is an 11th-century **crypt** with remains of frescoes by Taddeo Gaddi. Off to the right of the raised choir is the **sacristy,** which Spinello Aretino covered in 1387 with elaborate frescoes depicting the **"Life of St. Benedict" ★**. Off the left aisle of the nave is the 15th-century **Cappella del Cardinale del Portogallo ★★**, a collaborative effort by Renaissance artists to honor the Portuguese humanist Cardinal Jacopo di Lusitania. It's worth timing your visit to come here when the Benedictine monks are celebrating Mass in Gregorian chant (usually 5:30pm).

Around the back of the church is San Miniato's monumental **cemetery ★**, one enormous "city of the dead," whose streets are lined with tombs and mausoleums built in elaborate pastiches of every generation of Florentine architecture. It's a peaceful spot, soundtracked only by birdsong and the occasional tolling of the church bells.

Via Monte alle Croci/Viale Galileo Galilei (behind Piazzale Michelangiolo). ✆ **055-234-2731.** Free. Mon–Sat 9:30am–1pm and 3pm until dusk; Sun 3pm until dusk. Bus: 12 or 13.

Santa Felicita ★ CHURCH Greek sailors who lived in this neighborhood in the 2nd century brought Christianity to Florence with them, and this little church was probably the second to be established in the city, the first version of it rising in the late 4th century. The current church was thoroughly remodeled in the 1730s. The star works are in the first chapel on the right, the Brunelleschi-designed **Cappella Barbadori-Capponi**, with paintings by Mannerist master Pontormo (1525–27). His **"Deposition" ★★** and frescoed "Annunciation" are rife with his garish color palette of oranges, pinks, golds, lime greens, and sky blues, and exhibit his trademark surreal sense of figure.

Piazza Santa Felicita (on left off Via Guicciardini across the Ponte Vecchio). ✆ **055-213-018.** Free (1€ to illuminate chapel lights). Mon–Sat 9:30am–12:30pm and 3:30–5:30pm. Bus: C3 or D.

Santa Maria del Carmine ★★★ CHURCH Following a 1771 fire that destroyed everything but the transept chapels and sacristy, this Carmelite church was almost entirely reconstructed in high baroque style. To see the **Cappella Brancacci ★★★** in the right transept, you have to enter through the cloisters and pay admission. The frescoes here were commissioned by an enemy of the Medici, Felice Brancacci, who in 1424 hired Masolino and his student Masaccio to decorate it with a cycle on the "Life of St. Peter." Masolino probably worked out the cycle's scheme and painted a few scenes along with his pupil before taking off for 3 years to serve as court painter in Budapest, while Masaccio kept painting, quietly creating the early Renaissance's greatest frescoes. Masaccio eventually left for Rome in 1428, where he died at age 27; the cycle was completed between 1480 and 1485 by Filippino Lippi.

Masolino painted "St. Peter Preaching," the upper panel to the left of the altar, and the two top scenes on the right wall, which shows his fastidious, decorative style in a long panel of "St. Peter Healing the Cripple" and "Raising Tabitha," and his "Adam and Eve." Contrast this first man and woman, about to take the bait offered by the snake, with the **"Expulsion from the Garden"** ★★★, opposite it, painted by Masaccio. Masolino's figures are highly posed, expressionless models, while Masaccio's Adam and Eve burst with intense emotion. The top scene on the left wall, the **"Tribute Money"** ★★, is also by Masaccio, and showcases his use of linear perspective. The scenes to the right of the altar are Masaccio's as well; the **"Baptism of the Neophytes"** ★★ is among his masterpieces.

Piazza del Carmine. www.museicivicifiorentini.comune.fi.it. ✆ **055-276-8224.** Church free; Cappella Brancacci 6€. Mon and Wed–Sat 10am–5pm; Sun 1–5pm. Bus: D.

Santo Spirito ★ CHURCH One of Filippo Brunelleschi's masterpieces of architecture, this 15th-century church doesn't look like much from the outside (no proper facade was ever built). But the **interior** ★ is a marvelous High Renaissance space—an expansive landscape of proportion and mathematics in classic Brunelleschi style, with coffered ceiling, lean columns with Corinthian capitals, and the stacked perspective of arched arcading. Late Renaissance and baroque paintings are scattered throughout, but the best stuff lies in the transepts, especially the **Cappella Nerli** ★, with a panel by Filippino Lippi (right transept). The church's extravagant **baroque altar** has a ciborium inlaid in *pietre dure* around 1607—and frankly, looks a bit silly against the restrained elegance of Brunelleschi's architecture. The sacristy displays a wooden "Crucifix" that has, controversially, been attributed to Michelangelo.

Tree-shaded **Piazza Santo Spirito** ★ is one of the focal points of the Oltrarno, lined with cafes that see action late into the evening. Sometimes a few farmers sell their fruit and vegetables on the piazza.

Piazza Santo Spirito. ✆ **055-210-030.** Free. Mon–Tues and Thurs–Sat 10am–12:30pm and 4–5:30pm; Sun 4–5:30pm. Bus: C3, D, 11, 36, 37.

A Side Trip to Fiesole

Although it's only a short distance from Florence, **Fiesole** ★ is very proud of its status as an independent municipality. In fact, this hilltop village high above Florence predates its big neighbor in the valley below by centuries.

Etruscans from Arezzo probably founded a town here in the 6th century B.C., on the site of a Bronze Age settlement. *Faesulae* became the most important Etruscan center in the region, and although it eventually became a Roman town—conquered in 90 B.C., inhabitants built a theater and adopted Roman customs—it always retained a bit of otherness. Following the barbarian invasions, it became part of Florence's administrative district in the 9th century, yet continued to struggle for self-government. Medieval Florence settled things in 1125 by attacking and razing the entire settlement, save the cathedral and bishop's palace.

An oasis of cultivated greenery still separates Florence from Fiesole. Even with the big city so close, Fiesole endures as a Tuscan small town,

Fiesole Essentials

To get to Fiesole, take bus no. 7 from Florence. It departs from Via La Pira, to the right of San Marco. A scenic 25-minute ride through the greenery above Florence takes you to Fiesole's main square, **Piazza Mino.** The **tourist office** is at Via Portigiani 3 (www.fiesoleforyou.it; ✆ **055-596-1311**). From March through October it's open daily (Apr–Sept 9am–7pm, Mar and Oct 10am–6pm); from November through February, it's open Wednesday to Monday 10am to 3pm.

Fiesole's sights offer a single admission ticket, costing 12€ adults, 8€ visitors ages 7 to 18; a family ticket costs 24€. Prices are 2€ per person lower without the Museo Bandini, which is missable for all but ardent art lovers, and anyway only opens Friday through Sunday. All other sites are open the same hours as the tourist office, which doubles as the ticket office. For more information, visit **www.museidifiesole.it** or call ✆ **055-596-1293.**

mostly removed from Florence at its feet, and hence a perfect escape from summertime crowds. It stays relatively cool in summer, and while you sit at a cafe on Piazza Mino, sipping an iced cappuccino, the lines at the Uffizi and throng around the Duomo seem very distant indeed.

San Francesco ★ MONASTERY/MUSEUM The ancient high-point of the Etruscan and Roman town is now occupied by a tiny church and monastery. The 14th-century church has been largely overhauled, but at the end of a small nave hung with devotional works—Piero di Cosimo and Cenni di Francesco are both represented—is a fine "Crucifixion and Saints" altarpiece by Neri di Bicci. Off the cloisters is a quirky little **Ethnographic Museum,** stuffed with objects picked up by Franciscan missionaries, including an Egyptian mummy and Chinese jade and ceramics. Entrance to the church's painted, vaulted **crypt** is through the museum. To reach San Francesco, you will climb a sharp hill—pause close to the top, where a little balcony provides perhaps the best **view** ★★★ of Florence, and the wine hills of the Chianti beyond.

Via San Francesco (off Piazza Mino). ✆ **055-59-175.** Free. Daily 9:30am–noon and 2:30–5pm (6pm in summer). Bus: 7.

Teatro Romano (Roman Theater) ★ RUINS Fiesole's archaeological area is romantically overgrown and scattered with sections of columns, broken friezes, and other remnants of the ancient world. It is also dramatically sited, terraced into a hill with views over the olive groves and forests north of Florence. Beyond the **Roman Theater** ★ (which seated 1,500 in its day), three rebuilt arches mark the remains of 1st-century-A.D. **baths.** Near the arches, a cement balcony over the far edge of the archaeological park gives a good view of the best remaining stretch of Fiesole's 4th-century-B.C. **Etruscan walls.** At the other end of the park from the baths, the floor and steps of a 1st-century-B.C. **Roman Temple** were built on top of a 4th-century-B.C. Etruscan one dedicated to Minerva. To the left are oblong **Lombard tombs** from the 7th century A.D., when this part of Fiesole was a necropolis.

Via Portigiani 1. ✆ **055-596-1293.** For admission and hours, see "Fiesole Essentials," above. Bus: 7.

Organized Tours

To really get under the surface of the city, book an insightful culture tour with **Context Travel ★★** (www.contexttravel.com; ✆ **800/691-6036** in the U.S. or 06-96727371 in Italy). Led by academics and other experts in their field on a variety of themes, from the gastronomic to the archaeological and artistic, these tours are limited to six people and generally cost around 85€ per person. The quality of Context's walks is unmatched, and well worth the above-average cost.

Offerings from **CAF Tours** (www.caftours.com; ✆ **055-283-200**) include several themed walks and cooking classes costing from 28€ to over 100€. **I Just Drive** (www.ijustdrive.us; ✆ **055-093-5928**) offers fully equipped cars (Wi-Fi, complimentary bottle of Prosecco) plus an English-speaking driver for various themed visits; for example, you can book a private ride in a luxury Bentley or Mercedes up to San Miniato al Monte at dusk (1½ hr.; 129€). They also operate full-day and half-day private and group food and wine tours into the Chianti hills. **Viator.com** also has a range of locally organized tours and activities, reviewed by travelers.

Especially for Kids

You have to put in a bit of work to reach some of Florence's best views—and the climbs, up claustrophobic, medieval staircases, are a favorite with many kids. The cupola of **Santa Maria del Fiore** (p. 174), the **Palazzo Vecchio**'s (p. 183) Torre di Arnolfo, and the **Campanile di Giotto** (p. 174) are perfect for any youngster with a head for heights.

The best activities with an educational component are run by **Mus.e ★★** (www.musefirenze.it; ✆ **055-276-8224**), a program that offers child's-eye tours in English around the Palazzo Vecchio, led by guides in period costumes. Lively, affordable activities focus on life at the ducal court—pitched at children ages 4–7 ("The Turtle and the Snail", 4€ per person) or 10-plus ("At Court with Donna Isabella" and "Secret Passages", both 4€)—or take kids into the workshop to learn fresco painting (ages 8-plus, also 4€ each). Book online or at the desk next to the Palazzo Vecchio ticket booth.

When your youngsters simply need a crowd-free timeout space, head for the **Biblioteca delle Oblate,** Via dell'Oriuolo 26 (www.biblioteche.comune.fi.it; ✆ **055-261-6512**), where you'll find a library with books for little ones (including in English), as well as space to spread out, color, or draw. It's free and open 9am to 6:45pm, except for Monday morning and all day Sunday (closed 1 week mid-Aug). The Oblate's **cafe** (p. 221) is an excellent place to kick back.

There's only one game in town when it comes to spectator sports: *calcio*. To Italians, soccer/football is akin to a second religion, and an afternoon at the stadium can offer you more insight into local culture than a lifetime in the Uffizi. Florence's team, **Fiorentina ★** (nicknamed *i viola,* "the purples"), is often among the best in Italy's top league, *Serie A*. You can usually catch them alternate Sundays from September through May at the **Stadio Comunale Artemio Franchi**, Via Manfredo Fanti 4 (www.violachannel.tv). Book tickets online or head for an official ticket office on arrival (you must have a photo I.D.): There is a sales desk on the Mercato Centrale's upper floor (p. 219) and at Via dei Sette Santi 28R, open from 9:30am on match days. With kids, get seats in a Tribuna (stand) rather than a Curva, where the fanatical fans sit. To reach the stadium, take matchday-only bus no. 52 or no. 17 from Santa Maria Novella, or bus no. 20 from San Marco (10–15 min.). You can get kitted out in home colors at **Alè Viola,** Via del Corso 58R (✆ **055-295-306**), or at stalls around the ground on matchday.

You can skip the subtitles at an original 1920s movie theater right in the center, with films in their original language (usually English): **Odeon Firenze ★**, Piazza Strozzi (www.odeonfirenze.com; ✆ **055-214-068**).

Cycling is a pleasure in the riverside Parco delle Cascine: See p. 168 for bike rental advice. And remember: You are in the **gelato** capital of the world. At least one multiscoop gelato per day is the minimum recommended dose; see p. 215. Better still, plan to be in town during the **Gelato Festival** (www.gelatofestival.it) in late April.

WHERE TO STAY

Thanks to a rapidly growing stock of hotel beds, as well as national economic crises, the forces of supply and demand have brought hotel prices down…a little. Few hoteliers have increased rates in recent years, and many don't expect to anytime soon. Add the recent dollar appreciation against the euro, and you have a hotel market that is as favorable to North American visitors as it has ever been. That said, it is still hard to find a high-season double you'd want to stay in for much less than 100€.

Some of those price drops have been added back in taxes: Florence's government levies an extra 1€ to 1.50€ per person per night per government-rated hotel star, for the first 7 nights of any stay. It is payable on arrival, and is not usually included in quoted rates. Children up to age 12 are exempt from the tax.

Peak hotel season is Easter through early July, September through early November, and Christmas through January 6. May, June, and September are popular; January, February, and sometimes August are the months to grab a bargain—never be shy to haggle if you're coming then. **Booking direct** using phone, e-mail, or the hotel's own website, is often the key to unlocking the lowest rates or complimentary extras.

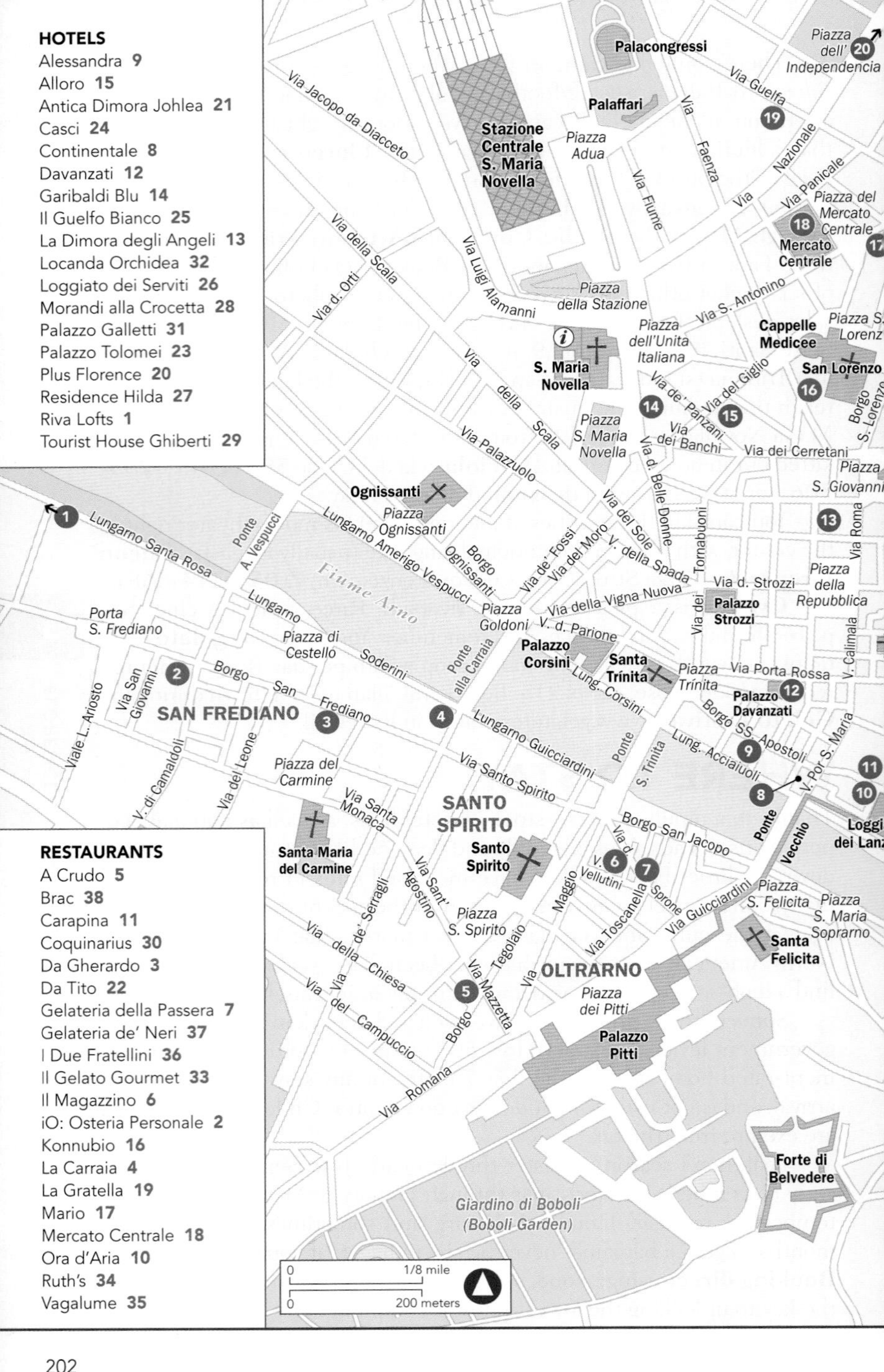
HOTELS
Alessandra 9
Alloro 15
Antica Dimora Johlea 21
Casci 24
Continentale 8
Davanzati 12
Garibaldi Blu 14
Il Guelfo Bianco 25
La Dimora degli Angeli 13
Locanda Orchidea 32
Loggiato dei Serviti 26
Morandi alla Crocetta 28
Palazzo Galletti 31
Palazzo Tolomei 23
Plus Florence 20
Residence Hilda 27
Riva Lofts 1
Tourist House Ghiberti 29
RESTAURANTS
A Crudo 5
Brac 38
Carapina 11
Coquinarius 30
Da Gherardo 3
Da Tito 22
Gelateria della Passera 7
Gelateria de' Neri 37
I Due Fratellini 36
Il Gelato Gourmet 33
Il Magazzino 6
iO: Osteria Personale 2
Konnubio 16
La Carraia 4
La Gratella 19
Mario 17
Mercato Centrale 18
Ora d'Aria 10
Ruth's 34
Vagalume 35
Palacongressi
Palaffari
Stazione Centrale S. Maria Novella
Piazza Adua
Piazza dell' Independencia
Via Guelfa
Via Nazionale
Via Faenza
Via Fiume
Via Panicale
Piazza del Mercato Centrale
Mercato Centrale
Via Jacopo da Diacceto
Via della Scala
Via d. Orti
Via Luigi Alamanni
Piazza della Stazione
Via S. Antonino
Piazza dell'Unita Italiana
Cappelle Medicee
Piazza S. Lorenz
San Lorenzo
Borgo S. Lorenzo
S. Maria Novella
Piazza S. Maria Novella
Via de' Panzani
Via del Giglio
Via dei Banchi
Via dei Cerretani
Piazza S. Giovanni
Via Palazzuolo
Via d. Belle Donne
Via Tornabuoni
Via Roma
Ognissanti
Piazza Ognissanti
Borgo Ognissanti
Lungarno Amerigo Vespucci
Lungarno Santa Rosa
Ponte A. Vespucci
Fiume Arno
Via de' Fossi
Via del Moro
Via del Sole
V. della Spada
Via d. Strozzi
Piazza della Repubblica
Via della Vigna Nuova
Palazzo Strozzi
Via dei
Piazza Goldoni
V. d. Parione
Palazzo Corsini
Santa Trinita
Piazza Trinita
Lung. Corsini
Via Porta Rossa
Palazzo Davanzati
V. Calimala
Porta S. Frediano
Lungarno Soderini
Piazza di Cestello
Borgo San Frediano
Ponte alla Carraia
Via San Giovanni
SAN FREDIANO
Lungarno Guicciardini
Borgo SS. Apostoli
Lung. Acciaiuoli
V. Por S. Maria
Viale L. Ariosto
V. di Camaldoli
Via del Leone
Piazza del Carmine
Via Santa Monaca
Via Santo Spirito
SANTO SPIRITO
Ponte S. Trinita
Ponte Vecchio
Loggia dei Lanzi
Santa Maria del Carmine
Santo Spirito
Borgo San Jacopo
Via d. Sprone
V. Vellutini
Via Maggio
Via Sant' Agostino
Via de' Serragli
Piazza S. Spirito
Via Toscanella
Via Guicciardini
Piazza S. Felicita
Piazza S. Maria Soprarno
Santa Felicita
Via della Chiesa
Via del Campuccio
Via Tegolaio
Via Mazzetta
Borgo
OLTRARNO
Piazza dei Pitti
Palazzo Pitti
Via Romana
Forte di Belvedere
Giardino di Boboli (Boboli Garden)
0 1/8 mile
0 200 meters

Florence Hotels & Restaurants
Giardino dei Semplici
San Marco
Piazza San Marco
Giardino della Gherardesca
Piazza Donatello
Santissima Annunziata
Galleria dell' Accademia
Piazza della SS. Annunziata
Ospedale degli Innocenti
Museo Archeologico
Palazzo Medici-Riccardi
Palazzo Pucci
Piazza Brunelleschi
Ospedale S. Maria Nuova
Teatro d. Pergola
Santa Maria Maddalena dei Pazzi
Piazza d'Azeglio
Duomo
Piazza del Duomo
Piazza S. M. Nuova
Sinogoga (Museo Ebraico)
Piazza Sant' Ambrogio
Bargello
Badia
Piazza S. Firenze
Teatro Verdi
Casa di Buonarroti
Piazza L. Ghiberti
Piazza Cesare Beccaria
Carceri delle Murate
Archivio di Stato
Palazzo Vecchio
Piazza S. Croce
Santa Croce
SANTA CROCE
Biblioteca Nazionale
Piazza Mentana
Piazza dei Cavalleggeri
Piazza Piave
Fiume Arno
Piazza G. Poggi
SAN NICCOLÒ
Piazza F. Ferrucci
Piazzale Michelangelo
Via S. Zanobi
Via XXVII Aprile
Via Gallo
V. S. Reparata
Via San Gallo
V. degli Arazzieri
Via Cesare Battisti
Via G. Capponi
Via Giuseppe Giusti
Via Pinti
Via G. La Farini
Via J. Nardi
Via B. Varchi
Viale Antonio Gramsci
Via Guelfa
Via Cavour
Via de' Ginori
Via Ricasoli
Via dei Servi
Via Laura
Via della Colonna
Borgo Pinti
Via L. C. Farini
Via degli Alfani
Via della Pergola
Via G. Carducci
Via dei Pucci
Via de' Martelli
Via M. Bufalini
Via dei Pilastri
Via dell'Oriuolo
Via S. Egidio
Via Fiesolana
Via de' Pepi
Via di Mezzo
Via della Mattonaia
Via A. Manzoni
V. d. Studio
Via del Proconsolo
Via del Corso
Borgo degli Albizi
Via Pietrapiana
Borgo la Croce
Via Dante Alighieri
Via de' Pandolfini
Via G. Verdi
V. M. Buonarroti
Via Allegri
Via F. Paolieri
Via Cimatori
Via Ghibellina
V. d. Vigna Vecchia
Via dell' Agnolo
Piazza della Signoria
Borgo de' Greci
Via de' Macci
Borgo Allegri
Uffizi
Via dei Neri
Via di San Giuseppe
Via della Giovine Italia
Via Pietro Thouar
Viale della Giovine Italia
Viale Giovanni Amendola
Via de' Benci
Borgo S. Croce
V. Magliabechi
Corso dei Tintori
Via de' Malcontenti
Lung. Gen. Diaz
Lungarno delle Grazie
Via Tripoli
Lung. della Zecca Vecchia
Lung. P. Giraldi
Ponte alle Grazie
Lungarno Torrigiani
Via de' Bardi
Lungarno Serristori
Via dei Renai
Via di S. Niccolo
Lungarno B. Cellini
Ponte A. Vespucci
Via dei Bastioni
Viale G. Poggi
Via di Belvedere
Via del Monte alle Croci
Viale Michelangiolo
21
22
23
24
25
26
27
28
29
30
31
32
33
34
35
36
37
38

To help you decide in which area you'd like to base yourself, consult "Neighborhoods in Brief," p. 165. Note that we have included parking information only for those places that offer it. As indicated below, many hotels offer babysitting services; however, these are generally "on request." At least a couple of days' notice is advisable.

Near the Duomo

MODERATE

La Dimora degli Angeli ★★★ This B&B occupies two levels of a grand apartment building in one of the city's busiest shopping districts. Rooms on the original floor are for romantics; bright wallpaper contrasts pleasingly with iron-framed beds and classic furniture. (Beatrice is the largest, with a view of Brunelleschi's dome—just.) The floor below is totally different, with sharp lines and leather or wooden headboards throughout. Breakfast is available at a local cafe—or if you prefer, you can grab a coffee in the B&B and use your token for a light lunch instead.
Via Brunelleschi 4. www.dimoredeicherubini.it. ✆ **055-288-478.** 12 units. 76€–198€ double. Breakfast (at nearby café) 12€. Parking 26€. Bus: C2. **Amenities:** Wi-Fi (free).

Near Piazza della Signoria

EXPENSIVE

Continentale ★★★ Everything about the Continentale is cool, and the effect is achieved without even a hint of frostiness. Rooms are uncompromisingly modern, decorated in bright white and bathed in natural light. Deluxe units are built into a medieval riverside tower, which have mighty walls and medieval-sized windows (that is, small). Standard rooms are large (for Florence), and there's a retro-1950s feel to the overall styling. Communal areas are a major hit, too: A relaxation room has a glass wall with a front-row view of the Ponte Vecchio. Top-floor **La Terrazza** (p. 221) serves Florence's best rooftop cocktails.
Vicolo dell'Oro 6R. www.lungarnocollection.com. ✆ **055-27-262.** 43 units. 153€–750€ double. Parking 35€. Bus: C3 or D. **Amenities:** Bar; concierge; spa; Wi-Fi (free).

Between San Lorenzo & San Marco

EXPENSIVE

Palazzo Tolomei ★★★ In its heyday, this palace was at the heart of Medici power. It even welcomed the painter Raphael as a guest in 1505 (probably in two rooms at the front, now Barocco 1 and 2). Guest rooms are all large, with Renaissance wooden ceilings and terracotta floors left untouched. Modern fittings—including leather sofas, soft mattresses, and florid crystal chandeliers—chime perfectly with a baroque redecoration completed in the 1600s, complete with ceiling frescoes by Alessandro Gherardini. The lower floor is given over to opulent public rooms, just as it would have been when it was the *piano nobile* of the family *palazzo*. These days you'll find a music room, art books, a welcoming host, and probably an open bottle of Tuscan red wine. Book direct for the best deal: perhaps a free airport transfer, free late checkout, or a discounted room rate.

Via de' Ginori 19. www.palazzotolomei.it. ✆ **055-292-887.** 8 units. 215€–395€ double (2 nights minimum at peak times). Rates include breakfast (in nearby cafe). Bus: C1. **Amenities:** Concierge; Wi-Fi (free).

MODERATE

Il Guelfo Bianco ★★ Decor in this former noble Florentine home retains its authentic *palazzo* feel, though carpets have been added for comfort and warmth. No two rooms are the same—stone walls this thick cannot just be knocked through—and several have antiques integrated into their individual schemes. Grand rooms at the front (especially 101, 118, and 228) have spectacular Renaissance coffered ceilings and masses of space. Sleep at the back and you'll wake to an unusual sound in Florence: birdsong. Under the same ownership, adjacent "farm-to-table" style bistro **Il Desco** (www.ildescofirenze.it; ✆ **055-288-330**) serves seasonal dishes made with organic ingredients. It's open to guests and nonguests alike.

Via Cavour 29 (near corner of Via Guelfa). www.ilguelfobianco.it. ✆ **055-288-330.** 40 units. 90€–280€ double, includes breakfast. Parking 27€–33€. Bus: C1, 14, 23. **Amenities:** Restaurant; bar; babysitting; room service; Wi-Fi (free).

INEXPENSIVE

Casci ★ The front part of the palace now occupied by the Casci was once composer Gioachino Rossini's Florence digs. This affordable, central hotel has long been a Frommer's favorite, and the partial pedestrianization of Via Cavour has made it an even more attractive base. Rooms follow a labyrinthine layout, split between Rossini's old *piano nobile* and a former convent to the rear, where the bigger rooms are located, including a couple of spacious family units. Rooms are simply decorated and some can be a little dark, but a rolling program of modernization (completed in 2016) installed new, light-toned furniture to counteract that. The welcome from some of Florence's friendliest family hoteliers is an unchanging feature.

Via Cavour 13 (btw. Via dei Ginori and Via Guelfa). www.hotelcasci.com. ✆ **055-211-686.** 25 units. 75€–160€ double, includes breakfast. Parking 22€–27€. Bus: C1, 14, 23. Closed 2 weeks in Dec. **Amenities:** Bar; babysitting; concierge; Wi-Fi (free).

Near Piazza Santa Trínita

MODERATE

Alessandra ★ This typical Florentine *pensione* transports you back to the age of the gentleman and lady traveler. Decor has grown organically since the place opened as a hotel in 1950; Alessandra is a place for evolution, not revolution. A pleasing mix of styles is the end result: some

rooms with carved headboards, gilt frames, and gold damask; others with eclectic postwar furniture, like something from a midcentury period movie set. A couple rooms have views of the Arno, while front-side rooms overlook Borgo SS. Apostoli, one of the center's most atmospheric streets.
Borgo SS. Apostoli 17. www.hotelalessandra.com. ✆ **055-283-438.** 27 units. 160€–180€ double, includes breakfast. Parking 25€. Bus: C3, D, 6, 11, 36, 37. Closed a few days around Christmas. **Amenities:** Wi-Fi (free).

Davanzati ★★ Although installed inside a historic building, the Davanzati never rests on its medieval laurels: There is a laptop and an iPad with cellular data in every room for free guest use around the city, and HD movies can be streamed to your TV. Rooms are simply decorated in the Tuscan style, with color-washed walls and half-canopies over the beds. Room 100 is probably the best family hotel room in Florence, full of nooks, crannies, and split-levels that give the adults and the kids a sense of private space. A free *aperitivo* for guests remains part of the Davanzati's family welcome.
Via Porta Rossa 5 (on Piazza Davanzati). www.hoteldavanzati.it. ✆ **055-286-666.** 27 units. 122€–211€ double, includes breakfast. Parking 26€. Bus: C2. **Amenities:** Bar; babysitting; concierge; use of nearby gym; Wi-Fi (free).

Between Santa Maria Novella & San Lorenzo

MODERATE

Alloro ★★ Officially a "bed-and-breakfast," this feels more like a small hotel, whose modern rooms inside a Renaissance palace overlook a silent inner courtyard—neatly soundproofing them against a noisy neighborhood. Rooms offer an excellent value for the price and location, with high ceilings, color-washed walls, and air-conditioning. Breakfast is a traditional spread of fresh fruit and pastries. A friendly ghost from the Renaissance era reputedly roams part of the palace; you're unlikely to get a discount if you spot him, but there's no harm in asking.
Via del Giglio 8. www.allorobb.it. ✆ **055-211-685.** 5 units. 85€–175€ double, includes breakfast. Bus: C1. **Amenities:** Concierge; Wi-Fi (free).

Garibaldi Blu ★★ The hotels of Piazza Santa Maria Novella are frequented by fashion models, rock stars, and blue-chip businessfolk. You can get a taste of that, for a fraction of the price, at this boutique hotel with attitude, opened in 2014. Each of the mostly midsize rooms is immaculate, and reflects the hotel's "warm denim" palette, with retro 1970s furniture, parquet floors, and marble bathrooms. It's well worth paying 30€ extra for a deluxe room at the front: These have much more space and a view over Florence's prettiest church facade, Santa Maria Novella itself. Occasional lifesize models of superheroes like Captain America dotted around the hotel add a touch of fun surrealism.
Piazza Santa Maria Novella 21. www.hotelgaribaldiblu.com. ✆ **055-277-300.** 21 units. 130€–350€ double, includes breakfast. Garage parking 35€–48€. Bus: C2, 6, 11, 22. **Amenities:** Bar; babysitting (prebooking essential); concierge; Wi-Fi (free).

INEXPENSIVE

Plus Florence ★ There's simply nowhere in Florence with as many services for your buck—including seasonal indoor and outdoor swimming pools—all in a price bracket where you are often fortunate to get an ensuite bathroom (and Plus has those, too). The best rooms in this large, well-equipped hostel are in the rear wing. Units here are dressed in taupe and brown, with subtle uplighting and space (in some) for up to four beds. The only minuses: a bland building and the location, between two busy roads. Light sleepers should request a room facing the courtyard.

Via Santa Caterina d'Alessandria 15. www.plushostels.com/plusflorence. ✆ **055-628-6347.** 240 units. 35€–125€ double. Bus: 20. **Amenities:** Restaurant; bar; concierge; gym; 2 pools; sauna; Wi-Fi (free).

Near San Marco & Santissima Annunziata

EXPENSIVE

Residence Hilda ★★ There's not a hint of the Renaissance here: These luxe mini-apartments are all bright-white decor and designer furnishings, with natural wood flooring, fiber Wi-Fi, hypoallergenic mattresses, Starck chairs, and modern gadgetry to keep everything running. Each is spacious, cool in summer, and soundproofed against Florence's background noise. Every apartment has a mini-kitchen, equipped for preparing a simple meal—ideal if you have kids in tow. Deluxe rooms were renovated in 2016, and the top-floor Executive unit now has a Nespresso machine, yoga mat, and an exercise bike. Unusual for apartments, all are bookable by the single night.

Via dei Servi 40 (2 blocks north of the Duomo). www.residencehilda.com. ✆ **055-288-021.** 12 units. 150€–450€ per night for 2-4 person apartments. Parking 31€. Bus: C1. **Amenities:** Airport transfer; babysitting; concierge; room service; Wi-Fi (free).

MODERATE

Antica Dimora Johlea ★★ There is a real neighborhood feel to the streets around this *dimora* (traditional Florentine home) guesthouse, which means evenings are lively and Sundays are quiet (although it's under a 10-min. walk to San Lorenzo). Standard-size rooms are snug; upgrade to a deluxe if you need more space, but there is no difference in the standard of decor, a mix of Florentine and earthy boho. Help yourself to coffee, a soft drink, or a glass of wine from the honesty bar and head up to a roof terrace for knockout views over the terracotta rooftops to the center and hills beyond. It is pure magic at dusk. No credit cards.

Via San Gallo 80. www.antichedimorefiorentine.it. ✆ **055-463-3292.** 6 units. 90€–220€ double, includes breakfast. No credit cards. Parking 25€. Bus: C1, 1, 6, 11, 14, 17, 23. **Amenities:** Bar; Wi-Fi (free).

Loggiato dei Serviti ★★ Stay here to experience Florence as the gentleman and lady visitors of the Grand Tour did. For starters, the building is a genuine Renaissance landmark, built by Sangallo the Elder in the 1520s. There is a sense of faded grandeur and unconventional luxury throughout—no gadgetry or chromatherapy showers, but you will find rooms with writing desks and lots of vintage ambience. No unit is small, but standard rooms lack a view of either Brunelleschi's dome or the perfect piazza outside. Air-conditioning is pretty much the only concession to the 21st century—and you will love it that way. Book direct for the best deals.

Piazza Santissima Annunziata 3. www.loggiatodeiservitihotel.it. ✆ **055-289-592.** 37 units. 120€–330€ double, includes breakfast. Valet parking 21€. Bus: C1, 6, 14, 19, 23, 31, 32. **Amenities:** Babysitting; concierge; Wi-Fi (free).

Morandi alla Crocetta ★★ Like many in Florence, this hotel was built in the shell of a former convent. Morandi alla Crocetta has retained the original convent layout, meaning some rooms are snug. But what you lose in size, you more than gain in character: Every single one oozes *tipico fiorentino.* Rooms have parquet flooring thrown with rugs and dressed with antique wooden furniture. Original Zocchi prints of Florence, from 1744, are scattered around the place. Superior rooms have more space and either a private courtyard terrace or, in one, original frescoes decorating the entrance to the former convent chapel, though the chapel itself is permanently sealed off. The hotel is set on a quiet street.

Via Laura 50 (1 block east of Piazza Santissima Annunziata). www.hotelmorandi.it. ✆ **055-234-4747.** 12 units. 90€–177€ double, includes breakfast. Parking 25€. Bus: 6, 19, 31, 32. **Amenities:** Bar; babysitting; concierge; Wi-Fi (free).

Tourist House Ghiberti ★ A pleasing mix of the traditional and the modern prevails at this backstreet guesthouse named after a famous former resident; the creator of the Baptistery's "Gates of Paradise" had workshops on the top floor of the *palazzo.* Rooms have plenty of space, with herringbone terracotta floors, whitewashed walls, and high, painted wood ceilings in a vaguely Renaissance style. There is a sauna and Jacuzzi for communal use, so you can soak away the aches and pains of a day's sightseeing; memory-foam mattresses should help with that, too. E-mail direct if you want to bag the best room rate.

Via M. Bufalini 1. www.touristhouseghiberti.com. ✆ **055-284-858.** 6 units. 64€–179€ double, includes breakfast. Parking 20€–30€. Bus: C1, 14, 23. **Amenities:** Jacuzzi; sauna; Wi-Fi (free).

Near Santa Croce

MODERATE

Palazzo Galletti ★★ Not many hotels within a sensible budget give you the chance to live like a Florentine noble. Rooms here have towering ceilings and an uncluttered arrangement of carefully chosen antiques. Most have frescoed or painted-wood showpiece ceilings. Bathrooms, in contrast, have a sharp, contemporary design, decked out in travertine and marble.

Aside from two street-facing suites, every room has a small balcony, ideal for a predinner glass of wine. If you're here for a once-in-a-lifetime trip, spring for the "Giove" or (especially) "Cerere"; both are large suites, and the latter has walls covered in original frescoes from the 1800s. Snag a free bottle of their own estate wine when you book direct and show this Frommer's guide. Via Sant'Egidio 12. www.palazzogalletti.it. ✆ **055-390-5750.** 11 units. 100€–170€ double; 170€–240€ suite, includes breakfast. Parking 30€–35€. Bus: C1, C2, 14, 23. **Amenities:** Wi-Fi (free).

INEXPENSIVE

Locanda Orchidea ★ Over several visits to Florence, this has been a go-to inn for trips on a tight budget, and a 2017 renovation has kept it on top of the game. Rooms are over two floors of a historic *palazzo*, the best of them rear-facing on a quiet, leafy courtyard where wisteria flowers each spring. Furniture is a fun mix of mismatched flea-market finds and secondhand pieces; tiled floors; and bold print wallpaper and fabrics. Bathrooms are shared (they have good water pressure), and there is no A/C or onsite breakfast. But for value, character, and welcome, this place is hard to beat.

Borgo degli Albizi 11 (close to Piazza San Pier Maggiore). www.hotelorchideaflorence.it. ✆ **055-248-0346.** 7 units. 42€–80€ double. Parking 18€–22€. Bus: C1 or C2. **Amenities:** Wi-Fi (free).

West of the Center

MODERATE

Riva Lofts ★★ The traditional Florentine alarm call—a morning mix of traffic and tourism—is replaced by birdsong when you awake in one of the stylish rooms here, on the banks of the River Arno. A former stone-built artisan workshop, Riva has had a refit to match its "loft" label: mellow color schemes, laminate flooring, floating staircases, marble bathrooms with rainfall showers, and clever integration of natural materials in such features as original wooden workshop ceilings. Noon checkouts are standard—a traveler-friendly touch. The center is a 30-minute walk, or jump on one of Riva's vintage-style bikes and cycle to the Uffizi along the Arno banks. Another standout feature in this price bracket: a shaded garden with outdoor plunge pool.

Via Baccio Bandinelli 98. www.rivalofts.com. ✆ **055-713-0272.** 10 units. 165€–255€ double, includes breakfast. Parking 20€. Bus: 6/Tram: T1 (3 stops from central station). **Amenities:** Bar; bike rental (free); outdoor pool; Wi-Fi (free).

Apartment Rentals & Alternative Accommodations

It's the way of the modern world: Global players in apartment rentals have overtaken most of the local specialists in Florence. Online agency **Cross Pollinate ★** (www.cross-pollinate.com; ✆ **800/270-1190** in

It's All Tripe

New York has the hot dog. London has pie and mash. Florence has... cow's intestine in a sandwich. The city's traditional street food, *lampredotto* (the cow's fourth stomach) stewed with tomatoes, has made a big comeback over the last decade, including on the menus of some fine-dining establishments. The best places to sample it are still the city's *trippai,* tripe vendors who sell it from vans around the center, alongside "regular" sandwiches. The most convenient vendors are in **Piazza de' Cimatori** and on **Via de' Macci** at Piazza Sant'Ambrogio. A hearty, nutritious lunch should come in around 4€. Most are open Monday through Saturday, but close in August, when Florentines flee their city.

U.S., 06/9936-9799 in Italy) has a Florence apartment portfolio worth checking. **GoWithOh.com ★** has a user-friendly website that incorporates verified guest feedback into its wide portfolio of high-quality apartments. **HomeAway.com,** TripAdvisor–owned **HolidayLettings.co.uk,** and **Airbnb** are also well stocked with central and suburban apartments.

An alternative budget option (and a unique perspective on your stay) is offered by staying in a **religious house ★**. A few monasteries and convents in the center receive guests for a modest fee, including the **Suore di Santa Elisabetta,** Viale Michelangiolo 46 (near Piazza Ferrucci; ✆ **055-681-1884**), in a colonial villa just south of the Ponte San Niccolò. Close to Santa Croce, the **Istituto Oblate dell'Assunzione,** Borgo Pinti 15 (✆ **055-2480-582**), has simple, peaceful rooms in a Medici-era building ranged around a courtyard garden. The easiest way to build a monastery and convent itinerary in Florence and beyond is via agent **MonasteryStays.com ★**. Remember that most religious houses have a curfew, generally 11pm or midnight.

Tip: For basic grocery shopping in the center, try **Conad City,** Via dei Servi 56R (✆ **055-280-110**), or any central branch of **Carrefour Express.** Both the **Mercato Centrale** and **Mercato di Sant'Ambrogio** offer farm-fresh produce (see "The Best Markets," p. 219).

WHERE TO EAT

Florence is well-supplied with restaurants, though in the most touristy areas (around the Duomo, Piazza della Signoria, Piazza della Repubblica, and the Ponte Vecchio), you must choose carefully. Many eateries are of below-average quality or charge high prices—sometimes both. The highest concentrations of excellent *ristoranti* and *trattorie* are around **Santa Croce** and across the river in the **Oltrarno** and **San Frediano.** There's also an increasing buzz around **San Lorenzo,** particularly since the top floor of the Mercato Centrale (see below) opened in 2014. The area's rep for catering to the lowest common denominator when it comes to visitors is quickly becoming a thing of the past. Bear in mind that menus at restaurants in Tuscany can change weekly or even (at some of the very best places) daily. The city has also become much more **gluten-savvy.** If you have any sort of food intolerance, don't be afraid to ask.

Reservations are strongly recommended if you have your heart set on eating anywhere in particular, especially at dinner on weekends.

Near the Duomo

MODERATE

Coquinarius ★★ TUSCAN There is a regular menu here—pasta; mains such as beef cheeks with red wine and beans; traditional desserts. But it's equally pleasurable just tucking into a couple of sharing plates and quaffing from the excellent wine list. Go for something from an extensive carpaccio list (beef, boar, octopus, swordfish) and maybe pair a *misto di salumi e formaggi* (mixed Tuscan salami and cheeses) with a full-bodied red wine, to cut through the strong flavors of the deliciously fatty and salty pork and Tuscan sheep's milk cheese, pecorino.

Via delle Oche 11R. www.coquinarius.com. ✆ **055-230-2153.** Main courses 13€–18€. Daily 12:30–3pm and 6:30–10:30pm. Bus: C1 or C2.

INEXPENSIVE

I Due Fratellini ★ LIGHT FARE This hole-in-the-wall has been serving food to go since 1875. The drill is simple: Choose a filling, pick a drink, then eat your fast-filled roll on the curb opposite or find a nearby piazza perch. There are around 30 fillings to choose from, including the usual Tuscan meats and cheeses—salami, pecorino, cured ham—and more flamboyant combos such as goat cheese and Calabrian spicy salami or *bresaola* (air-dried beef) and wild arugula. A glass of wine to wash it down costs from 2€. No credit cards. Lunchtime lines can be long.

Via dei Cimatori 38R (at corner of Via Calzaiuoli). www.iduefratellini.it. ✆ **055-239-6096.** Sandwiches 4€. Daily 10am–7pm. Bus: C2.

Near Piazza della Signoria

EXPENSIVE

Ora d'Aria ★★ CONTEMPORARY TUSCAN If you want to see what the latest generation of Tuscan chefs can do in a kitchen, this place should top your list. The mood is modern and elegant, but never stuffy. Dishes are subtle and creative, and combine traditional Tuscan ingredients in an original way. The menu changes daily, but expect the likes of pappardelle with mackerel ragù, artichokes, and thyme, or suckling pig with turnip greens and a garlic and lavender sauce. If you can't stretch the budget for dinner, book a table at lunch to taste simpler, cheaper

(15€–20€) dishes such as cold salad of salt cod with Pratese vermouth and sweet potato, served in full-size or half-price "tapas" portions. Reservations are essential.

Via dei Georgofili 11–13R (off Via Lambertesca). www.oradariaristorante.com. ✆ **055-200-1699.** Main courses 38€–45€ (at dinner); tasting menus 60€–150€. Tues–Sat 12:30–2:30pm; Mon–Sat 7:30–10pm. Closed 3 weeks in Aug. Bus: C3 or D.

Near San Lorenzo & the Mercato Centrale

Florence's best sandwich bar, **Sandwichic ★★**, Via San Gallo 3R (www.sandwichic.it; ✆ **055/281157**), keeps things simple, with freshly baked bread and expertly sourced ingredients including Tuscan cured meats and savory preserves. Try the likes of *finocchiona* (salami spiked with fennel), pecorino cheese, and *crema di porri* (a creamy leek relish). Sandwiches cost around 4.50€. It's open daily.

MODERATE

Konnubio ★★★ CREATIVE TUSCAN/VEGAN There's a warm glow (candles and low-watt lighting) about this place—it makes you instantly happy, and the cooking keeps you there. Ingredients are largely Tuscan, but combined creatively, such as in warm guinea hen salad with cream of roasted tomatoes, or a risotto of peas and cuttlefish. There's an extensive vegan menu, too, like curried cream of yellow squash with crispy tofu and mango. Under brick vaults and a covered courtyard, it could work for a romantic dinner; but you won't be out of place in a family group either. It feels like refined dining, but at a price point that gets you just a so-so bowl of pasta in many other places.

Via dei Conti 8R. www.konnubio.it. ✆ **055-238-1189.** Main courses 13€–27€. Daily noon–3pm and 7–11pm. Bus: C1.

La Gratella ★★ FLORENTINE/GRILL It doesn't look much—a workers' canteen on a nondescript side street—but looks don't matter much when you can source and cook meat like they do here. Star of the show is the *bistecca alla fiorentina*, a large T-bone-like cut grilled on the bone and brought to the table over coals. It is sold by weight and made for sharing; expect to pay about 50€. Pair this or any market-fresh meat on the menu with simple Tuscan sides like *fagioli all'uccelletto* (stewed beans and tomatoes). They cater to celiacs, too.

Via Guelfa 81R. www.lagratella.it/en. ✆ **055-211-292.** Main courses 12€–18€. Daily noon–3pm and 7–11pm. Bus: 1, 6, 11, 14, 17, 23.

INEXPENSIVE

Mario ★ TRADITIONAL FLORENTINE There is no doubt that this market workers' trattoria is now firmly on the tourist trail. But Mario's clings to the traditions and ethos it adopted when it first fired up the burners 60 years ago. Food is simple, hearty, and served at communal tables—"check in" on arrival and you will be offered seats together wherever they come free. Think *passato di fagioli* (bean puree soup) followed by traditional Tuscan beef stew, *peposo,* or *coniglio arrosto* (roast rabbit). No credit cards.

Via Rosina 2R (north corner of Piazza Mercato Centrale). www.trattoriamario.com. ✆ **055-218-550.** Main courses 8.50€–14€. Mon–Sat noon–3:30pm. Closed Aug. Bus: C1.

Mercato Centrale ★★ MODERN ITALIAN In 2014 the upper floor of Florence's produce market reopened as a bustling shrine to the best modern Italian street food. Counters sell dishes from all over Italy: pasta, vegetarian and vegan fare, authentic Neapolitan pizza, meats and cheeses, fresh fish, Chianina burgers and meatballs, and more. It works perfectly for families who can't agree on a dinner choice. Or just stop by for a drink and soak up the buzz: There's a beer bar (disappointing) and enoteca (superb), plus soccer games on the big screen.

Piazza Mercato Centrale. www.mercatocentrale.it. ✆ **055-239-9798.** Dishes 5€–14€. Daily 10am–midnight. Bus: C1.

Near San Marco & Santissima Annunziata

San Marco is the place to head for *schiacciata,* olive-oil flatbread loaded with savory toppings. You will find some of the best at **Pugi ★**, Piazza San Marco 9B (www.fornopugi.it; ✆ **055-280-981**), open 7:45am to 8pm Monday to Saturday, but closed most of August.

MODERATE

Da Tito ★★ TUSCAN/FLORENTINE Every night feels like party night at one of central Florence's rare genuine neighborhood trattorias. (For that reason, it's usually packed—book ahead.) The welcome and the dishes are classic Florentine, with a few modern Italian curveballs: Start, perhaps, with the *risotto con piselli e guanciale* (rice with fresh peas and cured pork cheek) before going on to a traditional grill such as *lombatina di vitella* (veal chop steak). The neighborhood location, a 10-minute walk north of San Lorenzo, and a mixed clientele keep quality very consistent.

Via San Gallo 112R. www.trattoriadatito.it. ✆ **055-472-475.** Main courses 10€–18€. Mon–Sat 12:30–3pm and 7–11pm. Bus: C1, 1, 7, 20, 25.

Near Santa Croce

MODERATE

Brac ★★ VEGETARIAN/VEGAN An artsy cafe-bookshop for most of the day, at lunch and dinner this place turns into one of Florence's best spots for vegetarian and vegan food. There are seasonal salads and creative pasta dishes, but a *piatto unico* works out best for hungry diners:

one combo plate loaded with three different dishes from the menu, perhaps pear carpaccio with Grana Padano cheese and a balsamic reduction; *tagliatelle* with broccoli, pecorino, and lemon; plus an eggplant and mozzarella *pane carasau* (Sardinian flatbread). The courtyard atmosphere is intimate and romantic, yet singletons won't feel out of place eating at the counter out front. Booking at dinner is a must.

Via dei Vagellai 18R. www.libreriabrac.net. ✆ **055-094-4877.** Main courses 10€–15€. Daily noon–midnight. Bus: C1, C3, 23.

Ruth's ★ KOSHER/VEGETARIAN Ruth's bills itself as a "kosher vegetarian" joint, but you will also find fish on the menu. It's small (around 12 tables), so book ahead to guarantee a table. The interior is cafe-like and informal, the menu likewise. Skip the Italian *primi* and go right for eastern Mediterranean *secondi* such as vegetarian couscous with harissa or fish moussaka, a layered bake of eggplant, tomato, salmon, and spiced rice served with salad and *caponata* (a cold sweet/sour vegetable preserve). A rabbi from the synagogue next door oversees kosher credentials.

Via Farini 2a. www.kosheruth.com. ✆ **055-248-0888.** Main courses 10€–18€. Sun–Fri 12:30–2:30pm; Sat–Thurs 7:30–10pm. Bus: 6, 19, 31, 32.

Vagalume ★★ MODERN ITALIAN The style is *"tapas fiorentine"*—there are no "courses" and no pasta, and you compile a dinner from a range of good-size dishes in any order you please. Dishes change daily, but could include the likes of a soufflé of Gorgonzola, hazelnuts, and zucchini; rabbit stewed in Vernaccia wine with olives; a "tarte tatin" of beetroot and burrata cheese; or a marinated mackerel salad with fennel and orange. To go with the modern menu, there's stripped-back decor, upcycled furniture, jazz-funk played in the background on an old vinyl record player, and an emphasis on beers, three on tap, plus a bottle list that is strong on European styles. The wine list is short but expertly chosen.

Via Pietrapiana 40R. www.facebook.com/vagalume.firenze. ✆ **055-246-6740.** Dishes 7€–14€. Daily 6pm–2am (Feb closed Tues). Bus: C2 or C3.

In the Oltrarno & San Frediano

EXPENSIVE

iO: Osteria Personale ★★★ CONTEMPORARY TUSCAN There's a definite hipster atmosphere, with the whitewashed brick and young staff, but a food ethos is ingrained, too. Ingredients are familiar to Tuscan cooking, but are often combined in a way you may not have seen before. The menu always has a good range of seafood, meat, and vegetarian dishes: perhaps tempura artichoke flowers stuffed with taleggio cheese and marjoram, followed by gnocchi with a white guinea-hen *ragù*, then roasted octopus with garbanzo-bean cream, cumin, and mint. Reservations are always advisable.

Borgo San Frediano 167R. www.io-osteriapersonale.it. ✆ **055-933-1341.** Main courses 15€–22€; tasting menus 40€ 4 dishes, 55€ 6 dishes. Mon–Sat 7:30–10pm. Closed 10 days in Jan and all of Aug. Bus: D or 6.

MODERATE

A Crudo ★★ CONTEMPORARY ITALIAN/RAW FOOD The name means "raw," which provides a clue to the strengths of this 2016 opening. A short carpaccio list might include the likes of venison with bitter citrus and pink peppercorn vinaigrette. But the real star is the meat tartare, done in traditional style as well as in such creative combos as Kathmandù (with lime and avocado) and Marinata (with gin and parsley). There's also vegetarian raw food tartare. A Crudo is a perfect example of modern Florence doing what it does best: tapping into food traditions and letting them breathe some 21st-century air.

Via Mazzetta 5. www.acrudo.com. ✆ **055-265-7483.** Main courses 10€–16€. Daily 12:30–3pm and 7pm–midnight. Bus: C3, D, 11, 36, 37.

Da Gherardo ★★ PIZZA This informal, cave-like restaurant is packed tight with tables for a reason: It's always busy. Pizzas arrive quickly from a wood-fired oven, in Naples style. Toppings go well beyond Neapolitan tradition, however—with *'nduja* (soft, spicy salami), four cheese, and zucchini on the menu—but the Marinara (tomato, garlic, oregano, basil) is hard to beat. Reservations are strongly advised, but if you forget, they do takeout, which you can munch around the corner in Piazza del Carmine.

Borgo San Frediano 57R. www.gherardopizzeria.com. ✆ **055-282-921.** Pizzas 4.50€–11€. Daily 7:30pm–1am. Bus: D or 6.

Il Magazzino ★ FLORENTINE A traditional *osteria* that specializes in the flavors of old Florence, it looks the part, too, with its terracotta tiled floor and barrel vault, chunky wooden furniture, and hanging lamps. If you dare, this is a place to try tripe or *lampredotto* (intestines), the traditional food of working Florentines, prepared expertly here in ravioli or meatballs, boiled, or *alla fiorentina* (stewed with tomatoes and garlic). The rest of the menu is carnivore-friendly too: Follow *tagliatelle al ragù bianco* (pasta ribbons with a "white" meat sauce made with a little milk instead of tomatoes) with *guancia di vitello in agrodolce* (veal cheek stewed with baby onions in a sticky-sweet sauce).

Piazza della Passera 3. ✆ **055-215-969.** Main courses 10€–18€. Daily noon–3pm and 7:30–11pm. Bus: C3 or D.

Gelato

Florence has a fair claim to being the birthplace of gelato, and has some of the world's best *gelaterie*—but many poor imitations, too. Steer clear of spots around major attractions with air-fluffed mountains of ice cream and flavors so full of artificial colors they glow in the dark. If you can see the Ponte Vecchio or Piazza della Signoria from the front door of the gelateria, you may want to move on. You might have to walk a block, or duck down a side street, to find a genuine gelato artisan. Trust us, you'll taste the difference. Opening hours tend to be discretionary: When it's warm, many places stay open to 11pm or beyond.

Carapina ★★ Militant seasonality ensures the fruit gelato here is the best in the center. ***Note:*** This branch usually closes at 7pm. Via Lambertesca 18R. www.carapina.it. ✆ **055-291-128.** Cone from 2.50€. Bus: C3 or D. Also at: Piazza Oberdan 2R (✆ 055-676-930).

Gelateria della Passera ★★ Milk-free water ices here are among the most intensely flavored in the city, and relatively low in sugary sweetness. Try the likes of pink grapefruit or jasmine tea gelato. Via Toscanella 15R (at Piazza della Passera). www.gelaterialapassera.wordpress.com. ✆ **055-291-882.** Cone from 2€. Bus: C3 or D.

Gelateria de' Neri ★ There's a large range of fruit, white, and chocolate flavors here, but nothing over-elaborate. If the ricotta and fig flavor is offered, you are in luck. Via dei Neri 9R. ✆ **055-210-034.** Cone from 1.80€. Bus: C1, C3, 23.

La Carraia ★★ It's packed with locals late into the evening on summer weekends—for good reason. The range is vast, the quality high. Piazza N. Sauro 25R. www.lacarraiagroup.eu. ✆ **055-280-695.** Cone from 2€. Bus: C3, D, 6, 11, 36, 37. Also at: Via de' Benci 24R (✆ 329-363-0069).

Il Gelato Gourmet di Marco Ottaviano ★★ It's all about the seasonal, produce-led flavors at this place. Choices may include Sicilian pistachio or Pastiera, based on a Neapolitan cake. Via Palmieri 34R (at Piazza di San Pier Maggiore). www.marcoottaviano.it. ✆ **055-234-1036.** Cone from 2€. Bus: C1 or C2.

SHOPPING

After Milan, Florence is **Italy's top shopping city**—beating even Rome. Here's what to buy: leather, fashion, shoes, marbleized paper, hand-embroidered linens, artisan and craft items including ceramics, Tuscan wines, handmade jewelry, *pietre dure* (known also as "Florentine mosaic," inlaid semiprecious stones), and antiques.

Standard Florentine **shopping hours** are Monday through Saturday from 9:30am to noon or 1pm and 3 or 3:30 to 7:30pm. Increasingly, shops stay open on Sunday and through the midafternoon *riposo,* or "nap." Larger stores and those around tourist sights have pretty much all gone that way already. Some small or family-run places close Monday mornings instead of Sundays.

Shopping for leather goods at an outdoor market.

Top Shopping Streets & Areas

AROUND SANTA TRÍNITA The cream of the crop of Florentine shopping lines both sides of elegant **Via de' Tornabuoni,** with an extension along **Via della Vigna Nuova** and other surrounding streets. Here you'll find the big Florentine fashion names like **Gucci** ★ (at no. 73R; www.gucci.com; ✆ **055-264-011**), **Pucci** ★ (at no. 22R; www.emiliopucci.com; ✆ **055-265-8082**), and **Ferragamo** ★ (at no. 5R; www.ferragamo.com; ✆ **055-292-123**), ensconced in old palaces or minimalist boutiques. Stricter traffic controls have made shopping on Via de' Tornabuoni a more sedate experience, though somewhat at the expense of surrounding streets.

AROUND VIA ROMA & VIA DEI CALZAIUOLI These are some of Florence's busiest streets, packed with storefronts offering mainstream shopping. It is here you will find the city's major department stores, **Coin,** Via dei Calzaiuoli 56R (www.coin.it; ✆ **055-280-531**), and **La Rinascente,** Piazza della Repubblica (www.rinascente.it; ✆ **055-219-113**), alongside quality clothing chains such as Geox and Zara. **La Feltrinelli RED,** Piazza delle Repubblica 26 (www.lafeltrinelli.it; ✆ **199-151-173**), is the center's best bookstore. A three-floor branch of upscale food-market minichain **Eataly,** Via de' Martelli 22 (www.eataly.net; ✆ **055-015-3601**), lies just north of the Baptistery. Online couture sales sensation **Luisa Via Roma** ★ (www.luisaviaroma.com) also has its physical store here, at Via Roma 21R.

AROUND SANTA CROCE The eastern part of the center has seen a flourishing of one-of-a-kind stores, with an emphasis on young, independent fashions. **Borgo degli Albizi** and its tributary streets are worth roaming.

Crafts & Artisans

Glassware from designer Marioluca Giusti.

Florence has a longstanding reputation for its craftsmanship. Although the storefront display windows along heavily touristed streets are often stuffed with cheap imports and mass-produced goods, if you search around you can still find handmade, top-quality items.

To get a better understanding of Florence's artisans, including a visit to a workshop, **Context Travel** (p. 200) runs a guided walk around the Oltrarno, Florence's traditional craft area. The "Made in Florence" walk costs 80€ and lasts 3 hours.

Madova ★ For nearly a century, this has been the best city retailer for handmade leather gloves, lined with silk, cashmere, or lambs' wool. You'll pay between 40€ and 60€ for a pair. Madova is the real deal, even this close to the Ponte Vecchio. Closed Sundays. Via Guicciardini 1R. www.madova.com. ✆ **055-239-6526.** Bus: C3 or D.

Marioluca Giusti ★★ The boutique of this renowned Florentine designer sells only his trademark synthetic glassware. The range includes colorful reinventions of cocktail and wine glasses, jugs, and tumblers—every piece both tough and chic. Via della Spada 20R. www.mariolucagiusti.it. ✆ **055-214-583.** Bus: 6 or 11. Also at: Via della Vigna Nuova 88R.

Officina Profumo-Farmaceutica di Santa Maria Novella ★★★ A shrine to scents and skincare, this is Florence's historic herbal pharmacy, with roots in the 17th century, when it was founded by Dominicans based in the adjacent convent of Santa Maria Novella. Nothing is cheap, but the perfumes, cosmetics, moisturizers, and other products are handmade from the finest natural ingredients and packaged exquisitely. Via della Scala 16. www.smnovella.it. ✆ **055-216-276.** Bus: C2.

Parione ★ This traditional Florentine stationer stocks notebooks, marbleized paper, fine pens, and handmade wooden music boxes. Via dello Studio 11R. www.parione.it. ✆ **055-215-684.** Bus: C1 or C2.

Scuola del Cuoio ★★ Florence's leading leather school is also open house for visitors. You can watch trainee artisans at work (Mon–Fri), then visit the small shop to buy the best soft leather. Portable items like wallets and bags are a good buy. Closed Sundays in off-season. Via San Giuseppe 5R (or enter through Santa Croce, via right transept). www.scuoladelcuoio.com. ✆ **055-244-534.** Bus: C3.

Food stall in the Mercado Centrale.

The Best Markets

Mercato Centrale ★★ The center's main market stocks the usual fresh produce, but you can also browse (and taste) cheeses, salamis and cured hams, Tuscan wines, takeout food, and more. This is picnic-packing heaven. It runs Monday to Saturday until 2pm (until 5pm Sat for most of the year). Upstairs is street-food nirvana, all day, every day; see p. 213. Btw. Piazza del Mercato Centrale and Via dell'Ariento. No phone. Bus: C1.

Mercato di San Lorenzo ★ The city's tourist street market is a fun place to pick up T-shirts, marbleized paper, or a city souvenir. Leather wallets, purses, bags, and jackets are another popular purchase—be sure to assess the workmanship, and haggle shamelessly. The market runs daily; watch out for pickpockets. In 2014 it was controversially ejected from part of its traditional home, in Piazza San Lorenzo, and now spreads around Piazza del Mercato Centrale; whether it will move back is as yet undecided. Via dell'Ariento and Via Rosina. No phone. Bus: C1.

ENTERTAINMENT & NIGHTLIFE

Florence has excellent, mostly free listings publications. At the tourist offices, pick up the free monthly ***Informacittà*** (www.informacitta.net), which is strong on theater, concerts, and other arts events, as well as one-off markets. Younger and hipper ***Zero*** (www.zero.eu/firenze), available free from trendy cafe-bars and shops, is hot on the latest eating, drinking, and edgy nightlife. ***Firenze Spettacolo,*** a 2€ Italian-language monthly sold at newsstands, is the most detailed and up-to-date listing of nightlife, arts, and entertainment. English-language magazine "The Florentine" publishes weekly events and listings at **www.theflr.net/weekly**.

If you just want to wander and see what grabs you, you will find plenty of tourist-oriented action in bars around the city's main squares. For something a little livelier—with a more local focus—check out **Borgo San Frediano, Piazza Santo Spirito,** or the northern end of **Via de' Macci,** close to where it meets Via Pietrapiana. **Via de' Benci** is usually buzzing around *aperitivo* time, and is popular with an expat crowd. **Via de' Renai** and the bars of San Niccolò around the **Porta San Miniato** are often lively too, with a mixed crowd of tourists and locals.

Performing Arts & Live Music

Florence does not have the musical cachet of Milan, Venice, Naples, or Rome, but there are two symphony orchestras and a fine music school in Fiesole, as well as great expectations for its new opera house (see below). The city's theaters are respectable, and most major touring companies stop in town. Get tickets to all cultural events online—they will send an e-mail with collection instructions—or buy in person at **Box Office,** Via delle Vecchie Carceri 1 (www.boxofficetoscana.it; ✆ **055-210-804**).

Many classical chamber music performances are sponsored by the **Amici della Musica** (www.amicimusica.fi.it; ✆ **055-607-440**), so check their website to see what is on while you are here. The venue is often the historic **Teatro della Pergola.**

Libreria-Café La Cité ★ A relaxed café-bookshop by day, after dark this place becomes a bar and small-scale live music venue. The lineup is eclectic, often offbeat or world music, one night forrò or swing, the next Italian folk or chanteuse. Borgo San Frediano 20R. www.lacitelibreria.info. ✆ **055-210-387.** Bus: C3, D, 6, 11, 36, 37.

Opera di Firenze ★★ This vast new concert hall and arts complex seats up to 1,800 in daring modernist surrounds on the edge of the Cascine Park. Its program incorporates opera, ballet, and orchestral music. The same venue hosts the **Maggio Musicale Fiorentino,** one of Italy's most prestigious music festivals. Piazzale Vittorio Gui. www.operadifirenze.it. ✆ **055-277-9350.** Tickets 10€–100€. Tram: T1.

St. Mark's ★ Operatic duets and full-scale operas in costume are the lure here. The program sticks to crowd-pleasers like "Carmen," "La Traviata," and "La Bohème" and runs most nights of the week all year. Via Maggio 18. www.concertoclassico.info. ✆ **340-811-9192.** Tickets 15€–35€. Bus: D, 11, 36, 37.

Volume ★ By day, it's a laid-back cafe and art space selling coffee, books, and crepes. By night, it's a buzzing cocktail bar with regular acoustic sets. Piazza Santo Spirito 5R. www.volumefirenze.com. ✆ **055-238-1460.** Bus: C3, D, 11, 36, 37.

Cafes

Florence no longer has a glitterati or intellectuals' cafe scene, and when it did—from the 19th-century Risorgimento era through 1950s *dolce vita*—it was basically copying the idea from Paris. Although they're often overpriced tourist spots today—especially around **Piazza della Repubblica**—Florence's high-toned cafes are fine if you want pastries served to you while you sit and people-watch.

Caffetteria delle Oblate ★ This relaxing terrace is popular with local families and students, and well away from the tourist crush (and prices) on the streets outside. As a bonus, it has a unique view of Brunelleschi's dome, and serves light lunch and *aperitivo*. Closed Monday morning. Top floor of Biblioteca dell'Oblate, Via del Oriuolo 24. www.caffetteriadelleoblate.it. ✆ **055-263-9685.** Bus: C1 or C2.

La Terrazza ★ The prices, like the perch, are a little elevated (3€–5€ for a coffee). But you get to enjoy your drink on a hidden terrace in the sky, with just the rooftops, towers, and Brunelleschi's dome for company. Top floor of La Rinascente, Piazza della Repubblica. www.larinascente.it. ✆ **055-219-113.** Bus: C2.

Procacci ★ The second you walk through the door, you're hit with the perfume of Procacci's specialty: *panini tartufati*, brioche rolls spread with truffle butter. Via Tornabuoni 64R. www.procacci1885.it. ✆ 055-211-656. Bus: C3.

Rivoire ★ If you are going to choose one overpriced pavement cafe in Florence, make it this one. The steep prices (6€ a cappuccino, 4.50€ for a small mineral water) help pay the rent of one of the prettiest slices of real estate on the planet. Piazza della Signoria (at Via Vacchereccia). www.rivoire.it. ✆ **055-214-412.** Bus: C2.

Wine Bars, Cocktail Bars & Craft Beer Bars

If you want to party into the wee hours, you will likely find Italian **nightclubs** rather cliquey. People usually go in groups to hang out and dance only with one another. There's plenty of flesh showing, but no meat market. Out in the 'burbs, **Tenax,** Via Pratese 46 (www.tenax.org; ✆ **335-523-5922**), attracts big-name DJs on Friday and Saturday nights.

Beer House Club ★★ Serving the best artisan beers from Tuscany, Italy, and farther afield. Their own line, brewed for the bar in nearby Prato, includes IPA, Imperial Stout, and Saison styles. Between 5 and 8pm, house beers are 5€ a pint instead of 6€. Corso Tintori 34R. ✆ **055-247-6763.** Bus: C1, C3, 23.

Cantinetta dei Verrazzano ★★ One of the coziest little wine and food bars in the center is decked out with antique wooden wine cabinets, in genuine *enoteca* style. The wines come from the first-rate Verrazzano estate, in Chianti (see p. 245). Closed Sunday evenings. Via dei Tavolini 18R. www.verrazzano.com. ✆ **055-268-590.** Bus: C2.

Diorama ★★ This tiny bar has a small terrace, Formica tables, craft beers (5€–7€), and a local vibe. Closed Mondays. Via Pisana 78R. www.dioramafirenze.com. ✆ **055-228-6682.** Bus: 6.

Lo Sverso ★★ New-breed craft cocktails and classics with a twist (like the rosemary Collins, with herb-infused gin), all at sub-10€ prices. There are a few outdoor seats under the loggia facing the market. Free snacks are offered from 6pm to 9pm. Via Panicale 7R. www.facebook.com/losverso.firenze. **No phone.** Bus: C1.

Mostodolce ★ Burgers, pizza, snacks, Wi-Fi, and sports on the screen—so far, so good. And Mostodolce also has its own artisan beer on tap, brewed just outside Florence at Prato (some are very strong). Happy hour is 3:30 to 7:30pm, when it is .50€ off a beer. Via Nazionale 114R. ✆ **055-230-2928.** Bus: 1, 6, 11, 14, 17, 23.

Cantinetta dei Verrazzano.

O' Café ★ An elegant, minimalist *aperitivo* spot. Pay 10€ to 14€ for a cocktail or glass of sparkling wine and help yourself to the buffet between 6:30 and 9pm every night. Live jazz plays from 9:15pm 3 nights a week in the adjoining Golden View Open Bar (essentially the same place). Via dei Bardi 56R. www.goldenviewopenbar.com. ✆ **055-214-502.** Bus: C3 or D.

Sant'Ambrogio ★ This fine wine and cocktail bar is in a lively part of the center, northeast of Santa Croce. It is popular with locals without being too achingly hip. In summer, everyone spills out onto the little piazza and church steps outside. Piazza Sant'Ambrogio 7R. No phone. Bus: C2 or C3.

Santino ★★ This snug wine bar stocks niche labels from across Italy, serving exquisite "Florentine tapas" (5€–10€) to munch while you sip. Via Santo Spirito 60R. ✆ **055-230-2820.** Bus: D, 11, 36, 37.

Terrazza Lounge at the Continentale ★★ There are few surprises on the list here—a well-made Negroni, Moscow Mule, Bellini, and the like—and prices are a little steep at 15€ to 18€ a cocktail. But the setting, on a rooftop right by the Ponte Vecchio, makes them practically a steal. The atmosphere is fashionable but casual (wear what you like) and staff is supremely welcoming. Arrive at sundown to see the city below start to twinkle. Closed in bad weather. Continentale Hotel, Vicolo dell'Oro 6R. ✆ **055-2726-5806.** Bus: C3 or D.

Uva Nera ★ Atmospheric little wine bar with vintage furniture, cold cuts at the counter, and organic wines by the glass. Borgo Ognissanti 25R. ✆ **055-012-1189.** Bus: C3, 6, 11.

6 TUSCANY

By Stephen Brewer

Generations of travelers have descended upon Italy's most popular region, and they still do. Little wonder. Even for Italians from other parts of the peninsula, Tuscany is the epitome of everything that's good about their country. Beguiling landscapes are carpeted with cypresses and vineyards. Medieval and Renaissance cities are some of Europe's great centers of civilization, and the food and wine is delicious. Even a short visit inundates a traveler with an embarrassment of riches. Renaissance artists famously left behind some of the world's greatest art and architecture in Tuscany—the Leaning Tower of Pisa, Piero della Francesca's frescoes in Arezzo, Ambrogio Lorenzetti's civic "Allegories" in Siena's Museo Civico.

Soaking up culture is certainly part of the allure, and the pleasures of the palate are just as noted. Even a simple meal can seem like a work of art in places as bountiful as the Val di Chiana and Val d'Orcia. Somehow it only makes sense that full-bodied red wines should come from towns as appealing as Montepulciano and Montalcino, and character-filled whites from proud little San Gimignano. Then there's all that iconic scenery, in landscapes like the rolling fields and pointy cypresses in the Crete Sienese or the vineyards of Chianti. Art, scenery, food, wine—you may come to agree that all the good things in life come together in Tuscany.

SIENA ★★★

70km (43 miles) S of Florence, 232km (144 miles) N of Rome

Florence's longtime rival, this medieval city of rose-colored brick seems to have come out on top in terms of grace and elegance. With steep, twisting stone alleys and proud churches, palaces, and crenellated public buildings draped across its gentle hillsides, Siena is for many admirers the most beautiful town in Italy. At its heart is a ravishing piazza, and from its heights rises a magnificent duomo of striped marble.

The city trumpets the she-wolf as its emblem, a holdover from its days as Saena Julia, the Roman colony founded by Augustus about 2,000 years ago (though the official Sienese myth has the town founded by the sons of Remus, younger brother of Rome's legendary forefather). Civic projects and artistic prowess reached their greatest heights in the 13th

FACING PAGE: **Piazza del Campo Square in Siena.**

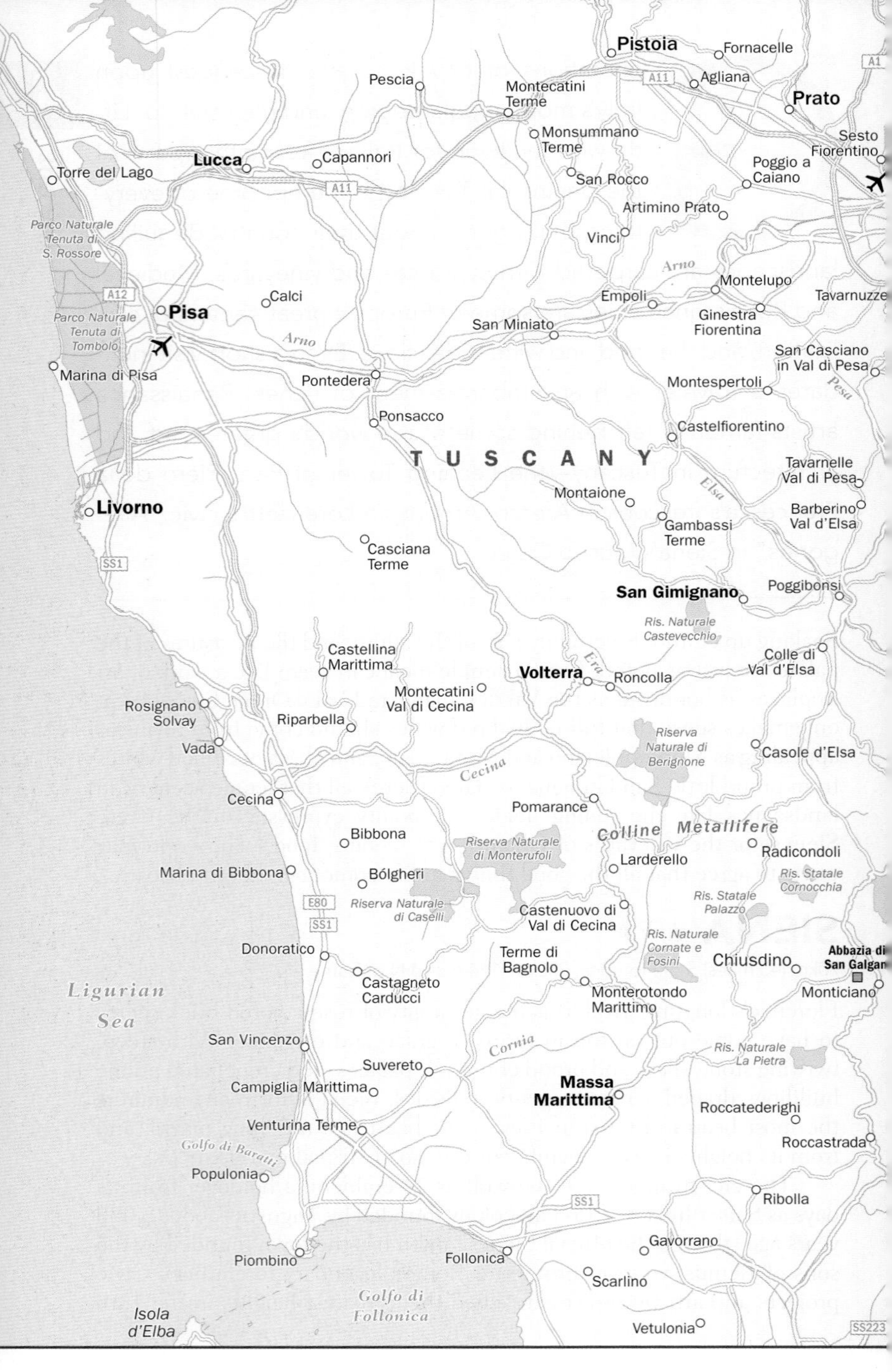
Pistoia
Fornacelle
A1
Pescia
Montecatini Terme
A11
Agliana
Prato
Monsummano Terme
Sesto Fiorentino
Lucca
Capannori
Poggio a Caiano
Torre del Lago
San Rocco
A11
Artimino Prato
Parco Naturale Tenuta di S. Rossore
Vinci
Arno
Montelupo
A12
Calci
Empoli
Tavarnuzze
Pisa
Ginestra Fiorentina
Parco Naturale Tenuta di Tombolo
San Miniato
Arno
San Casciano in Val di Pesa
Marina di Pisa
Pontedera
Montespertoli
Pesa
Ponsacco
Castelfiorentino
TUSCANY
Tavarnelle Val di Pesa
Elsa
Montaione
Barberino Val d'Elsa
Livorno
Gambassi Terme
Casciana Terme
SS1
San Gimignano
Poggibonsi
Ris. Naturale Castevecchio
Castellina Marittima
Era
Colle di Val d'Elsa
Volterra
Roncolla
Montecatini Val di Cecina
Rosignano Solvay
Riparbella
Riserva Naturale di Berignone
Vada
Casole d'Elsa
Cecina
Cecina
Pomarance
Colline Metallifere
Bibbona
Riserva Naturale di Monterufoli
Radicondoli
Larderello
Marina di Bibbona
Bólgheri
Ris. Statale Cornocchia
E80
Riserva Naturale di Caselli
Ris. Statale Palazzo
Castenuovo di Val di Cecina
SS1
Ris. Naturale Cornate e Fosini
Donoratico
Terme di Bagnolo
Chiusdino
Abbazia di San Galgan
Castagneto Carducci
Monterotondo Marittimo
Monticiano
Ligurian Sea
San Vincenzo
Cornia
Ris. Naturale La Pietra
Suvereto
Campiglia Marittima
Massa Marittima
Roccatederighi
Venturina Terme
Roccastrada
Golfo di Baratti
Populonia
Ribolla
SS1
Gavorrano
Piombino
Follonica
Scarlino
Golfo di Follonica
Isola d'Elba
Vetulonia
SS223

Tuscany
0
10 mi
0
10 km
Monte Falterona, Campigna, e Foreste Casentinesi
EMILIA-ROMAGNA
Vaglia
Vicchio
Rufina
Sieve
Fiesole
Florence (Firenze)
Pontassieve
Stia
Arno
Rignano sull'Arno
Vallombrosa
Poppi
Chiusi della Verna
Grassina
Bibbiena
Impruneta
Sto. Stefano a Tizzano
Pieve Santo Stefano
Reggello
San Polo in Chianti
Rassina
Caprese Michelangelo
Strada in Chianti
Pian de Sco
SS222
Figline Valdarno
Castelfranco di Sopra
SS71
Vicchiomaggio
Castello di Verrazzano
Area Naturale Protetta di Int. Locale Le Balze
Loro Ciuffenna
Greve in Chianti
Sansepolcro
Montefioralle
San Giovanni Valdarno
Valdarno
Capolona
Villa Vignamaggio
Ris. Naturale Reg. Valle dell'Inferno e Bandella
Castiglion Fibocchi
Anghiari
Panzano in Chianti
Giovi-Ponte alla Chiassa
Fontodi
Montevarchi
A1
Laterina
Castello di Volpaia
Levane
Chianti
Ris. Naturale Reg. Ponte a Buriano e Penna
Monterchi
Bucine
Radda in Chianti
Arezzo
Castellina in Chianti
Pergine Valdarno
Gaiole in Chianti
Battifolle-Ruscello
UMBRIA
Ambra
Val di Chiana
Quercegrossa
Rigutino
Monteriggioni
Castelnuovo Berardenga
Castiglion Fiorentino
Monte San Savino
Siena
E78
SS73
Rapolano Terme
Lucignano
Foiano dei Chiana
Cortona
Sovicille
SS326
Isola d'Arbia
SS71
Asciano
Terontola
SS223
Monteroni d'Arbia
Ombrone
Sinalunga
Ris. Naturale Alto Merse
Abbazia di Monte Oliveto Maggiore
Vescovado
Torrita di Siena
A1
Lago Trasimeno
Merse
Montepulciano Stazione
Buonconvento
Castiglione del Lago
Ris. Naturale Basso Merse
Montepulciano
San Quirico d'Orcia
Pienza
Ris. Naturale Farma
UMBRIA
Montalcino
Chianciano Terme
Panicale
Bagno Vignoni
Ris. Naturale Lucciolabella
Ris. Naturale Pietraporciana
Ombrone
Chiusi
Tavernelle
Abbazia di Sant'Antimo
Castiglione d'Orcia
Sarteano
Orcia
Piegaro
Cetona
Città della Pieve
Paganico
Radicófani
San Casciano dei Bagni
Campagnatico
Cinigiano
Arcidosso
Fabro
E78
Pianacastagnaio
Ficulle
SS2

and 14th centuries, when artists invented a distinctive Sienese style as banking and a booming wool industry made Siena one of the richest Italian republics. Then, in 1348, the Black Death killed more than half of the population, decimating the social fabric and devastating the economy. Siena never recovered, and much of the city has barely changed since, inviting you to slip into the rhythms and atmosphere of the Middle Ages.

Essentials

GETTING THERE

BY TRAIN Siena's **train station** is at Piazza Roselli, about 3km (1¾ miles) north and far below the city center. Trains connect Siena with **Florence** (usually 90 min.), with a change in Empoli; trains to and from Rome (3 to 4 hr.) require a change in Chiusi. To get into town, take the **no. 3, 8, or 10 bus** to Piazza Gramsci (buy your ticket, 1.20€, at the newsstand in the station). Don't take the buses that stop in front of the station, but go into the big brick shopping center across the street and take the escalator to the underground bus stop. Be sure to say *"Gramsci"* when you board, or you can end up in a far-flung district. You can also take a series of escalators up to town from the top floor of the shopping center—these too are poorly marked, but as long as you're going up you're moving in the right direction. You will be deposited onto Via Vittorio Emanule II, which you can follow through Porta Camollia to Piazza del Campo. ***Note:*** Siena's train station does not have a baggage storage office, though there is one at the bus station on Piazza Gramsci (see below).

BY BUS It's often easier and faster to travel between Siena and Florence and other towns by **bus** than it is by train. Buses let you off right in town at Piazza Gramsci, at the edge of the historic center: Tiemme (www.tiemmespa.it) express buses (*corse rapide;* around 25 daily; 75 min.) and slower buses (*corse ordinarie;* 14 daily; 95 min.) operate between **Florence**'s main bus station and Siena, and Siena is also connected with **San Gimignano** (at least hourly Mon–Sat, either direct or with a change in Poggibonsi; 65–80 min. not including layover), **Perugia** (two to four daily; 90 min.), and **Rome**'s Tiburtina station (five to nine daily; 3 hr.). A luggage storage office is tucked away in an arcade beneath Piazza Gramsci.

BY CAR Fast roads provide direct links from Florence, Arezzo, and Perugia; or from Florence, take the more scenic route, down the Chiantigiana SS222. From **Rome** get off the A1 north at the Val di Chiana exit and follow the SS326 west for 50km (31 miles). From **Pisa** take the highway toward Florence and exit onto the SS429 south just before

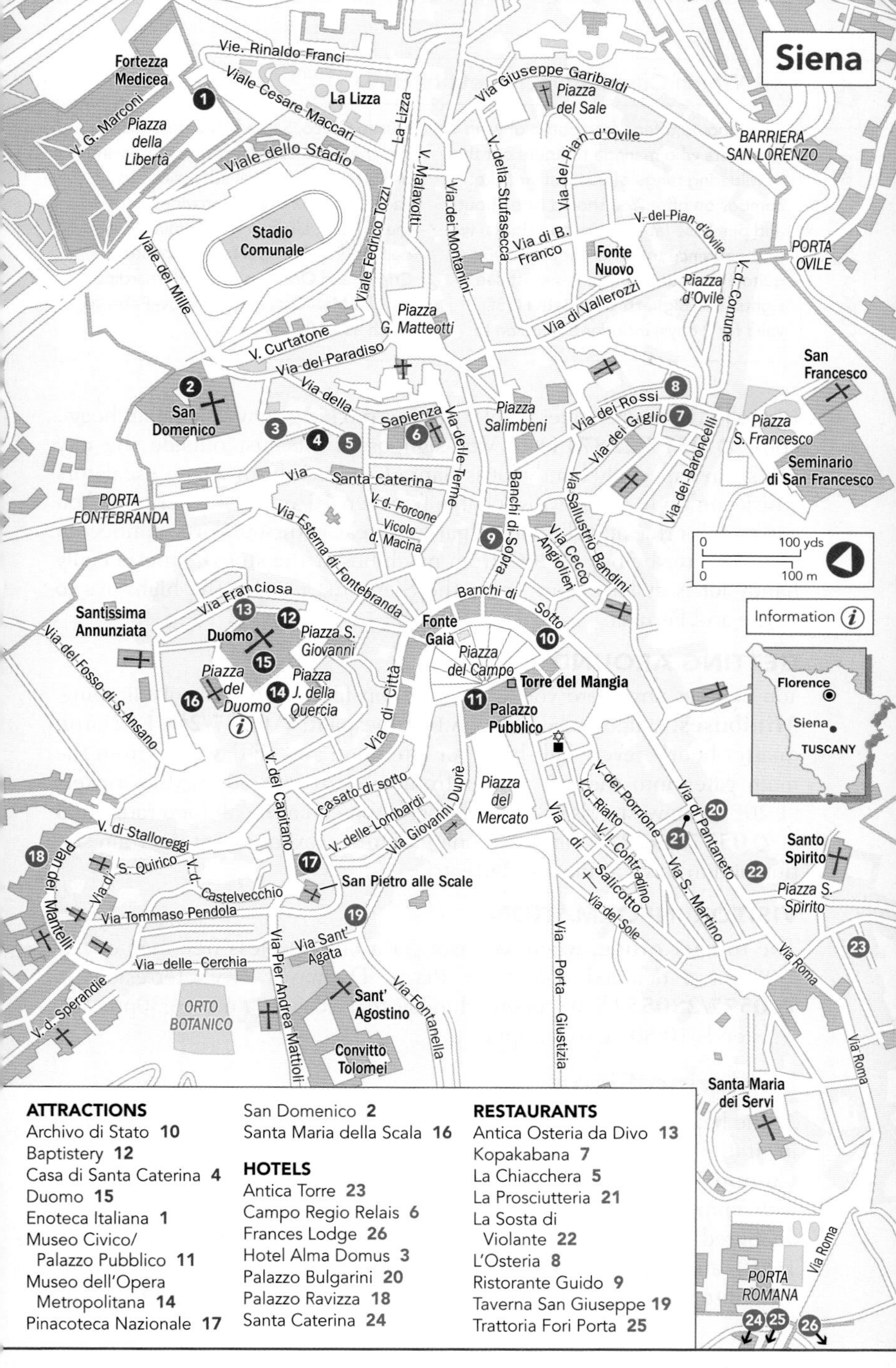

ATTRACTIONS

- Archivio di Stato **10**
- Baptistery **12**
- Casa di Santa Caterina **4**
- Duomo **15**
- Enoteca Italiana **1**
- Museo Civico/ Palazzo Pubblico **11**
- Museo dell'Opera Metropolitana **14**
- Pinacoteca Nazionale **17**
- San Domenico **2**
- Santa Maria della Scala **16**

HOTELS

- Antica Torre **23**
- Campo Regio Relais **6**
- Frances Lodge **26**
- Hotel Alma Domus **3**
- Palazzo Bulgarini **20**
- Palazzo Ravizza **18**
- Santa Caterina **24**

RESTAURANTS

- Antica Osteria da Divo **13**
- Kopakabana **7**
- La Chiacchera **5**
- La Prosciutteria **21**
- La Sosta di Violante **22**
- L'Osteria **8**
- Ristorante Guido **9**
- Taverna San Giuseppe **19**
- Trattoria Fori Porta **25**

Which Cumulative Tickets to Buy

Siena should offer a free bottle of wine to visitors who manage to figure out the bewildering range of cumulative ticket combos on offer. You should care about and purchase (at participating sights) two of them, since together they save you quite a few euros on Siena's must-see sights. The **Biglietti Cumulativi** (13€; valid for 2 days) includes admission to Museo Civico, Santa Maria della Scala, and the Torre del Mangia, a total savings of 15€ over individual admissions to each. The **Opa Si pass** provides entry to the Duomo, Libreria Piccolomini, Museo dell'Opera Metropolitana, Baptistery, Cripta, and Oratorio di San Bernardino for 15€ Mar–Oct) and 10€ Nov–Feb—as much as a 10€ savings.

Empoli (100km/62 miles total). There's **parking** (www.sienaparcheggi.com; ✆ **0577/228711**) in well-signposted lots just outside the city gates. An especially handy lot is Santa Caterina, from which escalators whisk you up to town. Most charge between 1€ and 1.60€ per hour. You can park for free at well-marked parking areas in the outskirts, connected to the center by bus (1.20€, from machines at the stops); an especially handy lot is at Due Ponti, near the Siena Est exit for the highways to Rome and Perugia.

GETTING AROUND

You can get anywhere you want to go on foot, with a bit of climbing. **Minibuses,** called *pollicini* (www.tiemmespa.it; ✆ **0577/204117**), run quarter-hourly (every half-hour Sat afternoon and all day Sun) from the main gates into the city center from 6:30am to 8:30pm. Buy tickets (1.20€) at newsstands or tabacchi-bars. You can also call for a radio **taxi** at ✆ **0577/49222** (7am–9pm only); there's a taxi queue at the train station and in town at Piazza Matteotti.

VISITOR INFORMATION

The **tourist office,** where you can get a fairly useless free map or pay .50€ for a detailed one, is at Piazza Duomo 1 (www.terresiena.it; ✆ **0577/280551**). It's open Monday to Friday 10am to 6:30pm and weekends 10:30am to 6:30pm.

Exploring Siena

At the heart of Siena is a serious contender for the most beautiful square in Italy—the sloping, scallop-shell-shaped **Piazza del Campo (Il Campo)**. Laid out in the 1100s on the site of the Roman forum, the welcoming expanse is a testament to the city's civic achievements; it's anchored by a crenellated town hall, the **Palazzo Pubblico** (1297–1310), and the herringbone brick pavement is divided by white marble lines into nine sections representing the city's medieval ruling body, the

Palio delle Contrade Race in the Piazza del Campo in Siena.

Council of Nine. A 19th-century replica of Jacopo della Quercia's 14th-century fountain, the **Fonte Gaia,** is on one side of the square (some of the restored, but badly eroded, original panels are in Santa Maria della Scala (see p. 237). The dominant public monument is the slender 100m-tall (328-ft.) brick **Torre del Mangia** (1338–48), named for a slothful bell ringer nicknamed Mangiaguadagni, or "profit eater." (There's an armless statue of him in the courtyard.) From the platform atop the tower's 503 steps, the undulating Tuscan hills seem to rise and fall to the ends of the earth (admission to tower 10€, mid-Oct to Feb 10am–4pm, Mar to mid-Oct 10am–7pm).

Archivio di Stato ★ MUSEUM Tucked into a 1469 Florentine Renaissance-style palazzo off the southeast corner of the Campo, this state archive displays such historic documents as Boccaccio's will and Jacopo della Quercia's contract for designing the Fonte Gaia fountain. Most riveting, however, is a remarkable set of wooden covers dating back to 1258 and made for the city's account books, the "Tavolette di Biccherna." They're painted with religious scenes, vignettes of daily working life, and important events in Siena's history.

Via Banchi di Sotto 52. ✆ **0577-241-745.** Free. Mon–Sat hourly viewings at 9:30, 10:30, and 11:30am

A DAY AT THE races

Siena lets its guard down every year, on July 2 and again on August 16, when the **Palio delle Contrade** transforms the Piazza del Campo into a racetrack, with hordes of spectators squeezing through the city's narrow alleyways to watch. This aggressive bareback horse race around the Campo involves 10 of Siena's 17 *contrade* (districts), chosen by lot to participate, and is preceded by a showy flag-waving ceremony and parade. The race itself is over in just 2 minutes. Frenzied celebrations greet the winning rider, and the day is rounded off with communal feasts in each district.

To witness the event, you'll end up standing for hours in the sun and waging battle to get to a toilet. An easier way to enjoy the experience is to settle for the trial races, also held in the Campo (starting June 29 and Aug 13). There's a crowd, but it's smaller and tamer. While trial races are not as fast and furious as the real thing, they are just as photogenic and fun to watch. There are usually six in the mornings (9am) and late evenings (7:45pm June, 7:15pm Aug).

Another way to view the Palio in comfort is to reserve a spot in the temporary stands, on one of the surrounding terraces, or even at a window overlooking the campo. You should reserve a year in advance and expect to pay at least 350€ and as much as 700€ a person. Among the travel agents handling arrangements is **2Be Travel Designers** (www.paliotickets.com).

Duomo ★★★ CATHEDRAL Much of the artistic greatness of Siena comes together in this black-and-white-marble cathedral, a magnificent showcase of Italian Gothic architecture begun in the 12th century and completed in the 13th century. You're likely to come away with a great appreciation for the Pisanos, father and son. Nicola was the principal architect of the church, until he fell out of favor with the group overseeing construction; young Giovanni did much of the carving on the facade, where an army of prophets and apostles appears around three portals (most of the originals are now in the Museo dell'Opera Metropolitana; see p. 235). Both worked on the pulpit, with sumptuously sculpted scenes of the life of Christ and the prophets and evangelists.

Beneath the pulpit spreads a flooring mosaic of 59 etched and inlaid marble panels (1372–1547), a showpiece for 40 of Siena's medieval and Renaissance artistic luminaries. Most prolific among them was Domenico Beccafumi, born into a local peasant family and adopted by his lord, who saw the boy's talent for drawing. Beccafumi studied in Rome but returned to Siena and spent much of his career designing 35 scenes for the flooring (from 1517–47); his richly patterned images are a repository of Old Testament figures. Matteo di Giovanni, another Sienese, did a gruesome Slaughter of the Innocents—a favorite theme of the artist, whose fresco of the same scene is in Santa Maria della Scala (see p. 237). Many of the panels are protected by cardboard overlays and uncovered only from mid-August to early October in honor of the Palio.

Umbrian Renaissance master Bernardino di Betto (better known as Pinturicchio, or Little Painter, because of his stature) is the star in the **Libreria Piccolomini,** entered off the left aisle. Cardinal Francesco Piccolomini built the library in 1487 to house the illuminated manuscripts of his famous uncle, a popular Sienese bishop who later became Pope Pius II. (Cardinal Piccolomini himself later became Pope Pius III—for a mere 18 days, before dying in office.) Pinturicchio's frescoes depict 10 scenes from the Pope Pius II's life, including an especially dramatic departure for the Council of Basel as a storm rages in the background.

In the **Baptistery** (not a separate building but beneath the choir), the great early Renaissance trio of Sienese and Florentine sculptors—Jacopo della Quercia, Lorenzo Ghiberti, and Donatello—crafted the gilded bronze panels of the baptismal font. Donatello wrought the dancing figure of Salome in the "Feast of Herod," and della Quercia did the statue of St. John that stands high above the marble basin.

Piazza del Duomo. www.operaduomo.siena.it. ✆ **0577/283048.** Opa Si Pass 15€ Mar–Oct and 10€ Nov–Feb includes Duomo, Libreria Piccolomini, Museo dell'Opera Metropolitana, Baptistery, Cripta, and Oratorio di San Bernardino. Duomo only 4€, except when floor uncovered 7€. Libreria Piccolomini only 2€. Baptistery only 4€. Mar–Oct Mon–Sat 10:30am–7pm, Sun 1:30–6pm; Nov–Feb Mon–Sat 10:30am–5:30pm, Sun 1:30–5:30pm.

Museo Civico/Palazzo Pubblico ★★★ MUSEUM Presiding over the Piazza del Campo, this great Gothic-style town hall houses some the city's finest artistic treasures. Siena's medieval governors, the Council of Nine, met in the **Sala della Pace,** and to help ensure they bore their duties responsibly, Ambrogio Lorenzetti frescoed the walls with what has become the most important piece of secular art to survive from medieval Europe. His 1338 "Allegory of Good and Bad Government and Their

Something New Under the Duomo

Siena's "newest" work of art is a cycle of frescoes painted between 1270 and 1275, discovered during excavation work in 1999. The colorful works are on view in a subterranean room called the **Cripta**, though it was never used as a burial crypt. Most likely the room was a lower porch for the Duomo (staircases lead to the nave), but it became a storeroom when the choir area above was expanded. What remains are fascinating fragments of scenes from the New Testament, full of emotion and painted in vibrant colors. Scholars are still trying to determine who painted what in the room. Admission is 8€, but the **Opa Si Pass** (see p. 230) also includes entry to the Duomo upstairs as well as other sights.

Effects on the Town and Countryside" provides not only a moral lesson but also a remarkable visual record of Siena and the nearby country as it appeared in the 14th century. Probably not by accident, the good-government frescoes are nicely illuminated by natural light, while scenes of bad government are cast in shadow and have deteriorated over the years. In a panorama on the good side of the room, the towers, domes, and rooftops of Siena appear much as they do today, with horsemen, workers, and townsfolk going about their daily affairs; in the countryside, genteel lords on horseback overlook bountiful fields. On the bad-government side, streets are full of rubble, houses are collapsing, and soldiers are pillaging; beyond the walls, fields are barren and villages are ablaze.

Among other frescoes in these rooms is Sienese painter Simone Martini's greatest work, and his first, a "Maestà" (or Majesty), finished in 1315 (he went over it again in 1321), in the **Sala del Mappamondo.** He shows the Virgin Mary as a medieval queen beneath a royal canopy, surrounded by a retinue of saints, apostles, and angels. The work introduces not only a secular element to a holy scene but also a sense of three-dimensional depth and perspective that later came to the fore in Renaissance painting. Mary's presence here in the halls of civil power reinforces the idea of good government, with the Virgin presiding as a protector of the city. Just opposite is another great Martini work (though the attribution has been called into question), the "Equestrian Portrait of

SIENA'S saintly SCHOLAR

Catherine Benincasa (1347–1380), one of 25 children of a wealthy Sienese cloth dyer, had her first vision of Christ when she was 5 or 6 and vowed to devote her life to God. She took a nun's veil but not the vows when a teenager, was wed "mystically" to Christ when she was 21, and became known for helping the poor and infirm. She and her followers traveled throughout central Italy promoting "the total love for God" and a stronger church. Not only did she found a woman's monastery outside Siena, she served as Siena's ambassador to Pope Gregory XI in Avignon. Encouraging his return to Rome, she continued to write him and other Italian leaders and to travel extensively, begging for peace and the reform of the clergy and the Papal States. She fasted almost continually, which eventually took such a toll on her health that she died at age 33. She was canonized as St. Catherine of Siena in 1461 by Pope Pius II—himself a native of Siena (see the Libreria Piccolomini, p. 233).

The stark, cavernous church of **San Domenico** in Piazza San Domenico (free admission; 9am–6:30pm daily) houses Catherine's venerated head, preserved in a gold reliquary, and her thumb. Her family home, the **Casa di Santa Caterina,** Costa di Sant'Antonio (© **0577/44177;** free admission; 9am–6pm daily), has been preserved as a religious sanctuary; the former kitchen is now an oratory with a spectacular 16th-century majolica-tiled floor.

The Duomo of Siena.

Guidoriccio da Fogliano." The depiction of a proud mercenary riding past a castle he has just conquered was part of a long lost "castelli," or "castles," fresco cycle that showed off Sienese conquests.

Palazzo Pubblico, Piazza del Campo. ✆ **0577/292226.** Cumulative ticket with Torre del Mangia and Santa Maria della Scala 20€ or 13€ with Santa Maria della Scala only; Museo Civico only 9€ adults without reservation, 8€ with reservation; 4.50€ students with reservation, 4€ without reservation; free for ages 11 and under. Nov–Mar 15 daily 10am–6pm; Mar 16–Oct daily 10am–7pm. Bus: A (pink), B.

Museo dell'Opera Metropolitana ★★ MUSEUM In 1339, Siena decided to show off its political, artistic, and spiritual prominence by expanding the Duomo. Work had just begun when the Black Death killed more than half the city's inhabitants in 1348, and the project ground to halt, never to be resumed—partly because it was later discovered that the foundations could not support the massive structure. The aborted nave of the so-called "New Duomo" has now been repurposed to house many of the church's treasures. Here you can see the glorious-if-worse-for-wear statues by Giovanni Pisano that once adorned the facade, as well as a 30-sq-m (323-sq-ft) stained-glass window made for the apse in the late 1280s, with nine colorful panels—beautifully illuminated to full effect in these new surroundings—depicting the Virgin Mary, Siena's four patron saints, and the four Biblical Evangelists.

Upstairs is the "Maestà" by Duccio di Buoninsenga, an altarpiece that was declared a masterpiece when it was unveiled in 1311, carried in a procession from the painter's workshop to the Duomo's altar. As a contemporary wrote, "all honorable citizens of Siena surrounded said panel with candles held in their hands, and women and children followed humbly behind." The front depicts the Madonna and Child surrounded by saints and angels, while the back once displayed 46 scenes from the lives of Mary and Christ. In 1711 the altarpiece was dismantled, and pieces are now in collections around the world. What remains here shows the genius of Duccio, who slowly broke away from a one-dimensional Byzantine style to imbue his characters with nuance, roundness, and emotion.

The **Facciatone,** a walkway atop the would-be facade of the "New Duomo," is the city's second most popular viewpoint, with a stunning perspective of the cathedral across the piazza and sweeping views over the city's rooftops to Siena's favorite height, the Torre del Mangia towering over the Campo.

Piazza del Duomo 8. www.operaduomo.siena.it. ✆ **0577/283048.** Opa Si Pass 15€ Mar–Oct and 10€ Nov–Feb, includes Duomo, Libreria Piccolomini, Museo dell'Opera Metropolitana, Baptistery, Cripta, and Oratorio di San Bernardino. Museum only, 7€. Mar–Oct Mon–Sat 10:30am–7pm, Sun 1:30–6pm; Nov–Feb Mon–Sat 10:30am–5:30pm, Sun 1:30–5:30pm.

Pinacoteca Nazionale ★ ART MUSEUM The greatest works of Sienese art have long since been dispersed to museums around the world. Even so, here you can still get an overview of the works of the city's major artists, especially those working in the 12th through the 16th centuries, nicely displayed in the Brigidi and Buonsignori palaces. What you'll notice is that while the Renaissance was flourishing in Florence, Siena held to its old ways—these works are rich in Byzantine gold and an almost Eastern influence in the styling.

Among the works by Duccio (of the famous "Maestà" in the Museo dell'Opera, p. 235) is an enchanting "Madonna and Child with Saints," in which a placid, otherworldly looking Mary holds a very wise-looking Jesus. Simone Martini (painter of Siena's other great "Maestà," in the Museo Civico, p. 274) did the wonderful "Agostino Novello" altarpiece, in which St. Augustine is shown performing all sorts of heroic deeds, such as flying over boulders to save a monk trapped in a ravine. In many of the panels you'll notice Sienese street scenes. Works by the Lorenzetti brothers include some charming landscapes by Ambrogio (artist of the "Allegory of Good and Bad Government" in the Palazzo Pubblico, p. 233); his "Castle on the Lake" is almost surrealistic, an architectural fantasy reminiscent of the 20th-century works of Giorgio di Chirico. Pietro's

"Madonna of the Carmelites," an altarpiece the artist executed for the Carmelite church in Siena, shows the Virgin and Child in a distinctly medieval setting, surrounded by members of the order in 14th-century garb, along with a typically Sienese landscape, complete with horsemen and planted hillsides. Domenico Beccafumi's cartoons, or sketches, for his floor panels in the Duomo are on the first floor.

Via San Pietro 29. ✆ **0577/286143.** 4€. Sun–Mon 9am–1pm; Tues–Sat 8:15am–7:15pm.

Santa Maria della Scala ★★★ MUSEUM One of Europe's first hospitals, probably founded around 1090, raised abandoned children, took care of the infirm, fed the poor, and lodged pilgrims who stopped in Siena on their way to and from Rome. These activities are recorded in scenes in the **Sala del Pellegrinaio** (Pilgrims' Hall), where colorful depictions of patients and healers from the Middle Ages looked down upon rows of hospital beds as recently as the 1990s. These are some of the finest secular works of the Middle Ages, color-rich 15th-century frescoes by Domenico di Bartolo and others, showing such scenes as surgeons dressing a leg wound or holding a flask of urine to the light, or caregivers offering fresh clothing to an indigent young man. One of Bartolo's panels encapsulates an orphan's lifetime experience at the hospital, as he pictures infants being weaned, youngsters being instructed by a stern-looking mistress, and a young couple being wed (young women raised in the hospital were given dowries). As these activities transpire, a dog and cat scuffle, foundlings climb up ladders toward the Virgin Mary, and wealthy benefactors stand on Oriental carpets.

You'll also see other frescoes and altarpieces commissioned by the hospital as it acquired considerable wealth over the centuries. One gallery houses some original panels from Jacopo della Quercia's 14th-century fountain in the Piazza del Campo, the Fonte Gaia. In the cellars is the dark and eerie **Oratorio di Santa Caterina della Notte,** where St. Catherine (see p. 259) allegedly passed her nights in prayer.

Piazza del Duomo 2. www.santamariadellascala.com. ✆ **0577/534571.** Cumulative ticket with Museo Civico and Torre del Mangia 20€ or 13€ with Museo Civico only; or 9€ adults, 8€ students. Mar 17–Oct 15 Mon–Wed 10:30am–4:30pm, Thurs–Sun 10:30am–6:30pm; Oct 16–Mar 16 daily 10:30am–4:30pm.

Where to Stay

Many hotels have discount arrangements with garages in the city center; around 15€ to 25€ per day is standard. When making parking arrangements with a hotel, though, check carefully to make sure the garage is not in a restricted zone, in which you are only allowed to drive once a day—meaning you can take the car out for a day trip but can't bring it back into the city later that day without incurring a fine.

EXPENSIVE

Relais la Suerva ★★ One of the world's most distinctive country-house hotels was once the country palace of Pope Julius II. He commissioned the Sistine Chapel, to give an idea of his lavish taste, and it's much in evidence in loggias, Italian gardens, a private church, and refined salons. The current owner, the Marquis Ricci, has added his own touches in elaborately decorated suites and rooms in the papal palace and an adjoining farm building, furnished with family antiques and enriched with colorful palettes, rich fabrics, decadently huge bathrooms, and centuries' worth of bibelots. The overall effect is design-magazine-worthy yet surprisingly welcoming and comfortable. You probably won't want to slouch around in your bathing suit in the swanky lounges (lined with 19th-century finery and other museum-worthy collectibles), but the hotel has a delightful pool and many relaxing corners. Siena and other Tuscan towns are within easy reach.

Via della Suvera 70, Pievescola Casole d'Elsa (28km/16 miles west of Sienna). www.lasuvera.it. ✆ **0577/960-300.** 36 units. From 350€ double. Closed Nov to mid Apr. **Amenities:** Restaurant; bar; pool; spa; Wi-Fi (free).

MODERATE

Campo Regio Relais ★★★ A "Room with a View" ambience pervades this stylish old house a 10-minute walk from the Campo. Two of the beautifully appointed rooms have spectacular views up a hillside crowned with the Duomo, one from its own sun-filled terrace, and all guests enjoy the same vista from an inviting sitting room/bar/breakfast room that also opens to a terrace. The old-fashioned *pensione* atmosphere is enhanced with modern updates that include lush fabrics and elegant furnishings, chic rather than staid. Amenities include an honesty bar, a library, attentive service, and excellent breakfast.

Via della Sapienza 25. www.camporegio.com. ✆ **0577/222073.** 6 units. 150€–450€ double. Rates include breakfast. Usually closed Jan to mid-Mar. **Amenities:** Library; Wi-Fi (free).

Frances' Lodge Relais ★★★ With the towers of Siena beckoning in the near distance, a pool glimmering in the garden, and lots of quiet corners nestled on a hillside planted with olive trees, this beautiful estate seems like a slice of heaven. Hosts Franco and Franca (Frances) Mugnai created this earthly paradise out of their ancestral home, and their richly hued rooms and suites are accented with family pieces and quirkily and charmingly decorated to be warm and rather exotic—Moroccan fabrics in one, a rose theme in another, all tucked away in old stone farm buildings. A hearty made-to-order breakfast is served in the garden; in bad weather the day begins in a lounge fashioned out of the old *limonaia* (lemon house), filled with kilims and vibrant art. The hosts require a 2-night minimum stay and request that guests be at least 18 years of age.

Strada di Valdipugna 2. www.franceslodge.it. ✆ **0577/42379**. 6 units. From 240€ double. Rates include breakfast. Closed mid-Nov to late Mar. **Amenities:** Bar; pool; Wi-Fi (free).

Palazzo Ravizza ★★ Generations of travelers have fallen under the spell of this 17th-century Renaissance *palazzo*, where high ceilings, oil paintings, highly polished antiques, and the gentle patina of age all suggest an era of grand travel. A large garden in the rear stretches towards green hills and can tempt anyone to give up sightseeing for a few hours and just relax; it's a popular cocktail spot for guests and Sienese alike. All the rooms are different, though most have wood beams and a surfeit of period detail, including some frescoes and coffered ceilings; furnishings throughout are comfortable and traditionally stylish. While this wonderful old place has the aura of a country hideaway, it's right in the city center, just a few streets below the Piazza del Campo.

Pian dei Mantellini 34 (near Piazza San Marco). www.palazzoravizza.it. ✆ **0577/280462.** 35 units. 105€–180€ double. Rates include breakfast. Free parking. Closed early Jan to early Feb. Bus: A (green, yellow). **Amenities:** Bar; babysitting; concierge; room service; Wi-Fi (free).

Santa Caterina ★★ You'll give up a city center location to stay here, but being just outside the walls—literally so, as this is the first house after Porta Romana, about a 10-minute walk from Piazza del Campo—has the advantage of making you feel like you are in the countryside. A large, shady garden enhances the feeling, and you can breakfast and enjoy a drink under the trees in good weather. For indoor lounging, there's a snug little bar, a well-upholstered lounge, and a glass-enclosed breakfast room. Most of the cozy rooms, with wood-beamed ceilings, simple wood furnishings, and old prints on the walls, face the back, where wide-sweeping views of the green Val d'Orcia seem to go on forever. One choice room has a little balcony; a few others are bilevel, with bedrooms tucked beneath the eaves. Ask for a rear-facing room (rather than a room facing the street), or you'll miss the wonderful view.

Via Enea Silvio Piccolomini 7. www.hscsiena.it. ✆ **0577/221105.** 22 units. 110€–130€ double. Rates include breakfast. Bus: A (red) or 2. **Amenities:** Babysitting; bikes; concierge; Wi-Fi (free).

INEXPENSIVE

Antica Torre ★ A 16th-century tower house dishes up no end of medieval atmosphere, with eight smallish rooms tucked onto four floors. If you don't mind the climb, the two on the top floor come with the advantage of views across the tile rooftops, and just treading on the old stone staircase is a pleasure. The rooms have plenty of character—with marble floors, brick and timbered ceilings, and handsome iron bedsteads—which for some guests may compensate for the fairly cramped quarters, small bathrooms, and lack of many hotel services. Continental breakfast (5€ extra) can get the day off to a rocky start, literally, as it's served downstairs in a rough-hewn stone vault.

Via di Fiera Vecchia 7. www.anticatorresiena.it. ✆ **0577/222255.** 8 units. 70€–99€ double. **Amenities:** Wi-Fi (free).

Hotel Alma Domus ★ This modern redo of the former drying rooms of a medieval wool works is run by the nuns of St. Catherine, who provide homey and spotless lodgings with a slightly contemporary flair. Set into the hillside below San Domenico church, near the Fontebranda (the oldest and most picturesque of the city's fountains), the place has the quiet air of a retreat—or a meditative, monastic calm, if you choose to see it that way—along with a great perk: city-view balconies in the more expensive rooms. Less expensive rooms do not come with views or air-conditioning. Breakfast is included, but it's a bit basic; you may prefer to walk up the hill and enjoy a cappuccino in the Campo.

Via Camporegio 37. www.hotelalmadomus.it. ✆ **0577/44177.** 28 units. 85€–120€ double. Rates include breakfast. Bus: A (red). **Amenities:** Wi-Fi (free).

Palazzo Bulgarini ★★ The converted *piano nobile* salons of an old palace aren't as opulent as they once were, but enough of the grandeur remains to elicit a gasp or two as you enter one of the six enormous guest rooms embellished with marble fireplaces, ceiling frescoes, and parquet floors. Furnishings are charmingly old-fashioned, and some better lighting would be a welcome luxury. Unchanged over the centuries are the views from the rear rooms over the Val d'Orcia, a stunning and a soothing surprise given the city-center location. Prices are extremely reasonable, all the more so since the surroundings are so genuinely palatial.

Via Pantaneto. www.bbpalazzobulgarini.com. ✆ **0577/152-4466.** 6 units. 75€–110€ double. Rates include breakfast. Bus: A (pink). **Amenities:** Wi-Fi (free).

Where to Eat

The **Enoteca Italiana** (www.enoteca-italiana.it; ✆ **0577/228843;** Mon noon–8pm; Tues–Sat noon–1am) in the 16th-century Fortezza Medicea di Santa Barbara is the only state-sponsored wine bar in Italy, in vaults that were built for Cosimo de' Medici in 1560. You can sample a choice selection of Italian wines by the glass and accompany your choices with small plates of meats and cheeses. For a snack or quick meal, step into **La Prosciutteria** on the corner Via Magialotti and Via Pantaneto (www.laprosciutteria.com; ✆ **0577/42026**), where you can quite literally pig out on a platter of Tuscan hams or a *porchetta* sandwich, served on tables out front or in a medieval cellar.

Every Italian city has a favorite *gelateria,* and Siena's is **Kopakabana,** at Via de' Rossi 52–54 (www.gelateriakopakabana.it; ✆ **0577/223744;**

mid-Feb to mid-Nov noon–8pm, later in warm weather), with flavors that include *panpepato,* based on the peppery Sienese cake.

EXPENSIVE

Antica Osteria da Divo ★★ CONTEMPORARY SIENESE It's hard to know what cuisine would best suit this almost-eerie setting of brick vaulting, exposed timbers, walls of bare rock, and even some Etruscan tombs—either some sort of medieval gruel or else something innovatively refined, which luckily is the direction this menu goes. Many of the offerings are uniquely Sienese, as in *pici alla lepre* (thick spaghetti in hare sauce), *sella di cinghiale* (saddle of wild boar braised in Chianti), or a breast of guinea fowl (*faraona*) roasted with balsamic vinegar. Such meals are well paired with vegetables, often caramelized onions or crisp roasted potatoes with herbs. Service is outstanding, and as befits one of the most romantic meals in town, the intimate spaces are beautifully candlelit at night.

Via Franciosa 25–29 (2 streets down from the left flank of the Duomo). www.osteriadadivo.it. ✆ **0577/284381.** Main courses 20€–24€. Wed–Mon noon–2:30pm and 7–10:30pm. Closed 2 weeks Jan–Feb. Bus: A (green, yellow).

MODERATE

La Sosta di Violante ★★ SIENESE This warm, friendly, rose-hued room is only a 5-minute walk from Piazza del Campo but far enough off the beaten track to seem like a getaway (*sosta* means rest or break, as in "take a break"). The surroundings attract a mostly neighborhood crowd that has come to count on the kitchen for excellent preparations of *papardelle, pici,* and other Tuscan pastas in rich sauces. Grilled Florentine steaks are another specialty, but so are many vegetarian choices, including delicious *fritelle di pecorino* (pecorino cheese fritters) and a cauliflower *(cavolfiore)* soufflé. Any civic-minded Sienese would get this reference to Violante, the Bavarian-born 18th-century duchess who, after the death of her Medici husband from syphilis, became a beneficent governor of Siena and divided the city into its famous present-day *contrade* (districts).

Via di Pantaneta 115. www.lasostadiviolante.it. ✆ **0577/43774.** Main courses 10€–17€. Mon–Sat 12:30–2:30pm and 7:30–10:30pm. Bus: A (pink).

Ristorante Guido ★★ SIENESE Italian celebs whose photos hang among etchings and paintings are among generations of diners who have enjoyed this wonderfully old-world place. Ristorante Guido seems to radiate hospitality from every brick in the cavernous, vaulted dining room. Waiters in crisp jackets and ties make a special occasion of meals that might include one of the housemade pastas—*pici fatti al cacio e pepe* (with cheese and pepper) is a house classic—and one of several variations of grilled Tuscan beef.

Vicolo Beato Pier Pettinaio 7. www.ristoranteguido.com. ✆ **0577/280042.** Main courses 12€–22€. Thurs–Tues noon–3pm and 7:30–10pm.

Taverna San Giuseppe ★★★ TUSCAN/GRILL A long, brick vaulted room from the 12th century is the setting for meals many travelers long remember as among the best they've had in Italy. It's a testament to the warmth and skill of the staff that, despite the popularity (reserve for dinner) and reputation among even the discerning Sienese, they work so hard to make diners feel at home and are justly proud of the Tuscan classics they bring out of the kitchen. *Picci,* the thick local pasta, with a ragu of *cinghiale* (wild boar), is surprisingly delicate, while ricotta-filled *gnudi* almost floats off the plate. Meals often begin with a complimentary glass of *Prosecco* and might end with a sweet on the house, bookends to an experience that in its entirety seems like a treat.
Via G. Dupré 132. www.tavernasangiuseppe.it. ✆ **0577/42286.** Main courses 10€–21€. Mon–Sat noon–2:30pm and 7–10pm. Bus: A (red).

Trattoria Fori Porta ★★ TUSCAN/GRILL The gate (*porta*) this chicly comfortable spot is just outside of (*fori*) is Porta Romana, making it a 15-minute walk from the Campo. The location slightly out of the center of things makes a meal here all the more authentic, served in two intimate dining rooms where plain wood tables on white-tile floors are offset by contemporary paintings and heavy beams. The Tuscan menu leans toward grilled steaks, with some innovative accompaniments, including a memorable trio of small onions stuffed with sausage, or the house version of a homey classic, braised cabbage rolls stuffed with pork.
Via Claudio Tomei 1. www.foriportasiena.it. ✆ **0577/2221000.** Main courses 11€–20€. Tues–Sun 7:30–11pm. Bus: A (red) or 2.

INEXPENSIVE

La Chiacchera ★★ SIENESE A hole in the wall is an apt description for this tiny, rustically decorated room tucked halfway along a steep alleyway. The climb can help work up an appetite or work off the large portions of *ribollita* (hearty bread and vegetable soup), *salsicce e fagioli* (sausage and white beans); or *tegamata di maiale* (a Sienese pork casserole). Good weather provides a unique dining experience on the street out front, where the legs of tables and chairs have been cut to accommodate the steep slope.
Costa di Sant'Antonio 4 (near San Domenico). www.osterialachiacchera.it. ✆ **0577/280631.** Main courses 7€–9€. Daily noon–3pm and 7pm–midnight. Bus: A (red).

L'Osteria ★★ TUSCAN/GRILL One of Siena's culinary treasures is this simple tile-floored, wood-beamed room where straightforward local cuisine is expertly prepared and served at extremely reasonable prices. Truffles occasionally appear in some special preparations, but for most of the year the short menu sticks to the classics—*pici al cinghiale* (pasta with wild boar sauce), tripe (*trippa*) stew, and thick steaks, accompanied by *fagioli bianchi* (white beans) and *patate fritte* (fried potatoes). Service can be brusque, but that's because nightly crowds keep the waiters hopping.

Via de' Rossi 79–81. ✆ **0577/287592.** Main courses 8€–17€. Mon–Sat 12:30–2:30pm and 7:30–10:30pm. Bus: A (red).

Shopping

Siena is famous for its *panforte,* a sweet, dense cake created by city bakers in the Middle Ages and sold in shops all over town. Made from candied fruit and nuts glued together with honey, it resembles a gloopy fruit cake. Each shop has its own recipe, with the most popular varieties being sweet Panforte Margherita and bitter Panforte Nero. Try a slice at **Drogheria Manganelli,** Via di Città 71–73 (✆ **0577/280002**), which has made its own *panforte* and soft *ricciarelli* almond cookies since the 19th century. Some Sienese would send you just as enthusiastically to the delectable and venerable **Nannini,** just off the Campo at Via Banchi di Sopra 24 (✆ **0577/303080**). The **Consorzio Agrario Siena,** Via Pianigiani 9 (www.capsi.it; ✆ **0577/2301**), showcases local wines, cheeses, pasta, even pastry, all from small Tuscan producers.

Tuscan vineyards.

Authentic Sienese ceramics feature only three colors: black, white, and the reddish-brown "burnt sienna," or *terra di Siena.* **Ceramiche Artistiche Santa Caterina,** at Via di Città 74–76 (✆ **0577/283098**), sells high-quality pieces, courtesy of Maestro Marcello Neri, who trained at Siena's premier art and ceramics institutions, and his son, Fabio.

A Side Trip into the Chianti

For many visitors to Italy, heaven on earth is the 167 sq. km (64 sq. miles) of land between Florence and Siena, known as the Chianti. Traversing the gentle hillsides on the SR222, the Chiantigiana is a classic drive, especially the stretch between Castellina in Chianti and Greve. Landscapes are smothered in vineyards and olive groves, punctuated by woodland and peppered with *case coloniche*—stone farmsteads with trademark square dovecotes protruding from the roofs.

First stop for wine lovers is **Radda in Chianti,** 36km (22 miles) north of Siena; the turnoff is just north of Castellina. This important wine center retains its medieval street plan and a bit of its walls. The center of town is the 15th-century **Palazzo del Podestà,** studded with the mayoral coats of arms of past *podestà.* **Porciatti** will give you a taste of traditional salami and cheeses at their *alimentari* on Piazza IV Novembre 1 at the gate into town (www.casaporciatti.it; ✆ **0577/738055**).

Seven kilometers (4⅓ miles) north of Radda on a secondary road is the **Castello di Volpaia ★★** (www.volpaia.com; ✆ **0577/738066**), a Florentine holding that was buffeted by Sienese attacks from the 10th to 16th centuries. The still-impressive central keep is all that remains, but it's surrounded by a 13th-century *borgo* (village) containing the Renaissance La Commenda church. The central tower has an enoteca for tastings and sales, plus award-winning olive oils and farm-produced white and red vinegars.

Back on the Chiantigiana (SR222), the next town is **Panzano in Chianti,** 12km (7 miles) north of Radda, known for its embroidery and a butcher, **Antica Macelleria Cecchini,** Via XX Luglio 11 (www.dariocecchini.com; ✆ **055/852020**). Dario Cecchini is fast becoming one of the most famous butchers in the world, entertaining visitors with classical music and tastes of his products while perhaps reciting the entirety of Dante's *Inferno* from memory.

Just north of Panzano, the SR222 takes you past the turnoff for Lamole. Along that road you'll find **Villa Vignamaggio ★★** (www.vignamaggio.com; ✆ **055/854661**), a russet-orange villa surrounded by elegant gardens where Lisa Gherardini, who grew up to pose for da Vinci's "Mona Lisa," was born in 1479. In 1404 the estate's wine was the first red wine to be referred to as "chianti." Book ahead at least a week to tour the cellar and gardens, sample the wines, or even stay overnight in atmosphere-laden rooms (from 180€ for a double).

Greve in Chianti, 8km (5 miles) north of Panzano on the SR222, is the center of the wine trade and the unofficial capital of Chianti. The central **Piazza Matteotti** is a rough triangle surrounded by a mismatched patchwork arcade—each merchant had to build the stretch in front of his own shop. Greve is the host of Chianti's annual September wine fair, and there are, naturally, dozens of wine shops in town. The best is the **Enoteca del Chianti Classico,** Piazzetta Santa Croce 8 (✆ **055/853297**). At Piazza Matteotti 69–71 is another famous butcher, **Macelleria Falorni** (www.falorni.it; ✆ **055/854363**), established in 1700 and still containing a cornucopia of hanging *prosciutti* and dozens of other cured meats, along with a decent wine selection. It's open daily.

The **Castello di Verrazzano** (www.verrazzano.com; ✆ **055/854243** or 055/290684), 6km (4 miles) northwest of Greve, is a significant stop for Americans: the ancestral home of the Verrazzano family, birthplace in 1485 of Giovanni Verrazzano, who discovered New York. The estate has been making wine since at least 1170; free tastings are offered daily at the roadside shop. Their "jewel" is a 100% sangiovese called Sasello, while the Bottiglia Particolare (Particular [Special] Bottle) is a Super Tuscan wine, at 70% sangiovese and 30% cab. Tours of the gardens and cellars run Monday through Friday (prebooking essential), and a rustic farmhouse inn, Foresteria Casanova, offers rooms from 94€ double.

From here it's 29km (17 miles) to Florence, or 50km (30 miles) back to Siena—allow a little over an hour without stops for the return trip.

WHERE TO STAY

Castello Vicchiomaggio ★★ A 700-year-old storybook castle, complete with a crenulated tower, has hosted Renaissance nobles, such luminaries as Leonardo da Vinci and the poet-biologist Francesco Redi, and modern-day visitors who enjoy a stay on a working wine estate set amid world-acclaimed vineyards. Large, character-filled apartments in the castle are tucked into turrets and medieval salons along twisting staircases and corridors, each filled with old-fashioned furnishings that are more homey than grand. An adjacent priory has been converted into six comfortable suites that surround a communal lounge. All share a shady formal garden and a swimming pool that hangs over the vineyards.

Via Vicchiomaggio, Greve in Chianti. www.vicchiomaggio.it. ✆ **055/854079.** 12 units. 130€–195€ double. Rates include breakfast. **Amenities:** Restaurant; pool; Wi-Fi (free).

Palazzo Leopoldo ★★ One of the grandest palaces in Radda in Chianti dates to the 15th century and was redone as a noble residence in the 18th century. Not much has changed since then. Guest rooms open

FEEL THE magic AROUND SIENA

If the Disney empire were to set up shop in Tuscany, it would have some ready-made stage sets near Siena. **Monteriggioni,** 14km (8½ miles) northwest of Siena along the SS2, is one of the most perfectly preserved fortified villages in all of Italy. The town was once a Sienese outpost, begun in 1213, where soldiers patrolled the walls and kept an eye out for Florentine troops from the towers—an image that Dante once likened to the circle of Titans guarding the lowest level of Hell. All 14 of these vantage points have survived, and you can climb up for a view (admission 3.50€, open Apr–Sept daily 9:30am–1:30pm and 2–7:30pm). A walk from one end of Monteriggioni to the other takes about 5 minutes—as you pass, note the stone houses and garden plots tucked against the walls, which once kept townsfolk nourished during times of siege. The **tourist office** is at Piazza Roma 23, 53035 Monteriggioni (www.monteriggioniturismo.it; ✆ **0577/304810**). Siena city buses 130A and 130R run out to Monteriggioni every hour.

The enchanting **Abbey of San Galgano,** in a grassy meadow on the banks of the River Merse, has a great "Sword in the Stone"–like back story. Galgano, born in Siena in 1148, was pursuing his career as a knight when he had a vision of the archangel Michael, who led him up a steep path to a circular temple outside the village of Montesiepi, where he met the 12 apostles. Moved by the vision, Galgano went off to Montesiepi, drove his sword into a stone to renounce his knighthood, and built a round stone hermitage. After his death in 1182, his simple dwelling was expanded into a spectacular rotunda, with a dome built of 24 alternating rows of brick and stone. This became the center of a community of Cistercian monks who were also great church builders (they designed the cathedral in Siena). The brothers later built a Gothic abbey down the hill, which, after the Black Death decimated their community, crumbled into an evocative ruin—you can prowl around it, admiring its high arches, carved capitals, and stone settings for long-vanished stained-glass windows. The saint's tomb is up the hill in the Hermitage; though his body long ago went missing, his sword remains in the stone, with only its handle protruding. The **abbey** (www.prolocochiusdino.it; ✆ **055/756700**) is outside the village of Chiusdino about 40km (25 miles) southwest of Siena via S73. It is open daily June to August 9am–8pm; March to May and September to October 9am to 7pm, and November to February 10am to 5pm. Admission is 2€.

off vaulted salons and have chunky beams, colorful frescoes, and comfy traditional furnishings to offer a satisfyingly historic, slightly regal ambience. Breakfast is served in the 18th-century kitchens, while a sunny terrace overlooks the nearby hills. A hedonistic **spa** is tucked beneath pleasant but slightly less atmospheric lodgings in an adjoining house.
Via Roma 33, Rada in Chianti. www.palazzoleopoldo.it. ✆ **0577/735605.** 22 units. 95€–150€ double. Rates include breakfast. **Amenities:** Restaurant; bar; pool; spa; Wi-Fi (free).

Wine barrels in a Montepulciano cellar.

MONTEPULCIANO ★★

67km (41 miles) SE of Siena, 124km (77 miles) SE of Florence, 186km (116 miles) N of Rome

Sipping a delicious ruby wine in a friendly hill town is a good reason to trek across the beautiful Tuscan countryside. There are few better places to aim for than Montepulciano, with its medieval alleyways, Renaissance palaces, and famous violet-scented, orange-speckled Vino Nobile di Montepulciano.

Montepulciano is also a good base for exploring other hill towns, especially nearby Pienza and Montalcino, and for making excursions into the Val d'Orcia, the enchantingly beautiful region of rolling green hills and stream-watered valleys.

Essentials

GETTING THERE Driving is the best method: From Siena, the most scenic route is south on the SS2 to San Quirico d'Orcia, where you get the SS146 eastbound through Pienza to Montepulciano.

Six Tiemme **buses** (www.tiemmespa.it; ✆ **0577/204111**) run daily from Siena (1½ hr.). Montepulciano is served by train, from Siena and

Chiusi, for example, but the station is about 15km (9 miles) outside of town, with infrequent bus connections. A taxi is about 25€ each way.

GETTING AROUND Montepulciano's Corso is very steep, but for those not up to the climb, little orange *pollicini* buses connect the junction just below the Porta al Prato and Piazza Grande in about 8 minutes. The official point of origin is "the fifth tree on the right above the junction." Tickets cost 1€ each way (buy them on the bus) and run every 20 minutes.

VISITOR INFORMATION Montepulciano's **tourist office** is in the parking lot just below Porta al Prato (www.prolocomontepulciano.it; **© 0578/757341**). It's open Monday to Saturday 9:30am to 12:30pm and 3 to 6pm (until 8pm in summer); in August it's open 9:30am to 8pm.

Exploring Montepulciano

It's all uphill from **Porta al Prato,** where the Medici balls above the gate hint at Montepulciano's long association with Florence. The steep climb up the Corso comes with a look at some impressive palaces. At no. 91 is the massive **Palazzo Avignonesi,** with grinning lions' heads, and across the street is the **Palazzo Tarugi** (no. 82). Both are by Vignola, the Renaissance architect who designed Rome's Villa Giulia. The lower level of the facade of the **Palazzo Bucelli** (no. 73) is embedded with a patchwork of Etruscan reliefs and funerary urns, placed there by 18th-century antiquarian scholar Pietro Bucelli, to show off his collection.

At the top of the street, the highest point in a very high town is **Piazza Grande.** You might recognize the 14th-century **Palazzo Comunale** from the movie *Twilight: New Moon*—it was filmed here, though the story was supposedly set in Volterra. One side of the piazza is taken up by the facade of the never-completed **Cattedrale di Santa Maria Assunta.**

A short and level walk north along Via Ricci brings you to **Piazza San Francesco,** where views extend south to Lago Trasimeno in Umbria and northeast across the golden folds of hills toward Siena.

Cattedrale di Santa Maria Assunta ★ CATHEDRAL Montepulciano's homely, bare-brick cathedral was erected in 1680 on the site of a much earlier church (only a relatively new 15th-century bell tower was left in place). The plan was to build a landmark worthy of its noble neighbors on Piazza Grande, but the city ran out of funds, and the exterior was never sheathed in marble as planned. Inside is Montepulciano's great work of art, a 1401 gold-hued altarpiece by Taddeo di Bartolo (1363–1422) of "The Assumption of the Virgin with Saints." This is one of the greatest works by Bartolo, one of Siena's post-Black-Death generation of artists. You can't get too close to the massive triptych soaring above the high altar, which is a shame, because the charm lies in the detail of the many various panels. The main sections show the death of the Virgin,

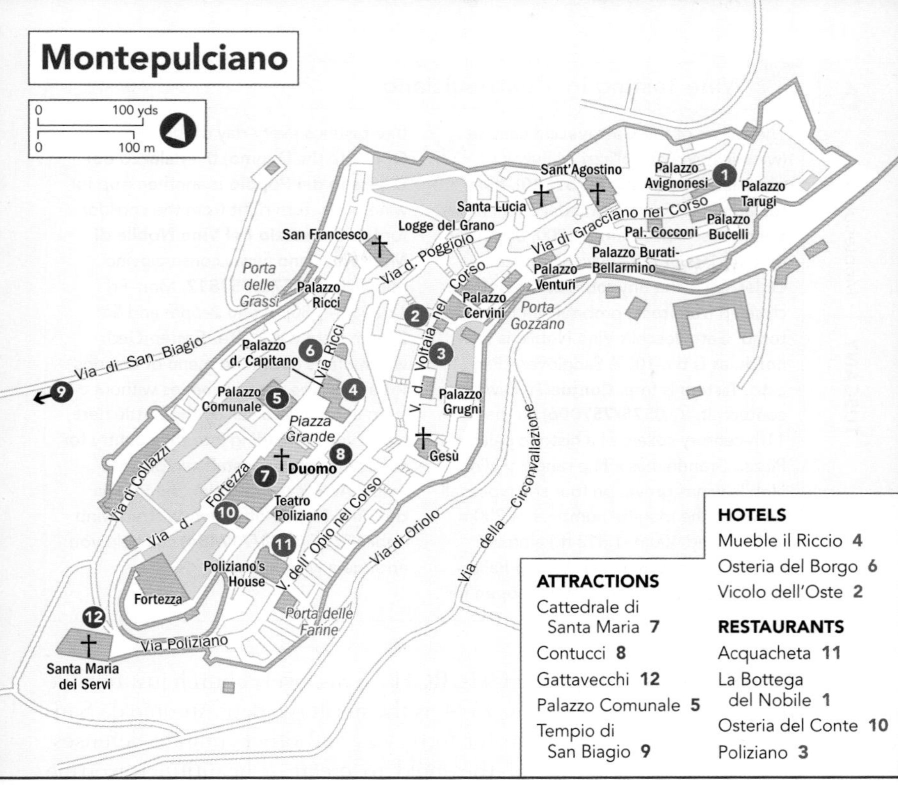

with the apostles by her bedside; her ascension into Heaven, as the apostles survey her empty tomb; and the Virgin's coronation, an extremely popular theme among 14th- and 15th-century Italian artists in which Christ crowns his mother as queen of Heaven. Surrounding these scenes are various adoring saints and episodes from the life of Christ. One charming vignette shows a child shinnying up a tree to get a better view of Christ entering Jerusalem.

The cathedral's other masterpiece are the remnants of a marble sculptural group by the Florentine architect and sculptor Michelozzo (1396–1472), crafted between 1427 and 1436 for the tomb of papal secretary Bartolomeo Aragazzi. The tomb was disassembled in the 17th century (some pieces were stolen and ended up in the Victoria and Albert Museum London). Look for a reclining, hooded statue of the deceased to the right of the central entrance door, and figures of fortitude and justice standing on either side of the high altar; leaning against a nearby pillar is the figure of St. Bartholomew, after whom Aragazzi was named. Piazza Grande. No phone. Daily 9am–12:30pm and 3:15–7pm. Free.

Wine Tasting in Montepulciano

The cellars of the **Gattavecchi** *cantine* (wineries), Via di Collazzi 74 (www.gattavecchi.it; ✆ **0578/757110**), burrowed under Santa Maria dei Servi, have been in use since before 1200, originally by the friars of the adjacent church. Older still is the tiny room at the bottom chiseled from rock, probably an Etruscan tomb. Gattavecchi's Vino Nobile is top-notch, as is the 100% Sangiovese Parceto. Tasting is free. **Contucci** (www.contucci.it; ✆ **0578/757006**), in the 11th-century cellars of a historic palace in Piazza Grande, has a fine range of Vino Nobile wines grown on four soil types, all between the magical numbers of 200m (656 ft.) and 400m (1,312 ft.) altitude. According to winemaker Adamo Pallecchi, this is crucial. The cantina is open for free tastings every day of the year. Opposite the Duomo, the **Palazzo del Capitano del Popolo** is another stop for wine buffs. Turn right from the corridor for the **Consorzio del Vino Nobile di Montepulciano** (www.consorziovinonobile.it; ✆ **0578/757812;** Mon–Fri 11:30am–1:30pm and 2–6pm and Sat 2–6pm from week after Easter–Oct), which offers a rotating menu of tastings for a small fee. Local wineries without a shop in town also sell by the bottle here, and if you're heading into the country for some wine touring, staff can provide maps. Across the corridor, the **Strada del Vino Nobile** office (www.stradavinonobile.it; ✆ **0578/717484)** can help you arrange a wine itinerary.

Tempio di San Biagio ★ CHURCH This lovely church just outside the town walls, completed in 1534, is the masterwork of Antonio da Sangallo the Elder. Best known for fortresses and other military defenses, here Sangallo broke out of the mold to create a beautiful travertine church on the plan of a Greek cross, with the four arms of equal length radiating from a central dome. Since the church is in the countryside with no other buildings nearby, it's easy to admire its classical unity. The interior is as refined as the exterior, but a bit dull at close inspection.
Via di San Biagio. No phone. Daily 9am–12:30pm and 3:30–7:30pm. Free.

Where to Stay

Meublé il Riccio ★★ This atmospheric 800-year-old palazzo near Piazza Grande, passed down through the innkeeper's family, lays on the charm—in the arcaded, mosaic-tiled courtyard, the antiques-and-art-filled salon and breakfast room, the homey lounge, and the rooftop terrace overlooking the landscapes of the Valdichiana far below. Some suites do justice to the surroundings with palatial expanses and terraces of their own, while other rooms are simpler and viewless but not without character. Carved wooden *ricci,* hedgehogs, which once emblazoned the 13th-century façade, make an appearance in all rooms. Ivana and Giorgio Caroti are on hand to dispense advice and make restaurant reservations, serving up delicious homemade pastries at breakfast and drinks throughout the day.

Via di Tolosa 21. www.ilriccio.net. ✆ **0578/757713.** 10 units. 100€–110€ double. Rates includes breakfast. **Amenities:** Bar; Wi-Fi (free).

Osteria del Borgo ★ Wood beams and exposed brickwork supply these bright, good-size rooms and apartments with rustic charm, while comfortably stylish furnishings and modern baths lend them a chic flair. The hilltop perch is just off Piazza Grande, so views from some rooms and the shared courtyard are expansive. A homey restaurant downstairs serves Tuscan specialties and spills out to a nice terrace in good weather.

Via Ricci. www.osteriadelborgo.it. ✆ **0578/716799.** 5 units. 90€–120€ double. Rates include breakfast and parking. **Amenities:** Restaurant; Wi-Fi (free).

Vicolo dell'Oste ★★ Tuscan chic prevails in this house on a narrow lane off the Corso, just below Piazza Grande. Wood-beamed ceilings set off streamlined modern furnishings, while deluxe touches such as large Jacuzzis are tucked into the corners of some rooms. Practical amenities include simple kitchens in several rooms. While there are no communal spaces, breakfast is served in a nearby cafe, and innkeepers Giuseppe and Luisa seem to always be near at hand to take care of your needs.

Via delle Oste. www.vicolodelloste.it. ✆ **0578/758393.** 5 units. 95€–110€ double. Rates include breakfast. **Amenities:** Wi-Fi (free).

Where to Eat

With a local wine that pairs especially well with hearty sauces and red meat, it's no accident that food in Montepulciano is typically Tuscan, relying heavily on game, beef from the Valdichiana, and thick pastas like hand-rolled *pici* topped with rich sauces. Aside from the town's many tasting rooms, you can also quaff the wine and taste local salamis and cheeses in an atmospheric old cafe, the late-19th-century **Poliziano,** on the Corso (number 27; ✆ **0578/758615**).

Acquacheta ★★★ SOUTHERN TUSCAN/GRILL If you're craving steak, you'll want to include a meal in this cellar eatery, where the emphasis is on local products. In a rustic dining room, long and narrow, seating is at shared tables, and meat is sold by weight and brought to your table by a cleaver-wielding chef for your approval before it goes onto the grill. A choice of pastas and sauces (mix and match as you please) are also available, as are hearty salads. Please don't ask for a separate wine glass—drinking water and wine from the same glass is an age-old tradition in simple eateries in these parts.

Via del Teatro 22 (down right side of Palazzo Contucci from Piazza Grande). www.acquacheta.eu. ✆ **0578/717086.** Main courses 7€–18€. Wed–Mon noon–3pm and 7:30–10:30pm. Closed mid-Jan to mid-Mar.

La Bottega del Nobile ★ TUSCAN It's a challenge to walk up the Corso without stopping at one of the many shops for a sip or two of wine, and this appealing tasting room and restaurant satisfies that temptation and much more, serving food and drink throughout the day. The upper floor is part cafe and part wine shop, representing the region's best producers. Snug, brick-walled cellars below are filled with tables where an affable young staff serves thick Tuscan steaks and hearty ragouts, and eagerly pairs just the right wine to complement each dish.

Corso 95. www.labottegadelnobile.com. ✆ **0578/757016.** Main courses 8€–16€. Daily noon–2:30pm and 7–9:30pm.

Osteria del Conte ★ SOUTHERN TUSCAN A trek to the top of town is rewarded with a delicious meal in this simple room, overseen by a mother-and-son team who are devoted to home cooking and warm hospitality. Put yourself in their hands with the set menu, which includes several local specialties and wine, or choose from a nice a la carte selection—the *pici all'aglione* (handmade spaghetti with garlic sauce) is a memorable first course, and most of the meats are grilled to order.

Via di San Donato 19. www.osteriadelconte.it. ✆ **0578/756062.** Main courses 9€–14€. Thurs–Tues 12:30–2:30pm and 7:30–9:30pm.

Wheels of cheese in Pienza market.

SIDE TRIPS FROM MONTEPULCIANO

Montepulciano, Montalcino, and Pienza are in the Crete Sienese, literally the "Sienese Clay Hills." You've probably seen iconic photographs of the terrain, which stretches south from Siena: lone farmhouses and pointy cypress trees in a stark landscape of golden rolling hills. You'll get a nice sense of the Crete Sienese on the drive between the three towns on SP 146. This is another face of Tuscany, quite different from the vineyard-clad hills of Chianti country, and at times the countryside seems forsaken, almost like the surface of the moon. Not that the landscapes aren't beautiful in their own way. The clay soil is planted with wheat, fava beans, and sunflowers, and, depending on the season, the expanses of golden grasses and yellow blooms enfold you in a most welcoming way.

PIENZA ★★

14km (9 miles) west of Montepulciano, 55km (34 miles) southeast of Siena

A 20-minute drive west of Montepulciano on the SS146, this lovely hilltown sits perched above the Val d'Orcia, with glorious landscapes of vineyards and wheat fields in every direction. Its narrow side streets are lined with shops selling the town's famous pecorino (sheep's milk cheeses) and honey. But Pienza has a unique noble heritage, dating to the mid-15th century, when it was rebuilt by humanist Pope Pius II and architect Bernardo Rossellino to be the ideal Renaissance town. Piazzas and palaces, spaces and perspectives, were to be designed to reflect Renaissance ideals of rationality and humanism, and to instill the populace with notions of peace and harmony. Rossellino's budget was 10,000 florins and he spent 50,000, but Pius was so pleased with the transformation of his birthplace that he scrapped the old name of Corsignano and named the town after himself. Sadly, Pius died soon thereafter, and most of his plans for palaces, churches, piazzas and well-ordered streets were never realized.

Park outside the town walls and follow the main street, **Corso Rossellino,** to the center of town: the splendid **Piazza Pio II**, the focal point of Pius's town-planning dream and a Renaissance stage set of architectural perfection. Here you'll find the two main buildings of Pius's ambitious dream: A church (the **Duomo)** and the pope's own residence (**Palazzo Piccolomini**). Pienza's **tourist office** is also here, inside the Palazzo Vescovile on Piazza Pio II, Corso Rossellino 30, 53026 Pienza (www.pienza.info; ✆ **0578/749905;** open Wed–Mon 10am–1pm and 3–6pm from Mid-March to Oct, weekends only the rest of the year).

Duomo ★ CATHEDRAL This light-drenched *domus vitrea* (literally "a house of glass") fulfilled Pius's notion that the church should symbolize enlightenment. The exterior represents Renaissance ideals of unity with a facade of three blind arches, atop which the pope immodestly placed his coat of arms. The interior was in part inspired by his travels in Germany, where he admired the local style of church architecture, hall churches lit by tall windows. For all of its perfection, the structure showed a serious flaw almost as soon as it was completed—the hillside on which it is built is unstable, and the foundations are slowly shifting (as you walk toward the rear, you'll notice the floor slightly slopes).

Piazza Pio II. No phone. Free. Daily 7am–1pm and 2:30–7pm.

Palazzo Piccolomini ★ HISTORIC SITE Pope Pius had to have a residence worthy of his lofty status, of course, and his dining room, bedroom, library, and other chambers are appropriately regal, and rather stuffy. The pope's descendants lived here until 1968, and nothing in the cavernous salons is very exciting (the dry-as-dust audio guide doesn't help, either). The bright spot is the palazzo's hanging garden and triple-decked loggia, reached through the painted courtyard; you can linger a while to take in the incredible views south over the Val d'Orcia. With a setting like this it's easy to see why Pius II, born Silvio Piccolomini into an impoverished branch of a noble Sienese family, wanted to return to this humble town of his birth after an event-filled life as a humanist scholar, itinerant diplomat, and pope from 1458 to 1464.

Piazza Pio II. www.palazzopiccolominipienza.it. ✆ **0578/74392.** 7€ adults, 5€ students and children 6–17, free for children under 5. Mid-Mar to mid-Oct Tues–Sun 10am–6:30pm; mid-Oct to mid Mar Tues–Sun 10am–4:30pm.

Where to Stay & Eat

La Bandita Townhouse ★★ While Pope Pius introduced the latest in Renaissance fashion to little Pienza, this stylish guesthouse does the same with 21st-century decor. Huge, loftlike guest quarters seem better suited to New York or Berlin than to a small Tuscan town (and it's telling that the elevator is the only one for miles around), but they certainly prove that contemporary chic can be comfortable. Even if you don't recognize the international designers of the steel frame beds, distressed leather armchairs, and slinky divans, you can appreciate the tastefully soothing surroundings and such luxuries as slipping effortlessly from a supremely comfortable mattress into a deep tub perched right alongside. Timeless pleasures include honey-colored stone walls and the view into the large garden and over the surrounding countryside. The dining room is furnished with refitted furnishings from a 1950s-era Florence school and sticks to straightforward takes on local cuisine, with some innovations that include hamburgers made from the best beef from the Val di Chiana.

Corso il Rossellino. www.la-bandita.com. ✆ **0578/749005.** 12 units. 250€–395€ double. Rates include breakfast. **Amenities:** Restaurant; bar; Wi-Fi (free).

La Casa di Adelina ★★★ Montichiello, a little walled village 10km (6 miles) east of Pienza, is an enchanting warren of piazzas and stone towers, and adding to the charm are these three rooms and three apartments (rooms and one attic apartment are in a grand old house on a central square, one apartment is in a nearby house, and another is in a medieval tower). All are full of antiques, family heirlooms, and tasteful vintage-modern and contemporary pieces. Guests share a large beamed lounge where a fire burns in the stove on chilly evenings and a breakfast with homemade pastries is served by affable host, Francesco. With a couple of shops and places to eat, the village is a good base for exploring the Val d'Orcia and some of Tuscany's most enticing towns.
Piazza San Martina 3, Montichiello. www.lacasadiadelina.eu. ✆ **0578/755167**. 6 units. 100€–140€ double. Rates include breakfast. Closed 2 wks. in Feb. **Amenities:** Lounge; Wi-Fi (free).

Trattoria da Fiorella ★★ TUSCAN An old stable is now an unusual and inviting dining room, with just eight or so tables on the main floor and a few on a balcony above. The setting seems almost theatrical, and the two friendly proprietor-brothers give the town's famous pecorino cheese the star treatment: *crespelle al forno ripiene con zucchini e pecorino fresco,* baked crêpes filled with zucchini and young pecorino cheese; *verdure grigliata con pecorino*, a nice assortment of vegetables topped with shaved cheese; and mixed pecorinos with honey and walnuts. Several hearty homemade pastas, some with sauces of *cinghiale* (wild boar), and grilled steak and pork also show off the local bounty.
Via Condotti 11. www.trattoriadafiorella.it. ✆ **0578/749045**. Main courses 8€–15€. Thurs–Tues noon–2:30pm and 7–9:30pm.

Trattoria Latte di Luna ★ TUSCAN Just about everyone who's in Pienza at mealtimes seems to squeeze through the narrow door of this family-run trattoria off a little square at one end of town. Home-cooked meals are prepared by mom in the kitchen and served by dad and daughter in the yellow stucco dining room. *Pici all'aglione* (with spicy tomato-and-garlic sauce) or *zuppa di pane* (a local variant on *ribollita,* with more cabbage) are stellar starters, followed by wild boar or suckling pig in season or grilled steaks any time. The dessert of choice is the house-made *semifreddo* flavored with walnuts and seasonal fruits and berries.
Corso Rossellino, next to Porta al Ciglio. ✆ **0578/748606.** Main courses 7€–16€. Wed–Mon 12:15–2:15pm and 7:15–9:15pm.

MONTALCINO ★★

23km (14 miles) west of Pienza; 28km (17 miles) west of Montepulicano; 40km (25 miles) south of Siena

Montalcino presents a warm welcome on the approach from the Ombrone River valley below, its medieval houses clinging higgley-piggley to precipitous alleys beneath prickly towers. Of course, if you know wine, you're aware that scenery is not the town's real calling card—that's Brunello di Montalcino, one of the world's most acclaimed reds, of which the town produces more than 3.5 million bottles a year, along with 3 million of its lighter-weight cousin, Rosso di Montalcino.

For many centuries, however, Montalcino wasn't concerned with wine at all, but with its shifting allegiances to the ever-battling rival powers of Florence and Siena. The little town was once known as the "Republic of Siena at Montalcino" for housing Sienese refugees after Florence conquered Siena in 1555 (see **La Fortezza**, below). Montalcino soon fell to Florence, however, and more or less languished until the 1960s, when the world began waking up to the fact that the local sangiovese grosso grapes—known as "Brunello" to the locals—yielded a wine to be reckoned with. Today Montalcino is flourishing, mostly because of the wine trade. As an added bonus, two fine medieval abbeys can be visited in the countryside nearby.

The **tourist office** is at Costa del Municipio (www.prolocomontalcino.it; ✆ **0577/849331;** daily 10am–1pm and 2–5:40pm, closed Mon Nov–Mar).

La Fortezza ★ HISTORIC SITE Built in 1361, this castle's moment arrived when the Sienese holed up here for 4 years after their city's final defeat by Florence in 1555 (ironically, the fortress had only recently been expanded and strengthened by Florence's Medici dukes). You can wander round the pentagonal walls and scale a ladder to the highest turret for a view across hills and dales all the way to Siena—but do so before you sample wine in the on-premise enoteca, perhaps the only tasting room in the world with ramparts.

Piazzale Fortezza. www.enotecalafortezza.it. ✆ **0577 849211.** 4€, 2€ children 6–17, includes Museo di Montalcino. Nov–Mar daily 10am–6pm; Apr–Oct daily 9am–8pm.

Sampling the Vino

Brunello di Montalcino is one of Italy's mightiest reds, a brawny wine that can hold its own with the rarest *bistecca alla fiorentina*. It's also the perfect accompaniment to game, pungent mushroom sauces, and aged cheeses. Brunello exudes the smell of mossy, damp earth and musky berries; it tastes of dark, sweet fruits and dry vanilla, and as the deep ruby liquid mellows to garnet, the wine takes on its characteristic complex and slightly tannic aspect. Although Montalcino has produced wine for centuries, its flagship Brunello is a recent development, born from late-19th-century sangiovese experiments. Most Brunellos are drinkable after about 4 to 5 years in the bottle; the complex ones are best after 10 years or so (few last beyond 30 years). Staff members at Montalcino's wine consortium **Consorzio del Vino Brunello di Montalcino** (www.consorziobrunellodimontalcino.it; ✆ **0577-848246**), Piazza Cavour 8, can provide info on local wines and steer you to vineyards that are open to the public.

Museo di Montalcino ★ ART MUSEUM Coming upon this small collection is a bit of a treat, as the cloisters of the church of Sant'Agostino house a trove of masterpieces that you wouldn't expect to find in such a small town. The painting galleries are devoted largely to Sienese artists, whose cold, Byzantine influences are not always immediately appealing. However, many were bold innovators of their times, in the years after the plague of 1348 killed more than half the population of Europe. The Virgin Mary, the favorite subject of early Renaissance painters, shows up in works of Bartolo di Fredi and Luca Tomme; Fredi's multi-panel painting of "The Coronation of Mary" is considered to be his masterpiece. The "Madonna dell'Unita (Madonna of Humility)," by Sano di Pietro (1406–1481), was quite radical in its time, showing Mary kneeling on a cushion rather than seated on her traditional throne. Andrea della Robbia's terracotta statue of St. Sebastian, who looks rather boyish and calm considering he's about to be shot full of arrows, brings the collection into the full flowering of the Renaissance in the late 15th century. A corny life-size model of an Etruscan warrior is the crowd-pleaser in the archaeological collection.

Via Ricasoli 31. ✆ **0577/846014**. 5€, children 3€, or included with Fortezza ticket. Tues–Sun 10am–1pm and 2–5:40pm.

A monk at Abbazia di Sant'Antimo.

Abbazia di Sant'Antimo ★★★ RELIGIOUS SITE This exquisite Romanesque abbey of pale yellow stone nestles serenely in a valley amid vines and olive groves at the foot of the village of Castelnuovo dell'Abate, 9km (6 miles) south of Montalcino. Legend has it that the first stone here was laid on the order of Charlemagne in A.D. 781, after an angel cured his plague-stricken entourage on a journey from Rome. While that story is debatable, the monastery does date to the 8th century and may have once housed the relics of namesake Saint Anthimus, an early Christian priest. Near the entrance is a charming medieval relief of the Madonna and Child, and carvings of mythological animals and geometric designs surround the doors. Inside the columned interior, the carving continues; look on the right side for an intricate depiction of Daniel in the lion's den. In the chapel, 15th-century frescoes by Giovanni di Asciano show scenes from the Life of St. Benedict, rich in earthy detail (one scene features two blatantly amorous pigs). The French monks who have inhabited the abbey since 1992 fill Sant'Antimo with their haunting Gregorian chant during six daily prayer services, open to the public, usually at 7am, 12:45pm, 3:30pm, 6pm, and 8:30pm. A well-marked cross-country hiking trail to the monastery from Montalcino takes about 2 hours. For a quicker return, ask for a bus timetable at Montalcino's tourist office.

Via Della Badia di Sant'Antimo, Castelnuovo dell'Abate. www.antimo.it. ✆ **0577–835659.** Free. Daily 10am–1pm, 3—6pm.

Monte Oliveto Maggiore ★★★ RELIGIOUS SITE The most famous of Tuscany's rural monasteries is set in the scarred hills of the Crete Senesi, 22km (13 miles) northeast of Montalcino. Founded in 1313 by a group of wealthy Sienese businessmen who wanted to devote themselves to the contemplative life, the Olivetan order built this red-brick monastic complex in the early 15th century. What draws most visitors today is one of the masterpieces of High Renaissance narrative painting: a 36-scene fresco cycle by Luca Signorelli and Sodoma illustrating the Life of St. Benedict. Signorelli started the job in 1497, before skipping town to work on Orvieto's Duomo, where he created his masterpiece, a "Last Judgment" (see p. 274). Antonio Bazzi, who arrived in 1505 and finished the cycle by 1508, is better known as "Il Sodoma" (probably a reference to his predilection for young men, although he was married at least three times and had as many as 30 children). Look for his self-portrait in scene 3—he's the richly dressed fellow with flowing black hair, accompanied by two pet badgers, a chicken, and a raven. To follow the cycle's narrative, start in the back left-hand corner, with a scene of the young Benedict, astride a spirited white horse, leaving his parents' home to study in Rome. The scenes are especially appealing because of their precise details of medieval life: Check out the construction crews in scene 11, or the harlots smuggled into the monastery in scene 19 (allegedly, the abbot made Sodoma add clothing to the nudes he'd first painted). Also inside the church are gorgeous choir stalls crafted in intarsia in 1505 by the monk Giovanni da Verona, showing city scenes with remarkably detailed perspective.

SP 451, Strada di Monte Oliveto. www.monteolivetomaggiore.it. ✆ **0577-707611**. Free. Daily 9:15am–noon and 3:15–6pm daily (until 12:30pm on Sun and 5pm in winter).

Where to Stay & Eat

Castello Banfi ★★★ One of Tuscany's leading wine producers houses guests in stylish luxury, in a repurposed little *borgo* pressed against

HOT SPOT: THE val d'orcia

If you're driving from Montalcino to Pienza, an easy side trip takes you to some sights nestled in the rippling hills of the Val d'Orcia. First stop is San Quirico d'Orcia, about 15km (9 miles) east of Montalcino on SR2. The 12th-century, honey-colored **Collegiata dei Santi Quirico e Giulitta** assaults you with a wealth of carved stone: capitals composed of animal heads, friezes of dueling fantasy creatures, and columns rising from the backs of stone lions. The church was once a popular stop for pilgrims on the Francigena road from Canterbury to Rome, who paused to venerate its namesake saints, a mother and son; when 3-year-old Quirico inadvertently scratched the face of the pagan governor of Taurus, he was thrown down a flight of stairs. Rather than being horrified, Giulitta was delighted that her little boy had become a martyr. Her calm acceptance of this show of might so angered the governor he had her ripped apart with hooks and beheaded. Just down the block in the main square, Piazza della Libertà, is the entrance to the **Horti Leonini,** a Renaissance Italianate garden (1580) with geometric box-hedge designs and shady holm oaks, originally a resting spot for pilgrims. It's a surprisingly sophisticated spot to come across in such a small, sleepy town and is open daily from sunrise to sunset. The town's tourist office is inside the Palazzo Chigi, Via Dante Alighieri, 53027 San Quirico d'Orcia (tel. **0577-897-211**), open April through October Thursday to Tuesday from 10am to 1pm and 3:30 to 6:30pm.

Five kilometers (3 miles) south and well signposted off the SS2 is **Bagno Vignoni,** little more than a group of houses surrounding one of the most memorable *piazze* in Tuscany. Instead of paving stones you'll find a steaming pool of mineral water, created when the Medici harnessed the hot sulfur springs percolating from the ground; it's lined with stone walls and finished with a pretty loggia at one end. Even St. Catherine of Siena, when not performing religious and bureaucratic miracles, relaxed here with a sulfur cure. To see the springs in their more natural state, as Roman legionnaires did, take the second turnoff on the curving road into town and pull over after about a km (half a mile), when you see the tiny sulfurous mountain on your right. The waters bubble up here in dozens of tiny rivulets, gathering in a pool at the bottom. You can also look down on the spectacle from the Pacro di Mulino at the edge of town. From both vantage points, there's a fairy-tale view of the **Rocca d'Orcia,** the 11th- to 14th-century stronghold and watchtower of the Aldobrandeschi clan, formidable toll collectors along the Francigena pilgrim road through these parts.

Should you wish to partake of the waters, head to **Antiche Terme di Bagno Vignoni,** Piazza del Moretto 12 (www.termedibagnovignoni.it; ✆ **0577–887635**), or **Piscina Val di Sole,** at the Hotel Posta Marcucci (www.piscinavaldisole.it; ✆ **0577–887112**), to soak away your cares.

the castle walls. What were once peasant cottages are these days extraordinarily luxurious suites and rooms fitted with stylish traditional furnishings, sumptuous fabrics and rare antiques, plus the latest in technological gadgetry. Aside from the polished and attentive service, guests enjoy such amenities as a swimming pool, a secluded rose garden, and two excellent restaurants. Also on the estate is a farmhouse where five large apartments provide a much more informal experience. Furnishings are comfortably rustic, and wide covered terraces overlook miles of vineyards. Guests are left to fend for themselves, though the kitchens are well stocked with estate wines and all the provisions for a satisfying breakfast.

Corso il Rossellino. www.castellobanfi.com. ✆ **0577/877505.** 14 borgo units, 5 farmhouse apartments. Borgo units from 350€, apartments from 150€ double. Rates include breakfast. **Amenities:** 2 restaurants; bar; pool (borgo suites only); Wi-Fi (free).

Fiaschetteria Italiana ★★ Montalcino's most popular drinking spot, in the center of town on Piazza del Popolo, was founded in 1888 by Ferrucci Biondi Santi, a pioneer in the development of Brunello. He modeled his establishment on Caffe Florian in Venice, which is why locals refer to the Art Deco establishment with red velvet sofas and marble-top tables as "The Florian." The square out front may not be as grand as the Piazza San Marco but it's certainly picturesque. Prince Charles is among the famous patrons who have quaffed the excellent Brunellos and other wines offered here. Snacks and light meals are available, and the coffee, almost as treasured as the wines, is hands-down the best for miles around.

Piazza del Popolo 6. www.caffefiaschetteriaitaliana.com. ✆ **0577/849-043.** Main courses 8€–12€. Daily 7:30am–11pm, closed Thurs Nov–Mar.

AREZZO ★

53km (32 miles) NE of Montepulicano

This lively little city on the eastern flanks of the Valdichiana is not nearly as well known or as often visited as its more famous Tuscan neighbors, but this doesn't mean that Arezzo doesn't have a lot to show off. Within a fairly unremarkable 20th-century perimeter (much of it built atop the rubble left by Allied bombings in World War II), you'll find an enticing medieval city of cobbled streets climbing to the charmingly lopsided Piazza Grande. An elegant loggia by native son Giorgio Vasari (author of the gossipy *Lives of the Artists*) anchors one side of the piazza, while the rest of the space seems to be rather casually draped across the slope, with slanting cobblestones and an irregular shape. The Duomo crowns the hilltop, while next it to the green expanse of the Parco del Prato, with airy views of the countryside, surrounds a ruined 16th-century fortress.

Arezzo's rich cultural life has left it with a number of art-filled churches. Famous natives of Arezzo include not only Vasari but Piero della Francesca, from nearby Sansepolcro, the poet Petrarch (1304–74), and actor and director Roberto Benigni, who filmed parts of his 1999

Antiques fair in the Tournament Square in Arezzo.

Oscar-winning *La Vita è Bella (Life Is Beautiful)* here.

Essentials

GETTING THERE Arezzo is just off the A1 autostrada, putting it within fairly easy reach of Florence and most Tuscan towns by car; there's also bus service (**Tiemme:** www.tiemmespa.it; ✆ **0575/39881**) from Siena. Arezzo is on a main north-south train line, with frequent service to and from Florence and Rome.

VISITOR INFORMATION There are several **tourist information offices** (www.arezzoturismo.it) in the center: at Piazza della Repubblica 28, ✆ **0575/377-678;** Palazzo Communale, Piazza Libertà 1, ✆ **0575/401-945;** San Sebastiano Church, Via Ricasoli, ✆ **0575/403-574;** and inside the Logge Vasari, Piazza Grande 13, ✆ **0575/182-4358.**

Basilica di San Francesco ★★★ CHURCH The timed-entry admission only lets you spend about 30 minutes in front of Piero della Francesca's "Legend of the True Cross," but that is reason enough to come to Arezzo. One of the greatest artists of the Renaissance painted

Treasure Hunters and Knights

Arezzo's famous **antiques fair** takes over the Piazza Grande and adjoining streets the first Sunday of each month and the preceding Saturday. More than 500 vendors come from around Italy to sell an appealing array of old furniture, silver, oil paintings, and other wares, at very good prices.

The **Giostra del Saracino,** a jousting contest between the four districts of the town, turns the clock back to medieval times twice a year in June and September. A lively procession through the streets to the accompaniment of trumpets and drums ends in Piazza Grande, where jousters on colorfully bedecked horses wield their lances against armor-plated dummies.

one of the world's greatest fresco cycles, in a league with the Sistine Chapel, between 1452 and 1466. The 10 panels are remarkable for their grace, narrative detail, compositional precision, perfect perspective, depth of humanity, and dramatic light effects—"the most perfect morning light in all Renaissance painting," wrote art historian Kenneth Clark. The full religious significance of the story may escape you, but with stalwart knights and fair ladies, the scenes seem like a medieval romance. The beauty is in the details: heaving bosoms, pouty lips, and dreamy eyes, along with some wonderful ancient and medieval finery. To each face, the artist rendered an aesthetic humanity that calls out to us from the plaster. You may have seen these frescoes in the film *The English Patient*, when Kip hoists Hana up to the frescoes by means of ropes and pulleys; we see her expressions of delight and wonder as she comes face

WHO DID SHE THINK SHE WAS, THE queen OF SHEBA?

The story Piero della Francesca chose to tell in the Basilica di San Francesco, the Legend of the True Cross, is a real doozy, even when it comes to complex religious fables that were so popular among Renaissance artists. The artist based his fresco cycle on a story included in Jacopo da Varazze's 1260 *Golden Legend*, a compilation of saintly lore that was a medieval bestseller and circulated as quickly as scribes could write out a manuscript. With the invention of the printing press in the 1450s, printers made fortunes selling copies in every European language.

As the story goes, Seth, son of Adam, planted on the grave of his father the seeds from the apple tree that had so consequentially led his parents into sin. Timbers from the tree were eventually made into a bridge, and, while crossing it, the Queen of Sheba, the much-mythologized ruler of an Arabic kingdom, recognized that the wood had special significance. She told Solomon, king of Israel, that a savior would one day be hung from the timbers and in so doing usurp the kingdom of the Jews. Solomon had the wood buried, but Romans discovered the beams and used them to crucify Christ. Two centuries later Roman co-emperor Constantine the Great saw the cross in a vision, emblazoned the image on his army's shields, defeated his co-emperor Maxentius to become sole ruler, and converted to Christianity. His mother, Helen, went in search of the true cross in Jerusalem, where she had unbelieving Jews thrown into a pit to die of hunger until they revealed the location of the cross. One man was dragged from the pit and revealed the whereabouts, then converted. Flash forward another few centuries and the cross was still working miracles, aiding what remained of the Eastern Roman Empire in its battles with the Persians. A tad convoluted and obscure? To us, certainly, but riveting as told by Piero della Francesca.

to face with Piero's colorful ladies and gents. You'll feel the same, even when earthbound and jostling for a good look with your co-viewers. Piazza San Francesco. www.pierodellafrancesca.it. ✆ **0575/352727.** Church free. Mon–Sat 8:30am–noon and 2:30–6:30pm, Sun 9:45–10:45am and 1–5pm. Della Francesca cycle 8€, 5€ students and children under 17. Timed-entry tickets (30 min) only; reservations required by phone, website, or in person. Mon–Fri 9am–7pm, Sat 9am–5:30pm, Sun 1–5:30pm.

Casa di Vasari (House of Vasari) ★★ HISTORIC HOUSE Giorgio Vasari was born in Arezzo in 1511, just as the Renaissance was flowering all around him. Though he never achieved the greatness of many of the other artists working around him, Vasari helped define the period—and may have even coined the term "Renaissance" for the creative period that led Europe out of the Dark Ages. An architect as well an artist—he designed the Palazzo degli Uffizi in Florence (see p. 176)—Vasari is best known for *Lives of the Most Excellent Painters, Sculptors and Architects,* a rather juicy account of the great masters, many of whom Vasari knew personally. He settled down here in his hometown in 1540 and set about frescoing the walls and ceilings of his gracious house with classical themes and portraits. Check out his playful fresco "Virtue, Envy, and Fortune" in which each of the three competing figures appears most prominent depending on where you're standing. In the Room of Celebrities, Vasari painted portraits of Michelangelo, Andrea del Sarto, and other notable contemporaries, surrounding himself with the cultural greats of his day. Vasari's copious correspondence, including 17 letters from Michelangelo, is sometimes on view. While the original furnishings are no longer in place, part of the beautiful garden remains, and like the rest of the house provides a glimpse of a cultured Renaissance lifestyle. Via XX Settembre 55. ✆ **0575/409040**. 4€, 2€ students and children under 17. Mon–Sat 8:30am–7:30pm, Sun 8:30–1:30pm.

Cattedrale di Arezzo ★ CATHEDRAL This big and austere Gothic barn, at the highest point in town, reveals some nice surprises once you step inside the coldly stark interior. First to catch your eye will be the stained-glass windows by Guillaume de Marcillat (1470–1529), a French master summoned to Rome to work for the popes, who spent the last 10 years of his life in Arezzo creating these seven magnificent windows. His colorful scenes include the Calling of St. Matthew, the Baptism of Christ, the Expulsion of Merchants from the Temple, the Adulteress, and the Raising of Lazarus along the right wall; and Saints Silvester and Lucy in the chapel to the left of the apse. (Lucy has a amazingly serene face, considering that she's about to have her eyes gouged out.) Another fine artwork is the robust Mary Magdalene portrayed in a fresco by Piero Della Francesca in an arch near the sacristy door. Take some time to inspect the stone-carved scenes on the tomb of Guido Tarlati, an Aretine bishop who died in 1327—though a man of the cloth, he seems to have been constantly at war, clad in armor and besieging. (He was eventually excommunicated.) In the chapel on the left near the entrance, a series of terracottas by della Robbia show the Assumption, the Crucifixion, and a Madonna and Child.

Piazza del Duomo. ✆ **0575/23991.** Free. Daily 7am–12:30pm and 3–6:30pm.

Santa Maria della Pieve ★★ CHURCH Most great churches are intended to draw the eye heavenward, but few achieve the effect quite as dramatically and almost playfully as this 12th-century arched facade. Three stacked arcades of beige stone subtly narrow as they rise above a five-arched lower floor and the street below; above it all rises a bell tower with five rows of windows. The effect is all the more powerful since the church is built on a slope, and the facade is often viewed from below.

Inside is an altarpiece by Pietro Lorenzetti, a Sienese artist who would eventually perish when the Black Death devastated the city in 1348. Like the church's facade, his work here is multitiered, with figures getting smaller on each successive layer. The paintings are unusually vivacious for the austere Sienese school. It is one of few medieval altarpieces to remain in situ in the church for which it was intended. Some of the remains of the town's patron saint, Donato—a 4th-century bishop of Arezzo—are here, too, in a beautiful gold reliquary.

Corso Italia 7. ✆ **0575/22629**. Free. Daily May–Sept 8am–7pm, Oct–Apr 8am–noon and 3–6pm.

Where to Stay

Antiche Mura ★ A tall, narrow old house just a few steps below the Duomo is tucked into the town walls and dates from the 1200s. Rock outcroppings, stone walls, glass walkways over ancient foundations, and an old olive press celebrate the heritage, while sleekly simple furnishings, bright white walls, and splashes of color add a distinctly contemporary flair. Each room is named and styled after a famous woman in literature or the movies, from Madame Bovary's period decor to the sensual reds used in the Marilyn Monroe room. Breakfast is served in a nearby bar.

Piaggia di Murello 35. www.antichemura.info. ✆ **0575/20410.** 6 units. 75€–95€ double. Rates include breakfast. Free parking nearby. **Amenities:** Wi-Fi (free).

Graziella Patio Hotel ★★ Decor in this old palace a stone's throw from the church of San Francesco is based on the travel essays of the late Bruce Chatwin. The gimmick actually works, adding romance and drama without sacrificing comfort, along with flourishes like huge bathtubs in the sitting/sleeping areas and a pleasantly contemporary lounge and breakfast room. The Colonial India room, with bright yellow walls and a four-poster bed, seems especially well-suited to the palatial surroundings, and the Moroccan room, with beautiful glazed-tile walls, is as colorful as

the town's famous frescoes. Three especially extravagant rooms are on a lower floor that opens to a hidden garden. One is equipped with a hot tub the size of a small swimming pool, and another has a huge sunken bathtub reached by a dramatic staircase behind the bed. Guests have use of a MacBook for the duration of their stay, and spa services are available.
Via Cavour 23. www.hotelpatio.it. ✆ **0575/401962.** 10 units. 135€–200€ double. Rates include breakfast. **Amenities:** Spa services; Wi-Fi (free).

Vogue Hotel ★★ With a name like this a hotel had better be stylish, and these good-size and gracious rooms deliver on the promise, bringing comfortable flair to centuries-old surroundings. Stone walls and beams accent rooms where huge soaking tubs are tucked behind glass headboards, enormous showers have windows, and sitting areas are set into alcoves. Traditional comforts include rich fabrics, fine carpets, and handsome wood furnishings. Some rooms also provide a timeless view of the town's towers and rooftops, and all the sights are just steps away.
Via Guido Monaco 54. www.voguehotel.it. ✆ **0575/24361.** 26 units. 120€–220€ double. Rates include breakfast. **Amenities:** Bar; Wi-Fi (free).

Where to Eat

In all but the worst weather, Aretines turn out for the evening *passeggiata*. Two prime spots to sit on a terrace and enjoy a pre-dinner glass of wine or aperitif while watching the comings and goings are **Caffe dei Costanti** in Piazza San Francesco (✆ **0575/1824075**) and **Caffe Vasari** (✆ **0575/21945**) under the Loggia overlooking Piazza Grande, a good place to perch even in the rain. The most popular place in town for a quick bite is **Dal Moro,** Via Cavour 68 (✆ **0575/043208),** with sandwiches and a huge selection of local cheeses and cold cuts.

Antica Osteria l'Agania ★★★TUSCAN On any given night half the town seems to be packed into these two floors of plain, brightly lit dining rooms, yet the waitstaff never seems daunted by the din or the crowds. Pastas are homemade from organic ingredients, produce is market fresh, and the meat is from local farms. Daily specials include such local favorites as *trippa* (tripe) and *grifi e polenta* (chunks of veal stomach in polenta), but lighter fare is usually available, too, and specials often include eggs topped with fresh asparagus or *tartufo* (dried truffles), especially tasty when accompanied with a Pinot Grigio. The house wine is excellent, and the house grappa puts the perfect finish on a meal.
Via Mazzini 10. www.agania.com. ✆ **0575/295381.** Main courses 7€–9€. Tues–Sun 12:30–2:30pm and 7:30–10:30pm.

La Torre di Gnicche ★★ TUSCAN/WINE BAR The emphasis here is on wine, with more than 30 choices available by the glass and hundreds by the bottle, and it's accompanied by a tempting choice of small plates and meals that might have you coming back more than once. A

huge selection of cheeses and salamis from local producers are available, as are many local favorites, such as *baccalà in umido* (salt-cod stew) and, in summer, *pappa al pomodoro* (a thick bread and tomato soup served at room temperature). The cluttered, bottle-lined room just off Piazza Grande is a nice hideaway on a chilly evening, and a few tables in the narrow lane outside are much in demand in warm weather.
Piaggia San Martino 8. www.latorredignicche.it. ✆ **0575-352-035.** Main courses 7€–11€. Thurs–Tues noon–3pm and 6pm–1am. Closed 2 wks in Jan.

Palazzo Comunale in Cortona.

Sottolemura ★ TUSCAN/PIZZERIA Arezzo has several nice family-oriented restaurants like this, but many Aretines claim the pizza served here in two big, friendly rooms and a large garden is the best in town. Some of the other dishes are formidable as well, including hefty pastas such as *rigatoni alla amatriciana* with a hearty and spicy tomato sauce, and a big choice of grilled meats. Even on a weeknight you'll be surrounded by boisterous families, and tables can be hard to snag on weekends when Sottolemura is a big favorite for get-togethers.
Via A. Sansovino 18. ✆ **0575/21403.** Main courses 8€–12€. Tues–Sun 7pm–11pm.

CORTONA ★★

34km (22 miles) S of Arezzo; 31km (19 miles) NE of Montepulciano

Draped across a green mountainside above terraced olive groves, austere-looking Cortona is a steep medieval city, where cut-stone staircases take the place of many streets. In recent years, the book and film *Under the Tuscan Sun* have brought waves of appreciative fans to town, but Cortona has survived the onslaught. The somber streets and stage-set piazzas are a bit more crowded in summer than they once were, but the town's appeal is as strong as ever and includes some significant art treasures and romantic misty views over the wide Valdichiana.

Note that if you arrive by **train,** the Camucia/Cortona train station (✆ **0575/603018**) is 5km (3 miles) below town in the workaday town of Camucia, where many services are located as well. **Buses** run from here to Cortona, but not as frequently as you'd wish—only once an hour at some periods during the day. Tickets are sold on the bus (1.60€).

In historic Cortona, you'll find a **tourist office** at Piazza Signorelli 9, in the courtyard beyond the Museo dell'Accademia Etrusca ticket office (www.cortonaweb.net; ✆ **0575/637223**).

Via Nazionale, known as the **Rugapiana** ("flat street," since it's the only one in town that even comes close to fitting that description), runs east-west through the medieval town to **Piazza della Repubblica,** presided over by a stern city hall loaded with towers, a stone staircase, and wooden balconies. On the northern corner the square opens into **Piazza Signorelli,** a lovely expanse named for the town's famous Renaissance artist, Luca Signorelli (1445–1523). This piazza was once the headquarters of Cortona's Florentine governors, whose coats of arms adorn the **Casali Palace** (now home to the excellent Etruscan museum). From here, streets lead down to the **Piazza del Duomo** and a treasure trove of art in the **Museo Diosceano.** Other streets climb steeply uphill from Piazza Signorelli to the **Basilica di Santa Margherita** and, even higher, to the hilltop **Medici Fortress.** You can, however, stay on level ground—as many strollers choose to do—and walk east along Via Nazionale to **Piazza Garibaldi.** This airy balcony at the edge of town extends into public gardens, where views look south to Lago Trasimeno in Umbria and west across the Valdichiana to Montepulciano and a little cafe serves a delicious snack of fried olives.

Basilica di Santa Margherita in Cortona.

Basilica di Santa Margherita ★ CHURCH High above the town, this 19th-century church with a red-and-white-striped interior would be quite forgettable if it were not for the intriguing story of its patron, Margaret of Cortona

(1247–1297), a follower of St. Francis. In her late twenties, Margaret—the former mistress of a lord from Montepulciano—devoted her life to caring for the sick and poor, establishing a hospital and order of nursing sisters. The 13th-century crucifix through which she carried on a prayer dialogue with God hangs in the church, and her embalmed body—to which the centuries have not been terribly kind—lies in full view in a lavish 14th-century tomb above the main altar.

Piazza Santa Margherita. ✆ **0575/603116**. Free. Apr–Oct daily 8–noon and 3–7; Nov–Mar 9–noon and 3–6.

Church of San Francesco ★ CHURCH This rather simple Romanesque church with its wood-raftered ceiling is the second Franciscan church ever built (the first, in Assisi, was begun around 1228, while this one dates to 1245). This church contains the tomb of Brother Elias of Cortona, who administered the Franciscan Order after Francis's death in 1226. It also houses three precious relics of St. Francis himself—his tunic, his manuscript of the New Testament, and a cushion he often used. On the high altar is the Reliquary of the Holy Cross, an ornate 10th-century ivory tablet containing a fragment of Christ's cross, presented to Elias by the Byzantine Emperor in 1244. The artist Luca Signorelli, who died in Cortona in 1523, is believed to be buried in the crypt.

Via Berrettini. ✆ **0575/603205.** Free admission. Daily 9am–5:30pm.

Fortezza di Girifalco ★ HISTORIC SITE It's all uphill to Cortona's rugged defenses, built in 1556 on the orders of Duke Cosimo di Medici (Cortona was a prosperous city under Medici rule). The torturous stepped ascent is enlivened by 15 modern mosaics depicting the Stations of the Cross, by the Futurist artist Gino Severini (1883–1966), a Cortona native. By the second time Christ falls, you'll feel like doing the same, though you can pause for a restorative drink at the bar by the Basilica Santa Margherita. The views from the four surviving bastions reward the climb, across the Valdichiana to Montepulciano, south toward Lago Trasimeno, and north toward Arezzo and the colossal Monte Amiata.

Viale Raimondo Bistacci. ✆ **0575/637235.** 3€. Hours vary; usually Sat–Sun 10am–7pm.

Museo dell'Accademia Etrusca ★ MUSEUM In pre-Roman Italy, Cortona was one of the 12 cities of the Etruscan confederation, and so many artifacts from that era were discovered nearby that an Etruscan Academy was founded in 1727. The collection is housed in the Palazzo Casali, a 13th-century mansion built for the city's governors. The original upper floors evoke the medieval period, while lower galleries have received a smart contemporary overhaul. The lower galleries tackle the

Etruscan and Roman history of Cortona, with lots of gold from excavated tombs and the enigmatic Cortona Tablet, a 200-word document inscribed in bronze. On the sprawling upper floors, the most intriguing object is a one-of-a-kind oil lamp from the late 4th century B.C., decorated with human heads, allegorical figures, and a few virile Pans playing their pipes, all surrounding a leering Gorgon's head on the bottom.

Piazza Signorelli 9. www.cortonamaec.org. ✆ **0575/637235**. 10€, 7€ children under 17, 3€ students. Apr–Oct daily 10am–7pm (closed Mon Nov–Mar).

Museo Dioscoceano ★ MUSEUM Almost every work in this small collection is a masterpiece. Pride of place, however, belongs to Fra' Angelico and Luca Signorelli. The Fra Angelico gem is an altarpiece from 1436 that offers a splendid "Annunciation," graced by his mastery of perspective and command of minute detail—notice the angel's precious garment embroidered in gold, the Virgin's elaborate robes, and the carpet of wildflowers (the new Eden) on which her house sits. Luca Signorelli, who was born in Cortona around 1450, is represented by a vividly detailed "Deposition" originally painted for the cathedral in Cortona in 1502. The painter instilled his figure of Christ with so much realism and passion, a legend soon began to circulate that he modeled the figure on his son, who had died of the plague that year. Signorelli's "Communion of the Apostles" (1512) in the same room shows the artist's strong sense of perspective and architectural space; notice Judas in the foreground, hiding the host in his purse—ashamed of his imminent betrayal, he can't swallow it. The museum is in a former Gesu church.

Piazza del Duomo. ✆ **0575-4027268.** 5€. Daily 10am–7pm (closed Mon Nov–Mar).

Where to Stay

Some of Cortona's most reasonably priced accommodations are in two convents just outside the city walls, **Casa Betania,** Via Gino Severini 50 (www.casaperferiebetania.com; ✆ **0575/630423**), and **Instituto Santa Margherita,** Viale Cesare Battisti 17 (www.santamargherita.smr.it; ✆ **0575/1787203**). Just a few minutes' walk from the town center, spartan but pleasant doubles at both begin at about 60€.

Hotel Italia ★ This 15th-century palace is not as grand as the neighboring San Michele, but the hospitality hits the same high notes, Piazza Signorelli is just steps away, and the relaxed ambience seems to come naturally, well-suited to small-town Cortona. The spacious high-ceiling rooms are plain but nicely atmospheric, with tasteful rustic wood furnishings, beamed ceilings, and other architectural flourishes. Only a few have views, but to enjoy those you only need linger over your coffee in the panoramic top-floor breakfast room or relax on the roof terrace.

Via Ghibellina 5–7. www.hotelitaliacortona.com. ✆ **0575/630254.** 17 units. 90€–120€ double. Rates include breakfast. **Amenities:** Wi-Fi (free).

Hotel San Michele ★★ In this 15th-century palazzo right in the center of town, the salons and high-ceilinged guest rooms, a few frescoed and paneled, are reminders of Cortona's long past as a prosperous and noble town. Tile-floored rooms are furnished in what might be described as "fading grandeur" style, and are quite appealing for it. Some have views over the valley below, while a choice few, including tower suites, have their own terraces. A roof terrace with the same vistas is open to all guests, as is a decidedly medieval-looking courtyard. The San Michele also operates **Residence Borgo San Pietro** (www.borgosanpietro.com; tel. **0575-612-402**), 4km (2½ miles) outside town in San Pietro a Cegliolo, with a countrified take on grand living in the 14 rooms and 5 apartments. A pool is set amid the 7 acres of olive trees and lavender.

Via Guelfa 15. www.hotelsanmichele.net. ✆ **0575/604348.** 42 units. 115€–135€ double. Rates include breakfast. **Amenities:** Bar; Wi-Fi (free).

Relais Il Falconiere ★★ When Riccardo Baracchi inherited a farm from his grandmother, he and his wife, Sylvia, created a stylish and sophisticated retreat, with antiques-filled rooms scattered among a villa and stone farmhouses. Beamed ceilings and terracotta floors accompany the rural setting, with a pool and gardens amid 20 acres of olive groves and vineyards. A luxurious spa with a walled garden enhances the sense of relaxation. Sylvia oversees one of the best restaurants in the area, serving refined Tuscan food in the refitted lemon house.

San Martino (3km/2 miles north of Cortona). www.ilfalconiere.it. ✆ **0575/612616.** 15 units. 250€–350€ double. Rates include breakfast. **Amenities:** Restaurant; bar; 2 swimming pools; spa; Wi-Fi (free) in public areas.

Relais la Corte dei Papi ★★★ The hospitable David Papi has converted his family's country house, dating from 1770, into a quiet and luxurious retreat in the valley just below Cortona. The former farm is well-suited to a romantic getaway, as many of the enormous suites are set up as spas, with sumptuous handcrafted furnishings surrounding pool-size soaking tubs and hydromassage showers that double as steam rooms. Surrounding the handsome stone buildings are lawns and flower gardens tended by David's lovely mom, Gabriella, and among them two outbuildings have been set up as guest cottages. A well-regarded restaurant overlooks the swimming pool and its surrounding terrace.

Via la Dogana 12. www.lacortedeipapi.com. ✆ **0575/614109.** 15 units. From 200€ double. Rates include breakfast. **Amenities:** Restaurant; bar; swimming pool; Wi-Fi (free).

Where to Eat

A walk usually includes a stop at **Molesini,** Piazza della Repubblica 3, or **Enoteca Enotria,** Via Nazionale 81, local institutions that will pour you a glass of wine and also offer a big selection of cheese, olive oil, and other local products. Enotria sells sandwiches, too, making the rustic room a popular hangout well into the late evening.

Ristorante la Loggetta ★★★ TUSCAN/GRILL You would probably be happy eating canned spaghetti while savoring the view over the Piazza della Repubblica from this restaurant's namesake loggia—or for that matter, dining under the enchanting stone-and-brick vaults inside. It's a moot point, however: The food here is very well done, and nicely, if rather stiffly, served. The kitchen is acclaimed for its preparations of beef from the Valdichiana, often served with a rich red-wine reduction.
Piazza di Pescheria. www.laloggetta.com. ✆ **0575/630575.** Main courses 9€–28€. Thurs–Tues 12:15–2:30pm and 7:15–9:30pm.

Trattoria Dardano ★ TUSCAN/GRILL Cortonans come to this simple, brightly lit room for meat—roasted here over a charcoal fire, with the emphasis on *bistecca alla fiorentina* from cattle raised in the valley below town (generally considered to be the best beef in Italy). *Pollo* (chicken), *anatra* (duck), *miale* (pork) and *faraona* (guinea hen) also go onto the flames. The heaping platters are usually preceded by *crostini neri* (little black toasts), with chicken liver, some local salamis, and often *ribollita*, the thick Tuscan soup, all accompanied by local wine.
Via Dardano 24. www.trattoriadardano.com. ✆ **0575/601944.** Main courses 8€–13€. Thurs–Tues noon–2:45pm and 6:40–10pm.

Trattoria la Grotta ★ TUSCAN For many regulars, any meal in this medieval, brick-vaulted dining room or in the tiny courtyard just off

The Valdichiana: The Big Valley

Cortona, Arezzo, and to the west, Montepulciano, nestle on the flanks of the Valdichiana (or Val di Chiana), a wide swath of farmland running north–south for some 100km (62 miles) through central Italy, roughly between Arezzo and Lago Trasimeno in Umbria. Etruscans settled the valley 2,500 years ago, leaving behind remnants of their sophisticated civilization in Cortona, Chiusi, and other centers of their 12-city confederation.

These early residents and subsequent settlers were plagued by malaria, spread by mosquitoes breeding in the low-lying wetlands. Leonardo da Vinci was among the medieval and Renaissance architects who set about draining the malaria swamps, a task not completed until the middle of the 19th century.

These days the valley supplies some of Italy's most prized beef, *bistecca alla fiorentina,* from Chianina cattle, along with no end of stunning views from Cortona and the other hill towns that overlook the green and golden folds of the landscape. You'll shoot through the valley on the A1 *autostrada* and the fast trains between Rome and Florence, and you'll get a nice close-up look on the 33-km (20-mile) drive between Cortona and Montepulciano.

Piazza della Repubblica must include the light-as-a-feather house gnocchi. All the pastas are housemade, and topped with rich, sweet sauces, while fresh, locally grown zucchini and artichokes are a light antidote for the deftly grilled steaks. The house wine is delicious and reasonably priced.

Piazza Baldelli 3. trattorialagrotta.it. ✆ **0575/630271**. Main courses 8€–18€. Wed–Mon noon–2pm and 7:30–11pm.

SAN GIMIGNANO ★★

42km (26 miles) NW of Siena, 52km (32 miles) SW of Florence

Let's just get the clichés out of the way, shall we?—"Manhattan of the Middle Ages" and "City of Beautiful Towers." There, it's said. As every brochure will tell you, in the 12th and 13th centuries more than 70 towers rose above the tile roofs of San Gimignano, built partly to defend against outside invaders but mostly as command centers and status symbols for San Gimignano's powerful families. A dozen towers remain, and as you approach across the rolling countryside, they do indeed appear like skyscrapers and give the town the look of a fantasy kingdom. Once inside the gates, you'll also better understand the reference to Manhattan, with visitors shoulder to shoulder in its narrow lanes, laying asunder the medieval aura you've come to savor. Almost everyone traveling the hilltown circuit makes a stop here, while bus tours pour in from Siena and Florence, and Italians arrive on weekend outings. If you want to be swept back to the Middle Ages, you're best visiting midweek in off-season, or late on weekday afternoons after the buses have headed home.

Essentials

GETTING THERE Approximately 30 daily **trains** run between **Siena** and **Poggibonsi** (one about every half hour, trip time: 25–40 min.), from where more than 30 buses make the 25-minute run to San Gimignano Monday through Saturday; only six buses run on Sunday.

Tiemme buses (www.tiemmepa.it; ✆ **0577/204111**) run at least hourly (fewer on Sun) for most of the day from both **Florence** (50 min.) and **Siena** (45 min.) to Poggibonsi. Many of those buses make an immediate connection with buses to San Gimignano (a further 20–25 min.; see above). From **Siena** there are also 10 direct buses (a 1¼ hr. journey) Monday through Saturday.

Arriving by **car,** take the Poggibonsi Nord exit off the **Florence-Siena** highway or the SS2. San Gimignano is 12km (7½ miles) from Poggibonsi. Parking is tight, and the *centro storico* is off-limits to most vehicles (including those of visitors). Read signs carefully, since many spots are reserved for residents, and at some parking is allowed for only

San Gimignano's medieval towers at twilight.

1 hour. The most convenient parking is at Parcheggio Montemaggio, outside the Porta San Giovanni (2€ an hour, 20€ a day). You can easily walk into town from here, but shuttle buses also take you up to Piazza della Cisterna (.75€, tickets sold on bus or at newsstand).

VISITOR INFORMATION The **tourist office** is at Piazza Duomo 1 (www.sangimignano.com; ✆ **0577/940008**). It's open daily March through October from 9am to 1pm and 3 to 7pm, and November through February from 9am to 1pm and 2 to 6pm.

Exploring San Gimignano

You'll see the town at its lively best if you come on a Thursday or Saturday morning, when the interlocking **Piazza della Cisterna** and **Piazza del Duomo** fill with market stalls. Piazza della Cisterna is named for the well at its center, a fairly ingenious device that for centuries was a repository for rainwater channeled from rooftops—a reliable and safe source of water that could not be tampered with or staunched by natural events occurring outside the city walls. For a refreshing break from the crowds, head up from the Duomo to the well-marked **Rocca e Parco di**

Montestaffoli. Filling the shell of the town's 14th-century fortress, this park provides greenery, quiet, and views over the town and countryside, all the better from the little tower in the far corner.

Collegiata ★★ CHURCH San Gimignano's main church is awash in frescoes, including one around the main door: a gruesome "Last Judgment" by Sienese artist Taddeo di Bartolo (1410) in which mean-looking little devils taunt tortured souls. Bartolo allegedly modeled some of the characters after townsfolk who rubbed him the wrong way. Much of the nave is also covered in the flat, two-dimensional frescoes of the Sienese school—a comic-strip-like Poor Man's Bible, illustrating familiar stories for the illiterate faithful in simple and straightforward fashion. The left wall is frescoed with 26 scenes from the Old Testament (look for the panel showing the Pharaoh and his army being swallowed by the Red Sea), and the right wall has 22 scenes from the New Testament (a very shifty-looking Judas receives his 30 pieces of silver for betraying Christ).

The best frescoes in the church are the two in the tiny Cappella di Santa Fina, where Renaissance master Domenico Ghirlandaio decorated the walls with airy scenes of the life of Fina—a local girl who, though never officially canonized, is one of San Gimignano's patron saints. Little Fina was so devout that when she fell ill with paralysis, she refused a bed and lay instead on a board, never complaining even when worms and rats fed off her decaying flesh. As you'll see in one of the panels, St. Gregory appeared and foretold the exact day (his feast day, March 12) on which Fina would die. She expired right on schedule and began working miracles immediately—all the bells in town rang spontaneously at the moment of her death. The second panel shows her funeral and another miracle, in which one of her nurses regained the use of her hand (paralyzed from long hours cradling the sick girl's head) when she laid it in Fina's lifeless hand.

Piazza del Duomo. ✆ **0577/940316.** 4€ adults, 2€ ages 6–18. Apr–Oct Mon–Fri 10am–7:30pm, Sat 10am–5:30pm, and Sun 12:30–7:30pm; Nov–Mar Mon–Sat 10am–5pm and Sun 12:30–5pm.

Museo Civico & Torre Grossa ★★ MUSEUM The late-13th-century home of the city government, Palazzo del Commune, is topped with San Gimignano's tallest tower, the aptly named Torre Grossa (Big Tower), finished in 1311. Your reward for a climb to the top will be views of the cityscape and rolling countryside of the Val d'Elsa, but save your 5€ and enjoy the same outlook for free by making the 5-minute climb uphill from Piazza del Duomo to the ruined Rocca.

Inside the **Camera del Podestà** (Room of the Mayor) are San Gimignano's most famous frescoes, Memmo di Filippuccio's "Scenes of Married Life." In one scene, a couple takes a bath together, and in the other, the scantily-clad fellow climbs into bed beside his naked wife. The great treasure in the adjoining painting gallery is the "Coppo di Marcovaldo Crucifix," an astonishingly touching work in which a vulnerably human figure of Christ is surrounded by six intricate little scenes of the Crucifixion. The artist Coppo, a Florentine soldier, was captured by the Sienese, who soon realized what a treasure they had in him; his masterpieces show a transition away from flat Byzantine style to more varied texture and three-dimensionality.

St. Fina's head (see the Collegiata, above) is in the **Tabernacle of Santa Fina** (1402), painted with scenes of the teenage saint's miracles. Taddeo di Bartolo, who did the terrifying "Last Judgment" in the Collegiata, painted the "Life of St. Gimignano (or Geminianus)" for this room. The town's namesake saint, St. Gimignano was a 5th-century bishop of Modena who conjured up a dense fog to save his flock from an attack by Attila the Hun. Hearing the news, the little town known as Silvia changed its name to San Gimignano. The saint cradles his namesake town in his lap, towers and all, offering his protection.

Piazza del Duomo. ✆ **0577/990312.** 6€ adults, 5€ ages 6–18 and 65 and over. Apr–Oct daily 9:30am–7pm; Nov–Feb daily 11am–5:30pm; Mar 10am–5:30pm.

Sant'Agostino ★ CHURCH An especially appropriate presence in this 13th-century church at the north end of town is St. Sebastian, the "saint who was martyred twice." In 1464, a plague swept through San Gimignano, and when it finally passed, the town hired the Florentine painter Benozzo Gozzoli to paint a thankful scene. (As a stop on trade and pilgrimage routes, the town would be decimated by the plague time and again, giving the townspeople a special affinity for St. Sebastian, who was also prone to repeated bad fortune.) The fresco shows St. Sebastian getting some divine help to fend off the arrows soldiers are shooting into his torso. In real life, the 3rd-century early Christian could not stay out of harm's way. When Sebastian proclaimed his faith, the emperor Diocletian ordered that he be taken to a field and shot full of arrows. Sebastian miraculously survived and was nursed back to health. Back on his feet, he stood on a step and harangued Diocletian as he passed in royal

Outdoor Art

Towers and medieval ambience aside, you'll also discover that San Gimignano is awash in frescoes—in churches, public buildings, and even outdoors. **In Piazza Pecori,** reached through the archway to the left of the Collegiata's facade, is a fresco of the "Annunciation," possibly painted in 1482 by the Florentine Domenico Ghirlandaio. The door to the right of the tourist office leads into a courtyard of the **Palazzo del Commune,** where Taddeo di Bartolo's 14th-century "Madonna and Child" is flanked by two works on the theme of justice by Sodoma, including his "St. Ivo"—an appropriate presence, given Ivo's role as patron saint of lawyers.

procession, and the emperor had him bludgeoned to death on the spot. Gozzoli also frescoed the choir behind the main altar with scenes from the life of St. Augustine, a worldly, well-traveled scholar who, upon having to make the decision to give up his concubine, famously prayed, "Grant me continence and chastity but not yet." The scenes are straightforward (without a great deal of religious symbolism) and rich in landscape and architectural detail.

Piazza Sant'Agostino. ✆ **0577/907012.** Free. Daily 7am–noon and 3–7pm (Nov–Apr closes at 6pm, and Jan to mid-Apr closed Mon mornings).

Where to Eat & Stay

San Gimignano's slightly peppery, dry white wine, **Vernaccia di San Gimignano,** is the only DOCG white wine in Tuscany, and it has quite a provenance, too: It's cited in Dante's *Divine Comedy.* A relaxing place to sip a glass or two is **diVinorum,** former stables with a small terrace at Via degli Innocenti 5 (✆ **0577/907-192**). At the famous **Gelateria di Piazza**, Piazza della Cisterna 4 (www.gelateriadipiazza.com; ✆ **0577/942244**), master gelato maker Sergio offers creative combinations like refreshing Champelmo, with sparkling wine and pink grapefruit, and *crema di Santa Fina,* made with saffron and pine nuts.

Chiribiri ★ ITALIAN This tiny vaulted cellar almost next to the walls seems more serious about what it sends out of the kitchen than do many of the pricier spots in the center of town. Ravioli with pumpkin, white beans and sage, beef in Chianti, wild boar stew, and other Tuscan classics are done well and served without fuss. ***Note:*** They don't take credit cards.

Piazzetta della Madonna 1. ✆ **0577/941948.** Main courses 8€–12€. Daily 11am–11pm.

Dorandò ★★ TUSCAN Three stone-walled rooms with brick-vaulted ceilings are the setting for San Gimignano's most elegant and best dining, though there's nothing fussy about the cooking. Ingredients and recipes are decidedly local—beef is done in a sauce of Chianti classic, local pork comes with an apple puree, and *cibrèo*, a rich ragout, comes with chicken livers and giblets scented with ginger and lemon. If you want to dine here during your trip, you'll need a reservation.

Vicolo dell'Oro 2. www.ristorantedorando.it. ✆ **0577/941862.** Main courses 20€–24€. Tues–Sun noon–2:30pm and 7–9:30pm (daily Easter–Sept). Closed Dec 10–Jan 31.

Hotel l'Antico Pozzo ★★★ When this 15th-century palazzo was a convent, the namesake "ancient well" served a grim purpose—young novices were dangled over the depths when they resisted *droit de seigneur*, the feudal rights of noblemen to have their way with young women living on their lands. That might not be the most inviting inducement to stay at a hotel, but the present incarnation just may be the best in town, and it's all about taste, elegance, and comfort. Reached by a broad stone staircase (or an elevator if you choose), rooms are filled with character, some beamed and frescoed, others with nice views of the town and Rocca. All are good-size and beautifully decorated, with classic furnishings that sometimes include canopied beds, along with fine prints and other appointments. A grassy garden in the rear is a welcome escape from the daytime crowds.

Via San Matteo 87. www.anticopozzo.com. ✆ **0577/942014.** 18 units. 90€–170€ double. Rates include breakfast. Closed part of Feb. **Amenities:** Bar; Wi-Fi (free).

La Cisterna ★ Behind the ivy-clad entrance on the town square, you'll find rooms that vary considerably in size and outlook—some of the smaller ones overlook a quaint courtyard, while larger rooms and suites may have balconies and views that extend for miles. Furnishings are simply and unobtrusively traditional Tuscan, with wrought-iron bedsteads and flourishes like arches, tile floors, and stone walls, although the surroundings—and the service, too—can seem a bit impersonal. The restaurant and terrace, along with a view-filled, glassed-in dining room upstairs, serve Tuscan food that is a lot better than you'd expect, given the presence of large tour groups that often pile in for lunch.

Piazza della Cisterna 24. www.hotelcisterna.it. ✆ **0577/940328.** 48 units. 100€–145€ double, includes breakfast. Closed Jan–Mar. **Amenities:** Restaurant, bar, Wi-Fi (free).

VOLTERRA ★★

29km (18 miles) SW of San Gimignano, 50km (31 miles) W of Siena

Volterra, in the words of D.H. Lawrence, perches "on a towering great bluff that gets all the winds and sees all the world." Volterra seems higher than any other Tuscan town, rising 540m (1,772 ft.) above the valley below. (You'll see the town long before you arrive.) Along its narrow ridge, a warren of medieval alleys falls steeply off the main piazza.

Lawrence came here to study the Etruscans, who took the 9th-century-B.C. town established by the Villanovan culture and, by the 4th century B.C. had turned it into Velathri, one of the largest centers in Etruria's 12-city confederation. Seeing their haunting bronzes and alabaster funerary urns is a compelling reason to venture here—that is, unless you're a fan of Stephanie Meyer's teen vampire trilogy, *Twilight,* in which case you're here to see the hometown of the Volturi vampire coven. Whatever brings you to Volterra, you'll soon find it's a terribly nice place to spend time and largely focused on day-to-day life rather than plying the tourist trade, unlike some of its Tuscan neighbors.

Essentials

GETTING THERE Driving is the easiest way to get here: Volterra is on the SS68 about 30km (19 miles) from the Colle di Val d'Elsa exit on the

A classic car race in the hilltown of Volterra.

Florence-Siena highway. From San Gimignano, head southwest on the road to Castel di San Gimignano, where you can pick up the SS68. You can park for free in a large lot below Porta Fiorentina, but you will pay a price—a climb up 350 steps to town.

From **Siena,** some 16 daily **Tiemme buses** (www.tiemmespa.it) make the 20- to 30-minute trip to **Colle di Val d'Elsa,** from which there are four daily buses to Volterra (50 min.). From **San Gimignano,** first take a bus to Poggibonsi (20 min.) then link up with those Colle di Val d'Elsa buses to Volterra. From **Florence,** take one of five daily buses (three on Sun) to Colle di Val d'Elsa and transfer there (2½–3 hr. total). Six to 10 **CPT buses** (www.cpt.pisa.it) run to Volterra Monday through Saturday from **Pisa** (change in Pontedera; 2–2½ hr. total).

VISITOR INFORMATION Volterra's helpful **tourist office,** Piazza dei Priori 19–20, 56048 Volterra (www.volterratur.it; ✆ **0588/87257**), offers both tourist information and free hotel reservations. It's open daily 9:30am to 1pm and 2 to 6pm. The office rents an audio guide (5€ for a handset) for an hour-long walk around town, providing some good tidbits about churches, palaces, and Etruscan and Roman remains along the way.

Exploring Volterra

The most evocative way to enter Volterra is through **Porta all'Arco,** the main 4th-century-B.C. gateway to the Etruscan city. Via die Priori leads steeply uphill from there to Volterra's stony medieval heart, the **Piazza dei Priori,** where the Gothic **Palazzo dei Priori** (1208–57) is said to be the first city hall in Tuscany, and the model for Florence's Palazzo Vecchio. A skull and crossbones outside the main hall handily sums up the medieval view of righteousness: "Remember divine judgement and you

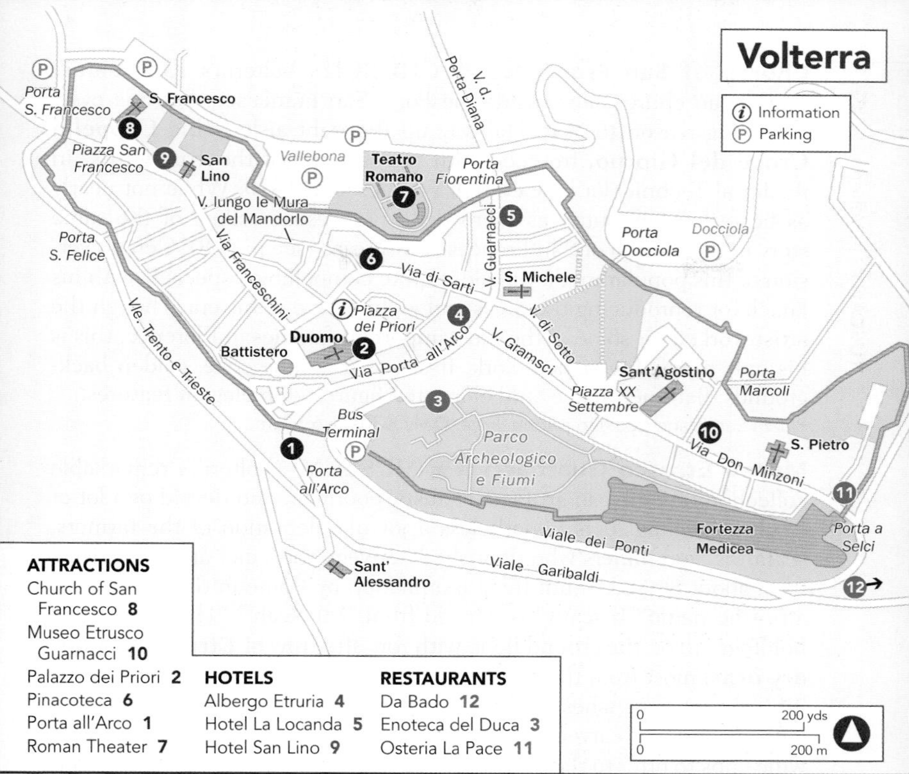

will not sin for all eternity." Two stone lions flanking the somber facade are symbols of the Florentines, who conquered Volterra in the early 14th century. Enjoy the view of the square with a coffee or glass of wine at one of the tables in front of Bar Priori; the hoodlike ornaments on the palazzo across Via dei Marchesi were installed to support canopies above shop stalls that lined the surrounding lanes during the Middle Ages. The squat tower in the eastern corner is festooned with a little pig (*porcellino*), hence its name, **Torre del Porcellino**. The beast is actually a boar, a symbol of strength for medieval residents—not only because of its robust heft but also because boars were plentiful in the surrounding woods and the mainstay of their diet (pasta with *ragù di cinghiale* and grilled boar are still menu favorites). A tolling of the bells once meant a death sentence had been carried out. Among the victims was 14th-century landowner Giusto Landini, who was stabbed and thrown out the windows of the Palazzo dei Priori after registering a complaint about a real-estate tax. Inside the modest-looking **Duomo** around the corner is a life-size "Deposition from the Cross," carved in wood around 1228 by anonymous Pisan masters and painted in bright colors. With their fluidity and emotional expressiveness, the figures look surprisingly contemporary.

Church of San Francesco ★ CHURCH Volterra's 13th-century Franciscan church, just inside the Porta San Francesco, has one overwhelming reason to visit: Halfway up the right aisle is the **Cappella Croce del Giorno,** frescoed with the "Legend of the True Cross" in medieval Technicolor by Cenni di Francesco in 1410. While not nearly as beautifully executed as Piero della Francesca's telling of the same story in the church of San Francesco in Arezzo (see p. 268), Cenni's version of this popular medieval tale is quite compelling, especially with his knack for reproducing the dress and architecture of his era. Though the artist worked for some of the most important families in Florence, this is his only remaining signed work. It shows a unique style: golden backgrounds, flattened space, and elongated figures with elegant features.
Piazza San Francesco. No phone. Free. Daily 8:30am–6:30pm.

Museo Etrusco Guarnacci ★★ MUSEUM Volterra's remarkable collection of Etruscan artifacts is dusty, poorly lit, and devoid of a lot of English labeling. It is nonetheless a joyful celebration of the farmers, seafarers, and miners who flourished between the Tiber and Arno rivers from about 800 B.C. until their assimilation by Rome in the 1st century A.D. (the name "Tuscany" is derived from "Etruscan"). The bulk of the holdings are on the ground floor, with row after row of **Etruscan funerary urns**, most from the 3rd century B.C., but some from as early as the 7th century B.C. Ashes were placed in these urns, which were topped with elaborately carved lids—finely dressed characters lounging with wine cups to offer to the gods, or horse and carriage rides into the underworld. One of the finest, the **Urna degli Sposi,** is a striking portrait of a husband and wife, somewhat dour-faced and full of wrinkles, together in death as in life. The Etruscans also crafted bronze sculptures, and one of the finest is a lanky young man with a beguiling smile known as the "Ombra della Sera (Shadow of the Evening)"—so called because the elongated shape looks like a shadow stretched in evening light.
Via Don Minzoni 15. ✆ **0588/86347.** 8€, or with 14€ Volterra Card. Mid-Mar to Oct daily 9am–7pm; Dec daily 9am–6pm; Nov and Jan to mid-Mar daily 10am–4:30pm.

Pinacoteca ★ MUSEUM While much of Volterra preserves the Etruscan, Roman, and medieval past, the town's worthy painting gallery transports you to the Renaissance with several standout paintings. Room 4 has a remarkably intact 1411 polyptych of the "Madonna with Saints" signed by Taddeo di Bartolo. The fellow in the red cape and beard in the tiny left tondo is the original Santa Claus, St. Nicholas of Bari. In room 11 is "Christ in Glory with Saints" (1492), the last great work of Domenico Ghirlandaio, one of the Florentine masters of the Renaissance. If you look hard, you can spot a giraffe being led along the road—an exotic animal that had only recently been acquired by the Medici for their menagerie. In Room 12 hangs a remarkably colored "Annunciation" (1491) by Luca Signorelli—note the great rush of feeling as the archangel bursts through the doorway to announce the news to Mary. In the same room is a "Deposition" (1521) by 26-year-old Rosso Fiorentino, a red-headed (and reportedly hot-headed) Florentine painter, who ended up going to France to work at the Chateau Fontainebleau. Painted in his odd color palette of flat grays and reds, it unusually portrays this solemn scene of Christ being taken off the cross as a swirl of action, with sashes flapping in the wind, workers scurrying up and down precarious-looking ladders, and the whole tragic event seeming frantic and disorganized.

Via del Sarti 1. ✆ **0588/87580.** 8€, or with 14€ Volterra Card. Mid-Mar to Oct daily 9am–7pm; Dec daily 9am–6pm; Nov and Jan to mid-Mar daily 10am–4:30pm.

Porta all'Arco ★★ HISTORIC GATE Volterra's greatest landmark is this huge, magnificent gate built by the Etruscans as early as the 3rd century B.C. in their 7km (4 mi) of city walls. The round arch contains a keystone that the Romans later incorporated into so much of their architecture. On the outside are mounted three basalt heads—features worn away by well over 2,000 years of wind and rain—said possibly to represent the Etruscan gods Tinia (Jupiter), Uni (Juno), and Menrva (Minerva). The gateway almost didn't survive World War II, when retreating German troops decided to blow it up to block the Allied advance through the city. Volterrans dug up the surrounding paving stones and temporarily plugged the opening, convincing the Germans not to destroy a gate that no one could pass through anyway.

Porta all'Arco. No phone. Free.

Roman Theater ★ ARCHAEOLOGICAL Take a stroll along Via Lungo le Mure, a walkway atop the medieval ramparts, to overlook the impressive remains of Volterra's Roman theater and baths, some of the best-preserved Roman remains in Tuscany. The theater dates back to the 1st century B.C., though parts of it were torn up for building materials during the construction of the medieval walls. The view from up here is the best way to see it all, and for free, but if you do want to wander among the stones, there's an entrance down on Viale Francesco Ferrucci.

Viale Francesco Ferrucci. ✆ **0588/86050.** 4€, or with 14€ Volterra Card. Mid-Mar to Oct and Dec daily 10:30am–5:30pm; Nov and Jan to mid-Mar Sat and Sun 10am–4:30pm.

Where to Stay

Staying within Volterra's city walls can be a transporting experience, especially in the evening when residents regain their historic town. Choices are fairly limited, so book ahead if you're planning a visit in the busy period of May through September.

Albergo Etruria ★★ The lounge and guest kitchen are homey touches, but the real attraction of this cozy lodging is the roof garden, a leafy retreat where the greenery is backed by the town's brick towers and tile rooftops. Parts of an Etruscan wall enhance the historic character of the old house, but rooms are charmingly up to date, filled with comfortable, attractive furniture handpicked by the friendly owners. The Piazza dei Priori is only a few steps from this stylish haven.

Via Matteotti 32. www.albergoetruria.it. ✆ **0588/87377.** 21 units. 69–99€ double. Rates include breakfast. **Amenities:** Wi-Fi (free).

Hotel La Locanda ★★ A location just inside the town walls makes this converted convent a good choice if traveling by car, since parking is just steps away. High-ceilinged rooms are done in soothing pastels, a few have massage showers and whirlpool tubs, and most pay homage to Volterra's medieval ambience with a patch or two of exposed stone and timber. The piazza and other sights are an easy walk away, and a quiet terrace tucked in the back offers a breath of fresh air.

Via Guarnacci 24. www.hotel-lalocanda.com. ✆ **0588/81547.** 18 units. 70€–110€ double. Rates include breakfast. **Amenities:** Restaurant; bar; Wi-Fi (free).

Hotel San Lino ★ There's a slightly utilitarian ring to the hallways and some of the guest rooms here, probably because for many centuries the 13th-century palazzo served as a cloistered convent. The enclosed gardens are still in place, and a little terrace looks across miles of countryside. There's also a small pool, the only one inside the city walls and reason enough to stay here in the summer. Some rooms are merely functional, while others are nicely turned out with a mix of modern and traditional furnishings. The best rooms overlook the gardens and sweeping landscapes beyond.

Via San Lino 6 (near Porta San Francesco). www.hotelsanlino.com. ✆ **0588/85250.** 44 units. 90€–110€ double. Rates include breakfast. **Amenities:** Restaurant; bar; pool; Wi-Fi (free).

Where to Eat

Da Bado ★★ TUSCAN Owner Giacomo's mom, Lucia, is in the kitchen of this favorite in the San Lazzero neighborhood, just outside the walls. She prepares a few daily choices that often include *zuppa volterrana* (bread and vegetable soup) and *baccalà rifatto* (pan-fried salted codfish stewed with tomatoes), along with *pappardelle alla lepre* (wide fettuccine with rabbit sauce) and other hearty pastas well suited to the homey, stone arched surroundings. Lucia also makes the jams that fill her delicious homemade tortes (cakes). A cafe in front serves coffee and pastries all day.

Da Bado. Borgo San Lazzero 9. ✆ **0588/80402.** Main courses 8€–13€. Thurs–Tues 12:30–2:30pm and 7:30–10:30pm.

Enoteca del Duca ★★ MODERN TUSCAN At Volterra's best restaurant, you'll have a choice of surroundings: the elegant, high-ceilinged dining room, a bottle-lined enoteca, or a pretty patio out back. Wherever you choose to enjoy them, the offerings are innovative and refined takes

crafty VOLTERRANS

The Etruscans made good use of the easily mined local stone, a translucent calcium sulfate known as **alabaster**—witness the hundreds of alabaster sarcophagi in the Guarnacci museum (see p. 280). Alabaster became a major industry in Volterra again at the end of the 19th century, when the material was much in demand for lampshades, with the rise of electric lighting. Today local artisans work alabaster into a mind-boggling array of objects, from fine art pieces to some remarkable kitsch.

Plaques around town denote the workshops of some of the best traditional artisans, where you will find only handworked items. Via Porta all'Arco has several fine shops, including internationally known **Paolo Sabatini**, at no. 45 (www.paolosabatini.com; ✆ **0588/87594**), whose alabaster sculptural pieces often combine wood and stone. The large **Rossi Alabastri** (www.rossialabastri.com; ✆ **0588/86133**) shop at Piazzetta della Pescheria shows off some especially distinctive lighting pieces, as well as alabaster bowls, fruits, and all sorts of other easily portable items. At **alab'Arte**, Via Orti S. Agostino 28 (www.alabarte.com; ✆ **0588/87-968),** near the Guarnacci museum, Roberto Cini and Giorgio Finazzo create sculptural pieces of museum quality—in fact, they are often called upon to help restore sculpture in churches and museums around Italy.

You'll find the work of many local artisans at the **Società Cooperativa Artieri Alabastro,** Piazza dei Priori 4/5 (✆ **0588/87590**), a sales showroom for smaller workshops. To learn more about the town's alabaster industry, visit the **Ecomuseo dell'Alabastro,** Piazzetta Minucci (✆ **0588/87580**; admission 8€ or with 14€ Volterra Card; daily 9:30am–7:30pm in summer, 10:30am–4:30pm in winter).

Alabaster isn't the only craft in town. **Fabula Etrusca,** Via Lungo le Mura del Mandorlo 10 (www.fabulaetrusca.it; ✆ **0588-87401**), sells intricate handmade jewelry based on original Etruscan designs. For prints created from hand-engraved zinc plates—another local specialty—visit **L'Istrice,** Via Porta all'Arco 23 (www.labositrice.it; ✆ **0588/85422**).

on Tuscan classics. All the salamis and cheeses are from local producers, *lavagnette* (homemade egg pasta) comes with a sauce of celery and pecorino pesto, and local beef is grilled to perfection. Some of the wines come from the owners' vineyards.

Via di Castello 2. www.enoteca-delduca-ristorante.it. ✆ **0588/81510.** Main courses 15€–25€. Wed–Mon 12:30–3pm and 7:30–10pm (also Tues dinner in summer).

Osteria La Pace ★ VOLTERRAN/TUSCAN No restaurant in Volterra can boast of such a long provenance, serving since 1600 and in the hands of the same family since 1939. The old brick walls and vaults look just as they must have 400 years ago, and the kitchen follows suit with perfectly prepared versions of such Volterra classics as tagliatelle with chestnuts and mushrooms and a hearty stew of wild boar.

Via Don Giovanni Minzoni 29. www.osterialapace.com. ✆ **0588/86511.** Main courses 7€–11€. Wed–Mon noon–11pm.

LUCCA ★★

72km (45 miles) W of Florence

Lucca is often called the forgotten Tuscan town. It's just far enough off the beaten track to be left out of package tours. But travelers have been waxing poetic about the place for a long time. In the 19th century, novelist Henry James called Lucca "a charming mixture of antique character and modern inconsequence"—the "inconsequence" bit meaning that Lucca, beautifully preserved within its 16th- and 17th-century walls, is much more a remnant of the past than a part of the modern world. The Etruscans were here as early as 700 B.C., and the Romans after them, and the city flourished as a silk center in the Middle Ages. No doubt such a long and colorful history inspired Lucca's native son Giacomo Puccini (1858–1924), composer of *Tosca, Madame Butterfly,* and *La Bohème,* some of the most romantic operas of all time. Lucca can seem like a stage set, and it's easy to look at the tiered facade of the church of San Michele and hear the strains of "O Mio Bambino Caro." Victorian art critic John Ruskin said it would be difficult to invent anything more noble.

Essentials

GETTING THERE Lucca is on the Florence-Viareggio **train** line, with about 30 trains daily (fewer on Sun) connecting with **Florence** (75–90 min.). A similar number of trains make the short hop to/from **Pisa** (30 min.). The **station** is a short walk south of Porta San Pietro.

By **car,** the A11 runs from Florence past Prato, Pistoia, and Montecatini before hitting Lucca. Inside the walls, you'll usually find a pay-parking space underground at **Mazzini** (enter from the east, through the Porta Elisa, and take an immediate right); aboveground parking areas surround the other gates as well, with rates from 1€ an hr.

Get in the Saddle

The popular way to get around Lucca, you'll soon learn, is on a bike. Enjoy the medieval lanes and squares on foot, but equip yourself with two wheels for a ride on the Passeggiata della Mura, atop the medieval walls. You can do so in style on one of the neon-green or Barbie-pink models from **Antonio Poli,** near the tourist office at Piazza Santa Maria 42 (www.biciclettepoli.com; ✆ **0583/493787;** daily 8:30am–7:30pm, closed Sun mid-Nov to Feb and Mon mornings year-round). On the same street, bikes are also available from **Cicli Bizzarri,** Piazza Santa Maria 32 (www.ciclibizzarri.net; ✆ **0583/496031;** Mon–Sat 8:30am–1pm and 2:30–7:30pm, plus Sun same hours Mar to mid-Sept). The going rates are 3€ an hour for a regular bike, 4€ to 4.50€ for a mountain bike, and 6.50€ for a tandem.

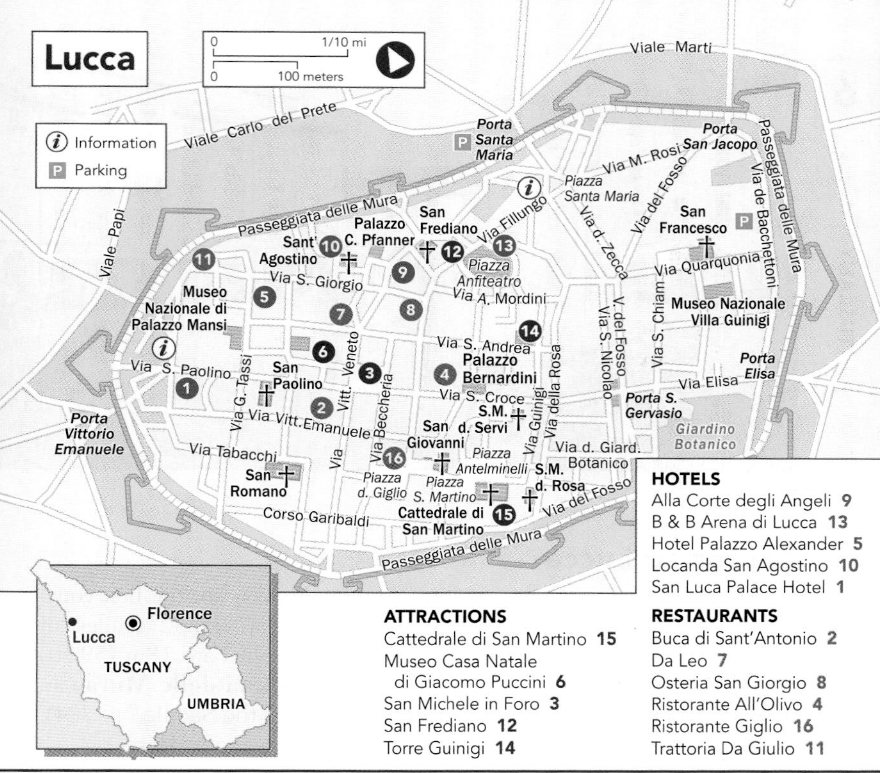

A **VaiBus** (www.vaibus.it) service runs hourly from Florence (70 min.) and from Pisa (50 min.) to Lucca's Piazzale Verdi.

GETTING AROUND A set of *navette* (electric **minibuses**) whiz down the city's peripheral streets, but the flat center is easily traversed on foot. But to really get around like a Lucchese, **rent a bike**—see the box "Get in the Saddle," p. 284, for rental information.

Taxis line up at the train station (✆ **0583/494989**), Piazzale Verdi (✆ **0583/581305**), and Piazza Napoleone (✆ **0583/491646**).

VISITOR INFORMATION The **tourist office** is inside the north side of the walls at Piazza Santa Maria 35 (www.luccaturismo.it; ✆ **0583/919931;** daily 9am–7pm, later in summer). The *comune* also has a small **local info office** on Piazzale Verdi (✆ **0583/442944**), which keeps similar hours. Depending on what you think about sharing the streets and squares with a multitude of costumed Darth Vaders and other fantasy figures, you might want to stay away from Lucca at the end of October. For a few days the city is overrun with as many as several hundred thousand attendees of the **Lucca Comics & Games** convention (www.luccacomicsandgames.com).

Piazza Anfiteatro in Lucca.

Exploring Lucca

Lucca has many remarkable architectural landmarks, but the first you'll notice are its incredibly intact city walls—more than 4km (2½ miles) of them, with 11 bastions and six gates; some stretches are 18m (59 ft.) wide. Topping the walls, the tree-shaded **Passeggiata delle Mura** can be circumnavigated on foot or by bike (see "Get in the Saddle," p. 284), as you peer across Lucca's rooftops toward the hazy mountains.

The most curious feature of Lucca's street plan is **Piazza Anfiteatro,** near the north end of Via Fillungo, the main shopping street. This semicircle of handsome medieval houses stands atop what were once the grandstands of a 1st- or 2nd-century-A.D. Roman amphitheater. Nearby, **Torre Guinigi** rises from the 14th-century palace of Lucca's iron-fisted rulers; notice that the tower is topped with a grove of ilex trees, one of many such gardens that once flourished atop the city's defensive towers. Climb the 230 steps for a spectacular view of Lucca's skyline, the snow-capped Apuan Alps and the rolling green valley of the River Serchio (3.50€ adults, 2.50€ children 6–12 and seniors 65 and over; open daily Apr–May 9am–7:30pm, June–Sept 9am–6:30pm, Oct and Mar 9:30am–5:30pm, Nov–Feb 9:30am–4:30pm).

The facade of **San Frediano,** Piazza San Frediano (✆ **0583/493627**), glitters with a two-story-tall 13th-century mosaic that depicts the Apostles watching Christ's ascent to heaven. Unlike most churches, San Fernando faces east, so the facade is a glittering spectacle when the mosaics catch the morning sun. As you stroll around town, especially along the main shopping street, **Via Fillungo,** notice how many shop-fronts display early-20th-century Art Nouveau signs etched in glass, adding a modern grace note to the city's medieval atmosphere. A splendid exception is the Renaissance cabinetry of fine wood and glass in front of **Carli,** at number 95, a gold and silver shop founded in 1651.

Cattedrale di San Martino ★★ CATHEDRAL Completed in 1070 to house one of the most renowned artifacts in Christendom, the Volto Santo (more on that below), Lucca's ornate Duomo does justice to its prized procession. On the facade, three arches open to a deep portico sheathed in marble; above it rise three tiers of arcaded loggias supported by dozens of little columns, each different. Legend has it that the Lucchese commissioned many artists to carve the columns, with the promise of hiring the best to do them all; they used all the entries and never paid anyone. A pair of binoculars will help you pick out the elaborate details of figures, animals, vines, and patterns in the loggias and on the portico. St. Martin, the former Roman soldier to whom the cathedral is dedicated, figures prominently—look for the statue of him ripping his cloak to give half to a beggar. A labyrinth is carved into the wall of the right side of the portico, for the faithful to make a figurative pilgrimage to the center of the maze, as if to Jerusalem, before entering the church. A Latin inscription reads, "This is the labyrinth built by Daedalus of Crete; all who entered therein were lost, save Theseus, thanks to Ariadne's thread."

Inside, the handsome sweep of inlaid pavement and the high altar are the work of the 15th-century Lucca native Matteo Civitali, as is the **Tempietto,** an octagonal, freestanding chapel of white and red marble in the left nave: This is where you'll find the famous **Volto Santo.** As the story goes, this crucifix was carved by Nicodemus, the biblical figure who helped remove Christ's body from the cross. Nicodemus, however, did not complete the face, fearing he could not do the holy visage justice. He fell into a deep sleep, and when he awoke he discovered a beautiful face miraculously carved on the crucifix (see "The Plot Thickens," below). The cathedral's other great treasure is the **Tomb of Ilaria Carretto Guinigi,** the young wife of Lucca ruler Paolo Guinigi, who died in 1405 at the age of 26; she lives on, accompanied by a little dog (a sign of her faithfulness) in a beautiful image carved by Jacopo della Quercia, the Sienese sculptor whose work so heavily influenced Michelangelo. An

The Plot Thickens

According to medieval legend, St. Nicodemus stashed the Volto Santo crucifix in a cave for safekeeping, where an 8th-century Italian bishop discovered it while on pilgrimage to the Holy Land (the location came to him in a dream). The bishop put the crucifix adrift in a boat, which magically washed up on the shores of northern Italy. Once again, the relic was set loose, this time in a driverless wagon pulled by two oxen, and all by itself it arrived in Lucca. First placed in the church of San Frediano, it miraculously moved itself to the cathedral. Throughout the medieval era, the Volto Santo and the legends attached to it attracted pilgrims from throughout Europe. On May 3 and September 13 to 14, the Lucchese walk in a candlelit procession from San Frediano to the cathedral, where the famous statue awaits them, dressed in gold and wearing a gold crown.

unseen presence is that of the great composer Giacomo Puccini, who was born nearby in 1858 and sang in the church choir.

Piazza San Martino. ✆ **0583/957068.** 3€ adults, 2€ children 6–14. Mon–Fri 9:30am–5:45pm (closes 4:45pm Nov–Mar), Sat 9:30am–6:45pm, Sun 9:30–10:45am and noon–6pm.

San Michele in Foro ★ CHURCH The magnificent facade of the Cattedrale di San Martino is matched, or even outdone for visual drama, by the delicately stacked arches and arcades of this 12th-century church, which rises above the site of Lucca's Roman forum. The show begins just above the main portal, where St. Michael slays a dragon as mythical creatures look on. Above that two lions flank a rose window, then begin four soaring tiers of little columns; these are inlaid with intricate carvings and topped with human heads, flowers, and animals. Above each row is a frieze on which real and mythical animals jump and run. The two top tiers are narrow and freestanding, capped by a statue of a bronze-winged **St. Michael the Archangel** flanked by two trumpeting cohorts. Lucchese claim to see a distinct glow emanating from St. Michael's right hand at sunset, created by a sapphire that, only according to legend, he wears on his finger. The interior is rather dull by comparison, although it is enlivened with a fine painting of "Sts. Roch, Sebastian, Jerome, and Helen" by Filippino Lippi in the right transept. The offspring of a notorious relationship between the painter Fra Filippo Lippi and a young nun, Lucrezia Buti, Filippino became one of the most accomplished painters of the late 15th century; his work shows the influence of his father as well as his teacher, Sandro Botticelli.

Piazza San Michele. ✆ **0583/48459.** Free. Summer daily 7:40am–noon and 3–6pm; winter daily 9am–noon and 3–5pm.

Where to Stay

Lucca has many B&B–style inns. For a complete listing, ask the tourist board for the handy booklet "Extra Alberghiero."

Alla Corte degli Angeli ★★ Some of the most charming accommodations in Lucca flow across four floors of this beautifully restored pink *palazzo* just off Via Fillungo, the main shopping street. It's hard not to fall for the gimmicky decor, which provides just the right touch of playful ambience in the smallish but extremely tasteful rooms. In each, colorful murals incorporate a flower, and rich draperies and upholstered headboards pick up the theme; a scattering of antique pieces and excellent lighting enhance the stylish comfort. Some of the good-size bathrooms have both showers and hydromassage tubs. A room on an upper floor ensures an extra amount of sunlight—third-floor Paolina, with two exposures, is an especially good choice.

Via degli Angeli 23 (off Via Fillungo). www.allacortedegliangeli.com. ✆ **0583/469204.** 10 units. 120€–210€ double. Rates include breakfast. Closed 2 weeks in Jan. **Amenities:** Bikes; concierge; Wi-Fi (free).

B & B Arena di Lucca ★★★ It's a stroke of good fortune that this parcel of prime real estate, an old apartment overlooking the Arena, welcomes guests, surrounding them with sublime views. Terracotta floors, oil paintings, and comfy sofas and chairs fill the shared lounge, while two high-ceilinged rooms also face the lively scene below from small balconies; two other rooms look onto the atmospheric Via del Anfiteatro. Hosts Alex and Livia treat guests as if they have come for a stay in a family home and serve a large breakfast by the kitchen hearth.
Via dell'Anfiteatro 16. www.bbarenalucca.com. ✆ **0339/678-6299.** 4 units. 100€–135€ double. Rates include breakfast. **Amenities:** Wi-Fi (free).

Bertolli Villas ★★★ Two beautiful villas tucked away on an olive estate in the hills surrounding Lucca are all about relaxing in comfortable and gracious style: Warmly decorated living rooms and bedrooms (each with private bath) are full of cushy armchairs, polished antiques, and colorful art. Olive groves and the mist-hung valley stretch beyond the large windows and terraces, and gardens surround sparkling pools. The villas can be rented in their entirety, as they often are during the summer, for a taste of the Tuscan good life, and at other times bedrooms in each are available for 2-night minimum stays, when guests share living areas and kitchens. Whichever way you enjoy this enticing taste of country life, the charming Flavia Bertolli Salom and her staff serve a breakfast of homemade cakes, prepare other meals on request, and go out of their way to treat their guests like friends who have come for a visit.
Via della Chiesa 13, San Colombano Alto (11km/7 mi. north of Lucca). www.bertolli villas.com. ✆ **340/761–9292.** 2 villas or 6 individual units. Villas from 1,200€ a week depending on season; rooms 120€ double. Rates include breakfast. **Amenities:** Kitchens; meals on request; pools; Wi-Fi (free).

Hotel Palazzo Alexander ★ Stepping into this 12th-century palace tucked into medieval streets feels a bit like walking onto an operatic stage set, and the feeling certainly doesn't let up as you settle in amid gilded and polished wood, reproduction antiques, old prints, and plush fabrics. You might have *putti* (cherubs) grinning down on you from the frescoed ceiling, while at the same time marble baths, Jacuzzi tubs in some rooms, excellent beds and fine linens, and other amenities are thoroughly up to date. Rooms are named after Puccini operas, and some of the especially charming suites have vaulted and beamed ceilings reminiscent of Rodolfo's *La Bohème* garret—that is, if the young poet had lived very, very well. Service is as memorable as the surroundings.
Via Santa Giustina 28. www.hotelpalazzoalexander.it. ✆ **0583/47615.** 9 units. From 80€ double. Rates include breakfast. **Amenities:** Bar; Wi-Fi (free).

Locanda San Agostino ★★ Three large, stylish, and atmospheric guest rooms are tucked away in a moody old palace. Four-poster beds, polished antiques, old oil paintings, and elegant wall coverings provide a character-filled and fairly luxurious ambience, as does the wisteria-shaded terrace and the raised hearth in the attractive lounge/breakfast room. The aptly named Teatro room comes with a big bonus: a private balcony with views over the ruins of a Roman theater.

Piazza San Agostino 3. www.locandasantagostino.it. ✆ **0583/467-884**. 3 units. From 130€ double. Rates include breakfast. **Amenities:** Wi-Fi (free).

San Luca Palace Hotel ★★ A sense of tasteful, old-world comfort begins in the downstairs hall and sitting room and continues into the large guest rooms, nicely done up with parquet floors and well-coordinated fabrics and draperies. Among the many nice flourishes are inviting table-and-chair arrangements in all the rooms and small "reading" alcoves with day beds in many. This old palace just inside the walls also has plenty of practical conveniences, including an easy-to-reach location (parking is adjacent) just a short stroll from the sights and train station. There's no in-house restaurant, but an extremely pleasant bar off the lobby serves light snacks.

Via San Paolino 103 (off Piazza Napoleone). www.sanlucapalace.com. ✆ **0583/317446.** 26 units. 85€ double. Rates include breakfast. **Amenities:** Bar; Wi-Fi (free).

Where to Eat

Lucca's extra-virgin olive oil appears on every restaurant table. An atmospheric 19th-century pastry shop, **Taddeucci,** Piazza San Michele 34 (www.taddeucci.net; ✆ **0583/494933**), is famous for *buccellato,* a Lucca specialty—a ring-shaped sweet bread flavored with raisins and fennel seeds. For a fortifying (and addictive) snack, stop by **Amedo Giusti,** Via Santa Lucia 18 (✆ **0583/496285**), where focaccia with many different toppings emerges piping hot from the oven. Sample Lucca's excellent DOC wines at **Enoteca Vanni,** Piazza San Salvatore 7 (www.enotecavanni.com; ✆ **0583/491902**). The atmospheric **Antica Bottega di Prospero,** Via Santa Lucia 13, will instill a deep appreciation of Lucca's sophisticated palate—it's stocked with local olive oils, vegetables, and an amazing array of dried beans and grains.

Buca di Sant'Antonio ★ LUCCHESE At least 3 centuries old, Lucca's most venerable dining room coasts a bit on its reputation these days, but sitting in the handsome surroundings amid copper pots and brass instruments is still a terribly pleasant experience—and usually requires a dinnertime reservation. Quietly formal service, with waiters in bow ties, and a welcoming glass of prosecco nicely accent a meal of traditional Lucchese dishes. The menu changes regularly, but usually includes such specialties as *farro alla garfagnana* (spelt, or barley, soup) and *coniglio in umido* (rabbit stew). A house dessert is *buccellato,* a ring-shaped confection named for the bread that sustained Roman legionnaires.

Via della Cervia 3 (a side alley just west of Piazza San Michele). www.bucadisantantonio.com. ✆ **0583/55881.** Main courses 15€. Tues–Sat 12:30–3pm and 7:30–10:30pm; Sun 12:30–3pm.

Da Leo ★★ LUCCHESE/TUSCAN It's a good sign when you have to veer off the well-beaten path to find a place, even better when anyone you ask along the way knows how to get there. The pleasantly old-fashioned room with plastic-draped tablecloths has been serving local classics for 50 years, and the *arrosto di maialino con patate* (roast piglet and potatoes), *coniglio* (rabbit), and other authentic Lucchese fare remain as good as ever. This is the place to try the typically Luccan *zuppa di farro,* a soup made with spelt, a barleylike grain cooked al dente. Via Tegrimi 1 (just north of Piazza San Salvatore). www.trattoriadaleo.it. ✆ **0583/492236.** Main courses 9€–16€. Daily noon–2:30pm and 7:30–10:30pm.

Osteria San Giorgio ★ LUCCHESE/TUSCAN This local favorite has a courtyard out front and comfortably informal rooms decorated with old photos, all tucked away on a quiet street near the Piazza Anfiteatro. The menu is geared to neighbors looking for a home-cooked meal: with several soups, including a hearty *farro alla luchesse* (beans and barley), *coniglio stufato con olive taggiasche e uva* (rabbit stew with olives and grapes), and a local seafood favorite, *baccalà alla griglia con ceci* (grilled cod with chickpeas). Servers seems to know just about everyone who comes in the door and extend a warm welcome to newcomers as well. Via San Giorgio 26. www.osteriasangiorgiolucca.it. ✆ **0583/953233.** Main courses 8€–13€. Daily noon–3pm and 7–10:30pm.

Ristorante All'Olivo ★ LUCCHESE/SEAFOOD This is where the Lucchese come when they're in the mood for fish. Taking a seat in one of its four comfortable and elegant little rooms—one with a fireplace, another like a covered garden—definitely elevates a meal to a special occasion. Seafood is brought in daily from the nearby Tuscan port of Viareggio and appears in a bounty of pastas, grilled platters, a nice choice of *antipasti di mare,* and a simply prepared catch of the day. Meat lovers will not be disappointed with the hearty roasts and grilled Tuscan steaks. Piazza San Quirico 1. www.ristoranteolivo.it. ✆ **0583/496264.** Main courses 12€–20€. Mon–Sat 12:30–2pm and 7:30–10pm.

Ristorante Giglio ★★ LUCHESE White tablecloths, fine china, and marble mantle pieces do justice to the setting in the 18th-century Palazzo Arnolfini, and even the well-laid tables on the terrace add a splash of elegance to quietly refined Piazza Giglio out front. The food is reassuringly Old World and traditionally Tuscan. Many Lucchese regulars would not think of dining anywhere else, or wavering from a meal of the house specials: tagliatelle topped with shaved white truffles, perfectly grilled beef tenderloin with porcini mushrooms, and for dessert, Lucchese *buccellato* (sweet bread) filled with ice cream and berries. Piazza del Giglio. ✆ **0583/494058.** Main courses 9€–20€. Thurs–Mon noon–2:30pm and 7:30–10pm; Tues and Wed 7:30pm–10pm.

O Mio Babbino Caro

While it's impossible to walk anywhere in Lucca without a Puccini aria or two wafting through your head, the maestro comes most vividly to life in Piazza Cittadella, commanded by his bronze statue. Puccini was born around the corner at 9 Corte San Lorenzo, where he lived until he left for Milan in his early 20s. The modest-yet-comfortable rooms of the **Museo Casa Natale di Giacomo Puccini** (www.puccinimuseum.org; ✆ **0583/584028**) are open for a look at scores, some random pieces of heavy furniture, and, most notably, the piano on which he composed many of his scores. Hours are March, April, and October daily 10am to 6pm; May through September daily 10am to 7pm; and November through February Wednesday to Monday 10am to 1pm and 3 to 5pm. Admission is 7€.

Trattoria Da Giulio ★★ LUCCHESE/TUSCAN You may have to go out of your way to find this local favorite, tucked away on back streets near the northwest corner of the city walls. Once there, it seems like everyone in town is on a first-name basis with the busy staff that dashes between the tables in the three brightly lit rooms. A long menu of local classics includes *salsicce con fagioli all'ucelletto*, sausage with beans in tomato sauce and sage; *tagliatelle alla contadina,* with fresh tomatoes, basil and oregano; and a few variations of *cavallo* (horsemeat, served raw, *tartara,* and otherwise). Excellent house wines are available by the pitcher.

Via delle Conce 25. ✆ **0583/55948.** Main courses 8€–13€. Mon–Sat noon–2:30pm and 6:30–10:30pm.

Entertainment & Nightlife

Every evening at 7pm from April through October, the Chiesa di San Giovanni hosts an opera recital or orchestral concert dedicated to hometown composer Giacomo Puccini, in a series called **Puccini e la sua Lucca (Puccini and His Lucca)** (www.puccinielasualucca.com). Tickets are 17€ (13€ for those 22 and under) and can be purchased all day inside San Giovanni. Just try listening to "Nessun Dorma" in this lovely church in the composer's hometown without chills running up your spine. Nearby Lago di Massaciuccoli is the backdrop for the summer **Puccini Festival ★** (www.puccinifestival.it; ✆ **0584/359322**), the biggest date in a local opera lover's calendar. Buy tickets at the seasonal ticket office at Viale Puccini 257a, in Torre del Lago, or online (35€–125€).

PISA ★★

85km (53 miles) south of Lucca, 76km (47 miles) W of Florence

It's ironic that one of the most famous landmarks in a country that has given Western civilization much of its greatest art and architecture is in

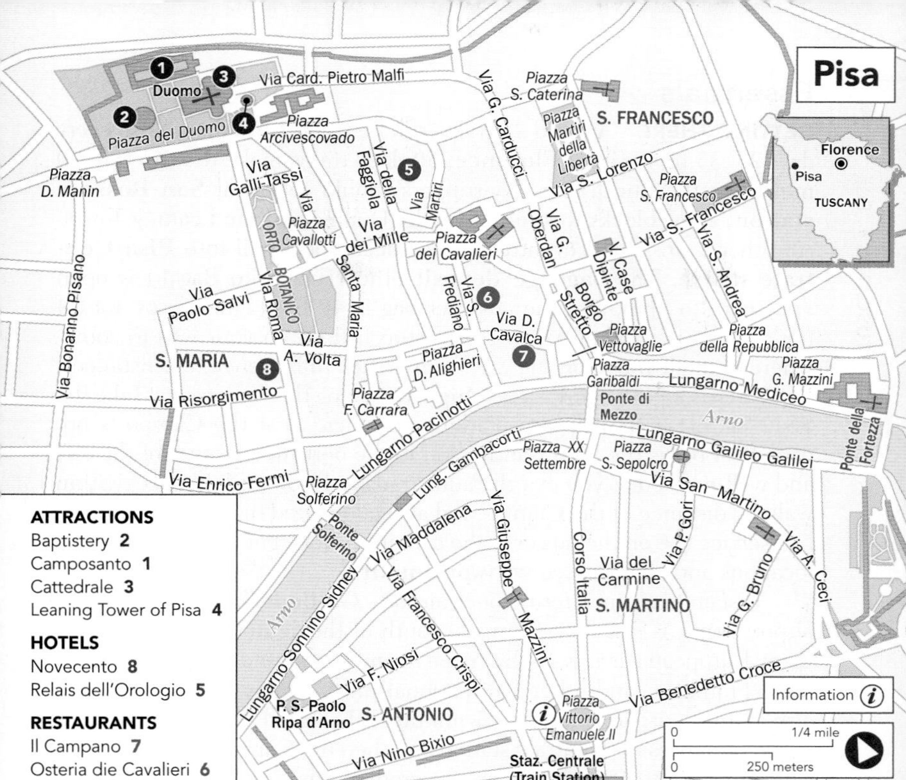

fact an engineering failure. Built on sandy soil too unstable to support so much heavy marble, Pisa's famous tower began to lean even while it was still under construction. Eight centuries later, however, the Leaning Tower puts Pisa on the map. Seeing it, maybe climbing it, and touring other landmarks on the Campo dei Miracoli (Field of Miracles) is probably why you come to this city near Tuscany's northwestern coast.

Pisa began as a seaside settlement around 1000 B.C. and was expanded into a naval trading port by the Romans in the 2nd century B.C. By the 11th century, the city had grown into one of the peninsula's most powerful maritime republics. In 1284, however, Pisa's battle fleet was destroyed by Genoa at Meloria (off Livorno), forcing Pisa's long slide into twilight. Florence took control in 1406 and, despite a few small rebellions, stayed in charge until Italian unification in the 1860s.

Today Pisa is lively and cosmopolitan, home to a university founded in 1343, one of Europe's oldest. Once away from the Campo dei Miracoli, however, there's not a whole lot to do but soak in the medieval and Renaissance ambience of this pleasant city, so you may want to join the ranks of day-trippers who visit from Florence or nearby Lucca.

Essentials

GETTING THERE Around 25 trains run between **Lucca** and Pisa every day (25–35 min.); from **Florence,** 50 daily trains make the trip (60–90 min.). On the Lucca line, day-trippers should get off at **San Rossore station,** a few blocks west of Piazza del Duomo and the Leaning Tower. All other trains—and eventually the Lucca one—pull into **Pisa Centrale** station. The **baggage deposit** office (Deposito Bagali) is open daily 6am to 9pm, and the cost per bag is 4€ for 12 hours, 6€ for 24 hours. This is handy if you want to stop in Pisa on your way to somewhere else—if you're on the way from Genoa to Florence, for instance.

There's a Florence-Pisa fast **highway** along the Arno valley. Take the SS12 or SS12r from Lucca. Parking anywhere near the Campo is not easy. Best bet is the Pietrasantina lot, in the northwest corner of the city and well-marked as you exit the autostrada at Pisa Nord; it's free, within walking distance of the Campo, and also connected by frequent shuttle-bus service (1€ on the bus or at the cafe in the lot). For details on parking locations and charges, see **www.pisamo.it**.

Tuscany's main international airport, **Galileo Galilei** (www.pisa-airport.com), is just 3km (2 miles) south of the center and is served by many European carriers, with service to and from London, Paris, Amsterdam, Frankfurt, and other international hubs. Trains zip you from the airport to Centrale station in 5 minutes; the LAM Rossa bus departs every 9 minutes for Centrale station and then the Campo. A metered taxi ride costs 10€ to 15€ (drivers accept credit cards).

GETTING AROUND **CPT** (www.cpt.pisa.it; ✆ **050/884284** or 800/012773 in Italy) runs the city's **buses.** Bus no. 4 and the LAM Rossa bus run from Pisa Central station to the Campo dei Miracoli. It's also an easy and pleasant 20-minute walk from the station to the Campo on a route that will take you through the heart of the medieval city. Head north from the station on Corso Italia toward the river, and from the other bank, Via Santa Maria into the Campo.

Taxis can be found on Piazza della Stazione and Piazza del Duomo. Call a radio taxi at ✆ **050/541600** or 055/555330.

VISITOR INFORMATION The main **tourist office** is at Piazza Vittorio Emanuele II 16 (www.pisaunicaterra.it; ✆ **050/42291;** daily 10am–1pm and 2–4pm). There's also an office near the Leaning Tower on Piazza del Duomo (✆ **050/42291;** daily 9:30am–5:30pm). Both offer a basically worthless map (with no street names) for free and sell a decent one for 3€.

Exploring Pisa

On a grassy lawn wedged into the northwest corner of the city walls, medieval Pisans created one of the most dramatic squares in the world.

Pisa's Leaning Tower.

Dubbed the **Campo dei Miracoli (Field of Miracles),** Piazza del Duomo contains an array of elegant buildings that heralded the Pisan-Romanesque style. A subtle part of its appeal, aside from the beauty of the white marble-sheathed buildings, is its spatial geometry. If you were to look at an aerial photo of the square and draw connect-the-dot lines between the doors and other focal points, you'd come up with all sorts of perfect triangles and tangential lines.

Aside from immersing yourself in this spectacle, take a little time to see the rest of the city, where much of the historic center is a well-preserved slice of the Middle Ages and Renaissance. A short walk from the Campo leads to the river along **Borgo Stretto,** a lively shopping street; just off the street is **Piazza delle Vettovaglie,** where a fish and vegetable market fills a Renaissance loggia every morning except Sunday, and **Piazza dei Cavalieri,** the seat of government when Pisa was one of the world's most powerful maritime republics. The presence of Cosimo I Medici, whose statue looks a little the worse for wear, is a reminder that Florence conquered Pisa in the early 1500s and the city never regained its might or glory. As you reach the river, pause in the middle of **Ponte di Mezzo** to look at the palazzo-lined banks; in the Middle Ages this graceful span, rebuilt many times, was lined with shops, like the Ponte Vecchio in Florence. Tidily wedged onto the south bank, downstream from the bridge, is the exquisite little **Chiesa di Santa Maria della Spina,** an extravagant Gothic masterpiece wrought by Pisa's leading Gothic sculptors, including Giovanni Pisano. From the south side of the bridge, shop-lined **Corso Italia** passes a graceful Florentine loggia and continues to the central train station.

Admission charges for the monuments and museums of the Campo are tied together in a complicated way. The cathedral is free. Any other single sight is 5€; any two sights cost 7€; and three cost 8€. Admission to the Leaning Tower is separate (see below). For more information, visit **www.opapisa.it**.

Baptistery ★★ CHURCH Italy's largest baptistery (104m/341 ft. in circumference), begun in 1153 and capped with a Gothic dome in the 1300s, is built on the same unstable soil as the Leaning Tower. The first

Camposanto Cemetery, with the chains that once protected Pisa's harbor.

thing you will notice is a decided tilt—not nearly as severe as that of the tower, but this ornate structure leans noticeably towards the cathedral. The unadorned interior is considered to be where the Renaissance, with its emphasis on classical style and humanism, began to flower, in the pulpit created by Nicola Pisano (1255–60). The sculptor had studied ancient Roman works that the Pisan navy brought back from Rome as booty, and the classic influence on his work is obvious—note the nude Roman god Hercules taking his place next to statues of St. Michael and St. John the Baptist. In scenes of the life of Christ, figures wear tunics and Mary wears the headdress of a Roman matron. If the baptistery is not too crowded, stand near the middle and say something loudly; the sound will reverberate for quite a while, thanks to the structure's renowned acoustics.

Piazza del Duomo. www.opapisa.it. ✆ **050/835011.** For prices, see above. Open daily, Apr–Sept 8am–8pm; Oct 9am–7pm; Nov–Feb 10am–5pm; Mar 9am–6pm. Bus: 4, LAM Rossa.

Camposanto ★ CEMETERY Pisa's cemetery, where the city's aristocracy was buried until the 1800s, was begun in 1278, when Crusaders began shipping back dirt from Golgotha (the mount where Christ was crucified). Giovanni di Simone (architect of the Leaning Tower) enclosed

the field in a marble cloister, and the walls were covered by magnificent 14th- and 15th-century frescoes, mostly destroyed by Allied bombings in World War II. One of the few remaining, a "Triumph of Death," inspired the 19th-century composer Franz Liszt to write his "Totentanz" ("Dance of Death"). Roman sarcophagi, used as funerary monuments, fared better (84 of these survive), as did the huge chains that medieval Pisans used to protect their harbor, which now hang on the cemetery walls.
Piazza del Duomo. www.opapisa.it. ✆ **050/835011.** For prices, see above. Same hours as the Baptistery; see above. Bus: 4, LAM Rossa.

Cattedrale ★★ CATHEDRAL Pisa's magnificent white marble cathedral will forever be associated with Galileo Galilei (1564–1642), a native son and founder of modern physics. Bored during church services, he discovered the law of perpetual motion (a pendulum's swings always take the same amount of time) by watching the swing of a bronze chandelier now known as the "Lamp of Galileo." (It's also said that Galileo dropped two wooden balls of differing sizes from the Leaning Tower; they hit the ground at the same time, thus proving that gravity exerts the same force on objects no matter what they weigh.) The exuberant cathedral, with its intricate tiers of arches and columns, is quite remarkable in its own right. Heavily influenced by Pisa's contact through trade with the Arab world, it has come to be the prime example of distinctive Pisan Romanesque architecture. Giovanni Pisano, whose father, Nicola, sculpted the pulpit in the Baptistery, created the pulpit here (1302–11), covering it with scenes from the New Testament. Now considered among the great masterpieces of Gothic sculpture, the relief panels were deemed too old-fashioned by the church's 16th-century restorers, who packed them away in crates until they were reassembled, rather clumsily, in 1926.
Piazza del Duomo. www.opapisa.it. ✆ **050/835011.** For prices, see above. Same hours as the Baptistery and Camposanto; see above. Bus: 4, LAM Rossa.

Leaning Tower of Pisa ★★★ ICON Construction began on the bell tower of Pisa Cathedral in 1173. Three stories into the job, it became apparent the structure was leaning distinctly, whereupon architects Guglielmo and Bonnano Pisano called off the work. A century later, Giovanni di Simone resumed the job, having quite literally gone back to the drawing board—he tried to compensate for the tilt by making successive layers taller on one side than the other, thus giving the tower a slight banana-like curve. Over the centuries engineers have poured concrete into the foundations and tried other solutions, all in vain. By the late 20th century the tower was in such serious danger of collapse, it was closed and braced with cables. Crews removed more than 70 tons of earth from beneath the structure, allowing it to slightly right itself as it settled. With a lean of only 4m (13 ft.), compared to a precarious 4.6m

(15 ft.) before the fix, the tower has been deemed stable for now and safe to climb once again. But before you do, take time to notice just how lovely the multicolor marble tower is, with eight arcaded stories that provide a mesmerizing sense of harmony as you look up its height.

The only way to climb the tower is to book a visit in the office on the north side of the piazza—or, for peak season, book online well in advance. Visits are limited to 30 minutes, and you must be punctual for your slot or you'll lose your chance to climb the 293 steps. Children under 8 are not permitted to climb the tower, and those 8 to 18 need to be accompanied by an adult (8 to 12s must hold an adult's hand at all times).

Piazza del Duomo. www.opapisa.it. ✆ **050/835011.** 18€. Same hours as the Baptistery, Camposanto, and Cattedrale; see above. Bus: 4, LAM Rossa.

Where to Eat & Stay

Most visitors comes to Pisa on a day trip, usually from Florence, which helps keep hotel prices down but also limits quality options. The low season for most hotels in Pisa is August. For pizza or *cecina* (a flatbread made of garbanzo-bean flour and served warm), stop in at **Il Montino,** in the historic center a block or so west of Borgo Stretto at Vicolo del Monte (✆ **050/598695**), a favorite slice stop for Pisans. At the end of Borgo Stretto, at number 11 in the riverside Piazza Garibaldi, is Pisa's best gelato shop, **Bottega del Gelato** (✆ **050/575467).**

Il Campano ★★ PISAN A meal in the simply furnished brick-and-stone rooms of an 18th-century tower house can be an evening-long event, as the kitchen makes everything to order. The *pappardelle alla lepre* (homemade pasta with hare sauce), *tagliata di scamerita di maiale* (grilled pork chops), the Florentine steaks, and everything else on the menu is well worth waiting for. It's an inviting place to spend a couple of hours or more, indulging in one or two of the bottles that line shelves.

Via Cavalca 19. www.ilcampano.com. ✆ **050/580585.** Main courses 10€–24€. Thurs 7:30–10:45pm; Fri–Tues 12:30–3pm and 7:30–10:45pm.

Osteria die Cavalieri ★ PISAN The "Restaurant of the Knights" operates out of stone rooms that date to the 12th century; the cooking is traditionally Tuscan but founded on the Slow Food principles of fresh and local. Being Pisa, this means seafood, including *tagliolini* with razor clams and a classic *baccala,* dried cod lightly battered and fried; some hearty meat choices, such as *pappardelle* with rabbit sauce, grilled steaks, and robust vegetable soups. You can get away with a one-dish meal here—in fact, it's encouraged at lunchtime, when a crowd of local office workers packs in.

Via San Frediano 16. www.osteriacavalieri.pisa.it. ✆ **050/580858.** Main courses 10€–18€. Mon–Fri 12:30–2pm and 7:45–10pm, Sat 7:45–10pm.

Novecento ★ These small and simple rooms set around a courtyard in an old villa are strictly contemporary, not an antique armoire in sight. Instead, Philippe Starck chairs and upholstered headboards are set against colored accent walls. A lush garden is filled with lounge chairs and quiet corners, and off to one side is the best room in the house, a self-contained, cottage-like unit. For guests desiring a bit more greenery, Pisa's Botanical Garden is just up the street. The Campo Santo is a 10-minute walk.

Via Roma 37. www.hotelnovecento.pisa.it. ✆ **050/500323.** 14 units. 60€–150€ double. Rates include breakfast. **Amenities:** Wi-Fi (free).

Relais dell'Orologio ★★ Maria Luisa Bignardi provided Pisa with its only truly remarkable place to stay when she converted her family mansion into refined yet relaxing guest quarters. The large garden and cozy top-floor "attic" lounge provide a relaxing refuge from the crowds in the Campo, just a 5-minute walk away. Guest rooms are filled with family heirlooms, some colorful architectural details, and lots of 21st-century conveniences, including excellent beds and marble bathrooms. Some of the rooms are quite small, though for a bit extra you can settle into a larger room or one overlooking the garden. Signora Bignardi also runs the 12-room **Relais dei Fiori,** Via Carducci 35 (www.relaisdeifiori.com; ✆ **050/556054**), where small but very attractive doubles start at 70€. At both, travelers 65 and older get a 20% discount in some periods.

Via della Faggiola Ugiccione 12–14. www.hotelrelaisorologio.com. ✆ **050/830361.** 21 units. 90€–180€ double. Rates include breakfast. **Amenities:** Restaurant; bar; Wi-Fi (free).

7

UMBRIA & THE MARCHES

By Stephen Brewer

It's easy to think of Umbria as second to Tuscany, its more-visited neighbor to the north, but that's a good thing—being slightly out of the limelight is one of the region's great assets. Perugia, Spoleto, Gubbio, and dozens of other noble hill towns are a little quieter than their Tuscan neighbors—a bit easier to enjoy, yet still filled with rival-worthy art treasures, from Giotto's famous fresco cycle in Assisi to Signorelli's horrifying view of Judgment Day in Orvieto. Even less visited are the rugged valleys of the Marches to the east, where charming towns like Urbino cling to hillsides in relative isolation. Umbrian landscapes are most memorably green, a picturesque mix of vineyards and olive groves, fertile valleys, and unspoiled forests, edged by the western Apennine mountains. All this mellow scenery befits a region often called *la terra dei santi* (land of the saints), in homage to St. Francis of Assisi and his followers, reminders of whom are everywhere.

PERUGIA ★★

164km (102 miles) SE of Florence, 176km (109 miles) N of Rome

Perugia is Umbria's capital, but it's most appealing in its guise of medieval hill town. Ancient alleys drop precipitously off **Corso Vannucci,** the cosmopolitan shopping promenade, and Gothic palaces rise above stony piazzas. The city produced and trained some of Umbria's finest artists, whose works fill the excellent art gallery. Thousands of students from Perugia's two universities impart a youthful energy, and Perugia's most famous product, chocolate, adds a sweet note to the town's appeal.

Essentials

GETTING THERE Two **rail** lines serve Perugia. The state railway connects with **Rome** (2–3 hr.; most trains require a change at Foligno) and **Florence** (2¼ hr.; most trains require a change at Terontola) every couple of hours. There are also hourly trains to **Assisi** (20–30 min.) and **Spoleto** (1 1/4 hr.). The station is a few kilometers southwest of the center at Piazza Vittorio Veneto (✆ **147/888088**) but well connected with buses to/from Piazza Italia (1€). Perugia's seven-stop, 3km (2-mile) long "minimetro" also makes the run from the station up to stops in the town

FACING PAGE: **San Martino district of Gubbio.**

Corso Vannucci, Perugia's main artery.

center (1.50€, buy tickets in machines). The station for the **Umbria Mobilità–operated regional railway** (✆ **800/512141**), Sant'Anna, is in Piazzale Bellucci (near the bus station). These tiny trains serve **Todi** every couple of hours.

SULGA lines (www.sulga.it; ✆ **075/5009641**) has one **bus** (Mon and Fri) from Florence (6pm; 2 hr.), six or seven daily from Assisi (30 min.) and Todi (40 min.), and around six a day from Rome (2½ hr.). Morning buses usually stop at the airport; the station is in Piazza Partigiani and connected to Piazza Italia by escalator. **Umbria Mobilità** (www.umbriamobilita.it; ✆ **800/512141**) buses connect Perugia with Assisi (six buses daily; 50 min.), Gubbio (six buses daily; 1 hr., 10 min.), and Todi (six buses daily; 1 hr., 15 min.).

Perugia is well connected by **road** to **Siena** (a little over an hour on the free Raccordo), Rome (about 2 hrs. via the A1 autostrada), and Assisi, Spoleto, and other Umbrian towns. While much of the *centro storico* is off-limits to nonresident drivers, well-marked parking lots are situated at the base of the hills over which old Perugia sprawls and are connected to the center via escalators. Some of the most convenient

Umbria
0 10 mi
0 10 km
Urbino
Ponte di Trajano
Pieve Santo Stefano
Urbania
Fermignano
Mercatello sul Metauro
Metauro
Caprese Michelangelo
Piobbico
Pergola
Sansepolcro
Anghiari
Apennines
Cagli
San Giustino
Arcevia
Selci Lama
Cantiano
Monterchi
Cittá di Castello
Sassoferrato
Pietralunga
Scheggia
E45
Morra
Montone
Trestine
Gubbio
Fabriano
TUSCANY
Osteria del Gatto
Umbertide
Monte Urbino
MARCHE
Cortona
Gualdo Tadino
SS71
Tiber
Terontola
Passignano sul Trasimeno
Monte Tezio
UMBRIA
SS3
Valfabbrica
Camerino
Monte Pennino
Lago Trasimeno
Magione
Corciano
Perugia
Serravalle di Chienti
Castiglione del Lago
San Feliciano
Petrignano
Topino
Nocera Umbra
Assisi
Bastia Umbra
Monte Subasio
Lago di Chiusi
Rivotorto
Torgiano
Chiascio
Panicale
SS77
Chiusi
Deruta
Cannara
Spello
Città della Pieve
Tavernelle
Piegaro
Visso
Gualdo Cattaneo
Foligno
Chiana
Bevagna
Marsciano
Montegabbiano
Montefalco
A1
Collazzone
Trevi
E45
Bastardo
Campello sul Clitunno
Fabro
San Venanzo
Ficulle
Monte Castello di Vibio
Castel Ritaldi
Norcia
Nera
Ponterio
Monte Peglia
Madonna di Lugo
Massa Martana
Paglia
Castel Viscardo
Todi
SS448
Fontanelle di Bardano
Spoleto
Cáscia
Orvieto
Lago di Corbara
Acquasparta
Castel Giorgio
Baschi
Castell dell'Aquila
Ferentillo
Guardea
Bolsena
San Gemini
Tiber
Bagnoregio
Montefranco
Leonessa
Lago di Bolsena
Lugnano in Teverina
Terni
Torreorsina
Amelia
Piediluco
SS2
Posta
Montefiascone
Lago di Piediluco
Giove
Narni
Marta
SS71
A1
Antroloco
Orte
SS3
Calvi dell'Umbria
Monti Sabini
Rieti
Viterbo
Magliano Sabina
LAZIO
Lago di Vico
Vetralla
Tiber
Civita Castellana

parking is at the underground pay lots at Piazza Partigiani, from which escalators take you up to Piazza Italia (with some amazing underground scenery along the route; see box p. 308). Rates are about 1€ an hour, though some hotels issue a card that allows you to park for 5€ a day, leaving and entering as you wish. For more about parking in Perugia, visit **www.sipaonline.it**.

Perugia's small **Aeroporto Internazionale dell'Umbria** (www.airport.umbria.it; ✆ **075/592141**), 10km (6 miles) east of the city, serves an increasing number of flights. **Ryanair** (www.ryanair.com) flights connect Perugia with London Stansted as well as Brussels. **Lufthansa** (www.lufthansa.com) flies between Perugia and Munich, a hub for ongoing international flights. Flights are usually met by a minibus outside the terminal, taking you to the Perugia train station and Piazza Italia (30–40 min.; 3.50€), but heading back there are just three buses per day, so check times in advance (just one bus Sat–Sun). Taxis to or from the airport cost around 25€.

VISITOR INFORMATION The **tourist office,** at Piazza Matteotti 18 (turismo.comune.perugia.it; ✆ **075/573-6458**), is open daily 8:30am to 6:30pm.

Exploring Perugia

Piazza Italia is like a balcony hanging over the hillside at one end of town. Among the somber, formidable banks and government buildings surrounding the expanse is the Provincia d'Umbria, the provincial offices, to your left as you face the airy, view-filled end of the square. The

Piazza IV Novembre.

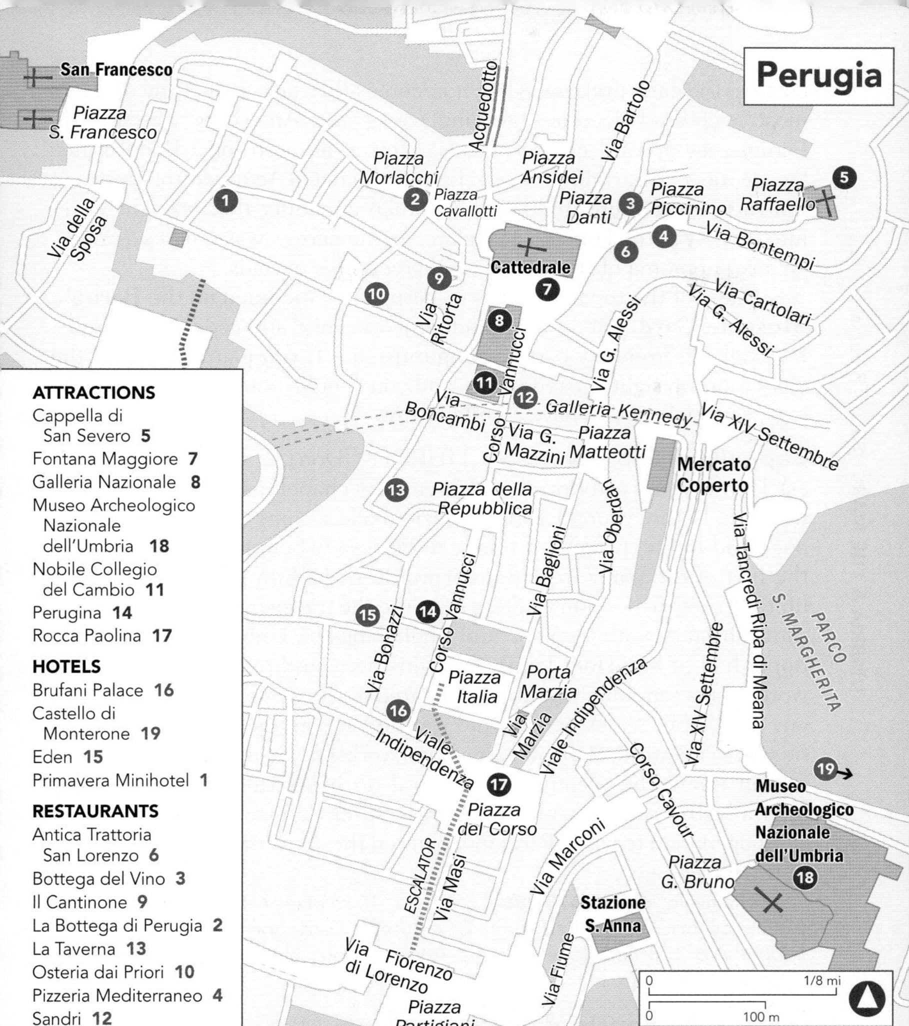

imposing porticos are more playful than they appear—a favorite game in town is to stand in a corner of one of the huge arches, place a companion in the corner diagonally across, and whisper—even the softest murmur travels as if transmitted over a phone. From Piazza Italia the sophisticated **Corso Vannucci** flows through the massive Palazzo dei Priori to **Piazza IV Novembre** and the cathedral. The square's focal point is really the elaborate **Fontana Maggiore,** with its carved panels and figures depicting saints and sinners crafted by Nicola Pisano and his son Giovanni in 1278 and 1280. It's especially entertaining to stroll up the corso in the early evening, when it becomes the stage set for one of Italy's most lively and decorous evening *passeggiate.* Anywhere you walk in Perugia, an upward glance reveals a tower, an arch, or a Renaissance facade decorated with marble figures. Via dell'Acquedotto, north of Piazza IV Novembre, follows the Roman aqueduct that brought water into the city to the Fontana Maggiore. As the narrow way crosses a ravine, an airy panorama of the old city and green hills unfolds.

Many of the top attractions in Perugia are included on the **Perugia Museum Card,** 13€ for one adult and one child and good for 48 hours. It's available from any participating museum. If you plan on visiting the city's four top sights, listed below, and you should, you'll realize a big savings, especially if you have a child in tow.

Cappella di San Severo ★ CHURCH Don't be fooled by the modest 18th-century exterior; the 14th-century chapel inside contains a real treasure. Before young Raphael Sanzio made a name for himself in Florence and Rome, he settled briefly in Perugia, where in 1504 he painted the first of the many frescoes that would make him famous in his own lifetime (not to mention vaulting him into the triumvirate of great Renaissance masters, with Da Vinci and Michelangelo). Unfortunately only the upper half of his "Holy Trinity" remains here, and that is damaged. The work seems touchingly modest compared to the complex "School of Athens" and other works he later did for the Vatican. As energetic in life as he was in his work, Raphael ran a huge workshop, had dozens of patrons, was in line to be a cardinal, and died on his 37th birthday, allegedly after a lustful session with his mistress. After Raphael's death, his then-septuagenarian teacher, Perugino, painted the six saints along the bottom of the fresco.

Piazza Raffaello. ✆ **075/573-3864.** 3€ adults, 1€ children 7–14, free for children 6 and under. Included on the Perugia City Museum Card. Apr–Oct Tues–Sun 10am–1:30pm and 2:30–6pm (open Mon in Apr and Aug); Nov–Mar Tues–Sun 11am–1:30pm and 2:30–5pm.

Galleria Nazionale dell'Umbria ★★★ MUSEUM The world's largest repository of Umbrian art covers 7 or so centuries and showcases dozens of artists. Pride of place belongs to the altarpieces by Perugino, who was born nearby in Città della Pieve and spent much of his career working in Perugia (he also studied alongside Leonardo da Vinci in Florence and executed frescoes in the Sistine Chapel in Rome). Among Perugino's works in Rooms 22–26 are delicate landscapes, sweet Madonnas, and grinning Christ childs that reveal his spare, precise style. Their divine beauty seems ironic, given that Perugino was openly anti-religion and had a fairly turbulent life—he was arrested in Florence for assault and battery and barely escaped exile; sued Michelangelo for defamation of character; and more than once was censored for reusing images and

Galleria Nazionale in the Palazzo dei Priori, Perugia.

lacking originality. He persevered, however, and worked prodigiously until his death at age 73, leaving a considerable fortune.

The museum's other showpiece is by Tuscan Piero della Francesca, who painted "Polyptych of Perugia" for the city's church of Sant'Antonio in 1470. The symmetry and realistic dimensions reflect the artist's other occupation as a mathematician; at the same time, his figures are robustly human. Della Francesca works sheer magic at the top of the piece, in a scene of the Annunciation, where an angel appears to Mary to tell her she will be the mother of the son of God. She's standing in a brightly lit cloister, and the illusion of pillars leading off into the distance is regarded as one of the greatest examples of perspective in Renaissance art.

Palazzo dei Priori, Corso Vannucci 19. ✆ **075/574-1247.** 8€ adults, free for children 17. Included on the Perugia City Museum Card. Daily 8:30am–7:30pm (closed 1st Mon of every month).

Museo Archeologico Nazionale dell'Umbria (National Archeological Museum of Umbria) ★ MUSEUM Etruscans stand out as the stars of the show among these ancient artifacts displayed in the former church, convent, and cloisters of San Domenico. Most riveting are the large tombs, brought from around the Tuscan/Umbrian region that 2,500 years ago was the heartland of an Etruscan 12-city confederation. To best appreciate the artistry of ancient masters, just wander along the porticos of the vast cloisters and enjoy the stories of everyday life that emerge in stone on the tombs that line the walls. A man with scales in hand, perhaps an architect, stands in front of a town gate; a young couple kisses; workers harvest grapes. One of the most fascinating pieces is the Sarcophagus dello Sperandio, from the tomb of a warrior. When discovered in 1843, it was surrounded by iron weapons. On one side, three men recline on a divan, enjoying a banquet as a slave serves them; in another long relief, men, women and animals (including heavily laden pack animals and collared dogs) follow one another in a procession, possibly a ceremonial parade or a migration from Chiusi to Perugia. It's believed that the sarcophagus was fashioned in Chiusi and brought to Perugia in heavy wagons along a rough, ancient track. The Cipo di

Perugia's Medieval Pompeii

Beneath Piazza Italia is some remarkable underground scenery. Around 1530 the Perugians rebelled against Pope Paul III over a tax on salt (to this day, Perugian bread is salt-free). In retribution, the Pope demolished more than a quarter of the city, building his **Rocca Paolina** atop the ruins. After Italian unification in 1860, locals ripped the castle to pieces and built Piazza Italia on top of that. Today, however, the vaults of the Pope's fort and the even older remains of medieval dwellings and streets are in full view beneath the piazza. You can clamber through doorless entrances, climb the remains of stairways, walk through empty rooms, and wander at will through the brick maze. Enter the underground city daily (free) from the escalators that connect the lower town's Piazza Partigiani, with its car park and bus station, and Piazza Italia (daily 6:15am–1:45am).

Perugia, from the 3rd century B.C., is the longest piece of Etruscan script ever discovered and is a land contract between two families, more proof that real estate is always a sound investment.

Piazza Giordano Bruno 10. ✆ **075/572-8599.** 4€ adults. Included on the Perugia City Museum Card. Daily 8:30am–7pm.

Nobile Collegio del Cambio ★★ MUSEUM The cubicles and fluorescent lighting of modern office life will seem even more banal after you visit the frescoed meeting rooms of Perugia's Moneychanger's Guild, one of the best-preserved "office suites" of the Renaissance. Perugino was hired in 1496 to fresco the Sala dell' Udienza (Hearing Room), perhaps with the help of his young student Raphael. The images merge religion (scenes of the Nativity and Transfiguration) with classical references (female representations of the virtues) and, most riveting of all, glimpses of 15th-century secular life.

Palazzo dei Priori, Corso Vannucci 25. www.collegiodelcambio.it. ✆ **075/572-8599.** 4.50€ adults, free for children 12 and under. Included on the Perugia City Museum Card. Mar–Oct Mon–Sat 9am–12:30pm and 2:30–5:30pm, Sun 9am–1pm; Nov–Feb Tues–Sat 8am–2pm, Sun 9am–12:30pm.

Where to Stay

Most Perugia hotels are flexible about rates, which often dive 40% to 50% below posted prices in the off season.

Brufani Palace ★★ Perugia's bastion of luxury commands one side of Piazza Italia, looming proudly over the valley below. Built in 1883 to host English travelers on the Grand Tour, the premises have not changed too much in the intervening years, except that the large, traditionally furnished rooms are now equipped with lavish marble bathrooms and lots of other amenities, including comfortable lounge chairs and sofas. Despite the grand surroundings, the real pleasures here are in the details:

fires burn in big stone hearths in the dining room and lounges; a swimming pool has been carved out of subterranean brick vaults, with see-through panels exposing Etruscan ruins beneath; and a large rooftop terrace is a perfect spot for a glass of wine at sunset.

Piazza Italia 12. www.brufanipalace.com. ✆ **075/573-2541.** 94 units. From 150€ double. Rates include breakfast. **Amenities:** Restaurant/bar; babysitting; concierge; small exercise room; indoor pool; room service; Wi-Fi (free).

Castello di Monterone ★★★ It's surprising just how inviting a medieval castle can be. That's partly because in the 19th century the Piceller family of musicians, artists, and archeologists made this 13th-century stronghold their home, creating lounges surrounding massive fireplaces and a beautiful cloister garden dotted with ancient artifacts. These days the many nooks and crannies have been converted to utterly charming guest rooms embellished with wide beams, stone walls, and handcrafted iron and wood furniture, and equipped with large marble bathrooms. Adding to the ambience is a library tucked away on a landing, a cozy lounge bar in the old hall, a swimming pool surrounded by lawns, and a roof terrace on the old battlements. Though the castle is nestled on a rural hillside, the center of Perugia is only 10 minutes away on a road used by the Etruscans and Romans.

Strada Monteville 3. www.castellomonterone.it. ✆ **075/572-4214.** 14 units. 135€–239€. Rates include breakfast. **Amenities:** Restaurant; bar; pool; Wi-Fi (free).

Eden ★ This comfortable little lair occupies the top floor of a 13th-century building in the city center (an elevator takes you up). The airy accommodations seem a world removed from the medieval city below. Furnishings are contemporary, with colorful accent walls and modern art; the compact bathrooms are up to date; and a pleasant breakfast room doubles as a sleek lounge. Outside the tall windows is an enticing jumble of rooftops, towers, and narrow stone lanes. The friendly management supplies an insightful self-guided city itinerary of their own design.

Via Cesare Caporali 9. ✆ **075/572-8102.** 12 units. 55€–95€ double. Rates include breakfast. **Amenities:** Wi-Fi (free).

Primavera Minihotel ★★ It's well worth the climb up the three flights of stairs to this aerie-like retreat, just down some twisty streets from Piazza della Repubblica. The high locale means that all the tall windows frame views of rooftops and the green valleys below. Rooms surround a welcoming lounge/breakfast room (breakfast costs extra), except for the best room in the house—a large rooftop double with a terrace. Some are furnished with Art Nouveau pieces, others with traditionally rustic furnishing and Deruta pottery, and all have hardwood floors and lots of timber, stone, and other architectural details.

Via Vincioli 8. www.primaveraminihotel.it. ✆ **075/572-1657.** 8 units. 65€–90€ double. **Amenities:** Wi-Fi (free).

Where to Eat

Perugia's youthful student population seems to subsist on pizza and *panini* (sandwiches), good news for the rest of us looking for a snack or light meal. Most popular among plenty of cheap *pizzerie* is **Mediterraneo,** at Piazza Puccini 11 (www.mediterraneopastaepizza.it; ✆ **075/572-4021**). Pizzas cost 6€ to 8€, and this friendly spot is open daily (Mon–Friday noon–2:30pm and 7pm–11pm; weekends 7–11pm). Top choice for a *panino* is **La Bottega di Perugia,** Piazza Francesco Morlacchi 4 (✆ **075/573–2963**), a friendly hangout whose young proprietors pride themselves on using only local Umbrian hams, greens, and other ingredients; *panini* cost about 4€ and can be washed down with wine or beer (Mon–Sat 10:30am–12:30am). Far more formal is the venerable **Sandri,** Perugia's oldest (opened in 1860) and most esteemed *pasticerria,* a suitably elegant and old-fashioned shop serving coffee, pastry, and light meals at Corso Vannucci 32 (✆ **075/572-4112;** Sun–Thurs 7:30am–9pm; Fri 7:30–11pm; Sat 7:30am–midnight).

Antica Trattoria San Lorenzo ★★ MODERN ITALIAN Everything here is local, right down to the Perugia-made pottery that sits on the candlelit tables. Chef/owner Simone Ciccotti sources his ingredients from producers in the nearby countryside. While his efforts are creative, they emphasize basic flavor in such creations as a "muffin" of caramelized onions and foie gras and a *millefeuille* of grilled vegetables with smoked mozzarella. The restaurant's namesake is not just a patron saint of Perugia but also the patron saint of chefs.

Piazza Danti 19a. www.anticatrattoriasanlorenzo.com. ✆ **075/527-1956.** Main courses 10€–18€. Daily 12:30–2pm and 7:30–10pm.

Bottega del Vino ★ UMBRIAN A snug, vintage-photo-lined room right off Piazza IV Novembre serves wines by the glass along with a nice assortment of Umbrian hams and cheeses—perfect for an evening *aperitivo* as all of Perugia promenades by the tables out front. The small lunch and dinner menus include salads and a couple of pastas, as well as a dish or two of the day, a steak, say, or roasted leg of lamb. Live jazz often plays into the wee hours, making this a popular after-dinner spot.

Via del Sole 1. ✆ **075/571-6181.** Main courses 13€. Tues–Sun noon–3pm and 7pm–midnight. Closed Jan.

Il Cantinone ★★ UMBRIAN/PIZZA Even a pizza seems like a meal fit for a medieval courtier in this softly lit, stone-walled, and brick-vaulted 14th-century cantina in a hidden courtyard around the corner from Piazza Maggiore. The excellent Umbrian fare befits the distinctively Old Perugia surroundings, with such hearty choices as homemade tagliatelle with duck ragù or wild boar sauce and locally sourced beef from the Val

The City of *Cioccolato* and Jazz

Perugia is a chocoholic's paradise. **Perugina,** Corso Vannucci 101 (✆ **075/573-4760**) has been making candy here since 1907 and now pumps out 120 tons of the sweet stuff a day, including 1½ million Baci (kisses), its gianduja-and-hazelnut bestseller. Perugia hosts a weeklong **Eurochocolate Festival** (www.eurochocolate.com) every year from mid- to late October. The highlight: a chocolate-carving contest, when the scraps of 1,000kg (455-lb.) blocks are handed out for sampling. **Umbria Jazz** (www.umbriajazz.com), one of Europe's top jazz festivals, draws top international names to town for 2 weeks in mid-July.

di Chiana topped with black truffles. And yes, they do serve pizzas, making this the most elegant pizzeria in town.

Via Ritorta. ristoranteilcantinoneperugia.com. ✆ **075/573-4430.** Main courses 8€–15€. Wed–Mon 12:30–2:30pm and 7:30–10:30pm.

La Taverna ★★ UMBRIAN For many Perugians, a tiny courtyard down a flight of steps from Corso Vannucci is the epicenter of good dining. In warm weather, tables fill the court; inside, barrel-vaulted ceilings shimmer with candlelight in evening, and the service and the cooking are similarly warm and down-to-earth. Everything, from bread to pasta to desserts, is made in-house and typically Umbrian: Pappardelle is sauced with a hearty ragù, *caramelle rosse al gorgonzola* (beet ravioli with gorgonzola) is made with local beets, and meats are seasoned with fresh herbs from the surroundings hillsides. Chef Claudio will make his way to your table at some point to ensure that everything is *tutto bene*.

Via delle Streghe 8 (near Corso Vannucci's Piazza Repubblica). ✆ **075/572-4128.** Main courses 9€–16€. Tues–Sun 12:30–2:30pm and 7:30–11pm.

Osteria dai Priori ★★★ UMBRIAN You'll pass through a wine shop and climb a flight of stairs to reach this welcoming brick-vaulted room with contemporary wood furnishings, where the emphasis is on age-old Umbrian recipes. A portion of slowly cooked beans *(fagiolina)* is paired with eggs and onions and bread salad; *gnoccconi* (large potato dumplings) are stuffed with fresh ricotta; slow-roasted pork shank *(stinco di mialale)* is served with crisp potatoes. The staff will eagerly walk you through the ever-changing menu and pair wines with each course.

Via dei Priori 39. www.osteriaapriori.it. ✆ **075/572-7098.** Main courses 9€–12€. Wed–Mon noon–3pm and 7:30–10:30pm.

Shopping

An easy excursion from Perugia is **Deruta,** a little hilltown 20km (12 miles) south via SS3bis, where residents have been making ceramics since the early Middle Ages. Some 300 studios make and sell ceramics all over town. The tourist office in Perugia can give you a list of shops.

GUBBIO ★★

39 km (24 miles) northeast of Perugia

Hands-down the most medieval-looking town in Umbria presents a crenelated skyline backed by forest-covered mountains. At this old town's stony heart is Piazza Grande, where the harsh expanse is softened from the south side by views of misty hills and the wide valley beneath them. When it comes to St. Francis lore, the proud and beautiful town is overshadowed by Assisi. Yet it was at Gubbio that the saint performed one of his most popular miracles, taming a wolf that was terrorizing the town (see Taverna del Lupo, below). In fact, here in Gubbio, the saint cast off his finery and put on the rough monk's habit, forsaking his worldly goods. Gubbio is also associated with another holy presence, Don Matteo, the priest detective of a wildly popular Italian TV series that was filmed in the town. The setting has since moved to Spoleto (see p. 327), but don't mention this to anyone in Gubbio, lest someone drops one of the geranium-filled pots adorning the stone balconies on your head. Also no longer here is the Gubbio Studiolo, a glorious room decorated with wood inlay that Duke Frederico da Montefeltro commissioned for his Ducal Palace in 1472. It's now in the Metropolitan Museum of Art in New York, and considered to be the finest Renaissance work in America.

GETTING THERE By **car,** the SS298 branches north from Perugia, off the E45, through rugged scenery. Faster but less scenic is the new four-lane SS318, connecting Perugia and Gubbio in about half an hour—making it all the easier to include this rewarding stop on an Umbrian itinerary. Gubbio is not served directly by **train,** though Fossato di Vico, 18km (11 miles) south, is on the Rome–Ancona line and served by trains that run about every 2 hours. Buses run from the station to Gubbio about every hour. Eight or nine daily **Umbria Mobilità buses** (www.umbria mobilita.it; ✆ **800/512141**) run between Gubbio and **Perugia;** they arrive at Piazza 40 Martiri (70 min.), named for citizens killed by the Nazis for aiding partisans during World War II.

VISITOR INFORMATION The **tourist office**, Via della Repubblica 15 (www.comune.gubbio.pg.it; ✆ **075/922-0693** or 075/922-0790), is open Monday to Friday 8:30am to 1:45pm and 3:30 to 6:30pm, Saturday 9am to 1pm and 3:30 to 6:30pm, and Sunday 9:30am to 1pm and 3 to 6pm; October through March, afternoon hours are 3 to 6pm. Staff hand out maps and, for 1€, sell a brief but handy walking guide to the town.

SPECIAL EVENTS Aside from engaging in the energetic springtime Corso dei Ceri (see Monte Igino, below), Gubbio lights up the **world's largest Christmas tree** on the slopes in December. Lights are laid out to form a shape 2,130 feet high and 1,100 feet wide at the base. The pope often does the honor of the tree-lighting ceremony, using a

Festa dei Ceri in the Palazzo dei Consoli in Gubbio.

computer in the Vatican palace. The town seems especially medieval the last weekend in May, when Eugubian *balestrieri,* or crossbow competitors, line up in Piazza Grande and face off with competitors from Sansepolcro, Tuscany.

Exploring Gubbio

To avoid the climb up to Piazza Grande, take the free elevator at the junction of Via Repubblica and Via Baldassini (daily 7:45am–7pm). As you stand in the piazza and take in the airy view over the valley below, turn around to admire the rambling, handsome Palazzo Ranghiasci behind you, on the north side. That the facade resembles an 18th-century neoclassical British country house is no accident. A nobleman of the time married an English lady and brought her back to Gubbio, where she languished in homesickness before fleeing. To lure his wife back, the heartbroken duke commissioned an architect to rebuild the front of his palace in the latest British fashion, but to no avail—his bride never returned. Note that one of the Greek-style columns has been clumsily replaced with bricks—that's a patch made after the Allies lobbed a shell into the piazza to dislodge the Nazi occupiers at the end of World War II. Approach the Fountain of the Madmen in Largo Bargello, a short walk west of the piazza along Via Consoli, with care; it's said that if you circle the monument three times you are sure to go mad.

Gubbio's sturdy **Duomo** and fortresslike **Palazzo Ducale** stand at the top of the town, where church and state could keep an eye on the citizens below. Life might not have been as grim as the expanses of heavy stone suggest—as you approach the ducal palace on Via Federico da Montefeltro, through a gate you'll see the **Botte dei Canonici** (Canon's Barrel), a humongous vessel capable of holding more than 5,000 gallons of wine. Monks in the monastery above, or so the story goes, could serve themselves by dipping a ladle through a trapdoor in the ceiling.

Museo del Palazzo dei Consoli ★★ MUSEUM The former home of the town government is a solidly Gothic-looking palace, with crenellations, a tower, and an imposing stone staircase that seems to demand you climb up from Piazza Grande. The main hall, where the medieval commune met, houses the sleep-inducing town museum, where one prize stands out amid the old coins and bits of pottery: the seven **Eugubine Tables**, inscribed on bronze from 200 to 70 B.C., which provide the only existing record of the Umbri language transposed in Etruscan and Latin letters—in other words, ancient Umbria's Rosetta Stone. A local farmer turned up the tablets while plowing his fields in 1444, and city officials convinced him to sell them for 2 years' worth of grazing rights. Be sure to find the secret corridor that leads from the back of the ceramics room to the Pinacoteca upstairs, via the medieval toilets.

Piazza Grande. ✆ **075/927-4298.** 5€ adults, 2.50€ children 7–25, free for children 7 and under and seniors. Apr–May daily 10am–1pm and 3–6pm; June Mon–Fri 10am–1pm and 3–6pm, weekends 10am–1:30pm and 2:30–6pm; July–Aug daily 10am–1:30pm and 2:30–6pm; Oct–Mar daily 10am–1pm and 2–5:30pm.

Monte Igino ★ PARK/GARDEN An open-air funicular whisks you to the top of this 908m (2,980-ft.) summit in about 5 minutes for yet more stupendous Umbrian views. On the ascent you can be glad you are not taking part in the May 15 **Corso dei Ceri,** when teams race up the mountainside carrying 15-foot-long wooden battering-ram-like objects called *ceri,* or "candles." The race is part of festivities honoring St. Ubaldo, the bishop who allegedly smooth-talked Frederick Barbarossa out of sacking the town in the 1150s and was sainted for his efforts. The saint's corpse is up here, too, languishing in a glass casket at the Basilica di Sant'Ubaldo, a 5-minute walk from the top station of the **Funivia Colle Eletto** (www.funiviagubbio.it; ✆ **075-927-3881**).

Funicular: Daily June 9:30am–1:15pm and 2:30–7pm; July and Aug 9am–8pm; early Sept 9:30am–7pm; late Sept 9:30am–1:15pm and 2:30–7pm; Oct 10am–1:15pm and 2:30–6pm; Nov–Feb 10am–1:15pm and 2:30–5pm; Mar 10am–1:15pm and 2:30–6pm; Apr–May 10am–1:15pm and 2:30–6:30pm. Round-trip tickets 5€ adults, 4€ children 4–13.

WHERE TO STAY & EAT

Grotta dell'Angelo ★ ITALIAN/UMBRIAN A barrel-vaulted dining room where locals have been gathering for the past 700 years or so is the place to sit in winter, while warm-weather dining is on a vine-shaded terrace. Wherever you eat, enjoy homemade gnocchi and other pastas, followed by sausages and other meats roasted over the open fire—the whole roast chicken stuffed with fennel is especially delicious.

Via Gioia 47. www.grottadellangelo.it. ✆ **075/927-3438.** Main courses 9€–14€. Wed–Mon 12:30–2:30pm and 7:30–11pm. Closed Jan 7–Feb 7.

Hotel Relais Ducale ★★★ Annexes of the palace of the dukes of Montefalco are as transporting as the Piazza Grande out front. Extremely comfortable guest rooms are scattered over several levels, with highly polished floors and well-tended traditional furnishings that befit the royal surroundings. Some have barrel vaulting and a few open to terraces, though are all within easy reach of delightful patios and shady nooks. Proprietors Daniela and Sean are on hand with a lot of personal attention and services that include a pickup at the train station in Fossato di Vico.

Via Galeotti 19. www.relaisducale.com. ✆ **075/922-0157.** 30 units. 80€–140€. Rates include breakfast. **Amenities:** Bar; room service; Wi-Fi (free).

Taverna del Lupo ★★ ITALIAN/UMBRIAN Around 1220, or so the story goes, a ferocious wolf *(lupo)* was menacing the good people of Gubbio, devouring them the moment they stepped outside the town gates. St. Francis, then living a monklike life of contemplation in Gubbio, went to the lair of the beast, tamed him, and led him back into the marketplace, where townsfolk promised to feed him in return for good behavior. A charming fresco depicting Francis and his tamed wolf is one of the many artworks on the stone walls of these former cellars, where, as the story goes, the animal would pop in for a meal. These days diners count on the refined surroundings for homemade tagliatelle with truffles and other local specialties, as well as the kitchen's famous *faraona al ginepro,* guinea hen roasted with juniper berries.

Via Ansidei 21. www.tavernadellupo.it. ✆ **075/927-4368.** Main courses 10€–18€. Daily noon–3pm and 7–10pm. Closed Jan 7–Feb 7.

A Side Trip to Urbino ★

One of the steepest hill towns in Italy is a time-capsule Renaissance city, a storybook compilation of towers, domes, and red-tile roofs. Though the glory days of this remote town wound down about 500 years ago, it's still prosperous and lively, and you'll be sharing the streets and squares with students at Urbino's famous university. The only easy way to get here easily from Gubbio is by car, 66km (40 miles) northeast through mountainous terrain on the SP3. The trip takes a slow hour, but the landscape puts on quite a show, its rippling hills carpeted with fields and forests and

GO jump IN THE LAKE

Lago Trasimeno, Italy's fourth-largest lake, washes up against the Tuscany–Umbria border between Cortona and Perugia. The shallow waters aren't quite a match for the beauty of Como and the other lakes up north, but Trasimeno is nonetheless a refreshing splash of blue amid olive groves and sunflower fields. It was also the site of a big moment in history: In 271 B.C., Hannibal, having breached the Alps, lured 16,000 Roman soldiers into an ambush on the northern shore and massacred them.

A well-equipped spot from which to enjoy the lake is **Castiglione del Lago,** 50km (30 miles) west of Perugia, where you can swim from a pebbly beach or do a bit of biking on shoreline paths; you can rent bikes for 8€ half a day, 10€ a day at **Cicli Valentini,** Via Firenze 68/B (ciclivalentini.it; ✆ **333/9678327;** open Sat–Sun 9am–1pm and 3:30–8pm). Hourly ferry trips of about half an hour cross the lake to picturesque **Isola Maggiore,** an especially nice place to take a dip in the cool waters, or to buy lace from the few local women who carry on the longstanding tradition. Stepping ashore on Isola Maggiore, you'll be following in the footsteps of St. Francis, who spent Lent of 1213 here. Allegedly, the saint even charmed the local fish—when Francis threw a pike given to him by a fisherman back into the lake, the creature swam alongside his savior until the saint gave him a special blessing.

topped with the occasional walled village. Stash your car in the large parking lot at Borgo del Mercatale (1.20€ per hr.), and then attack the steep cobblestone streets on foot.

Urbino's main draws are definitively art-related: It's the home of Raphael, the Renaissance painter of glorious frescos, and the outstanding art collection of Duke Frederico da Montefeltro in his magnificent palace.

Galleria Nazionale delle Marche Palazzo Ducale di Urbino ★★ MUSEUM Wise and worldly Duke Federico da Montefeltro (1422–82) paced the halls of this palace and contemplated his vast holdings from the study window, all the while dreaming up some of the most enlightened ideals of the Renaissance. One of the palace's most enchanting rooms is that study, beautifully paneled with intarsia depicting classical and humanistic writers as well as great religious thinkers. The duke famously came up with the concept of *sprezzatura*, the ideal of maintaining grace under pressure. Duke Federico and his son, Guidobaldo, oversaw a court that was so enlightened that Baldassare Castiglione set his 1507 bestseller, *Book of the Courtier*, in the palace's Hall of Vigils. Father and son were also patrons of some of the great artists of their day, whose works are among those hanging in the salons and staterooms. In keeping with the duke's enlightened notions is "Ideal City," attributed to Piero della Francesca. The artist's "Flagellation" is still among the palace's treasures and one of the Renaissance's finest accomplishments in perspective. Less lofty, subject-wise, is Paolo Uccello's similarly masterful work of perspective, "The Profanation of the Host," a piece of 15th-century anti-Semitic propaganda depicting a popular tale in which a pawnbroker attempts to cook the sacred communion wafer (believed to be transformed into the body of Christ during the Eucharist), as blood seeps under his door and attracts bailiffs.

Piazza Duca Federico. www.galleriaborghese.it ✆ **0722/2760.** 7.50€. Mon 8:30am–2pm; Tues–Sun 8:30am–7:15pm.

Raphael's Birthplace ★ MUSEUM One of the great artists of the High Renaissance (you can see his work at Cappella di San Severo in Perugia, p. 306, and his best efforts at the Vatican, p. 78) was born here in 1483. You can see his earliest known work, a modest boyhood fresco, "Madonna and Child," on one of the walls. Compare it to his "Portrait of a Young Woman," in the nearby Palazzo Ducale, which shows the genius of his mature style. The museum also holds works by Raphael's lesser-known father, Giovanni Santi, a court painter to the duke.

Via Rafaello 57. 3€. Mar–Oct Mon–Sat 9am–1pm and 3–7pm, Sun 10am–1pm; Nov–Feb Mon–Sat 9am–2pm, Sun 10am–1pm.

WHERE TO EAT

Taverna degli Artisti ★ ITALIAN These vaulted underground rooms, one with colorful frescoes, are the place to try *Strozzapretti con salmone, asparagi, funghi,* thick elongated pasta (the name means "priest choker") with a creamy sauce of salmon, asparagus, and mushrooms. It's an Urbino favorite that even locals claim is expertly done here. The other pastas and pizzas are excellent, too.

Via Bramante 52. ✆ **0722/2676.** Main courses 10€–15€. Daily 12:30–2:30pm and 7:30–10pm.

The World's Favorite Saint

For Christian pilgrims, the magic of Assisi is all about St. Francis, one of the patron saints of Italy (along with Catherine of Siena). Founder of one of the world's largest monastic orders, he is generally considered to be just about the holiest person to walk the earth since Jesus.

Born to a wealthy merchant, Francis was a spoiled young man of his time, until he did an about-turn in his early 20s and dedicated himself to a life of poverty. His humility, love of animals, and invention of the Christmastime crèche scenes have all helped ensure his legend. Francis traveled as far as Egypt (in an unsuccessful attempt to convert the sultan and put an end to the Crusades), but he is most associated with the gentle countryside around Assisi, where he spent months praying and fasting in lonely hermitages.

The Basilica di San Francesco, resting place of St. Francis of Assisi.

ASSISI ★★★

27km (17 miles) E of Perugia

St. Francis is still working miracles: His birthplace remains a lovely Umbrian hilltown, despite a steady onslaught of visitors. Many pilgrims come to pay homage to Francis at the Basilica di San Francisco, and almost as many are drawn by Giotto's frescoes celebrating the life of the saint. You'll find a blend of romance and magic in Assisi's honey-colored stone, the quiet lanes, and the mists that rise and fall over the Val di Spoleto below town. With its saintly presence and pleasing ambience, Assisi an essential stop on any Umbrian tour.

Essentials

GETTING THERE About 20 trains run daily from **Perugia** (25–30 min.). From **Florence** (2–3 hr.), trains run every 2 hours or so, though some require a transfer at Terontola. Trains arrive in the modern valley town of Santa Maria degli Angeli, about 5km (3 miles) from Assisi, with bus connections to Assisi every 20 minutes (1€), or **taxis** are available for about 15€ to 20€.

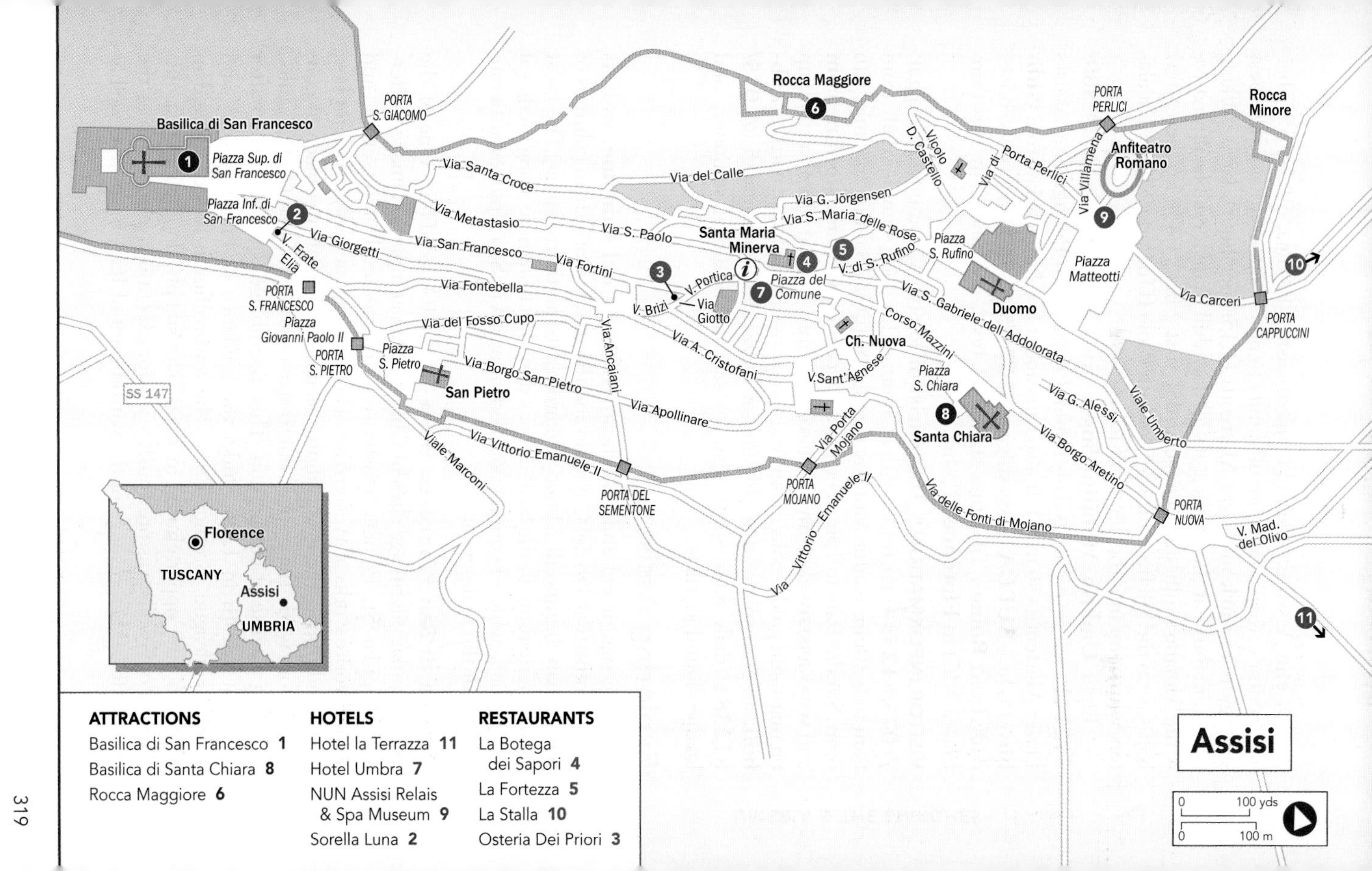

Basilica di San Francesco
Piazza Sup. di San Francesco
Piazza Inf. di San Francesco
PORTA S. GIACOMO
Rocca Maggiore
PORTA PERLICI
Rocca Minore
Anfiteatro Romano
Via Santa Croce
Via del Calle
Vicolo D. Castello
Via di Porta Perlici
Via Villamena
Via Metastasio
Via S. Paolo
Via G. Jörgensen
Via S. Maria delle Rose
Piazza S. Rufino
Via Giorgetti
Via San Francesco
Santa Maria Minerva
V. di S. Rufino
Piazza Matteotti
V. Frate Elia
Via Fortini
V. Portica
Piazza del Comune
Duomo
Via Carceri
PORTA S. FRANCESCO
Via Fontebella
V. Brizi
Via Giotto
Via S. Gabriele dell'Addolorata
PORTA CAPPUCCINI
Piazza Giovanni Paolo II
Via del Fosso Cupo
Corso Mazzini
Ch. Nuova
PORTA S. PIETRO
Piazza S. Pietro
Via Borgo San Pietro
Via Ancaiani
Via A. Cristofani
V.Sant'Agnese
Piazza S. Chiara
SS 147
San Pietro
Via Apollinare
Via G. Alessi
Viale Umberto
Santa Chiara
Via Porta Mojano
Via Vittorio Emanuele II
Viale Marconi
Via Borgo Aretino
PORTA DEL SEMENTONE
PORTA MOJANO
Via Vittorio Emanuele II
Via delle Fonti di Mojano
PORTA NUOVA
V. Mad. del Olivo
Florence
TUSCANY
Assisi
UMBRIA
ATTRACTIONS
Basilica di San Francesco 1
Basilica di Santa Chiara 8
Rocca Maggiore 6
HOTELS
Hotel la Terrazza 11
Hotel Umbra 7
NUN Assisi Relais & Spa Museum 9
Sorella Luna 2
RESTAURANTS
La Botega dei Sapori 4
La Fortezza 5
La Stalla 10
Osteria Dei Priori 3
Assisi
0
100 yds
0
100 m

By **car,** Assisi is 18km (11 miles) east of Perugia, off the SS75bis. The center's steep streets are off-limits to non-resident drivers. The best strategy is to **park** in Piazza Matteotti (1.15€ per hour), keep walking west, and finish at the basilica; it's all downhill. A dependable alternative is the Mojano multi-story garage (1.05€ first 2 hrs.; 1.45€/hr. thereafter) halfway up the hill from Piazza Giovanni Paolo II to Porta Nuova. Escalators whisk you into the center of town.

Eight **Umbria Mobilità buses** (www.umbriamobilita.it; ✆ **800/512141**) run seven times daily (Mon–Fri) between **Perugia** and Assisi's Piazza Matteotti (50 min.). It also runs about five buses a day from **Gubbio** (1¾ hr.). **SULGA** (www.sulga.it; ✆ **075/500-9641**) runs two buses daily from **Rome**'s Tiburtina station (3 hrs.), and one daily trip from Piazza Adua in **Florence** (2½ hrs.).

VISITOR INFORMATION The **tourist office** (www.comune.assisi.pg.it; ✆ **075/812534**) is on Piazza del Comune. It's open summer daily from 8am to 6:30pm; winter Monday through Saturday 8am to 2pm and 3 to 6pm; Sunday 9am to 1pm. The private websites **www.assisionline.com** and **www.assisiweb.com** also have good info. A good place to stock up on maps and guidebooks about Assisi and anywhere else on earth is **Zubboli,** an atmosphere-rich old shop at Piazza del Commune 5 (✆ **075/812381**; daily 8am–8pm); also for sale are beautiful stationery and leather-bound journals.

Exploring Assisi

Assisi's geographical and civic heart is **Piazza del Comune,** with its 13th-century Palazzo del Capitano and the stately Corinthian columns of the Roman Tempio di Minerva guarding its northern fringe. The most atmospheric route to the basilica goes downhill from here along medieval Via Portica, which becomes Via Fortini and Via San Francesco before arriving at the main event.

Basilica di San Francesco ★★★ RELIGIOUS SITE One of the most popular pilgrimage sites in Christendom combines homage to eternally popular St. Francis, masterworks of medieval architecture, and some favorite works of Western art. The basilica is actually two churches, lower and upper; the lower church is dark and somber, a place of contemplation, while the upper church soars into light-filled Gothic vaults, instilling a sense of celebration. This assemblage was begun soon after the saint's death in 1226, under the guidance of Francis's savvy and worldly colleague, Brother Elias. The lower church was completed in 1230, and the upper church in 1280. The steeply sloping site just outside the city walls was previously used for executions and known as the Hill of Hell. The presence of the patron saint of Italy, in spirit as well as in body, now makes this one of Italy's most uplifting sights. His kindness, summed up in his saying, "For it is in giving that we receive," seems to permeate the soft gray stones, and the frescoed spaces move the devout to tears and art lovers to fits of near-religious ecstasy.

The Lower Church Entered off Piazza Inferiore di San Francesco (the lower of the two squares abutting the church), the basilica's bottom half is a cryptlike church that is indeed, first and foremost, a crypt, housing the stone **sarcophagus of St. Francis,** surrounded by four of his disciples. An almost steady stream of the faithful files past the monument, many on their knees. Inside is the saint's remarkably intact skeleton. Most saints of the Middle Ages fell victim to the purveyors of relics, who made enormous profit dispensing bones, a finger here, a toe there. It's said that Brother Elias had the foresight to seal the coffin in stone, and it remained undetected until 1818. The dimly lit atmosphere is greatly enlivened by the presence of many rich frescoes, including Simone Martini's action-packed "Life of St. Martin" in the **Cappella di San Martino** (1322–1326). Martini displays his flair for boldly patterned fabrics and familiarity with detailed manuscript illumination. Martini was also, like St. Martin, a knight, which may have influenced his depictions of the saint—who was a Roman soldier—being investitured, ripping his cloak to share it with a beggar, and renouncing chivalry and weaponry in favor of doing good deeds. The imagery is not out of keeping with Francis, who as a youth dreamed of being a soldier.

Giotto and his assistants frescoed the **Cappella della Santa Maria Maddalena** with the "Life of St. Mary Magdalene" (1303–1309). An incredibly moving cycle of "Christ's Passion" (1316–1319) by Pietro Lorenzetti includes a hauntingly humane "Deposition," in which the young Sienese artist depicts a gaunt Christ and sorrowful Mary, displaying a naturalism and emotion not before seen in painting.

The Upper Church Entering the light-filled interior of the Upper Church, you'll first encounter **scenes of the New Testament** by Cimabue, the last great painter of the Byzantine style; some critics say only the faded and vaguely surreal "Crucifixion" (1277) is his, and the rest are by his assistants. In any case, it's rather ironic he's here at all. The artist was infamous for his stubbornness and difficult character (in the *Divine Comedy*, Dante places him in Purgatory among the proud, adding that "Cimabue thought to hold the field of painting, and now Giotto hath the cry.") It's Giotto who famously holds court in this church, with his 28-part fresco cycle on **"The Life of St. Francis,"** completed in the 1290s. Even nonreligious viewers love the scenes of the saint removing his clothing to renounce material processions, marrying poverty (symbolized by a woman in rags), and preaching to the birds (the subject of ubiquitous postcards for sale). Assisi itself is the star in the panel in which a humble man spreads his cloak before Francis, with the sturdy, easily recognizable palaces of Piazza del Comune as a backdrop.

Piazza Superiore di San Francesco. www.sanfrancescoassisi.org. ✆ **075/819001.** Free. Lower Church daily 6am–7pm; Upper Church daily 8:30am–7pm (churches close 10 min. earlier from Mar–Oct).

Basilica di Santa Chiara ★ CHURCH One of the first followers of St. Francis was a young woman, Chiara (Clare, in English), daughter of a count and countess, who was so swept away by the teachings of the zealot that she allowed him to cut her hair and dress her in sackcloth. She founded the order of the Poor Dames (now known as Poor Clares), whose members continue to renounce material possessions, and her remains lie in this vast, stark church on full view, her face covered in wax. Also in this church, the **Oratorio del Crocifisso** houses the venerated 12th-century crucifix from which the figure of Christ allegedly spoke to St. Francis and asked him to rebuild his church (the institution had by then become mired in corruption and warfare). As Clare lay ill on Christmas Eve 1252, she allegedly voiced regrets that she would not be able to attend services in the new Basilica di San Francisco. Suddenly, in a vision, she saw and heard the Mass clear as a bell and in color, a miracle for which in 1958 she was named the patron saint of television.

Piazza Santa Chiara. ✆ **075/812282.** Free. Daily 6:30am–noon and 2–7pm (6pm in winter).

Rocca Maggiore ★★ CASTLE This civic show of might is built of bleached yellow stone atop a steep hillside very high above the city. Some claim that a sharp-eyed observer can see all the way to the Mediterranean on a clear day, but that's probably an oxygen-deprivation vision induced by the climb through narrow medieval lanes and up the pine-scented hillside. Hyperbole aside, views across the Umbrian plain below are wonderful—quite a bit more exhilarating than the dull displays of costumes and weapons in the restored keep and soldiers quarters. Save the admission fee for a glass of wine when you get back down.

Piazzale delle Libertà Comunali, at the top of town, at the ends of Via della Rocca, Via del Colle, and the stepped Vicolo San Lorenzo off Via Porta Perlici. ✆ **075/815292.** 5:50€ adults; 3:50€ students, children 8–18; free for children 7 and under. Daily June–Aug 10am–8pm; Apr–May and Sept–Oct 10am–7pm; Nov–Feb 10am–3:45pm; Mar 10am–5:30pm.

Dress Appropriately

San Francesco and Santa Chiara have a strict dress code. Entrance is *forbidden* to those wearing shorts or miniskirts or showing bare shoulders. You also must remain silent and cannot take photographs in the Upper Church of San Francesco.

Where to Stay

Especially from Easter to fall, never show up in Assisi without a hotel reservation. Don't even *think* of showing up without a reservation on pilgrim-thronged **church holidays** or the **Calendimaggio,** a spring celebration the first weekend (starting Thurs) after May 1, with processions, medieval contests of strength and skill, and late-night partying—all in 14th-century costume, of course. At these times you may wind up stuck overnight in one of the bus-pilgrimage facilities 4km (2½ miles) away in Santa Maria degli Angeli. The official central booking office is **Consorzio Albergatori ed Operatori Turistici di Assisi,** Via A. Cristofani 22a (www.visitassisi.com; ✆ **075/816-566**).

For longer stays, the self-catering **Brigolante apartments,** located on Assisi's main Piazza del Comune (www.brigolante.com; ✆ **331/2222349**), are a good value.

Hotel la Terrazza ★★ The best of two worlds come together here in the countryside just outside the town walls—the basilica and other sights are a 20-minute walk away, while a pool, garden, and green surrounds provide a break from Assisi's stony streets and squares. The nicest rooms are in a low-slung outbuilding facing lawns on one side and views of the valley from balconies on the other, but those in a hotel section also open to gardens or balconies. Room decor is functionally comfortable, enlivened with colorful reproductions of Giotto's basilica murals over the beds, no doubt instilling dreams of doing saintly deeds.

Via Fratelli Canonichetti 1. www.laterrazzahotel.it. ✆ **075/812368.** 41 units. 110€–120€ double. Rates include breakfast. **Amenities:** Restaurant; bar; pool; spa; Wi-Fi (free).

Hotel Umbra ★ Assisi lodgings just don't get any homier than the Laudenzi family's traditional little inn, down a tiny alley from Piazza del Comune. A gate opens into a shady patio, and beyond are comfortable, if a bit outdated, guest rooms with vaulted ceilings, fresco fragments, and other historic remnants here and there, all nicely furnished with old-fashioned armoires and dressers. Views over rooftops to the valley below unfold through the tall windows, from the private terraces off a few choice rooms and the rooftop terrace. The dining room is one of the most pleasant places to eat in town and extends into a lovely garden.

Via Delgli Archi 6 (off west end of Piazza del Comune). www.hotelumbra.it. ✆ **075/812240.** 24 units. 85€–130€ double. Rates include breakfast. Closed mid-Jan to Easter. **Amenities:** Restaurant; bar; babysitting; concierge; room service; Wi-Fi (free).

NUN Assisi Relais & Spa Museum ★★ A dramatic change of pace from Assisi's heavily medieval aura is in full force at this contemporary redo of a centuries-old convent. Handsome guest quarters have all-white surfaces and bursts of color, accented with stone walls and arches, each room boldly turned out with Eames chairs, laminate tables, and high-tech lighting. A two-level suite with a hanging sleeping loft is focused on a massive 13th-century fresco of saints in the wilderness, bound to instill nighttime visions. A breakfast buffet and other meals are served in the refectory, and downstairs are hedonistic pleasures the former tenants could never have dreamed of: two pools, saunas and steam rooms, and a state-of-the-art spa.

Eremo delle Carceri 1A. www.nunassisi.com. ✆ **075/815-5150**. 18 units. From 260€ double. Rates include breakfast. **Amenities:** Restaurant; bar; concierge; indoor pools; room service; sauna; steam room; spa; Wi-Fi (free).

Sorella Luna ★ Recent renovations have given a 15th-century palace a contemporary slant, with a flower-filled terraced garden and glassed-in atriums. In the bright guest rooms, stone walls and wood beams offset the modern furnishings and tiled baths. The name refers to Clare (Sorella Luna), the follower of St. Francis whose church is on the other end of town. The Basilica di San Francisco is just down the street.

Via Frate Ella 5. www.hotelsorellaluna.it. ✆ **075/816194.** 13 units. 95€ double. Rates include breakfast. **Amenities:** Wi-Fi (free).

Villa Zuccari ★★★ If you have a car, you can easily visit Assisi from any number of smaller nearby towns. The little wine village of Montefalco, about 20 minutes south, is especially appealing, given the presence of dozens of wineries, vineyards, and this old estate, in the Zuccari family since the 16th century, where you will feel like a guest in a gracious Italian home. You will also be within easy reach of Spello, Trevi, Spoleto, Todi, and other hill towns that spill down the Umbrian hillsides. But you might be tempted to stay put on your own terrace or in the palm-shaded gardens surrounding the pool. Airy, light-filled bedrooms are large and comfortably equipped with soft armchairs, king-size beds, and nice antiques; the big bathrooms are sheathed in marble. Welcoming lounges are filled with books and pottery, and dinners are served in a vaulted room that glistens with terracotta tiles.

Locanda San Luca (just east of Montefalco). www.villazuccari.com. ✆ **0742/399402.** 34 units. From 120€ double. Rates include breakfast. **Amenities:** Restaurant; bar; pool; Wi-Fi (free).

Where to Eat

Several of Assisi's restaurants and bars serve a local flatbread called ***torta al testa,*** often split and stuffed with cheeses, sausages, and vegetables (spinach is popular). It's a meal in itself and a fast and cheap lunch. **La Botega dei Sapori,** a wine and food shop right on Piazza del Commune (no. 34) (✆ **075/812204**), serves platters of local meats and cheese and a delicious porchetta sandwich, accompanied by one of the excellent wines and served in a cozy tasting room or at a table on the piazza;

seating is limited, but if you wish, they'll fix a snack plate for you to take back to your hotel. They also ship wines, salamis, and other delicacies.

La Fortezza ★ UMBRIAN You don't have to veer far off the beaten track to find the Chiocchetti family's plain, stone-walled dining room, where the focus is on authentic Umbrian home cooking. Both body and soul benefit from their specialties, such as *cannelloni all'Assisiana* (fresh pasta sheets rolled with veal *ragù,* all baked under parmigiano) and *coniglio in salsa di mele* (rabbit roasted in a sauce of wine and apples).
Vicolo della Fortezza/Piazza del Comune (up the stairs near the Via San Rufino end). www.lafortezzaristorante.it. ✆ **075/812993.** Main courses 10€–13€. Fri–Wed 12:30–2:30pm and 7:30–9:30pm. Closed Feb and 1 week in July.

La Stalla ★★ GRILL/UMBRIAN The term "old barn" isn't often associated with good dining, but a meal in these rustic and rather raucous converted livestock stalls, with stone walls and low ceilings, can be the highlight of a trip to Assisi (even the servers seem to be having a good time). The pleasant, 15-minute walk out here will work up an appetite, so begin with the *assaggini di torta al testo,* samplers of Assisian flatbread stuffed with cheese, meat, and vegetables, then move through the selection of pastas to the simple servings of steak, pork and sausage skewers, chicken, and even potatoes that come off the grill. House wines complement the meals, and you can dine on a terrace in good weather.
Santuario della Carceri 24, 1½km (less than 1 mile) from center, direction Eremo. www.fontemaggio.it. ✆ **075/812317.** Main courses 8€–13€. Thurs–Tues noon–2:30pm and 7:30–10pm.

Osteria Dei Priori ★★★ UMBRIAN With cool jazz playing softly in the background and warm-hued brick vaults soaring above a red accent wall, it doesn't take long to feel at home at this appealing spot below Piazza Communale. The small, daily changing menu is just as enticing, with an emphasis on Umbrian classics made with the freshest local ingredients. Garden-grown eggplant appears in a delicious flan with *scamorza* (cow's milk cheese), and homemade *maccheroni* is served *alla Norcia,* with sausage and a light cream sauce. This welcoming place stays open through the winter, when many other Assisi restaurants close.
Via Giotto 4. ✆ **075/812149.** Main courses 8€–15€. Wed–Mon 12:30–3pm and 7:30–11pm.

A Side Trip to Spello ★

14km (9 miles) S of Assisi

You have a couple of couple of compelling reasons to make the short trip down SS75 from Assisi to this little hilltown of pink and honey-colored stone. It's beguilingly pretty, unspoiled, and relatively undiscovered, with none of the crowds that descend upon its more famous neighbor. Spello lies on the flanks of Monte Subasio and is guarded by walls that surround the *centro storico.* Then there's Pinturicchio, or "The Little Painter." He

The flower-lined streets of Spello.

created one of Umbria's great masterpieces, frescoes of the life of Christ tucked away in the Cappello Baglioni (see below). After admiring these color-saturated scenes, combining biblical references with an oft-cynical look at medieval life (notice the church treasurer with the bursting money bags witnessing the Annunciation), continue up to Via Cavour. The impressive **Porta Venere** is a Roman gate flanked by two 12-sided towers. The **tourist office** in Piazza Matteotti (www.comune.spello.pg.it; ✆ **0742/301-009**) is open daily 9:30am–12:30pm and 3:30–5:30pm.

Cappella Baglioni ★★ CHURCH/MUSEUM Spello's powerful Baglioni family decided to use this side chapel in the Santa Maria Maggiore church to generate some good press, and maybe some goodwill with the Almighty. They had been caught up in quite a debacle, when one branch of the family turned against the other in what became known as the Red Wedding. Family members were killed by rivalrous kinsmen, who were murdered in turn. To demonstrate the family's beneficence, survivor Troilio Bagnoli commissioned Pinturrichio to paint scenes from the boyhood of Christ. The color-filled frescoes are enchanting, filled with rich architectural detail and Umbrian landscapes. Pinturrichio himself appears in a portrait in the Annunciation scene, and Troilo Baglioni, looking unscathed, shows up in the Disputation in the Temple.
Piazza Matteotti. Free. Daily 8:30am–noon and 3–7pm.

Hotel Palazzo Bocci ★★ If rooms at the inns in Assisi are full or you prefer quieter surroundings, settle into Spello in style at the palace of a 15th-century merchant converted to its fairly splendid current state in the 18th and 19th centuries. The vaulted salons are suitably regal, filled with antiques and trompe l'oeil detailing, while guest rooms retain all the character you'd expect from such historic surroundings. Views from rooms in the rear are especially refreshing, looking over a large garden and terrace to the valley below town.
Via Cavour 17. www.palazzobocci.com. ✆ **0742/301021.** 130€–150€. Rates include breakfast. **Amenities:** Restaurant; bar; Wi-Fi (free).

Il Molino ★★ UMBRIAN A 13th-century olive mill has been bringing gourmands to Spello since the 1960s and still delights with its inspired use of local ingredients. Beef and lamb from the valley below is grilled over the fireplace, while ham from Norcia, asparagus and herbs from the mountains, and even beans from nearby farms show up in such pastas as cappeletti with beans and onion sauce and *zuppa di faro macinato,* soup with barley, beans, and cabbage. It's hard to pass up the chance to enjoy a meal in the series of arched, low-ceilinged rooms inside, though a seat on the terrace comes with a view of small-town life.
Piazza Matteotti. www.ilmolinodispello.com. ✆ **0742/651305.** Main courses 10€–24€. Wed–Mon 1–3pm and 7–10:30pm.

SPOLETO ★★

63km (39 miles) SE of Perugia

Spoleto feels like the center of the cultured world in June, when the **Festival dei Due Mondi** (a.k.a. **Spoleto Festival**) draws performers and audiences from all over the world. For most of the year, though, Spoleto is just another lovely Umbrian hilltown, a pleasant warren of steep streets and airy piazzas lined with artifacts from the Roman past and prosperous Middle Ages. Here is one of Italy's most beautifully situated cathedrals.

Cattedrale di Santa Maria Assunta in Spoleto.

Essentials

GETTING THERE Spoleto is a main **rail** station on the Rome-Ancona line, and 16 daily trains from **Rome** stop here (about 1½ hr.). From **Perugia,** take one of the 20 daily trains to Foligno (25 min.) to transfer to this line for the final 20-minute leg. From outside the station, you can take bus A, B, or C to Piazza Carducci on the edge of the old town, but it's an easy 10-minute walk.

By **car,** approach town on the old Roman Via Flaminia, now the SS3. There's usually plenty of parking, but the easiest option is to make for the Spoletosfera parking garage, signposted from the SS3's Spoleto Sud exit (1€ per hour). Escalators from the lot run up the hillside to the top of town, allowing you to get off at well-signposted levels (for Piazza della Libertà, the Duomo, and so on).

VISITOR INFORMATION The **information center** at Piazza della Libertà 7 (www.visitspoleto.it; ✆ **0743/220773**) hands out heaps of info and an excellent map. It's open daily (Mon–Fri 9am–1:30pm and 2–7pm; Sat 9am–1pm; and Sun 10am–1pm and 3:30–6:30pm).

Exploring Spoleto

You won't spend much time in the Lower Town, but a highlight is the 11th-century Romanesque **San Gregorio di Maggiore,** Piazza della Vittoria (✆ **0743/44140**). The church's namesake saint was killed at the nearby amphitheater in A.D. 304, as were a supposed 10,000 lesser-known martyrs whose bones reside beneath the altar. It opens daily from 8am to noon and 4 to 6pm, and admission is free.

Once you settle into town, you'll be able to figure out how to use the handy **moving walkway** that runs beneath the city and the network of **escalators,** all geared to avoiding steep uphill climbs; hotel staff will also usually help you plot a level course. **Piazza del Mercato,** the probable site of the old Roman forum, is a bustling spot in the Upper Town lined with grocers and fruit vendors' shops.

Casa Romana ★ HISTORIC HOME As a stop on the busy Via Flaminia route and an important wine supplier, Spoletium was fairly prosperous in the Roman world. Enough of this patrician's home remains, including frescoes and mosaics, to give an idea of what the good life was like for a Roman occupant in the 1st century A.D. The resident was obviously well-to-do, though there's no proof for the claim that it was Vespasia Polla, the mother of the Emperor Vespasian.

Via di Visiale. ✆ **0743/234350.** 3€ adults, 2€ ages 15–25 and seniors 65 and over, 1€ children 7–14, free for children 6 and under. Thurs–Tues 10:30am–5:30pm.

Cattedrale di Santa Maria dell'Assunta ★★ CATHEDRAL Spoleto's almost playfully picturesque cathedral was consecrated in 1098, barely 40 years after Frederick Barbarossa, Holy Roman Emperor, razed the entire town in retaliation for the citizens' lack of support in his ongoing wars against the papacy. The church seems to defy the brutality of that catastrophe, set in a broad piazza at the bottom of a flight of

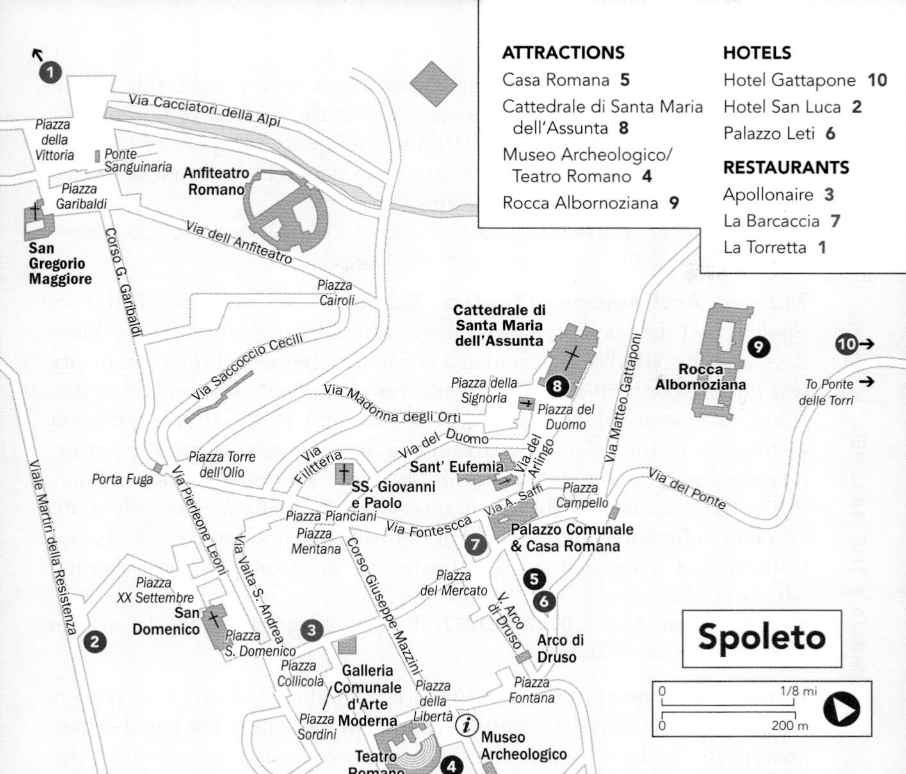

monumental steps. White marble and golden mosaics on the dazzling facade are framed against a gentle backdrop of a forested hill. Inside, the apse is graced with frescoes of the "Life of the Virgin," largely from the brush of Filippo Lippi, one of the more colorful characters of his time. An ordained priest, Filippo shirked his duties and was eventually given permission to paint full-time. Though he worked frequently and was a favorite of the Medicis, he was chronically impoverished, supposedly because he spent so much money on women. The commission to come to Spoleto must have been a plum for the artist, then close to 60. His engaging scenes of the Virgin being visited by the Archangel and holding her sweet-looking infant betray nothing of the turbulence in his life—he was fighting to get dispensation to marry a young nun, Lucrezia Buti, who had borne his son, Filippino Lippi (who would soon match his father's greatness as a painter). Both Lippis appear in the Domition of the Virgin scene, Filippo wearing a white habit with young Filippino, as an angel, in front of him. Fillippo died before he completed the frescoes; his assistants finished the task. The cause of his death was suspected to be poison, perhaps administered by Lucrezia's family or yet another paramour. He is buried beneath a monument on the right side of the transept, which his son Filippino designed at the request of Lorenzo de' Medici. In the Cappella delle Reliquie (Reliquary Chapel), on the left aisle, is a rare treasure—a letter written and signed by St. Francis. (Assisi has the only other bonafide signature.)

Piazza del Duomo. ✆ **0743/231063.** Free. Daily 8:30am–12:30pm and 3:30–5:30pm (until 7pm Apr–Oct).

Museo Archeologico/Teatro Romano ★ MUSEUM/RUINS Spoleto had the good fortune to more or less flourish through the Dark Ages and the Middle Ages, and as a consequence most of the Roman city was quarried or built over. The monastery of St. Agata was built atop this splendid theater, which wasn't recognized until 1891. After a thorough restoration in the 1950s, the theater is the evocative venue for performances during the Spoleto Festival. Much of the original orchestra flooring is intact, as is an elaborate drainage system that was allegedly quite efficient in flushing out the blood of slain animals and martyrs. Busts and statuary that once adorned the theater are on display in the adjoining Museo Archeologico.

Via di Sant'Agata 18A. ✆ **0743/223277.** 4€ adults, 2€ ages 18–25, free for children 17 and under. Daily 8:30am–7:30pm.

Rocca Albornoziana ★★ CASTLE Cardinal Albornoz, a power-hungry zealot tasked with rebuilding and strengthening the papal states, arrived in Spoleto in the mid-14th century and commissioned the Umbrian architect Matteo Gattapone to build a fortress. The site was perfect—atop a high hill above the town and, as history would prove, virtually impregnable. The walled-and-moated castle became famous in the 20th century as one of Italy's most secure prisons, where members of the Red Brigades terrorist organization were routinely incarcerated. The fortunate ones might have had a view through their cell windows of the majestic **Ponte delle Torri**, a 232m- (760 ft.) long aqueduct built in the 13th century on Roman foundations. Its arches span a deep, verdant gorge, 90m (295 ft.) above the Tessino river. The current occupant of the fortress is the **Museo Nazionale del Ducato di Spoleto** (✆ **0743/223055**)—and you needn't feel guilty about skipping its numbing collection of sarcophagi, mosaics, and statuary (and a visit is

Spoleto's Big Bash

Spoleto's be-all and end-all annual event bridges the end of June and early July. The **Spoleto Festival** (www.festivaldispoleto.it) offers 3 weeks of world-class drama, music, and dance held in evocative spaces like an open-air restored Roman theater and the piazza fronting the Duomo. A secondary **Spoleto Estate** season runs from just after the festival through September.

costly). The views of the town and Umbrian countryside from the grounds are free, and well worth the ride up, via a series of escalators and elevators.

Piazza Campello. ✆ **0743/224952.** 8€ adults, 7€ ages 15–25, 4€ children 7–14, free for children 6 and under. Tues–Sun 8:30am–7:30pm (last ticket 6:45pm).

Where to Stay

Accommodations are tight during the Spoleto Festival; reserve by March if you want to find a good, central room.

Hotel Gattapone ★ From the street, this unexpected hideaway beneath the Rocca Albornozina looks like a relatively modest 19th-century villa. But step inside and all is polished wood, free-floating staircases, and leather couches facing windows overlooking the Ponte dei Torre and green Monteluco hillsides. There's a cinematic, 1960s Antonioni-film feel to the place. Guest rooms have slightly dated but well-maintained contemporary furnishings mixed with traditional pieces, and huge bay windows hang over the same stunning views. Some guests comment that the air-conditioning is vintage, too, and anyone with mobility issues should keep in mind that there's no elevator and rooms and lounges flow for several floors down the hillside.

Via del Ponte 6. www.hotelgattapone.it. ✆ **0743/223447.** 15 units. From 90€ double. Rates include breakfast. **Amenities:** Bar; Wi-Fi (free).

Hotel San Luca ★★ A 19th-century tannery at the far edge of the city next to the Roman walls lends itself well to its current incarnation. A book-lined lounge, where canaries chirp in an antique cage and a fire crackles in cold months, faces a large courtyard, and so do many rooms; others overlook a rose garden to the side. The unusually large quarters are all different, a mix of traditional and contemporary pieces with a smattering of antiques, plus extremely large and well-equipped marble bathrooms. Sights and restaurants are about a 5-minute walk away, and the attentive staff will map out a route that involves the least amount of climbing. The easy-to-reach in-house garage is a real rarity in Spoleto.

Via Interna delle Mura 21. www.hotelsanluca.com. ✆ **0743/223399.** 35 units. From 90€ double. Rates include breakfast. **Amenities:** Bar; babysitting; bikes; concierge; room service (bar); Wi-Fi (fee).

Palazzo Leti ★★ An entrance through a Renaissance garden that opens to the Tessino gorge announces that this beautifully restored 13th-century palace of the Leti family is a pretty special place. Views of the gorge and green Monteluco hills are the focal point of most rooms, though a few overlook a medieval alley that has its own charm; all have period furniture and rich fabrics, plus couches and armchairs in the larger rooms and wood beams, granite hearths, and vaulted ceilings throughout. Anna Laura and Giampolo, who restored the palace from a dilapidated pile, are a friendly presence and provide all sorts of helpful advice.

Via degli Eremiti 10. www.palazzoleti.com. ✆ **0743/224930.** 12 units. 140€–200€ double. Rates include breakfast. **Amenities:** Bar; bikes; spa; Wi-Fi (free).

Where to Eat

For some gastro-shopping, visit **Bartolomei Orvieto** at 97 Corso Cavour (www.oleificiobartolomei.it; ✆ **0743/344550**), where you can sample the products before buying. **Colder Gelateria** (✆ **0743/235015;** daily 12:30pm–midnight) serves some of the best gelato (notably the "bread and chocolate" flavor) in Umbria, created by local artisans Crispini.

Apollonaire ★ UMBRIAN The low wood ceilings, stone walls, and beams are traditional holdovers from a 12th-century Franciscan monastery, but the menu is innovative and adventurous—contemporary Spoletan, if the food world has invented such a term. Dishes rely on fresh local ingredients and traditional recipes but have that extra twist: *Strangozzi* (the local long, rectangular wheat pasta) is topped with a pungent sauce of cherry tomatoes and mint; herb-roasted rabbit is served with black olive sauce; and pork filet mignon is topped with a sauce of pecorino cheese and pears soaked in Rosso di Montefalco.

Via Sant'Agata 14 (near Piazza della Libertà). www.ristoranteapollinare.it. ✆ **0743/225676.** Main courses 12€–24€. Thurs–Tues noon–3pm and 7pm–midnight. Closed Feb.

La Barcaccia ★ UMBRIAN Despite the name (the "Old Boat"), these brightly lit rooms are firmly planted on an airy square near the top of the town. Some nautical prints and paintings carry out the theme, but, except for some Adriatic fish choices, the menu is firmly landlocked in Umbrian classics. This is the place to strangle the priest, that is, enjoy the *strangozzi alla spoletina* (with peppery tomato sauce), named for rebellious clergy who broke with the papacy in the 14th century. Some of the tasty vegetarian dishes include *scamorza,* a cow's milk cheese similar to mozzarella, baked with radicchio.

Piazza Fratelli Bandiera 4. www.ristorantelabarcaccia.it. ✆ **0743/225082.** Main courses 9€–16€. Wed–Mon 12:30–2:30pm and 7–10:30pm.

La Torretta ★★ UMBRIAN In two welcoming rooms in a medieval tower, brothers Stefano and Elio Salvucci extend a genuine welcome and a nice selection of Umbrian dishes. The *tris di antipasti al tartufo estivo* (trio of truffle-based appetizers) is a memorable way to work up to beautifully seasoned pork or beef grilled over a wood fire. The kitchen also makes a light-as-air truffle omelet, a memorable break from heavier *secondi*.

Via Filitteria 43. www.trattorialatorretta.com. ✆ **0743/44954.** Main courses 9€–16€. Wed–Mon 12:30–2:30pm and 7:45–10:45pm (closed Sun evening).

Getting Active

Aside from climbing Spoleto's steep streets, you can exercise your legs with a scenic walk along the Giro dei Condotti. The well-marked 6km (4-mile) route begins just below the Rocca and starts out with a bang—a vertigo-inducing crossing of the Ponte delle Torri, with views into the deep valley far below. From there the trail crosses a forested hillside, with more views back to the bridge and the town, before descending through olive groves into the valley. The only gear you'll need for the fairly easy trek are comfortable walking shoes and a camera.

ORVIETO ★★

87km (54 miles) W of Spoleto, 86km (53 miles) SW of Perugia

Walking through the streets of Orvieto, you might be pleased to discover that nothing much has changed in the past 500 years. Adding to the magic is what might be Italy's most beautiful cathedral, covered in dazzling mosaics and statuary and rising above an airy piazza. The final coup de grace is the fact that the entire town is set atop a volcanic outcropping some 315m (1,033 ft.) above the green countryside. This impenetrable perch ensured that Etruscan "Velzna" was among the most powerful members of the *dodecapoli* (Etruscan confederation of 12 cities). The lofty setting continues to make Orvieto seem a world apart.

Essentials

GETTING THERE Fourteen **trains** on the main **Rome-Florence** line stop at Orvieto daily (1 hr., 45 min. from Florence; 1 hr., 20 min. from Rome). From **Perugia,** take the train to Terontola (16 trains daily) to transfer to this line heading south toward Rome (1¼ hr. total train time).

Orvieto's **station** is in Orvieto Scalo in the valley. To reach the city, cross the street and take the **funicular** (www.atcterni.it; 1€, every 10 min. 7:20am–8:30pm).

Orvieto is easy to reach by **car,** especially from southern Tuscany: It's right by the A1. The main link to the rest of Umbria is the SS448 to Todi (40 min.). You can leave your car in the large lot behind the train station off Piazza della Pace and take the funicular up to town or, if you want to get a bit closer, in the garage at Campo della Fiera, just outside the Porta Romana. From there take an elevator/escalator system up to Piazza San Giovanni or Piazza Ranieri.

VISITOR INFORMATION The **tourist office** is opposite the Duomo at Piazza Duomo 24 (www.comune.orvieto.tr.it; ✆ **0763/341772**). It's open Monday to Friday 8:15am to 1:50pm and 4 to 7pm, Saturday 10am to 1pm and 3:30 to 7pm, and Sunday from 10am to noon and 4 to 6pm.

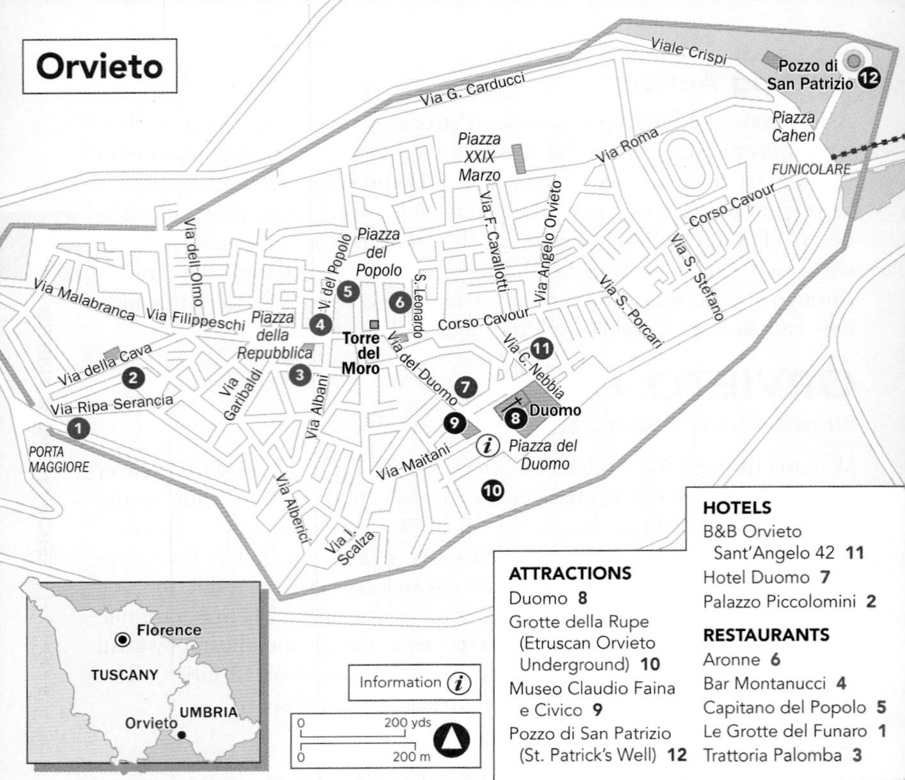

Exploring Orvieto

Life in Orvieto transpires along the animated Corso Cavour, cutting through the center of town. If you take the funicular up from the lower town, and you should, you'll begin your walk through Orvieto at the eastern end of the street. In the very center of town rises the **Torre del Moro,** a 13th-century show of civic might that provided views across the territory the medieval city controlled, stretching east to the Apennines and west to the Mediterranean. You can still take in the spectacle with an ascent that combines an elevator ride and a climb up 171 steps (open Mar–Apr and Sept–Oct daily 10am–7pm; May–Aug daily 10am–8pm; Nov–Feb daily 10:30am–1pm; 3€). The tower's bell is a familiar presence in Orvieto, having rung every 15 minutes for the past 700 years. Just to the north is **Piazza del Popolo,** where the Capitano del Popolo (Captain of the People) administered from the formidable, crenelated Palazzo del Popolo. The square is filled with market stalls on Thursday and Saturday mornings. Via del Duomo stretches south from the tower before emerging in front of Orvieto's masterwork, one of the most celebrated cathedrals in Italy.

Orvieto's other great wonder is the volcanic plug upon which it sits. To look at the city's tufa foundations, take a hike along the rupe, a path that encircles the base of the cliff. A landmark along the way is the **Necropoli Etrusca di Crocifisso del Tufo** (Etruscan Necropolis), where ancient Etruscan tombs are laid in a streetlike grid in subterranean caverns (3€; daily 8:30am–5:30pm). The tourist office can supply a map, Anello delle Rupe. You can also appreciate this unique setting with a stroll along the high ramparts that fringe the edges of town. Some of the most accessible are at the west edge of town, just beyond the church of Sant'Agostino.

Exploring Orvieto's narrow cobbled lanes.

Duomo ★★ CATHEDRAL Orvieto's pièce de résistance is a mesmerizing assemblage of spikes and spires, mosaics and marble statuary—and that's just the facade. The rest of the bulky-yet-elegant church is banded in black and white stone and seems to perch miraculously on the edge of the cliffs that surround the town. The church is wider at the front than at the back, designed to create the optical illusion upon entering that it is longer than it actually is. The facade has been compared to a medieval altarpiece, and it reads like an illustrated Catechism. On the four broad marble panels that divide the surface, Sienese sculptor and architect Lorenzo Maitani (who more or less designed the church) and others carved scenes from the Old and New Testament. On the far left is the story of creation, with Eve making an appearance from Adam's rib; on the far right, Christ presides over the Last Judgment, as the dead shuffle out of their sarcophagi to await his verdict. Prophets and the Apostles surround a huge rose window, and Mary appears in lush mosaics inlaid in fields of gold.

Capella del Coporale In 1263, a Bohemian priest, Peter of Prague, found himself doubting transubstantiation, the sacrament in which the communion bread, or host, is transformed into the body of Christ during mass. He went to Rome to pray on St. Peter's tomb that his faith be strengthened and, stopping in Bolsena, just below Orvieto, was saying Mass when the host began to bleed, dampening the corporal, or altar cloth. Pope Urban IV had the cloth brought to him in Orvieto, and a few decades later, Pope Nicholas IV ordered the cathedral built to house the relic. Frescoes in the chapel tell the story of the miracle, and the exquisite enamel reliquary that once held the cloth remains in place.

Cappella San Brizio The cathedral's other treasure is one of the Renaissance's greatest fresco cycles. The lofty themes are temptation, salvation, damnation, and resurrection, though the scenes are rich in everyday humanity. The works allegedly inspired Michelangelo, who came to Orvieto and filled sketchbooks before starting the Sistine Chapel. Fra' Angelico (the "Angelic Friar") began the series in 1447, and Luca Signorelli completed the works that have come to be considered his masterpiece in 1504. Both artists appear in a magnificent panel of the "Sermon of the Antichrist," in which the devil coaxes a Christ impostor to lure the faithful to damnation. Signorelli looks handsome and proud, with his long blonde hair, as he gets revenge on the mistress who jilted him, portraying her as the worried recipient of funds from a money lender (for prostitution services, some conject).

To the right of the altar is "The Entrance to Hell" and "The Damned in Hell," in which devils torment their victims, a man raises his fists to curse God as he sees Charon crossing the Styx for him, and bodies writhe in agony. Signorelli gets revenge again in his depiction of a winged devil leering toward a terrified blonde on his back—the ex-mistress, of course. If a bit of relief is in order, you need only look at the "Elect in Heaven," where the saved look quite content in their assurance of eternal salvation.

Piazza del Duomo. www.museomodo.it. ✆ **0763/341167.** 3€, free for children 10 and under. Apr–Oct Mon–Sat 9:30am–7pm, Sun 1–5:30pm (6:30pm July–Sept); Nov–Mar Mon–Sat 9:30am–1pm, 2:30–5pm (Sun to 5:30pm).

Grotte della Rupe (Etruscan Orvieto Underground) ★★ HISTORIC SITE More than 1,200 artificial and natural caverns have been found in the *pozzolana* (a volcanic stone powdered to make cement mix) and *tufa* rock upon which Orvieto rests. Guided tours explore 15m (45 ft.) below Santa Chiara convent, reached by a steep climb up and down 55 steps, along a narrow rock-hewn passage. The caverns have been used as Etruscan houses, water wells, ceramic ovens, pigeon coops, and cold storage (the temperature is a constant 14°C/58°F). Medieval citizens considered the tunnels safe refuges in times of siege, and residents took shelter in them during World War II Allied bombings, but most unwisely—a direct hit would have annihilated the soft rock.

Grotte della Rupe: Piazza Duomo 23 (next to the tourist info office; open daily 10:30am–5:30pm). www.orvietounderground.it. ✆ **0763/344891.** Guided tours only, 45 min.–1 hr., 6€ adults, 5€ students and seniors. Tours daily at 11am and 12:15, 3, 4, and 5:15pm; tours only Sat–Sun in Feb.

Museo Claudio Faina e Civico ★ MUSEUM A palace next to the cathedral houses what began as a private collection in 1864. Interestingly, some of the most stunning pieces are not Etruscan, but Greek:

St. Patrick's Well in Orvieto.

Attic black-figure (6th-c.-B.C.) and red-figure (5th-c.-B.C.) vases and amphorae from Athenian workshops (including some by Greek master Exekias from 540 B.C.) that were bought by discriminating Etruscan collectors. You'll see the resemblance to Etruscan black *bucchero* ware from the 6th and the 5th century B.C.

Piazza del Duomo 29. www.museofaina.it. ✆ **0763/341-11** or 0763/341216. 5€ adults; 3€ ages 7–12, seniors 65 and over, and families of 4 or more. Apr–Sept daily 9:30am–6pm; Oct–Mar daily 10am–5pm (closed Mon Nov–Mar).

Pozzo di San Patrizio (St. Patrick's Well) ★ HISTORIC SITE Orvieto's position atop a rocky outcropping made it a perfect redoubt in time of siege, easy to defend but with one big drawback—a lack of water. When Pope Clement VII decided to hole up in Orvieto in 1527 to avoid turbulence in Rome, he hired Antonio Sangallo the Younger to dig a new well. Sangallo's design was unique: He dug a shaft 53m (175-ft.) deep and 14m (45-ft.) wide, accessible via a pair of wide spiral staircases that form a double helix and are lit by 72 internal windows. Mule-drawn carts could descend on one ramp and come back up the other without colliding. You can climb down, too, though it's a trek up and down 496 steps, and there's nothing to see at the bottom but, well, a well. A few steps up and down will introduce you to the concept, and give you time to

Orvieto's Liquid Gold

The plains and low hills around Orvieto grow the grapes—verdello, grechetto, and Tuscan varietals trebbiano and malvasia—that go into one of Italy's great wines, a pale straw-colored DOC white called simply **Orvieto Classico.** A well-rounded and fragrant white (often with a hint of crushed almonds), it goes great with lunch. Most Orvieto Classico you run across is *secco* (dry), but you can also find bottles of the more traditional *abboccato* (semidry/semisweet), *amabile* (medium sweet), and *dolce* (sweet) varieties. To visit a vineyard, pick up a copy of the "Strada dei Vini" brochure at the tourist office; it lists the wineries along with the hours.

contemplate the name. It's a reference to St. Patrick's Purgatory, a pilgrimage site in Ireland where Christ allegedly showed St. Patrick a cave and told him it was an entrance to hell.

Viale San Gallo (near the funicular stop on Piazza Cahen). ✆ **0763/343768.** 5€ adults, 4€ students. May–Aug daily 9am–7:45pm; Mar–Apr and Sept–Oct daily 9am–6:45pm; Nov–Feb daily 10am–4:45pm.

Where to Stay

The upper town has few places to stay, so book ahead—especially on weekends, when Romans flock to Orvieto for a small-town getaway.

B&B Orvieto Sant'Angelo 42 ★★★ From the moment you step into the stone-floored foyer you'll feel right at home in Giulia Donato's pretty house on a narrow street off the Corso. In a lounge/breakfast room, a couch and chairs surround a huge hearth, and up a stone staircase are high-ceilinged guest rooms, two large doubles and two suite-size triples. Bathrooms are large (with deep tubs in the larger rooms), beds are luxurious, and handsome traditional pieces complement highly polished floors and mellow old beams and stones. Top-floor rooms come with a perk: little step-out balconies looking across rooftops to the distant hills.

Via Sant'Angelo 42. www.bborvieto.com. ✆ **0763/341-959.** 95{eu]–110€ double. **Amenities:** Lounge; Wi-Fi (free).

Hotel Duomo ★★ These snug quarters just a few steps from the Duomo (viewable from some rooms with a lean out the window) are not only extremely comfortable—with lots of modern built-in wood furnishings and excellent lighting—but also surprisingly quirky. A local artist, Livio Orazio Valentini, did the decor and hung his surrealistic paintings in the hallways, lounges, and rooms, complementing them with colorful upholstery and carpets to match the tones. He also created sculptural light fixtures that hang over many of the desks. The effect is slightly bohemian and quite homey, and the ambience is topped off nicely with a pleasant garden to one side of the hotel.

Vicolo dei Maurizio 7. www.orvietohotelduomo.com. ✆ **0763/341887.** 18 units. 100€–130€ double. Rates include breakfast. **Amenities:** Wi-Fi (free).

Palazzo Piccolomini ★★ Orvieto's most luxurious and character-filled rooms are in a 16th-century *palazzo,* resurrected from a dilapidated wreck 30 years ago. The stone and vaulted subterranean breakfast room and a couple of frescoed salons whisk you into the past, but most of the guest rooms are done in contemporary Umbrian chic: wood and tile floors, dark furnishings, and crisp white walls with neutral-tone accents, all very soothing. Some rooms have sitting areas or open to terraces, or are two-level, though the real prize here is a room of any size with a countryside view (only those on the upper floors have them).

Piazza Ranieri 36 (2 blocks down from Piazza della Repubblica). www.palazzopiccolomini.it. ✆ **0763/341743.** 32 units. From 100€ double. Rates include breakfast. **Amenities:** Restaurant; babysitting; concierge; room service; Wi-Fi (free in public areas).

Where to Eat

Orvieto's favorite pasta is *umbrichelli,* simple flour-and-water spaghetti rolled out unevenly by hand and somewhat chewy—similar to the *pici* of southern Tuscany, but not as thick. To sample a glass (or buy a bottle) of Orvieto Classico (accompanied by a *panino*), drop by the **Cantina Foresi,** Piazza Duomo 2 (✆ **0763/341611**). Ask to see the small, moldy cellar carved directly into the *tufa.* Top choice for an excellent casual meal is **Aronne,** Corso Cavour 101 (✆ **0763/340014**), a bright and appealing gastronomia run by Christian Manca, part of the mother-son team whose Trattoria del Moro Aronne is around the corner; cheeses, salamis, *panini,* and several daily hot dishes are served in two friendly rooms, accompanied by local wines. **Bar Montanucci** is a popular spot for snacks and drinks at Corso Cavour 23 (www.barmontanucci.com; ✆ **0763/341262**), with playful wooden sculptures, a large rear terrace, and a huge selection of chocolates, some house-made.

Capitano del Popolo ★★★ UMBRIAN Chef/proprietor Valentina Santanicchio grew up on a farm just outside of Orvieto, and she brings together her passion for cooking, commitment to locally grown ingredients, and flair for presentation in a former bakery on the town's market square. Leather couches and upholstered chairs are scattered around an all-day cafe up front, while in back, the dining room has vintage]']50s cabinets and tables topped with crisp linens and fresh flowers. Valentina prides herself on a *carbonara* that rivals the best in Rome, and along with spicy boar ragùs and other Umbrian classics she cooks dishes seldom encountered on Italian menus, like sweetbreads.

Piazza del Popolo 7–9. ✆ **320/928-7474.** Main courses 8€–12€. Daily 8am–11pm.

Le Grotte del Funaro ★ UMBRIAN A *funaro* (ropemaker) had his workshop in these grottoes carved into the cliff's *tufa* a thousand years ago, and you can almost see him at work in the shadowy recesses of the cavelike rooms. You can sit outside in good weather or better yet—so you don't miss the atmosphere inside—ask for one of the few window seats. You'll dine simply and well on grilled meats, the house specialty (including a *grigliata mista* of suckling pig, lamb, sausage, and yellow peppers), as well as excellent pizzas.

Via Ripa Serancia 41 (at the west end of town near Porta Maggiore). www.grottedelfunaro.it. ✆ **0763/343276.** Main courses 10€–13€; pizza 5.50€–8.50€. Tues–Sun noon–3pm and 7pm–midnight. Closed 1 week in July.

Trattoria Palomba ★★ UMBRIAN This is the kind of place you'll want to linger, for a long lunch after a morning of sightseeing or a comfy evening dinner—a meal here deserves leisurely appreciation. Black Umbrian truffles top many of the homemade pastas, most notably *umbrichelli al tartufo*, tossed with egg yolk and parmigiano. The signature dish, *palomba,* or wild dove, is roasted in a delicious sauce of capers, rosemary, olives, and a hint of anchovies. Any of the meat dishes, including beef in a red wine sauce, are similarly satisfying, and paired with a nice selection of wines. Reserve ahead.

Via Cipirano Menente 16. ✆ **0763/343395.** Main courses 10€–16€. Thurs–Tues noon–2pm and 7:30–10pm.

Shopping

With so many visitors wandering its streets, Orvieto has some especially tempting shops. **Orogami** (www.orogami.com; ✆ **0763/344206**) sells a distinctive line of gold jewelry, including playful pieces like a medallion mimicking the rose window in the Duomo (Via del Duomo 14/16). The showroom of internationally acclaimed ceramicist **Marino Moretti** at Via del Duomo 55 (www.marinomoretti.it; ✆ **0763-361663**) sells tiles, dinnerware, and other modern takes on traditional designs. **Federico Badia** is a young shoemaker who keeps the craft alive in his workshop at Via Garibaldi 27 (http://federicobadiashoes.com), fashioning made-to-order shoes, purses, bags, and belts from fine leather, all by hand.

8

BOLOGNA & EMILIA-ROMAGNA

By Stephen Brewer

A lot of travelers zip through this northernmost stretch of central Italy as they hurry along the well-worn path between Florence and Venice. Which is good news for anyone wishing to slow down long enough to visit—you will find appealing towns and cities that are a little less crowded and more engaged in everyday Italian life than other more popular stops on the Italian tourism circuit. The region has treasure troves of art and culture, and another bright side to its personality as well: It's almost hedonistically devoted to fine food.

Bologna is one of Europe's largest remaining medieval enclaves, its old palaces are filled with art, and its stony piazzas host an animated street life revved up by students at Europe's oldest university. Parma proudly shows off its famous hams and cheeses, its musical traditions, and its art. Ravenna is awash in glittering Byzantine mosaics, and Ferrara is a time capsule of the Renaissance. It's easy to get from one place to the other by train—Bologna makes a handy base for exploring the entire region—and once you reach these old cities, the preferred mode of transport is bicycle.

BOLOGNA ★★

151km (94 miles) SW of Venice, 378km (234 miles) N of Rome

It's easy to love a city so enamored of food that it's nicknamed *La Grassa* (the Fat); so devoted to scholarship (home of Europe's oldest university, founded in 1088) that it's called *La Dotta* (the Learned); and so noted for its fiery liberal politics that it's known as *La Rossa* (the Red). There are plenty of other reasons to like Bologna. The lively city of more than a million residents is built around one of the Europe's largest and best-preserved medieval cores, an attractive swath of palaces and towers, grand piazzas, and narrow lanes all easily traversed on foot. Quirky museums and art-filled churches seem all the more appealing amid the animated street life of the Quadrilatero, the medieval town center where shop windows brim with the region's famous hams and cheeses. You don't even have to carry an umbrella in Bologna, because 24 miles of sidewalks are covered with handsome loggias.

PREVIOUS PAGE: **Students in front of Bologna University.**

The Quadrilatero, Bologna's medieval heart.

Essentials

GETTING THERE

BY PLANE The international **Aeroporto Guglielmo Marconi** (www.bologna-airport.it; ✆ **051-6479615**) is 6km (3¾ miles) north of the city center and served by such domestic carriers as Alitalia and Meridiana; all the main European airlines also fly to this airport, including Ryanair (London-Stansted), EasyJet, and British Airways (both London-Gatwick. A **bus** (marked aerobus; aerobus.bo.it) runs daily (6am–12:15am) every 15 to 30 minutes from the airport to Bologna's rail station (Stazione Centrale). A one-way ticket costs 6€ (pay the driver), and the trip usually takes 20 minutes.

> **Sidewalk Porticos: Staying Dry in Bologna**
>
> Almost 40km (25 miles) of porticos cover the sidewalks of Bologna, providing the Bolognese with a venue to stroll and strut during the evening *passeggiata,* no matter how inclement the weather. Most are high enough to accommodate a man on horseback, as mandated by a 14th-century city ordinance. It's said they were originally built to duplicate the porticos of the ancient Greek academies, giving students a place to walk and ponder; they also allowed residents to extend the upper stories of their homes over the sidewalks, helping ease a medieval housing crunch. Showiest is the 3.5km (2 mi.) stretch of porticos, supported by 666 arches, that climb a green hillside to the **Santuario della Madonna di San Luca** (www.sanlucabo.org). Inside is a painting of Mary attributed to Luke the Evangelist; outside, the views of the city and surrounding countryside are riveting.

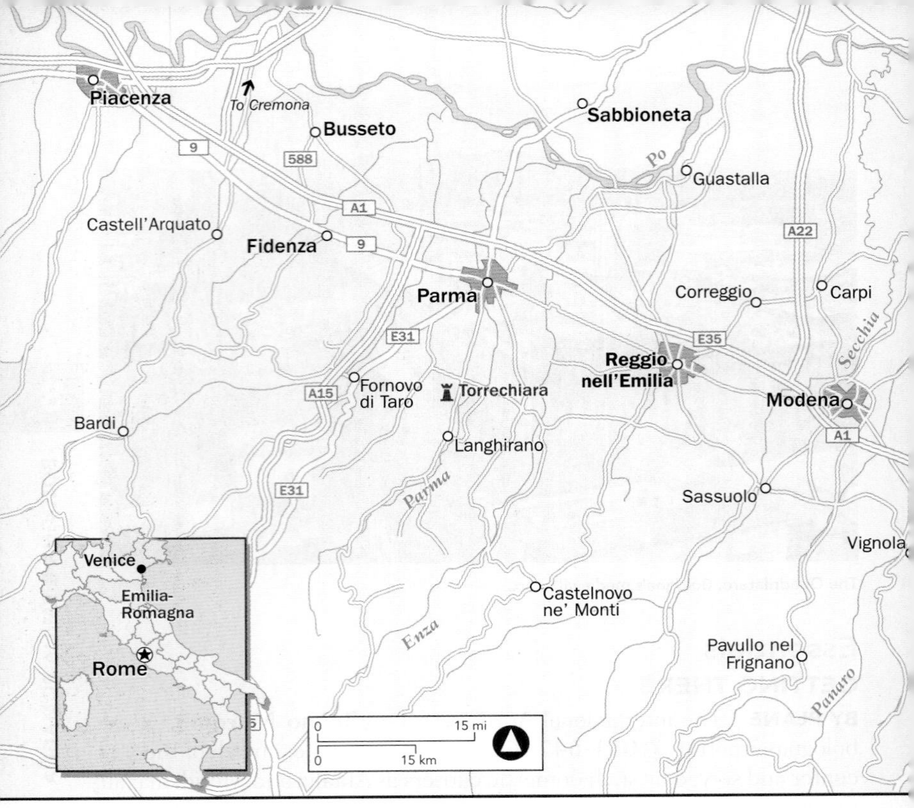

BY TRAIN Bologna's **Stazione Centrale** is at Piazza Medaglie d'Oro 2 (✆ **892021**). High-speed trains arrive hourly from Florence (trip time: about 30 min.) and Milan (about 1 hr.). Regional trains connect Bologna with other cities in the region. Most service between Bologna and Florence and Milan is now via high-speed train, and only a very few slower and less expensive trains run on these routes. Bus nos. A, 25, and 30 run between the station and the historic core of Bologna, Piazza Maggiore. Expect to pay around 6€ for taxi trips into the center. You can make the walk easily from the station to Piazza Maggiore down Via dell'Indipendenza in about 15 minutes, mostly under covered loggias.

BY CAR If you are driving in from Florence, continue north along A1 until reaching the outskirts of Bologna, where signs direct you to the city center. From Milan, take A1 southeast along the Apennines. From Venice or Ferrara, follow A13 southwest. From Rimini, Ravenna, and the towns along the Adriatic, cut west on A14. See the note on p. 353 about driving and parking in Bologna; if you have a choice, it's much easier to arrive in Bologna without a car.

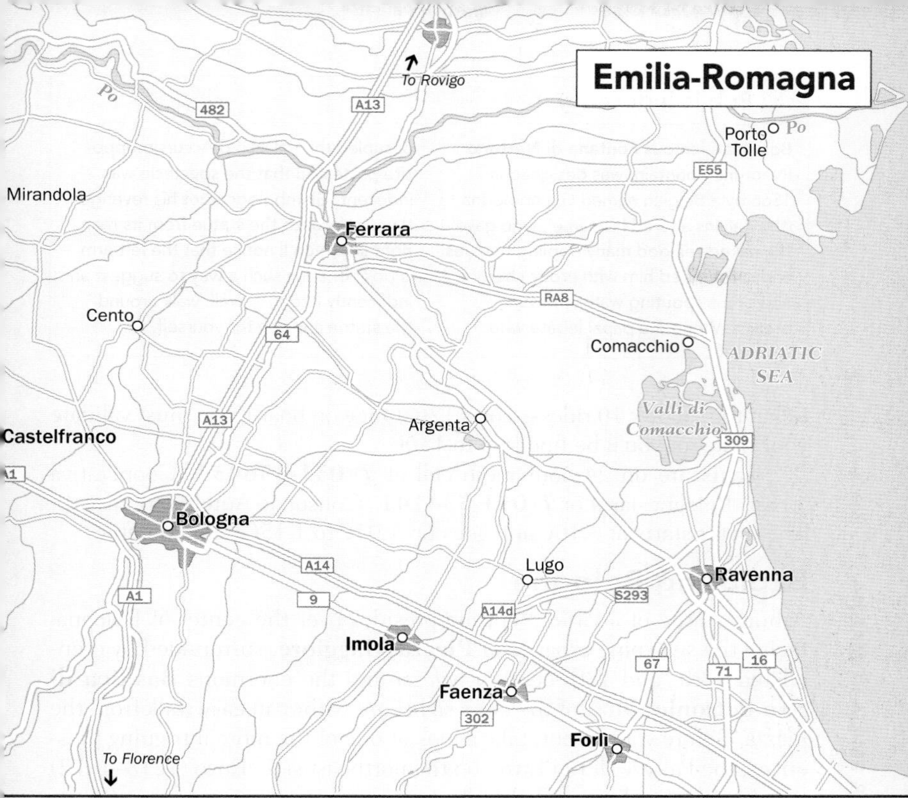

VISITOR INFORMATION The **tourist office** (www.bolognawelcome.com; ✆ **051-239660**) at Piazza Maggiore in the Palazzo del Podestà, is open Monday through Saturday 9am to 7pm and Sunday 10am to 5pm. There is another office at the airport, in the arrivals hall (✆ **051-6472113;** open Mon–Sat 9am–7pm and Sun and holidays 9am–4pm). These offices hand out free city maps, bus maps, and guides to sights and what's happening around the city.

GETTING AROUND Central Bologna is easy to cover **on foot;** most of the major sights are in and around Piazza Maggiore, and most of the sidewalks are famously covered. **City buses,** operated by **TPER** (Trasporto Passeggeri Emilia-Romagna; www.tper.it), leave for most points from Piazza Nettuno or Piazza Maggiore in the city center and the train station. You can buy tickets at one of many booths and *tabacchi* in Bologna, or use machines on the buses. Tickets cost 1.50€ from a machine at stops or on the bus (exact change required), or 1.30€ if you buy in advance from a *tabacchi,* and are valid for 1 hour. A **day-ticket** valid until midnight on the day of validation cost 5€ and a **city pass**—a single

Public Indecency

Bologna's famous **Fontana di Nettuno** (Neptune Fountain) was designed in 1566 by a Belgian named Giambologna (the Italians altered his name), who gave the naked sea god many rippling muscles and surrounded him with erotic cherubs and sirens spouting water from their breasts. When the papal legate who occupied the Palazzo d'Accursio opposite protested that the spectacle was indecent, Giambologna got his revenge: If you approach the statue from its rear right side, you'll notice that the left arm is positioned in such a way to suggest an indecently large . . . well, walk around the statue and see for yourself.

ticket that allows 10 rides—costs 12€. Once on board, you must validate your ticket or you'll be fined up to 150€.

Taxis are on 24-hour radio call at ✆ **051-356455** (Cooperativa Taxisti Bolognesiare) or ✆ **051-534141** (Consorzio Autonomo Taxisti). The meter starts at 3.10€ and goes up 1.05€ to 1.15€ per kilometer.

Exploring Bologna

A huge statue of a virile Neptune presides over the center of Bologna, facing the sweeping expanse of **Piazza Maggiore,** surrounded by crenellated 12th- and 13th-century *palazzi* and the enormous **Basilica di San Petronio.** Most of the city's sights are within an easy walk from the piazza. Before you set out, take a look at one of the more intriguing presences, the Palazzo di Rei Enzo, on the northeast side. Enzo (1218–1272) was king of Sardinia and the illegitimate son of German Emperor Frederick II. The papal-supporting Guelphs defeated the Ghibellines, who supported the Holy Roman Empire. Enzo, aligned with the Ghibellines, was imprisoned in this grim-looking palace until his death 23 years later. He didn't exactly languish in a dungeon—he was known for his lavish feasts, romantic conquests, and a foiled escape attempt when his blonde hair, protruding from a basket, proved a dead giveaway.

Local appetizers at a market in Bologna.

Basilica di San Domenico ★★

CHURCH Spanish-born St. Dominic, founder of the Dominican order and patron saint of astronomers, lived only 3 years in

HOTELS
Albergo delle Drapperie **13**
Alberta D Bed and Breakfast **22**
Art Hotel Commercianti **18**
Art Hotel Orologio **20**
Hotel Accademia **8**
Hotel Metropolitan **5**
Hotel Porta San Mamolo **25**
Hotel Roma **19**
Hotel Touring **26**

RESTAURANTS
All'Osteria Bottega **21**
Caminetto d'Oro **6**
Casa Monica **24**
Drogheria della Rosa **28**
Gelatauro **29**
Il Rovescio **23**
Montegrappa da Nello **4**
Trattoria Anna Maria **9**
Trattoria dal Biassanot **7**

ATTRACTIONS
Basilica di San Domenico **27**
Basilica di San Petronio **16**
Basilica di Santo Stefano **14**
Fontana di Nettuno **17**
Le due Torri **12**
Museo Civico Medievale **3**
Museo d'Arte Moderna di Bologna (MAMbo) **1**
Museo per la Memoria di Uscita **2**
Palazzo dell'Archiginnasio **15**
Pinacoteca Nazionale di Bologna **10**
San Giacomo Maggiore (Church of St. James) **11**

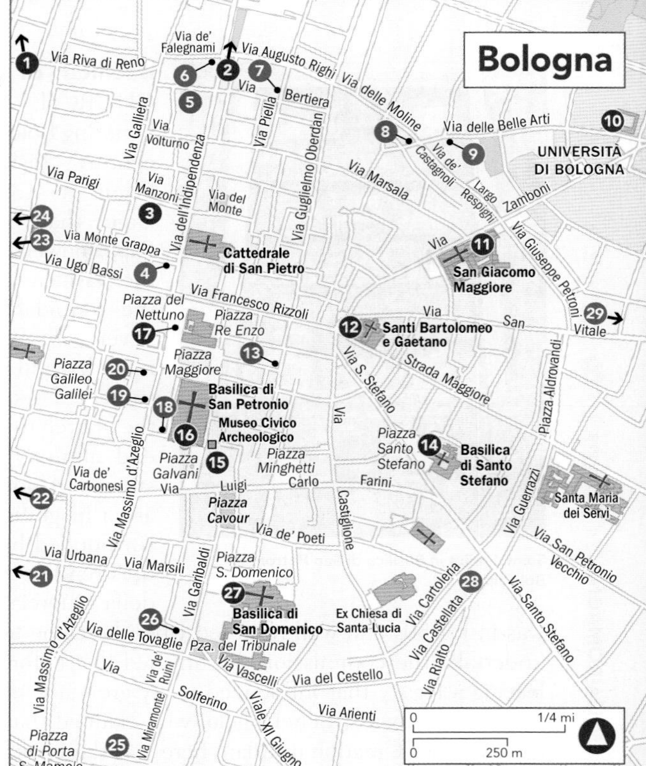

Bologna, but he rests forever here in a shrine designed by the 13th century's greatest sculptor, Nicola Pisano. Raised in wealth, Dominic aligned himself with the poor as a young student. To feed the starving, he sold his belongings, including his manuscripts, saying, "Would you have me study off these dead skins, when men are dying of hunger?" In Bologna he encouraged his followers "to have charity, to guard their humility, and to make their treasure out of poverty." The saint traveled from one end of Europe to the other before dying in 1221 on a bed of sackcloth; now he lies beneath elaborate carvings depicting his colorful life, the work of Arnolfo di Cambio. In the 15th century Nicolo di Bari added a canopy, carved with images of saints and evangelists, and was so proud of his work that he changed his name to Nicolo di Arca. A young Michelangelo, arriving in Bologna in 1495 when his patrons, the Medici, were expelled from Florence, added transcendent renderings of two other Bologna saints, Petronius and Proculus (who appears to be the prototype for his "David"). Bologna-born Guido Reni topped off the shrine in 1615 with a ceiling fresco depicting Dominic entering heaven.

Piazza San Domenico 13. ✆ **051-6400411.** Free. Mon–Sat 9am–noon and 3:30–6pm; Sun 3:30–5pm. Bus: A, 16, 30, 38, 39, 59.

Saints' relics in Basilica di San Petronio, Bologna.

Basilica di San Petronio ★ CHURCH The massive church honoring Bologna's patron, the 5th-century bishop Petronio, was begun in 1390, designed to be larger than St. Peter's in Rome. Papal powers cut off funding and the basilica remains unfinished—the formidable brick walls were never sheathed in marble as intended and transepts are severely truncated (look down either side of the church to see where extensions end abruptly in the surrounding streets). Among the few flourishes are a magnificent central doorway surrounded by Old Testament figures rendered in marble by Jacopo della Quercia of Siena. The artist was in his 50s and well-regarded when he came to Bologna in 1425 to undertake the commission; he finished just before his death in 1438, leaving a legacy that influenced many great artists of the Renaissance. Among them was Michelangelo, who claimed that della Quercia's rendering of the Creation of Adam here was the inspiration for his Genesis in the Sistine Chapel.

In the **Cappella Bolognini,** the fourth on the left as you enter, Giovanni da Modena painted a fresco cycle between 1408 and 1420 depicting scenes from the life of Petronio. Scenes of Hell from Dante's Inferno include a startling depiction of Satan eating and excreting doomed souls and Mohammed being devoured by devils in Hell (Al-Qaida operatives and other terrorists have twice in recent years tried to blow up the church in retaliation for the alleged defamation). The stark interior is enlivened ever so slightly at noon when a shadow indicating the day of the year makes an appearance on a meridian line in the left aisle; designed by Bologna's famed 17th-century astronomer Giovanni Domenico Cassini, the world's longest sundial stretches for 70m (231 ft.).

Piazza Maggiore. www.basilicadisanpetronio.it. ✆ **051-225442.** Free; 2€ for Cappella Bolognini. Daily 7:45am–1pm and 3–6pm. Bus: A, 11, 13, 14, 17, 18, 19, 20, 25.

Basilica di Santo Stefano ★★ CHURCH Bologna's most storied religious site is actually seven churches, a stone maze of medieval apses, romantic porticos, and courtyards awash in legend. Petronio, the 5th-century bishop of Bologna, allegedly founded the church on the remains

Le Due Torri, near Piazza Maggiore.

of a Roman temple to the earth goddess Isis. He was originally laid to rest here in the **Church of the Sepulcher**, where pregnant Bolognese women would circle his tomb 33 times—once for every year of Christ's life—stopping at every turn to crawl through a low door to say a prayer before the saint's remains (his body has been since been reunited with his head in the Basilica di San Petronio). The mothers-to-be moved on to the **Church of the Trinity** to pray before a fresco depicting a very pregnant Madonna stroking her belly. The **Church of Vitale and Agricola** is devoted to two other popular Bolognese saints and the city's first Christian martyrs, the 4th-century nobleman Agricola and his devoted slave; a cross near the tomb is said to be the one Agricola was holding when he was crucified, though it dates from much later. Similarly, a marble basin in the **Cortile di Pilato** (Courtyard of Pilate), alleged to be the one in which Pontius Pilate washed his hands after condemning Christ to death, actually dates to the 8th century; a statue atop a nearby column pays homage to the rooster who crowed three times when Peter denied knowing Jesus. It's said that Dante used to sit in the Romanesque **cloister** and reflect during his exile in Bologna. Look at the carved capitals atop the pillars, with their grotesque imagery of swiveling heads and men crushed beneath boulders—perhaps Dante found inspiration here for the hellish scenes of the *Divine Comedy.*

Via Santo Stefano 24. www.abbaziasantostefano.it. ✆ **051-223256.** Free. Daily 9am–noon and 3:30–6:30pm. Bus: 11, 13, 90, 96.

Le Due Torri ★★ MONUMENT/MEMORIAL It's been estimated that in the 12th and 13th centuries as many as 100 stone towers rose above the rooftops of Bologna, reaching heights of 100m (330 ft.). They were probably built as places of refuge and for offensive purposes and implied no small amount of wealth, since it took as long as 10 years and enormous expense to erect such towers, which required successively thinner layers of stone and masonry on the upper levels. Some 20 towers remain, and the most famous are these two slender medieval skyscrapers that lean tipsily but poetically just east of Piazza Maggiore. The **Garisenda** rises 49m (162 ft.) and leans about 3m (10 ft.) from perpendicular; the **Asinelli** stands 102m (334 ft.) tall and inclines almost 2.5m (8 ft.). Garisenda is off limits, but a climb up Asinelli's 500 steps reveals Bologna's finest aerial panorama, a sea of red-tile roofs and the green hills beyond.

Piazza di Porta Ravegnana. 3€. Daily Apr–Sept 9am–7pm; Oct 9am–6pm; Nov–Mar 9am–5pm. Last entry 20 min. before closing. Bus: 11, 13, 14, 19, 25, 27.

Museo Civico Medievale ★ MUSEUM Treasures of Middle Ages Bologna collected in the salons of the magnificently medieval Palazzo Ghisilardi include rare illuminated manuscripts and a bronze statue of Pope Boniface VIII that Manno Bandini da Siena crafted in 1302 on behalf of the city to thank the pontiff for stepping in to resolve some particularly nasty local disputes. Most riveting are a courtesan's shoes and other commonplace artifacts of everyday life in the Middle Ages. Ordinary funeral slabs provide such telling glimpses as a relief of a supine professor with his hands resting on a book, as if he has fallen asleep while reading, while statues show off the haircuts and clunky headgear of the times. With a little imagination it's easy to think these men and women are accompanying you on your wanderings through the loggias and squares of what is one of Italy's most intact medieval cities.

Palazzo Ghisilardi, Via Manzoni 4. www.museibologna.it/arteanticaen. ✆ **051-2193930.** 5€ adults, 3€ students and children 15–17, free for children 14 and under. Tues–Fri 10am–3pm; Sat–Sun and holidays 10am–6:30pm. Bus: A, 11, 20, 27, 28.

Museo d'Arte Moderna di Bologna (MAMbo) ★ MUSEUM This is the city's showcase for the avant-garde, with an emphasis on post–World War II art. The standout is the collection of works by Bolognese artist Giorgio Morandi (1890–1964), who once said, "What interests me most is expressing what's in nature, in the visible world"—an understatement given his deceptively straightforward still lifes, which seem almost abstract in their minimalism. Morandi's studio has been reconstructed here, and you can also visit his apartment at Via Fondazza 36 (✆ **051-649-6653;** by appointment; free admission), converted to stark galleries where his personal effects and the vases, utensils, and other objects he painted are on view. In the larger museum, another standout piece is Renato Guttuso's "I Funerali di Togliatti" (1972), awash in red flags, which depicts the funeral of the leader of the communist party, surrounded by images of other left-wing luminaries.

Via Don Minzoni 14. www.mambo-bologna.org, ✆ **051-6496611.** 6€ adults, 4€ students and children 6–17, free for children 5 and under. Tues, Wed, and Sun 10am–6pm; Thurs–Sat 10am–7pm. Bus: A, 11, 20, 27, 28.

Museo per la Memoria di Uscita ★★ MUSEUM In this haunting installation, artist Christian Boltanski commemorates the crash of a Bologna–Palermo flight off the eponymous Sicilian island on June 27, 1980, with wreckage of the DC-9 and lighting and sound effects. Victims are commemorated with 81 lights blinking off and on against the black ceiling while from 81 speakers come snippets of ordinary conversation. Most effective of all is the shattered aircraft, allegedly shot down by an Italian military missile when it was mistaken for a Libyan spy plane. The incident was the subject of an extensive cover-up and investigation.

Via di Saliceto 3/22. www.museomemoriaustica.it. ✆ **051-377680.** Free. Fri–Sun 10am–6pm.

Palazzo dell'Archiginnasio ★★ HISTORIC SITE It's no accident that one of the grander buildings of Bologna University, completed in 1563, is adjacent to the basilica of San Petronio. Pope Pius IV commissioned a central hall to house the university faculties on this site, in order to prevent the basilica from expanding and surpassing St. Peter's in Rome in size. Corridors and staircases decorated with the family crests lead to the **Teatro Anatomico,** a handsome lecture hall paneled in spruce where tiers of stiff wooden benches surround a marble slab. The Spellati, two skinless bodies carved in wood, support a canopy above the lecturer's chair; Apollo, god of medicine, gazes down from the ceiling; and statues of Hippocrates and other august physicians line walls. A curious statue of a physician holding a nose pays homage to Gaspare Tagliacozzi, a pioneer of rhinoplasty (aka "nose job"), a procedure that was much in demand in an era when noses were routinely cut off for punishment or revenge. The most looming presence, though, is a secret panel behind which sat a church inquisitor, spying on classes to make sure procedures did not waiver from church protocol for cadavers—all organs had to remain *in situ* and intact, ready for Judgment Day.

Piazza Galvani. www.archiginnasio.it. ✆ **051-276811.** 3€. Mon–Fri 10am–6pm; Sat 10am–7pm; Sun 10am–2pm. Bus: A or 29B.

Pinacoteca Nazionale di Bologna ★★ MUSEUM Beginning in the late 18th century, the former St. Ignatius monastery began to house altar pieces and other works gathered from religious institutions throughout Bologna. The collection grew considerably after 1815 when many works the French had carted off to the Louvre were returned to Bologna after the fall of Napoleon. Among the great works is Raphael's "St. Cecilia in Ecstasy" (Gallery 15), in which the saint, patron of music, is portrayed holding a lute with other instruments strewn at her feet, rapturously listening to a heavenly choir. The museum's emphasis is on works by Emilian and Bolognese artists. Guido Reni (1575–1642), who was born and is buried in Bologna, dominates Gallery 24 with his "Massacre of the Innocents," a terrifying visualization of scripture in which two muscular, knife-wielding soldiers set upon a group of screaming women and children. An especially amiable presence is that of Bologna's own Carracci family in Gallery 23. The three artists—brothers Agostino and Annibale and their cousin Lodovico—opened a famous academy in Bologna in the 1580s. Lodovico is better known as a teacher than as an artist. Agostino's masterpiece is "The Communion of St. Jerome," but the work for which he became best known was "I Modi" (The Way), a highly erotic series of engravings. His brother Annibale was the greater and more passionate painter, as is clear in his darkly moving "Mocking of Christ."

Via delle Belle Arti 56. www.pinacotecabologna.beniculturali.it. ✆ **051-4209411.** 6€ adults, 3€ ages 18–25, free for children 17 and under. Tues–Wed 9am–1:30pm, Thurs–Sun 2pm–7pm. Bus: 20, 28, 36, 37, 89, 93, 94, 99 (to Porta San Donato).

San Giacomo Maggiore (Church of St. James) ★ CHURCH Members of Bologna's most powerful 15th-century family are laid to rest in the **Cappella Bentivoglio.** Their likenesses appear in frescoes by Lorenzo Costa, who came to Bologna in the 1480s before moving on to Mantua (see p. 488), where he achieved his greatest fame. "Madonna Enthroned" is an especially telling window into the lives of the family, who were continually plotting and plotted against and were finally expelled from Bologna under papal edict. Giovanni II Bentiviglio, who was eventually excommunicated and imprisoned in Rome, kneels with his wife next to the Madonna, as his children look on, the lot of them giving thanks for the discovery of a conspiracy to overthrow them.

A Little-Known Treasure

Nicolo dell'Arca, famous for his carvings on Bologna's tomb of St. Dominic, crafted another lesser-known but delightful work in the Church of Santa Maria della Vita, just off Piazza Maggiore at Via Clavature 8. His Compianto sul Cristo Mortois a set of life-size terracotta figures taking Christ from the cross; the expressions on the faces of the lamenters are etched in grief, and the grouping is one of the most humane and moving religious images you'll encounter—even though they're clumsily shored up with wood to prevent earthquake damage. The chapel with the work is open Tuesday through Sunday 10am to 6:30pm), and admission is 3€.

"Triumph of Death" shows a ghastly procession in which death, represented by a scythe-wielding skeleton, is seated on a chariot drawn by oxen. Anton Galeazzo Bentivoglio, who fell out of favor with the papacy and was beheaded in 1435, lies in a tomb designed by Jacopo della Quercia. For an eerie thrill, follow the left-side chapels about halfway down until you come to a terrifyingly realistic-looking effigy of the corpse of Christ, encased in glass and complete with lash marks, oozing wounds, and plenty of blood.

Piazza Rossini, Via Zamboni. ✆ **051-225970.** Free. Daily 7:30am–12:30pm and 3:30–6:30pm (from 8:30am Sat and Sun). Bus: C.

Where to Stay

Bologna hosts four to six major trade fairs a year, during which times hotel room rates rise dramatically. You'll save a lot of money if you choose another time to visit (fair dates vary yearly; check with the tourist office). Bologna has a booming bed-and-breakfast scene, as well as many short-term rental apartments. A good place to browse offerings is **Airbnb.com**.

An important note on driving and parking: Parts of central Bologna (Via Ugo Bassi, Via Rizzoli, and Via Indipendenza) are closed to cars almost entirely, and large parts of the central city are entirely off-limits to traffic on Sundays, when you will have to park outside the center. Other areas are closed to cars without special permits from 7am to 8pm daily (including Sun and holidays). If your hotel is in a limited traffic zone, you will be allowed to drive in to unload your bags, but only if you've first registered with the police. When booking a room, present your car registration number, which the hotel will then provide to the police to ensure that you are not fined for driving in a restricted area. If you're planning to drive into Bologna, ask about these restrictions when booking, and also ask where to find nearby parking facilities. Best yet, come to this easily walkable city without a car.

MODERATE

Art Hotel Commercianti ★★ You can't stay any closer to San Petronio than this atmosphere-rich *palazzo*—in the best rooms and suites you can lie in bed, sit on a leafy terrace, or even soak in a deep tub while admiring the church's exquisite brickwork and statuary. Exposed timbers and fresco fragments lend a medieval aura to the decor, though many of the furnishings are plush and contemporary, with comfy armchairs and couches that invite you to relax after forays to the surrounding sights. In the lower-level breakfast room, a morning buffet is served beneath vaulted arches that show off the hotel's 13th-century origins.

Via de' Pignattari 11. www.art-hotel-commercianti.it. ✆ **051-7457511.** 34 units. 140€–185€ double, includes breakfast. Parking 28€ per day. Bus: 11, 13, 20, 30. **Amenities:** Bar; babysitting; bikes; room service; Wi-Fi (free).

Art Hotel Orologio ★★ This tall, narrow old house has been an inn for a couple of centuries and takes its name from the adjoining clock tower. The comfy surroundings have more nooks and crannies than the surface of Mars, and no two of the traditionally furnished guest rooms are the same. Most rooms are done in soothing, deep-hued wall coverings, and many have nice touches like little writing nooks. The higher you get, the more likely your room or suite has a glimpse of nearby Piazza Maggiore, or at least a tower and dome or two. Most of the sights and the lively market streets of the Quadrilatero (see below) are just steps away.

Via 4 Novembre 10. www.art-hotel-orologio.it. ✆ **051-7457411.** 33 units. 110€–152€ double, includes breakfast. Parking 28€ per day. Bus: 11, 13, 20, 30. **Amenities:** Bar; room service; Wi-Fi (free).

Hotel Metropolitan ★★★ This stylish haven is just a few steps off Via Indipendenza but a world removed, an oasis of calm and comfort. Soothing whites and neutral shades offset Indonesian antiques and other Asian pieces in the lobby and breakfast room and extend to the contemporary guest rooms upstairs. All rooms have large mosaic-tiled bathrooms, many have small sitting rooms, and several have terraces. In addition to a rooftop terrace, five airy, two-room suites open off a leafy roof garden planted with olive trees; they're some of the most restful accommodations in the city center. Piazza Maggiore and most city sights are an easy walk away. The hotel also rents out modern and well-equipped apartments near Piazza Maggiore; rates range from 100€ to 400€ per day depending on the size of the apartment and time of year.

Via Dell'Orso 6. www.hotelmetropolitan.com. ✆ **051-229393.** 50 units. 120€–170€ double, includes breakfast. Parking 20€ a day. Bus: A, 11, 20, 27, 28. **Amenities:** Restaurant; bar; babysitting; room service; Wi-Fi (free).

Hotel Porta San Mamolo ★★ Most of these rather romantic rooms surround a leafy courtyard, bringing the sense of a country retreat to the heart of Bologna—Piazza Maggiore is only a 15-minute walk away. Nice-sized, tile-floored rooms are done in soothing creams and warm golds and reds, with furnishings that are vaguely Florentine in style and offset with exposed beams, vaulted ceilings, and other architectural details. A few rooms have large terraces; others open directly into the garden. Breakfast is served in an airy, greenhouse-like pavilion that seems summery even during the gray Bolognese winter.

Vicolo del Falconi 6–8. www.hotel-portasanmamolo.it. ✆ **051-583056.** 43 units. 119€–172€ double, includes breakfast. Parking 20€ per day. Bus: 29B or 52. **Amenities:** Bikes; room service; Wi-Fi (free).

Hotel Roma ★★ What this old Bologna fixture lacks in chic style it makes up for with plenty of old-school charm and hospitality and a wonderful location just off Piazza Maggiore. Downstairs lounges and a small bar are gracious and welcoming, and the no-nonsense guest rooms upstairs are large and pleasantly done with brass beds and gleaming wooden floors; many open to small terraces overlooking the surrounding streets, and many of the large tiled bathrooms are windowed. The excellent in-house restaurant, **C'era Una Volta**—which translates as "Once Upon a Time"—offers Bolognese classics served by crisply uniformed waiters.

Via Massimo d'Azeglio 64. www.hotelroma.biz. ✆ **051-226322.** 86 units. From 120€ double, includes breakfast. Parking 20€ per day. Bus: 11, 13, 20, 30. **Amenities:** Restaurant; bar; bikes; room service; Wi-Fi (free).

Hotel Touring ★★ A rooftop terrace overlooking tile roofs and domes to the hills that surround Bologna is perfect for a few hours of quiet relaxation, an *aperitivo,* or even a soak in the hot tub. Guest rooms are all geared to quiet comfort, done in soothing cream colors and functional furnishings, while those on the third and floors have a great amenity: city-view terraces or balconies. A ground-floor reading room warmed by a fireplace is a perfect spot in which to curl up in cooler weather. Relaxed as the surroundings are, Piazza Maggiore and the main sights are an easy stroll away.

Via De' Mattuiani 1/2. www.hoteltouring.it. ✆ **051/584305.** From 130€ double, includes breakfast. **Amenities:** Bar; garage (parking 25€); Wi-Fi (free).

INEXPENSIVE

Albergo delle Drapperie ★ This centuries-old guesthouse is smack in the middle of the bustling market streets and steps from Piazza Maggiore. Top-floor rooms, the largest and best, have vaulted ceilings, wooden beams, gables, window seats that double as extra beds, and other touches. Lower-floor rooms are smaller and furnished with not much more than beds, though they're enlivened with homey iron bedsteads and the occasional fresco or coffered ceiling. You'll have to do some climbing to reach any of these rooms, as well as the lobby and breakfast room. The Drapperie also rents out apartments in a nearby building.

Via della Drapperie 5. www.albergodrapperie.com. ✆ **051-223955.** 21 units. 75€–85€ double, includes breakfast. Bus: A, 11, 20, 27, 28. **Amenities:** Wi-Fi (free).

Alberta D Bed and Breakfast ★★★ What must be some of the homiest lodgings in Bologna are scattered across two floors of a sophisticated and rambling home in a former medieval hospital. Three of the character-filled units face a tranquil inner courtyard, set up for warm-weather lounging, and three others are part of a separate, large upstairs apartment with shared kitchen (the apartment can also be rented in its entirety). Much of the furniture is antique or vintage, accented by chic accessories, and Alberta and her son, Pierfrancesco, are welcoming and helpful hosts. A filling breakfast includes Alberta's home-baked breads and cakes, homemade jams, fresh juices, and fine hams and cheeses.

Via Sant'Isaia 58. www.albertadbedandbreakfast.com. ✆ **051-333479.** 6 units. From 65€ double, includes breakfast. Bus: 21. **Amenities:** Sauna; Wi-Fi (free).

Hotel Accademia ★ The neighborhood is a bit scruffy, but one of the few hotels in the university district is surrounded by lively clubs, bars, and affordable student-oriented *osterie*. Large guest rooms have high ceilings and are spiffily up to date, with polished wooden floors, blond furniture, muted colors, and shiny bathrooms—many with that ever-so-rare fixture in less-expensive Italian hotels, a bathtub. The colorful street life can be a late-night curse—ask for a room facing the quiet courtyard in back.

Via delle Belle Arte 6. www.hotelaccademia.com. ✆ **051-232318.** 28 units. 100€–120€ double, includes breakfast. Parking 15€ per day. Bus: A, 11, 20, 27, 28. **Amenities:** Bikes; Wi-Fi (free).

Where to Eat

If there's one city in Italy where you really should indulge your appetite, it's Bologna. As capital of Italy's most productive agricultural region, Bologna has been a food center for centuries. Specialties include locally raised beef, exquisitely cured meats, fresh pastas, truffles, and hearty sauces—far more than just the rich meat sauce or the Americanized sandwich meat that was named after the city.

If you've got room left after dinner, a favorite Bologna post-prandial attraction is **Gelatauro,** Via San Vitale 98 (www.gelatauro.com; ✆ **051-230049;** Mon 9am–8pm, Tues–Thurs 8:30am–11pm, Fri–Sat 8:30am–midnight, Sun 9:30am–11pm), run by three brothers and known for its organic gelato, including a divine concoction made from Sicilian oranges.

EXPENSIVE

Caminetto d'Oro ★★ BOLOGNESE/ITALIAN Despite the sleekly contemporary appearance of the formal dining room and a more casual bistro to one side, the Carrati family has been feeding Bologna for 80 years, from premises that were once a bakery. A decades-old oven is still used to bake their own delicious breads, which are all made, along with the pasta, using wheat flour from a mill near Modena. The *tagliatelle al ragu* here is renowned—and a favorite of the many performers and theatergoers from the nearby Arena del Sole. This is also the best place in town for a steak; the T-bones from local Romagnola cattle are seared on soapstone.

Via de'Falegnami 4. www.caminettodoro.it. ✆ **051-263494.** Main courses 10€–22€. Mon–Sat 12:30–2:30pm and 7:30–10:30pm. Bus: C.

Montegrappa da Nello ★★ BOLOGNESE This Bologna institution occupies several cozily paneled subterranean rooms just off Piazza Maggiore. Crisply uniformed waiters who seem to have been here since the place began serving in 1948 will lead you through the specialties, which include the house signature dish, *tortellini Montegrappa,* served in a cream-and-meat sauce. *Funghi porcini* and truffles appear in many of the classics, including a fragrant veal scallopine in truffle sauce. The kitchen also prepares daily specials with some surprising variations of Bolognese standards, such as spinach tortellini with chicken filling. Meals should begin with a platter of buttery prosciutto and end with a selection of cheeses, all washed down with one of the fine wines from local vineyards. Forgo dining on the small terrace in the dreary lane out front and enjoy the ambience in the cheerful rooms downstairs; to ensure a table down there, reserve for dinner.

Via Montegrappa 2. www.ristorantedanello.com. ✆ **051-236331.** Main courses 10€–17€. Daily noon–3pm and 7–11:30pm. Closed 1 week in Jan or Feb and all of Aug. Bus: A, 11, 20, 27, 28.

MODERATE

Casa Monica ★★ BOLOGNESE/VEGETARIAN Tucked away in what looks like a converted garage at the western edge of the historic center is this pleasant, low-key dining room, an oasis of calm and refinement. Deep rose hues and warm lamplight give the contemporary surroundings a welcoming glow, and the cuisine might be a sought-after break from heavier Bolognese fare. Many choices are vegetarian, including creamy risottos and an airy flan *di zucca* (squash), and several main courses are fish. Even the desserts are deceptively light. This transporting spot is only a 15-minute walk or a short cab or bus ride away from Piazza Maggiore.

Via San Rocco 16. www.casamonica.it. ✆ **051-522522.** Main courses 10€–18€. Daily 7:30–11pm. Bus: 13 or 96.

Drogheria della Rosa ★★★ BOLOGNESE/ITALIAN This former apothecary looks much as it always has, except that now wine bottles are mixed in among the old-fashioned jars on the wooden shelves. Just as the premises once dispensed medicines, chef/owner Emanuele Addone dishes out down-to-earth Bolognese cooking, with an emphasis on market-fresh ingredients. There's no menu, but a waiter, often Emanuele himself, will guide you through the daily offerings and suggest wines to match. A meal usually begins with a plate of prosciutto and a glass of Prosecco. Tortellini are stuffed with zucchini blossoms or eggplant puree. Filet mignon is roasted to perfection and drizzled with balsamic vinegar from Modena; guinea fowl is done beautifully with a honey sauce. Desserts, including a mascarpone with chocolate shavings, are sumptuous, but leave a bit of room—some of the best gelato in Bologna is dispensed around the corner at **La Sorbetteria Castiglione,** at Via Castiglione 44.

Via Cartoleria 10. www.drogheriadellarosa.it. ✆ **051-222529.** Main courses 9€–18€. Mon–Sat 12:30–3pm and 8–10:30pm. Closed Aug 10–27 and 1st week of Jan. Bus: C, 11, 13.

Il Rovescio ★ BOLOGNESE/VEGETARIAN The name of this rustic-looking little room just off bar- and *osterie*-lined Via Pratello translates roughly as "upside down" or "backwards," and the concept applies to some unusual takes on traditional Bolognese cuisine. All the food is locally sourced, and the menu changes frequently to reflect what's fresh in season and, a real rarity in Bologna, often includes many vegetarian choices—grilled radicchio on a bed of polenta, say, or crepes filled with caramelized squash. Meat presentations, such as little ginger-laced meatballs on a bed of pureed peas, can be surprising, too. Rovescio keeps very late hours, making it a good choice for night-owl diners. It also operates a **bio-pizzeria** next door, where only organically grown ingredients are used in the kitchen.

Via Pietralata 28. ✆ **051-523545.** Main courses 10€–18€. Daily 7pm–3am. Bus: C, 11, 13.

Trattoria dal Biassanot ★★★ EMILIAN The wood beams, lace tablecloths, warm service, and other grace notes of this welcoming bistro (the name roughly means "night owl") do justice to the expertly prepared Bolognese classics that emerge from the kitchen. Light-as-a-feather *tagliatelle* with Bolognese sauce has a reputation as one of the best in a city that's famous for the dish, but all of the handmade pastas and succulent sauces are excellent; even the bread is housemade and delicious. Put yourself in the hands of the kitchen and opt for the very reasonably priced tasting menu, wine included. After a meal, walk down Via Piella to see one of Bologna's lesser-known but more intriguing sights, the **Finestra,** a shuttered window that surprisingly opens to a view over a canal, one of many that once flowed through the city.

Via Piella 16a. www.dalbiassanot.it. ✆ **051-230644.** Main courses 8€–15€; fixed-price menu 25€. Tues–Sat noon–3pm and 7–11pm, Sun noon–3pm. Closed Aug. Bus: 19, 27, 94.

INEXPENSIVE

All'Osteria Bottega ★★★ BOLOGNESE/ITALIAN In this unassuming storefront, the simple tables are covered with butcher paper, and pride of place belongs to the bright red meat slicer and the meats and cheeses on display. These find their way into *affetati misti* and delicious pastas, followed by roast rabbit and other hearty main courses. Owner Danielle Minarelli is on hand to enthuse about the daily offerings and will guide you through one of your most memorable meals in Italy. Reservations are recommended, especially for dinner.

Via Santa Caterina 51. ✆ **051-585111.** Main courses 8€–14€. Tues–Sat 12:30–2:30pm and 8–10:30pm. Bus: 11 or 13.

Trattoria Anna Maria ★ BOLOGNESE Photographs of Sophia Loren, Marcello Mastroianni, and legions of other celebrities line the walls of these high-ceilinged, welcoming rooms, but everyone in Bologna knows that the real star is Anna Maria, who has been serving her freshly made pasta for 30 years. *Tortellini in brodo,* parcels of pasta filled with minced pork and floating in chicken broth, and *taglietelle* with a hearty Bolognese sauce are her signature dishes, but the lasagnas are memorable, too. Anna Maria will probably find her way to your table at some point during your meal to make sure you've eaten every bite, but that won't be an issue.

Via Bella Arti 17/A. www.trattoriannamaria.com. ✆ **051-266894.** Main courses 10€–18€. Tues–Sat noon–3pm and 7–11pm. Bus: 11, 13, 20, 29B, 30, 38, 39.

Shopping

The shopping delights of Bologna revolve around—what else?—food.

The **Quadrilatero** is the gastronome epicenter of Bologna, where you can snack your way through its venerable food shops on a warren of lanes behind Piazza Maggiore. At **Tamburi,** one of Italy's most lavish food shops, Via Caprarie 1 (tamburini.com; ✆ **051-232-226**), a selection of pastas, meats and fish, soups and salads, vegetables, and sweets is accompanied by 200 wines by the glass. **La Baita,** Via Pescherie Vecchie 3A (✆ **051-223-940**), lets you choose from a dizzying selection of hams and cheeses and enjoy them in a busy mezzanine dining room. **Eataly** (Via degli Orefici 19; www.eataly.it; ✆ **051-095-2820**), Bologna's outpost of the chain that includes gourmet shops in New York and Chicago, sells cookbooks as well as cheese, hams, and other products and wine, consumed picnic-style at indoor and outdoor tables. The covered marketplace across the way has been converted into the **Mercato di Mezzo** (Via Clavature; ✆ **051-232919)** and houses small bars and food stands; in the evenings many offer free snacks to accompany drinks.

Osteria del Sole, Vicolo Ranocchi 1D (osteriadelsole.it; ✆ **348-225-6887;** closed Sun), is an invitingly rundown room with a novel twist on the bring-your-own policy—you bring the food, they supply the wine for 2€ a glass. Good places to shop for your DIY meal are the enticing **Salumeria Simoni,** Via Drapperie 5/2A (www.salumeriasimoni.it; ✆ **051-231-880**), and **Enoteca Italiana,** Via Marsala 2/B (www.enoteca italiana.it; ✆ **051-235-989**)—at both you can dine well on cheese and meat platters, sandwiches, and other dishes You might want to throw in a pastry from **Atti,** Via Caprarie 7 (www.paoloatti.com; ✆ **051-220425**).

Bologna's central food market, **Mercato delle Erbe,** is a few blocks west of this area, at Via Ugo Bassi 25 (www.mercatodelleerbe.it); it's open Monday to Wednesday 7am to 1:15pm and 5:30 to 7:30pm, Thursday and Saturday 7am to 1:15pm, and Friday 7am to 1:15pm and 4:30 to 7:30pm.

Maybe it's not unexpected that Bologna has many famous chocolatiers. **Majani,** Via de' Carbonesi 5 (✆ **051-234302**), claims to be Italy's oldest sweets shop, making confections since 1796. **Roccati,** Via

A BREAK FROM THE ART circuit

Modena, 40km (25 miles) NW of Bologna, is equally well known for its elegant marble cathedral, balsamic vinegar, and cars. The prosperous little city is in the center of what's known as La Terra dei Motori, the "Land of Motors." A car enthusiast who's been patiently traipsing through museums and churches might be delighted to learn that all of Italy's famed sports-car manufacturers are located here—and open to the public. It's possible to make the pilgrimage by public transport, but not easily, and you certainly couldn't do the whole circuit in a day. Besides, a car buff will probably want to rent a car anyway, right? As an alternative, **Motorstars** (motorstars.org; ✆ **059-921667**) provides a full day of touring, with transport from Bologna and lunch, for 220€.

Museo Ferrari, Via Dino Ferrari 43 (www.ferrari.com; ✆ **0536-943204**), in Maranello (18km/11 miles from central Modena), pays homage to the magnificent cars that Enzo Ferrari began turning out in 1929; vintage and current models are on display. Admission is 13€, and it's open daily May to September from 9:30am to 7pm (until 6pm Oct–Apr). Tours run at 12:30pm and 1:30pm; buy tickets in advance on the website.

Maserati, founded in Bologna in 1914, is now based in Modena, and 20 vintage models are parked permanently at the **Museo Panini** (www.paninimotormuseum.it), in the Modena suburb of Cittanova (on the SS9). Highlights include a rare Maserati Tipo 6CM from the 1930s and a Maserati A6G/54 from the 1950s. To visit you must make an appointment by written request (using a form on the website). The museum is open March to October (closed Aug), Monday to Friday from 9:30am to 12:30pm and from 3:30 to 6:30pm, and Saturday from 9:30am to 12:30pm. Admission is free.

A visit to the **Museo Lamborghini** (www.lamborghini.com; ✆ **051-681-7611**), Via Modena 12, in the company's hometown of Sant' Agata Bolognese, between Bologna and Modena, can include a tour of the factory for 40€ (students 30€). Otherwise, to see the cars and other displays, admission is 15€ (students 10€). The museum is usually open Monday to Friday 10am to 12:30pm and 1:30 to 5pm, but call ahead to confirm.

Clavature 17A (www.roccaticioccolato.com; ✆ **051-261-964**), is run by a husband-and-wife team that makes the *gianduja* (hazelnut and cognac-filled chocolate) their ancestors once concocted for the princes of Savoy.

Entertainment & Nightlife

Bologna's large student population keeps late hours in bars, clubs, and *osterie,* many clustered near the university on Via Zamboni and Via delle Belle Arti. Bolognese of all stripes, even those who plan to turn in early, stop at bars all over town for an *aperitivo,* when a glass of wine or a cocktail comes with snacks, usually served "all you can eat" buffet style.

Camera a Sud ★ Three shabby-chic rooms in the Jewish ghetto are part coffeehouse, part wine bar and late-night hangout, and popular any time of the day. Via Valdonica 5. www.cameraasud.net. ✆ **051-0951448.** Mon–Sat noon–1am, Sun 5pm–1am.

Cantina Bentivoglio ★★ You'll hear some of the best jazz in Bologna in the cellars of a 16th-century *palazzo* near the university, and select from one of the more than 500 labels that fill the wine racks. Via Mascarella 4B. www.cantinabentivoglio.it. ✆ **051-265416.** Daily 8pm–2am. Lunch Mon–Fri 12:15–2:45pm.

Le Stanze ★ Cocktails are accompanied by a lavish buffet (it comes with the cost of a drink plus 1€), but the real feast here is visual—the atmospheric premises occupy the heavily frescoed salons and 17th-century chapel of an aristocratic palace. Via del Borgo di San Pietro www.lestanzecafe.com. ✆ **051-228767.** Mon–Sat 11am–1am.

Nu Lounge Bar ★★ Hip young professionals check out each other (and themselves in the huge mirrors) while enjoying martinis under the porticos in the Quadrilatero. Via dei Musei 6. ✆ **051-222532.** Daily noon–2:30am.

Osteria de Poeti ★ Bologna's oldest *osteria*, feeding students since around 1600, not only dishes up cheap pastas and hearty *secondi* but live jazz and folk music as well, set against a mellow background of brick arches. Via Poeti 1. www.osteriadepoeti.com. ✆ **051-236166.** Tues–Fri 12:30–2:30pm and 7:30pm–2:30am, Sat–Sun 7:30pm–2:30am.

FERRARA ★★

52km (32 miles) N of Bologna, 100km (62 miles) SW of Venice

It's not that quiet, elegant Ferrara hasn't had some big moments. The powerful Este family controlled the city on the Po River for almost 4 centuries. Painters, composers, and poets came to town under their patronage and made Ferrara one of Europe's great capitals of culture. Lucrezia Borgia, notorious femme fatale of the Renaissance, arrived by ceremonial barge in 1502 to marry Prince Alfonso Este. They and the other Estes built pleasure pavilions and gardens and expanded their holdings

Ferrara by Bike

Ferrara is known in Italy as a *città della bicicletta,* because just about everyone in town, regardless of age, gets around on two wheels. The flat streets and squares lend themselves to easy pedaling, and the medieval walls are topped with trees, lawns, and a wide path that's ideal for cycling. Views of the city and surrounding farmlands are terrific, and if you want to go farther afield, well-marked bike paths lead into the Po Delta. Many hotels offer guests free use of bikes, or you can rent them from the lot outside the train station (2.50€ an hour, 10€ a day).

into the Addizione, a model city of the Renaissance crisscrossed with straight, palace-lined avenues. By the end of the 16th century, however, the Estes were gone—and Ferrara has looked pretty much the same ever since. That, of course, is its appeal. In what's essentially a time capsule, the Estes' castle and palaces and encircling walls, and proud old convents and churches are the backdrop for everyday life in an attractive provincial city.

Essentials

GETTING THERE Ferrara is on the main **train** line between Bologna and Venice, with service to and from both cities twice an hour (30–45 min. from Bologna; 1–1½ hrs. from Venice). Ravenna is an hour away, with hourly departures all day. From the train station it's an easy 20-minute walk to the Duomo, but you can also take the frequent no. 1 or 9 bus to Piazza Travaglio (1.30€; buy your ticket at the bus office inside the train station or at a tobacco shop; www.tper.it). You may also rent a **bike** at the station and get around the way most locals do (see "Ferrara By Bike," p. 361).

Cyclists on Via Giuseppe Mazzini in Ferrara.

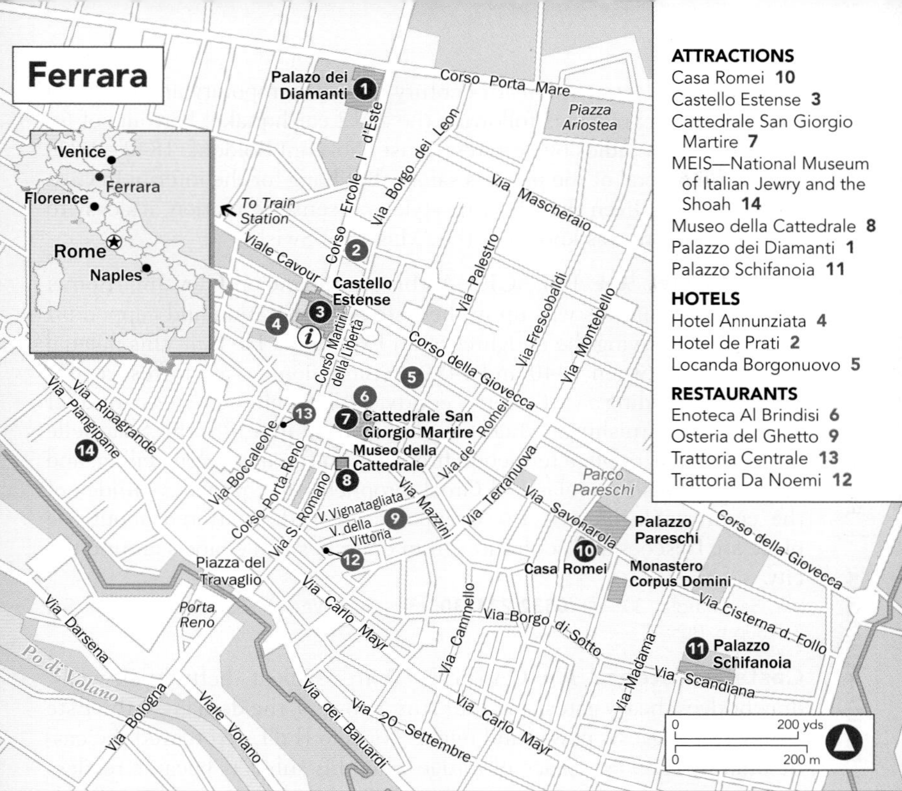

If you have a **car** and are coming from Bologna, take A13 north. From Venice, take A4 southwest to Padua and continue on A13 south to Ferrara.

VISITOR INFORMATION The helpful **tourist office** is inside the Castello Estense, Piazza del Castello (www.ferraraterraeacqua.it; ✆ **0532-299303**). It's open Monday to Saturday from 9am to 1pm and 2 to 6pm, Sunday 9:30am to 1pm and 2 to 5pm.

Exploring Ferrara

The **Castello Estense** is pretty much the center of town, with the **Cattedrale San Giorgio Martire** and twisting lanes of the medieval town just to the southeast. **Corso Ercole I d'Este,** flanked by beautiful *palazzi,* leads north into the Renaissance city and past **Palazzo dei Diamanti** to the city walls. The city's most atmospheric medieval lane is narrow, cobblestoned **Via delle Volte,** darkened with arched, upper-story passageways that once linked merchants' houses with their riverside warehouses. Renaissance-era **Palazzo Massari,** Corso Porto Mare

9, housing collections of 19th-century and contemporary art, is closed for extensive renovations following the 2012 earthquake. Portraits of *fin de siècle* society ladies by Ferrarese artist Giovanni Boldoni (1842–1931) usually fill several of the palace's salons, but hang for the interim in Castello Estense. Given their flowing style and sense of motion, it's easy to see why Boldoni was known as the "Master of Swish."

Casa Romei ★★ PALACE Ambitious financier Giovanni Romei managed to work his way up in the Este administration and capped off his rise by marrying the daughter of an Este duke. He built this palatial townhouse between 1440 and 1450, commissioning lavish frescoes for salons surrounding a vast interior courtyard. Though the Estes carted off most of the furnishings when they left Ferrara in 1598, the Sala delle Sibille, with its original terracotta fireplace, coffered wooden ceiling, and images of the sibyls (classical Greek prophetesses), provides an idea of the comfortable lifestyle the occupants enjoyed. Scattered about the place are frescoes and sculptures from churches and chapels around the city.

Via Savonarola 30. ✆ **0532-234130.** 3€. Sun–Wed 8:30am–2pm; Thurs–Sat 2–7:30pm. Bus: 11.

Castello Estense ★★ CASTLE With its moat, hefty brick walls, drawbridges, heavy gates, and four sturdy towers, the domain of the Este family still suggests power and might. Niccolò II d'Este ordered the castle built in 1385 as a place of refuge when his subjects became restless after a series of tax increases, and quite literally tore one of his officials to pieces. A long elevated gallery links the castle to the family's onetime residence, now the Palazzo Municipale, next door. Duke Niccolò d'Este III forever made the castle a place of infamy when, in 1425, he used a contrivance of mirrors to catch his 20-year-old wife, Parisina d'Este, *in flagrante delicto* with his illegitimate son, Ugolino. He promptly had the pair taken to the dungeons and beheaded; Robert Browning tells the story in his poem "My Last Duchess." (Ironically, Niccolò himself boasted of sleeping with 800 women, and a popular rhyme of the time was "left and right of the river Po, everywhere there are children by Niccolò.") Young Lucrezia Borgia, with her reputation for adultery, incest, and a poisoning or two, took up residence in 1502 as the wife of Duke Alfonso d'Este, who kept his half-brother, Giulio, in the dungeons for 53 years for plotting to overthrow him. Elderly Giulio allegedly created quite a stir when he finally emerged onto the streets of Ferrara in the clothing he had brought with him into his cell half a century before. For all their perfidy, the Estes also hosted one of the finest courts in Europe and cultivated the Renaissance arts and humanities. Their refined tastes come to the fore in the frescoed **Salone dell'Aurora** (the Salon of Dawn) and

Salone dei Giochi (the Salon of Games), and an *orangerie* that continues to flourish on terraces high above the city. Take a walk up the innovative ramplike spiral staircase ascending from the courtyard that allowed the dukes to ride their horses right up to their quarters.

Largo Castello. www.castelloestense.it. ✆ **0532-299233.** 8€ adults, 6.50€ children ages 11–18, free for ages 10 and under. Jan–May and Sept daily 9:30am–5:30pm; June daily 9:30am–1:30pm and 3–7pm; July–Aug Tues–Sun 9:30am–1:30pm and 3–7pm; Oct–Dec Tues–Sun 9:30am–5:30pm. Bus: 1, 7, 9, 11, 21.

Cattedrale San Giorgio Martire ★ CATHEDRAL The faithful did not even have to step beyond the magnificent 12th-century porch of Ferrara's cathedral to understand that salvation was a pretty dicey affair. In exquisite carvings above the entryway, the dead creep out of their tombs as an angel weighs sins and good deeds on a scale; as if to prove that the odds are against salvation, a devil mischievously tugs on the evil side so it skews toward sin. The saved, gloriously crowned and robed, proceed toward Heaven, where they are welcomed into the lap of Abraham; the naked damned slouch down to Hell to be tormented by sneering devils. In the vast interior—redone in dark baroque style after an 18th-century fire—look for a fresco by Guercino ("the squinter") portraying the martyrdom of St. Lawrence. When Roman authorities demanded that Lawrence, an early church deacon, turn over ecclesiastic treasures, he brought them the poor, saying "Behold in these poor persons the treasures which I promised to show you." As punishment Lawrence was tied to a spit and burned over a roaring fire. After the good-natured saint roasted for a time, he allegedly said, "I'm well done, turn me over," a wisecrack that has earned him a place as patron of chefs and cooks. The **cathedral museum,** housed in the former San Romano church and monastery opposite the church, is well stocked with works by Ferrara's leading 15th-century painter of the Este court, Cosmé Tura. Most arresting among them is "St. George and the Princess," an intense portrayal of Ferrara's patron saint savagely trying to do away with a dragon to save a damsel in distress. The tale was a popular part of religious tradition as well as a romantic legend of chivalry, so it may well have satisfied both the Estes' spiritual and courtly aspirations.

Piazza della Cattedrale. ✆ **0532-207449.** Church free. Mon–Sat 7:30am–noon and 3–6:30pm; Sun 7:30am–12:30pm and 3:30–7:30pm. Museum: 6€ adults, 3€ for students, children 17 and under free; 7€ joint admission with Palazzo Schifanoia. Tues–Sun 9am–1pm and 3–6pm. Bus: 11.

Palazzo dei Diamanti ★ MUSEUM The facade of the Estes' most remarkable residence comprises 8,500 spiky, diamond-shaped, white marble blocks, creating an architectural spectacle that shimmers in the light and seems to be constantly in movement. The *palazzo* stands at the

Ferrara's Piazza Trento Trieste.

intersection of two monumental avenues that were the main thoroughfares of the Addizione that Ercole d'Este laid out in the late 15th century, doubling the size of Ferrara and making the city into a Renaissance showplace. The **Pinacoteca Nazionale** occupies the first floor of the *palazzo* and provides a handy overview of the School of Ferrara, especially the trio of old masters who flourished under the Estes—Cosmé Tura, Francesco del Cossa, and Ercole de' Roberti (whose brilliance comes to light in the excellent free audio guide tour). Pride of place belongs to Tura's "Martyrdom of St. Maurelius," in which the subject, an early bishop of Ferrara, calmly kneels as his executioner swings a sword above his neck and some decidedly cheerful-looking *putti* look on from a cloud.

Corso Ercole d'Este 21. www.palazzodiamanti.it. ✆ **0532-205844** or 0532-244949. Pinacoteca 4€ adults, free for children 17 and under. Mon–Thurs 9am–1pm and 2pm–5pm, Fri 9am–2pm. Bus: 3C or 4C.

Palazzo Schifanoia ★★★ HISTORIC HOME The Estes retreated for leisure to several pleasure palaces around Ferrara, including this one enlarged by Duke Borso d'Este between 1450 and 1471. Schifanoia translates roughly as "chasing away tedium," and the concept comes to the fore in the **Salone dei Mesi (Salon of the Months),** where a mesmerizing cycle of frescoes represents the 12 months—or did, as only a few remain intact. Each is divided into three horizontal bands: The lower bands show scenes from the daily life of courtiers and people, with Duke Borso frequently making an appearance astride a horse; the middle bands illustrate signs of the zodiac; and the upper sections depict gods and goddesses associated with each sign. In this collaboration of the masters of the Ferrarese school of painting—del Cossa, de' Roberti, and Tura—characters of those distant times seem to come alive and step out of the scenes (one figure actually does, perching on the edge of the frame as if he's about to jump into the room). Men ride horses, harvesters pick grapes, women do needlework and play lutes. The artists even dug some skeletons out of the Este closet: In a mythical scene depicting Mars and Venus caught in a net as they make love, their clothing is laid beside the bed in such a way as to suggest a decapitated man and woman—a sly reference to the fate of the adulterous Ugolino and Parisina d'Este. Via Scandiana 23. ✆ **0532-244949.** 6€ adults, 3€ for students, free for 17 and under; 7€ joint admission with Museo della Cattedrale. Tues–Sun 9am–6pm. Bus: 1, 7, 9, 21.

Where to Stay

Hotel Annunziata ★★ The setting, across from Castello Estense, is medieval, and Casanova spent the night here when the place was a simple inn. But once inside the doors, you'll feel like you've been transported from old Ferrara into a Milanese showroom for contemporary style. The white color scheme strays into grays and beige here and there, even the occasional burst of red or orange, but for the most part this place is all about sleek lines, soothing neutrals, and minimalist calm, all extremely

Lucrezia Borgia, A Woman Misjudged?

With their penchant for murder, the Borgias are still one of history's most notoriously dysfunctional families, 500 years after their Renaissance heyday. Lucrezia was born into the clan in 1480, the illegitimate daughter of Cardinal Rodrigo Borgia, soon to be Pope Alexander VI. By the time she was 20, she had a child, allegedly fathered by her brother Cesare, and had been married twice—one husband fled for his life when the Pope decided Lucrezia needed to make a more politically advantageous alliance, another was strangled as he lay recovering from knife wounds (both attacks arranged by Cesare). With this sullied reputation, Lucrezia got a chilly reception when she arrived in Ferrara in 1500 as the new bride of Duke Alfonso d'Este. However, she proved herself to be a brilliant conversationalist and a patron of the arts. She is said to have carried on a passionate affair with the poet Pietro Bembo, but she was also known to be a loving wife and attentive mother. She died just before her 39th birthday, after giving birth to her fifth child.

comfortable and relaxing. In the large and bright guest rooms, the best with castle views, high-tech lighting and snowy linens contrast with wood floors and the occasional timbered ceiling, and bathrooms are luxurious. Six stylish apartments with kitchenettes are located in a 14th-century annex.

Piazza Repubblica 5. www.annunziata.it. ✆ **0532-201111.** 27 units. 100€–125€ double, includes breakfast. Bus: 1, 7, 9, 11, 21. **Amenities:** Restaurant; bar; babysitting; bikes; room service; Wi-Fi (free).

Hotel de Prati ★★ This welcoming inn is nicely appointed throughout with polished antiques and wrought-iron bedsteads in bright, quiet rooms that are enlivened with colorful paintings by local artists. Timbered beams and old archways show off the house's centuries-old origins, and the refined, old-world air extends to the gracious service provided by the de Prati family, who have been running the place for three generations. A few smaller rooms are set up for single travelers, while a suite opens to a sunny terrace overlooking the surrounding rooftops.

Via Padiglioni 5. www.hoteldeprati.com. ✆ **0532-241905.** 28 units. 95€ double, includes breakfast. Bus: Bus: 3C or 4C. **Amenities:** Bikes; Wi-Fi (free).

Locanda Borgonuovo ★★★ This lovely old house, converted from a 17th-century convent and just down a cobblestone street from the *castello,* could set the gold standard for B&Bs everywhere. The four rooms are furnished with family pieces, including some serious antiques, and share a flowery courtyard; one especially large double has an extra bed and a kitchenette. An excellent breakfast is served in the family living room, and the gracious hosts lend bikes and dispense advice about the best ways to enjoy their beloved Ferrara. They also rent a few one- and two-bedroom apartments in an adjoining building

Via Cairoli 21. www.borgonuovo.com. ✆ **0532-211100.** 75€–100€ double, includes breakfast. Bus: 4C or 7. **Amenities:** Bikes; Wi-Fi (free).

Where to Eat

You'll get a good intro to Ferrara's gastronomic pleasures on a stroll down Via Cortevecchia, a narrow brick lane near the cathedral where traditional *salumerias* such as Marchetti at no. 35 (✆ **0532-204800**) sell the city's famous *salama da suga*, handmade sausages. The food stalls of the **Mercato Comunale,** at the corner of Via Santo Stefano and Via del Mercato, are also good grazing grounds. Look for *coppia Ferrarese*, sourdough bread stretched into intertwining rolls that resemble two sets of legs (hence the name, "the couple"). In restaurants, the pasta to try is *cappellacci di zucca*—round pasta stuffed with squash, served *al burro e salvia* (with butter and sage sauce) or *al ragu* (with meat sauce).

The Jews of Ferrara

Ferrara's Jewish heritage dates to the Middle Ages, with a Jewish community flourishing here when the Este family controlled the city. The social prominence of Ferrara's 20th-century Jews and their sad fate is the subject of Giorgio Bassani's novel *The Garden of the Finzi-Contini,* brought evocatively to the screen in director Vittorio de Sica's 1970 film. Ferrara's excellent **Jewish Museum,** encompassing two synagogues in an old palazzo at Via Mazzini 95, was severely damaged in the 2012 earthquakes and has been closed ever since, with a reopening date still to be determined. Ferrara is also the future home of **MEIS—National Museum of Italian Jewry and the Shoah** (www.meisweb.it), under development in a former prison and a new pavilion at Via Piangipane 81; a small part of Ferrara's collection is on view in the complex Tuesday through Friday, 10am to 1pm and 3pm to 5pm, and Sunday, 10am to 6pm.

Enoteca Al Brindisi ★ FERRARESE It would be easy for this atmospheric little place—probably the oldest wine bar in the world, dating from 1435—to rest on its laurels. Titian was a regular, Copernicus is said to have lived upstairs while studying for his degree in 1503, and it looks like some of the dusty bottles stacked above the cramped tables have been around ever since. Locals (some of whom look like they've been around awhile, too) still pack the place, and waiters take earnest pride in recommending Italian wines, accompanied by a short menu of *cappellacci di zucca* (squash ravioli) and a few other local specialties.

Via Adelardi 11. www.albrindisi.net. ✆ **0532-471225.** Main courses 7€–10€. Daily 11am–1am. Bus: 11.

Osteria del Ghetto ★ FERRARESE/SEAFOOD From a simple storefront on the narrow cobblestone lanes of Ferrara's centuries-old Jewish ghetto, a staircase leads to two homey upstairs rooms enlivened with colorful murals. A small selection of pasta and meat dishes is available, but clearly the kitchen's passion is for fish—a fresh catch is usually on the menu, as is fried calamari and shrimp, rich fish soup, *spaghetti alle vongole,* seafood salads, and other choices to tempt you away from the region's meat-heavy staples.

Via Vittoria 26/28. www.osteriadelghetto.it. ✆ **0532–764–936.** Main courses 8€–16€. Tues–Sun 12:30–2:30pm and 7:30–10:30pm. Bus: 2.

Trattoria Centrale ★★ FERRARESE It's not the ambience that will pull you in—instead, the white walls, bright lighting, and sepia-toned photos of Ferrara landmarks provide a plain backdrop for delicious takes on local classics, usually served with a warm smile by the owner himself. Delicious, dumplinglike *cappellacci* are done just right here, and it's best to try a few of the house-made pastas in assortments that include four kinds of light-as-a-feather tortellini stuffed with meat, pumpkin, Taleggio cheese, and ricotta.

Via Boccaleone 8. ✆ **0532-470-940.** Main courses 8€–12€. Tues–Sun 12:30–2:30pm and 7:30–10:30pm.

Trattoria Da Noemi ★★ FERRARESE The surroundings date to 1400, with a pleasant old-world decor that befits the provenance and gracious service. The menu leans to Ferrarese classics—some residents say no one does them better. This is the place to become acquainted with *cappellacci di zucca*, the city's signature dish, little pockets of light egg pasta stuffed with roasted butternut squash with hints of nutmeg and parmigiano. Much of the meat-heavy *secondi* features local beef grilled over a wood fire. The house *semifreddo,* a delicious half-frozen custard with pistachio and walnuts or mint, is the perfect finish.

Via Ragno 31. www.trattoriadanoemi.it. ✆ **0532-769–070.** Main courses 8€–24€. Wed–Mon 12:15–2:30pm and 7–11pm. Bus: 2 or 11.

RAVENNA ★★

74km (46 miles) E of Bologna, 145km (90 miles) S of Venice, 130km (81 miles) NE of Florence

It's hard to believe that Ravenna was the epicenter of the Western World for a brief spell, when it was the capital of the Western Roman Empire from A.D. 402 to A.D. 476. Those rulers and the fathers of the early Christian church, and then the Goths and Byzantines who followed them, carpeted Ravenna's churches and monuments in glittering mosaics to create an artistic legacy that rivals the splendors of Venice and Istanbul. (The poet Dante, who's buried here, described Ravenna's mosaics as "the sweet color of Oriental sapphires.") Set amid the marshy landscapes of Emilia-Romagna's coastal plain, this once glamorous and powerful city is a bit off the beaten path but well worth the effort to reach.

Ravenna's Piazza del Popolo with Orologio tower and Palazzo del Governo.

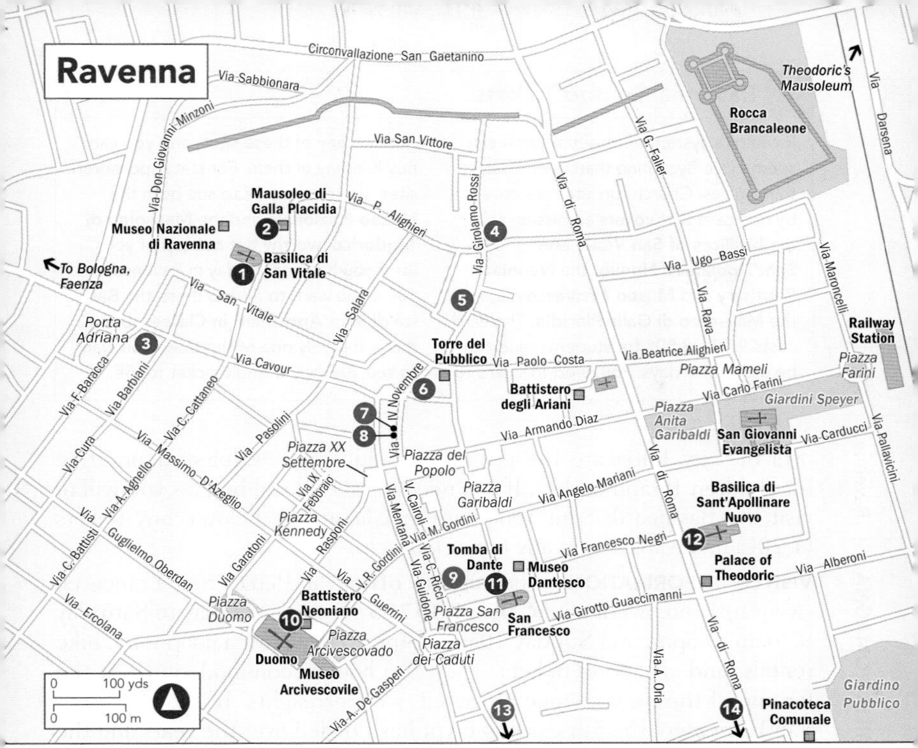

Ravenna

HOTELS

Albergo Cappello **6**
Casa Masoli **5**
Hotel Centrale Byron **8**
Hotel Diana **4**
M Club **3**

RESTAURANTS

Cà de Ven **9**
Cinema Alexander **13**
La Bella Venezia **7**

ATTRACTIONS

Basilica di Sant'Apollinare in Classe **14**
Basilica di Sant'Apollinaire Nuovo **12**
Basilica di San Vitale **1**
Battistero Neoniano (Neonian Baptistery) and Museo Arcivescovile **10**
Dante's Tomb **11**
Mausoleo di Galla Placidia **2**

Essentials

GETTING THERE With hourly **trains** that take only 1 hour, 20 minutes from Bologna, Ravenna can easily be visited on a day trip. There's also frequent service from Ferrara (1 hr., 15 min.), which has connections to Venice. The train station is a 10-minute walk from the center at Piazza Fernini (✆ **892021**).

If you have a **car** and are coming from Bologna, head east along A14. From Ferrara, take the S16.

GETTING AROUND Ravenna operates a useful bicycle rental system; keys provided by the tourist office give you unlimited access to bikes all

Ravenna Combo Tickets

Ravenna's system of museum cards can seem more Byzantine than the mosaics themselves. Church-run sites are covered by one card that covers admission to the **basilicas of San Vitale and Sant'Apollinare Nuovo,** the **Neonian Baptistry** and **Museo Arcivescovile,** and the **Mausoleo di Galla Placidia.** The card costs 9.50€ (8.50€ for students) and can be used for 7 days. You need this card to get into any of these sites, and you can buy it at any of them. For state-sponsored sites, you can pay 8€ to see both the **Museo Nazionale** and the **Mausoleo di Teodorico** (worthy but not top of your list if you have only a day in Ravenna) or 10€ if you want to add to those the **Basilica di Sant'Apollinare in Classe**—but if this is the only one of the three you want to see, just buy a single ticket for 5€.

over the city. Rates are 10€ per day for adults and 9€ for students (free for children 10 and under). If you need to take a local **bus** (as you will to visit the Basilica di Sant'Apollinare in Classe; see below), buy tickets (1.20€) in advance from any bar or *tabacchi*.

VISITOR INFORMATION The **tourist office** at Piazza San Francesco (www.turismo.ravenna.it; ✆ **0544-35755**) is open Monday to Saturday 8:30am to 6pm, and Sunday 10am to 4pm. They offer a good map, bike rentals, and attraction tickets. They also book accommodations. At the far end of the piazza is one of the city's eeriest sights: In the church of San Francesco, the 5th-century crypt has flooded over the years and the mosaics on the submerged floor shimmer in the light (daily 8am–1pm and 4–7pm; admission is free).

Exploring Ravenna

The elegant, Venetian-looking **Piazza del Popolo** was laid out in the late 15th century, when Venice ruled the city. From here you can easily walk to all of the sights, with the exception of Sant'Apollinare in Classe, for which you'll want to take a bus or drive.

Basilica di Sant'Apollinare in Classe ★★ CHURCH What is now a landlocked suburb surrounded by pine groves about 6km (3¾ miles) south of the city was at one time the port of the capital of the Western Roman Empire. This huge 6th-century church—dedicated to St. Apollinare, the first bishop and patron of Ravenna—befits the city's onetime importance. Apollinare allegedly landed in Ravenna sometime in the 2nd century and converted the locals. In a dazzling array of brilliantly hued mosaics, he is shown in prayer, surrounded by lambs (his flock) against a gentle background of rocks, birds, and plants, including the pines that still grow outside the church. (Lord Byron used to ride here with his Ravennese mistress, Teresa Guiccioli.) Above Apollinaire is a depiction of the Transfiguration, when Christ became radiant and began shining with bright rays of light; he is represented as a golden cross on a starry blue background, while Peter, James, and John, the three disciples who were present at the event, are shown as lambs. Some especially touching mosaics on the right of the church shows three Old Testament figures who made sacrifices to God: Abel, Melchizedek, and Abraham.

Via Romea Sud 224, Classe. www.soprintendenzaravenna.beniculturali.it. ✆ **0544-473569.** 5€ adults, 2.50€ ages 18–25, free for children 17 and under. Daily 8:30am–7:30pm. Bus: 4 from rail station or Piazza Caduti (1.30€).

Basilica di Sant'Apollinare Nuovo ★★ CHURCH The church that Emperor Theodoric built in the first part of the 6th century for followers of Arianism, a Christian sect, seems to be in perpetual motion. On the left side of the nave, reserved for women, 22 female saints and martyrs approach Mary and the Christ child as they receive gifts from the three magi. On the right side, 26 male martyrs led by St. Martin approach a bearded Christ. Above these processions are 26 charmingly rendered scenes from the life of Christ, including one of Christ standing on shore and calling to Peter and Andrew in their small fishing boat, asking them to be his disciples. Mosaics near the door provide a picture-postcard view of the old city, including Theodoric's palace and the port city of Classe. Look for the detached hand and forearm wrapped around a column of Theodoric's palace—it was once part of a portrait of Theodoric's court that was removed when the church became a Catholic basilica.

Via di Roma. www.ravennamosaici.it. ✆ **0544-541688.** Cumulative ticket 9.50€ adults, 8.50€ students, free for children 10 and under. Apr–Sept daily 9am–7pm; Mar and Oct daily 9:30am–5:30pm; Nov–Feb daily 10am–4:30pm.

Basilica di San Vitale ★★★ CHURCH The emperor Justinian (who never visited Ravenna and ruled instead from Constantinople) completed this octagonal church—richly ornamented with intensely green, blue, and gold mosaics—in 540 as a symbol of his power. Endowed with a halo to indicate his role as head of church and state, Justinian stands next to a clean-shaven Christ, perched atop the world, flanked by saints and angels. Looking on are Justinian's two most important adjuncts, his empress, Theodora, and a bald Maximianus, bishop of Ravenna. Theodora's presence suggests her immense influence and rapacious rise to power. Born into the circus, she became known for her beauty and was a famous actress and courtesan when she caught Justinian's eye. She became such a force in running the empire that in 532, not long before the completion of the church, she ordered that 30,000 insurgents be gathered up, brought to the Hippodrome in Constantinople, and slaughtered.

Via San Vitale 17. www.ravennamosaici.it. ✆ **0544-215193.** Cumulative ticket 9.50€ adults, 8.50€ students, free for children 10 and under. Apr–Sept daily 9am–7pm; Mar and Oct daily 9am–5:30pm; Nov–Feb daily 9:30am–4:30pm.

Battistero Neoniano (Neonian Baptistery) and Museo Arcivescovile ★ CHURCH/MUSEUM Ravenna's oldest monument was erected by Bishop Ursus around 400, to accompany a long-ago destroyed basilica on the site of an ancient Roman bath. The eight sides of this octagonal structure represent the 7 days of the week, as set out in Genesis, plus the day of the Resurrection, when Christ gave mankind eternal life. Bishop Neon embellished the structure at the end of the 5th century, adding the intensely colored blue, green, and gold mosaics that spread over the dome, showing John the Baptist baptizing Christ in the River Jordan, surrounded by the 12 Apostles carrying crowns as a sign of celestial glory. Many of the marble panels in the walls were taken from the Roman bathhouse—that structure, like the sunken baptistery, was originally at street level, which has risen more than 3m (10 ft.) over the intervening centuries. The private oratory of the 5th-century bishops of Ravenna is adjacent and now part of the Museo Arcivescovile; Christ is portrayed in mosaics in a way he is rarely seen elsewhere, as a victorious warrior in battle garb standing on a snake. The treasure in the warren of cramped little galleries is the bishops' throne, maybe the finest bit of ivory work in the world.

Mosaics in the Neonian Baptistery in Ravenna.

Piazza del Duomo. www.ravennamosaici.it. ✆ **0544-215201.** Cumulative ticket 9.50€ adults, 8.50€ students, free for children 10 and under. Apr–Sept daily 9am–7pm; Mar and Oct daily 9:30am–5:30pm; Nov–Feb daily 10am–4:30pm.

Mausoleo di Galla Placidia ★★ MONUMENT One of the most powerful women of the Byzantine world was the daughter and granddaughter of Roman emperors, sister of one ruler of the Western Roman Empire, and widow of another. Captured by the Visigoths during the sack of Rome in 410, she married King Athaulf, moved with his barbarian hordes to Barcelona, was traded back to the Romans for grain when Athaulf was murdered, and then married co-emperor Constantius, with whom she had a son, Valentinian III. When Constantius died and Valentinian became emperor at the age of 6, Galla acted as regent and in that capacity ruled the Western world for 12 years. Though she's most likely buried in Rome, her mausoleum here is crowned with a dome decorated with mosaics, vivid with hues of peacock blue, moss green, Roman gold, eggplant purple, and burnt orange. They're especially moving for their simplicity and spirituality—doves drink from fountains, as the faithful are nourished by God; a purple-robed Christ is surrounded by lambs, as the Heavenly king is surrounded by the faithful; and 570 tiny gold stars, suggesting life eternal, twinkle in the cupola. Soft light filtered by alabaster infuses everything with an otherworldly luminosity.

Via Fiandrini Benedetto. www.ravennamosaici.it. ✆ **0544-541688.** Cumulative ticket 9.50€ adults, 8.50€ students, free for children 10 and under. Apr–Sept daily 9am–7pm; Mar and Oct daily 9am–5:30pm; Nov–Feb daily 9:30am–4:30pm.

Tomba di Dante (Dante's Tomb) ★ MONUMENT The author of the *Divine Comedy* settled in Ravenna in 1318, having traveled restlessly throughout Italy after he was exiled from his native Florence in 1302, when he fell out of political favor. He died of marsh fever here on September 14, 1321. This simple marble tomb, erected in 1780, is inscribed with a harsh reprimand to the Florentines, who are still clamoring for the body's return: "Here in this corner lies Dante, exiled from his native land, born to Florence, an unloving mother."

Via Dante Alighieri. ✆ **0544-33662.** Free. Daily 10am–6:30pm (Oct–Mar closes 4pm).

Where to Stay

Ravenna's hotels do a slow business off-season (anytime outside of summer); rates come down accordingly and are usually open to some negotiation.

Albergo Cappello ★★ An old palace in the center of town retains enough damask, Murano chandeliers, stone fireplaces, and impressive old furnishings to make any guest feel like an aristocrat. But it's wise not to identify with one former high-born inhabitant, Francesca da Polenta, made famous in Dante's *Divine Comedy* as the cheating wife whose husband catches her with her lover and strangles both. Most of the seven large, high-ceilinged rooms are suites that open off salons on the piano nobile, while a few less grand but similarly character-filled quarters for commoners are tucked into a wing in the rear. Breakfast is served in a morning room downstairs amid a charming bestiary of forest creatures, while a handsome, beamed wine bar serves well into the evening.

Via IV Novembre 41. www.albergocappello.it. ✆ **0544-212114.** 7 units. 100€–120€ double, includes breakfast. **Amenties:** Bar; restaurant; Wi-Fi (free).

Casa Masoli ★★★ An 18th-century *palazzo* near the city center exudes a familial and slightly bohemian ambience. Two splendid suites at the front of the house are especially grand and cavernous—one retains the original brick vaulting, another frescoes and a marble tub—but high ceilings, tall windows, and wood-veneered bathrooms lend all the rooms a big dose of grandeur; those in the back face a surprisingly verdant garden. Scattered antiques, comfy lounge chairs and couches, and framed lithographs are friendly touches, as is the generous breakfast buffet with lots of homemade fare served in a frescoed salon.

Via Girolamo Rossi 22. www.casamasoli.it. ✆ **0544-217682.** 7 units. 70€–130€ double, includes breakfast. **Amenities:** Wi-Fi (free).

Hotel Centrale Byron ★ From 1819 to 1821 Lord Byron shared a nearby palace with his lover, Contessa Teresa Guiccioli, and her husband, and Ravenna has been milking the incident ever since. This hotel—one of several establishments in town named for the Romantic poet—is a lot less evocative than its name suggests, but it is wonderfully located a stone's throw from most of the sights, a few steps from Piazza del Popolo, and an easy stroll from the train station. Constant updating has given the rooms a contemporary patina more geared toward comfort than character, with some welcome touches that include soundproofing and excellent lighting.

Via IV Novembre 14. www.hotelsravenna.it. ✆ **0544-212225.** 54 units. 75€–110€ double, includes breakfast. **Amenities:** Bar; room service; Wi-Fi (free).

Hotel Diana ★ Tucked away slightly off the beaten path at the edge of the city center, these large, bright, and simply furnished rooms (many with extremely large windowed bathrooms) are a good base for exploring and especially handy for motorists, with several easy-to-reach garages nearby. Downstairs, an English-speaking staff dispenses recommendations with genuine enthusiasm, and a generous buffet breakfast is served on a large, glass-enclosed patio.

Via Girolamo Rossi 47. www.hoteldiana.ra.it. ✆ **0544-39164.** 33 units. 70€–95€ double, includes breakfast. **Amenities:** Bikes; Wi-Fi (free).

M Club ★★★ Keeping in step with the quiet elegance of old Ravenna, these bright quarters at the edge of the historic center are stylish and welcoming, crisscrossed with heavy beams and filled with a tasteful mix of antiques, oil paintings, French and Italian prints, and family memorabilia. Large windows open to Hadrian's Gate across the square out front or a quiet garden in back. While the six distinctively decorated rooms are set up for relaxing in private (the suite has a monastery table long enough to host a banquet), lounges are inviting as well.

Via Baracca. www.m-club.it. ✆ **333-955-6466.** 5 units. 80€–130€ double, includes breakfast. **Amenities:** Bikes; Wi-Fi (free).

Where to Eat

Ravenna's **Mercato Coperto** (near the center of town on Piazza Andrea Costa), once an attraction in itself, is closed for renovation and is slated to reopen, well, at some point. In the meantime, **Gastronomia Marchesini,** an elegant food store at Via Mazzini 2 (✆ **0544-212309**), is a good place to load up on regional hams and cheeses; it operates a reasonably priced self-service restaurant upstairs and a full-service restaurant above that. **Profumo di Piadina,** 24 Via Cairoli, tops warm-from-the oven *piadina* (flatbread) with prosciutto, creamy *squaquerone* (cheese), and other locally produced ingredients that you can eat on the go or enjoy at one of the few tables.

Ca' de Ven ★★ ROMAGNOLA A 16th-century guesthouse and former spice warehouse with frescoed ceilings and lots of paneling and exposed timbers makes a delightful stop for lunch or a light dinner. Heavier fare is offered, but the emphasis here is on *piadina,* the local flatbread, and that's the way to go. It's served with a dozen or so fillings or, even better, by itself warm from the oven with a selection of cured meats and *squaquerone,* a delicate soft cheese. There's also a huge selection of wine by the glass. At lunch and in early evening you'll rub elbows at communal tables with what seems like half the population of Ravenna, so enjoy the familiar atmosphere and ignore the sometimes-brusque service.

Via Corrado Ricci 24. www.cadeven.it. ✆ **0544-30163.** *Piadine* about 4€; main courses 11€–15€. Tues–Sun 11am–11pm.

Cinema Alexander ★ ITALIAN/SEAFOOD A former church became a movie house in the 20th century, and the vast, double-height hall where vintage movie posters hang beneath ancient beams combines the sacred and the profane, meanwhile providing a sophisticated setting for refined dishes. Ravenna's proximity to the sea comes to the fore in beautifully sauced fresh fish, and in nice combinations like fusilli with tuna and pork or calamari couscous; meat dishes lean toward roasted game birds and some unusual local preparations, such as veal cheeks with potato and lemon puree. Service is friendly and attentive, as soft jazz and mellow renditions of movie themes float through the space.

Via Bassa del Pignataro 8. www.ristorantealexander.it. ✆ **0544-212967.** Main courses 15€–28€. Tues–Sun 12:30–2:30pm and 7:30–11:30pm (closed Sun in summer).

La Bella Venezia ★ ROMAGNOLA The name suggests a certain airy elegance, and the cream-colored walls and light, starched tablecloths in this small room off the Piazza della Popolo deliver on the promise. Despite the name, don't expect Venetian specialties: This restaurant's menu is typically and deliciously Romagnolese. The kitchen is much

respected for its *cappelletti alla romagnola* (cap-shaped pasta stuffed with ricotta, roasted pork loin, chicken breast, and nutmeg, and served with meat sauce) and other homemade pastas, including simple ravioli with butter and sage, and risotto with fresh seasonal vegetables. Everything on the small menu is prepared with finesse and served with the kind of old-world flair that keeps a local clientele coming back.
Via IV Novembre 16. www.bellavenezia.it. ✆ **0544-212-746.** Main courses 10€–15€. Mon–Sat 12:15–2:15pm and 7:30–10:15pm.

PARMA ★

457km (283 miles) NW of Rome, 97km (60 miles) NW of Bologna, 121km (75 miles) SE of Milan

This prosperous little city on the Roman Via Emilia, about an hour north of Bologna, delivers a slice of the good life. Residents are surrounded by art-filled palaces and churches bestowed upon them by the Renaissance Farnese family and later Marie-Louise, wife of Napoleon. They enjoy the music of their own Giuseppe Verdi in a grand opera house, and when it comes to food, elegant Parma has given the world some of the finest hams and cheeses ever. You can easily fill a very satisfying day or two here, enjoying beautiful monuments, listening to music, stepping in and out of tempting food shops, and sitting down to some memorable meals.

Essentials

GETTING THERE Parma is served by the Milan-Bologna **rail** line, with hourly trains arriving from Milan (trip time: 1 hr. on frequent fast trains, 1½ hr. on the less-frequent but less-expensive slower trains). From Bologna, trains depart for Parma every 30 minutes or so (a little under an hr.). There are a few direct trains a day from Florence (2 hr.); most journeys will require a change in Bologna. For information and schedules, go to www.trenitalia.com.

If you have a **car** and are starting out in Bologna, head northwest along A1. Don't drive into the old town without first contacting your hotel—without a special pass you'll be fined 90€. You can park on the street, outside the restricted area, where you see blue lines (not blue and white lines), or aim for the official parking lots: Goito, Toschi, Duc, Dus, and Via Abbeveratoia (around 1€–1.70€ per hour).

VISITOR INFORMATION The **tourist office** at Piazza Garibaldi 1 (www.turismo.comune.parma.it; ✆ **0521-218889**) is open daily 9am to 7pm.

Exploring Parma

It's easy to explore Parma on foot, since most of the sights surround Piazza del Duomo and Palazzo della Pilotta and are within easy walking distance of the train station.

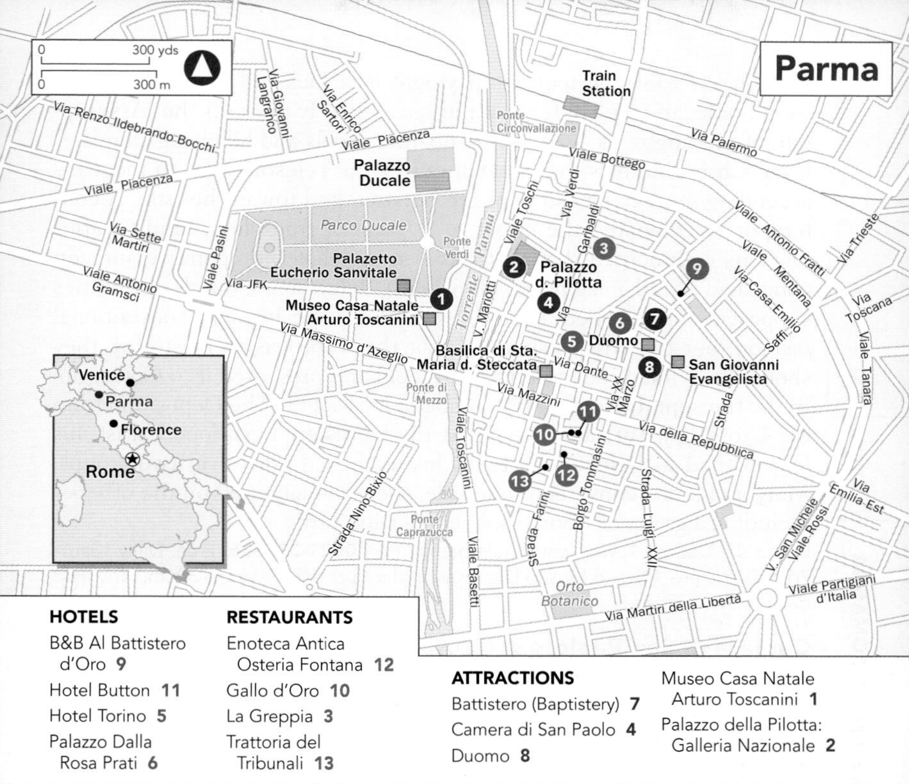

Battistero (Baptistery) and Duomo ★★★ CATHEDRAL The moment you walk into the Piazza del Duomo, you're in for a wallop of delightful visual storytelling. To one side rises the elegant **baptistery,** primarily the work of Italy's great Romanesque master Benedetto Antelami and begun in 1196. Octagonal in shape, it has four open loggias and tiers of 16 slender columns—all playing off the number eight, the sign of the Resurrection. Alternating bands of white and pink marble represent purity and the blood of Christ; carvings above the entrance are scripture in stone (look for the sequence depicting King Herod pulling his beard in rage, Salome dancing, and St. John losing his head). Inside, 13th-century frescoes depict the zodiac, the months and seasons, and the life of Christ with an overwhelming explosion of color and complex medieval iconography; there are some remarkably tender scenes, too, including one in which the Virgin Mary shields children huddled below her with her robe.

Two stone lions guard the entrance to the adjacent **Duomo,** one crushing a serpent (the devil), the other a lamb (symbol of sacrifice) under their paws. Inside are two of Parma's greatest treasures. Correggio, the master of light and color, spent 8 years painting the cupola; after finishing in 1530, he took his payment in a sack full of small change, went home, and died of fever at the age of 40. He presents the "Assumption of the Virgin" as a sea of free-floating angels and billowing clouds. A leggy Christ tumbles in a freefall out of the celestial light to meet his ascending mother, whose arms are outstretched toward her son. A contemporary compared the effect to a "hash of frogs' legs," and Charles Dickens commented that this was a scene that "no operative surgeon gone mad could imagine in his wildest delirium." Church authorities supposedly approached Titian to redo the dome in more conventional fashion, but the artist responded that the work was so masterful, they should have filled the structure with gold and presented it to Correggio. In the transept to the right is a somber bas-relief of "The Deposition from the Cross," by Antelami, creator of the baptistery next door. Christ, his face bathed in sadness, stretches his elongated arms over two groups, Mary and pious converts to one side, the unenlightened on the other—including a group of Roman soldiers playing cards.

Piazza del Duomo 1. www.cattedrale.parma.it. ✆ **0521-235886.** Free. Daily 10am–7pm. Battistero: 8€ with Museo Diocesano. Mar–Oct daily 10am–6:30pm; Nov–Feb daily 10am–4:30pm.

Camera di San Paolo ★★ CONVENT San Paolo was one of many well-endowed convents where women of means who, for one reason or another, could not marry spent their lives in relative comfort. When, around 1519, the cultured abbess Giovanna di Piacenza wanted to fresco her private dining room, she had the means to hire Correggio, who presented her with vivid mythological scenes, cherubs, astrological references, and an image of Diana, goddess of the hunt. The subject matter may well have been a conversation piece for the intellectuals who frequently gathered at the abbess's table, though the meaning of the representations remains a mystery. What is known is that church authorities later sealed off the chamber—the absence of religious subjects and the presence of so many bare-bottomed *putti* was considered profane.

Via Melloni 3 (off Strada Garibaldi). ✆ **0521-533221.** 2€ adults, 1€ ages 18–25, children 17 and under free. Mon–Fri 8:30am–2pm, Sat 8:30am–6pm.

Palazzo della Pilotta: Galleria Nazionale ★★ MUSEUM Like many Italian cities, Parma became a great center of the Renaissance under the stewardship of one family, the Farneses, whose members included popes, cardinals, and the dukes of Parma. They began their fortresslike Palazzo della Pilotta in the 1580s and remained there until the last heiress, Elisabetta, married King Philip of Spain and decamped for Madrid in 1714. The Hapsburg princess Marie-Louise (1791–1847), second wife of Napoleon and great-niece of France's Marie-Antoinette, was awarded the duchy a century later, and she made it her business to gather art treasures from the city in the palace the Farneses had left empty; she also collected works from villas and churches throughout

Italy, confiscated when her husband marched down the peninsula. Badly damaged by Allied bombs in World War II, the restored palace now houses the Galleria Nazionale. It's not too surprising that the collection with connections to the Vienna-born duchess includes such northern artists as Hans Holbein, Brueghel, and Van Dyck, though Parma artists steal the show. Correggio's "Madonna della Scodella (With a Bowl)" portrays Joseph as an elderly, caring man and the Madonna as a young woman looking adoringly at her infant son; "St. Jerome with the Madonna and Child" also represents age, youth, and love—a gentle ode to tenderness. Napoleon supposedly wanted to cart these delightful canvases off to the Louvre, but Marie-Louise insisted they remain in Parma. Parmigianino's alluring "Turkish Slave" is clearly the portrait of a well-kept young woman, dressed in gold-threaded finery, and everything about her—turban, cheeks, eyes, breasts—is beautifully rounded. "La Scapigliata" (aka the "Female Head") is one of the most celebrated works by the Italian master of the Renaissance, Leonardo da Vinci. The palace's other treasure is the **Teatro Farnese,** a wooden theater the Farneses had built, along the lines of Palladio's theater at Vicenza, to impress the Medicis. It's been used only times, including an inaugural event in 1639 when the section in front was flooded for mock naval battles.

Piazzale della Pilotta 15. www.gallerianazionaleparma.it. ✆ **0521-233309.** 10€ adults, 5€ ages 18–25, free for children 17 and under; includes Teatro Farnese. Tues–Sat 8:30am–7pm, Sun 8:30am–2pm.

Where to Stay

B&B Al Battistero d'Oro ★★★ It's easy to slip into the Parma good life in this elegant 19th-century house just behind the Duomo, where Patrizia Valenti's sprawling and tasteful apartment surrounds a courtyard. The hostess puts up her guests in a delightful ground-floor room with a private entrance and another large bedroom off a back corridor, welcoming them also into her bright and handsomely furnished living room and polished dining room, where she serves a delicious breakfast. She also offers a modern studio apartment in a nearby house. All rooms are beautifully equipped with fine linens and handy amenities (fridges in the rooms and a kitchenette in the apartment), and Patrizia is on hand to dispense advice on getting the most out of her native Parma.

Borgo delle Salina 7. www.albattisterodoro.com. ✆ **338-4904697.** 3 units. 130€ double, includes breakfast. **Amenities:** Wi-Fi (free).

Hotel Button ★★ The Cortesa family has been welcoming guests to this 17th-century *palazzo* for more than 40 years, providing lots of advice and dispensing excellent coffee from the small lobby bar. The premises have long ago been stripped of any of their historic provenance, and the current reincarnation, with floral wallpaper and dark furnishings, seems like a relic from the mid-20th century. You might be charmed by the extra-large rooms and old-fashioned ambience (as we are) or find the

place to be a bit stuffy and out of date, but you can't quibble with the excellent location in the heart of old Parma just off Piazza Garibaldi.
Borgo delle Salina 7. www.hotelbutton.it. ✆ **0521-208039.** 40 units. 85–105€ double, includes breakfast. **Amenities:** Babysitting; bar; Wi-Fi (free).

Hotel Torino ★ A couple of handsome and homey lounges off the lobby and a sprightly, patio-like breakfast room do justice to one of Parma's best lodging locations, in the old center just down the street from Piazza del Duomo. Guest rooms are a bit more banal, though the muted tones and neutral furnishings are soothing, and the small spaces are streamlined with lots of handy built-ins for stashing gear; some of the singles closely resemble ships' cabins. Parking in a small garage handily tucked beneath the hotel is available for a small fee.
Borgo Angelo Massa. www.hotel-torino.it. ✆ **0521-281046.** 39 units. From 85€ double, includes breakfast. **Amenities:** Bar; Wi-Fi (free).

Palazzo Dalla Rosa Prati ★★★ Clichéd as it sounds, you really will be living like royalty in this magnificent *palazzo* on a corner of the Piazza Del Duomo, sharing quarters with the Marquis Dalla Rosa Prati and his family, who still occupy part of the premises. They have converted one wing of the palace to seven sprawling, handsomely furnished suites, all with kitchenettes, and another section to 10 large apartments. In the suites, huge wooden bedsteads, massive armoires, and other polished antiques augment the largely 18th-cenutry surroundings; the real scene stealers are the pink baptistery next door, practically abutting some of the tall windows, and the stone expanses of the piazza. Apartments are tasteful but functional, have one or two bedrooms, and provide travelers with generous space to spread out. Suites are accessible by elevator, while reaching the apartments requires a climb up a grand but long staircase.
Strada al Duomo 7. www.palazzodallarosaprati.com. ✆ **0521-386429.** 17 units. From 150€ double, includes breakfast. **Amenities:** Bar; cafe; Wi-Fi (free).

Where to Eat

Topping the tasting list in Parma is *parmigiano* cheese, made from the milk of cows raised just outside town and aged for at least 12 months. A meal often begins and ends with a small wedge, and it's grated over pastas and fresh vegetables, used as a filling in crepes, and generally makes its way into almost every course. Then there's ham. Parma gourmands do not settle for any old *prosciutto.* The cut of choice is *culatello,* from the right hind leg—if you observe a pig sitting down, you'll see this part carries less weight, and hence becomes less sinewy. *Culatello* is the antipasto of choice. You can purchase ham and cheese all over town; an especially attractive and aromatic shop is **Salumeria Garibaldi,** Via Garibaldi 42 (www.specialitadiparma.it; ✆ **0521-235606;** Mon–Sat

HITTING THE high NOTES

Duchess Marie-Louise, who beneficently ruled Parma from 1814 to 1847, built the **Teatro Reggio,** Via Garibaldi 16, near Piazza della Pace (www.teatroregioparma.org; ✆ **0521-039399**). Opened in 1829, it is still considered one of the world's finest music theaters, hosting an opera season that rivals Milan's. Most appreciated are the works of **Giuseppe Verdi,** composer of "Il Trovatore" and "Aïda" and other perennially popular classics. Verdi was born outside Parma in 1813 and later settled with his mistress, the soprano Giuseppina Strepponi, in the **Villa Verdi,** in nearby Busseto. The villa shows off their personal effects, pianos, portraits, and the bed upon which the maestro died in Milan in 1901 (✆ **0523-830210;** 9€; Tues–Sun 9:30–11:45am and 2:30–6:15pm/2–4:30pm Nov–Mar). Parma celebrates the maestro each October during the **Verdi Festival,** with concerts and operatic performances in the Teatro Reggio and other venues.

Arturo Toscanini, the greatest orchestral conductor of the first half of the 20th century, was born in Parma in 1867. The rooms of his birthplace, **Museo Casa Natale Arturo Toscanini,** Via Rodolfo Tanzi 13, are filled with his scores, photos, and other personal effects (www.museotoscanini.it; ✆ **0521-285-499;** 2€; Wed–Sat 9am–1pm and 2–6pm; Sun 2–6pm).

8am–8pm). You might also want to visit the cheese production operations at **Consorzio del Parmigiano Reggiano** (www.parmigiano reggiano.com; ✆ **0521-2927000**), at Via Gramsci 26; call or e-mail to make an appointment.

Enoteca Antica Osteria Fontana ★ PARMIGIANA Cheap nibbles and a huge selection of wine by the glass draw a local crowd to this plain room with a long bar and battered wooden tables. Grilled *panini* are on offer, but the real treats are the morsels of *parmigiano* dribbled with balsamic vinegar from Modena, slices of prosciutto, and *crostini*, pieces of bread topped with everything from pesto to chicken livers.

Via Farini 24. ✆ **0521-286037.** Sandwiches and snacks from 4€. Tues–Sat noon–2:30pm and 8–10:30pm.

Gallo d'Oro ★ PARMIGIANA Parma's formidable food scene becomes decidedly more relaxed at this almost bohemian, bric-a-brac-filled trattoria just off Piazza Garibaldi. A young crowd seems to appreciate the old local traditions: Lambrusco, a slightly sparkling red, is the wine of choice, and *cavallo* (horse) and *coniglio* (rabbit) are served a few different ways. Those who want to sample the local cuisine a bit less adventurously can work their way through *tortelli ripieni* (pasta stuffed with cheese and vegetables), *ravioli alla zucca* (pumpkin), and a long list of other delicious local pastas, all homemade.

Borgo della Salina 3. www.gallodororistorante.it. ✆ **0521-208846.** Main courses 8.50€–11€. Mon–Sat noon–3pm and 7–midnight; Sun noon–3pm.

La Greppia ★★ PARMIGIANA/ITALIAN Looking toward the window at one end of the simple dining room, you'll see into the kitchen and notice that the staff is largely female. In the *donnas'* hands you'll be treated to exquisite dishes, some of which you've probably never encountered before—pears poached in red wine with a dense cream sauce is the house antipasto, the pastas are all homemade and often filled with the freshest local vegetables, and the secondi menu is heavy with slow-cooked goat, *trippa alla parmigiana* (tripe), and other regional favorites. The homemade *tortas,* filled with marmalade and a miraculous mélange of other ingredients, are irresistible. Service does the cuisine justice.
Via Garibaldi 39. ✆ **0521-233686.** Main courses 18€–28€. Wed–Sun noon–2:30pm and 7:30–10:30pm.

Trattoria del Tribunali ★★★ PARMIGIANA/ITALIAN Two floors of dining rooms that stretch beyond counters hung with hams are often filled to bursting, usually with locals who love the homey atmosphere and well-priced cuisine. They rely on the kitchen for such staples as huge platters of prosciutto and some distinctly local fare, such as horse-meat hash. More familiar choices range from delicious pastas, such as *tortelli* (pasta pockets) stuffed with pumpkin or ricotta, to steaks with Barolo and veal stuffed with *parmigiano*. A veteran staff never seems too flustered to be friendly, even during the usual lunchtime and evening rushes. It's a good idea to reserve, especially on weekend nights.
Vicolo Politi 5. www.trattoriadeltribunale.it. ✆ **0521-285527.** Main courses 8€–12€. Daily noon–3pm and 7–11pm.

9

VENICE

By Stephen Keeling

No place in the world quite looks like Venice. This vast, floating city of grand *palazzi,* elegant bridges, gondolas, and canals is a magnificent spectacle, truly magical when approached by sea for the first time, when its golden domes and soaring bell towers seem to rise straight from the sea. While it can sometimes appear that Venice is little more than an open-air museum where tourists always outnumber locals—by a large margin—it is still surprisingly easy to lose the crowds. Indeed, the best way to enjoy Venice is to simply get lost in its labyrinth of narrow, enchanting streets, stumbling upon a quiet *campo* (square), market stall, or cafe far off the beaten track, where even the humblest medieval church might contain masterful work by Tiepolo, Titian, or Tintoretto.

The origins of Venice are as muddy as parts of the lagoon it now occupies, but most histories begin with the arrival of refugees from Attila the Hun's invasion of Italy in 453 A.D. The mudflats were gradually built over and linked together, channels and streams eventually becoming canals. By the 11th century, Venice had emerged as a major independent trading city, and by the 13th century its seaborne empire (which included Crete, Corfu, and Cyprus) was held together by a huge navy and commercial fleet. Despite being embroiled with wars against rival Italian city Genoa and the Turks, the next few centuries were golden years for Venice, when booming trade with the Far East funded much of its grand architecture and art. Although it remained an outwardly rich city, by the 1700s the good times were over, and in 1797 Napoleon dissolved the Venetian Republic. You'll gain a sense of some of this history touring **Piazza San Marco** and **St. Mark's Basilica,** or by visiting the **Accademia,** one of Italy's great art galleries. But only when you wander the back *calli* (streets) will you encounter the true, living, breathing side of Venice, still redolent of those glory days.

ESSENTIALS

Getting There

BY PLANE You can fly to Venice nonstop from North America via **Delta Airlines** (www.delta.com) from Atlanta (late June–Aug only) and New

 PREVIOUS PAGE: **Venice's Grand Canal and the Basilica Santa Maria della Salute.**

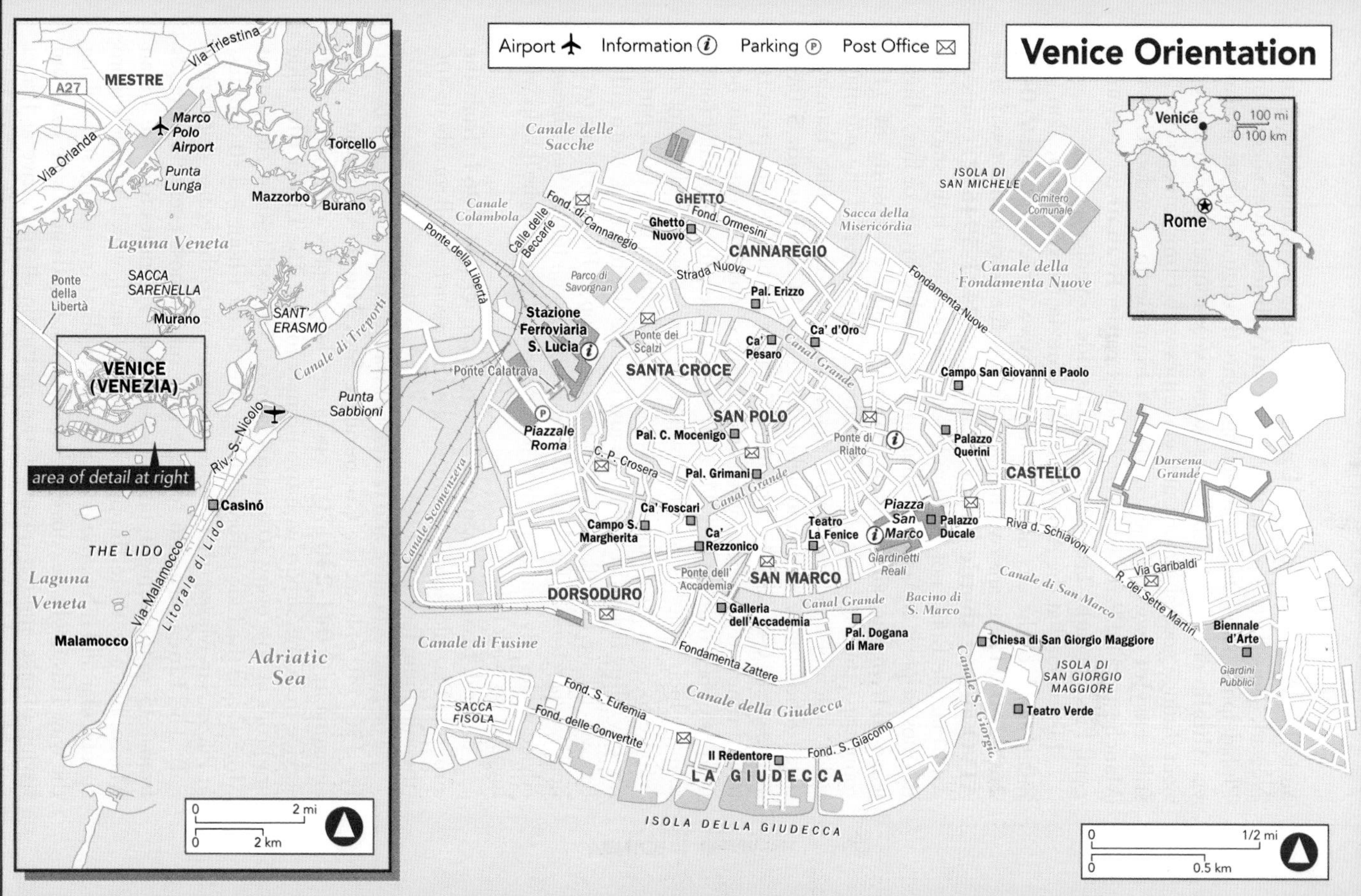
Venice Orientation
Airport
Information
Parking
Post Office
MESTRE
A27
Via Triestina
Via Orlanda
Marco Polo Airport
Punta Lunga
Torcello
Mazzorbo
Burano
Laguna Veneta
Ponte della Libertà
SACCA SARENELLA
Murano
SANT' ERASMO
Canale di Treporti
VENICE (VENEZIA)
area of detail at right
Punta Sabbioni
Riv. S. Nicolò
Casinó
THE LIDO
Via Malamocco
Litorale di Lido
Laguna Veneta
Malamocco
Adriatic Sea
0 2 mi
0 2 km
Canale delle Sacche
Canale Colambola
Fond. di Cannaregio
Calle delle Beccarie
Ponte della Libertà
GHETTO
Ghetto Nuovo
Fond. Ormesini
CANNAREGIO
Sacca della Misericórdia
Strada Nuova
Parco di Savorgnan
Pal. Erizzo
Stazione Ferroviaria S. Lucia
Ponte dei Scalzi
Ca' Pesaro
Ca' d'Oro
Canal Grande
Ponte Calatrava
SANTA CROCE
Piazzale Roma
SAN POLO
Pal. C. Mocenigo
C. P. Crosera
Pal. Grimani
Ponte di Rialto
Canale Scomenzera
Ca' Foscari
Campo S. Margherita
Ca' Rezzonico
Teatro La Fenice
Piazza San Marco
Palazzo Ducale
Giardinetti Reali
Ponte dell' Accademia
SAN MARCO
DORSODURO
Galleria dell'Accademia
Canal Grande
Pal. Dogana di Mare
Bacino di S. Marco
Canale di Fusine
Fondamenta Zattere
Canale della Giudecca
SACCA FISOLA
Fond. S. Eufemia
Fond. delle Convertite
Il Redentore
Fond. S. Giacomo
LA GIUDECCA
ISOLA DELLA GIUDECCA
ISOLA DI SAN MICHELE
Cimitero Comunale
Canale della Fondamenta Nuove
Fondamenta Nuove
Campo San Giovanni e Paolo
Palazzo Querini
CASTELLO
Darsena Grande
Riva d. Schiavoni
Canale di San Marco
Via Garibaldi
R. dei Sette Martiri
Biennale d'Arte
Giardini Pubblici
Chiesa di San Giorgio Maggiore
ISOLA DI SAN GIORGIO MAGGIORE
Canale S. Giorgio
Teatro Verde
Venice
Rome
0 100 mi
0 100 km
0 1/2 mi
0 0.5 km

York-JFK (Apr–Sept only), via **United Airlines** (www.united.com) from Newark (June–late Sept), or via **American Airlines** (www.aa.com) from Philadelphia (Apr–Oct); connecting flights through Rome are available via **Alitalia** or a number of other airlines year-round. You can also connect through several major European cities with European carriers. No-frills **easyJet** (www.easyjet.com) flies from Berlin, London-Gatwick, Manchester, and Paris, while rival budget carrier **Ryanair** (www.ryanair.com) flies to nearby **Treviso** (a 1-hr. bus ride to Venice).

Flights land at the **Aeroporto di Venezia Marco Polo,** 7km (4¼ miles) north of the city on the mainland (www.veniceairport.it; ✆ **041-2609260**). There are two bus alternatives for getting into town. The **ATVO airport shuttle bus** (www.atvo.it; ✆ **0421-594672**) connects with Piazzale Roma not far from Venice's Santa Lucia train station (and the closest point to Venice's attractions accessible by car or bus). Buses leave to/from the airport about every 30 minutes, costing 8€ (15€ roundtrip); the trip takes about 20 minutes. Buy tickets at the automatic ticket machines in the arrivals baggage hall, or the Public Transport ticket office (daily 8am–midnight). The local **ACTV bus no. 5** (actv.avmspa.it; ✆ **041-2424**) also costs 8€, takes 20 minutes, and runs two to four times an hour depending on the time of day; the best option here is to buy the combined ACTV and "Nave" ticket for 14€ (valid for 90 min.), which includes your first *vaporetto* ride at a slight discount (the "vaporetto" is the seagoing streetcar of Venice, which goes to all parts of the city). Buy tickets at machines just outside the terminal. With either bus, you'll have to walk to or from the final stop at Piazzale Roma to the nearby *vaporetto* stop for the final connection to your hotel. (See *vaporetto* advice under "By Train," below.) It's rare to find porters who'll help with luggage, so pack light.

A **land taxi** (www.radiotaxivenezia.com; ✆ **041-5964**) from the airport to Piazzale Roma (where you get the *vaporetto*) will run about 40€ (the minimum fare is 8–11€).

The most evocative and traditional way to arrive in Venice is by sea. For 15€ (14€ online), the **Cooperative San Marco/Alilaguna** (www.alilaguna.it; ✆ **041-2401701**) operates a large *motoscafo* (shuttle boat) service from the airport with two primary routes. The **Linea Blu** (blue line) runs almost every 30 minutes from 6:15am to 12:30am, stopping at Murano and the Lido before arriving, after about 1 hour and 30 minutes, in Piazza San Marco (this service continues on to the cruise ship terminal). The **Linea Arancio** (orange line) runs almost every 30 minutes from 7:45am to midnight, taking 1 hour and 15 minutes to arrive at San Marco, but gets there through the Grand Canal, which is much more spectacular and offers the possibility to get off at one of the stops along the way. This might be convenient to your hotel and could save you from having to take another means of transportation. If you arrive at Piazza San Marco and your hotel isn't in the area, you'll have to make a connection at the *vaporetto* launches. (If you're booking a hotel in advance, ask for specific advice on how to get there.)

A good alternative is **Venice Shuttle** (www.venicelink.com; daily 8am–10:30pm; minimum 2 people for reservations), a shared water taxi (they carry 6–8 people) that will whisk you from the airport directly to many hotels and most of the major locations in the city for 25€ to 32€ (add 6€ after 8pm). You must reserve online in advance.

A **private water taxi** (20–30 min. to/from the airport) is convenient but costly—there is a 110€ fee (big discounts available at www.venicelink.com) for up to five passengers with one bag each (plus 10€ more for each extra person up to a maximum of 10, 5€ for each extra suitcase, and another 20€ for 10pm–7am arrivals). It's worth considering if you're pressed for time, have an early flight (taxis run 24 hrs.), are carrying a lot of luggage (a Venice no-no), or can split the cost with a friend or two. The taxi may be able to drop you off at the front (or side) door of your hotel, or as close as it can maneuver given your hotel's location (check with the hotel before arriving). Your taxi captain should be able to tell you before boarding just how close he can get you. Try **Corsorzio Motoscafi Venezia** (www.motoscafivenezia.it; ✆ **041-5222303**) or **Venezia Taxi** (www.veneziataxi.it; ✆ **041-723112**).

BY TRAIN Trains from Rome (3¾ hr.), Milan (2½ hr.), Florence (2 hr.), and all over Europe arrive at the **Stazione Venezia Santa Lucia.** To get there, all must pass through a station marked Venezia-Mestre. Don't be confused: Mestre is a charmless industrial city that's the last major stop on the mainland (some trains also stop at the next station, Venezia Porto Marghera, before continuing to Venice proper). Occasionally trains end in Mestre, in which case you have to catch one of the frequent 10-minute shuttles connecting with Venice; it's inconvenient, so when you book your ticket, confirm that the final destination is Venezia Santa Lucia.

On exiting, you'll find the Grand Canal immediately in front of you, with the docks for a number of *vaporetti* lines to your left and right. Head to the booths to your left, near the bridge, to buy tickets. The most useful routes are the two lines plying the Grand Canal, from docks farther to the right: the no. 2 express (from bay "D"), which stops only at the San Marcuola, Rialto Bridge, San Tomà, San Samuele, and Accademia before hitting San Marco (30 min. total); and the slower no. 1 (from bay "E"), which makes 13 stops before arriving at San Marco (a 36-min. trip). Both leave every 10 minutes or so, but before 9am and after 8pm, the no. 2 sometimes stops short at Rialto, meaning you'll have to disembark and hop on the next no. 1 or 2 that comes along to continue to San Marco.

Note: The *vaporetti* go in two directions from the train station: left down the Grand Canal toward San Marco—which is the (relatively) fast and scenic way—and right, which also eventually gets you to San Marco (at the San Zaccaria stop) if you are on the no. 2, but takes more than twice as long because it goes the long way around Dorsoduro (and serves mainly commuters). If you get the no. 1 going to the right from the train station, it will go only one more stop before it hits its terminus at Piazzale Roma. Make sure the *vaporetto* you get on is heading left.

BY BUS Although rail travel is more convenient and commonplace, Venice is serviced by long-distance buses from all over mainland Italy and some international cities. The final destination is Piazzale Roma, where you'll need to pick up *vaporetto* no. 1 or no. 2 (as described above) to connect you with stops in the heart of Venice and along the Grand Canal.

BY CAR The only wheels you'll see in Venice are those attached to luggage. **No cars are allowed,** or more to the point, no cars could drive through the narrow streets and over the footbridges—even the police, fire department, and ambulance services use boats. You can drive across the Ponte della Libertà from Mestre (on the mainland) to Venice, but you can go no farther than Piazzale Roma at the Venice end, where many garages eagerly await your euros (and in high season are often full). The **Autorimessa Comunale garage** (www.avmspa.it; ✆ **041-2727301**) charges 26€ for a 24-hour period, while **Garage San Marco** (www.garagesanmarco.it; ✆ **041-5232213**) costs 30€ for 24 hours. From

Night market in Venice's Cannaregio neighborhood.

A Note on Addresses

Within each *sestiere* is a most original system of numbering the *palazzi*, using one continuous string of 6,000 or so numbers. The format for addresses in this chapter is, where possible, the number with the actual street or *campo* on which you'll find that address. But official mailing addresses (and what you'll see written down in most places) are simply the *sestiere* name followed by the building number, which isn't especially helpful—for example, San Marco 1471 may not necessarily be found close to San Marco 1473. Many buildings aren't numbered at all.

Piazzale Roma, you can catch *vaporetti* lines 1 and 2, described above, which go down the Grand Canal to the train station and, eventually, Piazza San Marco.

Visitor Information

TOURIST OFFICES The most central **tourist office** lies in the arcade at the western end of Piazza San Marco (Calle Larga de l'Ascensione 71F), near Museo Correr (daily 9am–7pm; ✆ **041-2424**). There are also offices at the Piazzale Roma garages (first floor; daily 7:30am–7:30pm), the train station (opposite platforms 2 and 3; daily 7am–9pm), and in the arrivals hall at Marco Polo Airport (daily 8:30am–7pm). See also **www.turismovenezia.it** or **www.veneziaunica.it.**

The monthly magazine ***Un Ospite di Venezia*** (www.unospitedivenezia.it) is a useful source of information; most hotels have free copies. Also very useful is ***VeNews*** (www.venezianews.it), published monthly and sold at newsstands all over the city.

City Layout

Even armed with the best map or a hefty smartphone data plan, expect to get a little bit lost in Venice, at least some of the time (GPS directions are notoriously unreliable here). View it as an opportunity to stumble upon Venice's most intriguing corners. Keep in mind as you wander hopelessly among the *calli* (streets) and *campi* (squares) that Venice wasn't built to make sense to those on foot, but rather to those plying its canals.

Venice lies 4km (2½ miles) from terra firma, connected to the mainland at Mestre by the Ponte della Libertà, which leads to Piazzale Roma. Snaking through the city like an inverted S is the **Grand Canal,** the wide main artery. Central Venice refers to the built-up block of islands in the lagoon's center, the six main *sestieri* (districts) that make up the bulk of the tourist city. Greater Venice includes all the inhabited islands of the lagoon—central Venice plus Murano, Burano, Torcello, and the Lido.

The Neighborhoods in Brief

SAN MARCO The central *sestiere* is anchored by the magnificent Piazza San Marco and St. Mark's Basilica to the south and the Rialto Bridge to the north; it's the most visited (and most expensive) of the *sestieri*. This is the commercial, religious, and political heart of the city and has been for more than a millennium. Although you'll find glimpses of the real Venice here, ever-rising rents have nudged residents to look for housing in the outer neighborhoods: You'll be hard-pressed to find a grocery store, for example. This area is laced with first-class hotels—so we give you suggestions for staying in the heart of Venice without going broke.

CASTELLO This quarter, whose tony waterside esplanade Riva degli Schiavoni follows the Bacino di San Marco (St. Mark's Basin), begins just east of Piazza San Marco, skirting Venice's most congested area to the north and east. Riva degli Schiavoni can sometimes get so busy as to seem like Times Square on New Year's Eve, but if you head farther east in the direction of the Arsenale or inland away from the *bacino,* the crowds thin out, despite the presence of such major sights as Campo SS. Giovanni e Paolo and the Scuola di San Giorgio.

DORSODURO You'll find the residential area of Dorsoduro on the opposite side of the Accademia Bridge from San Marco. Known for the Accademia and Peggy Guggenheim museums, it is the largest of the *sestieri* and was known as an artists' haven until rising rents forced much of the community to relocate elsewhere. Good neighborhood restaurants, a charming gondola boatyard, the lively Campo Santa Margherita, and the sunny quay called le Zattere all add to its character and color.

SAN POLO This mixed bag of residential corners and tourist sights stretches northwest of the Rialto Bridge to the church of Santa Maria dei Frari, and the Scuola di San Rocco. The hub of activity at the foot of the bridge is due in large part to the Rialto Market—some of the city's best restaurants have flourished in the area for generations, alongside some of its worst tourist traps. The spacious Campo San Polo is the main piazza.

SANTA CROCE North and northwest of the San Polo district and across the Grand Canal from the train station, Santa Croce stretches all the way to Piazzale Roma. Its eastern section is one of the least-visited areas of Venice—making it all the more desirable for curious visitors. Less lively than San Polo but just as authentic, it feels light-years away from San Marco. The quiet and lovely Campo San Giacomo dell'Orio is its heart.

CANNAREGIO Sharing the same side of the Grand Canal with San Marco and Castello, Cannaregio stretches north and east from the train station to include the old Jewish Ghetto. One-quarter of Venice's ever-shrinking population of 60,000 lives here. Most of the city's one-star hotels are clustered about the train station—not a dangerous neighborhood but not one known for its charm, either. The tourist-shop-lined

Vaporettos (water buses) ply Venice's main canals.

Lista di Spagna, which starts just to the left of the train station, morphs into Strada Nova and provides an uninterrupted thoroughfare to the Rialto bridge.

LA GIUDECCA Located across the Giudecca Canal from the Piazza San Marco and Dorsoduro, La Giudecca is a tranquil working-class residential island where you'll find a youth hostel and a handful of hotels (including the deluxe Cipriani, one of Europe's finest).

LIDO DI VENEZIA This slim, 11km-long (6¾-mile) island, the only spot in the Venetian lagoon where cars circulate, is the city's beach and separates the lagoon from the open sea. The landmark hotels here serve as a base for the annual Venice Film Festival.

Getting Around

Aside from traveling by boat, the only way to explore Venice is by walking—and by getting lost repeatedly. You'll navigate many twisting streets whose names change constantly and don't appear on any map, and streets that may very well simply end in a blind alley or spill abruptly into a canal. You'll also cross dozens of footbridges. Treat getting bewilderingly lost in Venice as part of the fun, and budget more time than you'd think necessary to get wherever you're going.

Burano Island in Venice.

STREET MAPS & SIGNAGE The map sold by the tourist office (5€) and free maps provided by most hotels don't always show—much less name or index—all the *calli* (streets) and pathways of Venice. Pick up a more detailed map (ask for a *pianta della città* at news kiosks—especially those at the train station and around San Marco or most bookstores). The best is the highly detailed **Touring Club Italiano map,** available in a variety of forms (folding or spiral-bound) and scales. Almost as good, and easier to carry, is the simple and cheap 1:6,500 folding map put out by Storti Edizioni.

Still, Venice's confusing layout confounds even the best navigators. You're better off just stopping every couple of blocks and asking a local to point you in the right direction (always know the name of the *campo*/square or major sight closest to the address you're looking for, and ask for that).

As you wander, look for the yellow signs (well, *usually* yellow) whose destinations and arrows direct you toward five major landmarks: **Ferrovia** (the train station), **Piazzale Roma** (the parking garage), **Rialto** (one of four bridges over the Grand Canal), **San Marco** (the city's main square), and the **Accademia** (the southernmost Grand Canal bridge).

BY BOAT The various *sestieri* are linked by a comprehensive *vaporetto* (water bus/ferry) system of about a dozen lines operated by the **Azienda del Consorzio Trasporti Veneziano** (ACTV; actv.avmspa.it; ✆ **041-5287886**). Transit maps are available at the tourist office and most ACTV ticket offices. It's easier to get around the center on foot; the

CRUISING THE canals

A leisurely cruise along the **Grand Canal ★★★** (p. 402) from Piazza San Marco to the train station (Ferrovia)—or the reverse—is one of Venice's must-dos. It's the world's most unusual Main Street, a watery boulevard whose *palazzi* have been converted into condos. Lower water-lapped floors are now deserted, but the higher floors are still coveted by the city's titled families, who have inhabited these glorious residences for centuries; others have become the dream homes of privileged expats, drawn as irresistibly as the romantic Venetians-by-adoption who preceded them—Richard Wagner, Robert Browning, Lord Byron, and (more recently) Woody Allen.

As much a symbol of Venice as the winged lion, the **gondola ★★★** is one of Europe's great traditions, incredibly and inexplicably expensive but truly as romantic as it looks (detractors who write it off as too touristy have most likely never tried it). The official, fixed rate is 80€ for a 40-minute gondola tour for up to six passengers. The rate bumps up to 100€ from 7pm to 8am (for 40 minutes), and it's 40€ for every additional 20 minutes (50€ at night). That's not a typo: 150€ for a 1-hour evening cruise. ***Note:*** Although the price is fixed by the city, a good negotiator at the right time of day (when business is slow) can sometimes grab a small discount for a shorter ride. And at these ridiculously inflated prices, there is no need to tip the gondolier. You might also find discounts online.

Aim for late afternoon before sundown, when the light does its magic on the canal reflections (and bring a bottle of Prosecco and glasses). If the price is too high, ask visitors at your hotel or others lingering about at the gondola stations if they'd like to share it. Though the price is "fixed," before setting off establish with the gondolier the cost, time, and route (back canals are preferable to the trafficked and often choppy Grand Canal). They're regulated by the **Ente Gondola** (www.gondolavenezia.it; ✆ **041-5285075**); call if you have questions or complaints.

And what of the **serenading gondolier** immortalized in film? Frankly, you're better off without. But if warbling is de rigueur for you, here's the scoop. An ensemble of accordion player and tenor is so expensive that it's shared among several gondolas traveling together. A number of tour operators (and on-line brokers such as www.viator.com) book evening serenades for around 40€ per person.

Venice has 12 gondola stations, including Piazzale Roma, the train station, the Rialto Bridge, and Piazza San Marco. There are also a number of smaller stations, with *gondolieri* in striped shirts standing alongside their sleek 11m (36-ft.) black wonders looking for passengers. They all speak enough English to communicate the necessary details. And remember, if you just want a quick taste of being in a gondola, you can take a cheap *traghetto* across the Grand Canal.

vaporetti mostly serve the Grand Canal, outskirts, and outer islands. The crisscross network of small canals is the province of delivery vessels, gondolas, and private boats.

A ticket for 75 minutes of travel (after validation) on a *vaporetto* is a steep 7.50€, while the 24-hour ticket is 20€. Most lines run every 10 to 15 minutes from 7am to midnight, and then hourly until morning. Most

COME HELL OR high WATER

During the tidal *acqua alta* (high water) floods, Venice's lagoon rises until it engulfs the city, leaving up to 1.5 to 1.8m (5–6 ft.) of water in the lowest-lying streets. Piazza San Marco, as the lowest point in the city, goes first. As many as 50 floods a year have been recorded since they first started keeping track in the late 1700s. Significant *acqua alta* can begin as early as late September or October, but usually takes place November to March. The waters usually recede after just a few hours. Walkways are set up around town, but wet feet are a given and locals tend to wear high-topped wading boots. A complex system of hydraulic gates—the Modulo Sperimentale Elettromeccanico or just "MOSE"—is being constructed out in the lagoon to cut off the highest of these high tides (controversial because of its environmental impact), and is expected to be operational sometime in 2018.

vaporetto docks have timetables posted. You can buy tickets at Venezia Unica offices, authorized retailers that display the ACTV/Venezia Unica sticker in town, and usually at the dock itself, though not all of these have machines or kiosks that sell tickets. If you haven't bought a pass (p. 408) or tickets beforehand, you'll have to settle up with the conductor onboard (look for him immediately on boarding—he won't come looking for you) or risk a stiff fine of at least 60€ (plus ticket price and admin fees), no excuses accepted. Also available are 48-hour tickets (30€), 72-hour tickets (40€) and 1-week tickets (60€). If you're planning to stay in Venice for a week or more and intend to use the *vaporetto* service a lot, it makes sense to pick up a **Venezia Unica city pass** (see "Venice Discounts," on p. 408), with which you can buy *vaporetto* tickets for just 1.50€. You must validate (stamp) all tickets in the yellow machines at the docks before getting aboard.

BY TRAGHETTO Just four bridges span the Grand Canal, and to fill in the gaps, *traghetti* skiffs (oversize gondolas rowed by two standing *gondolieri*) cross the Grand Canal at several intermediate points. Stations were traditionally located at the end of streets named Calle del Traghetto, and indicated by a yellow sign with the black gondola symbol. These days only a handful operate regularly, primarily at San Tomà, Santa Maria del Giglio and Santa Sofia (check with a local if in doubt). The fare is 2€ (locals pay just 0.50€), which you hand to the gondolier when boarding. Most Venetians cross standing up. Try the Santa Sofia crossing (daily: 7:30am–6:30pm Oct–Mar, 7:30am–7pm Apr–Sep) that connects the Ca' d'Oro and the Pescheria fish market, on the Grand Canal just north of the Rialto Bridge—the gondoliers expertly dodge water traffic at this point of the canal, where it's the busiest and most heart-stopping.

BY WATER TAXI *Taxi acquei* (water taxis) charge high prices and aren't for visitors watching their euros. Trips in town are likely to cost at least 40€ to 70€, depending on distance, time of day, and whether you've booked in advance or just hired on the spot. Each trip includes allowance for up to four to five pieces of luggage—beyond that there's a surcharge of 3€ to 5€ per piece (rates differ slightly according to company and how you reserve your trip). Plus there's a 20€ supplement for service from 10pm to 7am, and a 5€ charge for taxis on-call. Those rates cover up to four people; if any more squeeze in, it's another 5€ to 10€ per extra passenger (maximum 10 people). Taking a water taxi from the train station to Piazza San Marco or any area hotels costs around 80€ (the Lido is 90€), while the fixed fee to the airport is 105€ (for up to four people). Taxis to Burano or Torcello will be at least 120€. Note that only taxi boats with a yellow strip are the official operators sanctioned by the city. You can book trips with **Consorzio Moscafi Venezia** online at **www.motoscafivenezia.it** or call ✆ **041-5222303.**

Six water-taxi stations serve key points in the city: the Ferrovia, Piazzale Roma, the Rialto Bridge, Piazza San Marco, the Lido, and Marco Polo Airport.

[Fast FACTS] VENICE

Consulates See chapter 16.

Doctors & Hospitals The **Ospedale Civile Santi Giovanni e Paolo** (✆ **041-5294111**), on Campo Santi Giovanni e Paolo in Castello, has English-speaking staff and provides 24/7 emergency service (*vaporetto:* Ospedale).

Internet Access Most hotels, hostels, and bars offer free Wi-Fi. Venice also offers citywide Wi-Fi through the **VeniceConnected** (www.veneziaunica.it) network of 200 hotspots. Buy packages online (5€/24 hr., 15€/3 days, or 20€/7 days); access codes are then sent via e-mail. Internet cafes are now very rare in Venice.

Mail The most convenient post offices are: **Venezia Centro** at Calle de la Acque, San Marco (✆ **041-2404149;** Mon–Fri 8:25am–7:10pm and Sat 8:25am–12:35pm); **Venezia 4** at Calle de l'Ascension 1241, off the west side of Piazza San Marco (✆ **041-2446711**; Tues–Fri 8:25am–1:35pm and Sat 8:25am–12:35pm); and **Venezia 3** at Campo San Polo 2012 (✆ **041-5200315;** same hours as Venezia 4).

Pharmacies The city's pharmacies take turns staying open all night. To find out which one is on call in your area, ask at your hotel or check the signs posted outside all pharmacies.

Safety Generally speaking, Venice is one of Italy's safest cities. Be aware of petty crime like pickpocketing on the crowded *vaporetti*, particularly the tourist routes, where passengers are more intent on the passing scenery than on watching their bags. Venice's often deserted back streets are virtually crime-free, though occasional tales of theft have circulated.

EXPLORING VENICE

Venice is notorious for changing and extending the opening hours of its museums and, to a lesser degree, its churches. Before you begin your exploration of Venice's sights, ask at the tourist office for the season's list of museum and church hours. During peak months, you can enjoy extended museum hours—some stay open until 7pm or even 10pm—but unfortunately these hours are not released until sometime around Easter. Little is done to publicize the info, so you have to do your own research.

San Marco

Basilica di San Marco (St. Mark's) ★★★ CATHEDRAL One of the grandest, and certainly the most exotic of all cathedrals in Europe, **Basilica di San Marco** is a treasure heap of Venetian art and all sorts of booty garnered from the eastern Mediterranean. Legend has it that **St. Mark,** on his way to Rome in the 1st century a.d, was told by an angel his body would rest near the lagoon that would one today become Venice. Hundreds of years later, the city fathers were looking for a saint of high stature to replace their original patron St. Theodore, more in

Byzantine mosaics adorn the Basilica di San Marco.

keeping with their lofty aspirations. In 828 the prophecy was fulfilled when Venetian merchants stole the remains of St. Mark from Alexandria in Egypt (supposedly the body was packed in pickled pork to avoid the attention of the Muslim guards). Today the high altar's green marble canopy on alabaster columns is believed to cover the remains of St Mark and continues to be the focus of the basilica, at least for the faithful.

Modeled on Constantinople's Church of the Twelve Apostles, the original shrine of St. Mark was consecrated in 832, but in 976 the church burned down. The present incarnation was completed in 1094, then extended and embellished over the years it served as the doge's personal church. Today San Marco looks more Orthodox cathedral than Roman Catholic church, with a cavernous interior gilded with Byzantine mosaics added over 7 centuries, covering every inch of ceiling and pavement.

For a closer look at the most remarkable ceiling mosaics and a better view of the Oriental-carpet-like patterns of the pavement mosaics, pay the admission to go upstairs to the **Museo di San Marco** (enter in the atrium at the principal entrance); this was originally the women's gallery, or *matroneum,* and includes access to the outdoor **Loggia dei Cavalli**. Here you can admire a panoramic view of the piazza below and replicas of the celebrated ***Triumphal Quadriga***, four gilded bronze horses dating from the 2nd or 3rd century A.D.; the Roman originals were moved inside in the 1980s for preservation. (The word *quadriga* actually refers to a car or chariot pulled by four horses, though in this case there are only the horses.) The horses were transported to Venice from Constantinople in 1204, along with lots of other loot from the Fourth Crusade.

The basilica's greatest treasure is the altarpiece known as the **Pala d'Oro (Golden Altarpiece),** a Gothic masterpiece encrusted with over 2,000 precious gems and 83 enameled panels. It was created in 10th-century Constantinople and embellished by Venetian and Byzantine artisans between the 12th and 14th centuries. Second to the Pala d'Oro in importance is the 10th-century **"Madonna di Nicopeia,"** a bejeweled icon also purloined from Constantinople and exhibited in its own chapel. Also worth a visit is the **Tesoro (Treasury),** a collection of crusaders' plunder from

Know Before You Go

The guards at St. Mark's entrance are serious about forbidding entry to anyone in inappropriate attire—shorts, sleeveless shirts, cropped tops, and skirts above the knee. Note also that you cannot enter the basilica with luggage, and that photos and filming inside are forbidden. With masses of people descending on the cathedral every day, your best bet for avoiding the long lines is to come early in the morning. Although the basilica is open Sunday morning for anyone wishing to attend Mass, non-worshippers cannot enter merely to tour the site.

Basilica di San Marco 21
Bridge of Sighs (Ponte dei Sospiri) 23
Campanile di San Marco 20
Contarini del Bovolo 13
Fondaco dei Tedeschi 11
Galleria Giorgio Franchetti alla Ca' d'Oro 10
Gallerie dell'Accademia 8
Giardini 24
Il Ghetto (The Jewish Ghetto) 5
Museo Correr 17
Museo Ebraico di Venezia 6
Palazzo Ducale 22
Peggy Guggenheim Collection 9
Piazza San Marco 18
Punta della Dogana 16
Rialto Bridge 12
San Sebastiano 4
Santa Maria della Salute 15
Santa Maria Gloriosa dei Frari 2
Scuola di San Giorgio degli Schiavoni 25
Scuola Grande dei Carmini 3
Scuola Grande di San Rocco 1
Squero di San Trovaso 7
SS. Giovanni e Paolo 26
Teatro La Fenice 14
Torre dell'Orologio 19
SANTA CROCE
SAN POLO
DORSODURO
Canàl Grande
Canale della Giudecca
Campo S. Geremia
S. Geremia
Riva da Biásio
Palazzo Giovanelli
Fònd. d. Turchi
Palazzo Donà-Balbi
S. Zan Degolà
Ca' Tron
S. Stae
Ca' Pesaro
Pal. Mocenigo
Calle d. Tintòr
S. Simeòn Grande
S. Giacomo dell'Orio
Campo S. Giacomo dell'Oro
Palazzo Gradenigo
Campo N. Sáuro
S. Maria Máter Domini
Pal. Zane
S. Cassiar
Rio d. S. Cassiano
Palazzo Soranzo-Cappello
Fond. Rio Marin
Pal. Grioni
Calle d. Chiesa
Rio di S. Agostino
Pal. Muti Baglioni
Scuola Grande di S. Giovanni
Pal. Zane Collalto
Palazzo Albrizzi
Pal. Molin Cappello
Pal. Molìn
Rio di S. Polo
S. Giovanni Evangelista
Pal. Donà d. Rose
Pal. Corner
Campo S. Polo
Pal. Soranzo
Ex Convento dei Frari
Palazzo Zen
Campo d. Frari
San Polo
S. Rocco
Frari
Rio di San Polo
Pal. Papadopoli
Scuola Grande di San Rocco
Palazzo Centani (Museo Goldoni)
Pal. Dona
Pal. Grimani
Pal. Layard
Palazzo Barbarigo
Rio d. Frescada
S. Pantalòn
S. Tomà
Pal. Civràn-Grimani
S. Ángelo
Rio Ca' Foscari
Calle Foscari
Pal. Balbi
Pal. Cornèr Spinelli
Pal. Fortuny
Palazzo Mocenigo
Campo Santa Margherita
Ca' Foscari
Pal. Contarini d. Figure
Rio di S. Angelo
Oratorio dell'Annunciata
Campo S. Ángel
Palazzo Foscarini
Palazzo Moro-Lin
Pal. Grassi
Saliz S. Samuele
C. Crosera
Pal. Nani
Cărmini
Ca' Rezzonico
S. Samuele
San Samuele
S. Stefano
Pal. Zenóbia
Ist. Sup. d'Arte Applicata
Palazzo Malipiero
Campo S. Barnaba
S. Bárnaba
Ca' Rezzonico
Campo S. Stefano
S. Maurízio
Rio Malpaga
Pal. Stern
Ca' del Duca
Rio del Duca
C. Vetturi
Rio di S. Vidal
Pal. Morosini
Pal. Loredan
Rio di Santissimo
S. Maria d. Giglio
S. Sebastiano
Pal. Falier
Pal. Contarini degli Scrigni
Pal. Bárbaro
Pal. Pisani
Palazzo Cornèr d. Ca' Granda
Ponte dell'Accademia
Accademia
Pal. Molìn
Gallerie dell' Accademia
Palazzo Contarini dal Zaffo
S. Maria d. Gíglio
S. Trovaso
Rio di S. Trovaso
Pal. Centani
Pal. Venièr dei Leoni (Guggenheim)
S. Basílio
Pal. Molìn
Pal. Nani
Pal. Giustiniàn
Rio di S. Vio
S. Maria d. Visitaz.
S. Agnese
Fond. Bragadin
Gesuati
Záttere

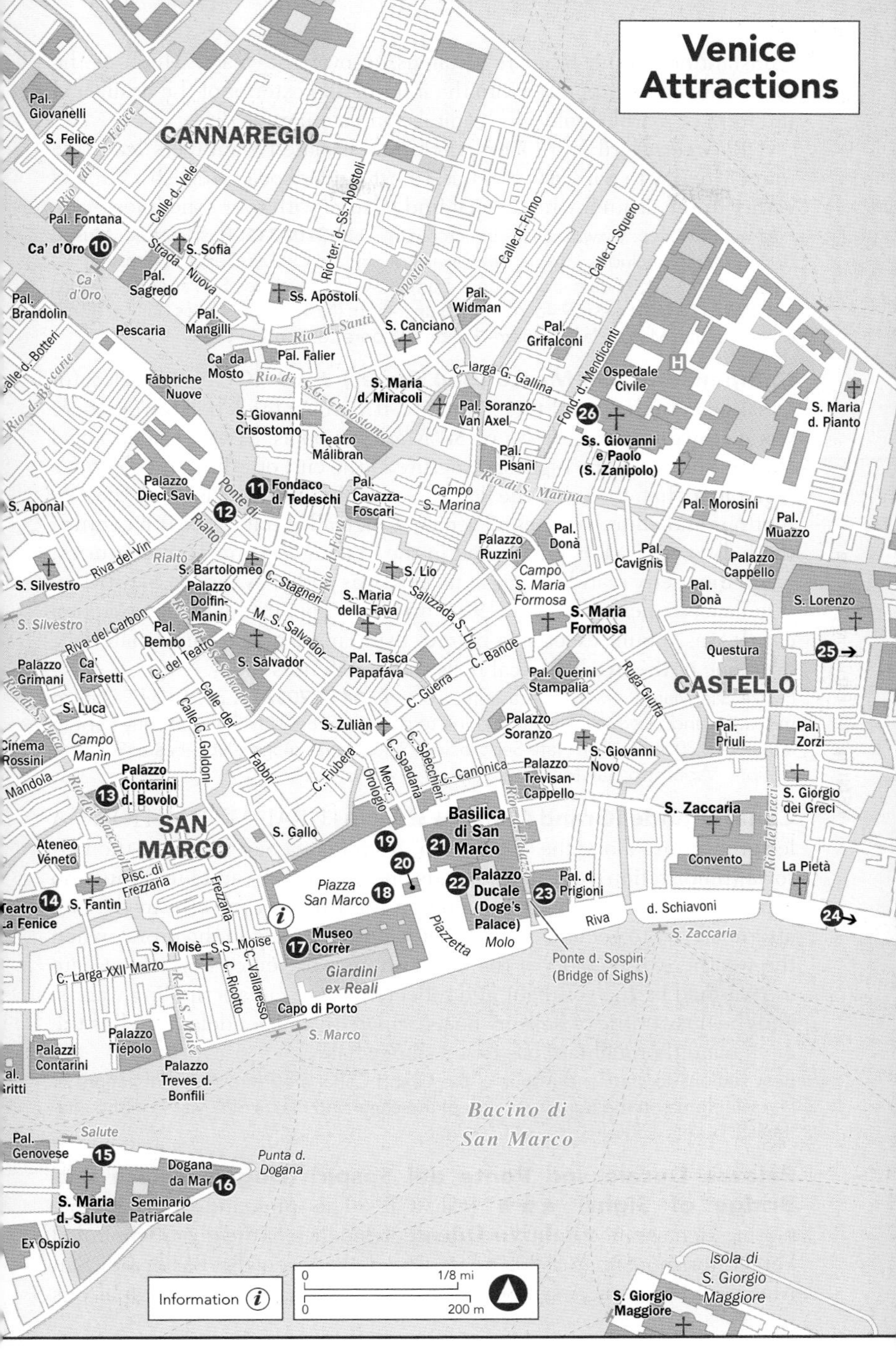
Venice Attractions
CANNAREGIO
SAN MARCO
CASTELLO
Ca' d'Oro 10
Fondaco d. Tedeschi 11
Ponte di Rialto 12
Palazzo Contarini d. Bovolo 13
Teatro La Fenice 14
15
16
Museo Corrèr 17
Piazza San Marco 18
19
20
Basilica di San Marco 21
Palazzo Ducale (Doge's Palace) 22
23
24
25
26
Ss. Giovanni e Paolo (S. Zanipolo)
S. Maria d. Miracoli
S. Maria Formosa
S. Zaccaria
S. Maria d. Salute
S. Giorgio Maggiore
Ponte d. Sospiri (Bridge of Sighs)
Bacino di San Marco
Isola di S. Giorgio Maggiore
Information
0 1/8 mi
0 200 m

Constantinople and other relics amassed over the years. Much of the loot has been incorporated into the interior and exterior of the basilica in the form of marble, columns, capitals, and statuary.

Between April and October, church-affiliated volunteers lead free tours Monday to Saturday at 11am (most guides speak English). Groups gather in the atrium, where you'll find posters with tour schedules.

Piazza San Marco. www.basilicasanmarco.it. ✆ **041-2708311.** Basilica free; Museo di San Marco (includes Loggia dei Cavalli) 5€, Pala d'Oro 2€, Tesoro (Treasury) 3€. Basilica Mon–Sat 9:30am–5pm, Sun 2–5pm (Nov–Easter closes Sun at 4pm). Tesoro and Pala d'Oro Mon–Sat 9:45am–5pm, Sun 2–5pm (Nov–Easter closes daily at 4pm). Museo di San Marco daily 9:45am–4:45pm. *Vaporetto:* San Marco.

Campanile di San Marco (Bell Tower) ★★★ ICON An elevator whisks you to the top of this 97m (318-ft.) brown brick bell tower where you get awe-inspiring views of St. Mark's cupolas. With a gilded angel atop its spire, it is the highest structure in the city, offering a pigeon's-eye panorama that includes the lagoon, neighboring islands, and the red rooftops and church domes of Venice. Originally built in the 9th century, the bell tower was reconstructed in the 12th, 14th, and 16th centuries, when the pretty marble loggia at its base was added by Jacopo Sansovino. It collapsed unexpectedly in 1902, miraculously hurting no one except a cat. It was rebuilt exactly as before, using most of the same materials, even one of the five historical bells that it still uses today.

Piazza San Marco. www.basilicasanmarco.it. ✆ **041-2708311.** 8€. Daily: Easter to mid-June and Oct 9am–7pm; mid-June to early Sept 8:30am–9:30pm; early Sept to late Sept 8:30am–8:15pm, late Sept to Sept 30 8:30am–7:45pm; Nov–Easter 9:30am–5:30pm. *Vaporetto:* San Marco.

Canal Grande (Grand Canal) ★★★ NATURAL ATTRACTION A leisurely cruise along the "Canalazzo" from Piazza San Marco to the Ferrovia (train station), or the reverse, is one of Venice's (and life's) must-do experiences (see box, p. 395). Hop on the **no. 1 *vaporetto*** in the late afternoon (try to get one of the coveted outdoor seats in the prow), when the weather-worn colors of the former homes of Venice's merchant elite are warmed by the soft light and reflected in the canal's rippling waters, and the busy traffic of delivery boats, *vaporetti,* and gondolas that fills the city's main thoroughfare has eased somewhat.

Best stations to start/end a tour of the Grand Canal are Ferrovia (train station) or Piazzale Roma on the northwest side of the canal and Piazza San Marco in the southeast. Tickets 7.50€.

Palazzo Ducale and Ponte dei Sospiri (Doge's Palace and Bridge of Sighs) ★★★ PALACE The pink-and-white marble Gothic-Renaissance **Palazzo Ducale,** residence of the doges who ruled Venice for more than 1,000 years, stands between the Basilica di San Marco and the sea. A symbol of prosperity and power, the original was destroyed by a succession of fires, with the current building started in 1340, extended in the 1420s, and redesigned again after a fire in 1483. If you want to understand something of this magnificent place, the history of the 1,000-year-old maritime republic, and the intrigue of the government that ruled it, take the **Secret Itineraries tour ★★★** (see "Secrets of the Palazzo Ducale," p. 404). Failing that, at least download the free iPhone/Android app (see the website) or shell out for the audioguide tour (available at entrance, 5€) to help make sense of it all. Unless you can tag along with an English-speaking tour group, you may otherwise miss out on the importance of much of what you're seeing.

The 15th-century **Porta della Carta (Paper Gate)** opens onto a splendid inner courtyard with a double row of Renaissance arches (today visitors enter through a doorway on the lagoon side of the palace). The self-guided route through the palace begins on the main courtyard, where the **Museo dell'Opera** contains assorted bits of masonry preserved from the palazzo's exterior. Beyond here, the first major room you'll come to is the spacious **Sala delle Quattro Porte (Hall of the Four Doors),** with a worn ceiling by Tintoretto. The **Sala dell'Anticollegio** is where foreign ambassadors waited to be received by the doge and his council. It is covered in four works by Tintoretto, and Veronese's **"Rape of Europa" ★★**, considered one of the palazzo's finest. It steals some of the thunder of Tintoretto's "Mercury & the Three Graces" and **"Bacchus and Ariadne" ★★**—the latter considered one of his best by some critics. The highlight of the adjacent **Sala del Collegio** (the Council Chamber itself) is the spectacular cycle of **ceiling paintings ★★** by Veronese, completed between 1575 and 1578 and one of his masterpieces. Next door lies the most impressive of the interior rooms, the richly adorned **Sala del Senato (Senate Chamber),** with Tintoretto's ceiling painting "The Triumph of Venice." After passing again through the Sala delle Quattro Porte, you'll come to the Veronese-decorated **Stanza del Consiglio dei Dieci (Room of the Council of Ten),** the Republic's dreaded security police. It was in this room that justice was dispensed and decapitations ordered. Formed in the 14th century to deal with emergency situations, the Ten were considered more powerful than the Senate and feared by all. In the **Sala della Bussola (the Compass Chamber),** notice the **Bocca dei Leoni (Lion's Mouth),** a slit in the wall into which secret denunciations and accusations of enemies of the state were placed for quick action by the much-feared Council.

The main sight on the next level down—indeed, in the entire palace—is the **Sala del Maggior Consiglio (Great Council Hall).** This enormous space is animated by Tintoretto's huge **"Paradiso" ★** at the far end of the hall above the doge's seat. Measuring 7×23m (23×75 ft.),

secrets OF THE PALAZZO DUCALE

The **Itinerari Segreti (Secret Itineraries) ★★★** guided tours of the Palazzo Ducale are a must-see for any visit to Venice of more than 1 day. The tours offer an unparalleled look into the world of Venetian politics over the centuries and are the only way to access the otherwise restricted quarters and hidden passageways of this enormous palace, such as the doges' private chambers and the torture chambers where prisoners were interrogated. The tour must be reserved in advance online (www.palazzoducale.visitmuve.it), by phone (toll-free within Italy ✆ **848-082-000,** or from abroad 041-4273-0892), or in person at the ticket desk. Tours often sell out at least a few days ahead, especially from spring through fall. Tours in English are daily at 9:55am, 10:45am and 11:35am, and cost 20€ for adults, 14€ for children ages 6 to 14 and students ages 15 to 25. There are also tours in Italian at 9:30am and 11:10am, and French at 10:20am and noon. The tour lasts about 75 minutes.

it is said to be the world's largest oil painting; together with Veronese's gorgeous **"Il Trionfo di Venezia" ("The Triumph of Venice") ★★** in the oval panel on the ceiling, it affirms the power emanating from the council sessions held here. Tintoretto also did the portraits of the 76 doges encircling the top of this chamber; note that the picture of the Doge Marin Falier, who was convicted of treason and beheaded in 1355, has been blacked out—Venice has never forgiven him. Tours culminate at the enclosed **Ponte dei Sospiri (Bridge of Sighs),** built in 1600, which connects the Ducal Palace with the grim **Palazzo delle Prigioni (Prison).** The bridge took its current name in the 19th century, when visiting northern European poets romantically imagined the prisoners' final resignation upon viewing the outside world one last time before being locked in their fetid cells. Some of the cells still have the original graffiti of past prisoners, many of them locked up interminably for petty crimes.

San Marco, Piazza San Marco. www.palazzoducale.visitmuve.it. ✆ **041-2715911.** Admission only with San Marco Museum Pass (19€; see "Venice Discounts," p. 408). For an Itinerari Segreti (Secret Itineraries) guided tour in English, see "Secrets of the Palazzo Ducale," p. 404. Daily 8:30am–7pm (Nov–Mar until 5:30pm). *Vaporetto:* San Marco.

Rialto Bridge ★★ ICON This graceful arch over the Grand Canal, linking the San Marco and San Polo districts, teems with tourists and overpriced boutiques. Until the 1800s, it was the only bridge across the Grand Canal, originally built as a pontoon bridge at the canal's narrowest point. The 1444 incarnation was the first to include shops, interrupted by a drawbridge in the center. In 1592, the current graceful stone span was finished to the designs of Antonio da Ponte, who beat out Sansovino,

Palladio, and Michelangelo with plans that called for a single, vast, 28m-wide (92-ft.) arch in the center to allow trading ships to pass.
Ponte del Rialto. *Vaporetto:* Rialto.

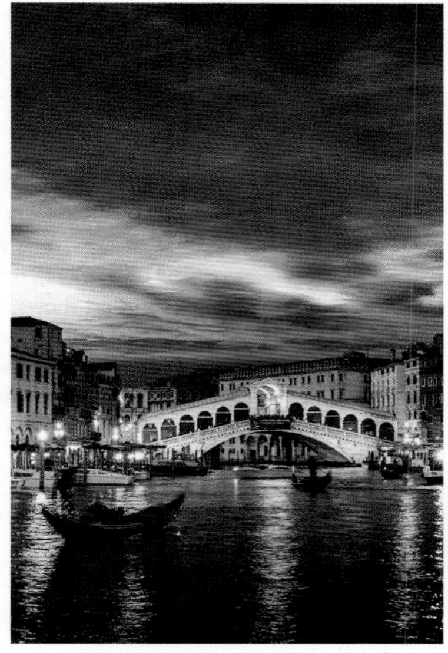
The Rialto Bridge at sunset.

Scala Contarini del Bovolo ★★ STAIRCASE Artfully restored and opened in 2016, this is one of the city's newest attractions. Part of a palazzo built in the late 15th century, this multi-arch spiral staircase leads to a belvedere with fabulous views of Venice. Halfway up, the **Tintoretto Room** contains the rare portrait of Lazzaro Zen, an African who converted to Christianity in Venice in 1770, as well as a preparatory painting by Tintoretto of his monumental "Paradise" (the final version is in the Palazzo Ducale).
Corte Contarini del Bovolo 4299, San Marco. www.scalacontarinidelbovolo.com. ✆ **041-3096605.** Admission 7€; audioguide 1€. Daily 10am–1:30pm and 2–6pm. Vaporetto: Rialto.

Teatro La Fenice ★★★ OPERA HOUSE One of Italy's most famous opera houses (it ranks third after La Scala in Milan and San Carlo in Naples), La Fenice was originally completed in 1792 but has been rebuilt twice after devastating fires; in 1837 and most recently in 2004. Self-guided tours take in the opulent main theater, ornate side rooms, the gilded "royal box," and a small exhibit dedicated to soprano Maria Callas.
Campo San Fantin 1965, San Marco. www.teatrolafenice.it. ✆ **041-2424.** Admission 10€. Daily 9:30am–6pm.Vaporetto: Giglio.

T Fondaco dei Tedeschi ★★ PALAZZO This 16th-century palazzo was converted into a posh department store in 2016, centered on an elegant courtyard and a roof deck with quite possibly Venice's greatest view: the Rialto, Grand Canal, and all the city's bell towers laid out before you.
Calle de Fontego dei Tedeschi, Ponte di Rialto, San Marco. www.dfs.com/en/venice. ✆ **041-3142000.** Daily 10am–8pm (roof deck free).Vaporetto: Rialto.

Torre dell'Orologio (Clock Tower) MONUMENT As you enter the magnificent **Piazza San Marco,** it's one of the first things you see, standing on the north side, the centerpiece of the stately white **Procuratie Vecchie** (the ancient administration buildings for the Republic). The

Renaissance clock tower was built between 1496 and 1506, and the clock mechanism still keeps perfect time (although most of the original workings have been replaced). On the top, two bronze figures, known as "Moors" because of the dark color of the bronze, pivot to strike the hour. Visits are by guided tour only (included in the price of admission).

The Biennale

Venice hosts the latest in contemporary art and sculpture from dozens of countries during the prestigious **Biennale d'Arte ★★★** (www.labiennale.org; ✆ **041-5218711**), one of the world's top international art shows. It fills the pavilions of the **Giardini** (public gardens) at the east end of **Castello** and at the **Arsenale**, as well as in other spaces around the city from May to November every odd-numbered year (usually open Tues–Sun 10am–6pm). Tickets cost around 25€, 20€ for those 65 and over, and 15€ for students and all those 26 and under.

Piazza San Marco. www.torreorologio.visitmuve.it. ✆ **848-082000** or 041-42730892. 12€, 7€ for children ages 6–14 and students ages 15–25; ticket also good for the Museo Correr, the Museo Archeologico Nazionale, and the Biblioteca Nazionale Marciana (but not Palazzo Ducale). Tours (1hr) in English Mon–Wed 10am and 11am, Thurs–Sun 2pm and 3pm (must be reserved in advance); tours start at the Museo Correr ticket office. There are also tours in Italian and French. *Vaporetto:* San Marco.

Castello

Basilica SS. Giovanni e Paolo ★ CHURCH This massive Gothic church was built by the Dominican order from the 13th to the 15th century and, together with the Frari Church in San Polo, is second in size only to the Basilica di San Marco. An unofficial Pantheon where 25 doges are buried (a number of tombs are part of the unfinished facade), the church, commonly known as Zanipolo in Venetian dialect, is also home to many artistic treasures. The brilliantly colored "**Polyptych of St. Vincent Ferrer**" (ca. 1465), attributed to a young Giovanni Bellini, is in the right aisle. You'll also see the mummified foot of St. Catherine of Siena—considered a holy relic—encased in glass near here. Visit the **Cappella del Rosario ★**, through a glass door off the left transept, to see three restored ceiling canvases and one oil painting by Paolo Veronese, particularly "The Assumption of the Madonna."

Anchoring the large and impressive *campo* outside the church, a popular crossroads for this area of Castello, is the **statue of Bartolomeo Colleoni ★★**, the Renaissance *condottiere* (mercenary) who defended Venice's interests at the height of its power until his death in 1475. The 15th-century sculpture by the Florentine **Andrea Verrocchio** is considered one of the world's great equestrian monuments.

Campo Santi Giovanni e Paolo 6363. www.basilicasantigiovanniepaolo.it. ✆ **041-5235913.** Admission 3.50€. Daily 7:30am–7pm (open to tourists Mon–Sat 9am–6pm and Sun noon–6pm). *Vaporetto:* Rialto.

Scuola di San Giorgio degli Schiavoni ★★ MUSEUM One of the most mesmerizing spaces in Europe, the tiny main hall of this *scuola* once served as a meeting house for Venice's Dalmatian community (Dalmatia is a region of Croatia—*schiavoni* means "Slavs"). Venetian *scuole,* or schools, were guilds that brought together merchants and craftspeople from certain trades or similar religious devotions. Built beside its sister church, San Giovanni di Malta, in the early 16th century, the scuola is most famous for the awe-inspiring painting cycle on its walls, created by Renaissance master **Vittore Carpaccio** between 1502 and 1509. The paintings depict the lives of the Dalmatian patron saints George (of dragon-slaying fame), Tryphon, and Jerome; in the upper hall (Sala dell'Albergo) is Carpaccio's masterful "Vision of St. Augustine."

Calle dei Furlani 3259A. ✆ **041-5228828.** Admission 5€. Mon 2:45–6pm, Tues–Sat 9:15am–1pm and 2:45–6pm, Sun 9:15am–1pm. *Vaporetto:* Rialto.

Dorsoduro

Gallerie dell'Accademia (Academy Gallery) ★★★ MUSEUM Along with San Marco and the Palazzo Ducale, the **Accademia** is one of the city's highlights, a magnificent collection of European art and Venetian painting from the 14th to the 18th centuries. Visitors are currently limited to 300 at one time, so lines can be long in high season—advance reservations are essential. There's a lot to take in here, so buy a catalog in the store if you'd like to learn more—the audio guides are a little muddled and not worth 6€. Note also that Da Vinci's iconic **Vitruvian Man** ★★★, one of the museum's prize holdings, is an extremely fragile ink drawing and rarely displayed in public.

Rooms are laid out in rough chronological order, though on-and-off again renovations mean some rooms may be off-limits when you visit (call ahead to check on specific paintings; the website is not updated regularly). The following artworks should be on display somewhere in the museum, though locations may change. Visits normally begin upstairs on the first floor, where room 1 (the grand meeting room of the Scuola Grande di Santa Maria) displays a beautifully presented collection of lavish medieval and early Renaissance art, primarily religious images and altarpieces dating from 1300 to 1450.

The giant canvases in room 2 include Carpaccio's "Presentation of Jesus in the Temple," and works by Giovanni Bellini (one of Bellini's images of St. Peter lies in room 3).

Rooms 6 to 8 feature Venetian heavyweights Tintoretto, Titian, Veronese, and Lorenzo Lotto, while Room 10 is dominated by Paolo Veronese's mammoth **"Feast in the House of Levi"** ★★. Vast Tintoretto canvases make up the rest of the room. Opposite is Titian's last painting, a "Pietà" intended for his own tomb.

VENICE discounts

Venice offers a somewhat bewildering range of passes and discount cards. We recommend buying an **ACTV travel card** (p. 394) and combining that with one of the first two passes listed below: The more complex Venezia Unica card scheme is convenient once you've worked out what you want online, but doesn't save you much money, and its main components are only valid for 7 days. However, the Venezia Unica website (www.veneziaunica.it) is now also a one-stop shop for all the passes listed below.

The **Museum Pass** (www.vivaticket.it) grants admission to all the city-run museums over a 6-month period—it also lets you skip any ticketing lines, a useful perk in high season. The pass includes the museums of St. Mark's Square (Palazzo Ducale, Museo Correr, Museo Archeologico Nazionale, and the Biblioteca Nazionale Marciana) as well as the Museo di Palazzo Mocenigo (Costume Museum), the Ca' Rezzonico, the Ca' Pesaro, the Museo del Vetro (Glass Museum) on Murano, and the Museo del Merletto (Lace Museum) on Burano. The Museum Pass is available online (for an extra 0.50€), or at any of the participating museums and costs 24€ for adults, and 18€ for students under 30 and kids aged 6–14. The **Chorus Pass** (www.chorusvenezia.org) grants admission to every major church in Venice, 18 in all, for 12€ (8€ for students under 30), for up to 1 year. For 24€, the **Chorus Pass Family** gives you the same perks for two adults and their children up to 18 years old.

The **Venezia Unica card** (www.veneziaunica.it) combines the above passes, transport, discounts, and even Internet access on one card via a "made-to-order" online system, where you choose the services you want. The most useful option is the **All Venice City Pass**, which combines the Museum Pass and Chorus Pass plus free entry to the Jewish Museum and discounts on temporary exhibits for 39.90€ for 7 days (29.90€ for ages 6–29). You can also buy various transportation packages and Wi-Fi access (from 5€ for 24hr.). Once you've paid, you'll be able to simply print out a voucher to use at museums and sights in Venice; to use public transport you must collect tickets by entering your booking code at one of the ACTV automatic ticket machines or by visiting one of the official Points of Sale in in the city (there's one in the train station open 7am to 9pm).

For visitors between the ages of 6 and 29, the **Rolling Venice** card (also available at www.veneziaunica.it) is valid until the end of the year in which you buy it, costs just 6€, and entitles the bearer to significant (20%–30%) discounts at participating restaurants (but only applies to cardholder's meal) and a similar discount on ACTV travel cards (22€ for 3 days). Holders of the Rolling Venice card also get discounts in museums, stores, hotels, and bars across the city (it comes with a thick booklet listing everywhere you're entitled to get discounts).

Room 11 contains work by Tiepolo, the master of 18th-century Venetian painting, and several paintings by Tintoretto.

Room 19 has traditionally contained the monumental cycle of nine paintings by Carpaccio illustrating the **Story of St. Ursula ★★**; most of these continue to undergo restoration, with "Arrival in Cologne" the only one likely to be displayed for some time.

The sculpture garden at the Peggy Guggenheim Collection.

Room 20 is filled by Gentile Bellini's cycle of **"The Miracles of the Relic of the Cross"** ★, painted around 1500.

While renovations are ongoing, room 23 will contain some of the museum's most famous paintings, including a gorgeous "St. George" by Mantegna, Della Francesca's "St. Jerome," a "St. John the Baptist" by Antonio Viviani, plus a series of Bellini Madonnas and his monumental "Martyrdom of St. Mark." Pride of place goes to Giorgione's enigmatic and utterly mystifying **"Tempest"** ★★.

Finally, room 24 is adorned with Titian's "Presentation of the Virgin," actually created to hang in this space.

Campo della Carità 1050, at foot of Ponte dell'Accademia. www.gallerieaccademia.org. ✆ **041-5200345.** Admission 12€ adults (during temporary exhibitions the price of admission is subject to change); free on first Sunday of the month (check in advance). Reservations by phone or online incur a 1.50€ charge. Daily 8:15am–7:15pm (Mon until 2pm). *Vaporetto:* Accademia.

Peggy Guggenheim Collection ★★ MUSEUM It's one of the best museums in Italy when it comes to American and European art of the 20th century, but you might find the experience a little jarring given its location in a city so heavily associated with the High Renaissance and the baroque. Nevertheless, art aficionados will find some fascinating work here, and the galleries occupy Peggy Guggenheim's wonderful former home, the 18th-century Palazzo Venier dei Leoni, right on the Grand Canal. Guggenheim purchased the mansion in 1949 and lived here, on and off, until her death in 1979. Highlights include Picasso's extremely abstract "Poet," and his more gentle "On the Beach," several works by Kandinsky ("Landscape with Red Spots No. 2" and "White Cross"), Miró's expressionistic "Seated Woman II," Klee's mystical "Magic Garden," and some unsettling works by Max Ernst ("The Kiss," "Attirement of the Bride"), who was briefly married to Guggenheim in the 1940s. Also look for Magritte's "Empire of Light," Dalí's "Birth of Liquid Desires," and a couple of gems from Pollock: his early "Moon Woman," which recalls Picasso, and "Alchemy," a more typical "poured" painting. The Italian Futurists are also well represented here, with a rare portrait from Modigliani ("Portrait of the Painter Frank Haviland").

Fondamenta Venier dai Leon 704. www.guggenheim-venice.it. ✆ **041-2405411.** Admission 15€ adults; 13€ 65 and over, and those who present an Alitalia ticket to or from Venice dated no more than 7 days previous; 9€ students 26 and under and children ages 10–18. Wed–Mon 10am–6pm. *Vaporetto:* Accademia (walk around left side of Accademia, take 1st left, and walk straight ahead following the signs).

San Sebastiano ★★ CHURCH Lose the crowds as you make a pilgrimage to this monument to **Paolo Veronese,** his parish church and home to some of his finest work. Veronese painted the coffered nave ceiling with the florid "Scenes from the Life of St. Esther." He also decorated the organ shutters and panels in the chancel in the 1560s with scenes from the life of St. Sebastian. Although Veronese is the main event here, don't miss Titian's sensitive "St. Nicholas" (just inside the church on the right). Veronese's sepulchral monument (with bust by Mattia Carneri) is to the left of the altar. The real highlight is the sacristy (go through the door under the organ), a tiny jewel box of a room adorned with more wonderful Veronese paintings of the "Coronation of the Virgin" and the "Four Evangelists."

Campo San Sebastiano. ✆ **041-2750462.** Admission 3€. Mon–Sat 10:30am–4:30pm. *Vaporetto:* San Basilio.

Santa Maria della Salute (Church of the Virgin Mary of Good Health) ★ CHURCH Known as "La Salute," this crown jewel of baroque architecture proudly reigns at a commercially and aesthetically important point, almost directly across from the Piazza San Marco, where the Grand Canal empties into the lagoon. The first stone was laid in 1631 after the Senate decided to honor the Virgin Mary for delivering Venice from a plague that had killed around 95,000 people. It was built from the revolutionary plans of a young, relatively unknown architect, Baldassare Longhena, who dedicated the next 50 years of his life to

Entrance to Santa Maria della Salute church.

overseeing its progress (he would die 5 years before its completion). Today the dome of the church is an iconic presence on the Venice skyline, recognized for its exuberant exterior of volutes, scrolls, and more than 125 statues. The most revered image inside is the **Madonna della Salute,** a rare black-faced sculpture of Mary brought back from Candia in Crete in 1670 as war booty. The otherwise sober interior is enlivened by the **sacristy,** with a number of important ceiling paintings and portraits by **Titian.** On the right wall of the sacristy, which you have to pay to enter, is Tintoretto's **"Marriage at Cana" ★**, considered one of his best paintings.

Campo della Salute 1. ✆ **041-5225558.** Church free; sacristy 3€. Daily 9am–noon and 3–5:30pm. *Vaporetto:* Salute.

Scuola Grande dei Carmini ★★ CHURCH The former Venetian base of the Carmelites, finished in the 18th century, is now a shrine of sorts to **Giambattista Tiepolo,** who painted the ceiling of the upstairs hall between 1739 and 1744. It's a magnificent sight. Tiepolo's elaborate rococo interpretation of "Simon Stock Receiving the Scapular" is now fully restored, along with various panels throughout the building.

Campo San Margherita 2617. www.scuolagrandecarmini.it. ✆ **041-5289420.** 5€. Daily 11am–5pm (Nov–Mar until 4pm). *Vaporetto:* San Basilio.

Squero di San Trovaso ★★ HISTORIC SITE One of the most intriguing sights in Venice is this small *squero* (boatyard), which first opened in the 17th century. Just north of the Zattere (the wide, sunny walkway that runs alongside the Giudecca Canal in Dorsoduro), the boatyard lies next to the Church of San Trovaso on the narrow Rio San Trovaso (not far from the Accademia Bridge). It is surrounded by Tyrolean-looking wooden structures (a rarity in this city of stone) that are home to the multigenerational owners and original workshops for traditional Venetian boats. Aware that they have become a tourist site themselves, the gondoliers don't mind if you watch them at work from across the narrow Rio di San Trovaso, but don't try to invite yourself in.
Dorsoduro 1097 (on the Rio San Trovaso). *Vaporetto:* Zattere.

San Polo & Santa Croce

Basilica Santa Maria Gloriosa dei Frari ★★ CHURCH Known simply as "i Frari," this immense 14th-century Gothic basilica was built by the Franciscans and is the largest church in Venice after San Marco. It houses a number of important artworks, including two Titian masterpieces: the **"Assumption of the Virgin" ★★** over the main altar, painted when the artist was in his late 20s, and "Virgin of the Pesaro Family" in the left nave, for which Titian's wife posed for the figure of Mary (and died soon afterward in childbirth). Don't miss Giovanni Bellini's **"Madonna & Child" ★★** over the altar in the sacristy, of which novelist Henry James wrote, "It is as solemn as it is gorgeous." The grand **mausoleum of Titian** is on the right as you enter the church, opposite the incongruous 18th-century monument to sculptor **Antonio Canova**, shaped like a pyramid—designed by Canova himself, this was originally supposed to be Titian's tomb.
Campo dei Frari 3072. www.basilicadeifrari.it. ✆ **041-2728611.** 3€, audio guide 2€. Mon–Sat 9am–6pm; Sun 1–6pm. *Vaporetto:* San Tomà (walk straight ahead on Calle del Traghetto and turn right and immediately left across Campo San Tomà; walk straight ahead, on Ramo Mandoler then Calle Larga Prima, and turn right when you reach beginning of Salizada San Rocco).

Scuola Grande di San Rocco (Confraternity of St. Roch) ★★★ MUSEUM Like many medieval saints, French-born St. Rocco (St. Roch) died young, but thanks to his work healing the sick in the 14th century, his cult became associated with the power to cure the plague and other serious illnesses. When his body was brought to Venice in 1485, this *scuola* began to reap the benefits, and by 1560 the current complex was completed. Work soon began on more than 50 paintings by **Tintoretto**, and today the *scuola* is primarily a shrine to the masterful Venetian artist. You enter at the **Ground Floor Hall (Sala Terrena),** where the paintings were created between 1583 and 1587, led by one of the most frenzied "Annunciations" ever made. The "Flight into Egypt" here is undeniably one of Tintoretto's greatest works. Upstairs is the

Great Upper Hall (Sala Superiore), where Old Testament scenes cover the ceiling. The paintings around the walls, based on the New Testament, are generally regarded as a master class of perspective, shadow, and color. In the **Sala dell'Albergo,** an entire wall is adorned by Tintoretto's mind-blowing "Crucifixion" (as well as his "Glorification of St. Roch," on the ceiling, the painting that actually won him the contract to paint the *scuola*). Way up in the loft, the **Tesoro** (Treasury) is a tiny space dedicated primarily to gold reliquaries containing venerated relics such as the fingers of St. Peter and St. Andrew, and one of the thorns that crowned Christ during the crucifixion.

Campo San Rocco 3052, adjacent to Campo dei Frari. www.scuolagrandesanrocco.org. ✆ **041-5234864.** 10€ adults (includes audio guide); 8€ ages 18–26; 18 and under free. Daily 9:30am–5:30pm. *Vaporetto:* San Tomà (walk straight ahead on Calle del Traghetto and turn right and immediately left across Campo San Tomà; walk straight ahead on Ramo Mandoler, Calle Larga Prima, and Salizada San Rocco, which leads into the *campo* of the same name—look for crimson sign behind Frari Church).

Cannaregio

Galleria Giorgio Franchetti alla Ca' d'Oro ★★ MUSEUM This magnificent palazzo overlooking the Grand Canal, the "golden house," was built between 1428 and 1430 for the noble Contarini family. Baron

Kayaking the canal at Cannaregio.

Galleria Giorgio Franchetti alla Ca' d'Oro is an intimate art museum on the Grand Canal.

Giorgio Franchetti bought the place in 1894, and it now serves as an atmospheric gallery for his exceptional art collection (mostly early Renaissance Italian and Flemish). The highlight is **"St. Sebastian" ★★** by Paduan artist Andrea Mantegna, displayed in its own marble side chapel. The so-called "St. Sebastian of Venice" was the third and final painting of the saint by Mantegna, created around 1490 and quite different to the other two (in Vienna and Paris); it's a bold, deeply pessimistic work, with none of Mantegna's usual background details to detract from the saint's suffering. Don't miss also the three panels from Carpaccio's "Stories of the Virgin" series on the first floor.

Strada Nuova 3932. www.cadoro.org. ✆ **041-520-0345.** 8.50€, plus 1.50€ reservation fee (higher during special exhibitions). Mon 8:15am–2pm; Tues–Sun 8:15am–7:15pm. *Vaporetto:* Ca' d'Oro.

Museo Ebraico di Venezia (Jewish Museum of Venice) ★ MUSEUM/SYNAGOGUE In the heart of the Ghetto Nuovo, the Jewish Museum contains a small but precious collection of artifacts related to the long history of the Jews in Venice, beginning with an exhibition on Jewish festivities in the first room; chandeliers, goblets, and spice-holders used to celebrate Shabbat, Shofàrs (ram's horns) and a

Séfer Torà (Scroll of Divine Law). The second room contains a rich collection of historic textiles and a rare marriage contract from 1792. A newer area explores the immigration patterns of Jews to Venice, and their experiences once here. But for many, the real highlight is the chance to tour three of the area's five historic synagogues: **German** (Scuola Grande Tedesca), founded in 1528; **Italian** (Scuola Italiana), founded in 1575; **Sephardic** (Scuola Levantina), founded in 1541 but rebuilt in the 17th century; **Spanish** (Scuola Spagnola), rebuilt in the first half of 17th century; and the baroque-style **Ashkenazi** (Scuola Canton), largely rebuilt in the 18th century. The ones you visit depends on which synagogues are being used; the Levantina and the Spanish are the most lavishly decorated, with one usually included on the tour. Ladies must have shoulders covered and men must have heads covered; no photos.

Cannaregio 2902B (on Campo del Ghetto Nuovo). www.museoebraico.it. ✆ **041-715359.** Museum 8€ adults, 6€ children and students ages 6–26; museum and synagogue tour 12€ adults, 10€ children and students ages 6–26. Museum Sun–Fri 10am–7pm (Oct–May until 5:30pm); synagogue guided tours in English hourly 10:30am–5:30pm (Oct–May last tour 4:30pm). Closed on Jewish holidays. *Vaporetto:* Guglie.

Giudecca & San Giorgio

Il Redentore ★★ CHURCH Perhaps the masterpiece among Palladio's churches, Il Redentore was commissioned by Venice to give thanks for being delivered from the great plague (1575–77), which claimed over

IL GHETTO AND THE JEWS OF VENICE

Jews began settling in Venice in great numbers in the 15th century, and the Republic soon came to value their services as moneylenders, physicians, and traders. In 1516, however, fearing their growing influence, the Venetians forced the Jewish population to live on an island with an abandoned foundry (*ghetto* is old Venetian dialect for "foundry"), and drawbridges were raised to enforce a nighttime curfew. By the end of the 17th century, as many as 5,000 Jews lived in the Ghetto's cramped confines. Napoleon tore down the Ghetto gates in 1797, but it wasn't until the unification of Italy in 1866 that Jews achieved equal status. Il Ghetto remains the spiritual center for Venice's ever-diminishing community of Jewish families, with two synagogues and a Chabad House; it's said that anywhere from 500 to 2,000 Jews live in all of Venice and Mestre, though very few now live in the Ghetto. Aside from its historic interest, this is also one of the less touristy neighborhoods in Venice (although it has become something of a nightspot) and makes for a pleasant and scenic place to stroll. Venice's first kosher restaurant, **Gam Gam,** opened here in 1996, at 1122 Ghetto Vecchi on the canal (www.gamgamkosher.com; ✆ **366-2504505**), close to the Guglie *vaporetto* stop. Owned and run by Orthodox Jews, it is open Sunday to Thursday noon to 10pm, Fri noon to 2 hours before Shabbat (sunset), and Saturday from 1 hour after Shabbat until 11pm (excluding summer).

a quarter of the population (some 46,000 people). The doge established a tradition of visiting this church by crossing a long pontoon bridge made up of boats from the Dorsoduro's Zattere on the third Sunday of each July, a tradition that survived the demise of the doges and remains one of Venice's most popular festivals.

The interior is done in austere but elegant Palladian style. The artworks tend to be workshop pieces (from the studios or schools of Tintoretto and Veronese), but a fine "Baptism of Christ" by Veronese himself is in the sacristy (accessed through a door in the last chapel on the right).

Campo del Redentore 195, La Giudecca. ✆ **041-523-1415.** 3€. Mon–Sat 10:30am–4:30pm (Mon closes at 4pm). *Vaporetto:* Redentore.

San Giorgio Maggiore ★★ CHURCH This church sits on the little island of San Giorgio Maggiore across from Piazza San Marco. It is one of the masterpieces of Andrea Palladio, the great Renaissance architect from nearby Padua. Most known for his country villas built for Venice's wealthy merchant families, Palladio designed this church in 1565 and it was completed in 1610. To impose a classical front on the traditional church structure, Palladio designed two interlocking facades, with repeating triangles, rectangles, and columns that are harmoniously proportioned. Founded as early as the 10th century, the church had its interior reinterpreted by Palladio with whitewashed stucco surfaces, an unadorned but harmonious space. The main altar is flanked by two epic paintings by Tintoretto, "The Fall of Manna," to the left, and the more noteworthy **"Last Supper" ★★** to the right, famous for its chiaroscuro. Accessed by free guided tour only (usually Apr–Oct only, times vary), the adjacent Cappella dei Morti (Chapel of the Dead) contains Tintoretto's "Deposition," and the upper chapel contains Carpaccio's St. George Killing the Dragon". To the left of the choir is an elevator that you can take to the top of the 1791 campanile—for a charge of 6€—to experience an unforgettable view of the island, the lagoon, and the Palazzo Ducale and Piazza San Marco across the way.

On the island of San Giorgio Maggiore, across St. Mark's Basin from Piazza San Marco. ✆ **041-5227827.** Free. Daily 9am–7pm Apr–Oct, 8:30am–6pm Nov–Mar. *Vaporetto:* Take the Giudecca-bound *vaporetto* (no. 2) on Riva degli Schiavoni (San Marco/San Zaccaria) and get off at the 1st stop, San Giorgio Maggiore.

Exploring Venice's Islands

Venice shares its lagoon with three other principal islands: **Murano, Burano,** and **Torcello.** Guided tours of the three are operated by a dozen agencies with docks on Riva degli Schiavoni/Piazzetta San Marco (all interchangeable). The 3- and 4-hour tours run 20€ to 35€, usually include a visit to a Murano glass factory, and leave daily around 9:30am and 2:30pm (times change; check in advance).

You can easily visit the islands on your own using the *vaporetti*. Line nos. 4.1 and 4.2 make the journey to Murano from Fondamente Nove (on the north side of Castello). For Murano, Burano, and Torcello, Line no. 12 departs Fondamente Nove every 30 minutes; for Torcello change to the shuttle boat (Line 9) that runs from Burano, timed to match the arrivals from Venice. The islands are small and easy to navigate, but check the schedule for island-to-island departures and plan your return so that you don't spend most of your day waiting for connections.

MURANO ★★

The island of Murano has long been famous throughout the world for the products of its glass factories. The **Museo del Vetro (Museum of Glass),** Fondamenta Giustinian 8 (www.museovetro.visitmuve.it; ✆ **041-739586**), charts the history of the island's glassmaking and is definitely worthwhile if you intend to buy a lot of glassware. Daily hours are 10am to 6pm (Nov–Mar to 5pm), and admission is 10€ for adults and 7.50€ for children 6 to 14 and students 25 and under.

Dozens of *fornaci* (kilns) offer free shows of mouth-blown glassmaking almost invariably hitched to a hard-sell tour of the factory outlet store. These retail showrooms of delicate glassware can be enlightening or boring, depending on your frame of mind. Almost all the places will ship their goods, but that often doubles the price. On the other hand, these pieces are instant heirlooms.

Murano is also graced by two worthy churches (both free admission): the largely 15th-century **San Pietro Martire ★** (Mon–Sat 9am–5:30pm, Sun noon–5:30pm), with paintings by Veronese and Giovanni Bellini, and the ancient **Santa Maria e Donato ★** (Mon–Sat 9am–6pm, Sun 12:30–6pm), with its intricate Byzantine exterior apse, 6th-century pulpit, stunning mosaic of Mary, and a fantastic 12th-century inlaid floor.

BURANO ★★★

Lace is the claim to fame of tiny, historic Burano, a craft kept alive for centuries by the wives of fishermen waiting for their husbands to return from the sea. Sadly, most of the lace sold on the island these days is made by machine elsewhere. The local government continues its attempt to keep Burano's centuries-old lace legacy alive with subsidized classes. It's still worth a trip to stroll the back streets of the island, whose canals are lined with the brightly colored, simple homes of the Buranesi fishermen—quite unlike anything in Venice or Murano. **Butter biscuits,** known as *buranelli,* are another famous island product—expect to be offered them in almost every store.

While you're there, visit the **Museo del Merletto (Museum of Lace Making),** Piazza Galuppi 187 (www.museomerletto.visitmuve.it;

✆ **041-730034**), to understand why something so exquisite should not be left to fade into extinction. It's open Tuesday to Sunday 10am to 6pm (Nov–Mar to 5pm); admission is 5€ adults, and 3.50€ for children 6 to 14 and students 25 and under.

TORCELLO ★★

Torcello is perhaps the most charming of the islands, though today it consists of little more than one long canal leading from the *vaporetto* landing to a clump of buildings at its center.

Torcello boasts the oldest Venetian monument, the **Basilica di Santa Maria dell'Assunta ★★★**, whose foundation dates from the 7th century (✆ **041-2702464**). It's famous for its spectacular 11th- to 12th-century Byzantine mosaics—a "Madonna and Child" in the apse and a monumental "Last Judgment" on the west wall—rivaling those of Ravenna's and St. Mark's basilicas. The cathedral is open daily 10:30am to 6pm (Nov–Feb to 5pm), and admission is 5€ (audio guide an extra 2€). Also of interest is the adjacent 11th-century **Santa Fosca** (free admission), a Byzantine brick church with a plain interior, and the **Museo di Torcello** (✆ **041-730761**), showcasing archeological artifacts from the Iron Age to medieval period, many found on the island. The church closes 30 minutes before the basilica, and the museum is open Tuesday to Sunday 10:30am to 5:30pm (Nov–Feb to 5pm). Museum admission is 3€. You must buy tickets for all attractions at the Basilica entrance.

Peaceful Torcello is uninhabited except for a handful of families and a population of feral cats, and is a favorite picnic spot. You'll have to bring the food from Venice—there are no stores on the island and only a handful of bars/trattorias plus one rather expensive restaurant, the **Locanda Cipriani** (Wed–Mon noon–3pm and 7–9pm; closed Jan to mid-Feb; ✆ **041-730150,** www.locandacipriani.com), which opened in 1935 and is definitely worth a splurge. Once the tour groups have left, the island offers a very special moment of solitude and escape.

THE LIDO

Although a convenient 15-minute *vaporetto* ride away from San Marco, Venice's **Lido beaches** are not much to write home about and certainly no longer a chic destination. For swimming and sunbathing there are much better beaches nearby—in **Jesolo,** to the north, for example. But the parade of wealthy Italian and foreign tourists and Venetian families who still frequent the Lido is an interesting sight indeed.

The Lido has two main beach areas. **Bucintoro** is at the opposite end of Gran Viale Santa Maria Elisabetta (referred to as the Gran Viale) from the *vaporetto* station Santa Elisabetta. It's a 10-minute stroll; walk straight ahead along Gran Viale to reach the beach. **San Nicolò,** about

THE film FESTIVAL

The **Venice International Film Festival ★**, in late August and early September, is the most respected celebration of celluloid in Europe after Cannes. Films from all over the world are shown in the **Palazzo del Cinema** on the Lido as well as at various venues—including the *campi.* Ticket prices vary, but those for the less-sought-after films are usually modest. Visit www.labiennale.org/en/cinema for details.

1.5km (1 mile) away, can be reached by bus B. Loungers and parasols can be rented for 10€–20€ per person (per day) depending on the time of year (it's just 1€ to use the showers and bathrooms). Keep in mind that if you stay at any of the hotels on the Lido, most have some kind of agreement with the different *bagni* (beach establishments).

Vaporetto line nos. 1, 2, 5.1, 5.2, and LN cross the lagoon to the Lido from the San Zaccaria–Danieli stop near San Marco. Note that the Lido becomes chilly, windswept and utterly deserted from October to April.

Organized Tours

Because of the sheer number of sights to see in Venice, some first-time visitors like to start out with an organized tour. Although few things can really be covered in any depth on these overview tours, they're sometimes useful for getting your bearings. **Avventure Bellissime** (www.tours-italy.com; ✆ **041-970499**) coordinates a plethora of tours (in English), by boat and gondola, though the walking tours are the best value, covering all the main sights around Piazza San Marco in 2 hours for 25€ (discounts available online). For something with a little more bite (literally), **Urban Adventures** (www.urbanadventures.com; ✆ **348-9808566**) runs enticing *cicchetti* tours (2.5 hr.) for 80€.

For those with more energy, learn to "row like a Venetian" (yes, standing up), at **Row Venice** (www.rowvenice.org; ✆ **347-7250637**), where 1½-hour lessons take place in traditional, hand-built "shrimp-tail" or *batele coda di gambero* boats for 85€ for up to 2 people.

Especially for Kids

It goes without saying that a **gondola ride** (p. 395) will be the thrill of a lifetime for any child (or adult). If that's too expensive, consider the far cheaper alternative: a **ride on the no. 1 *vaporetto*** (p. 402).

Judging from the squeals of delight, **feeding the pigeons in Piazza San Marco** could be the high point of your child's visit to Venice, and it's the ultimate photo op. Purchase a bag of corn and you'll be draped in fluttering and flapping pigeons in a nanosecond.

carnevale A VENEZIA

Carnevale traditionally was the celebration preceding Lent, the period of penitence and abstinence prior to Easter; its name is derived from the Latin *carnem levare*, meaning "to take meat away." Today Carnevale in Venice builds for 10 days until the big blowout, Shrove Tuesday (Fat Tuesday), when fireworks illuminate the Grand Canal, and Piazza San Marco becomes a giant open-air ballroom for the masses. The festival is a harlequin patchwork of musical and cultural events, many free of charge, appealing to all ages, tastes, nationalities, and budgets. Musical events are staged in some of the city's dozens of *piazze*—from reggae and zydeco to jazz and baroque. Book your hotel months ahead, especially for the two weekends prior to Shrove Tuesday. Check **www.carnevalevenezia.com** for details.

A jaunt to the neighboring **island of Murano** (p. 417) can be as educational as it is recreational—follow the signs to any *fornace* (kiln), where a glassblowing performance of the island's thousand-year-old art is free entertainment. But be ready for the sales pitch that follows.

Take the elevator to the **top of the Campanile di San Marco** (p. 402) for a scintillating view of Venice's rooftops and cupolas, or get up close and personal with the four bronze horses on the facade of the Basilica San Marco. The view from its **outdoor loggia** is something you and your children won't forget. Scaling the **Torre dell'Orologio** (p. 405) or the bell tower at **San Giorgio Maggiore** (p. 416) is also lots of fun.

The **winged lion,** said to have been a kind of good luck mascot to St. Mark, patron saint of Venice, was the very symbol of the Serene Republic and to this day appears on everything from cafe napkins to T-shirts. Keep a running tab of who can spot the most flying lions—you'll find them on facades, atop columns, over doorways, as pavement mosaics, on government stamps, and on the local flag.

WHERE TO STAY

Few cities boast as long a high season as that of Venice, which begins with the Easter period. May, June, and September are the best months weather-wise so the most crowded. July and August are hot (few of the one- and two-star hotels offer air-conditioning; when they do, it usually costs extra). Hotels are more expensive here than in any other Italian city, with no apparent upgrade in amenities. The least special of those below are clean and functional; at best, they're charming and thoroughly enjoyable, with the serenade of a passing gondolier thrown in for good measure. Some may even be your best stay in all of Europe.

Note: Always reserve your lodging in advance, even in the off-season. If you haven't booked, come as early as you can on your arrival day, definitely before noon.

SEASONAL CONSIDERATIONS Most hotels observe high- and low-season rates, and high-end hotels generally adapt their prices to availability. In the prices listed below, **single figures represent rack rates,** because the price varies too widely depending on availability, and you can usually get a room for much less, even in high season.

Self-Catering Apartments

Anyone looking to get into the local swing of things in Venice should opt for a short-term rental apartment. For the same price or less than a hotel room, you could have your own one-bedroom apartment with a washing machine, A/C, and a fridge to keep your prosecco cold. Properties of all sizes and price ranges are available for stays of 3 nights to several weeks.

It's standard practice for local rental agencies to collect 30% of the total rental amount upfront to secure a booking. When you check in, the balance of your rental fee is normally payable in cash only, so make sure you have enough euros in hand. Upon booking, the agency should provide you with detailed check-in procedures. Normally, you call a cell or office phone when you arrive in Venice, and then the keyholder meets you at the property. Although most apartments provide a list of nearby shops and services, be sure to ask for a few numbers to call in case of an emergency. Beyond that, you're on your own, which is what makes an apartment stay a great way to do as the Venetians do.

RECOMMENDED AGENCIES

Airbnb (www.airbnb.com) is now a major player in Venice, with more than 300 properties listed from just 30€ per night. **Couchsurfing** (www.couchsurfing.com) is also popular and generally safe in Venice, though take the usual precautions using the apartment-swapping service. **Cities Reference** (www.citiesreference.com; ✆ **06-48903612**) is the best traditional rental agency for Venice, with around 230 properties listed. The company's no-surprises property descriptions come with helpful information and lots of photos. **Cross Pollinate** (www.cross-pollinate.com; ✆ **06-99369799**) is a multi-destination agency with a decent roster of personally inspected apartments and B&Bs in Venice, created by the American owners of the Beehive hotel in Rome (p. 134). **GowithOh** (www.gowithoh.com; ✆ **800/567-2927** in the U.S.) is a hip rental agency that covers 13 European cities, including Venice. The website is fun to navigate and lists more than 190 apartments for rent in the city. **Rental in Venice** (www.rentalinvenice.com; ✆ **041-718981**) has an alluring website—with video clips of the apartments—and the widest selection of midrange and luxury apartments in the prime San Marco zone (there are less expensive ones, too).

Ai Tagliapietra 19
Ai Due Fanali 4
Al Piave 18
Al Ponte Antico 14
Antiche Figure 3
Arcadia 6
B&B San Marco 21
Bernardi 13
Ca' Barba B&B 11
Casa Verardo 17
Corte Di Gabriela 10
Falier 2
Galleria 8
Locanda Fiorita 9
Locanda Orseolo 16
Metropole 20
Moresco 1
Pensione Accademia 7
Pensione Guerrato 12
San Geremia 5
Violino d'Oro 15
Parco Savorgnàn
Campo S. Geremia
S. Geremia
Calle Priuli dei Cavaletti
Rio Terà Lista di Spagna
Riva da Biásio
Canàl Grande
Palazzo Giovanelli
Fònd. d. Turchi
Ca' Tron
S. Stae
Palazzo Donà-Balbi
S. Zan Degolà
Stazione Venezia–Santa Lucia
Calle d. Tintòr
Ca' Pesaro
Pal. Mocenigo
S. Simeòn Grande
S. Giacomo dell'Orio
Campo S. Giacomo dell'Orio
S. Simeòn Piccolo
Palazzo Gradenigo
Campo N. Sáuro
S. Maria Máter Domini
Rio d. S. Cassiano
Pal. Zane
S. Cassiar
Ferrovia
Palazzo Soranzo-Cappello
Fond. Rio Marin
SANTA CROCE
Pal. Grioni
Calle d. Chiesa
Ponte Calatrava
Giardini Papadopoli
Rio di S. Agostino
Pal. Muti Baglioni
Scuola Grande di S. Giovanni
Pal. Zane Collalto
Palazzo Albrizzi
Pal. Molin Cappello
Pal. Molin
Rio di S. Polo
S. Giovanni Evangelista
Pal. Donà d. Rose
SAN POLO
S. Nicolò di Tolentino
Pal. Corner
Campo S. Polo
Pal. Soranzo
Ex Convento dei Frari
Palazzo Zen
Palazzo Marcello
Campo d. Frari
San Polo
S. Rocco
Frari
Rio di San Polo
Pal. Papadopol
Scuola Grande di San Rocco
Palazzo Centani (Museo Goldoni)
Pal. Dona
Pal. Layard
Pal. Grimani
Palazzo Barbarigo
S. Pantalòn
Rio d. Frescada
S. Tomà
Pal. Civràn-Grimani
S. Ángelo
Rio Ca' Foscari
Calle Foscari
S. Tomà
Pal. Cornèr Spinelli
Pal. Fortuny
Pal. Balbi
Palazzo Mocenígo
Campo Santa Margherita
Ca' Foscari
Pal. Contarini d. Figure
Oratorio de Annunciat
Rio di S. Angelo
Palazzo Moro-Lin
Campo S. Ángel
Pal. Grassi
Saliz S. Samuele
C. Crosera
Pal. Nani
Ca' Rezzonico
S. Stefano
S. Samuele
San Samuele
Palazzo Malipiero
Campo S. Barnaba
S. Bárnaba
Ca' Rezzonico
Campo S. Stefano
S. Maurízio
Rio Malpaga
Pal. Stern
Ca' del Duca
Rio del Duca
C. Vetturi
Rio di S. Vidal
Pal. Morosini
Pal. Loredan
Pal. Falier
Rio d. Santissimo
S. Maria d. Giglio
Pal. Contarini degli Scrigni
Pal. Bárbaro
Pal. Pisani
DORSODURO
Palazzo Cornèr d. Ca' Granda
Accademia
Ponte dell'Accademia
Canàl Grande
S. Maria d. Giglio
Gallerie dell' Accademia
Palazzo Contarini dal Zaffo
Rio di S. Trovaso
S. Trovaso
Pal. Molin
Pal. Nani
Pal. Centani
Pal. Giustiniàn
Rio di S. Vio
Pal. Venièr dei Leoni (Guggenheim)
S. Maria d. Visitaz.
S. Agnese
Fond. Bragadin
Gesuati
Záttere

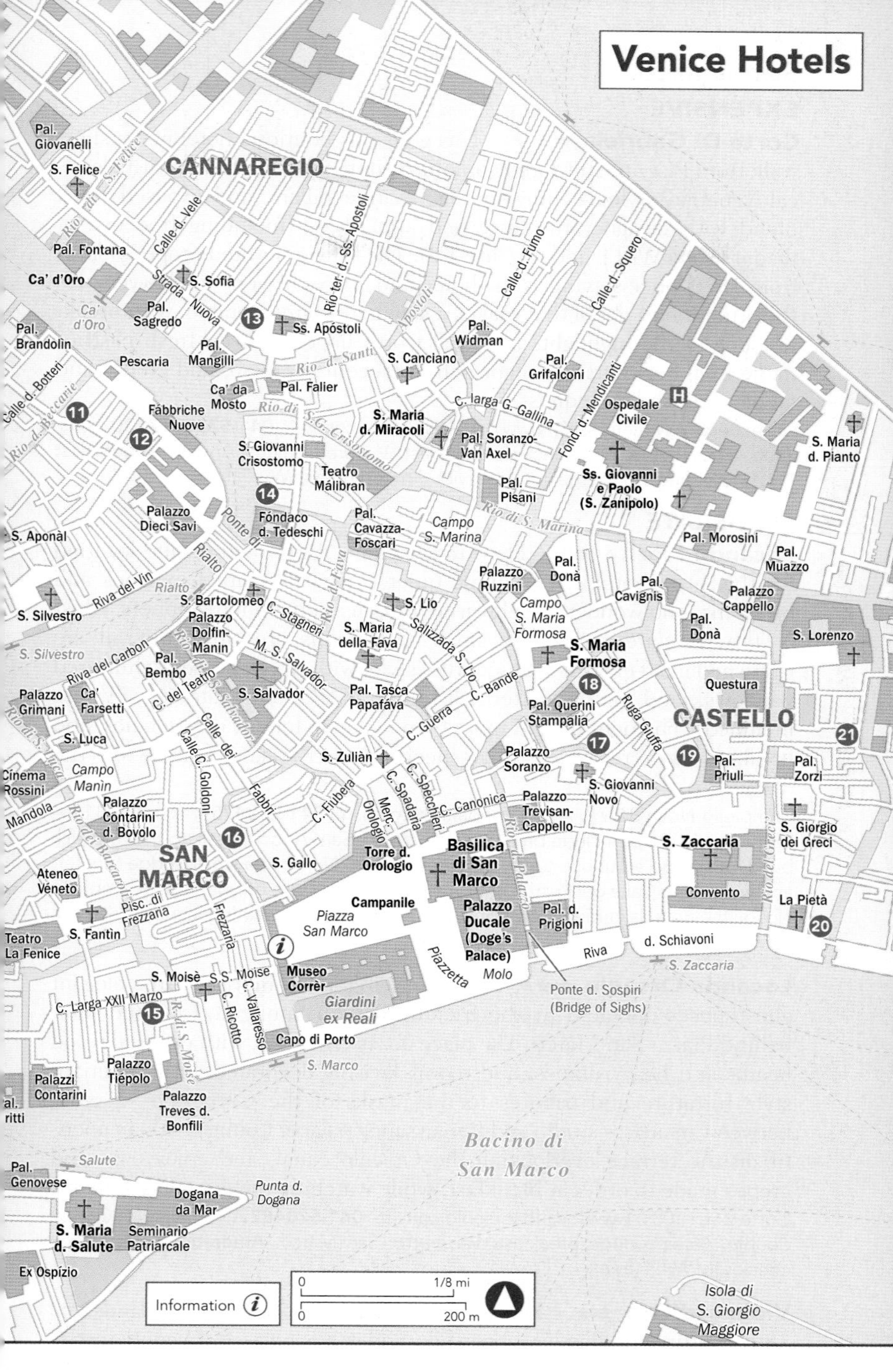
Venice Hotels
CANNAREGIO
SAN MARCO
CASTELLO
Bacino di San Marco
Information
0 1/8 mi
0 200 m
Pal. Giovanelli
S. Felice
Pal. Fontana
Ca' d'Oro
S. Sofia
Strada Nuova
Pal. Sagredo
Pal. Brandolin
Pescaria
Pal. Mangilli
Ss. Apóstoli
Ca' da Mosto
Pal. Falier
Fàbbriche Nuove
S. Giovanni Crisostomo
Teatro Málibran
Fóndaco d. Tedeschi
Palazzo Dieci Savi
S. Aponàl
S. Silvestro
Riva del Vin
Rialto
Ponte di Rialto
S. Bartolomeo
Palazzo Dolfin-Manin
Pal. Bembo
Riva del Carbon
Palazzo Grimani
Ca' Farsetti
S. Salvador
S. Luca
Cinema Rossini
Campo Manìn
Palazzo Contarini d. Bovolo
Ateneo Véneto
S. Fantìn
Teatro La Fenice
S. Moisè
C. Larga XXII Marzo
Palazzo Tiépolo
Palazzi Contarini
Palazzo Treves d. Bonfili
Pal. Genovese
S. Maria d. Salute
Dogana da Mar
Punta d. Dogana
Seminario Patriarcale
Ex Ospízio
S. Canciano
Pal. Widman
S. Maria d. Miracoli
Pal. Soranzo-Van Axel
Pal. Grifalconi
Ospedale Civile
S. Maria d. Pianto
Ss. Giovanni e Paolo (S. Zanipolo)
Pal. Pisani
Pal. Cavazza-Foscari
Campo S. Marina
S. Lio
S. Maria della Fava
Pal. Tasca Papafáva
Palazzo Ruzzini
Pal. Donà
Campo S. Maria Formosa
S. Maria Formosa
Pal. Querini Stampalia
Pal. Morosini
Pal. Muazzo
Pal. Cavignis
Palazzo Cappello
S. Lorenzo
Questura
S. Zulià n
Palazzo Soranzo
S. Giovanni Novo
Pal. Priuli
Pal. Zorzi
Palazzo Trevisan-Cappello
S. Zaccaria
S. Giorgio dei Greci
Convento
La Pietà
Torre d. Orologio
Basilica di San Marco
Campanile
Piazza San Marco
Palazzo Ducale (Doge's Palace)
Pal. d. Prigioni
Museo Corrèr
Piazzetta
Molo
Giardini ex Reali
Capo di Porto
S. Marco
Riva d. Schiavoni
Ponte d. Sospiri (Bridge of Sighs)
Isola di S. Giorgio Maggiore
11
12
13
14
15
16
17
18
19
20
21

San Marco

EXPENSIVE

Corte Di Gabriela ★★★ This gorgeous boutique hotel just a short walk from Piazza San Marco combines contemporary design with classical Venetian style—ceiling murals, marble pillars, and exposed brick blend with designer furniture and appliances (including free use of iPads, strong Wi-Fi, and satellite TV). The fully renovated property dates from 1870, once serving as the home and offices of Venetian lawyers. It's the attention to detail that makes a stay here so memorable, with breakfast one of the highlights and well worth lingering over: fresh pastries made by the owners the night before, decent espresso, and crepes and omelets cooked on request.

Calle degli Avvocati 3836. www.cortedigabriela.com. ✆ **041-5235077.** 10 units. 280€–460€ double. Rates include breakfast. *Vaporetto:* Sant' Angelo. **Amenities:** Bar; babysitting; concierge; room service (limited hours); Wi-Fi (free).

MODERATE

Locanda Fiorita ★★ Hard to imagine a more picturesque location for this little hotel, a charming, quiet *campiello* draped in vines and blossoms—no wonder it's a favorite of professional photographers. Most of the standard rooms are small (bathrooms are tiny), but all are furnished in an elegant 18th-century style, with wooden floors, shuttered windows, and richly patterned fittings (A/C and satellite TV are included). The helpful staff more than make up for any deficiencies, and breakfast is a real pleasure, especially when taken outside on the *campiello.*

Campiello Novo 3457a. www.locandafiorita.com. ✆ **041-5234754.** 10 units. 110€–185€ double. Rates include breakfast. *Vaporetto:* Sant'Angelo (walk to the tall brick building and go around it, turning right into Ramo Narisi; at a small bridge turn left and walk along Calle del Pestrin until you see a small piazza on your right [Campiello Novo]; the hotel is immediately opposite). **Amenities:** Babysitting; concierge; room service; Wi-Fi (free).

Locanda Orseolo ★★★ This enticing inn comprises three elegant guesthouses operated by the friendly Peruch family and located right behind Piazza San Marco. The place oozes character, with exposed wood beams and heavy drapes, and rooms lavishly decorated with Venetian-style furniture and tributes to the masks of the Carnevale—a cross between an artist's studio and Renaissance palace. Lounge with an aperitif on the terrace overlooking the Orseolo canal, and enjoy eggs and crepes made to order at breakfast, while watching the gondolas glide by.

Corte Zorzi 1083. www.locandaorseolo.com. ✆ **041-5204827.** 15 units. 150€–240€ double. Rates include breakfast. *Vaporetto:* San Marco. **Amenities:** Babysitting; concierge; Wi-Fi (free).

Violino d'Oro ★★ The relatively spacious rooms in this handsome 18th-century building have been adorned in a neoclassical Venetian style with exposed wooden beams, crystal chandeliers, and heaps of character. Most rooms overlook the romantic San Moisè canal, and Piazza San Marco is just a 5-minute stroll. At this price point (with incredible deals in low season), it's reassuring to know you get A/C, satellite TV, and an elevator. Breakfast is an event, a vast spread of homemade cakes and muffins paired with one of the best cappuccinos in the city.

Calle Larga XXII Marzo 2091. www.violinodoro.com. ✆ **041-2770841**. 26 units. 114€–214€ double. Rates include breakfast. *Vaporetto:* San Marco–Vallaresso (walk up Calle di Ca' Vallaresso, turn left on Salizada San Moisè and cross the footbridge; the hotel is across the *campiello* on the left). **Amenities:** Bar; concierge; room service; Wi-Fi (free).

Castello

EXPENSIVE

Metropole ★★★ This five-star behemoth with a waterfront location is part luxury hotel, part eclectic art museum, with antiques, Asian artworks, and tapestries dotted throughout. But it's no dusty grand dame; on the contrary, it's a chic boutique hotel with rooms furnished with a classic Oriental theme. The building has an incredible history, beginning life in the Middle Ages as the Ospedale della Pietà, serving as a charitable institution for orphans and abandoned girls, and later a music school (Vivaldi taught violin here in the early 1700s). After it was converted into a hotel in 1895, Sigmund Freud was an early guest, along with Thomas Mann, who allegedly wrote parts of *Death in Venice* here.

Riva degli Schiavoni 4149. www.hotelmetropole.com. ✆ **041-5205044.** 67 units. 192€–450€ double. Rates include breakfast. *Vaporetto:* San Zaccaria (walk along Riva degli Schiavoni to the right; the hotel is next to La Pietà church). **Amenities:** Restaurant; bar; babysitting; concierge; room service; Wi-Fi (free).

MODERATE

Al Piave ★★ Al Piave is a cozy, old-fashioned family-run hotel just 5 minutes from Piazza San Marco. Rooms are simply but attractively furnished with richly woven rugs, marble floors, and some of the original wood beams exposed (some come with a terrace, while the family suites are a good value for groups). Bathrooms are relatively big, and the A/C is a welcome bonus in the summer, but there are no elevators, so be prepared if you get a higher floor. Outside of peak months (July, Sept), Piave is an exceptionally good value, given its proximity to the *piazza*.

Ruga Giuffa 4838. www.hotelalpiave.com. ✆ **041-5285174.** 20 units. 117€–250€ double. Rates include breakfast. Closed Jan 7 to Carnevale. *Vaporetto:* San Zaccaria (find Calle delle Rasse beyond Palazzo Danieli; walk to the end of the street; turn left and then immediately right; continue to Ponte Storto, cross and continue to Ruga Giuffa—hotel is on left). **Amenities:** Babysitting; concierge; Wi-Fi (free).

Casa Verardo ★★★ Tucked away across a small bridge in the warren of central Castello, this enchanting property occupies a 16th-century *palazzo,* converted to a hotel in 1911. Rooms sport an old-fashioned Venetian style, with Florentine furniture, hand-painted beds, and colorful textiles (antiques and paintings are scattered throughout), but updated with A/C and satellite TV. Some rooms have a view over a canal, others over the shady courtyard and the city. A panoramic terrace on the top floor is a pleasant spot for an aperitif. They'll also take you to Murano for free, but you have to find your own way back.

Calle Drio La Chiesa 4765 (at foot of Ponte Storto). www.casaverardo.it. ✆ **041-5286138.** 25 units. 90€–300€ double. Rates include breakfast. *Vaporetto:* San Zaccaria (walk straight on Calle delle Rasse to Campo SS. Filippo e Giacomo; cross the *campo* to Calle della Sacrestia, then Calle Drio La Chiesa to Ponte Storto, and look for hotel on left). **Amenities:** Bar; babysitting; concierge; room service; Wi-Fi (free).

INEXPENSIVE

Ai Tagliapietra ★★★ This cozy B&B is run by the amicable Lorenzo, who works hard to make your stay a memorable one. It's a real bargain in this part of town. Rooms are basic, but spotless, modern, and relatively spacious with private bathrooms. The small, shared kitchenette is available for guests' use (with refrigerator and free tea). Lorenzo will usually meet you at San Zaccaria, give you a map, print your boarding passes, and generally organize your trip if you desire, making this an especially recommended budget option for first-time visitors.

Salizada Zorzi 4943. www.aitagliapietra.com. ✆ **347-3233166.** 4 units. 75€–110€ double. Rates include breakfast. *Vaporetto:* San Zaccaria (walk straight on Calle delle Rasse to Campo SS. Filippo e Giacomo; cross the *campo* to Calle della Sacrestia; take the first left; cross Salita Corte Rotta and continue to Salizada Zorzi). **Amenities:** Wi-Fi (free).

B&B San Marco ★★★ With just three double rooms, this exquisite B&B in a peaceful, residential neighborhood fills up fast, so book ahead. It's a comfortable, charming yet convenient option, the kind of place that makes you feel like a local, but not too far from the main sights. Your hosts are the bubbly Marco and Alice Scurati, who live in the attic upstairs, happy to provide help and advice. Rooms overlook the Scuola di San Giorgio degli Schiavoni and offer wonderful views of the canal and streetscapes nearby, and are furnished with antique furniture. Two rooms share a bathroom; the third has private facilities. Breakfast is self-service in the shared kitchen; yogurts, pastries, espresso, cappuccino, juice, and tea.

Fondamenta San Giorgio dei Schiavoni 3385. www.realvenice.it. ✆ **041-5227589.** 3 units. 70€–135€ double. Rates include breakfast. Closed Aug and Jan 7 to Carnevale. *Vaporetto:* San Zaccaria (walk on Calle delle Rasse to Campo SS. Filippo e Giacomo; cross the *campo* to Calle della Sacrestia, cross the canal; take a left at Campo S Provolo on Fondamenta Osmarin; turn left where the canal ends at a larger canal, and walk to bridge that connects to Calle Lion; at the street's end turn left along the canal; this is Fondamenta San Giorgio dei Schiavoni). **Amenities:** Wi-Fi (free).

Dorsoduro

EXPENSIVE

Moresco ★★★ An incredibly attentive staff, a decadent breakfast that includes prosecco (to mix with orange juice, ahem), and lavish 19th-century Venetian decor away from the tourist hubbub make this a popular choice. Rooms seamlessly blend Venetian style with modern design. Some have a terrace (with canal or garden views), while others have spa bathtubs; all have flatscreen TVs. If the weather cooperates, take breakfast in the courtyard garden to really soak up the ambience. The hotel is a 5- to 10-minute walk from Piazzale Roma and the train station, but you'll have a number of bridges and stairs to negotiate along the way.

Fondamenta del Rio Novo 3499, Dorsoduro. www.hotelmorescovenice.com. ✆ **041-2440202.** 23 units. 190€–370€ double. Rates include breakfast. *Vaporetto:* Ferrovia/Piazzale Roma (from the train station walk southwest along Fondamenta Santa Lucia, cross Ponte della Costituzione and turn left onto Fondamenta Santa Chiara; cross Ponte Santa Chiara and turn right onto Fondamenta Papadopoli, continuing across Campiello Lavadori then along Fondamenta del Rio Novo). **Amenities:** Bar; concierge; free trips to Murano; room service; Wi-Fi (free).

MODERATE

Galleria ★★ Just around the corner from the Accademia, right on the Grand Canal, this hotel occupies a 19th-century *palazzo* in one of the city's most inviting locations. It's been a hotel since the 1800s, hosting poet Robert Browning in 1878, and maintains an 18th-century theme in the rooms, with wood furniture and rococo decor. Hosts Luciano and Stefano serve a simple breakfast in your room. The smallest rooms here really are tiny, and there is no A/C (rooms are supplied with fans when it gets hot), but the fridge of free water and sodas is a lifesaver in summer.

Dorsoduro 878a (at foot of Accademia Bridge). www.hotelgalleria.it. ✆ **041-5232489.** 9 units, 6 with bathroom. 120€–290€ double. Rates include breakfast. *Vaporetto:* Accademia (with Accademia Bridge behind you, hotel is just to your left). **Amenities:** Babysitting; concierge; room service; Wi-Fi (free in public areas).

Pensione Accademia ★★ This spellbinding hotel with a tranquil blossom-filled garden has a fascinating history. The Gothic-style Villa Maravege was built in the 17th century as a family residence, but served as the Russian Embassy between World Wars I and II before becoming a hotel in 1950. If that's not enticing enough, rooms are outfitted with Venetian-style antique reproductions, wood furnishings, handsome tapestries, and A/C, with views over the Rio San Trovaso or the garden. Breakfast is served in your room, in the dining hall, or on the patio.

Fondamenta Bollani 1058. www.pensioneaccademia.it. ✆ **041-5210188.** 27 units. 157€–255€ double. Rates include breakfast. *Vaporetto:* Accademia (turn right down Calle Gambara, which becomes Calle Corfu, which ends at a side canal; walk left to cross over the bridge, and then turn right back toward the Grand Canal and the hotel). **Amenities:** Bar; babysitting; concierge; room service; Wi-Fi (free).

San Polo

MODERATE

Ca' Barba B&B ★★ What you'll remember most about Ca' Barba may well be the host, Alessandro, who usually meets guests at the Rialto *vaporetto* stop; inspires daily wanderings with tips, maps, and books; and provides fresh breads and pastries from the local bakery for breakfast. Of the four rooms (reservations are essential, with the best rates on airbnb.com), no. 201 is the largest and brightest, with a Jacuzzi tub (no. 202 also has one). All rooms come with antique furniture, 19th-century paintings, wood-beamed ceilings, LCD TVs, A/C, and strong Wi-Fi.

Calle Campanile Castello 1825. www.cabarba.com. ✆ **041-5242816.** 4 units. 77€–150€ double. Rates include breakfast. *Vaporetto:* Rialto (walk back along the Grand Canal, and turn left at Calle Campanile Castello). **Amenities:** Concierge; Wi-Fi (free).

Pensione Guerrato ★★★ Dating, incredibly, from 1227, this is definitely one of the city's most historic places to stay. The building's long history—it was once the "Inn of the Monkey," run by nuns, with the original structure mostly destroyed by fire in 1513—is worth delving into (the owners have all the details). Rooms are simply but classically furnished, with wood floors, exposed beams, A/C, and private baths—many with original frescos that may date from the medieval inn. Note that some rooms are on the sixth floor—and there's no elevator.

Calle Drio La Scimia 240a (near the Rialto Market). www.hotelguerrato.com. ✆ **041-5227131.** 19 units. 100€–145€ double. Rates include breakfast. Closed Dec 22–26 and Jan 8–early Feb. *Vaporetto:* Rialto (from the north side of the Ponte Rialto, walk through the market to the corner with UniCredit Banca; go 1 more short block and turn right onto Calle Drio La Scimia). **Amenities:** Babysitting; concierge; Wi-Fi (free).

Santa Croce

EXPENSIVE

Antiche Figure ★★★ The most convenient luxury hotel in Venice lies directly across the Grand Canal from the train station, a captivating 15th-century *palazzo* adjacent to an ancient gondola workshop. History aside, this is a very plush choice, with rooms decorated in neoclassical Venetian style, with gold leaf, antique furniture, red carpets, silk tapestries, and Murano glass and chandeliers, but also LCD satellite TVs and decent Wi-Fi. With the soothing nighttime views across the water it's certainly a romantic choice, and the staff is worth singling out—friendly and very helpful. There is an elevator, just in case you were wondering.

Fondamenta San Simeone Piccolo 687. www.hotelantichefigure.it. ✆ **041-2759486.** 22 units. 190€–315€ double. Rates include breakfast. *Vaporetto:* Ferrovia (from the train station you just need to cross the Scalzi Bridge on your left and take a right). **Amenities:** Restaurant; bar; babysitting; concierge; room service; Wi-Fi (free).

MODERATE

Ai Due Fanali ★★ Originally a wooden oratory frequented by fishermen and farmers (later rebuilt), this beguiling hotel features small but artsy rooms, even for Venice: Headboards have been hand-painted by a local artist, exposed wood beams crisscross the ceiling, vintage drapes add a cozy feel, and work by 16th-century Mannerist painter Jacopo Palma the Younger adorns the public areas. Bathrooms are embellished with terracotta tiles and Carrera marble. The location is close to the train station, and the roof terrace is the best place to soak up a city panorama (breakfast is served here). It's incredibly popular—book months ahead.

Campo San Simeon Profeta 946. www.aiduefanali.com. ✆ **041-718490.** 16 units. 145€–235€ double. Rates include breakfast. Closed most of Jan. *Vaporetto:* Ferrovia (cross Scalzi Bridge over the Grand Canal; continue straight, taking 2nd left to Campo San Simeon Profeta). **Amenities:** Bar; concierge; room service; Wi-Fi (free).

INEXPENSIVE

Falier ★ This tranquil budget hotel is in a quiet neighborhood, next to the Frari Church and just a 10-minute walk from the train station. Rooms are fairly compact (potentially cramped for some), but par for this price point in Venice, and all are air-conditioned. The elegant garden is a great place for the continental breakfast (you can also have it in the dining room), featuring warm croissants, cheese, a selection of yogurts and cereals, plus teas, coffee, and fruit juices. The hotel provides free entrance to the Venice casino and a free tour of a Murano glass factory, but the friendly English-speaking staff will also set you up with all manner of other tour options.

Salizada San Pantalon 130. www.hotelfalier.com. ✆ **041-710882.** 19 units. 70€–170€ double. Rates include breakfast. *Vaporetto:* Ferrovia. (From the train station, cross Scalzi Bridge, turn right along the Grand Canal and walk to the first footbridge; turn left before crossing and follow the smaller canal to Fondamenta Minotti; turn left, and the street becomes Salizada San Pantalon.) **Amenities:** Concierge; Wi-Fi (free).

Cannaregio

EXPENSIVE

Al Ponte Antico ★★★ Yes it's expensive, but this is one of the most exclusive hotels in Venice, steps from the Rialto Bridge, with a private wharf on the Grand Canal—to indulge your James Bond fantasy, look no further. Part of the attraction is size. The hotel has only seven rooms, and the attention to lavish detail is astounding. Rococo wallpaper, rare tapestries, elegant beds, and Louis XV–style furnishings make this place seem like Versailles on the water. The building was originally a 16th-century *palazzo;* one of the many highlights is the charming balcony where breakfast is served, and where Bellinis are offered in the evenings.

Calle dell'Aseo 5768. www.alponteantico.com. ✆ **041-2411944.** 7 units. 280€–340€ double. Rates include breakfast. *Vaporetto:* Rialto (walk up Calle Large Mazzini, take the 2nd left and then cross Campo San Bartolomeo; walk north along Salizada S.G. Grisostomo to Calle dell'Aseo on the left). **Amenities:** Bar; concierge; room service; Wi-Fi (free).

BACARI & CICCHETTI

One of the essential culinary experiences of Venice is trawling the countless neighborhood bars known as ***bacari,*** where you can stand or sit with *tramezzini* (small, triangular white-bread half-sandwiches filled with everything from thinly sliced meats and tuna salad to cheeses and vegetables), and ***cicchetti*** (tapas-like finger foods, such as calamari rings, fried olives, potato croquettes, or grilled polenta squares), traditionally washed down with a small glass of wine, Veneto prosecco, or a spritz (a cocktail of Prosecco and orange-flavored Aperol). All of the above will cost approximately 1.50€ to 6€ if you stand at the bar, as much as double when seated. Bar food usually sells out by late afternoon, so while it can make a great lunch, don't rely on it for dinner. A concentration of popular, well-stocked bars can be found along the **Mercerie** shopping strip that connects Piazza San Marco with the Rialto Bridge, the always lively **Campo San Luca** (look for Bar Torino, Bar Black Jack, or the character-filled Leon Bianco wine bar), and **Campo Santa Margherita.**

MODERATE

Arcadia ★★★ This sensational, modestly advertised boutique hotel set in a 17th-century *palazzo* has an appealing blend of old and new: The theme is Byzantium east-meets-west, a mix of Venetian and Asian style, but rooms are full of cool modern touches: rainfall showers, A/C, flatscreen TVs, bathrobes, and posh toiletries, with a lobby crowned with a Murano glass chandelier. It's a 5-minute walk from the train station.

Rio Terà San Leonardo 1333, Cannaregio. www.hotelarcadia.net. ✆ **041-717355.** 17 units. 120€–270€ double. Rates include breakfast. *Vaporetto:* Guglie (take a left into the main street Rio Terà San Leonardo; Arcadia is just 30m [98 ft.] on the left). **Amenities:** Bar; concierge; room service; Wi-Fi (free).

INEXPENSIVE

Bernardi ★★ This hotel is an excellent deal, with small, basic but spotless rooms in a 16th-century *palazzo* (the superior rooms are bigger), owned and managed by the congenial Leonardo and his wife, Teresa. Most rooms come with one or two classical Venetian touches: Murano chandeliers, hand-painted furniture, exposed wood beams, and tapestries. The shared showers are kept very clean (11 rooms have private baths), and fans are provided in the hot summer months for the cheaper rooms with no A/C. Breakfast is very basic, however, and note that the more spacious annex rooms, which have air-conditioning (nearby the main building) don't appear to get good Wi-Fi coverage.

Calle de l'Oca 4366. www.hotelbernardi.com. ✆ **041-5227257.** 18 units, 11 with private bathroom. 55€–130€ double. Rates include breakfast. *Vaporetto:* Ca' d'Oro (walk to Strada Nova, turn right to Campo SS. Apostoli and turn left and take 1st left onto Calle de l'Oca). **Amenities:** Concierge; room service; Wi-Fi (free).

San Geremia ★ This excellent budget option is just 10 minutes from the train station. Rooms are simple but adequate, with most featuring A/C and views across the canal or *campo.* Note that there is no elevator (some rooms are up three flights of stairs), and breakfast is not provided (but you get 50% off breakfast next door). The rooms have no TVs but do have strong Wi-Fi. The dorm rooms are a good deal at just 21€ to 25€ per night (for guests under 35 only). Cash only.

Campo San Geremia 283. www.hotelsangeremia.com. ✆ **041-715562.** 20 units, 14 with private bathroom. 60€–130€ double. Closed the week of Christmas. *Vaporetto:* Ferrovia (exit train station, turn left onto Lista di Spagna, and continue to Campo San Geremia). **Amenities:** Babysitting; concierge; room service; Wi-Fi (free).

WHERE TO EAT

Eating cheaply in Venice is not easy, though it's by no means impossible. The city's reputation for mass-produced menus, poor service, and overpriced food is, sadly, well warranted, and if you've been traveling in other parts of the country, you may be a little disappointed here. Having said that, everything is relative—this is still Italy, after all—and you'll find plenty of excellent dining options in Venice. As a basic rule, value for money tends to increase the farther you travel away from Piazza San Marco, and anything described as a *menù turistico,* while cheaper than a la carte, is rarely any good in Venice (exceptions noted below). Note also that compared with Rome and other points south, Venice is a city of early meals: You should be seated by 7:30 to 8:30pm. Most kitchens close at 10 or 10:30pm, even though the restaurant may stay open later.

The Rialto fish market.

San Marco

EXPENSIVE

Bistrot de Venise ★★★ VENETIAN It may look a bit like a wood-paneled French bistro, but the menu here is old-school Venetian, specializing in rare wines and historical recipes from the

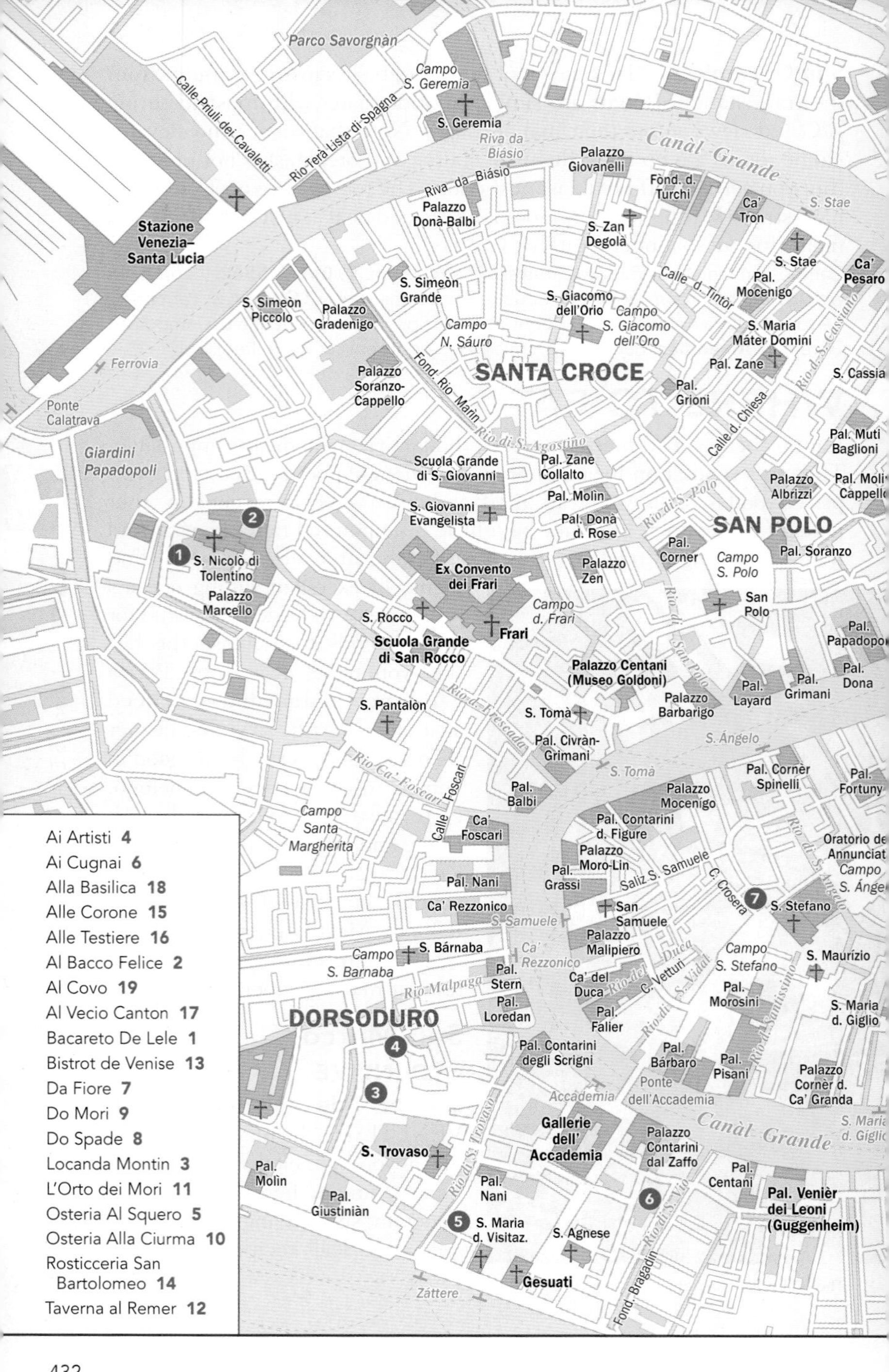
Parco Savorgnàn
Campo S. Geremia
S. Geremia
Calle Priuli dei Cavaletti
Rio Terà Lista di Spagna
Riva da Biàsio
Canàl Grande
Palazzo Giovanelli
Fond. d. Turchi
Ca' Tron
S. Stae
Riva da Biàsio
Palazzo Donà-Balbi
S. Zan Degolà
Stazione Venezia–Santa Lucia
Calle d. Tintòr
S. Stae
Ca' Pesaro
Pal. Mocenigo
S. Simeòn Grande
S. Giacomo dell'Orio
Campo S. Giacomo dell'Orio
S. Simeòn Piccolo
Palazzo Gradenigo
Campo N. Sáuro
S. Maria Máter Domini
Rio d. S. Cassiano
Ferrovia
Palazzo Soranzo-Cappello
Fond. Rio Marin
SANTA CROCE
Pal. Zane
S. Cassia
Pal. Grioni
Calle d. Chiesa
Ponte Calatrava
Giardini Papadopoli
Rio di S. Agostino
Pal. Muti Baglioni
Scuola Grande di S. Giovanni
Pal. Zane Collalto
Pal. Molìn
Rio di S. Polo
Palazzo Albrizzi
Pal. Moli Cappell
S. Giovanni Evangelista
Pal. Donà d. Rose
SAN POLO
S. Nicolò di Tolentino
Ex Convento dei Frari
Palazzo Zen
Pal. Corner
Campo S. Polo
Pal. Soranzo
Palazzo Marcello
San Polo
S. Rocco
Campo d. Frari
Frari
Rio di San Polo
Scuola Grande di San Rocco
Pal. Papadopo
Palazzo Centani (Museo Goldoni)
Pal. Dona
Pal. Grimani
Pal. Layard
Palazzo Barbarigo
Rio d. Frescada
S. Pantalòn
S. Tomà
Pal. Civràn-Grimani
S. Ángelo
Rio Ca' Foscari
Calle Foscari
S. Tomà
Pal. Cornèr Spinelli
Pal. Fortuny
Pal. Balbi
Palazzo Mocenígo
Campo Santa Margherita
Ca' Foscari
Pal. Contarini d. Figure
Rio di S. Angelo
Oratorio de Annunciat
Palazzo Moro-Lin
Pal. Grassi
Saliz S. Samuele
C. Crosera
Campo S. Ánge
Pal. Nani
Ca' Rezzonico
S. Samuele
San Samuele
S. Stefano
Palazzo Malipiero
Campo S. Barnaba
S. Bárnaba
Ca' Rezzonico
Campo S. Stefano
S. Maurízio
Rio Malpaga
Pal. Stern
Ca' del Duca
Rio del Duca
C. Vetturi
Rio di S. Vidal
Pal. Morosini
Pal. Loredan
Pal. Falier
Rio d. Santissimo
S. Maria d. Giglio
DORSODURO
Pal. Contarini degli Scrigni
Pal. Bárbaro
Pal. Pisani
Palazzo Cornèr d. Ca' Granda
Accademia
Ponte dell'Accademia
Canàl Grande
S. Maria d. Giglio
Gallerie dell' Accademia
Palazzo Contarini dal Zaffo
S. Trovaso
Rio di S. Trovaso
Pal. Molìn
Pal. Centani
Pal. Nani
Pal. Venièr dei Leoni (Guggenheim)
Pal. Giustiniàn
Rio di S. Vio
S. Maria d. Visitaz.
S. Agnese
Gesuati
Fond. Bragadin
Zàttere
Ai Artisti 4
Ai Cugnai 6
Alla Basilica 18
Alle Corone 15
Alle Testiere 16
Al Bacco Felice 2
Al Covo 19
Al Vecio Canton 17
Bacareto De Lele 1
Bistrot de Venise 13
Da Fiore 7
Do Mori 9
Do Spade 8
Locanda Montin 3
L'Orto dei Mori 11
Osteria Al Squero 5
Osteria Alla Ciurma 10
Rosticceria San Bartolomeo 14
Taverna al Remer 12

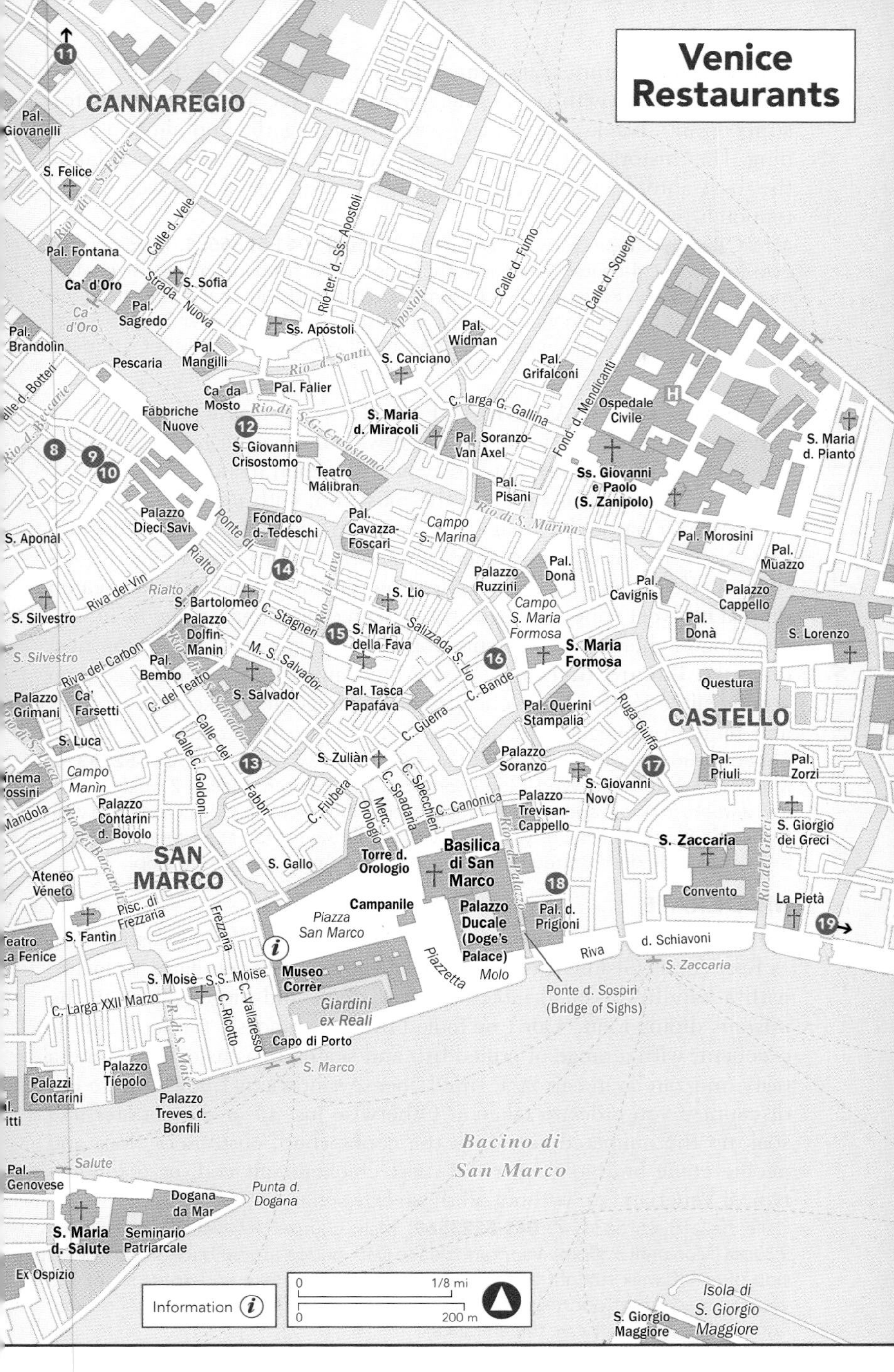
Venice Restaurants
CANNAREGIO
SAN MARCO
CASTELLO
S. Felice
Pal. Fontana
Ca' d'Oro
S. Sofia
Pal. Sagredo
Pescaria
Pal. Mangilli
Ss. Apóstoli
S. Canciano
Pal. Widman
Pal. Grifalconi
Ospedale Civile
S. Maria d. Miracoli
Ca' da Mosto
Pal. Falier
Fábbriche Nuove
S. Giovanni Crisostomo
Teatro Málibran
Pal. Soranzo-Van Axel
Pal. Pisani
Ss. Giovanni e Paolo (S. Zanipolo)
S. Maria d. Pianto
Palazzo Dieci Savi
Fóndaco d. Tedeschi
Pal. Cavazza-Foscari
Campo S. Marina
Pal. Morosini
S. Aponàl
S. Lio
Palazzo Ruzzini
Pal. Donà
Pal. Cavignis
Palazzo Cappello
S. Silvestro
S. Bartolomeo
Palazzo Dolfin-Manin
S. Maria della Fava
Campo S. Maria Formosa
S. Maria Formosa
S. Lorenzo
Pal. Bembo
S. Salvador
Pal. Tasca Papafáva
Questura
Palazzo Grimani
Ca' Farsetti
Pal. Querini Stampalia
S. Luca
S. Zuliàn
Palazzo Soranzo
S. Giovanni Novo
Pal. Priuli
Pal. Zorzi
Campo Manìn
Palazzo Contarini d. Bovolo
Palazzo Trevisan-Cappello
S. Zaccaria
S. Giorgio dei Greci
S. Gallo
Torre d. Orologio
Basilica di San Marco
Ateneo Véneto
Campanile
Piazza San Marco
Palazzo Ducale (Doge's Palace)
Pal. d. Prigioni
Convento
La Pietà
S. Fantin
Riva d. Schiavoni
S. Moisè
Museo Corrèr
Piazzetta
Molo
Ponte d. Sospiri (Bridge of Sighs)
Giardini ex Reali
Capo di Porto
Palazzo Tiépolo
Palazzi Contarini
Palazzo Treves d. Bonfili
Bacino di San Marco
Pal. Genovese
Dogana da Mar
Punta d. Dogana
S. Maria d. Salute
Seminario Patriarcale
Ex Ospízio
Information
0 1/8 mi
0 200 m
Isola di S. Giorgio Maggiore
S. Giorgio Maggiore

14th to 18th centuries. It's gimmicky but it works; think fennel soup, homemade pasta with goose sauce and pine nuts, and almond-crusted sturgeon in a black grape sauce, with a yellow garlic and almond pudding. The "historical" tasting menu is a splurge, but we recommend it as the best introduction. Whatever you opt for, expect service to be topnotch.

4685 Calle dei Fabbri. www.bistrotdevenise.com. ✆ **041-5236651.** Main courses 28€–36€; classic 4-course Venetian tasting menu 70€; historical 5-course Venetian menu 100€. Daily: Restaurant noon–3pm and 7pm–midnight; bar 10am–midnight. *Vaporetto:* Rialto (turn right along canal, cross small footbridge over Rio San Salvador, turn left onto Calle Bembo, which becomes Calle dei Fabbri; Bistrot is about 5 blocks ahead).

Da Fiore ★★ TRATTORIA/VENETIAN A classy but laid-back Venetian trattoria (not to be confused with the posher *osteria* with the same name). The menu features typical Venetian dishes like squid-ink pasta, but the specials here are the most fun, with *moeche* (local soft-shell crab) a particular treat (the two main seasons are Mar–Apr and Oct–Nov). Desserts are another specialty, with all sorts of sugary *golosessi* on offer, from *buranelli* to *zaletti* (cornmeal cookies, typically eaten dipped in sweet wine or chocolate), and an exceptional *sgroppino al limone* (lemon sherbet). Make sure you visit the bar and *cicchetteria* next door, the **Bacaro di Fiore** (Wed–Mon 9am–10pm), which has been around since 1871, serving cheap wine and finger food like fried sardines and squid, fried vegetables, and crostini with creamed cod.

Calle delle Botteghe 3461, off Campo Santo Stefano. www.dafiore.it. ✆ **041-5235310.** Main courses 15€–29€. Wed–Mon noon–3pm and 7–10pm. Closed 2 weeks in Jan and 2 weeks in Aug. *Vaporetto:* Accademia (cross bridge to San Marco side and walk to Campo Santo Stefano; as you are about to exit the *campo* at northern end, take a left onto Calle delle Botteghe; also close to Sant'Angelo *vaporetto* stop).

MODERATE

Rosticceria San Bartolomeo ★★ DELI/VENETIAN Also known as Rosticceria Gislon, this no-frills spot is incredibly popular with locals, with a handful of small tables and bar stools and bigger tables in the upstairs dining room. Don't be fooled by appearances—the food here is excellent, with a range of grilled fish and seafood pastas on offer, and a tasty "mozzarella in carrozza" (fried cheese sandwich; 1.90€). There is a discount if you order to takeout. Otherwise just sit at the counter and soak up the animated scene, as the cooks chop, customers chat, and people come and go. Order the roast chicken, salt cod, or polenta—typical Venetian fare without all those extra charges.

Calle della Bissa 5424. ✆ **041-5223569.** Main courses 10€–24€. Daily 9:30am–9:30pm (Mon until 3:30pm). *Vaporetto:* Rialto (with bridge at your back on San Marco side of canal, walk straight to Campo San Bartolomeo; take underpass slightly to your left marked sottoportego della bissa; the *rosticceria* is at the 1st corner on your right; look for gislon above the entrance).

Castello

EXPENSIVE

Al Covo ★★ SEAFOOD/VENETIAN For years, this high-quality Venetian restaurant from Diane and Cesare Benelli has been deservingly popular with American food writers (and TV chefs such as Anthony Bourdain), so expect to be eating with plenty of fellow tourists. It features two cozy dining rooms adorned with art (plus some outdoor seating in summer), but it's the food that takes center stage here: fresh fish from the lagoon or the Adriatic, fruits and vegetables from local farms, and meat sourced from esteemed Franco Cazzamali Butchers. The pasta, desserts, and sauces are all homemade. Begin with Venetian *saor,* sweet and sour fish and shellfish, or fried zucchini flowers, followed by fresh monkfish with pancetta on a celeriac fondue, or deep-fried scampi, calamari, and baby sole. Diane's desserts might include rustic pear and prune cake with a grappa-cinnamon sauce or green apple sorbet with Calvados.

Campiello della Pescheria 3968. www.ristorantealcovo.com. ✆ **041-5223812.** Reservations required. Main courses 25€–38€. Fri–Tues 12:45–3:30pm (kitchen closes 2pm) and 7:30pm–midnight (kitchen closes at 10pm); Closed usually in Jan and 10 days in Aug. *Vaporetto:* Piazza San Marco; walk along Riva degli Schiavoni toward Arsenale and take 3rd narrow street left (Calle della Pescaria) after Hotel Metropole.

Alle Corone ★★★ SEAFOOD/VENETIAN This is one of Venice's finest restaurants, an elegant 19th-century dining room inside the Hotel Ai Reali and overlooking the canal. Start with a selection of Venetian cicchetti before moving on to grilled scallops with black truffle, or main courses such as baked turbot with black olives, seared tuna with poppy seeds, or roast lamb with thyme, potatoes, and artichokes. To finish, the rosemary panna cotta with apple and ginger jam is spectacular. Reservations recommended.

Campo della Fava 5527 (Hotel Ai Reali). www.hotelaireali.com. ✆ **041-2410253.** Main courses 28.50€–32.50€. Daily noon–2:30pm and 7–10:30pm. *Vaporetto:* Rialto (walk east along Calle Larga Mazzini, turn left on Merceria then right on Calle Stella until you reach the hotel).

Alle Testiere ★★★ ITALIAN/VENETIAN This tiny restaurant (with only nine tables) is the connoisseur's choice for fresh fish and seafood, with a menu that changes daily and a shrewd selection of wines. Dinner is served at two seatings (reservations are essential), where you choose from appetizers such as swordfish carpaccio or clams that seem to have been literally plucked straight from the sea. The fresh fish fillets with aromatic herbs are always an exceptional main choice, but the pastas—like smoked ravioli with prawns and curry, or spaghetti with clams—are superb. Finish off with homemade peach pie or chestnut pudding. In peak season, make reservations at least 1 month in advance, and note that you'll have a less rushed experience in the second seating.

Calle del Mondo Novo 5801. www.osterialletestiere.it. ✆ **041-5227220.** Main courses 27€; many types of fish sold by weight. Tues–Sat noon–3pm and 2 seatings at 7 and 9:30pm. *Vaporetto:* Rialto or San Marco. Look for Salizada San Lio (west of Campo Santa Maria Formosa), and from there ask for Calle del Mondo Novo.

MODERATE

Al Vecio Canton ★ ITALIAN/PIZZA Venice is not known for pizza, partly because fire codes restrict the use of traditional wood-burning ovens, but the big, fluffy-crusted pies here—made using natural mineral water—are the best in the city. They also do a mean T-bone steak, cooked tableside on a granite slab, accompanied by truffle or red pepper sauce, and some of the pastas are pretty good, too—stick with seafood versions like cuttlefish, the seasonal *moeche* (soft-shell crabs), and *schie,* small gray shrimp from the lagoon. Wash it all down with the drinkable house wine, or for a change, tasty craft beers from Treviso-based 32 Via dei Birrai.

Calle Ruga Giuffa 4738a (at the corner of Corona Leonardo). www.veciocanton.it. ✆ **041-5287143.** Pizza 7€–15€. Main courses 14€–22€. Wed–Mon noon–3pm and 6:30–10:30pm. *Vaporetto:* San Zaccaria (head down road on the left side of Hotel Savoia e Jolanda to Campo San Provolo; take Salizada San Provolo on the north side of the *campo,* cross 1st footbridge on your left, and pizzeria is on 1st corner on left).

INEXPENSIVE

Alla Basilica ★ VENETIAN Considering its location around the corner from the Doge's Palace and St. Mark's, lunch here is a phenomenally good deal. Don't expect romance—it's a noisy, canteenlike place. Simple, freshly prepared meals include a pasta course like lasagna or *spaghetti con ragu,* a meat or fish main (think grilled pork chops or *dentice al vapore con zucchini grigliate,* steamed red snapper with grilled zucchini), and vegetables for just 16€. Add a liter of extremely drinkable house wine for just 10€. Basilica is a favorite of local workers and English is rarely spoken; practice your Italian here.

Calle degli Albanesi 4255, Castello. www.allabasilicavenezia.it. ✆ **041-5220524.** Lunch set menu 16€. Wed–Mon noon–3pm. *Vaporetto:* San Marco (as you disembark, the entrance to Calle degli Albanesi is a short walk to the left).

Dorsoduro

EXPENSIVE

Ai Artisti ★★★ VENETIAN This unpretentious, family-owned *osteria* and *enoteca* is one of the best dining experiences in Venice, with a menu that changes daily according to market offerings (because the fish market is closed on Monday, no fish is served that day). Grab a table by the canal and feast on stuffed squid, pan-fried sardines, and an amazing, buttery veal *scallopini,* or opt for one of the truly wonderful pastas. The tiramisu and chocolate torte are standouts for dessert. What's likely to stay with you in addition to the food is the impeccable service; servers are happy to guide you through the menu, and offer brilliant suggestions for wine pairing. It's a tiny place, so reservations are recommended. Fondamenta della Toletta 1169A. www.enotecaartisti.com. ✆ **041-5238944.** Main courses 25€–28€. Mon–Sat 12:45–2:30pm and 2 seatings at 7–9pm and 9–11pm. *Vaporetto:* Accademia (walk around Accademia and turn right on Calle Gambara to where it ends at Rio di San Trovaso, turn left on Fondamenta Priuli; take the 1st bridge onto a road that leads into Fondamenta della Toletta).

Locanda Montin ★★ VENETIAN Montin was the famous ex-hangout of Peggy Guggenheim in the 1950s, and has been frequented by Jimmy Carter, Robert De Niro, and Brad Pitt, among many other celebs. But is the food still any good? Well, yes. Grab a table in the wonderfully serene back garden (completely covered by an arching trellis), itself a good reason to visit, and sample Venetian classics like sardines in *saor* (a local marinade of vinegar, wine, onion, and raisins), and an exquisite *seppie in nero* (cuttlefish cooked in its ink). For a main course, it's hard to beat the crispy sea bass *(branzino)* or legendary monkfish, while the lemon sorbet with vodka is a perfect, tart conclusion to any meal. Fondamenta di Borgo 1147. www.locandamontin.com. ✆ **041-5227151.** Main courses 18€–27€. Daily 12:15–2:30pm and 7:15–10pm (closed on Wed Nov–Apr). *Vaporetto:* Ca'Rezzonico (walk straight along Calle Lunga San Barnaba, then turn left along Fondamenta di Borgo).

MODERATE

Ai Cugnai ★★ VENETIAN The name of this small trattoria means "at the in-laws," and in that spirit the kitchen knocks out solid home-cooked Venetian food, beautifully prepared and popular with locals and hungry gondoliers. The *spaghetti vongole* here is crammed with sea-fresh mussels and clams, the *caprese* and baby octopus salad are perfectly balanced appetizers, and the house red wine is a top value. Our favorite is the sublime spaghetti with scallops, a slippery, salty delight. There are just two small tables outside, so get here early if you want to eat alfresco. Calle Nuova Sant'Agnese 857. ✆ **041-5289238.** Main courses 14€–26€. Tues–Sun noon–3:30pm and 7–10pm. *Vaporetto:* Accademia (head east of bridge and Accademia in direction of Guggenheim Collection; restaurant will be on your right, off the straight street connecting the 2 museums).

INEXPENSIVE

Osteria Al Squero ★★★ WINE BAR/VENETIAN This enticing *osteria* with perhaps the most beguiling view in Venice is opposite the Squero di San Trovaso (p. 412). Sip coffee and nibble *cicchetti* while observing the activity at the medieval gondola boatyard and workshop, on the other side of the Rio di San Trovaso. It's essentially a place for a light lunch or *aperitivi* rather than a full meal. Snack on delights such as Carnia smoked sausage, *baccalà* (cod) crostini, anchovies, blue cheese, tuna, and sardines in *saor* for a total of around 15€ to 16€ per person. Spritz from 2.50€.

Fondamenta Nani 943–944. ✆ **335-6007513.** *Cicchetti* 1.20–2.50€ per piece. Tues–Sun 7am–8pm. *Vaporetto:* Zattere (walk west along the waterside to the Rio di San Trovaso and turn right up Fondamenta Nani).

San Polo

MODERATE

Do Spade ★ VENETIAN It's tough to find dining this authentic so close to the Rialto Bridge these days, but Do Spade has been around since 1415. Most locals come for the *cicchetti*, small plates such as fried calamari, meatballs, mozzarella, and salted cod (1.50–3.50€) and decent Italian wines (3€ a glass); you can sit on benches outside if it's too crowded indoors. The more formal restaurant section is also worth a try, with seafood highlights including a delicately prepared monkfish, scallops served with fresh zucchini, and rich seafood lasagna. The seasonal pumpkin ravioli is one of the best dishes in the city.

Sottoportego do Spade 860. www.cantinadospade.com. ✆ **041-5210574.** Main courses 12€–25€. Daily 10am–3pm and 6–10pm. *Vaporetto:* Rialto Mercato (with your back to Grand Canal, walk up Ruga Vecchia San Giovanni and turn right on Ruga dei Spezieri; at the end turn left on Calle de le Beccarie O Panataria, and then take 2nd right onto covered Sottoportego do Spade).

INEXPENSIVE

Do Mori ★★★ WINE BAR/VENETIAN Serving good wine and *cicchetti* since 1462, Do Mori is above all a fun place to have a genuine Venetian experience, a small, dimly lit *bàcari* that can barely accommodate 10 people standing up. Sample the baby octopus and ham on mango, lard-smothered *crostini,* and pickled onions speared with salty anchovies, or opt for the *tramezzini* (tiny sandwiches). Local TV (and BBC) star Francesco Da Mosto is a regular, but note that this institution is very much on the well-trodden tourist trail—plenty of *cicchetti* tours stop by in the early evening. Local wine runs 3€ to 4€ per glass.

Calle Do Mori 429 (also Calle Galeazza 401). ✆ **041-5225401.** *Tramezzini* and *cicchetti* 1.80€–3.50€ per piece. Mon–Sat 8am–8pm (June–Aug closed daily 2–4:30pm). *Vaporetto:* Rialto Mercato (with your back to Grand Canal, walk straight up Ruga Vecchia San Giovanni and turn right on Calle Galeazza).

Osteria Alla Ciurma ★★★ WINE BAR/VENETIAN With a dining room decked out like a traditional Venetian boat, this *cicchetteria* offers some of the freshest seafood snacks in the city, washed down with quality wines, spritz, and Prosecco—they source their fish straight from the daily market just around the corner. Mouth-watering *cicchetti* include cod fillets, fried zucchini flowers, fried artichokes, and shrimp wrapped in bacon. Sandwiches and lunch specials (noon–3pm) are also available.

Calle Galeazza 406. ✆ **340-6863561.** *Cicchetti* 1.50€–2.50€ per piece. Mon–Sat 9am–3pm and 5:30–9pm; Sun 10:30am–3pm (May–Sept only). *Vaporetto:* Rialto Mercato (with your back to Grand Canal, walk straight up Ruga Vecchia San Giovanni and turn right on Calle Galeazza).

Santa Croce

MODERATE

Al Bacco Felice ★ ITALIAN This quaint, friendly neighborhood restaurant is convenient to the train station and popular with locals, with a real buzz most evenings. Stick with the basics and you won't be disappointed—the pizzas, pastas, and fish dishes are always outstanding, with classic standbys *spaghetti alle vongole,* pasta with spicy *arrabbiata,* and *carpaccio* of swordfish especially well done. The meal usually ends with complimentary plates of Venetian cookies, a nice touch.

Santa Croce 197E (on Corte dei Amai). ✆ **041-5287794.** Main courses 15€–28€. Mon–Fri noon–3:30pm and 6:30–midnight; Sat and Sun noon–midnight. *Vaporetto:* Piazzale Roma (keeping the Grand Canal on your left, head toward train station; cross the small canal at the end of the park and immediately turn right onto Fondamenta Tolentini; when you get to Campo Tolentini turn left onto Corte dei Amai).

INEXPENSIVE

Bacareto Da Lele ★★★ WINE BAR/VENETIAN This tiny hole-in-the-wall *bacaro* is worth seeking out for its fresh snacks, sandwiches, and *cicchetti*. Tiny glasses or *ombras* of wine and prosecco are just 0.60€–1.50€)—there are no seats, so do as the locals do and grab a space on the nearby church steps while you sip and nibble. Opt for a tiny porchetta or bacon and artichoke panini (around 2.50€), antipasti plates (cheese and salami) or a freshly baked crostini for 1€–2€. Expect long lines here in peak season—the secret is definitely out.

Campo dei Tolentini 183. No phone. *Cicchetti* 1.50€–2.50€ per piece. Mon–Fri 6am–8pm, Sat 6am–2pm. *Vaporetto:* Piazzale Roma (walk left along the Grand Canal, past the Ponte della Costituzione, into the Giardino Papadopoli; turn right on Fonadmenta Papadopoli then left. Cross the park at the 1st bridge; the next canal should be the Rio del Tolentini, with the campo across the bridge and Da Lele on the southwest corner).

Cannaregio

EXPENSIVE

L'Orto dei Mori ★★ VENETIAN Traditional Venetian cuisine is cooked up here by a young Sicilian chef, so expect some differences to the usual flavors and dishes. Everything on the fairly small menu is exceptional—the *baccalà* (salted cod) especially so—and the setting next to a canal is enhanced by candlelight at night. The place can get very busy—the waiters are normally friendly, but expect brusque treatment if you turn up late (or early) for a reservation. Dinner is usually served in two seatings, one early (7–9pm) and one late, so waiters will be reluctant to serve those who arrive early for the second sitting—even if a table is available, you'll be given water and just told to wait.

Campo dei Mori 3386. www.osteriaortodeimori.com. ✆ **041-5243677.** Main courses 19€–26€. Wed–Mon 12:30–3:30pm and 7pm–midnight, usually in 2 seatings (July–Aug closed for lunch Mon–Fri). *Vaporetto:* Madonna dell'Orto (walk through *campo* to the canal and turn right; take 1st bridge to your left, walk down the street and turn left at canal onto Fondamenta dei Mori; go straight until you hit Campo dei Mori).

INEXPENSIVE

Taverna al Remer ★★ VENETIAN Eating on a budget in Venice doesn't always mean panini and pizza. This romantic *taverna* overlooks the Grand Canal from a small, charming piazza, and while the a la carte options can be pricey, the secret is to time your visit for the buffets. The 20€ weekday lunch is a fabulous deal: a choice of two fresh pastas plus a buffet of antipasto that includes vegetables, salads, cold cuts, a choice of two or three quality hot dishes (such as Venice-style liver with polenta or pan-fried squid), a choice of desserts, and coffee, water, and a quarter liter of wine per person. The evening *aperitivo* is an even better deal, from just 5€ for as much smoked meat, sausage, salads, seafood risotto, and pasta as you can eat, plus one Aperol spritz, Bellini, vino, or Prosecco. Normal service resumes after the buffet is cleared, with live music (Latin, soul, jazz) most nights at 8:30pm, but as long as you order a few drinks, it's fine to stick around and take in the scene.

Cannaregio 5701 (off Salizada S. Giovanni Grisostomo). www.alremer.it. ✆ **041-5228789.** Lunch buffet 20€ weekdays only; aperitivo (5:30–7:30pm) from 5€. Mon, Tues, and Thurs–Sun noon–2:30pm and 5:30pm–midnight. *Vaporetto:* Ca' d'Oro or Rialto (heading south on Salizada S. Giovanni Grisostomo, look for a narrow passage on the right, just beyond the Ponte S. Giovanni footbridge).

Gelato

Is the gelato any good in Venice? Italians might demur, but by international standards, the answer is most definitely yes. As always, gelato parlors aimed exclusively at tourists are notorious for poor quality and extortionate prices, especially in Venice. Avoid places near Piazza San Marco altogether. Below are two of our favorite spots in the city.

Il Doge ★★ GELATO Contender for best gelato in Venice, Il Doge has a great location at the southern end of Campo Santa Margherita. These guys use only natural, homemade flavors and ingredients, from an exceptional spicy chocolate to the house specialty, Crema de Doge, a rich mix of eggs, cream, and oranges. Try a refreshing *granita* in summer.

Campo Santa Margherita 3058, Dorsoduro. www.gelateriaildoge.com. ✆ **041-5234607.** Cones & cups 1.50€–5.50€. Daily 11am–10pm. *Vaporetto:* Ca'Rezzonico.

EATING cheaply IN VENICE

You don't have to eat in a fancy restaurant to enjoy good food in Venice. Prepare a picnic, and while you eat alfresco, you can observe the life in the city's *campi* or the aquatic parade on its main thoroughfare, the Grand Canal.

Mercato Rialto Venice's principal open-air market has two parts, beginning with the **produce section,** whose many stalls unfold north on the San Polo side of the Rialto Bridge. Vendors are here Monday to Saturday 7am to 1pm (some stay later). Behind these stalls a few permanent food stores sell cheese, cold cuts, and bread. At the market's farthest point, the covered **fish market** is still redolent of the days when it was one of the Mediterranean's great fish bazaars. The fish merchants take Monday off and work mornings only.

Campo Santa Margherita Every Tuesday through Saturday from 8:30am to 1pm, a number of open-air stalls set up shop on this spacious Dorsoduro *campo*, selling fresh fruit and vegetables. A conventional supermarket, **Punto Simply** (Mon–Sat 8:30am–8pm, Sun 9am–2pm), is just off the *campo* in the direction of nearby Campo San Barnaba, at no. 3019.

San Barnaba This is where you'll find Venice's heavily photographed **floating market** (mostly fruit and vegetables) operating from a boat moored just off San Barnaba at the Ponte dei Pugni in Dorsoduro. This market is open daily from 8am to 1pm and 3:30 to 7:30pm, except Wednesday afternoon and Sunday.

The Best Picnic Spots Given its aquatic roots, you won't find much in the way of green space in Venice (if you are desperate for green, walk 30 min. past San Marco along the water, or take a *vaporetto* to the **Giardini Pubblici,** Venice's only green park, but don't expect anything great). A much more enjoyable alternative is to find one of the larger *campi* that have park benches, such as **Campo San Giacomo dell'Orio,** in the quiet *sestiere* of Santa Croce. The two most central: **Campo Santa Margherita** (*sestiere* of Dorsoduro) and **Campo San Polo** (*sestiere* of San Polo).

The **Punta della Dogana (Customs House)** near La Salute Church in Dorsoduro is a prime viewing site at the mouth of the Grand Canal. Pull up on the embankment here and watch the flutter of water activity against a canvaslike backdrop deserving of the Accademia Museum. In this same area, another superb spot, **Campo San Vio** (near the Guggenheim), is directly on the Grand Canal and even boasts two benches and the possibility to sit on an untrafficked small bridge.

A bit farther afield, you can take the *vaporetto* out to Burano and then no. 9 for the 5-minute ride to the near-deserted island of **Torcello.** If you bring a basketful of bread, cheese, and wine you can do your best to reenact the romantic scene between Katharine Hepburn and Rossano Brazzi from the 1955 film *Summertime.*

La Mela Verde ★★ GELATO The popular rival to Il Doge for best scoop in the city, with sharp flavors and all the classics done sensationally well: pistachio, chocolate, *nocciola* and the mind-blowing lemon and basil. The overall champions: *mela verde* (green apple), like creamy, frozen fruit served in a cup, and the addictive tiramisu.

Fondamenta de L'Osmarin 4977, Castello. www.gelaterialamelaverde.it. ✆ **349-1957924.** Cones or cups from 1.75€. Daily 11am–10pm. Usually closed mid-Nov to mid-Feb. *Vaporetto:* Zaccaria.

SHOPPING

In a city that for centuries has thrived almost exclusively on tourism, remember this: **Where you buy cheap, you get cheap.** Venetians, centuries-old merchants, aren't known for bargaining. You'll stand a better chance of getting a good deal if you pay in cash or buy more than one item. In our limited space below, we've listed some of the more reputable places to stock up on classic Venetian items.

Shopping Streets & Markets

A mix of low-end trinket stores and middle-market-to-upscale boutiques line the narrow zigzagging **Mercerie** running north between Piazza San Marco and the Rialto Bridge. More expensive boutiques make for great window-shopping on **Calle Larga XXII Marzo,** the wide street that begins west of Piazza San Marco and wends its way to the expansive Campo Santo Stefano near the Accademia. The narrow **Frezzaria,** just west of Piazza San Marco and running north-south, offers a grab bag of bars, souvenir shops, and tony clothing stores like Louis Vuitton and Versace. There are few bargains to be had; the non-produce part of the **Rialto Market** is as good as it gets for basic souvenirs, where you'll find cheap T-shirts, glow-in-the-dark plastic gondolas, and tawdry glass trinkets. The **Mercatino dei Miracoli** (© **041-2710022**), held only six times a year in Campo Santa Maria Nova (Cannaregio), is a fabulous flea market with all sorts of bric-a-brac and antiques sold by ordinary Venetians—haggling, for once, is acceptable. It usually takes place on the second Saturday or Sunday of March, April, May, September, October, and December, from 8:30am to 8pm. The **Mercatino dell'Antiquariato** (www.mercatinocamposanmaurizio.it) is a professional antiques market in Campo San Maurizio, San Marco; it takes place 4 to 5 times a year (usually Mar–Apr, May, Sept, Oct, and Dec; check the website for dates).

Glassblower making a vase in Murano.

Arts & Crafts

Venice is uniquely famous for local crafts that have been produced here for centuries and are hard to get elsewhere: the **glassware** from Murano, the **delicate lace** from Burano, and the ***cartapesta* (papier-mâché) Carnevale masks** you'll find in endless *botteghe* (shops), where you can watch artisans paint amid their wares.

Now here's the bad news: There's such an overwhelming sea of cheap glass gewgaws that buying Venetian glass can become something of a turnoff (shipping and insurance costs make most things unaffordable; the alternative is to hand-carry anything fragile). Plus, there are so few women left on Burano willing to spend countless hours keeping alive the art of lace-making that any pieces not produced by machine in China are sold at stratospheric prices; ditto the truly high-quality glass (although trinkets can be cheap and fun). The best place to buy glass is Murano itself—the **"Vetro Artistico Murano"** trademark guarantees its origin, but expect to pay as much as 60€ for just a wineglass.

Carnevale masks and costumes in Venice.

Atelier Segalin di Daniela Ghezzo ★★ Founded in 1932 by master cobbler Antonio Segalin and his son Rolando, this old leather shoe store is now run by Daniela Ghezzo (the star apprentice of Rolando), maker of exuberant handmade shoes and boots, from basic flats to crazy footwear designed for Carnevale (shoes from 650€–1,800€). It's open Monday to Friday 10am to 1pm and 3pm to 7pm, and Saturday 10am to 1pm. Calle dei Fuseri 4365, San Marco. www.danielaghezzo.it. ✆ **041-5222115.** Vaporetto: San Marco.

Il Canovaccio ★ Remember the creepy orgy scenes in Stanley Kubrick's film *Eyes Wide Shut*? The ornate masks used in the movie were made by the owners of this vaunted store. All manner of traditional, feathered, and animal masks are knocked out of their on-site workshop. It's open daily 10am to 7:30pm. Calle delle Bande 5369 (near Campo Santa Maria Formosa), Castello. ✆ **041-5210393.** Vaporetto: San Zaccaria.

Il Grifone ★★★ Toni Peressin's handmade leather briefcases, bound notebooks, belts, and soft-leather purses have garnered quite a following, and justly so—his craftsmanship is magnificent (he makes everything in the workshop out back). Items start at around 25€. His shop is usually open Tuesday and Friday 10am to 6pm, and Wednesday, Thursday, and Saturday 10am to 1pm and 4 to 7pm. Fondamenta del Gaffaro 3516, Dorsoduro. www.ilgrifonevenezia.it. ✆ **041-5229452.** Vaporetto: Piazzale Roma.

La Bottega dei Mascareri ★★ High-quality, creative masks—some based on Tiepolo paintings—crafted by the brothers Sergio and Massimo Boldrin since 1984. Basic masks start at around 15€ to 20€, but you'll pay over 75€ for a more innovative piece. The smaller, original branch lies at the foot of the Rialto Bridge (San Polo 80; ✆ **041-5223857**). Both locations tend to open daily 9am to 6pm. Calle dei Saoneri 2720, San Polo. www.mascarer.com. ✆ **041-5242887.** Vaporetto: Rialto.

Marco Polo International ★ This vast showroom, just west of the Piazza San Marco, displays quality glass direct from Murano (although it's more expensive than going to the island yourself), including plenty of easy-to-carry items such as paperweights and small dishes. It opens daily 10am to 7pm. Frezzaria 1644, San Marco. www.marcopolointernational.it. ✆ **041-5229295.** Vaporetto: San Marco.

Venini ★ Convenient, classy, but incredibly expensive, Venini has been selling quality glass art since 1921, supplying the likes of Versace and many other designer brands. Its **workshop** on Murano is at Fondamenta Vetrai 50 (✆ **041-2737211**). Both locations tend to open Monday to Saturday 9:30am to 5:30pm. Piazzetta Leoncini 314, San Marco. www.venini.it. ✆ **041-5224045.** Vaporetto: San Marco.

Interior of Teatro La Fenice.

ENTERTAINMENT & NIGHTLIFE

If you're looking for serious nocturnal action, you're in the wrong town—Verona and Padua are far livelier. Your best bet is to sit in moonlit Piazza San Marco and listen to the cafes' outdoor orchestras, with the floodlit basilica before you—the perfect opera set—though this pleasure comes with a hefty price tag. Other popular spots include **Campo San Bartolomeo,** at the foot of the Rialto Bridge (a zoo in high season), and **Campo San Luca.** For low prices and low pretension, the absolute best place to go is **Campo Santa Margherita,** a huge open *campo* between the train station and the Accademia Bridge.

Visit one of the tourist information centers for current English-language schedules of the month's special events. The monthly *Ospite di Venezia* is distributed free or online at **www.unospitedivenezia.it** and is extremely helpful but usually available only in the more expensive hotels.

Performing Arts & Live Music

Venice has a long and rich tradition of classical music; this was, after all, the home of Vivaldi. People dressed in period costumes stand around in heavily trafficked spots near San Marco and Rialto passing out brochures advertising classical music concerts, so you'll have no trouble finding up-to-date information.

Santa Maria della Pietà ★★ The so-called "Vivaldi Church," built between 1745 and 1760, holds concerts throughout the year, mostly performed by lauded ensemble **I Virtuosi Italiani;** check the website for specific dates. Tickets are usually 28–30€. Riva degli Schiavoni 3701, Castello. www.chiesavivaldi.it. ✆ **041-5221120.** Vaporetto: San Zaccaria.

Teatro La Fenice ★★★ The opera season runs late November through June, but there are also classical concerts and ballet. Tickets are expensive for the major productions (66€–80€ for the gallery and 90€–220€ for a decent seat); budget travelers can opt for obstructed-view seats (35€) or listening-only seats (from 15€). Campo San Fantin 1965, San Marco. www.teatrolafenice.it. ✆ **041-2424.** Vaporetto: Giglio.

Cafes

For tourists and locals alike, Venetian nightlife mainly centers on the many cafes in one of the world's most beautiful *piazze:* Piazza San Marco. It is also a most expensive and touristed place to linger over a spritz, but it's a splurge that should not be dismissed too readily.

Caffè dei Frari ★★★ Established in 1870, this inviting bar and cafe overlooking the Frari church has walls still adorned with the original Art Nouveau murals and an antique wooden bar. The seafood is especially good here, and a handful of excellent German beers are on tap. Open Tues–Sat 9am–10pm and Sun and Mon 9am–4pm. Fondamenta dei Frari 2564, San Polo. ✆ **041-5241877.** Vaporetto: San Tomà.

Caffè Florian ★★ Occupying prime *piazza* real estate since 1720, this is one of the world's oldest coffee shops, with a florid interior of 18th-century mirrors, frescoes, and statuary. Sitting at a table, expect to pay 9.50€ for a cappuccino, 19€ for a Bellini (prosecco and fresh peach nectar in season), and 12.50€ for a spritz—add another 6€ if the orchestra plays (Mar–Nov). Standing at the bar is much cheaper (5€ for a cappuccino, 8.50€ for a Bellini and so on). Open Mon–Thurs 10am–9pm, Fri & Sat 9am–11pm, and Sun 9am–9pm. Piazza San Marco 56. www.caffeflorian.com. ✆ **041-5205641.** Vaporetto: San Marco.

Caffè Lavena ★★ Said to be Wagner's favorite cafe (look for the plaque inside), and the hangout of fellow composer Franz Liszt in the 19th century, Lavena lies on the opposite side of the *piazza* to Florian and was founded just a few decades later in 1750. Expect the same high prices and surcharges here (cappuccino 11.50€, cocktails 19.50€), though as with Florian, if you stand and drink at the bar you'll pay much less than sitting at a table (espresso is just 1.20€). Open daily 9:30am–midnight (closed Tues in winter). Piazza San Marco 133–134. www.lavena.it. ✆ **041-5224070.** Vaporetto: San Marco.

Il Caffè (aka Caffè Rosso) ★★★ Established in the late 19th century, Il Caffè has a history almost as colorful as its clientele, a mix of students, aging regulars, and lost tourists. This old-fashioned, no-nonsense cafe/bar has reasonably priced drinks and sandwiches, and lots of seating on the *campo*. Open Mon–Sat 7am–1am. Campo Santa Margherita 2963, Dorsoduro. www.cafferosso.it. ✆ **041-5287998.** Vaporetto: Ca'Rezzonico.

Birreria, Wine & Cocktail Bars

Although Venice boasts an old and prominent university, dance clubs barely enjoy their 15 minutes of popularity before changing hands or closing down (some are open only in summer). Young Venetians tend to go to the Lido in summer or mainland Mestre. Evenings are better spent lingering over a late dinner, having a pint in a *birreria,* or nursing a glass of *Prosecco* in one of the pricey outdoor bars and cafes in Piazza San Marco or Campo Santa Margherita.

Al Prosecco ★★ Get acquainted with all things bubbly at this smart *enoteca,* a specialist, as you'd expect, in Veneto Prosecco. It features tasty *cicchetti* and a gorgeous terrace overlooking the *campo* below. Most drinks run 3€ to 5€. Open Mon–Sat 10am–10:30pm (closes at 8pm in winter; closed Aug and Jan). Campo San Giacomo da l'Orio 1503, Santa Croce. www.alprosecco.com. ✆ **041-5240222.** Vaporetto: San Stae.

Caffè Centrale ★★ This super-hip bar and restaurant (with iPad menus) is located in the 16th-century Palazzo Cocco Molin, a short walk from Piazza San Marco. It has an intriguing selection of local and foreign beers (5.50€–7.50€) and a big cocktail list (10€–15€)—cover is an extra 4€ per person. Get a table by the canal or lounge on one of the comfy leather sofas. Open daily 7pm–1am. Piscina di Frezzaria 1659, San Marco. www.caffecentralevenezia.com. ✆ **041-8876642.** Vaporetto: Vallaresso.

Harry's Bar ★ Possibly the most famous bar in Venice (and now a global chain), Harry's was established in 1931 by Giuseppe Cipriani and frequented by the likes of Ernest Hemingway and Charlie Chaplin. The Bellini was invented here in 1948 (along with *carpaccio* 2 years later); you can sip the signature concoction of fresh peach juice and *Prosecco* for a mere 22€. Go for the history but don't expect a five-star experience—most first-timers are surprised just how ordinary it looks inside. It also serves very expensive food, but just stick to the drinks. Open daily 10:30am–11pm. Calle Vallaresso 1323, San Marco. www.harrysbarvenezia.com. ✆ **041-5285777.** Vaporetto: Vallaresso.

Margaret DuChamp ★★ This popular student and *fashionista* hangout has plenty of chairs on the *campo* for people-watching, cocktails, and a spritz or two (spritz is 3€). It also serves decent *panini* (5€) and *tramezzini* (2€ at the table, or 1.50€ at the bar) and has free Wi-Fi. Open Wed–Mon 9am–2am. Campo Santa Margherita 3019, Dorsoduro. ✆ **041-5286255.** Vaporetto: Ca' Rezzonico.

Paradiso Perduto ★★ "Paradise Lost" is the most happening bar in this neighborhood, crammed with students and featuring occasional live jazz or blues (full concerts every Mon and every first Sun of the month), great *cicchetti* (piled in mountains at the bar), and cheap(ish) wine. Some people come to dine on the tasty seafood, but it's usually too busy and noisy to enjoy a proper meal here—stick to the drinks and the snacks. Open Thurs–Mon noon to midnight (closed Tues–Wed). Fondamenta della Misericordia 2540, Cannaregio. www.ilparadisoperduto.wordpress.com. ✆ **041-720581.** Vaporetto: Madonna dell'Orto.

DAY TRIPS FROM VENICE

If you only have 3 days or so, you will probably want to spend them in the center of Venice. However, if you are here for a week—or on your second visit to the city—head over to the mainland to see some of the old towns that lie within the historic Veneto region.

Padua ★★★

40km (25 miles) W of Venice

Tucked away within the ancient heart of **Padua** lies one of the greatest artistic treasures in all Italy, the precious Giotto frescoes of the **Cappella degli Scrovegni.** Although the city itself is not especially attractive (it was largely rebuilt after bombing during World War II), don't be put off by the urban sprawl that now surrounds it; central Padua is refreshingly bereft of tourist crowds, a workaday Veneto town with a large student population and a small but intriguing ensemble of historic sights.

ESSENTIALS

GETTING THERE The most efficient way to reach Padua is to take the **train** from Santa Lucia station. Trains depart every 10 to 20 minutes, and take 26 to 49 minutes depending on the class (4.15€–17€ one-way). Padua ("Padova" in Italian) station is a short walk north up Corso del Popolo from the Cappella degli Scrovegni and the old city.

VISITOR INFORMATION The **tourist office** at the train station is usually open Monday to Saturday 9am to 7pm and Sunday 10am to 4pm (www.turismopadova.it; ✆ **049-2010080**). The office in the old city at Vicolo Pedrocchi is open Monday to Saturday 9am to 7pm.

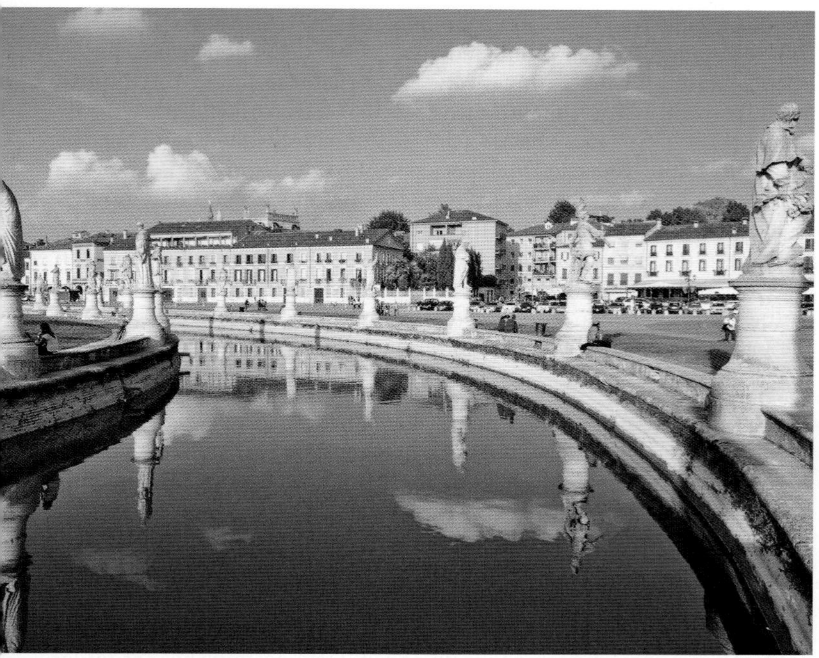

A tranquil scene in Padua.

EXPLORING PADUA

The one unmissable sight in Padua is the **Cappella degli Scrovegni ★★★** (www.cappelladegliscrovegni.it; ✆ **049-2010020;** daily 9am–7pm; check website for 7–10pm openings) at Piazza Eremitani, an outwardly unassuming chapel commissioned in 1303 by Enrico Scrovegni, a wealthy banker. Inside, however, the chapel is gloriously decorated with a cycle of frescoes by Florentine genius **Giotto,** depicting the lives of the Virgin Mary and Jesus and culminating in the Ascension and Last Judgment. Seeing Giotto's work in the flesh is spine-tingling; this is where he makes the decisive break with Byzantine art toward the realism and humanism that would define the Italian Renaissance.

Entrance to the chapel is limited, involving groups of 25 visitors spending 15 minutes in a climate-controlled airlock, used to stabilize the temperature, before going inside for another 15 minutes. To visit the chapel you must **make a reservation at least 24 hours in advance.** You must arrive 45 minutes before the time on your ticket. Tickets cost 13€ (6€ for kids ages 6–17 and students under 27).

If you have time, try and take in Padua's other historic highlights. The vast **Palazzo della Ragione** on Piazza del Erbe (Tues–Sun

Feb–Oct 9am–7pm, Nov–Jan 9am–6pm; 6€) is an architectural marvel, the cavernous town hall completed in 1219 and decorated by frescoes by Nicola Miretto in the 15th century. Pay a visit also to the **Basilica di Sant'Antonio** (www.santantonio.org; ✆ **049-8225652;** daily Apr–Oct 6:20am–7:45pm, Nov–Mar 6:20am–6:45pm; free admission) on the Piazza del Santo, the stately resting place of **St. Anthony of Padua,** the Portuguese Franciscan best known as the patron saint of finding things or lost people. The exterior of the church is a bizarre mix of Byzantine, Romanesque, and Gothic styles, while the interior is richly adorned with statuary and murals. Don't miss **Donatello**'s stupendous equestrian statue of the Venetian *condottiere* **Gattamelata** (Erasmo da Narni) in the piazza outside, the first large bronze sculpture of the Renaissance.

WHERE TO EAT

Padua offers plenty of places to eat, and you'll especially appreciate the overall drop in prices compared to Venice. It's hard to match the location of **Bar Nazionale ★★**, Piazza del Erbe 40 (Mon and Sat 7am–10:30pm, Tue, Thurs, Fri 7am–11:30am, Wed 7am–midnight, and Sun 9am–9:30pm), on the steps leading up to Palazzo della Ragione, but it's best for drinks and snacks (excellent *tramezzini*) rather than a full meal. For that, make for **Osteria dei Fabbri ★**, Via dei Fabbri 13, just off Piazza del Erbe (www.osteriadeifabbri.it; ✆ **049-650336;** Mon–Sat noon–3pm and 7–11pm), which cooks up cheap, tasty pasta dishes for under 15€.

Verona ★★

115km (71 miles) W of Venice

The affluent city of **Verona,** with its gorgeous red and peach-colored medieval buildings and Roman ruins, is one of Italy's major tourist draws, though its appeal owes more to **William Shakespeare** than real history. He immortalized the city in his (totally fictional) *Romeo and Juliet, The Two Gentlemen of Verona*, and partly, *The Taming of the Shrew*. In spite of its popularity with visitors, Verona is not Venice; it's a booming commercial center with vibrant science and technology sectors.

ESSENTIALS

GETTING THERE The best way to reach Verona from Venice is by **train.** Direct services depart every 30 minutes and take anywhere from 1 hour and 10 minutes to 2 hours and 20 minutes, depending on the type of train you catch (tickets range from 9€–27€ one-way). From Verona station (Verona Porta Nuova), it's a 15-minute walk to the historic center.

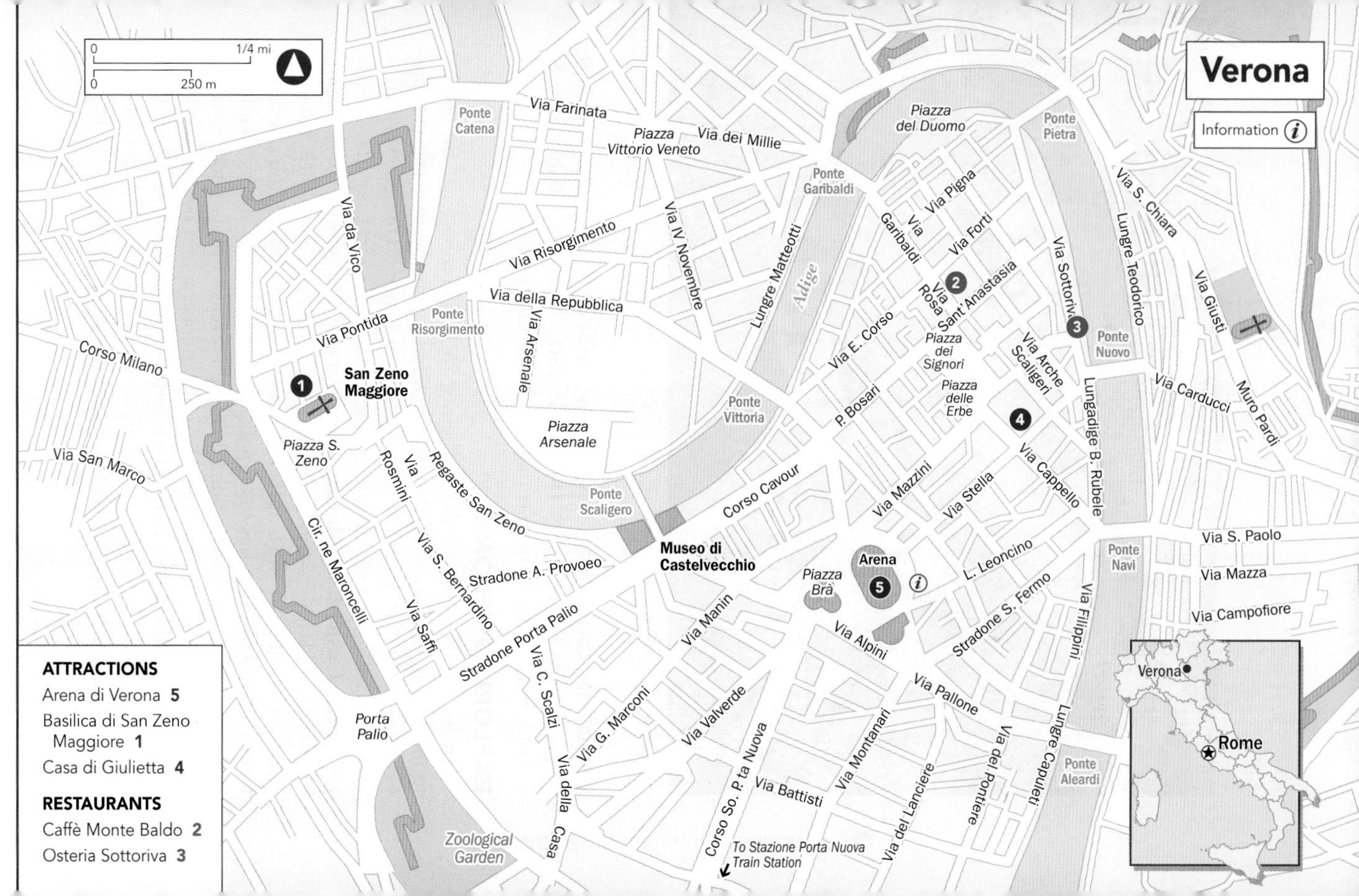
Verona
Information
0
1/4 mi
0
250 m
ATTRACTIONS
Arena di Verona 5
Basilica di San Zeno Maggiore 1
Casa di Giulietta 4
RESTAURANTS
Caffè Monte Baldo 2
Osteria Sottoriva 3
Rome
Verona
Via Farinata
Ponte Catena
Piazza Vittorio Veneto
Via dei Millie
Piazza del Duomo
Ponte Pietra
Ponte Garibaldi
Via Pigna
Via Garibaldi
Via Forti
Via S. Chiara
Lungre Teodorico
Via Giusti
Via da Vico
Via Risorgimento
Via IV Novembre
Lungre Matteotti
Adige
Via Sottoriva
Via Rosa
Sant'Anastasia
Via della Repubblica
Via Arsenale
Via Pontida
Ponte Risorgimento
Via E. Corso
Piazza dei Signori
Via Arche Scaligeri
Ponte Nuovo
Via Carducci
Muro Pardi
Corso Milano
San Zeno Maggiore
Piazza delle Erbe
Lungadige B. Rubele
Ponte Vittoria
P. Bosari
Piazza Arsenale
Piazza S. Zeno
Via Rosmini
Regaste San Zeno
Via San Marco
Via Cappello
Via Mazzini
Via Stella
Ponte Scaligero
Corso Cavour
Cir. ne Maroncelli
Via S. Bernardino
Museo di Castelvecchio
Stradone A. Provoeo
Arena
Piazza Brà
L. Leoncino
Via S. Paolo
Ponte Navi
Via Mazza
Via Saffi
Stradone Porta Palio
Via Manin
Via Alpini
Stradone S. Fermo
Via Campofiore
Via Filippini
Via C. Scalzi
Via Pallone
Porta Palio
Via G. Marconi
Via Valverde
Via della Casa
Corso So. P. ta Nuova
Via Montanari
Via Battisti
Via del Lanciere
Via del Pontiere
Lungre Capuleti
Ponte Aleardi
Zoological Garden
To Stazione Porta Nuova Train Station

City of Verona.

VISITOR INFORMATION The **tourist office** at Via Degli Alpini 9 (www.tourism.verona.it; ✆ **045-8068680;** Mon–Sat 10am–1pm & 3–5pm; Sun 10am–2pm) has maps and tour information.

EXPLORING VERONA

"Two households, both alike in dignity, in fair Verona . . ." So go the immortal opening lines of *Romeo and Juliet,* ensuring that the city has been a target for lovesick romantics ever since. Though Verona is crammed with genuine historic goodies, one of the most popular sites is the ersatz **Casa di Giulietta,** Via Cappello 23 (Mon 1:30–7:30pm, Tues–Sun 8:30am–7:30pm; 6€), a 14th-century house (with balcony, naturally), said to be the Capulets' home. In the courtyard, the chest of a bronze statue of Juliet has been polished to a gleaming sheen, thanks to a legend claiming that stroking her right breast brings good fortune. **Juliet's Wall,** at the entrance, is quite a spectacle, covered with the scribbles of star-crossed lovers; love letters placed here are taken down and, along with 5,000 letters annually, answered by the Club di Giulietta (locally based volunteers). There's not much to see inside the house.

Once you've made the obligatory Juliet pilgrimage, focus on some really amazing historic ruins. The 1st-century **Arena di Verona ★** (Mon 1:30–7:30pm and Tues–Sun 9am–7:30pm; 10€), in the spacious Piazza Bra, is the third largest classical arena in Italy after Rome's Colosseum and the arena at Capua—it could seat some 25,000 spectators and still hosts performances today (see www.arena.it).

Statue of Juliet with love notes, Casa di Giulietta.

To the northwest on Piazza San Zeno, the **Basilica di San Zeno Maggiore ★★** (www.basilicasanzeno.it. Mar–Oct Mon–Sat 8:30am–6pm, Sun 12:30–6pm; Nov–Feb Tues–Sat 10am–1pm and 1:30–5pm, Sun 12:30–5pm; 2.50€) is the greatest Romanesque church in northern Italy. The present structure was completed around 1135, over the 4th-century shrine to Verona's patron saint, St. Zeno (who died in 380). Its massive rose window represents the Wheel of Fortune, while the lintels above the portal represent the months of the year. The highlight of the interior is "Madonna and Saints" above the altar, by Mantegna.

WHERE TO EAT

Even in chic Verona, you'll spend less on a meal than in Venice. The most authentic budget restaurant is **Osteria Sottoriva,** Via Sottoriva 9 (**✆ 045-8014323;** Thurs–Tues 11am–11pm), one of the most popular places in town for lunch or dinner; try the *trippa alla parmigiana* (braised tripe) or the hopelessly rich gorgonzola melted over polenta (main courses 8€–15€). **Caffè Monte Baldo,** Via Rosa 12 (**✆ 045-8030579;** Sun–Thu 10:30am–midnight, Fri–Sat 10:30am–1am), is an old-fashioned cafe transformed into a trendy *osteria,* serving classic pastas and scrumptious *crostini* with wine in the evenings.

Treviso ★★

30km (19 miles) N of Venice

Long overshadowed by Venice, **Treviso** is a small, prosperous city of narrow, medieval streets, Gothic churches, and an enchanting network of canals, replete with weeping willows and waterwheels (it's known as "piccola Venezia" or "little Venice"). Giotto's follower **Tomaso da Modena** (1326–79), one of northern Italy's lesser-known artistic geniuses, frescoed many of its churches, and its maze of back streets makes for pleasant, often tourist-free exploring. Fashion giant Benetton was founded here in 1965; the city also claims to have invented tiramisu.

Treviso's Buranelli Canal.

ESSENTIALS

GETTING THERE The fastest way to reach Treviso is to by **train** from Santa Lucia station. Trains run two to four times an hour from Venice (30–40 min.). Tickets start at 3.40€ one-way. From Treviso Centrale station it's an easy 10 to 15-minute walk to Piazza dei Signori, north across the River Sile (follow signs to "Centro"). Note also that Ryanair budget flights to Venice actually arrive at Treviso airport.

VISITOR INFORMATION The **tourist office** at Via Fiumicelli 30 (www.visittreviso.it; ✆ **0422-547-632**) is open Monday from 10am to 1pm, Tuesday to Saturday 10am to 5pm, and Sunday 10am to 4pm.

EXPLORING TREVISO

The **Piazza dei Signori ★** is the historic heart of Treviso. The square is anchored by the **Palazzo del Podestà,** rebuilt in the 1870s with a tall clock tower, and the **Palazzo dei Trecento,** the 13th-century town council hall, now home to chic Bar Beltrame beneath the arches. Just beyond the square, on adjacent Piazza San Vito, sits a handsome pair of medieval churches: **Santa Lucia ★**, with a superb Tomaso da Modena fresco of the "Madonna del Pavegio" in the first shrine on the right, and **San Vito ★** (www.santaluciatreviso.it; ✆ **0422-5457200;** both daily 8am–noon; free admission), with its Byzantine-style frescoes from the 13th century. Historic **Via Calmaggiore,** lined with posh boutiques, runs northwest from Piazza dei Signori towards the cathedral. The relatively dull neoclassical facade of the **Duomo ★** (Mon–Sat 7:30am–noon & 3:30–7pm; Sun 8am–1pm & 3:30–8pm; free admission) is from 1836, but it's flanked by Romanesque lions that, along with its seven Venetian-Byzantine style green copper domes, are remnants of the cathedral's 12th-century origins. The crypt is the most compelling part of the interior, with the tombs of the city's bishops amid a forest of columns and fragments of 14th-century frescoes and mosaics. The highlight in the main body of the cathedral is a fine altarpiece, the "Malchiostro Annunciation" by Titian, from 1520.

A short stroll southwest from the Duomo, the massive brick 13th- to 14th-century Italian Gothic church of **San Nicolò ★** (daily 8am–noon & 3:30–6pm; free admission) houses some intriguing Gothic frescoes. Tomaso da Modena and his school decorated the huge round columns with a series of saints, notably St. Jerome, St. Agnes, and St. Romuald. Antonio da Treviso painted the absolutely gargantuan St. Christopher—his .9m-long (3-ft.) feet strolling over biting fish—in 1410.

East of Piazza dei Signori, across the **Buranelli**, the most attractive of Treviso's canals, lies the wide Canale Cagnan Grande, whose island hosts a **pescheria** (fish market) Monday to Saturday.

Farther east is a deconsecrated church that's now an enjoyable museum. The highlight of **Museo di Santa Caterina** (www.museicivicitreviso.it; ✆ **0422-658442**; Tues–Sun 9am–12:30pm and 2:30–6pm; 5€, special exhibitions can raise ticket price to 14€), on Piazzetta Mario Botter, is another fresco cycle by Tomaso da Modena, the "Story of the Life of Saint Ursula" (detached from a now-destroyed church and preserved here). There's also cache of local archaeological finds plus minor works by Titian, Lorenzo Lotto, and Francesco Guardi.

To the south, the 15th-century church of **Santa Maria Maggiore** (daily 8am–noon and 3:30–6pm; free admission) houses a venerated image of Mary (the "Madonna Granda"), a frescoed "Madonna and Child" originally painted in Byzantine style (probably pre–9th century), and later touched up by Tomaso and members of his school.

WHERE TO EAT

Treviso has some excellent restaurants, but its real claim to fame is as the home of **tiramisu**. Legend has it that the addictive dessert was created at restaurant **Le Beccherie,** Piazza Ancilotto 9 (www.lebeccherie.it; ✆ **0422-540871;** daily noon–2:15pm and 7–10:15pm), in the 1960s. The claim has been disputed over the years, but the restaurant is still open and still knocks out an exceptional tiramisu (the "classico" is 6€). In fact, just about every menu in town features tiramisu, as well as Treviso's other culinary specialty, **radicchio** (bitter red lettuce).

The bars and cafés around the **pescheria**, particularly along Via Palestro, are always buzzing, and perfect for sampling good-value local cuisine. It's hard to beat the **Hosteria Dai Naneti ★★**, Vicolo Broli 2 (www.dainaneti.it. ✆ **3403-783158**; Mon–Fri 9am–2:30pm &

5:30–9pm, Sat 9:30am–2pm and 5:30–9pm, Sun 11am–2pm and 5–8pm; May–Sept closed Sun), for atmosphere, a cozy tavern, deli and cheese shop where you can grab a delicious baguette and glass of wine, or just snack at the bar for around 5€ (standing room only).

For a full meal in the center, reserve a table at **Trattoria All'Antico Portico ★★**, overlooking the church at Piazza Santa Maria Maggiore 18 (www.anticoportico.it; ✆ **0422-545259;** Mon 9am–4pm, Wed–Sun 9am–11pm), which serves local specialties such as radicchio risotto and *baccalà alla veneziana* (salt cod); main courses are 15€ to 18€.

MILAN, PIEDMONT & THE LAKES

By Michelle Schoenung

10

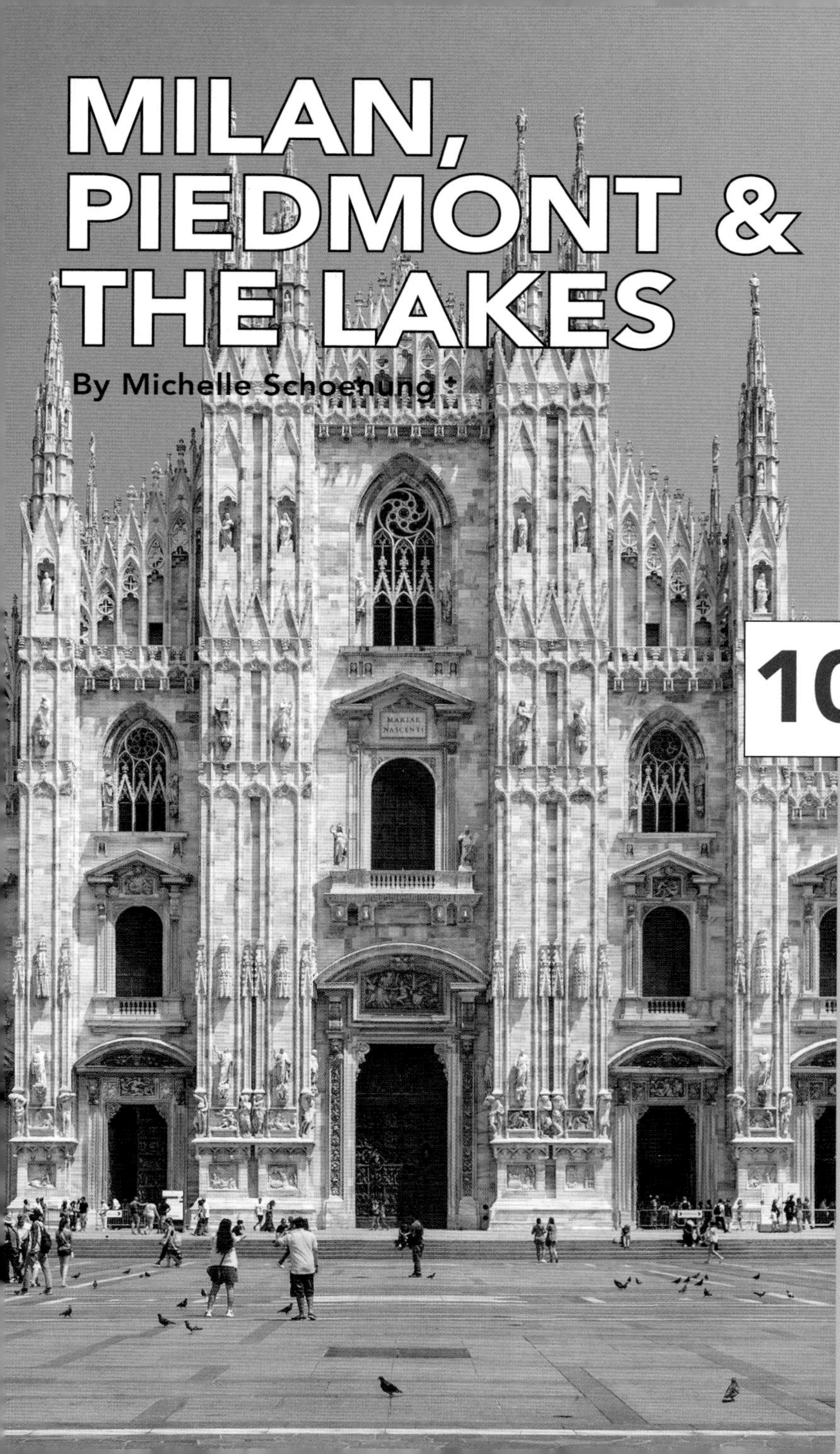

Lombardy and Piedmont are the powerhouses of northern Italy, thanks to the sprawling but charming cities of Milan and Turin, thriving on the industries that drive these regions forward. Agriculture plays its part here, from the rice fields of the eastern Lombardy plains to the hilly vineyards and hazelnut groves of Piedmont. The beauty of the lakes between Milan and the Alps have been a source of inspiration for writers and artists for centuries. Many of the lakes are an hour or so of the city, making them a favorite destination for the Milanese and tourists alike.

MILAN (MILANO) ★★★

552km (342 miles) NW of Rome, 288km (179 miles) NW of Florence, 257km (159 miles W of Venice) 140km (87 miles) NE of Turin, 142km (88 miles) N of Genoa

Milan—or Milano, as the Italians say it—is elegant, chaotic, and utterly beguiling. Traffic chokes the streets, and it can be bitterly cold in winter and stiflingly hot in summer, yet its architecture is majestic and the robust Northern Italian cuisine warming. It's a world-class stop on the international fashion stage, the banking capital of Italy, and a wealthy city of glamorous people and stylish shopping streets.

And Milan has history. As well as the Roman ruins, the soaring Duomo and its majestic piazza, the galleries are stuffed with priceless artworks, and there are ancient churches, medieval castles, Renaissance palaces, and amazing contemporary architecture to admire.

Massive changes were made to the city in preparation for 2015's World's Fair, known as **Expo Milano.** The city still continues to undergo somewhat of an urban and cultural Renaissance. A whole new skyline boasts innovative towers by international starchitects, the already efficient public transportation system continues to expand, new museums continue to crop up, and the city has an overall sense of renewed vitality.

Essentials

GETTING THERE

BY PLANE Both of Milan's major airports are operated by **SEA** (www.seamilano.eu; ✆ **02-232-323**). **Milan Malpensa,** 45km (28 miles) northwest of the city, is Milan's major international airport. The

 PREVIOUS PAGE: **Milan's Duomo.**

Malpensa Express train (www.malpensaexpress.it; ✆ **02-7249-4949**), costs 13€ one way (or 20€ roundtrip) and leaves from Terminal 1 with a 30-minute run half-hourly to Cadorna train station, or hourly to Stazione Centrale (45 min). Buses run directly to Stazione Centrale, a 50-minute journey, with five trips per hour, for 10€ one-way or 16€ round-trip; they're operated by **Malpensa Shuttle** (www.malpensa shuttle.it; ✆ **02-5858-3185)** or **Autostradale** (www.autostradale.it; ✆ **02-3008-9000**). By taxi, the trip into town costs a wallet-stripping 100€ and takes about 50 minutes. It's the only option after midnight.

Milan Linate, 7km (4.5 miles) east of the center, handles European and domestic flights. **Air Bus** (www.atm-mi.it; ✆ **02-48-607-607**) makes the 25-minute trip by bus every 30 minutes between 6am and midnight to Stazione Centrale for 5€. A roundtrip ticket costs 9€. City bus no. 73 leaves every 10 minutes for the San Babila Metro stop downtown and takes 25 minutes. The express no. X73 is faster and departs every 20 minutes between 7am and 8pm. Tickets for both are 1.50€. A trip into town by taxi costs roughly 20€.

Malpensa Shuttle buses also connect Malpensa and Linate airports with five daily runs between 9:30am and 6:20pm. The trip takes 90 minutes and costs 13€ (roundtrip 26€).

BY TRAIN Milan is one of Europe's busiest rail hubs. Trains travel every half-hour to Bergamo (1 hr.), Mantua (2 hr.), and Turin (1 hr. by the AV high-speed train). **Stazione Centrale** is a half-hour walk northeast of the center, with easy connections to Piazza del Duomo by Metro, tram, and bus. The station stop on the Metro is Centrale F.S. Multilingual automatic ticket machines accept cash and credit cards but *not* debit cards. You may need to validate your ticket in the machines at the beginning of the track as you get on your train, especially if you don't have an e-ticket.

Stazione Centrale is Milan's major station, but trains also serve **Cadorna** (Como and Malpensa airport), and **Porta Garibaldi** (Lecco and the north). All these stations are on the green Metro Linea 2.

BY BUS Long-distance buses are useful for reaching the ski resorts in Valle d'Aosta. Most bus services depart from Lampugnano bus terminal (Metro: Lampugnano) although some originate in Piazza Castello (Metro: Cairoli). **Autostradale** (www.autostradale.it; ✆ **02-5858-7304**) operates most of the bus lines and has ticket offices in front of Castello Sforzesco on Piazza Castello, open daily 9am to 6pm, and in front of the Duomo in Passageway 2 next to the TIM mobile phone store, open weekdays 8:30am to 6pm and weekends 9am to 4pm. **Savda** (www.savda.it; **0165-367-011**) runs five daily buses (more in the winter) between Milan Lampugnano and Aosta (2½ hr.; 17€) or Courmayeur (3½ hr.; 19.50€).

BY CAR The **A1 autostrada** links Milan with Florence (3 hr.) and Rome (6 hr.), while the A4 connects Milan with Verona (2 hr.) and Venice (2½ hr.) to the east and Turin (1 hr.) to the west.

GETTING AROUND

BY TRAIN Milan's most famous sights are within walking distance of each other, but the public transport system, an integrated system of **Metro, trams,** and **buses,** run by **ATM** (www.atm.it; ✆ **02-48-607-607**), is a cheap and effective alternative to walking. The Metro closes at midnight (Sat at 1am), but buses and trams run all night. Metro stations are well signposted; trains are speedy, safe, and frequent—they run every couple of minutes during the day and about every 5 minutes after 9pm. Tickets for 90 minutes of travel on Metro, trams, or buses cost 1.50€. A 24-hour unlimited travel ticket is a better value at 4.50€ and a 2-day ticket goes for 8.25€. Tickets are available at newsstands and Metro stations (all machines have English-language options; the 24-hr. ticket option is listed under "Urban"). Stamp your ticket when you board a bus or tram—there is a 35€ fine (more if not paid on the spot) if you don't. If you would like to know more, visit the ATM information offices in the Duomo Metro, Stazione Centrale, and Cadorna, all open Monday to Saturday, 7:45am to 8pm and on Sundays from 10:15am to 1:15pm and from 2pm to 5:30pm.

Lines 1 (red, with stops at Cairoli for Castello Sforzesco and Duomo for Galleria Vittorio Emanuele II and the Duomo) and **3** (yellow, with a stop at Via Montenapoleone) are the most useful for sightseeing.

BY CAR Driving and parking in Milan are not experiences to relish. First of all, you'll have to pay the Area C congestion charge of 5€ to enter the *centro storico* Monday to Friday 7:30am to 7:30pm. On top of that, the one-way system is complicated, some streets are reserved for public transport only, and there are many pedestrianized areas. Hotels will make parking arrangements for guests—take advantage of that.

BY TAXI Taxis are located in major *piazze* and by major Metro stops. There is a taxi stand in Piazza del Duomo and outside Castello Sforzesco; a journey between the two will cost around 7€. Hotel reception staff can call a taxi for you; otherwise, a reliable company is **Taxiblu** at ✆ **02-4040.** Meters start at 3.30€ and prices increase by 1.09€ per kilometer. Expect surcharges for waiting time, luggage, late-night travel, and Sunday journeys.

BY BIKE With the streets of the *centro storico* largely pedestrianized, Milan is a good city for cycling, with a handy bike-sharing program, **BikeMi** (www.bikemi.com), that is so popular you can't always find bikes at some stations. The tariff for the pass is typically convoluted: For

Milan's Parco Sempione.

4.50€ a day or 9€ a week, you can buy a pass that allows 30 minutes of free travel. The next 2 hours are charged at 0.50€ per 30 minutes (or fraction of it) up until 2 hours, and thereafter your time is charged at 2€ per hour or fraction of it. There are also now electric bikes, which cost slightly more to rent. Pick up one of the distinctive custard-yellow bikes at racks from outside Castello Sforzesco and the Duomo as well as at tram, bus, and metro stops. Buy your pass online; at the **ATM Points** at Centrale, Cadorna, Garibaldi, and Duomo stations from 7:45am to 8pm Monday to Saturday; or by calling © **02-48-607-607.**

ON FOOT The attractions of the *centro storico* are all accessible on foot. From Piazza del Duomo, Via Montenapoleone is a 10-minute walk through Piazza della Scala and along Via Manzoni, and it is a 10-minute walk to Castello Sforzesco. Santa Maria delle Grazie and "The Last Supper" are a 30-minute stroll from Piazza del Duomo.

VISITOR INFORMATION

The main **tourist office (called IAT for Informazione e Accoglienza Turistica)** is in Galleria Vittorio Emanuele on the corner of

Piazza della Scala (www.visitamilano.it; ✆ **02-8845-5555**). It's open Monday to Friday 9am to 7pm, Saturday 9am to 6pm, and Sunday 10am to 6pm.

CITY LAYOUT

Milan developed as a series of circles radiating out from the central hub, Piazza del Duomo. Within the inner circle are most of the churches, museums, and shops of the *centro storico*. **Parco Sempione** and Leonardo's "The Last Supper" are to the west in a posh neighborhood. The slightly grungy yet hip cafe-filled districts of **Porta Ticinese** and **Navigli** lie directly south, with genteel **Brera** and its classy stores and restaurants slightly to the north. The **Quadrilatero d'Oro (Golden Quadrilateral)** is the mecca of Milanese fashion and is northeast of the Duomo, although **Via Tortona** near the Navigli is quickly developing as a funky shopping option. A burgeoning new **financial district** is growing between Porta Garibaldi and Centrale stations, while the towers of **CityLife** have taken over the old fairgrounds area (the newer fairgrounds are located in the city of Rho right outside Milan).

[Fast FACTS] MILAN

ATMs/Banks Banks with multilingual ATMs are all over the city center. Opening hours are roughly Monday to Friday 8:30am to 1:30pm and 3 to 4pm, with major branches opening Saturday morning for a couple of hours. Central branches may also stay open through lunch.

Business Hours Most stores in central Milan are open Tuesday to Saturday, 9:30am to 7:30pm, with a half-day Monday (3:30–7:30pm). Most shops close on Sundays and some still close for lunch between 12:30pm and 3:30pm.

Consulates see chapter 16.

Crime For police emergencies, dial ✆ **112.** There is a police station in Stazione Centrale but the **Questura** is at the main station**,** just west of the Giardini Pubblici at Via Fatebenefratelli 11 (✆ **02-62-261;** Metro: Turati).

Dentists **Excellence Dental Network** at Via Mauro Macchi 38 near Stazione Centrale (www.excellencedentalnetwork.com; ✆ **02-7628-0498**) has English-speaking staff.

Doctors The **Centro Medico Santagostino** has a series of reasonably priced clinics throughout the city and a team of doctors with 40 different specialties. Call or make an appointment online. (www.cmsantagostino.it/en; ✆ **02-8970-1701**).

Drugstores Pharmacies rotate 24-hour shifts. Signs in most pharmacies post the schedule. The **Farmacia Stazione Centrale** (✆ **02-669-0735**) in Stazione Centrale is open 24 hours daily and the staff speaks English.

Emergencies All emergency numbers are free. Call ✆ **112** for a **general emergency;** this connects to the **Carabinieri,** who will transfer your call as needed; for the **police,** dial ✆ **113;** for a **medical emergency** or an ambulance, call ✆ **118;** for the **fire department,** call ✆ **115.**

Hospitals The **Ospedale Maggiore Policlinico** (✆ **02-55-031**) is a 5-minute walk southeast of the Duomo at Via Francesco Sforza 35 (Metro: Duomo or Missori). Most of the medical personnel speak some English.

Internet The free **Open Wi-Fi Milano** network has hundreds of hotspots all over the city, with Internet access for phones, tablets, and laptops. In addition, many Milanese hotels, bars, and cafes offer free Wi-Fi. Throughout the city, branches of the **Arnold Coffee** (www.arnoldcoffee.it) American-style coffee bars offer free Wi-Fi.

Post Office The main post office, **Poste e Telecommunicazioni,** is at Via Cordusio 4 (✆ **02-7248-2126;** Metro: Cordusio). It's open Monday to Friday 8:20am to 7:05pm and Saturday 8:30am to 12:35pm. The post office in Stazione Centrale is open Monday to Saturday 8:20am to 7:05pm. Other branches are open Monday to Saturday 8:30am to 1:30pm.

Safety Milan is generally safe, although public parks and the area around Stazione Centrale are best avoided at night.

Exploring Milan

Dress modestly when visiting Milan's churches: no short shorts for either sex, women must have their shoulders covered, and skirts must be below the knee. The dress code at the Duomo is particularly strict.

Castello Sforzesco ★ MUSEUM Although it has lived many lives under several different occupiers and been restored many times, this fortified castle is the masterpiece of Milan's two most powerful medieval and Renaissance dynasties, the Visconti and the Sforza. The Visconti built the castle (and the Duomo) in the 14th century before the Sforzas married into their clan, eclipsed their power, and took the castle in the 1450s, transforming it into one of the most gracious palaces of the Renaissance. Sforza *capo* Ludovico il Moro and his wife, Beatrice d'Este, helped make Milan one of Italy's Renaissance centers by commissioning works by Bramante, Michelangelo, and Leonardo.

The castle's most recent restoration was by architect Luca Beltrami at the end of the 19th century; it opened as a museum in 1905. Today it contains a dozen museums, known collectively as the Musei del Castello Sforzesco. Many of the Sforza treasures are on view in the miles of rooms that surround the castle's labyrinthine courtyards and corridors. They include a *pinacoteca* with works by Bellini and Correggio plus Mannerists Ribera and Ricci.

Milano Discount Card

The **MilanoCard** (www.milanocard.it) offers a great deal on sightseeing at just 7€ for 24 hours, 13€ for 2 days, or 19€ for 3 days. You get a lot for your buck, including free travel on all public transportation, discounts in some stores and restaurants, and free or reduced entry to more than 20 museums and galleries. Each card is valid for one adult and a child under 10.

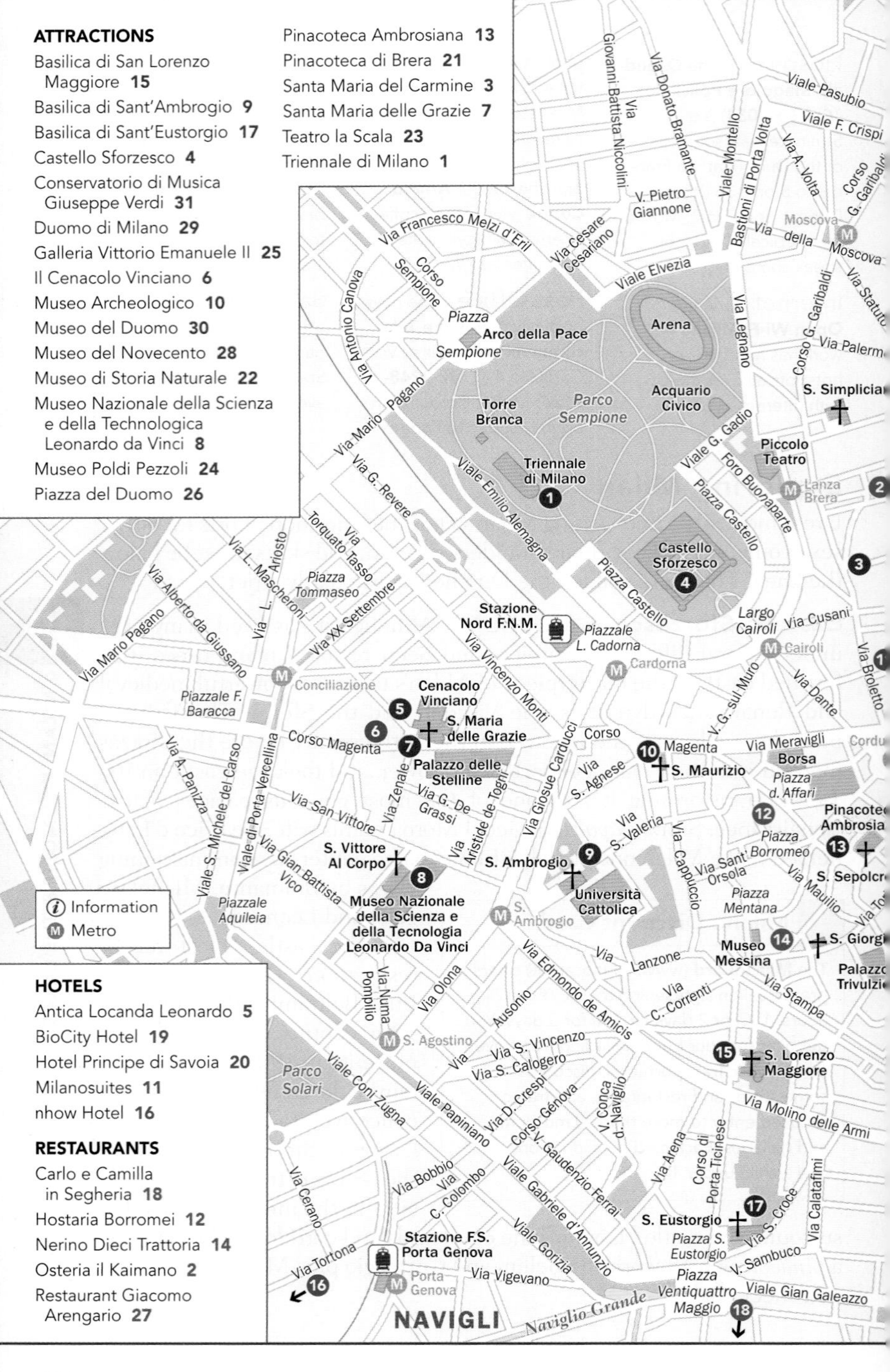

ATTRACTIONS
Basilica di San Lorenzo Maggiore 15
Basilica di Sant'Ambrogio 9
Basilica di Sant'Eustorgio 17
Castello Sforzesco 4
Conservatorio di Musica Giuseppe Verdi 31
Duomo di Milano 29
Galleria Vittorio Emanuele II 25
Il Cenacolo Vinciano 6
Museo Archeologico 10
Museo del Duomo 30
Museo del Novecento 28
Museo di Storia Naturale 22
Museo Nazionale della Scienza e della Technologica Leonardo da Vinci 8
Museo Poldi Pezzoli 24
Piazza del Duomo 26
Pinacoteca Ambrosiana 13
Pinacoteca di Brera 21
Santa Maria del Carmine 3
Santa Maria delle Grazie 7
Teatro la Scala 23
Triennale di Milano 1
HOTELS
Antica Locanda Leonardo 5
BioCity Hotel 19
Hotel Principe di Savoia 20
Milanosuites 11
nhow Hotel 16
RESTAURANTS
Carlo e Camilla in Segheria 18
Hostaria Borromei 12
Nerino Dieci Trattoria 14
Osteria il Kaimano 2
Restaurant Giacomo Arengario 27
Information
Metro
Arco della Pace
Piazza Sempione
Arena
Parco Sempione
Torre Branca
Acquario Civico
Triennale di Milano
Piccolo Teatro
Castello Sforzesco
Stazione Nord F.N.M.
Piazzale L. Cadorna
Cenacolo Vinciano
S. Maria delle Grazie
Palazzo delle Stelline
S. Maurizio
Borsa
S. Vittore Al Corpo
S. Ambrogio
Università Cattolica
Museo Nazionale della Scienza e della Tecnologia Leonardo Da Vinci
Museo Messina
S. Lorenzo Maggiore
S. Eustorgio
Stazione F.S. Porta Genova
Parco Solari
NAVIGLI
Naviglio Grande
Moscova
Lanza Brera
Cairoli
Cardorna
Conciliazione
S. Ambrogio
S. Agostino
Porta Genova
Corso Magenta
Via San Vittore
Viale Papiniano
Piazza Ventiquattro Maggio

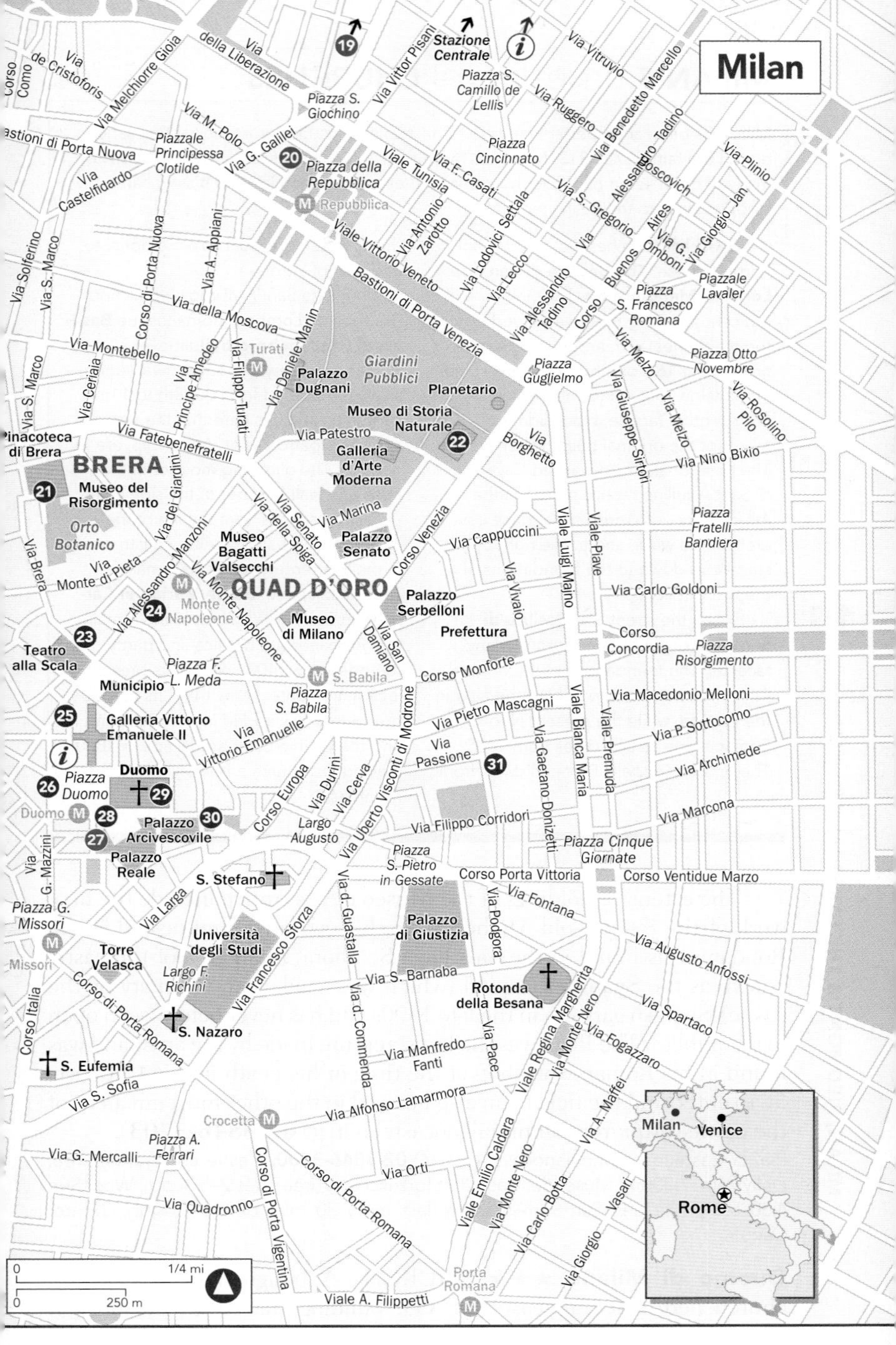
Milan
Stazione Centrale
Piazza S. Camillo de Lellis
Piazza S. Giochino
Piazzale Principessa Clotilde
Piazza della Repubblica
Repubblica
Piazza Cincinnato
Piazzale Lavaler
Piazza S. Francesco Romana
Piazza Guglielmo
Piazza Otto Novembre
Giardini Pubblici
Palazzo Dugnani
Planetario
Museo di Storia Naturale
Galleria d'Arte Moderna
Turati
Pinacoteca di Brera
BRERA
Museo del Risorgimento
Orto Botanico
Museo Bagatti Valsecchi
Palazzo Senato
QUAD D'ORO
Palazzo Serbelloni
Prefettura
Monte Napoleone
Museo di Milano
Teatro alla Scala
Piazza F. L. Meda
Municipio
S. Babila
Piazza S. Babila
Galleria Vittorio Emanuele II
Piazza Duomo
Duomo
Palazzo Arcivescovile
Palazzo Reale
Largo Augusto
Piazza S. Pietro in Gessate
S. Stefano
Piazza G. Missori
Missori
Torre Velasca
Università degli Studi
Largo F. Richini
S. Nazaro
S. Eufemia
Palazzo di Giustizia
Rotonda della Besana
Piazza Fratelli Bandiera
Corso Concordia
Piazza Risorgimento
Piazza Cinque Giornate
Crocetta
Piazza A. Ferrari
Porta Romana
Via Vitruvio
Via Ruggero
Via Benedetto Marcello
Via Alessandro Tadino
Via Boscovich
Via Plinio
Via Giorgio Jan
Via G. Omboni
Buenos Aires
Via S. Gregorio
Via F. Casati
Viale Tunisia
Via Lodovici Settala
Via Lecco
Via Antonio Zarotto
Via Vittor Pisani
Via della Liberazione
Via Melchiorre Gioia
Via de Cristoforis
Corso Como
Bastioni di Porta Nuova
Via M. Polo
Via G. Galilei
Via Castelfidardo
Via Solferino
Via S. Marco
Corso di Porta Nuova
Via A. Appiani
Viale Vittorio Veneto
Bastioni di Porta Venezia
Via della Moscova
Via Montebello
Via Ceriaia
Via Principe Amedeo
Via Filippo Turati
Via Daniele Manin
Via Patestro
Via Fatebenefratelli
Via dei Giardini
Via Alessandro Manzoni
Via della Spiga
Via Senato
Via Marina
Corso Venezia
Via Borghetto
Via Melzo
Via Giuseppe Sirtori
Via Rosolino Pilo
Via Nino Bixio
Viale Luigi Maino
Viale Piave
Via Cappuccini
Via Vivaio
Via Carlo Goldoni
Via Brera
Via Monte di Pietà
Via Monte Napoleone
Via San Damiano
Corso Monforte
Via Macedonio Melloni
Viale Bianca Maria
Viale Premuda
Via P. Sottocomo
Via Archimede
Via Marcona
Via Pietro Mascagni
Via Passione
Via Gaetano Donizetti
Via Vittorio Emanuelle
Corso Europa
Via Durini
Via Cerva
Via Uberto Visconti di Modrone
Via Filippo Corridori
Corso Porta Vittoria
Corso Ventidue Marzo
Via Fontana
Via Podgora
Via Augusto Anfossi
Via G. Mazzini
Via Larga
Via Francesco Sforza
Via d. Guastalla
Via d. Commenda
Via S. Barnaba
Via Spartaco
Viale Regina Margherita
Via Monte Nero
Via Fogazzaro
Via Pace
Via Manfredo Fanti
Corso di Porta Romana
Corso Italia
Via S. Sofia
Via Alfonso Lamarmora
Via A. Maffei
Viale Emilio Caldara
Viale Monte Nero
Via Carlo Botta
Via Giorgio Vasari
Via G. Mercalli
Via Orti
Via Quadronno
Corso di Porta Vigentina
Viale A. Filippetti
0 1/4 mi
0 250 m
Milan
Venice
Rome

MILAN'S time-travel CHURCHES

Milan has been an important center of Christianity since Emperor Constantine sanctioned the faith in A.D. 313. Milan has more than 100 churches, and, like the Duomo, many of them lie on pagan foundations. In these, layer upon layer of history can be stripped back to their early remains.

Two such churches are on Corso di Porta Ticinese. **The Basilica di San Lorenzo Maggiore** was built in the 4th century, using rubble removed from the amphitheater nearby, at the same time as the 16 Corinthian columns standing outside. The church now has a 16th-century facade, but inside, fragments of the original building survive: The octagonal, white-washed Cappella di Sant'Aquilino retains pieces of the 4th-century gold mosaic that once covered all the walls, and to the right of this, stairs lead down to the foundations of the first basilica.

Down the street, the **Basilica di Sant'Eustorgio** has undergone many facelifts. The foundations of the original 4th-century church are behind the altar in the basilica, while the present Neo-Romanesque facade dates from 1865. The ornate Cappella Portinari dates from the 15th century, built as a memorial to St. Peter of Verona.

In Piazza Sant'Ambrogio you'll find the sublime Lombard Romanesque **Basilica di Sant'Ambrogio.** Built over a Roman cemetery, the church was extensively remodeled from the 8th to 11th centuries, and it is here that the remains of Milan's patron saint, Ambrogio, are housed. The glittering mosaics in the apse and wall frescoes in the side chapels show scenes from the life of the saint, and a great gold altar constructed in the 9th century holds his remains.

The church of **Santa Maria del Carmine** in Brera was built over the remains of a Romanesque basilica and partly remodeled in 1400; most of its present incarnation dates from 1447. Its baroque presbytery was added in the 17th century and the Gothic-Lombard facade in 1880, making the church a true stylistic mishmash.

The extensive holdings of the Museo d'Arte Antica include the final work of the 89-year-old Michelangelo; his evocative, unfinished "Pietà Rondanini" is found in the Sala degli Scarlioni, in an area of the castle known as the Spanish Hospital (which was used as an infirmary by the castle's Spanish garrison in the late 1500s and has never before been open to the public). The Pietà was the last sculpture made by the artist and was found in his Roman workshop at the time of his death in 1564. It costs 5€ to enter, and the ticket can also be used in the other museum areas of the castle (http://rondanini.milanocastello.it; ✆ **02-8846-3703**).

Piazza Castello. www.milanocastello.it. ✆ **02-8846-3700.** Castle courtyards: Free. Daily 7am–7:30pm. Musei del Castello Sforzesco: 5€ (free Tues 2–5:30pm; Wed–Sun 4:30–5:30pm). Tues–Sun 9am–5:30pm (last entry 30 min. before closing). Metro: Cairoli.

Duomo di Milano ★★★ CHURCH Although there has been a church here since at least A.D. 355, building started on the present exterior of Milan's magnificent Gothic Duomo in the late 14th century, during the reign of Gian Galeazzo Visconti (1351–1402). Marble slabs for the facade were transported from quarries bordering Lake Maggiore into the city along the Navigli canals. It was consecrated in 1418, but the enormous dome wasn't added until the 16th century and the Duomo was not deemed complete until 1965, when the mammoth cast-bronze doors were finally finished. The cathedral dominates the vast, traffic-free **Piazza del Duomo** (see p. 471). Able to accommodate 40,000 people, it is one of the world's largest churches (St. Peter's in Rome, p. 76, takes the record), with an embellished gable facade encrusted with flying buttresses plus over 3,000 statues and gargoyles. Pinnacles bristle on the domed roof, topped by a 5m (16-ft.) gilded figure of the Virgin Mary, known as **La Madonnina** and regarded as Milan's lucky mascot.

The interior of the Duomo is surprisingly serene, despite the hordes of tourists who pour in daily. The floors are of complex patterned marble reflecting sunlight as it streams through jewel-like stained-glass windows. Rows of 52 marble columns divide the space into five cavernous aisles, and the side chapels are dotted with Renaissance and Mannerist tombs.

In the crypt, the **Battistero di San Giovanni alle Fonti** reveals the remains of the octagonal 4th-century foundations of the original church (ticket included in admission to the Museo del Duomo, though opening times vary), which is almost certainly where Sant'Ambrogio, patron saint and Bishop of Milan in A.D. 374, christened the great missionary St. Augustine. Pride of place in the crypt goes to the ornate gilded tomb of San Carlo Borromeo, Archbishop of Milan and leader of the Counter-Reformation, who died in 1584.

Piazza del Duomo. www.duomomilano.it. ✆ **02-7202-2656.** 2€. Daily 7am–7pm for worshippers and 8am to 6pm for visitors. Metro: Duomo.

spying **ON MILAN**

Take the trip up to the roof of the Duomo (www.duomomilano.it) for spine-tingling views across the rooftops of Milan and, on a clear day, to the Alps beyond. Elevators (13€) are found on the church's northeast corner, while stairs to the top (8€) are on the north flank. As well as the panorama, you can get up close to the Gothic pinnacles, saintly statues, and flying buttresses, as well as the spire-top gold statue of **"La Madonnina"** (the little Madonna), the city's beloved good-luck charm. The elevator is open daily 9am to 6:30pm (last ticket sold at 6pm).

Other sneaky viewpoints over the Duomo include the food market on the top floor of department store **La Rinascente** (see p. 482) and the posh **Restaurant Giacomo Arengario** at the **Museo del Novecento** (see p. 470).

Galleria Vittorio Emanuele II ★★ SHOPPING MALL Milan's most elegant shopping arcade links the Piazza del Duomo with Piazza della Scala, site of the famous opera house. The gallery is entered through an enormous neoclassical triumphal archway leading to a shopping mall blessed with ornate marble flooring and a massive octagonal glass dome. Inside, the arcade is lined with grand cafes such as **Biffi** and **Savini,** where the local elite gather to dine after a night at the opera. Designer stores here include Gucci, Versace, Prada, Louis Vuitton, and Swarovski.

Galleria Vittorio Emanuele II was the masterpiece of Bolognese architect Giuseppe Mengoni, who designed it in the 1870s to mark the unification of Italy under King Vittorio Emanuele II; mosaic and fresco decorations incorporate patriotic symbols and coats of arms of various Italian cities. Mengoni never saw his magnus opus flourishing—he died in a fall from scaffolding the day before it opened in 1878. Today giggling crowds gather under the dome to spin around on one heel on the private parts of a little mosaic bull in the floor, a legendary good-luck ritual.
Piazza del Duomo. Open 24 hrs. Metro: Duomo.

Museo Archeologico ★★ MUSEUM Milan's beautifully curated archaeology museum is set in a series of airy galleries housed among the cloisters, towers, and courtyards of the 8th-century convent of Monastero Maggiore of San Maurizio. Subdivided into exhibitions including Ancient Milanese, Greek, and Etruscan displays, the museum is built around the remains of a villa and a section of the 4th-century Roman walls that once fortified Milan. Roman Milan was known as Mediolanum; this area of

Navigli Grande canal in Milan.

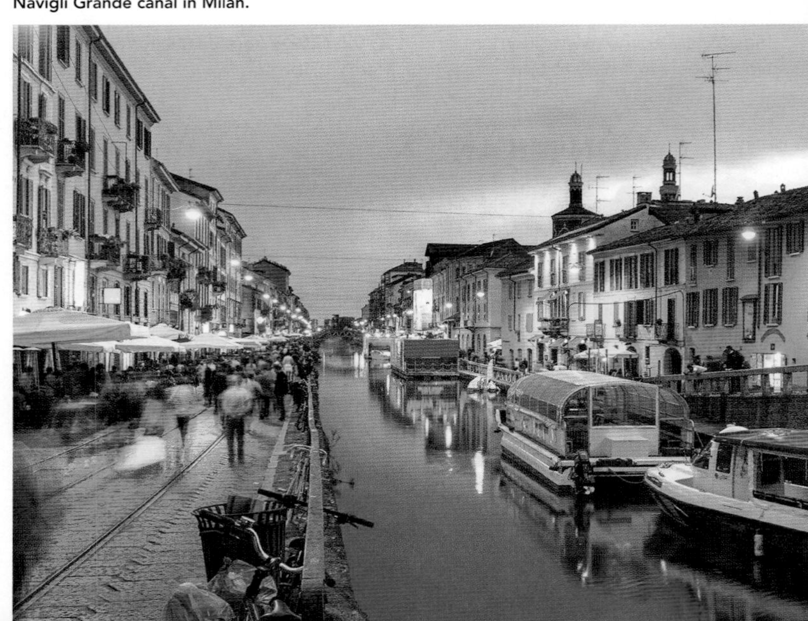

cruising **THE CANALS**

Explore Milan's **Navigli** area (*navigli* means canals), the perfect spot for a relaxed drink, people-watching, and a late-night supper, by taking Metro Line 2 to Porta Genova. Crowded and full of life, these few streets are refreshingly casual in ambience after the dressy obsession of the city center—it's one of the few places in Milan where you will see punks, hippies, and Goths or find vintage stores.

Building of the canals started in the late 13th century, initially to transport marble slabs from quarries along Lake Maggiore (see p. 499) to build the Duomo. The Naviglio Grande was Europe's first major canal and remains an engineering marvel of the medieval era. Used to import food, commodities, and trade goods, the canals were crucial to Milan's infrastructure until the 1970s, when road transport won out. Take a boat tour of the canals to peek into Milan's industrial heritage; **Navigli Lombardi** (www.naviglilombardi.it; ✆ **02-667-9131**) runs daily tours.

the city is particularly rich in ruins dating back to the time when it was capital of the Western Roman Empire. Most of the treasures exhibited were excavated locally.

The museum now incorporates a glimpse inside a third-century defense tower, with traces of medieval frescoes on its rounded walls portraying Jesus showing his stigmata to St. Francis. Highlights include the 1st-century B.C. **mosaic pavement** unearthed nearby in 1913; the stunning, gleaming 4th-century **Trivulzio Diattreta Cup,** made of the finest hand-blown glass; and the busts of various emperors from Caesar onwards.

Corso Magenta 15. www.comune.milano.it. ✆ **02-8844-5208.** 5€ adults. Free Tues after 2pm. Tues–Sun 9am–5:30pm. Metro: Cadorna.

Museo del Duomo ★★★ MUSEUM This museum is on the ground floor of the Palazzo Reale. Enter on the left side of the courtyard, to the right of the Duomo as you look at the facade. Incredible treasures from the Duomo are displayed here in an imaginatively curated exhibition, leading visitors on a chronological journey through the life of both Milan and its cathedral. Highlights among the carved cherubs, angels, and Renaissance Madonnas include a room full of startling gargoyles, ethereal 15th-century stained-glass works, scale wooden models of the cathedral, and the original supporting structure of **"La Madonnina"** (see p. 467), who has adorned the Duomo rooftop since 1774. Perhaps the standout piece is **"Jesus and the Moneylenders"** by Tintoretto, rediscovered by happy accident in the Duomo sacristy after World War II.

Piazza del Duomo 12. http://museo.duomomilano.it. ✆ **02-7200-3768.** 6€, 3€ under 26 and seniors. Tues–Sun 10am–6pm. Metro: Duomo.

Museo del Novecento ★ MUSEUM This museum of 20th-century art is next door to the Palazzo Reale. It features a circular concrete passageway, which winds up to the museum entrance on the third floor. The undisputed star of the collection is Giuseppe Pellizza da Volpedo's painting **"The Fourth Estate"** (1901), which is free for all to admire in the passageway outside the museum. Otherwise the collection showcases Italian modern art from Futurist to Arte Povera, making the case that Italy's contribution to the world of art did not end at the Renaissance. Brilliant bursts of genius include the magnificent **"Philosopher's Troubles"** (1926) by Giorgio de Chirico and the moving **"Thirst"** (1934) by sculptor Arturo Martini, so stick with it. One of the best things about this museum? The views of the Duomo and the piazza down below.
Via Marconi 1. www.museodelnovecento.org. ✆ **02-8844-0461.** 5€ adults, free for those under 25 and the disabled. Temporary exhibitions may have extra fees. Mon 2:30–7:30pm, Tues–Sun 9:30am–7:30pm (Thurs, Sat until 10:30pm). Metro: Duomo.

Museo Nazionale della Scienza e della Tecnologica Leonardo da Vinci ★★ MUSEUM This cavernous science museum comprises the former monastery of San Vittore Olivetan, plus three modern additions and outdoor spaces. While recent renovations have made the exhibits more interactive and fun, the floor plan is still immensely confusing, and it's a big museum; pick up a brochure so you don't miss the highlights. These include a clutch of Leonardo's anatomical drawings and not-so-batty designs for flying machines on the top floor, a display of 20th-century technology that will shock teenagers for how rudimentary it is, and a mini-submarine visit (book in advance: ✆ **02-4855-5330**; Tues and Thurs after 1:30pm; 18€–10€ to enter the museum and 8€ for the tour of the submarine; the submarine tour can't be purchased on its own). The Air and Water Building has lots of airplanes and boats to explore, and a railway track is full of locomotives.
Via San Vittore 21. www.museoscienza.org. ✆ **02-485-551.** 10€ adults, 8€ under 25, 5€ seniors. Guided tour in English 65€ for 1 hour. Tues–Fri 9:30am–5pm, Sat–Sun 9:30am–6:30pm. Metro: Sant'Ambrogio.

Museo Poldi Pezzoli ★★ ART GALLERY This wonderfully eclectic art collection was the life's work of aristocrat Gian Giacomo Poldi Pezzoli, who donated his cache of art and decorative arts to the city in 1879. It is now elegantly displayed in his luxurious former *palazzo*. The ornate rooms of the ground floor feature Oriental rugs, ancient armor, and rare books. Up the carved marble stairs the riches continue, through extravagant rooms adorned with family portraits, Murano glass, and Limoges china. Scenes from *The Divine Comedy* are featured in stained glass, and gilded pistols sit side by side with precious jewelry.

The stars of this wonderful show are the intricate **Armillary Sphere,** crafted by Flemish clockmaker Gualterus Arsenius in 1568 to illustrate contemporary theories of planetary movement, and the **Renaissance paintings** by Botticelli and Piero della Francesca in the Golden Room.

The clock room, which features 150 watches and clocks from the Renaissance to the late 1800s, has high-tech elements like touchscreen media devices that allow visitors to learn more about the pieces.

Via Manzoni 12. www.museopoldipezzoli.it. ✆ **02-794-889.** 10€ adults; 7€ seniors and students 11–18; free under 10. Audio guides 5€. Wed–Mon 10am–6pm, closed Tues. Metro: Montenapoleone.

Piazza del Duomo ★★ PIAZZA The Piazza del Duomo has been the beating heart of Milan since the city was taken over by the Romans in 222 B.C. and known as Mediolanum. This vast traffic-free piazza sees local life passing to and fro daily, added to by the bustle of tourists peering up at the majestic Duomo while dodging pigeons and street sellers pushing cheap souvenirs. From here a tangle of narrow streets branch off in all directions through the city's *centro storico* (historic center). The square took on its present form following the Unification of Italy in 1861, when the medieval buildings were replaced by splendid neoclassical buildings designed by Giuseppe Mengoni (1829–1877), also architect of the **Galleria Vittorio Emanuele II.** (see p. 468)

The piazza is home to the superb **Museo del Duomo** (see p. 469), temporary art exhibitions in the **Palazzo Reale** (www.palazzorealemilano.it; ✆ **02-0202**), and 20th-century Italian art in the **Museo del Novecento** (see p. 470).

Metro: Duomo.

Pinacoteca Ambrosiana ★★ ART GALLERY Founded in 1609 to display the collections of the pious Cardinal of Milan Federico Borromeo, this gallery is housed in the Europe's second-oldest public library (after the Bodleian in Oxford). While the emphasis is on Italian art from the 15th to 20th centuries, some Dutch work is also exhibited.

Despite a confusing layout encompassing courtyards, passageways, stairwells, and any number of tiny exhibition rooms, the gallery is well worth visiting for four outstanding artworks: **"Portrait of a Musician"** by Leonardo da Vinci (1490); the cartoon for **"The School of Athens"** by Raphael (1510); Caravaggio's charming **"Basket with Fruit,"** from around 1599; and Titian's **"Adoration of the Magi"** (ca. 1550).

Leonardo's original **"Codex Atlanticus"** is in the Biblioteca Ambrosiana next door along with other rare manuscripts; drawings from the "Codex" can be seen in the Sacristy of Bramante in Santa Maria della Grazie. Leonardo's entire life as an artist and scientist can be found in this extraordinary collection.

Piazza Pio XI. www.ambrosiana.eu. ✆ **02-806-921.** Pinacoteca and Leonardo's Codex Atlanticus 15€ adults, 10€ for those under 18 and over 65, free for children 14 and under. Pinacoteca only 10€. Tues–Sun 10am–6pm. Metro: Duomo or Cordusio.

Pinacoteca di Brera ★★★ ART GALLERY Milan's, and indeed Lombardy's, premier art collection resides in a 17th-century Jesuit college, wrapped around a two-story arcaded courtyard. This peerless collection romps in a circular tour through Italian art from medieval to Surrealism in 38 roughly chronological rooms. Along the way are splendid Renaissance altarpieces, Venetian School and baroque paintings, gloomy Mannerist works, and the odd piece by Picasso and Umberto Boccioni.

Although the collection is not immense, it is of exquisite quality; just some of the breathtaking highlights include Piero della Francesca's sublime **Montefeltro Altarpiece** (1474); the ethereal **"Dead Christ"** by Andrea Mantegna (1480); Caravaggio's superb, if mournful, 17th-century **"Supper at Emmaus"** (1601); and Raphael's **"Marriage of the Virgin"** (1504), which was beautifully restored in the glass-walled, temperature-controlled restoration rooms that are open to the public.

Of the secular works in the gallery, standout pieces include Francesco Hayez's **"The Kiss"** (1859) and artist Giovanni Fattori's pastoral scenes, which lead the way for the late-19th-century Macchiaioli School of Italian Impressionists. Moving the collection all the more up to date are works by the Italian playboy artist Amedeo Modigliani and sculptor Marino Marini.

Via Brera 28. http://pinacotecabrera.org. ✆ **02-722-632-64.** 10€ adults, 7€ seniors and students under 18. Audio guide 5€. Tues–Wed and Sat–Sun 8:30am–7:15pm, Thurs 8:30am–10:15pm. Free every first Sun of the month. Metro: Lanza.

Santa Maria delle Grazie ★★ CHURCH The delightful Lombard Renaissance church of Santa Maria delle Grazie is often ignored in the mad scramble to see Leonardo da Vinci's world-renowned "Last Supper" in the *cenacolo* (refectory) of the Dominican convent attached to the church. Started in 1465–1482 by Guiniforte Solari (ca. 1429–1481), the church was subsequently enlarged when the Sforza duke Ludovico il Moro (see p. 463) decided to make it his family mausoleum. He commissioned Leonardo da Vinci to paint the "Last Supper," and asked Donato Bramante, the leading architect of the Lombard Renaissance, who also helped design St Peter's in Rome, to add the terracotta-and-cream choir in 1492. Inside the church itself, a clash of styles is evident between Solari's frescoed Gothic nave and Bramante's airy, somber choir.

Piazza Santa Maria delle Grazie. www.grazieop.it. ✆ **02-467-6111.** Free. Mon–Sat 7am–noon, 3–7:30pm (4–7:30pm summer); Sun 7:30am–12:30pm, 4pm–9pm. Metro: Cadorna or Conciliazione.

Santa Maria delle Grazie, Il Cenacolo Vinciano ★★★ CHURCH Milan's greatest art treasure is also one of the most famous on earth, in part thanks to Dan Brown's blockbuster novel *The Da Vinci Code*. Painted for Ludovico il Moro by Leonardo da Vinci between 1495 and

Seeing "The Last Supper"

Unsurprisingly, Leonardo's "The Last Supper" is on almost every tourist's itinerary of Milan. And with only 30 people allowed in to the Cenacolo Vinciano at a time, it is a challenge to get a ticket if you don't book well in advance. Try the official website first, www.cenacolovinciano.net, or call ✆ **02-9280-0360** (tickets are 10€ from the website, plus a 2€ booking fee; children under 18 enter free but still pay the 2€ fee) **3 months** before you are due to visit. Present your e-tickets at the booking office outside the Cenacolo in Piazza Santa Maria delle Grazie at least 20 minutes before your allotted time slot. And remember that the Cenacolo is not in the church of Santa Maria delle Grazie itself, but in the refectory behind it, with a separate entrance of its own.

If you've missed the opportunity to snag a ticket in advance, many tour companies guarantee admission to "The Last Supper" as part of their guided tours of the city, which range from 40€ to 70€ (see "Organized Tours," below).

Don't miss **Leonardo's Vineyard Museum** across the street in the Casa degli Atellani, where da Vinci lived while he was painting "The Last Supper." It is said that he would go back to the house at the end of the day and, given he came from a family of winemakers, tend to his vines in the garden to unwind (www.vignadileonardo.com; ✆ **02-481-6150**). The small vineyard has been revived today, and visitors can tour it and the noble palazzo. Tickets are 10€ for adults and 8€ for those aged 6 to 18.

1497, "The Last Supper" adorns the back wall of the refectory in the Dominican convent attached to Santa Maria delle Grazie (see p. 472). Leonardo's masterpiece depicts Christ revealing that one of his disciples will soon betray him; horror and disbelief are etched into every face, while Jesus remains calm and resigned. As we look at the fresco, Judas sits to the left of Jesus, leaning away from him with the bag of silver clearly visible in his right hand. Is that Mary Magdalene sitting between him and Jesus? (Most historians think it's actually St. John, who was typically depicted as a particularly beautiful youth.) Wherever you stand on the issue, there is no doubt that "The Last Supper" is one of the world's most poignant and beautiful works of art.

In experimenting with his painting technique, Leonardo applied tempera straight on to the walls of the refectory. As a result, his work began to deteriorate virtually on completion. It suffered several ham-fisted restoration attempts in the 18th and 19th centuries and survived target practice by Napoleon's troops, not to mention a period exposed to the open air after Allied bombing in WWII. The latest cleanup of the fresco was completed in 1999, and while the colors are muted, they are thought to resemble Leonardo's original. The famous fresco is now climate-controlled for preservation, and groups of only 30 at a time are allowed in to view it, in preallocated periods of 15 minutes.

Piazza Santa Maria delle Grazie 2. www.cenacolovinciano.net, ✆ **02-9280-0360.** 10€ adults, children under 18 are free but a 2€ booking fee applies to all tickets. Tues–Sun 8:15am–7pm. Metro: Cadorna or Conciliazione.

Triennale di Milano ★★★ MUSEUM Located at the north end of Parco Sempione by the Torre Branca, this sleek temple of contemporary design features on-trend temporary exhibits ranging from modern craftsmanship to retrospectives on Italian design icons. An internal bridge on the second floor was designed by Michele de Lucchi out of bamboo planks. It leads from the exhibition spaces into the Triennale Design Museum, which has oft-changing displays of modern Italian design classics. The **DesignCafé** on the main floor is the venue of choice on Sundays for smart Milanese and their immaculately turned-out offspring.

Viale Alemagna 6. www.triennale.org. ✆ **02-724-341.** Design Museum 8€ adults. Most temporary exhibitions costs 8€. For 10€ you can visit the Design Museum as well as all temporary exhibitions in the museum. There is a range of discounts for students, seniors, and children. Tues–Sun 10:30am–8:30pm. Metro: Cadorna or Cairoli.

Organized Tours

Among the scores of companies offering guided tours of Milan and Lombardy, here are three of the best. **Viator** (www.viator.com; U.S. ✆ **702/648-5873**) offers private guided tours of Milan with hotel pickups as well as sightseeing tours by Segway, plus jaunts out to the lakes Como and Maggiore. **Zani Viaggi** (www.zaniviaggi.it; ✆ **02-867-131**) leads specialist tours to the revered turf of San Siro Stadium (see below) and the shopping outlets of northern Lombardy, while **Local Milan Tours** (www.localmilantours.com; U.S. ✆ **866/663-7017**) can organize trips around La Scala (see p. 483) and day trips as far afield as Venice.

Outdoor Activities

Milan is a densely populated urban sprawl where green space is rare and precious. The largest park is the 47-hectare (116-acre) expanse of **Parco Sempione** behind Castello Sforzesco. It is one of the "green lungs" of the city, the favorite place of well-heeled Milanese to walk their dogs along shady pathways sheltered by giant chestnuts; it is here that lovers come to moon around the ornamental lakes. The **Giardini Pubblici** on Bastioni di Porta Venezia is another haven, a firm favorite with families at the weekend for its little fair. Joggers circuit the park, and in winter there's ice-skating on the ornamental ponds. **Parco Solari** and **Gardaland Waterpark** (see p. 476) have swimming pools, and **Idroscalo** (see p. 475) near Linate offers every outdoor activity from sailing and swimming to climbing or tennis. The **Lombardy lakes** all offer the chance for watersports, cycling, and hiking. For sports fanatics, San Siro Stadium (www.sansiro.net; ✆ **02-4879-8201**) and **Monza F1 racetrack** (see p. 476) are open for tours.

Especially for Kids

Despite being world-renowned as a hub of high finance, fashion, and design, Milan is after all an Italian city—and all Italians dote on children. The city's rather formal facade belies its many family-friendly attractions, museums, *gelaterie*, and play parks, and everywhere you go, your *bambini* will be worshipped, hugged, and multilaterally adored.

Where to start? Chief among attractions that all kids will love is the ride up to the **Duomo rooftop** (see p. 514) for views across the red rooftops of the city and the new skyscraper district, all the way to the Alps. The **Museo Nazionale della Scienza e della Tecnologica Leonardo da Vinci** (see p. 470) is stuffed full of fun, interactive activities for kids. Children ages 4 to 11 can be distracted by the play area Sforzinda in the **Castello Sforzesco's** (see p. 463) 14th-century dungeons while parents explore the decorative arts. A picnic lunch and a run in the adjoining **Parco Sempione** is a welcome respite from cultural overload.

The **Museo dei Bambini** (Via Enrico Besana 12; www.muba.it; ✆ **02-4398-0402**) doesn't have a permanent collection, but offers creative and educational workshops for children ages 2 and up. Opening times and cost of workshops vary, but tend to run around 10 euros.

Another great green public space is the **Giardini Pubblici Indro Montanelli** (see p. 482). Here there are playgrounds, roundabouts, and a little electric train that chugs around the park. The Corso Venezia side of the park is home to the **Museo di Storia Naturale** (www.comune.milano.it/museostorianaturale; ✆ **02-8846-3337;** Tues–Sun 9am–5:30pm; admission 5€, children under 18 enter free), where you can take the kids to see dinosaur skeletons and the carcasses of massive bugs. **Parco Solari** (www.milanosport.it/impianto/28/solari/110; ✆ **02-469-5278;** Via Montevideo 20) has an indoor pool.

The newly restored **Darsena,** the historic port of the canal network in the Navigli area, offers plenty of stimulation for the little ones. It's a great place to sit down with a picnic or gelato and watch the boats go by, either in one of the seating areas or at the cafes along the water.

Near the Linate airport, just east of the city center, the **Idroscalo** park (Via Circonvallazione Idroscalo 29, Segrate; www.idroscalo.info; no phone) features a manmade lake that was originally created for seaplanes to land. This area has now been turned into a park and is open daily (summer 7am–9pm; winter 7am–5pm).

Most restaurants will happily rustle up a child's portion of pasta and tomato sauce, and if all else fails, it's usually easy to bribe any child with a visit to one of Milan's delicious ice cream shops; try **Biancolatte** (Via Turati 30; ✆ **02-6208-6177**) for dark-chocolate ice-cream cakes and

FUN IN THE theme parks

Italy's version of Disneyland, **Gardaland,** is located a couple of hours from Milan in Castlenuovo del Garda (see p. 507), but plenty of other options lie closer to the city. If you are looking to beat the heat in the summertime, there's the **Acquatica** waterpark (Via Gaetano Airaghi 61; www.acquaticapark.it; ✆ **02-4820-0134**) located on the far western outskirts of town. It has splashy water slides, rides, and picnic areas. It opens at the end of May and closes the end of August. To get there, take the new lilac line of the subway (also called MM5) to the San Siro stop, then either bus 80 (toward Quinto Romano) or the 423 bus (toward Settimo Milanese), which stops directly in front of the water park. The park is open daily 10am to 7pm. An all-day ticket costs 18€ adults and 12€ for children under 12 (on Sun, adult tickets are 20€). Children under 100cm tall enter for free. Enter after 2:30pm for slightly reduced tickets. Pools are 8€ on the weekend, and parking is 2€.

About 30 minutes northeast of Milan in the direction of Bergamo, the **Leolandia** amusement park (Via Vittorio Veneto 52, Capriate San Gervasio; www.leolandia.it) has rides and games for kids of all ages, as well as the delightful Minitalia, a replica of the major cities and monuments in Italy. More compact and manageable than the main Gardaland, it may be better suited to smaller children, with features such as Peppa Pig World, Thomas the Train Engine and Masha and the Bear. Tickets purchased at the park cost 32€, but can be half that online. Children up to 89cm (about 3 ft.) enter free. Leolandia opens in late March and stays open through Halloween. In early spring and fall, it's open only weekends; in June and July it's open Wednesday to Sunday; and in August it's open daily. The Z301 bus from Milan to Bergamo, managed by **Nord Est Trasporti** (www.nordesttrasporti.it; ✆ **800-905-150**), stops near Leolandia, at Capriate San Gervasio.

Rinomata Gelateria (Ripa di Porta Ticinese 1; ✆ **02-5811-3877**) in the Navigli area for one of the most traditional ice-cream cones in town.

Outlying Attractions

Autodromo Nazionale Monza ★★ RACING CIRCUIT Spread along the River Lambro in Lombardy, and 15km (10¼ miles) northeast of Milan, Monza is an appealing city with a central core reminiscent of a mini Milan, as well as a sprawling park that is famous throughout Europe. It also has a majestic early-Gothic Duomo and photogenic piazzas backed by lots of greenery. Sadly, the *centro storico* is usually bypassed in favor of this 10km (6.2-mile) Formula One racetrack, the epicenter of car-mad Italy's hopes and dreams. The home of the Italian Grand Prix since 1922, Monza track is now open to any and all who fancy being a racing driver for the day. Race-training sessions are held daily, with half-hour slots available for would-be champions to try out their skills on the track.

Rallies, races, and special events take place all year round. Check the website for tickets and event details.

Via Vedano 5, Monza. www.monzanet.it. ✆ **039-24-821.** Accessible by train (15 min.) from Centrale and Garibaldi stations.

Certosa di Pavia ★★★ CHURCH Located a few miles north of the town of Pavia, this awesome Carthusian monastery is well worth a day trip. It was originally commissioned in 1396 as a mausoleum for Milan's ruling Visconti family (see p. 467), but after their dynastic downfall, the Sforza family took over, refurbishing per their exorbitant tastes. The highly intricate Renaissance facade is the swan song of master 15th-century architect Giovanni Antonio Amadeo, who also worked on the **Basilica di Santa Maria Maggiore in Bergamo** (see p. 486). The monastery contains the ornate tomb (but not the bodies) of Ludovico del Moro and his wife, Beatrice, who together shaped the Milanese Renaissance (see p. 463). A tour takes in the peaceful cloisters, monks' cells, and refectory, but the highlight is the decorative church, its swaths of frescoes, the *pietra dura* altar, and the massive **mausoleum** of Gian Galeazzo Visconti.

Via Del Monumento 4, Certosa di Pavia. www.museo.certosadipavia.beniculturali.it. ✆ **0382-925-613.** Admission and guided tours by donation. Tues–Sun. May–Aug 9–11:30am, 2:30–6pm; Mar and Oct 9–11:30am, 2:30–5pm; Apr and Sept 9–11:30am, 2:30–5:30pm; Nov–Feb 9–11:30am, 2:30–4pm. Metro Line 3 to Certosa, then a 10-minute walk.

Where to Stay

Milan is northern Italy's largest commercial center, big on banking and industry, and for years its hotels have tended to chase expense-account customers, often to the detriment of tourists and families. The winds of change are blowing, however. A recent wave of cozy, independent *locandas* and *albergos,* as well as design-conscious boutique hotels, have come along to complement the grand old institutions.

Note that prices are often higher during the week than on the weekend, and room rates really soar when the fashion and design crowd hits town (late Feb, mid-May, and late Sept).

EXPENSIVE

Hotel Principe di Savoia ★★ This grand Beaux Arts institution is part of the Dorchester Collection of famous hotels that has been expanding at a rapid clip. Every conceivable guest whim is swiftly addressed, and a stay here is truly a luxurious respite from the hustle and bustle of the city outside. Guests have access to serene gardens, a soothing top-floor spa, a quality restaurant, an elegant bar, and opulent, suitably sumptuous rooms and suites. The presidential suite even has its own private indoor swimming pool. Not surprisingly this luxury comes at a price, but for a bit of old-fashioned glamour, there's nowhere else like it. This property is strategically located near both Stazione Centrale and the up-and-coming CityLife district, making tony Corso Como a short walk away over Milan's answer to New York City's High Line.

Piazza Della Repubblica 17. www.dorchestercollection.com/en/milan/hotel-principe-di-savoia. ✆ **02-623-01.** 301 units. 220€–510€ double; 325€–4,700€ suite. Metro: Repubblica. **Amenities:** restaurant; bar; concierge; room service; babysitting; spa; gym; indoor pool; Wi-Fi (free).

Milanosuites ★★★ Set in a charming 18th-century townhouse tucked away discreetly in the appealing rabble of streets between the Castello Sforzesco and Piazza del Duomo, the former Antica Locanda dei Mercanti had a thorough facelift and re-emerged as the elegant, light-filled Milanosuites. The glamorous suites are graced with parquet floors and simple white furnishings. All have living rooms and some have kitchenettes. Families can book a suite with two bedrooms. The property also has a communal breakfast area (breakfast usually costs extra depending on the rate you select) and a lounge.

Via San Tomaso 6. www.milanosuites.it. ✆ **02-8909-6849.** 5 units. 285€–395€ suite. Metro: Cordusio or Cairoli. **Amenities:** Concierge; room service; Wi-Fi (free).

nhow Milan ★★ A boutique hotel popular with the fashion and design set (who descend upon it during Milan's fashion weeks and the Salone del Mobile furniture fair), the nhow is part of a chain intent on providing stylish, well-priced accommodation. It all feels a bit soulless, however. The sleek reception area, with an orange color scheme straight from the 1960s, is only outdone by the lime-green furnishings in the minimalist bar, sometimes inhabited by gossiping models. Glass elevators whiz up to rooms decorated in white and bright solid colors; the standard rooms are compact with walk-in showers. The fourth floor is the preserve of stylish, loft-style suites with views over Milan's Zona Tortona fashion district. If you aren't an early riser, never fear. Breakfast is served until 3pm (and you can request to have it in your room, except on the day you are checking out).

Via Tortona 35. www.nhow-milan.com. ✆ **02-489-8861.** 246 units. 189€–289€ double; 419€–2,200€ suite. Rates include breakfast. Metro: Porto Genova. **Amenities:** Restaurant; bar; spa; gym; Wi-Fi (free).

MODERATE

Antica Locanda Leonardo ★★★ Located steps from where "The Last Supper" hangs in Santa Maria delle Grazie church, this lovely *albergo* in a 19th-century building overlooks a tranquil courtyard garden. It's like stepping into a family home. Rooms have been extensively revamped but retain a wonderfully traditional feel, with heavy antique headboards and dressers, gilt mirrors, and elegant draperies; each one is unique. Fortunately, bathrooms have been brought up to 21st-century standards, but the cozy lounge and breakfast room remain delightfully of a former age. The more expensive courtyard-facing rooms, many with tiny balconies, deflect the late-night noise on Corso Magenta. The hotel is in a perfect location in old Milan for seeing all of the city's major sights. Corso Magenta 78. www.anticalocandaleonardo.com. ✆ **02-4801-4197.** 16 units. 120€–340€ double. Rates include breakfast. Metro: Concilliazione, Cardorna. **Amenities:** Concierge; Wi-Fi (free).

INEXPENSIVE

BioCity Hotel ★★★ This fab little "organic city hotel" housed in a brightly colored villa from the 1920s offers the best value for accommodation in Milan. It's all a budget hotel should be: small and pristine, with a miniscule bar and breakfast room and a tiny terrace out back—*and* it's eco-friendly. Guest rooms are stylish—each one painted in colors inspired by nature that don't clash with the modern, technological touches—with big bathrooms almost fit for a four-star hotel. The limited reception area manages to squeeze in a little lounge that's furnished with edgy pieces. Operated by genial, well-informed owners, the BioCity is a few minutes' walk from Stazione Centrale, though as in many Italian cities, you may not want to linger around the train station late at night. This gem of a hotel is close to metro line 3, which zips straight into the *centro storico*.

Via Edolo 18. www.biocityhotel.it. ✆ **02-6670-3595.** 17 units. 85€–199€ double. Rates include breakfast. Metro: Sondrio. **Amenities:** Bar; Wi-Fi (free).

Where to Eat

Milan has thousands of eateries, from pizzerias to grand old cafes, Michelin-starred restaurants in highfalutin' surroundings to corner bars with a great selection of *aperitivo*-time tapas, *gelaterie* and traditional *osterie*. Avoid the obvious tourist traps: any place that has a menu showing photos of the dishes.

Cocktail hour starts at around 6:30pm. Around that time, a tapas-like spread of olives, crudités, cold pasta dishes, rice, salads, salamis, and breads make its appearance in every city bar worth its salt. This is when the Milanese appear, as if by magic, from shopping or work, to meet up for cocktails, a bitter Campari, or a glass of prosecco. By the time *aperitivo* hour is over, thoughts turn towards supper and the restaurants start to fill up. This phenomenon takes place all over Milan.

EXPENSIVE

Carlo e Camilla in Segheria ★★ MODERN ITALIAN Celebrated chef Carlo Cracco's innovative bar and restaurant located in an old

sawmill outside the *centro storico* is a favorite with foodies and hipsters. The restaurant and cocktail bar has a sparse yet warm post-industrial feel with one long communal table for up to 65 people and large chandeliers hanging from the ceiling. Come for a truly unique cocktail (some say these are the best drinks in town, and that is saying a lot—mixology culture has taken Milan by storm) or stay for dinner with modern Italian food that is clean, fresh, and "not too cerebral." The menu here changes with the seasons but what doesn't change are the clean flavors and theatrical details. Try spaghetti with anchovies, lime, and coffee or the salmon "cube" with a yogurt and lemongrass sauce.
Via G. Meda 24. www.carloecamillainsegheria.it. ✆ **02-837-3963.** Main courses 15€–25€. Daily 6pm–2am. Metro: Romolo, though Tram 3 from the Duomo gets you closer to the restaurant because it passes right in front.

MODERATE

Hostaria Borromei ★★ LOMBARDY This Milanese staple not far from the Duomo is a favorite for its down-home vibe and hearty Lombardian fare (with some southern dishes thrown into the mix as well). Book in advance for weekend dining, especially for a seat on the vineyard terrace when the weather is warm. The menu features polenta, homemade pastas (such as "mamma's" tagliatelle pasta with tomato sauce, meatballs, and peas), saffron risotto, the famed veal *osso bucco*, and plenty of seafood. Cheeses and traditional desserts such as *tiramisu* and *panna cotta* round off a winning experience in a lively atmosphere.
Via Borromei 4. www.hostariaborromei.com. ✆ **02-8645-3760.** Main courses 13€–44€. Mon–Fri 12:30–2:45pm and 7:30–10:45pm; Sat 7:30–10:45pm. Metro: Cordusio or Duomo.

Osteria il Kaimano ★★ NORTHERN ITALIAN This casual, pleasantly chaotic *osteria* is a good choice among the variety of restaurants and bars in the Brera district. The menu of pasta and pizza staples may not be vastly different from the other Brera dining options—**Sans Egal** (Vicolo Fiori 2; www.sansegal.it; ✆ **02-869-3096**) and **Nabucco** (Via Fiori Chiari 10; www.nabucco.it; ✆ **02-860-663**) are also good choices—but here the atmosphere and warm service shine. Strong choices include the zucchini flowers stuffed with ricotta for starters, and Neapolitan-style pizzas that continually slide out of the wood-burning oven. Given the translated menu posted outside, it might look like a tourist trap, but the food (and abundance of locals who frequent the place) tells another story. A terrace on the street for dining in warm weather becomes a favorite gathering spot of smokers in winter.
Via Fiori Chiari 20. ✆ **02-8050-2733.** Main courses 15€–40€. Daily noon–2:30pm, 6–11:30pm. Metro: Lanza Brera.

Upscale shopping in Milan.

Nerino Dieci Trattoria ★★ MEDITERRANEAN This extremely popular *trattoria* (call at least a month in advance for dinner reservations; it's a bit easier to get in for lunch) not far from the Duomo and the *centro storico* offers up solid Italian fare, with a focus on seafood, at reasonable prices. While the open kitchen and neon lettering on the wall may not be typical of most traditional Italian restaurants, this spot has plenty of cozy little corners that make it more suited to a romantic meal than a big family dinner. Mussels are served in a variety of creative ways (with ginger and orange, say, or gorgonzola cheese), and mains are traditional yet creative. Try risotto with chanterelles, pear, and Taleggio cheese, or fresh tuna in a pistachio crust. The lunch menu, including a main course, dessert, and water, wine, or other beverage, is a steal at 9€.

Via Nerino 10. www.nerinodieci.it ✆ **02-3983-1019.** Main courses 9€–15€. Mon–Fri noon–2:30pm, 7:30–11pm; Sat 7:30–11pm. Closed Sun. Metro: Lanza Brera.

Shopping

Milan is known the world over as one of the temples of high fashion, with the hallowed streets **Montenapoleone** and **Spiga** in the

Quadrilatero d'Oro, the most popular places of wallet-stripping worship. Here D&G, Prada, Gucci, Hermès, Louis Vuitton, Armani, Ralph Lauren, Versace, and Cavalli all jostle for Milan's minted fashionistas. The area around Porta Nuova (at the top of Corso Como) is also starting to become a luxury-shopping district. More reasonable shopping areas include **Via Torino** and **Corso Buenos Aires,** where midrange international brands proliferate; if you're clever you can also pick up a designer bargain at outlet store **Il Salvagente** (Via Fratelli Bronzetti 16; ✆ **02-7611-0328**).

Fashion is one Milanese obsession, food is another, and the *centro storico* has many superb delis from which to purchase the purest of olive oils and the finest cheeses. **Peck** (Via Spadari 9; ✆ **02-802-3161**) is still the number-one gourmet spot, although competition is keen from the **Eataly** megastore in Piazza XXV Aprile (www.eataly.it) for all Italian comestibles. The **top floor of the La Rinascente department store** in Piazza del Duomo (see below) is another haven for foodies, with its Obika mozzarella bar and fine selection of packaged Italian goods (as an added bonus, you get a close-up view of the Duomo). Opened in 2015, the **Mercato del Duomo** (www.ilmercatodelduomo.it; ✆ **02-8633-1924)** in Piazza del Duomo aims to be a "gourmet cathedral" directly across from the actual cathedral. It has a food market (a good place to grab focaccia or a quick lunch on the run) and various coffee bars, wine bars, aperitif spots, and a high-end restaurant.

English-language books are sold at **Feltrinelli Librerie, Mondadori Multicenter,** and **Rizzoli** (all in and around Piazza del Duomo or inside the galleria). English-language newspapers can be found on most major newsstands around the *centro storico*.

MILANO MARKETS

Everybody loves a bargain, and there's no better place to find one than at the colorful, chaotic **Viale Papiniano market** (Metro: Sant'Agostino). Its sea of stalls is open Tuesday and Saturday; some flog designer seconds, others leather basics. **Flea markets** spring up on Saturdays along the Alzaia Naviglio Grande (Metro: Porta Genova) and Fiera di Sinigaglia (Metro: Porta Genova), and on Sundays at San Donato Metro stop. During the Christmas season, holiday markets (complete with ice skating) pop up in different parts of the city, from Piazza Gae Aulenti (Metro: Garibaldi) to the Castello Sforzesco (Metro: Cairoli) to the area behind the Museum of Natural History (Metro: Palestro) in the Giardini Pubblici Indro Montanelli, which is focused on activities for children. A large **food market** at the Piazza Wagner Metro is open every morning except Sunday.

Nightlife & Entertainment

Unless you're heading for the Ticinese and Navigli, Milan is a dressy city and generally looks askance at scruffy jeans and sneakers after dark. When many people don't dine until well after 10pm, it's not surprising that clubs and bars stay open until the very wee hours.

Milan has its share of glitzy clubs and cocktail bars, but most explode on the scene and disappear just as quickly. A few spots that appear to be in for the long haul include the vine-covered cocktail terrace at **10 Corso Como** (www.10corsocomo.com; ✆ **02-2901-3581**), the evergreen dance club **Hollywood** (www.discotecahollywood.it; ✆ **02-6555-318**), and mega-club **Plastic** at Via Gargano 15 (✆ **02-5410-0161**—typically open weekends only). A newer kid on the block, **Ceresio 7 Pools & Restaurant** (www.ceresio7.com; ✆ **02-310-392-21**) offers a novel setup: a chic, sleek rooftop lounge with two pools where one can enjoy a cocktail while enjoying amazing views of the city.

North of Parco Sempione, **Chinatown** is a great area to explore for the dim sum restaurants concentrated around Via Paolo Sarpi.

A venerable Milan institution, the **Conservatorio di Musica Giuseppe Verdi** has two stages for classical concerts, at Via Conservatorio 12 (www.consmilano.it; ✆ **02-762-110).** And Milan is forever associated with the grand old dame of opera, **Teatro Alla Scala,** perhaps the world's favorite opera house. La Scala is all decked out with sumptuous red seats, boxes adorned with gilt, and chandeliers dripping crystal. Tickets are hard to come by, so book well in advance of the opera season, which kicks off on December 7 each year. Book online at www.teatroallascala.org, pay by phone with a credit card (✆ **02-860-775**—not exactly the easiest option because you're required to fax documentation), or buy your tickets direct from La Scala's booking office in the Galleria del Sagrato, Piazza del Duomo, open daily from noon to 6pm (closed Aug). The ticket office at the opera house (Via Filodrammatici 2) releases **discounted last-minute tickets** for that evening's performance 2½ hours before the curtain goes up; get there promptly if you want a ticket.

BERGAMO ★★

47km (29 miles) northeast of Milan.

Bergamo is a city of two distinct characters. The ancient **Città Alta** is a beautiful medieval and Renaissance town perched on a green hill. **Città Bassa,** mostly built in the 19th and 20th centuries, sits at the feet of the upper town and concerns itself with 21st-century life. Visitors tend to focus on the historic upper town, a place for wandering, soaking in the rarified atmosphere, and enjoying the lovely vistas from its belvederes.

Essentials

GETTING THERE **Trains** arrive from and depart for Milan Stazione Centrale hourly (50 min.; 5.50€). **Buses** to and from Milan are run by **Nord Est Trasporti** (www.nordesttrasporti.it; ✆ **800-905-150**) and run at least hourly, with more at commuter times; travel time is an hour and fares are 3.10€. The Z301 bus leaves from Milano Lampugnano station.

If you are **driving,** Bergamo is linked to Milan via the A4. The trip takes under an hour if traffic is good. ***Note:*** It's difficult to park in the largely pedestrianized Città Alta—park instead in Città Bassa and take the **funicular** (see below) up to the historic area.

VISITOR INFORMATION The **Città Bassa tourist office** is close to the train and bus stations at Viale Papa Giovanni XXIII 57 (✆ **035-210-204**); it's open daily 9am to 12:30pm and 2 to 5:30pm. The **Città Alta office** is at Via Gombito, 13 (✆ **035-242-226**), right off Via Colleoni, and is open daily 9am to 5:30pm.

CITY LAYOUT Piazza Vecchia, the Colleoni Chapel, and most major sights are in the **Città Alta,** which is dissected by **Via Colleoni.** To reach **Piazza Vecchia** from the funicular station at **Piazza Mercato delle Scarpi,** it's a 5-minute stroll along **Via Gombito.** The Accademia Carrara is in the Città Bassa.

GETTING AROUND Bergamo has an efficient **bus system** that runs throughout the Città Bassa and to points around the Città Alta; tickets are 1.30€ for 75 minutes of travel and are available from the machines at the bus stops outside the train station or at the bus station opposite.

To reach the Città Alta from the train station, take bus no. 1 or 1A (clearly marked Città Alta on the front) and make the free transfer to the **Funicolare Bergamo Alta,** run by ATB Bergamo (Largo Porta Nuova; www.atb.bergamo.it), connecting the upper and lower cities. It typically runs every 7 minutes from 7am to 1:20am.

Exploring the Città Bassa

Most visitors scurry through Bergamo's lower, newer town on their way to the Città Alta, but you may want to pause long enough to explore its main thoroughfare, **Corso Sentierone,** with its mishmash of architectural styles (16th-century porticos, the Mussolini-era Palazzo di Giustizia, and two mock Doric temples); it's a pleasant place to linger over espresso at a sidewalk cafe. The **Accademia Carrara** (Piazza Giacomo Carrara 82, www.lacarrara.it; ✆ **035-234-396**) is worth a peek for its fine

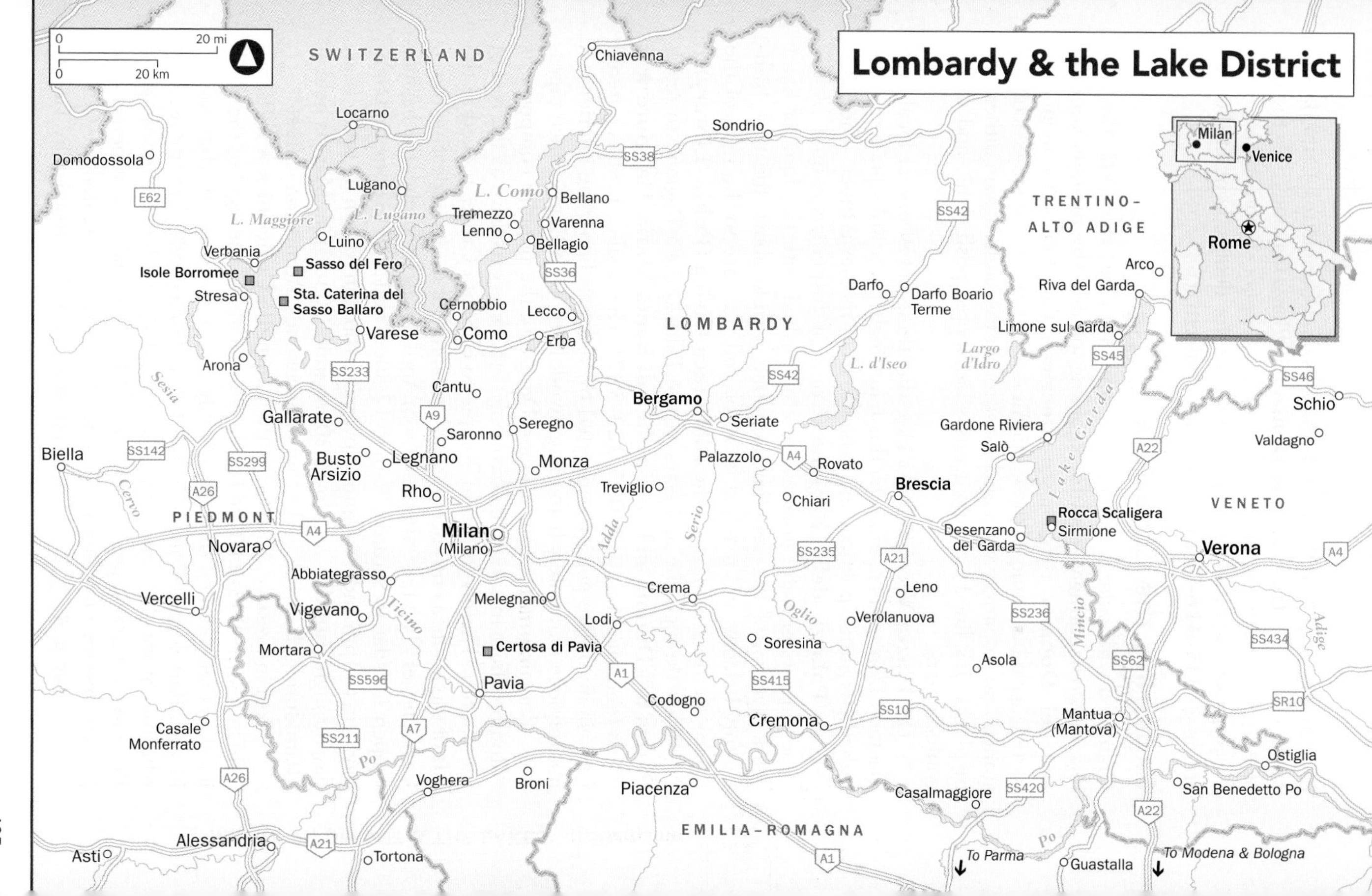
Lombardy & the Lake District
0
20 mi
0
20 km
SWITZERLAND
Milan
Venice
Rome
TRENTINO-
ALTO ADIGE
LOMBARDY
PIEDMONT
VENETO
EMILIA-ROMAGNA
Chiavenna
Locarno
Sondrio
Domodossola
Lugano
L. Como
Bellano
L. Maggiore
L. Lugano
Tremezzo
Lenno
Varenna
Bellagio
Luino
Verbania
Sasso del Fero
Isole Borromee
Stresa
Sta. Caterina del
Sasso Ballaro
Cernobbio
Lecco
Varese
Como
Erba
Arona
Darfo
Darfo Boario
Terme
Arco
Riva del Garda
Limone sul Garda
Largo d'Idro
L. d'Iseo
Lake Garda
Sesia
Cantu
Bergamo
Seriate
Gallarate
Seregno
Saronno
Busto
Arsizio
Legnano
Monza
Palazzolo
Rovato
Gardone Riviera
Salò
Schio
Valdagno
Biella
Cervo
Rho
Treviglio
Chiari
Brescia
Rocca Scaligera
Sirmione
Desenzano
del Garda
Milan
(Milano)
Novara
Verona
Adda
Serio
Abbiategrasso
Vercelli
Vigevano
Ticino
Melegnano
Crema
Leno
Lodi
Oglio
Verolanuova
Mincio
Adige
Mortara
Certosa di Pavia
Soresina
Asola
Pavia
Codogno
Cremona
Mantua
(Mantova)
Casale
Monferrato
Po
Ostiglia
Voghera
Broni
Piacenza
Casalmaggiore
San Benedetto Po
Alessandria
Asti
Tortona
To Parma
Guastalla
To Modena & Bologna
E62
SS38
SS42
SS36
SS45
SS46
SS233
A9
SS142
SS299
A26
A4
A22
SS235
A21
SS236
SS434
SS62
A1
SS415
SS596
SS10
SR10
SS211
A7
SS420
A21

collection of Raphaels, Bellinis, Botticellis, and Canolettos. Città Bassa's 19th-century **Teatro Gaetano Donizetti** (Piazza Cavour 15) is the hub of Bergamo's lively cultural scene, with a fall opera season and a winter-to-spring season of dramatic performances; for details, contact the theater at ✆ **035-416-0611** (www.teatrodonizetti.it).

Exploring the Città Alta

Crammed with *palazzi,* monuments, and churches, the Città Alta centers on two hauntingly beautiful adjoining squares, **the piazzas Vecchia** and **del Duomo.** Bergamasco strongman Bartolomeo Colleoni (see p. 486) gave his name to the Città Alta's delightful main street, cobblestoned and so narrow you can almost touch the buildings on either side in places. It's lined with gorgeous shoe shops, posh delis, and classy confectioners.

The **Piazza Vecchia** looks like something out of one of local hero Gaetano Donizetti's opera sets; this hauntingly beautiful square was the hub of Bergamo's political and civic life from medieval times. The 12th-century **Palazzo della Ragione** (Court of Justice) was built by the Venetians; its graceful arcades are embellished with the Lion of Saint Mark, symbol of the Venetian Republic, visible above the tiny 16th-century balcony and reached by a covered staircase to the right of the palace. Across the piazza is the **Biblioteca Civica (Public Library).**

Walk through the archways of the Palazzo della Ragione to reach **Piazza del Duomo** and the **Basilica di Santa Maria Maggiore ★★** (www.fondazionemia.it; ✆ **035-223-327**). The basilica itself is entered through an ornate portico supported by Venetian lions; the interior is a masterpiece of ornately baroque giltwork hung with Renaissance tapestries. Bergamo native son Gaetano Donizetti, the popular composer, is entombed here in a marble sarcophagus that's as excessive as the rest of the church. The oft-forgotten Tempietto of Santa Croce, tucked to the left of the basilica entrance, is worth seeking out for its endearing fresco fragments of "The Last Supper." From April through October the basilica is open Tuesday to Saturday 9am to 12:30pm and 2:30 to 6pm, and Sunday 9am to 1pm and 3 to 6pm; November through March it's open Tuesday through Saturday 9am to 12:30pm and 2:30 to 5pm. Mass is held at 10am during the week and 11am on weekends. Admission is free.

Most impressive, however, is the **Cappella Colleoni ★★★** (Piazza del Duomo; ✆ **035-210-061;** free admission), to the right of the basilica doors and entered through a highly elaborate pink-and-white marble facade. Bartolomeo Colleoni was a Bergamasco *condottiero* (mercenary) who fought for the Venetians; as a reward for his loyalty he was given Bergamo as his own private fiefdom in 1455. His elaborate funerary chapel was designed by Giovanni Antonio Amadeo, who created the Certosa di Pavia (see p. 477). Colleoni lies beneath a ceiling frescoed by Tiepolo and surrounded by statuary. Cappella Colleoni is open March to October daily 9am to 12:30pm and 2 to 6:30pm; and November to February Tuesday to Sunday 9am to 12:30pm and 2 to 4:30pm.

Where to Stay & Eat

The charms of Bergamo's Città Alta are no secret, and hotel rooms are in great demand over the summer, so make reservations well in advance. If you're staying in Milan, the city is an easy hour's journey from Stazione Centrale, making it a perfect day trip.

Hotel Piazza Vecchio ★★ Located steps from the Piazza Vecchio in the historic Città Alta, this ancient townhouse is full of historical touches. Rooms are all simply furnished, but each has beamed ceilings, brightly colored details, and a sleek new bathroom. The rooms at the back of the hotel, which overlook a labyrinth of alleyways and rooftops, are quieter. The hotel allows you to combine your stay in Bergamo with a visit to the San Pellegrino hot springs if you so wish. Ask about package deals.

Via Colleoni 3. www.hotelpiazzavecchia.it. ✆ **035-253-179.** 13 units. 150€–310€ double. Rates include breakfast. **Amenities:** Wi-Fi (free).

Caffè del Tasso ★ CAFE This charming spot on the atmospheric main piazza of the Città Alta has been in business since 1476. Today it has the rather cozy air of a 1950s teashop, but it also serves very good food at lunch and dinner. Service is smart, and they're generous with their *aperitivo* snacks. The gelateria next door does a brisk trade in summer, while an early evening drink on the terrace on warm nights is just a step away from heaven.

Piazza Vecchia 3. ✆ **035-237-966.** Main courses 10€–18€. Open daily 8am–midnight.

Osteria della Birra ★★ ORGANIC BREWPUB A great find in the Città Alta, this restaurant offers a simple menu of *piadine* (flatbread) and *panini* stuffed full of local cured hams and artisanal cheeses. Many of the breads are baked with beer, including savory beer-infused muffins. Part of the Elav microbrewery, it is all about the beer here (don't expect to find wine on the menu). It's run by a bunch of enthusiastic beer lovers keen to promote their organic brew and their largely organic produce.

Piazza Mascheroni 1/c. www.osteriadellabirra.it. ✆ **035-242-440.** Main courses 8€–17€. Mon–Sun noon to 2am.

Caffè della Funicolare ★ CAFE This characteristic spot located in the upper terminal of the funicular serves coffee, wine, beer, basic snacks, and more elaborate meals. In the last few years, this café has tried to expand its lunch and dinner menu to include more complex dishes made with quality ingredients. Try to get a table on the terrace, which is heated for dining "outdoors" even in the cold months, looking straight down over Bergamo Bassa for some of the best views in the upper town.

Via Porta Dipinta 1. www.caffedellafunicolare.it. ✆ **035-210-091.** Main courses 9€–20€, sandwiches 5€ and up. Daily 8am–2am.

MANTUA (MANTOVA) ★★★

158km (98 miles) E of Milan, 62km (38 miles) N of Parma, 150km (93 miles) SW of Venice

One of Lombardy's best-kept secrets, Mantua is in the eastern reaches of the region, making it a fairly easy side trip from Milan. Like its neighboring cities in Emilia-Romagna, Mantua owes its beautiful Renaissance monuments to one family, in this case the Gonzagas, who conquered the city in 1328 and ruled benevolently until 1707. Avid collectors of art, the Gonzagas ruled through the greatest centuries of Italian art, and today you can encounter their treasures in the **Palazzo Ducale;** in their summer retreat, the **Palazzo Te;** and in the churches and piazzas that grew up around their court.

The Palazzo Ducale, the **Galleria Museo Palazzo Valenti Gonzaga**, and other monuments were recently restored, while Mantegna's famous **Camera degli Sposi** (see p. 490) reopened in 2015 following earthquake damage in 2012.

Essentials

GETTING THERE Six direct **trains** depart daily from Milan Stazione Centrale (1 hr. 50 min.; 11.50€). There are nine daily trains from Verona (30–40 min.; 3.95€).

The speediest highway connections from Milan are via the A4 autostrada to Verona, then the A22 from Verona to Mantua (about 2 hrs.).

VISITOR INFORMATION The **tourist office** at Piazza Mantegna 6 (www.turismo.mantova.it; ✆ **0376-432-432**) is open on weekends from 9am to 5pm and 9am to 1:30pm and 2:30 to 5pm during the week (until 6pm in spring and summer). It's just to the right of the basilica of Sant'Andrea.

CITY LAYOUT Mantua is tucked onto a fat finger of land surrounded on three sides by the **Mincio River,** which widens into a series of lakes, prosaically named **Lago Superiore, Lago di Mezzo,** and **Lago Inferiore.** Most sights are within an easy walk of one another in the compact center, which is a 15-minute walk northwards from the lakeside train station.

Exploring Mantua

Mantua is a place for wandering along arcaded streets and through cobbled squares with handsomely proportioned churches and *palazzi*.

The southernmost of these squares is **Piazza delle Erbe (Square of the Herbs)** ★, so named for its produce-and-food market. Mantua's civic might is clustered here in a series of late-medieval and early Renaissance structures that include the **Palazzo della Ragione (Courts of Justice)** and **Palazzo del Podestà (Mayor's Palace)** from the 12th and 13th centuries, and the **Torre dell'Orologio,** topped with a 14th-century astrological clock. Also on this square is Mantua's earliest religious structure, the **Rotonda di San Lorenzo,** a miniature round church from the 11th century. The city's Renaissance masterpiece, **Basilica di Sant'Andrea** (see below), is off to one side on Piazza Mantegna.

To the north, Piazza delle Erbe transforms into **Piazza Broletto** through a series of arcades; here a statue honors the poet Virgil, who was born in Mantova in 70 B.C. The next square, **Piazza Sordello,** is vast, cobbled, rectangular, and lined with medieval *palazzi* and the 13th-century Duomo. Most notable is the massive hulk of the **Palazzo Ducale** (see below), which forms the eastern wall of the piazza. To enjoy Mantua's lakeside views and walks, follow Via San Giorgio from the **Piazza Sordello** and turn right on to Lungolago dei Gonzaga, which leads back into the town center.

Tip: The **Mantova Card** costs 20€ (8€ for those ages 12 to 18) and allows access to 10 city museums and the Palazzo Ducale museums in Sabbioneta, as well as free bus transportation and discounts in various local shops. Visit **www.mantovacard.it** for more details.

Basilica di Sant'Andrea ★★ CHURCH A graceful Renaissance facade fronts this 15th-century church by architect Leon Battista Alberti. The grandest church in Mantua, it is topped by a dome added by Filippo Juvarra in the 18th century. Inside, the vast classically proportioned space is centered on the church's single aisle. Light pours in through the dome, highlighting the carefully crafted *trompe l'oeil* painting of the coffered ceiling. The Gonzagas' court painter Andrea Mantegna—creator of the Camera degli Sposi in the **Palazzo Ducale** (see below)—is buried in the first chapel on the left. The crypt houses a reliquary containing the blood of Christ, which was allegedly brought here by Longinus, the Roman soldier who thrust his spear into Jesus's side; this is processed through town on March 18, the feast of Mantua's patron, Sant'Anselmo. Piazza Mantegna. www.santandreainmantova.it. Free. Daily 8am–noon, 3–7pm.

Museo di Palazzo Ducale ★★ PALACE The massive power base of the Gonzaga dynasty spreads over the northeast corner of Mantua, incorporating Piazza Sordello, the Duomo, the Castello San Giorgio, and the Palazzo Ducale. Together they form a private city connected by corridors, courtyards, and staircases filled with Renaissance frescoes and ancient Roman sculptures. Within the walls of this fortress-cum-family-palace lies the history of Mantua's most powerful family and what remains of the treasure trove they amassed over the centuries. Between their skills as warriors and a knack for marrying into wealthier houses, the Gonzagas acquired power, money, and the services of some of the top artists of the time, including Pisanello, Titian, and Mantegna.

The most fortunate of many opportunistic unions was in 1490, between Francesco II Gonzaga and aristocratic Isabella d'Este from Ferrara. She commissioned many of the complex's art-filled apartments.

The Palazzo Ducale offers up a glorious maze of gilded, frescoed, marbled rooms, passageways, corridors, secret gardens, follies, and elaborate *intaglio* furniture. Standouts among all the excess include the Arturian legends adorning **the Sala del Pisanello**, painted by Pisanello between 1436 and 1444; the **Sale degli Arazzi** (Tapestry Rooms) hung with copies of Raphael's tapestries in the Vatican; the **Galleria degli Specchi** (Hall of Mirrors); **Appartamento dei Nani** (Apartments of the Dwarfs), where a replica of the Holy Staircase in the Vatican is built in miniature; and the **Galleria dei Mesi** (Hall of the Months). The incomparable **Camera degli Sposi,** located in the north tower of the Castello San Giorgio, is the masterpiece of Andrea Mantegna, taking 9 years to complete. Commissioned by Ludovico III Gonzaga, it features portraits of members of his family and provides an intriguing glimpse into late 15th-century court life.

Piazza Sordello, 40. www.mantovaducale.beniculturali.it. ✆ **0376-224-832.** 7.50€ for the Palazzo Ducale Museum; 12€ for the Castello San Giorgio, Corte Vecchia and Freddi Collection; 7.50€ for the Corte Vecchia and apartment of Isabella d'Este. All free on the first Sunday of every month. Tues–Sun 8:15am–7:15pm. Last entry at 6:20pm.

Palazzo Te ★★ PALACE This glorious summer palace, designed by Giulio Romano between 1525 and 1535, took a decade to complete. Built for Federico II Gonzaga, the sybaritic son of Isabella d'Este, this splendid Renaissance palace was his retreat from court life, and it was designed to indulge his obsessions. A tour leads through a series of lavishly adorned apartments, decorated by the best artists of the day. Gonzaga's enthusiasms for love and sex, astrology, and horses are evident throughout, from the almost 3-D effect in the **Hall of the Horses** to the sexually overt frescoes by Romano in the elaborate **Chamber of Amor and Psyche.** The greatest room in the palace, however, is a metaphor for Gonzaga power: In the **Sala dei Giganti (Room of the Giants),** Titan is overthrown by the gods in a dizzying display of *trompe l'oeil* that gives the illusion that the ceiling is falling inwards. The Palazzo Te is also home to the **Museo Civico,** whose collections include the Gonzaga family's coins, medallions, 20th-century portraits by Armando Spadini, and a few Egyptian artifacts.

Viale Te 13. www.palazzote.it. ✆ **0376-323-266.** 12€ adults, 8€ seniors, 4€ ages 12–18 and students, free for those under 11. Mon 1–6:30pm; Tues–Sun 9am–6:30pm (hours may be extended in summer). The palazzo is a 20-min. walk from the center along Via Principe Amedeo.

Frescoed ceilings in Mantua's Palazzo Te.

MORE MANTUA MUSEUMS

En route from the center of town to Palazzo Te, you'll pass **Casa del Mantegna ★,** the house and studio of Andrea Mantegna, now an art gallery (Via Acerbi 47, ✆ **0376-360-506;** Tues–Sun 10am–1pm, Tues–Wed 3–6pm, Sat–Sun 3–6pm; admission free). Close by in the stark white Palazzo Sebastiano, the **Museo della Città ★** (Largo XXIV Maggio 12; www.museodellacitta.mn.it; ✆ **0376-367-087**; Mon 1–6pm, Tues–Sun 9am–6pm; admission 12€) gallops through the history of Mantua. Among its many architectural fragments is an impressive bust of Francesco Gonzaga, who commissioned the palace in 1507.

Just to the left of the Palazzo Ducale's main entrance, in the old market hall at the corner of Piazza Sordello, the **Museo Archeologico Nazionale di Mantova** houses in one giant space all sorts of local discoveries of Bronze Age, Greek, Etruscan, and Roman pottery, glassware, and utensils (www.museoarcheologicomantova.beniculturali.it; ✆ **0376-320-003;** admission 4€, age 17 and under free; Nov–Mar Tues–Sun 8:30am–1:30pm; Apr–Oct Tues, Thurs, Sat 2–7pm, Wed, Fri, Sun 8:30am–1:30pm.).

The lovely baroque interior of the **Teatro Bibiena ★★** is also worth a peek for its rows of luxurious boxes. Find it at Via Accademia 47

(✆ **0376-327-653;** admission 2€, 17 and under free; Tues–Sun 10am–1pm and 3–6pm, except Sat–Sun 10am–6pm mid-Mar to mid-Nov.)

For a change of pace—if you can catch it open, which is usually on weekends—the **Galleria Storica dei Vigili del Fuoco** (Fire Engine Museum) ★ at Largo Vigili del Fuoco 1 (www.museovigilidelfuoco.it; ✆ **0376-227-71**) has plenty of historic engines to distract from ancient art. Call beforehand to check opening times.

Where to Eat & Stay

Like Milan, Mantua sees many expense-account business travelers during the week, with families and tourists flocking in for the weekends and over summer, so book rooms in the town center well ahead of time.

Caffè Modi ★ ITALIAN Named for the artist Amedeo Modigliani, whose moody portrait dominates the restaurant, Modi is a friendly stop on the tourist circuit around Piazza Sordello. It may not look like much from the outside, but once inside it's a pleasant surprise. Chill music, gramophones, and threadbare armchairs lend a bohemian charm to the place. The menu offers the usual lineup of local pasta dishes (like pumpkin tortellini in a butter sage sauce) along with *insalatone* (big salads), but it's all well presented and tasty. If the place is quiet, the lovely, laid-back owner will come and chat—mostly about her enthusiasm for the works of Modigliani. In warm weather, grab a table outside.

Via San Giorgio 4. ✆ **0376-181-0111.** Main courses 10€–17€. Wed–Mon noon–midnight, sometimes later on weekends.

Lo Scalco Grasso ★★ MODERN ITALIAN This contemporary bistro with minimalist decor is owned by a young chef who likes to push boundaries. It's a sophisticated choice: The restaurant offers a modern take on classic dishes from Mantua alongside creative plates—the common theme is a focus on quality and seasonality. Expect beautifully crafted dishes featuring vegetables—local pasta stuffed with squash, delicate risotto, or perhaps a superb chickpea soup flavored with squid—alongside menu items like tartare of veal, beef cheek, and local delicacy *stracotto d'asino* (donkey stew). Lovely wines are available by the glass or bottle, and little bites of specialties are happily produced for guests to sample before ordering. The space is small so reservations are a must.

Via Trieste 55. ✆ **349-374-7958.** Main courses 18€–30€. Tues–Sat noon–2:30pm and 7:30–10pm; Mon 7:30–10pm (later on weekends).

Osteria dell'Oca ★★★ LOMBARDY The restaurant "of the goose" is crammed nightly with locals enjoying vibrant cooking at truly amazing prices. This is a rustic family-run Italian restaurant at its very best: noisy, happy, and joyous. Some of the best dishes on the menu are the sharing plates of *peccati di gola* ("forbidden delights"), local salamis and pancetta with a wedge of creamy polenta, lard, and beetroot salsa. If you are looking for true local specialties, try the pumpkin pasta with butter and sage or *agnoli* (like a tortellini) pasta in broth with a splash of wine. Only three wines are served, in thick carafes. Opt for the white from local vineyards rather than the *lambrusco,* which is quite sweet. This generous outpouring of food is rounded off with complimentary coffees and the thick hazelnut *digestivo della casa*. Reservations recommended.

Via Trieste 10. www.osteriadellocamantova.com. ✆ **0376-327-171.** Main courses 12€–17€. Wed–Sat and Mon 12:15–2:30pm and 7:15–11:30pm; Sun 12:15–2:30pm.

Casa Poli ★★★ Hidden behind the facade of a 19th-century mansion, this boutique hotel, which aims to offer the "elegance of a hotel, and the atmosphere of home," is packed nightly with both business and leisure travelers. It's easy to see why. Guest rooms are spotless and chicly pared down in contemporary style, with funky lights, bright splashes of color, and equally cool bathrooms. The lounge is full of arty books, and the summer courtyard is a great spot to while away an hour over an evening *aperitivo*. The breakfast buffet is abundant and of higher quality than what you find in many Italian hotels. It's the staff that really makes this place shine; they're chatty and informal, and willing to go the extra mile to please guests.

Corso Garibaldi 32. www.hotelcasapoli.it. ✆ **0376-288-170.** 27 units. 105€–170€ double, includes breakfast. **Amenities:** Bar; concierge; Wi-Fi (free).

Residenza Bibiena ★★ Tucked away in a pretty corner of Mantua's *centro storico* 5 minutes from the Palazzo Ducale, this cozy B&B, located in a traditional townhouse, has a pleasing air of old-school charm. The rooms are simply furnished with wooden furniture and tiled floors enlivened by warm color schemes and pretty linens. A buffet breakfast is served in the property's hall. There are now also four additional rooms at the Residenza Bibiena Deluxe (featuring slightly more modern accommodations, especially the bathrooms), a few doors down at Piazza Arche 8. Some of the rooms in these two properties have terraces and even lake views.

Piazza Arche, 5. www.residenzabibiena.it. ✆ **331-508-0876.** 8 units between the two properties. 80€ double. Rates include breakfast. **Amenities:** Wi-Fi (free).

Shopping & Entertainment

The favored shopping streets in Mantua radiate off Piazza delle Erbe, a delightful cluster of cobbled and arcaded streets sheltering delis stuffed with local cheeses, hams, fresh pasta, and olive oils. **Corso Umberto, Via Verdi,** and **Via Oberdan** are lined with posh boutiques, smart shoe shops, and bookstores. There's a **farmers' market** on Lungorio IV di Novembre on Saturday, and come lunchtime the lines outside the delicatessens form as happy patrons leave with beautifully packaged goodies. It's perfect fodder for a picnic in the lakeside gardens along Lungolago dei Gonzaga.

Mantua is a cultured city with ample theater and classical concerts; there are regular recitals at cute little **Teatro Bibiena** (see p. 491) and a full program of films and concerts at **Mantova Teatro** in the Piazza Cavallotti (www.teatrosocialemantova.it). A chamber-music festival is held every May, and the **Festivaletteratura** literature festival is a poplar draw in September.

LAKE COMO ★★★

Como (town): 65km (40 miles) NE of Milan; Menaggio: 35km (22 miles) NE of Como and 85km (53 miles) N of Milan; Varenna: 50km (31 miles) NE of Como and 80km (50 miles) NE of Milan

Life is slower around the northern Italian lakes than in fast-paced Milan. The city of Como is an ideal base for drawing breath and kicking back. Sitting on the southwestern tip of Lake Como, the city is essentially a center of commerce with a miniscule medieval quarter and a pretty waterfront. Tourists flock to Como for its ancient heritage, fine churches, and lake views. From here, frequent ferry service hops around the lake, visiting its many romantic lakeshore villas and villages.

Essentials

GETTING THERE **Trains** run from Milan's Stazione Central and Porta Garibaldi half-hourly to Como San Giovanni; the trip takes 1 hour and costs 4.80€. One-hour trains from Milan Cadorna arrive at Como Nord Lago (just off the lakefront promenade, near the ferry point) and cost 4.80€.

VISITOR INFORMATION The **regional tourist office** at Piazza Cavour 17 (www.lakecomo.com; ✆ **031-269-712**) has info on hotels, restaurants, and campgrounds around the lake. The office is open Monday to Saturday 9am to 1pm and 2 to 5pm. You'll also find tourist offices open in summer in several of the small towns around the lake; in **Tremezzo** at Via Regina 3 (✆ **0344-40-493**); in **Varenna** at Via IV Novembre 7 (www.varennaturismo.com; ✆ **0341-830-367**); and in **Bellagio** at Piazza Mazzini (www.bellagiolakecomo.com; ✆ **0341-950-204**).

GETTING AROUND Como is the jumping-off point for most adventures on Lake Como, which is criss-crossed by regular **ferry routes:** It takes 4 hours to travel from one end to the other, with many stops along the way. The most popular are **Tremezzo, Menaggio, Bellagio,** and timeless **Varenna** (see p. 496). Single fares from Como are 10.40€ to Bellagio; a day pass costs 23.30€. Tickets cannot be purchased online. The ferry terminal, run by **Navigazione Lago di Como,** is on the esplanade at Via per Cernobbio 18 (www.navigazionelaghi.it; ✆ **800-551-801**).

Como ★★

Como's tiny *centro storico* is dominated by the flamboyant **Duomo ★★** (Piazza Duomo; www.cattedraledicomo.it; ✆ **031-331-2275**), which combines Gothic and Renaissance architecture for two very different facades; long, narrow windows and a Gothic stained-glass rose window mark the western end, with a seamless apse and baroque dome added in 1744 by architect Filippo Juvarra at the eastern end. The Duomo is free, and open daily 7:30am to 7:30pm (Sun from 7:30am to 9:30pm).

Two blocks south of the Duomo, the 12th-century **San Fedele ★** basilica (www.parrocchiasanfedelecomo.it; free admission; daily 8am–noon, 3:30–7pm), stands above a charming square of the same name. Parts of the five-sided church, including the altar, date from the 6th century, and there are some fine frescoes along the right-hand side aisle.

Como's main street, **Corso Vittorio Emanuele II,** cuts through the medieval quarter and has plenty of upmarket boutiques and classy delis. If you have time, take the 10-minute **funicular ride** from Lungo Lario Trieste up to hilltop **Brunate ★★,** which has a cluster of excellent restaurants and bars. The funicular runs up a steep cliffside, with glorious views of Lake Como glinting below; at the top are wooded hiking trails that lead up to Bellagio. The funicular ticket office is at Piazza de Gasperi 4 (www.funicolarecomo.it; ✆ **031-303-608;** daily 6am–10:30pm; funicular runs until midnight on Sat and in summer). Tickets are 3€ adults, 2€ for kids under 12 (children under 110cm in height travel free). Trains depart from both ends of the line every 30 minutes.

Lake Como's Waterfront Villages

The romantic waterfront villages of Lake Como, with their cute clusters of yellow and pink houses, majestic *palazzos,* and lush lakeside gardens, are easily explored by ferry (see p. 499) or by car. Here are a few of the highlights, going clockwise round the lake.

LENNO ★★★ For centuries Lake Como was the playground of privileged Lombardian aristocrats, and quite honestly, not much has changed. **Villa del Balbianello** at Lenno (Via Comoedia 5; www.visitfai.it/villadelbalbianello; ✆ **0344-56-110**) is one of the best-known of their fabulous villas, with ornate landscaped gardens and a 16th-century palace sitting high on a peninsula over the lake. (You may recognize it from its recent brush with fame in the Bond movie *Casino Royale*.) The interior is full of priceless French furniture complemented by eclectic artwork from the travels of its former owner, explorer Guido Monzino, who died in 1988 and left the villa to the Italian National Trust. Garden entrance is 10€ adults, 5€ children 4 to 12; garden and villa (with compulsory 60-minute tour) is 20€ adults, 10€ children 4 to 12. It is a bit of a walk to reach the villa from the center of Lenno, so if you'd like to take a boat across the lake and be let out right at the villa's dock, the cost is about 8€ roundtrip. It's open mid-March to mid-November 10am to 6pm (closed Mon and Wed).

Varenna, one of Lake Como's charming villages.

TREMEZZO ★★ On the western side of Lake Como, Tremezzo was the 19th-century retreat of the Italian aristocracy; today it is lorded over by the exceptionally expensive **Grand Hotel Tremezzo** (www.grandhoteltremezzo.com; ✆ **0344-42-491**) and its wonderfully stylish beach. The plush gardens, museum, and rich art collections of the ornate 17th-century **Villa Carlotta** are open to the public (Via Regina 2; www.villacarlotta.it; ✆ **0344-404-05;** 10€ adults, 8€ seniors, 6€ students; open late Mar to mid-Oct 9am–7:30pm [last entry 6pm]; late Oct to mid-Mar 10am–6pm [last entry 5pm], though hours can vary over holiday weekends).

BELLANO ★ Most people stop in Bellano on the eastern shores of Lake Como to visit the **Orrido** (✆ **338-5246-716;** 3€ adults, 2.50€ seniors and under 14), a deep gorge cut out of the cliffs by the River Pioverna as it tears down the hillside. A nighttime trip down the floodlit gorge is a rare and eerie treat, and one that appears to be under threat from hydroelectric plans expected to reduce the flow of the torrent. Opening times vary seasonally but are roughly April to June and September 10am to 1pm and 2:30 to 7pm; and July to August 10am to 7pm and 8:45 to 10pm.

VARENNA ★★★ Adorable Varenna gives Bellagio a run for its money as the prettiest village on Lake Como, with a tumble of pink and terracotta houses in a labyrinth of narrow, cobbled streets, and smart villas clustered around the shoreline. Its winding lakeside path hangs over the water, with bars, shops, and art galleries looking over the lake. Linger a while over a glass of Prosecco and watch the sun go down over the glittering water.

BELLAGIO ★★★ Photogenic Bellagio is the most popular destination around Lake Como and has just about remained on the right side of overtly touristic. The shady lakefront promenade is lined with chic hotels, bars, and cafes. Pretty medieval alleyways ascend from the lake in steep steps and are lined with souvenir stores selling pricey handmade leather accessories. Regardless of the multitude of tourists, this is still a lovely place to linger for lunch overlooking the lake.

Where to Eat & Stay

With Como's fame has come a paucity of decent moderately priced hotels, although there are still plenty of options around the lake. If you're looking for a splurge, Cernobbio is home to one of Italy's most exclusive and expensive hotels: the **Villa d'Este** (see below). The local cuisine draws heavily on the lake, and polenta is as popular here as pasta.

The colorful streets of Bellagio.

Da Pietro ★★ PASTA/PIZZA Como's gorgeous Piazza del Duomo has a strip of restaurants all in a row that are fairly interchangeable, but Da Pietro makes for a nice family pit stop for a lunch or dinner of decently cooked pasta or vast, crisp pizzas. It's also a good spot if you just want a coffee in the day or an aperitivo in the early evening. Here you are paying for the view of the Duomo and a scene that is buzzing night and day.

Piazza Duomo 16, Como. ✆ **031-264-005.** Main courses around 12€. Daily 11am–3pm and 6:30–11pm.

Splendide Ristorante ★★★ REGIONAL ITALIAN You would be hard-pressed to find a prettier spot on the whole of Lake Como than this geranium-filled terrace of the Hotel Excelsior Splendide in Bellagio. Perched over the shimmering waters of the lake, the restaurant showcases local dishes, from polentas and pasta to prawns sizzled in garlic, and fresh lake trout. If you are looking for a quick meal, coffee, or gelato, you can also stop in at the hotel's lounge, which also offers wonderful views from the veranda. Via Lungo Lario Manzoni 28, Bellagio. www.hsplendide.com. ✆ **031-950-225.** Main courses 10€–40€. Mar–Nov noon–2:30pm.

La Polenteria ★★★ REGIONAL ITALIAN The ethos behind La Polenteria is to utilize whatever is in season; be it snails, venison, wild boar, and fish fresh from the lake to porcini mushrooms, or, in fall, pasta flavored with chestnuts or chocolate. You may find the occasional soup on the menu, but beyond the regional specialty polenta that accompanies many of the dishes (as the name of the restaurant suggests), vegetarians may find they have little to choose from here. All desserts are homemade. Booking is advisable because this restaurant, despite only being open on weekends, is often full, and is off the beaten path. Via Scalini, 66, Brunate. www.lapolenteria.it. ✆ **031-336-5105.** Main courses 8€–30€. Fri 7:15–10:30pm, Sat–Sun 12:15pm–2:30pm, 7:30–10:30pm.

Hotel du Lac ★★ With one entrance right on Varenna's charming waterfront and the other hidden away in its equally photogenic tangle of alleyways, the Hotel du Lac is housed in an elegant 19th-century villa offering prized views across Lake Como. The romantic theme continues inside with marble pillars and wrought-iron staircases, roomy (for Europe) bedrooms decked out in white with touches of green, gold, and red, and modern bathrooms. Via del Prestino 11, Varenna. www.albergodulac.com. ✆ **0341-830-238.** 16 units. Doubles 190€–280€ Rates include breakfast. Closed mid-Nov to Feb. **Amenities:** Restaurant (lunch only); bar; Wi-Fi (free).

Hotel Paradiso sul Lago ★★★ This great *albergo* has had a total overhaul and is now powered by voltaic panels, making it one of the first eco-hotels around Lake Como. Right at the top of the village of Brunate above Como town, it's in a little *piazza* surrounded by restaurants and is on the edge of pleasingly untamed countryside. The rooms are simple, clean, and functional, but the main selling points are the amazing hilltop views over Lake Como from some of the guest rooms, the breakfast room, and the panoramic terrace with swimming pool and Jacuzzi. The drive up the hill is a bit tricky, but you can always take the cable car. Be sure to book a room with lake views. Via Scalini 7, Brunate. www.hotelparadisocomo.com. ✆ **031-364-099.** 12 units. 120€–169€ double, includes breakfast. **Amenities:** Restaurant; cafe; bar; outdoor pool; shuttle service; Wi-Fi (free).

Nest on the Lake ★★ This cute little B&B is in a tranquil lakeside spot in Lezzeno, minutes from Bellagio. Bedrooms are a calming white;

some have fourposter beds and all have wrought-iron balconies. A decent self-service breakfast is offered, and owners Raffa and Costantino are incredibly helpful, always at the ready to recommend restaurants and organize tours. A self-catering apartment sleeps up to four people. The minimum stay is 3 nights in summer. The town of Lezzeno is a great base for taking hikes and getting out on the lake for waterskiing and wakeboarding.

Via Sostra 17/19, Lezzeno. www.nestonthelake.com. ✆ **031-914-372.** 5 units. 100–110€ double, includes breakfast. 120€–140€ apartment. **Amenities:** Solarium; Wi-Fi (free).

Villa d'Este ★★ Set in an ornate Renaissance *palazzo* dating from 1568 and overlooking the water amid verdant parklands, the Villa d'Este is quintessential Lake Como. This property sees a constant procession of major celebs and minor royalty arriving by speedboat or helicopter to luxuriate in the abundance of sports facilities, the array of fine dining options, and refined rooms furnished with priceless antiques. As befits one of the most exclusive hotels in the world, two revamped private villas guarantee complete seclusion from the hoi polloi.

Via Regina 40, Cernobbio. www.villadeste.com. ✆ **031-3481.** 152 units. 500€–760€ double; 880€–990€ junior suite, includes breakfast. Closed mid-Nov to mid-Mar. **Amenities:** 3 restaurants; 3 bars; nightclub; indoor and outdoor pools; spa; concierge; Wi-Fi (free).

LAKE MAGGIORE ★★

Stresa: 90km (56 miles) NW of Milan

Maggiore lies west of Como, a long, thin wisp of a lake protected by mountains and fed by the River Ticino, which flows on to Milan. Roughly a quarter of the northern section of the lake stands in Switzerland, including the city of Locarno and its delightful satellite resort of Ascona. **Stresa** is the largest town on the Italian side, a timeless resort on the western shoreline, famed for its setting opposite the **Isole Borromee.** Regular **ferries** span Maggiore, with frequent stops on the way from **Arona,** south of Stresa; the most popular include **Luino** for its massive market, and **Laveno** for cable-car rides up to mountain peaks (see p. 503).

ESSENTIALS

GETTING THERE Stresa is linked with Milan Stazione Centrale and Porta Garibaldi by 20 **trains** a day. Journeys take about an hour and cost 8.60€.

Boats arrive at and depart from Piazza Marconi, Stresa. Many lakeside spots can be reached from Stresa, with most boats on the lake

Isola Bella, Lake Maggiore.

operated by **Navigazione Laghi** (www.navlaghi.it; ✆ **800-551-801**). The lake's main ferry office, however, is at the lake's southern tip in **Arona,** at Viale Baracca 1; from there, ferries to Stresa take 40 minutes and cost 6.20€.

The A8 runs west from Milan to Sesto Calende, near the southern end of the lake; from there, follow Route SS33 up the western shore to Stresa. The trip takes just over an hour, but much longer with summer traffic.

VISITOR INFORMATION Stresa's **tourist office** is at the ferry dock on Piazza Marconi (www.stresaturismo.it; ✆ **0323-30-150**) and is open daily 10am to 12:30pm and 3 to 6:30pm (mid-Oct to mid-Mar closed Sat afternoons and Sun). For hiking information, ask for the booklet "Percorsi Verdi."

Stresa & the Islands

The biggest town on the Italian side of Maggiore, elegant Stresa is the springboard to the Isole Borromee (Borromean Islands), the tiny baroque jewels of the lake. Now a genteel tourist town, Stresa captured the hearts of 19th-century aristocracy, who settled in grandiose villas strung along the promenade. Just back into the tangle of medieval streets, **Piazza Cadorna** is a mass of restaurants that spill out into the center of the square in summer. There's a food and craft market on summer Thursday afternoons on the promenade, and a lido and beach club on the lakefront.

The three **Isole Borromee** (www.isoleborromee.it) are named for the aristocratic Borromeo family who has owned them since the 12th century. Public **ferries** leave for the islands every half-hour from Stresa's Piazza Marconi; a 17€ **daily pass** is the most economical way to visit the Bella, Pescatori, and Madre islands all in one day.

ISOLA DEI PESCATORI ★★ Pescatori is stuck in a medieval time warp, with ancient fishermen's' houses clustered together on every inch of the tiny island. Wander the cobbled streets as they reveal tiny churches, art galleries, souvenir shops, pizza and pasta restaurants, and, at every turn, a glimpse of the lake beyond. It's an entrancing place to explore, but be warned: The prices are extortionate and the crowds frustrating.

ISOLA BELLA ★★★ The minute islet of Bella is dominated by the massive baroque **Palazzo Borromeo** with its formal Italianate gardens. It makes for an absorbing tour, with conspicuous displays of wealth evident in the rich decor and exquisite furnishings. The terraced gardens are dotted with follies and have spectacular views across Maggiore. Of special interest are the ornate grottoes where the Borromeos went to stay cool, or the painting gallery, hung with 130 of the most important works the Borromeos collected over the centuries. Admission is 16€ adults and 8.5€ ages 6 to 15, which includes admission to the gardens and the painting gallery. It's open mid-March to mid-October 9am to 5:30pm.

ISOLA MADRE ★★ The largest and most peaceful of the islands is Isola Madre (30 min. from Stresa), overspread with exquisite flora in the 3.2-hectare (8-acre) **Orto Botanico.** Pick up a map at the ticket office to identify all the rhododendrons, camellias, and ancient wisteria. Many a peacock and fancy pheasant stalk across the lawns of another 16th-century **Borromeo palazzo,** which is filled with family memorabilia and some interesting old puppet-show stages. Admission to the garden and palace is 13€ adults and 6.5€ ages 6 to 15. It's open March to October 9am to 5:30pm.

Around Lake Maggiore

Beyond Stresa, Maggiore offers natural beauty and architectural wonders as well as lively towns, markets, and cable car rides up into the mountains.

ARONA ★★ As well as having the lake's main ferry office (see p. 500), this sophisticated town at the southern end of Lake Maggiore is a shopping magnet, with its charming **Via Cavour** lined with elegant boutiques and expensive delicatessens. The giant bronze **statue of Carlo Borromeo** (see p. 467), who was born in Arona in 1538, is located just outside of town. It's so huge, you can even climb inside and gaze out at the lake through Carlo's eyes (www.statuasancarlo.it; ✆ **0322-249-669;** admission 6€; mid-Mar to Oct daily 9am–noon and 2–6pm, open all day Sun).

Massive bronze statue of San Carlo Borromeo, erected between 1614 and 1698 in Arona.

LUINO ★★ On the western shore of Lake Maggiore just a few miles from the Swiss border, Luino is home of one of northern Italy's most popular **street markets**, with more than 350 stalls taking over the town every Wednesday. Here you'll find spices, piles of salami, grappas, olive oils, as well as the hand-tooled leather belts and bags for which the region is famous. Visitors from Milan can catch the train to Luino from Milan's Stazione Centrale or Stazione Porta Garibaldi in under 2 hours (7.90€), while extra ferries (www.navlaghi.it) serve the town every Wednesday.

Italy's Medieval Oligarchs

The all-powerful Borromeo family were Lombardian aristocrats who loomed large in Milanese politics and religion for 200 years. They regarded the vast tracts of land around the southern end of Lake Maggiore as their personal fiefdom, where they built castles, monuments, and palaces. The family spawned several archbishops of Milan, including Federico (1564–1631) and Carlo (1538–1584), a singularly wily individual who was canonized in 1610 for his support of the Counter-Reformation against papal infallibility. A great bronze statue of Carlo stands in Arona, looking out across the lake to his former family home, Rocca Borromeo at Angera.

SASSO DEL FERO ★★★ East of Laveno, make for Laveno Mombello, and take the 16-minute **cable-car** trip (www.funiviedellagomaggiore.it; ✆ **0332-668-012;** 10€ roundtrip) up the lush Val Cuvia to the Poggia Sant'Elsa viewpoint atop **Sasso del Ferro**, towering 1,062m (3,484 ft.) over Lake Maggiore. You'll find truly breathtaking panoramas, looking west to the snow-capped Alps or south over the lakes Varese, Monate, and Comabbio. If the conditions are right, there'll be plenty of paragliders, and the hills are traversed with hiking trails. Leave time to relax over a prosecco in the **Ristorante Albergo Funivia** (see below). Times vary according to the weather, but the cable car generally runs April to October (Mon–Fri 11am–6:30pm; Sat–Sun 11am–10:30pm).

SANTA CATERINA DEL SASSO BALLARO ★★★ Just south of Reno on the southeastern leg of Maggiore, beneath an inconspicuous car park in Piazza Cascine del Quiquio, an elevator descends to the magical hermitage of **Santa Caterina del Sasso Ballaro** (Via Santa Caterina 13, Leggiuno; www.santacaterinadelsasso.com; ✆ **0332-647-172).** Founded in the 13th century, this Dominican monastery sits photogenically against a sheer rock face, clinging to an escarpment 15m (49 ft.) above the lake. The serene complex of soft pink stone is embellished with Renaissance arches and pretty cobbled courtyards. Don't miss the 14th-century frescoes of biblical scenes in the chapel, which were hidden under lime during the Italian suppression of the monasteries in the 1770s and only rediscovered in 2003. The gift shop sells honey, candles, and soaps made by the monks. Admission is free, but donations are accepted (open Apr–Oct 9am–noon and 2:30–6pm, Nov–Mar Sat–Sun 9am–noon and 2–5pm).

Where to Eat & Stay

There are many hotels scattered around Maggiore eager to grab the tourist dollar: some good, some bad, many indifferent. The two listed here are exceptional, at opposite ends of the price spectrum. Just like the hotels in the area, food quality varies wildly; pick your restaurants in touristy Stresa with care.

Albergo Funivia ★★ This basic hotel located on the Poggia Sant'Elsa belvedere is only accessible by the Sasso del Ferro cable car (see above). What it lacks in charm, it makes up for in beautiful views over Lake Maggiore towards the Alps from the balconies in every room. It's best for summer visits when good weather is almost guaranteed. The restaurant serves a simple local menu and the terrace is always packed on sunny days. Little can beat sitting out there after dark and watching the lights around the lake glittering in the distance.

Via Tinelli, 15, Località Poggio Sant Elsa, Laveno Mombello. www.funiviedellagomaggiore.it. ✆ **0332-610-303.** 14 units. Doubles 100–120€. Rates include breakfast. **Amenities:** Bar; restaurant; Wi-Fi (free).

Grand Hotel des Iles Borromee ★★★ The vast, over-the-top Belle Epoque exterior of this majestic old hotel in Stresa faces Lake Maggiore with its manicured and landscaped gardens. The interior lives up to the exterior, too; all is hushed, ornate, and gilded, opulent as a mini-Versailles. Doubles with garden views are (relatively) staidly decorated with plush marble bathrooms, while the fabulously glitzy Hemingway Suite (the famous writer actually stayed there twice—once right after the war and again in 1948), which includes three bedrooms, a living room, four bathrooms, and a terrace overlooking the lake, is almost blinding in its marble, silk, stucco, and gilt design. There's a blissful spa and a gourmet restaurant with a lakeview terrace.

Corso Umberto I 67, Stresa. www.borromees.it. ✆ **0323-938-938.** 172 units. 185€–410€ double; 400€–3,300€ suite. Rates include breakfast. **Amenities:** Restaurant; bar; concierge; spa; sauna; indoor pool; 2 outdoor pools; personal trainer; gym; helicopter pad; Wi-Fi (free).

Ristorante Piemontese ★★ NORTHERN ITALIAN This fine-dining restaurant is definitely a cut above the myriad pasta/pizza places that haunt the town center. This is where all the Italian locals go to dine in Stresa. Here, the Bellossi family is serious about food and wine, with a focus on Piedmontese ingredients and wine, as the name would suggest. Dishes such as porcini risotto, a snail omelet, fresh pasta with meat sauce, and duck confit are presented in elegant and romantic surroundings, with fish and game options changing according to season. Finish off with a selection of pungent local cheeses. In warmer months, you can dine outside in a shaded courtyard.

Via Mazzini 25, Stresa. www.ristorantepiemontese.com. ✆ **0323-302-35.** Main courses 12€–28€. Tues–Sun 7:30–10:30pm. Closed Dec–Jan.

Ristorante Verbano ★★ SEAFOOD Although many of the restaurants on the Isole Borromee are overpriced and underwhelming, Verbano is the exception. For once on this touristy little island, the service is exemplary; you won't feel rushed and the waitstaff is courteous and informed. Its position is sublime, overlooking Isola Bella's Palazzo Borromeo (see p. 501), with lake waters lapping around the terrace—this would make a romantic proposal spot—and the food is pretty good, too. Chef Patrick Merletti puts the focus on traditional Italian dishes while relying on modern cooking techniques. As one would expect, lake fish is heavily featured on the menu here. The restaurant is a popular spot for wedding receptions and special events, so make sure to call ahead to reserve (also because if you aren't already on the island, you'll need to take a ferry or reserve a taxi boat to get there).

Via Ugo Ara 2, Isola Pescatori. www.hotelverbano.it. ✆ **0323-304-08.** Main courses 15€–30€. Daily noon–2:30pm and 7–10pm (winter closed Wed). Closed Jan.

LAKE GARDA (LAGO DI GARDA) ★★

Sirmione: 130km (81 miles) E of Milan, 150km (93 miles) W of Venice; Riva del Garda: 170km (105 miles) NE of Milan, 199km (123 miles) NW of Venice

Lake Garda is the largest and easternmost of the northern Italian lakes, with its western flanks lapping against the flat plains of Lombardy and its southern extremes in the Veneto. In the north, its deep waters are backed by Alpine peaks. Garda's shores are green and fragrant with flowery gardens, groves of olives and lemons, and forests of pines and cypress.

Lake Garda and the Sarca River.

Essentials

GETTING THERE Regular **trains** run from Milan Stazione Centrale and stops at Desenzano del Garda (fares start at 9.20€). From here it's a 20-minute bus ride to Sirmione; buses make the trip every half-hour for 2€).

Hydrofoils and ferries operated by **Navigazione Laghi** (www.navlaghi.it; ✆ **800-551-801**) ply the waters of the lake. One to two hourly ferries connect Sirmione with Desenzano del Garda in season (20 min. by ferry, 3€); less frequently October to April.

Sirmione is just off the A4 between Milan and Venice. From Venice the trip takes about 1½ hours, and from Milan a little over an hour. There's ample parking in Piazzale Monte Baldo.

VISITOR INFORMATION **Sirmione**'s tourist office is at Viale Marconi 8 (www.comune.sirmione.bs.it; ✆ **030-374-8721**). There is also a tourism kiosk at Viale Marconi 2 just before the bridge into the old part of town. In **Riva del Garda**, the tourist office is on the lakefront at Largo Medaglie d'Oro 5 (www.gardatrentino.it/en; ✆ **0464-554-444**). There's also a tourist office in **Gardone Riviera** at Corso Repubblica 8 (✆ **030-3748-736**). For all, hours vary depending on the season.

GETAWAY TO gardone RIVIERA

Halfway up the western shore of Lake Garda, this little resort—easily accessible by ferry or bus from Desenzano del Garda—offers visitors a gorgeous backdrop for a little relaxation. Oleanders dot the paved promenade, and the charming *centro storico* (Gardone Sopra) is filled with enticing bars and restaurants.

Uphill from Gardone Sopra, the **Heller Garden** (Via Roma 2; www.hellergarden.com; ✆ **0336-410-877**) is a tropical paradise founded by Arthur Hruska, a botanist who was also dentist to the ill-fated Tsar Nicholas II of Russia. Hruska planted this botanical haven in the 1900s, and 8,000 rare palms, orchids, and tree ferns now thrive here, thanks to the town's mild, sheltered climate. Today the gardens are curated by Austrian artist André Heller, whose sculptures can be found scattered among the water features, cacti, and bamboo copses. The garden is open March to October daily from 9am to 7pm; admission is 11€, 5€ for ages 6 to 11.

Gardone Riviera's other highlight is the **Vittoriale degli Italiani** (Via Vittoriale 12; www.vittoriale.it; ✆ **0365-296-511**), the wildly ostentatious and bizarrely decorated villa home of Gabriele d'Annunzio, Italy's most notorious poet and sometime war hero. He bought this hillside estate in 1921 and died here in 1936; a visit pays tribute to d'Annunzio's hedonistic lifestyle rather than his fairly awful poetry. The claustrophobic rooms of this madcap mansion are stuffed with bric-a-brac and artifacts from his colorful life, including mementos of his long affair with actress Eleonora Duse. The patrol boat D'Annunzio commanded in World War I, a museum containing his biplane and photos, and the poet's hilltop mausoleum are all found in the formal gardens that cascade down the hillside. The villa is open daily; in summer from 9am to 8pm and winter from 9am to 5pm. Admission ranges from 8€ to 16€, depending on which parts you visit. Children 6 and under enter for free. Tours are available in Italian only.

Sirmione

Perched on a promontory swathed in cypress and olive groves on the southernmost edge of Lake Garda, photogenic Sirmione has been a popular spot since the Romans first discovered hot springs here. Despite the onslaught of summer visitors, this historic town manages to retain its charm. Sirmione has lakeside promenades and pleasant beaches and is small enough for everything to be accessible on foot. It is chiefly famous for its thermal springs, castle, and northern Italy's largest Roman ruins.

The moated, fortified **Rocca Scaligera ★★★** (✆ **030-916-468**) was built on the peninsula's narrowest point and today dominates the *centro storico*. Built in the late 13th century by the Della Scala family, who ruled Verona and many of the lands surrounding the lake, the castle is worth a visit for its sweeping courtyards, turreted towers, dungeons, and views across Lake Garda. It's open Tuesday to Saturday 8:30am to 7:30pm, and from 8:30am to 2pm on Sundays; admission is 5€, ages 18 to 25 2.50€.

Rocca Scaligera castle in Sirmione.

From the castle, it's a 15-minute walk (or take the open-air tram from Piazza Piatti) along Via Vittorio Emanuele from the town center to the tip of Sirmione's peninsula and the **Grotte di Catullo ★★** (✆ **030-916-157**), romantically placed ruins with views across the lake. Built around A.D. 150, the remains are thought to represent two sizeable aristocratic villas. A small museum of Roman artifacts from the site includes jewelry and mosaic fragments (Piazzale Orti Manara 4; 6€ adults, 3€ 18–25; opening times vary, but are generally Apr–Sept Tues–Sat 8:30am–7:30pm, Sun 9:30am–6:30pm; Mar–Oct Tues–Sat 9am–5pm, Sun 8:30am–2pm).

The massive amusement park **Gardaland** (www.gardaland.it; ✆ **045-6449-777**) is half an hour's drive east of Sirmione at Castelnuovo del Garda. This huge resort includes two hotels and an aquarium and is generally thronged during school vacation periods, but if Disneyland-type places are your thing, you may want to check it out.

Riva del Garda

The northernmost settlement on Lake Garda is a thriving Italian town with medieval towers, Renaissance churches and *palazzi,* and narrow cobblestone streets where everyday business proceeds in its alluring way. Note that Riva del Garda becomes a cultural oasis in July, when the town hosts the international **Largo di Garda Festival** of classical music (www.mrf-musicfestivals.com). Riva del Garda's **Old Town** is pleasant, although the only notable historic attractions are the 13th-century **Torre d'Apponale** (2€, those 16 and under are free) in Piazza III Novembre, which is open in summer for visitors to climb its 165 steps for views across the lake, and the moated lakeside castle, **La Rocca.** Part of the castle now houses an unassuming civic museum (www.museoaltogarda.it ✆ **0464-573-869**; open daily 10am–6pm, closed on Mon; typically

out and about ON LAKE GARDA

Riva Del Garda's main attraction is the lake, lined with plush hotels and a waterside promenade that stretches for several miles past parks and pebbly beaches. The water is warm enough for swimming May to October, and air currents fanned by the mountains make Riva and neighboring Torbole the windsurfing capitals of Europe. Kitesurfing, kayaking, and sailing are all popular pastimes.

A convenient point of embarkation for a lake outing is the beach next to **La Rocca** castle, where you can rent rowboats or pedal boats for about 10€ per hour; from March through October, the concession is open daily 8am to 8pm.

Check out the sailing and windsurfing at **Sailing du Lac** at the luxurious **Hotel du Lac et du Parc** (see p. 509), where windsurf equipment can be rented for 52€ per day or 22€ for an hour. Lessons start at 69€ for 2 hours. Dinghy lessons are available from 69€ for 2 hours, rental from 30€ per hour. The school is open from mid-April to mid-October 8:30am to 6:30pm.

Lake Garda is also renowned for mountain biking; there are more than 80 routes around the lake and up into the Alpine foothills. At **Happy Bike,** Viale Rovereto 72 (www.happy-bike.it; ✆ **347-943-1208**, open daily 9am to 7pm), you can rent a mountain bike for 14€ per day, or grab an eco-friendly electric bike for 49€ per day.

closes in Dec, Jan, and sometimes Feb; admission 5€ adults, 3€ ages 15–26 and over 65, children 14 and under free).

Where to Stay & Eat

Sirmione and Riva del Garda have a choice of pleasant, moderately priced hotels, all of which book up quickly in July and August, when rates go up. The local cuisine features fish from the lake and lots of pasta.

Osteria Al Torcol ★★ ITALIAN Consistently regarded as *the* standout restaurant in Sirmione and one of the best on Lake Garda, Torcol serves up good strong, flavorful Italian dishes that are artfully presented. Though the food can tend toward nouvelle cuisine at times, the decor is more old-world, with a wooden interior packed with bottles of local wines (many available by the glass) and a serving staff that makes reliable suggestions. Signature dishes include fresh *tagliolini* with pistachio and shrimp as well as a choice of fresh fish of the day. Book in advance if you want to eat outside on the rustic patio or at one of the lovely tables out front.

Via San Salvatore 30, Sirmione. ✆ **030-990-4605.** Main courses 13€–30€. Open May–Sept daily 12:30–3pm, 7:30–10:30pm; Oct–Jan Sat–Sun 12:30–3pm, 7:30–10:30pm; Feb–Apr Sat–Sun 7:30–10:30pm.

Trattoria Riolet ★ ITALIAN Located a bit off the beaten path (you will need to drive there or take a trek uphill from town), this spot is as popular with Gardone locals as it is with summer visitors. The Riolet offers unsurpassed views over Lake Garda from its hilltop aerie. Although the cuisine might be basic—think pasta al pesto, chicken kebabs cooked over the open fire and served with polenta, and lots of grilled fish—everything is fresh and as tasty as could be. There's no menu and options can be limited, so take a leap of faith and follow your waiter's advice when ordering—and be sure to enjoy a carafe or two of the local wines. It can get crowded, especially when the weather is nice, so call ahead to reserve a table.
Via Fasano Sopra 47, Gardone Riviera. ✆ **0365-205-45.** Thurs–Tues 7–10:30pm. Main courses 8€–25€.

Hotel du Lac et du Parc ★★★ Set in lush gardens, this massive, family-friendly resort has swimming pools, spas, and every conceivable luxury. Leading down to a little beach at the lake, the grounds contain 33 bungalows and two luxurious blocks of apartments, still leaving ample space for the hotel. Despite the size of the property, the service still feels personal, and attention to detail can be seen everywhere. The gym, spas, and pools are spotless, the rooms are cheery and tasteful—ask for one overlooking the palm trees and rare plants of the park—and the breakfast buffet is five-star. If you find the cuisine in the **La Capannina** restaurant to be overly fussy, there are plenty of dining options in Riva del Garda itself, just a 15-minute walk away.
Via Rovereto 44, Riva del Garda. www.dulacetduparc.com. ✆ **0464-566-600.** 159 units in main hotel. 103€–229€ double; 170€–655€ suites, includes breakfast. Closed Jan to mid-Apr. **Amenities:** 2 restaurants; 3 bars; 2 outdoor pools; indoor pool; gym; spa; sauna; gardens; babysitting; kids' club; water sports; concierge; room service; Wi-Fi (free).

Hotel Eden ★ Once home of American poet Ezra Pound, this pink-stucco lakeside hotel is a stone's throw from the picturesque *centro storico* of Sirmione. Today, it has been modernized as a "design hotel." It is decked out in a bright and modern way with jazzy public spaces and vivid wallpaper; the breakfast room leads to a shady terrace overlooking the lake, and a swimming pier juts out over the water. Some rooms have splashy touches here and there to liven up the simple furnishings. Ask for a lakeview room—it can get a little noisy at night at the back of the hotel.
Piazza Carducci 19, Sirmione. www.hoteledensirmione.it. ✆ **030-916-481.** 30 units. 115€–190€ double, includes breakfast. Closed Nov–Easter. **Amenities:** Restaurant; bar; concierge; room service; Wi-Fi (free).

TURIN (TORINO) ★★★

669km (415 miles) NW of Rome, 140km (87 miles) E of Milan

It's often said that Turin is the most French city in Italy. The reason is partly historical and partly architectural. From the late 13th century until Italy's unification in 1861, Turin was the capital of the **House of Savoy.** These wealthy aristocrats were as French as they were Italian, with estates that extended into the present-day French regions of Savoy and the Côte d'Azur. Under the Savoys, Francophile 17th- and 18th-century architects razed much of the city and its Roman foundations, replacing them with broad avenues and grandiose buildings. As a result, Turin is one of Europe's great baroque cities, befitting a one-time capital of the nation. These days, thanks in part to the 2006 Winter Olympics and another makeover for the 150th anniversary of Italian unification in 2011, Turin has transformed itself from an industrial power into a vibrant city of museums, enticing cafes, beautiful squares, and designer shops. This sophisticated city is deservedly gaining a reputation as a go-to destination in northeast Italy.

Essentials

ARRIVING Domestic and international **flights** land at **Turin Airport** (www.aeroportoditorino.it; ✆ **011-567-6361**), about 13km (8 miles) northwest of Turin. Direct **trains** (www.gtt.to.it; ✆ **011-57-641**) run from the airport to GTT Dora Railway Station every 30 minutes between 5am and 11pm; the 3€ trip takes 19 minutes. **SADEM buses** (www.sadem.it) serve the airport and the main train stations, Porta Nuova and Porta Susa (40 min.; 6.50€ from the ticket office, 7.50€ on board). **Taxis** into town take about 30 minutes and cost 30€ to 50€, depending on the time of day.

Turin's main **train** station is **Stazione di Porta Nuova** on Piazza Carlo Felice. There is regular daily **Trenitalia** (www.trenitalia.com; ✆ **89-20-21**) service from Milan. The fastest trains take 1 hour, with fares averaging 29€ (though advance-purchase fares can be as low as 9€). Slower trains take up to 2 hours, with fares of 12€ to 17€. **Stazione di Porta Susa** connects Turin with local Piedmont towns and is the terminus for the TGV service to Paris; four trains a day make the trip in under 6 hours for around 98€, but there are often specials for as low as 29€ each way.

Turin's main **bus terminal** is **Autostazione Bus,** Corso Vittorio Emanuele II 131 (www.autostazionetorino.it). Buses connect Turin to Courmayeur, Aosta, Milan, and many small towns in Piedmont. A 2-hour **SADEM** (www.sadem.it) bus service to Milan Malpensa Airport costs 22€ each way.

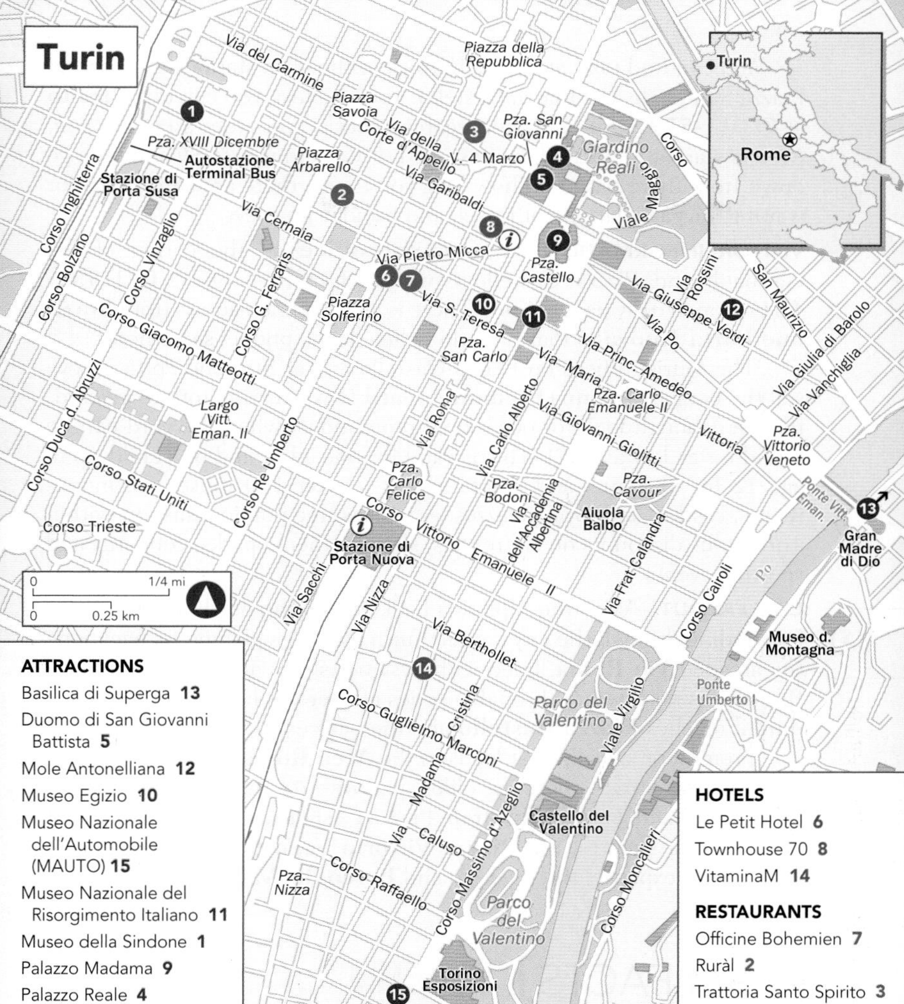

Turin is at the hub of the autostrade grid. The A4 connects Turin with Milan in 90 minutes. Journey time on the A5 to Aosta is around 90 minutes.

GETTING AROUND All the main sights of Turin are well within walking distance of each other. There's also a vast network of GTT trams and buses as well as one metro line (www.gtt.to.it; ✆ **011-57-641**). The historic Linea 7 tourist tram trundles around a circular route from Piazza Castello. Tickets on public transportation are available at newsstands for 1.50€ and are valid for 90 minutes. All-day tickets are 5€ and last 24 hours. There is no need to drive in the city center.

You can find taxis at stands in front of the train stations and around Piazza San Carlo and Piazza Castello. To call a taxi, you can dial **Pronto** at ✆ **011-5737**, but all hotel reception desks will order a taxi for you. Meters start at 3.50€ and increase by 1.44€ per km up to 8€ and then go down from there based on how long you travel; there are surcharges for waiting, luggage, late-night travel, and Sunday journeys.

VISITOR INFORMATION The **tourist office** on the corner of Via Garibaldi and Piazza Castello (www.turismotorino.org; ✆ **011-535-181**) is open daily 9am to 6pm. There is also a branch across from **Stazione Porta Nuova** in Piazza Carlo Felice (same phone; same hours).

The tourist offices on Piazza Castello and at Stazione Porta Nuova sell the bargain **Torino+Piemonte Card** (www.turismotorino.org/card) for 28€ (though look for occasional promotions, when the card can be found for as low as 23€). This is valid for one adult and one child up to age 12 for 48 hours and grants access to over 180 museums, monuments, castles, and royal palazzos, as well as free public transport within Turin, plus discounts on car rentals, ski lifts, theme parks, concerts, and sporting events.

CITY LAYOUT With the Alps as a backdrop to the north and the River Po winding through the city center, Turin has as its glamorous backbone the arcaded **Via Roma**, lined with designer shops and grand cafes. Via Roma runs northwards through a series of ever-lovelier baroque squares until it reaches **Piazza Castello** and the palaces of the Savoy nobility.

From here, a walk west leads to the **Area Romano**, a mellow jumble of narrow streets that's the oldest part of the city. Its edge is marked by Via Garibaldi. Or turn east from Piazza Castello along Via Po to one of Italy's largest squares, the **Piazza Vittorio Veneto** and, at the end of this elegant expanse, the River Po and **Parco del Valentino.**

[Fast FACTS] TURIN

ATMs/Banks There are banks with multilingual ATMs all over the city center. Opening hours are roughly Monday to Friday 8:30am to 1:30pm and 2:30 to 4:30pm.

Business Hours Stores are open Monday to Saturday from 9am to 1pm and 4 to 7:30pm.

Consulates See chapter 16.

Dentists Dr. Marco Capitanio at Via Treviso 24/G (www.marcocapitanio.com; ✆ **347-157-8802**), speaks fluent English.

Doctors The Medical Center at Corso Einaudi, 18/A (www.medical-center.it; ✆ **011-591-388**) has some English-speaking staff.

Drugstores The centrally located main pharmacy in Turin is the **Farmacia Centrale,** Corso Roma 24 (✆ **011-538-271**); it is open daily 9am to 6:30pm (closed Mon). Outside is an updated list of local drugstores with extended hours or open all night. The website **www.farmaciediturno.org** (search for Torino) gives updated opening hours of most of Turin's central pharmacies.

Emergencies All emergency numbers are free. Call ✆ **112** for a **general emergency**; this connects to the **Carabinieri,** who will transfer your call as needed; for the **police,** dial ✆ **113;** for a **medical emergency** or an ambulance, call ✆ **118;** for the **fire department,** call ✆ **115.**

Hospitals **Ospedale Mauriziano Umberto I,** Largo Filippo Turati 62 (www.mauriziano.it; ✆ **011-508-1111**).

Internet Many Turin cafes, bars, restaurants, and hotels now have Wi-Fi. Try, for example, **Busters Coffee** (www.busters coffee.it) at Via Cesare Battisti 7/L near Piazza Castello and the University of Turin, with other locations cropping up throughout the city.

Police In an emergency, call ✆ **113.** The central police station (Questura Torino) is near Stazione di Porta Susa at Corso Vinzaglio 10 (✆ **011-558-81**).

Post Office Turin's **main post office,** just west of Piazza San Carlo at Via Alfieri 10 (✆ **011-506-0265**) is open Monday to Friday 8:20am to 7:05pm and Saturday from 8:30am to 12:35pm. A list of central post offices and opening times can be found at www.poste.it/ufficio-postale.

Safety Turin is a relatively safe city, but use the same precautions you would in any large city. Avoid the riverside streets along the Po when the late-night crowds have gone home.

Palazzo Reale, Turin.

Exploring Turin

The stately arcades of **Via Roma,** Turin's premier shopping street, were designed in 1714 by Filippo Juvarra. This chic thoroughfare runs from the circular **Piazza Carlo Felice,** ringed with outdoor cafes and constructed around formal gardens, north into **Piazza San Carlo,** quite possibly Italy's most beautiful square. In summer Piazza San Carlo is Turin's harmonious outdoor *salone,* its arcaded sidewalks lined with big-name fashion stores and elegant cafes, including the genteel **Caffé Torino** (www.caffe-torino.it; ✆ **011-545-118**). In the center of the piazza prances a 19th-century equestrian statue of Duke Emanuele Filiberto of Savoy. Two 17th-century churches**, San Carlo** and **Santa Cristina**, face each other like bookends at the southern entrance to the square.

At the far north end of Via Roma, the **Piazza Castello** is dominated by **Palazzo Madama** (see p. 518), named for its 17th-century inhabitant, Christine Marie of France, who married into the Savoy dynasty in 1619. Farther north still stands the massive complex of the **Palazzo Reale** (see p. 519), residence of the Savoy dukes from 1646 to 1865.

Duomo di San Giovanni Battista ★ CHURCH One of the few pieces of Renaissance architecture in baroque-dominated Turin, this otherwise uninspiring 15th-century cathedral is famous as the resting place of the **Turin Shroud** (see below). The linen cloth is preserved in an aluminum casket in the temperature-controlled, air-conditioned **Cappella della Sacra Sindone** and closed off from human contamination (and public view) with bulletproof glass. The casket is adorned with a crown of thorns; the faithful come in droves to worship at the

History of the Turin Shroud

The Turin Shroud is allegedly the linen cloth in which Christ was wrapped when he was taken from the cross—and to which his image was miraculously affixed. The image on the cloth is of a bearded face—remarkably similar to the depiction of Christ in Byzantine icons—and a body marked with bloodstains consistent with a crown of thorns, a slash in the rib cage (made by the Roman centurion Longinus; see p. 489), what appear to be nail holes in the wrists and ankles, and scourge marks on the back from flagellation. Carbon dating results are confusing; some suggest that the shroud was manufactured around the 13th or 14th centuries, while other tests imply that those results were affected by the fire that all but destroyed it in December 1532. Regardless of scientific skepticism, the shroud continues to entice the faithful to worship at its chapel in the Duomo di San Giovanni Battista and the mystery remains unsolved—just how was that haunting image impregnated onto the cloth?

chapel, which is the last one in the left-hand aisle. To learn about the history of the shroud, head for the **Museo della Sidone** (see p. 517).
Piazza San Giovanni. www.duomoditorino.it. ✆ **011-436-1540.** Free. Mon–Fri 7am–12:30pm, 3–7pm; Sat–Sun 8am–12:30pm, 3–7pm. Bus: 11, 12, 51, 55, 56, 61, 68. Trams: 4, 13, 15, 18.

Mole Antonelliana & Museo Nazionale del Cinema ★★★ MUSEUM Turin's most peculiar building was once the tallest in Europe, begun in 1863 as a synagogue but then hijacked by the city fathers to become a monument to Italian unification (at the time, Italy was ruled by the House of Savoy from their base of power in Turin). The Mole has a squat brick base supporting several layers of pseudo-Greek columns, topped by a steep cone-like roof and a skinny spire, all of it rising 167m (548 ft.) above the streets. It is now home to Italy's National Film Museum.

Little by little, the museum is being updated with interactive displays, mobile tagging, digital captions, and augmented-reality features. The first exhibits track the intriguing development of moving pictures, from shadow puppets to risqué peep shows and flickering images of galloping horses filmed by Eadweard Muybridge in 1878. The display uses clips, stills, posters, and props to illustrate aspects of movie production, from *The Empire Strikes Back* storyboards to the creepy steady-cam work in *The Shining*. There are plenty of buttons to push and lots of hands-on action to keep kids happy.

The highlight of a visit is the ascent through the roof of the museum's vast atrium and up 85m (279 ft.) inside the tower to the 360-degree observation platform at the top. This experience affords a stunning view of the gridlike streets of Turin and its backdrop of snowy Alpine peaks. Some choose to bypass the museum and only do the panoramic elevator for a cost of 7€ (5€ if you have the Torino+Piemonte card). Lines form on weekends, so try to come early if you can.

Eataly has partnered with the museum to offer an **Eataly + Caffè Vergnano** museum café, which has the same hours as the museum and is open to the public without paying admission fees.
Via Montebello 20. www.museocinema.it. ✆ **011-8138-561.** Museum and panoramic elevator: 14€, 11€ seniors and students up to age 26, 8€ ages 6–18, free under 5. Museum only: 10€, 8€ seniors and students up to age 26, 3€ ages 6–18, free under 5. Elevator only: 7€; 5€ students, seniors, those with the Torino+Piemonte card, and ages 6–18. Tues–Fri & Sun 9am–8pm, Sat 9am–11pm. Multilingual guided tours by advance booking. Bus: 18, 55, 56, 61, 68. Tram: 13, 15, 16.

Museo Egizio (Egyptian Museum) ★★ MUSEUM Turin's magnificent Egyptian collection is one of the world's largest—no surprise, since it was also the world's *first* Egyptian museum, thanks to the Savoy kings and their explorers Bernardino Drovetti and Ernesto Schiaparelli, who voraciously hoarded Egyptian ephemera until the early 1900s, when attitudes reversed against such cultural plundering. After a massive renovation that doubled the exhibition space, there is now an innovative system of escalators to lead visitors seemingly on a path along the Nile over the three levels of displays. The layout not only reconstructs Egyptian cultural and funereal elements down to the smallest details, it also tells the history of the archeological expeditions undertaken as well as that of the museum and its collections. There are artifacts from all eras of ancient Egypt, including a papyrus "Book of the Dead." One of the most captivating exhibits is the exquisitely painted wooden sarcophagi and mummies of Kha and Merit, an aristocratic couple whose tomb was discovered in 1906. Visitors can choose from among different museum itineraries. The family tour, for example, lasts 90 minutes and includes an iPod-like device (for free with the regular price of admission) so visitors can listen to additional information at relevant stops along the way. If you reserve your visit ahead of time online, you will be able to beat the lines and crowds. Some say this is the most important collection of Egyptian artifacts outside of Cairo, so it's definitely a must-visit when in Turin.

Via Accademia delle Scienze 6. www.museoegizio.it. ✆ **011-440-6903.** 13€ adults, 9€ ages 15–18, 1€ ages 6–14, free for children 5 and under. Mon 9am–2pm, Tues–Sun 8:30am–7:30pm. Bus: 55, 56. Tram: 13.

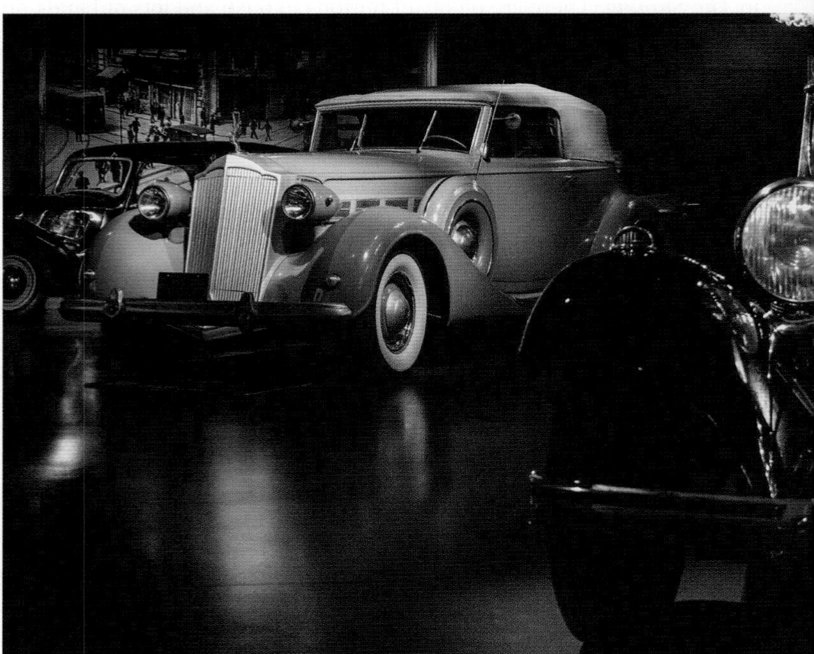

Vintage cars at the Museo Nazionale dell'Automobile.

Museo Nazionale dell'Automobile (MAUTO) ★★★ MUSEUM Not surprisingly in a city that spawned Fiat, the car is king at this whizzy, innovative museum. Located south of the Parco del Valentino, MAUTO features Alfa Romeos and lots of bright-red Ferraris with displays that start with vintage cars from the days when road travel was only for the very wealthy. The exhibition then progresses through to factory-line mass production. Displays also highlight the social, financial, and environmental impact that combustion engines have had on the planet. The different areas of the museum include "Automobiles and the 20th century," "Automobiles and Man," and "Automobiles and Design." You don't need to be a car buff to appreciate the lovely lines of a Maserati, and this is the perfect place to bring kids who have traipsed around one too many baroque *palazzo*. Is the museum has a café, a documentation center/archive, and a shop on the *piazza*—a futuristic covered courtyard that serves as the impressive entrance to the venue.

Corso Unità d'Italia 40. www.museoauto.it. ✆ **011-677-666.** 12€ adults, 8€ children 6–18 and seniors, free for children under 6. Mon 10am–2pm; Tues 2–7pm; Wed–Thurs, Sun 10am–7pm; Fri–Sat 10am–9pm. Metro: Lingotto.

Museo Nazionale del Risorgimento Italiano (National Museum of the Risorgimento) ★★★ MUSEUM On the Piazza Carignano—one of the most majestic in a city full of splendid corners—the equally handsome redbrick *palazzo* of the same name acquired huge national importance as the sometime home of Italy's first king following the country's Unification in 1861. Originally built between 1679 and 1685 by baroque maestro Guarino Guarini, the palace now houses the Museo del Risorgimento. At its heart is the ornate circular chamber where Italy's first parliament met. While this museum's focus is on days gone by, the fascinating way it presents the past is quite innovative for an Italian museum. There's a refreshing amount of multilingual signage and labeling, audio guides, video guides, and interactive touchscreens. The museum has more than 30 artfully decorated rooms that detail the military campaigns that led to Unification, both from an Italian and a European perspective; even non-Italians can easily appreciate the stirring drama of these years. Uniforms, vivid paintings, weapons, maps, and correspondence reveal feats of great derring-do as we are led through the Italy of the 19th century from Napoleon to Garibaldi. A recently renovated library holds a wealth of historical documents in its archives.

Via Accademia delle Scienze 5. www.museorisorgimentotorino.it. ✆ **011-562-1147.** 10€ adults, 8€ seniors, 5€ students, 2.50€ primary school, free 6 and under and for those with the Torino Card. Tues–Sun 10am–6pm. Bus: 11, 12, 27, 51, 51, 55, 56, 57. Tram: 13, 15.

Museo della Sindone (Holy Shroud Museum) ★★ MUSEUM Considering the Turin Shroud's hefty status as one of the world's most famous religious relics, it is refreshing to see that the endearing little museum dedicated to the scientific research into it doesn't try to offer any kind of special effects. A visit kicks off with a 15-minute film about the shroud (offered in five languages), its provenance, and the various theories and mysteries surrounding it. Visitors wander through a series of rooms with numbered exhibits chronicling the shroud's history from the first mention in 1204, to the fire that nearly destroyed it in Chambéry in 1532, to its arrival in Turin with the House of Savoy in 1578, and the modern-day carbon-testing sagas. The tour finishes in the richly ornamented chapel of Santo Sudario, a private place of worship for the Savoy dukes, where a copy of the shroud is displayed over the gleaming, gilded altar. The shroud itself is not displayed here (it is in the royal chapel of the Duomo, usually out of public view; see above). Log on to www.sindone.org to find out when the shroud will next be taken out and displayed; advance reservations are required to see the shroud during its brief public displays. It was last shown in 2015 and is typically taken out for public viewing every few years, making the time ripe for it to be displayed again—though the decision to do so is usually made by the reigning pope.

Via San Domenico 28. www.sindone.it. ✆ **011-436-5832.** 6€ adults, 5€ students and children aged 12 and under, and seniors. Daily 9am–noon and 3–7pm.

Palazzo Madama—Museo Civico di Arte Antica (Civic Museum of Ancient Art) ★ MUSEUM Looking like a mashup of two architectural styles, Palazzo Madama dominates Piazza Castello; its medieval facade faces eastward, while the westward facade is its baroque addition, created by the architect Filippo Juvarra in the 18th century when he was giving Turin its elegant arcaded facelift. Once inside this massive structure, you'll discover it incorporates a Roman gate and tower; courtyards, apartments, and towers from the medieval castle; and several Renaissance additions. Juvarra also added a monumental marble staircase to the interior, most of which is given over to the all-encompassing collections of the Museo Civico di Arte Antica. Just as the building has two styles, the museum's purpose is twofold as well: It focuses on the history of the building along with Turin's collections of art from past eras. The holdings cover four mammoth floors and focus on the medieval and Renaissance periods, which are shown off well against the building's austere, stony interior. On the top floor you'll find one of Italy's largest collections of ceramics, but it's all rather disorganized in layout. The star of the show here is Antonello da Messina's sublime "Portrait of a Man," hidden away in the Treasure Tower at the back of the building. Like many of Turin's museums, Palazzo Madama is trying to step up its innovation game and encourages visitors to post pictures from inside the collections. Audio guides, available for 3.50€, offer more in-depth information for about 100 works. If you need a break, the Caffè Madama on the first floor offers modern-day treats as well as hot chocolate and pastries inspired by the royal period of the city.

Piazza Castello. www.palazzomadamatorino.it. ✆ **011-443-3501.** 10€ adults, 8€ student and seniors, free under 18. Mon, Wed–Fri 10am–6pm; Sat 11am–7pm; Sun 10am–7pm. Closed Tues. Bus: 11, 12, 51, 55, 56, 61, 68; Trams: 4, 13, 15, 18.

Palazzo Reale (Royal Palace) & Armeria Reale (Royal Armory) ★
PALACE Overshadowing the north side of the Piazza Castello, the residence of the House of Savoy was begun in 1646; the family lived here up until 1865. Designed by the architect Amedeo di Castellamonte, the palace reflects the ornate tastes of European ruling families of the time, while its sheer size offers some indication of the wealth of these oligarchs. This Savoy palace gives the flamboyant frippery of Versailles a run for its money, with throne rooms, ballrooms, and apartments hung with priceless Gobelins tapestries and lavishly adorned with silk walls, sparkling chandeliers, ornate wooden floors, and gilded furniture.

The east wing of the *palazzo* houses the **Armeria Reale,** one of the most important arms and armor collections in Europe, especially of weapons from the 16th and 17th centuries. It also has a unique collection of stuffed horses, which look ready to leap into battle at any moment.

Behind the palace are the formal **Giardini Reali (Royal Gardens),** laid out in part by André Le Nôtre, who designed the Tuileries in Paris and the gardens at Versailles.

The Savoy royal family had an even keener eye for paintings than for baroque decor, amassing a collection of 8,000 works of art. The collection's highlights are on display in the **Galleria Sabauda** in the Palazzo Reale's New Wing. (This is a few minutes' walk from the main *palazzo.*) The exhibition kicks off with early Piedmont and Dutch religious works, plus a moody Rembrandt self-portrait and two massive paintings by van Dyck: "The Children of Charles I" (1637) and a magnificent equestrian portrait of Prince Thomas of Savoy (ca. 1634).

Now permanently housed in the basement beneath the Galleria Sabauda, the **Museo Archeologico**'s thoughtfully designed exhibition tells the story of Turin's development from Roman through medieval times. Incorporated into the museum are a section of Roman wall, remnants from the theater nearby, and a mosaic only discovered in 1993.

The **Biblioteca Reale** (Royal Library) is also part of the Palazzo Reale complex; it's free to enter and you'll find it on the right of the main entrance. Founded in 1831, it houses 200,000 rare volumes as well as ancient maps and prints. On the opposite side of the gates is the fine **church of San Lorenzo,** designed by master architect Guarino Guarini in 1666. Its plain facade belies a lacy dome and frothy interior.

A Glimpse into Roman Turin

Close to Turin's Duomo (see p. 514) and partly incorporated into the Museo Archeologico (see p. 486) stand two landmarks of Roman Turin: the remains of a theater and fragments of wall, as well as the **Porta Palatina,** a Roman-era city gate, flanked by twin 16-sided towers on Piazza San Giovanni Battista. The **Area Romana** west of the Piazza Castello is the oldest part of the city, a charming web of streets occupied since ancient times.

Keep in mind that new security rules prohibit visitors from bringing in large bags (backpacks, duffel bags, and luggage) and the palazzo currently offers no place to check these items for safekeeping.

Piazzetta Reale 1. www.ilpalazzorealeditorino.it. ✆ **011-436-1455.** Palazzo and all exhibitions: 12€ adults, 6€ ages 18–25, free for children and seniors. Free for all on the first Sun of the month. Tues–Sun 9am–7pm; last admission 6pm. Museo Archeologico closed Sun morning. Bus: 11,51, 55, 56, 68; Trams: 4, 13, 15, 18.

Outlying Attractions

Basilica di Superga ★★ CHURCH Half the fun of a visit to this lovely basilica is the 6.5km (4-mile) journey northeast of the city center on a narrow-gauge railway through the lush countryside of the Parco Naturale della Collina di Superga. The church was built as thanksgiving to the Virgin Mary for Turin's deliverance from the French siege of 1706. Prince Vittorio Amedeo II commissioned Filippo Juvarra, the Sicilian architect who designed much of Turin's elegant center, to build the magical baroque confection on a hill high above the city. The eye-catching exterior, with its beautiful colonnaded portico, elaborate dome, and twin bell towers, is actually more appealing than the ornate but gloomy interior, a circular chamber ringed by six chapels. Many scions of the House of Savoy are buried here in the Crypt of Kings beneath the main chapel.

Strada della Basilica di Superga, 73, www.basilicadisuperga.com. ✆ **011-899-7456.** Basilica: free. Open summer Mon–Fri 9am–noon and 3–6pm, Sat–Sun 9am–noon and 3–7pm; winter Mon–Fri 9am–noon and 3–5pm, Sat–Sun 9am–noon and 3–6pm. Take the "Tranvia a Dentiera" tramway from Stazione Sassi (6€ roundtrip) to the Superga stop, which is a short walk from the basilica. Bus: 61 from side of Ponte Vittorio Emanuele I opposite Piazza Vittorio Veneto.

Palazzina di Caccia di Stupinigi ★ PALACE Yet another Savoy family home is found at Stupinigi, just a few miles southwest from Turin. More great work commissioned in 1729 from the architect Filippo Juvarra resulted in a sumptuous, ornately decorated hunting lodge surrounded by royal forests. Built on a humungous scale, the palace's wings fan out from the main house, topped by a domed pavilion. Every bit as lavish as the apartments in the Savoys' city residence, Palazzo Reale (see

p. 519), the interior is stuffed with furniture, paintings, and bric-à-brac assembled from their myriad residences, forming the **Museo d'Arte e Ammobiliamento (Museum of Art and Furniture).** Wander through the acres of apartments to understand why Napoleon chose this for his brief sojourn in Piedmont in 1805 while on his way to Milan to be crowned emperor. Outstanding among the many, many frescoes are the scenes of a deer hunt in the King's Apartment and the triumph of Diana in the grand salon. The elegant gardens and surrounding forests provide lovely terrain for a jaunt.

Piazza Principe Amedeo 7, Stupingi, Nichelino. www.ordinemauriziano.it/palazzina-di-caccia-stupinigi. ✆ **011-620-0634**. 12€, seniors and children age 6–18 8€, children under 6 free]. Tues–Fri 10am–5:30pm; Sat 10am–6:30pm. It's 8.5km (5¼ miles) southwest of the city center.

Reggia di Venaria Reale ★★★ PALACE Completing the triumvirate of glitzy Savoy households around Turin, the Venaria was constructed in the mid-17th century to a design by Amedeo di Castellamonte, but sure enough Filippo Juvarra also had a hand in it. This massive complex, its stables, and the awesome formal gardens are now a UNESCO World Heritage Site. Venaria offers a great family-oriented day out with loads of outdoor summer activities as well as a glimpse into the extraordinarily privileged lives of the Savoy family. The Fountain of the Stag dances to music in the lake outside the *palazzo;* on the grounds are follies aplenty and the mock-Roman Fountain of Hercules. Exhibitions in the house include the "Peopling the Palaces" light show conceived by film director Peter Greenaway, who also had a hand in the exhibitions at the Museum of Cinema (see p. 525) in Turin.

Piazza della Repubblica 4, Venaria Reale (10km/6¼ mi northwest of the city center). www.lavenaria.it. ✆ **011-499-2333.** 25€ for palace, gardens, and activities, 5€ for gardens only, with many price options in between. Tues–Fri 9am–5pm; Sat–Sun 9:30am–6:30pm (last admission 1 hr. before closing). Bus: 11 from Piazza Repubblica. A Venaria Express bus runs Tues–Sun (40 min.), with stops at Stazione Porta Nuova, on Via XX Settembre, and at Stazione Porta Susa.

Organized Tours

Several tour companies run trips around Turin and Piedmont. **Viator** (www.viator.com; U.S. ✆ **702-648-5873** or Italy ✆ 199-241-489) offers an underground tour of the city's catacombs and guided tours of the Barolo region (see p. 532). A hop-on, hop-off bus service run by **Torino City Sightseeing** (www.torino.city-sightseeing.it; ✆ **011-535-181**) circles the major attractions, while **Delicious Italy** (www.deliciousitaly.com) showcases the food stores and restaurants that earn Turin its gourmet reputation.

Where to Stay

Turin has seen a recent injection of private capital into the hotel scene, and as a result, many boutique hotels have opened, giving travelers an alternative to the faceless frumpery of many of the city's older hotels.

Le Petit Hotel ★★ While it is unassuming from outside, the Petit Hotel offers simple bedrooms with spotless, functional bathrooms for business and pleasure travelers alike. What it lacks in luxury, it makes up for in reasonable prices and a central address. The hotel is a 10-minute walk from both the Porta Nuova and Porta Susa train stations, and very close to Palazzo Madama and the Egyptian museum and many other sites. A casual restaurant offers pizza and pasta staples, though there are better places to eat around the neighborhood. The colorfully furnished breakfast room offers a buffet of breads, cheeses, fruit, and pastries. For those looking for more privacy, the hotel also has some slightly more modern self-catering apartments that come in standard and deluxe versions. No parking is available on-site, but the hotel can set you up with parking in a nearby garage.

Via San Francesco d'Assisi 21. www.lepetithotel.it. ✆ **011-561-2626.** 79 units. Doubles 89€–129€; apartments 150€–220€. Rates include breakfast. **Amenities:** Restaurant; Wi-Fi (5€ for 3 hr.).

Townhouse 70 ★★★ Discreetly located (with very little signage outside) and just steps from Piazza Castello and the Palazzo Reale (see p. 519), the Townhouse could not be better placed for sightseers. As part of a small chain of luxury hotels based in Milan, this is a smooth, urbane property, with a tiny *aperitivo* bar tucked in one corner of reception and a breakfast room that has only one massive table, where smart businessmen and families all sit down together. Rooms are spacious for a hotel that is so centrally located and feature soothing dark colors; bathrooms have massive showers. Quieter bedrooms look over an internal courtyard (where you can grab a cocktail in warmer weather), but keep in mind that privacy could be a concern if you keep your shutters open.

Via XX Settembre 70. 70.townhousehotels.com. ✆ **011-1970-0003.** 48 units. Doubles 151€–170€. Rates include breakfast. **Amenities:** Bar; concierge; room service (7–10am); Wi-Fi (free).

VitaminaM ★★★ This tiny B&B with just two rooms has a funky interior design meant to represent the sophisticated city home of a modern art lover. The rooms are flooded with light, with silver and red color schemes, and the bathrooms are surprisingly luxurious. Book well ahead; this is one of the hottest tickets in town. The one drawback is that the B&B is four floors up with no elevator, though someone is always available to help with your bags. The B&B is very close to the Porta Nuova station in a residential area where street parking is available (1.30€ per hour Mon–Sat during the day; parking free at night and on Sun) if you come by car. A library full of books is available to guests, and musical instruments are available as well upon request. Expect little touches like chocolates on your pillow and homemade jams at breakfast. The artsy team behind VitaminaM now has other Vitamina properties in Milan and Rome.

Via Belfiore 18. www.vitaminam.com. ✆ **347-1526-130.** 2 units. 100€–120€ double; add an additional bed for 30€. Rates include breakfast. **Amenities:** Wi-Fi (free).

Where to Eat

Turin's gourmet reputation outshines other Italian cities renowned for their gastronomy. Many restaurants are strong advocates of the Slow Food movement, and a glance at a menu will tell you whether ingredients are local; look for porcini mushrooms and truffles in season. Wine lists feature Barolo, Barbera, and Barbaresco reds and sparkling Asti whites. Turin is also home to the world's largest food and wine fair, the **Salone del Gusto** (www.salonedelgusto.com), which runs every 2 years in September or October.

Officine Bohemien ★★ PIEDMONT With walls covered in black-and-white posters, this offbeat restaurant down a side street in the center of town is casual and slightly edgy. With its delightful young staff, the atmosphere here is laidback. The bar sells Piedmont wines, French or Belgian beers, and cocktails, while jazz plays in the background; frequent live-music events are held here. Lunch sees offerings of staple pasta dishes such as pasta *al pomodoro* or big salads at really good prices; dinner is a little more sophisticated (like taglioni pasta with gorgonzola cheese, blueberries, and walnuts) or gnocchi in an avocado pesto with pecorino cheese from Sardinia. There are also platters of grilled and smoked meats, regional cheeses, and fruits and vegetables, which are all sourced locally. Bread is made fresh daily.

Via San Camillo de Lellis (formerly known as Via Mercanti) 19. www.officinebohemien.it. ✆ **011-764-0368.** Main courses 8€–12€. Mon–Fri noon–3pm, 7:30–10:30pm (no dinner service on Mon); Sat 7:30–10:30pm; closed Sundays

Ruràl ★★★ MODERN PIEDMONT This minimalist restaurant located on the corner of two streets in a residential neighborhood a short walk from the historic city center is an award-winning proponent of the Slow Food ethos (born in nearby Bra). The menu has upped the gastronomic game in Turin. Its deceptively simple white and blond-wood interior strikes a classy note; the clientele is smart and the service friendly and informed. Chefs emerge from the open-plan kitchen to discuss dishes with customers. A great sharing plate of rabbit, veal "tonnato" (creamy sauce flavored with tuna), sausage, carpaccio, and tartare showcases typical Piedmont specialties, and the wine list offers plenty of regional reds and whites. It's obvious that everybody involved in this project is obsessive about food and proud to present the best of Piedmontese rural cuisine. The restaurant's empire has expanded in the city to include two *"latterie"* (shops selling cheese and other delights featured in the restaurant) and a clothing shop called Ruràl Dress, with pieces for men and women chosen just as carefully as the produce in the restaurant.

Via San Dalmazzo 16. www.ristoranterural.it. ✆ **011-2478-470.** Main courses 15€–25€. Tues–Sat 12:30pm–2:30pm and 7:30–10:30pm, Sun 12:30pm–2:30pm.

Trattoria Santo Spirito ★★ SEAFOOD Thanks to its prime location in a bustling piazza not far from Palazzo Reale in the heart of the Area Romana, this trattoria could be mistaken for a tourist trap. But Santo Spirito is well loved by locals and tourists alike, especially for its seafood. It serves up vast platters of mussels, tuna carpaccio, simply grilled fish, and delicious fettucine served with lobster. Portions are huge, so don't be tempted to over-order. It is testament to the standard of cooking here that this place has thrived since 1975 in a city where restaurants open and close every day. This may not be haute cuisine, but it is great home cooking with fresh ingredients and strong flavors. It offers separate "land" and "sea" tasting menus for 40€. In summer, tables spread onto the piazza; in winter a cozy fire blazes inside and heaters warm the loggia. The restaurant can get quite crowded, and the space inside can be tight, so it's best to call ahead for a table.

Shaken, not Stirred

Turin gave the world the aperitif vermouth, which was invented in 1786 by Antonio Benedetto Carpano; the brands Martini and Cinzano are still made in the Piedmont region. Order a glass at the gorgeous **Art Nouveau Caffè Mulassano** at Piazza Castello 15 (www.caffemulassano.com; ✆ **011-547-990**), or come early to enjoy coffee and tempting cannoli or dainty fruit tarts at the ornate marble counter.

Largo IV Marzo 11. www.trattoriaspiritosanto.com. ✆ **011-4360-877.** Daily 12:30–3:30pm, 7:30pm–midnight. Main courses 9€–25€, tasting menus 40€.

Outdoor Activities

Turin's beautiful playground is **Parco del Valentino,** which cradles the left bank of the River Po between the Ponte Umberto I and the Ponte Isabella. Its first incarnation was in 1630, when it was the private garden of the Savoy dukes, but the park was much extended in the 1860s and opened to the public. It's a romantic place to stroll among the botanical gardens, flowerbeds, and manicured lawns. The massive **Castello del Valentino,** built in 1660, was the pleasure palace of Christine Marie of France (see p. 514); it is closed to the public. The castle forms an incongruous backdrop to the **Borgo Medievale** (see p. 525), a riverside

Rowers on the River Po, flowing through Turin.

replica of a 15th-century Piedmontese village. It's a pleasant walk to the city center along Corso Emanuele Vittorio II, or you can hop Tram 9.

There are half a dozen rowing clubs on the Po; Reale Societa Canottieri Cerea (www.canottiericerea.it) is the oldest. Jogging and cycling routes follow the riverside pathways.

A little farther afield, it takes around an hour to reach the hiking trails of the **Gran Paradiso** national park (see p. 535). Turin is also an hour away from the ski resorts of **Valle d'Aosta** (see p. 535) in the Alps, and it's just a little farther to the sandy beaches of the **Riviera delle Palme** to the south.

Especially for Kids

There's plenty for kids to do in Turin. The **Parco del Valentino** (see above) has lots of open spaces to run around in, plus free admission to the open-air **Borgo Medievale,** a mock-Piedmontese village built for the Italian General Exposition in 1884 (Viale Virgilio 107; www.borgomedioevaletorino.it; ✆ **011-4431-701**; open 9am–7pm [8pm in summer]). Most youngsters will be intrigued by the **Museum of Cinema** at the Mole Antonelliana (see p. 515), or at least the trip up the Mole's tower to see the city lying far below. The **Museo Nazionale dell'Automobile** provides an antidote to Turin's baroque attractions.

If all else fails, pop into **Caffè Fiorio** (Via Po 8; ✆ **011-8173-225**) for some delicious gelato or, in cooler months, Turin's famous hot chocolate.

Shopping & Nightlife

Turin's high-end shopping area is quite simply one of the most beautiful in the world. The arcaded **Via Roma** does full justice to the exquisite fashions of Gucci, Armani, Ferragamo, Max Mara, and so on. At the end of Via Roma, the glass-roofed **Galleria Subalpina,** which links Piazza Castello with Piazza Carlo, competes with Milan's Galleria Vittorio Emanuele II for sheer opulence in its three levels of art galleries, antiquarian bookstores, and cafes. For those whose pockets may not be quite so deep, **Via Garibaldi, Corso XX Settembre,** and the surrounding streets together offer midrange international brands at reasonable prices.

The windows of Italian food shops are always a thing of joy, and the specialist delis and confectioners of Turin are no exceptions. **Confetteria Stratta** (Piazza San Carlo 191; ✆ **011-547-920**) and **Pasticceria Gerla** (Corso Vittorio Emanuele II 86) are known for their extravagant pastries, cakes, and *gianduiotti* (chocolate with hazelnuts). Turin is famous for its quality confectionery—the city produces 40%of Italy's **chocolate**. Turin also has a branch of **Eataly** (see p. 515), the current mecca for gourmet Italian fare, at Via Nizza 230, a little out of the center in Lingotto.

Most newsagents in Turin have English-language newspapers, and the two branches of **Feltrinelli** (Piazza Castello 19, ✆ **011-541-627** or Stazione Porta Nuova ✆ **011-563-981**) sell multilingual books.

Nightlife in the city that invented the vermouth *aperitivo* is sophisticated, and, as in Milan, it starts in the cafes and bars and finishes very, very late. Squeeze in with the Torinese at **Caffè Platti** (Corso Vittorio

The Markets of Turin

The **produce market** in and around Porta Palazzo takes over the gigantic Piazza della Repubblica Monday to Friday 7am to 2pm and Saturday until 7:30pm. A bustling **flea market** takes place in the warren of streets behind the Porta Palazzo every Saturday, among the antique shops on Via Borgo Dora. The second Sunday of every month, the same spot is the scene of an **antiques market,** the continuously expanding **Gran Balon** (www.balon.it), with more than 250 dealers from across northern Italy. Come December, a **Christmas market** sets out its stalls in Via Borgo Dora. Turin has many stores specializing in rare books and old prints, and these also sell their wares from stalls along the Via Po.

Emanuele II 72; ✆ **011-454-6151**) for a vermouth, and pick from the plates of enticing little pizzas made on the premises. Choose a Slow Food restaurant for dinner, and then join models and footballers to dance at **Kogin's** (Corso Sicilia 6; ✆ **011-661-0546**). In summer, head for the Murazzi embankment along the River Po for live bands and DJs in late-night dance clubs.

Dance, opera, theater, and musical performances (mostly classical) are on the agenda all year long—check www.visitatorino.com—but September is the month to really enjoy classical music in Turin, when more than 60 classical concerts are staged around the city during the month-long **Settembre Musica** festival (www.mitosettembremusica.it), which is hosted jointly with Milan. Beyond the festivals you'll find classical concerts at **Auditorium della RAI,** Via Rossini 15 (www.orchestrasinfonica.rai.it; ✆ **011-810-4653**) and dance performances and operas staged at the city's venerable **Teatro Regio** (www.teatroregio.torino.it; ✆ **011-8815-557**).

THE PIEDMONT WINE COUNTRY ★★

South of Turin, the Po valley rises into the rolling hills of Langhe and Roero, flanked by orchards and vineyards. You'll recognize the region's place names from the labels of its first-rate wines, among them **Asti Spumanti, Barbaresco,** and **Barolo.** And vines are not all that flourish in this fertile soil—truffles top the list of the region's gastronomic delights, along with rabbit and game plus excellent cheeses.

Asti ★★★

Asti: 60km (37 miles) SE of Turin, 127km (79 miles) SW of Milan

The Asti of sparkling-wine fame is a bustling working city, but it has many treasures to uncover in its history-drenched *centro storico*—medieval towers (there were about 120 at one time), Renaissance palaces, and piazzas provide the perfect setting in which to sample the town's most famous product, which flows readily in the local *enoteche* and cantinas.

ESSENTIALS

GETTING THERE Up to four **trains** per hour link Asti with **Turin Porta Nuova** (35 min; 5.25€) via **Trenitalia** (www.trenitalia.com; ✆ **89-20-21**). **Arfea** (www.arfea.it; ✆ **0131-225-810**) runs **buses** from Turin Autostazione to Asti; the trip takes 1 hour. By car, Asti can be reached in less than an hour from Turin via Autostrada 21.

VISITOR INFORMATION The **APT tourist office** is near the train station at Piazza Alfieri 34 (✆ **0141-530-357**). It's open Monday to

Saturday 9am to 1pm and 2:30 to 6:30pm; Sunday 9am to 1pm and 1:30pm to 5:30pm.

EXPLORING ASTI

Asti's historic heart is centered on three adjoining squares: **Piazza Libertá,** the vast **Campo del Palio,** and the grand arcaded **Piazza Alfieri.** Each year on the third Sunday of September, the area is mobbed for the **Palio,** Asti's annual horse race (www.comune.asti.it/pagina875_il-palio-di-asti.html; ✆ **0141-399-0577**), now held in Piazza Alfieri (originally it was in Campo del Palio). Like the similar race in the Tuscan city of Siena (see p. 232), Asti's Palio begins with a colorful medieval pageant through the town and ends with a wild bareback ride around the triangular Piazza Alfieri. First staged around 1273, the race coincides with Asti's other great festival, the **Douja d'Or** (www.doujador.it), a weeklong bacchanal celebrating the grape harvest.

Behind **Piazza Alfieri** stands the Romanesque-Gothic redbrick **Collegiata di San Secondo** (www.comune.asti.it; ✆ **0141-530-066;** daily 7:30am–7pm). This church has two distinctions: it houses the Palio Astigiano, the prestigious banner awarded to the winning jockey at the Palio, and it also contains the tomb of St. Secondo, patron saint of both the race and the town. A Roman officer who converted to Christianity in A.D. 119, Secondo was martyred for his faith, beheaded in roughly the spot where his tomb now stands.

From Piazza Alfieri, the charming and largely pedestrianized **Corso Alfieri** bisects the old town and is lined with Renaissance *palazzi*. At the eastern end is the church of **San Pietro in Consavia** (✆ **0141-399-489;** Tues–Sun 10am–1pm, 3–6pm, or until 7pm in summer) with a 10th-century Romanesque baptistery that was once a place of worship for the Knights of the Order of St. John. The archeology located inside San Pietro in Consavia has recently been renovated. At the western extreme of Corso Alfieri you'll find the rotund **church of Santa Caterina,** abutting the medieval red-and-white brick-topped **Torre Rossa**.

Asti's 15th-century **Cattedrale di Santa Maria Assunta** (✆ **0141-592-924;** daily 8:30am–noon, 3–5:30pm) is also at the western end of town in Piazza Cattedrale. Its austere exterior hides the gaudy excesses of the interior; every inch of the church is festooned with frescoes by late-15th-century artists, including Gandolfino d'Asti.

Being the agricultural and gourmet hotspot that it is, Asti is blessed with two **food markets.** The larger is held Wednesdays and Saturdays (part of a street market with all kinds of wares that lasts all day, but the food stands are only there from 7:30am–1pm) in the Campo del Palio and spills over into neighboring piazzas, with stalls selling cheeses, herbs, flowers, oils, and wines. The covered **Mercato Coperto** on Piazza della

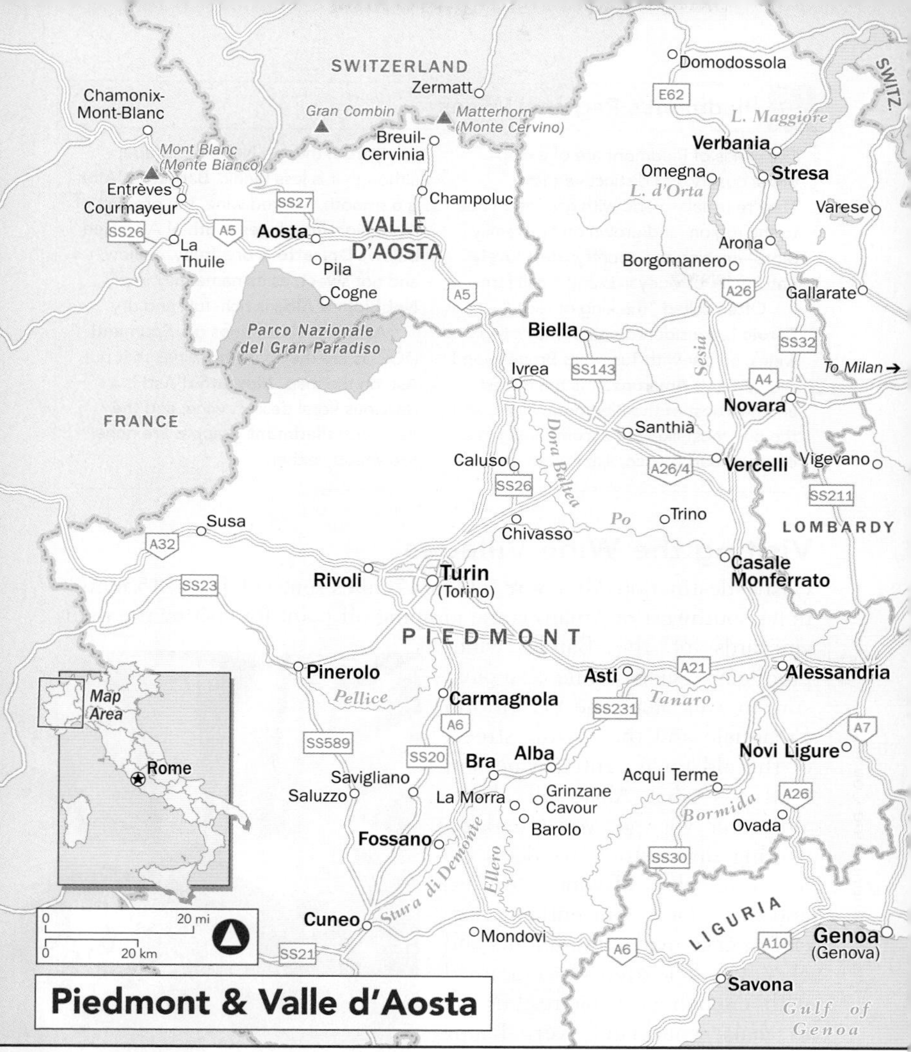

Piedmont & Valle d'Aosta

Libertà is open daily except Sunday (Mon–Wed and Fri 8am–1pm, 3:30–7:30pm; Thurs 8:30am–1pm; Sat 8am–7:30pm). Look for white truffles, *bagna cauda* (a fondue-like dip served warm and made with ingredients like olive, oil, butter, garlic, and anchovies), *robiola* cheeses, *amaretti* biscuits, and *nocciolata* (hazelnut and chocolate spread). The region's famous Asti Spumante DOCG sparkling wines can be bought from *cantinas* and *enoteche* in the town center and direct from some vineyards—a list is available from the **tourist office** at Piazza Alfieri 34 (see p. 527).

Piedmont's Regional Wines

The wines of Piedmont are of exceptional quality and distinctive taste. They're usually made with grapes unique to the region, and grown on tiny family plots—making the countryside a lovely patchwork of vineyards and small farms.

Often called "the king of reds," **Barolo** is considered one of Italy's top wines, on par with Tuscany's Brunello and the Veneto's Amarone. It is the richest and heartiest of the Piedmont wines, and the one most likely to accompany game or meat. **Barbaresco,** like Barolo, is made solely from the red Nebbiolo grape, although it is less tannic. **Barbera d'Alba** is a smooth, rich red wine, the product of the delightful villages south of Alba (see below). **Dolcetto** is dry, fruity, mellow, and not sweet, as its name may imply. **Nebbiolo d'Alba** is rich, full, and dry.

As far as white wines go, **Spumanti** DOCGs are the sparkling wines that put Asti on the map. **Moscato d'Asti** is a delicious floral dessert wine, and the fiery local **Piedmont** *grappas* are none too shabby either.

Visiting the Wine Villages

Gastro-destination **Alba ★★** (60km/37 miles south of Turin; 155km/96 miles southwest of Milan) is the jumping-off point for visiting the many vineyards of the Barolo wine-producing region. While it's a pleasure to walk along the Via Vittorio Emanuele and the narrow streets of the old town center, wine and food are what Alba's all about. Wherever you go, you'll end up peering into store windows to admire displays of wines, truffles, and the calorific but enticing *nocciolata* cake made of hazelnuts and chocolate. The streets are crammed with enough enticing restaurants to make gourmands very happy indeed (see p. 532).

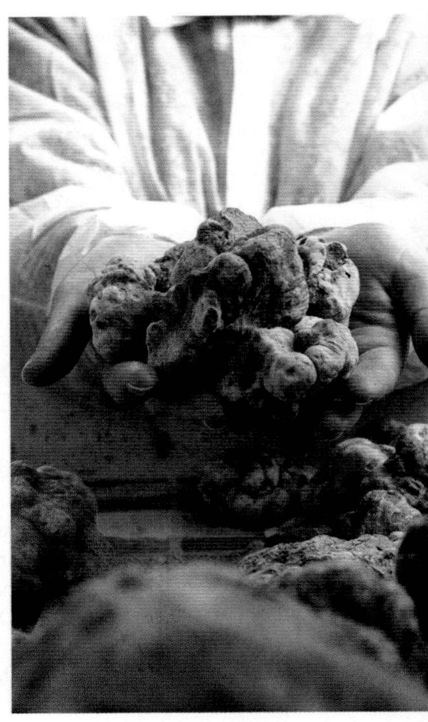

Precious white truffles from Alba.

Just to the south of Alba lie some of the Piedmont's most enchanting wine villages, sitting on hilltops among orderly rows of vines. The best way to see these villages is to drive; hire cars in Turin from **Avis,** Via Lessona Michele 30 (www.avisautonoleggio.it; ✆ **011-774-1962**), **Hertz,**

The village of Barolo and Castello Falletti, surrounded by vineyards.

at Corso Turati 37 (www.hertz.it; ✆ **011-502-080**), or **Sixt,** at Via Mongrando 48 (www.sixt.it; ✆ **011-888-768**). Before you head out on the small country roads, provide yourself with a good map and a list of vineyards from the tourist office in Asti (see p. 527).

The main road through the wine region is the SS231, which runs between Alba and Asti. It is, however, a fast, busy, and unattractive highway; you'll want to turn off it to explore Piedmont's rustic backwaters among hazelnut groves and vineyards.

One such enchanting drive heads south from Alba to the wine villages of the **Langhe hills** (follow signs out of town for Barolo on the SP3). After 8km (5 miles), take the right turn for **Grinzane Cavour,** a hilltop village built around a castle harboring the **Enoteca Regionale Piemontese Cavour** (www.castellogrinzane.com; ✆ **0173-262-159**), which is open daily from 9:30am to 7pm (until 6pm Nov–Mar). Here you can sample local wines from over 300 labels; the fine restaurant is perfect for lunch.

Return to the main road, turn left, and after 4km (2½ miles) south, take the right fork to **La Morra,** perched among vineyards with panoramic views over the rolling, vine-clad countryside. La Morra has several cafes and restaurants in which to taste the local vintages. The **Cantina Comunale di La Morra** at Via Alberto 2 (www.cantinalamorra.com; ✆ **0173-509-204**) represents local growers, selling Barolo, Nebbiolo, Barbera, and Dolcetto. It's open daily (except Tues) 10am to 12:30pm and 2:30 to 6:30pm.

The tourist office is located at Piazza Martiri 1 (www.lamorraturismo.com; ✆ **0173-500-344**), and is open on Monday and Tuesday 9:30am to 1:30 p.m. and Friday, Saturday, and Sunday 10am to 6pm. It is closed on Wednesday and has reduced hours in the winter.

Barolo is a handsome little village dominated by two ancient castles; it's 5km (3 miles) along the SP58 from La Morra. Here, too, you'll find a choice of restaurants and shops selling world-renowned red wines from local vineyards. Among these is **Castello Falletti** (www.enotecadelbarolo.it; ✆ **0173-56-277;** Thurs–Tues 10am–5pm), with a wine bar and an *enoteca* offering tastings in its cavernous cellars. They even offer Barolo and chocolate pairings.

Where to Eat & Stay

As well as a few decent urban hotels, the Barolo region is the land of the *agriturismo,* with options to stay on wine estates in the hills of Langhe. Restaurants don't come much classier than the best of the Piedmont.

Ristorante al Castello di Marc Lanteri ★★★ GOURMET Housed in the fairy-tale castle at Grinzane Cavour along with an *enoteca* selling the best of the region's wines, this renowned restaurant showcases the food of Michelin-starred chef Marc Lanteri, who took over the kitchen in late 2015. Lanteri, a French chef born on the Italian border, considers his cuisine to be representative of Franco-Piedmont style, with some influences from nearby Liguria. If you truly want to get into the Piedmontese spirit, try the chef's whole-grain egg tagliatelle with snails and aromatic herbs. The atmosphere is quite elegant. The chef's American wife, Amy, is the restaurant's sommelier.

Via Castello 5, Grinzane Cavour. www.castellogrinzane.com. ✆ **338-700-1914.** Main courses 18€–26€. Tasting menus from 50€ without wine pairings or 80€ with wine pairings. Mon 12:30–2:30pm, Wed–Sun 12:30–2:30pm, 7:30–10pm. Closed Jan.

Hotel Castello d'Asti ★★ Don't be put off by the slightly workaday street; this hotel is a find. Tucked into a lush courtyard garden to the northwest of the *centro storico*, the Castello is in a historic townhouse with an elegantly updated interior. The spacious rooms are decorated in soft shades of black and cream with luscious marble bathrooms. The suites are especially large, and all have their own balconies overlooking the gardens or the Asti-style courtyard. Downstairs there's a lively bar and the intimate **Cambiocavallo** restaurant serving innovative Piedmontese cuisine (with some Sicilian influences, considering the chef is from Sicily) and offering a wide selection of wines.

Via G Testa 47, Asti. www.hotelcastelloasti.com. ✆ **0141-351-094.** 11 units. 125€–155€ double; 175€–235€ suite. Rates include breakfast. Closed Jan. **Amenities:** Restaurant; bar; room service; Wi-Fi (free).

La Cascina del Monastero ★★★ Perfectly situated for exploring the Barolo wine region, this beautiful 16th-century family-run estate is part rustic B&B and part winery, all just minutes away from La Morra (see p. 531). Converted from an outbuilding of soft stone and arcading, the suites and apartments are beautifully furnished with Italian antiques and brass beds. Exposed stone walls, beams, and wooden floors add to the ambience of the place, while bathrooms have every modern convenience. The property boasts a sun terrace, and the unusual spa has a sauna in what appears to be a massive wine barrel. Best of all, you get the chance to taste the estate's wines. The "Langhe-style" breakfast kicks off the day in fine style. For those interested in cooking classes, the B&B partners with two local restaurants to offer a 3-hour afternoon course that includes wine tasting. A camping area is available amid lovely scenery near the main house.

Cascina Luciani 112A, Frazione Annunziata, La Morra. www.cascinadelmonastero.it. ✆ **0173-509-245.** 10 units. 130€–145€ double; 135€–150€ apartment. Rates include breakfast. Closed Jan and sometimes Feb. **Amenities:** Playground; spa; outdoor pool; room service; sauna; Wi-Fi (free).

Palazzo Finati ★★ This hotel offers a taste of old-fashioned luxury. Located in a *palazzo* within easy reach of Alba's shops and gourmet restaurants, the Finati has a choice of individually designed rooms, some with frescoed ceilings and terraces overlooking the inner courtyard. Rooms can be connected for family stays. The breakfast buffet includes fresh pastries, fruit, local cheeses, and cured meats, all served in an elegant brick-ceilinged, barrel-vaulted dining room.

Via Vernazza 8, Alba. www.palazzofinati.it. ✆ **0173-366-324.** 9 units. 150€–180€ double, 170€–250€ suite, includes breakfast. **Amenities:** Wi-Fi (free), parking.

AOSTA ★★ & VALLE D'AOSTA ★★★

Aosta: 113km (70 miles) N of Turin, 184km (114 miles) NW of Milan; Courmayeur-Entrèves: 35km (22 miles) W of Aosta, 148km (92 miles) NW of Turin

Tucked up against the French and Swiss borders in northwest Italy, the Aosta Valley is a land of harsh, snow-capped peaks, lush pastures, thick forests, waterfalls cascading into mountain streams, and romantic castles clinging to wooded hillsides. A year-round stream of skiers, hikers, cyclists, and nature lovers flock to this tiny Alpine region north of Turin for the scenery, outdoor adventure, and rustic gastronomy.

Aosta

ESSENTIALS

GETTING THERE Aosta is served by 20 **trains** a day to and from **Turin** (2 hr., change in Ivrea or Chivasso; tickets 9€) aboard **Trenitalia** (www.trenitalia.com; ✆ **89-20-21**). **Bus service** to Aosta is much less handy: Only a few buses travel from Turin Porta Nuova per day (most change in Ivrea), and even the direct trip takes 2 hours, the indirect route more than 3. However, a SAVDA bus conveniently connects Aosta hourly to **Courmayeur** (1 hr., 3.50€) and other popular spots in the valley.

Autostrada A5 from Turin shoots up the length of Valle d'Aosta en route to France and Switzerland via the Mont Blanc tunnel; there are numerous exits in the valley. The trip from Turin to Aosta normally takes about 90 minutes, but traffic can be heavy on weekends in the ski season.

VISITOR INFORMATION The **tourist office** in Aosta (Piazza Porta Praetoria 3; www.lovevda.it; ✆ **0165-236-627**) dispenses a wealth of information on hiking trails, ski lifts and passes, bike rentals, and rafting trips. It's open daily 9am to 7pm.

EXPLORING AOSTA

An appealing mountain town with an ancient heart, Aosta—nicknamed "the Rome of the Alps"—is surrounded by snowcapped peaks and steeped in a history that goes back to Roman times. Although you're not going to find much pristine Alpine quaintness here in the Valle d'Aosta's busy tourist center, you will find Roman ruins, medieval bell towers, and chic shops. Aosta's **weekly market** day is Tuesday, when stalls selling food, clothes, and crafts fill the Piazza Cavalieri di Vittorio Veneto.

Well-preserved city walls date from the days when Aosta was one of Rome's most important trading and military outposts. A **Roman bridge** spans the River Buthier, and two Roman gates arch gracefully across the Via San Anselmo. The **Porta Pretoria** forms the western entrance to the Roman town and the **Arco di Augusto** the eastern entrance. The **Teatro Romano** and the ruins of the **amphitheater** are north of the Porta Pretoria; the ruins of the **forum** are in an adjacent park. The theater and forum are open generally from 9am to 6pm (typically closed for a few hours in the afternoon in the winter), and admission is free. Architectural fragments from these monuments that were found during excavations are displayed in Aosta's **Archaeological Museum** at Piazza Roncas 12 (✆ **0165-275-902;** free admission; open daily 9am–7pm, in fall and winter Tues–Sun 10am–1pm, 2–5pm).

Summer hiking in Courmayeur.

The Valle d'Aosta

Most visitors to the Valle d'Aosta come here for the outdoor activities rather than to sightsee; the region has some of Italy's best hiking trails. In summer, climbers, cyclists, and ramblers head for the untamed **Parco Nazionale del Gran Paradiso** (see "Italian Wilderness," see below). In winter, the meadows and alpine forests around **Cogne** boast some of the region's best cross-country skiing. There's an **ice rink** in Aosta called **Art on Ice** at Corso Lancieri di Aosta 47 (www.artoniceaosta.it; ✆ **0165-415-66**), and if you're after something a bit different, consider **dog sledding** (www.dogsledman.com) near Courmayeur.

Most visitors, however, come for the **downhill skiing** and **snowboarding** destinations of **Courmayeur, Breuil-Cervinia,** and the **Monte Rose** ski area around the resort towns of Champoluc and Gressoney. There are trails for all levels, from gentle nursery slopes to black runs and mogul fields. Expert skiers are best off at high-altitude **La Thuile** for excellent off-trail

Italian Wilderness

The little town of Cogne is the gateway to one of Europe's finest parcels of unspoiled wilderness, **Parco Nazionale del Gran Paradiso.** Once the hunting grounds of King Vittorio Emanuele II, this vast and lovely national park—Italy's oldest—encompasses the jagged peaks of **Gran Paradiso** (4,061m/13,323-ft. high), five valleys, and some 703 sq. km (271 sq. miles) of forests and pastureland. Many Alpine beasts roam wild here, including the ibex (curly-horned goat) and the elusive chamois (small antelope), both of which are nearly extinct in Europe. Humans can roam these wilds via a vast network of well-marked **hiking trails**. Cogne is also well-respected for its 80km (50 miles) of challenging **cross-country (Nordic) skiing trails;** check www.funiviegranparadiso.it for details. The park's main **visitor center** is at Via Alpetta, Ronco Canavese (www.pngp.it/en; ✆ **011-860-6233 or 348-762-5890**). Admission is free.

UP AND OVER mont blanc

Riding high over Mont Blanc—Europe's tallest mountain at 4,811m (15,784 ft.)—has to be one of the most awe-inspiring experiences in the Italian Alps. It's an enchanted journey passing over glaciers and steep ravines, mountain lakes, and snowy peaks on the Italian side of the Vallée Blanche.

For years, this epic trek involved three changes of cable car, starting from the little ski village of **La Palud** (3km/1.75 miles above Courmayeur) and ascending through **Le Pavillon** and **Rifugio Torino** to the viewing terrace at **Punta Helbronner** (3,462m/11,358 ft.), in the heart of the Mont Blanc Massif. From here it was possible to take the cable car down to **Aiguille de Midi** on the French side of Mont Blanc, and then the Panoramic Mont-Blanc Gondola on into the party-loving resort of **Chamonix**.

But all that changed in 2015 when a new, vastly improved cable-car service, **Skyway Monte Bianco** (www.montebianco.com), launched. Run by Funivie del Monte Biano, the system has sleek rotating gondolas departing from a swish new station at **Pontal d'Entrèves** (near the entrance to the Mont Blanc tunnel) on a high-speed connection up to Punta Helbronner for a bird's-eye view of Monte Bianco and the surrounding peaks of Gran Paradiso and Monte Cervinia (Matterhorn). This new service offers breathtaking views, but be prepared to pay for them.

A roundtrip ticket from Pontal (Courmayeur) to Punta Helbronner is 48€ for adults (free for children 7 and under) and 36€ one way, while roundtrip from Pontal to Pavillon du Mont-Fréty—the midway point, which has a restaurant and shopping area—costs 27€ and 18.50€ one way. Stopping at the midway point is an option for those who want to enjoy the views but may suffer from altitude sickness at the very top at Punta Helbronner.

If you do venture all the way to Chamonix in your travels, the best way back to Courmayeur is to take the SAVDA/SAT bus service through Mont Blanc tunnel. Six buses run each way, and the journey takes 45 minutes (www.sat-montblanc.com or www.savda.it; tickets 15€, discounts available for children under age 12).

powder and heli-skiing. The ski season kicks off in early December and, weather permitting, runs through April. Altogether there are 800km (500 miles) of ski runs available under the **Valle d'Aosta ski pass;** multi-day passes cost from 138€ for 3 days up to 485€ for 2 weeks. One child under age 8 skis free with each adult who buys the pass. More details are available at www.skilife.ski or www.lathuile.it.

Where to Eat & Stay

In the ski season, many hotels in Valle d'Aosta expect guests to eat on the premises and stay 3 nights or more, but are more flexible outside busy tourist times.

The Valle d'Aosta is the land of mountain food—hams and salamis, creamy polenta—and buttery Fontina is the cheese of choice.

The Skyway Monte Bianco ascends Mont Blanc.

Hostellerie du Cheval Blanc ★★ This is no traditional wooden chalet, but if you're after family comforts and town-center convenience—in addition to Alpine views and a garden—the modern design of the Cheval Blanc (meaning "white horse") fits the bill. The hotel is designed around a massive atrium with stylish leather sofas and Oriental rugs. The hotel boasts two restaurants. **Le Petit** is fairly expensive, but the **Brasserie** lends itself to early suppers with kids. The rooms are conventionally decorated in muted shades, and the bathrooms come in highly ornate marble, most with baths as well as showers. Skiers will appreciate that a winter shuttle runs to the cable car up to Pila, while the pool and sauna provide perfect après-ski relaxation before a night of fun in the bars of Aosta. Guests have access to a gym and wellness center with indoor swimming pool, Jacuzzi, two saunas, and massage rooms (massages and other treatments are available at additional cost).

Rue Clavalité 20, Aosta. www.chevalblanc.it. ✆ **0165-239-140.** 55 units. 130€ doubles; 180€–200€ suite, includes breakfast. **Amenities:** 2 restaurants; bar; children's playroom; indoor pool; gym; sauna; spa; room service; Wi-Fi (free).

Osteria da Nando ★★ FONDUE This cheery terracotta-colored *osteria* is a true family affair, run by the Scarpa family since 1957. Over

the years, it has become one of Aosta's most popular restaurants for its fondues in many guises, from *bourguignonne* served with tender beef filet to *raclette* served with creamy Fontina cheese and chunks of chewy bread, alongside the classic Piedmontese dish of *bagna cauda* (anchovy fondue). The restaurant changes its menu each season and is continuously aiming to use local ingredients. A seven-course tasting menu can be ordered with wine pairings. Desserts are a little basic, such as French-style crèpes and gateaux, but the wine selection is impressively local.
Via Sant'Anselmo 99. Aosta. www.osterianando.com. ✆ **0165-44-455.** Main courses 12€–25€. Daily (closed Tues) noon–2pm, 7:30–10pm. Closed 2 weeks late June to early July.

Ristorante La Palud ★★ PIZZA/SEAFOOD This buzzing pizzeria/restaurant has the look of a sophisticated mountain chalet, offering impressive Monte Bianco and glacier views. Thanks to its position near the tunnel into France, it is nearly always packed, which means you should always reserve in advance. It is popular not just for the location, but also for its enormous pizzas, creamy polenta dishes, and fresh fish brought up from the Ligurian coast on Fridays. Desserts are prepared daily by the pastry chef. In summer, sit outside on the flower-filled terrace; in winter, huddle around the open fire and admire the drifts of snow piled up outside.
Strada la Palud 17, Courmayeur. www.ristorantepizzerialapalud.com ✆ **0165-89-169.** Main courses 10€–25€. Mon–Sun noon–3:30pm, 7:30–10:30pm.

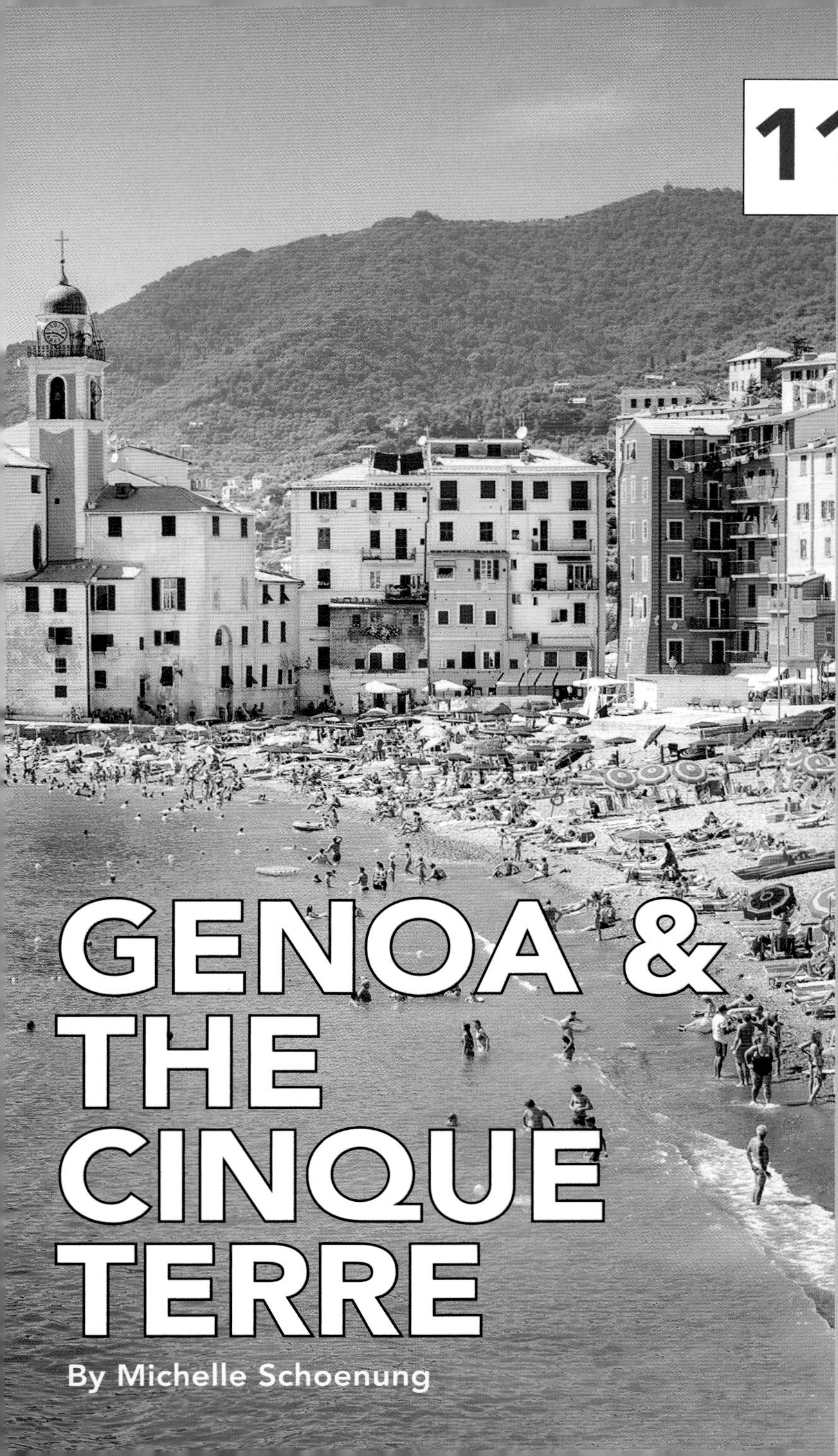

11

GENOA & THE CINQUE TERRE

By Michelle Schoenung

Hugging the Mediterranean coastline from the French border to the tip of Tuscany lies a crescent-shaped strip of land that makes up the region of Liguria. The pleasures of this region are no secret. Since the 19th century, world-weary travelers have been heading for Liguria's resorts, such as San Remo and Portofino, to enjoy balmy weather and a sapphire-blue sea. Beyond the beach, the stones and tile of fishing villages, small resort towns, and proud old port cities bake in the sun, and hillsides are fragrant with the scent of bougainvillea and pines.

Liguria is really two coasts. First, the "white sand" stretch west of Genoa known as the **Riviera di Ponente (Setting Sun)** is studded with fashionable resorts, many of which, like San Remo, have seen their heydays fade but continue to entice visitors with palm-fringed promenades and a gentle way of life. The rockier, more rugged, but also more colorful fishing-village-filled stretch to the southeast of Genoa, known as the **Riviera di Levante (Rising Sun),** extends past the posh harbor of Portofino to the ever popular villages of the Cinque Terre.

The province's capital, Genoa, is Italy's busiest port, an ancient center of commerce, and one of history's great maritime powers. Despite its rough exterior, it is an underrated gem filled with architectural delights, Italy's largest historic center, and a sense of "real Italy" that has become hard to come by in many of the country's more popular cities.

GENOA (GENOVA) ★★

142km (88 miles) S of Milan, 501km (311 miles) NW of Rome, 194km (120 miles) E of Nice

With its dizzying mix of old and new, **Genoa** is as multilayered as the hills it clings to. It was and is, first and foremost, a port city: an important maritime center for the Roman Empire, boyhood home of Christopher Columbus (whose much-restored house still stands near the medieval walls), and, fueled by seafaring trade that stretched to the Middle East, one of the largest and wealthiest cities of Renaissance Europe.

PREVIOUS PAGE: **Beach in Camogli.**

The Italian Riviera
To Turin
Bra
Alba
Acqui Terme
A26
E25
A7
E62
To Milan
To Parma
Ovada
Busca
A6
E716
PIEDMONT
Ligurian
Busalla
Apennines
EMILIA-ROMAGNA
A15
E33
Casella
Montebruno
Masone
Torriglia
Rezzoaglio
LIGURIA
Cabanne
Borgo Val di Taro
Cuneo
Cairo Montenotte
Voltri
Mondovi
Arenzano
Pegli
GENOA
SP225
Borzonasca
Millesimo
Varazze
Nervi
Recco
Rapallo
E74
Albisola
Camogli
S. Margherita Ligure
Varese Ligure
Savona
S. Fruttuoso
Chiavari
Maritime Alps
SP428
SP1
Portofino
SP523
TUSCANY
Gulf of Genoa
Paradiso
A10
Spotorno
Sestri Levante
Noli
Moneglia
SP1
Brugnato
Finale Ligure
Varigotti
Deiva Marina
Riviera di Levante
Tigullio
A12
Toirano
Loano
Levanto
Monterosso
E80
Monesi
Mendatica
Borghetto S. Spirito
Vernazza
FRANCE
SP453
Corniglia
La Spezia
Sarzana
Pieve di Teco
Albenga
Riviera delle Palme
Cinque Terre
Manarola
Triora
Riomaggiore
Lerici
Andora
Alassio
Portovenere
Tellaro
Carrara
SP64
Laigueglia
Baiardo
Cervo
Riviera di Ponente
Oneglia
Diano Marina
Dolceacqua
Taggia
Imperia
Giardini Botanici Hanbury
A10
Ventimiglia
Arma di Taggia
Liguria Sea
Venice
Genoa
The Italian Riviera
San Remo
Menton
Bordighera
Riviera di Fiori
San Remo
Florence
Monte Carlo
Nice
MONACO
Rome
0
20 mi
0
20 km

Genoa's Via XX Settembre.

Genoa began as a port of the ancient Ligurian people at least by the 6th century B.C. and by the early Middle Ages had become a formidable maritime power, conquering the surrounding coast and the mighty outlying islands of Corsica and Sardinia. Genoa established colonies throughout North Africa and the Middle East, and made massive gains during the Crusades. With bigger success came bigger rivals, and Genoa locked commercial and military horns with Venice, which eventually took the upper hand in the late 1300s. Genoa increasingly fell under the control of outsiders, and though self-government returned for a while in the 16th century, sea trade was shifting to Spain and eventually to its American colonies. Genoa's most famous son, Columbus, had to travel to Spain to find the financial backing for his exploration across the Atlantic.

It's easy to capture glimpses of Genoa's former glory days on the narrow lanes and dank alleys of the portside Old Town, where treasure-filled palaces and fine marble churches stand next to laundry-draped tenements and brothels. The other Genoa, the modern city that stretches for miles along the coast and climbs the hills, is a city of international business, peaceful parks, and breezy belvederes from which you can enjoy fine views of this colorful metropolis and the sea.

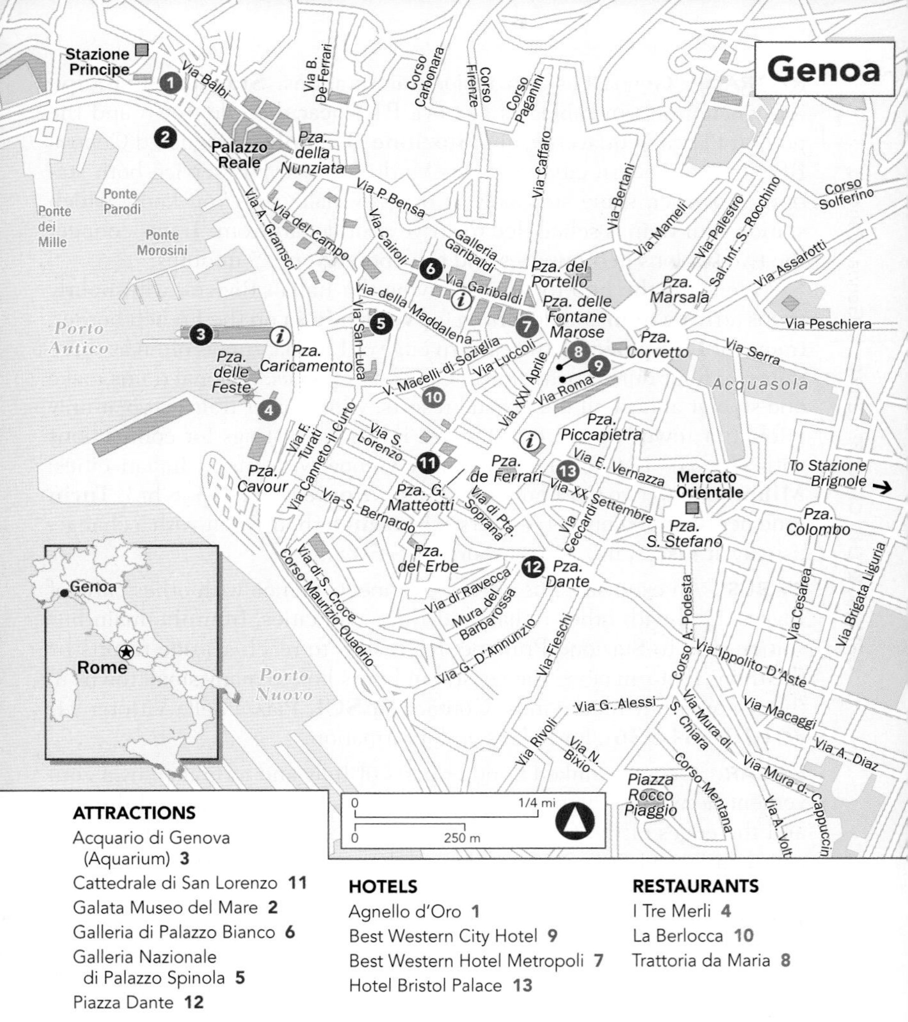

Essentials

GETTING THERE

BY PLANE Flights to and from most European capitals serve **Cristoforo Colombo International Airport,** just 6.5km (4 miles) west of the city center (www.airport.genova.it; ✆ **010-60-151**). **Volabus** (www.amt.genova.it; ✆ **010-558-2414**) connects the airport with the Principe and Brignole train stations, with buses running the 30-minute trip once or twice an hour from 5am to 10pm; buy tickets on the bus (6€, includes a transfer to or from the city transportation network).

BY TRAIN Genoa has two major train stations: **Stazione Principe** (designated on timetables as Genova P.P.) near the Old Town and the port on Piazza Acquaverde, and **Stazione Brignole** (designated Genova BR.) in the modern city on Piazza Verdi. Many trains service both stations; however, some stop only at one, so make sure you know which station your train is scheduled to arrive at or depart from. Trains connect the two stations in 5 minutes and run about every 15 minutes.

Genoa is the hub for trains serving the Italian Riviera, with hourly trains arriving from and departing for **Ventimiglia** on the French border; trains for **La Spezia,** at the eastern edge of Liguria, run as often as three trains an hour during peak times. Check timetables: regional trains make one stop at almost all the coastal resorts, while faster trains stop at only a few (for towns in this chapter, see individual listings for connections with Genoa). Lots of trains connect Genoa with major Italian cities: **Milan** (one to two per hour; 1½–2 hrs.), **Rome** (hourly; 5–6 hr.), **Turin** (one per hour; regional: 1¾–2 hrs.), **Florence** (hourly but with a change, usually at Pisa; 3 hr.), **Pisa** (hourly; 1½–3 hrs.).

BY BUS An extensive bus network connects Genoa with other parts of Liguria, and with other Italian and European cities, from the main bus station next to Stazione Principe. It's easiest to reach seaside resorts by the trains that run along the coast, but buses link to many small towns in the region's hilly hinterlands. Contact **PESCI,** Piazza della Vittoria 94r (✆ **010-564-936**), for tickets and information.

BY CAR Genoa is linked to other parts of Italy and to France by a convenient network of highways. Genoa has lots of parking around the port and the edges of the Old Town, so you can usually find a spot easily. It can be pricey (1.50€–2.50€ an hour), though in some lots you don't pay for the overnight hours.

BY FERRY Genoa connects to several other major Mediterranean ports, including Barcelona, as well as Sardinia and Sicily by ferry (www.traghettitalia.it). Most boats leave and depart from the Stazione Marittima (✆ **010-089-8300**), which is on a waterfront roadway, Via Marina D'Italia, about a 5-minute walk south of Stazione Principe. For service to and from the **Riviera Levante,** check with **Tigullio** (www.traghettiportofino.it; ✆ **0185-284-670**) or Golfo Paradiso (www.golfoparadiso.it; ✆ **0185-772091**); there's almost hourly service from 9am to 5pm daily in July and August.

VISITOR INFORMATION

The **main tourist office** is on **Via Garibaldi 12r** across from the beautiful city hall (www.visitgenoa.it; ✆ **010-557-2903**), open daily 9am to 6:20pm. There are also branches near the Porto Antico in Via al Porto Antico 2, open daily from about 9am to 6pm with longer hours in the summer months; and **Cristoforo Colombo airport,** open daily 9am to 1pm and 1:30 to 5:30pm.

GETTING AROUND

Given Genoa's labyrinth of small streets (many of which cannot be negotiated by car or bus), the only way to traverse much of the city is on foot—and you'll need a good map. The tourist office gives out terrific maps, but you can also buy an audio guide with map that really helps you navigate the small *vicoli* or alleyways. Genovese are usually happy to direct visitors, but given the geography with which they are dealing, their instructions can be complicated.

BY BUS Bus tickets (1.50€) are available at newsstands and at ticket booths, *tabacchi* (tobacconists, marked by a brown and white T sign), and at the train stations; look for the symbol **AMT** (www.amt.genova.it; ✆ **010-558-2414**). Otherwise, tickets cost 2.50€ on board on nights and weekends. You must stamp your ticket when you board. Bus tickets can also be used on the funiculars and public elevators that climb the city's steep hills surrounding the ancient core of the town. Tickets good for 24 hours cost 4.50€, or 9€ for four people (two people travel for free).

Genoa Takes to the Sea

Every June, an ancient tradition continues when Genoa takes to the sea in the **Regata delle Antiche Repubbliche Marinare,** rowing against crews from its ancient maritime rivals, Amalfi, Pisa, and Venice, who host the event in turn. Another spectacular—though more modern—regatta takes place every April: the **Millevele,** or Thousand Sails, when Genoa's bay is carpeted with the mainsails and spinnakers of nautical enthusiasts from around the world.

BY TAXI Metered taxis, which you can find at cabstands, are a convenient and safe way to get around Genoa at night. For instance, you may well want to consider taking a taxi from a restaurant in the Old Town to your hotel or to one of the train stations (especially Stazione Brignole, which is a bit farther out). Cabstands at Piazza della Nunziata, Piazza Fontane Marose, and Piazza de Ferrari are especially convenient to the Old Town, or call a **radio taxi** at ✆ **010-5966.**

BY SUBWAY The city's nascent subway system is a work in progress, with only eight stops on a single line between the new Brignole station and a suburb to the northwest called Certosa (there are convenient stops in between at Stazione Principe and at Dinegro close to the ferry port). The tickets are the same as those used for the bus.

CITY LAYOUT

Genoa extends for miles along the coast, with neighborhoods and suburbs tucked into valleys and climbing the city's many hills. Most sights of interest are in the **Old Town,** a fascinating jumble of old *palazzi,* shabby tenements, cramped squares, and tiny lanes and alleyways clustered on the eastern side of the old port. The city's two train stations are located on either side of the Old Town. As confusing as Genoa's topography is,

A Market Cornucopia

The sprawling **Mercato Orientale,** Genoa's boisterous indoor food market, evokes the days when ships brought back spices and other commodities from the ends of the earth. An excellent place to stock up on olives, herbs, fresh fruit, and other Ligurian products, it is held Monday through Wednesday 7:30am to 1pm and 3:30 to 7:30pm and Thursday through Saturday from 7:30am to 7:30pm with entrances on Via XX Settembre and Via Galata (about halfway between Piazza de Ferrari at the edge of the Old Town and Stazione Brignole). The district just north of the market (especially Via San Vincenzo and Via Colombo) is a gourmand's dream, with many bakeries, *pasticcerie* (pastry shops), and stores selling pasta and cheese, wine, olive oil, and other foodstuffs.

wherever you are in the Old Town, you are only a short walk or bus or taxi ride from one of these two stations.

Stazione Principe is the closest, just to the west; from **Piazza Acquaverde,** in front of the station, follow **Via Balbi** through **Piazza della Nunziata** and **Via Bensa** to **Via Cairoli,** which runs into Via Garibaldi (the walk will take about 15 min.). **Via Garibaldi,** lined with a succession of majestic *palazzi,* forms the northern flank of the Old Town and is the best place to begin your explorations. Many of the city's most important museums and monuments are on and around this street, and from here you can descend into the warren of little lanes, known as ***caruggi,*** that lead through the heart of the city and down to the port.

From **Stazione Brignole,** walk straight across the broad, open space to Piazza della Vittoria/Via Luigi Cadorna and turn right to follow broad **Via XX Settembre,** one of the city's major shopping avenues, due west for about 15 or 20 minutes to **Piazza de Ferrari,** which is on the eastern edge of the Old Town. From here, **Via San Lorenzo,** accessed by exiting the southwest corner of the square, will lead you past Genoa's cathedral and to the port. To reach Via Garibaldi, go north from Piazza de Ferrari on **Via XXV Aprile** to **Piazza delle Fontane Marose.** This busy square marks the eastern end of Via Garibaldi.

[FastFACTS] GENOA

Bookstores Genoa's best source for English-language books and other media is **Feltrinelli,** Via Ceccardi 16, near Piazza De Ferrari, just off of Via XX Settembre (www.lafeltrinelli.it; ✆).

Crime Genoa is a relatively safe city, but some of the very small alleyways of the Old Town near the port can be sketchy at night, and even during the day they can sometimes make you feel unsafe. Wait for other people, preferably locals, before entering little-trafficked alleyways and avoid any street that makes you feel uneasy. In an **emergency,** call ✆ **113.** There is a **police station** on the cusp of the Old Town and the port at Via Balbi 38/B (✆ **010-254-871**).

Drugstores Pharmacies keep extended hours on a rotating basis; dial ✆ **192** to learn which ones are open late in a particular week. Usually open overnight are **Pescetto,** Via Balbi 185r (✆ **010-261-609**), across from Stazione Principe; and **Europa,** Corso Europa 676 (✆ **010-380-239**).

Emergencies The general emergency number is ✆ **113;** for an ambulance, dial ✆ **118.** Both are free calls.

Holidays Genoa's patron saint, San Giovanni Battista (Saint John the Baptist), is the same as Turin's and is honored on June 24. For a list of official state holidays, see p. 35.

Hospitals The **Ospedale San Martino,** Largo Rosanna Benzi 10 (✆ **010-5551**), offers a variety of medical services.

Luggage Storage The luggage storage office in Stazione Principe is along track 11 and is open daily 8am to 8pm; the fee is 6€ per piece of baggage for the first 5 hours. In Stazione Brignole the storage office is on the ground floor (same hours and rates as Principe).

Post Office Genoa's main post office is at **Via Dante 4/b** (✆ **010-531-8781**). This office is open Monday through Friday 8:20am to 7:05pm, and on Saturdays from 8:20am to 12:35pm, while the other offices around town—including those at the two train stations and the airport—have shorter hours.

Telephone The area code for Genoa is ✆ **010.**

Exploring Genoa

Acquario di Genova (Aquarium of Genoa) ★★★ AQUARIUM Europe's largest aquarium is Genoa's biggest draw and a must-see for travelers with children. The structure alone is remarkable, resembling a ship and built alongside a pier in the old harbor; it's about a 15-minute walk from Stazione Principe and 10 minutes from Via Garibaldi. Inside, more than 50 aquatic displays re-create Red Sea coral reefs, pools in the tropical rainforests of the Amazon River basin, and other marine ecosystems that provide a home for sharks, seals, dolphins, penguins, piranhas, and just about every other kind of water creature. Look for the tiny orange frogs the size of a thumbnail from Madagascar. Descriptions are posted in English, and there's a 3-D film on ocean life (ask for printed English narration). Lines can get long, so come early.

Ponte Spinola (at the port). www.acquariodigenova.it. ✆ **010-23451.** 2€ adults, 21€ seniors 65 and over, 15€ children 4–12. Mon–Fri 9:30am–7:30pm; Sat–Sun 9:30am–8:30pm (July–Aug daily until 10:30pm). Bus: 1-8 and 12-15. Metro: Darsena.

Cattedrale di San Lorenzo ★ CATHEDRAL The austerity of this church's black-and-white-striped 12th-century facade is enlivened ever so slightly by fanciful French Gothic carvings around the portal and the presence of two stone lions. A later addition is the bell tower, completed in the 16th century. In the frescoed interior, chapels house two of Genoa's most notable curiosities: Beyond the first pilaster on the right is

Genoa's Gothic Cattedrale di San Lorenzo.

a still-unexploded shell fired through the roof from a British ship during World War II; and in the Cappella di San Giovanni (left aisle), a 13th-century crypt contains what crusaders returning from the Holy Land claimed to be relics of John the Baptist. The adjoining treasury appears to specialize in fabled tableware of doubtful provenance: the plate upon which Saint John's head was supposedly served to Salome, a bowl allegedly used at the Last Supper, and a bowl thought at one time to be the Holy Grail. Less storied but nonetheless magnificent gold and bejeweled objects reflect Genoa's medieval prominence as a maritime power. Entrance to the treasury is only by guided tour in Italian, but it's still worth seeing what is inside, even if the extent of your Italian is *gelato* and *pizza*.

Piazza San Lorenzo. ✆ **010-254-1250.** Cathedral free; treasury 6€ adults, 5€ seniors and students. Cathedral: Mon–Sat 9am–noon and 3–6pm. Treasury: By half-hour guided tour only, Mon–Sat 9am–noon and 3–6pm. Bus: 1, 7, 8, 17, 18, 19, 20.

Galata Museo del Mare (Museum of the Seas) ★★ MUSEUM
Located on "museum row" along the port, the Galata museum is a must-see. Visiting the Galata is like embarking on a voyage—despite its

modern appearance from renovations when the museum opened in 2004, the building itself is the oldest surviving construction of the dockyard from the old Republic, where Genovese galleys were built during the 17th century. You enter into the gallery dedicated to the old port with paintings and artifacts of the period, and then it's on to the full-scale reproduction of a Genovese "attack ship," with fun artifacts and props that will engage all ages. Billing itself as the largest and most innovative maritime museum in Europe, the Galata aims to combine old and new.

Ponte Parodi (at the port). www.galatamuseodelmare.it. ✆ **010-234-5655.** 12€ adults, 10€ seniors 65 and over, 7€ children 4–12. Mar–Oct daily 10am–7:30pm; Nov–Feb Tues–Fri 10am–6pm, Sat–Sun 10am–7:30pm (last entry 1 hr. before closing). Bus: 1-8 and 12-15. Metro: Darsena (a 10-min. walk or hop on the 1€ shuttle).

Galleria di Palazzo Bianco (White Palace) ★★ MUSEUM The White Palace can be considered the oldest and, at the same time, the most recent of the magnificent *palazzi* along ritzy Via Garibaldi, also known as the Strada Nuova (and a UNESCO World Heritage site). Although it was built during the mid-16th century by Luca Grimaldi, a scion of one of the most important Genovese families, the gorgeous white facade one sees today was reconstructed in the 18th century. Maria Durazzo Brignole-Sale de Ferrari donated the palace and her art collection to the city in 1884. It now displays an impressive collection of art, heavy on painters of the Spanish and Flemish schools and including works by Van Dyck, Rubens, Filippino Lippi, Veronese, and Caravaggio. The museum's most notable holding is the "Portrait of a Lady," by Lucas Cranach the Elder.

Via Garibaldi 11. www.museidigenova.it/it/content/palazzo-bianco. ✆ **010-557-2193.** 9€ adults; includes entrance to Palazzo Rosso and Palazzo Tursi. Oct 11–Mar 26 Tues–Fri 9am–6:30pm; Sat–Sun 9:30am–6:30pm. Mar 28–Oct 8 Tues–Fri 9am–7pm; Sat–Sun 10am–7:30pm. Bus: 18, 20, 35, 37, 39, 40, 41, 42.

Galleria Nazionale di Palazzo Spinola ★ MUSEUM Another prominent Genovese family, the Spinolas, donated their palace and magnificent art collection to the city in 1958. Not only is the art collection

A Cumulative Ticket

Admission to Genoa's major **palaces and art galleries** is grouped together on the **Card Musei** (12€ for 1 day, 20€ for 2 days; or 15€ and 25€ including unlimited use of the city's public transport), which includes entrance to the principal palaces, the Museo Sant'Agostino, San Lorenzo, the Galleria Nazionale di Palazzo Spinola, the Museo di Palazzo Reale, and a handful of other museums around town, plus discounts to the aquarium, the Galata museum, and movie theaters. Pick it up at any city museum, the airport tourist office, or in one of several bookstores downtown (www.visitgenoa.it).

something to behold, the centuries-old home itself is a wonderful example of how Genovese aristocrats really lived, among frescos and mirrored galleries. As in Genoa's other art collections, you will find masterworks that range from native artists like Strozzi, da Messina, Reni, Giordano, and De Ferrari, to van Dyck and other painters of the Dutch and Flemish schools, whom Genoa's wealthy were fond of commissioning to paint their portraits.

Piazza Pellicceria 1. www.palazzospinola.beniculturali.it. ✆ **010-270-5300.** 4€ adults, 2€ ages 18–25, free for those under 18 or 65 and over, or pay 12€ for a Card Musei cumulative ticket (see box below). Tues–Sat 8:30am–7:30pm; Sun 1:30–7:30pm. Bus: 1, 18, 20, 34.

Via Garibaldi, Genoa.

Piazza Dante ★ Though most of this square just south of Piazza de Ferrari is made up of 1930s-era office buildings, one end is bounded by the reconstructed **Porta Soprana ★★**, a twin-towered town gate built in 1155. The main draw, though, is the small **house** (rebuilt in the 18th c.), standing a bit incongruously in a tidy little park below the gate, said to have belonged to **Christopher Columbus's father,** who was a weaver and gatekeeper (whether young Christopher lived here is open to debate).

Bus: 14, 35, 42, 44.

Via Garibaldi ★★ Many of Genoa's museums and other sights are clustered on and around this street, also known as Strada Nuova, one of the most beautiful in Italy. Here Genoa's wealthy families built palaces in the 16th and 17th centuries. Aside from the collections housed in the **Galleria di Palazzo Bianco** (see above), the street contains a wealth of other treasures. The **Palazzo Podesta,** at no. 7, hides a beautiful fountain in its courtyard, and the **Palazzo Tursi** (no. 9), which houses municipal offices, displays artifacts of famous locals: letters written by Columbus and a violin of Nicolo Paganini (still played on special occasions).

Palazzo Tursi entrance included in price of admission to the Galleria di Palazzo Bianco. Oct 11–Mar 26 Tues–Fri 9am–6:30pm; Sat–Sun 9:30am–6:30pm; Mar 28–Oct 8 Tues–Fri 9am–7pm Sat–Sun 10am–7:30pm. Bus: 20, 32, 33, 35, 36, 41, 42.

Where to Stay

Despite the draw of the aquarium and its intriguing Old Town, Genoa is still geared more to business travelers. A pleasant boom of new quality accommodations has sprouted up, however, as the city starts to become more tourist-friendly. It is best to avoid hotels in the heart of the Old Town, especially around the harbor, as many are a little sketchy. Keep in mind, Genoa books up solid during its annual boat show, the world's largest, in October. The upper end of the price range listed below in most cases applies only the week of the boat show; the maximum the rest of the year is considerably lower, sometimes as much as 25%.

EXPENSIVE

Hotel Bristol Palace ★ This 19th-century *palazzo* has maintained the opulent oval staircase and beautiful stained-glass dome that have helped make it one of Genoa's most regal hotels. Located in the middle of the city's shopping district and mere steps from Genoa's most famous museums and historic palazzos, it is surprisingly quiet and perfectly located for exploring the sights. The **Ristorante Giotto** on the second floor serves sophisticated local cuisine at lunch and dinner most days of the week. An outdoor dining terrace adds even more appeal to this oasis-like lodging in the city center. Check the website for special rates, especially during the weekends, as standard rates are quite high.

Via XX Settembre 35. www.hotelbristolpalace.com. ✆ **010-592-541.** 133 units. 130€–470€ double; 249€–699€ junior suite. Rates include breakfast. **Amenities:** Restaurant; bar; babysitting; bikes; concierge; room service; Wi-Fi (free).

MODERATE

Best Western Hotel Metropoli ★★ The location of this hotel right in the center of the action may be its best selling point. On the corner of a lovely square and a pedestrian-only street in the historic center amid *palazzos* from the 16th century, Hotel Metropoli offers very good lodging with modern amenities, a robust breakfast buffet, and helpful service. Guest rooms are soundproofed, clean, and comfortable, with refurbished bathrooms. Family rooms have bunk beds and game consoles, and rooms especially meant for women come complete with professional-grade hair dryers, a L'Occitane beauty kit, and combination wellness packages.

Piazza delle Fontane Marose. www.hotelmetropoli.it. ✆ **010-246-8888.** 48 units. 93€–246€ double; 99€–260€ triple. Rates include breakfast. **Amenities:** Bar; room service; Wi-Fi (free).

Best Western City Hotel ★★ This nondescript building just off the city's main shopping street is actually a very nice, modern, and well-equipped 4-star hotel. Rooms have brightly colored contemporary decor, flatscreen TVs, and sleek built-ins; family rooms include bunk beds. Rooms on the upper floors have fantastic views of the city and port.

Breakfasts are hearty. A small wellness "corner" open to all guests has a sauna, Turkish bath, salt room, and shower with chromotherapy features.

Via San Sebastiano 6. www.bwcityhotel-ge.it. ✆ **010-584-707.** 64 units. 95€–275€ double. Rates include breakfast. **Amenities:** Bar; room service; Wi-Fi (free).

INEXPENSIVE

Agnello d'Oro ★ This former convent is now a low-cost *locanda.* It is just a few blocks away from Stazione Principe and on the edge of the Old Town, which can be viewed from the hotel terrace. Ferry and cruise-ship terminals are within easy walking distance. Most of the rooms are very basic but some still retain the building's original 16th-century character, with high ceilings (rooms numbered in the teens) or vaulted ones (rooms numbered under 10). Some top-floor rooms come with the added charm of balconies and views over the Old Town and harbor (best from no. 56). The owner is friendly and helpful with sightseeing tips. There are cheaper online rates that don't include breakfast, and if you are willing to pay ahead of time, that will shave even more off the rate.

Via Monachette 6, off Via Balbi. www.hotelagnellodoro.it. ✆ **010-246-2084.** 17 units. 70€–100€ double; 160€ for 4 people in 3-bedroom apt. **Amenities:** Bar; concierge; room service; Wi-Fi (free).

Where to Eat

I Tre Merli ★★ LIGURIAN/SEAFOOD This stylish restaurant overlooks the old port in a high-ceilinged room that's all black-and-white columns and exposed stone walls, nicely in line with the local architecture.

Fast . . . and Oh, So Good

All over Genoa you'll find shops selling **focaccia,** Liguria's answer to pizza, a sort of thick flatbread often stuffed or topped with cheese, herbs, olives, onions, vegetables, or prosciutto. Many of these *focaccerie* also sell ***farinata,*** a chickpea fritter that usually emerges from the oven in the shape of a big round pizza. Just point and make a hand gesture to show how much you want. Prices are by weight, and in most cases a piece of either will cost about 1.50€ to 3€. Most focaccia (especially the ones with cheese) and all *farinata* are better warm, so if the piece you are getting looks like it has been there awhile, ask them to warm it up.

A favorite spot for both snacks, near Stazione Principe, is **La Focacceria di Teobaldo ★**, Via Balbi 115r (daily 8am–8pm). **Focacceria di Via Lomellini ★**, Via Lomellini 57/59 in the heart of the Old Town (Mon–Sat 8am–7:30pm), has great *focaccia di Recco* (also called *focaccia al formaggio),* a super-thin focaccia filled with cheese and the specialty of the nearby town of Recco. Follow up with something sweet at **Fratelli Klainguti** (Piazza Macelli di Soziglia 98; ✆ **010-860-2628**). At Porto Antico, get your focaccia fix (you *will* be addicted after your first taste) at **Il Localino,** Via Turati 8r (Tues–Mon 8am–8pm; closed Wed).

Local seafood stars in dishes such as *fritua* (fried fish, squid, and shrimp with crisp vegetables and fried sage). Cheese *focaccia* comes with artichokes or arugula and Parma ham. On nice days, enjoy the terrace with sea views. I Tre Merli also operates a small wine bar and *"affittacamere"* (rooms for rent) in Camogli (see p. 560).

Calata Cattaneo 17. www.itremerli.it. ✆ **010-246-4416**. Main courses 16€–20€. Daily noon–3pm and 7:30–11pm.

La Berlocca ★ GENOVESE This bright and cozy trattoria serves good food and wine at decent prices. It is located in the historic center just a few steps from the port. The food is typically Ligurian with a focus on seafood and vegetables. Dishes are thoughtfully prepared, relying on recipes handed down throughout the generations. Special items are "off menu." Try the signature *buridda,* a traditional dish of salted cod, tomatoes, and herbs. There's also a variety of homemade pasta dishes.

Via dei Macelli di Soziglia 47r. www.laberlocca.com. ✆ **010-796-3333.** Main courses 8€–20€. Tues–Sat noon–3pm and 7–11pm and until midnight on Fri and Sat; Sun lunch only, with reservation. Closed last week of July to 3rd week of Aug.

Trattoria da Maria ★★ LIGURIAN Follow the nondescript alleyway to this simple trattoria, which also happens to be one of Genoa's most famous eateries, in business for decades (unfortunately, Maria has retired and is no longer in the kitchen). At the Trattoria da Maria, you dine side by side with lawyers, construction workers, students, and tourists. Pay no mind to the unattractive decor, and concentrate on the great dishes this Genovese institution has to offer. The handwritten menu changes daily, and the staff may not speak English—so your Italian will really get a workout here. Enjoy flavorful, no-nonsense dishes such as the near-perfect pesto, stuffed anchovies, and fish sautéed in white wine.

Vico Testadoro 14r (just off Via XXV Aprile). ✆ **010-581-080.** *Primi* and main courses 5€–9€. Fixed-price menu 10€; add 2.50€ for dessert. Mon–Sat noon–3pm and 7–9:15pm.

Entertainment & Nightlife

The Old Town, some parts of which are sketchy in broad daylight, is especially unseemly at night. Confine late-hour prowls in this area to the well-trafficked streets such as Via San Lorenzo and Via Garibaldi. On the edges of the Old Town, good places to walk at night are around the waterfront, Piazza Fontane Marose, Piazza de Ferrari, and Piazza delle Erbe, where many bars and clubs are located.

Genoa has two major venues for culture: the restored **Teatro Carlo Felice,** Piazza de Ferrari (www.carlofelice.it; ✆ **010-589-329**), home to Genoa's opera company, and the modern **Teatro Stabile di Genova** (www.teatrostabilegenova.it; ✆ **010-53-421**), on Piazza Borgo Pila near Stazione Brignole, which hosts concerts, dance, and other programs.

THE RIVIERA DI PONENTE: SAN REMO

140km (87 miles) W of Genoa, 56km (35 miles) E of Nice

Gone are the days when Tchaikovsky and the Russian empress Maria Alexandrovna joined a well-heeled mix of *nobili* strolling along San Remo's palm-lined avenues. They left behind an onion-domed Orthodox church, a few grand hotels, and a casino, but **San Remo** is a different sort of town these days. It's still the most cosmopolitan stop on the Riviera di Ponente, as the stretch of coast west of Genoa is called, catering mostly to sun-seeking Italian families in the summer and, in winter, Milanese who come down to escape the fog and chilly temperatures of their city.

If you've got a few extra days, base yourself in San Remo and explore farther along the coast, all the way to the French border. Train connections are good, and the coastal SS1 road links several charming towns. Highlights include the quiet resort town of **Bordighera** (12km/7.5 miles west of San Remo); one of Europe's finest gardens, **Giardini Hanbury** (28km/20 miles west of San Remo, just past Ventimiglia); and the inland village of **Dolceacqua** (23km/14 miles northwest of San Remo), with its well-preserved medieval core and abandoned castle.

Essentials

GETTING THERE **Trains** run hourly between San Remo and Genoa (about 2hr.). If you're arriving by train, note that San Remo's newer underground railway station, built in 2001, is a bit of a hike from the center of town and the old port. Trains from Genoa continue west for another 20 minutes to Ventimiglia on the French border. Some trains continue on into France; at Ventimiglia you can change onto one of the twice-hourly trains across the border to **Nice,** 50 minutes west.

The fastest **driving route** in and out of San Remo is Autostrada A10, which follows the coast from the French border (20 min. away) to

A Day at the Beach

The pebbly beach below the Passeggiata dell'Imperatrice is lined with beach stations, where many visitors choose to spend their days: It's easy to do, because most provide showers, snack bars, beach chairs, lounges, and umbrellas. Expect to spend up to 15€ for a basic lounge, but more like 20€ for a more elaborate sunbed arrangement with umbrella. ***Note:*** As is standard at most European resort towns without "public" sections of beach (which are usually not very nice anyway), you cannot go onto the beach without paying for at least a lounge chair.

The seaside resort town of San Remo.

Genoa (about 45 min. away). The slower coast road, SS1, cuts right through the center of town.

FESTIVALS Since the 1950s, the **Sanremo Festival** (mid- to late February; www.sanremo.rai.it) has been Italy's premier music fest, sort of an Italian Grammy Awards. It's spread out over several days with live performances by Italian pop stars, international headliners, and plenty of up-and-comers. Hotels book up and down the coast (and into France) months in advance. Call the tourist office to try to score tickets.

Exploring San Remo

San Remo's two main thoroughfares are **Via Roma** and **Corso Matteotti.** Corso Matteotti runs between **Piazza Colombo,** with its flower market, and the **casino** (see p. 556), passing through the heart of the bustling, pedestrian-only business district. Here you can shop, sit in cafes, and do a bit of true Italy people-watching. Midway along Corso Matteotti, turn north on **Via Feraldi** to reach the charming older precincts of town. From **Piazza Mercato,** Via Montà leads into the medieval quarter, **La Pigna,** set on a hill shaped like a pinecone (*la pigna* in

Italian). Aside from a few restaurants, La Pigna is a residential quarter, with tall old houses overshadowing narrow lanes that twist and turn up the hillside, with the park-enclosed ruins of a **castle** at the top.

VISITING THE CASINO

San Remo's white palace of a **casino** (www.casinosanremo.it; ✆ **0184-5951**), set intimidatingly atop a long flight of steps across from the old train station and enclosed on three sides by Corso degli Inglesi, is the hub of the local nightlife scene. You can't step foot inside without being properly attired (jacket for gents Oct–June; in general, avoid track suits, shorts, T-shirts, and flip-flops for the entire casino) and showing your passport. You must be 18 or older to enter. Poker tables start at 2€ games, but the more serious tables attract high-rollers from the length of the Riviera. Gaming rooms are open daily 2:30pm to 2:30am (Fri and Sat nights 3pm–3:30am). Things are more relaxed in the rooms set aside for slot machines, where there is no real dress code. It's open Sunday to Thursday 10am to 2:30am and Friday and Saturday 10am to 3:30am.

Where to Eat & Stay

Ristorante L'Airone ★ LIGURIAN/PIZZA This cute and always busy restaurant and pizzeria, on a pedestrian street in the center of town (exactly halfway between the Ariston Theater and the casino), serves consistently good food at decent prices. The menu focuses on traditional Ligurian dishes, such as *spaghetti alla vongole* (with clams) and *pasta al pesto,* but the thin-crust pizza is also excellent. The restaurant has been recently renovated and interiors are cozy, but you can also dine in the small garden or in the piazza that fronts the restaurant. There are several four-course menus just for children. This restaurant is quite popular, so reservations are recommended, especially for dinner.

Piazza Eroi Sanremesi 12. www.ristorantelairone.it. ✆ **0184-541-055.** Main courses 7.50€–17€. Sat–Wed noon–2:30pm; Fri–Wed 7:30–11:30pm.

Hotel Villa Maria ★★ Villa Maria offers comfort and quality in a lovely residential setting. Located on the hillside just above the casino, and not far from the beach, it is also a stone's throw from the Empress's Promenade and a new biking and walking path. The hotel's reasonable rates make the somewhat outdated style of the guest rooms forgivable. Originally three separate villas, the spacious, almost regal hotel and its many salons recall the heydays of the 1920s, '30s, and '40s. Several of these public rooms open to a nicely planted terrace. Pleasant gardens are filled with roses that flourish all year in the mild climate. Some rooms have balconies facing the sea. Because room sizes vary considerably, ask about what's available when booking or ask to see a few upon arrival. The hotel can also set up private olive oil– or wine-tasting sessions.

Corso Nuvoloni 30. www.villamariahotel.it. ✆ **0184-531-422.** 38 units, 36 with private bathroom. 60€–170€ double. Rates include breakfast. **Amenities:** Restaurant; concierge; room service; Wi-Fi (free in common areas).

Royal Hotel ★★★ This sprawling seafront resort within walking distance of the old town is a mix of old-world charm and luxury. Most of the rooms have sea views and are tastefully decorated. The gardens and seawater pool are spectacular and allow some reprieve from the sun and heat during the summer months. The buffet breakfast is particularly abundant. Along with the 5-star luxury designation comes jaw-dropping prices—even in the off-season. The website offers various package deals throughout the year to make this "kingdom of luxury" slightly more affordable. Families traveling in the high season will appreciate the kids' club offered in that period, where children can play and do activities while parents relax or take advantage of the many sports on offer.
Corso Imperatrice 80. www.royalhotelsanremo.com. ✆ **0184-5391.** 126 units. 248€–665€ double. Rates include breakfast. **Amenities:** 3 restaurants; bar; 24-hour room service; babysitting; kid's club; concierge; room service; Wi-Fi (free).

THE RIVIERA DI LEVANTE: CAMOGLI, SANTA MARGHERITA LIGURE & PORTOFINO ★★

Camogli: 26km (16 miles) E of Genoa; Santa Margherita Ligure: 31km (19 miles) E of Genoa; Portofino: 38km (24 miles) E of Genoa; Rapallo: 37km (23 miles) E of Genoa

Hugged by mountains that plunge into the sapphire-colored sea, the coast east of Genoa, the **Riviera di Levante (Shore of the Rising Sun),** is more ruggedly beautiful and less developed than the Riviera Ponente. Three of the coast's most appealing towns are within a few kilometers of one another, clinging to the shores of the Monte Portofino Promontory east of Genoa: **Camogli, Santa Margherita Ligure,** and little **Portofino.**

Essentials

GETTING THERE One to three **trains** per hour ply the coastline, connecting Genoa with Santa Margherita (25–30 min.) and Camogli (30–45 min.); the trip between Camogli and Santa Margherita takes 5 minutes by train. To get to **Portofino**, take the train to Santa Margherita and then take a taxi or bus 82 (www.atpesercizio.it; ✆ **0185-373-303**), a 25-minute ride via a beautiful coastal road (service every 30 min. to an hr.; 1.80€).

In summer, **boats** operated by Golfo Paradiso (www.golfoparadiso.it; ✆ **0185-772-091;** roundtrip tickets are 4€–35€, depending on the route) run from Camogli to Portofino and Genoa. **Tigullio ferries** (www.traghettiportofino.it; ✆ **0185-284-670**) make hourly trips from Santa Margherita to Portofino (15 min; 11€ roundtrip), for example In summer, a boat runs several days a week to the Cinque Terre (27€–30€). Hours of service vary considerably with the season; schedules are posted on the docks at Piazza Martiri della Libertà.

Camogli bay.

The fastest **car** route into the region is Autostrada A12 from Genoa (exit at Recco for Camogli), which takes about 40 minutes to either Camogli or Santa Margherita. Route SS1 along the coast from Genoa is much slower but more scenic. ***Note:*** Parking is a challenge in Camogli and Portofino in the summer, and traffic quickly gets clogged on the tiny road between Santa Margherita and Portofino. If you're coming by car, park it in Santa Margherita and take the bus or boat to Portofino.

VISITOR INFORMATION **Camogli**'s tourist office is across from the train station at Via XX Settembre 33 (www.camogliturismo.it; ✆ **0185-771-066**). In **Santa Margherita**, the tourist office is in Piazza Vittorio Veneto (www.smlturismo.it; ✆ **0185-287-485**). The **Portofino** tourist office is at Via Roma 35 (www.turismoinliguria.it; ✆ **0185-269-024**). All are open daily in summer (Portofino's office is closed Mon); expect shorter hours in winter, and a lunchtime closure between noon and 3.

Camogli ★

Camogli remains delightfully unspoiled, an authentic Ligurian fishing port with tall houses in pastel colors facing the harbor and a nice swath of beach. Given also its excellent accommodations and eateries, Camogli is a lovely place to base yourself while you explore the Riviera Levante. It's also a restful retreat from which you can visit Genoa, which is only 30

Getting Festive in Camogli

Camogli throws a well-attended annual party, the **Sagra del Pesce ★★**, on the second Sunday of May, when the town fries up thousands of sardines in a 3.6m-diameter (12-ft.) pan and passes them around for free—a practice accompanied by an annual outcry in the press about health concerns and even accusations that frozen fish is used.

The first Sunday of August, Camogli stages the lovely **Festa della Stella Maris ★**, during which a procession of boats sails to Punta Chiappa, a spot of land about 1.5km (1 mile) down the coast, and releases 10,000 burning candles. Meanwhile, the same number of candles is set afloat from the Camogli beach. If currents are favorable, the burning candles will come together at sea, signifying a year of unity for couples who watch the spectacle.

minutes away. Some say Camogli's name is derived from *"Ca de Mogge,"* or "House of the Wives" in the local dialect, so-named for the women who held down the fort while their husbands went to sea. Another possibility is that it comes from *"Ca a Muggi,"* or "clustered houses," particularly apt when you are out swimming in the sea and turn to look up at the town's wonderful mass of colorful buildings.

EXPLORING CAMOGLI

Camogli is clustered around its delightful waterfront, from which the town ascends via steep, staircased lanes to Via XX Settembre, one of the few streets in the town proper to accommodate cars (this is where the train station, tourist office, and many shops and other businesses are located). Adding to the charm of this setting is the fact that the oldest part of Camogli juts into the harbor on a picturesque little point (once an island). Here ancient houses cling to the little **Castel Dragone** and the **Basilica di Santa Maria Assunta** (**© 0185-770-130**), originally built in the 12th century but much altered through the ages; its overwhelming baroque interior is open daily 7:30am to noon and 3:30 to 7pm.

Most visitors, though, are drawn to the pleasant **seaside promenade ★** that runs the length of the town. You can swim from the pebbly beach below, and you can rent a lounge chair from one of the few beach stations for about 15€—highly recommended in the summer months, when finding even a small piece of pebbly sand is nearly impossible.

WHERE TO EAT & STAY

Bar Primula ★ CAFE/LIGHT FARE This Camogli institution is a must-visit thanks to its prime position along the *lungomare* (promenade). The outdoor tables allow for great people-watching, and patrons can be seen overflowing from the front terrace day and night. Pasta and main courses are served at lunch and dinner, but Primula is best for simple foods like panini, salads, gelato, and early-evening *aperitivo*.

Via Garibaldi 140. **© 0185-770-351.** Pizzas/main courses 9€–15€. Daily 9am–1am.

Hotel Cenobio dei Dogi ★★ The spectacular position of this resort, combined with the beautifully manicured grounds and old-world charm of the main building, make this Camogli's most popular (and most expensive) hotel. Rooms come in various shapes and sizes (and there's a big difference in size and style between standard and classic rooms) and, for the most part, are tastefully decorated in a mix of tradition and island flair. The large pool area and private beach—one part terraced stone, one part pebbles—are gorgeous and inviting. This is an especially popular destination for honeymoons and romantic getaways. Ask about the cooking classes offered by the chefs from the hotel restaurants.

Via Cuneo 34. www.cenobio.it. ✆ **0185-7241.** 108 units. 200€–480€ double includes breakfast and beach facilities. **Amenities:** 2 restaurants, 2 bars; babysitting; concierge; outdoor saltwater pool; tennis courts; watersports rentals; Wi-Fi (free).

La Camogliese ★★ This hotel is really basic, but it's affordable and perfectly located at the entrance of the old village. It is convenient to the beach and the train station. The large, bright rooms have simple furniture and comfortable beds; a few have balconies that require a slight twist of the head to take in the sea view (the best views are from rooms 3 and 16B). Bathrooms are small even by Italian standards, but they are adequate. Don't stay here to lounge in your room or the hotel's communal areas, but do come for the price and location (which make the hotel fill up fast, especially on weekends and in the summer—book early). The hotel can reserve parking nearby if you come by car.

Via Garibaldi 55. www.lacamogliese.it. ✆ **0185-771-402.** 21 units. 70€–130€ double, includes breakfast. 2- to 4-night required minimum stay. **Amenities:** Babysitting; concierge; exercise room; outdoor pool; room service; Wi-Fi (free).

Locanda I Tre Merli ★ This tiny wine bar (with rooms to let) is right on Camogli's charming harbor. Each of the five cozy guest rooms has a lovely view of the harbor. Warm, fresh focaccia is served in the morning with sublime cappuccino along with yogurt and other sweet and savory options; simply specify the night before what you want for breakfast in the morning. When the weather warms, breakfast is served outside—a real slice of true Italian seaside life, with boats coming and going, fishermen unloading their catch, and families and small children playing football along the walkway. Be patient with the small staff, and focus on what brought you here—the beautiful setting and ambience. A small wellness area with a hot tub offers a wonderful view of the port, but the large window also allows guests of the wine bar to see inside, which may be a bit awkward. If you come by car, this hotel right on the port is probably the least convenient option in town. Parking is available at the top of the hill in a very small lot that can be a tight squeeze.

Via Scalo 5. www.locandaitremerli.com. ✆ **0185-770-592.** 5 units. 170€–250€ double; 210€–250€ triple, includes breakfast. **Amenities:** Bar; Wi-Fi (free).

Focaccia by the Seaside

It might be the perfect seaside setting, or perhaps there is something in the water, but no matter the reason, Camogli has some of the best focaccia in all of Liguria. Along Via Garibaldi, the promenade above the beach, are many *focaccerie* to choose from, and though it's hard to go wrong with any of them, **Revello,** at no. 183 (closest to the church, stands out. There, Tino carries on the tradition passed down by his uncle, who first began pulling focaccia out of the oven here in 1964. Revello is open daily from 10am to 6pm (later in the summer months). You can enjoy your loot on one of the few benches outside. **O'Becco,** next door, also makes some mean focaccia—special mention goes to the version with fresh anchovies, parsley, garlic, and olive oil—and **U Caruggiu,** at the other end of Via Garibaldi, has kamut focaccia on the weekends.

Vento Ariel ★★ SEAFOOD We love the old port setting of this popular restaurant almost as much we love its food. From the main part of the promenade, make your way through the medieval archway connecting the *lungomare* to the old port and you'll find the restaurant nestled in the corner facing the *gozzi* (fishing boats of the old harbor). Seafood is done right at this "sea-to-table" restaurant. Some of the succulent dishes include *patè di seppie* (cuttlefish mousse), *acchiuge ripiene* (stuffed anchovies), and oven-baked fresh fish from the gulf blanketed in salt (the salt is removed before serving). Some of the pasta dishes are now made from kamut flour, and there are also options here for those who don't eat seafood. The wine list is extensive and contains some local, hard-to-find bottles of Vermentino and Pigato, plus the wonderful whites of Liguria. If you can, grab a table outside to drink in the local ambience as well. Reservations are highly recommended.
Calata Porto 1. www.ventoariel.it ✆ **0185-771-080.** Main courses 12€–28€. Daily noon–2:30pm and 8–11pm.

Santa Margherita Ligure ★

Santa Margherita had one brief moment in the spotlight at the beginning of the 20th century when it was an internationally renowned resort. Fortunately, the seaside town didn't let fame spoil its charm, and now that it's no longer as well known as its glitzy neighbor Portofino, it could be the Mediterranean retreat of your dreams. A palm-lined harbor, a decent beach, and a friendly ambience make Santa Margherita a fine place to settle down for a few days of sun and relaxation.

EXPLORING SANTA MARGHERITA

Life in Santa Margherita centers on its palm-fringed **waterfront,** a pleasant string of marinas, docks for pleasure and fishing boats, and pebbly beaches, in some spots with imported sand of passable quality.

Landlubbers congregate in the cafes that spill out into the town's two seaside squares, Piazza Martiri della Libertà and Piazza Vittorio Veneto.

The train station is above the waterfront, and a staircase in front of the entrance will lead you down into the heart of town. Santa Margherita's landmark of note is its namesake **Basilica di Santa Margherita** (open daily 7:30am–noon and 3–6:30pm), on Piazza Caprera and well worth a visit to view the extravagant, gilded, chandeliered interior.

One of the more interesting daily spectacles in town is the **fish market** on Lungomare Marconi from 8am to 12:30pm. On Friday, Corso Matteotti, Santa Margherita's major street for food shopping, becomes an open-air **food market.**

WHERE TO EAT & STAY

Grand Hotel Miramare ★★★ This once private villa turned top-notch hotel is pure Riviera elegance. Just a 10-minute walk from the town center along the busy road to Portofino, this hotel oozes class and money with carefully restored antique furniture and crystal chandeliers. The rooms are large, and most have parquet floors and charming stucco decorations on the walls and ceilings. The fifth-floor suites are larger, a bit more modern, and have balconies overlooking the Gulf of Tigullio. A lovely (but steep) park rises behind the hotel, from which you can take a pleasant hiking trail to Portofino and enjoy fantastic views of land and sea. You can also relax at the small, private pebble beach across the busy road. The **e'SPAce** wellness center offers another kind of relaxation indoors and even in a gazebo area in the park for outdoor treatments.

Via Milite Ignoto 30. www.grandhotelmiramare.it. ✆ **0185-287-013.** 84 units. 220€–600€ double. Rates include breakfast. **Amenities:** Restaurant, 3 bars; babysitting; concierge; outdoor heated saltwater pool; room service; spa services; watersports rentals, Wi-Fi (free).

Hotel Metropole ★★ This popular family-run hotel is just above the port and a 5-minute stroll from the town center. Some accommodations are in the main, modern building while others are in the preferable Villa Porticciolo, a dusty red villa right on the beach; rooms are smaller in the latter, but they're graced with 19th-century stuccoes, and the sea practically laps up against the building. All rooms have large terraces or balconies. The fourth floor is made up of junior suites and one double with sloped ceilings. Several rooms can be joined to make family suites, and there's daycare and a kids' play area at the beach. An outdoor seawater pool is located in the upper part of the large park that serves as the hotel's grounds. The small private beach includes a sunbathing terrace and a private boat launch. The hotel prides itself on being especially pet-friendly. Full- and half-board meal plans are available.

Via Pagana 2, Santa Margherita Ligure (GE). www.metropole.it. ✆ **0185-286-134.** 58 units. 120€–360€ double, includes breakfast. **Amenities:** 2 restaurants; bar; babysitting; exercise room; swimming pool; sauna; watersports rentals, Wi-Fi (free).

AN excursion TO SAN FRUTTUOSO

Much of the **Monte Portofino Promontory** can be approached only on foot or by boat (see below), making it a prime destination for hikers. If you want to combine some excellent exercise with magnificent glimpses of the sea through a lush forest, arm yourself with a map from the tourist offices in Camogli, Santa Margherita Ligure, Portofino, or Rapallo, and set out. You can explore the upper reaches of the promontory or aim for the **Abbazia di San Fruttuoso** (✆ **0185-772-703**), a medieval abbey surrounded by a tiny six-house hamlet and two pebbly beaches. It is about a 90-minute hike from Portofino.

Once you reach San Fruttuoso, you may well want to relax on the pebbly beach and enjoy a beverage or meal at one of the seaside bars. You can tour the stark interior of the abbey for 6.50€ (open June to mid-Sept daily 10am–5:45pm; May Tues–Sun 10am–5:45pm; Mar–Apr and Oct Tues–Sun 10am–3:30pm; and Nov–Feb Sat–Sun 10am–3:45pm). Despite these official hours, the abbey tends to close whenever the last boat leaves. Should you have your scuba or snorkeling gear along, you can take the plunge to visit **Christ of the Depths,** a statue of Jesus erected 15m (49 ft.) beneath the surface to honor sailors lost at sea.

You can also visit San Fruttuoso with one of the **boats** that run almost every hour during the summer months from Camogli. A round-trip costs 13€ (9€ one-way if you then plan to head southward from the abbey) and takes about 30 minutes. For more information, contact **Golfo Paradiso** (www.golfoparadiso.it; ✆ **0185-772-091**). ***Note:*** Hourly (in summer) **Tigullio boats** (www.traghetti portofino.it; ✆ **0185-284-670**) run to San Fruttuoso from Portofino (20 min.; 8.50€–12.50€ roundtrip), Santa Margherita (35 min.; 11€–15.0€ roundtrip), and Rapallo (50 min.; 11€–17€ roundtrip). Bear in mind that the seas are often too choppy to take passengers to San Fruttuoso, because docking there can be tricky. In that case, there are private boats you can take—smaller, rubber crafts capable of bad-weather landings—though these are expensive: From Portofino, you will likely be charged 100€ for up to 12 people.

La Paranza ★★ GENOVESE/LIGURIAN Although the ambience here is nothing special, locals say this is one of the best restaurants in town. One meal at this family-run trattoria will show you why. The menu is filled with delicious, innovative dishes, from the *bianchetti fritti* (fried baby sardines) to grilled-to-perfection fresh fish. They also serve a selection of Ligurian classics, such as homemade trofie pasta with pesto, green beans, and potatoes.

Via Jacopo Ruffini 46. www.laparanzasantamargherita.it ✆ **0185-283-686.** Main courses 12€–30€. Sun–Sat 12:30–2:20pm and 7:30–10:30pm. Closed Nov.

Portofino ★★★

Portofino is almost too beautiful for its own good—in almost any season, you'll be rubbing elbows on Portofino's harborside quays with day-tripping mobs, as well as Italian industrialists, international celebrities, and a lot of rich-but-not-so-famous folks who consider this little town to be the epicenter of the good life. If you make an appearance in the late afternoon when the crowds have thinned out a bit, you are sure to experience what remains so appealing about this enchanting place—its indelible beauty.

Colorful, exclusive Portofino.

EXPLORING PORTOFINO

The one thing that won't break the bank in Portofino is the spectacular scenery. Begin with a stroll around the stunning **harbor,** lined with expensive boutiques, eateries, and colorful houses set along the quay with steep green hills rising behind them. One of the most scenic walks takes you uphill for about 10 minutes along a well-signposted path from the west side of town just behind the harbor to the **Chiesa di San Giorgio** (✆ **0185-269-337**), built on the site of a sanctuary Roman soldiers dedicated to the Persian god Mithras. It's open daily 9am to 7pm.

From there, continue uphill for a few minutes more to Portofino's 15th-century **Castello Brown** (www.castellobrown.com; ✆ **010-251-8125**), which has a lush garden and great views of the town and harbor below. It costs 5€ and is open daily 10am to 6pm in the spring and fall (often open until 7pm in summer), and the rest of the year on Saturday and Sunday from 10am to 5pm.

For more lovely views on this stretch of coast and plenty of open sea, go even higher up through lovely pine forests to the ***faro*** (lighthouse).

From Portofino, you can also set out for a longer hike on the paths that cross the **Monte Portofino Promontory** to the Abbazia di San Fruttuoso (see "An Excursion to San Fruttuoso," p. 563). The tourist office provides maps.

WHERE TO EAT & STAY

Portofino's charms come at a price. Its few hotels are expensive enough to put them in the "trip of a lifetime" category, and the harborside restaurants can take a serious chunk out of a vacation budget as well. An alternative is to enjoy a light snack at a bar or one of the many shops selling focaccia, and wait to dine in Santa Margherita or one of the other nearby towns.

Belmond Hotel Splendido ★★★ Recently rebranded as part of the Belmond collection of luxury hotels, Splendido has been the Italian Riviera's #1 resort for more than 100 years. It has hosted Bogart and Bacall, Taylor and Burton, and, many more members of the rich and famous club than you can count. The former monastery turned 5-star luxury hotel is located in the heart of Portofino and surrounded by verdant gardens; the structure and grounds are spectacular. Nearly all of the 64 guest rooms, including 35 suites, have balconies with spectacular views across the picturesque harbor. Those looking for a wellness-based stay can choose a "sensorial journey," which includes, among other things, a welcome kit and 300€ in spa credit per stay. Be warned: The hotel's room rates may make your heart stop momentarily.

Salita Baratta 16. www.hotelsplendido.com. ✆ **0185-267-801.** 64 units. 425€–2,000€ double, includes breakfast. Closed mid-Dec to March or April. **Amenities:** 3 restaurants; bar; concierge; room service; wellness center; saltwater infinity pool; tennis court; access to hotel's motorboat; Wi-Fi (free).

Hotel Nazionale ★★ Location and price are the main two reasons to choose this hotel for your stay in Portofino. Rooms are fairly basic with minimal decoration, but you are right on the harbor and paying about one-third of what you would at any other hotel in the village. Several of the rooms are lofted suites with bedrooms upstairs. We highly recommend splurging for one of the five junior suites, which enjoy views of the harbor. Though the hotel has no elevator, luggage service is provided. Hotel staff can also help with excursions to San Fruttuoso or the Cinque Terre. The hotel's restaurant, **Da Nicola,** serves up typical Ligurian cuisine and pizza as well as delightful views.

Via Roma 8. www.nazionaleportofino.com. ✆ **0185-269-575.** 12 units. 190€–375€ double, includes breakfast. Closed mid-Dec to Mar. **Amenities:** Restaurant; bar; concierge; room service, Wi-Fi (free).

Ristorante Puny ★★ LIGURIAN Located on the *piazzetta* in front of the harbor, this colorful restaurant is in the middle of it all, so book well in advance. It's especially known for the freshness of its seafood, with a lengthy menu of tasty Ligurian dishes including *pappardelle al portofino* (large flat noodles with a mix of tomato and pesto sauce), the heavenly *pesce al forno* baked in bay leaves, or the famed *risotto al curry e gamberi* (curried rice with tiny shrimp). Be prepared to pay a small fortune for the location, view, food, and being part of the scene. While this is a favorite haunt of well-heeled locals and tourists, Puny maintains a welcoming, cozy feel.

Piazza Martiri dell'Olivetta 5. ✆ **0185-269-037.** Main courses 20€–30€. Mon–Wed and Fri–Sun 12:30–3:30pm and 7:30–11pm. Closed Jan–Feb.

THE CINQUE TERRE ★★★

Monterosso, the northernmost town of the Cinque Terre: 93km (58 miles) E of Genoa

Rocky coves, dramatic cliffs, and Apennine ridges are the spectacular backdrop to the Cinque Terre (Five Lands), a region that consists of five fishing and wine-making villages dramatically perched along a 11-mile stretch of Italy's Ligurian coast. Terraced vineyards and olive groves climb slopes that are largely inaccessible by road, but have become a hiker's haven stretching southeast from Monterosso al Mare to Vernazza, Corniglia, Manarola, and Riomaggiore.

Not too surprisingly, these charms have not gone unnoticed, and American tourists have been coming here in increasing numbers. From May to October (weekends are worst), you are likely to find yourself in a long procession of like-minded, English-speaking trekkers making their way down the coast, or elbow-to-elbow with day-trippers from cruise ships. Even so, the Cinque Terre manages to escape the hubbub that afflicts so many coastlines, and even a short stay here is likely to reward you with one of the most memorable seaside visits of a lifetime.

Essentials

GETTING THERE Cinque Terre towns are served only by local **train** runs. Coming from Florence or Rome, you will likely have to change trains in nearby La Spezia, which has one or two local trains per hour (6–8 min. to the smaller towns). From Pisa, there are about six daily trains to La Spezia (1¼ hr.); from Genoa, there are one or two direct trains per hour to La Spezia, stopping in Monterosso (1 hr., 40 min. from Genoa) and sometimes Riomaggiore (15 min. farther south).

The fastest **driving** route is via Autostrada A12 from Genoa; get off at the Corrodano exit for Monterosso. The drive from Genoa to Corrodano takes less than an hour, while the much shorter 15km (9¼-mile) trip from Corrodano to Monterosso (via Levanto) follows a narrow road and can take half an hour. Coming from the south or Florence, get off Autostrada A12 at La Spezia and follow cinque terre signs.

Navigazione Golfo dei Poeti (www.navigazionegolfodeipoeti.it; ✆ **0187-732-987**) runs a **ferry service** from the Riviera Levante towns, April to November, though these tend to be day cruises stopping for anywhere from 1 to 3 hours in Vernazza (see description below) before returning.

GETTING AROUND The best way to see the Cinque Terre is to devote a whole day and hoof it along the trails. See "Exploring the Cinque Terre," below, for details.

Local **trains** make frequent runs (two–three per hr.) between the five towns; some stop only in Monterosso and Riomaggiore, so check the posted *partenze* schedule at the station first to be sure you're catching a

RIVIERA runners-up

While Portofino and the Cinque Terre get their just accolades, it would be a shame to overlook some other lovely seaside destinations that also make a great base for exploring the area. When the Cinque Terre is drowning in tourists (a common occurrence May–Sept), these alternatives offer as much beauty, a bit more breathing room, and more options in terms of accommodations—some better in fact!

Set on opposites sides of the stunning Gulf of Poets lie the picturesque seaside medieval villages of **Portovenere** (tourist info: ✆ **0187-790-691**) and **Lerici** (tourist office: ✆ **0187-969-164**). Once archrivals—Portovenere belonged to Genoa and Lerici to Pisa—both built imposing fortresses to protect themselves from the enemy (and pirates!). These incredible edifices still remain along with charming, colorful homes backing up to olive-tree-covered hills. The beautiful harbors hold local fishing boats and yachts alike. One can easily take the spectacular ferry ride up to the Cinque Terre in less than an hour.

To the north of the Cinque Terre and only a 5-minute train ride from Monterosso is the sunny seaside town of **Levanto** (tourist info: www.levanto.com; ✆ **0187-808-125**) with its large sand beach, lovely historic center, and lodging options ranging from campsites to 4-star hotels.

A few train stops more, you arrive at **Bonassola, Moneglia,** and **Sestri Levanto** (tourist info: www.sestri-levante.net; ✆ **0185-478-530**) with its breathtaking "Bay of Silence"; any of these towns offer nice beaches and colorful town centers.

local. One-way tickets (2€) between any two towns are available—or you can buy a day ticket good for unlimited trips for 12€, meaning you can use it to town-hop; however, you'd have to use it six times in one day to make it worth your while, so evaluate whether it makes more sense to buy individual tickets.

A narrow, one-lane coast road hugs the mountainside above the towns, but all the centers are closed to cars. Parking is difficult and, where available, expensive. Riomaggiore and Manarola both have small **public parking facilities** just above their towns and minibuses to carry you and your luggage down. If you can manage to find parking in the garage before the beginning of the pedestrian zone in Monterosso (this is what they refer to as the "Loreto" lot, because it is the name for this part of town, and the garage doesn't have an official address but is where Strada Provinciale 38 meets Via Roma; there is another lot in an area of town called Fegina, but it's farther away), the price is 2€ per hour or 18€ per day though prices go down for longer stays. One of the priciest options is the garage in Riomaggiore at the beginning of the town's ZTL (limited-traffic zone where the pedestrian area starts) area. It costs about 23€ per day and there's no guarantee you will find a space. Some people park along the side of the road, and there are areas where parking is free for a few hours (you will need to have a "parking disk" to show the time you arrived), but if you overstay your time, you risk a hefty fine.

From the port in Monterosso, **Navigazione Golfo dei Poeti** (www.navigazionegolfodeipoeti.it; ✆ **0187-732-987**) makes eight to ten trips a day between Monterosso and Riomaggiore (25-min. trip), all stopping in Vernazza and half of them stopping in Manarola as well. A daily ticket for all of the Cinque Terre is 25€, so that you can take as many boats as you like over the day. One-way tickets tend to cost around 5€ and roundtrip tickets for the different villages cost 7€. Children 6 to 11 get a bit of a discount depending on the type of ticket.

VISITOR INFORMATION The Cinque Terre **tourist office** is underneath the train station of Monterosso, Via Fegina 38 (www.prolocomonterosso.it; ✆ **0187-817-506**). It's open Easter through September daily 9am to 5pm; hours are reduced the rest of the year. Even when it's closed, you will usually find a display of phone numbers and other information, from hotels to ferries, posted outside the office.

Additional useful websites for the region include **www.cinqueterre.it** and **www.parconazionale5terre.it.**

Exploring the Cinque Terre

Aside from swimming and soaking in the atmosphere of unspoiled fishing villages, the most popular activity in the Cinque Terre is **hiking from one village to the next ★★★** along centuries-old goat paths. Trails plunge through vineyards and groves of olive and lemon trees, hugging seaside cliffs and affording heart-stopping views of the coast and romantic little villages in the distance. The well-signposted walks from village to village range in difficulty and length, but as a loose rule, they get longer and steeper—and more rewarding—the farther north you go.

Depending on your pace, and not including eventual stops for focaccia and *sciacchetrà,* the local sweet wine, you can make the trip between **Monterosso,** at the northern end of the Cinque Terre, and **Riomaggiore,** at the southern end, in about 4½ hours. You should decide whether you want to walk north to south or south to north. Walking south means tackling the hardest trail first, which you may prefer, because you'll get it out of the way and things will get easier as the day goes on. Heading north, the trail gets progressively harder between townsa route you might prefer if you want to walk just until you tire and then hop on the train.

A **Cinque Terre Card** (7.50€ adults, 4.50€ children under 12) provides 1-day access to the trails, free use of bathrooms along the trails, reduced-price admission to local museums, and use of Wi-Fi at public hotspots. Check www.parconazionale5terre.it/Ecinque-terre-card.php for updated info.

Walking path above Manarola in the Cinque Terre.

For the past few years, Italy has been outlining plans to limit the number of daily visitors to this UNESCO World Heritage site. Those wanting to hike the Cinque Terre trails would be required to buy tickets ahead of time. In addition, there is supposed to be a dedicated app where visitors can check "traffic" on the trails in real time. As of press time, the plan had not been officially announced.

The walk from **Monterosso to Vernazza** is the most arduous and takes 1½ hours, on a trail that makes several steep ascents and descents (on the portion outside Monterosso, you'll pass beneath funicular-like cars that transport grapes down the steep hillsides). The leg from **Vernazza to Corniglia** is also demanding and takes another 1½ hours, plunging into some dense forests and involving some lengthy ascents, but is probably the prettiest and most rewarding stretch. Part of the path between **Corniglia and Manarola,** about 45 minutes apart, follows a level grade above a long stretch of beach, tempting you to break stride and take a dip. From **Manarola to Riomaggiore,** it's easy going for about half an hour along a partially paved path known as the Via dell'Amore, so named for its romantic vistas (great at sunset).

Because all the villages are linked by rail, you can hike as many portions of the itinerary as you wish and take the train to your next destination. Trails also cut through the forested, hilly terrain inland from the coast, much of which is protected as a nature preserve. The tourist office in Monterosso can provide maps.

The beach at Monterosso.

MONTEROSSO ★★★

The Cinque Terre's largest village seems incredibly busy compared to its sleepier neighbors, but it's not without its charms. Monterosso is actually two towns—a bustling, character-filled Old Town built behind the harbor, and a relaxed resort that stretches along the Cinque Terre's **only sand beach.** This is where you'll find the train station and the tiny regional tourist office (upon exiting the station, turn left and head through the tunnel for the Old Town; turn right for the newer town).

The region's most famous art treasure is here, housed in the **Convento dei Cappuccini,** perched on a hillock in the center of the Old Town: a "Crucifixion" by Anthony van Dyck, the Flemish master who worked for a time in nearby Genoa (convent open daily 9am–noon and 4–7pm). You will find the most modern conveniences in Monterosso, but you'll have a more "rustic" experience if you stay in one of the other four villages.

VERNAZZA ★★★

Vernazza may just be the quintessential, postcard-perfect seaside village. Tall, colorful houses (known as *terratetti*) cluster around a natural harbor, where you can swim among the fishing boats; above them a **castle** stands high atop a rocky promontory that juts into the sea (the castle, which is nothing special, is open Mar–Oct daily 10am–6:30pm; admission 1.50€). The center of town is waterside **Piazza Marconi,** itself a sea of cafe tables. The only Vernazza drawback is that too much good press has turned it into the Cinque Terre's mecca for American tourists.

CORNIGLIA ★

The quietest village in the Cinque Terre is isolated by its position midway down the coast, its hilltop location high above the open sea, and its hard-to-access harbor. Whether you arrive by boat, train, or the trail from the south, you'll have to climb some 300 steps to reach the village proper (arriving by trail from the north is the only way to avoid these stairs), an enticing maze of little walkways shadowed by tall houses.

Once there, though, the views over the surrounding vineyards and up and down the coastline are stupendous—for the best outlook, walk to the end of the narrow main street to a belvedere that is perched between the sea and sky. Corniglia is the village most likely to offer a glimpse into life in the Cinque Terre the way it was decades ago.

MANAROLA ★

Manarola is a near-vertical cluster of tall houses that seems to rise piggyback up the hills on either side of the harbor. In fact, in a region with no shortage of heart-stopping views, one of the most amazing sights is the descent into the town of Manarola on the path from Corniglia: From this perspective, the hill-climbing houses seem to merge into one another to form a row of skyscrapers. Despite these urban associations, Manarola is a delightfully rural village where fishing and winemaking are big business. The region's major **wine cooperative,** Cooperativa Agricoltura di Riomaggiore, Manarola, Corniglia, Vernazza e Monterosso, made up of

Vernazza.

300 local producers, is here; call ✆ **0187-920-435** for information about tours of its modern (established 1982) facilities. Try to reserve at least 3 days before your visit.

RIOMAGGIORE ★

Riomaggiore clings to the rustic ways of the Cinque Terre while making some (unfortunate) concessions to the modern world. The old fishing quarter has expanded in recent years, and Riomaggiore now has some sections of new houses and apartment blocks. This blend of old and new is a bit of a shame. The village center still looks like something from 50 years ago, bustling and prosperous in a charming setting, while the "new side" of town feels like a half-effort at maintaining the old mostly in color. A credit to both sides is that many of the lanes end in seaside belvederes.

From the parking garage, follow the main drag down; from the train station, exit and turn right to head through the tunnel for the central part of town (or, from the station, take off left up the brick stairs to walk the Via dell'Amore to Manarola).

That tunnel and the main drag meet at the base of an elevated terrace that holds the train tracks. From here, a staircase leads down to a tiny fishing harbor, off the left of which heads a rambling path that, after a few hundred meters, leads to a pleasant little **beach** of large pebbles.

Where to Stay

Gianni Franzi ★★ The owner of a local trattoria in Vernazza has 23 rooms in two different buildings; some come with a bathroom, others with excellent views up the coast. Most involve a steep climb to reach, so keep that in mind. Call ✆ **0187-821-003** to book, or when you arrive in town, stop by the trattoria's harborside bar (if you arrive on a Wed when the trattoria is closed, there is usually somebody there in the afternoon to take care of new arrivals, or else call ✆ **393-900-8155**). Breakfast is served on a roof deck with a wonderful view of the sea, up high as if seated on the bow of an oceanliner.

Restaurant address: Piazza G. Marconi 5, Vernazza (SP). www.giannifranzi.it. ✆ **0187-821-003** or 393-900-8155. 23 units. 65€–150€ double (some with shared bathrooms). Rates include breakfast. Closed from around Jan 10–Mar 10. **Amenities:** Restaurant; bar; garden/terrace; Wi-Fi (free).

Il Giardino Incantato ★★ This charming family-run B&B is in a converted 16th-century villa just off Via Roma in Monterosso's old village, and a stone's throw from the town beach and the pier from where boats arrive and depart. The three rooms and a junior suite are lovingly decorated with terracotta tiles, wood-beamed ceilings, and wrought-iron beds. Next to the villa is a lovely garden with lemon trees, lavender, and colorful flowers where breakfast is served, weather permitting. It is a tranquil and relaxing refuge in a town that can be quite busy in high season. Given that the house is full of antiques and other precious objects, if you are traveling with children, this B&B isn't for you.

Via Mazzini 18, Monterosso al Mare (SP). www.ilgiardinoincantato.net. ✆ **0187-818-315.** 4 units. 180€–200€ double. Rates include breakfast. Closed early Nov to Apr. **Amenities:** Garden.

Hotel Porto Roca ★★★ Considered the Cinque Terre's only resort, this 4-star hotel in Monterosso is spectacularly positioned upon the cliffside overlooking the village, cemetery, and blue sea below. Most of the rooms are small and in need of an update, but once you step out onto your private balcony suspended above the Mediterranean, you can easily forgive the hotel's shortcomings. The pleasant restaurant serves typical Ligurian dishes, and the cliffside patio offers the best seat in town on when the weather is nice. Prices are high even for a "back, small non-sea-view" room; we suggest splurging if you can to enjoy the full experience. There's space on the beach for guests, with free umbrellas and deck chairs. The infinity pool offers sea views, and a small wellness area is a relaxing spot after a day spent hiking the trails.

Via Corone 1, Monterosso al Mare (SP). www.portoroca.it. ✆ **0187-817-502.** 43 units. 240€–695€ double; 430€–510€ for a 4-person family room. Rates include breakfast. Closed Nov–Mar. **Amenities:** Restaurant; bar; concierge; spa/beauty center; pool; room service; Wi-Fi (free).

La Mala ★★★ This stylish four-room *locanda* in Vernazza has a chic minimalist, beachy feel. The rooms are not large but they are well-designed and -equipped, sunny, and come with great views (sea, village, and/or harbor view). Bathrooms are clean and modern. Room 26 has a small living area that can accommodate a third bed, making it ideal for families. Room 31 is large and bright, seemingly suspended in the air between the sea and sky. Guests can enjoy the communal seaside terrace, the perfect spot for a sunset *aperitivo*. There is no reception area, so you will be expected to call (or find) the owner, Gian Battista, upon your arrival in the village. Someone will meet you in town and help with your bags. There's no breakfast room; instead you are provided with vouchers for a simple Italian breakfast (such as a cappuccino and brioche) at a local bar. The draw here: the views.

Via San Giovanni Battista, Vernazza. www.lamala.it. ✆ **334-287-5718.** 4 units. 140€–220€ double. Rates include basic breakfast. Closed Jan 10 to Mar. **Amenities:** Wi-Fi (free).

La Torretta ★★★ Besides La Mala in Vernazza (see above), this charming lodge in Manarola is perhaps the only other "chic retreat" in the Cinque Terre. La Torretta (named for the fact that it is located in an ancient tower) offers lovely rooms and suites in varied sizes, several with sea views and balconies, and all with nice in-room amenities, such as luxurious toiletries. Our favorite rooms are the Design Suite in the main building and the Panoramic Suite in the annex, just a short walk from the main building. Despite the fairly steeps price (and position on the hill), rooms go quickly here during high season, so best to book way ahead of time. Fortunately, a luggage transfer service means guests don't have to lug their own bags up the hill from the train station.

Vico Volto 20, Manarola. www.torrettas.com. ✆ **0187-920-327.** 11 units. 230€–300€ double. 400€–900€ suites. Rates include breakfast. Closed Nov. **Amenities:** Solarium; Wi-Fi (free).

Ostello Cinque Terre ★ Don't expect luxury here, but a good clean bed and bath at more than reasonable prices make this hostel sell out weeks before the high season. Located in the center of Manarola near the church, it's an alternative in an area with few budget lodgings. Linens and blankets are included in your stay, but towels can be rented for 2€. The hostel restaurant, the **Osteria Du Vin Bun,** is open sporadically. Wi-Fi can be spotty outside of the small reception area. Guests are expected to be out of the rooms from 10am to 1pm so the staff can clean.

Via Riccobaldi 21, Manarola. www.hostel5terre.com. ✆ **0187-920-039.** 21€–28€ for beds in 6-bed dorm rooms, 55€–70€ for a room with 2 single beds and private bathroom, or 132€–162€ for 6-bed family room with private bathroom. 2-night minimum stay. Closed mid-Nov to mid-Mar. **Amenities:** Kayak, bike, and snorkel rental; pay laundry; Wi-Fi (free).

Where to Eat

Osteria a Cantina de Mananan ★★ LIGURIAN Locals and tourists alike flock to this tiny eatery in an old wine cellar carved into the stone of an ancient house in Corniglia. Given that the restaurant has very few tables and often only does one seating per meal, you will want to call ahead (and bring cash; credit cards are not accepted). You may even be asked to share a table with other diners. The menu puts the focus on fresh local ingredients, like vegetables from the nearby terraced gardens and seafood from local fishermen. Dishes are simple yet tasty. Try grilled and rolled vegetables stuffed with mozzarella, fresh anchovies stuffed with herbs, or the house specialty, *coniglio* (rabbit) roasted in a white sauce.

Via Fieschi 117, Corniglia. ✆ **0187-821-166.** Main courses 10€–15€. Tues–Sun 12:30–2:30pm and 7:30–9:30pm; closed Mon. Closed No, Mon–Fri in Dec, and part of Jan–Feb.

Ristorante Belforte ★★★ LIGURIAN Being perched on a medieval watchtower overlooking the Mediterranean makes for a pretty fantastic setting. Feasting on traditional Ligurian dishes makes the experience at this upscale restaurant in Vernazza worth the wait (even if you reserve ahead of time). Notable dishes include the *antipasto di mare,* a selection of six to eight small bites of seafood (we love the *cozze ripiene,* stuffed mussels, when they are in season), and the *spaghetti alla Bruno,*

with mussels, clams, and shrimp. Anchovies (served in a variety of ways) are also a house specialty. The wine list offers a selection of reds and whites meant to pair well with seafood. If you are able to nab the single table on a small balcony at sunset, you are in for a romantic treat!
Via Guidoni 42, Vernazza. www.ristorantebelforte.it. ✆ **0187-812-222.** Main courses 16€–30€. Wed–Mon noon–3:30pm and 7–10pm. Closed Nov–mid-March.

Ristorante Miky ★ SEAFOOD This family-run restaurant in Monterosso is considered one of the best—and most expensive—in the Cinque Terre. In addition to the friendly service and the tasty, beautifully presented dishes, you can dine in a lovely garden with the smell of lemon and rosemary in the air. House specialties include an excellent seafood sampler platter (including, among other things, red prawns with an avocado sauce; shrimp with almond, zucchini, and fennel; and a cold lobster salad), monkfish ravioli, and *pesce al sale*, fresh fish covered in coarse salt (the salt is removed before the fish is served) and slowly cooked in a wood-burning oven. Many pasta and rice dishes are served in large terracotta plates that give them a unique flavor. All dishes are artfully presented, adding to the already charming ambience. It's not cheap, but the food and setting make it worthwhile. Enjoy the homemade *limoncello* offered at the end of your meal, and you can even buy jars of the family's homemade pesto or marmalade to take with you. Reservations are highly recommended.
Via Fegina 104, Monterosso al Mare. www.ristorantemiky.it. ✆ **0187-817-608.** Main courses 12€–25€. Daily noon–3pm and 7:30pm–late. Closed Nov–Mar.

12

NAPLES & POMPEII

By Stephen Brewer

12

B*ienvenuti al sud*—welcome to the south. Your first encounter with southern Italy, for better or worse, will probably be Naples. If you've enjoyed the grandeur of Venice, the elegance of Florence, and the awesomeness of monumental Rome, be prepared for a bit of a shock. Naples lives up to its reputation for dirt and grime, delights with its energy and good cheer, and surprises with the sophistication of its monuments and museums. It can be overwhelming, but that's part of the city's allure. And Naples is just the beginning.

There's so much more right around Naples—some of the most extensive remains of the ancient world in Herculaneum and Pompeii; the favorite playgrounds of the rich on Capri and along the Amalfi coast; the natural, ominous wonders of Mt. Vesuvius and the Campo Flegrei; plus miles of coastline and hillsides carpeted with olive groves and orange and lemon orchards. You might want to think of Naples and Campania as Italy on overdrive. Hang on and enjoy the ride.

NAPLES ★★

219km (136 miles) SE of Rome

In Naples, Mt. Vesuvius looms to the east, the fumaroles of the Campo Flegrei hiss and steam to the west, and the isle of Capri floats phantom-like across the gleaming waters of the bay. For all the splendor and drama of this natural setting, one of Italy's most intense urban concoctions is the real show. Naples shoots out so many sensations that it takes a while for visitors to know what's hit them.

Everything seems a bit more intense in Italy's third-largest city, the capital of the south. Dark brooding lanes open to palm-fringed piazzas. Laundry-strewn tenements stand cheek by jowl with grand palaces. Medieval churches and castles rise above the grid of streets laid out by ancient Greeks. No denying it, parts of the city are squalid, yet the museums are packed with riches.

It seems that most of life here transpires on the streets, so you'll witness a lot. The pace can be leisurely in that southern way, and amazingly hectic. When you partake—in a meal, in a *passegiata,* or just in a simple

FACING PAGE: **Piazza del Plebiscito.**

HOTELS

Art Resort Gallery Umberto **15**

Chiaia Hotel de Charme **8**

Correra 241 **22**

Costantinopoli 104 **24**

Decumani Hotel de Charme **28**

Grand Hotel Parker's **2**

Grand Hotel Vesuvio **5**

Hotel Il Convento **17**

Hotel Piazza Bellini **25**

Robby's House **39**

San Francesco al Monte **19**

RESTAURANTS

Europeo di Mattozzi **16**

Il Buongustai **38**

La Campagnola **35**

Nenella **18**

Pizzeria Da Michele **30**

Pizzeria Gino Sorbillo **36**

Rosiello **1**

Squistezze/La Stanza del Gusto **26**

Tandem **29**

Zi Teresa **7**

ATTRACTIONS

Cappella di Sansevero **34**

Castel dell'Ovo (Castle of the Egg) **6**

Castel Nuovo **13**

Castel Sant'Elmo **21**

Catacombs of San Gennaro (St. Januarius) **41**

Certosa di San Martino (Carthusian Monastery) **20**

Chiesa del Gesù Nuovo **27**

Chiesa di San Gregorio Armeno **33**

Galleria Umberto I **12**

Il Duomo Cattedrale di Santa Maria Assunta **37**

Museo d'Arte Contemporanea Donna Regina (MADRE) **40**

Napoli Sotterranea **9**

National Archaeological Museum (Museo Archeologico Nazionale) **23**

National Museum & Gallery of the Capodimonte (Museo e Gallerie Nazionale di Capodimonte) **42**

Palazzo Zevallos Stigliano **14**

Pio Monte della Misericordia **31**

Royal Palace (Palazzo Reale) **10**

San Lorenzo Maggiore **32**

Teatro San Carlo **11**

Villa Comunale **4**

Villa La Floridiana & Museo Nazionale della Ceramica Duca di Martina **3**

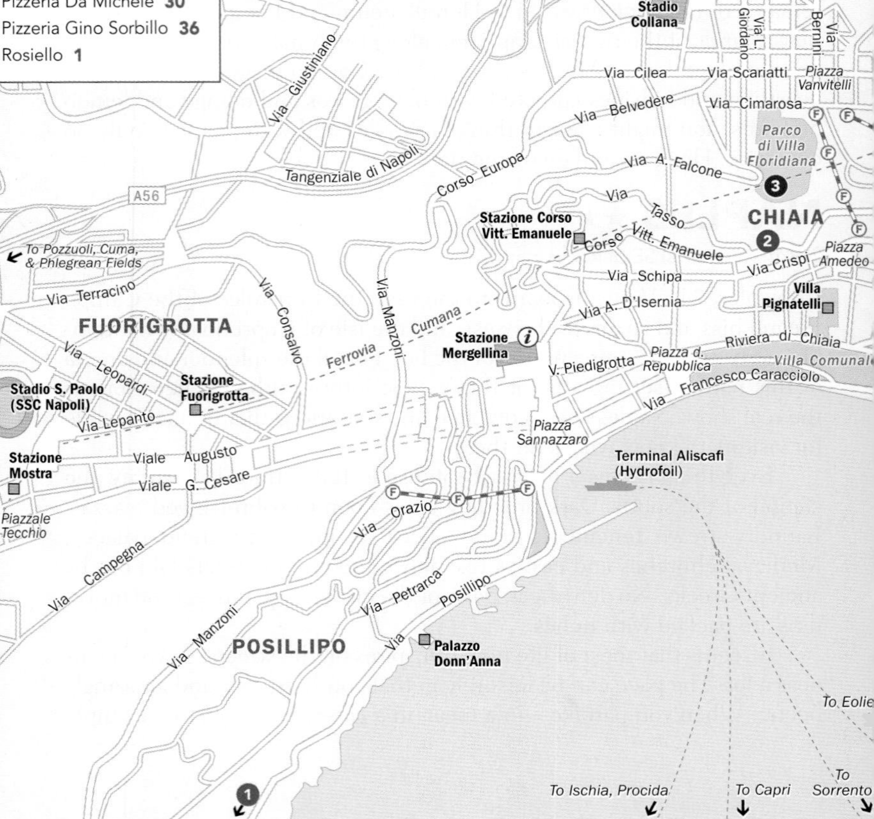

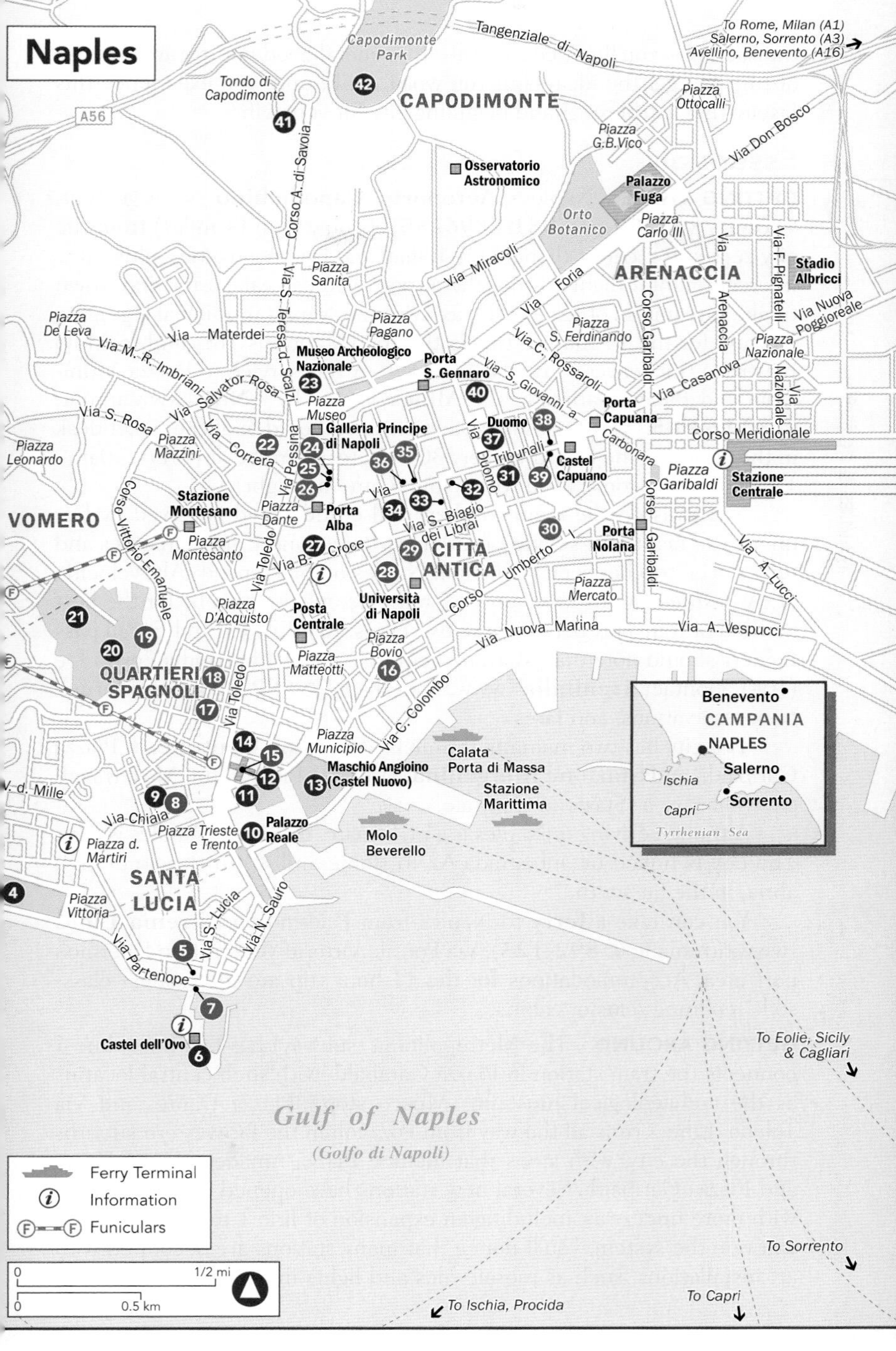
Naples
Capodimonte Park
Tangenziale di Napoli
To Rome, Milan (A1)
Salerno, Sorrento (A3)
Avellino, Benevento (A16)
Tondo di Capodimonte
CAPODIMONTE
A56
Piazza Ottocalli
Via Don Bosco
Piazza G.B.Vico
Corso A. di Savoia
Osservatorio Astronomico
Palazzo Fuga
Orto Botanico
Piazza Carlo III
Via S. Teresa d. Scalzi
Piazza Sanita
Via Miracoli
Via Foria
ARENACCIA
Stadio Albricci
Via Arenaccia
Via F. Pignatelli
Via Nuova Poggioreale
Piazza De Leva
Via Materdei
Piazza Pagano
Piazza S. Ferdinando
Corso Garibaldi
Via M. R. Imbriani
Museo Archeologico Nazionale
Porta S. Gennaro
Via C. Rossaroli
Piazza Nazionale
Via Nazionale
Via Salvator Rosa
Piazza Museo
Via S. Giovanni a Carbonara
Via Casanova
Via S. Rosa
Galleria Principe di Napoli
Duomo
Porta Capuana
Corso Meridionale
Piazza Leonardo
Piazza Mazzini
Via Correra
Via Pessina
Via Duomo
Via Tribunali
Castel Capuano
Piazza Garibaldi
Stazione Centrale
Corso Vittorio Emanuele
Stazione Montesano
Piazza Dante
Porta Alba
Via
Via S. Biagio dei Librai
VOMERO
Piazza Montesanto
Via Toledo
Via B. Croce
CITTÀ ANTICA
Corso Umberto
Porta Nolana
Via A. Lucci
Università di Napoli
Piazza Mercato
Piazza D'Acquisto
Posta Centrale
Via Nuova Marina
Via A. Vespucci
Piazza Bovio
Piazza Matteotti
QUARTIERI SPAGNOLI
Via C. Colombo
Benevento
CAMPANIA
NAPLES
Salerno
Ischia
Sorrento
Capri
Tyrrhenian Sea
Piazza Municipio
Calata Porta di Massa
Maschio Angioino (Castel Nuovo)
Stazione Marittima
V. d. Mille
Via Chiaia
Piazza Trieste e Trento
Palazzo Reale
Molo Beverello
Piazza d. Martiri
SANTA LUCIA
Piazza Vittoria
Via S. Lucia
Via N. Sauro
Via Partenope
Castel dell'Ovo
To Eolie, Sicily & Cagliari
Gulf of Naples
(Golfo di Napoli)
Ferry Terminal
Information
Funiculars
To Sorrento
0
1/2 mi
0
0.5 km
To Ischia, Procida
To Capri

transaction—you'll notice the warmth, general good nature, and a sense of fun. You get the idea—but you won't really, until you experience this fascinating, perplexing, and beguiling city for yourself.

Essentials

GETTING THERE Naples's **Aeroporto Capodichino** (www.gesac.it; ✆ **081/7896259** and **081/7896255**), is only 7km (4 miles) from the city center. It receives flights from Italian and European cities, plus a few intercontinental flights. From the airport, you can take a taxi into town (make sure it is an official white taxi with the Naples municipal logo); the flat rate for the 15-minute trip to the train station is 16€, and to Molo Beverello (for ferries to the islands) 19€. A bus service to Piazza Municipio and Piazza Garibaldi, the **Alibus,** is run by **ANM** (www.anm.it; ✆ **800/639-525;** 4€ one-way; buy tickets on board or at the ticket desk in the airport). The bus runs every 30 minutes from the airport (6:30am–11:50pm) and from Piazza Municipio (6am–midnight).

Naples is on the main southern rail corridor and is served by frequent and fast **train service** from most Italian and European cities and towns. The trip between Rome and Naples on high-speed (AltaVelocità, or AV) express trains takes only 87 minutes, making this by far the best method of transport between the two cities. Rail Europe and Eurail pass holders should note that AV trains require a reservation and an extra fee (10€). Contact **Trenitalia** (www.trenitalia.it; ✆ **892-021**) for information, reservations, and fares.

The city has two main rail terminals: **Stazione Centrale,** at Piazza Garibaldi, and **Stazione Mergellina,** at Piazza Piedigrotta. Most travelers will arrive at Stazione Centrale.

Although driving *in* Naples is a nightmare, **driving** *to* Naples is easy. The city is linked by autostrada A2 to Rome and A3 to Reggio di Calabria, in the far south.

You can take a **ferry** to Naples from Palermo on **Tirrenia Lines** (www.tirrenia.it; ✆ **892-123**), Via Pontile Vittorio Veneto 1, in Palermo's port area. Accommodations for the 11-hour trip are in business-class-style reclining seats or cabins.

GETTING AROUND The Metropolitana (subway) has two lines: line 1 connects the train station in Piazza Garabaldi with such central locatins as the archaeological museum (Museo stop), Piazza Dante, and Via Toledo. Line 2 runs all the way from Pozzuoli in the far western suburbs through the city, with stops that include Piazza Amadeo, Montesanto, and Piazza Garibaldi. Several new stations have opened in recent years, with more underway, including an expansion of line 1 to the airport. As you ride the system, you'll notice that many stations are decorated with art installations, such as mosaic tiles and lights in the Toledo station in shades of blue that become deeper and more intense as you descend; psychedelic colors and shapes in the Università station are intended to immerse you in the digital age. You might also find yourself using two urban railway networks to get to major attractions. The Circumvesuviana leaves runs from a station adjacent to the main train station in Piazza Garibaldi and runs southeast around the Bay of Naples to Oplontis, Pompeii, Herculaneum, and Sorrento. The Ferrovia Cumana runs from Piazza Montesanto to Pozzouli and other towns in the Campi Flegrei.

Handy **bus** routes include the R lines (R1, R2, R3, R4), with frequent stops at major tourist attractions (the R4, for example, connects the archaeological museum and Catacombs of San Gennaro), and the electric minibuses (marked e) that skirt the historic district.

Four **funiculars** take passengers up and down the steep hills of Naples. The **Funicolare Centrale,** one of the world's longest (about a mile) and busiest funiculars, connects the central city to Vomero. Daily departures (6:30am–12:30am) are from Piazzetta Duca d'Aosta just off Via Roma.

One-way fare for the subway, buses, and funiculars is 1.50€, daily tickets (Biglietto Giornaliero) are 4.50€ (valid until midnight the day they are validated), and weekly tickets (Biglietto Settimanale) are 16€. You can buy tickets at newsstands, tobacco shops, and from machines in most Metro and funicular stations and at some bus stops; you must validate tickets in the electronic ticket machines in stations or on the bus.

Taxis are an excellent, relatively inexpensive way to get around the city, and are very reliable and strictly regulated. Official taxis are painted white and marked by the comune di napoli. Inside is a sign listing official flat rates to the seaports, central hotels, and top attractions; don't fret if your driver doesn't use the meter—*not* using the meter is legal for all rides that have established flat rates. Taxis do not cruise but are found at the many taxi stands around town, or, for an extra 1€ surcharge, can be requested by phone (✆ **081/444-444** or **081/555-5555**).

As for **driving** around Naples, we have one word: *Don't.* If you're tempted, take a look at the cars on the street. In the rest of Italy, even the simplest models are kept in pristine condition; here, cars look like they've been used in demolition derbies. Car theft is common.

Walking is an excellent way to get around the city center, where sights are fairly close together, but remember: For Neapolitan drivers, red lights are mere suggestions; cross busy streets carefully, and stick with a crowd if possible. Always look both ways when crossing a street, because a lot of drivers scoff at the notion of a one-way street. The zebra stripes (white lines) in the street, indicating where pedestrians have the right of way, mean absolutely nothing here.

VISITOR INFORMATION The **Ente Provinciale per il Turismo,** Piazza dei Martiri 58 (✆ **081/4107211;** bus: 152), is open Monday to Friday 9am to 2pm, with another office at Stazione Centrale (✆ **081/ 268779;** Metro: Garibaldi; Mon–Sat 9am–7pm). The **AASCT** (www.inaples.it) maintains two excellent tourist information points: Via San Carlo 9 (✆ **081/402394**) and Piazza del Gesù (✆ **081/5512701**), both open daily (Mon–Sat 9:30am–6:30pm; Sun 9:30am–2pm). Any of these offices can give you a free map, an essential piece of gear when navigating Naples.

The confoundingly complex **Campania Card** (www.campaniartecard.it; ✆ **800-600601** or 06-3996–7650) can save you money if you plan to make the rounds of churches, museums, and archaeological sites. The standard **Napoli Artecard** (21€) gives you free admission to three attractions, a discount of 50% at the fourth, discounts at other attractions, free use of public transportation, and discounts to shops and restaurants. It's for sale at participating sites and at the Campania Card stand at Napoli Centrale train station.

[FastFACTS] NAPLES

Consulates

See chapter 16.

Drugstores

Several pharmacies are open weekday nights and take turns on weekend nights. A good one is located in the Stazione Centrale (Piazza Garibaldi 11; ✆ **081/ 440211;** Metro: Piazza Garibaldi).

Emergencies

If you have an emergency, dial ✆ **113** to reach the police. For medical care, dial ✆ **118,** but only in an emergency. To find the local **Guardia Medica Permanente** (a doctor on call), ask for directions at your hotel.

Safety

The Camorra-related crime for which Naples is infamous will have little bearing on your visit. Street crime is another story and it's best to err on the side of caution in this city with catastrophically high unemployment, a big drug problem, and lots of dark, empty streets. If you have a money belt, by all means use it. Also use common sense. *Do not* carry a lot of cash, wear expensive jewelry, walk around with a fancy camera hanging from your neck, place your smartphone on cafe tables, or plunge down dark, deserted lanes at night. *Do* leave your valuables in a safe at your hotel (most rooms are equipped with them). When going out for a meal or excursion, carry only as much cash as you are going to need and only the credit card you will be using. Beware of pickpockets in crowds and on the subways and commuter trains—they're crafty. Do not carry a wallet in your back pocket, of course, or even in your inside jacket pocket, where someone brushing against you can easily get to it. When walking, carry any bags on the side away from the street to thwart thieves whizzing past on motorbikes.

Naples' atmospheric streets.

Exploring Naples

Large as Naples is, it's easy to get to the sights you want to see on foot, letting you experience one of the city's greatest allures—its street life. From Piazza Trento e Trieste, with the magnificent **Teatro San Carlo** and **Galleria Umberto I**, Via Toledo/Via Roma leads north. To the left is the Quartieri Spagnoli, a neighborhood of tightly packed narrow lanes, while to the right, just beyond Piazza Dante, is the atmospheric historical center of the city, where many of the churches you want to see face airy piazzas. At the northern end of Via Toledo, about a 10-minute walk beyond Piazza Dante, is the celebrated archaeological museum.

SANTA LUCIA AND THE SEAFRONT

Not surprisingly, some of the city's most magnificent squares and public monuments are clustered near the seafront. **Piazza del Plebiscito ★★,** the most beautiful square in Naples, is surrounded by an elegant assemblage of neoclassical landmarks. Among them is **the Royal Palace (Palazzo Reale) ★**, with 30 grandiose yet strangely vacuous rooms where Neapolitan royalty ruled and entertained in the 18th and 19th centuries (www.palazzorealenapoli.it; ✆ **081/5808111**; palace 4€; courtyard and gardens free; Thurs–Tues 9am–7pm; bus: R2 or R3). Two Neapolitan kings survey the cobblestones from the backs of their steeds: the forward-thinking Carlo III (1716–1788) and the treacherous Ferdinando I (1423–1494). It's said you will be blessed with good fortune if you turn your back to the Palazzo Reale, close your eyes, and walk backwards between the two kings.

As every Neapolitan knows, the ancient Roman poet Virgil placed an egg under the foundations of the city's outrageously picturesque seafront **Castel dell'Ovo (Castle of the Egg) ★★,** Borgo Marinari (off Via Partenope), and when it breaks, a great disaster will befall the city. Considering earthquakes, eruptions of nearby Mt. Vesuvius, plague

The Castel dell'Ovo and Borgo Morinaro.

outbreaks, and wars, it's probably safe to assume the egg is no longer intact. The castle is enchanting even without such legends, squeezed onto a tiny island the Greeks first settled almost 3 millennia ago and a royal residence from the 13th through 20th centuries (© **081/7954593**; free admission; Mon–Sat 8am–6pm; Sun 8am–2pm; bus: 152, C25, 140, or E5 to Via Santa Lucia). The little lanes beneath the thick walls are lined with the houses of Borgo Marinaro, now occupied by pleasant bars and pizzerias. For Neapolitans, a walk across the stout bridge onto the island is a favorite Sunday afternoon outing.

The best view of **Castel Nuovo ★** is from the Piazza Municipo, with vistas of the castle's towers and crenellations, and the white-marble Triumphal Arch of Alfonso I of Aragona squeezed between two turrets. As you take in the sight, consider the plight of prisoners who once shared their dungeons with crocodiles imported from Egypt for the express purpose of snacking on the doomed souls. You can also enjoy the water-spouting lions and sea monsters of the square's **Fontana del Nettuno ★★.** This marble showpiece of dolphins, tritons, and sea god Neptune himself are partly the work of Pietro Bernini, whose greatest creation is the Fontana della Barcaccia at the bottom of the Spanish Steps in Rome.

Galleria Umberto I ★★ LANDMARK Shopping malls have only gone downhill since elegant glass-and-iron landmarks like this were all the rage in the late 19th century. The café- and shop-lined gallery modeled after the older Galleria Vittorio Emanuele II in Milan saw its best days in the years before World War I, though Neapolitans are once again waking up to the pleasures of shopping beneath the glass dome and vaulted wings. If the place works its magic on you, as it is sure to do, dip into *The Gallery,* a novel by John Hone Burnes (1916–1953) about American GIs in Naples after World War II. Much of the action transpires in the Galleria, though the sad, poignant vignettes and dire views of the human condition might not be the best prelude to an upbeat shopping experience.

4 entrances: To the right off Via Toledo as you come from Piazza del Plebiscito, Via Giuseppe Verdi, Via Santa Brigida, and Via San Carlo. Bus: R2 or R3 to Piazza Trieste e Trento.

Beautifully tiled floors of the Galleria Umberto.

Villa Comunale ★★ PARK/GARDEN Time was the public was only allowed into the seaside gardens of the royal family once a year, on September 8, the Fiesta di Piedigrotta. That changed with the proletarian sentiments that swept in with the unification of Italy in 1869, and a good thing, too. Following the paths through greenery and past statues and fountains for a km (½ mile) or so from Piazza Vittoria on the east to Piazza della Repubblica on the west is one of the city's great delights. The Bay of Naples shimmers to the south, and many of its denizens—octopi, squid, and sea urchins—now reside in tanks at the **Anton Dohrn Zoological Station.** The renowned German naturalist established the aquarium in 1874. A popular **antiques market** takes over a corner of Villa Communale on the 3rd and 4th weekends of each month from 8:30am to 1pm; contact the tourist office (p. 582) for info.

Park: Piazza Vittoria. Daily 7am–midnight. **Aquarium:** ✆ **081/5833111.** Free. Tues–Sun 9am–5pm. Bus: C82 or R2.

CITTA ANTICA (HISTORICAL CENTER)

This warren of many tight lanes, a few avenues, and some boisterous piazzas is also known as the Decumani, and just as often as Spaccanapoli (that's the name of the street that runs straight through the center of the neighborhood, as it has ever since the Greeks established a colony here). Roughly, the heart of Naples extends north from seaside Castel Nuovo to the Museo Archeologico Nazionale, and east from Via Toledo and Quartieri Spagnoli to the Porta Nolona Fish Market.

Cappella di Sansevero ★★ MUSEUM Only in Naples would a room as colorful, fanciful, mysterious, beautiful, and macabre as this exist. Prince Raimondo di Sangro of Sansevero remodeled his family's funerary chapel in the 18th century, combining the baroque style then in fashion with his own love of complex symbolism and intellectual quests. Neapolitan sculptor Giuseppe Sanmartino crafted "Christ Veiled Under A Shroud," in which a thin transparent covering seems to make Christ's flesh look even more tormented. (Antonio Canova, the Venetian sculptor, came to Naples a century later and said he would give 10 years of his life to have created something so beautiful.) The prince's father lies beneath a statue of "Despair on Disillusion," in which a man disentangling himself from a marble net suggests a troubled soul seeking relief—provided by the winged boy who represents intellect. Prince Raimondo's mother, who died at age 20, lies beneath a statue of "Veiled Truth," in which a woman holds a broken tablet, symbol of an interrupted life. Raimondo himself is surrounded by colorful floor tiles arranged in a complex maze, symbol of the quest to unravel the secrets of life. Downstairs are two skeletal bodies in which the circulatory systems are perfectly preserved and brightly colored, allegedly with the injection of a substance the prince devised (and the subjects are probably not, as legend has it, the prince's unwilling servants, whom he supposedly scarified in the interest of science).

Via Francesco De Sanctis 19 (near Piazza San Domenico Maggiore). www.museosansevero.it. ✆ **081/5518470.** 7€. Daily 9:30am–6:30pm. Closed May 1 and Easter Monday. Metro: Dante.

Chiesa del Gesù Nuovo ★ CHURCH The princes of Salerno built what was once their palace in 1470, requesting that the facade be done in *bugnato a punta di diamante*, or ashlar, a technique that uses stones that are regularly cut to create a perfectly uniform appearance. The princes lost the palace a century later thanks to their political shenanigans, and the Jesuit order bought it and converted the stately salons into a church. In due time they, too, were evicted, but not before enlivening the interior with opulent frescoes and marble work. On an interior wall a fresco by Francesco Solimena (1657–1747) is as dramatic as the exterior. Solimena was a mediocre painter who compensated for his lack of genius with flamboyance. His "Expulsion of Heliodorus from the Temple" is a colorful swirl of flowing draperies and churning robes. The altar of the chapel of the Visitation is the final resting place of Naples' most popular modern saint, Giuseppe Moscatti (1880–1927), a devout physician and biochemist famous for his ability to heal impossible cases. The so-called "Holy Physician of Naples" is believed to still be working miracles. His shrine is often thronged with the ill and injured seeking his help, and it's said that many have been cured on the spot.

Piazza del Gesù. www.gesunuovo.it. ✆ **081/5578111.** Free. Mon–Sat 7am–1pm and 2:15–7:30pm; Sun 7am–1:45pm and 4:15–7:30pm. Bus: R1, R2, R3, or R4. Metro: Dante.

Chiesa di San Gregorio Armeno ★★ CHURCH When nuns fleeing persecution in Asia Minor came to Naples in the 8th century, they brought with them the relics of St. Gregory, an Armenian bishop. Over the centuries they built suitable surroundings for the saint, who now rests in a sumptuous baroque church bursting at the seams with gold leaf and elaborate marble carvings. Stepping into the church, described as "a room of paradise on earth," is like walking into one of the elaborate nativity scenes, *presepi*, that vendors sell up and down the street outside. Neapolitan master Luca Giordano tells the story of the nun's flight with their precious cargo in a series of dramatic frescoes, "The Embarkation, Journey and Arrival of the Armenia Nuns with the Relics of St Gregory" (1671–84). Gregory, however, is upstaged by one of the nuns, Santa Patrizia, whose dried blood is said to liquefy every Tuesday. The cloisters, on the other hand, are an oasis of tranquility.

Via San Gregorio Armeno 44 (btw. Via San Biagio dei librai and Via dei Tribunali, 3 short blocks west of Via Duomo). Free. Daily 9:30am–noon. Metro: Piazza Cavour.

EVERY DAY IS christmas

Among the many delights of Naples are the *presepi*, nativity scenes that pop up everywhere, any time of the year, and, not surprisingly, come out in force at Christmas. St. Francis of Assisi allegedly commissioned the first *presepe* in the 13th century, and Naples elevated the scenes to high art, bolstered by the patronage of King Charles III in the 18th century. City craftsmen still go to town, carving figures in wood and firing them in ceramics, fitting them with tailored clothing, and setting the Holy Family and their retinue on typical Naples streets. In addition to mainstays like Mary, Joseph, and the baby Jesus, the Neapolitan repertoire often expands to soccer stars and other celebrities. Settings can be a lot more elaborate than a humble manger, too: medieval town squares, rusticated villages with thatched cottages, elaborate caves that look like some troglodyte fantasy. On **Via San Gregorio Armeno,** dozens of shops sell figures beginning at about 15€. You can also buy a complete scene for anywhere from 100€ to well into five digits, or have one made with figures of your own family and favorite celebrities (as many Neapolitans do). Be aware that pickpockets flock to the street like sheep to a Bethlehem hillside to prey on distracted window-shoppers. Among the most reputable shops are **Gambardella Pastori,** Via San Gregorio Armeno 40 (✆ **081/5517107**); **Giuseppe Ferrigno,** Via San Gregorio Armeno 10 (✆ **081/5523148**); and **Amendola,** Via San Gregorio Armeno 51 (✆ **081/5514899**).

Handmade *presepi* figurines.

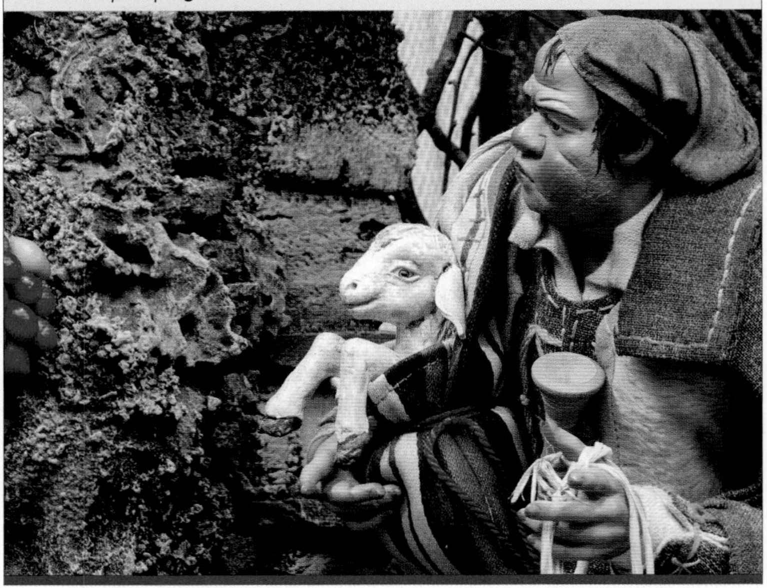

Il Cattedrale di Santa Maria Assunta ★★ CATHEDRAL Three times a year—the first Saturday in May, September 19, and December 16—all of Naples squeezes into the great cathedral that King Carlo I d'Angio dedicated to San Gennaro in the 13th century. On these dates the dried blood of the city's patron saint liquefies, or sometimes doesn't. Not doing so foretells terrible events for Naples, such as an outbreak of the plague in 1528 or the earthquake in 1980 that killed 2,000 residents. The rest of the year the blood is kept in a vault inside an altar in the **Canella di San Gunnar,** where a reliquary houses the head that soldiers of the Emperor Diocletian severed from the rest of the bishop's body around 305. Within the cathedral are Naples' two oldest remaining places of worship: The **Capella di Santa Restituta** was the city's 4th-century basilica and is supported by a forest of columns from a Greek temple; and the **Capella di San Giovanni in Fonte** was a 5th-century baptistery; if you crane your neck and squint (binoculars or a telescopic lens come in handy) you can make out some endearingly rendered frescoes in the dome.

Via del Duomo 147. ✆ **081/449097.** Cathedral free; archaeological zone 3€. Mon–Sat 8am–12:30pm and 4:30–7pm; Sun 8am–1:30pm and 5–7:30pm. Metro: Piazza Cavour.

Museo d'Arte Contemporanea Donna Regina (MADRE) ★ ART MUSEUM It's not New York's Guggenheim or London's Tate Modern, but the **Palazzo Regina** in the middle of medieval and baroque Naples provides a dramatic counterpoint for works by contemporary artists such as Anish Kapoor and Richard Serra. Painter Francesco Clemente, who was born in Naples, decorated two rooms in colorful tile floors and frescoes replicating ancient symbols of the city. Conceptual sculptor Kapoor transformed a room into a white cube with rich blue pigments on the floor that seem to draw you into the bowels of the earth; he also designed the entrance to the Monte S. Angelo subway station to resemble Dante's entrance to the underworld (and perhaps sympathizing with riders that commuting can be hell). Across town, the **Palazzo delle Arti Napoli (PAN)** (Via dei Mille 60; palazzoartinapoli.net; ✆ **081/7958604**) houses rotating exhibits of contemporary art.

Via Settembrini 79 (btw. Via Duomo and Via Carbonara). www.madrenapoli.it. ✆ **081/19313016.** 7€ Wed–Sun, free Mon. Mon and Wed–Sat 10:30am–7:30pm; Sun 10:30am–8pm. Bus: E1. Metro: Cavour.

Napoli Sotterranea ★★ ARCHAEOLOGICAL SITE These guided tours of the city's ancient water works are wildly popular and a surefire hit with kids. Some 2,000 years ago, Romans dug huge cisterns beneath the city and connected them with a system of tunnels. Neapolitans used the ancient water supply well into the 19th century, when cholera

BAD BOY WITH A brush

The painter Caravaggio arrived in Naples in 1606, fleeing authorities in Rome after he killed a man in a fight over a debt. With his taste for gambling, prostitutes, young boys, rowdiness, and drunkenness, the tempestuous artist must have felt right at home in Naples. The city was then the second largest in Europe after Paris, with 350,000 inhabitants, more than a few of whom shared Caravaggio's predisposition for recklessness. His sumptuous canvases, with their realistic portrayals of saints and martyrs and dramatic use of light, have become emblematic of the city's emotion-filled baroque style. Three Caravaggio works are in Naples.

The dark, moody, and chaotic "Seven Acts of Mercy" altarpiece is in the chapel of the **Pio Monte della Misericordia,** Via Tribunali 253 (✆ **081/446944;** Metro: Dante), a fraternity founded by nobles in 1601 to loan money to the poor. As you pick out the merciful acts—St. Martin in the foreground giving his cloak to the beggar is easy (clothing the naked)—you'll probably only detect six. But look again at the scene of the old man sucking at the breast of the young woman: That counts as two, visiting prisoners and feeding the hungry. Classicists might recognize the pair as the Roman Cimon, who was sentenced to death by starvation; his daughter, Pero, secretly suckled him, and this act of family honor won him his release. In the painting gallery upstairs are works by the so-called Cabal of Naples, a notorious triumvirate as colorful as Caravaggio that included the painters Belisario Corenzio, Jusepe de Ribera, and Batistello Caraciollo. They would destroy the works of interlopers who accepted commissions they thought were rightfully theirs, sometimes even poison their competitors, or simply harass them to the point that remaining in Naples was impossible. The chapel and gallery are open Thursday to Tuesday 9am to 2pm; admission is 7€.

Located in the **Capodimonte gallery** (p. 594), the "Flagellation of Christ" depicts two brutish tormentors whipping a nearly naked Christ with almost rote determination; a third is in the foreground, preparing his scourge to join in the action. Lighting emphasizes the arms in action and Christ's twisted, suffering body, providing an almost-hard-to-witness depiction of cruelty in action. This is one of two flagellation scenes Caravaggio painted while he was in Naples.

The "Martyrdom of St. Ursula" hangs in the **Palazzo Zevallos Stigliano** (Via Toledo 185; ✆ **081/425011;** Metro: Montesanto), the lavish headquarters of the Banco Intesa Sanpaolo. Ursula appears unfazed as the king of the Huns, from whom she has just refused an offer of marriage, shoots an arrow into her breast at point-blank range (given that, as legend has it, the 11,000 virginal handmaidens accompanying Ursula had just been beheaded, she could not have been terribly surprised at the cruel reaction of her jilted suitor). Caravaggio himself looks on from the background. This was his last painting and the last image we have of him—he died of fever while returning to Rome a couple of months later. The *palazzo* is open Tuesday to Sunday 10am to 6pm (Sat until 8); admission is 5€.

outbreaks necessitated purer sources. The emptied cisterns came in handy as quarries, as part of an escape route from the Palazzo Reale, and as WWII bomb shelters (some wartime furnishings and graffiti remain). Adding to the mix is a Greek theater that's been unearthed amid the subterranean network. Tours last about 60 minutes and include English commentary. Exit points vary, but usually you climb out of the dark up a long staircase and emerge into the courtyard of an ordinary-looking apartment house—a good illustration of this city's age-spanning layers. Aside from climbing stairs, you'll also be asked to squeeze through a very tight passage (not recommended for the claustrophobic or the overweight). Don't confuse this tour with the excursion through the archaeological excavations beneath the church of San Lorenzo Maggiore (see below). Vico S. Anna di Palazzo, 52. www.lanapolisotterranea.it. ✆ **081/400256.** 9€, 6€ children under 10. English tours Thurs 9pm; Sat 10am, noon, 4:30pm, and 6pm; and Sun 10am, 11am, noon, 4:30pm, and 6pm.

National Archaeological Museum (Museo Archeologico Nazionale) ★★★ MUSEUM The echoey, dusty, gloomy galleries of the rundown Palazzo degli Studi provide one of the world's great time-travel experiences, from grimy modern Naples back to the ancient world. Two treasure troves in particular should not be missed. The superb **Farnese Collection** of Roman sculpture shows off the pieces snapped up by the enormously wealthy Roman Cardinal Alessandro Farnese, later Pope Paul III (1543–1549), who was at the top of the Renaissance game of antiquity hunting. His remarkable collection was inherited by Elisabetta Farnese, who married Philip V of Spain and whose son and grandson became kings of Naples and brought the collection here in the 18th century. Among Cardinal Farnese's great prizes was the **Ercole Farnese,** a huge statue of Hercules unearthed at the Baths of Caracalla in Rome. The superhero son of Zeus is tuckered out, leaning on his club after completing his 11th Labor. He looks troubled, and who can blame him? After slaying monsters and subduing beasts, he's just learned he has to go back into the fray again, descend into Hell, and bring back Cerberus, the three-headed canine guardian. It's a magnificent piece, powerful and wonderfully human at the same time. Carved out of one piece of

The Ercole (Hercules) Farnese.

marble, the colossal **"Toro Farnese,"** 4m (13-ft.) high, is the world's largest-known sculpture from antiquity and was also unearthed at the Baths of Caracalla. Cardinal Farnese hired a team of Renaissance masters, Michelangelo among them, to restore it. The intricate and delicate work depicts one of mythology's greatest acts of satisfying revenge, when the twin brothers Amphion and Zethus tied Dirce—who had imprisoned and mistreated their mother, Antiope—to the horns of a bull that will drag her to her death.

On the mezzanine and upper floors are mosaics, frescoes, and bronzes excavated from Pompeii and Herculaneum. Seeing these everyday objects from villas and shops hauntingly brings the ruined cities to life. Some, such as baking equipment and signage, are quite mundane, touchingly so; many, such as the bronze statues of the "Dancing Faun" (on the mezzanine), the "Drunken Faun" (top floor), and five life-size female bronzes known as "Dancers" (top floor) show off sophisticated artistry. Most of the mosaics, on the mezzanine, are from the House of Faun, one of the largest residences in Pompeii. The million-plus-piece floor mosaic, "Alexander Fighting the Persians," depicts the wavy-haired king of Macedonia astride Bucephalos, the most famous steed in antiquity, sweeping into battle against King Darius III of Persia, who's looking a bit concerned in his chariot. The **Gabinetto Segretto** (Secret Room; also on the mezzanine) displays some of the erotica that was commonplace in Pompeii. Some works are from brothels, among them frescoes that show acts lively yet predictable and some bestial, and others include phallus-shaped oil lamps and huge phalluses placed at doorways to bring fertility and good fortune. We might titter at the bulges under togas, but they weren't necessarily intended to be pornography and rather suggest the libertine attitudes of the time.

Piazza Museo 19. cir.campania.beniculturali.it/museoarcheologiconazionale. ✆ **081/4422149.** 12€. Daily 9am–7:30pm. Metro: Museo or Cavour.

San Lorenzo Maggiore ★★ CHURCH The most beautiful of Naples's medieval churches seems to inspire great literature. Petrarch, the medieval master of Italian verse, lived in the adjoining convent in 1345, and it was here on Holy Saturday 1338 that Boccaccio (author of *The Decameron*) supposedly first laid eyes on his muse, Maria d'Aquino. The daughter of a count but rumored to have been the illegitimate daughter of Robert of Anjou, king of Naples, Maria was married but preferred refuge in a convent to life with her debauched husband. For Boccaccio, it was love at first sight; he nicknamed her La Fiametta (Little Flame), wooed her with his romantic epic "Filocoppo," and eventually won her over and convinced her to become his mistress (she jilted him for another man a few years later). You can ponder 14th-century romance as you stroll the delightful cloisters, then descend a staircase to witness more of the city's multilayered history: Excavations of the buried La

Neapolis Sotterrata have unearthed streets from the Greco-Roman city lined with bakeries and shops, an entire covered market, and an early Christian basilica.

Piazza San Gaetano, Via Tribunali 316. ✆ **081/290580.** Church free. Mon–Sat 8am–noon and 5–7pm. Excavations: 9€. Daily 9:30am–5:30pm. Metro: Piazza Cavour.

VOMERO

Life in Naples never really becomes *too* gentrified, but it calms down quite a bit in the hilltop enclave of the Napoli *bene* (the city's middle and upper classes). The trip up here from the center is on the Centrale and Montesanto funiculars.

Certosa di San Martino (Carthusian Monastery) ★★ The Carthusian monks who took up residence high atop the Vomero hill in 1368 obviously knew something of the good life. Their view is still the best in Naples, across the city and the bay to Mt. Vesuvius. Over the centuries they hired the city's best artists to embellish their environs. Foremost among them, the fractious architect and sculptor Cosimo Fanzago (1591–1678) created the pièce de la resistance, an enormous central courtyard/cloisters that is a masterpiece of the baroque, a grand assemblage of statue-lined porticoes facing a broad lawn. Lest the monks got too comfortable in their earthly surroundings, a gallery of skulls reminded them of their inevitable fate. As if to reinforce the point, in surrounding chapels the Spanish painter Jusepe de Ribera (1591–1652) executed ghoulish scenes of martyrdom and suffering, so realistically portrayed with wounds, wrinkles, and writhing agony that he's been said to partake in "the poetry of the repulsive." As you wander the vast monastery, now housing the **Museo Nazionale di San Martino ★★**, it's easy to see why royal administrators were so appalled by the monks' lavish lifestyle that they threatened to cut off state subsidies.

The museum is a repository of all things Neapolitan: paintings, prints, sculpture, artifacts, and the standout, the *presepi* (Nativity scenes) for which the city has an undying affection (see p. 588). None outshine the 750-piece Cuciniello Presepe, equipped with a lighting system that simulates the cycle of a day from dusk to nightfall. Even larger is the full-size model of the Great Barge used by King Charles of Bourbon in the 1700s, housed amid models and artifacts that honor the city's role as a maritime power. The Gothic cellars are filled with sculpture, including an astonishing St. Francis of Assisi by Giuseppe Sanmartino, who so artfully crafted "Christ Veiled Under A Shroud" in the Cappella di Sansevero.

Largo San Martino 8. ✆ **081/5781769.** 6€. Thurs–Tues 8:30am–7:30pm; ticket booth closes 90 min. earlier. Closed Jan 1 and Dec 25. Metro: Vanvitelli and then bus V1 to Piazzale San Martino. Bus: C28, C31, or C36 to Piazza Vanvitelli. Funicular: Centrale to Piazza Fuga or Montesanto to Morghen.

Villa La Floridiana & Museo Nazionale della Ceramica Duca di Martina ★★ MUSEUM When King Ferdinand I returned to Naples in 1815 after 10 years of exile, he brought with him a Italian/Spanish wife, Lucia Migliaccio, the duchess of Floridia. Their wedding, just months after the death of Ferdinand's first wife, Queen Marina Carolina of Austria, created an international scandal. The duchess did not care for court life or for Naples, and Neapolitans didn't care for her, so Ferdinand bought her this magnificent retreat on the Vomero hill with gardens and views that would make anyone surrender to the city's charms. The villa now houses the 6,000-plus ceramics collection of another noble Neapolitan, Placido de Sangro, the duke of Martina. Items of interest include King Ferdinand's walking stick, with a glass top that contains a portrait of Lucia; it was said this was the only way the powerless, morganatic queen would ever appear in court.

Via Cimarosa 77. ✆ **081/5788418**. 2€. Wed–Mon 8:30am–2pm; ticket booth closes 1 hr. earlier. Bus: C28, C32, or C36. Funicular: Chiaia to Cimarosa. Metro: Vanvitelli.

FARTHER AFIELD

Catacombs of San Gennaro (St. Januarius) ★ RELIGIOUS SITE Naples's popular patron San Gennaro was once buried here, forever lending his name to this two-story underground cemetery, used from the 2nd through 11th centuries. Some of the city's earliest frescoes are here, including one depicting a haloed San Gennaro with Mt. Vesuvius on his shoulders. Even earlier is a charming 2nd-century scene with Adam and Eve. Guides (most speak English) will lead you past the frescoed burial niches and early basilicas carved from the *tufa* rock, providing fascinating insights into the city's long past—with a special nod to Sant'Agrippino, a 3rd-century bishop once interred here, who is almost as popular among Neapolitans as San Gennaro. As you emerge from the lower level of this city of the dead you'll be in Rione Sanità, another world entirely—very much a city of the living. In the 16th and 17th centuries, Neapolitans who became ill were once banished to the neighborhood to protect the health (*sanità*) of those living within the city walls. One of the more esteemed later residents was early-18th-century architect Ferdinando San Felice, who built an elegant palazzo at Via Sanità 127; step inside the courtyard for a look at his magnificent double staircase. If you continue down Via Sanità you'll be in Piazza Cavour, at the edge of the historic center, within a few minutes.

Via Capodimonte 13. www.catacombedinapoli.it. ✆ **081/7443714.** 8€. Tours (in English) Mon–Sat on the hour 10am–5pm; Sun 10am–1pm. Bus: 24 or R4.

National Museum & Gallery of the Capodimonte (Museo e Gallerie Nazionale di Capodimonte) ★ MUSEUM Italy has many better art collections, and the trip here inevitably involves a change

Souvenir shop in Naples.

of buses or a taxi ride. That said, there's plenty to lure you out to the former hunting preserve of the Bourbon kings. For one, the *bosco reale* (royal woods) is one of the few parks in Naples, and sharing the greenery with picnicking families can be a refreshing change of scenery. The core of the collection is from Elisabetta Farnese, the duchess of Parma, who handed down the family's paintings to her children and grandchildren after she became Queen of Spain. They in turn brought them back to Italy when they became kings of Naples. By the time the works got here, many of the best had found their way into other collections; what remains includes a roster of Italian and Northern masters, but often secondary works. In fact, the museum's two standout pieces have nothing to do with the Farneses. Caravaggio's dramatic "Flagellation of Christ" was brought here in the 1970s, not long after another Caravaggio was stolen from an oratorio in Palermo. In the contemporary galleries Andy Warhol's "Mount Vesuvius" is an almost-corny comic-book depiction of an eruption that renders the mountain as an age-old icon of volatility. Upstairs, in the Royal Apartments, there's enough Sèvres and Meissen to put together a royal feast of epic proportions. The Capodimonte ceramics were fired right here on the grounds throughout the 18th century.

Palazzo Capodimonte, Via Miano 1; also through the park from Via Capodimonte. cir.campania.beniculturali.it/museodicapodimonte. ✆ **081/7499111.** 8€; 7€ after 2pm. Thurs–Tues 8:30am–7:30pm. Bus: R4 (from the Archaeological Museum).

Where to Stay

Where you stay in Naples makes a difference—as in, enjoyable stay versus "I never want to set foot in this hellhole again." You want a safe neighborhood close to the sights, and our suggestions below meet that criterion. Some good business-oriented hotels have opened near the train station, but this area is not all that convenient or, for that matter,

Campania is famous for its pizza.

particularly savory after dark. Naples hotels often post special rates on their website, especially in summer, which is low season in the city.

EXPENSIVE

Grand Hotel Parker's ★★ Naples' oldest grand hotel has been welcoming guests since 1870, when Prince Grifeo decided to transform his palace into a posh stopover where travelers on the Grand Tour could enjoy a bit of Neapolitan luxury. The name comes from British naturalist George Bidder Parker, who bought the enterprise in 1899 while working on the gardens in the Villa Communale (see above). Through wars, earthquakes, and other ups and downs the tradition continues, and this lovely old place on a hillside above the bay is still all about quiet refinement. Lounges are floored with rich marble and hung with a museum-worthy art collection, while the stylish guest rooms all open to balconies and are soothingly done in both traditional and contemporary touches. Choicest rooms overlook the bay, but for guests deprived of the spectacle, an airy top-floor lounge and dining area and an expansive roof terrace make the most of the views. Four so-called superior rooms are an especially good value, compensating for the lack of sea views with lots of extra space and cushy couches and big armchairs in which to stretch out.

Corso Vittorio Emanuele 135. www.grandhotelparkers.it. ✆ **081/761–2474.** 82 units. 180€–230€ double. Rates include breakfast. Bus 128; Metro: Piazza Amedeo; Montesanto or Centrale funiculars to Corso Vittorio Emanuele. **Amenities:** Restaurant; 2 bars; room service; spa; roof terrace; garage parking (25€); Wi-Fi (free).

Grand Hotel Vesuvio ★★ Old-world glamour holds sway in this famed waterfront hostelry that pampers the rich and famous with a Grand Tour–worthy experience, plus all the 21st-century amenities, including a spiffy spa. Expanses of shiny parquet, handsome old prints, fine linens on firm beds, and classic furnishings give the large, very comfortable rooms sophisticated-yet-understated polish. The big perk, though, is the view of the bay, the Castel dell'Ovo, and Mt. Vesuvius outside glass doors that open to balconies off many rooms. You'll get the same eyeful from the rooftop restaurant and the bright salon where a lavish breakfast buffet is served. High-season prices are geared to the budgets of celebrities and dignitaries, though seasonal rates and occasional specials bring the experience of a stay here within reach of the rest of us.

Via Partenope 45 (off Via Santa Lucia by Castel dell'Ovo). www.vesuvio.it. ✆ **081/7640044.** 160 units. 180€–320€ double. Most rates include breakfast. Bus: 152, 140, or C25. **Amenities:** 2 restaurants; bar; fitness center; indoor pool (for a fee); room service; spa; Wi-Fi (free).

MODERATE

Art Resort Gallery Umberto ★ As if the location were not dramatic enough, an upper floor of accommodations in the city's 1890s Art Nouveau–style glass shopping arcade is almost over the top with plush interiors. The painted headboards, swag draperies, and gilded furniture are not for minimalists, but for a Neapolitan experience it's hard to beat the dash of theatricality, or the location (none better for shoppers). Many of the rooms face the interior of the *galleria* (but just below the glass roof, so quite bright) while others look out over an adjoining piazzetta, and a choice few have little balconies. All guests can enjoy the large interior terrace high above the tile-floored arcades far below.

Galleria Umberto 1. www.artresortgalleriaumberto.it ✆ **081/497-6224.** 16 units. 120€–170€ double. Rates include breakfast. Bus: R2. **Amenities:** Bar; concierge; Wi-Fi (free in lobby and some rooms).

Chiaia Hotel de Charme ★ With its bright shops and bars, spiffy, pedestrian-only Via Chiaia may be the city's friendliest address, and this warmly decorated inn in an old noble residence does the location justice. Some smaller rooms face interior courtyards and have snug, shower-only bathrooms, while many of the larger ones on the street side (with double panes to keep the noise down) have large bathrooms with Jacuzzi tubs. Decor throughout is sufficiently traditional and regal to suggest the *palazzo's* aristocratic provenance, and services are more wholesome than they were when the place was an upscale brothel. Pastries and snacks are laid out in the sitting room in the afternoon and evening, the buffet breakfast is generous, and the staff is good at recommending restaurants and providing directions.

Via Chiaia 216. www.chiaiahotel.com. ✆ **081/415555.** 33 units. 75€–135€ double. Rates include breakfast. Bus: R2. **Amenities:** Bar; concierge; Wi-Fi (free in lobby and some rooms).

Costantinopoli 104 ★★ This 19th-century Art Nouveau palace is set in a palm-shaded courtyard that's mere steps from the archaeological museum but a world away from the noisy city—it even has a small swimming pool for a refreshing dip. Contemporary art and some stunning stained glass grace a series of salons; some rooms are traditionally done with rich fabrics and dark wood furnishings, others are breezily contemporary. The choicest rooms are on the top floor and open onto a sprawling roof terrace—a magical retreat above the rooftops and definitely what you should ask for when booking.

Via Santa Maria di Costantinopoli 104 (off Piazza Bellini). www.costantinopoli104.it. ✆ **081/5571035.** 19 units. From 140€ double. Rates include breakfast. Metro: Museo. **Amenities:** Pool; room service; Wi-Fi (free).

Decumani Hotel de Charme ★★ The heart-of-Naples neighborhood outside the huge portals can be gritty, but these are sprucely regal lodgings, on the piano nobile of the *palazzo* of the last bishop of the Bourbon kingdom, Cardinal Sisto Riario Sforza. Guest rooms surround a vast, frescoed ballroom-cum-breakfast room; all have plush draperies and fabrics and a few antiques complementing hardwood floors and timbered ceilings. Larger rooms include sitting areas and face the quiet courtyard, while many of the smaller, street-facing doubles share small terraces.

Via San Giovanni Maggiore Pignatelli 15 (off Via Benedetto Croce, btw. vias Santa Chiara and Mezzocannone). www.decumani.com. ✆ **081/5518188.** 22 units. 135€–170€ double. Rates include breakfast. Metro: Piazza Dante. **Amenities:** Wi-Fi (free).

Hotel Piazza Bellini ★★ The archaeological museum and lively Piazza Bellini are just outside the door of this centuries-old palace, but a cool contemporary redo softens the edges of city life. An outdoor living room fills the cobbled courtyard, and the rooms, which range across several floors, are minimalist chic with hardwood floors, neutral tones and warm-hued accents, sleek surfaces, and plenty of space for storage, plus Philippe Starck chairs and crisp white linens. Some of the rooms have terraces and balconies, a few are bilevel, and some with limited views are set aside as "economy"—but rates for any room in the house are reasonable and make this mellow haven an especially good value.

Via Costantinipoli 101. www.hotelpiazzabellini.com. ✆ **081/451732.** 48 units. 95€–125€ double. Rates include breakfast. Metro: Piazza Dante or Piazza Cavour. **Amenities:** Bar; concierge; Wi-Fi (free).

San Francesco al Monte ★★ This ex-Franciscan convent just above the Spanish quarter and halfway up the San Martino hill makes the monastic life seem pretty appealing. The hillside location is a handy refuge above the fray but an easy walk or funicular ride away from the sights, and views from all rooms and several airy glassed-in and outdoor lounges sweep across the city to the bay. The monastic tenants left behind a chapel, a refectory, secret stairways, and lots of atmospheric nooks and crannies. Their cells have been turned into large, tiled guest rooms and sprawling suites. In the contemplative monk's garden, shaded walkways are carved out of the cliffside and a swimming pool and outdoor bar on the heights above are welcome perks in summer.

Corso Vittorio Emanuele 328. www.sanfrancescoalmonte.it. ✆ **081/4239111.** 45 units. 140€–170€ double. Rates include breakfast. Metro: Piazza Amedeo; Montesanto or Centrale funiculars to Corso Vittorio Emanuele. **Amenities:** Restaurant; bar; pool; room service; Wi-Fi (free).

INEXPENSIVE

Correra 241 ★★ Follow a narrow side street, enter the rear courtyard of an old palazzo, and walk up a ramp into a former factory tucked into a tufa cliff. The old workrooms and storage lofts have been converted into cheerful lodgings furnished with contemporary flair. The yellow concrete floors, rock walls, colorful artwork, even an Etruscan-Greco aqueduct leading off the lobby befit a city that's legendary for its quirky pockets. There's no such thing as standard accommodations here: Some rooms are lit by skylights only and others by windows high up on double-height walls; still others are two story—you may want to ask about your room's distinct features when you book. Wherever you settle, you'll be only steps from the archaeological museum, but, with a rear courtyard setting, enjoying that rare amenity in Naples: quiet.

Via Correra 241. http://lifestylehotel.it/correra. ✆ **081/1956-2842.** 21 units. 65€–85€ double. Rates include breakfast. Metro: Dante. **Amenities:** Bar; parking (20€); Wi-Fi (free).

Hotel Il Convento ★ If you want to experience a slice of Neapolitan life—as in laundry flapping outside your window—this is the place for you. While the narrow Spagnoli streets outside teem with neighborhood color and bustle, a 17th-century former convent provides all sorts of cozy ambience, with lots of wood beams, brick arches, and terracotta floors. Two rooms have their own planted rooftop terraces, and two others spread over two levels. Main artery Via Toledo is just two short blocks away, taking the edge off comings and goings at night. An eager staff will steer you to neighborhood restaurants and shops.

Via Speranzella 137/a. www.hotelilconvento.com. ✆ **081/403977.** 14 units. 85€–140€. Rates include breakfast. Bus: R2 to Piazza Municipio. Small pets allowed. **Amenities:** Bar; fitness room and sauna; room service; Wi-Fi (free).

Robby's House Bed & Breakfast ★ This is definitely not a place for everyone, or for that matter, for anyone looking for a private bath, a sense of style, any hint of luxury, or TVs or other standard amenities. But the good-size, very frugally furnished rooms in a rambling apartment are ridiculously inexpensive and an excellent value for the basic comfort they offer in a prime city-center location. They're safe and spotlessly clean and an easy walk from the train station and many sights. All have little balconies overlooking one of those narrow, laundry-hung Neapolitan streets. Guests share two antiseptic bathrooms. The attentive host, Robby, likes to advise on what to see in his native Naples—if only he would ditch the harsh overhead lights and invest in some reading lamps. The website photos give a candid assessment of what to expect in terms of decor and style. Payment is cash only, due upon arrival.

Via S. Nicola dei Caserti 5 (off Via Tribunali). www.robbyshouse.com. ✆ **081/454546.** 5 units. From 35€ double. Rates include breakfast. Metro: Piazza Garibaldi or Piazza Dante. **Amenities:** Laundry service (fee); Wi-Fi (free).

Where to Eat

Neapolitans love to eat, and you'll love dining here, too. What's not to like about a cuisine in which pizza is a staple? Other dishes to look for include *mozzarella in carrozza* (fried mozzarella in a "carriage"), in which mozzarella is fried between two pieces of bread and topped with a sauce of the chef's design, often with tomatoes and capers; *gnocchi alla sorrentina,* little pockets of potato pasta filled with mozzarella and topped with tomato sauce; *ragu,* a meat sauce cooked for hours and served atop pasta; *parmigiana di melanzane* (eggplant parmesan)—the ubiquitous dish of fried eggplant, tomato sauce, mozzarella, parmigiano, and basil originated here—*crocchè di patate* (fried potatoes), mashed with herbs, cheese, sometimes salami, lightly coated in breadcrumbs and fried; and *pasta e fagioli,* beans and pasta, nothing could be more Neapolitan. Think, too, of seafood—any kind, especially *cozze,* mussels, often served *alla marinara* (simmered in tomato sauce)—and *polpette,* succulent little meatballs.

For a sampling of street food—especially the above-mentioned *crocchè di patate* and *arancini,* fried rice balls—stop by the stand on the ground floor of **Matteo,** a venerable pizzeria at Via Tribunali 94 (✆ **081/455262**), open Monday to Saturday 9am to midnight.

EXPENSIVE

Rosiello ★★★ NEAPOLITAN/SEAFOOD It's a cab ride or long bus trip out to this retreat, on a hilltop above the sea in swanky and leafy Posillipo, but the trek is worth it. Ask your hotel to make reservations and help arrange transport, because a meal on the terrace here is one of the city's great treats. Everything comes from the seas at your feet or the restaurant's extensive vegetable plots on the hillside; even the cheese is local. These ingredients find their way into seafood feasts that might include risotto *alla pescatora* (with seafood) and *pezzogna all'acquapazza* (fish in a light tomato broth), but even a simple pasta here, such as *scialatielli con melanzane e provola* (fresh pasta with local cheese and eggplant), is elegant and simply delicious.

Via Santo Strato 10. www.ristoranterosiello.it. ✆ **081/7691288.** Main courses 10€–25€. Thurs–Tues 12:30–4pm and 7:30pm–midnight (May–Sept open daily). Closed 2 weeks each Jan and Aug. Bus: C3 to Mergellina (end of line), and then 140.

Squistezze/La Stanza del Gusto ★★ CREATIVE NEAPOLITAN Chef Mario Avallone prepares some of the most innovative food in town, and he offers it two ways: In a casual, ground-floor cheese bar/*osteria* (**Squistezze**) and in a simple-but-stylish upstairs restaurant. Downstairs, daily offerings are written on blackboards and include the best lunch deal in town—a main course, dessert, wine, water, and coffee for 13€. You can pair cheese and *salumi* (cured meats) with carefully chosen wines or what is probably the city's largest selection of craft beers, or tuck into salads and unusual specialties, such as *arancino di mare,* a fresh take on classic fried rice balls, in this case concealing a core of seafood. Upstairs, locally sourced ingredients find their way into tasting menus that start at 35€; don't miss the *variazione di baccalà,* an amazing presentation of salt cod prepared in several different ways.

Via Santa Maria di Costantinopoli 100. www.lastanzadelgusto.com. ✆ **081/401578.** Main courses (upstairs restaurant) 14€–20€. Mon–Thurs 11am–11:30pm; Fri–Sat 11am–midnight. Closed 3 weeks in Aug. Metro: Piazza Dante or Museo.

MODERATE

Europeo di Mattozzi ★★ NEAPOLITAN/PIZZA/SEAFOOD Just about every Neapolitan ranks this attractive center-of-town eatery as a favorite. Walls covered with copper pots, framed photos, and oil paintings provide welcoming surrounds suggesting that dining here is serious business. Even connoisseurs claim the pizzas here are the best in town, and if one of the large pies doesn't suffice as a starter, choose from *zuppa di cannellini e cozze* (bean and mussel soup) or *pasta e patate con provola* (pasta and potatoes with melted local cheese). Seafood *secondi* are the house specialties and include *ricciola all' acquapazza* (a local species in a light tomato and herb broth) and *stoccafisso alla pizzaiola* (dried codfish in a tomato, garlic, and oregano sauce). Reservations are a must on weekends.

Via Marchese Campodisola 4. ✆ **081/5521323.** Main courses 12€–18€. Mon–Wed noon–3:30pm; Thurs–Sat noon–3:30pm and 8pm–midnight. Closed 2 weeks in Aug. Bus: R2 or R3 to Piazza Trieste e Trento.

Tandem ★ NEAPOLITAN Take a seat in the simple room or on the pleasant little terrace on the lane outside and linger over the house specialty, ragu. A lot of locals stop by this friendly, almost-funky little spot for their fix of the city staple, which comes with meat (three or four kinds, slow-cooked) or vegetarian, which is a bit of a desecration. It's served over spaghetti or a choice of other pasta, or by itself with thick slices of bread for dunking, along with carafes of the house wine.

Via Paladino 51.www.tandem.napoli.it. ✆ **081/4074833.** Reservations recommended Fri–Sat. Main courses 10€–18€. Mon–Fri noon–3:30pm and 7–11:30pm and Sat–Sun noon–4pm and 7pm–midnight. Metro: Piazza Dante.

Zi Teresa ★★ NEAPOLITAN/SEAFOOD Neapolitans know the Borgo Marinaro tourist traps to avoid, but they flock to this bright room in the shadow of Castel dell'Ovo to soak in the sea views while enjoying excellent fish. This 125-year-old institution is wildly popular for family gatherings, when the kitchen sends out huge platters of seafood grills and *frittura mista*. The decor has a nautical twist, and if that doesn't make the point, the fleet of boats bobbing by the huge terrace will.

Via Borgo Marinaro 1. www.ziteresa.it. ✆ **081/764-2565.** Main courses 9€–20€. Bus: 152, C25, 140, E5 to Via Santa Lucia. Tues–Sat 12:15–10:30pm; Sun 12:15–5:30pm; closed Mon.

INEXPENSIVE

La Campagnola ★ NEAPOLITAN Students, professors, and neighborhood regulars eat at this plain, homey wine shop/trattoria almost every day, or at least stop by for a glass of the house wine and a plate of fried artichokes or other appetizer. The chalkboard menu changes daily and ranges through Neapolitan home-style favorites like *parmigiano di melanzane* and *vitello limone*. The pizzas are perfect starters, and a meal usually ends with a plate of *zeppole* (fried donuts), courtesy of the house.

Via Tribunale 47. ✆ **081/459034.** Main courses 7€–10€. Tues–Sun noon–3pm and 7–11pm. Metro: Dante.

Il Buongustai ★ NEAPOLITAN/PIZZA To get away from the crowds on Via Tribunali, walk towards its eastern end, where a neighborhood vibe takes over. A favorite with locals on this part of the street is no-frills and always busy, with a takeaway counter out front and a small dining room in the rear. A huge selection of pizzas, including one that can be made with your choice of toppings (not common in Italian *pizzerie*) is served alongside *fritturina* (fried vegetables and other bits), *brushchetti*, and choices from a *tavola calda* (hot table), with grilled sausages, meatballs, and whatever else the chef is making that day.

Via Tribunali 201. ✆ **081/446768.** Pizzas and main courses 4€–8€. Daily noon–3pm and 7–11pm.

Nenella ★ NEAPOLITAN The guys at this Spagnoli favorite will make you feel like one of the regulars who crowd into the covered terrace or plain white room for the satisfying home cooking. Stick to the specials, listed on a board and recited by one of the busy waiters—*pasta e patate* (pasta and potatoes), maybe some fried fish or roasted pork, and salads of fresh greens. Even with wine, a meal here won't cost more than 12€ or 15€ a head.

Vico Lungo Teatro 103–105. ✆ **081/414338.** Main courses 6€–8€. Mon–Sat noon–3pm and 7–11pm. Metro: Montesanto.

Pizzeria Da Michele ★★★ PIZZA According to about half the residents of Naples, this no-frills, zero-ambience place serves the best pizza in town—the other half would vote for Sorbillo (see below). Take a number at the door and prepare to wait for a table—the place is always packed. But you won't have to wait long for one of the enormous and simply delicious pizzas that come in just two varieties, *margherita* or *marinara* (toppings are for snobs, say the guys behind the counter): They emerge from the oven in a mere 20 seconds, an act of wizardry that keeps the tables turning quickly. No credit cards accepted.

Via Sersale 1. www.damichele.net. ✆ **081/5539204.** Pizza 5€–7€. Mon–Sat 11am–11pm. Metro: Garibaldi.

Pizzeria Gino Sorbillo ★★★ PIZZA Don't let the crowds out front put you off, and don't let one of the other pizza places on Via Tribunali lure you in (also confusingly called Sorbillo, set up by other family members). Just make your way through the crowd, give your name to the friendly, bemused woman with the clipboard, and enjoy the partylike atmosphere on the street out front as you wait for a table. The wait is never as long as you think it might be, and once inside you'll probably be ushered to the vast, upstairs dining room where a long menu of pizzas is accompanied by a palatable house wine. This attractive place is the Ritz compared to serious contender Michele (see above). The Quattro Stagione (Four Seasons) pizza defies Michele's no-topping policy with its quadrants of mushrooms, salami, prosciutto, and cheese.

Via Tribunali 32. www.sorbillo.it. ✆ **081/0331009.** Pizza 5€–7€. Daily noon–3:30 and 7pm–midnight. Metro: Dante.

Shopping

Via Toledo and **Galleria Umberto I** still hold their own as mainstays of Naples shopping, though the clothing and accessories shops tend to

Sweet-Tooth Heaven

On top of their many other sterling qualities, Neapolitans make delicious sweets. Clam-shaped *sfogliatelle,* filled with ricotta cream, is the city's unofficial pastry, available at bars and pastry shops all over the city. *Il baba* are little cakes soaked in rum or limoncello syrup and often filled with cream; *delizia al limone* is sponge cake soaked with lemon or limoncello syrup, filled with lemon pastry cream, and iced with lemon-flavored whipped cream; and dark, flourless *torta* Caprese, topped with powdered sugar, the chocolate cake of choice.

Scaturchio, Piazza San Domenico Maggiore 19 (www.scaturchio.it; ✆ **081/5517031**), makes some of the best *sfogliatelle* in town and also serves excellent coffee. Another popular stop for a coffee and a sweet is **Il Vero Bar del Professore** at Piazza Trieste e Trento, 46 (www.ilverobardelprofessore.com; ✆ **081/403041**). Naples' ice cream parlors dispense some of the best gelato in the country; **Gelateria della Scimmia,** Piazza della Carità 4 (✆ **081/5520272**) is a mandatory stop. The city's revered temple of chocolate, **Gay-Odin** (www.gay-odin.it) has elegant shops throughout the city, dispensing chocolate *cozze* (mussels) and chocolate-wrapped coffee beans alongside much-lauded gelato. A convenient central location is at Via Benedetto Croce 61 (✆ **081/551-0794).**

be a little less elegant than those in **Chiaia.** There, big Italian fashion names have outlets along the Riviera di Chiaia, Via Calabritto, Via dei Mille, Via Filangeri, Via Poerio, and Piazza dei Martiri.

The city is justly famous for hand-crafted goods. Heading the list are *presepi,* the nativity scenes crafted and sold along **Via San Gregorio Armeno** (see p. 588). Another shop selling handcrafted figurines is **La Scarabatto,** in the historic center at Via die Tribunali 50 (www.lascarabattola.it; ✆ **081/291735**), where the output includes traditional folk figures and contemporary ceramics.

The lively **Mercato di Porta Nolano** stretches around Piazza Nolano, south of the train station (Metro: Porta Nolano). Stalls burst with seafood and local produce and all manner of other foodstuffs; they operate daily until 6pm Monday to Saturday and 2pm on Sunday (pickpockets have a field day here, so watch your effects). Every third Saturday and Sunday of each month from 8am to 2pm (except in Aug), a fiera ***antiquaria*** (antiques fair) is held in the Villa Comunale di Napoli on Viale Dohrn.

Opening hours for stores in Naples are generally Monday to Saturday from 10:30am to 1pm and from 4 to 7:30pm.

Entertainment & Nightlife

Neapolitans make the best of balmy evenings by passing the time on cafe terraces. Top choice is the oldest cafe in Naples, with a Liberty-style interior from the 1860s, the elegant **Gran Caffè Gambrinus,** Via

Chiaia 1, in Piazza Trento e Trieste (✆ **081/417582**). Another very popular spot is **La Caffetteria,** Piazza dei Martiri 25 (✆ **081/7644243**), a good stop for evening *aperitivi.*

OPERA & CLASSICAL MUSIC The great Naples-born tenor Enrico Caruso (1873–1921) appeared only once at his hometown's sumptuous opera house, in 1901—he was booed off the stage and vowed never to return. The venerable **Teatro San Carlo,** Via San Carlo 98 (www.teatrosancarlo.it; ✆ **081/7972412** or 081/7972331), has been kinder to other performers and composers. The world's oldest opera house, inaugurated on November 4, 1737, has welcomed Rossini, Bellini, Verdi, Puccini, and a veritable who's who of opera greats. The house still stages world-class opera, along with dance and orchestral works, Tuesday through Sunday, December through June. Tickets cost between 30€ and 100€. Guided tours 7€ are available daily 10:30am, 11:30am, 12:30pm, 2:30pm, 3:30pm, and 4:30pm.

The **Centro di Musica Antica Pietà dei Turchini,** Via Santa Caterina da Siena 38, at the base of the Vomero hill near the Vittorio Emanuele funicular stop (www.turchini.it; ✆ **081/402395**), is a music conservatory that is well known for concerts of early music, though the repertoire extends to other music as well. Concerts are held in the church of Pietà dei Turchini, beneath paintings by some of Naples' great baroque masters, and in a hall that was once an orphanage where young charges were instructed in singing and musical composition. Star pupils included Alessandro Scarlatti (1660–1725) and Giovanni Pergolesi (1710–1736).

Another great venue is the **Associazione Alessandro Scarlatti,** Piazza dei Martiri 58 (www.associazionescarlatti.it; ✆ **081/406011**), which stages chamber music concerts at Castel Sant'Elmo and other venues; tickets prices range from 15€ to 25€.

Trianon Viviani, near the train station (Metro Garibaldi) at Piazza Vincenzo Calenda 9 (www.teatrotrianon.it; ✆ **081/2258285**) focuses on traditional Neapolitan song and theater; the concert season usually starts in April, with performances Thursday through Sunday.

BARS & CLUBS This is a port, a cosmopolitan city, and a university town all rolled into one, so the Neapolitan nighttime scene is eclectic and lively. **Piazza Bellini,** near the university at the edge of the historical center, is an especially lively destination. Lined with books and old photos, the cozy rooms of the deservedly popular **Intra Moenia,** Piazza Bellini 7 (www.intramoenia.it; ✆ **081/290–988**; daily from morning to late), are a gathering spot for coffee, light meals, and drinks. **Cammarota Spritz,** Vico Lungo Teatro Nuovo 31 (daily), might be Naples' most popular bar, where a mob assembles outside (actually, there's no inside at this street stall) for the 1€ drinks served in plastic cups. **Archeobar,** Via Mezzocannone 101/Bis (✆ **081/1917-8862**), is friendly to students and sightseers alike, with a lively downstairs room and a quieter, book-lined room upstairs where patrons chat quietly and, gasp, even read. **Kestè,** near the university at Largo San Giovanni Maggiore 26 (www.keste.it; ✆ **081/551-3984**), is a dance club and bar with a huge terrace where the youth of Naples peacock around.

Enoteche, or wine bars, provide wines by the glass and the bottle, along with some food and often a relaxed atmosphere. The best are **Enoteca Belledonne,** Vico Belledonne a Chiaia 18 (www.enotecabelledonne.com; ✆ **081/403162;** closed Sun), with a local Chiaia vibe; **Barril** (Via Giuseppe Fiorelli 11, www.barril.it, ✆ **081/4362**), serving wine in chic rooms and a garden; and **Trip** (Via Giuseppe Martucci 64; www.tripnapoli.com; ✆ **081/1956-8994**).

AROUND NAPLES

To the west of Naples are the weird volcanic landscapes and evocative ancient ruins of the **Campo Flegrei,** the Phelgraean Fields. To the east are two of the world's most famous and well-preserved ancient cities, **Herculaneum** and **Pompeii,** and the volcano that doomed them, **Vesuvius.** You can visit any of these fabled places easily on a day trip and be back in Naples in time for a *passeggiata* and dinner.

Campo Flegrei (The Phlegraean Fields) ★★

On this seaside peninsula just west of Naples, volcanic vents steam and hiss, and ruined villas testify to ancient hedonism. Whatever drama natural phenomena and mere mortals fail to provide, mythic characters and oracles seem to spring to life and pick up the slack. Our alphabet was invented here, when the Latin language officially adopted the characters used for written communication in Cuma. Nero murdered his mother, the ambitious and villainous Agrippina, outside Baiae, the Palm Beach of the ancient world, where Caesar relaxed and Hadrian breathed his last. Away from Pozzuoli and other busy seaside towns, moonlike landscapes are interspersed with lush hillsides carpeted in olive groves and orange and lemon orchards, adding an eerie beauty to the mix.

GETTING THERE & AROUND

A day exploring this strange, mythic landscape begins in seaside Pozzuoli, reached from Naples by Line 2 of the Metropolitana (subway) or via the **Cumana Railroad** (www.unicocampania.it; ✆ **800-053939**), starting from Piazza Montesanto. The Metropolitana station in Pozzuoli is above the main town, near the Anfiteatro Flavio; the Cumana Railroad station is near the seafront and town center, just around the corner from the spectacular Serapeo ruins. From Pozzuoli, **SEPSA buses** (www.sepsa.it;

✆ **081/7354965**) run to the Solfatara, while the Cumana Railroad and bus connections will get you to Baia, Lago d'Averno, and Cuma—train to Lucrina and bus from there to Baia, train to Torregaveta and bus from there to Cuma.

As you may have discerned, getting around the Campo Flegrei requires some logistics. You can spend a full, rewarding day in Pozzuoli, leaving the other sights for another day or trip. Unless you have a yen to dive through the underwater ruins at Baiae or consult the Sybil at Cuma, you can get a good sense of the Campo Flegrei without venturing beyond Pozzuoli. In that case, take Line 2 of the Metropilitana (with city-center stops near the train station in Piazza Garibaldi, Piazza Cavour, and Montesanto) to Pozzuoli. Begin with a visit to the Anfiteatro Flavio and walk or take the bus from there to the Solfaterra. Return to the Pozzuoli seafront for lunch and a visit to the Serapeo and, if it's open, the newly excavated Rione Terra. If you have the time and stamina, and if the sights are still open, you could continue to Baia or Cumae and return to Naples on the Cumana railway from one of those places.

POZZUOLI ★★

23km (14 miles) West of Naples

Screen legend Sophia Loren was born in this seaside town in 1934, contributing a bit of color to a place already steeped in lore. The Greek colony of Dicearchia, founded in 530 B.C., became the Roman Puteoli in 194 B.C. You will soon sniff out the origin of the name—from the Latin *putere,* "to stink," from the sulfurous springs surrounding the town. Or possibly, and a little more kindly, the name comes from the Greek *pyteolos*, or "little well." Roman emperors preferred the harbor to the one at Partenope (Naples). Among them was Caligula, who performed his famous stunt at Puteoli: He road his horse across a floating bridge of boats to Baiae, defying the soothsayer who said he had "no more chance of becoming Emperor than of riding a horse across the Gulf of Baiae."

Puteoli was also a busy hub for cargo ships from all over the Roman world, and dockworkers unloaded grain from Egypt, Sicily, and other outposts of the empire and reloaded them with marble, mosaics, and other exports. Among the voyagers who disembarked here was St. Paul, sometime around A.D. 60. He'd sailed across the Mediterranean from Caesarea, in present-day Israel, where he'd been imprisoned. From Puteoli he traveled up the Appian Way to Rome to stand trial for alleged crimes in Asia Minor and was later freed.

The town also became famous for *pozzolana,* volcanic ash that reacts with water to form a substance like concrete that allowed engineers to build the huge dome of Rome's Pantheon. The barbarian Alaric destroyed the Roman town in A.D. 410, but the acropolis, on a tufa-stone promontory pushing into the sea, continued to be inhabited throughout the Dark

Ages and a modern town grew up around and on top of in the following centuries. This storied past, the ancient monuments, volcanic landscapes, and sweeping views over the sea and the islands of Ischia and Procida make Pozzuoli a lot more interesting and appealing than an otherwise scrappy suburban town has any right to be.

Anfiteatro Flavio (Flavian Amphitheater) ★★ RUINS More than 20,000 spectators could squeeze into the many rows of seats in this theater from the last part of the 1st century, the third-largest arena in the Roman world. So much remains that it seems like a crowd is about to mill in for the next gladiatorial show. The handiwork of the theater's engineers, who also built the coliseum in Rome, includes subterranean staging areas with "mechanics" that hoisted wild beasts up to the field of slaughter and pumped in water to flood the arena for mock naval battles. Among the unfortunate victims of the sophisticated works was Januarius, or San Gennaro, the patron saint of Naples. A painting by Artemisia Gentileschi (1593–1656), a surprisingly successful female artist of the Neapolitan baroque, shows the composed bishop withstanding the attacks of a ferocious boar. Actually, the saint didn't have much to worry about. According to legend, the beasts released to devour him fell submissively at his feet. Alas, Gennaro was later beheaded on the crater floor of the nearby Solfatara volcano. Gentileschi's painting, "The Martyrdom of San Gennaro at Puzzuoli" is in the Museo Nazionale di Capodimonte in Naples (see p. 594).

Via Nicola Terracciano 75. www.cir.campania.beniculturali.it. ✆ **081/5266007**. 2€ or 4€ combined ticket that also includes Serapeo, Parco Archeologica di Baia, Castello di Baia, and Scavi di Cuma, and is valid 2 days). June–Sept Wed–Mon 9am–7pm; Oct–May Wed–Mon 9am–4pm, last admission 3pm.

Rione Terra ★★ ARCHAEOLOGICAL SITE The Greek city that the Romans named Puteoli sits on a promontory above the sea. The area was built upon over the millennia and inhabited until the 1980s, when "bradyseism," a settling and rising of unstable volcanic ground, rendered living in the district unsafe and, with the bursting of sewer lines, nonhygienic. Excavations beneath crumbling houses from the 16th and 17th centuries has revealed the ancient town, and visitors can now walk down gridlike Roman streets past the foundations of shops, taverns, houses, and slave quarters. It's easy to envision day-to-day life in Puteoli: grooves in the pavement in front of doorways are tracks on which wooden screens were pulled shut at night; the remnants of lead pipes are from a sophisticated water system fed by aqueducts. The showpiece is a magnificent Greek/Roman temple, incorporated into the baroque Duomo. Columns and marble walls have been uncovered, and the ancient structure now houses a glass-fronted chapel that reveals the many layers of its past.

Access from Via Duomo. www.comune.pozzuoli.na.it. ✆ **081/1993-6286**. By guided tour only, often in English, 3€. Weekends 9am–5pm.

Serapeo ★★ RUINS The discovery of a statue of the Greco-Egyptian god Serapis in the 18th century led to centuries of confusion. Serapis was a popular cult figure in the ancient world, a master of abundance and resurrection. A Serapeum, or temple to the god, was a fixture of many Greco-Roman cities—though not, as was once believed, in Puteoli. Instead, the statue stood in a niche of a magnificent marketplace where shops ringed a marble-floored, arcaded courtyard. In the middle was a *tholos,* a raised round meeting hall decorated with sea creatures. Another mystery arose when 19th-century antiquarians discovered that columns in the marketplace were riddled with holes drilled by mollusks, a sign they had once been underwater. Subsequent investigations revealed that the culprit was bradyseism. Slow settling over long periods allows water to rush in, then the ground rises above sea level again—by as much as 6 feet in a decade, making living in Pozzuoli a fairly shaky business. In fact, a series of uplifts in the 1980s forced the evacuation of much of the town, damaged 8,000 buildings, and raised the seabed to the point that the harbor can no long accommodate large craft. As you wander around the site, you can see the telltale little holes in the marble columns that were once submerged in water.

Center; from the Cumana railway station, turn right and walk 1 block to the ruins. www.cir.campania.beniculturali.it. ✆ **081/5266007**. 2€ or 4€ combined ticket that also includes Anfiteatro Flavio, Parco Archeologica di Baia, Castello di Baia, and Scavi di Cuma and is valid 2 days. Wed–Mon 9am–1pm hour before sunset.

Solfatara ★★ PARK/GARDEN The ancients called this dormant volcano just 1km (½ mile) above the Anfiteatro Flavio "Forum Vulcani" and believed it to be the residence and workshop of the god Vulcan and an entrance to Hades. It's easy to see why: Lunar landscapes hiss, steam, bubble, and spew sulfurous clouds, and the ground beneath your feet can feel as hot as, well, hell. Despite the bubbling, steaming, and heavy stench of sulfur, the volcano has not erupted since 1198. It's quite safe to walk around the caldera floor on the well-marked paths, observing steaming fumaroles, breathing in the vapors, and taking in the ancient mysteries. For sheer drama, look up the slopes to the Bocca Grande, or Big Mouth, where fumaroles continually release steam at temperatures that reach 160°C (320°F). Meanwhile, in the middle of the crater, lakes of gassy mud sizzle at 250°C (482°F).

Via Solfatara 161; from the Pozzouli stop of line 2 of the Metropolitana, follow Via Oriana to Via Solfatara and turn right; from the Cumana railway station and town center, follow Via Rossini to Via Solfatara. www.solfatara.it. ✆ **081/5262341.** 6€. Daily 8:30am–1 hr. before sunset. From the entrance of the Anfiteatro Flavio, bus P9 and other routes go to Solfatara; from the amphitheater it's an easy walk of about 1km (½ mile) along Via Solfatara.

BAIA ★

6km (4 miles) Southwest of Pozzuoli

Many of the villas and thermal baths of this ancient spa town are now underwater, though enough remains on terra firma to suggest the grandeur of **Ancient Baiae** (the modern town dropped the last "e"). Julius Caesar, Nero, and other Roman elite once relaxed and debauched in Baiae's large villas, equipped with swimming pools and other luxuries. Seneca the Younger, the 1st-century philosopher and man of letters, called the place a "vortex of luxury." The poet Ovid said it was "a favorable place for love-making," while Horace chimed in, "No bay on Earth outshines pleasing Baiae." The town takes it name from Baio, the navigator of Odysseus, who is said to be buried somewhere in Baia.

Ancient Baiae was more luxurious than Herculaneum or Capri, other nearby retreats where wealthy Romans escaped the summer heat at home. Only Stabiae, east across the Bay of Naples, came close to creating such a paradise on earth. Under Augustus (reigned 27 B.C. to A.D. 14) Baiae became even more exclusive as imperial property. The town was also famed for its thermal baths, fed by sulfur springs believed to have medicinal properties. Some of the more salacious moments of Roman infamy transpired at Baiae—mostly because some amoral and hedonistic Romans spent a lot of time here. This is where, according to legend that probably obscures the factual record, the emperor Nero tried to kill his mother, Agrippina, by contriving to have a ceiling crash down on her bed. When that didn't work, he arranged to have her boat rammed at sea, but she swam ashore. The thwarted emperor finally sent a henchman to Baiae to stab the doomed woman. Poster girl for the town's debauchery may have been the allegedly sexually insatiable Messalina, third wife of the emperor Claudius. She is said to have snuck out of her Baiae villa in disguise at night to work at the town's brothel under the name She Wolf.

Ruins of temples, villas, and bathing establishments litter three grassy terraces above the bay. The ruins are not especially well marked nor well preserved. It's believed that a pile of stones near the top may have been the villa of Julius Caesar. He popped up to Rome for a meeting of the senate on the Ides of March 44 B.C. and the rest is history. His houseguest at the time was Cleopatra. Enough remains of the Terme di Baiae to show just how elaborate the bathing complexes were. Admission is free weekdays; Sat–Sun combined ticket is 4€ (includes Serapeo and Anfiteatro Flavio in Pozzuoli, Castello di Baia, and Scavi di Cuma; valid for 2 days). It's open Tuesday to Sunday 9am till 1 hour before sunset.

Much of the ancient town is underwater, preserved as the **Parco Archeologico Sommerso di Baiae (Underwater Archaeological Park of Baiae) ★★.** Mosaic flooring, statuary, fish ponds, and other ruins litter the seabed amid bubbling geysers and flourishing flora. You can view this undersea world on dives, by snorkeling, or on trips on glass-bottom boats. Dive centers and boat tours operate out of the port and Via Lucullo in Baia; expect to pay about 10€ for a boat trip, 20€ for a snorkeling tour, and 35€ for a guided dive. The office of the **Area Protteta di Baia** (www.areamarinaprotettabaia.eu; ✆ **081/523-2739**) can provide more info and a list of tour operators; it's at Via Lucullo 94.

Via Sella di Baia 22, Bacoli. www.cir.campania.beniculturali.it. ✆ **848/800228.**

Castello di Baia ★★ HISTORIC SIGHT/MUSEUM One of the most impressive landmarks in a town steeped in legend is the work of the Aragonese kings of Naples of the 16th century. Their massive complex of thick walls and defensive moats rises from a wave-buffeted headland that was once topped with the villa of Emperor Nero. The sea-facing battlements Neapolitan royalty built were meant to deter Barbary pirates from North Africa, who would pillage coastal towns and take captives to sell into the Ottoman slave market. More important, the unassailable stronghold with its sweeping views of the bay also ensured protection from the French navy, whose ships didn't stand a chance of sailing past the lookouts to land troops and invade Naples. Some of the vast rooms now house the **Museo Archeologico dei Campi Flegrei ★**, showing off statuary and other artifacts from Baia and the surrounding region. Most enchanting are the two nymphaeums, delightful, statue-lined porches that were once equipped with lavish fountains; one is said to have been from the villa of Emperor Claudius and rescued from the sea floor.

Via Castello 39. www.cir.campania.beniculturali.it. ✆ **081/5233797** or 848-800288. 2.50€ or combined ticket 4€ (includes Serapeo and Anfiteatro Flavio in Pozzuoli, Zona Archeologica in Baia, and Scavi di Cuma; valid for 2 days). Tues–Sun 9am–1 hr. before sunset.

CUMA ★

7km (4½ miles) Northwest of Lago d'Averno

The Greeks founded their first colony on mainland Italy at Cuma in the 8th century B.C., and Cuma grew into an important center of Greek farming operations in Campania. The settlers soon discovered they had a helpful neighbor: the Cumaean Sibyl, who, according to legend, passed on messages from Apollo. The god told Sibyl he would grant her one wish. She took a handful of sand and said she wanted to live as many years as the number of grains she held. Then came the catch: Apollo wanted her virginity in return. Sibyl refused, so Apollo gave her long life but not eternal youth. Over the centuries she withered away. She eventually became so small she could be kept in a jar, then only her voice remained—handy for uttering a last request, "I want to die." The Sibyl's chamber was a big draw for advice-seekers from around the ancient world. The Sibyl's inner chamber is at the end of a long, narrow tunnel cut through volcanic stone—131.5m (432 ft.) long, some 5m (16.5 ft.) high, and as wide as 2.4m (8 ft.) across. It's a mighty impressive entrance that can still send chills down the spine and likely reassured supplicants they were about to hear something gravely important.

Via Montecuma. www.cir.campania.beniculturali.it. ✆ **081/8543060.** 2.50€ or combined ticket 4€ (includes Serapeo and Anfiteatro Flavio in Pozzuoli, Zona Archeologica in Baia, and Castello di Baia; valid for 2 days). Daily 9am to 1 hr. before sunset.

WHERE TO EAT

Sileno ★ SEAFOOD/PIZZA You deserve a good meal after trudging through antiquities and volcanic landscapes, and it should center on fish or seafood, since Pozzuoli is a major port for fishing boats. Part of the catch comes direct to kitchens like the one at this modest place down the street from the Serapeo. It shows up in *linguine alle vongole* (with clams) and other straightforward but delicious pasta and risotto dishes, as well as platters heaped high with *fritto misto di pesce*, a fish fry.

Via Sacchini, 27/A, Pozzuoli. ✆ **081/526–2757.** Main courses 8€–14€. Wed–Mon 12:30–3:30pm and 7:30–11:30pm.

Vesuvius ★★

Towering, pitch-black Mount Vesuvius looms menacingly over the Bay of Naples. The volcano has erupted periodically since August 24, A.D. 79, when it buried Pompeii and Herculaneum in eruptions that released 100,000 times the thermal energy of the Hiroshima bomb. Less violent eruptions occurred in 1631, in 1906, and 1944. Mount Vesuvius is the only active volcano on mainland Europe, though another formidable volcanic summit, taller and more active Mount Etna, is only 560km (335 miles) away, on the east coast of Sicily.

The mountain still puffs steam every once in awhile, just to keep everybody on their toes. Volcanologists and geologists say that given the historic record, a major eruption is likely in the relatively near

Pompeii and Mount Vesuvius.

future. That is, it's a question of *when* rather than *if* the mountain will blow its top again, putting the 3 million people who live around the Bay of Naples at considerable risk. Especially vulnerable are the 600,000 residents who live in the so-called "red zone," the path of flowing lava and rocks expected to hurl through the sky at 100mph on the big day. That makes Vesuvius one of the most potentially deadly volcanoes in the world.

GETTING THERE The most convenient way to visit Vesuvius by public transportation from Naples or Sorrento is on the **Circumvesuviana railway train** (www.vesuviana.it; ✆ **800-053939** toll-free within Italy) to the Ercolano Scavi. There you can catch **Vesuvio Express** (www.vesuvioexpress.info) vans to the parking lot below the summit. Fares are 10€ round-trip, plus you'll pay another 10€ for admission to the park. Vans run every 45 minutes daily from 9:30am; the last bus makes the run up 2 hours before the park closes. You can also take the **Busvia del Vesuvio** (www.busviadelvesuvio.com; ✆ **340-935-2616**) for a ride on a bumpy back road up the mountain in a 4x4 vehicle that drops you at the summit parking lot; round-trip fare is 22€, including park admission, and the service runs April to October daily 9am to 3pm (sometimes later in July and Aug). Buy tickets at the train station. **Tram Via del Vesuvio** (Vesuvius Trolley Tram) also makes the trip up the mountain from a terminus near the train station; round-trip fare is 12€, plus park admission. Allow at least 1½ to 2 hours at the top.

By car, take the Torre del Greco exit from the A3 autostrada and follow the signs to Vesuvio. The road ends in the parking lot below the summit, where you'll pay 2.50€ to park. A taxi from Naples costs a flat rate of 90€ round-trip, including a 2-hour wait.

Funiculì, Funiculà

One way you *won't* be making the ascent up the mountain is on the Mt. Vesuvius Funicular, which once climbed to the summit from Pugliano, near Ercolano. It opened to great fanfare in 1880, when the song "Funiculì, Funiculà" was written to celebrate the event. Everyone from Connie Francis and the Grateful Dead to Luciano Pavarotti recorded the jaunty tune. The eruption of 1944 wiped out the tracks and sealed its fate; the ascent by road was by then more practical.

VISITOR INFORMATION The **Parco Nazionale del Vesuvio** (www.parconazionaledelvesuvio.it; ✆ **081/8653911**) maintains trails and other visitor facilities. All transportation gets you only as far as the park entrance at 1,017m (3,337 ft.) in altitude. You'll pay 10€ to continue on a fairly steep trail to the summit or explore the mountainside on other trails, none of which are wheelchair accessible. The entrance fee also includes admission to the observatory at 608m (1,994 ft.), the oldest such seismological/volcanological institution in the world, dating from 1841. The park is open daily November to March 9am to 3pm; April to

May 9am to 5pm; June to August 9am to 6pm; and Sept and October 9am to 5pm. The trail to the crater closes in extreme weather.

EXPLORING VESUVIUS

It might sound like a dubious invitation, but it's possible to visit the rim of the crater's mouth. As you look down into its smoldering core, you might recall that, a century before the A.D. 79 eruption that buried Pompeii, the escaped slave Spartacus, who boldly led an uprising against his Roman captors, hid in the hollow of the crater, which was then covered with vines. The menacing mountain is the centerpiece of 8,482-hectare (20,959-acre) **Parco Nazionale del Vesuvio (Vesuvius National Park) ★★★.** The park has laid out nine summit trails, each of them highlighting the lava flows and other geology underfoot all around you. Placards along the way explain the unique micro-environment of the volcanic summit, including many species of orchids and other amazingly tenacious vegetation. The ticket office hands out maps of the routes, also available in short version on the website, which range from easy 1-hour strolls to strenuous 8-hour hikes. The number 5 trail, Gran Cono, is the classic ascent to the top. A moderately difficult uphill walk of about half a mile leads from the parking area and ticket office near the summit to the 230-m (754-ft)-deep crater. The walk takes about 20 minutes, but forego any notions of being alone in empty volcanic landscapes—cafes and souvenir stands line the route. A guide will lead you around the rim, 650m (2,132 ft.) in diameter. Make sure the guide who approaches you is a bonafide ranger and not a shill looking for a tip; the guide service is free with the price of admission and mandatory. Wear sneakers; the lava underfoot can be hard on the feet, and bring a sweater or jacket, because it can be windy and surprisingly chilly on the heights. Once at the top, the view across Naples and the bay to the islands is so mesmerizing you might just forget how menacing Vesuvius really is. As a reminder, consider that

Ruins at Pompeii, with Mt. Vesuvius in the background.

before the A.D. 79 eruption, the mountain was more than twice as tall as its current 1,282m (4,206 ft.).

POMPEII & HERCULANEUM ★★★

On that fateful day, August 24, A.D. 79, the people of Pompeii, a prosperous fishing town, and Herculaneum, a resort just down the coast, watched Mount Vesuvius hurl a churning column of gas and ash high into the sky. It was only a matter of time before flows of superheated molten rock coursed through the streets of Herculaneum and ash and pumice buried Pompeii. In Herculaneum, volcanic debris quickly hardened into a layer of rock that fossilized everything—furniture, wooden beams, clothing, skeletons, graffiti, mosaics; in Pompeii, ash and rock fragments buried structures under a layer as deep as 12 meters (20 feet), preserving everything beneath it through the centuries.

Terrifying indeed for the ill-fated townsfolk, but lucky for us, the layers of ooze and ash preserved Pompeii and Herculaneum as time capsules. Pompeii is much more extensive than Herculaneum, with more to see, while Herculaneum provides an easier-to-manage, less crowded experience. With its gridlike streets and extensive remains, Pompeii provides an overview of a large Roman town, while Herculaneum, with its better-preserved houses and artifacts, gives an evocative glimpse into day-to-day life. You could see both in 1 day, and you might want to consider doing so if your time in the region is limited. However, get a good rest the night before, because seeing the sights involves lots of walking and possible sensory overload—you'll be taking in an enormous amount of information in a short amount of time. If you have to choose between the two, Pompeii provides the more sensational experience.

ESSENTIALS

GETTING THERE The **Circumvesuviana Railway** (www.vesuviana.it; ✆ **800-053939** toll-free in Italy) runs between Naples and Sorrento every half-hour from Piazza Garibaldi, with stops at the excavations. For Herculaneum, get off at Ercolano/Scavi (*scavi* means "archaeological excavation"). Herculaneum is 20 minutes from Naples and 50 minutes from Sorrento; the entrance is about 10 blocks from the station. Pompeii is about 40 minutes from Naples and 30 minutes from Sorrento; exit the train at Pompei-Scavi (note that the modern spelling drops the last "I" of the ancient name). The entrance is about 45m (150 ft.) from the station.

To reach either by **car** from Naples, follow the *autostrada* A3 toward Salerno. If you're coming from Sorrento, head east on SS. 145, where you can connect with A3 (marked napoli). Then take the signposted turnoffs for Pompeii and Herculaneum.

LOGISTICS Hours for both excavation sites are the same: April to October, they are open daily 8:30am to 7:30pm and November to March daily 8:30am to 5pm (last admission 90 min. before close). Admission to each is 11€, but a cumulative ticket (20€; good for 3 consecutive days) grants you access to both as well as to the nearby sites of Oplontis, Boscoreale, and Stabia. You can purchase it at the Circumvesuviana Railway Station, Piazza Garibaldi, in Naples, or at the sites.

Both sites can be crowded in the mornings, especially when tours arrive in force in July and August. Crowds thin out by early afternoon.

The ticket offices at both sites provide free maps and good, detailed booklets that will guide you through the sites. Inside the entrances at both you'll find **bookstores,** where you can purchase additional guidebooks to the ruins (available in English). Audio guides are good accompaniments to your visits. You can rent them at both sites for 7€, 10€ for two people (but sharing is not a particularly good idea), with a kids' version for 4€. Pompeii has a cafeteria inside the archaeological zone that's handy for sandwiches and drinks. At Herculaneum a good cafe/cafeteria is just outside the entrance. You can store your luggage at both sites (also at the train station in Pompeii), making it possible to work in a visit if you're traveling between Naples and Sorrento and the Amalfi Coast.

If you're visiting the sites on a sunny day, wear sunscreen and bring a bottle of water. For more details, visit **www.pompeiisites.org** or call **© 081/857-5111.**

Herculaneum (Ercalano)

10km (6 miles) southeast of Naples

Excavations began at Herculaneum in the early 18th century and continue to this day, with the fairly recent discovery of a beached boat full of desperate souls trying to make an escape by sea. Another 300 skeletons were found in vaulted stone boathouses on what would have been the town's beach; they were huddled in the shelters waiting to board boats and sail to safety when they were killed instantly by the poisonous vapors of a wall of heated gas and rock that swept through the town at 100mph. Although many questions about Herculaneum remain unanswered, it's known for certain that this glitzy seaside resort for elite Romans was about a third the size of Pompeii, with a population of about 4,000. Herculaneum had little commerce or industry, and its streets were lined mostly with elegant villas, along with a few apartment blocks for poor laborers and fishermen.

SCAVI DI ERCOLANO (HERCULANEUM ARCHAEOLOGICAL AREA) ★★★

The ruins of Herculaneum give the unsettling impression of a ghost town from which residents have only recently walked away. Many of the

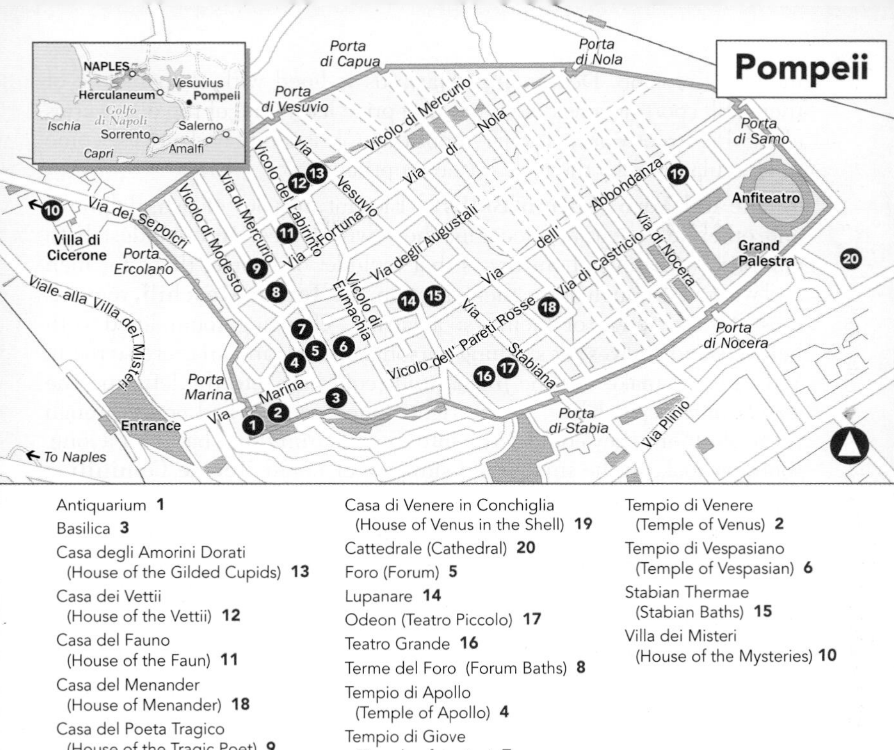

houses retain their second floors, making them seem more like residences than ruins. The volcanic mud that covered Herculaneum during the eruption of Vesuvius in A.D. 79 quickly hardened to a hard, rocklike material. While making excavations difficult, this semi-rock protected the structures underneath, and rather remarkably preserved wooden beams and floors along with furnishings, clothing, and other household objects. The ruins provide a wealth of rich and intriguing detail about building techniques, architecture, and domestic decoration in Roman times, and, of course, about daily life. The charred wood, staircases, and double-height houses here instill the sense of being in a real town, unlike the remote detachment you might experience in Pompeii and other ancient ruins. From the Ercolano-Scavi station, follow the signs for the scavi for about 10 blocks down the main street, Via IV Novembre; the entrance is about a 10-minute walk from the station. Plan to spend at least 2 hours.

Decumanus Maximus The excavations stretch from the town's main street to what was once the shoreline (now a kilometer to the west); the rest of the Roman town remains inaccessible beneath the buildings of modern Ercolano. Decumanus Maximus is lined with shops, some of them still sporting advertisements and price lists. One of the discoveries along this street was a crucifix, proof that Christianity had already come to Herculaneum by the time of the eruption.

Terme del Foro (Forum Baths) Elegant mosaics of fish, dolphins, and other sea creatures decorate the town's largest and grandest bath complex, with several entrances that include, of course, those for men and women. Enough of the men's section, the **Terme Maschili,** remains to show the range of facilities: a latrine, changing room lined with benches and shelves for stashing personal effects, and an exercise room. You can still make out the *frigidarium* (cold bath), to the left, and the *tepadarium* (tepid bath), to the right. Once patrons had gone through these ablutions they could settle into the *caldarium* (hot bath) for a long, soothing soak. In the smaller but similarly elaborate **Terme Feminili,** a mosaic of a naked Triton decorates the floor of the changing rooms.

Sedes degli Augustali (Hall of the Augustals) The Augustals were priests of a cult to Augustus, founder and first emperor of the Roman empire. These rooms with marble floors and elaborate wall paintings did justice to their elite status. Their custodian died in his sleep, in a small room that's still furnished with the bed where his skeleton was found.

Casa del Tramezzo di Legno (House of the Wooden Partition) Behind a perfect facade is a rarity in Roman houses, a double atrium. It probably just means that at some point the owner scraped together enough money to buy adjoining houses and merge them. He obviously worked hard: The house is named for a well-preserved wooden screen that separated part of the atrium from the *tablium,* a little room that served as an office.

Casa del Bella Cortile (House of the Beautiful Courtyard) The namesake courtyard seems almost medieval, with a wide stone staircase ascending to a landing on the second floor. Three skeletons that have been placed here are presumed to be those of a mother, father, and daughter trapped on the beach as they tried to flee.

Casa del Mosaico di Nettuno e Anfitrite (House of the Neptune and Anfitritis Mosaic) A bright blue mosaic of the sea god and his nymph is just one of many decorations in this house, whose owner likely operated the well-preserved shop next door. Carbonized wooden racks hold amphorae and masonry jars that were found on the counter, still filled with broad beans and chickpeas when they were unearthed.

Casa a Graticcio (House of the Latticework) This is one of the very few examples of working-class housing that has survived from antiquity; the name-giving lattices, though cheaply made of interwoven cane and plaster, are remarkably well preserved.

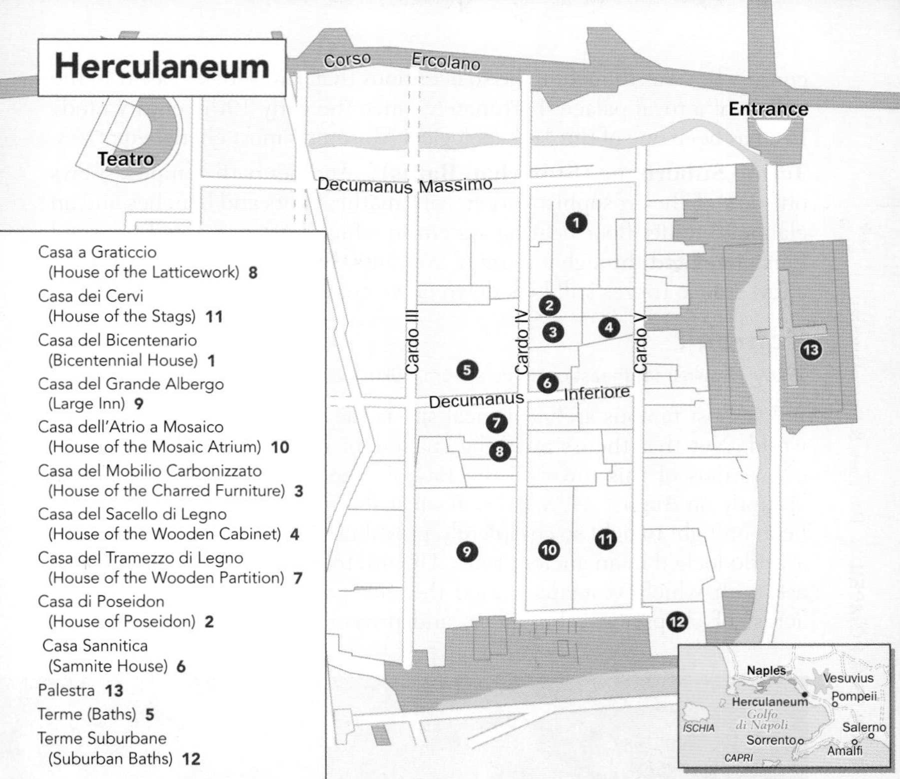

Casa dei Cervi (House of the Stags) One of the most elegant houses in town had terraces and porticos overlooking the sea. Decorations say much about its fun-loving inhabitants: Frescoes depict playful cherubs, while courtyards held statues of drunken satyrs and an inebriated, peering Hercules. The house is named for a statue of dogs attacking a pair of innocent, noble-looking deer, perhaps a commentary on the cutthroat politics and hard-edged social echelons of the Roman era.

Villa dei Papiri One of the grander seaside villas housed a huge library of 1,000-odd papyrus scrolls, badly charred but intact when they were uncovered during excavations (they're now in the library of the Palazzo Reale in Naples). The onetime home of Julius Caesar's father-in-law, consul Lucius Calpurnius Piso Caesoninus (100 B.C.–43 B.C.), has also yielded a treasure trove of nearly 90 magnificent bronze and marble sculptures, Roman copies of Greek originals that are now housed in the Archaeological Museum in Naples. Most famous among them is a sculpture of Pan, the half-man, half-goat god, caught in this marble having sex with a nanny goat. The oddly humane scene was unearthed in the 18th century but was thought to be so licentious that it was locked away in the cellars of a royal palace. Fortunately, since the early 19th century randy Pan has been one of the Archaeological Museum's most cherished prizes.

Terme Suburbane (Suburban Baths) Another bath complex shows off state-of-the art sophistication, with marble floors and benches and an elaborate under-floor heating system in which heat generated by wood fires circulated through a maze of conduits. In the *caldarium* (hot bath) a few stucco friezes still look down on visitors as they did on bathers.

Pompeii

19km (11 miles) southeast of Herculaneum, 30km (18 miles) southeast of Naples

Italy's most famous archaeological site is the Disneyland of the ancient world. Not that there's anything shallow or ersatz about the extensive excavations of this town on the Bay of Naples, where life stopped so abruptly on August 24, A.D. 79. It's just that no other ancient town has been brought to light so completely, providing an opportunity to step into a world locked in an ancient time. The 4m to 6m (13–20 ft.) of volcanic ash with which Vesuvius buried the city preserved 44 hectares (109 acres) of shops, civic buildings, and private houses. Ever since 1748

Architectural detail, Pompeii.

archaeologists have worked to painstakingly uncover the town, and the ruins provide the vicarious thrill of sharing space with residents of a lively, ancient Roman port.

How many people were living in Pompeii at the time of the eruption is not known. The city had been rocked by a major earthquake in A.D. 62 that, along with fires caused by toppled oil lamps, destroyed temples, houses, and public works. Repairs were still underway in A.D. 79, though many of the city's 11,000 recorded inhabitants had probably resettled elsewhere. The unfortunate Pompeians who remained behind are the most haunting presence at the site. The decaying bodies often left a mold inside the ash and lava that buried them. Excavators filled these empty spaces with plaster, and the eerie, lifelike casts lie in the Garden of the Fugitives and other places around town where the victims fell.

The entrance to the site is almost directly across the train station. Allow at least 4 hours for even a superficial visit.

SCAVI DI POMPEII (POMPEII ARCHAEOLOGICAL AREA) ★★★

Pompeii was a workaday town, and what stands out amid the ruins is a remarkable evocation of everyday life—streets, shops, bakeries, brothels, baths. The first thing you'll notice is the typical Roman plan of gridlike streets, on which stepping stones appear at every intersection. These were laid down to allow residents to cross the pavement even when the streets were being flushed with water, as they were at least once a day. Stones are spaced in just such a way to allow chariot wheels to roll past them. Raised sidewalks conceal water and sewage pipes, while glittering bits of marble mixed in with the volcanic pavement reflected light to make walking a little easier at night.

Unlike Herculaneum, with its seafront district of lavish villas, in Pompeii the wealthy usually lived among the working classes. Houses are interspersed with shops (which were often combined with dwellings) all over town. Also here are the remains of 25 street fountains, fed by a system of aqueducts and cisterns that fed lead pipes to keep baths, businesses, and homes supplied with fresh water.

PORTA MARINA The sight's main entrance is as busy now as it was back in the day, when this impressive gate, one of seven portals in the walls that surrounded the ancient city, opened to the seafront. Pompeii's docks did a brisk business importing and exporting goods that were often transported to and from Rome on the nearby Appian Way. The shimmering sea that once lapped the shoreline in front of the gate is nowhere to been: the sprawl of modern Pompei (one "I" in the modern spelling) now stands between the excavations and the sea, which has receded by about ½ km (¼ mile) over the centuries. The **Tempio de Venere** (Temple of

Venus), to the right of the entrance, has not fared as well as the gate; a lone column is all that attests to its onetime grandeur.

FORUM (FORO) Pompeii's marketplace, damaged in an earthquake 16 years before the eruption of Vesuvius, had not been repaired when the final destruction rained down. Columns still line the portico that surrounded a large, rectangular open space on three sides and opened to a covered meat and fish market, the **Macellum.** Facing the Forum are the **Basilica** (the city's largest single structure), a law court, exchange, and civic hall. The **Temple of Apollo** (Tempio di Apollo), with its columned portico, was the city's most important religious building. The **Granai del Foro** (Forum Granary) is now the repository for many of the plaster casts of victims made by 19th-century excavators (see above).

LUPANARE GRANDE (LARGE BROTHEL) Pompeii's most titter-inducing sight and prime photo op is a two-story brothel, just northeast of the forum off Via degli Augustali. Graphic wall paintings reveal what certainly appears to be a libertine attitude toward sex. It's easy to see why, correctly or not, the city is often associated with easy virtue. In the nearby Basilica, where many travelers stopped on a visit to Pompeii, a bit of graffiti loosely read, "If anyone is looking for some tender love in this town, keep in mind that here all the girls are very friendly." A list of prices is inscribed on the wall near the brothel. It's believed that Pompeii may have had dozens of such brothels. Many of the graphic works that once covered the walls of this one, the city's grandest pleasure palace, have been carted off to the Archaeological Museum in Naples, though many remain in place in the 10 small rooms equipped with stone beds.

VIA DELL'ABBONDANZA The town's main commercial street is rightfully named: the surrounding fields and vineyards kept Pompeii well supplied with an abundance of goods, as did a brisk trade with other Roman cities. This street was lined with shops, including **Fullonica Stephani** (Stephen's Laundry), and eateries where pots full of the daily offerings were kept on counters that are still in place. In most houses on the street, a shop is on the ground floor and the owner's apartment is on the second level. Many of the painted signs for bars and shops are in place, and walls of some shops are still covered with red writing promoting candidates in elections. Signs have also revealed the world's first known bit of slick advertising punditry, advertising Vesuvinum—a clever combo of Vesuvius and "vinum," the word for wine.

TRIANGULAR FORUM This large open area was the heart of the theater district. The beautiful **Teatro Grande**, carved out of a hillside of volcanic rock in the 2nd century B.C., could seat an audience of 5,000, while the smaller, 1st-century-B.C., 1,000-seat **Odeion,** or Small Theater, was used for music and mime shows. Audiences could step out between acts

A street and public fountain, Pompeii.

for a stroll along the columned **Quadriportico dei Teatri,** though the breezy walkway was later enclosed to serve as a barracks for gladiators. Nearby is the **Tempio di Iside** (Temple of Isis), one of the best-conserved temples to this goddess to survive from antiquity.

TERME STABIANE (STABIAN BATHS) One of the town's six public baths shows off the floor plan and arrangement of cold, tepid, and hot baths that were typical of these places, a mainstay of all Roman towns to provide a cleanse, relaxation, and socialization. The vaulted *apodyterium* (changing room) was the showpiece here, with fanciful wall paintings of playful nymphs. Looking at them might have brightened the day of the slaves who accompanied their masters to the baths and waited for them in the vast chamber with orders to keep an eye on their belongings.

CASA DI LOREIUS TIBURTINUS Election placards painted on the facade gave this large house its name: "Vote for Loreius" and "Vote for Tiburntinus." The name doesn't do justice to the owner, the well-off Octavius Quartio. He entertained his guests in a gardenlike *triclinium,* or dining room, where a delightful fresco depicts Pyramis and Thisbe. This lovely maiden and handsome youth of myth belonged to feuding families, and centuries later their doomed love inspired *Romeo and Juliet*.

GRANDE PALESTRA Sports events were held on this track and on the surrounding sports fields, while onlookers could escape the sun in the shade of an impressively long portico. A grandiose swimming pool was surrounded by plane trees (you can see the plaster casts of the stumps).

ANFITEATRO (AMPHITHEATRE) The oldest Roman amphitheater in the world, built in 80 B.C., could seat 1,000 people. It was the first Roman amphitheater to be built of stone, hence its longevity, and it set a standard for architectural quality that only the Coliseum in Rome outdid a century later. Especially enlightened were the entrances designed for crowd control, and the state-of-the-art latrines. The theater became known around the region for its gladiatorial contests, and the ancient counterparts of soccer hooligans packed in for events. Games were banned for 10 years after an A.D. 59 brawl between Pompeians and visitors from nearby Nuceria that left 10 dead—the action on the field obviously just wasn't gory enough for the blood-thirsty fans.

TERME SUBURBANE The city's four bathhouses are among the finest to survive from antiquity. This one is unusual in that men and women shared the facilities. Vividly colored frescoes in the changing rooms depict graphic sex acts and are the subject of ongoing controversy: Were they meant to advertise sexual services available on the upper floors or were they simply amusing decorations? These scenes and other so-called pornography from Pompeii shocked Francis I, king of the Two Sicilies. Coming across erotic artifacts on an 1819 visit to Archaeological Museum in Naples with his wife and daughter, he ordered many of them to be locked away in the museum's Gabinetto Segreto (Secret Cabinet) open only to "people of mature ages and respected morals."

CASA DEI VETTII (HOUSE OF THE VETTII) Pompeii's most elegant patrician villa was the ultimate bachelor pad, the home of wealthy merchants, the Vettii brothers. The huge phallus resting on a pair of scales at the entrance was not intended as a come-hither for female guests but a sign of good fortune—which the black-and-red Pompeian dining room with its frescoes of delicate cupids and colonnaded garden show the brothers had plenty of. Strong boxes imbedded in the floor suggest that they might have made at least part of their fortune as money lenders.

CASA DEL FAUNO (HOUSE OF THE FAUN) The sumptuous decor here is ancient proof that money and good taste can go together. Two of the great treasures of the Museo Archeologico Nazionale in Naples come from this huge spread, covering an entire city block, the biggest house in town. A bronze statue of a dancing faun decorated the *impluvium*, rain tank, used to collect water for the household. A much-celebrated "Battle of Alexander the Great" battle scene is one of many mosaics that decorated the lavish rooms.

VILLA DEI MISTERI (HOUSE OF THE MYSTERIES) A layer of ash ensured that this 90-room villa near the Porto Ercolano, just outside the walls (go along Viale alla Villa dei Misteri), retained its remarkable frescoes, the best still in place in Pompeii. Set against a background of a deep hue that's come to be known as Pompeian red, figures in the so-called Dionysiac Frieze are shown going through elaborate rituals that, scholars say, may be preparations for a wedding or initiation into a sect of Dionysus (Bacchus), one of many cults that flourished in Roman times.

13

SORRENTO & THE AMALFI COAST

By Stephen Brewer

The beautiful Sorrento peninsula and the Amalfi Coast have been tempting travelers ever since Ulysses sailed by. He filled the ears of his sailors with wax and tied himself to the mast of his ship to withstand the alluring call of the Sirens. Today, the pull of the sea and imposing rock-bound coast remain as compelling as they were in Homer's day. Even though besieged by tourists, graceful old Sorrento is a lovely place, perched high atop a cliff gazing across the sea toward the isle of Capri. The spectacular but nerve-racking Amalfi Drive heads vertiginously east, clinging to cliffs and rounding one bend after another until it comes to Positano, a tile-domed village hugging a near-vertical rock, then to Amalfi, a little seaside town that was once the center of a powerful maritime republic.

With transporting green hillsides, azure seas, and the enticing scent of lemon and frangipani, the charms of Sorrento and the Amalfi Coast are no secret. You'll do yourself a favor if you schedule a visit for the early spring or fall, before and after the summer crowds, and even then accept the fact that you will not have this slice of paradise to yourself.

SORRENTO ★★★

50km (31 miles) south of Naples

How does that old song, "Come Back to Sorrento," go? "*Vir 'o mare quant'è bello*"...or "See the sea how beautiful it is." You'll be humming a few bars, because the sea, the scented gardens, and sun-drenched vistas that have been luring visitors to this cliff-top town for millennia really are exquisite. Monuments are few and far between, but views from the town center Piazza Tasso or a trek down to Marina Grande, a fisherman's port, show off its irrepressible appeal. Sorrento provides easy access to Naples as well as such fabled places as Capri, Positano, Amalfi, and the ruins at Pompeii, and is usually thronged with happy holidaymakers who, at their best, provide pleasant company.

FACING PAGE: **Lemon candies in a stall in Sorrento.**

Choosing a Town

Just about everyone who visits Sorrento and the Amalfi Coast comes away with a favorite town to which they yearn to return. When choosing the place to put down your bags, it's hard to go wrong in this beautiful part of the world, but you may want to take some practical considerations into account. **Sorrento** is best situated as a base for exploring, given its excellent train, bus, and boat connections to Capri, Naples, Pompeii, and Herculaneum, and other towns. **Positano** is the most picturesque and resortlike, with the best (and most easily accessible) beaches, though getting in and out of town in high season on the traffic-choked coast road can be a nightmare (boats are a pleasant alternative). **Amalfi** provides small-town charm and gives you a two-fer—its beautiful neighbor **Ravello;** you can also avoid the worst of the coast traffic by approaching and leaving Amalfi from and to the east through Salerno, with its excellent train connections to Naples.

Essentials

GETTING THERE

BY TRAIN Sorrento is connected to Naples' Stazione Centrale by the **Circumvesuviana** railway (www.vesuviana.it; ✆ **800-053939**); the ride takes a little over an hour.

BY BUS **SITA** (www.sitabus.it; ✆ **089-405145**) offers frequent bus service, more often in summer than in winter, from Naples to Sorrento,

Marina Piccola, on Sorrento's seafront.

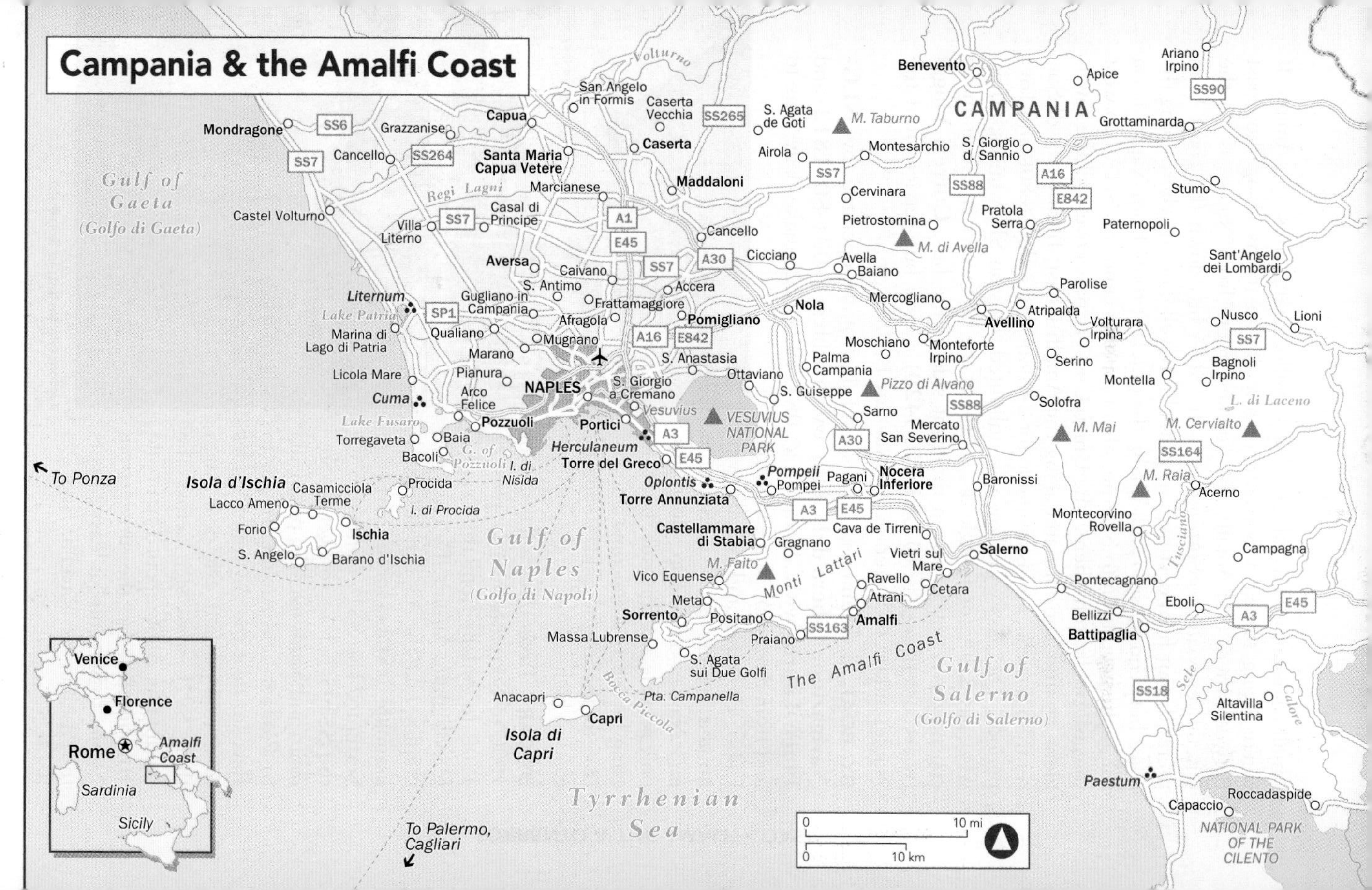

Campania & the Amalfi Coast
CAMPANIA
Gulf of Gaeta
(Golfo di Gaeta)
Gulf of Naples
(Golfo di Napoli)
Gulf of Salerno
(Golfo di Salerno)
Tyrrhenian Sea
The Amalfi Coast
To Ponza
To Palermo, Cagliari
NAPLES
Benevento
Caserta
Caserta Vecchia
Capua
Santa Maria Capua Vetere
Maddaloni
Aversa
Nola
Pomigliano
Avellino
Salerno
Pozzuoli
Portici
Herculaneum
Torre del Greco
Oplontis
Torre Annunziata
Pompeii
Pompei
Castellammare di Stabia
Sorrento
Positano
Praiano
Amalfi
Atrani
Ravello
Cetara
Vietri sul Mare
Cava de Tirreni
Nocera Inferiore
Pagani
Battipaglia
Paestum
Eboli
Capaccio
Roccadaspide
Altavilla Silentina
NATIONAL PARK OF THE CILENTO
Isola di Capri
Capri
Anacapri
Isola d'Ischia
Ischia
Procida
I. di Procida
Baia
Bacoli
Cuma
Liternum
Vesuvius
VESUVIUS NATIONAL PARK
M. Faito
Monti Lattari
M. Taburno
M. di Avella
Pizzo di Alvano
M. Mai
M. Raia
M. Cervialto
L. di Laceno
Mondragone
Castel Volturno
Cancello
Grazzanise
Villa Literno
Casal di Principe
Marcianese
San Angelo in Formis
Ariano Irpino
Apice
Grottaminarda
Stumo
Paternopoli
Sant'Angelo dei Lombardi
Lioni
Nusco
Bagnoli Irpino
Montella
Volturara Irpina
Serino
Solofra
Atripalda
Parolise
Campagna
Acerno
Montecorvino Rovella
Pontecagnano
Bellizzi
Baronissi
Mercato San Severino
Sarno
Vico Equense
Meta
Massa Lubrense
S. Agata sui Due Golfi
Pta. Campanella
Bocca Piccola
Sicily
Sardinia
Rome
Florence
Venice
Amalfi Coast
10 mi
10 km

Amalfi, Positano, and Salerno. For Ravello, change buses in Amalfi. If you're trying to reach Sorrento or any of the towns along the coast between there and Amalfi, the quickest route from Naples is via the Circumvesuviana to Sorrento and the SITA bus down the coast from there. If your final destination is Amalfi, Ravello, or anywhere along the coast between Salerno and Amalfi, the quickest route from Naples is via the high-speed train to Salerno (about an hour) and the SITA bus west toward Amalfi from there. The Unico Costiera pass covers all the towns along around Sorrento and along the Amalfi Coast, from Meta di Sorrento to Salerno, and is available for 24-hour and 3-day (6.80€ and 16€) periods. The pass will allow you unlimited rides on SITA buses; otherwise, pay 2.20€ for a single ticket. To get the best views on the dramatic coastal drive, get a seat on the right side of the bus. **Curreri Viaggi** (www.curreriviaggi.it; ✆ **081-8015420**) runs a bus service from the Naples airport to Sorrento; one-way fare is 10€.

BY BOAT In summer, ferries and hydrofoils operated by **NLG-Navigazione Libera del Golfo** (www.navlib.it; ✆ **081-8071812**) and **Linee Lauro** (www.alilauro.it; ✆ **081-4972222**) make daily runs to and from Sorrento, Naples, Ischia, Capri, Positano, and Amalfi, with limited service between Sorrento and Naples off-season. Boats not only provide a scenic ride, but traveling by sea is a welcome alternative to the traffic-choked coastal road in high season.

BY CAR **Taxis** offer a flat rate of 100€ to Sorrento from Naples; or 130€ to Amalfi from the Naples' Capodichino Airport. By **car** from Naples, take the A3, exit at Castellammare di Stabia for the SS145 to Sorrento. The SS163 branches off the SS145 before you get to Sorrento and heads over the peninsula to Positano and Amalfi. To get to Ravello, take the A3 from Naples to a well-marked exit near Angri then SP2b and SP1 across the mountains. Allow about 1 hour and 10 minutes for the drive from Naples to Sorrento; at least 2 hours to Positano or Ravello, and 2½ hours to Amalfi.

Limoncello tasting in Sorrento.

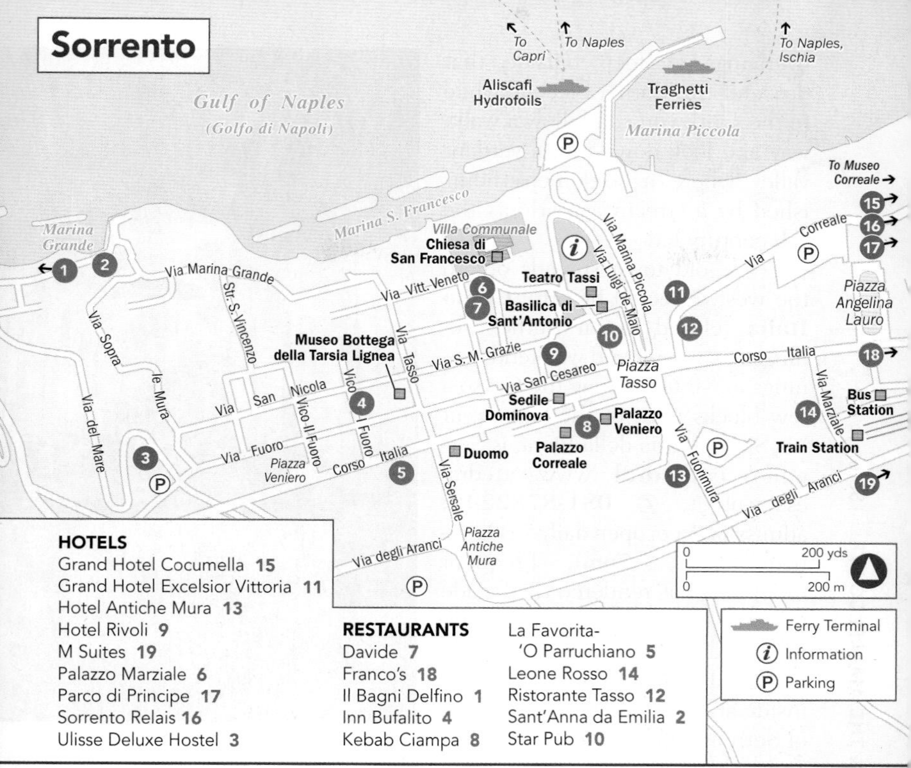

VISITOR INFORMATION Sorrento's **tourist office** is at Via de Maio 35, off Piazza Tasso (www.sorrentotourism.com; ✆ **081-8074033;** Mon–Fri 9am–4:15pm and Sat morning in summer). An information office is in the green caboose outside the train station (daily 10am–1pm and 3–7pm).

Exploring Sorrento

Sorrento is long and narrow, strung out along the top of seaside cliffs. Just about everything you want to see is an easy walk from the train station, with the exception of the two ports, which many residents opt to reach by bus. **Marina Piccola,** below Piazza Tasso (bus C or D, 1€), is the commercial port where ferries and hydrofoils dock; **Marina Grande,** below the town's western edge (bus D, 2€), is the old fishing port.

The center of town is sunny **Piazza Tasso.** Amid the piazza's cafes, glossy shops, and crowds of promenaders stands a statue of the namesake poet, Tarquato Tasso, who was born into a noble family in Sorrento in 1544. The piazza dramatically spans a deep gorge; the north end overhangs a steep hillside that descends to Marina Piccola, while to the south you can follow a walkway and look down into a verdant valley where a settlement flourished by a stream as early as the 5th century B.C.

The old town spreads out to the west, bisected by busy **Corso Italia** (closed to car traffic evenings in summer and weekend evenings in winter). Along the Corso a few blocks west of the square, at Via Santa Maria della Pieta, is Sorrento's **cathedral** (www.cattedralesorrento.it; ✆ **081-8782248;** admission free; open daily 7:30am–noon and 3–7pm). Frequent rebuilding has rendered the facade rather bland, except for an intriguing arcaded three-story campanile with embedded Roman columns; inside are doors inlaid with scenes of Sorrento life, a map of the town, and an enormous *presepe* (nativity scene), set on the streets of Naples with Mt. Vesuvius looming behind the manger. North of here are the quieter precincts around the gardens of the **Villa Communale.**

Sorrento's cathedral.

Chiesa di San Francisco ★ CHURCH Top choice for the most charming spot in Sorrento goes to the 14th-century Moorish cloisters of this church and convent, where an old pepper tree shades tufa-rock arches interspersed with elaborately capped columns. Inside the church, Francis is shown above the altar in a transcendent moment when, after weeks of fasting and praying, wounds opened on his hands, sides, and feet, bringing him close to the suffering Christ in body as well as in spirit. Piazza Francesco Saverio Gargiulo. Free. Daily 8am–1:30pm and 3:30–8pm.

Largo Dominova ★★ SQUARE For Sorrentines, this little square tucked away in the old quarter at the intersections of Via San Cesareo and Via P. R. Giuliani is the real heart of town. At one time that was truly the case: The town council used to meet in the 16th-century Sedile Dominova, an arched loggia with a green-tile cupola. The richly frescoed interior of trompe l'oeil columns and scenes of aristocratic life is now a gathering spot for retired workers. The old gents are used to visitors popping in for a look at their opulent surroundings, so don't be shy.

Marina Grande ★★ NEIGHBORHOOD Walking past a row of narrow houses squeezed along the quays between the steep hillside and the sea, you'll get a sense of Sorrento as an old-time fishing port. Even so, you'll have to contend with shills trying to lure you into restaurants with multi-language menus (a few restaurants here are excellent; see below). It's a nice walk from Sorrento down to the port; just follow the well-marked road from Piazza Vittoria; it eventually becomes a staircase and passes beneath a Greek gate—a reminder that Marina Grande was once a separate town that was vulnerable to pirate raids, a much riskier place to live than fortified Sorrento. You can take a dip here, but the small, pebbly beach is less than inviting (for better options, see p. 634). The scene is quite romantic in the evening, with moonlight illuminating a harbor full of bobbing boats. Should you have one *limoncello* too many while taking in the spectacle, hop on the D bus to get back up the hill.

Museo Correale di Terranova ★ MUSEUM A walk through these rather plain galleries carved out of an 18th-century villa introduces you to the good life as it's been enjoyed over the past few centuries in this part of the world. Counts Alfredo and Pompeo Correale donated to this museum the collectibles their family had amassed since 1500; the randomness of the assortment is its charm. Neapolitan paintings from the

Colorful Marina Grande.

17th through 19th centuries capture the scenic Sorrento views that have been inspiring travelers since the days of the Grand Tour. Inlaid intarsia furniture is from studios right here in Sorrento, and much of the porcelain was fired in kilns on the grounds of the Capodimonte palace in Naples (some especially delicate-looking pieces are from China and Japan, reflecting the 19th-century aristocratic craze for Far East arts). A lovely palm-shaded garden affords stunning views up and down the coast.

Via Correale 50. 8€. Mid-Apr to mid-Oct, daily 8am–1:30pm and 3:30–8pm, mid-Oct to mid-Apr, daily 8am–1:30pm.

Villa Communale ★★ PARK/GARDEN Views from one side of this delightful, palm-studded patch of greenery take in the port far below and a broad sweep of the bay of Naples. From the far side of the gardens you can take an **elevator** down to Marina Piccola (1€) or follow a well-marked lane and stairway down. A statue of St. Francis stands amid the cliffside gardens, looking as contented in the pleasant surroundings.

Tours

You can spend a pleasant day exploring the coast on cruises with **Marine Club** (www.marineclub.it; ✆ **081-8772621**), which run from Marina Piccola daily and usually include stops in Capri for swimming and in Positano and Amalfi. It's an excellent way to see the coast in high season without contending with traffic, supplying an affordable taste of *la dolce vita* along the coast (from 39€ per person). Round-trips take a full day.

Beaches

You can swim from a pebbly patch at Marina Grande or rent a beach chair at one of the beach clubs there, but for real sand, take the A bus from Piazza Tasso east to **Meta,** where the beach is often jammed with Neapolitans out for a day in the sun. A more appealing option is west of town, also reachable on the A bus from Piazza Tasso: **Bagno della Regina Giovanna** (Queen Giovanna's Bath) at Punta del Capo, the northwestern tip of the Sorrento Peninsula. Here a small rock-sheltered pool of clear water, reached on a path through citrus and olive groves, was once the private harbor of the ancient Roman Villa of Pollio Felice. Step through the ruins at the top of the cliff, where cultured man of letters Pollio Felice once entertained guests with readings of Virgil and Horace. Just beyond, also reached by the A bus, is **Marina di Puolo,** a little fishing port where you can swim in a sheltered cove.

Where to Stay

EXPENSIVE

Grand Hotel Cocumella ★★★ Of all Sorrento's grand hotels, this magically converted monastery is the most serene, set amid lush gardens

above the sea in elegant Sant'Agnello, a residential enclave at the eastern end of town. Rooms created from combined monk's cells are chic and sophisticated, mixing antiques with nice contemporary touches, offset with gleaming white tile floors. Some have sea-view terraces while others hang over orange-scented gardens, where a pool is tucked into the greenery. An elevator descends to the sea and a swimming platform.
Via Cocumella 7, Sant'Agnello. www.cocumella.com. ✆ **081-8782933.** 48 units. 340€–380€ double. Rates include breakfast. **Amenities:** Restaurant; bar; concierge; pool; beach; Wi-Fi (free).

Grand Hotel Excelsior Vittoria ★★★ The same family has been running Sorrento's most luxurious retreat since 1834, and the elegant lounges and vine-covered pergolas are little changed from the days of the Grand Tour. In fact, Oscar Wilde, Richard Wagner, and many other notable guests of the past could walk into one of the elegantly appointed guest rooms and feel right at home, though the modern bathrooms might make their heads spin. Choicest rooms have views over the Gulf of Naples; others, hardly a step down in luxury, face a luxuriant garden. Most open onto balconies or large terraces. A pool set amid palms and flowers is a welcome hideaway from the busy lanes outside the gate.
Piazza Tasso 34. www.exvitt.it. ✆ **081-8777111.** 105 units. 450€–595€ double. Rates include breakfast. **Amenities:** 2 restaurants; bar; concierge; pool; room service; spa; Wi-Fi (free).

Parco di Principe ★★ You'll be stepping into some colorful history when you walk onto these verdant grounds on a sea cliff at the edge of town. Jesuit friars once grew aphrodisiac plants here. In the early 19th century, Prince Leopold, Count of Syracuse, commissioned a villa where he could lead a life wholeheartedly devoted to pleasure away from his religiously fanatic wife. Tsar Nicholas II of Russia didn't make it in time to see the *dacha* built on the grounds for his visit a century later. In the 1960s, architect Gio Ponti (designer of Milan's Pirelli Tower) created what is an artistic statement as well as a stunning hotel, all about blue: blue sky and blue sea beyond the terraces and huge windows, blue tiles that carpet the floors. Even the upholstery on the impeccable Modernist chairs and couches is a blue that Ponti calibrated. It adds up to distinctive surroundings that are supremely comfortable and make you feel, as Ponti intended, as if you're floating between sea and sky.
Via Rota 44, Sant'Angello. www.royalgroup.it/parcodeiprincipi. ✆ **081/878-4644.** 96 units. 150€–275€ double. Rates include breakfast. **Amenities:** 2 restaurants; bar; pool; beach; spa; gym; Wi-Fi (free).

MODERATE

Hotel Antiche Mura ★★ An elegant Art Nouveau–style palazzo built on top of the town's former defensive walls reveals many surprises, including a huge garden filled with lemon trees surrounding a pool, as well as precipitous views from many rooms into the deep gorge that runs through Sorrento. Attractive public lounges flow over a couple of floors and include a conservatory-like breakfast room. Guest quarters are bright and cheerful, with colorful Vietri-tile floors; many have balconies facing the gorge or town, while some are tucked into the garden. Service is as gracious and welcoming as the surroundings.

Via Fuorimura 7 (entrance on Piazza Tasso). www.hotelantichemura.com. ✆ **081-8073523.** 46 units. 180€–250€ double. Rates include breakfast. **Amenities:** Bar; concierge; pool; Wi-Fi (free).

Hotel Rivoli ★ Convenience comes with high style at this strikingly revamped convent right in the center of town. A dramatic glass staircase floats up to airy, smartly decorated guest rooms and a rooftop breakfast room and terrace. Cozy, antiques-filled reading nooks open off the landings (there's also an elevator). You'll trade a pool and sea views for a center-of-town location—the pedestrian-only old town lanes are just outside the soundproofed windows, and the train station, port, and bus stops are nearby, making this a very handy base for exploring the coast.

Via Santa Maria delle Grazie 16. www.sorrentorivoli.com. ✆ **081-3654089.** 8 units. 120€–140€ double. Rates include breakfast. Discounts for longer stays. **Amenities:** Wi-Fi (free).

M Suites ★★★ You might be tempted to settle in for the whole season in these fashionable apartments on a hillside atop town. Each of the commodious one-bedroom units sleeps four and has a kitchen, terrace, and large bathroom with Jacuzzi tub. Antiques, Vietri tile floors, and paintings create rich surroundings inside, while extensive gardens and terraces are pillowed in flowers and lush foliage. Views extend across the peninsula to the sea. Guests have use of the pool and facilities at the Hotel Mediterraneo, down the hill in seaside Sant'Agnello.

Via Rubinacci 5. www.msuitesorrento.com. ✆ **081-3509956.** From 125€–150€ double; longer stay rates available. **Amenities:** 2 restaurants, 2 bars, pool at nearby Hotel Mediterraneo; Wi-Fi (free).

Palazzo Marziale ★★★ You can't help but feel a bit privileged in this character-filled old *palazzo* in the heart of town, as if you're visiting aristocratic relatives. In fact, this is the ancestral home of the proprietors, who have turned the stone-arched entrance court into a glassed-in lounge and furnished the huge guest rooms with old family prints and antiques, adding designer touches with deep color schemes and rich fabrics. All have queen- or king-size beds, sofas that double as extra beds, and enormous marble bathrooms. The cloisters of San Francesco and Villa Communale gardens are just across the street, as is an elevator to whisk you down to the port.

Piazza Francesco Saverio Gargiulo 2. www.palazzomarziale.com. ✆ **081/807-4406.** From 170€ double. Rates include breakfast. **Amenities:** Restaurant; bar; parking (18€); Wi–fi (free).

INEXPENSIVE

Masseria Astapiana Villa Giusso ★★ An ancient monastery turned noble residence in the hills outside Vico Equense is surrounded by parkland, olive groves, and vineyards, all set on 14 hectares (35 acres) overlooking the sea and the coast. Monks' quarters in the atmospheric old house are charmingly and comfortably done with plump armchairs, antiques, and wrought-iron beds, with a smattering of original frescoes and arched ceilings throughout. Breakfast is served in a vast tiled kitchen, and the grounds are laced with woodland paths, sunny terraces, and other quiet hideaways. Sorrento is 10km (6 miles) west.

Via Camaldoli 51. www.astapiana.com. ✆ **081-8024392.** 10 units. 90€–110€ double. Rates include breakfast. Discounts for longer stays. **Amenities:** Wi-Fi (free).

Sorrento Relais ★★ No sea views, no balconies, no grand hotel atmosphere—but this small, comfortable inn on the lower levels of an apartment house across the street from the Museo Correale di Terranova is appealing and an extremely good value. Compact, contemporary-style rooms are equipped with excellent beds and good lighting (a rarity in lower-priced Italian hotels) and artfully decorated with striped fabrics, bright colors, and quirky wall coverings. Mood lighting in the showers changes with the touch of a remote control and adds a little extra splash to the spiffy bathrooms. Rooms on the ground floor are bright despite the lack of views—those in the rear are blissfully quiet—though some decidedly less desirable accommodations are in the basement, where a decent breakfast is served in a large, convivial space.

Via Bernardino Rota 5. www.sorrentorelais.com. ✆ **081/1892-0834.** 7 units. 70€–99€ double. Rates include breakfast. **Amenities:** Lounge; Wi-Fi (free).

Ulisse Deluxe Hostel ★★ Hostel life takes on a glossy sheen in these chic, sprawling lounges and large, handsomely furnished guest rooms. A few quadruples remain true to the dormlike hostel image, but for the most part the emphasis is on quiet, hotel-standard comfort. Rooms lack a few thrills—no balconies or sweeping sea views—but white-tile floors shine, wood furnishings are polished to a high gloss, beds are firm (many are king-size), and extras include minibars and a luxury spa with steam room, sauna, and a large pool. The hillside perch is nicely located on the road down to Marina Grande, just west of the historic center.

Via del Mar 22. www.ulissedeluxe.com. ✆ **081-8774753.** 50 units. 80€–110€ double. Rates include breakfast. Discounts for longer stays. **Amenities:** Bar; spa; pool; Wi-Fi (free).

Where to Eat

For a quick meal and a meat fix, try the veal or chicken kebabs at **Kebab Ciampa,** Via Pieta 23 (www.kebabsorrento.com; ✆ **081-8074595**), which also serves falafel and meatballs. **Star Pub,** Via Luigi de Maio 17 (www.starpub.it; ✆ **081-8773618**), satisfies a hamburger craving, and also makes excellent salads that are meals in themselves, washed down with a well-curated selection of wines and beers. **Franco's,** Corso Italia 265 (✆ **081/877–2066**), is a local institution, always open (daily 8am–2am) and always crowded, making calzones, *piadine* (stuffed sandwiches), and pizzas in many varieties, served at communal tables.

The best gelato in town is at **Davide,** Via Padre Reginaldo Giuliani 39 (✆ **081-8072092;** closed Wed in winter), where the 60 flavors include deliciously creamy *noci di Sorrento* (Sorrento walnuts), rich *cioccolato con canditi* (dark chocolate cream studded with candied oranges), and *delizia al limone* (a delectable lemon cream).

MODERATE

Il Bagni Delfino ★★ SORRENTINE A meal here comes with a perk, the chance to swim off the adjoining pier. That's a good incentive to eat lightly from the snack food menu, though the heaping platters of fresh seafood are tempting—and a popular Sunday afternoon lunch choice, when locals come down to take in the sun and indulge in excellent cooking and friendly service.

Western end of port off Via Marina Grande. ✆ **081-8782038.** Main courses 12€–24€. Daily 12:30–3:30pm and 6:30–11pm. Closed Nov–Mar.

Inn Bufalito ★ SORRENTINE The approach here is to use only local products, especially buffalo meats and cheeses (buffalo-milk mozzarella is one of the region's most prized specialties). The brown-toned room gives off a rustic vibe, even though the menu and service are decidedly polished. Enjoy buffalo steaks or pasta with a heavy sauce of buffalo *ragu*, while a platter of cheeses and salamis is a nice light meal.

Vico I Foro 21. www.innbufalito.com. ✆ **081-3656975.** Main courses 12€–24€. Wed–Mon noon–3:30pm and 6:30–11pm. Closed Nov–Feb.

Ristorante 'o Parrucchiano La Favorita ★★ SORRENTINE This old-time Sorrento landmark dates back to 1868, when a former priest decided to get into the restaurant business (the name means "Priest's Place"). The vast, multilevel, greenhouse-like space opens to a vine-covered garden planted with potted citrus trees—guaranteed to give the grumpiest customer a festive dining experience. Tour groups pour in, but there's room for everybody, and the food is consistently good as members of a third generation of owners are on hand to ensure a memorable time. Some dishes, such as baked pasta crêpes stuffed with ricotta, mozzarella, and minced beef, have been on the menu since the start and only get better with time; recent innovations include some wonderful seafood pastas, like shrimp ravioli in clam sauce.

Corso Italia 71. www.parrucchiano.com. ✆ **081-8781321.** Main courses 10€–25€. Daily noon–3pm and 7–11:30pm (closed Wed mid-Nov–mid-Mar).

Ristorante Tasso ★★ SORRENTINE Sorrento prides itself on fresh seafood, and the catch is the focus in this casually elegant room that resembles a garden pavilion (and also has a large garden for alfresco dining). The choices change daily, with two reasonably priced set menus, though you can also dine a la carte. Surprisingly (given the classy surroundings), pizza is a specialty, one that many regulars say is the best this side of Naples.

Via Correale 11d. www.ristorantetasso.com. ✆ **081-8785809.** Main courses 12€–24€. Daily noon–4pm and 7–11:30pm.

INEXPENSIVE

Leone Rosso ★ SORRENTINE/PIZZA Sorrentines and their visitors crowd the terrace and rambling, bright rooms for simple, straightforward seafood dishes, offered in so many variations that you should put down the huge menu and simply ask one of the friendly, English-speaking waiters to recite the daily specials. That will likely include all sorts of fresh catch, expertly grilled, and heaping platters of *risotto alla pescatore* (seafood risotto) and *spaghetti alla vongole* (spaghetti with clams). Non-pescatarians can enjoy *gnocchi alla sorrentina,* little pockets of potato pasta filled with mozzarella and topped with tomato sauce, and a big choice of other land-based Sorrento classics. A meal usually ends with a complimentary *limoncello.*

Via Marziale 25. www.illeonerosso.it. ✆ **081/807-3089.** Main courses 7€–12€. Daily 11:30am–11:30pm.

An Acquired Taste?

Lunch and dinner in Sorrento and on the Amalfi Coast often ends with a *limoncello,* usually homemade and often complimentary. Almost every family in Campania has its own recipe, passed on for generations, for this potent and sweet liqueur. True *limoncello* is made from *sfusato di Amalfi,* a particular lemon that has obtained D.O.P. recognition (the stamp of controlled origin for produce, similar to D.O.C. for wine). The Amalfi lemon is large and light in color, with a sweet and very flavorful aroma and taste, almost no seeds, and a very thick skin.

Sant'Anna da Emilia ★ SORRENTINE The simple pleasures of this old boat shed in Marina Grande are well-known, so getting a table during the summer rush may require a long wait. Patience pays off with old-time classics such as *gnocchi alla Sorrentina* (Sorrento-style potato dumplings with cheese and tomato sauce) and *fritto misto* (deep-fried calamari and little fish). The best tables, of course, are on the pier outside. No credit cards are accepted.

Via Marina Grande 62. ✆ **081-8072720.** Main courses 9€–14€. Daily noon–3:30pm and 7:30–11:30pm (closed Tues in winter). Closed Nov–Feb.

Shopping

On a walk along *palazzo*-lined **Via San Cesareo**, you can easily stock up on all sorts of things you don't need, mostly emblazoned with the town's signature lemons. For a bottle of the town's ubiquitous *limoncello* liqueur, head out to the charming **Giardini di Cataldo,** just off Corso Italia near the train station (www.igiardinidicataldo.it; ✆ **081-8781888**); in a fragrant lemon and orange grove you can taste and buy *limoncello*, marmalade, and other products made on the premises.

For centuries, Sorrento craftspeople have been known for producing the beautiful inlaid wood designs known as intarsia. You can see fine examples at the **Museobottega della Tarsialignea,** Via San Nicola 28 (www.museomuta.it/muta/it; ✆ **081-8771942**), and can even order a custom-made piece of furniture if you're tempted. The 19th-century prints of old Sorrento are equally enticing (8€; Apr–Oct daily 9:30am–1pm and 4–8pm, Nov–Mar daily 9:30am–1pm and 3–7pm). **Gargiulo & Jannuzzi,** Piazza Tasso 1 (www.gargiulo-jannuzzi.it; ✆ **081-8781041**), sells fine intarsia, and you can visit the workshops for a demonstration.

Libreria Tasso, Via San Caesaro 96 (www.libreriatasso.com; ✆ **081-8071639**), stocks a good selection of English-language titles, from the latest thrillers to guidebooks.

Nightlife

Epicenter of nightlife in Sorrento is the lively terrace of the **Fauno Bar,** Piazza Tasso 13 (www.faunobar.it; ✆ **081-8781135**), popular for an *aperitivo* and people-watching throughout the day until late into the evening. The adjoining nightclub caters to a mature crowd willing to fork over the 25€ cover charge. Some popular casual bars, usually packed with an international crowd, are **Chantecler,** Via Santa Maria della Pietà 38 (www.chanteclers.com; ✆ **081-8075868**), and the **English Inn,** Corso Italia 55 (www.englishinn.it; ✆ **081-8074357**).

The **cloister of San Francesco,** Piazza Francesco Saverio Gargiulo, is the evocative setting for summertime concerts. Contact the tourist office (p. 631) for a schedule of events, including others staged at many restaurants and taverns in town. ***Sorrento Musical*** is a perennially popular revue of Neapolitan songs hosted by **Teatro Tasso,** Piazza Sant'Antonino (www.teatrotasso.com; ✆ **081-8075525**; tickets cost about 25€ depending on the show; 50€ including dinner).

THE SORRENTO PENINSULA

When Sorrento seems a little too crowded, it's easy to get away. For terrain that's a little wilder and more peaceful, you only need to travel south to the southwestern stretches of the Sorrento peninsula, where the ruggedly beautiful landscapes come with soul-soothing sea views.

Essentials

GETTING THERE **SITA buses** (www.sitabus.it; ✆ **089-405145**) serve towns on the Sorrento Peninsula. By **car,** SS145 leads west, then south for access to the peninsula.

VISITOR INFORMATION The **tourist office** in Sorrento (see above) has information on towns and activities, including hiking, on the Sorrento Peninsula. Another source for local information is the small tourist office in **Massa Lubrenese,** Viale Filangeri 11 (✆ **081-5339021**).

Sant'Agata sui Due Golfi ★★

7km (4½ miles) south of Sorrento

It won't take you too long to figure out where this hilltop village (at 300M, or 990 ft., you could almost say mountaintop) got the "two gulfs" part of its name. Look to the south, and you'll see the Gulf of Sorrento, Turn your head to the north, and there's the Gulf of Naples. It's also easy to see why the town was already famous in the days of the Roman Empire as the junction of trading routes across the peninsula. Artisans working on the 17th-century church of **Santa Maria delle Grazie** decided to try to outdo these views and created a ridiculously sumptuous altar with lots of marble, mother of pearl, and lapis lazuli (open 9am–1pm and 4pm–7pm). Nuns desiring less ostentatious surroundings settled in the **Convento del Deserto,** on a hillside 1km (half a mile) outside town; follow Corso Sant'Agata from the center. You'll only rarely be invited inside, but you're not missing much—the attraction is the **view** from the terrace, all the way to Ischia in the northwest down the coast to Paestum in the east. In the 19th century, especially before the road to Positano and Amalfi opened in the late 1830s, this was a major stop on the Grand Tour, as far along the coast as view-seekers could get. The terrace is generally open April through September daily 8am to noon and 5 to 7pm; and October through March daily 10am to noon and 3 to 5pm.

Marina del Cantone ★★

5km (3 miles) south of Sant'Agata Sui Due Golfi

This cove cut into the cliffs was known to the ancient Greeks as Hyeros Anthos, meaning "Sacred Flower." From Sant'Agata, follow the road down through Metrano then on to Nerano-Marina del Cantone; SITA buses from Sorrento (see above) make the run to and from Marina del Cantone throughout the day. The beach (mostly pebbles) is the longest for miles around, backed by houses and a few cafes and shops. You'll be part of a crowd here, especially on summer weekends when festive sunseekers come from as far away as Naples. Looming just offshore are Li Galli, an archipelago of tiny islets once owned by dancer Rudolf Nureyev.

They're also known as the Isole Sirenuse—home, legend has it, of the Sirens of *Odyssey* fame whose song lured sailors to their deaths.

Massa Lubrense ★★

5km (3 miles) west of Sant'Agata Sui Due Golfi

Quiet little Massa Lubrense was once a powerful rival to Sorrento for dominance over this coast. These days a position off the beaten track and firmly out of the limelight, along with considerable natural beauty, is its great asset. You'll want to pause long enough on Largo Vescovado to take in the dead-on view of the shimmering profile of Capri, just across the bay at this point, then step into the church of **Santa Maria delle Grazie** for a look at the colorful majolica floor; it's open daily 8am to noon and 4 to 8pm. Sparkling just below is the sea at Marina della Lobra, a steep 2-km (1 mile) descent that deposits you on a quiet little beach.

Punta Campanella ★★

9km (6 miles) south of Massa Lubrense

Lands End on the Sorrento Peninsula is this rocky point where a lighthouse guides ships through the treacherous Capri Narrows, the 3km (2 miles) of swift-moving waters between the peninsula and the famous island. Punta Campanella takes its name from the bell on **Torre Minerva,** a 14th-century watchtower that once warned of pirate incursions (*campanella* means "small bell"). It was built next to the ruins of a temple dedicated to Athena (called Minerva by the Romans). With some luck and divine guidance from the goddess of wisdom, ancient sailors could possibly make it through the rock-strewn narrows. Athena might have been kindly disposed to mortals, who surrounded her temple with olive groves to supply the oil they presented as offerings.

Getting Active

The peninsula is traversed by a network of 22 well-maintained **hiking** paths that crisscross valleys, meander atop seaside cliffs, and descend hillsides to secret coves for a total length of 110km (68 miles). The tourist office in Sorrento (see above) can provide you with maps.

One of the most scenic walks is from the village of Torca (2km/1 miles southeast of Sant'Agata sui Due Golfi), where Via Pedara becomes a dirt path that descends a cliff face past the ruins of the 12th-century abbey of San Pietro to a delightful cove. Just offshore are Li Gali islands, the very rocks where it's said the Sirens lured innocent mariners to their deaths.

Another walk descends from the village of Termini (5km/3 miles southwest of Sant'Agata sui Due Golfi) into the Vallone della Cala di Mitigliano, carpeted with olive groves and *macchia mediterranea*, typical Mediterranean vegetation that includes the beautifully scented *mirto*.

The trail then crosses a plateau with large boulders and the ruins of Torre di Namonte, a medieval watchtower, before beginning a steep descent toward the sea, with the profile of Capri looming ahead.

On the southern side of the peninsula, the seashore and offshore waters are protected as a marine park, **Area Marina Protetta di Punta Campanella** (www.puntacampanella.org; ✆ **081-8089877**). The most scenic way to see the unspoiled coast is to rent a **boat,** hugging the rocky shoreline as you pass hidden coves and stopping now and then for a swim. Marina del Cantone (see above) is the port of departure. Skipper Peppe takes day sailors out on his beautiful boat, *La Granseola* (www.lagranseola.com; ✆ **081-8081027**). Other seaworthy providers are **Cooperativa S. Antonio** (✆ **081-8081638)** and **Nautica 'O Masticiello** (www.masticiello.com; ✆ **081-8081443**).

Where to Eat

Don Alfonso 1890 ★★★ CREATIVE SORRENTINE The Iaccarino family has elevated their charming dining rooms to international fame, and the secret to their success soon becomes clear. A team of excellent chefs makes the most of local produce, with breads and pasta made in house and almost everything else coming from the family garden or a network of local suppliers, with owner and former chef Alfonso Iaccarino growing the vegetables, shopping, and ordering (his wife, Livia, oversees the dining room). Even the tomatoes here seem like exotic fruits, and they infuse dishes as simple-yet-transporting as ravioli filled with farmhouse cheese and served with tomato sauce and basil or a bouillabaisse with freshly caught fish. Tasting menus and *a la carte* choices are available, and lunch is served in a beautiful garden next to a swimming pool in summer. For many travelers, a meal here is reason enough to come to Sorrento. If you wish to prolong the experience, Don Alfonso 1890 Relais houses guests in nine elegant rooms, many with a glimpse of the sea and furnished with antiques (from 400€).

Corso Sant'Agata 11, Sant'Agata sui Due Golfi. www.donalfonso.com. ✆ **081-8780026.** Main courses 35€–45€; tasting menu 140€–155€. Wed–Sun 12:30–2:30pm and 8–10:30pm (June–Sept also Tues 8–10:30pm). Closed Nov–Mar.

Maria Grazia ★★ SORRENTINE/SEAFOOD Diners have relished the sea views and simple dishes at this waterfront institution for more than 50 years. The bare-bones room right across from boats moored along the pebbly beach lets you know what you can expect—fresh grilled octopus and just-caught fish, along with basic pastas that include the house specialty, *pasta con i cucuzzielli,* spaghetti in a light tomato sauce with baby eggplant, basil, and *caciocavallo* cheese. It's all delicious, washed down with the house white wine, and followed up with a limoncello or other homemade *digestivo.*

Marina del Cantone. ✆ **081-8081011**. Main courses 10€–18€. Mar–Dec daily noon–3pm and 7–10pm.

POSITANO ★★

16km (10 miles) E of Sorrento

Hugging a semi-vertical rock formation, Positano is the very essence of picturesque, an enticing collection of pastel-colored houses and majolica domes that spill down a ravine to the sea. Novelist John Steinbeck, after a visit in 1953, described it in words that still ring true: "It is a dream place that isn't quite real when you are there and becomes beckoningly real after you have gone. . . ." It's not surprising that Positano was the retreat for *la dolce vita* set in the 1960s and '70s. In midsummer, its throngs of admirers can seem like an invading horde, much like those that attacked the little kingdom back in the 9th to 11th centuries, when it was part of the powerful Republic of the Amalfis, rival to Venice as a sea power.

VISITOR INFORMATION The **tourist office** is at Via del Saracino 4 (www.aziendaturismopositano.it; ✆ **089-875067**), open Monday to Saturday 8:30am–2pm, and also from 3:30–8pm in July and August.

Positano's idyllic cityscape and shoreline.

Positano is famous for handcrafted sandals.

Exploring Positano

Whether you arrive by boat or bus, you're in for an uphill or downhill climb along narrow lanes and steep lanes (wear comfortable walking shoes). At some point you'll want to stay put, probably along the sea at **Marina Grande,** where the town's few fishermen still haul up their boats and ferries arrive and depart. Most of the pebbly shoreline is taken up with a beach, backed by restaurants and bars in what were once shipyards and storehouses when Positano was a naval power. From Marina Grande, **Via Positanesi d'America**, a cliff-side pedestrian promenade, stretches along the shore past the cape of **Torre Trasita** and a 13th-century lookout to the smaller and slightly more relaxing beach of **Fornillo.**

If you wander up the steps from Marina Grande you'll soon find yourself amid a souklike sprawl of shops shaded by bougainvillea-laced trellises. The majolica-domed **Collegiata di Santa Maria Assunta ★★**, Piazza Flavio Gioia (✆ **089-875480;** daily 8am–noon and 4–7pm), is Positano's main church, founded as a Benedictine monastery in the 13th century. The "Madonna Nera" (Black Madonna), a Byzantine-style icon above the altar, allegedly gave the town its name when a 12th-century pirate ship carrying the icon sailed into a violent storm. Sailors heard the Madonna on the icon saying "Posa, Posa" ("Put me down") and they took their ship to safety in what would become the harbor of Positano. A relief on the campanile outside shows a wolf nursing seven fish, a clue to how the town once made its living. If you're waiting for a bus at the western bus stop (on the Sorrento side of town), step into the small **Chiesa di Nuova,** Via Chiesa Nuova, for a look at the lovely majolica tile floor.

BEACHES

Positano has two beaches, **Spiaggia Grande** and the slightly quieter **Fornillo.** You can swim for free at both, or rent a lounger and umbrella for about 10€. To reach more idyllic settings, board any of the tour boats that set off from Spiaggia Grande for stops at coves along the coast, or rent a rowboat and poke along the rocky shoreline at your own pace.

Positano's Spiaggia Grande beach.

You can explore the cove-laced shoreline in a rental boat from **Lucibella** (✆ **089-875032**) for 35€ and 60€ per hour, without skipper, depending on the kind of boat and the duration of the rental. Many day sailors set their sights on **Li Galli (The Roosters) ★★**, the four small islands visible to the west of Marina Grande. According to Homer, the Sirens lived on the rocky outcroppings and lured mariners to their deaths on the rocky shoals with their enchanting songs. Sirens themselves were less than enchanting in the flesh, birdlike creatures (hence the name, Li Galli, "The Roosters") with human faces and the bodies of fish. If the light is right and you've had some wine on the voyage, it's easy to see how the rooster-shaped islets might have appeared to be Sirens rising out the sea mist. The island to head for is **Gallo Lungo,** where a medieval watchtower rises above a little beach. This is where Russian dancer Rudolph Nureyev settled a few years before his death of AIDS in 1993, transforming a villa built for another Russian ballet star, Léonide Messine (1896–1979), into an Aladdin's cave filled with rich mosaics and kilims.

GETTING ACTIVE

The 25km-long (15-mile) ***Via degli Incanti* (Trail of Charms)** hiking path winds between Positano and Amalfi through cultivated terraces and citrus groves. If you don't want to do the entire trail, you can catch the coast-road bus at any of the towns and settlements along the route.

Where to Stay

Small, guesthouse-style rooms offer a way to beat Positano's sky-high lodging prices. The tourist office has a full list of bed-and-breakfasts, home stays, and other moderately priced accommodations.

EXPENSIVE

San Pietro ★★★ One of the world's most fabled getaways is luxurious and enchanting, perched on its own promontory above the sea and the discreet retreat of royalty, movie stars, and just plain folks who want the vacation experience of a lifetime. Opulently tiled terraces cascade down the cliff face, laced with shaded nooks and crannies, perfectly poised for hours of relaxation (and the best setting in Positano for a cocktail, expensive but memorable). Facing the sea through huge windows and from private terraces, the large accommodations are a gracious mix of antiques, stylishly informal and comfortable pieces, and elaborate tiles and artwork. The pièce de résistance is the private beach, reached by an elevator that descends through the cliff. For those who want to venture farther, the hotel's private yacht takes guests on complimentary coast cruises, and a free shuttle plies the 2km (1 mile) to town. Many guests choose to stay put amid the hedonistic surroundings, with the glorious, view-filled terrace of **Il San Pietro** restaurant providing exceptional sustenance.

Via Laurito 2. www.ilsanpietro.it. ✆ **089-875455.** 60 units. 600€–680€ double. Rates include breakfast. 3 nights minimum stay in high season. Closed Nov–Mar. **Amenities:** Restaurants; bar; concierge; health club; pool; room service; sauna; spa; tennis court; Wi-Fi (free).

MODERATE

Hotel Buca di Bacco ★ The closest Positano comes to a beach hotel is this former fisherman's hut, much expanded and glorified over the years, and right on Marina Grande. The beachfront perch puts you in the center of the action, so convenience comes with a bit of noise, along with endless sea views from colorfully tiled balconies and terraces. Even rooms with partial or no sea views are a bit of a treat, with handsome antiques and comfy upholstered pieces set on tile floors to create a casual, gracious elegance that's typical of the Amalfi Coast. Three generations of the Rispoli family look after guests with care that extends to excellent meals in a sea-facing dining room and an informal snack bar.

Via Rampa Teglia 4. www.bucadibacco.it. ✆ **089-875699.** 46 units. 245€–450€ double. Rates include breakfast. Closed 2 weeks in winter. **Amenities:** Restaurant; bar; beach (public); babysitting; concierge; room service; Wi-Fi (free).

Palazzo Murat ★★ Gioacchino Murat, Napoleon's brother-in-law and king of Naples, built this enticing and vaguely exotic 18th-century baroque palace near Positano's small port as a summer getaway. It's still a retreat of royal magnitude, set amid a vast garden and orchard dripping with flowering vines and scented with lemons and jasmine. Five especially large rooms, filled with handsome antiques, are in the original palace, and others are in a new but extremely tasteful addition, where tile floors and traditional furnishings adhere to the historical ambience.

Most rooms have balconies, some with sea views; others overlook the surrounding greenery, the tile-domed church of Santa Maria Assunta, or the town. Buffet breakfast is served in the garden in good weather.

Via dei Mulini 23. www.palazzomurat.it. ✆ **089-875177.** 31 units. 250€–450€ double. Rates include breakfast. Closed Jan to week before Easter. **Amenities:** Restaurant; concierge; pool; room service; Wi-Fi (free).

INEXPENSIVE

Hotel Savoia ★★ You won't find a lot of luxurious amenities, but this hotel's great location right in the heart of Positano, steps from the beach, is coupled with pleasant decor—bright tile floors, comfortable beds, and attractive traditional furnishings. Some rooms have sea views, and others take in the sweep of the old town climbing the hillside. The old-fashioned ambience comes with a provenance: The D'Aiello family has been running this place since 1936, when Positano was a getaway for a select few, and that's how they treat their guests still.

Via Cristoforo Colombo 73. www.savoiapositano.it. ✆ **089-875003.** 42 units. 150€–190€ double. Rates include breakfast. **Amenities:** Bar; babysitting; concierge; room service; Wi-Fi (free).

La Fenice ★★★ All the charm and beauty of Positano comes to the fore in this little parcel of heaven clinging to a cliff on the outskirts of town. A stay requires a bit of walking and climbing, to and from the town center (about a 10-minute stroll) and on the gorgeous property itself, along shaded walkways and stone stairways through gardens and groves to the pool and private beach below—an amenity that's the pride of only a few other much more expensive retreats along the coast. Charming and simple whitewashed rooms, most with tiled terraces overlooking the sea, are tucked into a couple of villas and several cottages that descend the hillside amid lemon groves and grape vines. Owner Constantino Marino and his family live on the property and go out of their way to make guests feel at home, and that includes carting bags up and down the stairs and serving informal meals made with produce from the garden (meals served on request).

Via Giuglielmo Marconi 4. lafenicepositano.com. ✆ **089-875513.** 14 units. 140€–160€. Rates include breakfast. Cash only. **Amenities:** Pool; beach; Wi-Fi (free).

La Rosa die Venti ★★ Each of the humbly furnished, tile-floored rooms in this house high on a hillside in the quieter part of Positano comes with a big perk: a large planted terrace with a sea view. It's tempting to settle in here and stay put, but moving around town and the coast is easy to do; the beach at Fornillo is at the bottom of the hill, shops and restaurants are nearby, and it's an easy climb up to the bus stop or down to the harbor.

Via Fornillo 40. www.larosadeiventi.net. ✆ **089-875252.** From 170€ double. Rates include breakfast. **Amenities:** Wi-Fi (free).

Where to Eat

EXPENSIVE

Next 2 ★★ AMALFITAN Step through the iron gates into one of Positano's most sophisticated lairs. A softly lit courtyard with knockout sea views and a contemporary room of dazzling white linens and bright cushions is the setting for refined takes on local favorites made with fresh ingredients, many from the restaurant garden. Fried ravioli stuffed with ricotta and mozzarella is set on a bed of tomatoes plucked from the vine minutes before, while *fiori di zucchini* (zucchini flowers) are filled with ricotta, mozzarella, and basil and served with pesto sauce. Fresh fish is a specialty, paired with the same homegrown ingredients.
Via Pasitea 242. www.next2.it. ✆ **089-8123516.** Reservations recommended in season. Main courses 16€–25€. Daily 7–11pm. Closed Nov–Mar and Mon off-season.

MODERATE

Da Adolfo ★ AMALFITAN/SEAFOOD One of Positano's old-time favorites makes the most of its beachside location with a laidback ambience and an emphasis on fresh seafood. Sample some local specialties here, such as mozzarella *alla brace* (grilled on fresh lemon leaves), followed by a beautifully seasoned *zuppa di cozze* (mussel stew). Come for lunch and spend the afternoon, making use of the adjacent changing rooms, showers, and chair-and-umbrella rentals. Sooner or later, though, you'll have to face the 450 rugged steps up the hillside to the road—better yet, take the free water-shuttle service to Marina Grande.
Via Spiaggia di Laurito 40. www.daadolfo.com. ✆ **089-875022.** Main courses 10€–18€. Daily 1–4pm. Closed mid-Oct to early May.

Il Ritrovo ★★ AMALFITAN/PIZZA Just being in this mountainside village above Positano is a treat, far removed from the crowds and frenzy 450m (1,500 ft.) below. The airy terrace makes the most of the sea and mountain views, and the menu is inspired by both. *Grigliata mista* (grilled meat medley) and the chicken roasted with mountain herbs are hearty and excellent, as are the excellent pastas laden with fresh seafood. Chef Salvatore might come out and insist you follow up a meal with one of his homemade liqueurs. He shares his considerable skills in year-round cooking classes. You can take the SITA bus up from town, or the restaurant will send a car down for a free pickup.
Via Montepertuso 77, Montepertuso. www.ilritrovo.com. ✆ **089-812005.** Main courses 10€–20€; set-price menu 30€–40€. Thurs–Tues noon–3:30pm and 7pm–12:30am; open daily Apr to mid Oct. Closed Jan.

INEXPENSIVE

Il Grottino Azzurro ★ AMALFITAN/WINERY This modest little wine cellar opening onto the street near the top of the town is a favorite

with locals, who count on the kitchen for delicious renditions of simple recipes. *Manicaretti* (large ravioli) and cannelloni are filled with meat and baked with cheese and homemade tomato sauce (extra sauce served on the side), while *spaghetti alla vongole* is piled high with sweet, tender clams from local seas. A good choice of regional wines is on hand.
Via Guglielmo Marconi 158 (SS 163). © **089-875466.** Main courses 8€–16€. Thurs–Tues 12:30–3pm and 7:30–11pm (also Wed in summer).

Pupetto ★ AMALFITAN/PIZZA You can reach this lovely spot by elevator off the coast road above, but it's hard to beat the approach by the seaside footpath from Marina Grande. Once here, the lovely, lemon-scented terrace above Fornillo beach is the setting for a simple meal of grilled fresh fish or one of the many seafood pastas. Pizzas are served in the evening and light snacks during the day, when a seat beneath the bamboo awnings is a prime spot for a drink after a swim on the beach.
Via Fornillo 37. www.hotelpupetto.it. © **089-875087.** Main courses 12€–22€; pizza 7€–10€. Daily 12:30–3pm and 7:30–10pm. Closed Nov–Mar.

Shopping

Though Positano appears to have sold its soul to the devils of commerce, the endless rows of shops are curiously unenticing. If you can't resist, consider loungewear, a throwback to the '70s when Moda Positano was all the rage. The excellent **Sartoria Maria Lampo,** Viale Pasitea 12 (www.marialampo.it; © **089-875021**), is a holdover from those days. The town is famous for handcrafted sandals, often made while you wait. Top shoemakers are **D'Antonio,** Via Trara Genoino 13 (© **089-811824**); **Dattilo,** Via Rampa Teglia 19 (© **089-811440**); and **Safari,** Via della Taratana 2 (www.safaripositano.com; © **089-811440**).

Nightlife

You can still get a whiff of Positano's jet-set days at **Music on the Rocks,** Via Grotto dell'Incanto 51 (www.musicontherocks.it; © **089-875874**), a two-level dance club carved into the rocks above Spiaggia Grande; the upstairs terrace provides views and mellow piano music; dancing is in the cavelike disco beneath. Right on the beach, **La Buca di Bacco,** Via del Brigantino 35 (www.bucapositano.it; © **089-811461)** has been Positano's prime stop for a post-dinner drink for half a century.

Between Positano & Amalfi

You can easily get to a string of little towns that cling to cliffs along the coast by bus or by walking from one to the other on the ***Via degli Incanti* (Trail of Charms)** hiking path (see "Getting Active," above). With a generous profusion of porticos and domes, medieval **Praiano** and its adjacent twin, **Vettica Maggiore** (6km [4 miles] east of Positano)

Photo Op

If you're traveling by car or taxi, just west of Positano on SS 163 keep an eye out for the renowned **Belvedere dello Schiaccone.** It's the best lookout point on the Amalfi Drive, 200m (656 ft.) above sea level. The view extends across palm and citrus groves to the archipelago of Li Galli and Capo Sottile, with the splendid summit of Monte Sant'Angelo a Tre Pizzi in the background. According to the legend of Monte Sant'Angelo, the devil challenged the Virgin Mary to see who could pierce the rock face. The devil could only scratch the surface, but at the Virgin's touch the rock crumbled and the large opening that you see in one side of the peak appeared.

sit 120m (394 ft.) above sea level on the slopes of Monte Sant'Angelo as they drape seaward over the promontory known as Capo Sottile. It's said that "Whoever wants to live a healthy life spends the morning in Vettica and the evening in Praiano," which is probably just supposed to mean that this is a good place to spend a day. The little towns were the preferred summer residence of the Amalfi doges, who loved the beautiful views over Positano, Amalfi, and the Faraglioni of Capri, still the main draw. The settlements eventually merge into a sea-facing, majolica-paved piazza that seems more like the deck of a ship than it does a shelf of terra firma carved out of the hillside. Twin towns, twin harbors: East of Praiano is tiny, picturesque **Marina di Praia,** at the bottom of a deep chasm with a small pebbly beach and clear waters. To the west is a tiny slip of pebbles at **Marina Piccola,** tucked into a cove beneath olive groves (follow the signs for "Spiaggia" from the piazza).

Residents of gravity-defying **Furore,** 18km (11 miles) southeast of Positano, might have the strongest legs in Italy, since it's a climb of more than 500m (1,600 ft.) from one end of the town to the other, from the sea to a sky-high perch above. Down at sea level is the fjord of Furore, a deep cleft in the cliffs that provides a natural harbor. It's easy to see how the town got its name when water roars though the fjord with a fury. You can sit in one of the little waterside bars and consider the perils of coastal life as you sip one of the delicious wines from the town's highly acclaimed winery, **Cantine Marisa Cuomo,** Via Lama 14 (www.marisacuomo.com; ✆ **089-830348**). Meanwhile, the top of the village is perched high in the mountains above, safely out of reach of pirates who once raided the coast. Wherever you go, you'll do some climbing: It's 944 steps down to the harbor, and 3,000 steps from there to the top of town along the **Sentiero della Volpe Pescatrice** (Fox-Fish's Path) and the **Sentiero dei Pipistrelli Impazziti** (Mad Bats' Path).

Rambling little **Conca die Marini,** 2km (1 mile) east of Furore, is really just a hamlet of houses perched hillside along the coast road. It's hard to believe that the little harbor in the picturesque cove once bustled with enough boatbuilding to make the town richer than Amalfi. At one time 27 galleons were moored in the tiny harbor beneath Capo di Conca. For that matter, the views and Conca's out-of-the way quiet have been a lure for a long line of privacy-seeking celebs, among them Jackie O, Carlo Ponti, Princess Margaret of England, and the Queen of Holland.

Today Conca is best known as the jumping-off point for the **Emerald Grotto ★★.** Discovered in 1932, the town's famous sea cave gives Capri's Blue Grotto (see p. 678) a run for its money. The stalactites and stalagmites produce transcendent light effects, and an otherworldly blue-green aura envelops the grotto when the sun is high (best between noon and 3pm) and the sea is calm. You can reach the cave from Conca die Marini via an elevator from SS 163, or a long series of steps, then climbing into a rowboat. You can also take a boat from Amalfi, just 5km (3 miles) down the coast (trips usually 15€, including admission to the grotto). Admission is 6€, including the rowboat ride (open Mar–Oct daily 9am–7pm; Nov–Feb daily 9am–4pm).

While you're in Conca, take time to try Sfogliatella di Santa Rosa, a delicious pastry invented by 17th-century nuns at the local **Convento di Santa Rosa**. The enterprising sisters replaced the traditional ricotta-cheese filling of the popular Neapolitan *sfogliatella* with cream and a dash of *amarene*, candied sour cherries in syrup. And mamma mia!—the creation was a hit that you can still taste in pastry shops all over town.

AMALFI ★★

19km (12 miles) east of Positano

From the 9th to the 11th century, the seafaring Republic of Amalfi rivaled the great maritime powers of Genoa and Venice. Its capital, Amalfi, still enjoys some prominence today as a major resort on the Amalfi Drive. Set among lemon groves and olive trees on the slopes of the Lattari Mountains and the Bay of Salerno, where public beaches flank the harbor, Amalfi is a lovely town. Despite its popularity, Amalfi doesn't seem crushed by tourism as Positano does—at least not in the early morning and evening hours before and after the tour buses and boats descend. With its porticos, little squares, medieval streets, and green mountainsides on one side and blue sea on the other, it's a terribly pleasant place to spend some time and, to the delight of beach lovers, is surrounded by some the best stretches of sand on the coast.

GETTING THERE If you're coming to Amalfi from Positano by land, you'll take the famous Amalfi Drive (see p. 651). But if you're going right to Amalfi from Naples or somewhere else in Italy, you're better off taking the high-speed train to Salerno from Naples (see p. 668) and from there heading

Piazza Duomo in Amalfi.

west up the coast on the **SITA bus** (www.sitabus.it; ✆ **089-405145**). This is a convenient time-saver that eliminates the trip by train to Sorrento and the transfer to the bus for the long trip down the coast road. You can also take the SITA express bus that operates between Naples and Amalfi, though schedules are geared to workers rather than vacationers. Buses to Amalfi operate mornings and late afternoons on some days, but the return bus to Naples from Amalfi travels in the wee hours of the morning.

VISITOR INFORMATION The **tourist office** (www.amalfitouristoffice.it; ✆ **089-871107**) is in Palazzo di Città, Corso delle Repubbliche Marinare 19. It's open Monday to Friday 9am to 1pm and 2 to 6pm, Saturday 9am to noon. It's only open in the mornings in winter.

Exploring Amalfi

Just outside the old town walls, **Piazza Flavio Gioia** opens onto the harbor. It commemorates the local navigator who some say invented the compass around 1300 (a dubious claim, since sailors used rudimentary compasses, likely introduced by Arab navigators, long before). Let's just say he might have perfected the compass for marine use. It is fact that Amalfi sailors provided material for some of the first nautical charts of the Middle Ages and also came up with a maritime code, the **Tavole Amalfitane,** that was followed in the Mediterranean for centuries, with guidelines for everything from terms for haulage to conditions for the crew. This document is on view in the **Arsenale Marinaro** (see below).

That Amalfi was one of the most important ports and maritime powers in the world is illustrated in a tile panel in the Porta Marina, created by artist Renato Rossi in the 1950s, depicting Amalfi's commercial empire in the Middle Ages. Another ceramic piece, just up the Corso delle Repubbliche Marinare, this one from the 1970s, tells more of Amalfi's history, from its founding by Romans to the arrival of St. Andrew's body from Constantinople.

The medieval heart of Amalfi, a maze of covered porticos and narrow streets, stretches from **Piazza Duomo,** a lively cathedral square near the sea, into an increasingly narrow ravine. You can walk the length of town in 10 minutes or so, along Via Amalfi from Piazza Duomo up to the **Paper Museum** (see below). For much of the town's history, Via Amalfi was a rushing stream; you can still hear water gurgling beneath the pavement. To navigate the town as medieval residents once did, follow the **Rua Nova Mercatorum,** a tunnel-like alley that ends in a little piazza with a fountain, Capo di Ciuccio (Donkey's Head), so-called because the hard-working beasts could pause here and dip their muzzles into the cool water. A local family has decorated every inch of the rocky wall behind the basin with a year-round nativity scene.

Lemon tree terraces of Hotel Santa Caterina in Amalfi.

Arsenale Marinaro ★ HISTORIC SITE The Republic of Amalfi's power in the Mediterranean was maintained in this medieval shipyard, where galleys up to 40m (131 ft.) and powered by 120 oarsmen were built. The stone-vaulted boatsheds now house the solid-looking gold coins (*tari*) that Amalfi once minted and the documents with which the republic wielded its considerable legal clout. The spotlight here is on the 66-chapter **Tavole Amalfitane,** a maritime code that more or less established the laws of the high seas from the 13th to 16th centuries. Storms have erased much of the complex, but 10 of 22 piers retain some semblance of their former appearance.

Via Matteo Camera (off Piazza Flavio Gioia). 2€. Easter–Sept daily 9am–8pm.

Duomo ★★ CHURCH This monument to Amalfi's rich past, covered in black-and-white marble and rich mosaics, sits atop a monumental staircase just inland from the sea. The **Cloister of Paradise** (Chiostro del Paradiso) is decidedly Moorish, with a whitewashed quadrangle of interlaced arches and brightly colored geometric mosaics. Amalfi's medieval nobles are entombed in the sarcophagi littered around this exotic enclosure. The **Crypt** houses the remains of St. Andrew, Amalfi's protector saint. It was important for Amalfi to have a famous patron, just as Venice had St. Mark, so soldiers brought the remains of Andrew back from Constantinople at the end of the 4th Crusade, in 1206. Legend has it that Andrew has been working miracles ever since. After the pirate Ariadeno Barbarossa attacked Amalfi in 1544, his fleet was suddenly sunk in a giant sea surge. Andrew's other miraculous presence is in the form of a thick ooze, reverentially called "manna," that appears on this tomb every once in a while. The 18th-century baroque restoration with rich marbles and mundane frescoes is no match for the wonderfully fanciful facade and cloisters or the medieval austerity of an adjacent basilica, now housing a museum of gold chalices and other treasures.

Piazza del Duomo. Duomo: ✆ **089-871059.** Free. Nov–Feb daily 10am–5pm; Mar–Oct 9am–9pm. Museum and cloister: ✆ **089-871324.** 3€.

Museo della Carta (Museum of Paper) ★ HISTORIC SITE Among the many goods Amalfi's sailors and merchants brought back from their voyages was paper, a popular commodity throughout the Middle East that Arab traders had come across in China. From the 13th through the mid-19th centuries, Amalfi was one of Europe's largest exporters of

Evening stroll along Via Amalfi.

paper, produced in factories whose ruins now litter the Valle dei Mulini (Valley of the Mills) at the end of town. Water wheels once powered machines that beat linen, cotton, and hemp into fine parchment. In the remains of one of the once-thriving mills a guide shows off vintage machinery and the paper that is still sold in Amalfi shops. Nearby factories are evocative ruins that you can view from a path through the valley.

Palazzo Pagliara, Via delle Cartiere 24. ✆ **089-8304561.** www.museodellacarta.it. 4€. Nov–Mar Tues–Sun 10am–3pm; Apr–Nov daily 10am–6:30pm.

GETTING ACTIVE

Amalfi's **beaches** are two pebbly strips on either side of the harbor. For a large stretch of sand, take the footpath to **Atrani** (see below), a pretty village 1km (half a mile) along the coast, an easy 15-minute stroll eastward. Or, keep heading east to pretty little workaday **Minori,** surrounded by citrus groves at the mouth of a small stream, 2km (2 miles) east of Atrani. It's not nearly as famous as some of its glitzier neighbors, but little matter—Minori has an asset that's the envy of almost every town on the Amalfi Coast, a long, sandy beach. In fact, only the one in Maiori, separated from Minori by a rocky headland, is longer. SITA buses (www.sitabus.it; ✆ **089-405145**) run regularly to and from Amalfi to both towns.

From the harbor at Amalfi's **Marina Grande** you can rent **boats**—with or without a skipper—to explore the coast. **Cooperativa Sant'Andrea** (www.coopsantandrea.it; ✆ **089-873190**) offers regular service to the beaches of Duoglio and Santa Croce, only a few minutes' away; in summer, boats leave every 30 minutes between 9am and 5pm.

A popular **hike** from Amalfi is the easy walk along **Valle dei Mulini (Valley of the Mills)**. Follow Via Genova from Piazza del Cuomo until it turns into a picturesque trail through lush countryside to the **Mulino Rovinato (Ruined Mill),** about 1 hour away. Flour mills once thrived here, as did the paper mills. If you continue to climb the hill, you'll come to the **Vallone delle Ferriere**, where now-ruined *ferriere* (iron mills) operated into the 19th century. At the top of the valley is a waterfall; allow 2 hours to reach the falls from Amalfi. If you're really ambitious and have another 2 hours, continue from here up to Ravello (see below).

Where to Stay

EXPENSIVE

Hotel Luna Convento ★★ St. Francis himself founded this seaside monastery in 1222. The beautiful cloisters and transformed monks' cells and chapel also have a venerable history of hospitality as one of the first grand hotels on the Amalfi Coast, receiving guests since 1822. Among the famous guests were Norwegian playwright Henrik Ibsen, who wrote *A Doll's House* here in 1879. American playwright Tennessee Williams also spent time here, as did heads of state Otto von Bismarck and Benito Mussolini. Adding even more luster to the storied and atmospheric surroundings are a 15th-century Saracen watchtower, now housing a bar and standing guard over a little private beach and a large seawater pool. Most of the plain-yet-chic guest rooms, many carved out of former monks' cells, have sea views and some have terraces; all are embellished with nice art and antiques to enhance the historic provenance. Lounging in the sunny gardens that once supplied the monks' kitchens is yet another experience to savor at this unusual retreat.

Via Pantaleone Comite 33. www.lunahotel.it. ✆ **089-871002.** 48 units. 250€–340€ double. Rates include breakfast. **Amenities:** 2 restaurants; bar; babysitting; concierge; outdoor pool; room service; Wi-Fi (free).

Hotel Santa Caterina ★★★ One of the world's great getaways provides a stay of a lifetime while making guests feel right at home. Its comfortable yet unpretentious rooms and suites are set in gardens and citrus groves hovering above the water. Colorful Vietri tiles and handsome antiques add notes of elegance, while balconies and terraces make the most of the cliffside location. Glassed-in elevators and a winding garden path descend to a private beach and saltwater swimming pool, and memorable meals are served in a vine-covered, glassed-in dining room or on a seaside terrace. Several private bungalows with private pools tucked into citrus groves provide the ultimate hideaways.

Via Nazionale 9. www.hotelsantacaterina.it. ✆ **089-871012.** 49 units. 315€–770€ double. Rates include breakfast. Closed Nov–Mar. **Amenities:** 2 restaurants; bar; beach; concierge; gym; pool; room service; spa; Wi-Fi (free).

MODERATE

Residenza Luce ★★★ These attractive and comfortable rooms near the town center top the list for an affordable stay in Amalfi. Half of the handsomely decorated, tile-floored units are bilevel, with sleeping lofts tucked above living areas; many have balconies and all have large windows overlooking medieval lanes and squares. A sunny rooftop breakfast room overlooks the surrounding hills, while the beach and port are just steps away.

Via Fra Gerardo Sasso. www.residenzaluce.it. ✆ **089-871537.** 10 units. 90€–140€ double. Rates include breakfast. **Amenities:** Wi-Fi (free).

INEXPENSIVE

Albergo Sant'Andrea ★★ One of the most authentic ways to experience old Amalfi is from these tidy rooms smack dab in the center of town, right across from the Duomo. Views of that magnificent facade are the focal point of some of the guest rooms, while others look out to sea and, some, alas, into alleyways. For guests not looking for luxury, the location, the warm hospitality, immaculate surroundings, and some of the lowest rates on the Amalfi Coast might compensate for old-fashioned rooms that are well-maintained and good-size but decidedly bare bones. Piazza Duomo. www.albergosantandrea.it. ✆ **089-871145.** 8 units. 70€–90€ double. Rates include breakfast. **Amenities:** Wi-Fi (free).

Hotel Lidomare ★ One of Amalfi's few bargains is set on a small square just beyond the main street, providing pleasant, old-fashioned ambience in a 13th-century *palazzo*. You might find the enormous, high-ceilinged, tile-floored guest rooms either charmingly old-fashioned or a bit ramshackle, but many have sea views, and all are furnished with antiques and comfy old furnishings. Amalfi's beach is just steps away. Largo Piccolomini 9. ✆ **089-871332.** 15 units. 90€–145€ double. Rates include breakfast. **Amenities:** Wi-Fi (free).

Where to Eat

Amalfi is well suited to cafe sitting. On Piazza Duomo, the elegant **Bar Francese** (✆ **089-871049**) serves excellent pastries. Another sweet stop on the piazza is **Pasticceria Pansa** (✆ **089-871065;** closed Tues), concocting delicious pastries since 1830; try their *torta caprese* or sticky, lemon-flavored *delizia al limone*. **Gelateria Porto Salvo,** Piazza Duomo 22 (✆ **089-871636;** closed Jan–Mar), is one of the best *gelaterie* on this part of the coast—try the *mandorla candita* (candied almond) flavor. **Gran Caffè di Amalfi,** Corso Repubbliche Marinare (✆ **089-871047**), overlooks the sea, making it a prime spot for an *aperitivo*.

EXPENSIVE

Da Gemma ★ SEAFOOD/AMALFITAN Amalfi's old-time classic, in warm-hued rooms tucked behind the cathedral and in the hands of the Grimaldi family for several generations, holds high standards for the seafood it serves to a loyal and discerning clientele. The house *zuppa di pesce* is a meal in itself, prepared only for two. Equally memorable is the special pasta *paccheri all'acquapazza,* with shrimp and monkfish. The dessert of choice is *crostata* (pie with jam), made with pine nuts and homemade marmalades of lemon, orange, and tangerine. Reservations, especially on weekends, are a must.
Via Frà Gerardo Sasso 11. www.trattoriadagemma.com. ✆ **089-871345.** Main courses 16€–26€. Daily 12:30–2:45pm and 7:30–11pm (closed Wed Nov to mid-Apr). Closed 6 weeks Jan to early Mar.

La Caravella ★★★ MODERN AMALFITAN You'll leave today's world (along with sea views) behind when you step into this 12th-century palazzo in medieval Amalfi. Romantic dining rooms where candlelight plays off stucco walls adorned with patches of colorful frescoes are the

the stage-like setting for some of the best food on the coast, recognized when the restaurant became the first in Italy to win a Michelin star, way back in 1967. Ever since then the *dolce vita* set has made a beeline to the linen-covered tables, where Amalfi classics as simple as *scialatelli alla caravella* (handmade pasta in a tomato-seafood sauce) or *pezzogna* (fresh local fish) are enlivened with local lemons and mountain herbs. Reservations are a good idea, especially in summer, and refined as the food and the setting are, smart informal attire is acceptable; after all, this place is playful enough to embellish its tables with ceramic donkeys.

Via Matteo Camera 12. www.ristorantelacaravella.it. ✆ **089-871029.** Main courses 25€–35€; tasting menu 90€. Wed–Mon noon–2pm and 7:30–11pm. Closed Nov and Jan.

Ristorante Al Mare ★ PIZZA/AMALFITAN The bamboo-roofed, alfresco dining terrace just above the beach at the Santa Caterina Hotel (see above) is an alluring spot for a seaside lunch. The menu offers a nice choice of pizzas, grilled fish, and pastas that include the hotel specialty, *tagilolini limone*, homemade noodles with a lemon cream sauce. Prices aren't exactly in the beach-shack category, but it's hard to beat the magnificent surroundings for a dash of informal glamour.

Via Nazionale 9. www.hotelsantacaterina.it. ✆ **089-871012.** Main courses 20€–35€, pizzas from 20€. May–Oct daily 12:30–3:30pm.

MODERATE

L'Abside ★★ SEAFOOD/AMALFITAN If this charming small place were more formal you could call it a temple of gastronomy, since it occupies part of a former church. As is, the delightful, whitewashed and arched room adds even more charm to a delicious meal (also served on a terrace out front in good weather). Seafood and vegetables are so fresh that even a simple bruschetta with anchovies is memorable, as are the homemade pastas and garden-fresh salads.

Piazza dei Dogi. www.ristorantelabside.it. ✆ **089-873586.** Main courses 9€–20€. Daily 12:30–2:45pm and 7:30–11pm.

Il Tari ★ AMALFITAN/PIZZA The name (after the coin used in the days of the Amalfi Republic) and the setting (an old stable that's nicely done with white walls and colorful artwork) harken back to older times in Amalfi, as does the simple menu of traditional favorites. *Scialatielli* (long, fettuccine-like noodles) comes laden with mussels and other seafood (a trio of pastas with various sauces is served as a starter), and the fish soup with pasta and beans is an old Amalfi recipe. Excellent pizza is served at lunch and dinner, and set menus are a very good value.

Via P. Capuano 9. www.amalfiristorantetari.it. ✆ **089-871832.** Main courses 8€–19€. Wed–Mon noon–2:30pm and 7:30–10:30pm.

Around Amalfi: Atrani ★★

Pretty little Atrani is just 1km (half a mile) east along the coast, an easy 15-minute stroll eastward. Leaving town, follow the sidewalk along the main road until you come to a staircase (signposted for Atrani) up to a path that's really a series of alleyways between hillside houses; it soon drops down to the sea again. From the beach, a maze of vaulted alleys and stepped streets leads through a labyrinth of white houses to **Piazza Umberto I,** where more than a few window boxes put the final flourishes on the charming tableau. M.C. Escher (1898–1972), the Dutch artist who depicted scenes filled with intricate geometric patterns and complex perspective, loved Atrani and sketched it often; looking at the layer upon layer of connected, white-washed houses, it's easy to see why.

By the 12th century, Atrani had bounced back from Vesuvius eruptions and barbarian invasions to become the preferred residence of Amalfi aristocrats. In fact, Amalfi doges were crowned and buried in the 10th-century **church of San Salvatore de Bireto.** Inside, beyond the bronze doors pillaged from Constantinople, a plaque shows off two peacocks, signs of vanity and pride, something the rich little town once had aplenty.

The walk between Amalfi and Atrani is an excellent way to begin and end a meal, especially when the feast is as memorable as that served in **'a Paranza ★★,** Via Dragone 1–2 (www.ristoranteparanza.com. **© 089-871840),** an old-fashioned room off Atrani's main piazza. The antipasti should be part of any meal, from heavenly slices of fresh tuna to stewed octopus to grilled razor clams. Seafood reigns here, but other local favorites include *sarchiapone,* a long gourd stuffed with meat, or *melanzane con la cioccolata*—yes, that's right, eggplant with chocolate, deep fried and topped with walnuts and dried fruit. It's open Wednesday through Monday for lunch and dinner; entrees are 12€ to 23€.

RAVELLO ★★★

7km (4 miles) N of Amalfi

Clinging to a mountainside overlooking the sea, Ravello can seem like a world removed from the clamor down on the coast. This sense of escape, along with views and some of the world's most splendid gardens, has long made this aerie 1,000 feet above the coast a refuge for the rich and famous. Its eclectic group of admirers has included composer Richard Wagner, writers D.H. Lawrence and Gore Vidal, and actress Greta Garbo. Like they did, you'll come here not to do much other than stroll in the gardens, gaze at the coastline, and maybe relax for a few days in one of many villas converted into luxury hotels. Ravello is simply a beautiful, beautiful place, maybe more so than any other town in Italy.

The Wines of Campania

The wines produced in the harsh, hot landscapes of Campania seem stronger, rougher, and, in many cases, more powerful than those grown in gentler climes. Ones to try are *Lacryma Christi* (Tears of Christ), from a white grape that grows in the volcanic soil near Naples, Herculaneum, and Pompeii; *Taurasi*, a potent, full-bodied red also known as *Aglianico*; and *Greco di Tufo*, a pungent white laden with the odors of apricots and apples. *Falanghina*, one of the most popular white wine varieties, is produced from the famed Falernian grapes so favored by the ancient Romans. Another varietal of special interest is fruity *Piedirosso*, a dark red grape that is famously grown on the slopes of Vesuvius and the isle of Capri.

GETTING THERE The most convenient way up to Ravello from Amalfi is the **SITA bus** from Amalfi (www.sitabus.it; ✆ **089-405145**), running about every half hour. If you're driving from Naples or other places off the coast, you can avoid the traffic-choked coast road by taking the A3 to a well-marked exit near Angri then climbing over the mountains from the north on SP2b and SP1 before dropping into Ravello on the Valico di Chiunsi. When arriving by car, you can't go any farther than the large, well-marked public parking lot not far from the Duomo.

VISITOR INFORMATION Ravello's **tourist office,** Via Roma 18 (www.ravellotime.it), is open daily 9am to 7pm (to 6pm Nov–May). The town is largely **pedestrian,** with steep, narrow lanes and many stairs.

Exploring Ravello

The heart of town is **Piazza del Vescovado,** a terrace overlooking the valley of the Dragone, and the adjacent **Piazza del Duomo.** Climb up steep Via Richard Wagner (behind the tourist office) to reach **Via San Giovanni del Toro**, lined with some of Ravello's grandest medieval palaces, built as hilltop retreats for wealthy families of the Amalfi Republic and now housing some of Italy's most distinguished hotels.

Auditorium Niemeyer ★★ LANDMARK Ravello's most controversial landmark is also its newest, inaugurated in 2010 to critical architectural acclaim but the disdain of many residents and visitors. Naysayers find the sweeping, dazzling-white canopied white roof of Brazilian architect Oscar Niemeyer's auditorium sorely out of keeping with Ravello's medieval ambience. It's hard, though, not to admire the way the sinuous curves tuck so naturally into the hillside. And no one can complain about the pleasure of enjoying a concert while viewing the spectacle of sea and sky through the huge eye-shaped window.

Via della Repubblica 12. www.auditoriumoscarniemeyer.it. ✆ **346-737-8561.** Open for concerts and film screenings (check the Tourist Office for events).

Duomo ★★★ CHURCH All the glories of Ravello's past seem to come to the fore in the beautiful cathedral that Orso Papiro, first bishop of Ravello, founded in 1086. The 54 embossed panels of the 12th-century bronze doors, cast in Constantinople, were intended to delight the faithful with stories of Christ's miracles and other familiar Bible stories. Another piece of scripture comes to life in the beautiful mosaics of the **Ambone dell'Epistola ★★★,** a pulpit dating from 1130, which depict the story of Jonah being swallowed by the whale. Opposite is another pulpit resting atop twisting columns that in turn rise out of the backs of two regal-looking lions, with a mighty eagle perched atop the whole affair. Add to that a wonderful collection of Roman sarcophagi and columns, bits of medieval frescoes, and a titled floor that tilts gently toward the entrance, an artful attempt to enhance the perspective and visually enlarge the space. The cathedral's patron is honored in the **Cappella di San Pantaleone.** The physician saint was beheaded in Nicomedia (in present-day Turkey) on July 27, 305, and the blood housed in his reliquary is said to liquefy and come to a boil every year on the anniversary of his death.

Piazza del Vescovado. ✆ **089-85831. Duomo:** Free. Daily 9am–noon and 5:30–7pm. **Museum:** 2€. Summer daily 9am–7pm; winter daily 9am–6pm. Guided tours available.

Museo del Corallo ★ MUSEUM/SHOP For centuries, craftspeople around the Bay of Naples carved precious cameos and other objects out of coral. In fact, the earliest object in this stunning private collection is a 3rd-century-A.D. Roman amphora with a coral formation inside it. The 600 pieces here are the possessions of cameo craftsman Giorgio Filocamo, whose Camo workshops are attached to the museum. That he still toils is a tribute to his love for the art, since his antique pieces, such as a 17th-century coral Christ on the Cross, are coveted by museums around the world. Filocamo has carved cameos for Hilary Clinton, Pope John Paul II, and Princess Caroline of Monaco, and you can pick up one of his creations for yourself in the adjoining shop.

Piazza Duomo 9. www.museodelcorallo.com. ✆ **089-857461.** Free. Mon–Sat 9:30am–noon and 3–5:30pm.

Villa Cimbrone ★★★ GARDEN The Englishman Lord Grimthorpe, a dilettante, gardener, and erstwhile banker, created this grand villa in 1904, embellishing a crumbling 14th-century farmhouse with towers, turrets, and exotic Arabesque details (the villa is now a hotel). The lavish salons and gardens soon became associated with the 20th-century elite, few more elusive than Swedish actress Greta Garbo, who hid out here in 1937—not to be alone, but to be with her lover, the conductor Leopold Stokowski. The high point of the lavish gardens, quite literally, is the

A sweeping view from the Villa Rufolo garden.

Belvedere Cimbrone, where you'll have the dizzying sensation of being suspended between sea and sky. The writer and long-time Ravello resident Gore Vidal, who never really had anything very nice to say about anything or anybody, called the outlook "the most beautiful view in the world."

Via Santa Chiara 26. www.villacimbrone.it. ✆ **089-857459** (for hotel). Villa 6€ adults, 4€ children. Daily 9am–sunset. Last admission 30 min. before close.

Villa Rufolo ★★ GARDEN The 14th-century poet Boccaccio was so moved by this onetime residence of 13th-century merchant prince Landolfo Rufolo that he included it as background in one of his tales. In the mid-19th century, Scotsman Sir Francis Reid transformed the house into an exotic fantasy, with Moorish cloisters surrounded in part by interlacing arcs. The most famous visitor to the palace was Richard Wagner, who composed an act of *Parsifal* here in 1880 and used the surroundings for his *Garden of Klingsor,* home of the Flower Maidens. The Norman tower was renamed Klingsor's Tower in his honor. Paths wind through beds of rare plantings to lookout points high above the coastline, where the surreal scene of sea meeting sky in a wash of blue is as transporting as the house and gardens. The lower garden, known as the Wagner Terrace, is the setting for the **Concerti Wagneriani** during the summer Ravello festival.

Piazza Duomo. www.villarufolo.it. ✆ **089-857621.** 5€. Summer daily 9am–8pm; winter daily 9am–sunset. Last admission 15 min. earlier.

GETTING ACTIVE

Hikers can take heart in the fact that from Ravello it's all downhill—or mostly, since a popular hike is up the **Monastery of Saint Nicholas** at an altitude of 486m (1,594 ft.). From the center of Ravello, take the road to Sambuco for 1km (half a mile) and from there the trail up to the monastery. Plan on 2 hours for the 9km (6-mile) round-trip. Now, the downhill stretch: From the town center, take another footpath—actually, a series of steps and hidden alleys—that descends all the way down to seaside **Minori** (see p. 656). Start from the alley to the left of Villa Rufolo, next to the small fountain. It will take you past the 13th-century Annunziata church, then the church of San Pietro, before you reach the hamlet of Torello. From there the path descends through olive trees to Minori. The hike down takes a half-hour; the return trip double that.

Where to Stay

EXPENSIVE

Palazzo Avino ★★★ A 12th-century patrician palace strikes just the right balance between comfort and opulence, with enough antiques, Vietri ceramic floors, and fine linens to satisfy the most discerning guests. Views extending for miles up and down the coast make the most of Ravello's aerie-like position. They're enjoyed through huge windows in just about every room, on the rooftop terrace with two Jacuzzis, from the sumptuous gardens and pool that cascade partway down the cliff, and from the hotel's double-Michelin-starred, dinner-only **Rossellinis** (see below). A free shuttle takes guests to the **Clubhouse by the Sea** (open May–Sept), the hotel's beach club, with a small outdoor pool, a waterside terrace with lounge chairs and umbrellas, and a **casual restaurant.**

Via San Giovanni del Toro 28, Ravello. www.palazzoavino.com. ✆ **089-818181.** 44 units. 350€–710€ double. Rates include breakfast. Closed mid-Oct to Mar. **Amenities:** Restaurant, bar; concierge; gym; pool; room service; spa; Wi-Fi (free).

Hotel Palumbo ★★★ This popular stop on the 19th-century Grand Tour circuit (and a favorite of many 20th-century celebs) only seems to get better with age, holding its own against much glitzier competitors as a mainstay of old-world refinement. Beyond the bougainvillea-covered entryway is an exotic and rarefied world of columns, arches, exquisitely tiled floors, and finely upholstered, highly buffed furnishings. The ambience extends throughout the 12th-century palazzo and an adjacent annex, and many of the antiques-filled guest rooms open to terraces overlooking the coastline and the hotel's gardens and lemon groves. This isn't a place to pad around in your beach togs, but the nooks and crannies and citrus-scented walkways are such a romantic throwback you'll be happy to dress for the part.

Via San Giovanni del Toro 16. www.hotelpalumbo.it. ✆ **089-857244.** 21 units. 220€–480€ double. Rates include breakfast. Closed Jan and Feb. **Amenities:** Restaurant; bar; pool; Wi-Fi (free).

MODERATE

Hotel Rufolo ★★ Your postcards home might be a little more florid while staying at this ages-old villa in the heart of town, converted to a *pensione* for an arty set more than a century ago. American writer Gore Vidal lived in an adjacent villa at the end of the garden path, and D.H. Lawrence hid away in room 423 while writing *Lady Chatterley's Lover,* leading a monk-like life despite the scenes erupting on his pages. It's hard to live here like a monk these days: Rooms and suites are filled with fine old furnishings set on gleaming Vietri tile floors, a large pool sparkles in the verdant garden, and a hedonistic spa pampers guests. Then, too, of course, there are all those glorious views.

Via San Francesco 1. www.hotelrufolo.com. ✆ **089/857133.** 34 units. 290€–340€. Rates include breakfast. **Amenities:** Restaurant; bar; pool; spa; Wi-Fi (free).

INEXPENSIVE

Hotel Parsifal ★★ A convent-turned-holiday-getaway is hardly a rarity on the Amalfi Coast, but few offer good-value accommodations like these in such charming architectural surroundings. The cloisters, tiled hallways, fish pond, and flower-filled patios still exude a peaceful, contemplative air, just as the original 13th-century residents intended. Whitewashed rooms fashioned from the former monks' cells are plain and frugal enough to suit their former inhabitants and the slightly rickety, old-fashioned ambience is embellished with colorful tile floors and, from some rooms, sensational sea views. Meals in the friendly sea-view dining room may well remind you of the days when rooms came with board, an experience you may or may not care to relive.

Via Gioacchino D'Anna. www.hotelparsifal.com. ✆ **089-857144.** 17 units. 135€–210€ double. Rates include breakfast. **Amenities:** Restaurant; bar; concierge; Wi-Fi (free).

Where to Eat

EXPENSIVE

Rossellinis ★★★ CREATIVE AMALFITAN Meals in this elegant dining room and view-filled terrace come with credentials—two Michelin stars and a reputation as one of Italy's best. What might come as a surprise is an ambience that's not informal but far from stuffy—a sense that with food this good and prices this high, no one needs to be anything other than comfortable. Service is impeccable; the staff will gladly lead diners through Chef Mario Deleo's creative takes on local cuisine, infused with extra passion since he's from the region. Even the bread, with ham baked into it, is exceptional, as are such sublime creations as ravioli stuffed with squid or cod in an olive crust. Meals are paired with local wines and followed with mountain cheeses and sweets that, like everything else, are satisfying without being overwhelming.

Via San Giovanni del Toro 28 (in the Palazzo Avino, p. 664). www.palazzosasso.com. ✆ **089-818181.** Main courses 28€–32€; tasting menus from 120€. Daily 7:30–11pm. Closed Nov–Mar.

MODERATE

Cumpa' Cosimo ★★ AMALFITAN Netta Bottone runs the restaurant her family started back in 1929, serving generous portions of pastas (including an extravaganza with seven types of noodles topped with seven different sauces) and big platters of *frittura di pesce* (fish fry) and some very well-done lamb and veal dishes (Netta also runs the butcher shop next door). Artichokes and other vegetables are right out of nearby garden plots. Whatever you order, Netta herself may well serve it with a flourish and a kiss on the cheek.

Via Roma 44. ✆ **089-857156.** Main courses 11€–18€; pizza 6€–10€. Daily 12:30–3pm and 7:30–11pm. Closed Mon Nov–Feb.

INEXPENSIVE

Da Nino ★★ AMALFITAN/PIZZA Lemon groves and vineyards have long occupied the residents of **Tramonti,** about 12km (8 miles) inland from Ravello, and in their spare time they invented pizza—a claim that's shared by many others, for sure. But the pizzas here, once baked in communal bread ovens, are undeniably delicious and make the little village a bit of a culinary outpost. Local nuns added to the offerings when they came up with ***concierto,*** a bitter-sweet digestive liquor concocted from nine different mountain herbs and spices. You can try these local specialties at "Ninuccio" (little Nino). Whole-wheat crusts are topped for the most part with ingredients from the owners' farm, or at least from their neighbors. The salami and mozzarella are homemade, vegetables are homegrown, olive oil is from local groves, and the bread is oven-fresh.

Via Pucara 39, Tramonti. ✆ **089-855407.** Main courses 8€–15€; pizza from 7€. Wed–Mon noon–3:30pm and 7:30–11pm (also Tues in summer).

Pizzeria Vittoria ★★ PIZZA/AMALFITAN It's refreshing to know that life in Ravello can come down to earth, too, as it does in this friendly pizzeria near the Duomo. Thin-crust pies with a huge variety of toppings are the draw; even the classic Margherita seems like perfection, given that everything is fresh—tomatoes and basil from the garden, mozzarella from nearby farms, herbs from the mountains. Some simple pasta dishes are similarly delicious. The tile-floored rooms can be packed, even at lunch, so plan on eating early or late.

Via dei Rufolo 3. www.ristorantepizzeriavittoria.it. ✆ **089-857947.** Main courses 10€–15€. Daily 12:30–3pm and 7:30–10pm. Closed Nov–Mar.

Shopping

In addition to the cameo handiwork that might tempt you at the **Camo** workshops at the Museo del Corallo (see above), you'll encounter some beautiful ceramics at **Ceramiche d'Arte Carmella,** Via die Rufolo 16 (www.ceramichedartecarmela.com; ✆ **089-857303**). Many of the pieces are from Vietri down the coast, though works by other

Beautiful ceramics in Ravello.

local ceramicists are also on display. **Profumi della Costiera,** Via Trinita 37 (www.profumidellacostiera.it; ✆ **089-858167**), carries a remarkable selection of limoncello and other sweet liqueurs, while the in-town outlet of 150-year-old **Episcopio Winery,** operated by the Palumbo family, is in the Hotel Palumbo at Via Giovanni a Toro 16 (✆ **089-857244**).

Nightlife

Ravello's otherwise staid entertainment scene ramps up considerably in the summer, when the town hosts the internationally famous **Festival di Ravello** (www.ravellofestival.com; ✆ **089-858422**) from July through September. The focus is on classical music and includes the concerts of the **Festival Musicale Wagneriano,** held in July in the garden of **Villa Rufolo ★★**. Tickets run from 15€ to 130€.

THE RUINS OF PAESTUM ★★★

35km (22 miles) S of Salerno; 100km (62 miles) SE of Naples

South of Salerno, soaring seaside cliffs and forested mountains give way to a wide, flat agricultural plain. As uninspiring as the dull, grassy landscapes might seem, rising from them is an amazingly dramatic sight: three honey-colored temples, some of the best-preserved remains of the ancient world. The scene is especially lovely in spring and early summer, when poppies and wildflowers surround the ruins. Adding to a sense of timelessness is the presence of Italian water buffalo that have grazed the low-lying grasslands for the past 1,000 years or so. The huge, sluggish beasts are not only tried-and-true draught animals but also produce the milk that yields the region's deliciously creamy *mozzarella di bufala*.

Essentials

GETTING THERE **Trains** stop at two stations near the ruins: **Capaccio-Roccadaspide** and **Paestum,** only 5 minutes from each other. Either station is only about a 10- to 15-minute walk from the archaeological area, with Paestum being the more convenient. Via Porta Sirena leads from Paestum train station to Via Magna Grecia, which cuts through the middle of the archaeological site. The trip to either is about 30 minutes from Salerno and 90 minutes from Naples, though you can shorten the journey from Naples by taking the high-speed train to Salerno and connecting to the local train there. Contact **Trenitalia** (www.trenitalia.it; ✆ **892021** in Italy) for fares and information.

Paestum is well-connected to Salerno by **bus. BusItalia Campania** (www.fsbusitaliacampania.it; ✆ **089-252228** or 800-016659 toll-free within Italy) has regular service to Paestum from Naples and Salerno (both line 34), with both lines continuing on to Agropoli and Acciaroli, in the Cilento. **SITA** (www.sitabus.it; ✆ **089-405145**) runs from Salerno to Capaccio Scalo and Paestum; and **Autolinee Giuliano Bus** (www.giulianobus.com; ✆ **0974-836185**) has several lines between Naples, Salerno, and the Cilento, making stops in Paestum and Capaccio Scalo (lines 3, 4, 5, 6, 7, and 10).

By **car,** take autostrada A3, exit at battipaglia onto SS 18, and follow the brown signs for Paestum.

VISITOR INFORMATION You'll find a **tourist office** (www.infopaestum.it; ✆ **0828-811016**) at Via Magna Grecia 151, by the Archaeological Museum, near the entrance to the temples (daily 9am–1pm and 2–4pm).

Exploring the Ruins

While the forum and other parts of the town have been reduced to rubble, Paestum's three magnificent temples, excavated around 1750, are remarkably intact. So are parts of the circuit of massive defensive walls, 5m (16½ ft.) thick on average, 15m (50 ft.) high, and 4,750m (15,584 ft.) in length, with 24 square and round towers along their length. At the monumental western gate, **Porta Marina,** you can climb the walls and walk on the patrol paths, enjoying excellent views over the ruins and coast. Wear comfortable shoes and bring a hat and water. Allow at least an hour to see the temples and another hour for the museum (see below).

Archaeological Area of Paestum ★★★ The enclosed site contains the three temples (all built facing east) and a number of other ruins that were part of the sacred area at the center of the ancient Greek town. The **Via Sacra (Sacred Street)** runs arrow straight through the length of the site, connecting all three temples, its Roman pavement laid over the original Greek road. When it was built, the road continued for about 12km (7½ miles) to connect the Greek town of Poseidonia with the Sanctuary of Hera on the coast.

Tempio di Hera (Temple of Hera) ★★★ The oldest of Paestum's temples was built in 550 B.C. with a massive portico that's still supported by 50 columns. Worshippers attended rites in front, gathering around a partially ruined sacrificial altar and a square *bothros*, a sacrificial well where the remains were thrown. The temple is believed to have been part of a huge complex dedicated to Hera, wife and sister of Zeus and the goddess of fertility and maternity.

Tempio di Nettuno (Temple of Neptune) ★★★ The best example of a Doric temple in the world dates from around 450 B.C. and is lined in travertine stone that glows a magical gold hue when hit by the sun's rays. Perfect proportions lend a slender elegance, while thick, closely spaced columns give the temple a muscularity. It's the best preserved of Paestum's temples: only the roof and internal walls are missing. In front are two sacrificial altars; the smaller one is a Roman addition from the 3rd century B.C.

Tempio di Cerere (Temple of Ceres) ★★ The smallest of the three temples, at the northern end of the sight, was built at the end of the 6th century B.C., probably in honor of the Goddess Athena. Under the Romans it was dedicated to Ceres, their goddess of agriculture and fertility, and Christian tombs in the portico suggest later use as a church. Main entrance Via Magna Grecia 917; secondary entrance Porta della Giustizia (Justice Gate, off Via Nettuno; for ticket holders only). www.infopaestum.it. ✆ **0828-721113.** 9€. Daily 8:30am–7:30pm (last entry 60 min. earlier); closed 1st and 3rd Mon of month.

National Archaeological Museum of Paestum ★★ MUSEUM Star of the show among the artifacts from centuries of excavations is the sole figure of a young man taking a swan dive into a rushing stream from the so-called Tomb of the Diver, probably dating to around 470 B.C. The meaning of the simple, powerful image has long been the subject of debate, though the most reassuring suggestion is that the fellow is graciously making the transition from earth into the other world. The young man was clearly an athletic sort—flasks filled with the oil he used to prepare himself for wrestling matches were found next to a skeleton assumed to be his. Four other frescoes from the same tomb complex depict scenes of a symposium—more or less a drinking bash—probably to give the deceased a good send-off. These images are unique, the only tomb frescoes from the ancient period that depict human figures.

A frieze from the Sanctuary of Hera (see below) gives a close-up look at some of the mythological scenes that would have delighted a 6th-century-B.C. audience, such as the story of Hercules and the Kerkopes. As legend has it, the hero had fallen asleep when these two scamps snuck up and stole his weapons. Hercules awoke, captured the miscreants, and tied them upside down to a pole that he carried over his shoulder. The Kerkopes started laughing and Hercules demanded to know why. They told him they were laughing at his hairy backside, so he started laughing, and set the boys free (Zeus was less amused by their antics and later turned them into monkeys). Another delightful scene depicts two lithe and gleeful maidens running, their finely sculpted robes flowing around them—the joy of these images suggests just how light-hearted ancient Greek religion could be.

Via Magna Grecia 918 (across from the entrance to the temples). ✆ **0828-811023.** Included with admission to temples. Daily 8:30am–7:30pm (last entry 60 min. earlier). Closed 1st and 3rd Mon of month.

CAPRI ★★★

5km (3 miles) off the tip of the Sorrentine peninsula

Rugged, mountainous Capri (pronounced *Cap*-ry, not Ca-*pree*), just off the tip of the Sorrentine Peninsula, is one of the most glamorous and beautiful islands in the world. The legend-steeped, gossip-soaked out-cropping of limestone, a mere 4 square miles in size, has beguiled a long list of admirers. Emperor Tiberius ruled the Roman Empire from these pine- and rosemary-scented cliffs, and Russian novelist Maxim Gorky exiled himself to the island from 1906 to 1913. British music-hall star Gracie Fields used to belt out tunes for the likes of Maria Callas and Liz Taylor at her seaside hideaway on Marina Piccola. Poets Pablo Neruda and Rainer Maria Rilke took inspiration from the magical landscapes. The island is still a magnet for the rich, the famous, artists, eccentrics, and mostly, just plain folks. All delight in the same pleasures: stark-white villas; garden walls dripping with bougainvillea and hibiscus; azure seas lapping rugged coasts; a chorus of birdsong and a heady taste of the good life. The emperor Augustus was on to something when he called the island Apragopolis, or City of Sweet Idleness.

Crowd Control

Whether or not Capri's beauty will transcend the tourist crowds for you depends on your tolerance levels and when you come. Avoid summer weekends especially, when Neapolitans visit for the day and bronzed sun worshippers arrive from as far away as Rome. Actually, to enjoy the island at its best, you might want to forgo a summertime visit altogether and visit in spring or early fall. Note that the island shuts down almost entirely from November to May.

Essentials

GETTING THERE You can easily reach Capri from either Naples or Sorrento, and in summer there's also regular ferry service from Amalfi and Positano. Don't let the profusion of companies confuse you: At tourist

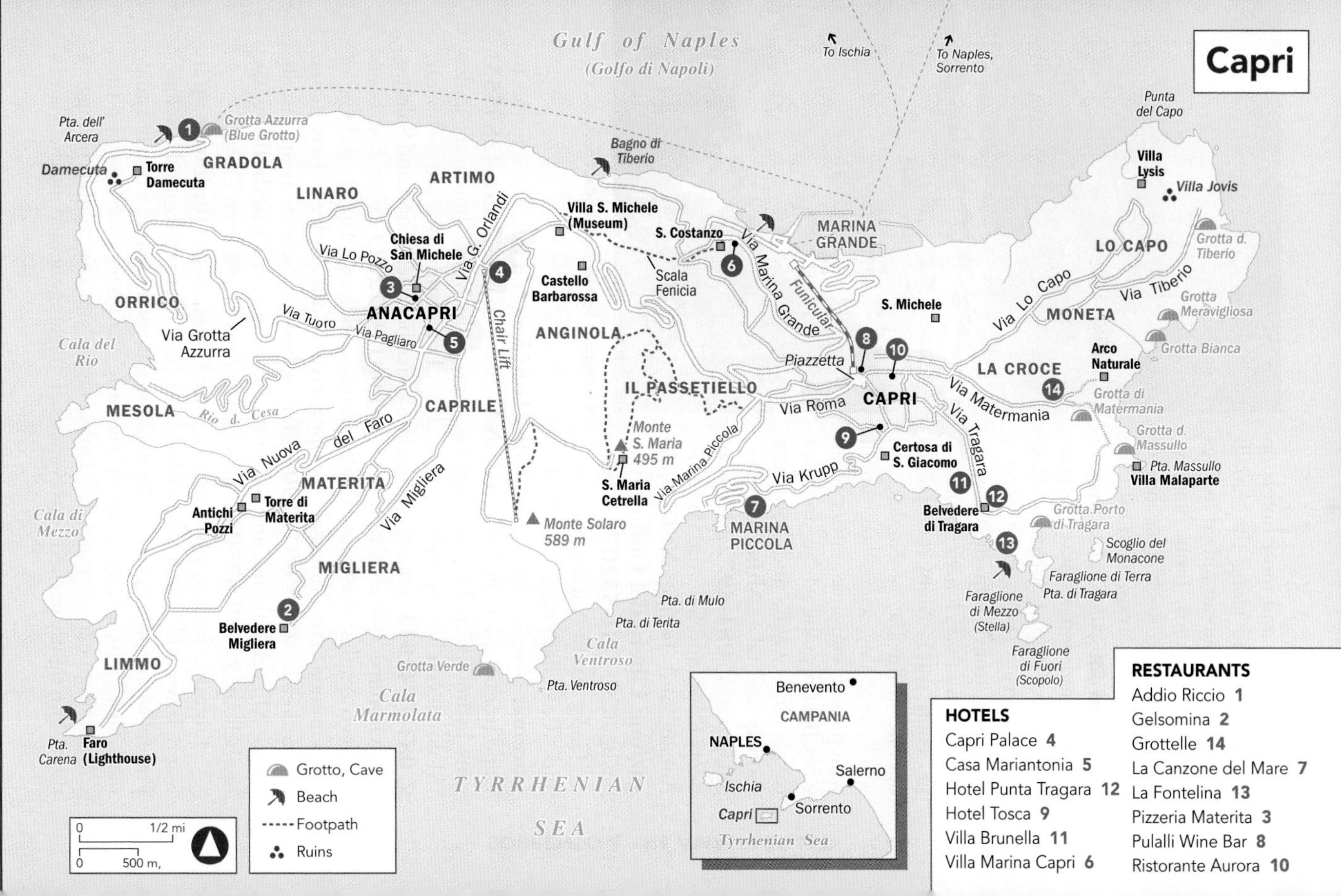

Capri
Gulf of Naples
(Golfo di Napoli)
To Ischia
To Naples, Sorrento
Punta del Capo
Pta. dell' Arcera
Grotta Azzurra (Blue Grotto)
Damecuta
Torre Damecuta
GRADOLA
LINARO
ARTIMO
Bagno di Tiberio
Villa Lysis
Villa Jovis
Villa S. Michele (Museum)
S. Costanzo
MARINA GRANDE
LO CAPO
Grotta d. Tiberio
Chiesa di San Michele
Via Lo Pozzo
Via G. Orlandi
Castello Barbarossa
Scala Fenicia
Via Marina Grande
Funicular
Via Tiberio
Via Lo Capo
Grotta Meravigliosa
ORRICO
Via Tuoro
ANACAPRI
Via Pagliaro
Chair Lift
S. Michele
MONETA
Via Grotta Azzurra
ANGINOLA
Arco Naturale
Grotta Bianca
Cala del Rio
Piazzetta
LA CROCE
IL PASSETIELLO
CAPRI
Grotta di Matermania
MESOLA
Rio d. Cesa
CAPRILE
Via Roma
Via Matermania
Via Tragara
Grotta d. Massullo
Via del Faro
Monte S. Maria 495 m
Certosa di S. Giacomo
Pta. Massullo
Villa Malaparte
Via Nuova
Via Marina Piccola
Via Krupp
MATERITA
Via Migliera
S. Maria Cetrella
Antichi Pozzi
Torre di Materita
Cala di Mezzo
Monte Solaro 589 m
MARINA PICCOLA
Belvedere di Tragara
Grotta Porto di Tragara
Scoglio del Monacone
MIGLIERA
Faraglione di Terra
Pta. di Tragara
Faraglione di Mezzo (Stella)
Pta. di Mulo
Pta. di Terita
Belvedere Migliera
Cala Ventroso
Faraglione di Fuori (Scopolo)
LIMMO
Grotta Verde
Pta. Ventroso
Cala Marmolata
Pta. Carena
Faro (Lighthouse)
Grotto, Cave
Beach
Footpath
Ruins
TYRRHENIAN SEA
0 1/2 mi
0 500 m,
Benevento
CAMPANIA
NAPLES
Salerno
Ischia
Sorrento
Capri
Tyrrhenian Sea
HOTELS
Capri Palace 4
Casa Mariantonia 5
Hotel Punta Tragara 12
Hotel Tosca 9
Villa Brunella 11
Villa Marina Capri 6
RESTAURANTS
Addio Riccio 1
Gelsomina 2
Grottelle 14
La Canzone del Mare 7
La Fontelina 13
Pizzeria Materita 3
Pulalli Wine Bar 8
Ristorante Aurora 10

offices, docks, and most hotels on the islands and along the Amalfi Coast you'll find simplified listings of ferry schedules. From Naples's Molo Beverello dock (take bus or taxi from the train station), the **hydrofoil** *(aliscafo)* takes just 45 minutes and departs several times daily (some stop at Sorrento). Regular **ferry** *(traghetto)* service departing from Porta di Massa is cheaper but takes longer (about 1½ hr. each way). Many companies operate in the Bay of Naples, and you'll probably care less about which one you use rather than what boat is going where you want to get and when, and how long the trip will take. **Alilauro** (www.alilauro.it; ✆ **081-4972222**) connects Capri and Salerno, Positano, Amalfi, and Ischia; **NLG-Navigazione Libera del Golfo** (www.navlib.it; ✆ **081-5520763**) runs to Capri from Naples, Sorrento, and Castellammare di Stabia. **Caremar** (www.caremar.it; ✆ **199-116655** within Italy) runs ferries to Capri from Naples and Sorrento; **SNAV** (www.snav.it; ✆ **081-4285555**) runs hydrofoils and catamarans to Capri from Mergellina and Naples (Molo Beverello) as well as to Ischia; **Travelmar** (www.travelmar.it; ✆ **081-7041911**) maintains regular service between Capri and Salerno; **Volaviamare** (www.volaviamare.it; ✆ **081-4972211**) runs fast boats between Naples, Sorrento, Amalfi, Positano, Salerno, Ischia, and Capri. In summer, Amalfi-based **Cooperativa Sant'Andrea** (www.coopsantandrea.it; ✆ **089-873190**) offers scheduled service from Amalfi, Capri, Minori, Salerno, and Sorrento; Positano-based **Lucibello** (www.lucibello.it; ✆ **089-875032**) also makes runs to and from Capri.

Beachgoers by Marina Grande, Capri.

From the harbor, you can take a **taxi, bus,** or the **funicular** up to Capri Town and bus or taxi to Anacapri (see "Getting Around," below). Porters will approach you at the dock, and if you're taking a bus or funicular, *don't be in a hurry to shoo them away.* Turn over your bags and they will soon appear in your hotel lobby, saving you the trouble of lugging them onto tightly packed conveyances or dragging them along the island's pedestrian-only lanes. These fellows are trustworthy, and the charge is well worth the 6€ to 8€ per piece of luggage (depending on size).

GETTING AROUND The island is serviced by funiculars, taxis, and buses. From the ferry dock in Marina Grande, take the funicular or a bus to **Capri Town** (1.80€ for either, buy tickets at the office near the funicular terminal, from newsstands or tobacco shops, or from the driver). A day pass for 7€ is valid for two funicular rides and unlimited bus service on the island. Buses also run between Capri and **Anacapri** about every 15 minutes throughout the day.

If you wish to explore further, there's a chair lift from Anacapri to the top of Monte Solaro (see below), and buses run between Anacapri and the Faro (lighthouse) at the far southwestern tip of the island or the Grotto Azzurra, on the northwestern coast.

The **funicolare,** run by **SIPPIC** (✆ **081-8370420**), is the picturesque means of transportation between Marina Grande—where the ferry and hydrofoil landings are—and the town of Capri, where it arrives in the heart of town, off Piazza Umberto I. Funiculars leave about every 15 minutes for the 5-minute ride.

The public **bus** system is excellent, but in high season, a ride in one of these diminutive vehicles can feel like being in the proverbial sardine can. **ATC** (part of SIPPIC, above) offers service between Marina Grande, Capri, Marina Piccola, and Anacapri, while **Staiano Autotrasporti** (www.staianogroup.it; ✆ **081-8372422**) offers service between Anacapri, Faro (Lighthouse), and Grotta Azzurra.

Taxis, usually readily available at the port and at taxi stands outside the towns, are expensive but a welcome alternative when you encounter long lines to board buses and the funicular. Taxi fares are about 15€ for the short ride from the port up to Capri; 15€ between Capri and Anacapri; and 20€ between Marina Grande and Anacapri. There are supplements for baggage (2€ per piece) and nighttime services.

Even when traveling by bus or the funicular, wear comfortable shoes. You'll do a lot of walking on Capri, where all but a few main roads are closed to cars. You can be environmentally friendly and patronize **Rent an Electric Scooter,** Via Roma 68 (✆ **081-8375863**), while gas-powered scooters are available from such outlets as **Antonio Alfano,** with two locations: Via Marina Grande 280 (✆ **081-8377941**) and Piazza Barile 26, Anacapri (✆ **081-8373888**).

VISITOR INFORMATION The **tourist office** is in Capri town on Piazzetta Italo Cerio (www.capritourism.com; ✆ **081-8375308**). April to October, it's open Monday to Saturday 8:30am to 8:30pm, Sunday 8:30am to 2:30pm; November to March, hours are Monday to Saturday 9am to 1pm and 3:30 to 6:30pm.

Exploring Capri

You'll soon discover that life on the island, quite literally, has its ups and down. From Marina Grande, the main harbor, you'll go up, via road or funicular, to Capri Town. The white houses of the island's main settlement rise and dip across hilly terrain on a saddle between the twin peaks of Monte Tiberio and Monte Solaro. Anacapri, the island's other town, is even higher, tucked onto the slopes of Monte Solaro. Getting down to the sea from these towns, and elsewhere on the island, often means descending the formidable, grotto-laced cliffs that ring the shoreline. More often than not you do so via paths and steps, hundreds of them, that often lead to viewpoints where you can catch your breath and take in views. The easiest, and often only, way to get around is on foot, and it would be hard to find a more inviting place on the planet to walk.

Capri Town ★★

Most visitors approach Capri's mountainside main town on the funicular railway that climbs steep slopes just behind the harbor. A traffic-choked road also makes the ascent, as does a footpath for the hearty. However you make the climb, as soon as you step into the enticing warren of narrow lanes lined with walled villa gardens you'll realize you're in a rather exotic place that's lofty in more ways than one. Town life radiates from the **Piazzetta,** a small square that at times is so full of visitors that it's called the "world's living room." While the crowd of Gucci-dressed beauties and swarthy Lotharios suggest a certain "see and be seen" glamour, the little square's **Palazzo Cerio** is sturdily medieval and the **Museo Caprense Ignazio Cerio** inside is decidedly down to earth, housing the island's repository of archaeological and geological finds (see below). Overlooking the scene is the pleasantly plain **Torre dell'Orologio,** rising above the old city gateway, and tucked next to it is the homey **church of Santo Stefano.**

If the square's collection of celebrities, jetsetters, obscure royals, and many pretenders starts to get on your nerves, remember that the island has attracted a jaded set

Dining alfresco in Capri Town.

for centuries. Early-20th-century novelist D.H. Lawrence grumpily referred to Capri as "a gossipy, villa-stricken, two-humped chunk of limestone, a microcosm that does heaven much credit, but mankind none at all." You might also want to remember that not too many centuries ago the hilly uplands that cradle the pretty white town were grazing land for the goats, *caprerae,* which gave the island its name.

It's easy to escape the fray, even in busy Capri Town. From the Piazzetta the old town's narrow streets lead west past glittering shops along vista-filled, pine-scented walkways to the more sedate **Certosa di San Giacomo** (see below). Just beyond are the **Giardini di Augusto ★★,** terraced public gardens that overlook the sea with panoramic views toward Monte Solaro, the Faraglioni, and Marina Piccola. German steel manufacturer and longtime visitor Friedrich Alfred Krupp (1854–1902) laid out the gardens to show off the island's rich flora. An unexpected presence amid the flowerbeds and viewpoints is that of Vladimir Lenin (1870–1924), the first leader of the Soviet Union. In 1908 the great revolutionary stayed on Capri as a guest of Russian writer Maxim Gorky, who lived here from 1906 to 1913. Gorky, a novelist and political activist, began his *Encyclopedia of Russian History* on the island and was living in the villa opposite the gardens, now the Villa Krupp hotel.

Certosa di San Giacomo ★ RELIGIOUS SITE The island's most imposing architectural landmark is this monastery. It was built by Count Giacomo Arcucci in the 14th century as a place to retire from the world. Arcucci's former employer, Queen Joanna I of Naples, provided the prime parcel of land and the funds. The count managed to remain on the good side of the queen, who was adept at political intrigue and whose husbands and lovers had a way of meeting grisly ends. Arcucci became a Carthusian monk, ending his days in solitary contemplation. The monks were not popular with the islanders, whose hunting and grazing lands the community confiscated, then added insult to injury by taxing them for ongoing improvements to the monastery. Things came to a nasty head when the brothers locked out islanders who showed up at their gates seeking refuge from the plague of 1653. The suffering populace retaliated by throwing the corpses of the victims over the monastery walls.

Ironically, the complex, perched poetically above the sea, is quite community-oriented these days, housing the island's public library and a high school. The cloisters are the evocative settings for concerts, and the garden that looks out into azure infinity is a favorite spot for romantic tête-à-têtes. The quirky **Museo Diefenbach** shows the works of painter Karl Wilhelm Diefenbach, an advocate of peace, free love, and nudism who lived on Capri from 1900 to 1913. He was a bit of an attraction himself, walking the paths barefoot in a white robe, his long gray hair flowing behind him.

Via Certosa. ✆ **081-8376218.** 4€. Tues–Sun, May 10am–6pm, June–Aug 10am–7pm, Sept–Oct 10am–5pm, and Nov–Dec 9am–2pm.

Villa Jovis ★★ ARCHAEOLOGICAL SITE From Capri Town, a comfortable 45-minute stroll of about 2.4km (1½ miles) ends with a steep climb to the northeastern tip of the island and the most sumptuous and best-preserved of the 12 villas the Roman emperor Tiberius (ruled 14 to 37 A.D.) built on Capri. The emperor spent the final 10 years of his reign on the island, partly because he was fond of the scenery and the views, but also because the sheer waterside cliffs and few closely guarded harbors made the island unassailable to assassins—an antidote to his increasing paranoia. Even then, the emperor had his bread imported from Positano, afraid the islanders would poison him. He installed elaborate baths, forcing his architects to adapt to the mountaintop location by devising an ingenious way to collect rainwater. Eight levels of walls and many staircases remain to suggest the size of the villa, probably covering about 1½ acres, with vast terraces and floors of reception halls and living quarters clinging to the craggy summit of Monte Tiberio. The covered Loggia Imperiale follows the cliff edge to the Salto di Tiberio, a 330m-high (1,083-ft.) precipice from which it's been said Tiberius used to hurl lovers who had fallen out of favor with him. Even his contemporaries fueled what's now believed to be nothing more than gossip. Take your mind off the grisly details to enjoy the views across the island and over the straits to the Sorrentine Peninsula.

Via Tiberio. www.capri.net. 2€. April–Oct, Wed–Mon 9am–6pm and Nov–Mar, Wed–Mon 10am–2pm.

Villa Lysis ★ ARCHITECTURAL SIGHT Of the many eccentric foreigners who have sought refuge on Capri, Baron Jacques d'Adelsward-Fersen (1880–1923) might be the most colorful character of all. When a scandal involving French schoolboys (and a subsequent prison stint) forced the dissolute baron to leave France in 1905, he came to Capri with his lover, the famous young Roman model of erotic photographers, Nino Cesarini. The house Fersen built on the heights just below Villa Jovis is a neoclassic fantasy of marble, columns, tilework, and gilt mosaics, with a motto etched in stone above the entrance proclaiming the premises to be a "shrine to love and sorrow." Lysis, from the Socratic dialogues, is a reference to homosexual love. The furnishings have long since been removed, but the blue-and-white majolica-tile lounge, the huge bedroom with three windows facing the Bay of Naples and three facing Monte Tiberio, and the many terraces all suggest that Fersen drowned his sorrows in the good life. And more than that: In the Chinese room in the basement, specially built for smoking opium, he succumbed to an overdose of cocaine while sipping Champagne.

Via Lo Capo. www.cittadicapri.it. ✆ **081-838-6111.** 2€. May, Sept, and Oct Thurs–Tues 10am–6pm; June–Aug Thurs–Tues 10am–7pm; Nov–Dec Thurs–Tues 10am–4pm.

MARINA PICCOLA ★★

The island's largest beach, on the southern shore, is nothing much, just a pebbly strip tucked picturesquely amid the rocky shorelines, but the water is clean and crystal clear. The pretty cove has been a focus of island life since the Romans harbored their boats here. In recent centuries fishermen have been sharing the space with visiting glitterati, who frequent the many little bathing establishments perched on the rocks to swim and lounge in the sun, but mostly just to be part of the island's social scene. Even the most jaded beachgoers can't help but to admire the views of the famous **Faraglioni,** three rock stacks jutting out of the sea nearby (see below). It's said that the outcropping that divides Marina Piccola neatly into halves is the very rock from which the Sirens tried to lure Ulysses and his crew onto the shoals and wreck their ships. That's a lot of mumbo-jumbo, of course, but the story adds even more romance to an already idyllic setting.

While buses make frequent runs between Capri Town and Marina Piccola, the classic approach is on Via Krupp, a steep path that descends the cliffs in a series of giddy switchbacks from the Gardens of Augustus at Capri Town. Friedrich Alfred Krupp had the walkway built at the turn of the 20th century so he could easily travel between his two yachts at Marina Piccola and his suite at the Quisisana Hotel in Capri Town. When word leaked out that Krupp also used the path to access the notorious Grotta di Fra Felice, a cave at the base of the cliff where gentlemen met to enjoy the sexual favors of island youth, he was eventually forced to leave Italy, and he committed suicide soon after. Falling rocks can render passage unsafe and the path is often closed for repairs.

Faraglioni ★★★ NATURAL WONDER Among Italy's most famous natural sights are these three rock stacks rising as high as 100m (330 ft.) from the sea off the island's southeastern coast. The outermost rock is home to a type of bright blue lizard, the *Podarcis sicula coerulea*, found nowhere else on the planet. It's believed that the blue color serves as camouflage that allows the little reptiles to blend in with the surrounding sky and water. Records suggest that ancient Roman aristocrats imported the colorful creatures from Greece to brighten up their island gardens. The middle stack, Faraglione di Mezzo, is punctured with a poetic little archway where waves have worn away part of the base. It's a popular game for anyone at the helm of a boat to navigate the opening. A shale ledge connects the rock closest to shore, Stella, to the island, and the base shelters two famous beaches with bathing establishments, La Fontelina and Da Luigi. Boats ferry customers back and forth to Marina Piccola, but a far more sporting way to reach the base of the rocks is on the hundreds of steps that descend from Punta Tragara.

PUNTA TRAGARA ★★★

Just 10 minutes beyond the Piazzetta, on pine-shaded paths, is a world far removed from the clamor and bling. The island's most dazzling walks are along this stretch of coastline on Via Tragara and its eastward continuation, Via Pizzolungo, skirting lush vegetation on the top of the cliffs and affording glimpses of spectacular seascapes through the trees. The enchanting paths intersect at the Punta Tragara lookout, a perch high above the sea and the Faraglioni. Among those who admired the views was poet-in-exile Pablo Neruda, who in 1953 stayed in a villa on Via Tragara as a guest of Edwin Cerio (see Museo Caprense Ignazio Cerio, above). Steps leading down to the Faraglioni from the viewpoint are informally known as the Neruda path; a plaque honors the poet at the top.

Isolated beyond Via Tragara atop Punta Massullo is Casa Malaparte, a boxlike villa that seems to grow out of the rock, with steps in the shape of an inverted pyramid leading to a rooftop terrace. It's the creation of freethinking, outspoken Curzio Malaparte, who curried favor with Fascists, communists, and even Italy's Allied liberators during the 1930s and WWII years. The house, still vilified by islanders for its harsh intrusion on protected lands, is the star of Jean-Luc Goddard's 1963 film *Contempt*. Its cold, vast spaces and vertigo-inducing perch high above the sea reflect the estrangement and sense of looming disaster between the couple, played by Brigitte Bardot and Michele Piccoli. The film might afford your only look at the interior; the house is now owned by the Ronchi Foundation and is open only occasionally for cultural events.

BLUE GROTTO (GROTTA AZZURRA) ★★★

Italy's tourist-trap extraordinaire can be beguiling, despite all the hassle a visit entails—the frenzy of climbing off a motorboat into a small rowboat, waiting for your turn to be rowed in, lying back, squeezing through a narrow opening, and being rowed out again just as you are beginning to enjoy the experience. The magical colors of the water and walls of this huge grotto are extraordinary, even more so than they appear in countless photographs. Little wonder that postcard writers have rhapsodized about the cave since it became part of the tourist circuit in the 19th century. (Actually, a small, ancient Roman dock and some statues retrieved from the seafloor suggest this outlet of a vast system of shoreline caverns was known long before then.) It's open daily 9am to 5pm. In summer, boats leave frequently from the harbor at Marina Grande, transporting passengers to the grotto's entrance for 17€ round-trip (that includes the fee for the rowboat that takes you inside). If you get to the entrance to the Blue Grotto under your own steam (via bus from Anacapri), you'll still pay 14€ to be rowed in. The boat trip out from Marina Grande is well worth the few extra euros, delivering sea-level views of the island's spectacular cliffs and rugged shoreline.

Anacapri ★★★

Capri's second town, perched on heights surrounded by vineyards, is a pleasant place where, once away from the main square, life transpires like you might have hoped it would on a small island in the Mediterranean. Your impression, as you arrive at the main squares, Piazza Monumentale and Piazza Vittoria, might be otherwise. This is where crowds gather to board buses down to the Blue Grotto, get onto the chairlift to be whisked up Monte Solaro, and make the short walk out to Villa San Michele.

Actually, you might be a bit shell-shocked by the time you squeeze out of the little orange bus that makes the trip along the island's narrow main road from Capri Town. The noisy vehicle zips along straightaways 1,000 feet above the sea, then grinds around switchbacks in first gear. You may well wonder where all those glamorous habitués of the Piazzetta cafes have gone as elderly housewives jab you with sharp elbows and knock you around with huge bags full of mysterious foodstuffs. Time was, the only way to get between Capri's two towns was on the **Scala Fenicia (Phoenician Staircase)**, a steep path (with no authenticated connection to the ancient peoples of its name) of 881 steps—and many superb views.

Wander off the square onto Via Orlandini and you'll soon be passing tailor shops and shoemakers. Villagers sit on benches in front of the **church of Santa Sofia,** and from the lively square streets meander into narrow lanes lined with vineyards, lemon groves, and gardens brimming with fragrant flowers. With some careful navigating you can walk to Punta Carena, about 2km (1 mile) beyond Anacapri at the southwestern tip of the island (the most scenic route follows Via Migliara to a coastal path, the **Sentiero die Forini,** or Path of the Forts; see Getting Active, below). The little cove beneath the Faro (lighthouse) is one of the nicest places on the island for a swim. From there, a bus takes you back to Anacapri. Another place to get away from the crowds is **Philosophers Park ★,** where paths wind through a parcel of hillside carpeted in scrub and broom lined with 60 ceramic plaques bearing inscriptions from the great philosophers (www.philosophicalpark.org; free admission; dawn–dusk). The easy, 20-minute walk out from Anacapri is along Via Migliara, flanked by gardens and vineyards. Just beyond the garden is the Belvedere Migliara, overlooking the southern coast.

Chiesa di San Michele ★★ CHURCH The 18th-century builders of this octagonal church made a wise decision when they decided to install a delightful **majolica floor,** now one of the island's most colorful manmade sights. Francesco Solimena (1657–1747), the undisputed master of Neapolitan baroque painting, did the design, full of his typical flamboyance, and Naples' finest ceramics master, Leonardo Chiaiese, executed the hand-painted tilework. Their minutely detailed assemblage re-creates the drama-filled moment when Adam and Eve are expelled from the Garden of Eden, as a unicorn, a goat, and other unlikely creatures look on. The final effect of the piece is so pleasing that no one's ever felt comfortable treading on the floor, creating some logistical problems. Pews were never installed, and worshippers and visitors are relegated to a wooden walkway around the perimeter. Those in the know head up the spiral staircase for a bird's-eye view of the multicolor scene. Piazza San Nicola. ✆ **081-837-2396.** 2€. Apr–Oct daily 9am–7pm, Nov–Mar 10am–2pm; closed first 2 weeks of Dec.

Monte Solaro ★★★ NATURAL WONDER Capri's highest peak soars to 590m (1,932 ft.), a magnet for view seekers who "ooh" and "ah" at the island and the Bay of Naples unfolding at their feet. You can hike up along fairly easy paths in about an hour (the easiest is the well-marked route that begins next to Villa San Michele). The chairlift **Seggiovia Monte Solaro** (capriseggiovia.it; ✆ **081-837-1428**) departs from Piazza Vittorria and whisks you to the top in just 12 minutes. Tickets cost 8€ one-way, 11€ round-trip, free for children 8 and under; hours are March and April daily 9:30am to 4pm; May through October daily 9:30am to 5pm; November through February daily 9:30am to 3:30pm. Emperor Augustus greets you at the top, his right arm outstretched as if he's claiming everything in the name of the Roman Empire.

Villa San Michele ★★★ HISTORIC HOUSE Swedish doctor and writer Axel Munthe built this remarkable and gracious house in the 19th century on the ruins of one of Tiberius's villas. He had the funds and inspiration to fulfill his wish that "My home shall be open for the sun and the wind and the voices of the sea—like a Greek temple—and light, light, light everywhere!" Perched on a ledge at the top of the Scala Fenicia entrance to Anacapri (see above), the spacious, airy rooms are filled with Munthe's art and antiques. An arbor-lined path leads to panoramic views across the bay. A sphinx looks out to sea—touching its well-worn hindquarters is said to bring good luck.

Munthe preferred San Michele to his residences in England and Sweden, though a devastating eye condition forced him to forgo the bright light of Capri for a time in the 1920s. In his absence he rented San Michele to the eccentric heiress Luisa Casati (1881–1957). The socialite famously said "I want to be a living work of art" and shocked islanders by doing so—walking around the island with leashed cheetahs and wearing live snakes as jewelry. Her lavish lifestyle at Villa San Michele and elsewhere left her $25 million in debt; she lived out her days in relative poverty in London. After successful eye surgery, Munthe returned to Capri, living many happy years here before returning to Stockholm during World War II as a guest of the royal family.
Viale Axel Munthe 34. www.villasanmichele.eu. ✆ **081-8371401.** 8€; Nov–Feb 9am–3:30pm; Mar 9am–4:30pm; Apr and Oct 9am–5pm; May–Sept 9am–6pm.

Beaches

Inviting as Capri's crystalline waters are, getting into them can be bit of a challenge. The most convenient place to get wet is **Marina Piccola,** where the pebbly beaches are accessible by bus from Capri Town. Also near Capri Town is **Bagni di Tiberio,** a nice, sandy stretch on the north side of the island about 1km (a half-mile) east of Marina Grande. Getting down from the cliff path and, especially, back up, requires a bit of a climb, though you can also get there and back in one of the little boats from Marina Grande for about 3€ each way. Other beaches are next to the Blue Grotto (Via Grotta Azzurra), accessible by bus from Anacapri; below the Faro (lighthouse) at **Punta Carena,** at the southwestern tip of the island, also reached by bus from Anacapri; and at the base of the **Faraglioni,** reached by hundreds of steps from the Via Tragara or by boat from Marina Piccola.

You can bring a towel and lounge on the beach and rocks at any of these places. Most are lined with beach clubs *(stabilimenti balneari)* that usually open mid-March to mid-November 9am to sunset, and charge about 20€ a day for use of a changing room, chair or lounge, and towels; you'll find snack bars at most, excellent restaurants at some (see "Where to Eat," below), and pools at a few.

Getting Active

Capri is heaven for walkers. The island is laced with paths that beckon anyone with a good pair of walking shoes, a sun hat, and a bottle of water. Some especially enticing routes just outside Capri Town take you across handsome, view-filled landscapes around Punta Tragara and to some of the island's most famous sights, including the Faraglioni and Villa Jovis (see above for all). A lesser traveled but no less exhilarating route is on the western side of the island, the **Sentiero die Forini (Path of the Forts).** The 5km (3-mile) walk between the Blue Grotto and Faro (lighthouse) at Punta Carena passes four small coastal fortresses erected over the centuries to keep pirates and foreign powers at bay. However busy the island might be, here you'll find yourself amid Mediterranean countryside and an almost inexhaustible supply of sparkling sea views.

A pleasant (and mostly downhill) walk is from the summit of Monte Salaro (see above) into the **valley of Cetrella.** You may opt to take the chairlift to the mountain's summit, saving your energy for the descent back to Anacapri through wooded countryside along paths once used by the Carthusian monks of the Certosa di San Giacomo (see above), who came out here to check on their herds. The path passes the aptly named **Villa Solitaria,** the onetime home of British novelist Compton Mackenzie (1883–1972). Mackenzie and his wife, Faith, lived on Capri from 1913 to 1920 and intermittently thereafter. The island's famous tolerance of homosexual foreigners, along with Faith's affair with the classical pianist Renata Borgatti, inspired Mackenzie's lesbian-themed 1928

Extraordinary Women. A less secular landmark is just down the path, where the little **hermitage of Cetrella** and its **church of Santa Maria** nestle in a verdant copse. The church is not often open, so check with the tourist office before setting out if a look inside at the double nave is high on your list of must-sees.

Where to Stay

EXPENSIVE

Capri Palace ★★★ If you find it hard to leave the island, a perfect place to give into temptation is this delightful getaway in Anacapri on the slopes of Monte Solaro. Everything here is geared to soothing relaxation: An expanse of green lawn surrounds the swimming pool, chic lounges are quiet and welcoming, and guest rooms are done in restful creams with rose-colored tile floors and white linens. Some suites have private pools, and some rooms look across the sea all the way to Vesuvius, but even the outlooks from rear rooms over the green flanks of Monte Solaro are relaxing. A shuttle bus runs to the port, Capri Town, and a delightful beach club with platforms that make it easy to dip into the Mediterranean.

Via Capodimonte 2, Anacapri. www.capri-palace.com. ✆ **081-9780111.** 79 units. 340€–1,250€ double. Rates include breakfast. Closed mid-Oct–mid-Apr. No children under 10 June–Aug. **Amenities:** 2 restaurants; bar; beach club; heated pool; room service; spa; Wi-Fi (free).

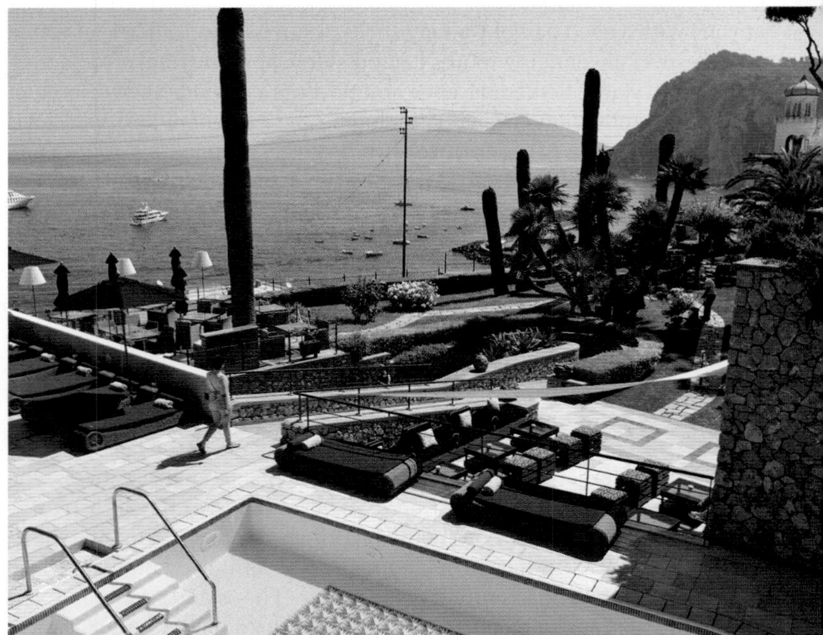

Views of the Marina Grande from Villa Marina Capri.

Hotel Punta Tragara ★★ French architect le Corbusier designed this multilevel villa in the 1920s, and Winston Churchill and Dwight Eisenhower are among those who have enjoyed falling asleep to waves lapping on the shore far below and waking up to birdsong. Each of the stylish quarters is different, some strikingly contemporary, others comfortingly traditional, though all are luxurious without being pretentious. All also open onto terraces, and most offer views of the Faraglioni. You can make the descent to the sea on the hundreds of steps outside the gate, or enjoy a swim in the two pools tucked into gardens.

Via Tragara 57, Capri Town. www.hoteltragara.com. ✆ **081-8370844.** 45 units. 450€–850€ double. Rates include breakfast. Closed Nov–Easter. **Amenities:** Restaurant; bar; concierge; gym; 2 pools; room service; spa; Wi-Fi (free).

Villa Marina Capri ★★ A view-filled perch above the marina is a romantic island getaway, where a late-19th-century villa is set amid lush gardens and sunny terraces. Rooms are quietly glamorous and named for the artists and bohemians who have landed on Capri over the years—but decor is firmly geared to soothing contemporary comfort. Most open to the outdoors and sea views, and a spa, restaurant, and notably attentive service are among the pampering amenities that also include free shuttle service to the port and Capri town.

Via Prov. Marina Grande 91. www.villamarinacapri.com. ✆ **081/837-6630**. 21 units. From 320€ double. Rates include breakfast. Closed late-Oct to Apr. **Amenities:** Restaurant; bar; pool; spa; free shuttle; Wi-Fi (free).

MODERATE

Casa Mariantonia ★★ A gracious old villa near the Church of San Michele commands some of the best real estate in Anacapri—a shady lemon grove, lawns, gardens, and a big swimming pool all right in the center of town. Four generations have been welcoming guests to the family home, which mixes traditional island architecture with contemporary touches for a relaxed but luxurious ambience. The family claims that great-grandmother Mariantonia invented *limoncello,* which may be a bit of a stretch. Even so, sipping the homemade elixir on a terrace next to the trees from whence it comes is a great Capri experience.

Via G. Orlandi 180, Anacapri. www.casamariantonia.com. ✆ **081-8372923.** 10 units. From 140€–190€ double. Rates include breakfast. Closed Jan–Mar. **Amenities:** Bar; pool; Wi-Fi (free).

Villa Brunella ★★ Flower-filled terraces spilling down the hillside from Via Tragara seem to pull you right into the magic of Capri, with eye-popping sea views from each of the airy, tile-floored guest rooms. Ambience hovers between cozy, old-fashioned Italian hospitality and romantic getaway, with some nice antiques and overstuffed armchairs in the bright rooms and plenty of bougainvillea-filled nooks and crannies on the pine-shaded grounds. A pool sparkles on a welcoming patio, and guests have access to a beach club at Marina Piccola. The **Terrazza Brunella**

provides excellent food in elegant surroundings for those occasions when even the short walk into town seems like an effort.

Via Tragara 24, Capri Town. www.villabrunella.it. ✆ **081-8370122.** 20 units. 190€–270€ double. Rates include breakfast. Closed Nov–Apr. **Amenities:** Restaurant; bar; pool; room service; Wi-Fi (free).

INEXPENSIVE

Hotel Tosca ★ You don't have to break the bank to stay on the island or even sacrifice style at this pretty little retreat on the quiet side of Capri Town, near the Gardens of Augustus. Many of the bright, whitewashed rooms have sea views, some have terraces, and all look out over lush gardens. Arches, vaulted ceilings, and tile floors help create the ambience of a simple-yet-tasteful island house. Breakfast is served on a breezy sea-view terrace.

Via Dalmazio Birago 5, Capri Town. www.latoscahotel.com. ✆ **081-8370989.** 11 units. 75€–165€ double. Rates include breakfast. **Amenities:** Wi-Fi (free).

Where to Eat

EXPENSIVE

Grottelle ★ CAPRESE A trek along the southern side of the island is rewarded with a stop at this out-of-the-way lair tucked onto a ledge above the Arco Naturale. A cave etched out of limestone cliffs and a panoramic terrace provide plenty of ambience, perhaps more memorable than the meal itself, though simple dishes like *zuppa di fagioli* (bean soup) and *spaghetti con pomodoro e basilica* (with fresh tomatoes and basil) are perfectly fine accompaniments to the views that extend across the sea to the Amalfi Coast. To find this memorable spot, wander east from Punta Tragara; it's about a 20-minute walk from the Piazzetta.

Via Arco Naturale 13, Capri. ✆ **081-8375719.** Main courses 15€–30€. Fri–Wed noon–3pm and 7–11pm. Closed Nov–Mar.

Ristorante Aurora ★★ CAPRESE You'll get a taste of Capri's high life at the island's oldest eatery, where photos of celebrities hang above the white banquettes. A few may also be sitting around you in the minimalist main dining room or on the terrace facing Capri Town's main thoroughfare. Despite all the glitz, the third generation of the D'Alessio family sticks to the basics, serving island classics like the trademark thin-crust *pizza all'acqua,* with mozzarella and hot peppers, *sformatino alla Franco* (rice pie in prawn sauce), and spaghetti *alle vongole* (clams).

Via Fuorlovado 18. ✆ **081–8370181.** Main courses 12€–22€. Apr–Dec noon–3:30pm and 7:30–11pm.

MODERATE

Gelsomina ★ CAPRESE The sparkling swimming pool is a tempting draw on a warm summer day at this countryside retreat outside Anacapri. Come for the day, to swim, have lunch, and maybe walk to the Belvedere della Migliera viewpoint just down the road. It's also a popular evening

spot. Dining is on a terrace overlooking the sea, and the food is a perfect complement to the low-key setting, with many ingredients plucked straight from the surrounding gardens. Homemade *ravioli di caprese* is light as a feather and stuffed with delicious ricotta from a local producer. Anacapri is about 15 minutes away on foot, on lanes that slice through vineyards and gardens. A free shuttle is available. Several modest **guest rooms** (115€–190€) are above the restaurant.
Via Migliara 72, Anacapri. www.dagelsomina.com. ✆ **081-8371499.** Main courses 10€–18€. Daily 12:30pm–3:30pm and 7–11pm. Closed Nov–Mar.

INEXPENSIVE

Pizzeria Materita ★ PIZZERIA/CAPRESE All the warmth of little Anacapri comes to the fore in this busy local favorite on an animated square overlooking the church of Santa Sofia. Pizzas from the wood-fired oven and the palatable house wine are crowd pleasers, though the simple pastas are solidly tasty, too. Busy waiters often come around with fresh fish that soon reappear perfectly grilled with island herbs.
Via Giuseppe Orlandi 140, Anacapri. ✆ **0181-8373375.** Main courses 8€–18€. Wed–Mon 12:30–3:30pm and 6:30–10:30pm.

Pulalli Wine Bar ★★ CAPRESE To find a hideaway in the jam-packed Piazzetta, just look up to this little terrace next to the clock tower. The bird's-eye view comes with wine, a selection of cheeses, or a full meal—the *risotto al limone* (lemon-flavored risotto) is especially transporting in this magical setting, all the more so since it's served in a hollowed-out lemon. To secure one of the seven tables in this coveted spot, it's best to reserve ahead.
Piazza Umberto I 4, Capri Town. ✆ **081-8374108.** Main courses 10€–25€. Wed–Mon noon–3pm and 7pm–midnight. Closed Nov to just before Easter.

A Meal and a Swim

Some of Capri's most beloved institutions are the *stabilmenti balneari,* beach clubs, where you can eat well and begin or end a meal with a swim and some lounging. A day at one of these charming places is, like so much else about Capri, a simple pleasure with a glamorous twist.

Addio Riccio ★★★ SEAFOOD The cliffside pavilion that serves as the informal beach bistro of the Capri Palace Hotel (see above) is done in soothing shades of blue and crisp white and hangs just above the Grotto Azzurra, bathed in the same mesmerizing light. The setting is so delightful that you won't want to leave after feasting on a fish lunch, and you don't have to—the top level is a sunning platform, filled with lounges and umbrellas, while, better yet, stairs and a path descend to wave-washed swimming platforms below. Lunch draws crowds even from the mainland, and dinner is also served in summer months, making this the prime spot on the island for a romantic evening. The kitchen turns out what's said to be the freshest seafood on Capri, such as turbot baked in a salt crust and a spaghetti with urchin roe that is so good you'll wonder why you've been missing out on this treat all your life. Buses from Anacapri to the Grotta Azzurra stop just outside the door, as do shuttles from the Capri Palace.

Via Gradola 4, Grotta Azzurra. www.capripalace.com. ✆ **081-8371380.** Main courses 20€–40€. Daily 12:30–3:30pm and 8–11pm. Closed Nov–mid-Apr.

La Canzone del Mare ★ SEAFOOD/CAPRESE The British music-hall star Gracie Fields came to Capri in the 1930s and decided she would be the happiest woman on earth if "one small blade of grass on this wonderful, gentle place could belong to me." She eventually bought Il Fortino, a house fashioned out of a ruined fort at Marina Piccola. Over the years she carved bathing platforms out of the rocks, installed a salt-water pool shaped like the island, and built terraces and lounges that would accommodate a restaurant, an American bar, and a few guest rooms, as well as living quarters that served as an informal retreat from life at her villa in Anacapri. Fields died of pneumonia after performing on the Royal Yacht anchored offshore, but her bathing establishment and restaurant still flourish. A meal of fresh vegetables and seafood pastas is lot more expensive than you might expect from the simple surroundings, but the atmosphere is fun and eccentric and Fields is still a presence. Five rooms named after famous former guests (like Elizabeth Taylor) provide sleeping quarters about as close to the sea as you'll find on Capri.

Via Marina Piccola 93. www.lacanzonedelmare.com. ✆ **081–8370104.** Main courses 20€–40€. Daily 12:30–3:30pm and 8–11pm. Closed Nov–Apr.

La Fontelina ★★ CAPRESE/SEAFOOD Many travelers spend the winter months dreaming of a summertime lunch on the rocks at the base of the Faraglioni, where a meal comes with a swim in one of Europe's most legendary seaside settings. A fruit-loaded Sangria is the house drink, the Caprese salad—with *mozzarella di bufala* and just-off-the-vine tomatoes—is legendary, and the fish is so fresh you might think it jumped right out of the sea and onto your plate. Lunch is the only meal served, and it's necessary to reserve for one of the two seatings, at 1 and 3pm. Most guests come early and hang around long after a meal to lounge on the rocks and dip into the crystalline waters.

Via Faraglioni. www.fontelina-capri.com. ✆ **081–8370845.** Main courses 20€–40€. Daily noon–7pm. Closed Nov–Mar. Closed Nov–Apr.

ISCHIA ★★

30km (18 miles) northwest of Capri; 42km (26 miles) northwest of Naples; 20km (13 miles) west of Pozzuoli

While Capri is swathed in glamor and sophistication, Ischia (pronounced EES-kee-a) is scented with sulfur, rising off hundreds of hot springs. These wellsprings have been the island's calling card ever since ancient Romans stepped ashore and discovered the pleasures of a long, soothing

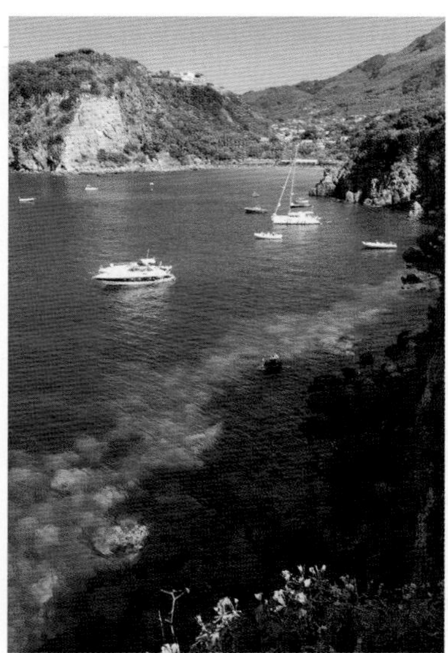

San Montano Bay from Mezzatore Hotel in Ischia.

soak. **Monte Epomeo,** the island's 788m-high (2,585-ft.) dormant volcano, still has enough life in it to feed the mineral hot springs, producing therapeutic muds that are the stock in trade for the island's 150 spas. As a result, Ischia is often called the "island of eternal youth," a moniker that more aptly describes the young Neapolitans who peacock around cafes and bronze themselves on the many beaches. Ischia is also known as the Isola Verde (Green Island), not, as some assume, for its verdant slopes, but for the green-tinged karst (limestone) that underlies much of the landscape. Even so, Ischia *is* refreshingly green with forests, orchards, and vineyards, and the towns along its 37km (23 miles) of shoreline are laidback, pleasant places that might lack the sophistication of Capri but for many admirers are all the better for it.

Essentials

GETTING THERE Ischia's three main harbors—**Ischia Porto** (the largest), **Forio,** and **Casamicciola**—are well connected to the mainland, with most ferries leaving from Pozzuoli and Naples's two harbors (Mergellina Terminal Aliscafi and Stazione Marittima). Both **ferry** and **hydrofoil** *(aliscafi)* services are frequent in summer but slow down during the winter, when the hydrofoil is sometimes suspended because of rough seas. **Caremar** (www.caremar.it; ✆ **199-116655** in Italy), **Medmar** (www.medmargroup.it; ✆ **081-3334411**), and **SNAV** (www.snav.it; ✆ **081-4285555**) offer ferry service from Naples, Pozzuoli, Capri, and Procida to Ischia Porto and Casamicciola. **Alilauro** (www.alilauro.it; ✆ **081-4972222**) runs hydrofoils from Naples (Mergellina and Molo Beverello) to Ischia Porto and to Forio; and **NLG-Navigazione Libera del Golfo** (www.navlib.it; ✆ **081-5520763**) operates hydrofoils from Salerno to Ischia. ***Note:*** In high season, car access to the island is restricted and car slots are limited; if you plan to bring your car, make your reservations well in advance.

GETTING AROUND Public transportation on Ischia is excellent, with a well-organized **bus** system with **EAV** (✆ **800-0539309** toll-free in Italy). One line circles the island in a clockwise direction (*circolare destra* marked cd), and the other counterclockwise (*circolare sinistra,* marked cs). A number of other lines crisscross the island. Tickets cost 2€ and are valid for 90 minutes (daily pass 6€); they are on sale at bars, tobacconists, and news kiosks. The tourist office can provide a printout of the bus schedule (see "Visitor Information," below).

Taxis wait at stands strategically located around the island, including Piazza degli Eroi (✆ **081-992550**) and Piazzetta San Girolamo (✆ **081-993720**) in **Ischia Porto;** Piazza Bagni (✆ **081-900881**) in Casamicciola; and Piazza Girardi in Lacco Ameno (✆ **081-995113**).

You can **rent motor scooters, bicycles,** and **cars** on the island from a number of agencies, including **Autonoleggio In Scooter** in Forio (www.autonoleggioinscooter.it; ✆ **081-998513** or 320-4218039) and **Island Center,** Via V. Di Meglio 161 in Barano (✆ **081-902525**).

VISITOR INFORMATION The **AACST tourist office** (✆ **081-5074231;** www.infoischiaprocida.it) is at Via Sogliuzzo 72, Ischia Porto, where you'll find free maps as well as information and brochures. In summer an information booth operates at Piazza Antica Reggia 11, Ischia Porto.

Exploring the Island

Ischia is large as far as its neighbors in the Bay of Naples go, about 46 sq. km (18 sq. miles). Most of its main settlements—Ischia Porto, Casamicciola, and Lacco Ameno—are on the north shore, with Forio on the west coast. Boats call at Ischia Porto, with the island's one great historic landmark, the **Castello Aragonese,** in adjoining Isola Ponte. The busy harbor of Ischia Porto is a volcanic crater that was landlocked until 1854, when Bourbon King Ferdinand II had a channel cut to the sea. He created one of the most thrilling sea entrances anywhere, as ferries and yachts navigate the impossibly narrow cut and emerge into a becalmed lake surrounded by colorful waterside cafes and green hillsides carpeted with the island's distinctive white, flat-roofed houses. **Casamicciola** is a famous spa town that's been devoted to the healing arts since the 17th century. Among the arthritic, gouty, and otherwise ailing travelers who found their way here, Norwegian playwright Henrik Ibsen came for a cure in the 1860s, with time off from treatments to read the works of philosopher Soren Kierkegaard and write his famous verse drama *Peer Gynt*. He's honored with a plaque in Piazza Marina, near a statue of King Vittorio Emanuele II. Lacco Ameno is the island's most sophisticated resort. Looming just offshore is the **Fungo,** a mushroom-shaped lump of wave-sculpted tufa that is as iconic to Ischia as the Faraglioni are to Capri. The arrival of Richard Burton and Elizabeth Taylor in 1963 to shoot the barge scenes from the blockbuster film *Cleopatra* ensured the town's celebrity. The quiet little backwater became a jet-set hotspot when newspapers around the world ran paparazzi photos of the adulterous lovers yachting and swimming offshore. Forio holds down the west coast and compensates for its lack of beauty with spectacular stretches of sand, a lively resort scene, and some extremely palatable wines from the surrounding vineyards. Wherever you settle, you won't be too far from the sights. A road follows the coast around the island, and buses make it easy to get from one town to the other.

Castello Aragonese (Aragonese Castle) ★★★ HISTORIC SIGHT Greeks settled this rocky islet as early as the 5th century B.C., building watchtowers to keep an eye on enemy fleets. The fortifications atop 91m (300-ft.) cliffs have been a plum for invaders ever since, from ancient Neapolitans and Romans to Goths to Normans. King of Naples Alfonso I gave the walled complex its present form in the mid-15th century as a defense against pirate raids, shoring up watchtowers and walls and installing churches, terraces, and squares that give the walled compound a village-like air. At one time some 17,000 people sheltered within the walls, among them nuns, monks, and soldiers. The British shelled the compound during the Napoleonic Wars, and did a pretty good job of it, though enough remains to give an idea of the onetime might of the citadel. Many churches still stand, in various states of repair. The frescoed crypt is about all that remains of the Cattedrale dell'Assunta, while the Chiesa dell'Immaculata and hexagonal San Pietro a Pantaniello are fairly intact. A somber if not downright macabre presence is the small Cimitero delle Monache Clarisse, attached to the island's convent. When the inhabitants breathed their last, they were left sitting on stone chairs as a reminder of what becomes of our earthly presence—the spooky-looking seating arrangement is still in place, minus the bones.

You can ponder all this as your make a circuit of the breezy ramparts, a vertigo-inducing lookout hundreds of feet above the crashing waves. An elevator whisks visitors up to the castle entrance, though the climb up the stairs and ramps provides a more authentic experience.

Piazzale Aragonese, Ischia Ponte. www.castelloaragoneseischia.com. ✆ **081-992834.** 10€ adults, 6€ youth 10–14; free for children 9 and under. Daily 9am–sunset.

Villa La Mortella ★★ GARDEN Sir William Walton (1902–1983), one of the greatest English composers of the 20th century, and his Argentine wife Susana Walton (1926–2010) settled on Ischia in 1949. Walton found the peace and light conducive to composition, and Susana became enchanted with the idea of creating a garden at their home, La Mortella (the Myrtles) on the west side of the Monte Vico promontory outside Forio. She worked with the great landscape designer Russell Page to landscape the Valley Garden, filling it with rare Mediterranean and South American species, great sweeps of orchids and other flowers, and fountains, ponds, and brooks. Walton could control the valves from his study and turned off the jets when the gurgling disturbed him. Lady Walton designed the sunny, view-filled Hill Garden as a tribute to her husband, working in the soil herself well into her later years. The exotic

Locals playing cards in Lacco Amena in Ischia.

romance of the gardens are an apt tribute to the Waltons, who married just a few months after meeting in Buenos Aires. Today, it's customary on a walk along the garden paths to wave at the palms, following Lady Walton's belief that "You have to wave at them when you go by because they think you haven't paid attention."

Via Francesco Calise 39. www.lamortella.it. ✆ **081-986220.** 12€ adults, 10€ children 8–16 and seniors over 60, 6€ children 5–7. Apr 1–Nov 15 Tues, Thurs, and Sat–Sun 9am–7pm.

BEACHES

Ischia has a commodity that's the envy of Capri and towns along the Amalfi Coast: long stretches of sand. It's especially pleasant in May and September, but in the dog days of summer the sands are jam-packed with a mixed crowd of islanders, day-tripping Neapolitans, and Germans and Russians drawn to Ischia by the combined allure of thermal baths and beaches. The island's most beautiful beach is **Spiaggia dei Maronti ★★★**, stretching for about 2km (1¼ miles) east of the village of Sant'Angelo. South of Forio is the **Spiaggia di Citara ★★**, with hot mineral springs that flow out to sea at its southern edge. The scenic beach on the bay of **San Montano ★★** is tucked onto the flanks of the promontory of Monte Vico near Laco Ammeno. On the south coast, just outside the little village of Sant'Angelo, is so-called **Fumarole beach.** Hot underground vapors heat the sand to such high temperatures that islanders come to bury chicken and fish in aluminum foil and splash around a bit as they wait for their food to cook. The sands also provide welcome relief to arthritis sufferers, who plonk down on the warm grains and let the heat penetrate their aching joints. Just offshore, geysers bubble up to create natural hot-tub-like pools. A flotilla of little boats ferry passengers from the town marina to this otherworldly seascape, about 5€ each way, and it's also easy to reach on a seaside path.

If you're staying in or near Ischia Porto or Ischia Ponte and can't wait to get in the water, your best bet is **Spiaggia dei Pescatori ★,** where local fishermen beach their boats; it's just west of the Aragonese Castle.

SPAS & THERMO-MINERAL TREATMENTS

Ischia's *terme,* or thermal baths, have been popular ever since ancient Greeks soaked their weary bones in the natural hot springs. Elaborate thermal parks are top among the island's many attractions. Most facilities offer slightly lower rates after midafternoon, so opt for a late entrance and a sunset soak. They also offer multi-day passes, for those who want to spend most of their time on Ischia quite literally in hot water.

Parco Termale Castiglione ★★ Low-key is not quite the right word for a place that splashes out with 10 pools, but they're tucked into tastefully designed seaside terraces laced with all sorts of quiet nooks and crannies. If the pool temperatures get to be a bit too relaxing—they range from 82° to 104°F (28°–40°C)—a stone jetty is poised for a dip in the sea. The absence of a beach, and the serious mud and thermal treatments, makes the park more popular with a sedate crowd than it is with families, so screaming kids aren't likely to disturb the peace.

Shore road, between Ischia Porto and Casamicciola. www.termecastiglione.it. ✆ **081-982551.** 28€ a day, 24€ after 1pm, 9€ children 2–12; 2€ more in Aug. Apr–Oct 9am–7pm.

Parco Termale Giardini Poseidon ★ Everything about Ischia's largest spa is over the top, with 22 pools, a large private beach, tropical gardens, and several restaurants. The kitsch runs high, including toga-bedecked statues. It's hard not to feel like a figure of ancient legend in the complex's nicest feature, an eons-old natural thermal cave etched out of a cliff. It's a toss-up who enjoys these surroundings more, Germans and their *kinder* or Italian families, so be prepared for a crowd.

Via Giovanni Mazzella, Citara Beach, near Forio. www.giardiniposeidon.it. ✆ **081-908-7111.** 32€ a day (35€ in Aug), 27€ after 1pm (30€ in Aug), 16€ children 4–11 (17.50€ in Aug). Apr–Oct, daily 9am–7pm.

Parco Termale Negombo ★★★ If you have time and/or inclination to visit only one thermal establishment on Ischia, make it this delightful spot on the island's most picturesque cove, San Montano.

Gorgeous gardens, laid out by botanist Duke Luigi Camerini, surround 12 pools and facilities that include saunas, steam rooms, and massage cabins. While waterfalls and luxuriant plantings provide a transporting getaway atmosphere, just as alluring is the beach of fine sand. You could happily spend a day traipsing back and forth between the warm pools and the refreshing sea, with some naptime in the shade next to one of the garden's beautiful, albeit ersatz, waterfalls.

San Montano beach, on the promontory of Monte Vico near Lacco Ameno. www.negombo.it. ✆ **081-986152**. 32€, 26€ after 1:30pm, 22€ after 3:30pm, children less than 4½ ft. and more than 3¼ ft. tall, 22€, 20€ after 12:30pm, 18€ after 3pm. Late Apr–mid-Oct, daily 8:30am–7pm.

Where to Stay & Eat

Albergo Il Monastero ★★ The labyrinth of stone-walled, arched passageways, courtyards, and arbor-shaded seaside terraces of this former monastery are enticing in themselves, all the more so since the old premises are set within Ischia's spectacular Aragonese Castle (p. 689). Whitewashed guest rooms carved out of former monks' cells are spacious and soberly stylish, with handsome furnishings and knockout sea views from most. A huge panoramic terrace atop the castle walls is the setting for breakfast and delicious dinners, fed by produce from the hotel's garden. ***Note:*** The hotel is only accessible by foot, and accommodations are reached by what can seem like endless staircases.

Castello Aragonese. www.albergoilmonastero.it. ✆ **081-992435.** 20 units. 120€–160€ double. Rates include breakfast. Closed mid-Oct–mid-Apr. **Amenities:** Restaurant; Wi-Fi (free).

Da Ciccio ★★ SEAFOOD A seat on the little terrace in front of a half-a-century-old island favorite comes with killer views of the Aragonese Castle (p. 689). That's about as showy as it gets as this little hole in the wall, where Ciccio and son Bruno focus on fresh seafood in memorably delicious preparations: thick mussel soup is steeped with mountain herbs and topped with fried bread, squid is stuffed with bread crumbs, raisins, and chopped fish, and linguine is laden with clams.

Via Luigi Mazzella 32, Ischia Ponte. ✆ **081-991686.** Main courses 10€–15€. Wed–Mon noon–2:30pm and 7–11pm.

Hotel della Baia ★ At this delightful little getaway tucked onto the myrtle-clad hillside above San Montano Bay, a lounge is shaded by lime trees, and all the simple-chic rooms open to bougainvillea-filled terraces. Just down the road are two of the island's best places to swim and lounge, a sandy beach in a beautiful cove and **Negombo,** the nicest of Ischia's thermal parks.

San Montano beach, on the promontory of Monte Vico near Lacco Ameno. www.negombo.it. ✆ **081-986150**. 16 units. 100€–120€ double, includes breakfast. **Amenities:** Bar; pool; beach; Wi-Fi (free).

La Brocca ★★ SEAFOOD Lacco Ameno might be the toniest town on the island, but simple old-time ways still hold sway at this no-frills spot facing the sea and Il Fungo. The friendly family could be the town's goodwill ambassadors as they rush between the dining room and terrace to serve straightforward and delicious preparations of fresh-off-the boat seafood. Any of the pastas *alla pescatora* (with seafood), washed down with a chilled carafe of the house white, deliver a memorable feast.
Via Roma 28, Lacco Ameno. ✆ **081-900051.** Main courses 8€–15€. Daily noon–2:30pm and 7–11pm.

Mezzatorre Resort & Spa ★★★ A former fortress at the end of a rocky promontory provides a sense of privileged escape. Survey the sea and the 17 acres of pine-scented gardens from one of the beautifully appointed rooms in the dark-red, 15th-century watchtower. All of the airy, view-filled accommodations are spectacular, including the spacious quarters in the modern annexes scattered among the gardens, stylishly done in bright Mediterranean color schemes and a chic mix of antiques and contemporary pieces. Thermal pools tucked onto seaside terraces, a hot springs and spa, and private beach ensure you can partake of a wellness regimen without ever leaving the property.
Via Mezzatorre, 80075 Forio. www.mezzatorre.it. ✆ **081-986111.** 60 units. 440€–580€ double. Rates include buffet breakfast. Free parking. Closed Nov–Apr. **Amenities:** 2 restaurants; bar; babysitting; concierge; health club; 3 pools; room service; spa; outdoor tennis courts; Wi-Fi (free).

BASILICATA & PUGLIA

By Stephen Brewer

14

South of Naples, the Mezzogiorno begins in earnest. The name, which literally means "midday," evokes rugged, sun-baked landscapes. But that doesn't begin to describe the riches you'll discover in the instep and heel of the Italian boot, or, officially, Basilicata and Puglia. Some of Italy's great architectural marvels are here, the *sassi* cave dwellings in Matera and the *trulli,* fairy-tale stone houses with cone-shaped roofs that only exist in Alberobello and around "white cities" of the surrounding Valle d'Itria. Lecce, meanwhile, is city of honey-colored stone chiseled into intricate baroque facades.

Outside these towns and cities, the landscapes are a sweep of groves, orchards, vineyards, and fields, often edged by beaches. It's estimated that more than 6 million olive trees carpet the southeast, yielding almost half the country's oil production, and almost any view is likely to take in gnarled trunks growing out of red earth. Where there's good olive oil, there's good wine and good food. The region's simple but delicious *cucina povera* (peasant cooking) will nicely fuel your explorations—and you'll never think of a fava bean with indifference again.

MATERA ★★

254km (158 miles) SE of Naples, 73km (44 miles) S of Bari

In Matera, it's all about caves. A vast honeycomb of thousands of caverns riddles the chalk cliffs above the gorge of the Gravina River. It's estimated that these caves have been inhabited for at least 9,000 years, making Matera the oldest continuously inhabited place on earth. The rugged landscapes appear to have been sheltering hunters and gatherers long before then, and the remains of a 150,000-year-old hominid have been found in a nearby cave. Excavations around the cathedral have unearthed 3,000-year-old ceramics, Greek and Byzantine coins, Roman houses, and the coffins of early Christians.

By the middle of the 20th century, some of Italy's poorest residents lived in the caves, with as many as 20,000 troglodytes eking out a miserable existence in what was a vast, unsanitary underground slum. Man and beast shared the dank, dark caves, a breeding ground for malaria, typhoid, and other diseases. Most of the cave dwellers were illiterate and starving. As Carlo Levi observed in his 1945 autobiographical novel *Christ Stopped at Eboli,* "I have never in all my life seen such a picture of poverty."

FACING PAGE: **Ancient town of Matera.**

Strategies for Getting There & Around

If you're **flying** into the southeast, all of the major towns are within easy reach of the **Bari and Brindisi airports** (www.aeroportidipuglia.it); both are served by low-cost flights from the rest of Europe. **Fast trains** from Rome and the north serve Bari (with connections to other major towns) and continue on to Lecce. It's possible to see many of the highlights of the southeast without driving; Lecce, Alberobello, Lecce, Martina Franca, Ostuni, and Trani—all places you'll want to see—are on rail lines. A **car,** of course, offers a lot more freedom of movement. Matera is about 3 hours southeast of Naples via the A3 and E847. Alberobello is 4 hours east of Naples (via the A16 and A14 autostrade to Bari) and 5 hours southeast of Rome, via the A1 autostrada south to Naples and then the A16 and A14 from there. From Bari to Lecce, it's 1½ hours on E55 and SS16.

Eventually the Italian government moved the cave dwellers to more sanitary housing on the ridge above the cliffs in modern Matera. By the mid-1980s, the rock-cut settlement was attracting attention for its unique beauty, and little wonder. Steep "streets" and meandering staircases run right over the rooftops of underlying houses. The pastiche of roofs, labyrinthine alleys, and endless stairways are one alluring, warm-hued jumble. Matera is so richly evocative of ancient Mediterranean civilization that it's been the location for many biblical films, most famously Pier Paolo Passolini's *The Gospel According to St. Matthew* (1964) and Mel Gibson's *The Passion of the Christ* (2004).

It's a sign of the times that one of the many restaurants that have opened in the caves offers Pasta Mel Gibson, a variation of the town's peasant classic with chili peppers and fried breadcrumbs. Other rock

Interior of an ancient cave house carved into tufa rock in Matera.

Basilicata & Puglia
Milan
Venice
Rome
ADRIATIC SEA
Gulf of Manfredonia
Gulf of Taranto
Gulf of Salerno
PUGLIA
BASILICATA
CAMPANIA
CALABRIA
MOLISE
Gargano Peninsula
Salentine Peninsula
Le Murge
Appennino Lucano
Appennino Campano
Lago di Lesina
Lago di Varano
Ofanto
Bradano
Basento
Peschici
Vieste
Rodi Garganico
San Nicandro Garganico
Monte Sant'Angelo
Lesina
Apricena
San Giovanni Rotondo
San Marco in Lamis
Manfredonia
Torremaggiore
San Severo
Margherita di Savoia
Barletta
Trani
Bisceglie
Giovinazzo
Bari
Mola di Bari
Polignano a Mare
Monopoli
Trinitapoli
Lucera
Foggia
San Ferdinando di Puglia
Andria
Molfetta
Bitonto
Triggiano
Rutigliano
Conversano
Orta Nova
Cerignola
Canosa di Puglia
Corato
Ruvo di Puglia
Bitetto
Grumo Appula
Castellana Grotte
Fasano
Castel del Monte
Cisternino
Ostuni
Carovigno
Brindisi
Alberobello
San Vito dei Normanni
Cassano delle Murge
Locorotondo
Martina Franca
Ceglie Messapica
San Pietro Vernotico
Gioia del Colle
Mesagne
Lavello
Santeramo in Colle
Altamura
Gravina in Puglia
Crispiano
Grottaglie
Oria
San Pancrazio Salentino
Lecce
Ariano Irpino
Melfi
Venosa
Mottola
Castellaneta
Massafra
Rionero in Vulture
San Giorgio Ionico
Manduria
Copertino
Otranto
Benevento
Laterza
Palagiano
Sava
Matera
Ginosa
Taranto
Lizzano
Galatina
Maglie
Pulsano
Montescaglioso
Nardò
Santa Cesarea Terme
Galatone
Avigliano
Potenza
Bernalda
Gallipoli
Matino
Avellino
Taurisano
Taviano
Tricase
Racale
Ugento
Campagna
Policoro
Santa Maria di Leuca
Salerno
Sala Consilina
Sorrento
Capaccio
Agropoli
Lauria
A14
SS89
SS17
SS16
SS655
SR1
SR6
SP231
SS96
A14
SS379
SS172
SS7
SS99
SS87
A16
RA 9
SS407
SS691
RA5
RA 2
A30
A3
SS18
SS106
SP430/a
SP430/b
0 25 mi
0 25 km

dwellings have been converted to hotels, where it's now possible to enjoy the experience of sleeping in a cave without having to share quarters with a donkey. The evocative spectacle of rugged dwellings stacked one atop another is drawing more and more travelers every year. This unique cave city is now a UNESCO World Heritage site, and in 2019 Matera will be in the spotlight as a European Capital of Culture, sharing that year's honor with Plovdiv, Bulgaria.

Essentials

GETTING THERE If you're traveling to Matera from Naples, the easiest way is **by car,** following the A3 south, then the E847 east through Potenza. The drive of 254km (158 miles) takes a little more than 2 hours. Four-times-a-day **bus service** with Marino (www.marinobus.it) takes about 4½ hours. **Trains** (www.trenitalia.com) run between Naples and the nearby town of Ferrandina, from where you take a bus to Matera. Trains run three times a day for trips of 4 to 5 hours. A private train line, **Ferrovie Appulo Lucane (FAL)** (ferrovieappulolucane.it), operates between Bari and Matera, arriving at Matera Centrale station, from which buses run down to the *sassi*. Trains run every 1 to 2 hours, and the trip takes about 1 hour and 30 minutes; trains do not operate on Sunday.

If you're arriving in the region by **air,** the closest airports are in Bari and Brindisi; information for both can be found at **www.aeroportidi puglia.it**. Matera is 73km (44 miles) south of Bari via SP236 and 136km (82 miles) northeast of Brindisi via E90 and SS7.

Pugliabus (pugliairbus.aeroportidipuglia.it) runs service between Bari airport and Matera 5 times a day. **Sitabus** (www.sitabus.it) operates between Matera and other towns throughout the southeast.

GETTING AROUND The only easy way to get around Matera is **on foot,** and be prepared for a lot of climbing. If you're arriving by car, make arrangements with your hotel for arrival and parking in advance. Most hotels have agreements with lots and garages in the modern town where you can park for a slight discount of about 12€ a day, and they'll usually drive you to a drop-off close to your hotel for about 5€. It's possible to drive to the bottom of Sasso Barisano and continue along Via Madonna delle Virtù into the bottom of Sasso Caveoso, though this is encouraged only to drop off bags, plus your hotel must supply your license plate number to the police in advance; even at that it's best to avoid this hair-raising trip and leave the car above. The dispatch number for **Matera taxi** is ✆ **334348.**

VISITOR INFORMATION Odd, given Matera's emergence on the tourist map, but the town has no government-run tourist office. Private agencies abound, though they're in business to sell you expensive and often unnecessary walking tours of the *sassi*. Hotels dispense maps and more. A good online resource is **www.sassiweb.it.** For excellent background on Matera, step into **Casa Noha,** Recinto Cavone 9 (www.fondoambiente.

Overlooking the Civita, or medieval heart of Matera.

it; ✆ **0835/335452**), where visual projections and a good soundtrack trace the city's history and its unique social and architectural heritage; the staff can also set you up with a free walking-tour app. It's open March to December daily 10am to 6pm; admission is 5€.

Exploring Matera

Matera is essentially divided into three districts. At the top of the ridge is the center of the modern town, where the Duomo stands amid squares and palaces in the Civita. Below spread the ***sassi*** (literally, "stones"), the cliff-hugging districts of cave dwellings. **Sasso Barisano** is to the north and **Sasso Caveoso** to the south, though the lanes and alleyways of one meander into the lanes and alleyways of the other.

The best way to appreciate the *sassi* is to plunge in and wander, following one of the well-marked stone staircases off Via Duomo in the Civita. At the foot of the cliff in each *sasso* is one street with a cluster of shops and cafes. In Sasso Barisano, it's **Via dei Fiorentino,** and in Sasso Caveoso, it's **Via Bruno Buozzi.** No need to rush down to these outposts of civilization, though. Along the way are wonky staircases, blind alleys, crumbling courtyards where a profusion of greenery flourishes amid the stone, and many remarkable vistas. Trying to find a specific address in the *sassi* can be as challenging as trying to find your way out of the maze of the Minotaur, but a few sights are worth seeking out.

The **Casa-Grotta di Vico Solitario ★,** off Via Bruno Buozzi in Sasso Caveoso, re-creates a dwelling from the 1950s, when the government cleared out the *sassi* and moved 20,000 residents to banal, albeit sanitary, quarters in modern Matera. The crude authentic furnishings include a ridiculously high bed that kept occupants well off the frigid stone floor and provided storage space beneath. Not in evidence is the filth that might have accompanied sharing tight quarters with pigs and donkeys, though a black-and-white film footage captures the district's dire poverty and squalor. The house is usually open daily from 9:30am to

9pm, and admission is 2€. Also in Sasso Caveoso is another remnant of the once-thriving community, **La Racolte delle Acque ★** (✆ **0340-6659107;** 3€; April–Oct daily 9:30am–1pm and 2 to 7pm; Nov–Mar daily 9:30am–1pm). This creepy underground network shows off the vast network of canals that channeled rainwater collected from streets and roofs into deep cisterns. Enter at Via Bruno Buozzi 67.

One of Matera's best-preserved rock church complexes, **Madonna delle Virtù e San Nicola dei Greci ★★,** is in Sasso Barisano on Via Madonna delle Virtù (✆ **377-4448885;** 5€; June–Sept daily 10am–8pm; Oct, April, and May daily 10am–1:30pm and 3–6pm; and Nov–Mar daily 10am–1:30). A labyrinth of 10th- and 11th-century frescoed chapels and living quarters, home to a community of nuns on one level and monks on another, twists and turns across several levels. At one point the low-slung caverns open to an almost majestic apse with a domed ceiling.

Some of the best views of the *sassi* are from the **Parco della Murgia Materana ★** (www.parcomurgia.it), where rocky pastureland rises and falls along the gorge of the Gravina River just below town. High ground affords sweeping views back toward the *sassi,* while the ravines are riddled with caves that have been used as churches, stables, and shepherds' shelters. Enter the park off Via Madonna delle Virtù.

Duomo ★ CHURCH The residents of the *sassi* are never out of sight of the city's soaring cathedral, completed in 1270 on high ground at the side of the cliff just above them. The faithful received a morality lesson from a wealth of carvings on the facade before they even stepped inside. A mermaid warms of the passions likely to steer us off a path of righteousness, while an eagle is poised to devour lesser, meeker animals, just as we are always prey to sin. Meanwhile, the Archangel Michael battles the dragon, standing in for the forces of evil, before an audience of the

Cave Art

The Palazzo Pomarici is a wonder in itself, a 16th-century palace with frescoed salons and—since it sits in the middle of the *sassi*—many cave rooms. These quarters are now the evocative setting for the **Museum of Contemporary Sculpture Matera (MUSMA),** showing off the work of an international roster of artists. The museum is in Sasso Caveoso on Via San Giacomo (www.musma.it; ✆ **0835-330582;** 5€; April–Sept daily 10am–2pm and 4–8pm; Oct–Mar daily 10am–2pm). The **Palazzo Lanfranchi,** in the Civita's Piazzetta Giovanni Pascoli, displays Neapolitan paintings and religious objects in the **Museo Nazionale d'Arte Medievale e Moderna della Basilicata** (www.basilicata.beniculturali.it; ✆ **0835-256211;** 3€; Thurs–Tues 9am–8pm). Standouts are the colorful paintings by Carlo Levi (1902–1975), the artist and political activist exiled to this region in the 1930s for his anti-fascist activities. Levi spent his time working alongside a physician, painting, and writing, and his autobiographical novel, *Christ Stopped at Eboli,* brought the region's poverty and squalid living conditions to world attention. Likewise, his hard-hitting paintings capture the hardships of peasant life.

Matera's Duomo.

town's medieval elite. Similarly moralistic frescoes that once covered the interior were destroyed in many renovations, though a terrifying 13th-century *Last Judgment* remains, to the right of the entrance. Archangel Michael makes another appearance, this time wielding his sword in hell, where serpents attack the damned. Among them are popes, monks, and kings, proof that no one escapes the final judgment. An antidote is the utterly charming 16th-century nativity scene in a side chapel, where shepherds and their flocks are set against a re-creation of Matera, looking like just the sort of place where Christ would be born.

Piazza del Duomo. Free. Daily 8am–12:30pm and 3:30–7:30pm.

Where to Stay

Alle Malve Bed & Breakfast ★ No one says a cave dwelling can't have a crisp, chipper vibe, and this ancient house that's partly dug into the hillside at the foot of Sassi Caveoso is downright cheerful. The many contemporary touches in the bright lounge and guest rooms include a sunken sitting area in front a crackling fire, a floating staircase, and large, state-of-the-art bathrooms. Papevero is an especially appealing room, with high, wooden ceilings and a large terrace.

Via Bruno Buozzi 102. www.bbmatera.allemalve.it. ✆ **0835-312816.** 4 units. 80€–150€ double, includes breakfast. **Amenities:** Wi-Fi (free).

Sextantio le Grotto della Civica ★★ If the Flintstones had hired a big-name decorator, they might have been treated to a design-magazine-worthy abode like these luxurious cave sanctuaries overlooking the Gravina River gorge at the edge of Matera. Furnishings are rustic chic, with authentically old pieces scattered around cavernous spaces where

soft light flickers off stone walls. Luxuries include freestanding tubs, fireplaces, and (in many rooms) terraces overlooking the sweep of green, rock-studded countryside. The attempt to re-create the look of a primitive cave dwelling without sacrificing creature comforts can seem a bit forced, but it's hard to quibble with the luxury of stepping out of bed onto a cave floor heated from beneath. Breakfast, drinks, and some meals are served in an ancient church hewn out of the rock.
Via Civita 28. legrottedellacivita.sextantio.it. ✆ **0835-332744.** 18 units. 150€–350€ double. Rates include breakfast. **Amenities:** Bar; cafe; Wi-Fi (free).

Fra I Sassi Residence ★★★ Of the many cave hotels in Matera, this beautiful enclave at the bottom of Sasso Barisano is one of the most welcoming. These are caves with a view, where well-designed cave rooms (some with sunken tubs) open onto a bright terrace that provides a front-row seat for the spectacle of cave dwellings clinging to the surrounding hillsides. It's one of the best vistas in town. The welcoming outdoor spaces are well supplied with loungers, the perfect perch for a drink, a nap, or just sitting and soaking in the textures. Breakfast is served in a reception room that does double duty as a bar/cafe.
Via D'Addozio 102. www.fraisassiresidence.com. ✆ **08365-336020.** 9 units. 89€–140€ double. Rates include breakfast. **Amenities:** Bar; Wi-Fi (free).

San Giorgio Hotel ★★ You will feel like a bonafide troglodyte—albeit a high-living one—in one of these well-done, well-equipped dwellings scattered throughout Sassi Barisano. Most have one or two bedrooms, and many are multilevel and, given their unusual settings, rich in arches, vaults, and other architectural details, including fireplaces and terraces in some. An accommodating staff serves breakfast in a pleasant room in the main house.
Via Fiorentini 259. www.sangiorgio.matera.it. ✆ **0835/334583.** 11 units. 120€–210€. **Amenities:** Wi-Fi (free).

Where to Eat

La Talpa ★★ BASILICATESE Matera's caves don't get any more inviting than these snug, white-walled rooms hung with old cooking implements and filled with cozy, gingham-topped tables. The homey setting is suited for such local dishes as *purea di fave con cicorielle di campo* (broad bean puree with chicory) or *cavatelli* with chickpea puree, arugula, porcini mushrooms, and tomatoes. Lamb and veal are grilled to perfection, and pizzas emerge from a wood oven at the back of the cave.
Via dei Fiorentini 167. www.latalparistorante.it. ✆ **0835-335086.** Main courses 9€–18€. Wed–Sun 1–3pm and 8pm–11pm.

Le Botteghe ★★ PUGLIAN At this house partly dug out of a cave and opening to a bright square in Sasso Barisano, the setting is refined and the cooking is a whole-hearted attempt to present the best of local cuisine. You will be encouraged, nicely so, to have a full meal, and it would be a shame not to do so—to try the "Orecchiette al Tegamino," ear-shaped pasta baked with ham, cheese, and tomatoes or one of the local pastas, then move on to the house specialty, expertly grilled meat. Even the house-baked bread, *pane di Matera,* is delicious.

Piazza San Pietro Barisano. ✆ **0835/344072.** Main courses 10€–22€. Mon–Sat 1–2:30pm and 8–11pm, Sun 8–11pm.

Oi Mari ★ BASILICATESE/NEAPOLITAN Many Italians might recognize the name that this convivial spot in Sasso Barisano shares with a famous Neapolitan serenade. That's not the only way this high, cheery cave, with nicely laid, candlelit tables tucked into natural nooks, takes its inspiration from Naples. The pizzas are reputed to be the best in town, and the cavernous space fills up nightly with eager enthusiasts. No need to settle for pizza alone, though. You can nicely stretch out a meal with heaping platters of *antipasto di mare,* with octopus, squid, and *baccala,* and a big choice of seafood pastas and meat dishes.

Via dei Fiorentini 66. www.oimari.it. ✆ **0835-346121.** Main courses 8€–18€. Mon–Fri 8pm–midnight; Sat–Sun 1–3pm and 8pm–midnight.

Trattoria Caveosa ★ BASILICATESE A convivial multilevel cave in the same-named *sasso* neighborhood is decorated with bold contemporary art but is wholeheartedly devoted to the pleasures of local, old-fashioned cuisine. The wholesome, straightforward preparations don't pretend to be anything other than *cucina povera,* poor man's grub, and fresh, local produce shows up in dishes like *strascinate con rape mollica fritta,* topped with broccoli, chili peppers, and breadcrumbs, or lamb fried with onions, tomatoes, mushrooms, and wild onions.

Via Bruno Buozzi 21. www.ristorantedelcaveoso.it. ✆ **0835-312374.** Main courses 6€–12€. Thurs–Tues 12:30–3pm and 7:30–11pm.

TRANI ★★

85km (51 miles) N of Matera

This little seaside city would bring a smile to the face of the most hardened traveler. A once-thriving medieval seaport, Trani has twisting lanes and airy piazzas lined with palaces and churches, all hewn from golden limestone that glows with just a tinge of pink when the sun hits it. Sooner or later the maze untangles alongside the shimmering blue waters of the Adriatic, where, from certain angles, one of the most dramatic cathedrals in Italy seems to rise right out of the waves. Trani is also a jumping-off point for Frederick II's remarkable **Castel del Monte** to the west and the beautiful **Gragano peninsula,** to the north.

Essentials

GETTING THERE Trani is just off the A14 autostrada, which follows the Adriatic coast between Bari and Rimini. If you're driving from Matera, head north to Altamura, then follow signs through Corato to Trani from there. Trani is on the direct **train line** that connects Bari and Brindisi with Rome.

Use Bari as your gateway to visit Trani and Castel del Monte; each of these sights lies less than an hour away from the Pugliese capital **by car** on well-signed and well-maintained highways. The Gargano promontory is at the northern tip of Puglia and can be reached in 2½ hours from Bari (take the A14 north to Foggia, then bear east on the SS89, toward Manfredonia). If driving to the Gargano from Rome (4 hrs.) or Naples (2¾ hrs.), do not go as far south as Bari; instead follow signs to Foggia and then Manfredonia. You can also fly into Foggia's **airport** (www.aeroportidipuglia.it).

GETTING AROUND You'll need a car to visit Castel del Monte with any ease, and the only way to explore the Gargano promontory is by car. To visit Castel del Monte, head south to Andria, where you'll begin to see signs for the castle; you want to be driving south, in the direction of Spinazzola. The trip takes about half an hour. From Trani, the Gargano gateway city is Manfredonia, about 80km (50 miles) north via SS 16 and SP 77. Once there, SS89 skirts the peninsula; expect at least half a day of slow driving to make the circuit. If you're planning to visit the castle on the way from Matera to Trani, Bari, or other coastal town, head to Altamura and from there to Gravina; in Gravina follow signs toward Spinazzola, and the castle will be signposted.

VISITOR INFORMATION Visit **www.viaggiareinpuglia.it** for information about Trani, Castel del Monte, and the Gargano. Trani has a **tourist office** at Piazza Trieste 10 (✆ **0883-588830**). On the Gargano, Vieste's tourist office is at Piazza J.F. Kennedy (✆ 0884-708806), and Peschici has an office at Via Magenta 3 (✆ 0884-915362).

Exploring Trani

For most of Trani's history, travelers approached the city by sea. Today you'll likely come into town through the scruffy outskirts sprawling across the flat Puglian plain—but you'll still want to head to the port. The enormous 13th-century Castello Svevo along the shoreline is proof of Trani's onetime power, street names like Via Synagoga are reminders of a large medieval Jewish population, and Via Cambio (Street of the Moneychangers) testifies to Trani's role as a major Mediterranean trading center. Trani was also a port for holy warriors setting off for the crusades; the Knights Templar, an elite corps of Christian soldiers from throughout Europe, received their blessings before embarking in the courtyard of the church of Ogisanti, on Via Ogisanti (usually closed, but the exterior is splendidly medieval).

Duomo ★★ The best place to savor first impressions of this towering, gleaming, Romanesque-style masterwork is from the east side of the entrance of Trani's round little port. From there, the **campanile** (bell tower), stretches 59m-high (194-ft.) toward the sky, while the church's tall limestone walls seems to be rooted not in the ground but in the sea. This dramatic union of sea and sky lifts the spirit long before you step

One of the eight octagonal towers in Castel del Monte, Trani.

foot in the church, an effect the architects and craftsmen who began work in 1097 no doubt had in mind. Their singular mission was to outdo Bari, their neighbor just down the coast. With the help of pirates, Bari had just removed the relics of St. Nicholas (of Christmastime fame) from Myra, in present-day Turkey. The town was building a basilica to house the remains, sure to be a big draw on the lucrative pilgrimage circuit. Trani had a new saint of its own, San Nicola Pellegrino (St. Nicholas the Pilgrim). The Greek shepherd boy, after a long sea voyage across the Adriatic, collapsed and died from exhaustion in front of the church of Santa Maria, upon which Trani's cathedral is built. Nicola was so pious that he spent all his waking hours continually reciting the phrase "Kyrie Eleison" ("Lord, have mercy"), a habit that those around him found less than ingratiating but won for him almost instant sainthood.

The origins of the 7th-century church of Santa Maria remain in the crypt, where the saint's tomb rests among a forest of columns. The main church above is a soaring display of arches, columns, and vaults, all luminously fashioned from golden limestone. Barisano da Trani, most famous for his reliefs of the doors in Monreale outside Palermo (see page 748) created the heavy doors. The 32 intricate bronze panels depict familiar biblical figures as well as dragons, lions, archers, and jugglers. In one panel the artist portrays himself, humbly at the feet of San Nicola. Piazza Duomo 9. ✆ **0883-494210.** Free admission. Daily 9am–8pm.

Around Trani

Castel del Monte ★ HISTORIC SIGHT This tall castle atop a small mount above the fertile Puglian plains comes into sight from miles away, just as the enlightened Frederick II, Holy Roman Emperor and King of Sicily, intended when he ordered construction in 1237. If the distinctive octagonal shape looks familiar, that may be because it appears on the 1-cent euro printed in Italy.

The castle's purpose has never been determined. What's not here, a moat or a circuit of curtain walls, casts doubt on its practicality as a defense, though the strategic hilltop position certainly ensured that an enemy could not approach without being spotted. Meanwhile, the octagonal shape with eight octagonal towers blends Islamic and Gothic influences to suggest engineering precision and reflects Frederick's passion for science and mathematics. Large trapezoidal rooms on two floors are warmed by fireplaces and imply a certain degree of luxury, fueling speculation that the castle was meant for entertaining or as a hunting lodge. A few fragments of mosaics, frescoes, and marble work remain, and it's known that a plumbing system fed by rainwater supplied baths and latrines. Poor souls languished in the cold chambers when Frederick's successors converted the castle to a prison.

18km (11 miles) south of Andria. www.casteldelmonte.org. ✆ **0883-569997.** Admission 5€. Mar–Sept daily 10:15am–7:45pm; Oct–Feb daily 9:15am–5:45pm.

Promontorio del Gargano ★★★ NATURAL WONDER Most of this thumb-shaped promontory is protected as the **Parco Nazionale del Gargano** (www.parks.it/parco.nazionale.gargano), with headquarters in Monte Sant'Angelo, 90km (55 miles) north of Trani. The mountainous interior of the peninsula, the spur of the Italian boot, is carpeted in part with the ancient oak and beech forest known as the Foresta Umbra that once covered much of Central Europe, while the coast is a magical seascape of cliffs, rocks, caves, islets, and sandy beaches. Come August, Italian families head in droves to low-key summertime-only resorts around the whitewashed towns of Vieste and Peschici. Residents of both towns spent many centuries fending off unwelcome visits from pirates and other invaders, and in the old town of Viestre, jutting into the Adriatic on a narrow promontory, in 1554 the Turks beheaded more than 5,000 men, women, and children on the Chianca Amara, the "bitter stone." The Gargano has long been on the tourist map, and not just for its beaches. Medieval crusaders are among the throngs who have made the pilgrimage to the cave of St. Michael the Archangel in Monte Sant'Angelo, the oldest shrine in Western Europe and the scene of three appearances by the archangel. Even more popular is the sanctuary of Padre Pio in San Giovanni Rotondo, where the beloved saint arrived shortly after he became a priest in 1916 and remained for 52 years. Associated with many miraculous events, he was canonized in 2002. His shrine, including a stunning church by modern architect Renzo Piano, is the second-most-visited Catholic pilgrimage site in the world, after Mexico City's Our Lady of Guadalupe, with 7 million pilgrims per year.

Where to Eat & Stay

B&B Palazzo Paciotti ★★ A restored palace in the old quarter near the cathedral oozes with Trani's long history, but beyond the rich stone facade the large, high-ceiling spaces on the third floor (with elevator) are spruce and modern. Low slung chairs are upholstered in white, beds framed in white steel are a sharp take on the four-poster, and modern bathrooms gleam with sparkling mosaic tiles. Breakfast is served in an upper-floor sunroom with terrace, shared with the slightly snazzier, slightly more luxurious Le Dimore del Re on another floor of the palace (for information, go to www.ledimoredeire.it).

Via della Giudea 41. www.palazzopaciotti.it. ✆ **340/238-8121**. 5 units. 80€–90€ double, includes breakfast. **Amenities:** Wi-Fi (free).

Corte in Fiore ★★★ SEAFOOD Cast aside any notions of an old fisherman's haunt, or for that matter the region's famous *cucina povera*, in these luxurious contemporary spaces. A few outdoor rooms meander through the courtyard of an old palace near the port, covered in winter, and always full of greenery offsetting the chic white furnishings. The menu is short and simple but a fish fancier's delight, with antipastos of fresh sashimi and sushi or a cooked selection of the chef's choice, depending on what's fresh that day; follow-ups are a few grilled choices and perfectly prepared seafood pastas and risottos.

Via Ognissanti 18. www.corteinfiore.it. ✆ **0883/508-402.** Main courses 12€–25€. Tues–Sun noon–2:30pm and 8–10:30pm.

THE VALLE D'ITRIA: *TRULLO* COUNTRY ★★

The Valle d'Itria can seem like a magical place, where stone, cone-shaped, fairytale-ish *trulli* poke above olive groves. *Trulli* are sprinkled over farms and fields throughout this part of Puglia, and in Alberobello, a little town at the heart of the Valle d'Itria, more than 1,600 of these beehive houses line the hilly, winding lanes. The scene looks like something out of a children's storybook and has earned UNESCO World Heritage Site status. Alberobello is just the beginning. The road winds south through the Valle d'Itria to a string of towns built of gleaming white stone and perched on hilltops.

Exploring the *trulli* of Alberobello, Puglia.

Alberobello ★★

Alberobello has 1,620 *trulli*, and the effect is whimsical, even a bit weird. Walking through the narrow streets you can't help but feel you've stepped into the pages of a fairy tale, or a scene from *The Hobbit*.

You'll be forgiven for making a crack or two, like "These are *trulli* charming" or "These are *trulli* ingenious" (see box). Just don't think you're being clever, because the residents of Alberobello have heard it all.

Most of the *trulli* of Alberobello date from the mid-16th century to the 19th century. The best explanation for their proliferation has to do with their ease of construction and the flexibility of the design, with stones are put in place without mortar. Local lore has it that the technique became popular because, when tax inspectors came around, residents could dismantle their *trulli* and erase any evidence of them. More likely is the possibility that since no mortar was used, the structures didn't qualify for full taxation. As you walk along the lanes, many ending in little cul-de-sacs, notice that the *trulli* are clustered together to allow for multi-room residences. Because of the nature of *trulli* construction, with thick stone walls supporting a conical roof, they could only be built as single-room structures. So, each conical roof corresponds with a single room below.

ESSENTIALS

GETTING THERE If you have a car, head south of Bari on S100 and then east (signposted) on S172. To find the *trulli,* follow Via Mazzini, which turns into Via Garibaldi, until you reach Piazza del Popolo. Turn left on Largo Martellotta, which will take you to the edge of the popular tourist area; the *trulli* are well signposted once you get to town. A parking lot off Largo Martellotta charges about 2€ an hour, payable in a machine that dispenses a ticket to place on your dashboard. Local **Ferrovia del Sud Est (FSE)** (www.fseonline.it) trains leave Bari every hour (every 2 hrs. on Sun) heading to Alberobello. The trip takes about 1¾ hours.

trulli INGENIOUS

The architecture of Puglia's famous *trulli* is specific to the Valle d'Itria, where the conical-roofed stone huts were used as sheds and shelters for farmers in the fields. Later the construction technique, in which stones and limestone slabs are piled one atop the other and no mortar is used, was used to build dwellings. In Alberobello, the *trullo* (from the Greek *troulos,* "dome") became the standard house type.

The gray roof "tiles" (slabs of limestone called *chiancarelle*) were dry-laid over an inner masonry cone. But some *trullari* (*trullo*-specialized masons) were more skilled than others: The smoother-roofed *trulli* are the work of expert *trullari,* while sloppy stonework bears testimony to the quick-and-dirty jobs by cut-rate masons or apprentices. The sculpted pinnacles or finials that top many *trulli* probably had no real meaning or function besides being ornamental business cards for the *trullaro* who built the house. Some *trulli* have artwork on the side of their roof, often symbols from pagan, Jewish, and Christian traditions. As you walk through Alberobello, look for such markings as a radiant orb, representing the sun and Christ, or a familiar heart shape with an arrow through it, a depiction of the heartache of the Virgin Mary.

VISITOR INFORMATION The main **tourist office** in Alberobello is north of the *trulli* zone on the central square of the modern town, at Piazza del Popolo 6 (✆ **080-4325171;** open Mon, Wed, and Thurs 8:30am–1pm, Tues and Fri 9am–1pm and 4–7:30pm).

EXPLORING THE TOWN

You need an hour or two to tour the *trulli*, starting from **Largo Martellotta.** This airy, pedestrian-only square separates the *centro storico*'s two *trulli* zones: Rione Monti, to the south, and Rione Aia Piccola, to the northeast. **Rione Monti** is the larger and busier of the two, and many of its *trulli* are now coffee bars and of course, gift shops. It's hard to resist leaving Alberobello without a small-scale replica of a *trullo,* crafted in the same type of stone that the town's builders used.

Once you've adjusted to the whimsy of so many curved walls and conical roofs, cross the square and walk up the hill into **Rione Aia Piccola.** This quiet residential quarter seems much more like a quaint village and provides a chance to get away from the crowds and appreciate the ancient and surreal aspect of the *trulli.* Aia Piccola occupies a hillside, and from here you'll get a great view across the valley to the spectacle of Monti's hundreds upon hundreds of densely packed *trulli.*

The most monumental house in town is the **Trullo Sovrano (Sovereign Trullo).** It's not in Aia Piccola or Monti but on the far northern edge of modern Alberobello in Piazza Sacramento (from Largo Martellotta, walk north into Piazza del Popolo and then follow Via Vittorio Emanuele north to Piazza Sacramento). This rare two-story *trullo* kcomprises 16 separate, joined structures surrounding a central *trullo* with a cupola. A prominent family built the compound, complete with stables, barns, and a farm court, in the late 18th century. It later became headquarters for a religious confraternity and today shows off *trulli* domestic life, with a bread-baking oven and some quaintly furnished rooms. It's open daily 10am to 1pm and 3 to 7pm. Admission is 1.50€.

WHERE TO EAT & STAY

While it's easy to see the appeal of staying in a setting as unique as the *trulli* zone, remember that you will essentially be stepping onto a Disney-like stage set, with thousands of selfie-taking gawkers trooping up and down the narrow streets. On the other hand, once the day-trippers leave, having the strange townscape almost to yourself is a magical experience. If this is something, sorry, you *trulli* want to experience, **Tipico Resort in Trulli** can set you up nicely in one of its 10 comfortably equipped *trulli* around town, all with spiffy bathrooms and other modern conveniences; rates begin at 70€ double and include breakfast. The office is at Via Brigata Regina 47 (www.tipicoresort.it; ✆ **080/432-4108**).

La Cantina ★★ PUGLIESE The Lippolis family has been satisfying local appetites since 1958. Their homey, stone-walled eatery just outside the *trulli* district is such an institution that the street out front is named for them. Offerings are *cucina povera* (simple, "poor" food) with some nice twists, and they're prepared in an open kitchen overseen by owner-chef Francesco. He usually sends out some delicious *bruschetta,* on thick local bread with rich olive oil and fresh tomatoes and mozzarella, perhaps followed by local *salumi* and *burrata*. The pork from nearby Martina Franca is grilled to perfection. La Cantina has only seven tables, so booking is essential, even in the winter.

Vico Lippolis 8. www.ilristorantelacantina.it. ✆ **080-4323473.** Main courses 9€–15€. Wed–Mon 12:30–2:30pm and 7:30–10:30pm. Closed 2 weeks in Feb and 2 weeks in July.

La Fontana 1914 ★ PUGLIESE For a quick bite on the main square, step into a butcher shop that also grills meat to order, serving platters and sandwiches in an informal, old-fashioned room off to the side. Chicken and chips is the top choice of the local kids who crowd in for a snack; another favorite is the *bombette,* pork shoulder wrapped around melted cheese and spiced with herbs. Salads are made with farm-fresh vegetables, and decent house wine is served by the glass or carafe.

Largo Martellotta 55. ✆ **380-3696969.** Main courses 5€–9€. Daily 8am–11pm.

Masseria Torre Coccaro ★★★ You can jump from one architectural experience to another with a 45-minute drive from Alberobello over to the coast, where this centuries-old *masseria*, a fortified farm compound, offers an experience as transporting as the *trulli*. Accommodations are tucked into haylofts, towers, and in the case of the cavernous Orange Garden suite, carved out of a rocky hillside. All surround citrus-scented gardens and a lake-like swimming pool. Dining is in an elegantly transformed stable block, where cooking lessons are among the many extras the hotel provides.

Contrada Coccaro 8, Savelletri di Fasano (Brindisi). www.masseriatorrecoccaro.com. ✆ **080-4829310.** 39 units. 285€–440€ double. Rates include breakfast. **Amenities:** Restaurant; bar; babysitting; bikes; exercise room; outdoor pool (heated Mar–Nov); room service; spa; Wi-Fi (free).

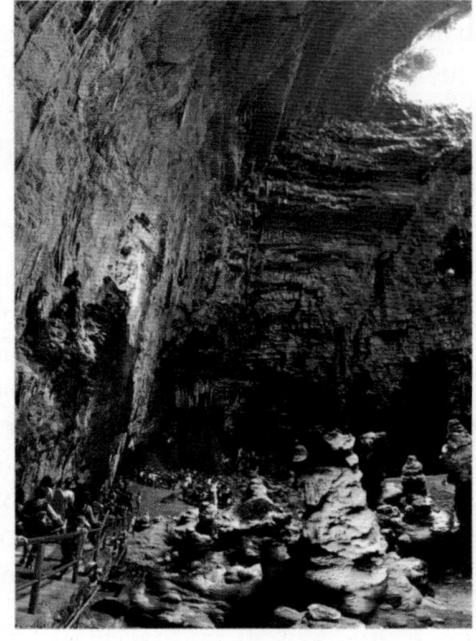

The Grave, a water-carved chamber in the Grotte di Castllana.

Trulli e Puglia B&B ★ We can't resist: These accommodations in the heart of the Monti quarter are *trulli* unique, with a cluster of well-restored *trulli* showing off the stonework and conical, beehive ceilings that make these dwellings so distinctive. Several are two stories, with sleeping lofts atop spiral staircases, and all sport rustic furnishings and wood finishes for a cozy atmosphere. All units have fridges and a few have kitchenettes, plus such modern conveniences as air-conditioning (not really necessary, given the thick walls and stone roofs) and surprisingly spacious, nicely appointed bathrooms. Innkeeper Mimmo and his staff provide a welcome that's as memorable as the architecture.

Via Monte San Michele 58. www.trulliepuglia.com. ✆ **080-7558539** or ✆ 347-5538539. 6 units. From 60€–70€ double. Rates include breakfast. **Amenities:** Bar; Wi-Fi (free).

A SIDE TRIP TO THE GROTTE DI CASTELLANA

The **Grotte di Castellana** is a vast network of caves, 3,350m (11,050 ft.) long and 125m (412 ft.) deep, that has been carved out over the centuries by water streaming through the limestone that underlies this part of Puglia. It's 17km (11 miles) north of Alberobello via SS172 and SS237.

An enormous tunnel leads into the **Grave,** a huge chamber lit by a skylight through which sunbeams and moonlight enter to flicker across the walls and floor. The vastness and eerie light have given rise to all sorts of legends of demons and lost souls floating through the depths. From the Grave, a series of paths winds through other underground rooms with names like **Corridoio del Serpent** and **Corridoio del Deserto,** filled with stalagmites and stalactites. At the end of the network of corridors is the majestic **Grotta Bianca**, where walls gleam with white alabaster and the rock formations are translucent. Visits are only by guided tours. Tours in Italian, English, French, and German run roughly every hour (and half-hour in summer) on a complex timetable that offers short (1 hr.) and long (2 hrs.) tours from 9am to 4pm, depending on the month, with longer hours in summer (www.grottedicastellana.it; ✆ **080-4998221**). From November to February, the caves are open by reservation only. Admission is 15€ for the long tour, 10€ for the short tour (the latter does not include the Grotte Bianca). Bring an extra layer: It's 15°C (59°F) in the caves year-round.

The White Cities

South of Alberobello and its cone-roofed *trulli* are a string of hilltowns that in look and feel seem a world removed from their famous neighbor but are distinctive nonetheless. Hewn out of light-colored stone, these towns are so glaringly bright in the sun that they're collectively known as the "white cities" and bring to mind Greece, southern Spain, and just as they should, southern Italy. Three of the most striking towns, **Locorotondo, Martina Franca,** and **Ostuni,** are near each other just south of Alberobello. It's easiest to reach them **by car,** heading south through the Valle d'Itria along SS172 to Locorotondo and Martina Franca, then east to Ostuni; the towns are all well signposted. You can also reach them **by train,** with 15 to 20 connections a day from Bari and Brindisi. Ostuni is on the main Italian state railways Adriatic line (www.trenitalia.com), while Locorotondo and Martina Franca are served by **Ferrovie del Sud Est** (www.fseonline.it).

LOCOROTONDO ★★★

8km (5 miles) S of Alberobello

As you approach this white and unabashedly cheerful little town you might think you're seeing a mirage: a ring of bright white houses with pointed gable roofs (called *cummerse*) crown the top of a hill. From a distance the scene looks a little like the rim rock you'd see in a Western American landscape, except, of course, for the domes of baroque churches rising above the rooftops. Once inside the gates the meaning of the town's name becomes clear: Streets of light-colored stone, flanked by white houses splashed with red geraniums, hug the contours of the hilltop in near-perfect concentric circles. Surrounding the circular maze are the old protective walls, skirted by a ring road from which you can see far across the plains below—a view that makes it clear why Locorotondo is known as the "balcony of the Valle d'Itria." Locorotondo is famous for its white wine. You can sample it in any of the restaurants and bars in town, or from the Cantina Sociale del Locorotondo, near the railway station below town on Via Madonna della Catena.

The town's **tourist office** is at Piazza Vittorio Emanuele 27 (✆ **080/431-3099**) and is usually open daily 9am–1pm and 4–7pm.

MARTINA FRANCA ★★★

6km (4 miles) S of Locorotondo, 14km (9 miles) S of Alberobello

This lively hilltown with its baroque finery and whitewashed back alleys was founded in the 10th century when coastal residents fled inland to escape Saracen attacks along the Adriatic and Ionian coasts. Tellingly, the *centro storico* is an intriguing tangle of medieval lanes that lead from one piazza to another. The labyrinthine layout may seem haphazard, but it was smartly devised as a means to confuse plunderers.

The **APT tourist office** is in Piazza Roma (www.martinafrancatour.it; ✆ **080-4805702**; Mon–Sat 9am–1pm and Tues and Thurs 4–7pm). You can't drive in Martina Franca's *centro storico* but you can park within a few blocks of the center on Via Giuseppe Aprile, Via Gabriele d'Annunzio, Piazza Francesco Crispi, Piazza Umberto, and Via Verdi.

At the center of town are two adjoining squares, **Piazza Plebiscito** and **Piazza Immacolata. Via Cavour**, leading south from Piazza Immacolata, is the main street of the Lama, the old quarter. Lining the handsome street are baroque *palazzi,* with fanciful arches and balconies, often crawling with stone cherubs. On and off Via Cavour and also north of Piazza Plebiscito and Piazza Immacolata is a tangle of whitewashed back streets, impossibly narrow passageways, and blind alleys. Some of the defense walls and towers still exist around the old city's perimeter, and the streets just below offer terrific views over the Valle d'Itria.

Rising above Piazza Plebiscito is the **Basilica di San Martino ★★** (✆ **080-4306536**), its facade richly adorned with baroque relief sculptures depicting episodes from the life of St. Martin. The most famous

Piazza Plebiscito and the Basilica di San Martino, Martina Franca.

scene has the saint, a Hungarian soldier who enlisted in the Roman legions, coming upon a poor beggar on a chilly November night and cutting his military cloak in half with his sword to keep the beggar warm. Martin's feast day on November 11th coincides with the grape harvest, earning him the honor of patron saint of wine. The first of the new wine is ready for tasting around San Martino's day, so on the 11th, it's said, *"ogni mosto e' vino"* ("every juice becomes wine"). Admission is free; the church is open daily 8am to 12:30pm and 4:30 to 8pm.

Also in the square is the **municipal clock tower,** erected in 1734, with a *meridiana* (sundial) inscribed on an eye-level plaque. In pretty, adjoining Piazza Immacolata, the landmark is century-old **Caffè Tripoli** (Via Garibaldi 25; ✆ **080-4805260**), where the specialty is *granita di caffè* (espresso with whipped cream). The town's culinary specialty is *capocollo di Martina Franca* (cured pork), cut from the top of the neck where it meets the shoulder, and cured with local wine, herbs, and wood smoke. Butcher/deli **Romanelli**, just off Piazza XX Settembre at Via Valle d'Itria 8–12 (✆ **080-4805385**), will let you sample its *capocollo* for free (along with *taralli* and red wine in paper cups, depending on the time of day), and you can buy sliced *capocollo* by the *etto* (100 grams).

OSTUNI ★★

24km E of Martina Franca, 35km SE of Alberobello

Other nearby towns may bill themselves as "white cities," but they're positively beige by comparison to gleamingly white Ostuni. Practically blinding in summer, and perched atop a commanding hill 8km (5 miles) above the Adriatic coast, Ostuni makes it clear you're close to Greece. Ancient Greeks, in fact, are among the dozens of invaders and occupiers who have come and gone over the past 2,500 years, though the mazelike streets and arched steps that tumble down hillsides are mostly medieval.

The **tourist office** at Corso Mazzini 6 (www.comune.ostuni.br.it; ✆ **083-1301268**) is open Monday to Saturday 10am to 1pm and 3:30 to 5:30pm, though hours vary.

Especially beneficent to Ostuni over the ages were two female rulers, Isabella of Aragon and her daughter, Bona Sforza, who in the 16th century made the city a cultured outpost and added walls and towers. Among the defenses were lookout towers along the coast, where beacon fires were lit to send warnings of approaching pirates. Sant'Oronzo, the patron of nearby Lecce and another benefactor, perches more than 60 feet atop La Colonna di Sant'Oronzo in Piazza della Libertà, at the foot of the hill to which the oldest part of town clings. His presence is a reference to a neighborly gesture in which he allegedly saved Ostuni from the plague in 1657 and again in 1771. The scene below the saint can seem a bit unholy on a warm weekend night, when everyone from miles around gathers in the piazza to chat, stroll, and sit in one of the cafes. From Piazza della Libertà, Via Cattedrale winds its way up and up through *la città Bianca* to the hilltop, Gothic-style **Duomo,** with a graceful, marble facade that swoops down into a gracious curve on one side; it's open daily 9am to 1pm and 3 to 7pm and admission is 1€. In a touching panel above a doorway to the left of the main entrance, Oronzo appears again, this time cradling Ostuni in his protective arms.

WHERE TO EAT & STAY

Villaggio In (Via Arco Grassi 8; www.villaggioin.it; ✆ **080-4805911**) rents spacious and well-furnished apartments in the heart of Martina Franca. Rates start at 75€ a day. All units have full kitchens.

La Tavernetta ★ PUGLIESE Step down off the busy street into this white- walled and arched cellar and you're transported to old Puglia, where waiters who have been here for decades dispense one traditional Pugliese classic after another—and at decidedly old-fashioned prices. House specialties include *fave e cicoria* (pureed fava beans with sautéed chicory), *orecchiette al ragu* (handmade ear-shaped semolina pasta with a robust sauce), and *braciole* (sliced veal stuffed with parsley, cheese, and garlic and simmered in tomato sauce).

Via Vittorio Emanuele 30, Martina Franca. ✆ **080-4306323.** Main courses 5.50€–15€. Tues–Sun 12:30–3pm and 7:30–11pm.

Osteria del Tempo Perso ★★ PUGLIESE Even in its centuries-old guise as a bakery, the *osteria* "of lost time" must have been charming, its rough-hewn walls carved out of a cave. Today the linen-topped tables spread into an adjoining room that's no less atmospheric, hung with old farm implements that dangle a little precariously among beautiful local ceramics. These colorful surrounds, just around the corner from the Duomo, are the setting for food that sticks close to local traditions, with lots of Adriatic seafood. Dishes you're not likely to find elsewhere include the house's own creation based on old recipes, *tegamino di funghi,* a casserole with bread, mushrooms, and zucchini flowers.

Via G. Tanzarella Vitale 47, Ostuni. www.osteriadeltempoperso.com. ✆ **0831-304819.** Main courses 7€–16€. Tues–Sun 12:30–2:30pm and 7:30–10:30pm. Also Mon in July–Aug.

Masseria La Rascina ★★ Tucked into a hillside between Ostuni and the sea, this old farmhouse is surrounded by manicured gardens and lawns and beautiful terraces set up for hours of lounging. Inn-type accommodations are in the main house, some opening off a quiet inner courtyard, while apartments with kitchens and outdoor dining areas are in bungalows on the grounds. Like the lounges, they are done in a tasteful mix of traditional, contemporary, and Asian pieces for an effect that's comfortable and soothing.

Strada Statale Adriatica (SP19, km 4.7), Rosmarina, Ostuni. www.larascina.it. ✆ **338-4331573.** 10 units. 100€–240€ double. Breakfast included with some rates; weekly rates available. **Amenities:** Bike rentals; swimming pool; Wi-Fi (free).

Pizzeria Casa Pinto ★★ PIZZERIA It's probably not much of an exaggeration to say that on weekend nights most of Locorotondo crowds into these tiny rooms, one of them taken up by a huge pizza oven. In bad weather waiting diners are shunted off to a little room across the lane. Tables are tucked into an almost cavelike vaulted cellar, and the pizzas are almost as distinctive, made with organic products. Some are topped so lightly with olive oil and cheese that they seem more like savory baked bread than pizza. Other toppings are more traditional, but any choice should be washed down with the town's signature white wine.

Via Aprile 23, Locorotondo. ✆ **34627/49859.** Pizzas 6€–8€. Wed–Mon noon–2:30 and 7:30–10:30pm.

The whitewashed facades of Ostuni.

Sotto le Cummerse ★★★ With its warm light stone and compact lanes and squares, Locorotondo might be one of the most welcoming towns anywhere. Visitors who want to hang around for awhile can live like a native in these 13 distinctive lodgings tucked into houses around the old

14

BASILICATA & PUGLIA | The Valle d'Itria: Trullo Country

town. All are different, ranging from simple ground-floor studios to multilevel suites; all are nicely furnished in traditional style and make the most of stone walls, fireplaces, and other vintage details. Many have terraces, as well as up-to-date bathrooms, some equipped with Jacuzzis. Breakfast is served in a welcoming room near the reception, where the accommodating staff is on hand well into the evening hours.

Via Vittorio Emanuele 138, Locorotondo. www.sottolecummerse.it. ✆ **080/431-3298.** 80€–240€ double. Rates include breakfast. **Amenities:** Wi-Fi (free).

LECCE ★★

113km (68 miles) SE of Alberobello, 40km (25 miles) SE of Brindisi, 408km (245 miles) SE of Naples

Sophisticated Lecce combines baroque architecture and urbane elegance with typically southern Italian radiance. The handsome old city center is clad almost entirely in the local golden limestone, lending an irresistible warmth, amplified by Lecce's fabulous baroque embellishments. *Il barocco leccese* was a particularly ebullient version of the 17th-century Italian predilection for architectural decoration. Because the local limestone is fairly soft and easy to chisel, sculptors covered church facades and civic palaces with saints, angels, and intricate details as if they were drawing on paper. While it's easy to describe the limestone as "buttery," "milky" might be more apt—milk was applied to the final work, and the lactose seeped into the pores of the stone and hardened it. Founded by Greeks more than 2,200 years ago, Lecce is also a city with a tangible ancient history, with a Roman theater and amphitheater and the bastions of the 16th-century Castello Carlo V (Castle of Charles V, the Habsburg Holy Roman Emperor).

Lecce calls itself the "Florence of the South," but that comparison misses the mark. Lecce's identity is southern Italian through and through. While the city is beautiful and proud, it doesn't have Florence's concentration of art-rich monuments. It is nonetheless an enjoyable place to amble and gawk; rather than tourism, the Leccesi are wrapped up in agriculture, especially the sale and distribution of olive oil and wine. Lecce is also a good base for making day trips around the rest of the Salento peninsula, much of which is within an hour's drive.

Baroque Lecce was built of golden limestone.

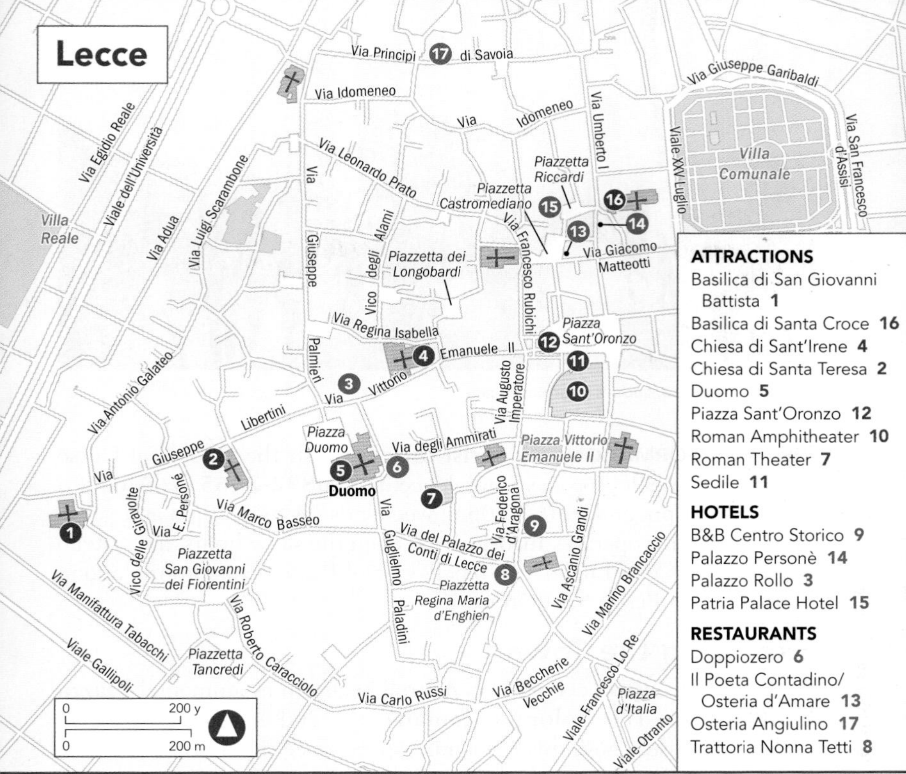

Essentials

GETTING THERE High-speed Frecciargento trains connect Lecce with Rome, via Bari, in a not-so-fast 5½ hours; faster service is expected to begin operating in 2018. Lecce is also connected to Bari and Brindisi by frequent **train** service. The journey from Bari takes about 1½ hours; from Brindisi it's a half-hour trip. Visit www.trenitalia.com or call ✆ **892021** in Italy for train schedules and information. Note that Lecce's train station is about 2km (1¼ miles) from the center of the old quarter; from the train station, buses 11, 12, and 14 run to Porta Napoli at the edge of the *centro storico*. The fare is 1.30€ and you can purchase tickets at newsstands; for more information, go to www.sgmlecce.it.

If you have a **car** and are arriving from the north, follow signs to Brindisi, then take state highway SS613 south to Lecce (38km/24 miles, or about a half-hour). Most of the center is closed to car traffic and parking is extremely limited; it's best to leave your car in one of the large lots in Piazza Muratore, Piazza Giuseppe Libertini, or elsewhere on the perimeter of the *centro storico*. You can most likely make parking arrangements with your hotel for one of these lots in advance of arrival.

Piazza Sant'Oronzo, Lecce's principal square.

VISITOR INFORMATION A **tourist office** is near the Duomo at Corso Vittorio Emanuele 16a (www.infolecce.it; ✆ **0832-246517**; Mon–Fri 9:30am–1:30pm and 3:30–7:30pm; weekends 10am–1:30pm and 3:30–7pm. The office operates **info-points,** open the same hours, at Castello Carlo V, Viale XXV Luglio, two blocks east of Piazza Sant'Oronzo, and in the Sedile, on Piazza Sant'Oronzo.

Exploring the Town

It's easy to explore Lecce on foot. A stroll begins in monumental **Piazza Sant'Oronzo**. The **Colonna Romana,** the 2nd-century-A.D. Roman column that rises above this welcoming space, once stood near its mate in Brindisi; together they marked the end of the Appian Way. Lightning toppled this column in 1528, and the Brindisians left it lying on the ground until 1661, when the citizens of Lecce bought it. St. Oronzo, the patron saint of Lecce, stands atop the capital. He's honored on August 26 and venerated for miraculously delivering Lecce from a plague in 1658.

At the southern side of the piazza are the remains of a **Roman amphitheater.** Archaeologists can't agree on the date of the structure—it's either Augustan (1st century B.C., thus predating the Roman Colosseum), or Trajanic-Hadrianic (2nd century A.D.). It would have accommodated 25,000 fans, who came to watch bloody fights between gladiators and wild beasts. The amphitheater is sometimes open for a look round, usually during the summer from 10am to noon and 3 to 7pm; admission is free. Also uncertain is the exact date of Lecce's nearby **Roman Theater,** tucked off Via Ammirati south of Piazza Sant'Oronzo. The half ellipse was also constructed sometime between the late 1st century B.C. and the early 2nd century A.D. and housed about 5,000 spectators for plays and concerts. You can step into the theater as part of a visit to the adjacent **Museo del Teatro Romano** (www.comune.lecce.it ✆ **0832-279196**; Mon–Sat 9:30am–1pm; admission 3€).

Perhaps the most striking presence in Piazza Sant'Oronzo is the odd but gracious **Palazzo del Seggio,** or **Il Sedile,** along the northwest curve of the amphitheater. The perfectly proportioned pavilion has an arched loggia on the ground floor and an arcaded terrace above. Built in 1592, Il Sedile was originally the seat *(sede)* of the city government. It now houses a branch of the tourist office.

To the west of Piazza Sant'Oronzo is a string of extravagantly baroque churches. To get an eyeful of their facades, follow Via Vittorio Emanuele and its continuation, Via Giuseppe Libertini, past the Duomo to the 18th-century Porta Rudiae. The **Chiesa di Sant'Irene,** the first church you come to on Via Vittorio Emanuele, was built in 1591 for the then-patron of Lecce. Priest-architect Francesco Grimaldi designed the church with the same flair he exhibited with his baroque landmarks in Naples and Rome, adorning the facade with columns, niches, statues, and a wolf from the town's coat of arms. Irene, who still stands above the portal, was demoted to regular-saint status when Oronzo saved Lecce from the plague in the 17th century. Lecce's first telegraph station was installed in the tower in the mid-19th century, while the somber nave became a communal meeting hall during the unification of Italy.

The column of St. Orontius of Lecce.

The 17th-century **Chiesa di Santa Teresa**, farther up on Via Libertini (✆ **0832/33269**), has also served multiple purposes, as a police barracks, a school, and a tobacco warehouse. These practical functions transpired behind a fanciful facade by master sculptor Giuseppe Zimbalo (see the Duomo and Santa Croce, below). Even though the facade was never finished, what's in place is an exuberance of columns and statuary, among them the two Saint Johns, the Baptist and the Evangelist. Inside is what might be the town's most macabre work of art, a lifelike statue of a bloodied, emaciated Christ that lies within a coffinlike glass box. By comparison, the **Basilica di San Giovanni Battista** a few steps up Via Libertini (✆ **0832/308540**) is a joyful place, where cherubs float through the light-filled interior. Admission to most of Lecce's churches is free, and they're generally open daily from 7am to noon and 3:30 to 7pm.

Basilica di Santa Croce ★★ CHURCH The *barocco leccese* hits fever pitch at Santa Croce (Holy Cross) basilica, where sculptors drew from religion, mythology, and local history to cram the facade with lions, angels, sea creatures, Turks, goddesses—hundreds of figures in all, crowding the columned tiers. Most significant might be those turbaned Turks, whose forces had been menacing Lecce and the rest of southern Europe for centuries but had been defeated at the Battle of Lepanto in 1571. The victory tipped the scales to ensure the dominance of Christianity in Europe, and in many esoteric ways, this expanse of masonry more or less celebrates Christian values. Even those strange-looking beasts and figures on the lower tiers represent the Christian forces that conquered the Turks, with the griffon standing in for the Republic of Genoa and Hercules for the dukes of Tuscany. It's unlikely that you're going to understand much of the iconography, but that really doesn't matter. Just stand in Via Umberto I out front and soak in the spectacle. The facade is the work of three generations of local masons; most notable is master Giuseppe Zimbalo (1620–1710), also known as Lo Zingarello, the "Tiny Gypsy." His son, Francesco, did the portals and some of the most beautiful work in the interior, with its forest of carved columns. Among his credits is the tomb of Saint Francesco di Paolo. Carvings depict scenes from the life of the local saint. Like his same-named role model from Assisi, the friar and cave-dwelling hermit was an animal lover, and in some of his most acclaimed miracles he restored life to a roasted lamb and a fried trout. He was also the envy of boatmen, since he could hoist up his robes to catch a breeze and sail across the sea. Via Umberto I. ✆ **0832/241957.** Free. 9am–noon and 3:30–7:30pm.

Duomo ★ CHURCH Lecce's cathedral stands in an almost completely enclosed square, a setting that is both dramatic and practical. In times of siege, residents would take refuge in the huge piazza, entered by narrow entrances that could be completely closed off. Despite doing double duty as a fortress, the square is remarkably playful. Giuseppe Zimbalo, one of the creators of Santa Croce (see above), also reworked the chiseled facade of the 12th-century Duomo, embellishing it with

Statues at the Basilica of Santa Croce (Church of the Holy Cross).

sculpted saints and other figures. High above the entrance is Lecce's patron St. Oronzo. Zimbalo also designed the adjacent **campanile** that towers 64m (210 ft.) above the piazza, ascending in tiers like a wedding cake. The **seminary,** across the square, has an extravagantly chiseled facade that could have been squirted out of a pastry tube and is the work of Giuseppe Cino, a student of Zimbalo. Adding to the exuberance is the **Bishop's Palace (Palazzo Vescovile),** still home to Lecce's archbishops, with its arches and saint-filled niches.

Piazza del Duomo. Via Vittorio Emanuele. http://cattedraledilecce.it. ✆ **0832-308557**. Free. Daily 7am–noon and 4–7pm.

Where to Stay

B&B Centro Storico ★★★ Every inch of the beautifully restored floor of a baroque palace is carefully tended by the two proprietor brothers, who extend the same attention to their guests. Centuries-old stone window frames are sculpted in such a way to capture maximum sunlight; expertly restored baroque ceilings form *volte a stella,* star-shaped vaults; sleeping lofts are tucked above gleaming wood floors in former salons turned suites. A mix of antiques and modern pieces add to the appeal of these character-filled and extremely comfortable spaces. Above is a rambling roof deck with a hot tub and a cottage-like guest room with its own private terrace. Breakfast is served in a nearby cafe.

Via A. Vignes 2. www.centrostoricolecce.it. ✆ **0832/242727.** 6 units. 60€–100€. Rates include breakfast. **Amenities:** Roof terrace; hot tub; Wi-Fi (free).

Palazzo Persone ★★★ It's easy to slip into the easygoing Leccese lifestyle in these wonderful rooms surrounding the courtyard of a palazzo in the heart of the old quarter. Rooms are a mix of centuries-old details—fireplaces, absurdly high beamed ceilings, and time-worn wood and tile—and midcentury furniture and contemporary touches. The welcome is as warm as the city's honey-colored stone. Breakfast is served in a pleasant cafe facing the lane out front, while a dining room incorporates part of a 16th-century synagogue and *mikveh* (ritual bath).

Viale Umberto I 5. www.palazzopersone.com. ✆ **0832-279968.** 6 units. 70€–90€ double. Rates include breakfast. **Amenities:** Bar; café; Wi-Fi (free).

Palazzo Rollo ★★ Stepping into the vine-covered courtyard of this 17th-century palace is like entering a world unto itself, the private domain of the Rollo clan for more than 200 years. In its current guise the old surroundings house guests in a magical warren of suites that are more homey than luxurious, with tile floors, old-fashioned furnishings, and almost endless nooks and crannies. Four ground-floor apartments off the courtyard have been fashioned out of stone-vaulted old storerooms. A luxuriant roof garden offers plenty of shady spots from which to take in the view over the bell tower next door and the *centro storico* rooftops.

Via Vittorio Emanuele II 14. www.palazzorollo.it. ✆ **0832-3017152.** 4 suites, 4 apartments. From 80€ double. Rates include breakfast. **Amenities:** Wi-Fi (free).

Patria Palace Hotel ★★ Lecce's bastion of luxury has been pampering guests since 1797, and these days does so in richly upholstered and carpeted rooms, where traditional furniture creates a clublike lair that's especially popular with traveling business folks and nobs. The old *palazzo* would be almost stodgy if it weren't for its neighbor, the flamboyant Santa Croce basilica. A few rooms have private terraces, while a roof garden is a perfect spot to enjoy a bottle of wine while contemplating the baroque surroundings.

Piazzetta Riccardi 13. www.patriapalacelecce.com. ✆ **0832-245111.** 67 units. 89€–131€ double. Rates include breakfast. **Amenities:** Restaurant; bar; concierge; room service; Wi-Fi (free).

Where to Eat

An almost mandatory stop in Lecce is **Natale,** at Via Trinchese 7A (www.natalepasticceria.it), for the best gelato and pastry in town.

Doppiozero ★ PUGLIESE Lecce shows off its most hip, urbane side in a cafe and deli where repurposed bottles light long communal tables and bottles of the local vintage are stacked to the high ceilings. Alongside them are big wheels of cheese, hams, long salamis, and vats of olive oil. These and other market-fresh ingredients, also available for takeaway purchases, find their way into sandwiches and deli boards, along with crostini, salads, soups, and a few daily pastas. The light fare is a hit with a youthful crowd that doesn't seem to mind the rushed service.

Via Paladini 2. www.emporiodoppiozero.com. ✆ **0832/521052.** Main courses 8€–12€. Daily 8am–midnight (closes at 4:30pm Mon in winter).

Il Poeta Contadino/Osteria d'Amare ★ PUGLIESE/SEAFOOD You'll be reminded that Lecce is almost on the Adriatic in this comfy little room with big glass windows facing Piazza Sant'Oronzo, where the freshest seafood shows up in a few well-done preparations each day, from sandwiches generously filled with filets of swordfish and fresh vegetables to basic pastas along the lines of *spaghetti alla vongole* (with clams). From the *"poeta contadino"* (poet farmer) side of the menu comes a nice selection of meat-and-vegetable-topped *bruschetti,* pastas with fresh vegetables, and other land-based, simple fare, all accompanied by good local wines by the glass.

Piazzetta Castromediano 8. ✆ **0348-0251133.** Main courses 8€–16€. Tues–Sun noon–2:30pm and 7–10pm.

Osteria Angiulino ★★ PUGLIESE These brightly tiled, vaulted rooms are Lecce's favorite outpost for *cucina povera,* but that really translates as the region's authentic cuisine. Many of the dishes are vegetarian, including an appetizer of green beans and fava beans, parboiled to perfect crunchiness. The *melanzane alla parmigiana* is a perfect meatless main-course follow-up. On the carnivorous side of the menu is horsemeat prepared in every way imaginable—as meatballs, chopped, fileted and topped with a green sauce, or in a savory stew. The house wine is as hearty and affordable as the cuisine.

Via Principe di Savoia 4. ✆ **0832-245146.** Main courses 5€–8€. Mon–Sat 1–2:30pm and 7–10pm.

Trattoria Nonna Tetti ★★ PUGLIESE The warm and inviting room with lots of tile and stone is another outpost for local cooking. The big menu also expands into the rest of Italy, but even so, the standouts are strictly Leccese, like *ricciareddhe* pasta with cherry tomatoes, garlic, and cheese or wild chicory with a purée of boiled fava beans.

Piazzetta Regina Maria 17. ✆ **0832-246036.** Main courses 8€–12€. Mon–Sat noon–2:30pm and 7–11pm.

Shopping

For a selection of local crafts, including *cartapesta* (papier-mâché), ceramics, and terracotta, step into **Mostra Permanente dell'Artigianato,** Via Francesco Rubichi 21 (✆ **0832-246758**). Works of dozens of local artists are on display in the cavernous space, from nativity figures to abstract sculpture to embroidered clothing. **Mamma Elvira Enoteca,** Via Umberto I 19 (✆ **0832-0169-2011**), is an especially welcoming bar/shop in Via Umberto I. It's a great place to introduce yourself to wines of the southeast. **Cartoleria Pantheon Lecce,** Via Giuseppe Libertini 69 (www.pantheon-lecce.com; ✆ **0832-521312**), whisks you off to Florence, so enticing are all the creamy leather goods. Wares range from iPhone cases and leather-bound diaries to briefcases and bags.

A Side Trip to Otranto ★★

The easternmost town in all of Italy, Otranto is on the Salento peninsula, the heel of the Italian boot. Two colors dominate here: the electric turquoise of the sea and the gleaming white of the old quarter. Reason enough to come is to walk the maze of streets in the medieval *borgo* and gaze out over the Adriatic from waterfront promenades—it's said that if you look hard enough on a clear day you can see all the way to Albania. The city shows off its colorful history in two landmarks (see below).

The **tourist office** is across from the fortress at Piazza Castello 8 (✆ **0836-801436**; daily 9am–noon and 3–6pm). By **car,** Otranto is about 45 minutes southeast of Lecce, via SS16. **Trains** operated by **Ferovia Sud Est (FSE)** (www.fseonline.it) run between Lecce and Otranto about every hour and a half; travel time is a little over an hour, with a change in Magile and sometimes a second change in Zollino.

Castello Aragonese ★ FORTRESS Otranto's 15th-century sea-facing fortress, surrounded in part by a moat filled with fearsome green water, looks mightier than it proved to be. The thick, squat fortifications failed to thwart an attack by the fleet of Mehmet the Conqueror, who landed nearby in 1480 and took the city in just 2 weeks. That's largely

Turquoise seas and gleaming white houses at Otranto.

because most of the garrison and townsfolk fled at the sight of the Turkish ships approaching by sea. Those who took refuge in the fortress poured boiling water over the ramparts, but to little avail. It's said that when the castle and the rest of the town was overrun, more than 800 of those captured chose to die rather than renounce Christianity, with the tailor Antonio Primaldi proclaiming, "since the Lord died on the cross for us, it is fitting that we should die for him." It's moving to see the skulls of the so-called Martyrs of Otranto stacked up in the Duomo and ponder their fate as you regard the glorious sea views from the ramparts. Other than those, the castle really doesn't have much to show off. If you've come here looking for the setting of Horace Walpole's famous gothic novel, *The Castle of Otranto,* you'll be disappointed—the fortress bears no likeness to the creepy dwelling of Walpole's imagination.

Piazza Castello. ✆ **0836-871308.** 2€. Jan–Feb and Nov–Dec Tues–Sun 10am–1pm and 3–5pm (Mar and Oct to 6pm); Apr–May daily 10am–1pm and 3–7pm; June and Sept daily 10am–1pm and 3–10pm; July–Aug daily 10am–midnight.

Cattedrale di Otranto ★★★ CHURCH Otranto's formidable 11th-century cathedral is built atop remains that some of the town's oldest inhabitants left behind. These include a village founded by the Messappi, an Indo-European tribe (as early as the 8th century B.C.); a Roman villa; and an early Christian church. Inside is a remarkable remnant from the Middle Ages, the **Tree of Life floor mosaic,** created by artisans under the direction of the monk-artist Pantaleone in the 1160s. The colorful tile work presents a compendium of world knowledge as might have been available to an erudite scholar in the 12th century. Laid out on the floor like a tree in genealogy diagrams, the trunk and branches cover much of the length and width of the church. Arthurian legend gets a nod,

Souvenir shops in the streets of Otranto.

as does Islam, then prevalent in southern Italy, and Alexander the Great, who blended so many ancient cultures. Some of the images are recognizable—Adam and Eve, Noah, the huntress Diana among your best shots at deciphering the vivid and complex symbolism, while strange-looking horse heads, mermaids, and couples riding fish remain beautiful yet mysterious. No such uncertainty surrounds the *beati martiri,* the skulls of the citizens beheaded during the Ottoman sack of Otranto in 1480. They line the walls of a spooky side chapel (see Castello Aragonese, above). Piazza Basilica. ✆ **0836-80272.** Free. Daily 7am–noon and 3–5pm (till 7pm summer).

BEYOND OTRANTO

Heading south from Otranto on SS173, the coast is quite rugged and the driving scenic. **Santa Cesarea Terme,** a spa town for more than 500 years, exploits the stinky sulfuric waters emerging from the underlying rock as an alleged cure for all kinds of maladies, mostly rheumatic. Take a soak in the thermal pools at the **Terme di Santa Cesarea** spa facility, Via Roma 40 (www.termesantacesarea.it; ✆ **0836-944070**). Admission to the pools is 5€; they're open 9am to 7pm, shorter hours in winter.

The very tip of the Salento's stiletto heel is **Santa Maria di Leuca.** The classic experience here is climbing up to the lighthouse and adjacent basilica, called **De Finibus Terrae** (End of the World), for a bracing, almost 360-degree panorama of the Adriatic and Ionian Seas.

SICILY

By Stephen Brewer

15

Sicily has been conquered, settled, and abandoned by dozens of civilizations, from the Phoenicians, Greeks, and Carthaginians in antiquity to the Arabs, Berbers, Moors, and Normans in the Middle Ages, to the Spanish and Bourbons in the Renaissance, and finally (at least nominally), modern Italy. It's an intricate and violent story that nonetheless left a fascinating legacy. Touring the relics of Sicily's tumultuous past can sometimes make you feel that you're visiting several different countries at once.

Though it's only separated from the mainland by the 5km-wide (3 miles) Stretto di Messina (Straight of Messina), the 25,708 sq. km. (9,926 sq. mile) island, the largest in the Mediterranean, has a palpable, captivating sense of otherness. Some Sicilians will refer to a trip to the mainland as "going to Italy." The island offers the full package of Italian travel experiences: evocative towns, compelling art, impressive architecture, and ruins older than anything in Rome. Alongside the jewels of Sicily's glorious Classical past (Agrigento, Siracusa, Segesta, Piazza Armerina) you'll see baroque cities rebuilt after devastating earthquakes (Noto and Ragusa)—and, sadly, hideous postwar concrete monsters.

The island's geographic palette goes from the arid, chalky southeast to the brooding slopes of Mt. Etna to the brawny headlands of Palermo and the gentle agricultural landscapes of the east—all surrounded by cobalt seas and beaches where you can swim from May to October. The colors and natural contrasts are shaped by the elements like nowhere else on earth; African and alpine fauna live spectacularly on the same island.

Then, of course, too, there are the Sicilians themselves: The descendants of Greek, Carthaginian, Roman Vandal, Arab, Norman, and Spanish conquerors. They can be welcoming yet suspicious, taciturn and at the same time garrulous, deeply tied to traditions yet yearning to break away from distasteful precedents. True to stereotypes, Sicilians are a passionate people, and their warmth can make even everyday transactions memorable.

Thousands of years of domination have created stark contradictions, but Sicilians have left an archaeological, cultural, and culinary legacy like no other in this world. In Goethe's words, "The key to it all is here."

FACING PAGE: **Isola Bella, Sicily.**

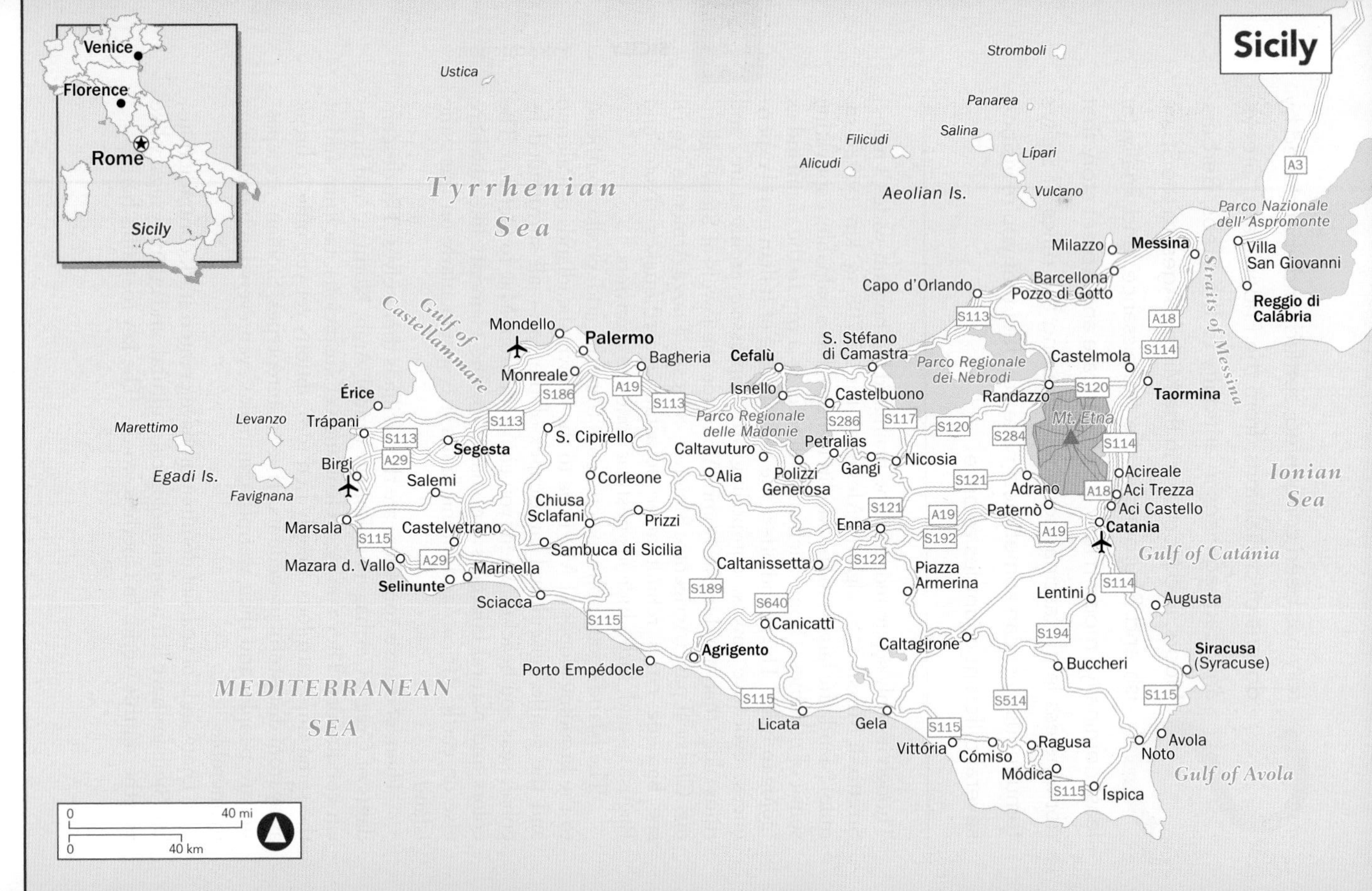
Sicily
Venice
Florence
Rome
Sicily
Tyrrhenian Sea
Ionian Sea
MEDITERRANEAN SEA
Straits of Messina
Gulf of Catánia
Gulf of Avola
Gulf of Castellammare
Aeolian Is.
Stromboli
Panarea
Salina
Lípari
Vulcano
Filicudi
Alicudi
Ustica
Egadi Is.
Marettimo
Levanzo
Favignana
Parco Nazionale dell'Aspromonte
Villa San Giovanni
Reggio di Calábria
Messina
Milazzo
Barcellona Pozzo di Gotto
Taormina
Castelmola
Randazzo
Mt. Etna
Adrano
Paternò
Acireale
Aci Trezza
Aci Castello
Catania
Augusta
Siracusa (Syracuse)
Lentini
Avola
Noto
Buccheri
Íspica
Ragusa
Módica
Cómiso
Vittória
Gela
Caltagirone
Piazza Armerina
Enna
Nicosia
Gangi
Parco Regionale dei Nebrodi
Capo d'Orlando
S. Stéfano di Camastra
Castelbuono
Petralias
Polizzi Generosa
Parco Regionale delle Madonie
Cefalù
Isnello
Caltavuturo
Alia
Caltanissetta
Canicattì
Licata
Agrigento
Porto Empédocle
Bagheria
Palermo
Mondello
Monreale
S. Cipirello
Corleone
Prizzi
Sambuca di Sicilia
Chiusa Sclafani
Sciacca
Marinella
Selinunte
Castelvetrano
Salemi
Segesta
Érice
Trápani
Birgi
Marsala
Mazara d. Vallo
A3
A18
A19
A29
S113
S114
S115
S117
S120
S121
S122
S186
S189
S192
S194
S284
S286
S514
S640
0
40 mi
40 km

PALERMO ★★★

233km (145 miles) W of Messina, 721km (447 miles) S of Naples, 934km (579 miles) S of Rome

In Palermo, street markets evoke Middle Eastern souks, and famous monuments bear the exotic artistic signature of the Arab-Norman 12th century, when the city was one of Europe's greatest cultural and intellectual centers. Palermo is Sicily's largest port, its capital, and a jumble of contradictions. Parts of some neighborhoods remain bombed out and not yet rebuilt from World War II; unemployment, poverty, traffic, crime, and crowding are rampant. Yet Palermo boasts some of the greatest sights and museums in Italy, and looming over it all is crown-shaped Monte Pellegrino, what Goethe called "the most beautiful headland on earth."

Even the mix of monuments can be baffling: Byzantine mosaics, rococo stuccoes, Islamic red domes, Catalonian-Gothic arches. Yet there is magic in its madness, and those who embrace it discover artistic gems and memorable vignettes of street life. You won't love every inch of this alluring yet hectic place, but you'll be swept away by much of it, and you may come away with the travel experience of a lifetime.

Essentials

GETTING THERE

BY AIR Palermo's dramatically situated **Falcone-Borsellino Airport** (a.k.a. Punta Raisi; www.gesap.it; ✆ **091-7020273**) is on the sea among tall headlands 25km (16 miles) northwest of the city center. Palermo is well served by flights from all over Italy and many European cities. In summer, **Meridiana** (www.meridiana.it) operates a few weekly nonstop flights between New York and Palermo. All the major rental car companies have operations here, although if you drive into Palermo with a

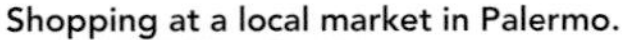
Shopping at a local market in Palermo.

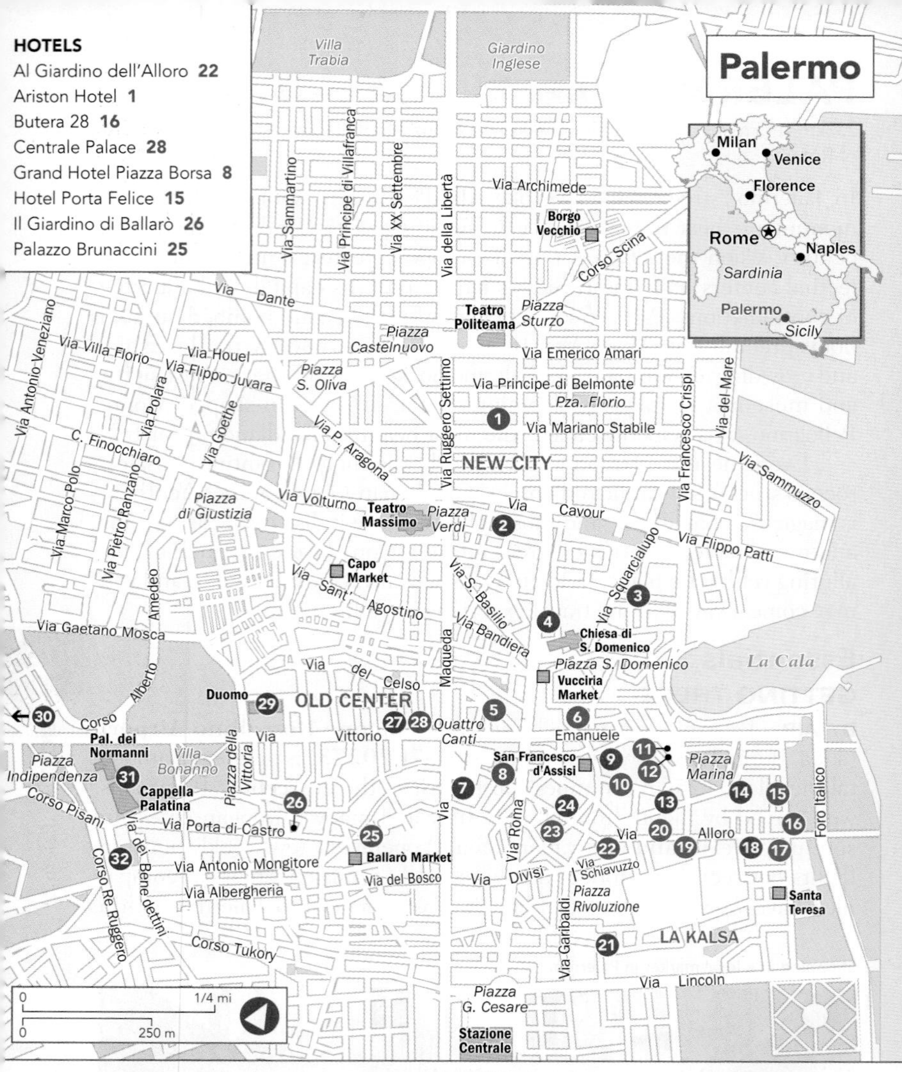

ATTRACTIONS

Catacombs of the Capuchins (Catacombe dei Cappuccini) **30**
Chiesa della Martorana/San Cataldo **7**
Duomo **29**
Galleria d'Arte Moderna **24**
Galleria Regionale della Sicilia (Regional Gallery)/Palazzo Abatellis **18**
Museo Archeologico Regionale "Antonino Salinas" (Regional Archaeological Museum) **2**
Oratorio del Rosario di San Domenico **4**
Oratorio di San Lorenzo **9**
Oratorio di Santa Cita **3**
Palazzo Chiaromonte Steri/ Museo dell'Inquizione **14**
Palazzo dei Normanni and Cappella Palatina **31**
Palazzo Mirto **13**
Palazzo Riso **27**
San Giovanni degli Eremiti **32**
Stanza al Genio **21**

RESTAURANTS

Antica Focacceria San Francesco **10**
Cana Enoteca **20**
Casa del Brodo **6**
Ferro di Cavallo **5**
La Cambusa **12**
Osteria dei Vespiri **23**
Ottava Nota **17**
Palazzo Sambuca **19**
Panineria Friggitoria Chiluzzo **11**

rental car, get clear directions and parking information from your hotel. An easier way to reach the center from the airport is with the **shuttle bus** run by **Prestia e Comandè** (www.prestiaecomande.it; © **091-580457**). The buses depart every half-hour from 5am to 12:30am (service from Palermo begins at 4am and ends at 10:30pm); the trip takes 45 minutes and costs 6.30€ one-way, 11€ round trip. In central Palermo, the several stops include points along Via Libertà, Teatro Politeama, the main train station, and Via Emerico Amari (port). A **train service,** the **Trinacria Express,** connects the airport with the main train station, but the "express" part is a bit of hyperbole: Service is slow at the best of times, often more than an hour, and the line is often nonoperational. Scheduled service from Palermo begins at 4:45am and ends just after 8pm, and from the airport service runs from 5:54am to 10:05pm; fare is 5.50€ each way. You can purchase tickets at desks in the station and airport or from machines near the platform. **Taxis** are plentiful; expect to pay about 50€ from the airport to town, but be sure to settle on a price before you set off. You can share a cab for about 7€—drivers will corral you as you exit the terminal. This is a safe and reliable option, though you will have to slip the driver a little extra to take you to your destination rather than dropping you nearby.

BY TRAIN If you're arriving in Palermo from another place in Sicily by **rail,** all trains come into Palermo Stazione Centrale, at the edge of the historic center. Trains to Sicily are operated by Italy's national rail company, **Ferrovie dello Stato** (www.trenitalia.com). Trains from mainland Italy come down through Calabria and across the Strait of Messina to Sicily on ferries equipped with railroad tracks on the cargo deck. It's a novel way to arrive in Sicily, but takes some time (the trip from Rome to Palermo is at least 11 hours, from Naples to Palermo 9–10 hours). Passenger rail service on the island is generally spotty and slow, with limited routes and antiquated, dirty coaches. The bus is almost always a better option, except on busy routes along the north coast between Palermo and Messina.

BY BUS **Buses** from elsewhere in Sicily arrive at a depot adjacent to the train station. Bus travel in Sicily is excellent, with good connections between most cities. Coaches are clean and modern, with comfortable, upholstered seats, A/C, and smooth suspensions. The main bus companies in Sicily are **Interbus** (www.interbus.it; © **091-6167919;** also known as **Etna Trasporti, Segesta,** and **Sicilbus,** depending on which part of Sicily you're in), and **Cuffaro** (www.cuffaro.info; © **091-6161510**), which operates buses between Palermo and Agrigento.

BY CAR The northeastern tip of Sicily is separated from mainland Italy by the 5km- (3-mile) wide Stretto di Messina (Strait of Messina), which is crossed by regular car ferries between the Calabrian port of Villa San Giovanni (just north of Reggio Calabria, essentially the "toe" of the Italian peninsula's boot) and the Sicilian city of Messina. From Messina, which lies on the well-maintained A20 and A18 autostrade, it's a straight shot west to Palermo (233km/145 miles; about 2 hrs.) or south to

Taormina (52km/32 miles; 45 min.), Catania (97km/60 miles; 1 hr., 15 min), and Siracusa (162km/100 miles; about 2 hrs.).

If you're planning to drive down from Naples or Rome, prepare yourself for a long ride: 721km (448 miles) south from Naples or 934km (580 miles) south from Rome.

BY SEA Palermo's large port is served by passenger ferries from the Italian mainland cities of Naples, Civitavecchia (near Rome), Livorno, and Genova, and from the Sardinian city of Cagliari. Nearly all are nighttime crossings, departing between 7pm and 9pm and arriving the next morning between 6am and 8am. Some of these ferries are tricked out like miniature cruise ships, with swimming pools, beauty salons, discos, and cabins in various configurations, from four-bunk dorms to private rooms. Ferries from Naples are the most numerous, operating daily year-round. The Naples–Palermo route is run by **SNAV** (www.snav.it; ✆ **081-4285555**), **Tirrenia Lines** (www.tirrenia.it; ✆ **892123** or 02-26302803), and **Grandi Navi Veloci** (GNV; www.gnv.it; ✆ **010-2094591**). The ferry trip takes 11 hours. From Civitavecchia, the port that cruise ships use when visiting Rome, **GNV** has ferries to Palermo that depart at 8pm, arriving in Palermo the next morning at 8am; GNV also operates ships between Genoa and Palermo. Schedules vary depending on weather conditions, so always call on the day of departure even if you've already confirmed your reservation.

GETTING AROUND

Walking is the best way to get around Palermo—distances are never great within the historic center. Buses run by **AMAT** (amat.pa.it; ✆ **091-350111**; 1.40€ per ride; all-day ticket 3.50€) take you to Palermo destinations outside the center (like the catacombs) or farther-flung locales (such as Mondello and Monreale). Bus tickets are sold at *tabacchi* and some newsstands.

VISITOR INFORMATION

The website of Palermo's tourism board is www.palermotourism.com. Official **tourist information offices** are located at Falcone-Borsellino (Punta Raisi) airport (✆ **091-591698;** Mon–Sat 8:30am–7:30pm) and in the city center near Teatro Politeama at Piazza Castelnuovo 35 (✆ **091-6058351;** Mon–Fri 8:30am–2pm and 2:30–6:30pm). Another city-run tourist office is in Piazza Bellini, near the church of San Cataldo (turismo.comune.palermo.it; ✆ **091-740-5908**; Mon–Thurs 8am–8pm, Fri 8:30am–6:30pm, Sat 9am–7pm, and Sun 9:30am–6:30pm).

The **Micro-Tourist Information Centre Palermo** (www.visitpalermo.it; ✆ **091-783-8185**) is a for-fee service with an office at Via Alloro 19 in the Kalsa district, where you can rent bikes or arrange kayaking and hiking excursions. The office also arranges some offbeat tours, such as a look at sites in Palermo where anti-Mafia activity has centered and a visit to artisan studios in the Kalsa district.

SAFETY

Palermo is home to some of the most skilled pickpockets on the continent. Police squads operate mobile centers throughout the town to help combat street crime, but **your best defense is common sense.** Don't flaunt expensive jewelry, cameras, or wads of bills and be especially careful on buses; routes to Monreale and Mondello, popular stops on the sightseeing circuit, are fertile ground for pickpockets. Women who carry handbags are especially vulnerable to purse snatchers on Vespas. Leave your valuables in a safe at your hotel (most rooms are equipped with them). When going out for a meal or excursion, carry only as much cash as you need and only the credit card you will be using, and leave the others behind. Do not carry a wallet in your back pocket, of course, or even in an inside jacket pocket, where someone (or a pair, as is often the case) brushing against you can easily get to it.

Neighborhoods in Brief

Palermo is divided into four historical districts, or *mandamenti,* that spread out from **Quattro Canti,** or Four Corners. Time was, and not too long ago, that it was unthinkable for Palermitani from one of these districts to marry someone from another. The actual name of the square is Piazza Vigliena, after the viceroy who commissioned it, and it marks the intersection of **Via Maqueda** (which runs north–south) and **Corso Vittorio Emanuele** (which runs east–west, east toward the seafront from here). The square is also known as Theater of the Sun, because at any given time of day, the sun will shine on one of the four corners. Each corner of the square is decorated with a niche in three tiers. The first tier of each contains a fountain and a statue representing one of the four seasons. The second tier of each niche displays a statue of one of the Spanish Habsburg kings, while the third tier of each niche has a statue of the patron saint of the neighborhood that begins here. Be careful not to back into the street when admiring this grimy but still beautiful assemblage—you might step into the path of a speeding Vespa.

ALBERGHERIA Located southwest of the Quattro Canti, this is the oldest of the four *mandamenti;* it is also known as the mandamento Palazzo Reale because the Phoenicians first laid the foundations of what would become the royal palace on the highest part of the city. The Albergheria is filled with tiny, dimly lit alleyways barely wide enough for a person to walk, and decaying buildings in dire need of repair. It's unsavory in some patches, despite the ever-growing presence of cafes. Still, there are some very exquisite corners—especially the splendid **Piazza Bologni,** with its noble palaces and statue of Charles V, and the historic market **Il Ballarò** extending from Piazza Bologni to Corso Tukory.

IL CAPO The northwestern neighborhood, enclosed within Via Maqueda, Corso Vittorio Emanuele, Via Papireto and Via Volturno, has a warren of tiny, winding streets and alleyways spread out behind the Teatro

Massimo. At its heart is the largest and the most bazaarlike of Palermo's markets, also called **Il Capo** (see p. 747). The Capo was once the headquarters of the secret society of the Beati Paoli, the legendary sect that robbed from the rich and gave to the poor; pickpockets still adhere to this age-old principle, so watch your wallet.

CASTELLAMMARE Owing its name to the castle that once overlooked the sea, this northeastern quadrant is bordered by Corso Vittorio Emanuele, Via Cavour, Via Roma, and Via Crispi. Though heavily bombed by the Allies during 1943, the neighborhood houses some spectacular palazzi and churches, such as the **Oratorio del Rosario di Santa Cita** and the **Oratorio di San Lorenzo** (p. 738). The centuries-old market **La Vucciria,** once the beating heart of Palermo, is here (see p. 747). Though only a smattering of the erstwhile vibrancy remains, you'll still see butcher shops (*carnizzerie*), fishmongers scaring shoppers with large heads of swordfish, precarious houses that look as though they might crumble at any time (some have in recent years), and hole-in-the-wall eateries that may seem shady but are often excellent. Night owls are rediscovering the Vucciria, and bars and inexpensive eateries are cropping up in the lanes and crumbling squares.

LA KALSA A thousand years ago, Arabs settled this southeast quadrant, bounded by Via Lincoln, Via Roma, Corso Vittorio Emanuele, and the Foro Italico. The neighborhood still has an exotic feel to it. Time was, even 10 years ago, when the quarter was so insalubrious that walking down the narrow lanes was risky business. Some patches have never been rebuilt after Allied air raids in 1943. The **Santa Maria dello Spasimo** (Via dello Spasimo; ✆ **091-6161486**) is a skeleton of a church, not a victim of bombs but never completed, where mature trees grow out of broken Gothic vaults. It's still wise to avoid emptier areas after dark, though these are rather rare these days, since restaurants and bars have opened in old *palazzi*. One of the finest art museums in Sicily, the **Galleria Regionale della Sicilia**, in the Palazzo Abbatellis, is on Via Alloro, while in the middle of Piazza Marina is a park shaded by centuries-old trees and cooled by breezes off the nearby sea.

NEW CITY As you head north along Via Maqueda, the streets grow broader but also more nondescript. The monumental **Teatro Massimo**, at Piazza Verdi, roughly marks the division between the Old City and the New City. Via Maqueda becomes Via Ruggero Séttimo as it heads north through the modern town, emptying into the massive double squares at Piazza Politeama, site of the **Teatro Politeama Garibaldi.** North of the square is Palermo's swankiest street, **Viale della Libertà,** running up toward the Giardino Inglese (the English Gardens). This is the area where the Art Nouveau movement triumphed, as is still visible in the kiosks at Piazza Castelnuovo and in Piazza Verdi, but many of these priceless edifices were torn down by unscrupulous builders to make way for ugly cement behemoths that in places mar the elegance of the neighborhood.

Exploring Palermo

Most of everything you want to see is within walking distance of the Quattro Canti, where Via Maqueda meets Via Vittorio Emanuele.

Catacombs of the Capuchins (Catacombe dei Cappuccini) ★ CEMETERY In 1599, the occupants of the adjoining Capuchin monastery discovered that the bodies of the brothers they placed in their catacombs soon became naturally mummified (with the aid of chemical infusions), and Sicilians began demanding to be buried along with them. In these chambers, the corpses of some 8,000 people in various stages of preservation now hang from walls and recline in open caskets. It would be easy to write the spectacle off as eerie (which it certainly is), but for the deceased and the loved ones they left behind, a spot here provided a bit of comforting immortality. Wearing their Sunday best, the dead are grouped according to sex and rank—men, women, virgins, priests, nobles, professors (possibly including the painter Velasquez), and children. This last grouping includes the most recent resident, 2-year-old Rosalia Lombardo, who died in 1920 and whom locals have dubbed "Sleeping Beauty." Giuseppe Tommasi, prince of Lampedusa and author of one of the best-known works of Sicilian literature, *The Leopard*, was buried in the cemetery next to the catacombs in 1957. His great-grandmother, the model for the Princess in the novel, is in the catacombs.

Capuchins Monastery, Piazza Cappuccini 1. www.palermocatacombs.com. ✆ **091-212117.** 3€. Daily 9am–noon and 3–6pm. Closed Sun afternoons Oct–late Mar. Bus: 327 from Piazza Indipendenza.

Chiesa della Martorana/San Cataldo ★★ CHURCH These two Norman churches stand side by side, separated by a little tropical garden. George of Antioch, Roger II's Greek admiral, founded Santa Maria dell'Ammiraglio in 1141; the church was later renamed **Chiesa della Martorana** for Eloisa Martorana, who founded a nearby Benedictine convent. The nuns gained the everlasting appreciation of Palermitans when they invented marzipan, and *frutta di Martorana*—in which marzipan is fashioned into the shape of little fruits—has outlived the order. George of Antioch, for his part, had a love of Byzantine mosaics and hired the North African craftsmen who had just completed their work on the **Cappella Palatina** (see p. 739) to cover this church's walls, pillars, and floors with stunning mosaics. Christ crowns Roger II, George appears in a Byzantine robe, and Christ appears again in the dome, circled by angels. The Arab geographer/traveler Ibn Jubayr visited Palermo in 1166 and called the church "the most beautiful monument in the world." In 1266 Sicilian nobles met here and agreed to offer the crown to Peter of Aragon, ending a bloody uprising against French rule known as the Sicilian Vespers. A baroque redo has rendered the interior a little less transporting than it was then, but it's still beautiful.

Maio of Bari, chancellor to William I, began the tiny **Chiesa di San Cataldo** next door in 1154, but he died before it was completed in 1160,

A colorful mosaic in La Martorana church in Palermo.

so the church was left unfinished. The red domes and the lacy crenellation around the tops of the walls are decidedly Moorish, while the stone interior, with three little cupolas over the nave, evoke the Middle Ages. Adjoining Piazza Pretoria is graced with the 16th-century **Fontana Pretoria,** where nymphs, god, and goddesses romp in a huge basin. Florentine sculptor Francesco Camilliani completed the monumental fountain for the garden of a Tuscan villa in 1555, but the work was sold to Palermo as a centerpiece of the city's new waterworks. The nakedness inspired Palermians to call the exuberant assemblage the "Fountain of Shame," as it's been known ever since. Nuns from a nearby convent took a stand against the indecent presence of so many naked males by having the noses lopped off (you can still see some clumsy reattachments)—to remove the members that actually offended the sisters meant acknowledging the presence of unthinkable indecency.

Piazza Bellini 2, adjacent to Piazza Pretoria. ✆ **091-616-1692.** La Martorana: Free. Mon–Sat 9:30am–1pm and 3:30–6:30pm; Sun 8:30am–1pm. San Cataldo: 2€. Tues–Fri 9am–5pm; Sat–Sun 9am–1pm. Bus: 101 or 102.

Duomo ★ CATHEDRAL All those who came, saw, and conquered in Palermo left their mark on this cathedral, an architectural pastiche that lies somewhere between exquisite and eyesore. It is, however, noble enough as befits the final resting place of Roger II, the first king of Sicily, who died in 1154, and other Norman–Swabian royalty. Neapolitan architect Ferdinando Fuga began a restoration in 1771 in an all-encompassing neoclassical style, adding a cupola that sticks out like a sore thumb on the original Norman design. You can still pick out some of the original elements: four impressive campaniles (bell towers) from the 14th century; the middle portal from the 15th century; and the south and north porticos from the 15th and 16th centuries.

Piazza Cattedrale. ✆ **091-334373.** Duomo: free; crypt and treasury: 1€ each. Mon–Sat 9:30am–5pm. Bus: 101, 104, 105, 107, 139.

Galleria Regionale della Sicilia (Regional Gallery)/Palazzo Abatellis ★★★ MUSEUM Competing for attention with this fine collection is the late-15th-century *palazzo* that houses it, built around two courtyards and beautifully restored in the 1950s. On display is an array of the arts in Sicily from the 13th to the 18th centuries, though it's hard to get beyond the gallery's most celebrated work, the **"Trionfo della Morte" ("Triumph of Death").** Dating from 1449 and of uncertain attribution, this huge study in black and gray is prominently displayed in a two-story ground-floor gallery (climb the stairs to the balcony for an overview). Death has never looked worse—a fearsome skeletal demon astride an undernourished steed, brandishing a scythe as he leaps over his victims (allegedly members of Palermo aristocracy, who were none too pleased with the portrayal). The painter is believed to have depicted himself in the fresco, seen with an apprentice praying in vain for release from the horrors of Death; the poor and hungry looking on have escaped such a gruesome fate for the time being. The precision of this astonishing work, including details of the horse's nostrils and the men and women in the full flush of their youth, juxtaposed against such darkness, suggests the Surrealism movement that came to the fore 400 years later.

The second masterpiece of the gallery, in room 4, is a refreshing antidote, and also quite modern-looking: the white-marble, slanted-eyed bust of **"Eleonora di Aragona,"** by Francesco Laurana, who captured this likeness of Eleanor, daughter of King Ferdinand I of Naples, shortly before she married Ercole d'Este in 1468 and became the duchess of Ferrara. Antonello da Messina's **"Annunciation"** stands out in room 11. It is probably the artist's most famous work, completed in 1476 in Venice. He depicts the Virgin as an adolescent girl, sitting at a desk with a devotional book in front of her, clasping her cloak modestly to her chest. She raises her hand, seemingly to us viewers but probably to Gabriel, who has just delivered the news that she is to be the mother of the son of God. Considering that news, her expression is remarkably serene. It's one of the most lovely and calming works anywhere.

Via Alloro 4, Palazzo Abatellis. www.regione.sicilia.it/beniculturali/palazzoabatellis. ✆ **091-623-0011.** 8€ adults, 4€ children; 10€ combined ticket with Palazzo Mirto (see below). Tues–Fri 9am–6:30pm and Sat–Sun 9am–1pm. Bus: 103, 105, 139.

Museo Archeologico Regionale "Antonino Salinas" (Regional Archaeological Museum) ★★★ MUSEUM The first thing to know about this stunning collection of antiquities is that you may not see it: The museum was closed indefinitely in 2011 for a much-needed renovation. You can, however, step into a few galleries surrounding the ground-floor courtyard; admission is currently free. When the museum is open in its entirety, possibly by late 2018, you will see a head-spinning repository of artifacts from the island's many inhabitants and invaders: Phoenicians, Greeks, Saracens, and Romans. The most important treasures in the museum, set in the former convent of the Filippini around a

THE oratories OF GIACOMO SERPOTTA

Some of Palermo's most delightful places of worship are oratories, private chapels funded by societies and guilds and usually connected to a larger church. Giacomo Serpotta, a native master of sculpting in stucco, decorated several oratorios in the early 18th century. Hours vary, but most are open Monday through Friday 10am to 1pm and 3 to 6pm, Saturday 10am to 1pm. You'll be charged 2€ admission, and your ticket is good for at least one other oratory.

Serpotta was a member of the Society of the Holy Rosary, and he decorated the society's **Oratorio del Rosario di San Domenico** (Via dei Bambinai; ✆ **091-332779**) with delightfully expressive putti (cherubs), who are locked forever in a playground of happy antics. His 3-D reliefs depict everything from the Allegories of the Virtues to the Apocalypse of St. John to a writhing "Devil Falling from Heaven." Anthony van Dyck, the Dutch master who spent time in Palermo in the 1620s, did the "Madonna of the Rosary" over the high altar.

Serpotta also worked on the **Oratorio di San Lorenzo** (Via dell'Immacolatella; ✆ **091-332779**) between 1698 and 1710, creating panels relating the lives of St. Francis and St. Lawrence to create what critics have admiringly called "a cave of white coral." Some of the most expressive of the stuccoes depict the martyrdom of Lawrence, who was roasted to death and nonchalantly informed his tormentors, "I'm well done. Turn me over." Caravaggio's last large painting, a "Nativity," once hung over the altar, but it was stolen in 1969 and never recovered.

The all-white **Oratorio del Rosario di Santa Cita** (Via Valverde 3; ✆ **091-332779**) houses Serpotta's crowning achievement: a detailed relief of the Battle of Lepanto, in which a coalition of European states defeated the Turks, more or less preventing the expansion of the Ottoman Empire into Western Europe and so defending Christianity against Islam. Serpotta's cherubs, oblivious to international affairs, romp up and down the walls and climb onto window frames.

lovely cloister, are metopes (temple friezes) from once-great Selinunte on the southern coast. Sumptuous, detailed marbles depict Perseus slaying Medusa, the Rape of Europa by Zeus, Actaeon being transformed into a stag, and other scenes that bring these myths vividly to life. Among the other artifacts—anchors from Punic warships and mirrors used by the Etruscans—is a rare Egyptian find: The **Pietra di Palermo** (Palermo Stone), a black stone slab dating from 2700 B.C. that is known as the Rosetta stone of Sicily. Discovered in Egypt in the 19th century, it was in transit for the British Museum in London when it was shuffled off to the corners of a Palermo dock. The hieroglyphics reveal the inscriber's attention to detail: a list of pharaohs, details of the delivery of 40 shiploads of cedarwood to Snefru, and flood levels of the Nile.

Piazza Olivella 24. www.regione.sicilia.it/bbccaa/salinas. ✆ **091-611-6805.** Closed temporarily except for some ground-floor galleries. Free admission currently. Sat–Sun 8:30am–1:30pm. Bus: 101, 102, 103, 104, 107.

Palazzo Chiaromonte Steri/Museo dell'Inquisizione ★ PALACE/MUSEUM The Inquisiton was put in force in Sicily from about 1600

Painting in the Hall of Weapons in the dungeons of the Inquistion, Palazzo Chiaromonte Steri.

to 1780 as a means for the church to stifle the aristocracy and control the populace. Accused were held in this palace, built in 1307 for the powerful Chiaromonte family, when it was headquarters of the Aragonese/Spanish viceroys of Sicily. The lower floors housed prisoners from all levels of society in miniscule, cagelike cells that were left untouched through the centuries, preserving a wealth of graffiti: hearts, caricatures, maps, initials, verse, and more left by the hapless souls who were left here to rot or worse, tortured and hung. An antidote to all this misery is a bright gallery that houses the exuberant *Le Vucciria,* a scene of the once-thriving nearby market saturated with color and realism, by Palermitano painter Renato Guttuso (1912–1987). Even more refreshing are views of the sea and the old city from the top-floor **Sala Magna,** with an elaborately painted ceiling that depicts scenes from the Bible and mythology. You can only visit on guided tours, offered in English.

Piazza Marina 61. ✆ **091-607-5306.** 5€, 3€ children 11 and under. Tues–Sat 9am–1pm and 2:30–6:30pm, Sun 10am–2pm.

Palazzo dei Normanni ★★ and Cappella Palatina ★★★ PALACE

The cultural influences of Sicily collide in this palace, which dates back to the 8th century B.C., when Punic administrators set up an outpost in the highest part of the city. In the 9th century A.D. the Arabs built a palace on the spot for their emirs and their harems, and in the 12th century the Normans turned what was essentially a fortress into a sumptuous royal residence. Here Frederick II presided over the early 13th–century court of minstrels and literati that founded the Scuola Poetica Siciliana, which marked the birth of Italian literature. Spanish viceroys took up residence in 1555, and today most of the vast maze of rooms and grand halls houses the seat of Sicily's regional government.

Entrance to the Cappella Palatina, Palazzo dei Normanni.

Arab–Norman cultural influences intersect most spectacularly

in the **Cappella Palatina**, a chapel covered in glittering Byzantine mosaics from 1130 to 1140. It was finished in time for the coronation of Roger II, who proved to be not only the most powerful of European kings but also the most enlightened. High in the cupola at the end of the apse is Christ Pantocrator (holding the New Testament in his left hand and making the blessing with his right hand), surrounded by biblical characters, some interpreted a little less piously than usual—Adam and Eve happily munch on the forbidden fruit, and rather than showing any remorse for their act of defiance, they greedily reach for a second piece. Shame prevails in the next scene, when God steps in reproachfully and the naked couple cover themselves. The mosaics are vibrant in the soft light, and the effect is especially powerful in scenes depicting water, as in the flood and the Baptism of Christ—the water actually appears to be shimmering.

Scenes on the wooden ceiling were done in a 3-D technique using small sections of carved wood, known in Arabic as *muqarnas*. A team of Egyptian carpenters and painters created the playfully secular scenarios of dancers, musicians, hunters, drinkers, even banqueters in a harem. They're best seen with binoculars or a telephoto lens.

Since this is the seat of government, visits to the **Royal Apartments** are escorted. Tours are almost always conducted in Italian; ask if there is an usher on duty who can speak English. The apartments are not open to the public when the Sicilian parliament is in session—meeting in the **Salone d'Ercole**, named for the mammoth 19th-century frescoes depicting the "Twelve Labours of Hercules" (perhaps an apt decoration for legislators wading through government bureaucracy). The fairly pompous staterooms from the years of Spanish rule give way to earlier remnants, among them the **Sala dei Presidenti,** a stark chamber hidden in the bowels of the palace for several centuries, completely unknown until 2002, when an earthquake revealed the untouched medieval relic. The **Torre Gioaria** (Tower of the Wind) is a harbinger of modern air-conditioning systems: A fountain in the middle of the

State-of-the-Art Art

This city that so richly evokes past conquerors and baroque grandeur also has a rich contemporary art scene, with a beachhead in the beautiful 18th-century Palazzo Riso, now home to the **Museum of Contemporary Sicilian Art,** Via Vittorio Emanuele 365 (www.poloartecontemporanea.it; ✆ **091-587717**; open Tues, Wed, and Sun 10am–7:30pm and Thurs–Sat 10am–11:30pm; admission 6€). The artists highlighted in the changing exhibitions are part of a long tradition of Sicily's presence on the contemporary art scene. Works of their predecessors, mostly late-19th and 20th-century Sicilian artists, fill a 15th-century Franciscan convent and an adjoining church, now the **Galleria d'Arte Moderna (GAM),** Via Sant'Ana 21 (www.gampalermo.it; ✆ **091-843-1605;** open Tues–Sun 9:30am–6:30pm; admission 7€, audio guide 4€). The galleries are best appreciated with the excellent English-language audio guide.

tower (since removed) spouted water that cooled the breezes coming from the four hallways. Much less hospitable are the **Segrete,** or dungeons, where the cold stone walls are etched with primitive scenes of Norman warships. The otherwise enlightened Frederick II is said to have taken his interest in science to perverse lengths in these chambers, where he shut prisoners in casks to see if their souls could be observed escaping through a small hole at the moment of death. Frederick was also fascinated by the stars and brought many astronomers and astrologers to his court. His Bourbon successors shared the interest and in 1790 added an astronomical observatory, still functioning, at the top of the **Torre Pisana.** From these heights in 1801 the priest Fra Giuseppe Piazza discovered Ceres, the first asteroid known to mankind.

Piazza del Parlamento. www.ars.sicilia.it. ✆ **091-626833.** 9€, free for children 17 and under; 7€ Tues–Thurs, when the Royal Apartments are closed due to Parliamentary meetings. Mon–Sat 8:15am–5pm; Sun 8:15am–12:15pm. Bus: 104, 105, 108, 109, 110, 118, 304, 309.

Palazzo Mirto ★★ HISTORIC SIGHT The streets of old Palermo are lined with palaces, though many are decrepit and others abandoned. Few are as beautifully maintained as the home of the princes of Lanza Filangieri, one of Sicily's oldest families. The last of the princes bequeathed his 17th-century home to the city in the 1980s, leaving behind the copious trappings of his aristocratic lifestyle: furnishings, statues, rococo fountains that splash on hidden patios, and elaborate tableware (including plates given away as party favors, decorated with costumed nobs who once danced the night away in the over-the-top ballroom). It's hard to imagine that life in the grandiose, tapestry-hung salons could have been terribly comfortable or very relaxed, especially for the modern-looking, fashionable 20th-century princes and princesses whose photos appear casually on ornate side tables. Then again, it would have been transporting to while away an evening in the smoking room decorated in painted-silk scenes of everyday life in China as a 19th-century artisan imagined it to be. As it is, the remarkably well-preserved palace affords a voyeuristic glimpse into long-vanished eras.

Via Merlo 2. ✆ **091-6167541.** Admission 6€ (combined ticket with Palazzo Abatellis 10€). Mon–Sat 9am–7pm; Sun 9am–1pm. Bus: 103, 105, 139.

San Giovanni degli Eremiti ★ CHURCH Palermo's most romantic landmark is a simple affair, part Arab, part Norman, with five red domes atop a portico, a single nave, two small apses, and a squat tower. As befits the humble Spanish recluse it honors, St. John of the Hermits, the church is almost devoid of decoration, though the surrounding citrus blossoms and flowers imbue the modest structure with an otherworldy aura. Adding to the charms of the spot is a Norman cloister, part of a Benedictine monastery that once stood here.

Via dei Benedettini 3. ✆ **091-651-5019.** 6€ adults; 3€ students, seniors, and children. Tues–Sat 9am–1pm and 3–7pm; Sun 9am–6:30pm. Bus: 109 or 318.

House of Tiles

One of Palermo's delightful hidden treasures is the **Stanza al Genio ★,** a collection of 2,300 historic tiles of Neapolitan and Sicilian manufacture. They cover every inch of a private apartment on the *piano nobile* of an old palace in the Kalsa district. An informative guide will walk you through the kitchen, dining room, and living room, explaining the glorious ceramics carpeting the walls and floors. The museum is at Via Garibaldi 11 (www.stanzealgenio.it; ✆ **340-097-1561**); call or write (stanzealgenio@yahoo.it) for an appointment. Admission is 7€.

Where to Stay

Palermo has some excellent hotels, with rates much lower than they are in Rome or Florence. For convenience and atmosphere, don't stay too far beyond the neighborhoods in the old center (see above).

EXPENSIVE

Centrale Palace ★★ A wonderful location steps from the Quattro Canti puts this much-redone yet still grand *palazzo* within easy reach of most sights. Public rooms, including a vast frescoed salon where breakfast is served, evoke the 1890s Belle Epoque when the 17th-century *palazzo* was first converted to a hotel. The good-size guest rooms are comfortably functional, with luxe touches like rich fabrics and mosaic-tiled bathrooms; double-pane windows in the front rooms keep the street noise at bay. A rooftop terrace with an airy dining room is a retreat from the city below, with views extending to Monte Pellegrino. You may want to linger here well into a warm summer night.

Via Vittorio Emanuele 327 (at Via Maqueda). www.centralepalacehotel.it. ✆ **091-336666.** 104 units. 140€–271€ double. Breakfast included in most rates. **Amenities:** 2 restaurants; bar; exercise room; sauna; room service; babysitting; Wi-Fi (free). Bus: 103, 104, 105.

Hotel Porta Felice ★ It's a sign that the old Kalsa district is on the upswing that this elegant and subdued retreat has risen amid a once derelict block of buildings just off the seafront. Marble-floored public areas are coolly soothing, while guest rooms are sleekly contemporary, with just enough antique pieces and expanses of hardwood to suggest traditional comfort. A rooftop bar and terrace is a welcome refuge, while the downstairs health spa is geared to ultimate relaxation.

Via Butera 35. www.hotelportafelice.it. ✆ **091-617-5678.** 33 units. 130€–240€ double. Rates include breakfast. **Amenities:** Bar; spa; Wi-Fi (free). Bus: 103, 104, 105, 118, 225.

MODERATE

Butera 28 ★★★ The 17th-century Lanza Tomasi Palace, facing the seafront, is the home of Duke Gioacchino Lanza Tomasi, the adopted son of Prince Giuseppe Tomasi di Lampedusa, author of one of the greatest works of modern Italian literature, *The Leopard.* The gracious duke and his charming wife, Nicoletta, have converted 12 apartments of their *palazzo* to short-stay apartments, filling them with family pieces and all the modern conveniences, including full kitchens and, every traveler's dream come true, washing machines. Apartments have one or two bedrooms; some have sea views and terraces, some are multilevel, and all have beautiful hardwood or tile floors and other detailing. The duchess also offers cooking classes, and she and the duke are on hand to provide a wealth of advice to help you get the most out of their beloved Palermo. Via Butera 28. www.butera28.it. ✆ **333-316-5432.** 12 units. From 80€ double. **Amenities:** Kitchens; Wi–Fi (free). Bus: 103, 104, 105, 118, 225.

Grand Hotel Piazza Borsa ★★ This conglomeration of three historic buildings seems to take in a bit of every part of Palermo's past—the banking floor and grand offices of the old stock exchange, a monastery, and a centuries-old *palazzo.* These elements come together atmospherically in surroundings that include a cloister, open-roofed atrium, paneled dining rooms, and frescoed salons. Guest rooms are a bit more businesslike, though large and plushly comfortable, with hardwood floors and furnishings that cross tradition with contemporary flair; the best have balconies overlooking the surrounding churches and palaces. A spa and exercise area includes a sauna and steam room.
Via dei Cartari 18. www.piazzaborsa.com. ✆ **091-320075**. 103 units. 120€–200€ double. Rates include breakfast. **Amenities:** Restaurant; bar; babysitting; concierge; spa; Wi-Fi (free). Bus: 103, 104, 105, 118, 225.

Palazzo Brunaccini ★★ Princess Lucrezia Brunaccini probably wouldn't recognize the home from which she reigned over 18th-century Palermo society, but her dignified old *palazzo* still commands a beautiful and tranquil piazza just steps from the madness of the Ballarò market. Salons and the airy guest rooms are a pleasant mix of traditional grandeur and clean-lined contemporary touches, with oil paintings, wall hangings, and antiques thrown into the mix. Many of the high-ceilinged rooms overlook the piazza and surrounding neighborhood from small terraces.
Piazza Lucrezia Brunaccini. www.palazzobrunaccini.it. ✆ **091-586904.** 18 units. 125€–145€ double. Rates include breakfast. **Amenities:** Restaurant; bar; Wi-Fi (free). Bus: 104, 105, 108, 109, 110, 118.

INEXPENSIVE

Al Giardino dell'Alloro ★★ This pleasant city-center getaway is tucked away from the fray of the surrounding Kalsa quarter, with brightly colored, nattily furnished rooms around a garden at the end of a little alley. Two resident felines are as friendly as owner/manager Donatella, who's on hand with a wealth of advice. The flower-filled patio seems like the most becoming place on earth after a day of exploring Palermo.
Vicolo San Carlo 8. www.giardinodellalloro.it. ✆ **091-6176904.** 5 units. 70€–85€ double. Rates include breakfast. **Amenities:** Wi-Fi (free). Bus: 103, 105, 139.

Ariston Hotel ★ The sixth floor of an apartment building near Teatro Massimo houses bright, airy rooms spread along a corridor off a comfortable lounge. Furnishings are of the basic wood-veneer modular variety and luxuries don't extend much beyond free coffee and tea, but the premises are spotless, owner/manager Giuseppe is a welcoming host, and a smattering of modern art hits just the right tasteful notes—all making this place an excellent value.

Via Mariano Stabile 139. www.aristonpalermo.it. ✆ **091-3322434.** 8 units. 59€–75€ double. **Amenities:** Wi–Fi (free). Bus: 101.

Il Giardino di Ballarò ★★★ The stables of the Palazzo Conte Federico were converted to a bakery more than a century ago, and now they've been revamped in the style of a casually luxurious country house, steps from the Ballarò market. In the downstairs lounges, plump couches surround a fireplace against a backdrop of old brick, arches, and columns, while a breakfast lounge and several guest rooms face a rear garden filled with banana trees and other exotic plantings. Two rooms are tucked under the eaves beneath huge skylights, and large family rooms have two bathrooms. The distinctive decor is enhanced with splashes of color, kilims, and contemporary art, all reflecting the refined taste of proprietor Annalise Correnti, whose two daughters are gracious and capable hosts.

Via Porta di Castro 75/77. www.ilgiardinodiballaro.it. ✆ **091-212215.** 7 units. 80€–110€. Rates include breakfast. **Amenities:** Bar; garden; Jacuzzi (use by arrangement); Wi-Fi (free). Bus: 104, 105, 108, 109, 110, 118.

Where to Eat

Palermitans dine well on fresh seafood and the other bounty of the city markets, and share a laudable appreciation for sweets. Legendary pastry shops like **Mazzara** (Via Generale Magliocco 19; ✆ **091-321443**) will fill you up with cassata, cannoli, *frutta martorana* (marzipan sweets), and gelato, while the opulent **Antico Caffè Spinnato** (Via Principe di Belmonte 115; www.spinnato.it; ✆ **091-583231**), established in 1860, is the place to linger over a pastry and coffee. In the Kalsa quarter, **Ciccolateria Lorenzo** (Via Quattro Aprile 7; ✆ **091-840846;** closed Mon.), has a wonderful selection of cakes and the best hot chocolate in Palermo; and the Riso di Paradise, a concoction of chocolate, rice, and whipped cream at **Antica Gelateria Patricola** (on the waterfront at Foro Umberto 1; ✆ **091-851223;** closed in winter) will bring you back daily.

Palermitani can put Americans to shame when it comes to a fondness for fast food, though the *cucina povera* (literally "poor man's cuisine") that street vendors and simple eateries sell is a delicacy in itself. Favorites are *arancine* ("little oranges"), saffron-flavored rice balls, usually filled with meat ragu or ham and mozzarella, rolled in bread crumbs, and fried. Other fried favorites are *cazzilli* (potato croquettes) and *panelle* (chickpea fritters).

EXPENSIVE

Osteria dei Vespiri ★ SICILIAN Several small, simple rooms occupy a quite corner of the Kalsa, on the lower floor of the beautiful Palazzo Valguarnera-Gangi (film buffs might enjoy a meal all the more knowing that the ballroom scene in The Leopard was filmed upstairs). The menu changes from osteria offerings in the winter to fanciful variations on fresh seasonal ingredients in the summer, when the main dining scene is on the terrace out front. Reasonably priced winter meals are available on set menus that feature such well-prepared basics as pasta alla Norma (with eggplant) and grilled meats, while summertime tasting menus are quite a bit fussier and more expensive but at their best stick to such Sicilian classics as softly roasted tuna and pasta with sea urchins.
Piazza Croce dei Vespiri. www.osteriadeivespri.it. ✆ **091-617-1631.** Winter menus from 25€, summer menus from 30€. Mon–Sat 1–3pm and 8–11pm. Bus: 103, 104, 105, 118, 225.

Ottava Nota ★★ SICILIAN "New Sicilian" is in full force at the most exciting of the restaurants that have opened in the once-derelict Kalsa district in recent years, where the sleek surroundings are the setting for creative takes on Sicilian classics. Tuna tartare is served with avocado, risotto is laced with leeks and tuna caviar, and eggplant meatballs are topped with tomato cream. Duck, beef, and fish are market fresh and beautifully prepared, but you may not want to go beyond the pastas with fresh seafood—linguine with scallops, risotto with shrimp, tagliatelle with sea urchins. The friendly, attentive service is strictly old-school, and a meal begins with a complimentary glass of Prosecco.
Via Butera 55. www.ristoranteottavanota.it. ✆ **091-616-8601.** Main courses 10€–20€. Mon 8–11pm; Tues–Sun 12:30–3:30pm and 8–11pm. Bus: 103, 104, 105, 118, 225.

Palazzo Sambuca ★★ SEAFOOD/SICILIAN While the beautifully restored Palazzo Sambuca in the Kalsa quarter is one of Palermo's great baroque landmarks, its ground floor namesake is white and chicly contemporary, with a couple of small, intimate dining rooms. A mother and son team oversees the kitchen while father and daughter tend to guests, serving Sicilian classics on a daily-changing menu. Fish and seafood are the focus—lightly fried baby squid, seafood risottos, simply grilled and baked fresh fish—but land-based classics, including expertly grilled steak, are given the same reverence and all are part of a warm and elegant experience.
Via Alloro 26. ✆ **091-507-6794.** Main courses 12€–24€. Mon–Sat noon–2:30pm and 7:30–10:30pm. Bus: 103, 104, 105, 118, 225.

MODERATE

Cana Enoteca ★ WINE BAR/ITALIAN The stone walls of these old rooms on the ground floor of a palazzo in the Kalsa are lined with bottles, from which a choice selection of wines is served by the glass or the bottle. The staff will help you pair drink selections with an impressive array of hams, cheeses, as well as six or so more substantial dishes of grilled meats and pastas on offer every evening.

Via Alloro 105. canaenoteca.it. ✆ **345-5934130.** Main courses 8€–12€. Daily 7–midnight. Bus 103, 104.

Casa del Brodo ★ SICILIAN With a setting in two plain rooms on the edge of the now sadly diminished Vucciria market, this century-old institution serves old Sicilian specialties that you might not encounter outside of home kitchens. *Fritelle di fava* (fava beans) are fried with vegetables and cheese; *carni bollite* is a tantalizing assortment of tender, herb-flavored boiled meats; and the *macco di fave* (meatballs and tripe) is a carnivore's delight. The namesake *brodo* (broth) is served several ways, best as tortellini in brodo, with housemade pasta. To sample Sicilian home cooking at its best, order one of the good-value fixed-price menus.

Corso Vittorio Emanuele 175. www.casadelbrodo.it. ✆ **091-321655.** Main courses 8€–16€; fixed-price menus from 20€. Wed–Mon 12:30–3pm and 7:30–11pm (closed Sun June–Sept). Bus: 103, 104, 105, 118, 225.

Ferro di Cavallo ★ SICILIAN Bright red walls seem to rev up the energy to high levels in this ever-busy favorite, but the buzz is really about the good, simple food served at very reasonable prices. A decent *antipasti* platter offers a nice sampling of *panelle* (fried chickpea fritters) and other street food, but go with the daily specials to get the full flavor of the kitchen. The preference is for beans and celery, broad beans and vegetables, meatballs in tomato sauce, boiled veal, and other classics. Service hovers between nonchalant and brusque, but the jovial atmosphere compensates, and you'll pay very little for your homey meal.

Via Venezia 20. www.ferrodicavallopalermo.it. ✆ **091-331835.** Main courses 7€. Mon–Sat 10am–3:30pm and 7:45–11:30pm. Bus: 103, 104, 105, 118, 225.

La Cambusa ★★ SICILIAN/SEAFOOD Palermitani have been coming to this Kalsa outpost to enjoy Sicilian favorites for decades, in good weather enjoying the beautiful Piazza Marina from the terrace out front and at other times dining in one of two plain dining rooms warmly decorated with paintings by local artists. The city's ties with the sea come to the fore in such classics as *zuppe di cozze* (mussels soup) and *bucatino fresco con le sarde* (homemade buccatini with fresh sardines), though land-based dishes include some excellent vegetarian choices, including a memorable *ravioli ricotta e pistachi,* ricotta and pumpkin ravioli, served in a mushroom sauce.

Piazza Marina. www.lacambusa.it. ✆**091-584574.** Main courses 9€–18€. Daily 12:30–3pm and 7–11pm (closed Wed in winter).

INEXPENSIVE

Antica Focacceria San Francesco ★ SICILIAN/SNACKS Palermo street fare is good anywhere you have it, but it's especially savory in this atmospheric, marble-floored institution founded in 1834. If you've shied away from buying a *panino con la milza* (bread roll stuffed with slices of boiled spleen and melted cheese) from a street vendor, you might want to

Do Some Market Research

You can't do justice to Palermo without swinging through one of its street markets. Nowhere is Palermo's multicultural pedigree more evident than at the stalls of the **Ballarò** (in Piazza Ballarò), **Capo** (from Via Porta Carini south toward the cathedral), and even the sadly declining **La Vucciria** (on Via Argenteria, north of Via Vittorio Emanuele and east of Via Roma). These open-air souks go on for blocks, hawking everything from spices to seafood to handicrafts to electronics. Delve even deeper into Palermo's market culture at the neighborhood **Borgo Vecchio** market (along Via Ettore Ximenes to Via Principe di Scordia) in the newer part of the city, northwest of Piazza Politeama. Antiques vendors with many unusual buys lie along the Piazza Peranni, off Corso Vittorio Emanuele.

jump in and try the delicious specialty here. You can also snack or lunch on *panelle* (deep-fried chickpea fritters), *ararancini di riso* (rice balls stuffed with tomatoes and peas or mozzarella), *focaccia farcita* (flat pizza with fillings), or other sandwiches, curtly dispensed from a busy counter. Via A. Paternostro 58. www.afsf.it. ✆ **091-320264.** Sandwiches 3€–5€. Daily 11am–11pm (closed Tues Oct–Mar). Bus: 103, 105, 225.

Panineria Friggitoria Chiluzzo ★★ Palermo's favorite stop for street food commands a corner of Piazza Marina where, even in the heat summer, a big vat of oil boils away to turn out *panelle* (fried chickpea fritters) and other food, plus sandwiches. *Pane e panelle,* in which the fritter is tucked between heavenly pieces of sesame bread, combines both and is especially popular, and the fried chicken here might make Colonel Sanders rethink his recipe. You can eat indoors in a bare-bones dining room, though in all but the worst weather the shady terrace out front is the better choice. A side window sells food to take away.
Piazza della Kalsa 10. Sandwiches and fried choices from 2.50€. Mon–Sat 8:30am–9:30pm (hours can vary). Bus: 103, 104, 105, 118, 225.

Entertainment & Nightlife

Palermo is a cultural center of some note, with an opera and ballet season running from November to July. The principal performance venue is the restored **Teatro Massimo ★★**, Piazza G. Verdi (www.teatro massimo.it; ✆ **091-6053111**), which boasts the third largest indoor stage in Europe. Francis Ford Coppola shot the climactic opera scene here for *The Godfather: Part III* (but poisonings, shootings, and stabbings aren't really a regular occurrence during performances, except on stage). Built between 1875 and 1897 in a neoclassical style, the theater was restored in 1997 to celebrate its 100th birthday. Tickets range from 10€ to 125€. The box office is open Tuesday to Sunday 10am to 3pm. ***Note:*** Teatro Massimo can be visited Tuesday through Sunday from 10am to 3pm. Visits cost 5€. Guided tours in English are given Tuesday through Saturday from 10am to 3pm (bus: 101-104, 107, 122, or 225).

The old **Vucciria market,** no longer the lively shopping souk it once was, is remerging as a nightlife scene. **Via Chiavettieri,** leading into the neighborhood off Via Vittorio Emanuele, is lined with bars where your aperitivo comes with free *cicchetti* (snacks). The decrepit old market square and lanes surrounding it are also lined with street-food outlets and bars, and the square fills up with tables on weekends—and during soccer matches, broadcast on a huge outdoor screen. The nearby seafront is the setting for the city's most distinctive nightlife locale, **Kursaal Kalhesa,** Foro Umberto I 21A (www.kursaalkalhesa.com; ✆ **340-157-3493**), housed in an ancient palazzo that meanders into caverns set into the old city walls. Music varies, but you can usually find a stone-walled nook filled with mellow jazz or lounge music. Some of the most sophisticated watering holes are in the New City. Few are more generous than **Graal,** several blocks beyond Teatro Massimo at Via Sant'Oliva 10 (✆ **091-333533**), where cocktails come with a cornucopia of appetizers: pasta, seafood, pizza, so much food you probably won't need dinner afterward.

Side Trips from Palermo

For many Palermitans, a warm summer day means one thing—a trip to **Mondello Lido,** 12km (7½ miles) west of Palermo, where Belle Epoque Europeans once came to winter. Their Art Nouveau villas face a sandy beach that stretches for about 2km (1¼ miles), though there's little or no elbow room in July and August. Bus no. 806 makes the 30-minute trip from a stop on Via Libertà next to the Giardino Inglese.

Should you wish to do more than lie on a beach, many other sights are within easy reach of Palermo.

MONREALE ★★★

10km (6 miles) S of Palermo

On the Mons Regalis overlooking the Conca d'Oro (the Golden Valley), this hilltop village would be just another of the many that dot this fertile area south of Palermo if it weren't for its majestic Duomo, one of Italy's greatest medieval treasures, carpeted in shimmering mosaics. The locals even have a saying, "To come to Palermo without having seen Monreale is like coming in like a donkey and leaving like an ass."

GETTING THERE The **AST bus** (www.aziendasicilianatrasporti.it; ✆ **840-000323**) leaves every hour or so throughout the day from Palermo's Piazza Giulio Cesare (Central Train station) and Piazza Indipendenza (2.10€ one-way). If you are **driving** (it's about a 30-min. drive), leave your vehicle at the car park at Via Ignazio Florio. From there take a cab or walk up the 99 steps that lead to the cathedral.

Exploring the Duomo

Duomo ★★ CATHEDRAL Legend has it that William II had the idea of this cathedral in a dream when, during a hunting expedition, he fell asleep under a carob tree. While slumbering, the Virgin Mary

Interior of the Cathedral of Monreale.

appeared to him, indicating where a treasure chest was located—and with this loot he was to build a church in her honor. Legends aside, William's ambition to leave his mark was the force behind the last—and the greatest—of Sicily's Arab-Norman cathedrals with Byzantine interiors. Best of all, the cathedral in Monreale never underwent any of the "improvements" that were applied to the cathedral of Palermo, so its original beauty was preserved.

For the most part, the exterior of the building is nothing remarkable. But inside, mosaics comprise 130 individual scenes depicting biblical and religious events, covering some 6,400 sq. m (68,889 sq. ft.), and utilizing some 2,200 kg (4,850 lb.) of gold. The shop in the arcade outside the entrance sells a plan of the mosaics with a legend detailing what's what, a mandatory aid to enjoying the spectacle; binoculars are also handy.

Episodes from the Old Testament are depicted in the central nave (a particularly charming scene shows Noah's Ark riding the waves) while the side aisles illustrate scenes from the New Testament. Christ Pantocrator, the Great Ruler, looks over it all from the central apse; actually, he gazes off to one side, toward scenes from his life. Just below is a mosaic of the Teokotos (Mother of God) with the Christ child on her lap, bathed in light from the window above the main entrance. Among the angels and saints flanking Teokotos is Thomas à Becket, the Archbishop of Canterbury who was murdered on the orders of William's father-in-law, Henry II (he is the second from the right).

Buried here is William II, also honored with a mosaic showing him being crowned by Christ. The heart of St. Louis, or Louis IX, a 13th-century king of France, rests in the urn in which it was placed when the king died during a crusade in Tunisia; the urn was transported to Sicily, at the time ruled by Louis's younger brother, Charles of Anjou.

The lovely cloisters adjacent to the cathedral are an Arabesque fantasy, surrounded by 228 columns topped with capitals carved with scenes from Sicily's Norman history. A splendid fountain in the shape of a palm tree adds to the romance of the place.

Piazza Guglielmo il Buono. ✆ **091-6404413.** Cathedral free; 2€ north transept and treasury; 2€ roof; 8€ cloisters, 4€ ages 18–25, free for children 17 and under. Mon–Sat 8am–1pm and 2:30–6:30pm, Sun 8am–1pm; Cloisters: daily 9am–7pm.

CEFALÙ ★★

81km (50 miles) E of Palermo

The former fishing village of Cefalù, anchored between the sea and a craggy limestone promontory, has grown into a popular resort, though it will never be a rival to Taormina. If you saw the Oscar-winning film *Cinema Paradiso,* you've already been charmed by the town, though the filmmakers wisely left out the hordes of white-fleshed northern Europeans who roast themselves on the crescent-shaped **beach**, one of the best along the northern coast. Towering 278m (912 ft.) above the beach and town is **La Rocca,** a massive and much-photographed crag. The Greeks thought it evoked a head, so they named the village Kephalos, which in time became Cefalù. It's a long, hot, sweaty climb up to the top, but once there, the view is panoramic, extending all the way to the skyline of Palermo in the west or to Capo d'Orlando in the east.

GETTING THERE From Palermo, some three dozen **trains** (www.trenitalia.com; ✆ **892021**) head east to Cefalù (trip time: 1 hr.). Trains pull into the Stazione Termini, Piazza Stazione (✆ **892021**). **SAIS buses** (✆ **091-617-1141**) run between Palermo and Cefalù.

By **car,** follow Route 113 east from Palermo to Cefalù; count on at least 1½ hours of driving time (longer if traffic is bad). Once in Cefalù, park along either side of Via Roma for free, or pay 1€ per hour for a spot within one of the two lots signposted from the main street; both are within an easy walk of the town's medieval core.

VISITOR INFORMATION The **Cefalù Tourist Office,** Corso Ruggero 77 (✆ **0921-421050**), is open Monday to Saturday 8am to 7:30pm, Sunday 9am to 1pm. It's closed on Sunday in winter.

Exploring Cefalù

Getting around Cefalù on foot is easy—no cars are allowed in the historic core. The city's main street is **Corso Ruggero,** which starts at Piazza Garibaldi, site of one of a quartet of gateways to the town.

Duomo ★★★ CHURCH Anchored on a wide square at the foot of towering La Rocca, the twin-towered facade of the Duomo forms a landmark visible for miles around. Legend has it that Roger II ordered the construction of this mighty church in the 12th century after his life was spared in a violent storm off the coast. In reality, he probably built it to flex his muscle with the papacy and show the extent of his power in Sicily. Inside are more mosaics, and even if you've become inured

The Old Town of Cefalù.

to the charms of these shimmering scenes in Palermo and Monreale, you're in for a bit of a surprise: This being a Norman church, Christ is depicted as a blond, not a brunette. In his hand is a Bible, a standard fixture in these images of Christ the Pantocrator (the Ruler), with the verse, "I am the light of the world; he who follows me shall not walk in darkness." Columns in the nave are said to be from the much-ruined Temple of Diana halfway up La Rocca (you can inspect the rest of the stony remains if you make the climb to the top).

Piazza del Duomo. ✆ **0921-922021.** Free. Summer daily 8am–noon and 3:30–7pm; off-season daily 8am–noon and 3:30–5pm.

Museo Mandralisca ★ MUSEUM There is only one reason to step into this small museum, and it's a compelling one: "Ritratto di un Uomo Ignoto" ("Portrait of an Unknown Man"), a 1470 work by the Sicilian painter Antonello da Messina. Seeing this young man with a sly smile and twinkling eyes—some say he was a pirate from the island of Lipari—is an experience akin to seeing the "Mona Lisa," and you won't have to fight your way through camera-wielding crowds to do so.

Via Mandralisca 13. ✆ **0921-421547.** 5€. Daily 9am–1pm and 3–7pm.

Where to Eat

For cakes and cookies, stop by **Pasticceria Serio Pietro,** V. G. Giglio 29 (✆ **0921-422293**), which also sells more than a dozen flavors of the most delicious gelato in town.

Osteria del Duomo ★★ SICILIAN/SEAFOOD A prime spot across from the Duomo with great views of the Rocca makes this a worthy stop, and the fresh seafood does justice to the locale. Seafood salads are a perfect choice for lunch on a summer's day, and piscivores will love the *carpaccio de pesce* (raw, thinly sliced fish). Carnivores can tuck into the similarly excellent carpaccio of beef. Reserve on weekends.

Via Seminario 3. ✆ **0921-421838.** Main courses 8€–16€. Tues–Sun noon–midnight. Closed mid-Nov to mid-Dec.

SEGESTA ★★★

75km (47 miles) SW of Palermo

The **Tempio di Segesta**, one of the best-preserved ancient Doric temples in Italy, proves yet again that the Greeks had a remarkable eye for where to build. Part of the ruined ancient city of Segesta, for millennia this beautiful structure in a lonely field overlooking the countryside has been delighting those lucky enough to gaze upon it. The temple was especially popular with 18th-century artists traveling in Sicily, whose paintings usually included herds of sheep and cattle surrounding the temple.

GETTING THERE From Palermo, three trains a day make the 1¾- to 2-hour journey. The station is about a 1km (½-mile) walk to the park entrance. It's more convenient to reach Segesta **by bus; Tarantola** (✆ **0924-31020**) operates four buses from Piazza Giulio Cesare (Central Train Station) in Palermo (journey time: 1¾ hour).

By **car,** take the autostrada (A29) running between Palermo and Trapani. The exit at Segesta is clearly marked. The journey takes a little under an hour from Palermo.

Exploring the Parco Archaeologico (Archaeological Park)

The archaeological site, which is outside the modern town of Calatafimi, is still the subject of study by archaeologists from around the world. There's a small, canopied eating area opposite the only cafe, where visitors can unwind or rest during their visit.

Parco Archaeologico Segesta ★★★ RUINS The **Tempio di Segesta (Temple of Segesta)** stands on a 304m (997-ft.) hill, on the edge of a deep ravine carved by the Pispisa River. Built in the 5th century B.C., it was never finished, its columns left unfluted and missing a roof. It's been suggested that the temple was actually a ruse, begun to impress diplomats from Athens who, it was thought, would see the project as a sign of the city's wealth and therefore ally with Segesta again Selinunte.

The Greek Temple of Segesta.

Red-Hot Lava & Sparkling Seas: Aeolian Island Escapes

The **Aeolian Islands** can seem like exotic getaways, even as close as they are to Sicily's civilized north coast (they're reached by ferries and hydrofoils from the port of Milazzo). The seven islands share sparkling waters and lava-etched landscapes, and each has its own devotees. Especially popular are **Vulcano,** a stomping ground for summertime partiers and known for black-sand beaches and thermal baths, and **Stromboli,** whose volcano sends red-hot lava tumbling down its slopes to meet the sea with a loud hiss.

Construction halted as soon as the delegation left town. Segesta's other great sight is the perfectly preserved **Teatro (Theater),** hewn out of rock at the top of 431m (1,414 ft.) Mount Barbaro (accessible by a hike of 4km [2½ miles] or by buses that run every half-hour; 1.50€). The *cavea* of 20 semicircular rows could seat 4,000 spectators, who enjoyed views across the surrounding farmland to the Gulf of Castellamare. Those stunning views surely competed with any performance—and still do, during summertime stagings of operas, concerts, and plays.

Parco Archaelogico Segesta. ✆ **0924-952356**. Admission 6€. Mar daily 9am–6:30pm; Apr–Sept daily 9am–7:30pm; Oct–Feb daily 9am–5pm. Ticket office closes 1 hr. before park closes.

TAORMINA ★★★

53km (33 miles) N of Catania, 53km (33 miles) S of Messina, 250km (155 miles) E of Palermo

Guy de Maupassant, the 19th-century French short-story writer, played the tourist shill and wrote, "Should you only have one day to spend in Sicily and you ask me 'what is there to see?' I would reply 'Taormina' without any hesitation. It is only a landscape but one in which you can find everything that seems to have been created to seduce the eyes, the mind and the imagination." Lots of visitors have felt the same way. The Roman poet Ovid loved Taormina, and 18th-century German man of letters Wolfgang Goethe put the town on the Grand Tour circuit when he extolled its virtues in his widely published diaries. Oscar Wilde was one of the gentlemen who made Taormina, as writer and dilettante Harold Acton put it, "a polite synonym for Sodom," and Greta Garbo is one of many film legends who have sought a bit of privacy here.

With its beauty and sophistication, Taormina has a surfeit of star quality itself. The town seems more international than Sicilian, and visitors often outnumber locals. Then again, perched precariously on a cliff between the sinister slopes of Mount Etna and the glittering Ionian Sea, its captivating alleyways lined with churches and *palazzi,* Taormina is almost over-the-top beautiful, and what is more Sicilian than that?

Shopping on Taormina's Corso Umberto I.

Essentials

GETTING THERE Taormina is well served by buses, most of which connect through Catania. Nine Taormina-bound buses run from Catania's Fontanarossa airport daily, stopping in downtown Catania before heading up the coast to Taormina. Travel time is about 1½ hours; tickets are about 5€ one-way. Schedules are available from **Interbus** (www.etnatrasporti.it). Taormina's bus station is on Via Pirandello, near Porta Messina, on the north end of town.

If you're arriving by **car** from Messina, head south along A18, following signs for Catania. From Catania, take the A18 north, toward Messina. Exit the autostrada at the Taormina exit, which lies just north of a series of highway tunnels. Find out if your hotel has parking and if there's a fee, and get very clear instructions about how to arrive—Taormina is a mind-boggling maze of tiny one-way streets and hairpin turns. Otherwise, take advantage of the large public **parking garages** just outside the old town, both clearly signposted with blue "P"s on all roads that approach Taormina. On the north side of town, **Parking Lumbi** (✆ **0942-24345**) charges 14€ per day (16€ per day in Aug) and has a free shuttle from the garage to the Porta Messina gate of Taormina proper. On the south end of town, **Parking Porta Catania** (✆ **0942-620196**) is another multilevel garage with slightly higher rates than Lumbi (15€ per day, 17€ per day in Aug) but with the advantage of being practically in town (it's just 100m/328 ft. from the Porta Catania city gate). Down by the beach at Mazzarò, in the vicinity of the lower cable-car station, is **Parking Mazzarò** (14€ per day, 16€ in Aug).

It's also possible to take the **train** to Taormina, on a line between Messina and Catania, each between 40 minutes and 1½ hours away, depending on the speed of your train. See **www.trenitalia.com** for schedules. Keep in mind that Taormina's train station, which is shared with the seaside town of Giardini-Naxos, is 1.6km (1 mile) away from town. From the station, you have to take a bus up the hill to Taormina (9am–9pm, every 15–45 min.; 2€ one-way), or a taxi (about 15€).

VISITOR INFORMATION The **tourist office** is in Palazzo Corvaja, Piazza Santa Caterina (✆ **0942-23243** or 0942-24941; Mon–Thurs 8:30am–2pm and 4–7pm; Fri 8:30am–2pm). Here you can get a free map, hotel listings, bus and rail timetables, and a schedule of summer cultural events staged at the **Teatro Greco** (Greek Theater; see p. 756).

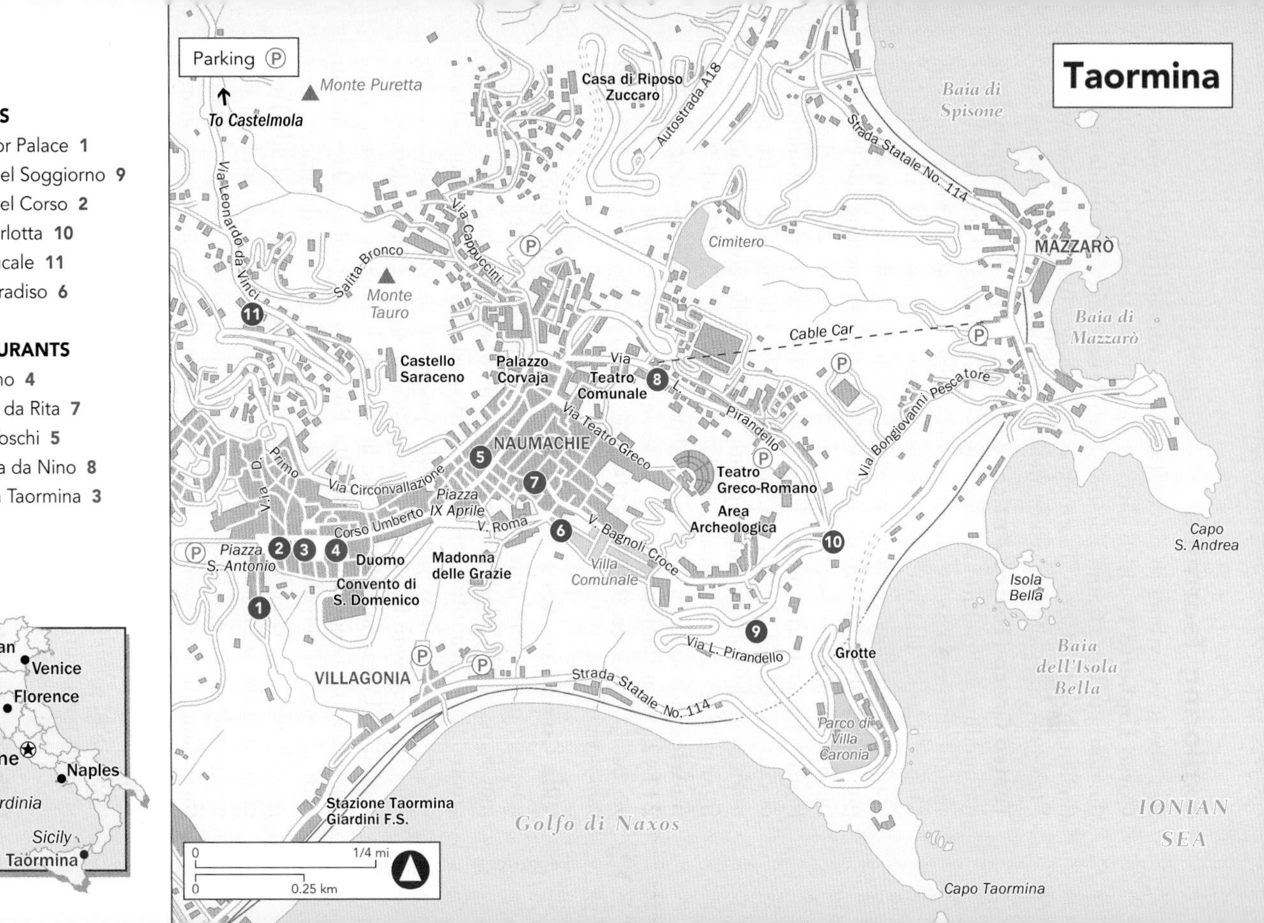

Taormina
HOTELS
Excelsior Palace 1
Hotel Bel Soggiorno 9
Hotel del Corso 2
Villa Carlotta 10
Villa Ducale 11
Villa Paradiso 6
RESTAURANTS
Il Duomo 4
Osteria da Rita 7
Tischi Toschi 5
Trattoria da Nino 8
Vecchia Taormina 3
Parking
To Castelmola
Monte Puretta
Via Leonardo da Vinci
Salita Bronco
Monte Tauro
Via Cappuccini
Casa di Riposo Zuccaro
Autostrada A18
Strada Statale No. 114
Baia di Spisone
Cimitero
MAZZARÒ
Baia di Mazzarò
Cable Car
Castello Saraceno
Palazzo Corvaja
Via Teatro Comunale
L. Pirandello
Via Bongiovanni Pescatore
NAUMACHIE
Via Teatro Greco
Teatro Greco-Romano
Area Archeologica
Via Circonvallazione
V.ia D. Primo
Piazza IX Aprile
Corso Umberto
V. Roma
V. Bagnoli Croce
Villa Comunale
Piazza S. Antonio
Duomo
Convento di S. Domenico
Madonna delle Grazie
Capo S. Andrea
Isola Bella
Via L. Pirandello
Grotte
Baia dell'Isola Bella
VILLAGONIA
Strada Statale No. 114
Parco di Villa Caronia
Stazione Taormina Giardini F.S.
Golfo di Naxos
IONIAN SEA
Capo Taormina
0 1/4 mi
0 0.25 km
Milan
Venice
Florence
Rome
Naples
Sardinia
Sicily
Taormina

Exploring Taormina

Just about everything to see in Taormina unfolds from the main drag, **Corso Umberto I**, which slices through town from Porta Messina, in the north, to Porta Catania, in the south. It only takes 15 minutes to walk the length of the Corso. Taormina is also a handy base for trips to Mount Etna—the high-altitude visitor areas are only about 1 hour away by car.

Teatro Greco (Teatro Antico) ★★★ RUINS With their penchant for building in beautiful settings, the Greeks perched the second-largest ancient theater in Sicily, after the one in Siracusa, on the rocky flanks of Mount Tauro. The backdrop of smoldering Mount Etna and the sea crashing far below certainly provided as much drama as any theatrical production. Romans rebuilt much of the theater, adding the finishing touches on what we see today in the 2nd century A.D., and put the arena to use for gladiatorial events. In ruin, but with much of the hillside *cavea,* or curved seating area, intact, the theater is still the setting for performances and film screenings, greatly enhanced by columns and arches framing the sea and volcano in the background. Check with **TaorminaArte**'s headquarters, Corso Umberto 19 (www.taoarte.it; ✆ **0942-21142**), or at the tourist office for exact dates and show times.

Via del Teatro Greco. ✆ **0942-21142.** 8€. Daily Apr–Sept 9am–7pm; Oct–Mar 9am–4pm.

Villa Comunale ★★★ PARK/GARDEN Of all the colorful characters who have spent time in Taormina, the one leaving the biggest mark may have been Lady Florence Trevelyan, who in the late 19th century created these beautiful gardens, now the park also known as Parco Duca di Cesarò. Lady Trevelyan allegedly was asked to leave Britain after an entanglement with Edward, Prince of Wales, son of Queen Victoria. She settled in Taormina, married, and lived quite happily in the lovely, adjacent villa that is now the hotel **Villa Paradiso** (see below). Her liaison with a farmer, much of it conducted amid these groves and terraces, supposedly inspired D.H. Lawrence's "Lady Chatterley's Lover." Lady Trevelyan built the stone and brick pavilions in the park for birdwatching and entertaining—it's too bad the gates are swung shut at sunset, because these fanciful follies would be perfect for whiling away a hot summer night. During the day, the 3 hectares (7½ acres) of groomed terraces provide a nice respite from the busy town, filled as they are with luxuriant vegetation, cobblestone walkways, picturesque stone stairways, and a sinuous path lining the park's eastern rim with superb views over the sea.

Via Bagnoli Croce. No phone. Free. Daily 8:30am–7pm (6pm in winter).

Where to Stay

The hotels in Taormina are some of the best in Sicily. All price ranges are available, with lodgings ranging from army cots to sumptuous suites. If you're driving to a hotel at the top of Taormina, call ahead to see what arrangements can be made for your car. Ask for exact driving directions

MEET mighty MOUNT ETNA

Warning: Always get the latest report from the tourist office before setting out for a trip to Mount Etna. Adventurers have been killed by a surprise "belch" (volcanic explosion). Mount Etna remains one of the world's most active volcanoes, with sporadic gas, steam, lava, and ash emissions from its summit.

Looming menacingly over the coast of eastern Sicily, Mount Etna is the highest and largest active volcano in Europe. The peak changes in size over the years but it currently soars 3,324m (10,906 ft.). Etna has been active in modern times: In 1928, the little village of Mascali was buried under lava, and powerful eruptions in 1971, 1992, 2001, and 2003 caused extensive damage to facilities nearby. Throughout the year, episodes of spectacular but usually harmless lava fountains, some hundreds of meters high, are not uncommon, providing a dramatic show for viewers in Taormina.

Etna has figured in history and in Greek mythology. Empedocles, the 5th-century-B.C. Greek philosopher, is said to have jumped into its crater in the belief that he would be delivered directly to Mt. Olympus to take his seat among the gods. It was under Etna that Zeus crushed the multiheaded dragon Typhoeus, thereby securing domination over Olympus. Hephaestus, god of fire, made his headquarters in Etna, aided by the single-eyed Cyclops. The Greeks warned that when Typhoeus tried to break out of his prison, lava erupted and earthquakes cracked the land. That must mean that the monster nearly escaped on March 11, 1669, one of the most violent eruptions ever—it destroyed Catania, about 27km (17 miles) away.

Etna is easy to reach by car from Taormina. The fastest way is to take the E45 autostrada south to the Acireale exit. From here, follow the brown etna signs west to Nicolosi, passing through several smaller towns along the way. From Nicolosi, keep following the etna signs up the hill toward **Rifugio Sapienza** (1,923m/ 6,307 ft.), the starting point for all expeditions to the crater. The faux-Alpine hamlet here has tourist services and cheap and ample parking, and is the base station of the **Funivia del Etna** cable car (www.funiviaetna.com; ✆ **095-914141;** daily 9am–4:30pm), which takes you to the **Torre del Filosofo** (Philosopher's Tower) station at 2,900m (9,514 ft.). You can also hike up to the station, but it's a strenuous climb and takes about 5 hours. The final ascent to the authorized crater areas at about 3,000m (9,843 ft., as close to the summit as visitors are allowed) is via *Star Wars*-ish off-road vehicles over a scrabbly terrain of ash and dead ladybugs (dead ladybugs are everywhere on Mount Etna). Conditions at the crater zone are thrilling, but the high winds, exposure, and potential sense of vertigo are not for the faint of heart.

The round-trip cost of getting to the top of Etna, including the cable car ride, the off-road vans, and the requisite authorized guide at the crater zone, is about 55€. Etna is not a complicated excursion to do on your own, but if you'd prefer to go with a tour, Taormina is chock-full of agencies that organize Etna day trips.

as well as instructions on where to park—the narrow, winding, one-way streets can be bewildering once you get here.

EXPENSIVE

Villa Carlotta ★★★ This 1920s stone villa vaguely resembling a castle is tucked away at the edge of town. It's another creation of Andrea and

Rosaria Quartucci, who work their magic at **Villa Ducale** (below). A wall of Byzantine catacombs adds an air of mystery, but what wins you over is the classic-yet-contemporary style and wonderful sense of privacy and comfort. Most of the warm-hued, stylish rooms have terraces and sea views, and many overlook the luxuriant rear gardens where a swimming pool is tucked into the greenery. As at Villa Ducale, service is personalized and attentive, and a shuttle bus makes a run down to the beach. Villa Carlotta also operates the **Taormina Luxury Apartments** (www.taorminaluxuryapartments.com), just up the street.

Via Pirandello 81. www.hotelvillacarlottataormina.com. ✆ **0942-626058.** 23 units. 200€–350€ double. Rates include breakfast. Parking 10€. Closed Jan–early Mar. **Amenities:** Restaurant; concierge; health club; pool; Wi-Fi (free).

Villa Ducale ★★★ Andrea and Rosaria Quartucci have fashioned a family villa into a warm and stylish getaway perched high on a hillside above the town, with flower-planted terraces, Mediterranenan gardens, and extraordinary eagle's-nest views that extend as far as Calabria. Distinctive rooms and suites, in the villa and a house across the road, are done in Sicilian chic, with extremely comfortable furnishings set against warm hues that play off terracotta floors; they are enlivened with beams, arches, and other stylish architectural details, equipped with luxurious baths, and fitted out with fine linens and works by local artists. Service is exceedingly warm and personal, and a lavish buffet breakfast and complimentary sunset cocktails, accompanied by a spread of Sicilian appetizers, are served on a living-room-like terrace; lunch and dinner are available on request. The hotel has no pool, but there's a Jacuzzi, and a shuttle makes a run to a private beach (and also to town).

Via Leonardo da Vinci 60. www.villaducale.com. ✆ **0942-28153.** 15 units. 240€–400€ double. Rates include buffet breakfast. Parking 10€. Closed Jan–early Mar. **Amenities:** Jacuzzi; room service; Wi-Fi (free).

MODERATE

Excelsior Palace ★ This is not a palace, really, but a sprawling pink grand hotel from the early 20th century tucked into one end of town just off Corso Umberto. Rooms here have not been upgraded since, well, since a time when burnt-orange bathroom tiles and floral carpets were all the rage. They're well maintained, though, and every one has a view—many of Mt. Etna and the coastline—and many have little balconies with just enough room for two chairs. Though the place is often filled with groups, service is attentive and old-world, with waiters in ties and jackets serving cocktails in frumpy lounges full of overstuffed couches and armchairs. The magnificent garden is the best amenity, draped over a promontory above the town and sea and the setting for a magnificently perched swimming pool—making this a top summertime choice.

Via Toselli 8. www.excelsiorpalacetaormina.it. ✆ **0942-23975.** 85 units. From 75€–125€ double. Rates include breakfast. **Amenities:** Restaurant; bar; concierge; pool; Wi-Fi in public areas (free).

Hotel Bel Soggiorno ★★ You could be nowhere but Sicily in this rather grand old villa surrounded by lush gardens that tumble down a hillside, filled with lemon and orange trees, exotic flowers, and sweeping coastal vistas. Tile-floored guest rooms are plain but comfortable, with handsome iron bedsteads and simple wooden furniture. All open through French doors to balconies and, in many cases, huge terraces. What has to be the friendliest staff on the island serves a generous breakfast in a beautiful orangerie and on an adjoining patio. As bucolic as the surroundings are, the center of town is an easy 10-minute walk away.

Via Luigi Pirandello 60. www.belsoggiorno.com. ✆ **0942-23342.** From 110€ double. Rates include breakfast. **Amenities:** Bar; gardens; Wi-Fi (free).

Villa Paradiso ★ Lady Florence Trevelyan, who created the beautiful gardens that are now the Villa Communale, lived in this villa until her death in 1907. It then passed to the Martorana family, three generations of whom have proven to be outstanding hoteliers. Family antiques, comfy armchairs and couches, and paintings (many presented by guests over the years) fill lounges and bright, handsomely decorated guest rooms, where balconies and sun-drenched sitting alcoves face the sea. Breakfast and dinners are served in a top-floor, glassed-in restaurant, **Settimo Cielo** (Seventh Heaven), which it really seems to be. Between June and October, the hotel offers free shuttle service and free entrance to the Paradise Beach Club, about 6km (4 miles) to the east, in the seaside resort of Letojanni.

Via Roma 2. www.hotelvillaparadisotaormina.com. ✆ **0942-23921.** 37 units. 130€–210€ double. **Amenities:** Restaurant; bar; room service; Wi-Fi (fee).

INEXPENSIVE

Hotel del Corso ★ You'll forgo spas, pools, and other chic luxuries in these basic lodgings right in the heart of town, on Corso Umberto near the Duomo, but you won't give up views of the sea and Mt. Etna. They fill the windows of many of the rooms and spread out below the top floor lounge, breakfast room, and sun terrace; some rooms have less dramatic but pleasing views of the town. Black-and-white terrazzo floors, iron bedsteads, and soothing neutral colors add a lot of spark to the comfortable guest rooms, a few of which have small balconies. Book well in advance, especially on weekends, when this good-value property fills up fast.

Corso Umberto 328. www.hoteldelcorsotaormina.com. ✆ **0942-628698.** 15 units. 70€–110€ double. Rates include breakfast. **Amenities:** Wi-Fi (free).

Where to Eat

The ultimate Sicilian summer refreshment, the sorbet-like *granita,* is perfect at **Bam Bar,** not far from the Grand Hotel Timeo at Via di Giovanni 45 (✆ **0942-24355**). Specialties are the almond *(mandorla)* or white fig *(fico bianco),* but there are usually a dozen or more flavors to choose from.

MODERATE

Il Duomo ★★ SICILIAN The decor leaves something to be desired, with harsh lighting and a green-and-orange color scheme—to avoid it, choose a table near the large window overlooking the Duomo, or better yet in good weather, on the side terrace. Fortunately, the food takes no such liberties in taste, sticking to traditional Sicilian recipes, with some well-conceived modern twists. This is the best place in town to try pasta con sarde (with sardines and breadcrumbs); the fish is fresh and nicely enlivened with capers, tomatoes, and olives.

Vico Ebrei. www.ristorantealduomo.it. ✆ **0942-625656.** Main courses 10€–16€. Tues–Sun 12:30–3pm and 7:30–10:30pm.

Tischi Toschi ★★★ SICILIAN/SEAFOOD A warm-hued yellow room facing a little piazza and decorated with old ceramics is the setting for creative takes on old Sicilian classics. Even *pasta alla Norma* (with eggplant and ricotta) seems like a work of art here, and is topped with a grilled eggplant. Venture further into some dishes you might not find in many other places, such as *insalata di pesce stocco*, a salad made from dried cod, raw fennel, and tomato dressed with olive oil and parsley, and *sarde a beccafico*, sardines stuffed with pine nuts and fennel and served with lemon and orange. Don't miss the delicious fried artichokes, and end a meal with the heavenly, refreshing lemon jelly.

Via F. Paladini 3. ✆ **339-3642088.** Main courses 10€–18€. Daily noon–3pm and 6:30–11pm.

Vecchia Taormina ★★ SICILIAN One of Taormina's longtime favorites keeps a steady stream of regulars happy with what are reputed to be the best pizzas around. The *pizza alla Norma,* the ingredients of the classic eggplant-laden pasta on a flaky crust, makes good on the claim. The kitchen also does nice versions of spaghetti con vongole (with clams), or topped with fresh sardines and breadcrumbs, as well as other classics, serving them in two cozy rooms and a delightful outside terrace.

Vico Ebre 3. ✆ **0942-625589**. Main courses 10€–15€. Thurs–Tues 7:30–10:30pm.

INEXPENSIVE

Osteria da Rita ★★ SICILIAN Taormina needs more easygoing eateries like this pleasant little place tucked away between the Corso and Villa Communale. Pizzas, sandwiches, salads, omelets, and a few pasta dishes—including heaping platters of spaghetti carbonara and pasta alla Norma—are served in a small, plain room and on a picture-perfect piazzetta out front. Service is friendly and prices are reasonable.

Via Calapitrulli 3. ✆ **0942-680888.** Main courses 7€–13€. Daily noon–3pm and 7:30–10:30pm.

Trattoria da Nino ★ SICILIAN Good, no-nonsense Sicilian *cucina casalinga* (home cooking) is the recipe for success in this unpretentious, brightly lit room (with an airy terrace in warm weather) across from the upper station of the cable car. Pastas are housemade (deliciously delicate gnocchi, little potato dumplings, are served *alla Norma,* with eggplant and ricotta), and the fish is fresh and served simply grilled. Nino's is a local institution, a 50-year veteran of the Taormina dining scene, and it's always packed; they don't take reservations for groups of fewer than six. Via Pirandello 37. www.trattoriadanino.com. ✆ **0942-21265.** Main courses 8€–18€. Daily noon–3pm and 6:30–11pm.

Outdoor Pursuits

To reach the best and most popular beach, **Lido Mazzarò,** you have to go south of town via a cable car (✆ **0942-23605**) that in theory but often not practice leaves from Via Pirandello every 15 minutes (3€ each way, 10€ day ticket) in spring and summer between 7:45am and 8pm (from 8:45am on Monday). The soft, finely pebbled beach is one of the best equipped in Sicily, with bars, restaurants, and hotels. You can rent beach chairs, umbrellas, and watersports equipment at kiosks from April to October. To the right of Lido Mazzarò, past the Capo Sant'Andrea headland, is the region's prettiest cove, where twin crescents of beach sweep out to the minuscule **Isola Bella** islet.

North of Mazzarò, the long, wide beaches of **Spisone** and **Letojanni** are more developed but less crowded than **Giardini,** the large resort beach south of Isola Bella. A local bus leaves Taormina for Mazzarò, Spisone, and Letojanni; another heads down the coast to Giardini.

Shopping

Shopping is all too easy in Taormina—just walk along **Corso Umberto I.** Ceramics are one of Sicily's most notable handicrafts, and Taormina's shops are among the best places to buy them on the island, as the selection is excellent. **Giuseppa di Blasi,** Corso Umberto I 103 (✆ **0942-24671**), has a nice range of designs and specializes in the highly valued "white pottery" from Caltagirone. Mixing the new and the old, **Carlo Panarello Antichità,** Corso Umberto I 122 (✆ **0942-23910**) offers Sicilian ceramics (from pots to tables) and also deals in eclectic antique furnishings, paintings, and engravings.

Side Trips from Taormina

CASTELMOLA ★★

Taormina gets high praise for its gorgeous views, but for connoisseurs of scenic outlooks, the real show takes place in the village of Castelmola, an eagle's nest 3km (2 miles) northwest of Taormina, and about 300m (1,000 ft.) feet higher. The Ionian Sea seems to stretch to the ends of the earth from up here, and you'll be staring right into the northern flanks of Mt. Etna. For the full experience, make the trip up on foot, following routes that begin at Porta Catania and Porta Messina (the tourist office or any hotel desk can give you directions); the Porta Messina trail passes a section of the Roman aqueduct and the Convento dei Cappuccini, where you can pause for a breather. Either route involves an hour or so of fairly strenuous walking, but once at the top, stop at Castelmola's **Bar Turrisi** (Piazza Duomo 19; ✆ **0942-28181;** daily 10am–1am, until 3am weekends) for a glass of *vino alla mandorla* (almond wine) and a look at its peculiar art collection. If that's more walking than you care to do, you can also drive up to Castelmola (park below the village and walk in) or take an orange bus that runs more or less hourly from Porta Messina (2.20€ round-trip).

GOLE DELL'ALCANTARA ★★

In a series of narrow gorges on the Alcantara (Al-*cahn*-ta-rah) river, rushing ice-cold water fed by snow melt on Mt. Etna darts and dashes over fantastically twisted volcanic rock, creating a scenic spectacle that's especially refreshing on a hot day. The basalt rock formations were sculpted into these wild shapes thousands of years ago by cool water flowing over molten debris during eruptions on Etna. The gorge is now protected as **Parco Fluviale dell'Alcanta** (www.parcoalcantara.it; ✆ **0942-985010**), though ticket booths, turnstiles, and elevators into the gorge lend an amusement-park aura. Get away from the crowds with a hike along the riverbed, stopping now and then to lounge on flat riverside rocks and wade and even swim in the chilly water. From October to April, only the upper area of the park, with an overlook trail above the gorge, is open. It costs 8€ to enter the park (open daily 7am–7:30pm). Amenities include a gift shop, cafeteria, picnic areas, and toilets. You can reach the Gole dell'Alcantara by car from Taormina in 35 minuntes or you can take **Interbus** (www.interbus.it; ✆ **0942-625301**) for the 1-hour trip, with several daily runs from Taormina (6€ roundtrip). Organized excursions (from 25€) to the gorges are also offered by tour operators in Taormina, often in conjunction with a visit to Mount Etna.

SIRACUSA ★★

This small, out-of-the-way southern city packs a one-two punch. Siracusa was one of the most important cities of Magna Graecia (Greater Greece), rivaling even Athens in power and influence. The still-functioning Teatro Greco, where Aeschylus debuted his plays, is one of many landmarks of this ancient metropolis. Ortigia, the quaint historical center spreading over its own island, belongs to a much later time, when palaces and churches were built in baroque style after the earthquake of 1693.

Siracusa might seem far removed, but in making the trip to the southeast coast you'll be following in the illustrious footsteps of the scientist Archimedes, statesman Cicero, evangelist St. Paul, martyr St. Lucy, painter Caravaggio, and naval hero Admiral Lord Horatio Nelson, all of whom left a mark on this rather remarkable place.

Essentials

GETTING THERE Siracusa is 1½ hours south of Taormina on the A18. It's 3 hours southeast of Palermo on the A19 and A18, and 3 hours east of Agrigento on the SS540, A19, and A18. Siracusa is also well connected with the rest of Sicily by bus and train, though buses are more efficient and frequent than trains. **Interbus buses** (www.etnatrasporti.it) run almost hourly between Siracusa and Catania and several times a day between Siracusa and Palermo. Train travel usually requires a change in Catania; for details, contact www.trenitalia.com ✆ **892021.** Both trains and buses arrive in Siracusa at the station on Via Francesco Crispi, between the Parco Archeologico (Archaeological Park) and Ortigia.

GETTING AROUND You won't need a car, just your own two feet and perhaps a few bus or cab rides to see the best of Siracusa proper. However, if you're using Siracusa as a base for exploring southeastern Sicily, you may arrive here by car—in which case, inquire about parking with your hotel or rental agency before arriving.

VISITOR INFORMATION The **tourist office,** at Via San Sebastiano 43 (✆ **0931-481232**), is open Monday to Friday 8:30am to 1:30pm and 3 to 6pm, Saturday 8:30am to 1:30pm. There's another office in the historic center at Via della Maestranza 33 (✆ **0931-65201**); it's open Monday to Friday 8:15am to 2pm and 2:30 to 5:30pm, Saturday 8:15am to 2pm.

Exploring Siracusa

Ortigia Island is Siracusa's *centro storico,* a mostly pedestrian zone where narrow alleys lined with romantic 18th-century *palazzi* spill onto Piazza del Duomo. The ancient ruins are a good half-hour walk north of Ortigia along Corso Gelone.

ORTIGIA ISLAND ★★★

The historic center of Siracusa is an island only about 1 sq. km (¾ sq. mile), with breezy, palm-shaded seaside promenades fringing its shores. Most of the island is baroque, with grandiose palaces and churches lining narrow lanes and flamboyant piazzas, though Ortigia was settled in ancient times. According to myth, Leto stopped on the island to give

Siracusa's Ortigia Island.

birth to Artemis, one of the twins she conceived with Zeus; she continued on her way and delivered Apollo on the Greek island of Delos.

The first landmark you'll come to after you cross Ponte Umbertino from the mainland is the **Temple of Apollo,** the oldest Doric temple in Sicily. The Apollion would have measured 58m × 24m (190 ft. × 79 ft.) when it was built in the 6th century B.C. It later served as a Byzantine church, then a mosque, then a church again under the Normans and is now an evocative ruin, with the temple platform, a fragmentary colonnade, and an inner wall rising in the middle of Piazza Pancali.

The **Piazza del Duomo,** certainly one of the most beautiful squares in Sicily, is all about theatrics—a sea of white marble softened by pink oleander and surrounded by flamboyant palaces with elaborate stone filigree work and wrought-iron balconies. The Duomo itself (open daily 8am–noon and 4–7pm) is frothily baroque, almost too playful to be religious. The two tiers of Doric columns that define its remarkable facade were once part of Siracusa's 5th-century-B.C. Temple of Athena, one of the best-known sights of the ancient world, built to mark a Greek victory over the Carthaginians. Cicero, the Roman orator and traveler, reported that the temple was filled with gold, the doors were made of gold and ivory, and a statue of Athena atop the pediment was visible for miles out to sea. Romans made off with the gold, but a statue of the Virgin stands atop the pediment as Athena once did. Other ancient columns are present in the apse of the church, which was first fashioned from the temple around the 7th century.

On the south side of the square is the pretty church of **Santa Lucia alla Badia,** its tall, marble baroque facade embellished with twisted columns, pediments, and a wrought-iron balcony. Lucia, a plucky 4th-century Siracusan virgin, is the city's patron. Born of wealth, from an early age she adapted Christian principles and was determined to give her worldly goods to the poor. Her piety and generosity annoyed the young man to whom she had once been betrothed, and out of spite for seeing Lucia's sizable dowry squandered in such a way, the youth denounced her to Roman authorities. Lucia was condemned to prostitution, but refused to be dragged off to a brothel. Authorities tied her to a pillar and lit a fire beneath her, but she proved to be flame-resistant. Finally, a soldier plunged a sword into her throat. You'll see depictions of this gruesome act throughout Siracusa and the rest of Sicily, where the saint is very popular (tamer versions show the saint holding the sword that killed her).

Also on Piazza del Duomo is an entrance to the **Hypogeum** (no phone; 3€; Tues–Sun 9am–1pm and 4–8pm), a network of underground chambers and corridors dug as air-raid shelters in World War II.

A spring feeds **Fonte Aretusa,** a lovely shoreline spot where papyrus grows in a shallow pool that supplied Siracusa with fresh water for millennia. Classical myth, however, tells a different story: The nymph Aretusa was bathing in a river in Greece when the river god Alpheus took a liking to her. She asked for help in avoiding his advances, and Artemis, goddess of the wilderness and protectress of young women, turned her into a river that emerged here. Not to be thwarted, Alpheus followed suit, and the two of them bubble forth for eternity.

The elegant 13th-century palace **Galleria Regionale Palazzo Bellomo,** Via Capodieci 16 (✆ **0931-69511;** 8€; Tues–Sat 9am–7pm, Sun 2–7:30pm), houses Sicilian works from the Middle Ages through the 20th century, including two great masterpieces. Antonello da Messina's **"Annunciation"** (1474) shows the artist's remarkable attention to detail: Tall windows, beams, columns, the Virgin's bed, and a blue-and-white vase compose an intricately rendered interior, with bright light infusing the spaces. The scene is typical of the Flemish paintings that were popular in Naples, where Messina studied when he left his native Sicily as a teenager. Caravaggio's **"Burial of St. Lucia"** was commissioned in 1608, when the artist had just escaped from a prison in Malta and come to Siracusa. Note how, with his characteristic lighting, the artist highlights the muscular gravediggers, showing their brute strength, while the mourners seem small and meek in the background. A shaft of light falls on Lucia's face and neck, showing the stab wound that killed her; she is a study in serenity, having entered the heavenly kingdom.

THE ANCIENT RUINS ★★★

Of all the Greek cities of antiquity that flourished in Sicily, Siracusa was the most important, a formidable competitor of Athens. In its heyday, the city dared take on Carthage and even Rome. Sprawling Greek and Roman ruins are these days surrounded by an unremarkable section of the modern city. To reach the ruins, walk north along Corso Gelone (or better yet, take bus no. 1, 3, or 12, or a cab from Ortigia's Piazza Pancali) or take buses 11, 25, or 26 from the front of Siracusa's central train station.

Castello Eurialo ★ RUINS Part of a massive, 27km- (16-mile) long defense system, this 4th-century-B.C. fortress is surrounded by three trenches, connected by underground tunnels. These supposedly impregnable defenses were never put to the test: Siracusa fell to the Romans in 212 B.C. without a fight, because the entire garrison was celebrating the feast of Aphrodite. It was here, legend has it, that the Greek mathematician Archimedes famously cried "Eureka!" having discovered the law of water displacement while taking a bath. The evocative ruin overlooking the Siracusan plain is the best-preserved Greek castle in the Mediterranean. The defenses are at the far end of the archaeological zone, about 5km (3 miles) outside the city center near a village called Belvedere; buses 25 and 26 pass the entrance.

Piazza Eurialo 1, off Viale Epipoli in the Belvedere district. ✆ **0931-481111.** 4€; 10€ with Parco Archeologico and Museo Archeologico. Daily 9am–5:30pm.

Catacombe di San Giovanni ★★ RUINS Spooky subterranean chambers, installed in underground aqueducts that had been abandoned by the Greeks, contain some 20,000 ancient Christian tombs. They are entered through the Church of San Giovanni, now in ruin but holy ground for centuries; it was the city's cathedral until it was more or less leveled by an earthquake in 1693. St. Paul allegedly preached here when he stopped in Siracusa around A.D. 59, and a church was erected in the 6th century to commemorate the event. The Cripta di San Marciano (Crypt of St. Marcian) honors a popular Siracusan martyr, a 1st-century-A.D. bishop who was tied to a pillar and flogged to death on this spot. Piazza San Giovanni, at end of Viale San Giovanni. No phone. 5€. Tues–Sun 9:30am–12:30pm and 2:30–4:30pm. Closed Feb.

Museo Archeologico Regionale Paolo Orsi (Paolo Orsi Regional Archaeological Museum) ★★★ MUSEUM One of Italy's finest archaeological collections shows off artifacts from southern Sicily's prehistoric inhabitants through the Romans, showcasing pieces in stunning modern surrounds. Amid prehistoric tools and sculptures are the skeletons of a pair of dwarf elephants, as intriguing to us as they were to the ancients: It's believed that the large central orifice (nasal passage) of these skeletal beasts inspired the myth of the one-eyed Cyclops. Early Greeks left behind a (much-reproduced) grinning terracotta Gorgon that once adorned the frieze of the temple of Athena (see Duomo, above) to ward off evil. You'll also see votive cult statuettes devoted to Demeter and Persephone—mother and daughter goddesses linked to fertility and the harvest. Legend had it that Hades, god of the underworld, abducted Persephone in Sicily and carried her down to his realm; with a bit of negotiating between angry Demeter and the other gods, it was agreed that Persephone could return to Earth but must descend to resume her duties as queen of the underworld for part of the year, when in her absence winter descends upon the lands above. The museum's most celebrated piece is the **Landolina Venus,** a Roman copy of an original by the great classical Greek sculptor Praxiteles. The graceful and modest goddess, now headless, rises out of marble waves; French writer Guy de Maupassant called her "the perfect expression of exuberant beauty." In the gardens of the Villa Landolina in Akradina, Viale Teocrito 66. www.siracusaturismo.net. © **0931-464022.** 8€ or 13.50€ with Parco Archeologico della Neapolis. Tues–Sat 9am–6pm; Sun 9am–1pm.

Parco Archeologico della Neapolis ★★★ RUINS Many of Siracusa's ancient ruins are clustered in this archaeological park at the western edge of town, immediately north of Stazione Centrale.

The **Teatro Greco ★★★** (Greek Theater) was hewn out of bedrock in the 5th century B.C., with 67 rows that could seat 16,000 spectators. It was reconstructed in the 3rd century B.C., appears now much as it did then, and is still the setting for ancient drama in the spring and early summer. Tickets are 30€ to 70€. Contact **INDA,** Corso Matteotti 29, Siracusa (www.indafondazione.org; © **0931-487200**).

Only the ancient theaters in Rome and Verona are larger than the **Anfiteatro Romano,** created around 20 B.C. Gladiators sparred here, and a square hole in the center of the arena suggests that machinery was used to lift wild beasts from below. Historical evidence suggests that the arena could be flooded for mock sea battles called *naumachiae;* pumps could also have flooded and drained a reservoir in which crocodiles are said to have fed on the corpses of victims killed in the games. The Spanish carted off much of the stonework to rebuild city fortifications when they conquered Siracusa in the 16th century, but some of the seats remain—the first rows would have been reserved for Roman citizens, those right above for wealthy Siracusans, and the last rows for the hoi polloi.

What is now a lush grove of lemon and orange trees, the **Latomia del Paradiso** (Quarry of Paradise) was at one time a fearsome place, vast, dark, and subterranean—until the cavern's roof collapsed in the great earthquake of 1693. Originally prisoners were worked to death here to quarry the stones used in the construction of ancient Siracusa. Certainly the most storied attraction in the park is the **Orecchio di Dionisio** (Ear of Dionysius). The Greeks created this tall and vaguely ear-shaped cave by digging into the cliff, simply to expand the limestone quarry for water storage—but something about this huge cavern has always inspired more dramatic accounts. One legend, completely unfounded, claims the cave's occupants were Athenians captured by Dionysus' mercenaries during the Peloponnesian Wars; supposedly he liked the way the cave's acoustics amplified their screams as they were tortured. Almost as fascinating is the well-documented purpose of the **Ara di Ierone** (or, Altar of Heron): Fifth-century B.C. Greeks built the altar, 196m (636 ft.) long and 23m (75 ft.) wide and approached by enormous ramps, for the sacrifice of 450 bulls at one time.

Via Del Teatro (off the intersection of Corso Gelone and Viale Teocrito), Viale Paradiso. www.siracusaturismo.net. ✆ **0931-66206.** 10€ or 13.50€ with the archaeological museum. Daily Apr–Sept 9am–7:15pm (until 4:30pm on certain summer evenings when performances are held in the theater); Oct–Feb 9am–4:30pm; Mar 9am–5:30pm.

A Gigantic Teardrop Runs Through It

The tallest building in Siracusa is the bizarre **Santuario della Madonna delle Lacrime** (Our Lady of Tears Sanctuary, Via Santuario 33; ✆ **0931-21446;** free admission; daily 8am–noon and 4–7pm), a monstrous cone of contemporary architecture (built in 1993) halfway between Ortigia and the archaeological zone. Meant to evoke a sort of angular teardrop and rising 74m (243 ft.) with a diameter of 80m (262 ft.), it houses a statue of the Madonna that supposedly wept for 5 days in 1953. Alleged chemical tests showed that the liquid was similar to that of human tears. Pilgrims flock here, and you'll see postcards of the weepy Virgin around Siracusa. In the interior, vertical windows stretch skyward to the roof. A charlatan TV evangelist and his congregation would not look out of place here.

Where to Stay

The best place to stay in Siracusa is Ortigia, with enough character, charm, and comfortable choices to keep the most discerning traveler happy. A good agency for apartments in Ortigia is **Case Sicilia** (www.casesicilia.com; ✆ **339-298-3507**). For villas, **Think Sicily** (www.thinksicily.com) has a carefully edited list of well-equipped properties in and around Siracusa.

Algilà Ortigia Charme Hotel ★ A slightly exotic air pervades this old stone palace at the edge of the sea. Built around a peaceful inner courtyard with a splashing fountain, it's accented throughout with carefully restored stone work and wooden beams, offset by beautiful multicolor tiles and other rich details. Rooms combine conventional luxury with all the modern amenities, plus a surfeit of four-poster beds, antiques, and tribal kilims; many have sea views. The in-house restaurant serves Sicilian classics and seafood beneath a beautiful wooden ceiling.
Via Vittorio Veneto 93. www.algila.it. ✆ **0931-465186.** 30 units. 174€–400€ double. Rates include breakfast. **Amenities:** Restaurant; room service; Wi-Fi (free, in lobby).

Approdo delle Sirene ★★ This natty little inn occupies two floors of a seaside apartment house, beautifully refashioned as light-filled quarters with a slightly nautical flair, as becomes the sparking blue water just beyond the tall windows. In the contemporary guest rooms, polished wood floors offset handsome furnishings, striped fabrics, and bold colors. Several rooms have French doors opening to small balconies, though some rooms are sky-lit only—flooded with light but without views. The sunny breakfast room/lounge and terrace provide plenty of panoramas, however. The hosts, mother and son Fiora and Friedrich, are a hospitable on-the-scene presence and can arrange all kinds of tours and excursions. They even have free bikes available for guests' use.
Riva Garibaldi 15. www.apprododellesirene.com. ✆ **0931-24857.** 8 units. 80€–130€ double. 2-night minimum stay June–Aug. Rates include breakfast. **Amenities:** Bikes; Wi-Fi (free).

Domus Mariae Benessere Guest House ★ The Ursiline sisters who still occupy a wing of this seaside convent have found their calling as innkeepers. The large, bright rooms border on vaguely luxurious, with plush headboards on extremely comfortable beds, attractive rugs on tile floors, and lots of counter and storage space in the large bathrooms. Some rooms have sea views, while others face an atrium-like courtyard. The surprising indulgences given the surroundings include a lovely roof terrace and a lower-level spa, with a small pool and Jacuzzi. An in-house restaurant serves a rather monastic buffet breakfast as well as a well-prepared dinner of healthful Mediterranean fare.
Via Veneto 89. www.domusmariaebenessere.com. ✆ **0931-24854.** 21 units. From 60€ double. Rates include breakfast. **Amenities:** Bikes; pool; spa; Wi-Fi (free).

Henry's House ★★ The namesake Henry was a now departed friend of the owners, and he could not have a nicer legacy than this lovely seaside palazzo at the southern edge of Ortigia. Several terraces, including a few private spaces off some of the rooms, look over the sea, while salons filled with antiques and artifacts are also atmospheric. Guest quarters are tucked away on several floors and have beams, tile floors, and character-filled furnishings that lend the aura of a private home.
Via del Castello Maniace 68. www.hotelhenryhouse.com. ✆ **0931-21361.** 14 units. 140€–160€, includes breakfast. **Amenities:** Bar; room service; Wi-Fi (free).

Hotel Gutkowski ★★★ Two old houses facing the sea at the edge of Ortigia are warm, hospitable, and capture the essence of southern Italy—Sicilian hues on the walls, colorful floor tiles, and views of the blue water or sun-baked roofs of the old city. Each room is different, some with balconies, some with terraces, and furnishings are functional but chosen to provide restful simplicity—old Sicilian and vintage mid-century pieces offset by contemporary tables and bedsteads. A rooftop terrace serves as an outdoor living room for much of the year, and the bar serves regional wines and one or two well-prepared dishes in the evenings for guests only.
Lungomare Vittorini 26. www.guthotel.it. ✆ **0931-465861.** 25 units. From 80€ double, includes breakfast. **Amenities:** Bar; Wi-Fi (free).

Where to Eat

Caseificio Borderi, tucked in among piles of fresh fish in Ortigia's morning market at 6 Via die Benedictis (✆ **329-9852500**), is a required stop on the food circuit for its huge selection of house-made cheeses, cured meats, olives, and wine; the staff hands out samples and makes delicious sandwiches (4€), paired with excellent wines by the glass.

Archimede ★★ SEAFOOD/PIZZA This Siracusa institution has been serving meals since 1938, and in these whitewashed, vaulted dining rooms since 1978; it's remained a favorite for a night out, even when the surrounding neighborhood moldered in neglect. Specialties veer toward Sicilian classics: spaghetti with *ricci* (sea urchin), tagliolini al *nero di seppie* (pasta with cuttlefish ink), and *pesce all'acqua pazza* (fish cooked with garlic, tomatoes, capers, and olives). Many fans claim that no one in Sicily makes them better. The kitchen is also equipped with a wood-fired oven that turns out what many Siracusans consider to be the best pizza in town, available in different sizes, including one that's a perfect starter.
Via Gemmallaro 8. www.trattoriaarchimede.it. ✆ **0931-69701.** Main courses 12€–24€. Mon–Sat 12:30–3:30pm and 7:30–11:30pm.

Darsena ★★ SEAFOOD The name means "dock," and the town piers line the harbor just across the street from this brightly lit room and terrace out front. Several generations of Siracusans have counted on Darsena for the freshest fish in town, displayed on ice in cases near the

entrance. A waiter will bring some of the just-caught offerings around for your inspection, then take it back to the kitchen to be grilled or roasted to your preference. *Riccio,* sea urchin, and other local specialties are served raw and in a long, long list of deftly prepared seafood pastas.
Riva Giuseppe Garibaldi. www.ristorantedarsena.it. ✆ **0931-61522.** Main courses 9€–18€. Tues–Sun 12:30–2:30pm and 7:30–10:30pm; closed Mon.

Don Camillo ★★ SIRACUSAN/SEAFOOD This top contender with Archimede (see above) for long-time Siracusa favorite is slightly more formal, with lots of polished antiques offsetting the handsomely tiled floors and rows of vintage wines. House specialties, like spaghetti *delle Sirene* (with sea urchin and shrimp in butter) and *tagliata al tonno* (with sliced tuna), have been drawing loyal regulars here for years. On weekends especially, join the many Siracusan families who fill the vaulted rooms decorated with vintage photos of Ortigia.
Via Maestranza 96. www.ristorantedoncamillosiracusa.it. ✆ **0931-67133.** Main courses 14€–24€. Mon–Sat 12:30–3pm and 8–10:30pm.

L'Osteria da Seby ★ SIRACUSAN/SEAFOOD Oil paintings and exposed stone create a warm setting that, despite its attempt at being rustic, is a bit more formal than the food warrants. What's best about this friendly place, a favorite of guests from hotels on the nearby waterfront, is the straightforward *osteria* fare: seafood pastas and risottos, mixed grills, and well-done standards such as scallopini in lemon sauce.
Via Mirabella 21. www.losteriadaseby.it. ✆ **0931-1815619.** Main courses 9€–18€. Tues–Sun noon–3pm and 7–11pm.

Side Trips from Siracusa

Several beaches are easy to reach from Siracusa, and a visit to the 18th-century *centro storico* of **Noto** is an easy half-day excursion. Plan a full day to visit the remarkable Roman mosaics outside Armerina.

BEACHES NEAR SIRACUSA

Some of the best, most unspoiled shoreline in all of Italy is on Sicily's southeastern coast. **Fontane Bianche** is the closest beach to Siracusa, 15 minutes away. It's an almost-square bay with laidback beach clubs and luxurious deep sand. **Lido di Noto,** 15 minutes from the baroque hill town of Noto, is a lively beach with great waterfront restaurants. Half the beach is private beach clubs (where you pay around 10€ for day use of a lounge chair, umbrella, and shower facilities), and half is free public access. Between Noto and Pachino is the **Vendicari Nature Reserve,** where beaches are small and hard to find but the scenery is beautiful. Thousands of migratory birds nest here every year. A few miles south of the autostrada on SP19, park at the Agriturismo Calamosche to reach **Calamosche.** It's a 15-minute walk along a nature path to the intimate cove, framed by rock cliffs and sea caves. The water is a calm, perfectly dappled teal. **Isola delle Correnti ★★**, a little over an hour south of

Calamosche Beach.

Siracusa at the southeastern tip of the island, is one of the best beaches on Sicily. It's a bit more windswept and wavy than the other spots. On a clear day, you can see Malta, just 100km (60 miles) to the south.

NOTO ★★★

31km (19 miles) SW of Siracusa

Dubbed the "Stone Garden" because of its sheer beauty, this little town has a main street, Corso Vittorio Emanuele, lined with rich-looking buildings of golden stone, some of the most captivating on the island. What's more, Noto is set amid olive groves and almond trees on a plateau overlooking the Asinaro Valley, providing lovely outlooks.

Essentials

GETTING THERE Take the A18 autostrada south for 27km (17 miles), then exit and head north up a hill, following blue signs toward Noto. Near town, follow the yellow signs toward Noto's *"centro storico"* (brown "Noto Antica" signs lead to the ruins of the old city, some distance from town.) The drive from Siracusa takes 35 minutes. It's also easy to reach Noto by bus (55 min. each way; 6€ round-trip), with either **AST** (www.aziendasicilianatrasporti.it) or **Interbus** (www.interbus.it), which run a dozen buses per day from Ortigia or Siracusa train station. Buses arrive at Piazzale Marconi, a 5-minute walk from the *centro storico.*

VISITOR INFORMATION The **tourist office**, Via Gioberti 13 (✆ **0931-836503**), is open May to September daily 9am to 1pm and 3:30 to 6:30pm; and October to April Monday to Friday 8am to 2pm and 3:30 to 6:30pm.

Freshly picked almonds in Noto.

Exploring Noto

This hill town on the flanks of Mount Alviria was a flourishing place in the late 17th century, having outgrown its medieval core and expanded into streets lined with palaces and convents. On January 11, 1693, it all came tumbling down when the strongest earthquake in Italian history leveled Noto and much of southeastern Sicily. The ruins of that old city can be seen at the **Noto Antica** archaeological site outside town.

The good to come out of such a devastating tragedy, however, is that Noto was rebuilt—not on the same site but on the banks of the River Asinaro, and not haphazardly but in splendid, unified baroque style. Noto is a stage set of honey-colored limestone, with curvaceous facades, curling staircases, and wrought-iron balconies. You will be surrounded by all this theatricality on a walk down **Corso Vittorio Emanuele III.** In addition to baroque fantasies, this street is also the setting, at number 125, of the **Caffe Sicilia,** a richly atmospheric old-fashioned place that many aficionados claim makes the best *granita* and *gelato* on the island (✆ **0931-835013**). Things hit an architectural high note on a side street, **Via Nicolaci,** with the beautiful elliptical facade of the **Chiesa di Montevirgine,** and the playful **Palazzo Villadorata,** where expressive maidens, dwarves, lions, and horses support the balconies.

Work on the 18th-century landmarks is ongoing, while much of the rest of the town seems to languish in disrepair—suggesting that in Noto the attitude is, "If it ain't baroque, don't fix it."

RAGUSA ★

79km (49 miles) SW of Syracuse.

Ragusa is a town divided, between modern Ragusa Superiore and baroque Ragusa Ibla, separated by a deep ravine, the Valle dei Ponti. The divide came about in 1693, when a powerful earthquake all but obliterated Ragusa Ibla, the original town, killing thousands. Despite efforts to rebuilt Ragusa Ibla as a planned town in exuberant baroque style, most of the wary residents decided to relocate to an adjacent ridge, calling their new settlement Ragusa Superiore. Today, Ragusa Superiore is the modern center of the sprawling, two-parted town, while Ragusa Ibla is a place to wander on quiet lanes and big piazzas enlivened with flamboyant baroque churches. From the twin towns, you'll often catch glimpses of the surrounding countryside, fields and orchards crisscrossed with low-lying, white dry-stone walls.

Essentials

GETTING THERE Three **trains** a day make the 2-hour trip to Ragusa from Siracusa. **AST buses** (www.aziendasiciliatrasporti.it; ✆ **0932-681818**) make the 3-hour run seven times daily. The train and bus stations are in Ragusa Superiore on Piazza del Popolo and adjoining Piazza Gramsci.

Ragusa Ibla.

By **car** from Siracusa, the quickest route takes you through Noto (p. 771) then southwest along Route 115 to the town of Ispica, at which point the highway swings northwest toward Ragusa.

VISITOR INFORMATION The **tourist office,** Via Capitano Bocchieri 33 (✆ **0932-221511**), is open Monday, Wednesday, and Friday 9am to 1:30pm and Tuesday and Thursday 9am to 1:30pm and 4 to 6pm.

GETTING AROUND If you don't want to make the steep descent from Superiore into Ibla, you can take city bus no. 3 departing from Piazza del Popolo. It's a hair-raising ride. The bus will let you off in Ibla at Piazza Pola or Giardini Iblei in the medieval and baroque town.

What to See & Do

The most scenic way to reach the old town is by taking the 242 steps of the Salita Commendatore that clamor down the hillside from Ragusa Superiore into Ragusa Ibla. You can take a breather along the way on a landing in front of the ruined **Santa Maria delle Scale** (St. Mary of the Steps), enjoying the views of the ochre-colored houses of Ragusa Ibla spreading out at your feet. The path eventually winds around to **Piazza del Duomo,** where a dramatically curved staircase leads to the sumptuous facade of **Cattedrale di San Giorgio ★★** (✆ **0932-220-085**), open daily 9am to noon and 4 to 7pm. Three tiers of columns and balconies are the piéce de resistance of architect Rosario Gagliardi, the master of the Sicilian baroque. Gagliardi's second-best work is just east, **Chiesa di San Giuseppe ★**, Via Torre Nuova 19 (✆ **0932-621779**), open daily 9am to noon and 4 to 6pm. The tall, convex facade rises in three tiers, embellished with columns and statues of saints. Inside, above a striking floor of black asphalt interspersed with majolica tiles, is one of Ragusa's most beloved paintings, the so-called "Our Lady of the Cherries." In an altarpiece portraying the Holy Family, Mary holds cherries in her apron, offering them to passersby. Just down the street are the beautiful public gardens, **Giardino Ibleo ★★**. Long avenues lined with palms are idyllic places to stroll, and stone benches are tucked into shady alcoves. At the edge of the gardens, a terrace opens to views across the Valley of Irminio. The gardens are free and open daily 8am to 8pm.

Where to Stay & Eat

Ragusa Ibla is where you will want to stay and probably eat, and options are improving all the time. A sign of a new wave of gentrification that's sweeping over the town is **I Banchi,** Via Orfanotrofio 39, a stylish bakery, food shop, wine bar, and casual eatery that would seem trendy even in Rome (www.ibanchiragusa.it; ✆ **0932-655000**).

Duomo ★★★ NEW SICILIAN/SEAFOOD If the baroque extravagance of this part of Sicily sweeps you away, you'll find the culinary complement at this famed spot, the creation of Chef Ciccio Sultano. The fussy parlorlike dining rooms, all dark polished wood and red velvet, suggest an extravagant experience, and nothing that emerges from the kitchen dispels the notion. Regional ingredients and age-old Sicilian traditions form the foundation for dishes that combine homemade pastas, local seafood, and fresh garden produce in remarkably innovative ways, such as a *cannolo* of creme fraiche, raw shrimp, and caviar, or in relatively down-to-earth preparations, like fresh pasta with bottarga (fish roe). You should leave financial concerns at the door, and the best way to indulge in the extravagance to the fullest is with one of the tasting menus.
Via Capitano Bocchieri 31, Ibla. www.cicciosultano.it. ✆ **0932-651265**. Main courses from 40€; tasting menus from 130€. Tues–Sat 1–2pm and 8–10:30pm, Sun 8–10:30pm.

Hotel Antico Convento ★★ The Capuchin monks who settled this convent in the 16th century had a good eye for location, enhanced even more in recent centuries with the addition of the town's beautiful public gardens, the Giardino Ibleo, which now surround the stone walls. The small monks' cells, converted to guest rooms, remain simple though not austere, with bright stone floors and handsome wooden built-ins, and they overlook a peaceful cloister, the gardens, or the valley below. A bar and restaurant spills into the cloister in warmer months.
Giardino Ibleo. Via Margherita 41. www.anticoconventoibla.it. ✆ **347-147-2915.** 24 units. From 80€ double. Rates include breakfast. **Amenities:** Restaurant; bar; Wi-Fi (free).

La Bettola ★★ SICILIAN The 1940s-era decor suggests simpler times, and the Sicilian classics that arrive at tables bedecked with red-checked tablecloths in the homey dining room and large terrace in front do little to shake off the throwback ambience. Daily offerings are listed on a chalkboard: homemade caponata, octopus salad, platters of spaghetti a la Norma, or simple grilled pork cutlets topped with fresh herbs.
Largo Camerina 7. ✆ **0932-653377.** Main courses 10€–15€. Mon–Sat 12:30–2:30pm and 7:30–11:30pm.

Locanda Don Serafino ★ SICILIAN The vaulted, rock-walled cellars, part of a very stylish hotel, are the evocative setting for a grand meal, and the mazelike rooms are wonderfully cool in the dog days of summer. The food is innovative yet more traditional and down to earth than the fancy decor and lavish table settings might suggest, relying on a bounty of fresh local ingredients. A rich *zuppa di pesce don Serafino* (fish soup) and such meat-heavy dishes as hare, roasted with mountain herbs, can be coupled with fresh fish steamed in zucchini leaves.

Via Orfanotrofio 39. www.locandadonserafino.it. ✆ **0932-220065.** Main courses 30€–35€. Wed–Mon 12:30–2:30pm and 5:30–11:30pm (closed lunch July–Aug.)

PIAZZA ARMERINA ★★★

134km (83) miles NW of Siracusa, 158km (98 miles) SE of Palermo

Travelers make a big effort to get to this dusty, sun-baked hilltown in the center of Sicily for one reason: To see the richest collection of Roman mosaics in the world, at the **Villa del Casale,** in the countryside 5km (3 miles) outside of town. From elevated walkways you'll gaze down upon wild beasts, superheroes, and the monsters of myth, depicted in glorious and colorful mosaic tableaux. The masterful ancient artistry is in a near-miraculous state of preservation, providing a fascinating window into 4th-century-A.D. preoccupations. More than that, these brilliant mosaic scenes are as entertaining as a good film, one in glorious Technicolor.

Essentials

GETTING THERE From Taormina, Siracusa, or anywhere in the east, take the A19 west from Catania, exit at Dittaino, and head south following blue signs for Piazza Armerina. From Palermo, take the A19 east and south, exit at Caltanissetta, then immediately look for signs for Piazza Armerina. (The route is SS626 south to SS122 east to SS117bis.) You can reach Piazza Armerina by **SAIS bus** (www.saisautolinee.it; ✆ **800-211020**); from Palermo (a 2-hr. trip) there are five buses a day, three on weekends; coming from Siracusa or other east coast towns, take a bus from Enna (40 min; 4 buses a day). Once in Piazza Armerina, take local bus B to the site (15 min; runs daily 9am–noon and 3–6pm). Taxis also eagerly await visitors.

VISITOR INFORMATION Admission to Villa Romana (Strada Provinciale 15; www.villaromanadelcasale.it; ✆ **0935-680036**) is 10€. It's open daily 9am to 7pm (until 5pm Nov–Mar).

Intricate mosaics at the Villa Romana del Casale in Piazza Armerina.

Exploring Villa Romana del Casale

Built between 310 and 340, this enormous villa of a rich and powerful landowner was the center of a vast agricultural estate. It was almost completely covered by a landslide in the 12th century, but this natural disaster turned out to be a blessing, because the mud preserved almost 38,000 square feet of mosaic flooring. Rediscovered in the 19th century, the villa was excavated and restored starting in the early 20th century.

The place must have been magnificent, more a palace than a mere villa, with 40 rooms, many of them clad in marble, frescoed, and equipped with fountains and pools. Heating the villa were *terme,* or steam baths (Rooms 1–7), with steam circulating through cavities in the floors and walls. The villa was built to impress, and the ostentation reached its zenith in mosaics of mythology, flora and fauna, and domestic scenes that carpeted most of the floors. Given the style and craftsmanship, they were likely the work of master artists from North Africa.

The villa's 40 rooms are arranged around a garden courtyard, or peristyle. Take time as you wander through the rooms simply to enjoy the mosaics, noticing the expressions, colors, and playfulness of many of these scenes. Remember, the mosaics were intended to delight visitors.

Corridors of the **peristyle** (Room 13) contain the splendid Peristyle mosaic, a bestiary of birds, plants, wild animals, and more domesticated creatures such as horses. Adjoining it, the **Palestra** (exercise area, Room 15) holds mosaics depicting a chariot race at Rome's Circus Maximus.

Along the north side of the peristyle is the **Sala degli Eroti Pescatori ★** (Room of the Fishing Cupids, Room 24), probably a bedroom. The occupant would have drifted off to a scene of four boatloads of winged cupids harpooning, netting, and trapping various fish and sea creatures.

Just past those rooms is the **Sala della Piccola Caccia** (*piccola caccia* meaning "small hunt," Room 25), where hunters in togas go after deer, wild boar, birds, and other small game as Diana, goddess of the hunt, looks on. In one scene the hunters roast their kill under a canopy.

The long hall to the east is the **Corridoio della Grande Caccia ★★★,** or Corridor of the Great Hunt (Room 28), measuring 65m (197 ft.) in length. The mosaics depict men capturing panthers, leopards, and other exotic animals, loading them onto wagons for transport, and finally onto a ship in an eastern-looking port. They're obviously bound for Rome, where they will be part of the games in the Colosseum.

A cluster of three rooms east of the north (right-hand side) end of the Grande Caccia corridor includes the **Vestibolo di Ulisse e Polifemo** (Vestibule of Ulysses and Polyphemus, Room 47), where the Homeric hero proffers a *krater* of wine to the Cyclops (here with three eyes instead of one, and a disemboweled ram draped casually over his lap) in hopes of getting him drunk. Adjacent is the **Cubicolo con Scena Erotica** (Bedroom with Erotic Scene, Room 46), where a seductress, with a side gaze and a nicely contoured rear end, embraces a young man.

Off the southwest side of the Grande Caccia corridor is one of the most amusing rooms of all, the **Sala delle Palestrite,** Room of the Gym Girls (Room 30). Their skimpy strapless bikinis would be fitting for a beach in the 21st century, but ancient literary sources tell us that this was actually standard workout apparel 1,700 years ago—the bandeau top was called the *strophium,* and the bikini bottom the *subligar.* The girls are engaged in various exercises—curling dumbbells, tossing a ball, and running.

South of the central block of the villa and peristyle, the **Triclinium** (Room 33) is a large dining room with a magnificent rendition of the Labors of Hercules. In the central apse, the mosaics depict the Gigantomachy (Battle of the Giants), in which five mammoth creatures are in their death throes after being pierced by Hercules' poison arrows.

AGRIGENTO & THE VALLEY OF THE TEMPLES ★★★

129km (80 miles) SE of Palermo

The evocative skeletons of seven temples of honey-colored stone, arranged on a long ridge and commanding views of the sea, comprise one of the most memorable sights of the ancient world—the embodiment of classical dignity. Colonists from Crete or Rhodes established Akragas in the 7th century B.C., and by the 5th century B.C. the city was one of the great Mediterranean powers, with close to 200,000 residents. The Greek poet Pindar described Akragas as the most beautiful city "inhabited by mortals" but commented that its citizens "feasted as if there were no tomorrow." The city poured part of its enormous wealth into temples erected along a ridge overlooking the sea, their bright pediments becoming well-known landmarks along southern sea routes. Carthage and Rome fought over the city for centuries until Akragas became part of the Roman Empire in 210 B.C. Tumbled by earthquakes, plundered for marble, and overgrown from neglect, today the temples are proud remnants of ancient grandeur.

Essentials

GETTING THERE Agrigento is about 2½ hours by **car** from either Palermo or Siracusa. From Palermo, cut southeast on the SS121, which becomes SS189 before it finally reaches Agrigento. From Siracusa, take the A18 autostrada north to Catania and the A19 west toward Enna; just past Enna, exit the A19 and follow signs south through Caltanissetta and down to Agrigento. The "coastal route" from Siracusa—taking the SS115 all the way—may look more direct on the map but is much more time-consuming, up to 5 hours on an often very curvy, two-lane road. Parking is below the temples, near the western section, Zeus, and eastern section, Collina dei Templi, entrances. A well-marked path leads along the ridge past the temples. A shuttle bus (3€ each way) connects the parking areas with the top of the site, though the walk is not terribly strenuous.

Bus connections between Palermo and Agrigento are fairly convenient: **Cuffaro** (www.cuffaro.info; ✆ **0922-403150**) runs nine buses per day and drops you right in front of the entrance to the archaeological site; the trip takes 2 hours and costs 8€ one-way or 13€ round-trip. Bus service is also possible from Siracusa, but it's at least 4 hours each way.

The main rail station, **Stazione Centrale,** is at Piazza Marconi (✆ **892021**); from there you have to take a cab or local bus (lines 1, 2, or 3) to the temples, 10 minutes away. The train trip from Palermo takes 2 hours; there are 12 trains daily. Train is not a practical option from Siracusa—the trip takes 6 hours, with a change in Catania.

VISITOR INFORMATION The **tourist office,** in the modern town at Piazzale Aldo Moro 7 (✆ **0922-20454**), is open Sunday through Friday 8am to 1pm and 3 to 8pm and Saturday 8am to 1pm. Another tourist office is at Via Empedocle 73 (✆ **0922-20391**), open Monday to Friday 8am to 2:30pm and Wednesday 3:30 to 7pm.

Exploring the Ruins

As you enter the valley surrounded by hills planted with olive and almond trees, you'll see that "valley of the temples" is a misnomer, as the temples are perched along a ridge. The park is divided into eastern and western zones, with entrances at each.

Parco Valle dei Templi ★★★ RUINS In the eastern zone are Agrigento's three best-preserved temples. **The Temple of Hercules (Tempio di Ercole)** is the oldest, dating from the 6th century B.C. At one time the temple sheltered a celebrated statue of Hercules, though it has long since been plundered. Gaius Verres, the notoriously corrupt 1st-century-B.C. governor of Sicily, had his eyes on the statue as he looted temples across the island, though there is no record of Verres getting this prize. Eight of 36 columns have been resurrected, while the others lie rather romantically scattered in the tall grass and wildflowers; they still bear black sears from fires set by Carthaginian invaders.

The Tempio della Concordia, Valley of the Temples, Agrigento.

The **Tempio della Co**[illegible]**lia (Temple of Concord)**, surrounded by 34 columns, has survived al[illegible] since its completion in 430 B.C. It was shored up as a Christian ba[illegible] 6th century, so was never plundered, and the soft soil its founda[illegible] help absorb the shock of earthquakes. The **Temple of Juno** [illegible]ral resiliency and was partly destroyed in an earthquake, thou[illegible] and sections of the colonnade have been restored. A long alta[illegible] for wedding ceremonies and sacrificial offerings.

The western zone would have been the setting of the largest temple in the Greek world, if the **Temple of Jove/Zeus (Tempio di Giove)** had ever been completed—and if what was built had not been toppled in earthquakes. A copy of an 8m- (26-ft.) tall telamon (sculpted figure of a man with arms raised) lies on its back amid the rubble; the original is the pride of the site's Museo Archeologico. Several such figures were used as columnlike supports on the temple; the German writer Goethe, who was much impressed with the massive 20m- (66 ft.) high columns, took home with him a prized painting of one of the temple carytids, a female figure similarly used for support. The **Temple of Castor and Pollux (Tempio di Dioscuri** or **Tempio di Castore e Polluce),** with four Doric columns intact, honors Castor and Pollux, the twins who were patrons of seafarers; Demeter, the goddess of marriage and of the fertile earth; and Persephone, the daughter of Zeus and the symbol of spring.

For more detailed explanations, in both Italian and English, of the many artifacts unearthed here, stop by the **Museo Archeologico** (Via dei Templi; ✆ **0922-40111;** admission 6€ or 13.50€ with archaeological park combo ticket; Mon 9am–1:30pm, Tues–Sat 9am–7:30pm), between the ruins and Agrigento town. However, after a long and dusty outing at the ruins, this isn't a mandatory stop.

Parco Valle dei Templi. www.lavalledeitempli.it. ✆ **0922-621611.** 13.50€, includes Museo Archeologico. Daily 8:30am–7pm. Separate admission 10€ for evening hours: July–Aug Mon–Fri until 9:30pm and Sat–Sun until 11pm.

Where to Stay & Eat

Ambasciata di Sicilia ★ SICILIAN One of the few reasons to venture into modern Agrigento is chance to enjoy a hearty meal at this old-fashioned favorite, a city institution since 1919. True to the name, the kitchen makes it a point to act as Sicilian ambassadors and introduce diners to the island's finest cuisine, specializing in delicious preparations of fresh fish, along with *linguine al'Ambasciata* (prepared with meat sauce, bacon, calamari, and zucchini). Meals are served in a small dining room crammed to the ceiling with marionettes and other colorful artifacts or on a breezy terrace overlooking the rooftops.

Via Gianbertoni 2, off Via Atenea. www.ristorantelambasciatadisicilia.it. ✆ **0922-20526.** Main courses 7€–12€. Sept–July Tues–Sun 12:30–3:30pm and 7–11:30pm; Aug daily 12:30–3:30pm and 7–11:30pm. Closed 2 weeks in Nov.

Hotel Villa Athena ★ An ...ury villa set in gardens within the Valley of the Tees ...e the best-located perch in all of Italy. Lookin... ...oncord, illuminated at night, is one of Sicily's ... and can be enjoyed from the balconies and even ...many of the rooms, done with smart traditional furnishings ...andsome fabrics. The beautiful garden, surrounding a pool, is also a prime spot to enjoy the view while enjoying a glass of wine.
Via Passeggiata Archeologica 33. www.hotelvillaathena.it. ✆ **0922-596288.** 27 units. 190€–330€ double. Rates include breakfast. Bus: 2. **Amenities:** Dining room; 2 bars; outdoor pool; room service; Wi-Fi (free).

SELINUNTE ★★★

122km (76 miles) SW of Palermo

This westernmost Greek colony was one of the most powerful cities in the world, home to 100,000 inhabitants, when the great Carthaginian general Hannibal virtually destroyed it in 409 B.C. He spared only the temples—not out of respect for the deities, but to preserve the loot they housed. Even in the context of those brutal times the wrath of the Carthaginians was abhorrent. An army of 100,000 men descended on the city with battering rams, and in an orgy of destruction raped, looted, plundered, and butchered, killing most of the inhabitants and enslaving the rest. Today the vast archaeological park comprises 270 hectares (670 acres), making it Europe's largest archaeological site. Selinunte is not just large, it's also a bucolic spot where you can walk amid the ruins, gaze out to sea, and ponder what life was like millennia ago. As you walk amid the wildflowers and smell the wild herbs, remember that the name of the town name comes from the Greek word *selinon,* meaning parsley.

GETTING THERE Selinunte is on the southern coast of Sicily and is most easily reached by **car.** From Palermo (about 2 hrs.), take the A29 autostrada and exit at Castelvetrano, following the signs thereafter.

If you prefer to take the **train** (www.trenitalia.it; ✆ **892021**) from Palermo, you can get off at Castelvetrano, 23km (14 miles) from the ruins. The trip from Palermo to Castelvetrano takes a little over 2 hours (you'll need to change trains); once at Castelvetrano, board a **bus** for the final lap of the journey to Selinunte. **Autoservizi Salemi** (www.autoservizisalemi.it; ✆ **0923-981120**), which also operates a service from Palermo to Castelvetrano, will take you to the archaeological park in 20 minutes.

VISITOR INFORMATION The **tourist office** at Via Giovanni Caboto (✆ **0924-46251**), near the archaeological park, is open Monday to Saturday 8am to 2pm and 3 to 8pm and Sunday 9am to noon and 3 to 6pm.

Exploring the Archaeological Park

Given the enormity of the area, allow yourself at least 4 hours to visit, preferably in the early morning. Bring drinks for your visit, as it can get hot under the sun. **Ecotour Selinunte** runs a hop-on, hop-off service to all the sites in the park on a train of golf carts. For details, visit www.selinunteservice.com or call ✆ **347-164-5862.**

Parco Archeologico Selinunte ★★★ RUINS The archaeological grounds have three designated zones: The East Hill and temples, the Acropolis and ancient city, and the Sanctuary of Demeter Malophorus. You will likely start your visit from the East Hill, adjacent to the main entrance. (Archaeologists are still trying to determine which deity each of the Doric temples was dedicated to—for now, they are simply denoted by letters of the alphabet.) The **East Hill** was the sacred district of the city, with three temples surrounded by an enclosure. Temple E, which was in all probability dedicated to Hera (Juno), was built between 490 and 480 B.C. and has a staggering 68 columns. The Metopes, the reliefs that are the pride and joy of the archaeological museum in Palermo, are from this temple. Temple F is the oldest of the trio, built between 560 and 540 B.C.; in its original state, it had a double row of six columns at the eastern entrance and 14 columns on either side. Temple G, now an impressive heap of rubble except for a lone standing column, was destined to be of colossal proportions if it had been completed in 480 B.C.; even so, it is the second largest temple in Sicily.

Atop a plateau, the **Acropolis,** a district of gridlike streets surrounded by defensive walls, was the center of social and political life. Here stood most of Selinunte's important public and religious buildings, as well as the residences of the town's aristocrats. Temple C, the earliest surviving temple of ancient Selinus, was built here in the 6th century B.C.; it stands surrounded by 14 of its resurrected 17 columns. From the Acropolis, you cross the now-dry Modione River to the **Sanctuary of Demeter Malophorus,** the ruins of several shrines to Demeter, goddess of fertility. The custom was for worshipers to place stone figurines in the shrines to honor Demeter; as many as 12,000 such figurines have been unearthed.

✆ **0924-46540.** Admission 6€. Daily 9am to 1 hour before sunset.

Acropolis of Selinunte.

MARSALA ★

31km (19 miles) S of Trapani, 124km (77 miles) SW of Palermo

This thriving little port on Cape Boéo, the westernmost tip of Sicily overlooking the Egadi Islands and Tunisia, is where the world-famous Marsala sweet wine is produced. You can sample some amber yellow Marsala in one of the town's quaint wine shops, or head through the hills along roads lined with prickly-pear cacti to a vineyard nearby. Townspeople sip the dark, vintage Marsala as a dessert wine with hard piquant cheese, fruit, or pastries. Famous product aside, Marsala is an elegant town with baroque palaces and churches, Roman ruins, a lively fish market, and a long sandy coastline stretching to the north and south.

Essentials

GETTING THERE **Trains** (www.trenitalia.it; ✆ **892021**) run daily between Marsala, Trapani, and Palermo. The journey takes 30 minutes from Trapani, up to 3 hours from Palermo. **AST Buses** (www.aziendasicilianatrasporti.it; ✆ **0923-21021)** for Marsala leave from Piazza Montalto in Trapani three times a day. The one-way trip takes 35 minutes. From Palermo**,** **Salemi** (www.autoservizisalemi.it; ✆ **0923-981120;**) runs several buses to the town center. The journey takes 1 hour, 45 minutes. By **car,** head south from Trapani along Route 115.

VISITOR INFORMATION The **tourist office,** at Via 11 Maggio 100 (✆ **0923-714097**), is open Monday to Saturday 8am to 1:45pm and 2 to 8pm and Sunday 9am to noon.

What to See & Do

Enter the city from the **Porta Garibaldi**, a massive arched gateway from the 1600s crowned by an eagle. Garibaldi is honored because it was at Marsala that the 19th-century freedom fighter and his red-shirted volunteers overthrew the Bourbon regime, paving the way for the independence of southern Italy. The road from the gate leads to **Via Garibaldi,** where it ends at the busy **Piazza della Repubblica,** the heart of the city. The square's 18th-century **Palazzo Senatorio,** now the Town Hall, is nicknamed "Loggia" for its flank of elegant arcades. Leading north from Piazza Repubblica is the main thoroughfare, **Via 11 Maggio**, flanked by the town's most splendid baroque palaces. To the northwest, facing the sea on the **Lungomare Boéo,** the archaeological museum stands amid many old *bagli,* Marsala wine warehouses. A little farther are the excavations of the ancient Lilybaeum, or the **Insula Romana,** an archaeological site containing the remains of a Roman villa that had a steam room, among other trappings, and well-preserved mosaics.

Chiesa Madre ★ CHURCH It's only fitting that Marsala's most imposing church is dedicated to Britain's St. Thomas à Becket, given the

English connections that brought the city such wealth over the centuries. Legend has it that a ship carrying materials to build a church dedicated to the saint was on its way to England when a storm forced it to seek shelter at Marsala. It's more likely that the cultlike popularity of the saint, murdered in Canterbury cathedral in 1170, had spread to Sicily when the church was founded in the 13th century. The most impressive decorative pieces in the three-aisle interior are also by outsiders, the 15th-century Gaginis. This Swiss family of sculptors worked their way down the Italian boot until they undertook commissions in Palermo and elsewhere around Sicily. Their best work here, by Domenico Gagini, is lovely *Madonna del Popolo* in the right transept.
Piazza della Repubblica. ✆ **0923-716295**. Free. Daily 7:30am–7pm.

Museo Archeologico Nave Punica–Baglio Anselmi ★★ MUSEUM A former wine warehouse (*baglio*) houses gold jewelry from ancient Mozia (see p. 785) while the showpiece is a well-preserved **Punic ship** (Punic being the Latin name for Carthage, the ancient kingdom in what is today's Tunisia). It's believed the ship, discovered in shallow waters in 1971, was constructed for the Battle of the Egadi Islands during the First Punic Wars between the Romans and Carthaginians in 241 B.C. and sank on its maiden voyage; some scholars argue that the vessel was not a warship but was used to carry cargo. Measuring 35m (115 ft.) long, the ship was manned by 68 oarsmen. Large sections remain, enough to suggest the sleekness and power of the wooden shell covered with sheets of lead fixed with bronze nails. They are on display along with bowls, plates, animal bones, cannabis leaves, and other material carried on board.
Lungomare Boéo. (✆ **0923-952535**). 3€ adults, 2€ children 17 and under. Daily 9am–7pm.

Museo degli Arazzi (Tapestry Museum) ★★ MUSEUM Eight Flemish tapestries, made in Brussels between 1530 and 1550, are the legacy of a bishop of Messina, who donated them to his hometown of Marsala. Tucked away for centuries, and at one point almost auctioned off, the exquisite silk and wool pieces once hung in the royal palace in Madrid. They depict scenes from the Roman wars against the Jews from A.D. 66 to A.D. 67, when troops of Flavius Vespasian occupied Jerusalem. The tapestries are kept in darkened rooms to avoid damage.
Via Garraffa 57. ✆ **0923-711327.** 4€. Tues–Sun 9am–1pm and 4–6pm.

Where to Stay & Eat

Grand Hotel Palace ★ The 19th-century estate of an English wine importer has been redone, but the premises retain a luxurious, old-world aura, so hushed and quiet you feel that even the statues might doze off and topple over. The most character-filled rooms are in the old house, but those in the new annex are fine, too. All are spacious and outfitted

The Wine that Put Marsala on the Map

On a dark and stormy night in 1770, English trader John Woodhouse was forced to anchor in Marsala. He headed for a tavern, downed some local wine, discovered it tasted similar to the Portuguese "Porto," and realized its commercial potential. Woodhouse began to mass-produce and export the wine. He got a big break when legendary Admiral Horatio Nelson developed a taste for Marsala and decided that the British Navy should allot sailors a glass per day. Around the same time, Joseph Whitaker, another English entrepreneur, inherited a vast vineyard in Marsala and further expanded the wine's reputation by exporting it to the United States. He also bought the island of Mozia (p. 785), where he founded an archaeological museum and published important studies of Tunisian birds. One more enterprising businessman entered the scene when Vincenzo Florio, from Palermo, purchased the Woodhouse wine empire in the mid-19th century and refined Marsala grapes. The Florios also exported tuna and were one of Sicily's most prominent families well into the 20th century. Sample Marsala at **Enoteca La Ruota** on Lungomare Boéo near the archaeological museum (number 36-A, ✆ **0923-715241**), while admiring the Stagnone lagoon lying in front of you.

with traditional furnishings; many have sea views. In the surrounding gardens, stately old trees are a backdrop for the swimming pool.

Lungomare Mediterraneo 57. www.grandhotelpalace.eu. ✆ **0923-719492.** 56 units. 100€–130€ double. Rates include breakfast. **Amenities:** Restaurant; bar; outdoor pool; room service; babysitting; Wi-Fi (free).

Villa Favorita ★★ An early-19th-century hunting lodge is a rather exotic retreat, tucked into lush gardens at the edge of historic Marsala. The fanciest guest rooms and suites are on the upper floors of an elegant villa, with wide-oak and tile floors and arched loggias opening onto a courtyard. Others are garden bungalows that resemble stone igloos—they're unusual but attractive, sort of an Italian take on glamping, divided into small sitting rooms and bedrooms with a cramped bathroom and scattered among greenery and shaded lanes surrounding a beautiful swimming pool. The atmosphere is casual and the grounds are full of many shady corners for relaxing. A pizza oven is fired up in the summer, and the restaurant serves well-done Sicilian dishes.

Via Favorita 23. www.villafavorita.com. ✆ **0923-989100.** 29 bungalows, 13 units in the main building. 85€–125€ double. Rates include breakfast. From the center of Marsala, take the SS115 toward Trapani. The hotel is signposted. **Amenities:** 2 restaurants; bar; outdoor pool; tennis court; Wi-Fi (free).

Trattoria Garibaldi ★ SICILIAN-SEAFOOD At this 50-year-old institution near the cathedral, four arched, colorful dining rooms serve local favorites with a well-deserved reputation for freshness. Seafood, simply grilled with spices or served atop couscous, has a decidedly North African flare, while *busiate* (the local homemade pasta) with fresh fish is specialty you probably won't encounter beyond the west coast.

Piazza dell'Addolorata 35. ✆ **0923-953006.** Main courses 7€–13€. Mon–Fri noon–3pm and 7:30–10pm; Sat 7:30–10pm; Sun noon–3pm.

Around Marsala

MOZIA ★★★

2km (1 mile) W of Marsala, 15 km (9 miles) SW of Trapani.

The tiny island of San Pantaleo in the Stagnone, a lagoon and nature reserve, is littered with the ruins of the ancient city of Motya (today's Mozia). The island, owned by the Whitakers, Marsala's winemaking family, is also a wonderful place to observe the pink flamingoes, curlews, and egrets that visit the lagoon. In summer the sparse landscape is abloom with white sea daffodil and sea lavender. **Arini and Pugliese ferries** (www.arinipugliese.com; ✆ **347-7790218**) runs a daily, year-round service to Mozia from Marsala and costs 5€ return, 2.50€ for schoolchildren and adults 65 and over.

Mozia was a stronghold of the Phoenicians, who eventually migrated to Carthage (present-day Tunisia), and by the 6th century B.C. the island settlement was surrounded by nearly 2.5km (11-2 miles) of defensive walls. In 397 B.C., Dionysius the Elder of Syracuse mounted a massive attack on the inhabitants, who retreated to Lilybaeum (now Marsala).

Footpaths meander among the scattered ruins, and the free island map (available at the boat landing) is essential in making sense of what can seem like not much more than the ruins of low walls here and there. Most intact are the **Casa dei Mosaici** (**House of Mosaics),** with scenes of animal life dating to the 4th to 3rd century B.C., and the Tophet, a Phoenician burial ground for victims of child sacrifice, where the gravestones, *stele*, are intricately carved. The best of the excavated artifacts are in the **Villa Malfitano** museum. The prize is a sensual marble statue of a young man in a wet tunic, the **Giovane di Mozia (Young Man of Mozia),** which dates to around 440 B.C.

THE EGADI ISLANDS

This archipelago of three islands (Favignana, Levanzo, and Marettimo) forms the westernmost point of Sicily and, served by ferry and hydrofoil from Trapani and Marsala, is a place to get away from it all. The islands are popular summertime retreats for swimming and scuba-diving, but the rest of the year their 4,600 inhabitants are left to live from the fruits of the sea, as they have done for centuries. Home to the largest tuna fishery in Sicily, the islands are famous for the annual *mattanza,* an age-old method of culling tuna by forcing them to swim into a long corridor of nets known as *camera della morte,* or chamber of death.

TRAPANI ★★

100km (62 miles) SW of Palermo, 14km (8⅔ miles) SW of Erice

The big draw along the most westerly stretch of Sicily is the coast from Trapani to Marsala (p. 782), lined with dazzling white salt pans. The flats are protected as a nature reserve populated by migratory birds, and the sight of vast stretches of white rock salt stretching into the blue horizon broken by red-and-white stone windmills is spectacular. The provincial capital, Trapani, is set below Mount Erice, and the old center on a sea-girt promontory is an atmospheric maze of medieval streets and squares.

Essentials

GETTING THERE Frequent **trains** from Palermo make the 2½-hour run to Trapani; there are also about a dozen per day from Marsala, taking 30 minutes. Trains pull in at the Piazza Stazione, where luggage storage is available (www.trenitalia.it; ✆ **892021**). **Terravision** (www.terravision.eu; ✆ **0923-981120**) operates **bus** service between Palermo and Trapani airport, where you can get a bus into the city center.

It's possible you'll be arriving by **plane. Vincenzo Florio Airport** at Birgi, 15km (9 miles) from the center of Trapani (www.airgest.it; ✆ **0923-842502**), is the island's third-largest and the main Ryanair hub for Sicily from the U.K. From here, take the buses that connect you to the city or to Palermo. **AST** (www.aziendasicilianatrasporti.it; ✆ **840-000323**) has an hourly service from the airport to Trapani at a cost of 5€. From Palermo by **car,** follow the A29 autostrada southwest into Trapani. From Marsala, head north along Route 115 to Trapani.

Trapani is a major embarkation point for **ferries** and **hydrofoils.** Most depart for the Egadi Islands of Marettimo, Levanzo, and Favignana. Service is also available to Ustica, Pantelleria, Civitavecchia near Rome, and even Tunisia in North Africa. Ferries depart from the docks near Piazza Garibaldi. Service is offered by **Ustica** (www.usticalines.it; ✆ **0923-22200**) or **Grimaldi** (www.grimaldi-lines.com; ✆ **0923-593673**).

VISITOR INFORMATION The **tourist office** (Via San Francesco d'Assisi (✆ **0923-545511**) is open Monday to Saturday 8am to 8pm and Sunday 9am to noon.

Exploring Trapani

The old town extends westward out to sea, with a typical North African style and feel in the labyrinth of narrow streets that wind toward the **Torre di Ligny,** built in 1671 on the tip of the peninsula. Many elegant baroque buildings line **Corso Vittorio Emanuele,** sometimes called Rua Grande, as it extends west from the **Palazzo Senatorio,** the 17th-century, pink-marble town hall. Adjacent 18th-century **Via Garibaldi** (also known as Rua Nova, or "New Road") is flanked with palaces and churches. One of them, the 17th-century baroque **Chiesa del Purgatorio,** houses the single greatest treasure in Trapani: The ***Misteri***, 20 life-size wooden figures from the 18th century depicting Christ's Passion and carried through town for Good Friday's **Processione dei Misteri** (Procession of the Mysteries). The church is open daily 8:30am to 12:30pm and 4 to 8pm but is often closed. **Via Torrearsa** leads down to a bustling ***pescheria* (fish market)** where tuna is traded; the valuable

Trapani's main street, Corso Vittorio Emanuele, and Palazzo Senator.

commodity is caught in nearby waters and traded with buyers from as far away as Japan. **Villa Margherita,** public gardens stretching between old and new Trapani, is an inviting oasis with fountains, banyan trees, and palms rustling in the sea breeze.

Santuario dell'Annunziata/Museo Regionale Pepoli ★ CHURCH/MUSEUM The cloisters of a 14th-century convent enclose a collection of archaeological finds and art, many of it salvaged by a local aristocrat, Count Pepoli. With his fine eye, the count found the best examples of coral carving, a popular Trapani tradition that local craftspeople pursued well into the early 20th century, when nearby coral beds were depleted. Many of the works, in which coral is often intermingled with silver filigree, are by local artisans Andrea and Alberto Tipa. Among their creations is a spectacularly elaborate *presepe* (nativity scene). Before leaving the premises, step into the convent's **Cappella della Madonna** to see a graceful, sculpted scene of the Virgin and Child, attributed to the 14th-century Tuscan master Nino Pisano.

Via Conte Agostino Pepoli 200. ✆ **0923-553269**). 4€, 2€ for children 12 and under. Mon–Sat 9am–1pm and Sun 9am–12:30pm.

Where to Stay & Eat

Trapani is a good place to try what's considered to be the oldest handmade pasta in the world, *busiati*. The curly, eggless pasta has a firm texture and mealy taste, and is good eaten with pesto sauce made Trapanese-style with cherry tomatoes. For the past 70 years, the favorite stop in town for quick bite has been **Pizzeria dal 1946,** Via Nunzio Nasi, with slices and pies to take out or eat in, in several atmospheric, always crowded rooms (Wed–Mon 11am–late; ✆ **0923-21464**).

Ai Lumi Tavernetta ★ SICILIAN The narrow, arched ground floor of a palazzo, filled with heavy rustic tables and chairs, is a cool retreat in which to enjoy Trapanese classics. Seafood is plentiful, as are such meat specialties as roast lamb in a citrus sauce and busiati, the thick local

pasta that seems like perfection itself when simply topped with tomato, basil, and pecorino. The terrace in front is one of the nicest places in Trapani to spend a summer evening. Upstairs are 12 pleasant, well-furnished rooms, some with kitchenettes, with doubles starting at 70€.
Corso Vittorio Emanuele 75. www.ailumi.it. ✆ **0923-872418.** Main courses 8€–18€. Sept–July Mon–Sat 7:30–11pm; Aug daily 7:30–11pm.

Ligny Bed and Breakfast ★★ Right at the edge of the sea at the end of the Old Town peninsula, an old palazzo offers high-ceilinged rooms, each with a panoramic terrace that takes in sweeping views of the gulf and Erice rising above the shores. Beaches, the port, and the town sights are within an easy walk. Iron bedsteads and some old family pieces add a homey touch to the rooms, up two flights of stairs; bathrooms are shower-only, and some are not en suite. Credit cards are not accepted.
Via Torre Ligny 114. www.ligny.it. ✆ **0923-1941515**. 5 units. 45€–80€ double. Rates include breakfast. No credit cards. **Amenities:** Wi-Fi (free).

Osteria La Bettolaccia SICILIAN Trapani's longtime favorite never disappoints, drawing big crowds (reserve if you can) to a couple of rambling, tile-floored rooms near the seafront. The kitchen prepares what many regulars claim is the best seafood couscous in Sicily, laden with calamari and a spicy sauce. Another favorite is spaghetti with swordfish, tuna, tomatoes, herbs, and breadcrumbs.
25 Via Enrico Fardella. ✆ **0923-21695.** Main courses 8€–15€. Mon–Fri 1–3pm and 7–11pm and Sat 1–3pm.

Around Trapani

Trapani is wedged between two especially scenic stretches of coastline. To the northeast is the dramatic headland at San Vito Lo Capo, with fine beaches and the Zingaro nature reserve. Stretching south of Trapani are coastal salt pans that have been harvested since antiquity.

RISERVA NATURALE DELLO ZINGARO & SAN VITO LO CAPO ★★

The most beautiful stretch of coastline in Sicily extends 12km/7½ miles north from the tiny town of Scopello (35km/21 miles) east of Trapani to the headland of San Vito Lo Capo. The beaches can be impossibly crowded in summer, but they're paradisiacal, much like those in the Caribbean. The alternating sand and pebble shores are etched with coves. The **Tonnara di Scopello,** at the edge of Scopello, is an especially idyllic spot to swim. The abandoned 13th-century tuna-processing plant is surrounded by wind-shaped rocks and faces a sparkling cove. Much of the land is set aside as the **Riserva Naturale dello Zingaro** (www.riservazingaro.it; ✆ **0924-35108**). The first designated wildlife area in Sicily covers nearly 1,600 hectares (3,954 acres) of Mediterranean maquis and coastline. Within the reserve is also the **Grotta dell'Uzzo,** a cave that served as a dwelling in Paleolithic times, and now is a refuge

Countryside of Trapani.

for six different types of bats (off-limits to all but sanctioned naturalists). Motorized vehicles are prohibited (the only transport is by mule).

THE SALT MARSHES ★★★

Stretching from Trapani to Marsala along route SP21, the salt pans skirting the coast have been harvested since antiquity. For millennia, salt was used as a preservative for perishable food and for the Romans as payment for mercenaries (the word "salary" is from the Latin *salaries* meaning "soldier's allowance for the purchase of salt"). The area is now protected as the **Riserva Naturale Orientata "Saline di Trapani e Paceco"** (www.wwfsalineditrapani.it; ✆ **0923-867700**), covering 1,000 hectares (2,471 acres). Visit in the late afternoon, against a terse evening sky that changes color as the sun goes down and as the migrating birds perform their spectacular in-flight choreographies.

ERICE ★★★

96km (60 miles) SW of Palermo, 14km (8⅔ miles) NE of Trapani, 45km (28 miles) NW of Marsala

The enchanting medieval city of Erice, high atop Mount Erice (743m/ 2,438 ft.), is all about views. On a clear summer's day, you can see west

Salt of the Earth

When the Carthaginians first landed in the area from North Africa they saw the potential for salt production and created basins from which to harvest the valuable commodity. The process exploits the high level of salinity in the seawater and the wind and sun that contribute to the evaporation process. In mid to late winter, water is pumped into the pans through a canal. Over the next few months the water is left to evaporate, when it assumes a reddish color dense with mineral pigment. Around July, just as the water reaches a sluggish consistency, the salt is raked, harvested, and brought onto dry land to complete the exsiccation process. What look like little salt huts line the road, covered in protective terracotta tiles. Once completely dry, the salt is cleansed of debris and packaged.

to the Egadi Islands, east to Mount Etna and south to Africa, glimpsing Tunisia's Cape Bon. Even the mist that often shrouds Erice doesn't diminish the spectacle. Seeing the city's towers and craggy rocks poking through a hazy blanket of gray is a memorable sight in itself.

Essentials

GETTING THERE From Trapani (see above), you have two public transport options. From Piazza Giovanni Paolo II you can take bus no. 21, leaving every 30 minutes and run by **ATM Trapani** (www.atmtrapani.it; ✆ **0923-559575**); pay the fare (1.20€) on the bus. Get off at the cable-car station on Via Capua in lower Erice and board the **funivia** (cableway; www.funiviaerice.it; ✆ **0923-560023**). It whisks you to the top in about 10 minutes at a cost of 9€ round-trip, 5.50€ one way (wheelchair accessibility available). ***Note:*** The cableway is usually closed Monday mornings for general maintenance, does not operate in inclement weather, and often is not up and running when you want it to be; check before going, but generally the service operates daily 8am to 11pm. You can also make the entire trip by **AST buses** (www.aziendasicilianatrasporti.it; ✆ **840-000323**), departing from Trapani's Piazza Montalto; service is daily 6:40am to 7:30pm, and the fare is 2.40€. The trip along winding, uphill turns lasts 50 minutes.

Discovering Erice

Erice is an atmospheric place, where you'll stop to perhaps admire an arch, a door, or a bell tower, as you wander its steep cobblestone streets flanked by churches and stone houses with elaborate baroque balconies packed with cascading geraniums. The city is famous throughout Sicily for its pastries, and you'll want to sample such delights as the tangy *dolci di Badia* cakes, made from almond paste and citron juice.

Whether you come up to Erice by road or cable car, you will arrive at **Porta Trapani,** one of three entrance gates of the city (the other two are Porta Spada and Porta Spagnola, farther north). The 12th-century Porta Trapani is imbedded in the Elymian-Punic walls, the extensive defensive barrier laid out by the Elymians (the ancient inhabitants of western Sicily) around 1200 B.C. and later fortified by the Carthaginians from North Africa to guard the city from attackers coming from the west.

Steep, cobblestone **Via Vittorio Emanuele** leads past churches and monasteries to the town high point and central square **Piazza Umberto I.** From there, Via Guarnotti leads through Piazza San Giuliano to the beautiful **Giardino del Balio,** surrounding the Norman-era **Castello Pepoli.** The cliffside promenade beneath the castle affords the most spectacular views in western Sicily, all the way to Tunisia, a distance of 170km (106 miles), on a clear day. The gardens are always open.

Castello di Venere (Castle of Venus) ★ RUIN The Normans who conquered Sicily in the 12th century built a massive mountaintop

Approaching Erice's 12th-century Castle of Venus.

castle, a majestic show of might, on the site of an ancient temple to Venus. Medieval towers and the ruins of walls still surround the compound, and through defensive slits and other openings you can look out over the plains of Trapani and the Egadi Islands, showing off the site's defensive advantage. Most intriguing are the rites of the onetime temple, where young women became slaves in a cult to Venus, goddess of love, and serviced male worshippers as part of their duties. This was an honorable profession that ended at the age 21, when the women were set free as desirable brides.

Erice. ✆ **366-6712832**. 4€, 2€ children 8–14, free for children 10 and under. Daily Nov–Feb 10am–4pm; Mar–May 10am–6pm; June to mid-July 10am–7p mid-July to mid-Sept 10am–8pm; mid-Sept to Oct 10am–7pm.

Chiesa Matrice (Royal Duomo of Erice) ★ CHURCH Rather ironically, Erice's 14th-century Duomo was constructed with stones from the ancient Temple of Venus, that temple of pagan hedonism where young maidens offered their services to supplicants. The campanile (bell tower) that rises 28m (92 ft.) next to the church also has an ancient past, built in the late 15th century atop a watchtower from the 2nd century B.C. Frederick of Aragon, who eventually lost Sicily to the Spanish, built the campanile so his sentries could watch for invading troops in the sea lanes far below. The church's porch, dubbed the "Gibbena" (from the Latin *agi bene,* meaning "act well"), is a later addition, built to accommodate penitents who were not allowed to partake in the Mass. They missed out on worshipping under the vaulted, arabesque ceiling in front of the enormous altarpiece of Carrara marble, depicting the life of Christ.

Piazza Umberto I. ✆ **0923-869123**), 2€, free for children 12 and under. Mon–Fri 9:30am–12:30pm and 3:30–5:30pm; Sat–Sun 9:30am–1pm and 3:30–6pm.

Where to Stay & Eat

Hotel Elimo ★ A 400-year-old palazzo in the heart of Erice's historic core welcomes guests in stone-walled lounges where a fire blazes in a hearth beneath beamed ceilings in the chilly months. Guest quarters are a bit more conventional, though comfortable, though some have views over the plains below, as do the restaurant and terrace.

Via Vittorio Emanuele 75. www.hotelelimo.it. ✆ **0923-869377.** 22 units. 110€ double; 185€ suite. **Amenities:** Restaurant; bar; Wi-Fi (free).

Hotel Moderno ★★ The "moderno" dates to the conversion of a 19th-century house just after World War II, though old-fashioned charm prevails. Antiques, brass, and wicker pieces lend a homey touch, and about a dozen rooms open onto private balconies or terraces. The view from the terrace, where breakfast can be taken in warm weather, is stunning, and the restaurant is excellent.

Via Vittorio Emanuele 67. www.hotelmodernoerice.it. ✆ **0923-869300.** 40 units. 80€–110€ double. Rates include breakfast. **Amenities:** Restaurant; bar; Wi-Fi (free).

Il Carmine ★★ This refurbished 15th-century convent still shows traces of monastic living in simple, no-frills rooms and shower-only bathrooms. Yet the spartan surroundings are loaded with character, and views into the gardens are as soothing as they were intended to be. A separate entrance ensures you won't disturb convent life.

Piazza del Carmine. www.ilcarmine.com. ✆ **0923-1941532**. 6 units. 70€–90€ double. Rates include breakfast. **Amenities:** Restaurant; Wi-Fi (free).

Monte San Giuliano ★★★ SICILIAN You'll navigate some steps and stone alleyways to reach this garden hideaway, where a table on the terrace or in the rustic dining room seems, like much of medieval Erice, far away from the modern world. The menu shows off Arab influences in the flavorful seafood couscous, with many nods to such local favorites as lamb with a pistachio crust and pasta with *sarde* (with sardines) or with *pesto alla Trapanese,* with garlic, basil, fresh tomatoes, and almonds.

Vicolo San Rocco 7. www.montesangiuliano.it. ✆ **0923-869595.** Main courses 8€–15€. Tues–Sun 12:15–2:45pm and 7:30–10pm. Closed Jan 7–21.

PASTRIES

Erice is renowned throughout Sicily for its pastries, refined by cloistered nuns from the 14th to the 18th century. Maria Grammatico, raised in the nearby San Carlo convent, became famous in Italy when she wrote her autobiography, *Bitter Almonds*. Her crunchy almond cookies, rum- or orange-filled marzipan balls, and confections fashioned from chocolate-covered almond paste at **Pasticceria Grammatico** (Via Vittorio Emanuele 14; ✆ **0923-869390**) are a modern legend. **Pasticceria San Carlo** (Via S. Domenico 18, ✆ **0923-869235**) does not enjoy the same celebrity status, but it's just as good and can supply you with a mixed assortment of cookies and other treats to fortify a walk around town.

16

PLANNING YOUR TRIP TO ITALY

By Donald Strachan

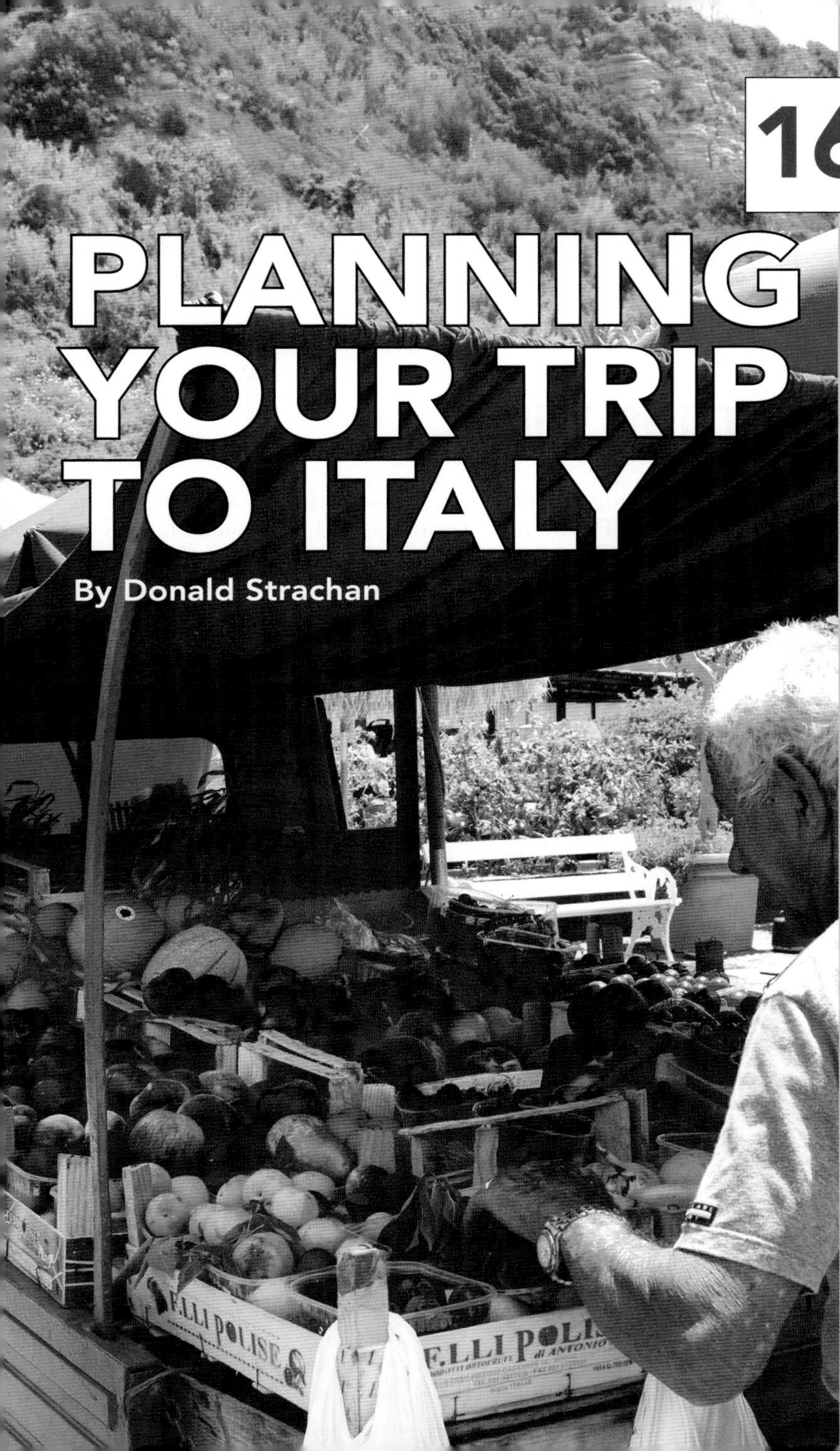

This chapter provides a variety of planning tools, including information on how to get to Italy, how to get around, and the inside track on local resources to tap. If you do your homework on festivals and events, pick the right place for the right season, and pack for the climate, preparing for a trip to Italy should be pleasant and uncomplicated. See also "When to Go," p. 34.

GETTING THERE

By Plane

If you're flying across an ocean, you'll most likely land at Rome's **Leonardo da Vinci–Fiumicino Airport** (FCO; www.adr.it/fiumicino), 40km (25 miles) from the center, or **Milan Malpensa** (MXP; www.milanomalpensa-airport.com), 45km (28 miles) northwest of central Milan. Rome's much smaller **Ciampino Airport** (CIA; www.adr.it/ciampino) serves low-cost airlines connecting to European cities and other destinations in Italy. It's the same story with Milan's **Linate Airport** (LIN; www.milanolinate-airport.com). For information on getting to central Rome from its airports, see p. 61; for Milan, see p. 458.

FLYING DIRECTLY TO VENICE, BERGAMO, BOLOGNA, PISA, OR PALERMO

Carriers within Europe fly direct to several smaller Italian cities. Among the most convenient for Italy's highlights are Venice's **Marco Polo Airport** (VCE; www.veniceairport.it), Bergamo's **Orio al Serio Airport** (BGY; www.orioaeroporto.it/en), Bologna's **Marconi Airport** (BLQ; www.bologna-airport.it), or Pisa's **Galileo Galilei Airport** (PSA; www.pisa-airport.com).

For information on getting into central Venice from the airport, see p. 386. For reaching Florence from Pisa Airport, see p. 162. Florence is also connected with Bologna Airport, by the **Appennino Shuttle** (www.appenninoshuttle.it; ✆ **348-9999651**). The direct bus runs 10 times each day and the journey takes between 80 and 90 minutes. Tickets cost 25€, 10€ ages 5 to 10, free ages 4 and under; book online ahead of time for a 5€ per adult, 2€ per child discount. Buses arrive at and depart from Piazzale Montelungo, between Florence's Santa Maria Novella rail station and the Fortezza da Basso. Central areas around San Lorenzo, Santa Maria Novella, and the Duomo are all an easy walk from there.

 PREVIOUS PAGE: **Fruit vendor in Ischia.**

Several services connect Bergamo's airport with Milan's Stazione Centrale, including **Orioshuttle** (www.orioshuttle.com; ✆ **035-330706**). The service runs approximately half-hourly all day, a little less frequently on weekends. Journey time is 50 minutes. Tickets cost from 4€ if you book online ahead of time.

For information on arriving in Sicily via Palermo's airport, see p. 729.

By Train

Italy's major cities are well connected to Europe's rail hubs. You can arrive in Milan on direct trains from **France** (Nice, Paris, Lyon) by **TGV** (**tgv.en.voyages-sncf.com/en**) or from **Switzerland** (**www.sbb.ch/en**). Connect at Milan to Venice or Florence or Rome (see "Getting Around," below). TGV services also connect France with Turin. Several routes connect **Vienna** with Italy via a comfortable overnight Austrian sleeper train. These **Nightjet** (www.nightjet.com) services visit Verona, Bologna, Milan, Florence, and Venice, among other places. Prices start from 39€ per person if you book ahead (up to 180 days is permitted); specially configured family couchette cabins start from 199€ for 1 to 2 adults and up to 4 children ages 14 and under. Three other Nightjet services connect Munich, Germany, with Rome, Milan, and Venice, respectively.

Thello (www.thello.com) also operates an overnight service connecting Paris with Milan and Venice. After crossing the Alps in the dead of night, the train calls at Milan, Brescia, Verona, Vicenza, and Padua, before arriving in Venice around 9:30am. For Florence, Rome, and points south, alight at Milan (around 6am) and switch to Italy's national high-speed rail lines; see below. Accommodation on the Thello train is in sleeping cars, as well as in six- and four-berth couchettes. Prices range from 35€ per person for the cheapest fare in a six-berth couchette to 290€ for sole occupancy of a sleeping car. It's worth paying the extra for private accommodations if you can.

Book in Italy; online at **Loco2** (www.loco2.com); or use an agent such as **Rail Europe** (www.raileurope.com; ✆ **800-622-8600**) or **International Rail** (www.internationalrail.com; ✆ **+44 871-231-0790**).

GETTING AROUND

By Car

Much of Italy is accessible by public transportation, but to explore vineyards, countryside, and smaller towns, you need a car. You'll get the **best rate** if you book your car far ahead of arrival. Try such websites as **Kayak.com**, **Rentalcars.com**, **Skyscanner.net,** and **Momondo.com** to compare prices across multiple rental companies and agents. Car rental search companies usually report the lowest rates available between 6 and 8 weeks ahead of arrival. Rent the smallest car possible and request a diesel rather than a gasoline engine, to minimize fuel costs. You must be

25 or older to rent from many agencies (although some accept ages 21 and up, at a premium price).

You also must have nerves of steel, a sense of humor, a valid domestic driver's license, and strictly speaking (for non-EU citizens), an **International Driving Permit.** Insurance on all vehicles is compulsory.

Note: If you're planning to rent a car in Italy during high season, you should **book further in advance.** It's not unheard of to arrive at an airport in June or July to find that every agent is all out of cars, perhaps for the whole week.

It can sometimes be tricky to get to the *autostrada* (fast highway) from the city center or airport, so consider renting or bringing a GPS-enabled device, or installing an offline sat-nav app on your phone. In bigger cities you will first have to get to the *tangenziale,* or beltway, which will eventually lead to your highway of choice. The beltway in Rome is known as the Grande Raccordo Anulare, or "Big Ring Road."

The going can be slow almost anywhere, especially on Friday afternoons leaving the cities and Sunday nights on the way back into town, and rush hour around any city can be epic. Driving for a day or so on either side of the busy *Ferragosto* (August 15) holiday is to be avoided *at all costs.* See **www.autostrade.it** for live traffic updates and a road-toll calculator.

Autostrada tolls can get expensive, costing approximately 1€ for every 15km (10 miles), which means that it would cost about 18€ for a trip from Rome to Florence. Although European fuel prices fell significantly in 2015–16, gas remains around 1.50€ *per liter* at time of writing, and has been climbing. (Diesel is usually around .15€ cheaper.) Add in the price of car rental, and it's often cheaper to travel by train, even for two people.

Before leaving home, you can apply for an **International Driving Permit** from the American Automobile Association (AAA; (www.aaa.com; ✆ **800/622-7070** or 650/294-7400). In Canada, the permit is available from the Canadian Automobile Association (CAA; www.caa.ca; ✆ **800/222-4357**). Technically, you need this permit and your actual driver's license to drive in Italy, though at the rental desk, your license itself generally suffices. Traffic police can fine you for driving without an IDP, however. Visitors from within the EU need only take their domestic driver's license.

Italy's equivalent of AAA is the **Automobile Club d'Italia** (ACI; www.aci.it). They're the people who respond when you place an emergency call to ✆ **803-116** for road breakdowns, although they charge for this service if you're not a member.

DRIVING RULES Italian drivers aren't maniacs; they only appear to be. Spend any time on a highway and you will have the experience of somebody driving up from behind insanely close, headlights flashing. Take a deep breath and don't panic: This is the aggressive signal for you to move to the right so he (invariably, it's a "he") can pass, and until you do he will stay mind-bogglingly close. On a two-lane road, the idiot who has swerved into your lane to pass someone in the opposing traffic expects you to veer obligingly over toward the shoulder so three lanes of traffic can fit. He would do the same for you. Probably. Many Italians seem to think that blinkers are optional, so be aware that the car in front could be getting ready to turn at any moment. It is compulsory to keep your headlights illuminated—set to dip—even during the day.

Autostrade are toll highways, denoted by green signs and prefaced with an *A,* like the A1 from Milan to Florence, Rome, and Naples. A few fast highways aren't numbered and are simply called *raccordo,* a connecting road between two cities (such as Florence–Siena and Florence–Pisa).

Strade statali (singular: *strada statale*) are state roads, sometimes without a center divider and two lanes wide (although sometimes they can be a divided four-way highway), indicated by blue signs. Their route numbers are prefaced with an *SS,* as in the SS11 from Milan to Venice. On signs, however, these official route numbers are used infrequently. Usually, you'll just see blue signs listing destinations by name with arrows pointing off in the appropriate directions. It's impossible to predict which of all the towns that lie along a road will be the ones chosen to list on a particular sign. Sometimes the sign gives only the first minuscule village that lies past the turnoff. At other times it lists the first major town down that road. Some signs mention only the major city the road eventually leads to, even if it's hundreds of kilometers away. It pays to study the map before coming to an intersection, to carry a GPS device, or to download an offline GPS app for your smartphone. The *strade statali* can be frustratingly slow thanks to traffic, traffic lights, and the fact that they bisect countless towns: If you're in a hurry to get where you're going, pay for the autostrada.

The **speed limit** on roads in built-up areas around towns and cities is 50 kmph (31 mph). On two-lane roads it's 90 kmph (56 mph), and on the highway its 130 kmph (81 mph). Italians have an astounding disregard for these limits. However, police can ticket you and collect the fine on the spot. The blood-alcohol limit in Italy is .05%, generally achieved with just two regular-size drinks; driving above the limit can result in a fine of up to 6,000€, a driving ban, or jail. The blood-alcohol limit is set at zero for commercial drivers and for anyone who has held a driver's license for under 3 years.

Safety belts are obligatory in both the front and the back seats; ditto child seats or special restraints for minors under 1.5m (5 ft.) in height, though this latter regulation is often ignored. Drivers may not use a handheld cellphone while driving—yet another law that locals seem to consider optional.

PARKING On streets, **white lines** indicate free public spaces, **blue lines** are pay public spaces, and **yellow lines** mean only residents are allowed to park. Meters don't line the sidewalk; rather, there's one machine on the block where you punch in coins corresponding to how long you want to park. The machine spits out a ticket that you leave on your dashboard.

If you park in an area marked *parcheggio disco orario,* root around in your rental car's glove compartment for a cardboard parking disc. With this device, you dial up the hour of your arrival and display it on your dashboard. You're allowed *un'ora* (1 hr.), *due ore* (2 hr.), or whatever the sign advises. If you do not have a disk, write your arrival time clearly on a sheet of paper and leave it on the dash.

Parking lots have ticket dispensers, but exit booths are not usually manned. When you return to the lot to depart, first visit the office or automated payment machine to exchange your ticket for a paid receipt or exit token, which you will then use to get through the exit barrier.

ROAD SIGNS A **speed limit** sign is a black number in a red circle on a white background. The **end of a speed zone** is just black and white, with a black slash through the number. A red circle on white, a black arrow pointing down, and a red arrow pointing up means **yield to oncoming traffic,** while a red-and-white triangle pointing down means **yield ahead.**

Many city centers are closed to traffic, and a simple white circle with a red border, or the words *zona pedonale* or *zona traffico limitato,* denotes a **pedestrian zone** (you can often prearrange to drive through and drop off baggage at your hotel); a white arrow on a blue background is used for Italy's many **one-way streets;** a mostly red circle with a horizontal white slash means **Do Not Enter.** Any image in black on a white background surrounded by a red circle means that image is **not allowed** (for instance, if the image is two cars next to each other, it means no passing; a motorcycle means no Harleys permitted; and so on). A circular sign in blue with a red circle-slash means **no parking.**

Gasoline (gas or petrol), *benzina,* can be found in gas stations along major roads and on the outskirts of town, as well as in 24-hour stations along the autostrada. Almost all stations are closed for the *riposo* and on Sundays (except for those on the autostrada), but most have machines that accept cash. All gas is unleaded. Diesel is *gasolio* (or simply *diesel*).

By Train

Italy, especially the northern half, has one of the best train systems in Europe with most destinations connected by rail. Consequently, the train is an excellent option if you're looking to visit the major sites without the hassle of driving. The vast majority of lines are run by the state-owned **Ferrovie dello Stato,** or FS (www.trenitalia.com; ✆ **892021**). A private operator, **Italo** (www.italotreno.it; ✆ **060708** or 892020) operates only on the Turin–Milan–Florence–Rome–Naples–Salerno high-speed line, plus the branch from Bologna north to Padua, Ferrara, and Venice.

Travel Times Between the Major Cities

CITIES	DISTANCE	(FASTEST) TRAIN TRAVEL TIME	DRIVING TIME
Florence to Venice	281km/174 miles	2 hr.	3 hr.
Florence to Milan	298km/185 miles	1 hr., 40 min.	3½ hr.
Milan to Venice	267km/166 miles	2 hr., 25 min.	3¼ hr.
Milan to Rome	572km/355 miles	2 hr., 55 min.	5½ hr.
Rome to Florence	277km/172 miles	1½ hr.	3 hr.
Rome to Naples	219km/136 miles	1 hr., 10 min.	2½ hr.
Rome to Turin	669km/415 miles	3 hr., 50 min.	6½ hr.
Rome to Venice	528km/327 miles	3hr., 25 min.	5½ hr.

Travel durations and ticket prices vary considerably depending on what type of train you are traveling on. The country's principal north–south high-speed line links Turin and Milan to Bologna, Florence, Rome, Naples, and Salerno. Milan to Rome, for example, takes under 3 hours on the quick train, and costs 89€—though you can find tickets as low as 19€ if you buy ahead and travel in off-peak hours. Rome to Naples takes 70 minutes and costs 44€ (walk-up fare) on the fast train, or you can spend 12€ for a trip on a slower train that takes just over twice as long. If you want to bag the cheapest fares on high-speed trains, try to **book around 100 to 120 days before your travel dates.** The **Italo newsletter** (and homepage) regularly advertises limited-time promo code discounts of up to 50% off its advanced fares—making them crazy cheap.

TYPES OF TRAIN The speed, cleanliness, and overall quality of Italian trains vary widely. The high-speed **Frecciarossa** (along with Italo's rival high-speed service) is the fastest of the fast. These trains mostly operate on the Turin–Milan–Florence–Rome–Naples–Salerno line, and run up to 300 kmph (186 mph)—and new FS equipment (Frecciarossa 1000) has a top speed of 400 kmph (249 mph). Frecciarossa services also run down Italy's eastern coast (Milan–Rimini–Ancona–Bari) and connect Milan with Venice (with stops in Verona and Vicenza). The cheapest class on both operators is perfectly comfortable, even on long journeys (although Business Class on the state railway is well worth paying a little extra for, especially if you can find a cheap advanced fare). These are Italy's premium rail services.

The **Frecciargento** uses similar, slightly downgraded hardware, and travels a little slower; it links Naples, Rome, Florence, Verona, and Venice at speeds of up to 250 kmph (155 mph). There are also Rome–Bari–Lecce, Rome–Bolzano, and Rome–Genoa Frecciargento services. Frecciargento trains have the usual two classes, First and Second. The **Frecciabianca** service isn't a genuine high-speed service, merely an upgraded train running on standard track. Useful routes include regular Milan–Venice trains.

Speed and cleanliness come at a price, with tickets for the high-speed trains usually costing around three times the slower "regional" train. With *Le Frecce* you **must make a seat reservation** when you buy a ticket. If you are traveling with a rail pass (see below), you must pay a 10€ supplementary fee to ride them and reserve a seat. Passes are not accepted (for now) on Italo trains.

Intercity (IC) trains are one step down, both in speed and in comfort; as with Le Frecce, seat reservations are compulsory on IC trains. The slower ***Regionale* (R)** and ***Regionale Veloce* (RV)** make many stops and can sometimes be on the grimy side of things, but they are also very cheap: A Venice–Verona second-class ticket will put you back only 9€, compared with 26€ on the high-speed service. There is no advantage in booking R or RV services ahead of travel.

Old *Regionale* rolling stock is also slowly being replaced, and comfort is improving. However, **overcrowding** is sometimes a problem on these standard services on Friday evenings, weekends, and holidays, especially in and out of big cities, or just after a strike. In summer, the crowding escalates, and many trains going toward a beach in August bulge like an overstuffed sausage.

TRAIN TRAVEL TIPS If you don't have a ticket with a reservation for a particular seat on a specific train, then you must **validate your ticket by stamping it in the little yellow box** on the platform before boarding the train. If you board a train without a ticket, or without having validated your ticket, you'll have to pay a hefty fine on top of the ticket or supplement, which the conductor will sell you. If you board a train without a ticket or realize once onboard that you have the wrong type of ticket, your best bet is to search out the conductor, who is likely to be more forgiving because you found her and made it clear you weren't trying to ride for free.

Schedules for all trains leaving a given station are still printed on yellow posters tacked up on the station wall (a similar white poster lists all the arrivals). These are good for getting general guidance, but keep your eye on the electronic boards and screens that update with delays and track *(binario)* changes. You can also get official schedules (and more train information, also in English) and buy tickets at www.trenitalia.com or www.italotreno.it, or at an online agent such as **Loco2** (www.loco2.com).

In big cities (especially Milan and Rome) and the tourist destinations (above all Venice and Florence), ticketing lines can be dreadfully long. Don't be scared of the **automatic ticket machines.** They are easy to navigate, allow you to follow instructions in English, accept cash and credit cards, and can save you the stress that comes with waiting in an interminably slow line. You can't buy international tickets at automatic machines. Rail **apps** for both Italo and Trenitalia offer paperless ticketing for high-speed trains. You can also just show a copy (paper or email) of your booking confirmation, which has a unique PNR code.

SPECIAL PASSES & DISCOUNTS To buy the **Eurail Italy Pass,** available only outside Europe and priced in U.S. dollars, contact **Rail Europe** (www.raileurope.com). You have 1 month in which to use the train a set number of days; the base number of days is 3, and you can add up to 5 more. For adults, the first-class pass costs $217, second class is $175. Additional days cost $40 to $45 more for first class, roughly $35 for second class. Up to two children ages 2 to 11 travel free with any adult passholder. For youth tickets (27 and under), a 3-day second-class pass is $143 and additional days about $30 each. Buying your pass early in the year is usually rewarded with an extra day's travel at no additional cost (such as pay for 3 days, get 4). Saver passes are available for groups of two to five people traveling together at all times, and amount to a savings of about 15% on individual tickets. There are also Italy–Austria, Italy–Greece, Italy–Spain, Italy–France, and launched in 2017, Italy–Switzerland rail pass combinations.

***Note*:** Booking rail travel online ahead of arrival will usually beat a rail pass on price, especially if you factor in the costs (and hassle) of making compulsory seat reservations on high-speed trains. However, because the cheapest online fares are nonrefundable, you gain some flexibility with a pass.

When it comes to regular tickets, if you're **25 and under,** you can buy a 40€ **Carta Verde (Green Card)** at any Italian train station. This gets you a 10% break on domestic trips (walk-up fares only) and 25% off international connections for 1 year. Present it each time you buy a ticket. An even better deal is available for anyone **61 and over** with the **Carta d'Argento (Silver Card):** 15% off domestic walk-up fares and 25% off international, for 30€ (the Carta d'Argento is free for those 76 and over). **Children 15 and under ride half-price** while kids under 4 don't pay, although they also do not have the right to their own seat. State railways also sometimes offer free tickets for children 15 and under traveling with an adult; ask about "Bimbi gratis" fares when buying (automatic machines will also offer this option, if it's available). The **Italo Family** fare, available at the station and online, includes free travel for up to three kids ages 14 and under accompanying an adult paying full fare (in Smart class only, Mon–Sat).

By Bus

Although trains are quicker and easier, you can get just about anywhere on the network of local, provincial, and regional bus lines. Keep in mind that in smaller towns, buses exist mainly to shuttle workers and schoolchildren, so the most runs are on weekdays, early in the morning, and usually again in midafternoon.

In a big city, the **bus station** for intercity trips is usually near the main train station. A small town's **bus stop** is usually either in the main square, on the edge of town, or just outside the main town gate. You should always try to find the local ticket vendor—if there's no office, it's invariably the nearest newsstand or *tabacchi* (signaled by a sign with a white t), or occasionally a bar—but you can usually also buy tickets on the bus. You can sometimes flag down a bus as it passes on a country road, but try to find an official stop (a small sign, sometimes tacked onto a telephone pole). Tell the driver where you're going and ask courteously if he'll let you know when you need to get off. When he says, *"È la prossima fermata,"* that means yours is the next stop. *"Posso scendere a…?"* (*Poh*-so *shen*-dair-ay ah…?) is "Can I get off at…?"

For details on urban bus transportation, see individual chapters. Perhaps the only longer-distance bus you will want to take while you are in Italy is the efficient **Florence–Siena** service; see "Siena," p. 228. However, if you are traveling on a tight budget, check **FlixBus** (www.flixbus.it; ✆ **02/947-59208**) intercity fares, which often significantly undercut train prices. A long-distance bus is *un pullman*.

By Plane

These days, the only internal air connection you will likely want to make is to the island of **Sicily.** From Milan, **easyJet** (www.easyjet.com) and **Alitalia** (www.alitalia.com) connect Malpensa Airport with both Palermo and Catania. **Meridiana** (www.meridiana.it) flies Milan Linate to both Palermo and Catania. **Ryanair** (www.ryanair.com) connects Bergamo, Bologna, Turin, and Pisa with Palermo, Trapani, and Catania. Direct **Rome** to Sicily routes are operated by Alitalia and Ryanair. Alitalia operates direct flights between **Venice** and Palermo. **Volotea** (www.volotea.com) also flies to Catania from Venice, Verona, Naples, Bari, and Genoa and connects Palermo with each of those five plus Turin.

[Fast FACTS] ITALY

Area Codes The **country code** for Italy is **39.** Former **city codes** (for example, Florence 055, Venice 041, Milan 02, Rome 06) are incorporated into the numbers themselves. Therefore, you must dial the entire number, ***including the initial zero,*** when calling from *anywhere* outside or inside Italy and even within the same town. For example, to call Milan from the United States, you must dial **011-39-02,** then the rest of the local phone number. Phone numbers in Italy can range anywhere from 6 to 12 digits in length.

Business Hours, Banks & ATMs General open hours for **stores, offices,** and **churches** are from 9:30am to noon or 1pm and again from 3 or 3:30pm (or later) to 7:30 or 8pm. The early afternoon shutdown is the *riposo,* the Italian siesta (in the downtown area of large cities, stores don't close for the *riposo*). Most stores close all day Sunday and some also on Monday (morning only or all day). Some services and business offices are open to the public only in the morning.

Traditionally, **state museums** are closed Mondays. Most of the large museums stay open all day long otherwise, though some close for *riposo* or are only open in the morning (9am–2pm is popular). Some churches open earlier in the morning, and the largest often stay open all day, though the last hour or so of opening is usually taken up with a service, when tourist visits are frowned upon. **Banks** tend to be open Monday through Friday 8:30am to 1:30pm and 2:45 to 4:15pm.

The easiest and best way to get cash is from an ATM, referred to in Italy as a ***bancomat.*** ATMs are prevalent in Italian cities, and while every town usually has one, it's good practice to fuel up on cash in urban centers before traveling to villages or rural areas.

Be sure to confirm with your bank that your card is valid for international withdrawal and that you have a four-digit PIN. (Some ATMs in Italy will not accept any other number of digits.) Also, be sure you know your daily withdrawal limit before you depart. ***Note:*** Many banks impose a fee when you use a card at another bank's ATM, and that fee can be higher for international transactions (up to $5 or more) than for domestic ones. In addition, the bank from which you withdraw cash may charge its own fee, although this is not common practice in Italy.

If at the ATM you get an on-screen message saying your card isn't valid for international transactions, don't panic: It's most likely the bank just can't make the electronic connection to check it (occasionally this can be a citywide epidemic). Try another ATM or another town.

Customs

Foreign visitors can bring along most items for personal use duty-free, including merchandise valued up to $450.

Disabled Travelers

Most of the top museums and churches have installed ramps at their entrances, and several hotels have converted first-floor rooms into accessible units. Other than that, you may find many charming parts of Italy tricky to tackle. Builders in the Middle Ages and the Renaissance didn't have wheelchairs or mobility impairments in mind when they built narrow doorways and spiral staircases, and preservation laws prevent Italians from being able to do much about this in some areas.

Public transportation is improving, however. There is generally better access for passengers in wheelchairs, particularly on modern local buses and new transit developments like Florence's tram. There are usually dedicated seats or areas for those with disabilities, and Italians are quick to give up their place for somebody who looks like they need it. **Trenitalia** has a special number that disabled travelers should call for assistance on the rail network: ✆ **199-303060.** Italo has dedicated wheelchair spaces on every train: Call ✆ **060708** for any station assistance you need.

Accessible Italy (www.accessibleitaly.com; ✆ **378-0549-941-111**) provides travelers with info about accessible tourist sites and places to rent wheelchairs, and also sells organized "Accessible Tours" around Italy.

Accomable (www.accomable.com) is an Airbnb-like agency connecting travelers with accessible properties for rent.

Doctors & Hospitals

See individual chapters for details of emergency rooms and walk-in medical services.

Drinking Laws

People of any age can legally consume alcohol in Italy, but a person must be 16 years old to be served alcohol in a restaurant or bar. Noise is the primary concern to city officials, so bars generally close by 2am, though alcohol is often served in clubs after that. Supermarkets carry beer, wine, and spirits.

Electricity Italy operates on a 220-volt AC (50 cycles) system, as opposed to the U.S. 110-volt AC (60 cycles) system. You'll need a simple adapter plug to make the American flat pegs fit the Italian round holes and unless your appliance is dual-voltage (as some hair dryers, travel irons, and almost all gadgets are), an electrical currency converter. You can pick up the hardware at electronics stores, travel specialty stores, luggage shops, and airports.

Embassies & Consulates The **Australian Embassy** is in Rome at Via Antonio Bosio 5 (www.italy.embassy.gov.au; ✆ **06-852-721**). The **Australian Consulate-General** is in Milan at Via Borgogna 2 (✆ **02-7767-4200**).

The **Canadian** Embassy is in Rome at Via Zara 30 (www.italy.gc.ca; ✆ **06-85444-2911**). The **Canadian Consulate** is in Milan at Piazza Cavour 3 (✆ **02-6269-4238**).

The **New Zealand Embassy** (www.nzembassy.com/italy; ✆ **06-853-7501**) is in Rome at Via Clitunno 44.

The **U.K. Embassy** (www.gov.uk/government/world/italy; ✆ **06-4220-0001**) is in Rome at Via XX Settembre 80a. The **British Consulate-General** is in Milan at Via San Paolo 7 (✆ **02-723001**).

The **U.S. Embassy** is in Rome at Via Vittorio Veneto 121 (http://italy.usembassy.gov; ✆ **06-46741**). There are also **U.S. Consulates General** in **Florence,** at Lungarno Vespucci 38 (http://florence.usconsulate.gov; ✆ **055-266-951**); in **Milan,** at Via Principe Amedeo 2/10 (http://milan.usconsulate.gov; ✆ **02-290-351**); and in **Naples,** in Piazza della Repubblica (http://naples.usconsulate.gov; ✆ **081-583-8111**).

Emergencies The best number to call in Italy with a **general emergency** is ✆ **112,** which connects you to the ***carabinieri*** who will transfer your call as needed. For the **police,** dial ✆ **113;** for a **medical emergency** and to call an **ambulance,** the number is ✆ **118;** for the **fire department,** call ✆ **115.** If your car breaks down, dial ✆ **116** for **roadside aid** courtesy of the Automotive Club of Italy. All are free calls, but roadside assistance is a paid service for nonmembers.

Family Travel Italy is a family-oriented society. A crying baby at a dinner table is greeted with a knowing smile, rather than a stern look. Children can almost always request discounted smaller portions, and sometimes even get a special treat from the waiter, but the availability of such accoutrements as child seats for cars and dinner tables is more the exception than the norm. (The former, however, is a legal requirement: Be sure to ask a rental car company to provide them.) There are plenty of parks, offbeat museums, markets, ice-cream parlors, and vibrant street-life scenes to amuse even the youngest children. Child discounts apply on public transportation, and at public and private museums.

Health You won't encounter any special health risks by visiting Italy. The country's public health care system is generally well regarded. The richer north tends to have better **hospitals** than the south.

Italy offers universal health care to its citizens and those of other European Union countries (U.K. nationals should remember to carry an EHIC: See **www.nhs.uk/ehic**). Others should be prepared to pay medical bills upfront. Before leaving home, find out what medical services your **health insurance** covers. ***Note:*** Even if you don't have insurance, you will be treated in an emergency.

Pharmacies offer essentially the same range of generic drugs available in the United States and internationally. Pharmacies are ubiquitous (look for the green cross) and serve almost like mini-clinics, where pharmacists diagnose and treat minor ailments, like flu symptoms and general aches and pains, with over-the-counter drugs. Carry the generic name of any prescription medicines, in case a local pharmacist is unfamiliar with the brand name. Pharmacies in cities take turns doing the night shift.

Insurance

Italy may be one of the safer places you can travel in the world, but accidents and setbacks can and do happen, from lost luggage to car crashes. For information on traveler's insurance, trip cancellation insurance, and medical insurance while traveling, please visit **www.frommers.com/tips**.

Internet Access

Internet cafes are in healthy supply in most Italian cities, though don't expect to find a connection in every small town. If you're traveling with your own computer or smartphone, you'll find Wi-Fi in almost every hotel, but if this is essential for your stay, make sure you ask before booking and certainly don't always expect to find a connection in a rural *agriturismo* (digital detox is often part of their appeal). In a pinch, hostels, local libraries, and some cafes and bars have web access. Several spots around Venice, Florence, Rome, and other big cities are covered with free Wi-Fi access provided by the local administration, but at these and any other Wi-Fi spots around Italy, antiterrorism laws make it obligatory to register for an access code before you can log on. Take your passport or other photo ID when you go looking for an Internet point. **High-speed trains** often have free Wi-Fi (but throttle Skype, video streaming, file sharing, and similar data-hungry services).

LGBT Travelers

Italy as a whole, northern Italy in particular, is gay-friendly. Homosexuality is legal, and the age of consent is 16. Same-sex civil unions became legal in 2016. Italians are generally more affectionate and physical than North Americans in all their friendships, and even straight men occasionally walk down the street with their arms around each other—however, kissing anywhere other than on the cheeks at greetings and goodbyes may draw attention. As you might expect, smaller towns tend to be less permissive than cities and beach resorts.

Italy's national associations and support networks for gays and lesbians are **ArciGay** and **ArciLesbica.** The national websites are **www.arcigay.it** and **www.arcilesbica.it**, and most cities have a local office. See **www.arcigay.it/sedi** for a map directory of local affiliates.

Mail & Postage

Sending a postcard or letter up to 20 grams, or a little less than an ounce, costs 1€ to other European countries, 2.20€ to North America, and a whopping 2.90€ to Australia and New Zealand. Full details on Italy's postal services are available at **www.poste.it** (some of it in English).

Mobile Phones

GSM (Global System for Mobile Communications) is a cellphone technology used by most of the world's countries that makes it possible to turn on a phone with a contract based in Australia, Ireland, the U.K., Pakistan, or almost every other corner of the world and have it work in Italy without missing a beat. (In the U.S., service providers like Sprint and Verizon use a different technology—CDMA—and phones on those networks also need GSM and/or 4G/LTE compatibility to work in Italy. Most current, high-end models do; older phones may not work.) Also, if you are coming from the U.S. or Canada, you may need a multiband "world" phone. All travelers should activate "international roaming" on their account, so check with your home service provider before leaving.

But—and it's a *big* but—using roaming can be very expensive, especially if you access the Internet on your phone. It is usually much cheaper, once you arrive, to buy an Italian SIM card (the fingernail-size removable plastic card found in all GSM phones that is encoded with your phone number). This is not difficult, and is an especially good idea if you will be in Italy for more than a week. You can **buy a SIM card** at one of the many cellphone shops you will pass in every city. The main service providers are **TIM** (www.tim.it), **Vodafone** (www.vodafone.it), **Wind** (www.wind.it), and **3** (www.tre.it). If you have an Italian SIM card in your phone, local and national calls may be as low as .10€ per minute, and incoming calls are free. Value prepaid data packages are available for each—usually with LTE/4G data speeds inclusive—as are nano-SIMs, as well as prepaid data bundles for iPads and other tablets. Not every network allows **tethering**—ask if you need it. Deals on each network change regularly; check the individual websites, or walk into a branded store or an electronics chain such as **Euronics** (www.euronics.it). ***Note:*** U.S. contract cellphones are often "locked" and will only work with a SIM card provided by the service provider back home, so check first that you have an unlocked phone.

Buying a phone is another option, and you shouldn't have too much trouble finding one for about 20€. Use it, then recycle it or eBay it when you get home. It will save you a fortune versus alternatives such as roaming or using hotel telephones.

Money & Costs

Frommer's lists exact prices in the local currency. The currency conversions quoted below were correct at press time. However, rates fluctuate, so before departing, consult a currency exchange website, such as **www.oanda.com/currency/converter**, to check up-to-the-minute rates.

Like many European countries, Italy uses the **euro** as its currency. Euro coins are issued in denominations of .01€, .02€, .05€, .10€, .20€, and .50€, as well as 1€ and 2€; bills come in denominations of 5€, 10€, 20€, 50€, 100€, 200€, and 500€. You'll get the best rate if you **exchange money** at a bank or one of its ATMs. The rates at "Cambio/change" exchange booths are invariably less favorable but still better than what you'd get exchanging money at a hotel or shop (a last-resort tactic only).

In any case, the evolution of international computerized banking and consolidated ATM networks has led to the triumph of plastic throughout Italy—even if cold cash is still the most trusted currency, especially in small towns and mom-and-pop joints, where credit cards may not be accepted. (It remains a good idea to carry some cash—small businesses may accept only cash or may claim their credit card machine is broken to avoid paying card fees.) **Visa** and **Mastercard** are almost universally accepted, and some businesses take **American Express,** typically at the luxe end. **Diners Club** tends not to be accepted in Italy. Be sure to let your bank know that you'll be traveling abroad to avoid having your card blocked after a few days of big purchases far from home. ***Note:*** Many banks assess a 1% to 3% "transaction fee" on **all** charges you incur abroad, whether you're using the local currency or your native currency.

Traveler's checks have gone the way of the Stegosaurus.

THE VALUE OF THE EURO VS. OTHER POPULAR CURRENCIES

€	Aus$	Can$	NZ$	UK£	US$
1	1.38	1.39	1.47	0.85	1.06

WHAT THINGS COST IN ROME (HOTEL PRICES ARE HIGH SEASON)

Bus ticket (from/to anywhere in the city)	1.50€
Double room at Capo d'Africa (very expensive)	185.00€–325.00€
Double room at Lancelot (moderate)	130.00€–216.00€
Double room at Mimosa (inexpensive)	59.00€–154.00€
Continental breakfast (cappuccino and croissant standing at a bar)	2.50€
Dinner for one, with wine, at Glass (very expensive)	75.00€–100.00€
Dinner for one, with wine, at La Barrique (moderate)	35.00€
Dinner for one, with wine, at Li Rioni (inexpensive)	15.00€
Small gelato at Fatamorgana	2.00€
Glass of wine at a bar	3.00€–7.00€
Coca-Cola (standing/sitting in a bar)	2.50€/4.50€
Cup of espresso (standing/sitting in a bar)	.90€/2.50€
Admission to the Colosseum and Forum	12.00€

Newspapers & Magazines "The New York Times International Edition" and "USA Today" are available at most newsstands in the big cities, and sometimes even in smaller towns. You can find the "Wall Street Journal Europe," European editions of "Time," the "Economist," and most of the major European newspapers and magazines at larger kiosks in the bigger cities.

Police For emergencies, call ✆ **112** or ✆ **113.** The *carabinieri* (✆ **112**; www.carabinieri.it) normally only concern themselves with serious crimes, but point you in the right direction. The *polizia* (✆ **113**; www.poliziadistato.it), whose city headquarters is called the *questura,* is the place to go for help with lost and stolen property or petty crimes.

Safety Italy is a remarkably safe country. The worst threats you'll likely face are pickpockets who sometimes frequent touristy areas and public buses; keep your hands on your camera at all times and your valuables in an under-the-clothes money belt or inside zip-pocket. Don't leave anything valuable in a rental car overnight, and leave nothing visible in it at any time. If you are robbed, you can fill out paperwork at the nearest police station *(questura),* but this is mostly for insurance purposes and perhaps to get a new passport issued—don't expect them to spend any resources hunting down the perpetrator. In general, avoid public parks at night. The areas around rail stations are often unsavory, but rarely worse than that. Otherwise, there's a real sense of personal security for travelers in Italy.

Senior Travel Seniors and older people are treated with a great deal of respect and deference, but few specific programs or concessions are made for them. The one exception is on admission prices for museums and sights, where those ages 60 or 65 and older will often get in at a reduced rate or even free. There are also special train passes and reductions on bus tickets (see "Getting Around," above). As a senior in Italy, you're *un anziano,* or if you're a woman, *un'anziana,* "elderly"—it's a term of respect, and you should let people know you're one if you think a discount may be in order.

Smoking Smoking has been eradicated from inside restaurants, bars, and most hotels, so smokers tend to take outside tables at bars and restaurants. If you're keen for an alfresco table, you are essentially choosing a seat in the smoking section; requesting that your neighbor not smoke may not be politely received.

Student Travelers

An **International Student Identity Card (ISIC)** qualifies students for savings on travel tickets, entrance fees, and more. The card is valid for 1 year. You can apply for the card online at **www.myisic.com** or in person at **STA Travel** (www.statravel.com; ✆ **800/781-4040** in North America). If you're no longer a student but are still 30 and under, you can get an **International Youth Travel Card (IYTC)** or an **International Teacher Identity Card (ITIC)** from the same agency, either of which entitles you to some discounts. Students will also find that many university cities offer ample student discounts and inexpensive youth hostels.

Taxes No sales tax is added to the price tag of purchases in Italy, but a 22% value-added tax (in Italy: IVA) is automatically included in just about everything, except food and a few specific goods and services, where rates of 4% and 10% apply. If government budget targets are missed, the 22% rate will rise to 24% in 2018 and 26% in 2019. Entertainment, transport, hotels, and dining are among a group of goods taxed at a lower rate of 10%. For major purchases, you can get IVA refunded. Several cities have also introduced an **accommodation tax.** For example, in Florence, you will be charged 1.50€ per person per night for a 1-star hotel plus 1€ per night per additional government-star rating of the hotel, up to a maximum of 10 nights. So, in a 4-star joint, the tax is 4.50€ per person per night. Children 9 and under are exempt. Venice, Rome, and several other localities also levy their own taxes. This tax is not usually included in a published room rate.

Tipping In **hotels,** service is usually included in your bill. In family-run operations, additional tips are unnecessary and sometimes considered rude. In fancier places with a hired staff, however, you may want to leave a .50€ daily tip for the maid and pay the bellhop or porter 1€ per bag. In **restaurants,** a 1€ to 3€ per person "cover charge" is automatically added to the bill, and in some tourist areas, especially Venice, another 10% to 15% is tacked on (except in the most unscrupulous of places, this will be noted on the menu somewhere; if unsure you should ask, è incluso il servizio?). It is not necessary to leave any extra money on the table, though it is not uncommon to leave up to 5€, especially for good service. Locals generally leave nothing. At **bars and cafes,** you can leave something very small on the counter for the barman (maybe 1€ if you have had several drinks), though it is not expected; there is no need to leave anything extra if you sit at a table, as they are likely already charging you double or triple the price you'd have paid standing at the bar. It is not necessary to tip **taxi** drivers, though it is common to round up the bill to the nearest euro or two.

Toilets Aside from train stations, where they cost about .50€ to use, and gas/petrol stations, where they are free (with perhaps a basket seeking gratuities for the cleaners), public toilets are few and far between. In an emergency, standard procedure is to enter a cafe, make sure the bathroom is not *fuori servizio* (out of order), and then order a cup of coffee before bolting to the facilities. It is advisable to always make use of the facilities in a hotel, restaurant, or museum before a long walk around town. Public toilets—and often those in bars, too—can be dirty, with no seat or toilet paper. It's best to carry a pack of tissues with you, especially if you're travelling with children or teens who are easily grossed-out.

Websites Following are some of our favorite sites to help you plan your trip: **www.italia.it/en** is the official English-language tourism portal for visiting Italy; **www.arttrav.com** is excellent for cultural travel, exhibitions, and openings, especially in Florence and Tuscany; **www.summerinitaly.com/planning/strike.asp** provides updates on the latest transport strikes; **www.prezzibenzina.it** finds the cheapest fuel close to your accommodations or destination (they also have a mobile app); **www.ansa.it** gets you Italian news, partly in English; and naturally, **www.frommers.com/destinations/Italy**, for more expert advice on the country.

Index

J

K

L

M

Q

T

U

V

Accommodations

Restaurants

PHOTO CREDITS

p. 1, agean / Shutterstock.com; p. 2, Luca Lorenzelli / Shutterstock.com; p. 3, Jorg Hackemann / Shutterstock.comp; p. 6, Vladimir Wrangel / Shutterstock.com; p. 7, Nattee Chalermtiragool / Shutterstock.com; p. 8, Viacheslav Lopatin / Shutterstock.com; p. 9, © photogolfer / Shutterstock.com; p. 11, oleandra / Shutterstock.com; p. 12, ELEPHOTOS / Shutterstock.com; p. 14, Efired; p. 15, Andriy Palanchuk / Shutterstock.com; p. 19, Roxana Bashyrova / Shutterstock.com; p. 20, Catarina Belova; p. 23, PaolikPhotos / Shutterstock.com; p. 27, © Mihai-Bogdan Lazar / Shutterstock.com; p. 30, © Matej Kastelic; p. 32, Boris Stroujko / Shutterstock.com; p. 35, Pecold / Shutterstock.com; p. 38, Cristian Puscasu / Shutterstock.com; p. 39, © Lucian Milasan / Shutterstock.com; p. 43, Mariia Golovianko / Shutterstock.com; p. 50, top, Vladimir Wrangel / Shutterstock.com; p. 50, bottom, © Raffaele Capasso; p. 53, Gaspar Janos; p. 54, © anshar; p. 58, Vladimir Korostyshevskiy; p. 59, Meghan Lamb; p. 60, Viacheslav Lopatin; p. 64, Elizabeth Heath; p. 74, © Janis Lacis; p. 76, WDG Photo / Shutterstock.com; p. 78, Genevieve Borden / Shutterstock.com; p. 90, © Nikonaft; p. 93, Elizabeth Heath; p. 97, Phant;

p. 104, © Jannis Tobias Werner / Shutterstock.com; p. 107, r.nagy / Shutterstock.com; p. 114, Catarina Belova; p. 120, Giordano Cantone / Shutterstock.com; p. 130, Courtesy of Inn at Spanish Steps; p. 139, Courtesy of Da Pancrazio; p. 140, Elizabeth Heath; p. 151, Northfoto / Shutterstock.com; p. 154, lornet / Shutterstock.com; p. 150, Marina99; p. 161, Alexander Cher; p. 166, onairda; p. 170, starmaro / Shutterstock.com; p. 174, littleting; p. 180, © starmaro / Shutterstock.com; p. 182, voe / Shutterstock.com; p. 184, Efired; p. 185, S.Borisov; p. 187, salajean; p. 193, Daniel M. Silva; p. 194, Karol Kozlowski; p. 217, gvictoria / Shutterstock.com; p. 218, g.sighele; p. 219, Diriye Amey / Shutterstock.com; p. 222, Alexandra; p. 224, Valery Rokhin / Shutterstock.com; p. 231, Migel / Shutterstock.com; p. 235, Eddy Galeotti / Shutterstock.com; p. 243, Shaiith; p. 247, Dmitriy Yakovlev; p. 252, Tania Zbrodko; p. 257, © gengish skan; p. 261, arkanto / Shutterstock.com; p. 266, Maciej Czekajewski / Shutterstock.com; p. 267, marcovarro / Shutterstock.com; p. 273, Sorin Colac; p. 278, Roberto Cerruti / Shutterstock.com; p. 286, eFesenko / Shutterstock.com; p. 295, 135pixels; p. 296, Patryk Kosmider / Shutterstock.com; p. 300, ValerioMei / Shutterstock.com; p. 302, Sonia Alves-Polidori / Shutterstock.com; p. 304, DiegoMariottini / Shutterstock.com; p. 307, Maurizio Zanetti; p. 313, , Buffy1982 / Shutterstock.com; p. 318, WDG Photo; p. 326, alexandro900; p. 327, Aksenya / Shutterstock.com; p. 335, canadastock; p. 337, Tatiana Popova; p. 341, posztos / Shutterstock.com; p. 343, bellena; p. 346, RossHelen / Shutterstock.com; p. 348, Zvonimir Atletic / Shutterstock.com; p. 349, © Matej Kastelic; p. 362, Alvaro German Vilela / Shutterstock.com; p. 366, Cividin / Shutterstock.com; p. 370, Alvaro German Vilela / Shutterstock.com; p. 374, vvoe / Shutterstock.com; p. 385, ESB Professional; p. 390, pio3 / Shutterstock.com; p. 393, Aleksandr Stepanov / Shutterstock.com; p. 394, bellena / Shutterstock.com; p. 398, © Anastazzo; p. 405, Rad Radu; p. 409, © Riccardo de Luca; p. 411, Mila Atkovska; p. 413, kavalenkava volha / Shutterstock.com; p. 414, Elzloy / Shutterstock.com; p. 431, jdpphoto / Shutterstock.com; p. 442, Timur Kulgarin; p. 443, william casey; p. 445, Miguel Mendez; p. 449, © Arseniy Krasnevsky; p. 452, Dudarev Mikhail; p. 453, kavalenkava volha; p. 454, milosk50; p. 457, Noppasin; p. 461, Claudio Divizia; p. 468, Mihai-Bogdan Lazar; p. 481, ValeStock / Shutterstock.com; p. 491, © pio3 / Shutterstock.com; p. 496, Rene Hartmann; p. 497, Anna-Mari West; p. 500, Roberto Binetti; p. 502, Joaquin Ossorio Castillo / Shutterstock.com; p. 505, Gaspar Janos; p. 507, mikolajn; p. 513, Claudio Divizia / Shutterstock.com; p. 516, © Max Bashirov; p. 525, © ROBERTO ZILLI / Shutterstock.com; p. 530, Red On; p. 531, PHB.cz (Richard Semik); p. 535, Fabio Lamanna / Shutterstock.com; p. 537, © Venturelli Luca / Shutterstock.com; p. 539, Boris Stroujko; p. 542, Yulia Grigoryeva / Shutterstock.com; p. 548, Leonid Andronov; p. 550, trabantos / Shutterstock.com; p. 555, Aleksandar Todorovic; p. 558, StevanZZ; p. 564, LianeM; p. 569, © Kert; p. 570, Shoriful Chowdhury; p. 571, iryna1; p. 576, Meghan Lamb; p. 583, Meghan Lamb; p. 584, b-hide the scene / Shutterstock.com; p. 585, Meghan Lamb; p. 588, © BrunoRosa; p. 591, Anna Pakutina / Shutterstock.com; p. 595, mkos83 / Shutterstock.com; p. 596, Meghan Lamb; p. 612, Ekaterina Pokrovsky; p. 614, b-hide the scene / Shutterstock.com; p. 620, anuwat1303; p. 623, Viacheslav Lopatin; p. 626, Meghan Lamb; p. 628, Meghan Lamb; p. 630, Meghan Lamb; p. 632, Meghan Lamb; p. 633, Meghan Lamb; p. 644, Meghan Lamb; p. 645, Meghan Lamb; p. 646, Meghan Lamb; p. 653, Meghan Lamb; p. 654, Meghan Lamb; p. 655, Meghan Lamb; p. 663, Meghan Lamb; p. 667, Meghan Lamb; p. 672, Meghan Lamb; p. 674, Meghan Lamb; p. 682, Meghan Lamb; p. 687, Meghan Lamb; p. 690, Meghan Lamb; p. 694, canadastock; p. 696, ermess; p. 699, Littleaom; p. 701, maudanros / Shutterstock.com; p. 705, Cristiano Palazzini; p. 707, Andrei Rybachuk / Shutterstock.com; p. 710, Giorgio Galeotti; p. 713, Emi Cristea; p. 715, Pug Girl; p. 716, AlenKadr / Shutterstock.com; p. 718, Eddy Galeotti / Shutterstock.com; p. 719, inavanhateren; p. 720, jorisvo; p. 724, leoks; p. 725, pio3 / Shutterstock.com; p. 726, andras_csontos / Shutterstock.com; p. 729, © Tupungato / Shutterstock.com; p. 736, Boris Stroujko; p. 739, top, Gandolfo Cannatella / Shutterstock.com; p. 739, bottom, futureGalore / Shutterstock.com; p. 749, vvoe / Shutterstock.com; p. 751, Littleaom; p. 752, robertonencini / Shutterstock.com; p. 754, andras_csontos / Shutterstock.com; p. 763, © Gurgen Bakhshetsyan; p. 771, top, Marco Ossino; p. 771, bottom, Marco Ossino; p. 773, Martin M303; p. 775, © lapas77 / Shutterstock.com; p. 778, © silky; p. 781, robertonencini; p. 787, Marco Crupi / Shutterstock.com; p. 789, Standret; p. 791, Avillfoto / Shutterstock.com; p. 793, Meghan Lamb.